Description vs. Explanation
Continuity vs. Change
Nature vs. Nurture
Data vs. Theory
Structure vs. Function
Organic vs. Mechanistic
Observation vs. Experiment
~~Stage vs. Continuity~~
Passive vs. Active
Subjective vs. Objective
Quantitative vs Qualitative
Contemporary vs Retrospective
Universals vs. Idiographic/Individual
Reductionism vs. Wholism
Unilateral influence vs. Reciprocal
                                           influence

DEVELOPMENTAL PSYCHOLOGY
AN ADVANCED TEXTBOOK
Third Edition

DEVELOPMENTAL PSYCHOLOGY
AN ADVANCED TEXTBOOK
Third Edition

Edited by
Marc H. Bornstein
Michael E. Lamb
National Institute of Child Health
and Human Development

LEA

LAWRENCE ERLBAUM ASSOCIATES, PUBLISHERS

1992   Hillsdale, New Jersey   Hove and London

Lawrence Erlbaum Associates, Inc., Publishers
365 Broadway
Hillsdale, New Jersey 07642

Library of Congress Cataloging-in-Publication Data:

Developmental psychology : an advanced textbook / edited by Marc H.
Bornstein and Michael E. Lamb. — 3rd ed.
      p.   cm.
   Includes bibliographical references and indexes.
   ISBN 0-8058-1007-2 (hard)
   1. Developmental psychology.   I. Bornstein, Marc H.   I. Lamb,
Michael E., 1953–
BF713.D465   1992
155 — dc20   91-37537
                                                                CIP

Printed in the United States of America
10   9   8   7   6   5   4   3   2   1

Contents

PART II: PERCEPTUAL AND COGNITIVE DEVELOPMENT

3. Perception Across the Life Span   155
Marc H. Bornstein

4. Cognitive Development   211
Deanna Kuhn

5. Information-Processing Approaches
to Cognitive Development   273
David Klahr

FOUNDATIONS OF DEVELOPMENTAL PSYCHOLOGY

The two chapters in the first section focus on the intellectual history of developmental psychology and the manner in which empirical research on development is conducted. In Chapter 1, Roger Dixon and Richard Lerner summarize the philosophical origins and history of developmental psychology. Like many other commentators, they place great emphasis on Charles Darwin's role in transforming what would become developmental psychology from a largely speculative and descriptive discipline into a theoretically grounded empirical science. Since Darwin's seminal contributions, developmental psychology has been the primary battleground for theorists attempting to elucidate development. Dixon and Lerner also explain shifts over time in both the definitions of development proposed within each type of theory and in the manner in which central issues in development (e.g., nature vs. nurture, continuity vs. discontinuity) are portrayed.

In Chapter 2, Donald Hartmann discusses the many ways in which evidence is gathered, analyzed, and understood by developmental psychologists. Developmental psychologists are methodologically eclectic and rely on systematic or unsystematic observations, interviews, questionnaires, and experiments to obtain data. They use an array of descriptive and inferential statistical techniques to analyze those data and reach conclusions based on them. Because most studies conducted by developmentalists involve children, a unique set of ethical issues also attend developmental research, and these too are discussed by Hartmann.

1 A History of Systems in Developmental Psychology

Roger A. Dixon
University of Victoria

Richard M. Lerner
Michigan State University

INTRODUCTION

A student beginning the advanced study of developmental psychology is probably all too aware of the vast array of theories, methods, and ideas present in the field. Such an array may suggest a picture of formidable complexity, or even anarchy. Closer inspection, however, reveals some identifiable clusters of theories, methods, and ideas, and shows that, although these clusters differ in important ways, they also share certain foci, themes, and — most important for the purposes of this chapter — historical roots. Accordingly, we examine some of the key historical bases of the principal modern systems of developmental psychology. In considering this history we examine early connections among what have evolved into major theoretical orientations toward development. In addition, we specify some major similarities and differences in these approaches to understanding development. By referring to the field's history, we are able to understand much of the contemporary scene in developmental psychology.

Our analysis of the history of developmental psychology reveals two major conceptual features of the field today. First, developmental psychologists are now more concerned with, and better prepared to address, the explanation of development (i.e., the specification of the causes or antecedents of development) as opposed to just the description of development (i.e., the depiction or representation of change). One prominent objective of developmental psychology is to explain what stays the same and what changes across life, and to specify the conditions under which such constancy (or continuity) and change (discontinuity) arise. Second, because it has been recognized that one's explanation of development derives from one's theory of development, developmental psychologists have begun to attend to one or more of the available systems of interpretation (e.g., Baldwin, 1980; Lerner, 1976, 1986). Much current, exemplary developmental research is aimed at theory development or model testing as opposed, for example, to the mere generation of developmental norms.

What led to these current trends? We begin this chapter by noting some of the recent events that are associated with today's emphasis on theory and explanation. Next we find that, although the current emphasis on theory has been associated with the recognition of the range of systems that may be used to account for development, there has also been a concern with appreciating, accepting, and explaining the presence of multiple viable theories of development. In other words, why is there more than one theory of psychological development? Are these theories compatible or incompatible with one another; are they in competition with one another? Although we see here that the answers to such questions depend on philosophical differences among psychologists, we observe that another answer exists.

Distinct in many important ways, each of today's major theoretical systems of developmental psychology can be linked historically to the intellectual context of the 19th century. Each system is connected to the historical and evolutionary theories of this period (e.g., those of Charles Darwin). Thus, one explanation for the presence of distinct theories of development is that different scientists devised their perspectives on development by emphasizing different aspects of such prominent accounts of historical change as Darwin's theory of evolution (Dixon & Lerner, 1985; White, 1968; Wolhlwill, 1973). We return to this point later. In addition to observing the existence of several relatively adequate "families" of developmental theories, we discuss the recent interest in the history of developmental psychology (e.g., Borstelmann, 1983; Cairns, 1983; Cavanaugh, 1981; Eckardt, Bringmann, & Sprung, 1985; Smuts & Hagen, 1986; White, 1985, 1983). Finally, we summarize the history and the major features of a life-span approach to developmental psychology. Let us turn now to the bases of the trend toward addressing issues of explanation.

SOME BASES OF THE CONTEMPORARY CONCERN WITH THE EXPLANATION OF DEVELOPMENT

In the early decades of this century, and continuing through at least the beginning of the 1940s, much of developmental psychology was descriptive and normative. Instrumental in promoting this emphasis was the research of Arnold Gesell (1880–1961). Gesell (1929, 1931, 1934, 1946, 1954)

Nature - nurture issue !

emphasized that maturationally based changes unfold independently of learning, and his research stressed the need for the careful and systematic cataloging of growth norms. His work provided the field with useful information about the expected sequence for, and normative times of, the emergence of numerous physical and mental developments in selected groups of infants and children (largely White, middle-class ones). Conceptually, Gesell's work is related to one side of what has been a continuing debate in the history of developmental psychology: the *nature–nurture* controversy. This controversy pertains to a consideration of where the sources of development lie, whether in inborn (or hereditary) mechanisms or in acquired (or learned) processes. By stressing that maturation rather than learning is the prime impetus for developmental change, Gesell (1929) was taking a nature, as opposed to a nurture, stance. Historically, other terms associated with the nature position are *preformationism, nativism,* and *innateness;* some terms associated with the nurture position are *learning, conditioning, experience,* and *socialization.*

It is important to recognize that the differences in views of the source of development are associated with differences regarding the nature–nurture issue because, although Gesell's (1929, 1931, 1934) work emphasized the descriptive and normative nature of the field, there was indeed work occurring in other areas of psychology that countered Gesell's emphasis (White, 1970). For example, some experimental psychologists stressed the applicability of learning principles to the study of childhood (e.g., Dollard, Doob, Miller, Mowrer, & Sears, 1939; Miller & Dollard, 1941; Watson, 1924). One consequence of this activity was to provide evidence that nurture-based learning phenomena, as opposed to nature-based maturational phenomena, could account for some features of children's behavior and development. These learning psychologists emphasized less the facts of development per se (e.g., "What is the age at which an infant sits, stands, walks, or has a two-word vocabulary?") than the explanation of those facts (e.g., "What mechanisms—nature or nurture—need to be referred to in order to explain these facts?").

This alternating emphasis between nature and nurture was furthered in the 1940s by events leading up to and including World War II (Lerner, 1983). Nazi persecution led many Jewish intellectuals to flee Europe, and many sought refuge and a new start for their careers in the United States. Many of these refugees were able to secure positions in American universities and associated institutions, despite the fact that they often brought with them ideas counter to those that were typical of the American scene (e.g., behaviorism and learning theory). For instance, although Freud himself settled in London (and died there in 1939), many psychoanalytically oriented psychologists, some trained by Freud or his daughter Anna, emigrated to North America (e.g., Peter Blos and Erik Erikson).

One reason that so many psychoanalytically oriented professionals were able to secure faculty positions in America may be related to the fact that the federal government was contributing large amounts of money to universities to support the training of clinical psychologists. Such psychologists were needed to conduct the testing of soldiers for both psychological and physical fitness (Misiak & Sexton, 1966). This infusion of psychoanalysis resulted in the introduction of a nature-based perspective into numerous psychology departments, some of which had been dominated by nurture-based theorists (Gengerelli, 1976). Nevertheless, the psychoanalytic orientation represented just one of many different theoretical accounts of human functioning — accounts that stressed either nature or both nature and nurture as sources of behavior and development — that were now making inroads into North American thinking.

For similar reasons, nativistic ideas about perception and learning, introduced by psychologists who believed in the holistic (integrative) aspects of behavior, began to appear more frequently on the North American scene. The gestalt (meaning "form," "shape") views represented by some Europeans (people like Max Wertheimer, Kurt Koffka, Wolfgang Köhler, Kurt Goldstein, and Kurt Lewin) were shown to be pertinent also to areas of concern such as brain functioning, group dynamics, and social problems (Henle, 1977; Sears, 1975). European perspectives relevant to human development also were being introduced. For the most part, as we see later, these views also emphasized maturational (nature) components and, to some extent, clinical, nonexperimental methods. Heinz Werner (e.g., 1948) and Jean Piaget (e.g., 1923a, 1923b) were especially influential.

The outcome of this cross-fertilization of ideas about development was to reinforce, if not redefine, the evolving ideas about development in North America. Any given behavior, patterns of behaviors, or systematic changes in behavior could be explained by a number of different theories, and the various theories were advanced by respected advocates often working in the same academic contexts (Gengerelli, 1976). Thus, in American departments of psychology, developmentalists were confronted with a range of perspectives.

We suggest that such fundamental differences in approaches to, and interpretations of, behavior may have led to more serious efforts to articulate one position over another. In this way, the pluralistic situation in American academia may have fostered or strengthened interest in issues surrounding the explanation of human development. That is, the simultaneous presentation of diverse interpretations further promoted a more serious concern with theories of development. In subsequent decades conceptual and historical reviews of "child development" or "child psychology" reflect this trend (e.g., Anderson, 1956; English, 1950; Frank, 1935, 1962). This focus on theoretical and explanatory concerns continued in the post-World War II era, into the late 1950s and 1960s. The pluralism of ideas about development is especially evident in the now-classic publication, *The Concept of Development,* a collection of thematic chapters edited by Dale Harris (1957).

In an early review of the history of developmental science, Bronfenbrenner (1963) noted that from the 1930s to the early 1960s there was a continuing shift away from studies involving the mere collection of data and toward research concerned with abstract processes and constructs. Some books and essays published during this period epitomized this trend by calling for the study of developmental processes and mechanisms (e.g., Harris, 1956, 1957; McCandless & Spiker, 1956; Spiker & McCandless, 1954). Accordingly, describing the status of the field in 1963, Bronfenbrenner wrote that "first and foremost, the gathering of data for data's sake seems to have lost in favor. The major concern in today's developmental research is clearly with inferred processes and constructs" (p. 527).

Similarly, in a review almost a decade later, Looft (1972) found a continuation of the trends noted by Bronfenbrenner. Looft's review, like Bronfenbrenner's, was based on an analysis of major handbooks of developmental psychology published from the 1930s to 1972. Looft noted that a shift toward more general concerns about integrating theoretical ideas occurred after World War II, and that the trend continued through 1963 (Bronfenbrenner, 1963) to 1972. As a case in point, we may note that the editor of a 1970 handbook (Mussen, 1970) pointed out: "The major contemporary empirical and theoretical emphases in the field of developmental psychology, however, seem to be on explanations of the psychological changes that occur, the mechanisms and processes accounting for growth and development" (p. vii).

Since the early 1970s, this trend toward increasing attention to the explanation of developmental processes has continued in a number of ways. For example, considerable interest has been focused on a variety of theories, on explanations, and on processes of development. Such foci have led to the recognition that there are many adequate ways (theories) of accounting for the facts (descriptions) of development. This pluralistic perspective implies further that theory and data should be evaluated in terms of each other. A second aspect of this trend toward increasing explanatory considerations may be seen in an examination of the most recent compilations of research and theory. For example, in the fourth edition of the *Handbook of Child Psychology,* the first volume (Mussen & Kessen, 1983) is devoted to historical, theoretical, and methodological issues, topics not even juxtaposed in a single section of previous editions. Other prominent collections, such as the *Advances in Child Development and Behavior* series (edited by H. W. Reese), the *Life-Span Development and Behavior* series (edited by P. B. Baltes, D. L. Feathermen, & R. M.

Lerner), and the *Handbook of the Psychology of Aging* (edited by J. E. Birren & K. W. Schaie) evince similar trends.

The interest in conceptual and methodological issues has itself generated considerable scholarship. In particular, the theoretical and metatheoretical bases on which individual development is studied and interpreted became a focus of investigation (e.g., Overton, 1984, 1991; Overton & Reese, 1973; Reese, 1976; Reese & Overton, 1970; van Geert, 1991). Following the work of such philosophers as Kuhn (1970) and Pepper (1942), Reese and Overton (1970; Overton & Reese, 1973, 1981) identified two major philosophical models that provide the basis for many extant assumptions about human development. These models provide a set of assumptions, or metatheoretical ideas, about human nature and thereby influence lower order theoretical and methodological statements.

The two models discussed by Reese and Overton (1970) were termed *organicism* and *mechanism*. The organismic position stresses the qualitative features of developmental change and the active contribution of the organism's processes in these changes. The theories of Piaget (e.g., 1970) and to some extent of Freud (e.g., 1954) are examples of such organismically oriented approaches. In contrast, the mechanistic position stresses quantitative change and the active contribution of processes lying outside the primary control of the organism (e.g., in the external stimulus environment) as the major source of development. The behavioral analysis theories of Bijou (1976) and of Bijou and Baer (1961) are a major example of such mechanistically oriented approaches. We discuss these metatheories in greater detail later.

Again, on the basis of some established ideas in the philosophy and history of science, discussion occurred concerning the "family of theories" associated with each model (Reese & Overton, 1970). For instance, as we previously noted, there are at least two types of organismically oriented theories, those of Freud and those of Piaget. Although there are differences among family members (Freud emphasized social and personality development and Piaget emphasized cognitive development), there is greater similarity among the theories within a family (e.g., the common stress on the qualitative, stagelike nature of development) than there is between theories associated with different families (e.g., mechanistically oriented theories would deny the importance, indeed the reality, of qualitatively different stages of development). Due to the philosophically based differences between families of theories derived from the organismic and the mechanistic models, the period since the early 1970s has involved several discussions about the different stances regarding an array of key conceptual issues of development. Examples are the nature and nurture bases of development (Lehrman, 1970; Lerner, 1978; Overton, 1973); the quality, openness, and continuity of change (Brim & Kagan, 1980; Looft, 1973);

appropriate methods of studying development (Baltes, Reese, & Nessel-roade, 1977; Nesselroade & Baltes, 1979; Wohlwill, 1991); and ultimately, the alternative truth criteria for establishing the "facts" of development (Dixon & Nesselroade, 1983; Overton & Reese, 1973; Reese & Overton, 1970).

This awareness of the philosophical bases of developmental theory, method, and data contributed in the 1970s and 1980s to the consideration of additional models appropriate to the study of psychological development. In part, this consideration developed as a consequence of interest in integrating assumptions associated with theories derived from organismic and mechanistic models (Looft, 1973). For instance, Riegel (1973, 1975, 1976) attempted to apply a historical model of development that seemed to include some features of organicism (e.g., active organism) and some features of mechanism (e.g., active environment). However, there was an interest in continual, reciprocal relations between an active organism and its active context (and not in either element per se) and with these relations as they exist on all phenomenal levels of analysis. These interests were labeled in different ways in the human development literature. For example, such terms as *dialectical* (Riegel, 1975, 1976), *transactional* (Sameroff, 1975), *relational* (Looft, 1973), and *dynamic interactional* (Lerner, 1978, 1979) have been used. In a similar way, a number of theorists have explored the application of contextual and developmental contextual perspectives (Bei-lin, 1984; Lerner, 1986, 1989; Lerner, Hultsch, & Dixon, 1983; Rosnow & Georgoudi, 1986).

By the end of the 1970s, developmental psychology had evolved into a field marked by not one but several explanatory theories. This theoretical pluralism (or multiplicity of reasonable theoretical alternatives) continues to exist today (Cavanaugh, 1991; Dixon & Nesselroade, 1983). An interesting paradox exists, however, one that leads to both similarities and differences among the present major theoretical systems in developmental psychology. Although these systems differ in the superordinate philosophical models that they represent, as well as in their respective definitions of development, variables, and problems of interest, and their methods of research, to a great extent all share a common intellectual heritage: All have been influenced by theories of temporal progression or evolution, with perhaps the historically most notable exemplar being Darwinism.

In the next section of this chapter, we suggest that historical and evolutionary theories (particularly Darwinism) have provided some intellectual basis for five different theoretical systems in developmental psychology. This is the case despite the frequent misuse and misunderstanding of Darwinism evident in the early literature (cf. Charlesworth, 1986; Dixon & Lerner, 1985; Ghiselin, 1986). First, the influence of 19th-century evolutionary thought on the *organismic model* may be traced from the work of

G. Stanley Hall, James Mark Baldwin, Pierre Janet, and Arnold Gesell, to the continuing influential work of Jean Piaget and Heinz Werner. Second, the related *psychodynamic model* developed in a less direct fashion from the work of Sigmund Freud and Carl Jung to that of Erik Erikson. Third, Wilhelm Preyer and Sir Francis Galton, some of the later aspects of the work of G. S. Hall, and John B. Watson, contributed to the development of the *mechanistic model.* The *dialetical model,* influenced by G. W. F. Hegel and Karl Marx, was later developed more specifically by Lev S. Vygotsky and Klaus F. Riegel. *Contextualism* derived from the turn-of-the-century American pragmatic philosophers, most notably William James, Charles Sanders Peirce, John Dewey, and G. H. Mead. Thus, one way in which we can understand the present meaning of each of these different theoretical systems in developmental psychology is to appreciate some commonalities in their intellectual heritage and the historical trajectories they followed in developing away from one another. To understand the influence of evolutionary theories on developmental psychology it is useful first to consider the historical setting within which the most prominent evolutionary theory was developed.

EVOLUTIONARY THEORY AND THE EMERGENCE OF DEVELOPMENTAL PSYCHOLOGY

Early Work on the Concept of Development

It is impossible to understand either the genesis or the eventual impact of evolutionary theory (and in particular, Darwinism) without understanding the interest among 18th- and 19th-century intellectuals in the topic of history (Dixon & Lerner, 1985; Eiseley, 1958; Vidal, Buscaglia, & Vonèche, 1983; Wertheimer, 1985). In his intellectual history of the 19th century, Mandelbaum (1971) observed:

> It is generally agreed that one of the most distinctive features of nineteenth-century thought was the widespread interest evinced in history. The manifestations of this interest are not only found in the growth and diversification of professional historical scholarship, but in the tendency to view all of reality, and all of man's achievements, in terms of the category of development. (p. 41)

The category of development implies that an adequate understanding of any phenomenon (biological or philosophical) requires that it be considered in terms of its position in the present situation and its role in a continuous developmental or historical process. As Mandelbaum (1971) described it, the concern is not with the "nature of the event itself, [but] . . . with its place in some process of change" (p. 46). Events have no autonomous existence (and, especially, no independent meaning) outside of the role they play in the stream of history. In the human sciences, where the events of concern are sociohistorical in nature (e.g., wars and plagues), the province of general human history is indicated; where the events are of an individual nature (e.g., the onset of logical thinking, puberty, or marriage), the province of individual human history, or developmental psychology, is implied.

In general, during the late 18th and early 19th centuries, the concept of development received attention on two fronts, both of which helped to influence the emergence of developmental psychology. The thrust of the interest in the idea of development (and individual development in particular) was an ongoing attempt by researchers in a variety of disciplines to understand humanity in a temporal and historical context. On the philosophical front, this involved a dynamic, dialectical theory of history, such as the ideal philosophy of G. W. F. Hegel (1770–1831) and the material philosophy of Karl Marx (1818–1883). On the scientific front, the interest in development was manifested in two mutually influential areas of investigation. On the one hand, there were the notions of natural history informed by research in geology; of particular note in this regard was the gradual and developmental method of Sir Charles Lyell (1797–1875). On the other hand, there were various biological theories of evolution, especially those of Jean Baptiste de Lamarck (1744–1829), Charles Darwin (1809–1882), and Herbert Spencer (1820–1903; see Richards, 1987).

Prior to the 19th century, most efforts to understand human development did not result in sustained developmental psychologies. Many such efforts derived primarily from philosophical, literary, or theological domains. From Aristotle (384 B.C.–332 B.C.) through St. Augustine (354–430) to William Shakespeare (1564–1616) and Jean-Jacques Rousseau (1712–1778), many important thinkers wrote about the ages or stages of human life, often speculating on their unique needs and purposes (Dennis, 1972). It was not until the 18th and the early 19th century, however, that these theoretical perspectives were attached to systematically empirical investigations.

The 19th century has often been viewed as a formative period in the emergence of developmental psychology (Baltes, 1983; Cairns, 1983; Dixon & Lerner, 1985; Groffman, 1970; Reinert, 1979; Wertheimer, 1985). In addition to the influence of evolutionary theory, several advances occurred in this and in the late part of the preceding century. Especially notable early contributors include the following: (a) Dietrich Tiedemann (1748–1803), who, in 1787, produced the first psychological diary of the growth of a young child (see Murchison & Langer, 1927); (b) Friedrich August Carus (1770–1808), who endeavored to develop a comprehensive age-oriented science; (c) Carl Gustav Carus (1789–1869), who argued for the application of the developmental method to a broad range of psychological issues (Köhler, 1985); (d) Adolphe Quetelet (1796–1874), who produced highly advanced methods to disentangle the multiple influences on the course of human development; and (e) Johann Nikolas Tetens (1736–1807), who argued for natural scientific methods to guide the search for general laws regarding human development from birth to death (Müller-Brettel & Dixon, 1990; Tetens, 1777).

In addition, in the 19th century numerous "baby biographies" began to appear. Such ontogenetic observational studies often took the form of diaries written by scientist–parents describing the successive achievements of a child (often their own). For example, Darwin kept such a diary of his infant son's growth during the years from 1840 to 1841; this was not published, however, until 1877, when it appeared as an article, "Biographical Sketch of an Infant," in the journal *Mind* (Darwin, 1877). Many other baby biographies appeared around the turn of the century (e.g., Braunshvig & Braunshvig, 1913; Champneys, 1881; Hall, 1891b; Moore, 1896; Perez, 1878; Prior, 1895; Shinn, 1893–1899, 1900; Simpson, 1893; Sully, 1903). Shinn's (1893–1899, 1900) work with her niece was perhaps especially well known, for she made comparisons with the methods and results of other, similar research. This biographically oriented activity continued through (and in some cases beyond) the 1930s (Bühler, 1930; Dennis, 1949, 1951; Jaeger, 1985).

In the next subsection we describe more completely the impact of evolutionary theory on the study of psychological development (see Butterworth, Rutkowska, & Scaife, 1985; Lickliter & Berry, 1990). Before doing so, however, it may be useful to reiterate that developmental psychology did not arise solely as a function of evolutionary theory. As Peters (1965) suggested, evolutionary theory was useful in preparing the way for a scientific analysis of change (or progress) and of continuity, both between human and animal and between adult and child. But there was also a quite practical social influence that consisted of pressure applied by educational administrators and social planners concerned with the large-scale education of a growing population of children (see also Borstelmann, 1983). Such a development served to focus institutional attention on the practical issues of ontogenesis (Sears, 1975; Siegel & White, 1982). These practical concerns continued to be influential in the 20th century, as evidenced by the (a) founding of numerous child welfare and research centers (Frank, 1962; Sears, 1975), and (b) continued study of the application of developmental theories to human development intervention (e.g., Montada & Schmitt, 1982; Sigel, 1972; Turner & Reese, 1980).

Darwin and the Theory of Evolution

Charles Darwin played perhaps the exemplary role in the emergence of evolutionary thinking in the 19th century, but even he was not without intellectual antecedents (Eiseley, 1958). He was influenced by a number of different people, ideas, and experiences, but two major interrelated strands should be noted. On the one hand, Darwin gathered from his own family, his life history, and his early cultural context much of the intellectual disposition that is apparently necessary to effect a massive scientific revolution and to effect the precise kind of revolution with which he was associated (Gillespie, 1979; Gruber, 1974; Manier, 1978). On the other hand, Darwin was part of an intellectual lineage that stemmed from more formal or academic sources. For example, Darwin's views about evolution were influenced by the English geologist Sir Charles Lyell, who was among the first to view natural phenomena from a historical and developmental perspective.

Darwin's model of nature, and especially his theory of evolution, served as a conceptual impetus for many fields of scholarly inquiry, including biology, philosophy, and developmental psychology (Dewey, 1910, Dixon & Lerner, 1985; Lickliter & Berry, 1990; Toulmin & Goodfield, 1965; Vidal et al., 1983). It is also apparent that Darwin developed his theory in the context of the extant philosophical and scientific models of human behavior, activity, and development. It may be inferred that there was a bidirectional relation between Darwin's theory and the theoretical ideas that have shaped developmental psychology (Vidal et al., 1983). Given that evolutionary biology and developmental psychology have similar—if not parallel—missions, it is not surprising that Darwinism had a notable impact on the emergence of the latter.

Some selected features of Darwin's theory of evolution deserve specific attention. Darwin proposed a theory of evolution in which species development occurs in gradual, continual, and adaptive steps. In other words, Darwin (1859) believed that new species emerge gradually over long periods of time; thus, there is a continuous chain of being from our now-extinct ancestors to us, a chain built on the concepts of natural selection and survival of the fittest. We explain this theory briefly by noting the meaning of these key ideas.

The environment may be portrayed as placing demands on the members of a given species. In effect, it selects individuals who possess some characteristic that contributes, for example, to the successful gathering of available nourishment. If the individual has that characteristic, the individual will fit in with its environment, obtain nourishment, and survive. If not, it will either move to another ecological setting or die. The weakest or least adaptable members of the species are unable to reach maturity and therefore to mate (Morgan, 1902). Thus, the natural setting determines which characteristics of the organism will lead to survival, and will therefore be passed on genetically. This action of the natural environment, selecting organisms for survival, is termed *natural selection* (Loewenberg, 1957; Mayr, 1977).

Hence Darwin proposed the idea of *survival of the fittest*. Organisms that possess characteristics that fit the survival requirements for a particular environmental setting will survive in the sense of successfully passing on their genes. In other words, certain characteristics in certain settings have fundamental biological significance; that is, they allow the organism to survive. Naturally selected characteristics that meet the demands of the environment (and so allow survival) are adaptive, or functional, characteristics.

In an evolutionary sense, something is functional if it is adaptive; that is, if it has been naturally selected to aid survival (Gould & Vrba, 1982). Thus, the structure of an organism (its physical makeup, its constitution, its morphological or bodily characteristics) may be functional. Although Darwin emphasized the function of physical structures of species in 1859, he later (Darwin, 1872) pointed out that behavior too has survival value. Showing the emotion of fear when a dangerous bear approaches and being able to learn to avoid certain stimuli (e.g., poisonous snakes) and to approach others (e.g., food) are examples of behaviors that would be adaptive; they would further the individual's chances for survival.

Thus, mental activity and behavior also have a function (Stout & Baldwin, 1902). The function of behavior became the focus of much social scientific concern. This concern was reflected in the ideas of those interested in the evolution (phylogeny) of behavior. In addition, the idea was promoted that those behavior changes characterizing ontogeny could be understood on the basis of adaptation. Although occasionally misrepresented and misunderstood, the adaptive role of behavior thus became a concern providing a basis for all American psychology (White, 1968); it has played a major part in the ideas of theorists as diverse as James (1890), Hall (1904), Freud (1954), Piaget (1950), Erikson (1959), and Skinner (1938, 1950). Indeed, a functional and neofunctional view of developmental psychology continues to reflect this concern (e.g., Beilin, 1984; Dixon & Baltes, 1986).

Peters (1965) indicated that, prior to Darwin, emphasis was placed on differences between human and animal on the one hand, and adult and child on the other. After Darwin's argument for continuity in the former case, emphasis in human study shifted to the detection and consideration of similarities between adult and child. Peters (1965) summarized the sentiment of this period: "And if under the influence of theology, men had tended to say before Darwin: 'What a piece of work is man,' they would now tend to say, under the influence of biology: 'How wonderful are children and the beasts of the field' " (p. 732). Darwin (1871) suggested that there is substantial similarity (as well as dissimilarity) and continuity (as well as discontinuity) among several species and between the adult and child of a given species. For this reason, the absolute, ahistorical view of both present species and the adult form of a given species was called into question (Richards, 1982). Whether on the species or individual level, it became theoretically and methodologically important to consider a present form (or phenomenon) as having developed from a succession of earlier forms, and being likely to continue to develop into future forms. We refer to this perspective as the developmental tradition or approach. Although Darwin's own view emphasized continuous or gradual change, other evolutionary theories have emphasized discontinuous or qualitative change (e.g., Costall, 1986; Toulmin & Goodfield, 1965).

We now consider how the general impetus provided by the active intellectual milieu of the 19th century, and especially evolutionary theory, led to the multiplicity of theories we find in developmental psychology today.

ROOTS OF CONTEMPORARY THEORIES IN DEVELOPMENTAL PSYCHOLOGY

To some extent, all extant metatheoretical, and derivative theoretical, views about human development were influenced by, or progressed through, the prism of 19th-century historical or evolutionary thinking. We have noted that there are presently at least five major models of developmental psychology, and we suggest that these models share some strands of their heritage. Although there are originating figures for each of these models, there is no single originating figure for all of developmental psychology. Notably, however, Darwinism — whether accurately or inaccurately understood, whether accepted entirely or rejected in part — was considered by the major early representatives of many modern theories in the discipline (Angell, 1912; Dixon & Lerner, 1985; Kirkpatrick, 1909; Lickliter & Berry, 1990; Misiak & Sexton, 1966; Vidal et al., 1983; White, 1968; Wohlwill, 1973).

Some Important Caveats

There are a number of ways to represent the history of a complex science such as developmental psychology. Histories of sciences can be (and have been) written in numerous ways, ranging from conceptual histories (histories of ideas and concepts in which personalities may play a subservient role) to "great person" or "great event" histories (emphasizing the major characters or events populating the centuries). We have chosen a middle ground, in that we have adopted one broad conceptual organization of the field (the five major models) consistent with some recent theoretical treatments (e.g., Lerner, 1986). We have identified some (but not all) of the major thinkers active within each of the conceptual categories, and discussed briefly (a) their major ideas and research emphases, and (b) where they might fit in the chronological history of the model. A detailed history of each conceptual category would, of course, be a worthwhile endeavor, but this is beyond the mission of our chapter. Thus, our historical treatment of each of the metatheories is incomplete; learned observers of given models are advised that it is possible to note occasional omissions of people, ideas, or events. For example, our discussion of philosophers who contributed to the conceptual foundations of the various models of development has been curtailed (see Pepper, 1942; Reese & Overton, 1970).

On the other hand, we have tried to minimize the errors of commission. To this end, we would like to clarify our focus on the 19th century and, in particular, evolutionary theory as a "starting point" in the history of developmental psychology. Several important reservations should be noted.

First, we have already mentioned the fact that Darwin is by no means the original evolutionist (Richards, 1987; Ruse, 1979; Toulmin & Goodfield, 1965). He may be, however, the evolutionist with the single greatest influence on the emergence of a scientific developmental approach to studying humans. Second, and related to the first reservation, we have seen that several developmental psychologists antedated Darwin; for better or for worse, however, these figures were not major influences in the emergence of the field of developmental psychology. Third, we propose that the intellectual climate of historical or evolutionary thinking — a climate that, as we have seen, both preceded Darwin and gained impetus from him and that, in some ways, was epitomized by him — is an originative intellectual core of developmental psychology. This is not tantamount to suggesting that Darwin himself was the single generating figure in developmental psychology. For simplicity, on some occasions we generalize our use of the term *Darwinian* to indicate the temporalizing of scientific theories and methods that occurred during the rise of evolutionary thought.

Fourth, we do not propose that all present versions of developmental psychology embrace a Darwinian evolutionism, for, as we see later, this is simply not the case. Nevertheless, in the developmental tradition there is a stress on the history of the organism, a focus on the functional, adaptive features of behavioral and mental ontogeny, and an interest in the study of the role of the environment or context in such ontogeny (see Lerner, 1986). This is a tradition propagated in part by Darwin, and it is present in all current major systems. Thus, although the present (or even early) representatives of the existing models may not have produced (or even endorsed) developmental theories that are truly Darwinian (Dixon & Lerner, 1985; Ghiselin, 1986) an influence may still be identifiable. Indeed, the connection between what we see as key features of the developmental tradition—a tradition that is present in all five models of development—and the ideas propagated by Darwin allows us to argue for his seminal role.

Fifth, we should note that there were, of course, other sources of influence on today's developmental theories and metatheories. These other influences account for many specific features of the different approaches to developmental psychology. This is an important caveat, for some researchers may argue, for example, that Darwinian mechanisms are less active agents of change in adulthood (and thus less influential in the development of their field) than other more sociocultural or individual goal-directed models of change (some of which, indeed, predate Darwin). This latter qualification may apply especially to the recent life-span approach to developmental psychology, which we treat in a later section. In addition to 19th-century influences, the roots of this approach—like the roots of the models—may extend both to some of the earliest European developmental scientists mentioned previously and to philosophers of cultural and social change (Baltes, 1983; Collingwood, 1956; Nisbet, 1980; Toulmin & Goodfield, 1965). The influence of other philosophical traditions has also been explored (e.g., Chapman & Dixon, 1987; Harris, 1957).

Despite these disclaimers, we should note that other, earlier reviewers have also depicted Darwin as a point of origin for several of the major lines of thought in contemporary developmental psychology (White, 1968; Wohlwill, 1973). Indeed, White (1968) noted that each of these lines of thought apparently selected something different from the writings of the evolutionist, and it is partly due to this selection that they all developed in different fashions. As White noted, "Within 50 years after the publication of Darwin's *The Origin of Species* in 1859, the theory of evolution has crystallized its influence upon developmental psychology not once but several times. As often happens with a broad and powerful theory, different people took different messages from evolutionism and occasionally those messages could come into conflict" (1968, p. 187). Wohlwill's (1973) views about the originative nature of Darwin's thought are somewhat distinct from those of White in that Wohlwill stressed not Darwin's influence on developmental theories per se, but the contribution of Darwinian thinking to the development of metatheories. More recently, Richards (1987) delineated the many ways in which Darwinism was the fertile soil of evolutionary theories of human behavior.

Although we sketched the broad outlines of, and intellectual connections among the five metatheories in an earlier section, it is necessary to provide here a more detailed discussion in order to address each of the models separately. Although all models started with philosophers (and as, for example, *world views*), we concentrate on the developmental and empirical aspects stimulated during the 19th century. The first metatheoretical line of thought we consider is the *organismic* model. In addition to the influence of Darwin and such philosophers as Hegel, it developed out of the early work of G. Stanley Hall (1846–1924) and James Mark Baldwin (1861–1934), through Arnold Gesell (1880–1961) and Pierre Janet (1859–1947) to Jean Piaget (1896–1980) and Heinz Werner (1890–1964). A second, organismically oriented line of thought is the *psychodynamic*. Philosophically related to the work of F. W. Nietzsche (1844–1900), it stemmed from the work of Sigmund Freud (1856–1939) through Carl Jung (1875–1961) and Erik Erikson (b. 1902).

The third metatheoretical line, the *mechanistic* model, is philosophically related to the work of, for example, John Locke (1632–1704) and David Hume (1711–1776). It developed from the works of Wilhelm Preyer (1841–1897) and Sir Francis Galton (1822–1911) to the later works of G. Stanley Hall and the works of John B. Watson (1878–1958). A fourth line that is described has its principal roots in both the philosophy (Hegel, Marx) and the biology (Darwin) of the 19th century; it culminates in the *dialetical* model of developmental psychology as proposed by such Soviet psychologists as Lev S. Vygotsky (1894–1934) and A. R. Luria (1902–1977). Finally, a fifth line of thought, *contextualism,* may also be traced to Darwinism; this line was promoted by William James (1842–1910), Charles Sanders Peirce (1839–1914), John Dewey (1859–1952), and George Herbert Mead (1863–1931), the major figures of pragmatic philosophy. For heuristic purposes, we present the history of each model as a historical lineage; however, the lineages represent more the flow of ideas since Darwin than the impact of one individual on another.

Organicism

As described by Pepper (1942; see also Lerner, 1986; Overton & Reese, 1973; Reese & Overton, 1970), the organismic model was patterned after the view of biological growth that prevailed in the preceding century. That is, psychological development was thought to be goal-directed and teleological in character. Developmental change, according to this model, is characterized as qualitative rather than (or, in isolated cases, in addition to) quantitative, and as unidirectional and irreversible. Following the emphasis on qualitative changes, a stage pattern is often employed, resulting in a conception of development that is discontinuous and universal in sequence and pattern. The organism is seen as relatively active, constructing a relatively passive environment. The major figures in the emergence of this tradition of developmental psychology are thought to be linked, as shown in Row A of Fig. 1.1.

Tradition	19th Century Origins (Darwin, Evolutionary Theory, Historical Perspective)	Into the 20th Century	Late 20th Century
A. Organismic	●	(early) Hall < Baldwin / Gesell → Piaget, Werner → / Janet	Contemporary neo-Piagetians
B. Psychodynamic	●	Freud → Jung → Erikson → / Hall	Contemporary Ego and Depth Psychologists
C. Mechanistic	●	Galton / < Preyer (later) Hall → Watson →	Contemporary Mechanistic Psychologists
D. Dialectical	●	Marx → Vygotsky, Luria → Riegel → / Hegel	Contemporary Soviet and Dialectical Psychologists
E. Contextual	●	James / < Peirce Dewey → Mead, Bartlett →	Contemporary Contextual Psychologists

FIG. 1.1. Heuristic scheme representing the 19th-century origins of five metatheoretical traditions in developmental psychology.

G. Stanley Hall is one initial figure linking the elaboration of an organismically derived theory with Darwinian evolutionism. Hall organized the American Psychological Association and became its first president. He started the first American journal of psychology (aptly called *The American Journal of Psychology*), as well as the first scientific journal devoted to human development (first entitled *Pedagogical Seminary,* and then given its present name, *The Journal of Genetic Psychology*). Hall (1883) contributed one of the earliest papers on child psychology and also wrote the first text on adolescence (a two-volume work entitled *Adolescence,* 1904), as well as an often overlooked text on old age (*Senescence,* 1922). The latter testifies to his ground-breaking life-span perspective but is also an example of his later mechanistic tendencies.

One of the most prominent and influential psychologists at the turn of the century, Hall had his most specific (but not enduring) influence on developmental psychology. Hall saw development from a nativistic point of view. Although not many people (including his students) adopted his specific nature-based theory of development as such, some did follow the general developmental orientation he espoused (e.g., Arnold Gesell and Lewis Terman).

In devising his nature viewpoint, Hall was profoundly influenced by Darwin. In fact, fancying himself the "Darwin of the mind" (White, 1968), Hall attempted to translate Darwin's phylogenetic evolutionary principles into conceptions relevant to ontogeny. He did this by adapting ideas derived from those of the embryologist, Ernst Haeckel (1834–1919). Haeckel (1891) believed that an embryo's ontogenetic progression mirrored the phylogenetic history—the evolution—of its species. Thus, when one looks at the changes characterizing an individual member of a species as it progresses across its embryological period, one sees a recapitulation of the evolutionary changes of the species. In short, Haeckel was one of the prominent proponents of the notion that "ontogeny recapitulates phylogeny."

Hall applied to postnatal life the recapitulationist idea that Haeckel used for prenatal, embryological development. Arguing that during the years from birth to sexual maturity a person was repeating the history of the species, as had been done prenatally, Hall believed that the postnatal recapitulation was somewhat more limited than the prenatal (Gallatin, 1975). Furthermore, although an ardent evolutionist and a strong proponent of recapitulation theory, and so an exemplar of organismic theories, Hall nevertheless placed considerable emphasis on environmental, especially social, factors in later ontogenesis. That is, at separate points, recapitulation theory and environmental influences were incorporated into Hall's perspective, becoming one that encompassed the life span. In his attempt to extend the work of previous developmentalists beyond childhood, Hall (1904) argued that until adolescence the developing child repeats (through both play and fear) the evolution of human society. During adolescence, however, environmental factors increase their developmental significance (McCullers, 1969); this gives the latter part of Hall's ideas the mechanistic tone discussed later. Indeed, Hall believed that during adolescence genetic changes could be affected by the environment (Charles, 1970).

Arnold Gesell, whose work we described earlier, was for a time a student of Hall's at Clark University. Like Hall's other prominent student, Lewis Terman, Gesell was his heir but not his descendant (Kessen, 1965). That is, Gesell was an ardent student of child development and, although convinced of the importance of biological considerations, he distanced himself from Hall's recapitulationist ideas. Gesell's positive regard for Darwin's impact on developmental psychology can be read in his article "Charles Darwin and Child Development" (Gesell, 1939, 1948). In this article, Gesell paid tribute to Darwin's "perception of the gradual genesis of all living things, including the genesis of the human mind" (1948, p. 44). This "developmental outlook . . . led to profound revisions in the interpretation of childhood." The new revolutionary formulations, Gesell argued, influenced his own former teacher, G. S. Hall.

Gesell was a notable contributor to developmental psychology for at least three major reasons. First, his approach was consistent with the assumptions of organicism in that it focused on the biological, maturational, growthlike aspects of psychological development. In the 1920s, when the heredity–environment (or nature–nurture) issue was actively debated, Gesell (1928, 1929) argued for the predominance of nature (heredity), even adopting some teleological (goal-directed and -oriented) language. Second, Gesell, who was a thorough methodologist, was an assiduous observer of change patterns, and thus a prodigious contributor of normative growth tables and descriptions. Third, it should be noted that Gesell, as a methodologist, made at least two lasting contributions: (a) he was an early and active proponent of the use of "cinema records" (a forerunner of videotapes) in the study of children, and (b) he was an early advocate of twin studies in disentangling the influences of nature and nurture. For these reasons, Gesell continues to be remembered in contemporary treatments of the history (e.g., Cairns, 1983) and theories (e.g., Lerner, 1986) of developmental psychology.

Like Hall, James Mark Baldwin is difficult to classify in purely organismic terms. There are two major intellectual sources to Baldwin's (e.g., 1895, 1906) developmental psychology. Fundamentally a Darwinian evolutionist, he was also influenced by British empiricism and associationism (see Baldwin, 1913). The former influence is manifested most positively by Baldwin's devotion to a Darwinian psychology (Baldwin, 1909; Richards, 1987; Russett, 1976) and, less positively, by his endorsement of recapitulation theory, although some authors suggest that Baldwin managed to avoid a thorough parallelism between phylogeny and ontogeny (Reinert, 1979). Baldwin was influenced by Wilhelm Preyer's developmental study of his son's infancy, but also by the later birth of his own two children (Richards, 1987). The British influence is revealed through his stimulus–response system based on pleasure and pain. Baldwin saw the child as developing from the simple to the more complex, first through an instinctive biological stage and second through a plastic or learning stage. The social system, especially the interactions between the child and this system (Cairns & Ornstein, 1979), was seen as a critical feature of ontogenesis.

Although some of Baldwin's work appears to be antithetical to organismic theory, his endorsement of the development method (Baldwin, 1930), and his leadership (with G. S. Hall) of the developmental psychology movement, assure him a place in the history of organicism. Moreover, much of his work prefigures the assimilation–accommodation theory of Piaget (Broughton, 1981; Piaget, 1982; Reinert, 1979; Ross & Kerst, 1978) and has been firmly placed in the history of genetic epistemology, the theory of knowledge most appropriate to organismic thinkers (Wozniak, 1982). Several recent reviewers have explored the influence of Baldwin on Piaget (e.g., Broughton, 1981; Cahan, 1984; Cairns, 1980; see also several contributors to Broughton & Freeman-Moir, 1982). Although there is considerable overlap in the assumptions and approaches of Baldwin and Piaget, Cahan (1984) pointed also to some important differences. Both proffer models of developmental sequences (or stages), but Baldwin's approach was more attentive to the dialectical interplay between the social and individual aspects of intellectual development. This attention is not sufficient to remove him from the organismic camp, for he was less mechanistic and dialectical than his contemporaries. For example, his speculations on the biological nature of at least early behavioral development often led to criticism from (mechanistic) experimentalists who thought that his questionnaires and experimental studies were not a sufficient basis on which to found a developmental psychology. In complementary fashion, Baldwin expressed doubt that a mechanistic account would ever succeed.

Rather more isolated from mainstream developmental psychology than either Hall or Baldwin, Pierre Janet developed a historical (or developmental) clinical psychology (Mayo, 1952). He viewed the life course as a succession of adaptive moments, each of which could influence the long-range adjustment of the individual (Janet, 1930). An evolutionary concept of psychic tension, together with the developmental method of, for example, Baldwin, informed Janet's approach to the study of the development of human action and behavior (Sjövall, 1967). To understand the psychological conditions of adulthood, according to this approach, the investigator must also explore the childhood and adolescent history of the individual (Mayo, 1952). The mental life of the organism is seen as both active and passive (reflective). Piaget took courses from Janet, and it has been noted that Janet had an active appreciation of Baldwin (Mueller, 1976). Indeed, it may have been through Janet that Piaget was most influenced by Baldwin (Cairns & Ornstein, 1979; Mueller, 1976; Piaget, 1978). It should be noted that Janet also had an impact on Freud.

Although only some of Piaget's early work cites Baldwin (see Piaget, 1923a, 1923b, 1932), his later publications contain ample acknowledgment of Baldwin's influences (Cairns & Ornstein, 1979; Evans, 1973; Langer, 1969; Piaget, 1978, 1982; White, 1977; Wozniak, 1982). In an interview late in his life, Piaget acknowledged he had closely read Baldwin's main work (Vonèche, 1982). Among other things, Piaget may have taken from Baldwin an interest in such processes as imitation and play. Further, according to McCullers (1969), Piaget's early work contains some endorsement of a modified recapitulation theory (later termed *correspondence theory;* Gould, 1977). Like Baldwin, Piaget proposed a qualitative stage model of the development of the individual's interpretation of reality. But, as alluded to earlier, Piaget's stage model was more completely organismic than Baldwin's, for Piaget emphasized the active, unfolding nature of intellectual development. Nevertheless, numerous reviewers have noted that Piaget's (1972) developmental psychology was anticipated by Baldwin (Wozniak, 1982). Still, it is important to note that the early Piaget accords less emphasis to the influence of the social environment on an individual's development.

As noted earlier, Piaget's theory of the development of cognition was known in North America in the 1920s (Piaget, 1923a). It is unclear why his theory and research were generally ignored until the late 1950s (Flavell, 1963). Some observers have speculated that the reason may lie in the "clinical," nonexperimental nature of his research methods, his nonstatistical style of data analysis, or the abstract constructs with which he was concerned, all of which ran counter to predominant trends in the United States. Perhaps due to the European intellectual influences on American thinking occurring from events related to World War II, greater attention was given by Americans to the intellectual resources coming from and present in Europe. Thus, Piaget was "rediscovered," and in the 1960s achieved prominence in American developmental psychology. Indeed, his influence continues to the time of this writing, as a result both of further substantiation of portions of his theory, and of promoting discussions of alternative (but still organismic) theoretical conceptualizations (Brainerd, 1978; Chapman, 1988a; Kuhn, this volume; Overton & Newman, 1982; Siegel & Brainerd, 1977). For example, theoretical issues of the relation between cognitive development and epistemology (or theory of knowledge) have been explored by several contributors to books edited by Mischel (1971) and by Kitchener (1986). In addition, that oft-cited gap in Piaget's theory—pertaining to the relation between social and individual cognitive development—has been explored recently (e.g., Chapman, 1988b; Flavell & Ross, 1981; Overton, 1983; Wapner, Kaplan, & Cohen, 1973).

Due to Piaget's centrality in modern organismic metatheory, most of the introductory comments to this section are directly applicable to his developmental psychology (see also Kuhn, this volume). In the present context we cannot completely represent the thinkers who influenced him (they range from philosophers such as Hegel and Kant to biologists such as Lamarck and Darwin). Indeed, it should be noted that, partly because of his affinity to Hegel, some aspects of his thought are distinctly dialectical (Reese, 1986). Piaget wrote voluminously, and his work has served as a framework for his many followers in the United States and Europe (see Kuhn, this volume). His influence has been felt in educational practice (primarily dealing with young children), psychological research (on cognitive development through adolescence), and philosophy (e.g., epistemology). Although continually criticized, amended, and extended, the Piagetian organismic model has become somewhat institutionalized in contemporary developmental psychology (Liben, 1981). One unresolved issue is whether Piaget's (1983) theory is a life-span theory. Recently, some notable efforts have been made to examine the Piagetian perspective in terms of its application to adult cognitive development (e.g., Labouvie-Vief, 1980, 1982, 1986). A critical issue is whether there is additional qualitative (or structural) change after formal operations, the final stage in Piaget's model. Several more recent examples of this direction of theory and research may be found in Commons, Sinnott, Richards, and Armon (1989; see also Rybash, Hoyer, & Roodin, 1986).

Werner's (1948) orthogenetic principle—that development proceeds from a lack of differentiation to increasing differentiation, integration, and hierarchic organization—was anticipated by Baldwin and supported by embryology (Langer, 1969). His early work (e.g., his introductory book on developmental psychology, first published in German in 1926) was influenced by the developmental–holistic psychology of Felix Krueger (Baltes, 1983; Werner, 1948, 1957). In keeping with his conviction that it is not appropriate to systematize developmental theory (because it is a way of viewing behavior in general), Werner did not generate a methodical scheme of developmental psychology. In his later writing (e.g., 1957), he considered recapitulation theory (in particular, G. S. Hall's version) and rejected it. He was, however, willing to accept a parallel between evolutionary development and ontogenetic development, but not a one-to-one correspondence (see Brent, 1978). Nevertheless, his concept of development is clearly biological and maturational. The orthogenetic principle implies that development is directional and unilinear (Werner, 1957). Werner argues, as well, that any evolutionary or developmental process tends toward stabilization, thus adding a teleological (goal-oriented) component to his model. It is apparent, however, that Werner considered as well a number of contextual, nonorganismic factors to be influential in change (1957; see also Lerner, 1986; Wapner et al., 1973). For example, Wapner and colleagues examined the role of the physical environment in influencing individual development.

Although Freud was eclectic, his theoretical position (Freud, 1954) is, in many ways, an organismic one akin to that of Piaget (1970; see also Fast, 1985). Nevertheless, it is sufficiently distinct to merit attention as a line of thought independent of organicism per se (Wohlwill, 1973).

The Psychodynamic Tradition

The organismic, dynamic psychology of Sigmund Freud (1954) did not emerge until the last few years of the 19th century (Freud, 1910, 1938). Developmental change is viewed as qualitative and stagelike, proceeding through tension resolution from one stage to the next. Generally, a direction of development is implied; that is, there is an end state toward which development progresses. The psychodynamic tradition shares this teleological perspective with organicism. Unlike the typical organismic model, however, regression (movement back through earlier stages) is possible and, in some cases, frequent. The focus of attention is on emotional and personality development (especially abnormal personality), with only secondary interest given to cognitive progression (Wolff, 1960). The proposed line of influence is shown in Fig. 1.1 (Row B).

According to Groffman (1970), "The psychoanalysts were usually outsiders [to the developmental tradition]. As physicians they were confronted mainly with the psychological disorders of adult persons. . . . It is doubtful whether [Freud] was influenced by early developmental psychology" (p. 62).

Somewhat to the contrary, however, McCullers (1969) argued that Freud may have been influenced by G. S. Hall, especially in light of the former's active endorsement of recapitulation theory in such seminal works as *Totem and Taboo* (Freud, 1961; first published in 1913), *Introductory Lectures on Psychoanalysis* (Freud, 1966; first published in 1916), and *Moses and Monotheism* (Freud, 1939), and the fact that Freud visited Hall in 1909, at the 20th anniversary of Clark University (of which Hall was then president). This was the only time that Freud visited the United States, and it resulted in the establishment of a long-term correspondence between Hall and Freud (Freud, 1938). It appears that Freud was influenced by Darwin, at least in some respects; for example, he credited Darwin (along with the German philosopher and poet Goethe) for his decision to enter medical school (Jones, 1961; Schur, 1972).

Sulloway (1982) explored specifically the biological influences on Freud's theory of psychosexual development. Sulloway argued that Freud's former friend and colleague, Wilhelm Fliess (1858–1928) was instrumental in articulating the relevance of evolutionary theory to Freud. Again, like G. S. Hall, Freud was an adherent to Haeckel's recapitulation theory (the biogenetic law). Freud's endorsement of this law was in part a result of his early training as a biologist, at a time when this perspective was influential (Gould, 1977). Indeed, in his first year of medical school, Freud enrolled in a class on biology and Darwinism taught by Carl Claus, an adherent of Darwin and of Haeckel's theory (Schur, 1972). Although the biogenetic law was discredited as being justified more by Lamarckian than by Darwinian evolutionary theory (Gillispie, 1968; Lovejoy, 1968), Freud's developmental theories had already absorbed certain features. For example, Sulloway (1982) argued that the universal character of Freud's developmental theories can be attributed to his understanding of the biogenetic law. It was virtually impossible to abandon, even if he had wanted to, certain features of his theory that were influenced by biogenetic assumptions. Moreover, Sulloway asserted that it is possible

to trace many of the most basic psychoanalytic concepts to Freud's prior thinking along biological lines. Included among these psychobiological aspects of Freudian theory are the notion of infantile sexuality, particularly its polymorphously perverse and periodic (schubweise) nature; the theory of erotogenic zones; sexual latency; sublimation; reaction formation; critical stages in psychosexual development; and the theories of fixation, regression, the death instinct, and organic repression. (p. 212)

In addition, Groffman (1970) pointed out that although it was Quetelet who helped make it clear that behavioral changes were, in part, a result of the interaction between the individual and his or her social and cultural context, it was psychoanalysis that brought this relation into focus in developmental research. It is worth noting that such a characterization of environment–organism interaction (minus the Lamarckian view of inheritance) is not antithetical to Darwin's evolutionary theory (Lerner, 1986). Certainly Freud adopted a developmental approach to understanding his preferred domain of psychological phenomena. In addition, psychoanalytic theory delineates two major mechanisms (fixation and regression) through which early events influence or determine later behavior (Cairns & Ornstein, 1979).

Another potential, albeit indirect, Darwinian connection may also exist in that Sir Francis Galton (Darwin's cousin) appears to have anticipated Freud in one important way. Galton (1883) described mental operations and incidents that may appear in childhood and then lie dormant for years, until roused to consciousness. Alternatively, permanent traces of these incidents may continually influence the development of mental operations throughout life. This notion, which appeared prior to Freud, bears a striking resemblance to Freud's theory of the unconscious. It should be noted, however, that the notion of the unconscious had been around at least since the time of the philosopher, Arthur Schopenhauer (1788–1860), with a major 19th-century work devoted to this topic appearing first in 1868 with several subsequent editions (Hartmann, 1931). One other indirect linkage between Darwin and Freud can be noted. It has been claimed that Darwin influenced Baldwin, who in turn influenced Janet and Piaget. As it happens, Freud is a minor figure in this equation, for he shared a direct intellectual ancestor with Janet. Both Freud and Janet studied under Jean Martin Charcot (1825–1893) in Paris (Flugel, 1933).

Groffman, following C. Hall and Lindzey (1957), viewed Freud's psychosexual theory of development as partly mechanistic and partly Darwinian: "[Freud's] theory of personality development was basically a theory of the development of the libido, which he attempted to explain in terms of both a phylogenetic and ontogenetic process" (Groffman, 1970, p. 61). Significant events in the life course (or significant confrontations) disposed people to particular developmental paths.

One of Freud's early followers, Carl Jung, became one of his most distinguished critics, and one of the most notable contributors to psychodynamic developmental theory. According to Havighurst (1973), "Disciples of Jung generally claim that his personality theory was more 'developmental' than that of Freud" (p. 19). Although Havighurst (correctly) disputed the developmental claim with regard to Jung—calling Jung's theories more a "philosophy of life than a theory of life-span development" (1973, p. 61)— he did not question the aptness of the comparison. Jung's developmental psychology was more explicit, if not more refined, than Freud's.

Jung criticized both Freud's model of psychosexual development (as too reductionistic) and the Christian view of personal transformation (as lacking applicability to rational modern man), and proposed an individuation process consisting of four stages. Based on this rather teleological perspective, such development has as its goal the emergence of self. Jung, taking an explicit life-course perspective and also adopting a recapitulation view, was seen by McCullers (1969) as more closely parallel to Hall than to Freud.

Like Freud, Jung was a lifelong supporter of recapitulation theory (Gould, 1977; Jung, 1916). For Jung, few psychopathologies were developed during the childhood period of recapitulation. As did Freud, Jung had a potential source of Darwinian thinking inculcated through a reliance on the work of Galton. In his early work Jung employed the method of associative word reaction that had been invented by Galton and Wundt (Flugel, 1933). Whereas the latter two researchers were primarily interested in intellectual factors related to word association, Jung demonstrated that the affective dimension was also influential.

Jung was one of several major revisionists of Freudian psychodynamic theory. Other influential figures include Alfred Adler (1870–1937), Karen Horney (1885–1952), Eric Fromm (1900–1980), and Harry Stack Sullivan (1892–1949). Modern psychodynamic views of development are represented by Erik Erikson, who developed a life-span theory of personality. His theory, revolving around a set of sequential psychosocial tasks (note again the confrontation between organism and environment), is also a stage theory (see Emmerich, 1968; Erikson, 1950, 1959). His organismically oriented views have begun to influence some conceptions of cognition and adjustment in later adulthood. His view of wisdom, for example, suggests that wisdom is a virtue emerging after the successful mastery of earlier life tasks (Erikson, 1968). Although it is clearly clothed in developmental terms — because it may appear in earlier stages of life as an expression of the contingencies of that level of development — wisdom, like most concepts in the psychodynamic model, is largely restricted to the realm of personal and emotional development. Nevertheless, Erikson's perspective has inspired some generalized inquiry into the cognitive aspects of wisdom and other such potentially progressive forms of adult development (e.g., Clayton & Birren, 1980). Indeed, much psychodynamically inspired life-span developmental work has appeared in recent years. For example, both Levinson and colleagues (Levinson, Darrow, Klein, Levinson, & McKee, 1978) and R. Gould (1978) have made considerable progress in understanding the dynamics of personal change in adulthood.

Mechanism

The mechanistic model represents the organism as analogous to a machine in that it is composed of discrete parts interrelated by forces in a space–time field (see Overton & Reese, 1973; Pepper, 1942; Reese & Overton, 1970). Behavioral change or development depends on the level of stimulation, the kind of stimulation, and the history of the organism. The organism is seen as relatively passive (or reactive), whereas its environment is considered relatively active. In this way, behavioral functioning is a result more of environmental forces than of intrinsic (organismic, psychodynamic) causes. Moreover, behavioral change is more quantitative, additive, and continuous, than purposive, qualitative, and structural. The major figures in the progression of this model are shown in Row C of Fig. 1.1.

Preyer (1882, 1893), Galton (1883), and Watson (1924, 1926) were early figures in the emergence of the mechanistic view of the science of developmental psychology. Preyer's 1882 German publication, later translated as *The Mind of the Child,* was the first book devoted to a systematic consideration of the development of the mental faculties of the child. Despite the mixed reviews received by the book, responsibility for the advent of developmental psychology is often assigned to it (Eckardt, 1985; Hardesty, 1976; Reinert, 1979). Although he devoted much attention to patterns of physical development, Preyer also comments on such psychological phenomena as reflexes, language, spatial knowledge, and memory. Primarily a physiologist, Preyer was also influenced by extant work in psychoanalysis and evolutionary theory (Eckardt, 1985; Jaeger, 1982; Richards, 1987; Tobach, 1983, 1985). Late in his life, Preyer (1896) published a biography of Darwin, in which he extolled the discovery of the developmental method; that is, the attempt to understand current phenomena through an examination of the processes through which they came to be. The influence of evolutionary theory can be seen, however, not only in the developmental approach of his research, but also in the comparative methods he adopted. Preyer (1882) argued for intraindividual (longitudinal), interindividual (e.g., cross-sectional), and interspecies comparisons. The influence of the biology of the day can also be seen in Preyer's work insofar as it reflected consideration of several organismic features (e.g., maturational, nativistic thinking) as well as, to some extent, the biogenetic law.

Some observers have argued that, because of his wide range of influences and writings, Preyer was not a pure mechanist (Eckardt, 1985). Although this may be accurate, it is important to note that incorporating variables normally associated with a different model of development does not in itself make him less a mechanist. In contrast to the early G. S. Hall, Preyer emphasized individual differences in child development (Tobach, 1985). In addition, as a function of his interest in psychophysics, Preyer attended to the role of stimulus–experience relations in child development. Furthermore, as Dennis (1972) noted, Preyer's method of response management anticipates much of the reinforcement theory of modern mechanistic psychology. Although Preyer (1893) upheld a basically voluntaristic position, the organism must exert some effort to overcome immediate environmental contingencies.

Darwin's influence on the work of his cousin Sir Francis Galton is quite apparent. Galton's investigations of individual differences in psychology form an intellectual bridge between Darwinian evolutionism and individual psychology. His well-known work on heredity (e.g., Galton, 1978) is one of the earliest scientific formulations of one of the basic issues of developmental psychology, the nature–nurture question. Galton's (1876) early study, in which he used twins in an attempt to disentangle nature and nurture influences, is still considered a classic. Galton's consuming interest in this issue, however, was practical as well as theoretical and thus led to the founding of *eugenics,* the applied science of heredity (Hearnshaw, 1964; Kevles, 1985). In addition, his classic treatise on human development (Galton, 1883) contained an array of essays that anticipated both experimental and correlational developmental psychology (although some of his methods and statistics were apparently influenced by Quetelet). Galton's views on the predominance of nature (inheritance) over nurture in the development of mental traits was, according to Buss (1975), partly ascribable to the prevailing political orientation of the time, which, in effect, demanded a nature interpretation. As Bronfenbrenner and Crouter (1983) pointed out, Galton qualified carefully his nature-oriented conclusions. Indeed, Galton argued that nature is a more predominant influence than nurture only within a restricted range of environmental variation. Beyond that range, when more environmental factors are allowed to vary, nurture becomes considerably more influential (Bronfenbrenner & Crouter, 1983).

G. S. Hall, who wrote the introduction to the American edition of Preyer's (1888) *The Mind of the Child,* placed considerable emphasis in his later work on environmental, especially social, factors in postchildhood behavioral ontogenesis. Thus, at separate points in the life span, nature and nurture components were incorporated into Hall's perspective. As a developmental psychologist, Hall lacked a systematic program of thought. In this respect he fits neither the mechanistic nor the organismic model perfectly. Hall's somewhat loose eclecticism is revealed by his simultaneous attachment to correlational, experimental, and psychoanalytic traditions, in addition to his a priori dedication to recapitulation theory (Cairns & Ornstein, 1979). Regarding the latter, Hall actually represented the peak of the influence of recapitulation theory in psychology; as it was being increasingly discredited in embryology, the foundation of its application to psychology was crumbling (Gould, 1977; Thorndike, 1904).

Although John B. Watson is not normally identified as a developmental psychologist, he had a lasting impact on the emergence of behavioral (learning theory) developmental psychology. Watson was originally enamored of the psychology of John Dewey, and Dewey's work (as we note later in this chapter) was substantially influenced by evolutionary theory. As Richards (1987) pointed out, Watson's early work was in fact premised on some Darwinian principles. For Watson, of course, this did not last long, and his later work emphasized the behavioral theses for which he became famous. His atomistic, reductionistic framework (Watson, 1924), and his subsequent view of development as tantamount to cumulative learning (Watson, 1926), could hardly contrast more with the biological, organismic view of Baldwin and Piaget (Cairns & Ornstein, 1979). Further, Watson modified James' contextual interest in the stream of consciousness to a more empirical interest in stream of behavior (White, 1968).

Today, the mechanistic tradition in developmental psychology is best represented by those adopting a behavior-analytic approach to studying change across life, as for example in the work of Donald M. Baer and Sidney W. Bijou (see Reese, 1986, for a comparison of the Watsonian and Skinnerian views of behavioral psychology). The concepts, methods, and principles of behavior analysis (e.g., Skinner, 1953) were extended to child developmental psychology in a series of articles by Bijou and in a landmark text by Bijou and Baer (1961). As with all approaches to development, the behavior-analytic approach has evolved in the more than 30 years since Bijou and Baer's (1961) seminal work (see Lipsitt & Cantor, 1986). Such evolution can be observed by consulting the more recent versions of child development textbooks (Bijou, 1976; Bijou & Baer, 1978), as well as recent theoretical statements (e.g., Bijou, 1979; Morris, 1982; Reese, 1986; Spiker, 1986). Morris and Hursh (1982) indicated that behavior-analytic developmentalists have become increasingly concerned with metatheoretical issues (e.g., Bijou, 1979; Skinner, 1974), and in this regard they have examined the usefulness of key developmental concepts and issues such as those pertinent to the nature of change (continuous), the usefulness of age (descriptive) as a variable in developmental research, the model of the organism, and the role of the environment (Baer, 1970, 1973, 1976; Baltes & Lerner, 1980; Reese, 1980, 1986).

Similarly, Bijou (1979) appeared to distance the behavior-analytic approach from extreme positions on several issues fundamental to the mechanistic viewpoint. For example, he rejected both reductionism (explaining behavioral phenomena with, for instance, chemical phenomena) and a passive model of the organism. The rejection of a purely passive model of the organism is consistent with Skinnerian behaviorism (Reese, 1980, 1986; Skinner, 1974).

Despite the apparent movement toward the center among contemporary behavior analysts regarding developmental issues — and despite parallel movements among, for example, organicists — it is unlikely that harmonious relations between these two approaches will ever be established (Baer, 1982;

Molenaar & Oppenheimer, 1985; Reese, 1982a). (Indeed, the philosopher Pepper, 1942, warned against eclecticism among the world views.) Clear differences exist on a number of fundamental issues and assumptions (Baer, 1982; Lerner, 1986). However, it is possible to note several similarities between the mechanistic behavioral-analytic approach to studying individual development and some aspects of the contextual model (see following section and Morris, 1988).

The behavior-analytic approach to development is not the only one that can be identified within contemporary developmental psychology as consistent with a mechanistic tradition. Current applications to life-span developmental psychology of both the operant approach and learning theory can be seen in Hoyer (1980). Some cognitive social learning approaches to development (e.g., Bandura, 1977; Mischel, 1977) also have features consistent with a mechanistic orientation. These latter positions have also been revised, and they now include ideas pertinent to reciprocal, person–context interaction models of development (Bandura, 1978, 1986). As such, these cognitive social learning approaches share some common features with both dialecticism and contextualism.

Dialecticism

The dialectical materialism of the 19th century has significantly influenced one modern approach to developmental psychology. Under the contemporary dialectical model, the basic metaphor appears to be contradiction or conflict (Riegel, 1975, 1976; see also Datan & Reese, 1977). The activities of the individual are viewed as being in dynamic interaction with the activities of the environment. Some dialecticians represent the individual, like the society, as developing through a continuous process of thesis, antithesis, and synthesis (Wozniak, 1975a, 1975b). This perspective emphasizes the continuing nature of change, as well as the fact that change occurs at multiple levels (Reese, 1982b; Riegel, 1975, 1976; Tolman, 1983; Vygotsky, 1978). Thus, the interactional nature of individual and social development becomes a prime concern (Lerner, 1978; Overton, 1973; Riegel & Meacham, 1976). In addition, the dialectical model generally represents both the organism and the environment as inherently active. A schematic representation of the line of influence is presented in Row D of Fig. 1.1.

Although neither Hegel nor Marx proposed a specific program of individual development, their views on both ideational and social change have been adapted for the individual psychological level. Hegel was unquestionably an influence on Marx, although in certain respects his ideas were rejected by the much younger revolutionary. One important point of commonality between them is the dialectic itself. The influence of Darwin on Marx is difficult to assess completely, but some writers have suggested that Marx wanted to dedicate *Das Kapital* to the evolutionist (Berlin, 1978; but see also Fay, 1978). Further, it is known that Marx warmly inscribed a copy of the second edition of his magnum opus to Darwin (Huxley & Kettlewell, 1965). Marx's own intellectual companion, Friederich Engels (1820–1895), portrayed a certain intellectual kinship between Darwin and Marx in his notes read at the latter's graveside. Several of Marx's letters to Engels in the years immediately following the 1859 publication of Darwin's *Origins* indicated that he believed evolutionary thinking to be consonant with his own dialectical materialism (see Padover, 1978). This issue appears to have occupied several early socialist scholars (Richards, 1987).

In some respects, however, Marx's own evolutionism may have more closely resembled Spencer's or Lamarck's than Darwin's. Indeed, Richards (1987) noted a few isolated aspects of intellectual companionship between Marx and Spencer. Unlike Darwin's view of development, Marx wrote occasionally as though social change was directed toward an ultimate end state, and as though development occurred in a revolutionary rather than evolutionary manner. Nevertheless, both Darwin and Marx shared a concern, emerging on multiple fronts in the 19th century, with a historical and developmental perspective. It is this shared fundamental concern that forms a critical link between the two. This focus on change entailed developmental methods. It may not be widely known by students of developmental psychology that Marx believed his theory to be scientific, and strongly supported enlightened empirical enquiry.

After the Bolshevik revolution in 1917, dialectical psychology in the Soviet Union burgeoned. The most influential of these dialectical develop- mentalists was Vygotsky (1929, 1962, 1978). Through such junior col- leagues as A. R. Luria and A. N. Leontiev (e.g., Leontiev, 1978; Leontiev & Luria, 1968; Luria, 1971, 1976, 1979), a dialectical approach to psy- chology developed. Several features of this approach are notable. For example, it inherited from Marxism a strongly developmental orientation and a focus on individual activity (e.g., Leontiev, 1978). It may also be characterized as sociocultural in that it attends closely to the impact of cultural change (and extant cultural differences) on individual development (e.g., Luria, 1976). Luria (1979) recounted his own view on the emergence of many of these ideas in his history of Soviet psychology.

For both intellectual and political reasons, dialectical developmental psychology was not until recently a noticeable, much less a prominent, force on the American scene (Riegel, 1972). Thus, there is little explicit linkage between Soviet and American developmental psychology until after the mid-20th century. As this connection has become better drawn, several themes pertinent to a dialectical view of development have emerged. For example, Wozniak (1975a, 1975b) has described the following three laws of developmental change based on Marxist dialectics:

1. the unity and opposition of contradictory principles;
2. the possibility of transforming quantitative change into qualitative change and vice versa; and
3. the negation of a negation.

In turn, developmental psychology, when viewed dialectically, is understood as the study of the changing individual in a changing world (Riegel & Meacham, 1976).

However, as with the historical methods of Marx's dialectical materialism, the utility of the methods involved in a dialectical approach to the study of human development, insofar as they vary from more traditional methods, is an issue deserving further attention. Several efforts have been made to examine the implications of this approach for psychological research (e.g., see Datan & Reese, 1977; Hultsch, 1980; Lerner, Skinner, & Sorell, 1980). The implications of Soviet psychology for cross-cultural developmental research have been articulated by Michael Cole and colleagues (e.g., Cole, Gay, Glick, & Sharp, 1971; Laboratory of Comparative Human Cognition, 1983). In this research the cultural relativism of developmental patterns is emphasized.

The leading figure in contemporary developmental dialectics was Klaus F. Riegel. Because of this prominence and because his ideas allow us to present important distinctions between dialecticism and other models, we focus on his work. In many ways Riegel was both the intellectual leader of and catalyst for the exploration of the use of alternative models for the study of human development in the 1970s. This was the case, first, because he was a prolific and passionate writer—his book, *Psychology Mon Amour: A Countertext* (1978), being an excellent case in point—and, second, because he was editor of the journal *Human Development,* an important outlet for theoretical scholarship in the field of human development. In his theoretical work, Riegel stressed that (a) the primary goal of a developmental analysis was the study of change, not stasis, and (b) any level of organization—from inner–biological, through individual–psychological and physical–environmental, to the sociocultural—influences and is influenced by all other levels. Thus, Riegel (1975, 1976, 1979) "developmentalized" and "contextualized" the study of the person by embedding the individual within an integrated and changing matrix of influences derived from multiple levels of organization.

Riegel's model of dialecticism was an important instance of the growing interest in the interactive role of the changing physical and social context for human behavior and development during this period. Riegel's ideas, as well as those of Sameroff (1975), Looft (1973), Lerner (1978, 1979), and others (e.g., Baltes, 1979; Bronfenbrenner, 1977, 1979; Elder, 1974, 1975), were similar in their emphasis on change and context—and, to this extent, may be interpreted as being part of a common family of models. However, as scholarship about this family advanced it became increasingly clear that important distinctions existed among family members. Riegel (1976), himself, was at pains to argue that dialecticism constituted a model of development distinct from organicism. In his view, the dialectical theory of cognitive development differed from the one of Piaget (1950, 1970). For example, whereas Piaget proposed that after the development of formal operations no new cognitive structure emerged, Riegel argued that the dialectic resulted in a fifth, open-ended stage of cognitive development.

On the other hand, Riegel did not attend to the similarities and differences between the dialectical and contextual world views. The latter model, which we discuss in the following subsection, not only stresses the very features of human development emphasized by Riegel — change and context — but, as well, was attracting considerable attention in the literature at about the same time (Lerner et al., 1983). Notably, however, Riegel's (1975, 1976, 1979) ideas on context and change differed from those of other family members with respect to the format of change. The nature of dialectical change may be more compatible with the view of change found in organicism than that of contextualism (Dixon, Lerner, & Hultsch, 1991; but see also Tolman, 1991). Riegel (1979) may have been correct in stressing that postformal operational thought is possible (e.g., see Alexander & Langer, 1990), but his theoretical differences with Piaget (1950, 1970) may have been overdrawn.

Indeed, the congruence between organismic and dialectical views of change provides one key reason why the dialectical model of Riegel has not remained a conception of prime focus among developmental scholars. First, dialecticism, as presented by Riegel, is but one instance of a concern (shared by several models) with change and context. Second, Riegel's dialecticism may have rested on a view of change for which the integration of empirical data supporting multidirectionality and plasticity in human development is difficult (e.g., Baltes, 1987; Brim & Kagan, 1980; Lerner, 1984). To be sure, such data are never easy to incorporate into coherent scientific theories. Nevertheless, we now turn to a discussion of contextualism, a model that emphasizes context, change, multidirectionality, and plasticity.

Contextualism

Contextualism derives in part from pragmatic philosophers like Charles S. Peirce, William James, John Dewey, and George Herbert Mead. The contextual model of psychology was also influenced by such functional psychologists as James Rowland Angell, Harvey Carr, and, of course, James and Dewey. Much of the initial activity occurred in the early part of this century, and thus contextualism, as a philosophical position, is quite advanced (Pepper, 1942). It has been recently revived in psychology (e.g., Rosnow & Georgoudi, 1986) and adapted to such research areas as cognition and cognitive development (e.g., Dixon, 1986; Jenkins, 1974) and social and personality development (Blank, 1986; Lerner & Lerner, 1986; Sarbin, 1977). Its basic metaphor is change or the historic event. The individual and the social environment are viewed as mutually influential, acting on one another in dynamic interaction. The proposed line of influence is presented in Fig. 1.1 (Row E).

William James was considerably influenced by Darwin's natural selection theory of evolution (Richards, 1987). James' (1890) psychology was nonreductionistic in character; that is, he argued against the analysis (or reduction) of complex mental events into primitive or elementary parts. Instead, experience consists of a stream of events, each of which possesses a unique quality or meaning. The novelty of each event is assured by the stream metaphor. The implication James developed was that the meaning or significance of a mental event is inseparable from the context of its occurrence, which is itself in flux. Development is continuous, "without breach, crack, or division" (James, 1890, p. 237); it is composed of quantitative differences rather than qualitatively distinct stages. His approach to psychology may be characterized as historical in that "mental reaction on every given thing is really a resultant of our experience of the whole world up to that date" (p. 234).

As had Darwin, James viewed the human mind as both dynamic (active) and functional, continuously involved in the process of adaptation to a changing ecology. Both James and Peirce sought to infuse developmental change with the element of chance (e.g., Peirce's "tychism") so integral to the Darwinian hypothesis. Eschewing the directional or teleological focus of Lamarckian evolutionists and psychologists, these early contextualists sought to develop a generally nonteleologial, Darwinian-based developmental method. According to the Darwinian interpretation, a chance event, although not wholly determined by the past, does reflect the character of preceding events (Russett, 1976). In this way, teleological characteristics are avoided, but both novelty and developmental continuity are maintained (James, 1977).

The concept of function was critical to the early contextual approach to psychology; indeed, this concept represents a clear conduit through which Darwinian thinking entered into American psychology. The biological version of this concept suggested that anatomical structures, shaped as they were by natural selection, functioned so as to further the survival of the organism (Ghiselin, 1969). Early contextualists applied this concept to psychology in a straightforward manner (Bawden, 1910; James, 1890; Wiener, 1949). The mind, they argued, is an "organ" selected for its utility in promoting the successful adaptation of the complex changing human organism to the complex changing environment. This approach to psychology is often dated to John Dewey's (1896) classic paper "The Reflex Arc Concept in Psychology." However, even in his earlier work in psychology, Dewey had already demonstrated a strong dynamic and practical orientation to the study of mental phenomena. In this earlier period, however, Dewey cast developmental questions in the framework of a Hegelian *telos,* or necessary movement to a final end state. But Dewey soon fell under the influence of Darwinism (see Dewey, 1910) and his subsequent psychological writings stressed the developmental method, the continuous model of developmental change, as well as the Darwinian view of the dynamic organism–environment transaction (Russett, 1976). Like James, Dewey offered a relatively active organism (and active environment) model of this transaction. Finally, like so many of the early figures we have discussed, Dewey (1910) attributed the discovery of the historical (or developmental) method to Darwin.

No modern contextual developmental psychologist has produced a system as complete as that of James and his colleagues. Certainly, with the exception of areas pertinent to language development, Peirce and Mead have not had a major effect on contemporary developmental psychology. Indeed, with the exception of the work of F. C. Bartlett (1932) and perhaps Vygotsky (1962), a dialectician (discussed earlier) who at least cited James, contextual developmental psychology appears to have lain dormant for several decades. However, several prominent psychologists, normally associated with other models, espoused some tenets of contextualism. For example, Reese (1986) argued that Skinner's (e.g., 1974) philosophy of science is pragmatic (contextual), even though the model of the organism is mechanistic. Other notable mechanists or contextualists are J. R. Kantor (1888–1984) and E. C. Tolman (1886–1959). On the other hand, Lerner's (1986) developmental contextual perspective links contextualism to organicism and thus to such organicists as Werner (1948). Nevertheless, numerous psychologists have recently promulgated some aspects of contextual thinking and have attempted to articulate its methodological implications (Beilin, 1984; Bronfenbrenner, 1977; Bruce, 1985; Dixon & Hertzog, 1988; Dixon & Nesselroade, 1983; Hultsch & Pentz, 1980; Jenkins, 1974; Lerner et al., 1983; Petrinovich, 1979; Sarbin, 1977).

Lerner (1990) argued that the growing interest in contextualism during the 1970s and 1980s (e.g., Bandura, 1978, 1986; Jenkins, 1974; Mischel, 1977; Rosnow & Georgoudi, 1986; Sarbin, 1977) was associated with the recession of the other major models to the "back burner" of theoretical and empirical activity among developmentalists. Although interest in all models continues into the 1990s, contextualism is being actively explored and tested for its suitability as a model for the scientific study of human development.

To understand this view of the role of contextualism, it may be useful to compare it to neighboring models.

Pepper (1942) noted that contextualism is related to both mechanism and organicism. In focusing on the relation between contextualism and organicism, Lerner (1986) noted that both world views are nonreductionistic, involve the consideration of variables or events at multiple levels of organization, and are change-oriented. However, it is in this last similarity — change — that the two models diverge as well. The process of change is seen quite differently in the two perspectives. Within organicism change is often teleological (Lerner, 1986; Nagel, 1957). The final cause producing the goal-directedness of such change means that despite the "strands" (Pepper, 1942) of change that may exist over the course of life, development will eventually channel into a single direction; that is, despite individual differences in change that may exist at some earlier time in life, development will have a common (i.e., interindividually invariant) endpoint — be it the attainment of formal operational thought, the emergence of the ego crisis of integrity versus despair, or the development of postconventional moral reasoning. People may differ only in how fast or in how far they develop toward this universal endpoint. In other words, because of the telos of change, development follows a predetermined path; change, when seen from the perspective of the entire span of life, is thus unidirectional. Accordingly, individual differences are not as emphasized in such conceptions of development as they are in contextualism.

Contextualism, in contrast, embraces plasticity of change (i.e., systematic alteration in structure or function; see Lerner, 1984; Willis, 1990), multidirectionality of life-span development (Baltes, 1987), and increases across age in individual differences (Schaie, 1983). These themes are prominent in recent contextual scholarship (e.g., Baltes, 1987; Brim & Kagan, 1980; Elder, 1974; Featherman, 1983; Gollin, 1981; Hetherington, Lerner, & Perlmutter, 1988; Lerner, 1984, 1986; Magnusson, 1988; Riley, 1979; Sorensen, Weinert, & Sherrod, 1986). Such diversity is counterintuitive to some developmental scholars. In order to harness some of the natural dispersiveness of the model (Pepper, 1942), Lerner (1986, 1989; Lerner & Kauffman, 1985; Lerner & Tubman, 1989) explored a variant termed *developmental contextualism*. One feature of developmental contextualism is that it stresses that there is no single cause of the individual's functioning or development. Neither within-person variables (e.g., biological or psychological ones), nor interpersonal variables (such as peer group or personal relations), nor extrapersonal variables (such as institutional or environmental ones) are sufficient in and of themselves. Rather, the structure or pattern of relations among these levels of analysis produces the individual's behaviors; and changes in the form (the configuration) of these relations produce developmental change.

Other approaches to contextual developmental psychology may be noted. For example, Sarbin (1977) adapted the dramaturgical model of G. H. Mead (1934), one of the important figures in the development of contextualism. Assuming that individuals carry on their activities and interactions in an episodic, changing way, Sarbin argued for an *emplotment* methodology. That is, Sarbin suggested that psychologists develop a taxonomy of plots; action is temporal, occurring in historical, concurrent, and future contexts. Further examples of the application of contextualism to personality development may be found in Rosnow and Georgoudi (1986). For example, Lerner and Lerner (1986, 1989) described a contextual goodness-of-fit model of child temperament development, and Blank (1986) described a contextual approach to adult social development. With regard to cognition, Jenkins (1974) has argued for a contextual approach (reminiscent of both William James and F. C. Bartlett) to memory research. According to this view, a memory is not an item, a thing, or a spot in the cortex (all of which appear in some alternative accounts); nor is memory separable from other processes, much less the environment (as some accounts often suggest). Rather, "what memory is depends on context" (Jenkins, 1974, p. 786). As the context is ever-changing, so is the memory. Several other researchers have explored the relevance of a contextual approach to life-span cognitive development (e.g., Bruce, 1985; Dixon, 1986; Dixon & Hertzog, 1988; Neisser, 1978).

In summary, contextualism turns attention not only to the external context of psychological development, but also to the internal context (e.g., affective processes, motivation, other skills or schemata). It especially focuses attention on the coordination, interaction, or fusion (Tobach & Greenberg, 1984) of these aspects of the organism and context, and on opportunities for and constraints on change promoted by both organism and context. As with dialecticism, important empirical challenges remain for this model.

Summary

Contemporary developmental psychology is marked by a diversity of theoretical systems that are nevertheless linked by some commonalities in intellectual heritage. The contemporary scene in developmental psychology is not a static one. Indeed, to illustrate this dynamism, we turn now to a discussion of currently central life-span perspectives in developmental psychology. These perspectives have arisen in part as an attempt to integrate ideas from several of the models discussed earlier. They reflect a concern for both the developmental tradition in general, and for the major issues of development (such as nature–nurture) in particular. In the following section we focus on one of these life-span perspectives.

A LIFE-SPAN PERSPECTIVE WITHIN CONTEMPORARY DEVELOPMENTAL PSYCHOLOGY

Earlier, we noted that the developmental tradition, promoted by the contributions of evolutionary theory and the historical perspective of the 19th century, stresses the necessity of knowing something about an organism's history in order to understand the organism's present situation or behavior. This interest has naturally led to a concern with developmental processes throughout the life span. As the developmental tradition is present (albeit in different ways) in each of the five models we have discussed, a concern with life-span development has emerged from each. In this section, we focus on one version of the life-span perspective, one that arose in the late 1960s. This version derives from ideas consonant with several of the models discussed previously.

As this life-span perspective is related to the theoretical models of developmental psychology, it is reasonable to assume that there are some linkages between evolutionary thinking and the set of concepts found within this perspective (e.g., Dixon & Baltes, 1986; Lerner, 1984, 1986). These linkages, however, are qualified in a way that is similar to the historical connections between evolutionary theories and the models themselves. For example, the theoretical influence does not necessarily imply that the features of an individual's development across life are entirely the product of Darwinian mechanisms (e.g., natural selection). Especially in the postreproductive mature adult and aged years, it may be the social context (which is shaped by changing social institutions and cultural conditions) that provides primary impetus for the content and direction of life-span change (Featherman & Lerner, 1985; Lerner, 1984). The consequence of our evolutionary heritage is to have the potential for a period of life—indeed, a relatively extensive one—extending beyond the point of reproduction; however it is the social context, involving such elements as medical technology and institutional support for the health and welfare of the person, which across history has allowed the evolutionary potential for plasticity of functioning into late adulthood to be realized. Thus, social interactional factors supplement biological ones to provide the breadth and content of the human life course. This emphasis underscores the link between the life-span perspective we discuss in this section and the evolutionary thinking described earlier. Once again the notion of organism–environment dynamic interaction is emphasized.

What is this life-span perspective? Even the earliest proponents of this particular perspective (such as Paul Baltes, Hayne Reese, and Warner Schaie) argued that it does not constitute a theory, a collection of theories, or a metatheory of development; rather, it was said to offer a perspective on psychology based on the proposition that the changes (growth, development, aging) shown by people from the time of their conceptions, throughout their lives, and until the time of their deaths are usefully conceptualized as developmental (Baltes, Reese, & Lipsitt, 1980). This developmental conceptualization can occur without necessarily prejudging several fundamental assumptions and conceptual issues on which the models of development clearly differ.

The point of view currently labeled as *life-span developmental psychology* or as a *life-span view of human development* (Baltes, 1979; Baltes, Reese, & Lipsitt, 1980) became crystallized as a set of interrelated ideas about the nature of human development and change. In their combination, these ideas present a set of implications for theory building, for methodology, and for scientific collaboration across disciplinary boundaries. Among the key propositions about life-span development are *embeddedness* and *dynamic interaction* (Lerner, 1986; see also Baltes, 1987). From these propositions an interrelated set of implications may be derived, and these propositions and implications constitute key concepts in current life-span thinking.

The idea of embeddedness is that the key phenomena of human life exist at multiple levels of being (e.g., the inner-biological, individual-psychological, dyadic, social network, community, societal, cultural, outer-ecological, and historical). Thus, at any one point in time variables from any and all of these levels may contribute to human functioning. However, the reason it is important to have a perspective about human development that is sensitive to the influences of these multiple levels is that the levels do not function as independent domains; rather, the variables at one level influence and are influenced by the variables at the other levels. In other words, there is a dynamic interaction among levels of analysis. As such, each level may be a product and a producer of functioning and change at other levels (Lerner, 1986).

How can the dynamic interaction between person and environment emphasized in the life-span perspective be explained? Baltes and colleagues (1980) suggest three major influence patterns that affect this relation:

1. normative age-graded influences;
2. normative history-graded influences; and
3. non-normative, life-event influences.

Normative age-graded influences consist of biological and environmental determinants that are correlated with chronological age. They are normative to the extent that their timing, duration, and clustering are similar for many individuals. Examples include maturational events, such as menarche and the initiation of the growth spurt, and socialization events, such as entrance into parenthood. Normative history-graded influences consist of biological and environmental processes occurring at a particular historical time. They are normative to the extent that they are experienced by most members of a cohort. In this sense they tend to define the developmental context of a given cohort. Examples include historical events (epidemics and periods of economic depression or prosperity) and sociocultural evolution (changes in sex-role expectations, the educational system, and child-rearing practices). Several contributions to McCluskey and Reese (1984) explore the conceptual and methodological issues involved in research on such topics and describe the present state of empirical evidence. Both age-graded and history-graded influences covary with time. Non-normative, life-event influences — the third system — are not directly indexed by time because they do not occur for all people, or even for most people. In addition, when non-normative influences do occur, they are likely to differ across people in terms of their clustering, timing, and duration. Examples of non-normative events relevant to life-span development include accidents, illness, divorce, or death of a spouse.

Baltes and colleagues (1980) have speculated that these three sources of influence exhibit different profiles over the life cycle. Normative age-graded influences may be particularly significant in childhood and early adolescence, and again in old age, whereas normative history-graded influences are thought to be more important throughout adolescence and the years immediately following it; this is believed to reflect the importance of the sociocultural context as the individual begins adult life. Finally, non-normative, life-event influences are postulated to be particularly significant during middle adulthood and old age, reflecting increasing diversity among individuals produced by each person's experience of unique life events.

In summary, two of the key assumptions of this life-span perspective — embeddedness and dynamic interactionism — imply, first, that individual developmental phenomena occur in the context of the developmental and nondevelopmental changes at other levels of analysis. Second, the assumptions imply that developments and/or changes on one level both influence and are influenced by developments and/or changes at these other levels. There are at least three major implications of these ideas.

First, a potential for plasticity exists because changes at one level are reciprocally dependent on changes at other levels. This reciprocity suggests that there is always some possibility for altering the status of a variable or process at any or all levels of analysis. However, we must emphasize that this potential for plasticity is not construed by life-span developmentalists to mean that there are no limits or constraints on change. For instance, by virtue of its structural organization, a system delimits the range of changes it may undergo and such a structural constraint holds for any level of analysis. In addition, the possibility that developmental and nondevelopmental phenomena at one point in life may influence functioning at later points is explicitly recognized by life-span developmentalists in the concept of developmental embeddedness (Lerner, 1986).

Second, a potential for intervention derives from the plasticity of developmental processes. Given potential plasticity, it follows that means may be designed to prevent, ameliorate, or enhance undesired or nonvalued developments or behavior (Baltes, 1987; Willis, 1990). Third, the idea that the person is a producer of his or her own development arises because any level of analysis can influence phenomena at other levels of analysis. For individual psychological development this means that people may affect the social or physical context that affects them (Lerner, 1986).

This life-span perspective is often associated with a call for interdisciplinary research on human development. That is, attempts have been made to integrate ideas from the many disciplines involved in the study of human lives (e.g., anthropology, biology, sociology). The generality of the perspective—its tolerance for multiple metatheoretical positions and methodological approaches—promotes openness to such interdisciplinary contact but at the same time, it may generate ambiguity and controversy (e.g., Dannefer, 1984). Nevertheless, lifelong change occurs on multiple levels of analysis (e.g., biological, psychological, social), and changes on one level often influence changes on other levels. Therefore, some life-span psychologists argue that, given this complex set of change patterns, the student of human development is well served by collegial contact with neighboring disciplines.

Although this life-span perspective is often dated to the late 1960s, a number of historical observers (e.g., Baltes, 1979, 1983; Dixon & Nesselroade, 1983; Havighurst, 1973; Müller-Brettel & Dixon, 1990) have identified instances of precursors from much earlier periods: for example, the aforementioned Tetens (1777), Carus (1808), and Quetelet (1835). In the early 20th-century contributions from both Europe and the United States are noteworthy: for example, Sanford (1902); Hall (1922); Hollingworth (1927); Bühler (1933); and Pressey, Janney, and Kuhlen (1939). Work conducted by the Committee on Human Development at the University of Chicago (e.g., Havighurst, 1948; Neugarten, 1964; Neugarten & Guttman, 1958) was quite influential in bringing a multidisciplinary perspective to the study of individual and social development across life.

As interest burgeoned in multidisciplinary perspectives and, in particular, problems of adult development and aging, new theoretical (e.g., Baltes, 1987; Lerner, 1986) and methodological (e.g., Baltes et al., 1977; Nesselroade & Baltes, 1979) advances were required. The nature of a life-span orientation has become somewhat clearer through the publication of several conference proceedings, symposia, and a series of annual volumes, as well as numerous empirical and theoretical papers (e.g., Baltes, 1987; Baltes et al., 1980). For example, an annual series of conferences at West Virginia University on conceptual, methodological, and empirical issues has been held since 1969 (e.g., Baltes & Schaie, 1973; Datan & Ginsberg, 1975; Datan & Reese, 1977; McCluskey & Reese, 1984; Nesselroade & Reese, 1973). The annual research series, *Life-Span Development and Behavior* (edited by Baltes, Brim, Jr., Featherman, Lerner, & Perlmutter) began publication in 1978 (e.g., Baltes, 1978; Baltes & Brim, 1984; Baltes, Featherman, & Lerner, 1986).

Perhaps the greatest testimony to the impact of this series is that not only do numerous contributors to these and other volumes come from disciplines other than psychology, but that the following summary of this perspective applies as well to most of the other chapters in this particular textbook. The summary is: From the life-span perspective, the potential for developmental change is seen to be present across all of life; the human life course is held to be potentially multidirectional and necessarily multidimensional. In addition, the sources of the potentially continual changes across life are seen to involve both inner-biological and outer-ecological levels of the context within which the organism is embedded. Indeed, although it is an orientation to the study of development rather than a specific theory of development (Baltes, 1979a), life-span developmental psychology is disposed to a reciprocal model of organism–context relations. In this way, it establishes and maintains contact with such neighboring fields as life-course sociology.

CONCLUSIONS

Developmental psychology has come to be characterized by an emphasis on explanation and process, and by a concern with several theoretical systems and their philosophical bases. We have described how numerous early figures of developmental psychology drew sustenance from 19th-century evolutionary and historical perspectives, and then turned to face the fresh demands of their own context. These demands were sufficiently varied to propagate views about human development that today appear mutually distinct. Perhaps one of the greatest contributions of evolutionary theory to the emergence of developmental psychology derives from its accentuation of the underlying general issues pertaining to ontogeny. Among these abiding problems are such classical polarities as nature versus nurture (Lerner, 1978), continuity versus discontinuity of development (Brim & Kagan, 1980), and unidirectionality versus non- or multidirectionality of temporal progression (Lerner, 1986). All of these are addressed throughout this volume.

It is reasonable to assert that the structure of the five major contemporary developmental metatheories described in this chapter cut across these salient issues in qualitatively different ways. Thus, contemporary developmental theories may share a certain intellectual lineage, embrace a generalized historical or developmental approach to human phenomena, and at the same time represent relatively distinct metatheoretical positions. The commonality and diversity results in both (a) shared research questions and procedures, and (b) relatively specific methods and unique interpretations of developmental observations. This variation can be viewed as a vital ingredient of the intellectual vigor and excitement present in the contemporary study of human development across life.

ACKNOWLEDGMENTS

This chapter has been revised to reflect the historical coverage of an earlier chapter of the same name in earlier editions of this volume (by the present authors), and to summarize the contemporary life-span movement as covered in another chapter in the first edition of this collection (by P. B. Baltes and H. W. Reese). The chapter has benefited from several valuable discussions with, and commentaries by, Paul B. Baltes and Hayne W. Reese. The authors thank also Marc Bornstein and Michael Lamb for their many helpful suggestions on earlier drafts. Roger A. Dixon's work on this chapter was supported by a grant from the Canadian Network of Centres of Excellence (CARNET), and by an operating grant from the Natural Sciences and Engineering Research Council of Canada. Richard M. Lerner's work on this chapter was supported in part by an NICHD grant (HD23229).

REFERENCES

Alexander, C. N., & Langer, E. J. (Eds.). (1990). *Higher stages of human development: Perspectives on adult growth.* New York: Oxford University Press.

Anderson, J. E. (1956). Child development: An historical perspective. *Child Development, 27,* 181–196.

Angell, J. R. (1912). *Chapters from modern psychology.* New York: Longmans, Green.

Baer, D. M. (1970). An age-irrelevant concept of development. *Merrill-Palmer Quarterly, 16,* 238–245.

Baer, D. M. (1973). The control of developmental process: Why wait? In J. R. Nesselroade & H. W. Reese (Eds.)., *Life-span developmental psychology: Methodological issues.* New York: Academic Press.

Baer, D. M. (1976). The organism as host. *Human Development, 19,* 87–98.

Baer, D. M. (1982). Behavior analysis and developmental psychology: Discussant comments. *Human Development, 25,* 357–361.

Baldwin, A. L. (1980). *Theories of child development* (2nd ed.). New York: Wiley.

Baldwin, J. M. (1895). *Mental development in the child and the race.* New York: Macmillan.

Baldwin, J. M. (1906). *Mental development in the child and the race: Methods and processes* (2nd ed.). New York: Macmillan.

Baldwin, J. M. (1909). *Darwin and the humanities.* Baltimore: Review.

Baldwin, J. M. (1913). *History of psychology: A sketch and interpretation (Vol. 2). From Locke to the present time.* London: Watts.

Baldwin, J. M. (1930). [Autobiography]. In C. Murchison (Ed.), *A history of psychology in autobiography* (Vol. 1). Worcester, MA: Clark University Press.

Baltes, M. M., & Lerner, R. M. (1980). Roles of the operant model and its methods in the life-span approach to human development. *Human Development, 23,* 362–367.

Baltes, P. B. (Ed.). (1978). *Life-span development and behavior* (Vol. 1). New York: Academic Press.

Baltes, P. B. (1979a). Life-span developmental psychology: Some converging observations on history and theory. In P. B. Baltes & O. G. Brim, Jr. (Eds.), *Life-span development and behavior* (Vol. 2). New York: Academic Press.

Baltes, P. B. (1979b, Summer). On the potential and limits of child development: Life-span developmental perspectives. *Newsletter of the Society for Research in Child Development,* 1–4.

Baltes, P. B. (1983). Life-span developmental psychology: Observations on history and theory revisited. In R. M. Lerner (Ed.), *Developmental psychology: Historical and philosophical perspectives.* Hillsdale, NJ: Lawrence Erlbaum Associates.

Baltes, P. B. (1987). Theoretical propositions of life-span developmental psychology: On the dynamics between growth and decline. *Developmental Psychology, 23,* 611–626.

Baltes, P. B., & Brim, O. G., Jr. (Eds.). (1984). *Life-span development and behavior* (Vol. 6). Orlando, FL: Academic Press.

Baltes, P. B., Featherman, D. L., & Lerner, R. M. (Eds.). (1986). *Life-span development and behavior* (Vol. 7). Hillsdale, NJ: Lawrence Erlbaum Associates.

Baltes, P. B., Reese, H. W., & Lipsitt, L. P. (1980). Life-span developmental psychology. *Annual Review of Psychology, 31,* 65–110.

Baltes, P. B., Reese, H. W., & Nesselroade, J. R. (1977). *Life-span developmental psychology: Introduction to research methods.* Monterey, CA: Brooks-Cole.

Baltes, P. B., & Schaie, K. W. (Eds.). (1973). *Life-span developmental psychology: Personality and socialization.* New York: Academic Press.

Bandura, A. (1977). *Social learning theory.* Englewood Cliffs, NJ: Prentice-Hall.

Bandura, A. (1978). The self system in reciprocal determinism. *American Psychologist, 33,* 344–358.

Bandura, A. (1986). *Social foundations of thought and action: A social cognitive theory.* Englewood Cliffs, NJ: Prentice-Hall.

Bartlett, F. C. (1932). *Remembering.* Cambridge: Cambridge University Press.

Bawden, H. H. (1910). *The principles of pragmatism: A philosophical interpretation of experience.* Boston: Houghton Mifflin.

Beilin, H. (1984). Functionalist and structuralist research programs in developmental psychology: Incommensurability or synthesis? In H. W. Reese (Ed.), *Advances in child development and behavior* (Vol. 18). Orlando, FL: Academic Press.

Berlin, I. (1978). *Karl Marx: His life and his environment* (4th ed.). Oxford: Oxford University Press.

Bijou, S. W. (1976). *Child development: The basic stage of early childhood.* Englewood Cliffs, NJ: Prentice-Hall.

Bijou, S. W. (1979). Some clarifications on the meaning of a behavior analysis of child development. *Psychological Record, 29,* 3–13.

Bijou, S. W., & Baer, D. M. (1961). *Child development, Vol. 1: A systematic and empirical theory.* New York: Appleton-Century-Crofts.

Bijou, S. W., & Baer, D. M. (1978). *Child development: A behavior analysis approach.* Englewood Cliffs, NJ: Prentice-Hall.

Blank, T. O. (1986). Contextual and relational perspectives on adult psychology. In R. L. Rosnow & M. L. Georgoudi (Eds.), *Contextualism and understanding in behavioral science.* New York: Praeger.

Borstelmann, L. J. (1983). Children before psychology: Ideas about children from antiquity to the late 1800s. In P. H. Mussen & W. Kessen (Eds.), *Handbook of child psychology: Vol. 1. History, theory, and methods.* New York: Wiley.

Brainerd, C. J. (1978). The stage question in cognitive-developmental theory. *The Behavioral and Brain Sciences, 2,* 173–182.

Braunshvig, M., & Braunshvig, G. (1913). *Notre enfant: Journal d'un père et d'une mère* [Our child: Journal of a father and a mother]. Paris: Hachette.

Brent, S. B. (1978). Individual specialization, collective adaptation and rate of environmental change. *Human Development, 21,* 21–33.

Brim, O. G., Jr., & Kagan, J. (1980). Constancy and change: A view of the issues. In O. G. Brim, Jr., & J. Kagan (Eds.), *Constancy and change in human development.* Cambridge, MA: Harvard University Press.

Bronfenbrenner, U. (1963). Development theory in transition. In H. W. Stevenson (Ed.), *Child psychology. Sixty-second yearbook of the National Society for the Study of Education, part I.* Chicago: University of Chicago Press.

Bronfenbrenner, U. (1977). Toward an experimental ecology of human development. *American Psychologist, 32,* 513–531.

Bronfenbrenner, U. (1979). *The ecology of human development.* Cambridge, MA: Harvard University Press.

Bronfenbrenner, U., & Crouter, A. C. (1983). The evolution of environmental models in developmental research. In P. H. Mussen & W. Kessen (Eds.), *Handbook of child psychology: Vol. 1. History, theory, and methods.* New York: Wiley.

Broughton, J. M. (1981). The genetic psychology of James Mark Baldwin. *American Psychologist, 36,* 396–407.

Broughton, J. M., & Freeman-Moir, D. J. (Eds.). (1982). *The cognitive-developmental psychology of James Mark Baldwin.* Norwood, NJ: Ablex.

Bruce, D. (1985). The how and why of ecological memory. *Journal of Experimental Psychology: General, 114,* 78–90.

Bühler, C. (1930). *The first year of life.* New York: John Day.

Bühler, C. (1933). *Der Menschliche Lebenslauf als Psychologisches Problem* [The human life course as a psychological problem]. Leipzig: Hirzel.

Buss, A. R. (1975). The emerging field of the sociology of psychological knowledge. *American Psychologist, 30,* 988–1002.

Butterworth, G., Rutkowska, J., & Scaife, M. (Eds.). (1985). *Evolution and developmental psychology.* New York: St. Martin's.

Cahan, E. D. (1984). The genetic psychologies of James Mark Baldwin and Jean Piaget. *Developmental Psychology, 20,* 128–135.

Cairns, R. B. (1980). Developmental theory before Piaget: The remarkable contributions of James Mark Baldwin. *Contemporary Psychology, 25,* 438–440.

Cairns, R. B. (1983). The emergence of developmental psychology. In P. H. Mussen & W. Kessen (Eds.), *Child psychology: Vol. 1. History, theory, and methods.* New York: Wiley.

Cairns, R. B., & Ornstein, P. A. (1979). Developmental psychology. In E. Hearst (Ed.), *The first century of experimental psychology.* Hillsdale, NJ: Lawrence Erlbaum Associates.

Carus, F. A. (1808). *Psychologie. Zweiter Theil: Specialpsychologie* [Psychology. Second part: Differential psychology.] Leipzig: Barth & Kummer.

Cavanaugh, J. C. (1981). Early developmental theories: A brief review of attempts to organize developmental data prior to 1925. *Journal of the History of the Behavioral Sciences, 17,* 38–47.

Cavanaugh, J. C. (1991). On the concept of development: Contextualism, relative time, and the role of dialectics. In P. van Geert & L. P. Mos (Eds.), *Annals of theoretical psychology* (Vol. 7). New York: Plenum.

Champneys, E. H. (1881). Notes on an infant. *Mind, 6,* 104–107.

Chapman, M. (1988a). *Constructive evolution: Origins and development of Piaget's thought.* Cambridge: Cambridge University Press.

Chapman, M. (1988b). Contextuality and directionality of cognitive development. *Human Development, 31,* 92–106.

Chapman, M., & Dixon, R. A. (Eds.). (1987). *Meaning and the growth of understanding: Wittgenstein's significance for developmental psychology.* Berlin: Springer-Verlag.

Charles, D. C. (1970). Historical antecedents of life-span developmental psychology. In L. R. Goulet & P. B. Baltes (Eds.), *Life-span developmental psychology: Research and theory.* New York: Academic Press.

Charlesworth, W. R. (1986). Darwin and developmental psychology: 10 years later. *Human Development, 29,* 1–4.

Clayton, V. P., & Birren, J. E. (1980). The development of wisdom across the life span: A reexamination of an ancient topic. In P. B. Baltes & O. G. Brim, Jr. (Eds.), *Life-span development and behavior* (Vol. 3). New York: Academic Press.

Cole, M., Gay, J., Glick, J. A., & Sharp, D. W. (1971). *The cultural context of learning and thinking.* New York: Basic.

Collingwood, R. G. (1956). *The idea of history.* London: Oxford University Press.

Commons, M. L., Sinnott, J. D., Richards, F. A., & Armon, C. (Eds.). (1989). *Adult development: Comparisons and applications of developmental models.* New York: Praeger.

Costall, A. (1986). Evolutionary gradualism and the study of development. *Human Development, 29,* 4–11.

Dannefer, D. (1984). Adult development and social theory: A paradigmatic reappraisal. *American Sociological Review, 49,* 100–116.

Darwin, C. (1859). *On the origin of species.* London: John Murray.

Darwin, C. (1871). *Descent of man.* London: John Murray.

Darwin, C. (1872). *The expression of emotions in man and animals.* London: John Murray.

Darwin, C. (1877). Biographical sketch of an infant. *Mind, 2,* 285–294.

Datan, N., & Ginsberg, L. H. (Eds.). (1975). *Life-span developmental psychology: Normative life crises.* New York: Academic Press.

Datan, N., & Reese, H. W. (Eds.). (1977). *Life-span developmental psychology: Dialectical perspectives on experimental research.* New York: Academic Press.

Dennis, W. (1949). Historical beginnings of child psychology. *Psychological Bulletin, 46,* 224–235.

Dennis, W. (Ed.). (1951). *Readings in child psychology.* New York: Prentice-Hall.

Dennis, W. (Ed.). (1972). *Historical readings in developmental psychology.* New York: Appleton-Century-Crofts.

Dewey, J. (1896). The reflex arc concept in psychology. *Psychological Review, 3,* 357–370.

Dewey, J. (1910). The influence of Darwinism on philosophy. In J. Dewey (Ed.), *The influence of Darwin on philosophy and other essays on contemporary thought.* New York: Henry Holt.

Dixon, R. A. (1986). Contextualism and life-span developmental psychology. In R. L. Rosnow

& M. Georgoudi (Eds.), *Contextualism and understanding in behavioral science*. New York: Praeger.

Dixon, R. A., & Baltes, P. B. (1986). Toward life-span research on the functions and pragmatics of intelligence. In R. J. Sternberg & R. K. Wagner (Eds.), *Practical intelligence: Nature and origins of competence in the everyday world*. Cambridge: Cambridge University Press.

Dixon, R. A., & Hertzog, C. (1988). A functional approach to memory and metamemory development in adulthood. In F. E. Weinert & M. Perlmutter (Eds.), *Memory development across the life span: Universal changes and individual differences*. Hillsdale, NJ: Lawrence Erlbaum Associates.

Dixon, R. A., & Lerner, R. M. (1985). Darwinism and the emergence of developmental psychology. In G. Eckhardt, W. G. Bringmann, & L. Sprung (Eds.), *Contributions to a history of developmental psychology*. Berlin: Mouton.

Dixon, R. A., Lerner, R. M., & Hultsch, D. F. (1991). The concept of development in the study of individual and social change. In P. van Geert & L. P. Mos (Eds.), *Annals of theoretical psychology* (Vol. 7). New York: Plenum.

Dixon, R. A., & Nesselroade, J. R. (1983). Pluralism and correlational analysis in developmental psychology: Historical commonalities. In R. M. Lerner (Ed.), *Developmental psychology: Historical and philosophical perspectives*. Hillsdale, NJ: Lawrence Erlbaum Associates.

Dollard, J., Doob, L. W., Miller, N. E., Mowrer, O. H., & Sears, R. R. (1939). *Frustration and aggression*. New Haven: Yale University Press.

Eckardt, G. (1985). Preyer's road to child psychology. In G. Eckardt, W. G. Bringmann, & L. Sprung (Eds.), *Contributions to a history of developmental psychology*. Berlin: Mouton.

Eiseley, L. (1958). *Darwin's century*. Garden City, NY: Doubleday.

Elder, G. H., Jr. (1974). *Children of the great depression*. Chicago: University of Chicago Press.

Elder, G. H., Jr. (1975). Age differentiation and the life course. In A. Inkeles, J. Coleman, & N. Smelser (Eds.), *Annual review of sociology* (Vol. 1, pp. 165-190). Palo Alto, CA: Annual Reviews.

Emmerich, W. (1968). Personality development and concepts of structure. *Child Development, 39*, 671-690.

English, H. B. (1950). Child psychology. In J. P. Guilford (Ed.), *Fields of psychology: Basic and applied*. Princeton, NJ: Van Nostrand.

Erikson, E. H. (1950). *Childhood and society*. New York: Norton.

Erikson, E. H. (1959). Identity and the life cycle [Special Issue]. *Psychological Issues, I*.

Erikson, E. H. (1968). *Identity, youth and crisis*. New York: Norton.

Evans, R. I. (1973). *Jean Piaget: The man and his ideas*. New York: Dutton.

Fast, I. (1985). *Event theory: A Piaget-Freud integration*. Hillsdale, NJ: Lawrence Erlbaum Associates.

Fay, M. A. (1978). Did Marx offer to dedicate *Capital* to Darwin? *Journal of the History of Ideas, 39*, 133-146.

Featherman, D. L. (1983). Life-span perspectives in social science research. In P. B. Baltes & O. G. Brim, Jr. (Eds.), *Life span development and behavior* (Vol. 5, pp. 1-57). New York: Academic Press.

Featherman, D. L., & Lerner, R. M. (1985). Ontogenesis and sociogenesis: Problematics for theory and research about development and socialization across the life span. *American Sociological Review, 50*, 659-676.

Flavell, J. H. (1963). *The developmental psychology of Jean Piaget*. Princeton, NJ: Van Nostrand.

Flavell, J. H., & Ross, L. (Eds.). (1981). *Social cognitive development: Frontiers and possible futures*. Cambridge: Cambridge University Press.

Flugel, J. C. (1933). *A hundred years of psychology.* New York: Macmillan.

Frank, L. K. (1935). The problem of child development. *Child Development, 6,* 7–18.

Frank, L. K. (1962). The beginnings of child development and family life education in the twentieth century. *Merrill-Palmer Quarterly, 8,* 207–227.

Freud, S. (1910). The origin and development of psychoanalysis. *American Journal of Psychology, 21,* 181–218.

Freud, S. (1938). The history of the psychoanalytical movement. In A. A. Brill (Ed. and Trans.), *The basic writings of Sigmund Freud.* New York: Random House.

Freud, S. (1939). *Moses and monotheism* (K. Jones, Trans.). New York: Knopf.

Freud, S. (1954). *Collected works, standard edition.* London: Hogarth Press.

Freud, S. (1961). *Totem and taboo* (J. Strachey, Trans.). London: Routledge & Paul. (Original work published 1913)

Freud, S. (1966). *Introductory lectures on psychoanalysis* (J. Strachey, Trans., Ed.). New York: Liveright. (Original work published 1916)

Gallatin, J. E. (1975). *Adolescence and individuality.* New York: Harper & Row.

Galton, F. (1876). The history of twins as a criterion of the relative power of nature and nurture. *Anthropological Institute Journal, 5,* 391–406.

Galton, F. (1883). *Inquiries into human faculty and its development.* London: Macmillan.

Galton, F. (1978). *Hereditary genius: An inquiry into its laws and consequences.* New York: St. Martin's. (Original work published 1869)

Gengerelli, J. A. (1976). Graduate school reminiscence: Hull and Koffka. *American Psychologist, 31,* 685–688.

Gesell, A. (1928). *Infancy and human growth.* New York: Macmillan.

Gesell, A. L. (1929). Maturation and infant behavior pattern. *Psychological Review, 36,* 307–319.

Gesell, A. L. (1931). The individual in infancy. In C. Murchison (Ed.), *Handbook of child psychology.* Worcester, MA: Clark University Press.

Gesell, A. L. (1934). *An atlas of infant behavior.* New Haven: Yale University Press.

Gesell, A. (1939). Charles Darwin and child development. *Scientific Monthly, 49,* 548–553.

Gesell, A. L. (1946). The ontogenesis of infant behavior. In L. Carmichael (Ed.), *Manual of child psychology.* New York: Wiley.

Gesell, A. (1948). *Studies in child development.* Westport, CT: Greenwood.

Gesell, A. L. (1954). The ontogenesis of infant behavior. In L. Carmichael (Ed.), *Manual of child psychology* (2nd ed.). New York: Wiley.

Ghiselin, M. T. (1969). *The triumph of the Darwinian method.* Berkeley: University of California Press.

Ghiselin, M. T. (1986). The assimilation of Darwinism in developmental psychology. *Human Development, 29,* 12–21.

Gillespie, N. C. (1979). *Charles Darwin and the problem of creation.* Chicago: University of Chicago Press.

Gillispie, C. C. (1968). Lamarck and Darwin in the history of science. In B. Glass, O. Temkin, & W. L. Straus, Jr. (Eds.), *Forerunners of Darwin: 1745–1859.* Baltimore: Johns Hopkins University Press.

Gollin, E. S. (1981). Development and plasticity. In E. S. Gollin (Ed.), *Developmental plasticity: Behavioral and biological aspects of variations in development.* New York: Academic.

Gould, R. I. (1978). *Transformations: Growth and change in adult life.* New York: Simon & Schuster.

Gould, S. J. (1977). *Ontogeny and phylogeny.* Cambridge, MA: Harvard University Press.

Gould, S. J., & Vrba, E. (1982). Exaptation: A missing term in the science of form. *Paleobiology, 8,* 4–15.

Groffman, K. J. (1970). Life-span developmental psychology in Europe: Past and present. In

L. R. Goulet & P. B. Baltes (Eds.), *Life-span developmental psychology: Research and theory*. New York: Academic.

Gruber, H. E. (1974). *Darwin on man: A psychological study of scientific creativity*. New York: Dutton.

Haeckel, E. (1891). *Anthropogenie oder Entwicklungsgeschichte des Menschen* [Anthropogenie or developmental history of humans] (4th ed., 2 vols). Leipzig: Engelmann.

Hall, C. S., & Lindzey, G. (1957). *Theories of personality*. New York: Wiley.

Hall, G. S. (1883). The contents of children's minds. *Princeton Review, 11*, 249–272.

Hall, G. S. (1891a). The contents of children's minds on entering school. *The Pedagogical Seminary, 1*, 139–143.

Hall, G. S. (1891b). Notes on the study of infants. *The Pedagogical Seminary, 1*, 127–138.

Hall, G. S. (1904). *Adolescence: Its psychology and its relations to physiology, anthropology, sociology, sex, crime, religion, and education* (Vols. 1–2). New York: Appleton.

Hall, G. S. (1922). *Senescence: The last half of life*. New York: Appleton.

Hardesty, F. P. (1976). Early European contributions to developmental psychology. In K. F. Riegel & J. A. Meacham (Eds.), *The developing individual in a changing world*. Chicago: Aldine.

Harris, D. B. (1956, September 3). *Child psychology and the concept of development*. Presidential address to the Division of Developmental Psychology, American Psychological Association, Washington, DC.

Harris, D. B. (Ed.). (1957). *The concept of development*. Minneapolis: University of Minnesota Press.

Hartmann, E. von (1931). *Philosophy of the unconscious: Speculative results according to the inductive method of physical science*. London: Kegan Paul, Trench, Trubner.

Havighurst, R. J. (1948). *Developmental tasks and education*. New York: David McKay.

Havighurst, R. J. (1973). History of developmental psychology: Socialization and personality development through the life span. In P. B. Baltes & K. W. Schaie (Eds.), *Life-span developmental psychology: Personality and socialization*. New York: Academic Press.

Hearnshaw, L. S. (1964). *A short history of British psychology 1840–1940*. New York: Barnes & Noble.

Henle, M. (1977). The influence of gestalt psychology in America. *Annals of the New York Academy of Sciences, 291*, 3–12.

Hetherington, E. M., Lerner, R. M., & Perlmutter, M. (Eds.). (1988). *Child development in life span perspective*. Hillsdale, NJ: Lawrence Erlbaum Associates.

Hollingworth, H. L. (1927). *Mental growth and decline: A survey of developmental psychology*. New York: Appleton.

Hoyer, W. J. (Ed.). (1980). Conceptions of learning and the study of life-span development: A symposium. *Human Development, 23*, 361–399.

Hultsch, D. F. (Ed.). (1980). Implications of a dialectical perspective for research methodology. *Human Development, 23*, 217–267.

Hultsch, D. F., & Pentz, C. A. (1980). Encoding, storage, and retrieval in adult memory: The role of model assumptions. In L. W. Poon, J. L. Fozard, L. S. Cermak, D. Arenberg, & L. W. Thompson (Eds.), *New directions in memory and aging: Proceedings of the George A. Talland Memorial Conference*. Hillsdale, NJ: Lawrence Erlbaum Associates.

Huxley, J., & Kettlewell, H. B. D. (1965). *Charles Darwin and his world*. New York: Viking.

Jaeger, S. (1982). Origins of child psychology: William Preyer. In W. R. Woodward & M. G. Ash (Eds.), *The problematic science: Psychology in nineteenth-century thought*. New York: Praeger.

Jaeger, S. (1985). The origin of the diary method in developmental psychology. In G. Eckhardt, W. G. Bringmann, & L. Sprung (Eds.), *Contributions to a history of developmental psychology*. Berlin: Mouton.

James, W. (1890). *The principles of psychology* (Vol. 1). New York: Dover.

James, W. (1977). *A pluralistic universe*. Cambridge, MA: Harvard University Press.

Janet, P. (1930). [Autobiography]. In C. Murchison (Ed.), *A history of psychology in autobiography* (Vol. 1). Worcester, MA: Clark University Press.

Jenkins, J. J. (1974). Remember that old theory of memory? Well, forget it! *American Psychologist, 29,* 785–795.

Jones, E. (1961). *The life and works of Sigmund Freud*. London: Hogarth.

Jung, C. G. (1916). *Psychology of the unconscious*. London: Kegan Paul, Trench, Trubner.

Kessen, W. (1965). *The child*. New York: Wiley.

Kevles, D. J. (1985). *In the name of eugenics*. New York: Knopf.

Kirkpatrick, E. A. (1909). *Genetic psychology: An introduction to an objective and genetic view of intelligence*. New York: Macmillan.

Kitchener, R. F. (1986). *Piaget's theory of knowledge: Genetic epistemology and scientific reason*. New Haven: Yale University Press.

Köhler, U. (1985). The concept of development and the genetic method of C. G. Carus. In G. Eckhardt, W. G. Bringmann, & L. Sprung (Eds.), *Contributions to a history of developmental psychology*. Berlin: Mouton.

Kuhn, T. S. (1970). *The structure of scientific revolutions* (2nd ed.). Chicago: University of Chicago Press.

Laboratory of Comparative Human Cognition. (1983). Culture and cognitive development. In P. H. Mussen & W. Kessen (Eds.), *Handbook of child psychology: Vol. 1. History, theory, and methods*. New York: Wiley.

Labouvie-Vief, G. (1980). Beyond formal operations: Uses and limits of pure logic in life-span development. *Human Development, 23,* 141–161.

Labouvie-Vief, G. (1982). Dynamic development and mature autonomy: A theoretical prologue. *Human Development, 25,* 161–191.

Labouvie-Vief, G. (1986). Intelligence and cognition. In J. E. Birren & K. W. Schaie (Eds.), *Handbook of the psychology of aging* (2nd ed.). New York: Van Nostrand Reinhold.

Langer, J. (1969). *Theories of development*. New York: Holt, Rinehart & Winston.

Lehrman, D. S. (1970). Semantic and conceptual issues in the nature-nurture problem. In L. R. Aronson, E. Tobach, D. S. Lehrman, & J. S. Rosenblatt (Eds.), *Development and evolution of behavior: Essays in memory of T. C. Schneirla*. San Francisco: Freeman.

Leontiev, A. N. (1978). *Activity, consciousness, and personality*. Englewood Cliffs, NJ: Prentice-Hall.

Leontiev, A. N., & Luria, A. R. (1968). The psychological ideas of L. S. Vygotsky. In B. B. Wolman (Ed.), *Historical roots of contemporary psychology*. New York: Harper & Row.

Lerner, R. M. (1976). *Concepts and theories of human development*. Reading, MA: Addison-Wesley.

Lerner, R. M. (1978). Nature, nurture, and dynamic interactionism. *Human Development, 21,* 1–20.

Lerner, R. M. (1979). A dynamic interactional concept of individual and social relationship development. In R. L. Burgess & T. L. Huston (Eds.), *Social exchange in developing relationships*. New York: Academic.

Lerner, R. M. (Ed.). (1983). *Developmental psychology: Historical and philosophical perspectives*. Hillsdale, NJ: Lawrence Erlbaum Associates.

Lerner, R. M. (1984). *On the nature of human plasticity*. New York: Cambridge University Press.

Lerner, R. M. (1986). *Concepts and theories of human development* (2nd ed.). New York: Random House.

Lerner, R. M. (1989). Developmental contextualism and the life-span view of person–context interaction. In M. Bornstein & J. S. Bruner (Eds.), *Interaction in human development*.

Hillsdale, NJ: Lawrence Erlbaum Associates.

Lerner, R. M. (1990). Weaving development into the fabric of personality and social psychology—On the significance of Bandura's *Social foundations of thought and action*. *Psychological Inquiry, 1,* 92–95.

Lerner, R. M., Hultsch, D. F., & Dixon, R. A. (1983). Contextualism and the character of developmental psychology in the 1970s. *Annals of the New York Academy of Sciences, 412,* 101–128.

Lerner, R. M., & Kauffman, M. B. (1985). The concept of development in contextualism. *Developmental Review, 5,* 309–333.

Lerner, R. M., & Lerner, J. V. (1986). Contextualism and the study of child effects in development. In R. L. Rosnow & M. Georgoudi (Eds.), *Contextualism and understanding in behavioral science.* New York: Praeger.

Lerner, R. M., & Lerner, J. V. (1989). Organismic and social contextual bases of development: The sample case of adolescence. In W. Damon (Ed.), *Child development today and tomorrow.* San Francisco: Jossey-Bass.

Lerner, R. M., Skinner, E. A., & Sorell, G. T. (1980). Methodological implications of contextual/dialectic theories of development. *Human Development, 23,* 225–235.

Lerner, R. M., & Tubman, J. (1989). Conceptual issues in studying continuity and discontinuity in personality development across life. *Journal of Personality, 57,* 343–373.

Levinson, D. J., Darrow, C. N., Klein, E. B., Levinson, M. H., & McKee, B. (1978). *Seasons of a man's life.* New York: Knopf.

Liben, L. S. (1981). Individuals' contributions to their own development during childhood: A Piagetian perspective. In R. M. Lerner & N. A. Busch-Rossnagel (Eds.), *Individuals as producers of their development: A life-span perspective.* New York: Academic Press.

Lickliter, R., & Berry, T. D. (1990). The phylogeny fallacy: Developmental psychology's misapplication of evolutionary theory. *Developmental Review, 10,* 348–364.

Lipsitt, L. P., & Cantor, J. H. (Eds.). (1986). *Experimental child psychologist: Essays and experiments in honor of Charles C. Spiker.* Hillsdale, NJ: Lawrence Erlbaum Associates.

Loewenberg, B. J. (1957). *Darwin, Wallace and the theory of natural selection.* Cambridge, MA: Arlington.

Looft, W. R. (1972). The evolution of developmental psychology: A comparison of handbooks. *Human Development, 15,* 187–201.

Looft, W. R. (1973). Socialization and personality throughout the life span: An examination of contemporary psychological approaches. In P. B. Baltes & K. W. Schaie (Eds.), *Life-span developmental psychology: Personality and socialization.* New York: Academic Press.

Lovejoy, A. O. (1968). Recent criticism of the Darwinian theory of recapitulation: Its grounds and its initiator. In B. Glass, O. Temkin, & W. L. Straus, Jr. (Eds.), *Forerunners of Darwin: 1745–1859.* Baltimore: Johns Hopkins University Press.

Luria, A. K. (1971). Towards the problem of the historical nature of psychological processes. *International Journal of Psychology, 6,* 259–272.

Luria, A. R. (1976). *Cognitive development: Its cultural and social foundations* (M. Lopez-Morillas & L. Solotaroff, Trans.; M. Cole, Ed.). Cambridge, MA: Harvard University Press.

Luria, A. R. (1979). *The making of mind: A personal account of Soviet psychology.* Cambridge, MA: Harvard University Press.

Magnusson, D. (1988). *Individual development from an interactional perspective: A longitudinal study.* Hillsdale, NJ: Lawrence Erlbaum Associates.

Mandelbaum, M. (1971). *History, man, and reason.* Baltimore: Johns Hopkins University Press.

Manier, E. (1978). *The young Darwin and his cultural circle.* Dordrecht, Holland: Reidel.

Mayo, E. (1952). *The psychology of Pierre Janet.* Westport, CT: Greenwood.

Mayr, E. (1977). Evolution through natural selection: How Darwin discovered this highly unconventional theory. *American Scientist, 65,* 321–328.

McCandless, B. R., & Spiker, C. C. (1956). Experimental research in child psychology. *Child Development, 27,* 78–80.

McCluskey, K. A., & Reese, H. W. (Eds.). (1984). *Life-span developmental psychology: Historical and generational effects.* Orlando, FL: Academic Press.

McCullers, J. C. G. (1969). G. Stanley Hall's conception of mental development and some indications of its influence on developmental psychology. *American Psychologist, 24,* 1109–1114.

Mead, G. H. (1934). *Mind, self, and society.* Chicago: University of Chicago Press.

Miller, N. E., & Dollard, J. (1941). *Social learning and imitation.* New Haven: Yale University Press.

Mischel, T. (Ed.). (1971). *Cognitive development and epistemology.* New York: Academic Press.

Mischel, W. (1977). On the future of personality measurement. *American Psychologist, 32,* 246–254.

Misiak, H., & Sexton, V. S. (1966). *History of psychology in overview.* New York: Grune & Stratton.

Molenaar, P., & Oppenheimer, L. (1985). Dynamic models of development and the mechanistic–organismic controversy. *New Ideas in Psychology, 3,* 233–242.

Montada, L., & Schmitt, M. (1982). Issues in applied developmental psychology: A life-span perspective. In P. B. Baltes & O. G. Brim, Jr. (Eds.), *Life-span development and behavior* (Vol. 4). New York: Academic.

Moore, K. C. (1896). The mental development of a child. *Psychological Review Monograph,* (Supplement, Vol. 1, No. 3).

Morgan, C. L. (1902). Selection. In J. M. Baldwin (Ed.), *Dictionary of philosophy and psychology* (Vol. 2). New York: Peter Smith.

Morris, E. K. (1982). Behavior analysis and developmental psychology. *Human Development, 25,* 340–364.

Morris, E. K. (1988). Contextualism: The world view of behavior analysis. *Journal of Experimental Child Psychology, 46,* 289–323.

Morris, E. K., & Hursh, D. E. (1982). Behavior analysis and developmental psychology: Metatheoretical considerations. *Human Development, 25,* 344–349.

Mueller, R. H. (1976). A chapter in the history of the relationship between psychology and sociology in America: James Mark Baldwin. *Journal of the History of the Behavioral Sciences, 12,* 240–253.

Müller-Brettel, M., & Dixon, R. A. (1990). Johann Nicolas Tetens: A forgotten father of developmental psychology? *International Journal of Behavioral Development, 13,* 215–230.

Murchison, C., & Langer, S. (1927). Tiedemann's observations on the development of the mental faculties of children. *Journal of Genetic Psychology, 34,* 205–230.

Mussen, P. H. (Ed.). (1970). *Carmichael's manual of child psychology* (3rd ed.). New York: Wiley.

Mussen, P. H., & Kessen, W. (Eds.). (1983). *Handbook of child psychology: Vol. 1. History, theory, and methods.* New York: Wiley.

Nagel, E. (1957). Determinism in development. In D. B. Harris (Ed.), *The concept of development.* Minneapolis: University of Minnesota Press.

Neisser, U. (1978). Memory: What are the important questions? In M. M. Gruneberg, P. Morris, & R. H. Sykes (Eds.), *Practical aspects of memory.* New York: Academic Press.

Nesselroade, J. R., & Baltes, P. B. (Eds.). (1979). *Longitudinal research in the study of behavior and development.* New York: Academic Press.

Nesselroade, J. R., & Reese, H. W. (Eds.). (1973). *Life-span developmental psychology: Methodological issues.* New York: Academic Press.

Neugarten, B. L. (1964). *Personality in middle and late life.* New York: Atherton.

Neugarten, B. L., & Guttman, D. L. (1958). Age-sex roles and personality in middle age: A thematic apperception study. *Psychological Monographs, 72,* (470).

Nisbet, R. (1980). *History of the idea of progress.* New York: Basic.

Overton, W. F. (1973). On the assumptive base of the nature–nurture controversy: Additive versus interactive conceptions. *Human Development, 16,* 74–89.

Overton, W. F. (Ed.). (1983). *The relationship between social and cognitive development.* Hillsdale, NJ: Lawrence Erlbaum Associates.

Overton, W. F. (1984). World views and their influences on psychological theory and research: Kuhn–Lakatos–Lauden. In H. W. Reese (Ed.), *Advances in child development and behavior* (Vol. 18). New York: Academic.

Overton, W. F. (1991). The structure of developmental theory. In P. van Geert & L. P. Mos (Eds.), *Annals of theoretical psychology* (Vol. 7). New York: Plenum.

Overton, W. F., & Newman, J. L. (1982). Cognitive development: A competence-activation/utilization approach. In T. Field, A. Huston, H. Quay, L. Troll, & G. Finley (Eds.), *Review of human development.* New York: Wiley.

Overton, W. F., & Reese, H. W. (1973). Models of development: Methodological implications. In J. R. Nesselroade & H. W. Reese (Eds.), *Life-span developmental psychology: Methodological issues.* New York: Academic Press.

Overton, W. F., & Reese, H. W. (1981). Conceptual prerequisites for an understanding of stability-change and continuity-discontinuity. *International Journal of Behavioral Development, 4,* 99–123.

Padover, S. K. (Ed.). (1978). *The essential Marx: The non-economic writings.* New York: New American Library.

Pepper, S. C. (1942). *World hypotheses.* Berkeley: University of California Press.

Perez, B. (1878). *Les trois premières années de l'enfant [The child's first three years].* Paris: Ballieze.

Peters, R. S. (Ed.). (1965). *Brett's history of psychology.* Cambridge, MA: MIT Press.

Petrinovich, L. (1979). Probabilistic functionalism: A conception of research method. *American Psychologist, 34,* 373–390.

Piaget, J. (1923a). La pensée symbolique et la pensée de l'enfant [Symbolic thought and children's thinking]. *Archives of Psychology, 18,* 273–304.

Piaget, J. (1923b). *Le langage et la pensée chez l'enfant* [The language and thought of the child]. Neuchatel: Delachaux & Niestlé.

Piaget, J. (1932). *The language and thought of the child.* New York: Harcourt, Brace.

Piaget, J. (1950). *The psychology of intelligence.* London: Routledge & Kegan Paul.

Piaget, J. (1970). Piaget's theory. In P. H. Mussen (Ed.), *Carmichael's manual of child psychology* (Vol. 1). New York: Wiley.

Piaget, J. (1972). *Problèmes de psychologie génétique* [Problems of genetic psychology]. Paris: Denoel.

Piaget, J. (1978). *Behavior and evolution.* New York: Pantheon.

Piaget, J. (1982). Reflections on Baldwin. In J. M. Broughton & D. J. Freeman-Noir (Eds.), *The cognitive-developmental psychology of James Mark Baldwin: Current theory and research in genetic epistemology.* Norwood, NJ: Ablex.

Piaget, J. (1983). Piaget's theory. In P. H. Mussen & W. Kessen (Eds.), *Handbook of child psychology: Vol. 1. History, theory, and methods.* New York: Wiley.

Pressey, S. L., Janney, J. E., & Kuhlen, R. G. (1939). *Life: A psychological survey.* New York: Harper & Row.

Preyer, W. (1882). *Die Seele des Kindes* [The mind of the child]. Leipzig: Fernau.

Preyer, W. (1888). *The mind of the child: Part I. The senses and the will* (H. W. Brown, Trans.). New York: Appleton.

Preyer, W. (1893). *Mental development in the child* (H. W. Brown, Trans.). New York: Appleton.

Preyer, W. (1896). *Darwin: Sein Leben und Wirken.* Berlin: Ernst Hofman.

Prior, M. D. (1895). Notes on the first three years of a child. *Pedagogical Seminary, 3,* 339–341.

Quetelet, A. (1835). *Sur l'homme et le développement de ses facultés* [On man and the development of his faculties]. Paris: Bachelier.

Reese, H. W. (1976). Conceptions of the active organism (introduction). *Human Development, 19,* 69–70.

Reese, H. W. (1980). A learning theory critique of the operant approach to life-span development. *Human Development, 23,* 368–376.

Reese, H. W. (1982a). Behavior analysis and developmental psychology: Discussant comments. *Human Development, 25,* 352–357.

Reese, H. W. (1982b). A comment on the meanings of "dialectics." *Human Development, 25,* 423–429.

Reese, H. W. (1986). Behavioral and dialectical psychologies. In L. P. Lipsitt & J. H. Cantor (Eds.), *Experimental child psychologist: Essays and experiments in honor of Charles C. Spiker.* Hillsdale, NJ: Lawrence Erlbaum Associates.

Reese, H. W., & Overton, W. F. (1970). Models of development and theories of development. In L. R. Goulet & P. B. Baltes (Eds.), *Life-span developmental psychology: Research and theory.* New York: Academic.

Reinert, G. (1979). Prolegomena to a history of life-span developmental psychology. In P. B. Baltes & O. G. Brim, Jr. (Eds.), *Life-span development and behavior* (Vol. 2). New York: Academic Press.

Richards, R. J. (1982). Darwin and the biologizing of moral behavior. In W. R. Woodward & M. G. Ash (Eds.), *The problematic science: Psychology in nineteenth-century thought.* New York: Praeger.

Richards, R. J. (1987). *Darwin and the emergence of evolutionary theories of mind and behavior.* Chicago: University of Chicago Press.

Riegel, K. F. (1972). Influence of economic and political ideologies on the development of developmental psychology. *Psychological Bulletin, 78,* 129–141.

Riegel, K. F. (1973). Developmental psychology and society: Some historical and ethical considerations. In J. R. Nesselroade & H. W. Reese (Eds.), *Life-span developmental psychology: Methodological issues.* New York: Academic Press.

Riegel, K. F. (1975). Toward a dialectical theory of development. *Human Development, 18,* 50–64.

Riegel, K. F. (1976). The dialectics of human development. *American Psychologist, 31,* 689–700.

Riegel, K. F. (1978). *Psychology mon amour: A countertext.* Boston: Houghton Mifflin.

Riegel, K. F. (1979). *Foundations of dialectical psychology.* New York: Academic.

Riegel, K. F., & Meacham, J. A. (Eds.). (1976). *The developing individual in a changing world* (2 vols.). Chicago: Aldine.

Riley, M. W. (Ed.). (1979). *Aging from birth to death.* Washington, DC: American Association for the Advancement of Science.

Rosnow, R. L., & Georgoudi, M. (Eds.). (1986). *Contextualism and understanding in behavioral science.* New York: Praeger.

Ross, B. M., & Kerst, S. M. (1978). Developmental memory theories: J. M. Baldwin and Piaget. In H. W. Reese (Ed.), *Advances in child development and behavior* (Vol. 12). New York: Academic Press.

Ruse, M. (1979). *The Darwinian revolution*. Chicago: University of Chicago Press.

Russett, C. E. (1976). *Darwin in America: The intellectual response 1865-1912*. San Francisco: Freeman.

Rybash, J. M., Hoyer, W. J., & Roodin, P. A. (1986). *Adult cognition and aging*. New York: Pergamon.

Sameroff, A. J. (1975). Transactional models in early social relations. *Human Development, 18*, 65-79.

Sanford, E. C. (1902). Mental growth and decay. *American Journal of Psychology, 13*, 426-449.

Sarbin, T. R. (1977). Contextualism: A world view for modern psychology. In J. K. Cole & A. W. Landfield (Eds.), *Nebraska Symposium on Motivation* (Vol. 24). Lincoln: University of Nebraska Press.

Schaie, K. W. (1983). The Seattle Longitudinal Study: A 21-year exploration of psychometric intelligence in adulthood. In K. W. Schaie (Ed.), *Longitudinal studies of adult psychological development*. New York: Guilford.

Schur, M. (1972). *Freud: Living and dying*. New York: International Universities Press.

Sears, R. R. (1975). Your ancients revisited: A history of child development. In E. M. Hetherington (Ed.), *Review of child development research* (Vol. 5). Chicago: University of Chicago Press.

Shinn, M. W. (1893-1899). *Notes on the development of a child* (Vol. 1). Berkeley: University of California Press.

Shinn, M. W. (1900). *The biography of a baby*. Boston: Houghton Mifflin.

Siegel, A. W., & White, S. H. (1982). The child study movement: Early growth and development of the symbolized child. In H. W. Reese (Ed.), *Advances in child development and behavior* (Vol. 17). New York: Academic.

Siegel, L. S., & Brainerd, C. J. (Eds.). (1977). *Alternatives to Piaget: Critical essays on the theory*. New York: Academic Press.

Sigel, I. E. (1972). Developmental theory: Its place and relevance in early intervention programs. *Young Children, 27*, 364-372.

Simpson, W. G. (1893). A chronicle of infant development. *Journal of Mental Sciences, 39*, 378-389, 498-505.

Sjövall, B. (1967). *Psychology of tension: An analysis of Pierre Janet's concept of "tension psychologique" together with an historical aspect* (A. Dixon, Trans.). Norstedts, Sweden: Scandinavian University Books.

Skinner, B. F. (1938). *The behavior of organisms*. New York: Appleton.

Skinner, B. F. (1950). Are theories of learning necessary? *Psychological Review, 57*, 211-220.

Skinner, B. F. (1953). *Science and human behavior*. New York: Macmillan.

Skinner, B. F. (1974). *About behaviorism*. New York: Macmillan.

Smuts, A. B., & Hagen, J. W. (Eds.). (1986). History and research in child development. *Monographs of the Society for Research in Child Development* (Vol. 30, Nos. 4-5).

Sorensen, B., Weinert, E., & Sherrod, L. R. (Eds.). (1986). *Human development and the life course: Multidisciplinary perspectives*. Hillsdale, NJ: Lawrence Erlbaum Associates.

Spiker, C. C. (1986). Principles in the philosophy of science: Applications to psychology. In L. P. Lipsitt & J. H. Cantor (Eds.), *Experimental child psychologist: Essays and experiments in honor of Charles C. Spiker*. Hillsdale, NJ: Lawrence Erlbaum Associates.

Spiker, C. C., & McCandless, B. R. (1954). The concept of intelligence and the philosophy of science. *Psychological Review, 61*, 255-266.

Stout, G. F., & Baldwin, J. M. (1902). Adaptive (mental processes). In J. M. Baldwin (Ed.), *Dictionary of philosophy and psychology* (Vol. 1). New York: Peter Smith.

Sulloway, F. J. (1982). Freud and biology: The hidden legacy. In W. R. Woodward & M. G. Ash (Eds.), *The problematic science: Psychology in nineteenth-century thought*. New York: Praeger.

Sully, J. (1903). *Studies of childhood.* New York: Appleton.

Tetens, J. N. (1777). *Philosophische Versuche über die Menschliche Natur und ihre Entwicklung* [Philosophical research on human nature and its development]. Leipzig: Weidmanns Erben und Reich.

Thorndike, E. L. (1904). The newest psychology. *Educational Review, 28,* 217–227.

Tobach, E. (1983). The relationship between Preyer's concept of psychogenesis and his views of Darwin's theory of evolution. *Zeitschrift für Psychologie, 191* 387–395.

Tobach, E. (1985). The relationship between Preyer's concept of psychogenesis and his views of Darwin's theory of evolution. In G. Eckhardt, W. G. Bringmann, & L. Sprung (Eds.), *Contributions to a history of developmental psychology.* Berlin: Mouton.

Tobach, E., & Greenberg, G. (1984). The significance of T. C. Schneirla's contribution to the concept of integration. In G. Greenberg & E. Tobach (Eds.), *Behavioral evolution and integrative levels.* Hillsdale, NJ: Lawrence Erlbaum Associates.

Tolman, C. (1983). Further comments on the meaning of "dialectic." *Human Development, 26,* 320–324.

Tolman, C. W. (1991). For a more adequate concept of development with help from Aristotle and Marx. In P. van Geert & L. P. Mos (Eds.), *Annals of theoretical psychology* (Vol. 7). New York: Plenum.

Toulmin, S., & Goodfield, J. (1965). *The discovery of time.* Chicago: University of Chicago Press.

Turner, R. R., & Reese, H. W. (Eds.). (1980). *Life-span developmental psychology: Intervention.* New York: Academic Press.

van Geert, P. (1991). Theoretical problems in developmental psychology. In P. van Geert & L. P. Mos (Eds.), *Annals of theoretical psychology* (Vol. 7). New York: Plenum.

Vidal, F., Buscaglia, M., & Voneche, J. J. (1983). Darwinism and developmental psychology. *Journal of the History of the Behavioral Sciences, 19,* 81–94.

Vonèche, J. (1982). An interview conducted with Piaget: Reflections on Baldwin. In. J. M. Broughton & D. J. Freeman-Noir (Eds.), *The cognitive developmental psychology of James Mark Baldwin.* Norwood, NJ: Ablex.

Vygotsky, L. S. (1929). The problem of the cultural development of the child. *Journal of Genetic Psychology, 36,* 415–434.

Vygotsky, L. S. (1962). *Thought and language.* Cambridge, MA: MIT Press. (Original work published 1934)

Vygotsky, L. S. (1978). *Mind in society* (M. Cole, V. John-Steiner, S. Scribner, & E. Souberman, Eds.). Cambridge, MA: Harvard University Press.

Wapner, S., Kaplan, B., & Cohen, S. B. (1973). An organismic-developmental perspective for understanding transactions of men and environments. *Environment and Behavior, 5,* 255–289.

Watson, J. B. (1924). *Behaviorism.* New York: Norton.

Watson, J. B. (1926). What the nursery has to say about instincts. In C. Murchison (Ed.), *Psychologies of 1925.* Worcester, MA: Clark University Press.

Werner, H. (1948). *Comparative psychology of mental development.* New York: International Universities Press.

Werner, H. (1957). The concept of development from a comparative and organismic point of view. In D. B. Harris (Ed.), *The concept of development.* Minneapolis: University of Minnesota Press.

Wertheimer, M. (1985). The evolution of the concept of development in the history of psychology. In G. Eckhardt, W. G. Bringmann, & L. Sprung (Eds.), *Contributions to a history of developmental psychology.* Berlin: Mouton.

White, S. H. (1968). The learning–maturation controversy: Hall to Hull. *Merrill-Palmer Quarterly, 14,* 187–196.

White, S. H. (1970). The learning theory tradition and child psychology. In P. H. Mussen

(Ed.), *Carmichael's manual of child psychology* (3rd ed.). New York: Wiley.

White, S. H. (1977). Social proof structures: The dialectic of method and theory in the work of psychology. In N. Datan & H. W. Reese (Eds.), *Life-span developmental psychology: Dialectical perspectives on experimental research.* New York: Academic Press.

White, S. H. (1983). The idea of development in developmental psychology. In R. M. Lerner (Ed.), *Developmental psychology: Historical and philosophical perspectives.* Hillsdale, NJ: Lawrence Erlbaum Associates.

White, S. H. (1985). Presidential address: Developmental psychology at the beginning. *Developmental Psychology Newsletter, 7,* 27–39.

Wiener, P. P. (1949). *Evolution and the founders of pragmatism.* Cambridge, MA: Harvard University Press.

Willis, S. L. (Special Section Ed.). (1990). Cognitive training in later adulthood. *Developmental Psychology, 26,* 875–915.

Wohlwill, J. F. (1973). *The study of behavioral development.* New York: Academic Press.

Wohlwill, J. F. (1991). Relations between method and theory in developmental research: A partial-isomorphism view. In P. van Geert & L. P. Mos (Eds.), *Annals of theoretical psychology* (Vol. 7). New York: Plenum.

Wolff, P. H. (1960). The developmental psychologies of Jean Piaget and psychoanalysis. *Psychological Issues, 2,* (1, Monograph No. 5).

Wozniak, R. H. (1975a). A dialectical paradigm for psychological research: Implications drawn from the history of psychology in the Soviet Union. *Human Development, 18,* 18–34.

Wozniak, R. H. (1975b). Dialectics and structuralism: The philosophical foundations of Soviet psychology and Piagetian cognitive developmental theory. In K. F. Riegel & G. Rosenwald (Eds.), *Structure and transformation: Developmental aspects.* New York: Wiley.

Wozniak, R. H. (1982). Metaphysics and science, reason and reality: The intellectual origins of genetic epistemology. In J. M. Broughton & D. J. Freeman-Noir (Eds.), *The cognitive-developmental psychology of James Mark Baldwin: Current theory and research in genetic epistemology.* Norwood, NJ: Ablex.

2 Design, Measurement, and Analysis: Technical Issues in Developmental Research

Donald P. Hartmann
University of Utah

INTRODUCTION

This chapter is concerned with the technical aspects of developmental research; the substantive aspects — the findings and theory involving cognitive and social development — are addressed in the chapters that follow. These technical parts of research include at least the following topics: the design of studies, the measurement of variables, and the analysis of data, as well as ethical considerations. To the neophyte who has attempted to read the method and analysis sections of developmental papers, these "methodological" aspects of research appear to be bewildering, and infinitely varied in type, form, and perhaps function. To give but a few illustrations of studies differing in *design,* consider the following:

1. an anecdotal case study of the social interactions from birth through weaning of a litter of puppies;
2. a survey of the sexual practices of hundreds of high achieving and low achieving 13- to 19-year-old adolescents;
3. a laboratory experiment on touch-induced stress performed on 40 very low birth weight (premature) newborns;
4. systematic playground observations of the altruistic reactions of groups of mixed- and uniform-gender kindergarten children over the course of the school year;
5. a single-subject experiment run in a nursing-care facility on the short-term memory of an elderly lady; and

6. norms for a test of child social behaviors established on representative samples of male and female children in cohorts differing in 1.5 year intervals.

This brief list of studies suggests the widely varying nature of developmental investigations. Underlying this variation, however, are relatively tractable sets of dimensions involving design types and the validity threats the designs were intended to control, populations and methods of generating samples from them, and the like. So it is not the number of dimensions and their constituent parts that may be bewildering, but rather the ways in which these dimensions can be combined.

However complex the technical aspects of research may be — and they are, infrequently, extraordinarily complex — it is important to emphasize the dependence of research technology on the questions motivating the empirical investigation. The question to be answered should determine the most effective design, the most appropriate measures, and the most informative forms of analysis applied to the resulting scores. Questions determined by technical knowledge and expertness tend to be unsystematic, atheoretical, and of dubious use in advancing the science of development. The dependence of research technology on the substance of the experimental questions places an additional burden on investigators: They must find, or, if unavailable, develop the design, the measurement operations, and the methods of analysis that are uniquely suited to their research questions.

The aspects of design, measurement, and analysis presented in this chapter are not intended to qualify individuals to select, let alone develop, their own design, measurement, and analysis procedures. Each of these tasks typically requires a series of graduate courses. Instead, this chapter is intended to serve as a guide for those individuals who are seriously entering the domain of developmental research, to show them how design, measurement, and analysis work in this area of investigation by specifying commonly used methods, indicating major issues, noting more serious pratfalls, and suggesting where additional information might be obtained.

The section on design focuses on the four classes of validity threats, and how nonexperimental, quasi-experimental, and true experimental designs meet, or fail to meet, the challenges represented by these threats. Special attention is paid to design difficulties that plague developmental investigators, and to the traditional as well as the newer designs that have been developed in response to these difficulties.

In examining measurement issues, the purposes of measurement, the types of scores generated by developmental investigators, and the criteria used for judging the worth of these scores are discussed. Standardization, reliability, and validity criteria emerge as uniquely important for assessing the quality of scores. Many aspects of measurements — including the nature of the underlying constructs, accessible characteristics of target responses, relevant comparison standards for deciphering the meaning of scores, and available source of information — determine how scores are operationalized, as well as judged.

The section on analysis begins with a discussion of preliminary data analysis: methods of appropriately laundering data and developing an intimate familiarity with them. Formal statistical analysis is viewed as serving two interrelated functions: describing data by means of various indices of typical performance, variability, and relation; and testing whether the value of these indices varies from null values — that is, whether the data are statistically significant. A substantial number of techniques for serving these functions are described, with brief mention made of pitfalls and problems in their use and of the sources for learning more about them. These techniques of analysis accommodate the two major purposes of developmental research: assessing average performance as well as variation about the average, or individual differences. Univariate and multivariate analytic techniques for qualitative and quantitative data are described, and two, relatively new and increasingly popular, techniques, structural modeling and meta-analysis, are singled out for special attention. The analysis section ends with a discussion of the frequent misunderstandings of the results of statistical testing.

The chapter ends with a brief discussion of ethical issues in developmental research. The discussion is aimed at both general issues relevant to the integrity of science, such as honesty in the report of research findings, and those issues that more directly impact research subjects, including justifiable risk, invasion of privacy, and informed consent.

DESIGN

Science has three main purposes: the prediction of important criteria, the control of relevant outcomes, and the search for causal relations between independent and dependent variables. The substantive area of investigation determines the most important of these goals and the variables investigated. Once an investigator chooses the research question — and thereby defines the purposes of the research — a design must be constructed so that that question can be answered in as unambiguous a manner as is reasonable given the ethical, technological, and practical constraints under which we all must function. Design, then, involves the structure of investigations, the extent and means by which investigators exercise control over their independent, as well as other, variables that might be operating in the investigative context, so that appropriate conclusions can be drawn from the research.

Experimental design, then, is intended to guard against alternative or competing plausible interpretations of the phenomena under study. These competing interpretations have been construed as threats to the validity of the investigation. This section describes the most common of these validity threats, with particular attention directed to problems common to the research experiences of developmentalists. The solutions to these problems afforded by a variety of design variations, including true experimental, quasi-experimental, and nonexperimental designs are described. Special attention is paid to the designs defined by the developmental variables of age, cohort, and time of assessment, both in their traditional combination and in their newer and more complex combination in sequential designs. The section ends with a listing of suggested readings for readers who may want additional information on these issues.

Validity Threats

Campbell and his associates (Campbell & Stanley, 1963; Cook & Campbell, 1979) distinguished four classes of threats to the validity of investigations that developmental, as well as other, researchers must confront. These four classes, their definitions, and specific examples are given in Table 2.1, Panels A-D (see pp. 63, 65, 66, and 67; also see Huck & Sandler, 1979, for illustrations of many of the frequently discussed validity threats).

Statistical Conclusion Validity

Threats to statistical conclusion validity—or to the validity of the statistical tests—are easier to understand with at least some acquaintance with statistical decision theory. Table 2.2 illustrates a simple decision matrix that describes the decisions that might be made as a result of null hypothesis testing. Two decisions and two states of nature are shown: The decisions are to accept or to reject the null hypothesis; the states of nature are that the null hypothesis is either true or false. The resulting decision matrix shows two types of correct and two types of incorrect decisions. The incorrect decisions are referred to as either (a) Type I errors, which occur when a true null hypothesis is mistakenly rejected (with a probability equal to α—where α is the critical value required for rejection of the null hypothesis, traditionally set at either $p = .05$ or $p = .01$), and (b) Type II errors, which occur when a false null hypothesis is wrongly accepted (with a probability equal to β, where $[1 - \beta]$ = power).

Threats to statistical conclusion validity represented by Type I errors occur as a result of conducting numerous statistical tests on the same set of data, such as comparing each of $k = 6$ means to every other mean, resulting in $k(k - 1)/2 = 15$ comparisons. Unless the data analyst makes

TABLE 2.1: Panel A
Statistical Conclusion Validity Threats: Definition and Examples

Are the results of the statistical tests — acceptance or rejection of each of the null hypotheses — valid? *OR* Is statistical conclusion validity threatened by design or analytic weaknesses or errors?

Low Power: Is failure to reject a false null hypothesis (a Type II error) ascribable to the fact that the null hypothesis was true and there was no effect to be detected[1] or to low power? Low power might occur as a result of
1. inadequate sample size;
2. unreliable or weak measures;
3. weak or inconsistent manipulation of the independent variable;
4. poor experimental control (the presence of random irrelevancies in the investigative setting);
5. excessive subject heterogeneity;
6. weak statistics; and,
7. excessively small alpha levels.

Violation of the Assumptions of the Statistical Tests: Has an incorrect conclusion been drawn — either an incorrect rejection (Type I error) or an incorrect acceptance of the null hypothesis (Type II error) — because an important assumption of the statistical test has been violated?

Fishing Expeditions: Have Type I errors been inflated — sometimes referred to as probability pyramiding (Neher, 1967) — as a result of excessive, overlapping analysis of the data?

Notes: Additional threats to the four types of validities outlined in Panels A to D of Table 2.1 are given in Cook and Campbell (1979, Chapter 2).

[1] Strictly speaking no null hypothesis may be precisely true. Trivial differences may even be found for the null hypothesis such as that involving the equivalence in IQ of people living east of the Mississippi in comparison to those living west of the Mississippi (see Morrison & Henkel, 1970). The relevant difference to be detected is not *any* difference, but any difference large enough to be interesting to the investigator.

adjustments for the number of statistical tests conducted, Type I error mushrooms for the entire set of tests, and is clearly not equal to α. Additional threats represented by distortions of Type I error occur when certain kinds of statistical assumptions are violated (see, e.g., Gardner & Hartmann, 1984; Kenny & Judd, 1986; Kirk, 1982, chap. 2). Threats represented by Type II errors occur primarily when power (the probability of rejecting a false null hypothesis) is low, but also when statistical assumptions are violated.[1]

Internal Validity

Threats to internal validity (Panel B of Table 2.1), called confounds, are, with few exceptions, easily understood. One of the more knotty confounds is regression to the mean. Regression occurs when subjects are selected on

---

[1] Any factor that inflates Type I error, will, if the null hypothesis is false, decrease Type II error.

TABLE 2.2
A Matrix Illustrating Statistical Decision Theory

| | | State of Nature: H_o | |
		True	False
Investigator's Decision	Reject H_o	Type I Error (α)	Correct Rejection (Power)
	Accept H_o	Correct Acceptance	Type II Error (β)

Note: H_o refers to the null hypothesis.

the basis of the extremity of their scores, such as poor readers, highly distractible individuals, or insensitive mothers. If the measure used to select these extremely performing subjects is less than perfectly reliable — which is almost always true — they can be expected to score less deviantly on repeated assessment with the initial selection device or with *any other* assessment technique (Furby, 1973; Labouvie, 1982). Thus, as a group, poor readers will appear to be less poor in their reading performance on a second assessment of their reading performance simply because the (random) error component of their scores cannot be expected to be consistently poor — as they were likely to be on the initial assessment.

A second seemingly opaque class of confounds consists of ambiguity about the direction of causal influence. However, this threat to internal validity is recognizable by the old adage that "correlation does not imply causation." Even if all potential third variable causes can be excluded (the troublesome variable Z, when variables X and Y are investigated), it still may be plausible, particularly in nonexperimental investigations, that X (the putative independent variable) is caused by Y (the ostensible dependent variable) rather than the other way around.

Most threats to internal validity can be avoided by random assignment of subject to conditions, a critical method of control in psychological research, and a characteristic of true experiments. However, even randomization may not rule out some threats to internal validity, such as those represented in the last two paragraphs of Panel B of Table 2.1 (e.g., diffusion of treatments and resentful demoralization).

Construct Validity

In general, threats to construct validity occur when the variables, as operationalized, either underrepresent the intended constructs or include surplus components. For example, the construct *anxiety* that did not

TABLE 2.1: Panel B
Internal Validity Threats: Definition and Examples

Can the observed findings be attributed to the independent variable? *OR* Is internal validity threatened by some methodological confound?

History: Did some event intervene, say, between the pretest and the post-test that produced an effect that might be confused with an effect produced by the independent variable (IV)?

Maturation: Are the observed findings ascribable to the growth or other internal changes in the subject rather than to the IV?

Testing: Did the subject's familiarity with the assessment device produce the observed changes in the dependent variable (DV)?

Instrumentation: Did the measurement instrument itself change over the course of the study so that differences are a result of changes in the calibration of the instrument and not of changes produced by the IV?

Regression: Are observed changes due to the selection of deviant subjects based on their performance on an unreliable assessment device, and their scores moving toward the mean on repeated testing as a function of the combination of selection and unreliability, rather than as a result of changes produced by the IV?

Selection: Are observed differences attributable to preexisting differences in the individuals assigned to the groups compared, rather than to effects produced by differences in exposure to the IV?

Mortality: Are observed differences due to differential dropouts or attrition in the groups compared?

Interactions with Selection: Are the observed findings ascribable to the interaction of selection with, say, maturation (because of selection factors, groups of subjects are maturing at different rates) rather than to the effects of the IV?

Ambiguity About the Direction of Causal Influence: Is the causal connection from the presumed DV to the IV rather than the other way around?

Diffusion of Treatments, Compensatory Equalization of Treatments, or Compensatory Rivalry: Is the lack of observed differences a result of the fact that the nontreated subjects were either inadvertently exposed to the treatment, provided with compensatory treatments, or "worked harder" because they did not receive the favored treatment?

Resentful Demoralization: Was the effect observed attributable to the demoralized responding of subjects who thought that they received a less desirable treatment?

---

include physiological, ideational, and behavioral components might be faulted for construct underrepresentation. On the other hand, a paper-and-pencil measure of assertion that correlated highly with verbal IQ might be criticized for including surplus irrelevancies.

Construct validity threats can be sustained by either the independent variable (IV) or the dependent variable (DV). Consider, for example, the use of a single male and a single female model (an example of mono-operation bias—see Table 2.1, Panel C), in a study of the effects of model gender on the imitation of aggression. In this example, mono-operationalization of the IV might result in a unique characteristic of one of the models, such as attractiveness, producing an effect that is confused with a gender effect. A construct validity threat to DVs might occur when all of the outcome variables are assessed using a single method, such as self-

TABLE 2.1: Panel C
Construct Validity Threats: Definition and Examples

Do the critical variables in the study (the independent and dependent variables) measure the intended constructs? *OR* Is construct validity threatened by one or more methodological artifacts.

Inadequate Preoperational Explication of Constructs: Does the meaning of the construct as used in the investigation match the ordinary meaning of the construct as used in this area of study?

Mono-operational Bias: Have the critical variables in the study been operationalized in but one way, so that the results are a function of the particular operationalization employed?

Monomethod Bias: Have the operationalizations of a construct or constructs all used the same method, so that the results might be ascribable to overlapping method variance rather than overlapping construct variance?

Hypothesis-guessing: Are the results attributable to subjects acting consistently with their hypotheses about the study, or how they believe the experimenter wants them to behave (the Hawthorne effect)?

Evaluation Apprehension: Is some "subject effect" (Webber & Cook, 1972) such as fear of evaluation responsible for the observed changes in performance, rather than the IV?

Experimenter Expectancies: Are the results a function of the expectancies of the experimenter (e.g., Jung, 1971)—a treatment-correlated irrelevancy—which are somehow transmitted to the subject?

Confounding Constructs and Levels of Constructs: Is it the particular level of the IV that produced (or failed to produce) the observed effect, rather than the entire range of levels of the IV?

Interaction of Different Treatments: Is the effect observed a result of the particular combination or sequence of IVs employed, rather than of the pivotal treatment variable?

Interaction of Testing and Treatment: Does the putative effect of treatment require the use of pretesting—where subjects may be primed to respond in a particular manner?

Restricted Generalizability Across Constructs: Does the IV affect a range of outcome constructs, or instead, just the more-or-less narrow range of outcome constructs employed in the investigation?

---

report. In such cases of monomethod bias, relationships found between the outcome variables might be produced by the self-report method variance (Campbell & Fiske, 1959) that they share, rather than by actual interdependence of the constructs.

Construct validity threats include not only measurement artifacts, but other artifacts as well that distort the meaning of either the IV or DV. Among these are subject effects (e.g., evaluation apprehension and the distrusting subject) that produce atypical responding (Rosenthal & Rosnow, 1969), and experimenter effects such as expectancies that influence subjects in irrelevant ways (e.g., Jung, 1971), as well as the use of pretest assessments that sensitize the subjects, or a particular sequence or combination of treatments that modifies the effect of the target treatment.

TABLE 2.1: Panel D
External Validity Threats: Definition and Examples

Can the results of the investigation be generalized broadly? *OR* Is external validity threatened by contrived settings, unusual subjects, or other factors that limit the generality of the results of the study?

Interaction of Selection and Treatment: Are the results limited to the particular sample investigated, or can they be generalized to a broader range of subjects?

Interaction of Setting and Treatment: Are the effects produced applicable to other settings than the specific settings employed in the present investigation?

Interaction of History and Treatment: Can the results be generalized to other time periods, or are they limited to the particular historical circumstances in which the study was conducted?

External Validity

Issues of external validity are sometimes otherwise labeled—as issues of ecological validity, generalizability, or representativeness (e.g., Bronfenbrenner, 1977; Brunswik, 1953). Whatever label is attached, the primary concern is the extent to which the results of studies are applicable to individuals, settings, and times different from those existing during the conduct of the study. Generalizability is one of psychology's seminal issues, and requires continued vigilance. Are the results of research performed on North American samples of adolescents applicable to adolescents living in third-world countries? Are the findings of research conducted in the 1930s on the effects of nursery school applicable to nursery school experiences in the 1990s, when the nature of nursery schools, the caregivers who enroll their children in them, and the like, differ? Logical analysis should help us to answer such questions, although given the penchant of most scientists to define neither their sampling frames,[2] nor the historical contexts and setting events of their studies, extrapolating from present studies is at best an uncertain enterprise. Perhaps it is only with the aid of replication that questions of external validity will be answerable (e.g., Hersen & Barlow, 1984; Lykken, 1968).

No investigator can thwart all of these common validity threats as some requirements conflict with others. For example, the uniform application of treatments may increase statistical conclusion validity, but at the cost of external validity. No study has been, nor will any ever be, perfect. Basic researchers, those studying basic processes of development, may tend to

---

[2]Most investigators treat the *sampling* of study participants as an issue not worthy of serious consideration—as if any sampling method will do, whether it be convenience or accidental sampling, or involves snowballing (one subject recommends a second, etc.), coercion, or bribery. Unless it is implausible that subject variables could modify important conclusions drawn from the research, such an attitude seems scientifically perilous.

emphasize internal, construct, and statistical conclusion validity to the detriment of external validity, whereas applied researchers studying social policy issues may emphasize internal, external, and statistical conclusion validity at the cost to construct validity.

Seminal Design Issues for Developmental Investigators

All investigators, whatever their focus or interest, must confront these four classes of validity threats. In addition to these generic threats to the validity of research findings, there are other design concerns that are more or less the province of developmental investigators. These special issues, not surprisingly, concern the modifiability of the variables studied by developmentalists, the changing form of the phenomena they study, their subjects' limited ability to perceive or describe their experiences, the complexity out of which the behavior they study develops, and the dangerous causal biases held by them — as well as by many students of development.

Intractable Variables

Many of the important variables investigated by developmental researchers are relatively intractable. For example, a pivotal question to the field is the way heredity and environment conspire to produce behavior. But heredity cannot be manipulated, except in studies of infrahuman species, and environments are likewise generally not modifiable over broad sweeps or for extensive periods of an individual's life. Even that most popular of all developmental variables, age, has clear limitations. Age cannot be modified or manipulated, although individuals of various ages can be chosen for investigation. And although it is unquestionably useful to find that a phenomenon covaries with age, neither age — nor the related variable, time — are causal variables; changes occur in time, but not as a result of time. Instead, time or age are part of a context in which causal processes operate. Thus, in an important sense, the most studied developmental variable (see Miller, 1987) is causally impotent (Wohlwill, 1970).

Change

The study of development is foremost the study of change. Change has associated with it a variety of thorny technical problems (Rogosa, 1988). Among these is the fact that a construct may itself change in topography or other important characteristics with development. Thus, a measure of emotional control appropriate for one developmental level may be inappropriate for assessing emotional control during another phase of development. Furthermore, individuals vary in the timing of developmental changes. For some individuals, change may occur briefly and comparatively late; for others change may occur over more protracted periods of time, and early. A lack of sensitivity to temporal parameters of change may mean that the time period during which a process is most open to our inspection will be missed.

Limited Availability of Self-Reports

Unlike the sophisticated college student subjects often studied by cognitive psychologists, the subjects of many developmental investigations are unable to aid the investigator by describing their experiences—either because they are unaware of the relevant behaviors or processes, or because they do not have a communicative system that can be readily accessed (Messick, 1983). Other, oftentimes complex, methods must be used to address even limited aspects of the young child's mental and emotional experiences, or independent raters must be relied on to gain access to the more obvious manifestations of these experiences.

Complexity of Causal Networks

Many developmental phenomena are intricately embedded in a complex, interacting network of environmental and genetic–constitutional forces that defies simple analysis or study. In many cases, the factors of presumed importance—such as severe environmental deprivation—cannot be reproduced with humans because of obvious ethical concerns. As a result, investigators are forced to the laboratory where analogues of naturally occurring phenomena are created, and where complex, naturalistic conditions are greatly simplified. The consequences of these actions are that external and construct validity may be substantially strained.

Directional Causal Biases

Many developmentalists are biased in attributing causal agency to adults rather than children, to families rather than cultural factors, and (perhaps still) to environmental rather than biological determinants. The reasons for these biases are undoubtedly complex, and are not widely discussed—although the classic paper by Bell (1968) on the direction of effects in the socialization literature is widely cited and appears to have had an important impact on developmental research. Nonetheless, we must be cautious in imputing direction of causation, particularly so for findings that are produced by passive observational or ex post facto studies. Furthermore, we must also exercise constraint in not overemphasizing the causal importance of proximal variables (such as parents), while underplaying the role of more distal variables, such as unemployment, inequitable distribution of wealth, and the like. And finally, we must be wary of overstating the causal importance of currently politically correct causes, to the detriment of equally important but unpopular causes. We may, for example, be prone to attribute children's aggressive behavior to violence in television programming rather than to competitive learning environments in our educational institutions, when both factors are equally plausible and potent determinants of aggression.

Design Variations

Developmental investigators have employed a variety of design variations in response to the validity threats and problems already discussed. Many of the common variations are summarized in Table 2.3. As the note to that table suggests, a design chosen to answer one type of validity threat may actually facilitate another type of validity threat. For example, contrived settings have allowed investigators to exercise experimental control over unwanted sources of variation—but at the expense of external validity. The study of natural treatments promotes external validity, but the complexity and noise associated with these treatments often blurs their meaning or construct validity. The intensive study of a few individuals may allow investigators to capture the complexity of their target phenomena, but may raise questions of generalizability.

Perhaps the most important differences between families of designs are those based on the nature of the causal statement that the designs allow. Campbell and his associates (Campbell & Stanley, 1963; Cook & Campbell, 1979) distinguished three levels of investigation based on the causal implications of the designs: true experiments, quasi-experiments, and nonexperiments.

True Experiments

True experiments have both manipulation of the independent variable by the investigator and control of extraneous variables by random assignment of subjects to conditions. These designs, if conducted properly, allow investigators to make strong inferences regarding the causal effect exerted by the IV over the DV. Part A of Table 2.4 illustrates two true experimental designs: the simplest of all true experimental designs—and from which all other true experimental designs are derived—the experimental-control group design with posttests only, and the more complex, Solomon four-group design. Other true experimental designs are discussed by Campbell and Stanley (1963) and by the authors of other design texts (e.g., Neale & Liebert, 1980).

TABLE 2.3
The Advantages of Design Variations Intended to Solve Validity Threats and Other Design Concerns

	Vs	
Experimental Control		*Statistical Control*

Experimental Control

Nuisance variables are precluded from occurring by isolation or selection.

Improves internal validity by avoiding error variance.

Statistical Control

Nuisance factors are removed by statistical means (e.g., partial *r*).

Promotes internal validity by removing error variance.

Preserves external validity by not tampering with setting.

Contrived Settings

Modifies settings so that target behaviors occur and extraneous variables are controlled (e.g., laboratories).

Promotes internal validity by exercising tight control over nuisance variables.

Saves investigative time by decreasing dross rate.

Field Setting

Employs untampered settings for investigations.

Facilitates external validity by providing a natural context.

Provides estimates of naturally occurring rates of behaviors.

Artificial Treatments

Introduces ideal or protoypical forms of treatments.

Improves construct validity of causes by control over nature of IV.

Natural Treatments

Examines naturally occurring treatments.

Promotes external validity by studying natural variation.

Crossed Designs

Designs in which each level of every factor is paired with each level of every other factors (e.g., in an age by gender design, girls and boys are represented for each age group).

Allows for the assessments of interactions.

Nested Designs

Designs in which each level of every factor is not paired with each level of every other factor.

Improves efficiency by omitting treatment conditions of little interest.

Facilities content validity by precluding certain forms of multiple-treatment interference.

Within-Subjects' Designs

Uses each subject as own control.

Promotes statistical conclusion validity by controlling error variance.

Between-Subjects Designs

Control provided by random assignment of subjects to conditions.

May foster construct validity by avoiding multiple treatment interference.

Uses investigative time efficiently by allowing simultaneous study of many treatments.

Intensive (Idiographic) Designs

Designs in which one or a few subjects are intensively assessed, usually across time, as in a longitudinal or time-series study.

Furthers the study of performance across time.

Accommodates the complexity of performance.

Provides access to where the laws of behavior reside — in the individual.

Extensive (Nomothetic) Designs

Many subjects are assessed, but not often.

Makes efficient used of investigative time.

Provides normative performance information.

Note: The advantages of one alternative, typically, although not always, are the limitations of the other alternative.

TABLE 2.4

Illustrations of True Experimental, Quasi-Experimental, and Nonexperimental Designs

---

Panel A: True Experimental Designs
Experimental–Control Group Design Employing Posttest Only Assessments:
Group

Experimental	R:	X 0
Control	R:	0

Solomon Four-Group Design:
Group

Experimental	R:	0 X 0
	R:	X 0
Control	R:	0 0
	R:	0

Panel B: Quasi-experimental Designs
Interrupted Time-Series (ABA) Design:
Group (or Subject)

Unit 1: $0.....0\ X_10.....X_10\ 0.....0$

OR

$X_10.....X_10\ X_20.....X_20\ X_20.....X_10$

Interrupted Time-Series (Multiple Baseline) Design:
Group (or Subject)

Unit 1[a]	$0.....0\ X_10.....X_10$
Unit 2	$0\ 0.....0\ X_10.....X_10$
Unit 3	$0\ 0\ 0.....0\ X_10.....X_10$

Panel C: Nonexperimental Designs
One-Group, Pre- and Posttest Design:
Group

Experimental: 0 X 0

Note: By convention, R indicates random assignment of subjects to groups, 0 indicates an assessment, and X indicates a treatment. The separation of events by ..... indicates that the event may be repeated one or more times.

[a]Units can represent individuals, or treatment settings or behaviors for an individual. Individuals may be either a single individual or an aggregate of individuals such as a classroom of students (e.g., Gelfand & Hartmann, 1984).

Quasi-experiments

Quasi-experiments are investigations in which control procedures are instigated, but assignment to conditions is not random. In such cases, the thread connecting cause and effect is less susceptible to clear delineation, although some causal inferences are possible. Part B of Table 2.4 illustrates two quasi-experimental designs frequently used by applied behavior analysts, the ABA and Multiple Baseline Designs (Gelfand & Hartmann, 1984). With the ABA or interrupted time-series design, the subject is repeatedly observed under one treatment or control series (the repeated X₁O linkages), then another treatment is imposed and observation continues (the repeated

X_2O linkages). The initial treatment–observation phase is reinstituted (the second set of X_1O linkages), and in many cases, the second phase of treatment–observation (X_2O) is also reinstated. With the Multiple Baseline Design, treatment is successively introduced into each of two or more units (behaviors, subjects, or contexts) following a series of control observations. These and other quasi-experimental designs can, with the addition of special features, exclude many, or even all plausible alternative interpretations, and so allow strong causal inferences.

Nonexperimental Designs

Nonexperimental designs employ neither randomization nor adequate control conditions. Designs in this class generally provide a product that does not allow drawing secure causal inferences. Included in this group are case studies, one-group pre- and post-test designs (see Panel C of Table 2.4), and similar designs that are used primarily for hypothesis generation. Ex post facto and passive observational designs also are members of the nonexperimental design family (Meehl, 1970).[3] The lack of clarity regarding causal connections between the variables investigated in these designs is generally well known. Nonetheless, they serve the important role of *probing* (in contrast to *testing*) potential causal models. Certainly a causal model relating X and Y is probed if X and Y are found to be uncorrelated. But even then, one could argue that the relation was too complex to be revealed by the design, that the investigator made a poor decision in choosing the time delay between putative cause and effect (e.g., hunger is undoubtedly causally related to food intake, but self-reported hunger and observed food ingestion might only be correlated if eating was assessed for the meal immediately following the assessment of hunger), and so forth. Unfortunately, many traditional developmental designs are closer to the nonexperimental designs in the level of causal inference allowed than they are to true experimental designs.

Developmental Designs

Developmentalists traditionally have been concerned with two issues: the normative changes that occur in the developing individual and individual differences in these developmental functions. The pursuit of these goals generally involves the variable of age, and age typically has been investigated using either traditional cross-sectional or longitudinal designs.

Before discussing these, and other developmental designs, it seems useful

---

[3]In the past, these designs were sometimes referred to as "correlational designs." However, that is an unfortunate term, as correlations are statistical measures of association, not designs, and can be applied to the data from any of the three types of designs described earlier.

to examine three variables that distinguish the various developmental designs: cohort, age, and time of assessment. Cohorts are groups of subjects who are born in the same time period. Thus, we speak of the 1979 cohort, of the cohort born in the 1960s, and of the cohort of baby boomers. Age has its usual meaning, as does time of assessment.

As is soon apparent, the design-defining variables of cohort, age, and time of assessment are not independent. This lack of independence can be seen by specifying a cohort and a time of assessment in the matrix shown in Panel A of Table 2.5. Once the values for these two variables are specified, age — the variable specified in the body of the matrix — is not free to vary, but instead is fixed or determined. Herein lies one of the major problems with the designs derived from this matrix: The variables of cohort, age, and time of assessment in these designs are inherently confounded. Consider the cross-sectional design (shown in Panel B of Table 2.5).

Cross-sectional designs are those in which at least two cohorts are assessed at the same time of assessment. As a result, the cohorts differ in age. If DV performance in a cross-sectional study differs across the age groups, one would be tempted to attribute the performance difference to

TABLE 2.5
Simple Developmental Designs

Panel A			
		Time of Assessment	
Cohorts	*1975*	*1980*	*1985*
1960	15^{1b}	20^b	25
1965	10	15^{ac}	20
1970	5	10^a	15^c

Panel B			
		Cohort	
Cross-sectional Design:		*1965*	*1970*
Time of Assessment: 1980		15^1	10

Panel C			
		Age	
Longitudinal Design:		15	20
Cohort: 1960		1975^2	1980

Panel D			
		Time of Assessment	
Time-lagged Design:		*1980*	*1985*
Age: 15		1965^3	1970

[a]Cross-sectional Design.
[b]Longitudinal Design.
[c]Time-lagged Design.
[1]Age is given in the body of the table.
[2]Time of Assessment is given in the body of the table.
[3]Cohort is given in the body of the table.

age or development. However, note that the same variation in performance on the DV can also be attributed to cohort differences! Cohort differences might be produced by genetic variation (resulting from changes in migration patterns or exposure to radiation), or they might stem from environmental variation (such as educational reform associated with living during a somewhat different historical epoch). Each of the simple developmental designs diagrammed in Table 2.5 shares an analogous confound. These elementary developmental designs also share two other interpretive difficulties. First, the variables of cohort and time of assessment are *not* causally active—a status that has already been noted for age. At best, the variables of cohort, age, and time of assessment are *proxy* variables for the real causal processes that operate in time or are associated with cohort or time of assessment. Second, the variables of cohort, age, and time of assessment are not manipulated in these designs, nor are subjects randomly assigned to cohorts or ages, though they can be randomly assigned to times of assessment—although not after age and cohort are determined. Thus, the aspects of these developmental designs involving cohort, age, and time of assessment are not truly experimental. Indeed, the designs are nonexperimental (ex post facto), and the resulting data do not lend themselves to strong causal inferences regarding the effects of either age, cohort, or time of assessment.

Longitudinal designs are illustrated in Panel C of Table 2.5. These designs have been described as "the lifeblood of developmental psychology" (McCall, 1977, p. 341). Nonetheless, they confound age and time of assessment and are nonexperimental with respect to these two variables (e.g., Labouvie, Bartsch, Nesselroade, & Baltes, 1974). In addition, age and time of assessment are only proxies for active causal variables. We have already considered some of the causally active variables for which age could serve as a proxy; in the case of time of assessment, the casual variables may be events such as a turndown in the economy, the death of a prominent official, or a natural disaster.

A time-lagged design, the last of the simple developmental designs, is illustrated in Panel D of Table 2.5. The time-lagged designs confound the proxy variables of cohort and time of assessment and are nonexperimental with respect to these two variables as well.

Although these simple developmental designs suffer from a variety of interpretive problems, they provide valuable information to developmentalists as to whether standing on important DVs varies as a function of age, cohort, or time of assessment. Once such a discovery has been made, the search for the explanation—the underlying process responsible for the finding—can begin.

In an attempt to remedy some of the problems associated with these simple developmental designs, more complex developmental designs—

called sequential designs—have been developed (e.g., Schaie, 1965). These designs are illustrated in Table 2.6. Panel A displays a cohort × time of assessment matrix similar to the one shown in Table 2.5. In this case, however, the designs that are derived from the matrix are more complex that those derived from the matrix in Table 2.5. Each of the sequential designs (Panels B–D in Table 2.6) represents the crossing (see Table 2.3) of two of the three definitional variables of cohort, age, and time of assessment.

Consider the cross-sequential design (Panel B of Table 2.6), and see how the design is generated, and how its findings might be interpreted. The cross-sequential design—renamed the cohort × time of assessment design—represents the crossing of the two variables, cohort and time of assessment. That is, each level of the cohort variable is combined with each level of the time of assessment variable to generate the conditions included in the design. (In many design books, the × symbol represents the

TABLE 2.6
Complex (Sequential) Developmental Designs

Panel A

Cohort	Time of Assessment		
	1975	*1980*	*1985*
1960	15^{1b}	20^{bc}	25
1965	10	15^{abc}	20^{abc}
1970	5	10^{a}	15^{ac}

Panel B

Cohort × Time of Assessment Design	Cohort	
	1965	*1970*
Time of Assessment: *1980*	15^{1}	10
1985	20	15

Panel C

Age × Cohort Design	Age	
	15	20
Cohort: *1960*	1975^{2}	1980
1965	1980	1985

Panel D

Time of Assessment × Age Design	Time of Assessment	
	1980	*1985*
Age: *15*	1965^{3}	1970
20	1060	1965

[a]Cohort × Time of Assessment (Cross-sequential) Design.
[b]Age × Cohort (Cohort-sequential) Design.
[c]Time of Assessment × Age (Time-sequential) Design.
[1]Age is given in the body of the table.
[2]Time of Assessment is given in the body of the table.
[3]Cohort is given in the body of the table.

operation of crossing.) As depicted in Panel B of Table 2.6, this design is comprised of combinations of the more elementary developmental designs. At its minimum, the cohort × time of assessment design includes two short-term longitudinal designs (the 1965 cohort assessed at ages 15 and 20, and the 1970 cohort assessed at ages 10 and 15), two cross-sectional designs (10- and 15-year-olds assessed in 1980 and 15- and 20-year-olds assessed in 1985), and one time-lagged design (15-year-olds assessed in 1980 and 1985).

The cohort × time of assessment design can be compared to the cross-sectional design illustrated in Panel B of Table 2.5, which compared 10- and 15-year-olds when they were assessed in 1980. The presence of a second group of 15-year-olds (from the 1970 cohort assessed in 1985) assists in determining whether the performance of the 15-year-olds from the 1980 cohort is ascribable to age or to cohort differences. Furthermore, if the two cohorts of 15-years-olds respond similarly, the data might be treated analogously to the data obtained from a longitudinal design with age ranging from 10 through 20 years—but instead of requiring 10 years to conduct, the study only took 5 years!

The two remaining sequential designs, renamed the age × cohort design and the time of assessment × age design (as the two designs represent the crossing of the two variables included in their names) are shown in Panels C and D of Table 2.6. The interpretation of the data from these designs is analogous to those made for the cohort × time of assessment design (see Adams, 1978; Costa & McCrae, 1982).

Additional Concerns and References

Experimental design issues do not end with our brief discussion of generic and special developmental validity threats and problems, and design variations that have been developed to address these concerns. Additional topics, such as philosophy of science considerations underlying the choice of design, subject selection, and single-subject design strategies, also are major aspects of design that have been given, at best, short shrift in this chapter. Because of space considerations and perhaps idiosyncratic judgments of the author, these topics must be dependent on the initiative of the reader. To facilitate the reader's task, the following references are suggested. For general design issues, consult Achenbach (1978); Appelbaum and McCall (1983); Barber (1976); Carlsmith, Ellsworth, and Aronson (1976); Kazdin (1980); Meehl (1978); Miller (1987); Mussen (1960); Neale and Liebert (1980); Pedhazur and Pedhazur-Schmelkin (1991); Rosenthal and Rosnow (1969); and Vasta (1982). For additional information on the implications of the philosophy of science for design, see Braybrooke (1987), Cook and Campbell (1979, chap. 1), Kuhn (1970), and Popper (1959). For discussions of the critical issues of subject selection and assignment, refer to

Suen and Ary (1989, chap. 3) and Pedhazur and Pedhazur-Schmelkin (1991, chap. 15). Finally, for additional information on single-subject design, consult Barlow and Hersen (1984), Iwata et al. (1989), and Kazdin (1982).

MEASUREMENT

Measurement includes the operations that are used to obtain scores for subjects in developmental research. In developmental research, the scores provided by measurement operations assess DV performance, evaluate subject's IV statuses, and determine subjects' standings on other dimensions used to describe the research sample or to control for differences among individual subjects or groups of subjects. These research-related decision-making functions of measurement, or scaling as it is sometimes called, require that the resulting scores are both relevant and of high quality.

Issues of measurement quality are particularly acute in developmental investigations because of the vicissitudes of assessing subjects occupying the ends of the developmental spectrum. Youngsters in particular present problems "of establishing rapport and motivation; of ensuring that instructions are well understood; of maintaining attention; and, of coping with boredom, distraction, and fatigue" (Messick, 1983, p. 479). In addition, because of children's rapid changes in many cognitively based activities, it may be difficult to capture their transient performance levels. Furthermore, the meaning of test scores may change in concert with changes in the children's development. Thus, at one age, test scores may reflect understanding, and at a slightly later age primarily reflect motivation (e.g., Hofstaetter, 1954). As a result of these problems in measuring children's performance, developmental investigators have additional demands placed on them to demonstrate that their measures are of high quality.

The assessment of measurement quality, not surprisingly, depends on the nature of the research and the specific questions put forward for investigation. Nevertheless, certain criteria are generally relevant to judgments of quality, including whether or not the measurement device is applied in a standard fashion, and whether or not the resulting scores are replicable (reliable) and measure what they are supposed to measure—a notion that bears very close resemblance to the notion of construct validity, which we have already discussed. Still other criteria, such as the presence of a meaning zero point for the measurement scale, may be imposed by the nature of the statistical methods that are to be applied to the resulting scores.

Precisely how these criteria or standards are applied, and which are relevant, may also depend on various technical or theoretical considerations—sometimes referred to as measurement *facets* and *sources* (e.g., Messick, 1983). The facets include the nature of the characteristic assessed—whether they are stable traits or changing states, structures or functions, and competence or typical performance. Other facets involve whether the scores are used for interindividual (normative) or intraindividual (ipsative) comparisons, and depend for their interpretation on norms (norm-referenced) or on objective performance standards (criterion-referenced).

The sources of measurement include whether the assessment responses are based on self reports, constitute test responses, or are reports of performance in naturalistic settings by participant or independent observers. We briefly discuss scores—the products of measurement—and the criteria for evaluating scores, measurement facets, and sources of data. The section on measurement ends with an illustrative example involving the observation of children's social behavior, and sources for additional study.

Types of Scores

Scores come in a bewildering assortment of types. Most scores obtained from subjects in developmental research will be straightforward and understandable either from reading the description of the study's procedures or from examining the study's tables or figures. Examples include scores that are expressed in basic units of measurement such as length, frequency, and duration (see Johnston & Pennypacker, 1980), as well as aggregate scores resulting from the addition of item scores obtained on questionnaires and tests. These scores need not concern us further.

Other scores pose slight interpretive problems because they are constructions of the original scores—percentiles, and "alphabet scores" (T and z scores)—that come with additional interpretive baggage. These scores are often designed to meet the assumptions of statistical tests or to remedy some perturbation, such as skewness, in the original distribution of scores. Such scores are described in Table 2.7, as are the defects they are intended to remedy and the interpretive warnings with which they are associated.

Still other scores represent more complicated transformations of the original data—difference or growth scores, and age- or grade-equivalent scores; they must be treated with some caution. Perhaps the most troublesome of these prudence-demanding scores are simple difference scores, X(posttreatment or time 2) − X(pretreatment or time 1), used to index change over some period of development or as a result of treatment. Difference scores are often employed to assess change or growth, but are widely regarded as multiply flawed (e.g., Achenbach, 1978; Cronbach & Furby, 1970; Harris, 1963), but compare with Rogosa and his associates (e.g., Rogosa, 1988; Rogosa, Brandt, & Zimowski, 1982). Difference scores

TABLE 2.7
Transformed Scores, Their Purposes, and Qualifications to Their Interpretation

Transformation	Purpose	Interpretive Qualifications
$[X + 1]^{1/2}$, log X, arc sin X	Regularize (e.g., normalize) distributions for data analytic purposes	Interpretation must be applied to transformed scores
Proportion of X_1, X_2, etc.	Control for variation in subject productivity	All subjects have the same total score (across all variables)[a]
Standard score: $z = (X - M)/SD$	Control for disparate Ms and/or SDs for variables	All variables have Ms = 0 and SDs = 1.0[b]
Percentile rank of X	Reduce the disparity of extreme scores	All variables are given identical ranges (i.e., 1 to 99)

Note: X is the symbol for the original raw scores; M for the mean, and SD for the standard deviation.

[a]See the later discussion of ipsative scores.

[b]Distributions of standardized scores can be generated with any convenient mean and standard deviation. For example, if the transformed score distribution has a mean of 50 and a standard deviation of 10, the scores are referred to as T scores. T scores are generated by the following equation: $T = 50 + z(10)$.

suffer from problems of unreliability—even though the scores that are differenced may themselves be reliable! Difference scores are not "base free" as is sometimes believed, but are frequently negatively correlated with initial or prescores. Additional problems occur when the characteristic that is assessed itself changes across the period of assessment.

Other problematic scores are age- (or grade-) equivalent and age-adjusted scores, such as mental age (MA) and intelligence quotient (IQ). The former, age-equivalent scores are, of course, only as good as the normative groups on which they are based. In addition, they may vary in meaning at different locations on the measurement scale. For example, during periods in which skills and abilities are improving dramatically, the performance differences between adjacent age or grade groups may be appreciable; yet during periods of sluggish growth, performance differences between adjacent groups may be minimal. Consider the differences in mental ability between 2- and 5-year-old children and between 22- and 25-year-old adults. In the former case the differences are substantial; in the latter case they are trivial. Thus, developmental researchers need to exercise caution in interpreting differences expressed in age equivalents.

Age-adjusted scores such as IQ scores are not only encumbered by the surplus meanings attributed to them (e.g., that IQ scores are fixed, similar to the way eye color is fixed; see Hunt, 1961), but also by the special measurement properties shared by all such age-adjusted scores. Equal scores for children of different ages do not indicate equal skill or ability, but instead indicate equivalent statuses for the children in their respective age groups. Thus, groups of 8-year-olds and 10-year-olds with equal mean IQs of 115 do not have equivalent cognitive skills. Indeed, the 10-year-olds clearly are the more skillful. What the two groups of subjects do have in common is that they are both one standard deviation above their age-group means with respect to IQ (Anastasi, 1978). Age-adjusted scores, similar to age-equivalent scores, must be interpreted with care.

Criteria for Evaluating Scores

The quality of scores usually is judged by their conformity to standard psychometric criteria. These criteria include the standardization of administration and scoring procedures and the demonstration of acceptable levels of reliability and of validity (e.g., American Psychological Association [APA], 1985). Some of these criteria require modification as a result of the nature of the variable under investigation. For example, because many performance variables, such as children's social skills, are assumed to be consistent over at least a few weeks, scores that assess these variables must demonstrate temporal reliability or stability over that time period. On the other hand, a measure of some transient characteristic, such as mood, would be suspect if it produced scores displaying temporal stability over a 2-week period.

Standardization

Standardization is intended to ensure that procedurally comparable scores are obtained for all of the subjects who take part in assessments using the device. Thus, standardization requires the use of equivalent administrative procedures, materials—such as items for tests or questionnaires and the timing and setting for observations—and methods of recording responses and of arriving at scores. In addition, it may be necessary to provide directions on how to develop and maintain rapport, whether to terminate or modify instruction for subjects with special deficiencies or handicaps, when to present assessment materials and social commentary, and how to ensure that subjects understand necessary instructions (e.g., Miller, 1987). The absence of standardized procedures can introduce substantial noise into data and hence ambiguity into the interpretation of individual studies or even groups of studies as has occurred, for example, in the literature on the assessment of children's fears using behavioral avoidance tests or BATs (Barrios & Hartmann, 1988).

Reliability

Reliability concerns the dependability, consistency, or generalizability of scores (e.g., Cronbach, Gleser, Nanda, & Rajaratnam, 1972). Theoretical treatises on reliability decompose obtained scores (X) into at least two generic components: True or universe scores (X_t) and error scores (e_x).

$$X = X_t + e_x.$$

The true score portion of one's obtained score is the part that remains constant across time. This component is sometimes defined conceptually as the mean of an infinite number of measurements, or across all possible parallel forms of an instrument, or across all possible relevant measurement conditions (also sometimes referred to as facets) such as occasions, scorers, and the like. The error component is the portion of one's score that changes across time, and hence results in inconsistent performance. Inconsistent performance might be produced by any number of factors, including chance events such as the break of a pencil lead during a test of mathematical problem solving, temporary states of the subject (e.g., being ill, elated, or angry), or idiosyncratic aspects of the measurement instrument such as inconsistent observer behavior or scorer error (e.g., Cronbach, 1970). Unfortunately, the factors that produce consistent and inconsistent responding on measurement instruments vary depending on the way reliability is assessed. For example, illness during observations of playground aggression might produce consistent responding in any assessment of reliability that breaks up an observational session into temporal parts and examines the internal consistency of performance across those parts. On the other hand, illness will produce inconsistent responding if observations conducted during a child's first grade are compared with those conducted during his or her second grade, when the child is no longer ill.

As this discussion suggests, reliability may be assessed in a number of ways that differently divide obtained scores into true and error scores, including the following:

Internal Consistency. Internal consistency measures of reliability assess the consistency of performance across a measure's internal or constituent parts (e.g., its items). Internal consistency reliability is one of the only forms of reliability that does not require repeated administration or scoring of an instrument.[4]

Interobserver Reliability. Interobserver (or interscorer) reliability assesses the extent to which observers or scorers obtain equivalent scores when

---

[4]The Spearman-Brown Prophesy formula (e.g., Nunnally, 1978) allows estimation of the internal consistency of an instrument from information about its items. Consider a test containing $k = 20$ items that have average intercorrelations (r_{ij}) equal to .20. Absolutely speaking, these are low intercorrelations, but they would not be considered particularly low for test items. The internal consistency reliability, (r_{kk}), of the test $= kr_{ij}/[1 + (k - 1)r_{ij}] = .83$, a very respectable value that perhaps indicates that in the area of test construction one can make a silk purse out of a sow's ear. At least one can if one has enough sows!

assessing the same individual. Interobserver reliability is assessed or measured with agreement statistics (e.g., percent agreement or kappa) or with traditional reliability statistics (e.g., correlation coefficients).

Parallel-form Reliability. Parallel-form reliability determines the degree to which alternative (e.g., parallel) forms of an instrument provide equivalent scores. Parallel-form reliability is to tests as interobserver reliability is to direct observations.

Situational Consistency (Generalizability). Situational consistency indexes the extent to which scores from an instrument are consistent across settings. This form of reliability is analogous to the concept of the external validity of investigations.

Temporal Reliability (Stability). Temporal reliability measures the degree to which an instrument provides equivalent scores across time. Test–retest correlations frequently are used to assess stability.

Two types of reliability, internal consistency and interobserver (or interscorer) agreement, are required for most uses of assessment instruments. The scores obtained from an instrument composed of internally consistent parts assess a single characteristic or a set of highly interrelated characteristics. In contrast, assessment procedures containing internally inconsistent items, time periods, or analogous constituent parts measure a hodgepodge; as a result, scores obtained from them will not be comparable. Two subjects who obtain identical total scores on an internally inconsistent measure may perform very differently from one another on the instrument's parts.

Interobserver or interscorer reliability likewise is requisite for the minimal interpretability of scores. Without adequate agreement between observers or scorers, the very nature of the phenomenon under study is unclear (e.g., Hartmann & Wood, 1982, 1990). The remaining forms of reliability, situational consistency and temporal stability, are required when an investigator wishes to generalize, respectively, across settings and time. Such would be the case if, for example, infants' attachment to their mothers assessed in the laboratory at age 10 months was used to infer their attachment in the home at age 10 months (situational consistency or setting generalizability), or their attachment in the laboratory at age 24 months (temporal stability). Temporal stability is consistently found to be negatively correlated with the length of time between assessments. Indeed, the decreasing stability with increasing interassessment time (sometimes described as simplex in structure) has been observed so commonly in investigations of stability that it has assumed the character of a basic law of behavior. Over a standard time interval, temporal consistency typically increases with age during childhood (e.g., Jones, 1954). Brief temporal consistency often exceeds situational consistency (e.g., Mischel & Peake,

1983), although this finding is open to some dispute (e.g., Epstein & Brady, 1985).

Despite the quite different meanings of the various forms of reliability, they are often assessed in much the same manner — by correlating pairs of subjects' scores (e.g., Mitchell, 1979). The scores may be paired across items, observers, time, or settings depending on the type of reliability assessed. The statistics commonly used to summarize reliability data are noted in Table 2.8. The advantages and disadvantages of various statistics for summarizing reliability analyses are described in Hartmann (1982a, 1982b).

Reliability gains general importance because it places a very specific limit on an instrument's empirical validity,[5] the following topic.

Measurement Validity

Although all of the aforementioned psychometric criteria involve the interpretation or meaning of scores, validity is the psychometric criterion most directly relevant to their meaning. Instruments, and the scores that they produce, may have various forms of validity.

Face Validity.   Face validity refers to whether the instrument appears to be a valid measure of some construct, as would a measure of altruism that asked children about the amount of money they donated to starving Ethiopians. Except for its public relations value, face validity is the least important form of measurement validity.

Content Validity.   Content validity assesses the degree to which the content of the instrument constitutes a representative sample of some substantive domain such as junior life saving, social competence, or problem solving. This form of validity is particularly important for achievement tests and observational coding systems.

Factorial Validity.   This form of validity determines the extent to which an instrument taps some substantive construct or factor, and is most often determined for instruments developed using factor analysis (see factor analysis in the analysis section). Factorial validity is highly related to the notion of internal consistency as discussed in the section on reliability.

Predictive Validity.   Predictive validity indicates the degree to which the scores from an assessment device are useful for predicting certain future

---

[5]If validity is indexed by an instrument's correlation with a criterion (r_{xy}), and the instrument's reliability is expressed as r_{xx}, the upper limit of r_{xy} is $r_{xx}^{1/2}$. That is, $|r_{xy}| \leq r_{xx}^{1/2}$ — which is a form of the well-known correction for attenuation formula (e.g., Nunnally, 1978). Thus, a measuring instrument with $r_{xx} = .50$ could not expect to correlate greater than .707 with any criteria.

TABLE 2.8
Commonly Used Statistical Techniques for Summarizing Reliability Data

Statistical Technique	Primary Use
Coefficient Alpha (α)[a]	Describes internal consistency reliability. Ranges from .0 to +1.0.
Intraclass Correlation (ICC)	General method of summarizing reliability data. Accommodates a variety of data types and forms of reliability. ICC indicates the ratio of subject to total variance. Ranges from .0 to +1.0.
Kappa *(K)*	Summarizes the reliability of categorical data. An agreement statistic frequently recommended because it corrects for chance agreement. For more detail, see the section on analysis. K ranges from <.0 to +1.0.
Kuder–Richardson-20 and -21	Assesses the internal consistency reliability of a device composed of dichotomous items, such as true–false achievement tests.
Product Moment Correlation (r_{xx})	General method of summarizing reliability data. Accommodates various forms of data and types of reliability with one of its many variants. According to classic reliability theory, r_{xx} indicates the ratio of true score to total variance; $1 - r_{xx}$ indicates the proportion of error variance. Ranges from .0 to +1.0.
Raw Agreement	Most frequently used method of summarizing interobserver reliability data. Frequently criticized for its failure to correct for chance agreements.
Spearman–Brown Prophesy Formula	Used for estimating the internal consistency reliability of lengthened or shortened assessment devices. See footnote 4.

Note: For more extended lists of statistics used for summarizing reliability data, see Berk (1979), Fleiss (1975), and House, House, and Campbell (1981).
[a]Not to be confused with α, the level of significance chosen for testing a null hypothesis.

criteria, such as academic success. This form of validity is similar to concurrent validity (see following). Indeed, predictive and concurrent validity are sometimes referred to as various forms of "criterion-related validity." Criterion-related validity is typically assessed with a correlation coefficient. A correlation of $r = .5$ between predictor and criterion measures indicates that the percentage of variance that overlaps between the two is 25%. Percent overlap equals $100 \times r^2$ (cf. McNemar, 1969, pp. 152–153; Ozer, 1985; Steiger & Ward, 1987).

Concurrent Validity. Concurrent validity indicates an instrument's correspondence with an important, currently assessed criterion. A test with substantial concurrent validity may be preferred over the devise against which it is validated, if it is more efficient or less expensive than the criterion measure.

Construct Validity. An instrument's construct validity indicates the extent to which it assesses some theoretical construct, such as concrete operational reasoning, anxiety, or self-efficacy. Construct validity is perhaps the most basic, and at the same time most inclusive form of validity. The extent of an instrument's construct validity depends on the congruence between the pattern of results it provides and the theoretical superstructure for the construct it presumably measures (Cronbach & Meehl, 1955). The demonstration of congruence usually involves numerous sources of information. For example, the scores obtained from a construct valid measure of children's interpersonal self-efficacy expectations (Bandura, 1977) presumably would distinguish socially successful from less successful children; show reasonable temporal stability except when following treatments intended to improve children's self-efficacy expectations; and correlate modestly with traditional measures of intelligence and moderately with peer-based measures of popularity and self-perceived competence. The more extensive and collaborative the interconnections between theory and measure, the stronger the evidence of the validity of the measure for assessing the construct (e.g., Kerlinger, 1986).

Wise investigators provide evidence for the construct validity of their measures, evidence that is independent of the results of the study that uses the measures to answer substantive questions. The failure to do so may result in a serious interpretive dilemma, particularly if the investigation does not work out as predicted. Critics may ask: Did the assessment instrument inadequately assess the construct? Was the theory supporting the construct faulty? Or did the study itself contain fatal validity threats? Without independent support for the construct validity of the measures, it may not be possible to decide among these three vastly different choices.

Other Criteria

With some interpretations of scores, the standard psychometric criteria must be supplemented with additional quantitative requirements. These requirements may include that the scores have a meaningful zero point, that the differences between scores have direction, and that the differences between scores are scaled (e.g., Nunnally, 1978). For example, if the differences between popularity scores are scaled, interpretations such as "Suzy is as different from Chen in popularity as Sigerdur is from Abdul" are possible. If, in addition, the popularity scale has a meaningful zero point, interpretations such as "Ling is twice as popular as Danielle" also are possible. Whichever of these criteria are met establishes the level of measurement obtained by the instrument's scores. The level of measurement relates not only to the interpretations that can be applied to the scores, but also to the statistics that are most commonly used with them (e.g., Stevens, 1968). The typically distinguished levels of measurement, along with illustrations, interpretations, and statistics typically applied to them are summarized in Table 2.9.

Data Facets

Measurement specialists and personality theoreticians have described an array of conceptualizations or facets of measurement that concern developmental investigators. The more important of these facets concern the organization, stability, and content of the constructs assessed, the characteristic or property of the response that is targeted for assessment, and the standards against which scores are compared (Messick, 1983). These facets are generally noteworthy because they influence the planning, execution, analysis, and interpretation of developmental investigations. More specifically, they determine which of the psychometric standards are relevant to judging the adequacy of scores.

Nature of the Measurements

The variables that developmentalists assess in their empirical investigations invariably represent classes or categories. These categories may be narrow and seemingly simple, such as smiles or seat-in-desk (Bijou & Baer, 1960); or they may be broad and encompassing, such as dominance, achievement orientation, or aggression. These response categories may be conceptualized either as *traits* — relatively enduring, internally organized patterns of responding (e.g., Cattell, 1957), as *response classes* — sets of responses that are elicited and/or maintained by similar environmental contingencies (e.g., Skinner, 1971), or as *states* — relatively transient conditions of the organism (e.g., Hertzog & Nesselroade, 1987).

TABLE 2.9
Typically Distinguished Levels of Measurement

Level	Example	Interpretation	Typical Statistics
Nominal	Gender	= or ≠	Counts; chi square
Ordinal	Best friends	< or >	Centiles and rank-order correlations
Interval	Grade equivalent	differences are =, <, or >	Ms, SDs, rs, and ANOVAs; t and F
Ratio	Height	ratios	Geometric and harmonic means; coefficient of variation

Note: The interpretations and typical statistics appropriate for more primitive levels of measurement also are applicable to higher levels of measurement.

Whichever of these conceptualizations is adopted has implications for both the internal consistency and the temporal stability of the scores used in an investigation. For example, behaviors composing a trait should display internal consistency, temporal stability, and perhaps situational consistency as well, but only internal consistency would be expected of behaviors constituting a response class or state (Gewirtz, 1969).

The responses assessed also can be considered as *samples* of behavior of interest or as *signs* of some substrate not directly accessible (Goodenough, 1949). Children's eye contact, for example, might be a sample of an important aspect of social skill, or reflect the underlying trait of introversion. In the former case, the investigator must be concerned about the representativeness of the sample of eye contact obtained, and in the latter case about the extent to which eye contact correlates with other measures of introversion.

The substrate assessed need not be some relatively enduring, organized *structure,* such as a trait, but could instead be a *process* or function, such as social problem solving. And either children's competence or their performance on these structures or processes could be targeted for assessment. According to Messick (1983), "competence embraces the structure of knowledge and abilities, whereas performance subsumes as well the processes of accessing and utilizing those structures and a host of affective, motivational, attentional, and stylistic factors that influence the ultimate responses" (p. 484). The distinction between competence and performance is particularly important for developmental researchers, as it is tempting to imply that children are incompetent based on their inadequate performance. However, it may be erroneous to imply, for example, that young children do not have the concept of conservation because they fail to solve Piaget's water-glass problem, or that they do not have a particular linguistic structure because they do not use the structure in their spontaneous verbalizations (e.g., Flavell & Wohlwill, 1969). Instead, the failure may belong to the investigator, who did not elicit competent responses because of faulty selection of test stimuli or setting, or because of the use of inadequately motivating instructions (e.g., Overton & Newman, 1982).

Responses also can be conceptualized in terms of whether they assess behavior, attitudes and images, or physiological responding (Lang, 1968). This triple response *mode* distinction has been particularly useful for the assessment of the constructs of fear and anxiety, for example, which are construed as being represented in varying degrees by different individuals through the three modes (e.g., Barrios & Hartmann, 1988).

Response Characteristics

There are many properties of responses that could form the basis for scoring systems. Some of these properties are simple and easy to measure, such as number, duration, and amplitude. Other characteristics of responses are more complex, and must be inferred or judged by some standard that exists beyond the response itself, such as the correctness or the goodness of the response. In assessing correctness, scoring of responses usually occurs by comparing the responses to a list of acceptable alternatives, and a total score is obtained simply by accumulating all correct or partially correct responses. This is the procedure that is typically followed in scoring achievement and ability tests. Response goodness may be substantially more difficult to judge (e.g., Cronbach, 1970), and to summarize. To illustrate this difficulty, consider the situation in which children's block play is scored for the uniqueness of their constructions (Goetz & Baer, 1973). The children may use quite different building strategies, with some of them generating few, highly elaborated constructions, others many simple ones, and still others some mixture of these two strategies. Thus, a summary response score may need to be based on some weighting of response number, complexity, and uniqueness, even though the latter is of primary interest. This example illustrates an ubiquitous characteristic of performance—that responses differ not only in substance, but also in style. The stylistic aspects of responding initially captured the attention of measurement specialists because they were a nuisance; differences in style were targets of control as they colored judgments of substance. Later, when the ugly duckling had turned into the prince charming (McGuire, 1969, p. 20), and style became the focus of investigation, measurement specialists were faced with the opposite task—of assessing style untainted by substance! This latter focus on the manner or style of responding led to the creation of a number of major style constructs, including social desirability, cognitive tempo, and field dependence (e.g., Wiggins, 1973).

Comparison Standards

Because most scores are not meaningful in themselves, they must be compared to some standard in order to achieve meaning. Traditionally scores have acquired meaning by comparison with the average performance of some relevant group of subjects, called a norm group. Such scores, not surprisingly, are called *normative* scores. Typical standard scores and percentile ranks are normative scores. *Ipsative* scores, in contrast, are obtained by comparing the scores to other scores obtained by the same individual (Cattell, 1944).[6] The proportion scores obtained from observa-

---

[6]A somewhat related distinction is made between whether the methods and procedures of investigation are designed to discover general laws (the *nomothetic* approach) or designed to discover laws that may be unique to the individual (the *idiographic* approach); see, for example, Allport (1937) and West (1983). This distinction is one of those that separates behavioral assessment from more traditional branches of assessment (e.g., Hartmann, Roper, & Bradford, 1979).

tional measures of children's social behavior are ipsative scores; they indicate, for example, how the individual's total behaviors were apportioned to the observational categories. Ipsative scores can be perplexing and sometimes troublesome, first, because they have unusual statistical properties.[7] Second, ipsative scores pose very knotty problems of interpretation when investigators use both normative and ipsative comparisons. For example, one could be in the difficult position of having to explain how a child who scores consistently below par (normatively) on an IQ test could score higher (ipsatively) on the vocabulary subscale than another child scoring consistently above average (normatively) on the very same test.

Another possible method of inducing meaning in scores is to compare them with a criterion or a behavioral referent. Using this *criterion-referenced* approach, a child might be said to have mastered the ability to add two digit numbers or to have mastered 80% of the tasks necessary to replace the rear wheel of a bicycle. Instruments that are constructed with the intent of using criterion-referenced scoring have substantially different statistical properties than have instruments developed with the intent of employing normative scoring. The primary statistical differences between these two approaches to test construction are summarized in Table 2.10.

Sources of Data

Assessment data on the subjects of developmental studies come from a number of sources: from the subjects themselves, from objective tests, and from observations in more-or-less natural settings (e.g., Cattell, 1946). These three sources can be further subdivided. For example, self-reports can be open-ended or provided in response to standard questions, their content can be narrowly focused or far ranging, and they can be intuitively judged or formally scored.

Each of the sources of assessment information is associated with a relatively unique set of distortions. The presence of these method-specific distortions prompted Campbell and Fiske (1959) to propose that all scores should be conceived of as trait- or behavior-method units: Both the construct assessed and the method of measurement contribute to the resulting scores. As a consequence, total score variation is sometimes decomposed into two variance components: construct variance and method variance. In order to avoid research results that are limited in generality by method variance, investigators assess their major constructs with multiple measures that differ in method-specific variation (also see the section on threats to construct validity in the design section).

---

[7]For example, the mean of a set of k ipsative subscales is $1/k$, their average intercorrelation is $-1/(k-1)$, and their average correlation with a criterion is exactly zero (Hicks, 1970).

TABLE 2.10
Distinguishing Features of Criterion-referenced and Norm-referenced Assessment Instruments

Method	Purpose	Statistical Characteristics
Criterion-referenced	Determining what a child can do, or what a child knows	Truncated, sometimes dichotomous score distributions. Items have variable intercorrelations; many easy or difficult items
Norm-referenced	Determining how a child compares to other children	Highly variable, often normal score distributions. Items are moderately intercorrelated. No very easy or very difficult items

The primary distortions (contributors to method variance) associated with the three sources of assessment information are summarized in Table 2.11. It is important to note in interpreting this table that the distortions lose their unique associations with the sources, if, for example, the subject is aware of the purpose of an objective-test assessment, or is even aware that an observational assessment is underway. In these two cases, the distortions produced by deception, defensiveness, and impression management are shared by all three sources.

It is not uncommon in assessment research to confound mode (behavior, images or thoughts, and physiological responses) with source in examining

TABLE 2.11
Sources of Method Variance for Self-report, Objective-test, and Observational Sources of Assessment Data

	Sources of
Data	Distortions
Self-Report	Misinterpretations; atypical use of descriptors (differing "anchor points")
	Degree of relevant self-knowledge; self-observational skills; memory; verbal skills
	Reactive effects such as deception, defensiveness and impression management
Objective-Test	Cognitive styles such as impulsivity and field dependence
	Response styles such as acquiescence or position preferences (e.g., prefer first alternative)
	Instrumentation effects such as differential familiarity with various item formats and content selection biases
Observations	Observer biases and expectancies
	Observer distortions including memory loss and leveling (Campbell, 1958)
	Instrumentation effects such as halo error, leniency error, and central tendency errors (Guilford, 1954)
	Reactivity effects, such as avoidance of the observational setting

the consistency of responding in the three modes (e.g., Cone, 1979). For example, fearful behavior measured observationally might be compared with fearful images and physiological response assessed by means of self-report. It would not be surprising in these comparisons to find greater correspondence between self-reports of fearful images and physiological responses than between either of these two responses and observed fearful behavior. This pattern of responding may not reflect greater agreement or synchrony between imaginal and physiological response systems. Instead, it may be attributable to the self-report method variance shared by the imaginal and physiological response measures.

To illustrate the variety of issues associated with obtaining scores once a measurement source has been selected, the following section discusses the assessment of children's social behavior by means of observations.

Observations of Children's Social Behavior: An Illustration

Observational assessment of children's social behavior has a long history (e.g., Arrington, 1943), and continues to be popular in both child clinical and developmental investigations (e.g., Cairns, 1979; Lamb, Suomi, & Stephenson, 1979; Sackett, 1978a). Observations have been used to assess a variety of human (and infrahuman) social behaviors including infants' attachments (e.g., Ainsworth, Blehar, Waters, & Wall, 1978), children's play (Parten, 1932) and emotional expression (Ekman, 1972), and coercive parent–child interactions (Patterson, 1982). The popularity of this method is due, in part, to the inadequacies of other sources: Young children have limited capacity for describing their own behaviors and retrospective reports of their behavior by primary socializing agents such as their parents tend to be inaccurate (e.g., Goodwin & Driscoll, 1980). Other, more proactive reasons for the popularity of behavioral observations include their flexibility, simplicity, and wide range of applicability (Yarrow & Waxler, 1979). Methodological behaviorism also has emphasized the direct observation of behavior (Hartmann, 1984), as have current research interests in peer interactions and in the micro- or fine-grained analysis of children's social behavior (e.g., Messick, 1983; Wasik, 1984).

Choosing What to Observe

Before observations can be made of children's social behavior, the investigator must answer a series of questions involving the what, where, when, and how of the data collection system. The first question, logically, concerns the behaviors to be observed, and the answer obviously depends largely on the theoretical questions to be asked of the data (e.g., Reid,

Baldwin, Patterson, & Dishion, 1988). Investigators also must make other decisions regarding (a) whether the observation system is to catalog all responses—in which case it would be called exhaustive; (b) whether the response classes are to be mutually exclusive or can occur concomitantly (Sackett, 1978a); (c) the response characteristics that are to be assessed, such as frequency, duration, or quality; and (d) the level of inference required of the observers. As regards the last category, global or *molar* response categories such as "cooperative play," "kvetch," or "empathize" may require substantial inferences from the observers (Hutt & Hutt, 1970). As a result, observational systems using molar responses may require the use of unusually talented observers (Boice, 1983) who are trained extensively. In contrast, so-called molecular responses—responses narrowly defined in terms of sequences of movements—such as "smile" may require less observer training and nevertheless produce reliable data (e.g., Hawkins, 1982). This is so because of the greater objectivity and operational precision of molecular response definitions.

The Context of Observations

Next, investigators must select the context of their observations. Observations can be conducted in analog or laboratory settings, or in either tempered or untampered natural settings such as summer camps, playgrounds, and shopping centers (e.g., Cone & Foster, 1982). Observations conducted in natural settings have the advantage of ecological validity (Bronfenbrenner, 1979), but may be associated with excessive dross—time during which relevant behaviors are not occurring. Contrived settings usually make more efficient use of observer time, as investigators can structure their settings to ensure that the behaviors of interest occur with adequate frequency. However, as a consequence of structuring observational settings the inferences drawn may be specific to the data obtained in that setting (e.g., Kazdin, 1979).

If observations are conducted in natural settings, investigators may have the choice of using participant observers, such as teachers or counselors, instead of employing independent observers. The former have the advantages of convenience and of unobtrusiveness, but they may be less dependable, more subject to biases, and more difficult to train and evaluate than are independent observers (e.g., Nay, 1979). When behavior cannot be scored in situ—perhaps because the presence of observers would cause serious reactive effects or because the scoring system requires repeated exposure to the stream of behavior—observational data may be collected by means of video- or audio-recorder and scored later at the observers' convenience (e.g., Weick, 1968).

Next, unless data are collected by participant observers in institutional or home settings (so that observations can be conducted continuously), observation sessions must be scheduled. Haynes (1978) suggested that more (and perhaps longer) sessions are required when rates of the targeted behavior are low, variable, or changing in some systematic manner; when setting, or other contextual events vary; and when complex coding systems are used. Additional sessions or longer sessions also are required when more than one individual is being observed in the same setting, and when chains of behavior are studied (see Arrington, 1943).

Segmenting the Behavioral Stream

Investigators must also decide on how the behavioral stream will be described. The observations can be relatively unstructured or open (Wright, 1967) or clearly focused or closed. Illustrative of an open format are the running accounts, narrative recordings, or specimen records of activities, such as Barker and Wright's (1951) description of a day in a boy's life—a single day's record that required a 435-page monograph! Open methods have as their primary functions the generation of hypotheses and serving as a preliminary technique for the development of closed methods. Open methods also are useful when a set of observations later will be subject to a variety of scoring systems for quite different purposes.

Closed methods are sometimes called sampling procedures, perhaps because they refer to various methods of segregating or sampling the behavioral stream. Among the closed methods are real-time observations, event recording, scan sampling, and interval recording (Altmann, 1974).

Real-Time Recording. With this method, the frequency and duration of the targeted events are recorded as they are occurring. Because of the complexity of real-time recording, it either is limited to simple observation systems or else requires the aid of special equipment, such as a hand-held electronic recording device (e.g., Simpson, 1979). Such devices are virtual necessities for gathering the fine-grained (or microanalytic) data required for many forms of sequential analysis (Bakeman & Gottman, 1986).

Event Recording. This sampling method scores the initiation of events, and is appropriate when only the count of events or chains of events is of interest (Wright, 1960). Event sampling, also called frequency recording, the tally method, and trial scoring, may be unwieldy when either the initiation or the termination of behaviors is difficult to discriminate (e.g., with a behavior such as fooling around). Because event sampling or recording breaks up the continuity of behavior, it is sometimes supplemented with some form of narrative recording, particular during the early phases of investigation.

Scan Sampling.   Scan sampling, also referred to as instantaneous time sampling, momentary time sampling, and discontinuous probe-time sampling, refers to a technique that extracts brief snapshots from the behavior stream. The observer might glance at the subjects every 3 minutes and note whether preselected behaviors are included in each snapshot. This approach provides unbiased estimates of the duration of the targeted responses once the proportion of samples containing these responses is determined. Because of its simplicity, scan sampling can even be used when an entire group of children is observed for the occurrence of some response such as hitting or being near.

Interval Recording.   The final sampling method is also referred to as time sampling, one-zero recording, and the Hansen system. This method divides the observation period into brief intervals, each of which is scored if the behavior occurs during any portion of the interval. For example, an observation period might be divided into 6-second intervals, and each interval might be scored for whether a child is interacting primarily with a teacher, a peer, or is alone during the interval. Although popular (Kelly, 1977), interval recording is problematic as it provides biased estimates of both frequency and duration (for a review, see Hartmann & Wood, 1982, p. 115). The direction and extent of the bias varies as a function of the interval size and the behavior's frequency and range of durations (e.g., Ary, 1984). Ary and Suen (Ary & Suen, 1983; Suen & Ary, 1986) developed methods for retrieving frequency and duration data from interval recordings, but these methods may have limited utility.

If the questions motivating the investigation require knowledge of the order of occurrence of behaviors, their frequencies and durations, then real-time recording is required. However, if less complex information is required, simpler and less expensive methods of sampling the behavioral stream can be used. For example, if duration is unimportant, event recording should prove to be adequate. On the other hand, if frequency and order are not relevant to the investigative question, scan sampling should provide acceptable data. Finally, in some intervention programs, the (unknown) mixture of duration and frequency data provided by the interval method might be functional (Baer, 1986).

Ensuring the Quality of Observational Data

Unless observational data are of high quality, they may be of little use in investigations of children's behavior. Quality can be improved by means of a number of the methods already mentioned, including the use of objective and clear operational definitions of the target behaviors, and by gathering sufficient data for each subject (Hartmann, 1982a). Other important methods of ensuring that observational data will be of high quality are to select competent and motivated observers, to train them thoroughly, and to assess their performance regularly and unobtrusively (Boice, 1983; Yarrow & Waxler, 1979).

Once potential observers are selected, they must be trained. Hartmann and Wood (1990) described seven steps for training observers. The first step includes an introduction to the importance of objectivity and of ethical principles such as confidentiality in the conduct of observational research. Subsequent steps involve learning the observational manual, scoring enacted observations, learning the rules of courtesy and practicing in situ, and conducting retraining–recalibration sessions. In the final step, the post-investigative debriefing, the expectations of observers that might have affected their performance are assessed. As Reid (1982) suggested, maintenance of high observer morale throughout these steps is a critical component in ensuring high quality data.

Evidence that observers are adequately trained is disclosed in the results of interobserver reliability checks. (If an incontrovertible standard is available, such as a criterion videotape, observer accuracy as well as observer reliability can be assessed; see, e.g., Cone, 1981). These reliability checks require that two or more observers simultaneously and independently code the same stream of behavior, preferably without the observers being aware that reliability is being assessed. This latter requirement has been added since Reid (1970) demonstrated that announced *(overt)* reliability assessments can produce greatly inflated estimates of data quality in comparison to unannounced *(covert)* reliability checks. Interobserver reliability assessments should be conducted during observer training in order to reveal those behaviors that continue to produce disagreements and hence require additional training, and to indicate when the observers are ready to begin formal data collection. They also should be conducted periodically during regular data collection in order to determine if the observers have deteriorated in their performance and hence need further training (e.g., Taplin & Reid, 1973), and to provide a general assessment of the quality of the data.[8]

If both the investigator and the data collection system survive these steps, the data should be appropriate for data analysis. Data analysis is directed at answering the substantive questions that motivated the investigation. It is this topic to which we next turn. Students who require more specific information on the development of observational procedures for class projects might consult Boehm and Weinberg (1977), Gelfand and Hart-

---

[8]The methods of summarizing reliability assessment data so that they achieve these purposes are a matter of some controversy, and are beyond the scope of this chapter. The interested reader may consult Hartmann (1982a) for a moderately technical discussion of these issues.

mann (1984), or Mendinnus (1976). General information on measurement and scaling is available in Anastasi (1988), Crocker and Algina (1986), Cronbach (1984), and Nunnally (1978), and on behavioral observations in Hartmann and Wood (1990) and Suen and Ary (1989).

ANALYSIS

Analysis refers to those procedures, largely although not exclusively statistical in nature, that are applied to the products of measurement (scores) in order to describe them and assess their meaning. Methods of analysis, because they are equated with sometimes difficult and obscure aspects of mathematics, seem to distress students (and some professionals as well) more than any other aspect of scientific inquiry. This section discusses some of the technical aspects of statistical analysis—as well as more friendly graphic methods.

Once scores have been obtained, preliminary operations typically are performed on them so that they will be suitable for formal analysis. These operations include adjusting the data for missing scores and outliers (extreme scores that indicate either errors in handling data or atypical subject responding). These preliminary operations also include any additional measurement manipulations that need to be completed such as the construction of composite scores—difference scores, ratio scores, or total scores—and transformations of the scores in cases in which they fail to meet the assumptions of the statistical tests that will be performed on them. With intractable or otherwise troublesome data sets, these adjustments—sometimes referred to as cleaning or laundering the data—may occur repeatedly and at various points during the data analysis process.

Another important goal of preliminary analysis is to become familiar with the data through hands-on experience. This familiarization process often occurs as part of, preceding, or following adjustment of the data. It may involve careful study of frequency distributions and scrutiny of descriptive statistics calculated on the scores, such as measures of central tendency, variability, and correlation.

Once the data have become old friends, and their general meaning is understood, the investigator conducts formal inferential tests on them. These tests function as decision aids that supplement the binocular tests conducted during the familiarization stage. The statistical tests determine which of the hypothesized effects, as well as those merely noted, are unlikely a function of chance variation in the data; that is, are statistically significant or reliable.

The statistical analysis, whether intended to describe the data or to test hypotheses relevant to them, will differ depending primarily on the research question, and secondarily on the nature of the data. Most research questions can be conceived as belonging to one or both of two analytic classes. In one class are research questions that involve either the correlates of individual differences or the consistency of individual differences across time, settings, or behaviors. The data from these studies require some form of correlational (Pearsonian) analysis. Correlation analysis includes simple, part, partial, and multiple regression analysis, factor analysis, as well as structural equation modeling. In the other class are questions about longitudinal changes or cross-sectional differences in average performance. The data from these studies are subjected to some form of Fisherian analysis, such as the analysis of variance (ANOVA).[9]

As has already been indicated, scores differ in a variety of ways. Two of these dimensions have particular relevance for the selection of statistical tests. The first dimension is whether the scores are qualitative or quantitative in nature. Qualitative scores include binary (e.g., yes–no) and other few-categoried discrete scores, such as like–neutral–dislike scales. Quantitative scores are continuous and multipointed, and include ratio, interval, and near-interval scores such as ratings on 5-point Likert scales. Qualitative scores often require some form of contingency table analysis, not unlike common chi-square analyses, whereas quantitative scores usually are analyzed using some form of the ANOVA or traditional regression analysis.

The second dimension concerns the number and type of scores contributed by each sampling unit (sampling units usually are composed of individual subjects, but sometimes a dyad or a larger group such as a family or a classroom constitutes a sampling unit). If each sampling unit contributes one score, then a univariate analysis is performed; one score repeatedly assessed over time or setting, then a repeated-measures univariate analysis may be conducted; or multiple scores, ordinarily obtained during the same time period, then a multivariate analysis (MANOVA) is conducted.

These analyses require a wide variety of specific statistical tests, each of which has its assumptions, advantages, and pitfalls. Whatever the form of analysis, the ubiquitous $p < .05$ or $p < .01$ resulting from the analysis has a specific technical meaning that is critical to an understanding of hypothesis testing as it is currently practiced. Unfortunately, that meaning is widely misunderstood. These, and related issues, are addressed in this section.

---

[9]Both analytic classes are based on the general linear model (e.g., Kirk, 1982), however, the distinction between Pearsonian and Fisherian approaches to data analysis has been associated with design, subject matter, and other aspects of research strategy (Cronbach, 1957).

Preliminary Analyses

Adjusting Scores

Scores, like toddlers, require our constant vigilance and repeated intervention if they are to stay out of trouble. Some subjects will have missing scores, and we must decide whether estimated scores should be derived for them, or whether those subjects should be omitted from some or all of the analyses. Other scores may be incorrectly transcribed on data sheets or mistakenly entered into the computer. Most of these errors can be avoided if investigators emphasize accuracy in their scientific work, provide instructions in how to obtain error-free data, institute frequent accuracy checks, and provide incentive for accurate results (Hartmann & Wood, 1990).

Still other data inaccuracies may reflect subjects' misunderstandings of instructions, their incorrect use of answer sheets, or even faking or cheating on their part. If these and other errors cannot be avoided by suitable instructions or by performance monitoring, they might be detected — and either corrected or eliminated — if the erroneous data are sufficiently atypical. Unusual scores are detectable if they are substantially different in value from those of neighboring scores. For example, a child who scored 2 standard deviations either above or below his or her nearest scoring classmate on an observational assessment of aggression would certainly be a candidate for further investigation, and for possible removal from the data set. Incorrect scores also may be detectable because they represent an improbable pattern of responding. Examples include responding to the same question differently when it is asked twice; missing three very easy problems but answering correctly four, more difficult problems; and admitting to taking birth control pills by someone who indicates being a 10-year-old boy. Sieves for the detection of errors of this sort require close scrutiny of the data by members of the research team, perhaps supplemented by computer programs developed to detect unusual responses or patterns of responses (e.g., Hill, 1981; Mickey, 1981).

Still other adjustments may have to be made to the data before they are suitable for analyses. For example, it is not uncommon for scores to be combined or aggregated prior to major data analysis. The item, or other subpart scores may be combined based on purely theoretical considerations — all items measure the same construct, and so the item scores are simply summed to generate a composite total score. Instead, the item scores may be combined on empirical bases, including the item intercorrelations, their reliability, or their correlations with a criterion (see Nunnally, 1978, for a not entirely dispassionate discussion of these alternative empirical strategies for combining assessment information). Finally, and most often, scores are combined with an eye to both theoretical and empirical considerations. Simultaneously serving more than one criterion need not be troublesome, unless of course the criteria suggest opposite courses of action, as may happen when theoretically appropriate items are inconsistently correlated with one other. In that case, after suitable digging into the data in an effort to make sense of the inconsistencies, investigators must rely on their good judgment and perhaps the good judgment of their colleagues.

Another common preliminary manipulation of the data involves equating scores for differences in the opportunity to behave. For example, children may be evaluated on the number and kinds of errors they make in solving math problems, but may differ in the number of problems attempted. In such cases, investigators adjust scores by prorating, by shifting to proportion or percentage scores, or by employing other ratios such as rate per unit of time.

Still other transformations of scores, such as square root, log, and arc sin transformations may be required because the original scores violate the assumptions of statistical tests that will be performed on them. These transformations and their affects were outlined earlier in the section on measurement.

Following, as part of, or sometimes interspersed between such laundering operations, investigators are wise to construct graphs of their data and calculate descriptive statistics on them.

Becoming Familiar With Data

Informal or exploratory data analysis—consisting of constructing graphs, charts, and plots, and calculating simple descriptive statistics—is critically important to understanding the meaning of data. Indeed, some investigators argue that these procedures, particularly the scrutiny of graphic displays, constitute the primary method of judging the outcomes of experiments (e.g., Baer, 1977).

Whether these methods are primary, or merely contributory for judging the outcomes of experiments, there is little doubt of their importance. Unfortunately, it seems all too often that novice investigators omit all, or the greater portion of the preliminary stage of data analysis: The excitement of having completed data collection is quickly followed by the need to know if the data contain anything "statistically significant." And so the data are prematurely formally analyzed, perhaps using only standard or "canned" computer programs, with results that unnecessarily support the adage "garbage in, garbage out." This misplaced enthusiasm deprives investigators of the opportunity to experience a sense of intimacy with their data—the kinds of "hands on" experiences from which serendipitous findings and otherwise new perspectives are discovered. Unfortunately, there is not a large literature on the procedures useful for gaining familiarity with data, and so the procedures tend to be idiosyncratic and perhaps needlessly artistic in nature. Generally, however, they involve constructing graphic displays and calculating standard as well as quick and dirty descriptive statistics (e.g., Tukey, 1977).

Graphing Data. Useful graphic displays range from freehand sketches of univariate and bivariate frequency distributions to computer-crafted, publication-ready, three-dimensional drawings of multiple time series (see Parsonson & Baer, 1978). The concern during preliminary data analysis is not with beauty, however, but with utility. For example, when groups are being compared, simple bar graphs (see Fig. 2.1) of each group's performance can readily be drawn.

Each display might be checked for atypical performances (see Panel A of Fig. 2.1) if this has not already been done in some other way, and a decision made concerning how unusual respondents should be handled. Other aspects of the data also might be noted, such as the modality or peakedness of the distribution of scores (see the bimodal distribution in Panel A of Fig. 2.1), their symmetry (see the positively skewed distribution in Panel B of

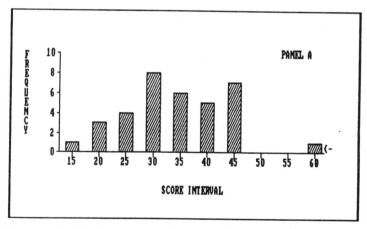

FIG. 2.1.   Univariate frequency distributions illustrating the presence of an outlier (Panel A), a bimodal distribution (Panel A), a positively skewed distribution with a pronounced floor effect (Panel B), and an approximately normal distribution in which the estimated and calculated values of the mean *(M)* and standard deviation *(SD)* are in reasonable agreement (Panel C).

Panel A. Illustration of a bimodal frequency distribution containing an outlier (see arrow). With the outlier, $M = 34.3$, $SD = 9.56$, and $N = 35$; without the outlier, $M = 33.5$, $SD = 8.57$, and $N = 34$.

Fig. 2.1), and whether floor and ceiling effects (also see Panel B of Fig. 2.1) are present. Bimodal distributions are found when a sample is composed of scores for two quite different types of subjects, such as a distribution of birth weights for a sample composed of term and preterm infants. Skewness, or lack of symmetry in the scores, might occur for a variety of reasons, including the presence of floor or ceiling effects. These latter forms of asymmetry are observed when the preponderance of subjects receives the lowest scores (floor effect) or the highest scores (ceiling effect) on the assessment instrument. In ability testing, the presence of a floor effect suggests that the test was too difficult for the subjects, and a ceiling effect suggests that the test was too easy for the subjects.

If the data are approximately normal in their distribution, both the mean and standard deviation can be readily estimated from graphic displays. The mean will lie approximately in the center of the distribution, and the standard deviation will be between one sixth and one half of the group's range, depending on the size of the sample (see the very handy Table 5.6 in Guilford, 1965, p. 81). With the data shown in Panel C of Fig. 2.1, the standard deviation for a sample of $N = 25$ is estimated to be 1/3.8 of the range of scores ($= 25/3.8 = 6.6$).

When investigations employ more than one dependent variable it often proves useful to cross-tabulate the scores or to sketch their bivariate frequency distribution (see Fig. 2.2). The resulting displays—sometimes referred to as scatter diagrams—can be examined for a number of disturbances, including the presence of outliers. When outliers are present, they can dramatically change the magnitude of the correlation between the

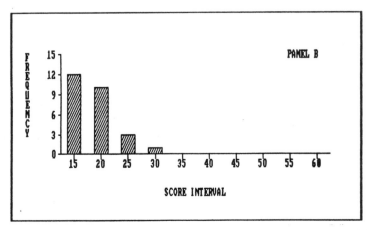

Panel B. Illustration of a positively skewed frequency distribution with a distinct floor effect. For this distribution, $M = 18.7$, $SD = 4.14$, and $N = 26$.

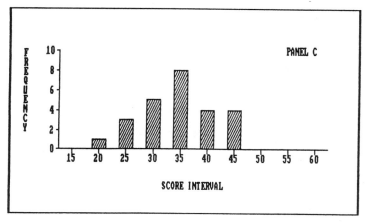

Panel C. Illustration of an approximately normal frequency distribution for which rules of thumb provide close approximations to the *M* and *SD* of the distribution. *M* = 34.6 (estimated *M* = 35), *SD* = 6.8 (estimated *SD* = range/3.8 = 25/3.8 = 6.6), *N* = 25.

variables. (Compare the value of *r* for the data in Panel A of Fig. 2.2 when the outlier is included, and when the outlier is excluded.)

Scatter diagrams also can be checked for the extent to which the regression between the variables is linear. Nonlinear regression is illustrated in Panel B of Fig.b 2.2. Because the product moment correlation *(r)* assesses the linear part of the relation between variables, *r* will underestimate the relations between variables that are nonlinearly related. Compare, for example, the value of *r* and of eta (the curvilinear correlation coefficient) for the data shown in Panel B of Fig. 2.2.

In addition to disclosing the presence of outliers and nonlinear regressions, scatter diagrams can indicate heteroscedasticity (unequal dispersion of scores about the regression line). Heteroscedasticity indicates that errors of predictions vary depending on the value of the predictor score. With the data displayed in Panel C of Fig. 2.2, Y-scores are less accurately predicted for individuals with high X-scores than for individuals with low X-scores. Scatter diagrams and other graphic plots serve both as important detection devices and judgmental aids in the hands of experienced investigators.

More on Descriptive Statistics. Means, standard deviations, and correlation coefficients are the most commonly used descriptive statistics. In addition, a number of other statistics are sufficiently common to deserve brief mention. First, we consider a number of the many descriptive statistics related to *r,* the correlation coefficient: part and partial correlation, kappa, and conditional probability.

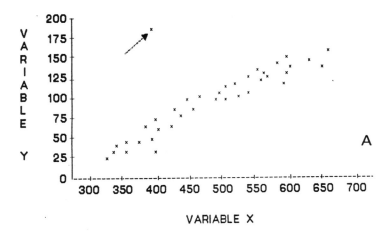

FIG. 2.2.   Bivariate frequency distributions illustrating an outlier (see arrow in Panel A), linear regression (Panel A), curvilinear regression (Panel B), homoscedasticity (Panel A and the regression of Y on X for Panel B), and heteroscedasticity (Panel C and the regression of X on Y for Panel B).

Panel A. Illustration of positive linear relation between variables X and Y. Outlier indicated by arrow. With the outlier included, $r = +.81$; with the outlier omitted, $r = +.94$. The dispersion of scores with each X-array is approximately normal (homoscedasticity). $N = 38$.

Part and *partial correlations* are ordinary product–moment correlations that deserve special names because of the nature of the scores to which they are applied: Either one (part) or both (partial) of the scores correlated are corrected for uncontrolled variation in a third variable. For example, in a 3-variable regression problem involving height, weight, and age, the correlation between height and weight, with age corrected, is called the partial correlation and is symbolized $r_{hw \cdot a}$. The partial correlation between height and weight is equal to the correlation between these two variables when calculated for subjects who all are at the mean age of the group. Partial correlation is used when the effects of a third variable, such as age in the aforementioned example, cannot be experimentally controlled. If age was partialed out of weight, but not out of height, the resulting correlation would be the part correlation between height and weight. This part correlation is symbolized $r_{h(w \cdot a)}$. Part correlations play an important role in multiple regression, as they indicate the overlap of the criterion with the unique portion of each of the predictors. Using the three variables of age, height, and weight, the distinctions between simple correlations, and part and partial correlations, are illustrated by the Venn diagram shown in Fig. 2.3.

Kappa (Cohen, 1960) is an agreement statistic that is used increasingly to summarize interjudge reliability data, particularly for observational data.

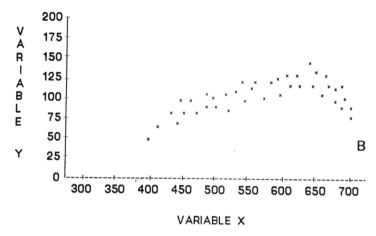

Panel B. Illustration of curvilinear relation between X and Y. The value of the linear correlation is +.54, whereas the value of eta, the curvilinear correlation, is +.94. The dispersion of scores within each X-array is approximately equal (homoscedasticity). $N = 40$.

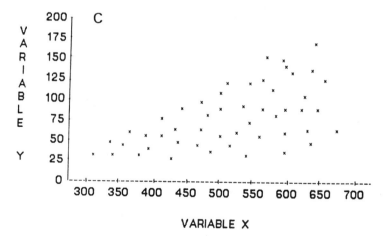

Panel C. Illustration of heteroscedasticity (unequal dispersion of scores within each X-array). $r = +.57$ and $N = 50$.

Assume that two observers each independently classified the same 200 10-sec observation intervals into whether a target child interacted with her peers, her teacher, or failed to interact. The resulting data might resemble those given in Fig. 2.4. A typical, older, and flawed method of summarizing these data is simply to tabulate the proportion of intervals for which the two observers agreed. For the data in Fig. 2.4, the observers agreed on 95 intervals scored as "interacted with peers," 25 intervals rated as "interacted

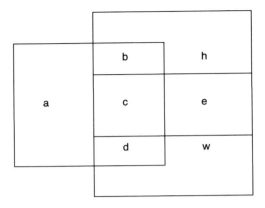

FIG. 2.3. Venn diagram illustrating the distinctions between simple correlations, and partial- and part-correlations. For the simple correlation between height and weight (r_{hw}), height is represented by (b + c + e + h), weight by (c + d + e + w), and the overlapping or correlation producing part by (c + e). For the partial correlation $(r_{hw \cdot a})$, height is now represented by only (e + h), weight by (e + w), and the overlap by (e). For the part correlation, $r_{h(w \cdot a)}$, height is again represented by (b + c + e + h), weight by (e + w), and the overlap by (e).

with teacher," and 40 intervals classified as "alone." These 160 intervals, when divided by 200 (the total number of intervals during which observations were taken), gives a proportion of agreement of .80. When kappa is calculated on these same data, a somewhat lower estimate of agreement is obtained, as kappa corrects for agreements that might have occurred by chance (e.g., Hartmann, 1977). Kappa is equal to

$(p_o - p_c)/(1 - p_c)$, where
p_o is the proportion of observed agreements, and
p_c is the proportion of chance agreements.

For the data in Fig. 2.4, p_o is .80, as we have already determined in the calculation of the simple agreement statistic, and p_c is equal to the sum of the expected values for each of the agreement cells in Fig. 2.4 divided by the total number of observation intervals (p_c = .4275).[10] Kappa is then equal to

$(.80 - 4275)/(1 - .4275) = .65.$

---

[10]The expected values are determined in exactly the same manner as they typically are for chi-square tables; that is, by summing the products of corresponding marginal values and dividing by N. For the data given in Fig. 2.4, the expected value for the agreement cell for "interacts with peers" is 120 × 110/200 = 66; for the agreement cell "interacts with teacher" is 30 × 30/200 = 4.5; and for the agreement cell "alone" is 50 × 60/200 = 15. Summing these values and dividing by N yields p_c = (66 + 4.5 + 15)/200 = .4275.

	Observer 1 Child Interacts With			
Observer 2	Peer	Teacher	No one	Totals
Child Interacts With — Peer	95	05	10	110
Teacher	05	25	00	30
No one	20	00	40	60
Totals	120	30	50	200 = N

FIG. 2.4. Joint, but independent observations of a child's interactions by Observer 1 and Observer 2 used to illustrate the calculation of interobserver reliability using Cohen's kappa. N = the number of observation intervals, not the number of subjects. The values in the principle diagonal cells — the cells for which like categories intersect for the two observers, and extending from upper left to lower right — represent observation intervals for which the observers agreed. The values in the off-diagonal cells represent disagreements between the two observers (e.g., the 10 entries in the cell defined by the first row and third column are those for which Observer 2 indicated that the child was interacting with her peers, but Observer 1 stated that she was alone).

The final common descriptive statistic related to r is the *conditional probability*. Conditional probabilities play an important role in analysis of fine-grained interactional data (e.g., Bakeman & Gottman, 1986; Gottman & Roy, 1989). These probabilities perhaps can best be understood by examining 2 × 2 table data, such as those shown in Fig. 2.5. The data in Fig. 2.5 describe the temporal patterning of talking by a mother and her child. These data can be summarized in various ways: by a correlation statistic such as the phi coefficient, or by means of a conditional probability. The conditional probability of the child talking given that her mother talked in the prior interval is equal to the joint probability that the child talked and the mother talked in the previous interval divided by the

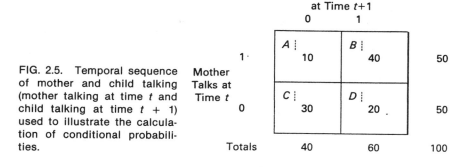

FIG. 2.5. Temporal sequence of mother and child talking (mother talking at time t and child talking at time $t + 1$) used to illustrate the calculation of conditional probabilities.

	Child Talks at Time $t+1$		
	0	1	
Mother Talks at Time t — 1	A 10	B 40	50
Mother Talks at Time t — 0	C 30	D 20	50
Totals	40	60	100

probability that the mother talked in the previous interval (e.g., Allison & Liker, 1982). For the example given in Fig. 2.5, the conditional probability of the child talking at time $t + 1$ given that her mother talks in the previous interval is equal to $(B/N)/[(A + B)/N] = B/(A + B) = 40/(10 + 40) = .80$. The conditional probability is often compared with its unconditional probability. The unconditional probability of the child talking is $(B + D)/(N) = (40 + 20)/(100) = .60$. Thus, the mother's talking in the previous interval increases the likelihood that the child will talk in the following interval from .60 to .80.

The final descriptive statistic, one similar to an ordinary variance, is the characteristic root or *eigen value*. Eigen values are to matrices what the variance is to a distribution of numbers. Not surprisingly then, eigen values (symbolized as gammas), are frequently encountered in multivariate analysis, where one deals with matrices of scores. For example, in principle component analysis, a factoring technique, the eigen value for each principle component may be thought of as the amount of variance in the original standardized variables associated with that principle component. And in multivariate analysis of variance the eigen value can be thought of as the variance between the group centroids. (A centroid is to multiple dependent variables what a mean is to a single dependent variable.)

Null Hypothesis Testing

Following the calculation of descriptive statistics, several methods are available to judge the significance of the statistics. Significance in this context refers to whether or not the effects of interest, which are presumably reflected in the data and in the summary descriptive statistics applied to the data, could have arisen by chance. The primary method that developmentalists use to judge the statistical significance of their results is null hypothesis testing. Preference for this method of assessing statistical significance exists despite the very substantial criticism directed at null hypothesis testing procedures (e.g., Meehl, 1978; Morrison & Henkel, 1970).

Null hypothesis testing is a multistep process (see Table 2.12) that begins with the development of two models or hypotheses about the data. One model, sometimes called the experimental model, contains the putative effect of interest to the investigator, such as treatment, age, or gender. The other model, often called the null or restricted model, does not contain this effect or states that the effect of interest equals zero. Null models or hypotheses often are stated in one of two forms. In one form of the null hypothesis, some effect or parameter is assumed to equal zero in the population under investigation. The parameter, for example, may be a simple correlation coefficient or a beta weight in a multiple regression

TABLE 2.12
Illustration of Null Hypothesis Testing

Step 1. An investigator explores the relation between the number of observed positive social requests and sociometric status in a group of 3-year-old children. The null hypothesis states the following about the population correlation, ρ:

$\rho = .00$. This null hypothesis is contrasted with an alternative hypothesis that states that $\rho \neq .00$

Step 2. α, the probability associated with rejection of the null hypothesis, is set at $p = .05$. Therefore, the obtained finding must have a probability of occurrence $\leq .05$ before the null hypothesis will be rejected and the alternative hypothesis accepted.

Step 3. The obtained correlation is tested with the z test for the significance of r using Fisher's r to $z_{r(zr)}$ transformation.

$z = (z_r - 0)/\sigma (z_r)$, and $\sigma (z_r) = 1/(N - 3)^{1/2}$.
With $r = .50$, and $N = 19$, $z_r = .549$ and $\sigma (z_r) = 1/(19 - 3)^{1/2} = .25$, so $z = (.549 - 0)/.25 = 2.20$

Step 4. The two-sided probability value associated with $z = 2.20$, according to the normal curve table, is approximately $p = .028$.

Step 5. Because $p = .028$ meets the criterion established in Step 2 where α was set at $p = .05$, the null hypothesis is rejected. Therefore, it is concluded that positive social requests and sociometric status are significantly correlated in 3-year-old children.

analysis (e.g., $\beta = 0$). In another form of the null hypothesis, the values of the parameter of interest for two or more populations are assumed to be equal. The parameters to be compared most often include population means or variances (e.g., $\sigma_a^2 = \sigma_b^2$).

In the second step of null hypothesis testing, the investigator decides how unlikely the obtained results must be before concluding that the null hypothesis is probably false. The logic implied here is that if the sample data are unlikely to have occurred under the null model, then that model must not be true. This step is sometimes referred to as "selecting an α level." α levels (or probabilities) of .05 or .01 are the conventional ones used in deciding whether to reject null models or hypotheses. However, it is important to add that the selection of α should be based on the consequences of making a Type I error versus the consequences of accepting a false null hypothesis (a Type II error), and not by convention. If the consequences of making a Type I error are substantial—say millions of dollars may be spent in changing an existing social policy—and the consequences of accepting a false null hypothesis are minor, a very, very small α level, such as .0001, might be employed.

In the third step, the investigator uses the sample data to compute the value of a test or inferential statistic. This test statistic measures the extent of the deviation of the sample data from those expected on the basis of the null hypothesis. Traditional univariate test statistics are the z (normal curve) test, the t test, the F test, and the chi-square test.

In the fourth step, the investigator determines the probability associated with the test statistic, often by reference to statistical tables or computer output. In order for these sources to provide appropriate probability values, the sample data must be consistent with a set of assumptions required by the statistical test. Although each statistical test has its own set of assumptions, some assumptions are common to many inferential tests. Typical among these shared assumptions are that scores (usually error or residual scores) must be distributed normally, homogeneously, and independently. Violation of these assumptions—particularly that of independence and to a lesser degree that of homogeneity—can result in highly erroneous probability values (e.g., Kirk, 1982; Lewis & Burke, 1949; Scheffé, 1959). In order to help ensure the correctness of probability values that result from the major statistical analyses, the tenability of critical assumptions should be formally tested (see, e.g., Kirk, 1982).

In the final step of null hypothesis testing, the probability value associated with the statistical test is compared with the alpha value selected by the investigator (see Step 2). As a result of this comparison, the null hypothesis, and the model on which it is based, is either accepted or rejected.

The statistical testing procedures just outlined differ in detail depending on a variety of considerations. These considerations include the descriptive statistic that answers the investigator's question. For example, questions answered by examining means may require different testing procedures than do questions concerned with variability or correlation. Another consideration involves whether each independent experimental unit[11] receives a score for a single dependent variable (univariate analysis), more than one score for a single dependent variable (repeated-measures analysis), or one or more scores for more than one dependent variable (multivariate analysis). Still another consideration is whether qualitative or quantitative data are tested for significance. The following sections address significance testing in these various circumstances. Because of the large number of combinations of circumstances involved, however, only those commonly occurring are discussed.

Qualitative Analysis

The analysis of categorical data, the most common form of qualitative data, typically has involved some form of chi-square analysis. Less fre-

---

[11]The number of independent experimental units (called units of analysis) usually, although not always, is equal to the number of subjects. Exceptions occur when the sampling units are themselves aggregates, such as dyads, families, or classrooms. In these exceptional cases, the responses of individual subjects may be dependent, and the independent experimental units are given by the number of dyads, families, or classrooms, respectively. When the number of units of analysis exceed the number of sampling units, one is often in imminent danger of lethally threatening statistical conclusion validity. See, for example, the discussion of dependency by Kenny and Judd (1986) and of "nested" subjects by Anderson and Anger (1978) and by Cairns (1983).

quently used are other nonparametric tests, such as Fisher's Exact Test, and parametric tests that are more appropriate for quantitative data. Chi-square tests serve a variety of uses in the statistical testing of categorical data. For example, they are used to determine whether proportions or frequencies differ from one another, whether categorical variables are correlated, and whether distributional assumptions, such as normality, hold. These uses of chi-square and of other traditional nonparametric testing procedures have been ably described in a number of books, including those by Conover (1971), Hollander and Wolfe (1973), Fienberg (1980), Fleiss (1973), and Siegel (1956), and are not cataloged here. Instead, some common errors made in these analyses are noted and then a number of relatively new methods for analyzing complex categorical data are described briefly.

Perhaps not surprising in view of their general utility, chi-square tests have long been a favorite for abuse. The sources of this abuse are clearly spelled out in a sequence of critical papers, including the classic papers by Lewis and Burke (1949, 1950) and the more recent paper by Delucchi (1983). Perhaps the most serious of the many errors made in the use of chi-square is violation of the independence assumption. This error occurs when investigators shift experimental units from subjects to the events engaged in by these subjects.

Consider a set of fictitious data gathered to assess a prediction derived from a theory of moral development: that 4-year-olds would cheat more frequently in turn-taking than would 6-year-olds. The data gathered to test this hypothesis might take the form of the number of violations of turn-taking observed during 10-minute samples of free play for 15 four- and 15 six-year-old children. If the number of cheating incidents totaled 40, and individual scores ranged from 0 to 3, some investigators might be tempted to conduct the chi-square analysis summarized in Part A of Fig. 2.6 (also see the data display in Panel A). It is apparent from inspection of this figure that the investigator has shifted experimental units from children ($N = 30$) to some combination of children and cheating incidents ($N = 40$). The 19 entries in cell A represent the number of incidents of cheating engaged in by the nine 4-year-old children who engaged in some cheating. It is difficult to argue that these cheating incidents were independent, as individual children contributed as many as three entries to this cell.

The correct display of the data is shown in Panel B of Fig. 2.6, maintaining children as the unit of analysis. The proper analysis of these data is given in Part B. As can be seen from this latter analysis, the two age groups do not differ significantly in the proportion of children who are observed cheating; that is, age and cheating are not significantly correlated in these data.[12] Comparing the results of the appropriate and inappropriate

---

[12]The analysis given in Fig. 2.6 is a test of the difference between independent proportions. That is, is the proportion of 4-year-olds who engage in cheating different from the proportion

	PANEL A AGE OF CHILD				PANEL B AGE OF CHILD		
CHEATING	4	6		CHEATER	4	6	
Occurrences	$A = 19$	$B = 6$	25	Yes	$A = 9$	$B = 6$	15
Nonoccurrences	$C = 6$	$D = 9$	15	No	$C = 6$	$D = 9$	15
Totals	25	15	40	Totals	15	15	30

Panel A. Chi square (χ^2) calculations based on $A = 19$ (see Panel A).

$$\chi^2 = \Sigma\Sigma[(o_{ij} - e_{ij})^2/e_{ij}],$$

where o_{ij} is the observed frequency in the ith row and jth column, e_{ij} is the expected frequency in the ith row and jth column and is equal to the product of the ith row frequency and the jth column frequency divided by N.

$$\chi^2 = [19 - (25 \times 25/40)]^2(25 \times 25/40) + 2 \times [6 - (25 \times 15/40)]^2/(25 \times 15/40)$$
$$+ [9 - (15 \times 15/40)]^2/(15 \times 15/40)$$
$$= 5.184, \text{ which, with 1 degree of freedom is associated with } p < .05.$$

Panel B. Chi square calculation based on $A = 9$ (see Panel B).

$$\chi^2 = 2 \times [9 - (15 \times 15/30)]^2/(15 \times 15/30)$$
$$+ 2 \times [6 - (15 \times 15/30)]^2/(15 \times 15/30)$$
$$= 1.20, \text{ which, with 1 degree of freedom is associated with } p > .20.$$

FIG. 2.6. Incorrect (Panel A) and correct (Panel B) data displays for cheating during turn-taking in 15 4-year-old and 15 6-year-old children, and incorrect (Part A) and correct (Part B) applications of chi-square analyses to these data. Note that even though some of the cells in the correct (Part B) analysis included small expected values, no correction for continuity was included. Recent research indicates that the correction usually is unnecessary as long as N exceeds 20; indeed use of the correction produces overly conservative probabilities (Delucchi, 1983).

analysis indicates that violating the independence assumption can produce serious distortions in chi-square probabilities. Similar distortions of chi-square probabilities have been noted by Gardner, Hartmann, and Mitchell (1982) in the analysis of dyadic time series data when an interacting dyad provides all of the data entries (see Fig. 2.5 for an example of data of this type).

The newer methods of analyzing categorical data are variously called log-linear analysis and (multidimensional) contingency table analysis. These approaches allow investigators to analyze complicated cross-classified categorical data, such as the data presented in Fig. 2.6 made more complex with the inclusion of additional IV or DVs. The analytic approach is similar to that used in the analysis of variance. As in ANOVA, a linear model is

of 6-year-olds who engage in cheating? As such, the analysis is one of the differences between independent means (as the two group proportions in this problem are really group means). The analyses can also be viewed as one of the correlation between group status (age) and cheating. Thus, in an important sense, differences between means and correlations are but two alternative ways of viewing data analysis.

developed that expresses a score as a function of main and interaction effects. Multidimensional contingency table analysis differs from ANOVA in that in the former case the *logarithm* of the putative effects are summed. Because the equation is linear in its log form, the approach is referred to as log-linear. In addition, testing procedures resemble those used with data from unbalanced ANOVA designs. That is, a hierarchical model testing procedure is followed in which an experimental model, simplified by the omission of one or more parameters, is tested. A small value of the test statistic indicates acceptance of this model, whereas a high value of the test statistic indicates that additional parameters must be included in the model. The test statistic used for multidimensional contingency table analysis is either the ordinary chi-square statistic or the likelihood ratio statistic, G^2. G^2 involves the logarithm of the ratio of observed and expected frequencies, rather than the squared discrepancy between observed and expected frequencies as does the ordinary chi-square test.

These techniques for analyzing multidimensional table data have the advantages of ANOVA: They provide omnibus tests of main and interaction effects in factorial investigations, allow for subsequent contrast tests, and control for Type I error rates. These advantages come with some cost, however. According to Appelbaum and McCall (1983), multidimensional contingency analysis requires large numbers of subjects, particularly when repeated-measures versions of this approach are used.

When these, as well as other methods of statistical analysis are used for the first time, the computer program as well as the user should be tested by replicating a textbook example. After an example from any of the standard texts — such as Fleiss (1981), Kleinbaum and Kupper (1978), or Landis and Koch (1979) — is successfully analyzed, the new data are ready for analysis. Additional useful material on multidimensional table analysis can be found in Bishop and Holland (1975) and Knoke and Burke (1980).

Quantitative Analysis

Often, data are multipoint and ordered, such as Likert scale data, and can be analyzed with one or another of the general methods of quantitative analysis. The more common of these are ANOVA and regression–correlation analysis. Both methods are based on the general linear model, in which a score is conceived of as a linear combination of main and interaction effects, plus error. While in many respects ANOVA and regression analysis can be thought of as alternative approaches to the analysis of quantitative data, certain problems are more closely tied to one approach than to the other. Consequently, the following material discusses the two approaches separately. However, it is important to recognize that the problems discussed under one or the other approach do not disappear when one shifts from regression analysis to the analysis of variance, or vice versa. The problems, such as lack of independence of the predictor variables (referred to as nonorthogonality in ANOVA), inflating Type I error by conducting many tests of significance on the same set of data, and the like must be dealt with whatever the form of analysis.

Regression Analysis

Regression analysis is the most general approach for the analysis of quantitative data. It accommodates data aimed at answering the two general types of questions asked by developmentalists: questions regarding group trends and those involving individual differences. Most readers will be familiar with the latter use of regression analysis, for example to explore the correlates of popularity in a group of 8-year-old children. That regression analysis also can evaluate group trends may be less familiar — but review the discussion of the data on cheating in 4- and 6-year-olds.

In both of its major applications, regression analysis is plagued with difficulties for the unwary. Many of these difficulties are primarily interpretive in nature, rather than involving problems in statistical testing. Nevertheless, they seem worthy of note, and the conditions responsible for these difficulties are summarized in Table 2.13. Additional information on the foibles associated with the interpretation of regression–correlation analysis can be found in McNemar (1969, chap. 10) and in Cohen and Cohen (1975).

The effects tested in regression–correlation analysis involve either correlation coefficients (bivariate rs or multiple Rs) or statistics such as path coefficients and beta weights that are a function of correlation coefficients. Tests of these statistics most often employ the F distribution (after Fisher), but in certain simple or unusual cases the t test or the normal curve (or z) test may be used (see the analysis conducted in Table 2.12).

As in many uses of statistical testing, problems occur when investigators are insufficiently sensitive to violations of independence assumptions when conducting statistical tests in conjunction with regression–correlation analysis. Nonindependence (dependence) affects statistical tests in regression analysis in at least two ways. First, tests may be conducted on nonindependent statistics from a regression analysis, but the testing procedure may only be appropriate for independent statistics. This may occur whenever investigators attempt to answer the generic question "Is X more highly correlated with Y than S is correlated with Z?" and both r_{xy} and r_{sz} are obtained from data from the same subjects. Because the data are obtained from the same subjects, such correlation coefficients are likely to be themselves correlated, and their testing requires adjustments to accommodate the dependency between the coefficients (Steiger, 1980).

TABLE 2.13
Disturbing Factors in Regression and Correlation Analysis

Disturbing Factors	*Consequences*
Unreliable measurement	Correlation is underestimated.
Restricted score range	Correlation typically underestimated.
Non-normal distributions	Maximum value $|r| < 1.0$ unless correlated variables are identically non-normal.
Small N to IV ratio	R overestimated; R regresses toward zero when cross-validated
Correlated IVs	$r(x_1y)^2$ does not give the proportion of variance in Y (the DV) uniquely associated with X_1; $\Sigma r(x_iy)^2$ does not equal R^2.
Highly correlated IVs (multicollinearity)	Beta weights (βs) unstable[a]

[a]Correlated IVs (called nonorthogonal IVs) also produce complicated issues of statistical testing when data are analyzed via ANOVA. The problem of correlated independent variables in the analysis of variance is discussed by Cohen (1968) and by Kahneman (1965). Appelbaum and his associates (Appelbaum & Cramer, 1974; Appelbaum & McCall, 1983) have presented methods of analyzing these data.

The second dependency problem occurs when the pairs of scores on which a correlation coefficient is calculated are not independent. (A similar problem was discussed with respect to the cheating data shown in Fig. 2.6.) This dependency problem occurs, for example, when more than one member of the family contributes pairs of scores to the correlation analysis, or when the same individual contributes all of the scores entering into the analysis.

A final problem in testing correlational statistics occurs when a large number of variables are intercorrelated, and the correlation between each pair of variables is tested for significance in the usual manner. When this is done, the probability of making one or more Type I errors (see Table 2.2) may approach 1.0. In order to avoid the problem of inflating Type I error with a large matrix of intercorrelations, the entire matrix is first tested to ensure that some significant covariation exists in the matrix as a whole. If that test proves to be significant, then statistical tests are conducted on the individual correlations with alpha adjusted so as to hold the probability of a Type I error for the entire collection of tests to some specified level (Larzelere & Mulaik, 1977). This procedure has the effect of using a much more conservative alpha for tests of significance conducted on the individual correlations.

The Analysis of Variance

ANOVA is most often the approach used to assess differences in means for the variables investigated in developmental research, such as age and time of measurement. ANOVA, like regression, is a general approach to data analysis that can accommodate the data from a wide variety of experimental designs. ANOVA can be used when all design facets involve (a) between-subject effects (e.g., completely randomized designs), (b) within-subject effects (randomized block or repeated-measures designs), or (c) both within- and between-subject effects (mixed or split-plot designs). ANOVA procedures also can be applied when additional measured variables are included to statistically control unwanted sources of variation (the analysis of covariance or ANCOVA), and when the design employs multiple dependent variables (MANOVA).

The analysis of variance is illustrated with a 4 (age) × 2 (gender) × 3 (time of measurement) split-plot factorial design shown in Part A of Table 2.14. The analysis of the data from that design might be used to test whether the means for the groups defined by age, gender, and time of testing alone, and in combinations, vary significantly. The latter tests of combinations of variables are referred to as tests of interactions. The tests performed require that the subject scores that are used in the analysis meet certain assumptions, including those of normality of score distributions, of homogeneity (equivalence) of variance, and of "homogeneity" of covariance or correlation between the repeated measures. ANOVA is relatively robust (insensitive) to violations of the former assumptions as long as each group contains approximately the same number of subjects, and sample sizes are not very small (e.g., Glass, Peckham, & Sanders, 1972). It is not robust, however, to violations of the requirement concerning the correlation between the repeated measures (Kirk, 1982). This requirement is likely to be violated whenever more than two times of testing are employed. This is so because the essence of the assumption is that all of the repeated measures are equally correlated. However, scores almost always correlate more highly with measures that are adjacent in time, and less highly with temporally more remote measures. Hence, with even three repeated measures, the correlations between Time 1 and Time 2 scores and between Time 2 and Time 3 scores are likely to exceed the correlation between Time 1 and Time 3 scores.

When the assumption of homogeneity of covariance is violated, the probability values obtained from ordinary statistical testing are too small (i.e., the effects appear to be more significant than they are). A number of procedures have been developed to remedy the biasing of probability values when this assumption may be violated, the most popular of which is the procedure developed by Geisser and Greenhouse (1958).

The Geisser–Greenhouse adjustment was applied to all of the within-subject tests conducted in Part B of Table 2.14. That is, the degrees of freedom used in calculating the probability values for the tests were reduced by dividing the usual degrees of freedom by the degrees of freedom

TABLE 2.14

Schematic Design and ANOVA Summary Table for an Age × Sex × Time of Testing Factorial Design

Part A. Design Schematic:

Age	Gender	Testing Period 1	2	3
4	Girl ($n = 5$)			
	Boy ($n = 5$)			
6	Girl ($n = 5$)			
	Boy ($n = 5$)			
8	Girl ($n = 5$)			
	Boy ($n = 5$)			
10	Girl ($n = 5$)			
	Boy ($n = 5$)			

Part B. ANOVA Summary Table:

Source	Degrees of Freedom (df)	MS	F	p	
Between Subjects					
Age (A)	$a - 1 = 4 - 1 = 3$	25.0	5.00	$<.01$	
Gender (B)	$b - 1 = 2 - 1 = 1$	5.5	1.10	$>.25$	
A × B	$(a - 1)(b - 1) = 3$	10.0	2.00	$<.25$	
Error (S/A × B)	$ab(n - 1) = 32$	5.0			
Within Subjects					
Assessments (D)	$d - 1 = 3 - 1 = 2$	8.4	3.36	$<.05$	$(<.10^a)$
D × A	$(d - 1)(a - 1) = 6$	10.0	4.00	$<.01$	$(<.05^b)$
D × B	$(d - 1)(b - 1) = 2$	2.8	1.12	$>.25$	$(>.25^a)$
D × A × B	$(d - 1)(a - 1)(b - 1) = 6$	3.1	1.24	$>.25$	$(>.25^b)$
Error (D × S/A × B)	$ab(n - 1)(d - 1) = 64$	2.5			

[a]Tested with 1 and 32 degrees of freedom (Geisser–Greenhouse correction).
[b]Tested with 3 and 32 degrees of freedom (Geisser–Greenhouse correction).
Note: MS indicates "mean square." The lower case letters in the source table equal the number of levels for the source indicated in the corresponding upper case letter. For example, there are 4 ages, so the source age (A) has four levels (a = 4). In generating F tests, age, gender, and time of testing are considered fixed so that all between-subject and within-subject effects are tested with their respective subject−S/A × B or D × S/A × B−error terms (Kirk, 1982).

associated with the repeated measure $(d - 1)$. The resulting statistical tests indicate that age and the interaction between age and time of assessment significantly determine performance.

The interaction between age and time of assessment is shown in Fig. 2.7. From an inspection of this figure, it can be discerned that the interaction, revealed by a lack of parallelism of the four data lines, is largely due to the performance of the two older age groups of children in comparison with that of the two younger age groups of children. That is, the 8- and 10-year-olds slightly deteriorate in performance across time, whereas the 4-

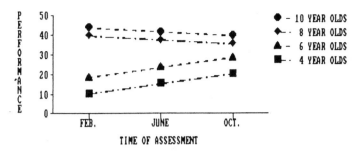

FIG. 2.7. Illustration of the interaction between age and time of assessment for the design shown in Table 2.14.

and 6-year-olds improve somewhat with each repetition of the assessment procedures.

The standard tests conducted by ANOVA can be supplemented (and sometimes replaced) by other statistical tests under at least two sets of circumstances. First, additional tests usually are conducted to determine exactly which level(s) of a factor differ from which other level(s) following a significant ANOVA test involving more than one degree of freedom. (More than one degree of freedom means that more than two means are being compared.) The procedures used for these follow-up tests involve some form of trend test, test of simple main effects, or other comparisons between combinations of means. Generically, these tests are referred to as multiple comparison tests. Their intent is to determine which specific levels of the independent variables included in the omnibus test are significantly different, while maintaining some control of Type I error rate produced by conducting multiple tests of significance on a set of data. (See the related discussion in the "Regression Analysis" section.) Of course, neither these, nor any other form of significance testing are appropriate for "test hopping"—that is, hopping from one inferential testing procedure to another until "significant" results are found.[13]

Many multiple comparison tests are available, including the Dunnett D' test, Tukey's HSD test, Scheffe's S test, and the Newman-Keuls test (Games, 1971). The selection among tests is based on a number of considerations, including whether the comparisons were planned prior to data analysis (a priori comparisons) or are selected after examining the data (a posteriori comparisons or fishing expeditions), whether pairwise or more complex comparisons among means are conducted, and whether all condi-

---

[13]A subtle and common, but nonetheless illegitimate variant of test hopping involves switching the form of the data as well as the method of analysis. For example, an investigator interested in differences in prosocial behavior between children of different ages may initially analyze donation rate data with a t test, and finding the test insignificant, switch to a chi-square analysis conducted on the transformed data of whether or not each child donated.

tion means are contrasted with a control group mean (see, e.g., Kirk, 1982, Table 3.61).

The second basis for not relying on omnibus tests from ANOVA relates to a message previously noted in this chapter: that the analysis should suit the question. And the standard tests performed by ANOVA may not adequately evaluate the comparison between means that are involved in an a priori hypothesis. Consider the interaction illustrated in Fig. 2.8 among the four levels from a 2 × 2 completely randomized factorial design. (In a completely randomized design, all effects involve between-subjects comparisons.) Using standard ANOVA tests, the variation associated with this interaction would be split between the main effects of age and of gender, and the age × gender interaction. All of the tests of these effects may be insignificant, yet a contrast written specifically for this expected pattern of interaction might be highly significant. And, of course, this is exactly the approach that should be taken with atypical a priori hypotheses: The contrast for the expected effect should be constructed and then tested. These a priori contrast tests may be conducted prior to, or even instead of, the traditional ANOVA tests (Rosenthal & Rosnow, 1985).

In addition to these general issues associated with the use of ANOVA, specific concerns accrue to the use of special, commonly used, ANOVA designs. Two of these designs are hierarchical ANOVA and ANCOVA.

Hierarchical Designs.   Formally, hierarchical designs are those in which the levels of one factor are nested within the levels of another factor. The design would be hierarchical, for example, if both second- and fourth-grade girls and boys were taught spelling using mnemonic devices, but different procedures were used for the second graders and for the fourth graders. Such obvious examples of nesting (think of the grades as nests, and the mnemonic devices as eggs within the nests) are unlikely to be mistakenly analyzed. Mistakes do occur, however, when a nuisance variable such as

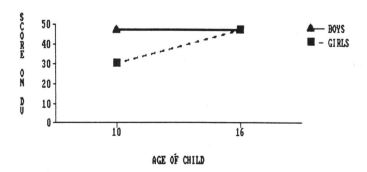

FIG. 2.8. Illustration of a predicted interaction between gender and age not adequately assessed using standard omnibus ANOVA tests.

classroom, play group, or family is nested within an experimental factor. Consider the case in which child aggression comprised the dependent variable, the design factor concerned whether aggression was disregarded ("put on extinction") or interpreted, and children were assessed and treated within play groups. In this example, a particularly aggressive group member might instigate counteraggression from other group members. As a result, the scores for all or most members of this play group would be elevated, scores for members within the group likely would be interdependent, and play group membership may be a substantial source of nuisance variation. Thus, the dependency between scores for members of a group and the effect of the group itself must be accommodated in the data analysis — or else serious inferential errors may be made. Various methods for integrating nested variables into the statistical analysis are discussed by Anderson and Anger (1978) and by Kraemer and Jacklin (1979); also see Kirk (1982).

Analysis of Covariance.   ANCOVA is involved when one or more measured variables are used to control unwanted sources of variance through statistical means in any of the standard ANOVA designs. (This is not unlike the method of statistical control served by partial correlations.) For example, in an experiment on methods of teaching reading, children's IQ scores might be used as a covariate to reduce naturally occurring differences in reading potential for the children participating in the experiment. Because unwanted sources of variability can be reduced statistically when they cannot be controlled experimentally, ANCOVA is a popular means of increasing statistical power or sensitivity. However, its use requires strict attention to a rigorous set of requirements (e.g., Huitema, 1980).

Two particularly serious problems can occur as a result of using ANCOVA incorrectly: One problem results from violating the ANCOVA assumptions; the other occurs when ANCOVA is asked to perform roles for which it is ill suited. The ANCOVA assumption that can be particularly problematic when violated is the assumption of independence between treatment and scores on the covariate. In the reading example mentioned above, the IQ scores must be independent of treatment. And that probably means that they must be obtained prior to implementation of the treatment for reading — when it is impossible for the treatment to have affected the IQ scores. The second problem occurs when investigators employ ANCOVA to adjust for initial differences between preexisting treatment groups, such as classrooms. Such a selection strategy — *choosing* groups that either have been treated or untreated — is a clear violation of random assignment procedures. Furthermore, initial biases typically cannot be undone by ANCOVA procedures (Overall & Woodward, 1977).

Multivariate Extensions

Various multivariate extensions of ANOVA and regression analysis are used by developmental investigators. There follows—in alphabetical order—a brief description of each of the more popular of these extensions, their primary functions or uses, their most common problems, and where interested readers can find out more about them. Before they are described, it is important to note a few similarities among the various multivariate techniques. Most important, all of the multivariate procedures apply *weights to the subjects' scores on the original set of measured variables to form one or more new composite variables; the weights are selected to optimize some function.* For example, if the newly constructed composite variable is Y, the original variables are X_a through X_e with optimum weights *a* through *e,* then the composite score for the ith individual is given by

$$Y_i = aX_{ai} + bX_{bi} + cX_{ci} + dX_{di} + eX_{ei},$$

where, for example, X_{ai} is the ith individual's score on variable X_a.

This process is similar to forming the composite variable, total score, for a classroom achievement test. The total score is based on a linear combination of weighted item scores. The item scores may be weighted in order to maximize individual differences in performance on the test—or an approximation to this, weighting each item 1.0, is more likely used. In multivariate analysis, the weights may be selected, for example, to maximize the correlation between two sets of variables (canonical correlation), to minimize the number of independent dimensions necessary to characterize a set of variables (factor analysis), or to maximize the differences between two or more groups (discriminant analysis).

All multivariate techniques also share a number of common weaknesses. Foremost among these weaknesses is that they eschew perfectly, or near perfectly, correlated variables. Perfectly correlated variables comprise one case of problem to multivariate analysis called *linear dependency.* Highly correlated variables pose a slightly different problem called *multicollinearity.* Both conditions are undesirable for all forms of multivariate analysis. Second, multivariate procedures require substantial numbers of subjects. As the ratio of variables to subjects approaches 1.0, the optimizing algorithm used to generate weights increasingly exploits chance relationships in the data. As a consequence, the results of the study will not replicate.

Canonical Correlation.   The aim of canonical correlation is to explore the interrelations between two sets of variables. It is the multivariate analog of bivariate correlation. Instead of single predictor and criterion variables, canonical correlation is used when sets of predictor and criterion variables are obtained. The technique generates composite scores from a weighted linear combination of the set of predictor variables and of the set of criterion variables; the weights are selected to maximize the correlation between the two composite scores. The linear combinations of variables generated by this procedure are called canonical variates; hence, the correlation between canonical variates is called a canonical correlation. Following the construction or extraction of the first canonical variates from the predictor and criterion sets of variables and the calculation of their correlation, additional canonical variables may be extracted and correlated. The weights used in forming these subsequent canonical variates are chosen with an additional criterion: The new variates must be independent of the canonical variates already constructed.

Canonical correlation is used when an investigator intends to explore the relations between sets of variables in separate domains, for example, between nursery school children's social interactional behaviors and their performance on cognitive tasks. Unless the ratio of subjects to variables in such an investigation is quite large, say 10:1, the specific optimum weights used are unlikely to cross-validate in subsequent investigations. Additional information on canonical correlation can be found in Thompson (1984), and in the multivariate textbooks by Marascuilo and Levin (1983) and by Tabachnick and Fidell (1989).

Discriminant Analysis.   The purpose of discriminant analysis is to assign individuals to the group to which they belong. Assignments are based on the individual's standing on one or more weighted linear composites of their scores on a set of predictor variables. The weights are selected so that the predictor variables maximize differences between the groups. For example, a discriminant analysis might be used to assign children to popular, neglected, or rejected groups based on composite scores formed by weighting their scores on the scales of the Child Behavior Checklist (Achenbach & Edelbrock, 1981). This problem, involving as it does classification into one of three groups, requires the construction of two (one less than the number of groups) composite variables.

The composite variables formed in discriminant analysis are called discriminant functions. Typical discriminant analysis output provides the weights for the predictor variables that are used in constructing the discriminant functions; that is, the weights for the variables that aid in the prediction of group membership. The output also includes information on which categories individual children are assigned to based on their scores on the discriminant functions, as well as the proportion of children correctly classified. The standard multivariate texts previously mentioned, as well as the manuals for standard computer data analysis software such as BMDP

(Dixon et al., 1985), SAS (1985), and SPSS^x (1986) can be consulted for additional information on discriminant analysis.

Factor Analysis.   Factor analysis, and related techniques such as principle component analysis, have as their purpose the discovery of the minimum dimensions underlying a set of variables. Investigators may be interested, for example, in the number of dimensions underlying performance on the subtests of the WISC-R, or underlying endorsement of the items included in the Child Behavior Checklist. These dimensions, referred to as factors or components, are constructed by forming weighted linear composites of the original variables (e.g., subtest or item scores). The weights applied to the variables in the construction of each factor vary depending on the factoring technique used. In general, however, the weights are chosen to explain the maximum variation in the entire set of variables as yet unexplained. Thus, the weights assigned the variables in the construction of the first factor are chosen so as to maximize the correlations of that factor with the original variables. The weights for the variables in the construction of the second factor are chosen so that factor has the highest correlations with those parts of the original variables not accounted for by the first factor, and so forth.

After factors are extracted, they often are rotated. Rotation refers to the transformation of factors by modifying the weights for the variables from which they were constructed. The purpose of rotation is to facilitate description, and hence understanding of the factors extracted from a set of data. In Fig. 2.9, the two original factors extracted (I and II) from eight verbal and quantitative tests were rotated (counterclockwise) some 30° to promote understanding of the factors. The original factors (labeled I and II) are hodgepodges of verbal and quantitative abilities; the new factors (labeled I' and II') appear to be relatively pure measures of verbal and quantitative skills, respectively. Readers interested in learning more about factor analysis and related techniques can consult the articles by Comrey (1978) and by Rummel (1967), and the readable texts by Gorsuch (1983) and McDonald (1985).

Multivariate Analysis of Variance.   MANOVA is a straightforward generalization of ANOVA to investigations employing more than one dependent variable. For example, if the age × gender × repeated assessment problem described in Table 2.14 included two or more DVs, rather than just one DV, MANOVA would be the appropriate method of analysis of the data. Furthermore, the MANOVA summary table would closely resemble in form Panel B of Table 2.14, the ANOVA summary table. The primary difference between ANOVA and MANOVA is that the latter forms

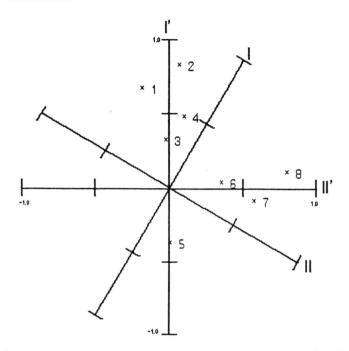

FIG. 2.9. Illustration of rotation to achieve improved interpretability of factors. The correlations between the original eight variables and the factors, I and II, are indicated by finding the coordinates of the xs used to represent the eight variables. For example, variable 1 (see x 1) has correlations of about |.5| with both factors I and II. The original factors were rotated approximately 30° counterclockwise to form the new factors, I' and II'. As a result, the five verbal tests (numbered 1 through 5) defined the first rotated factor (I'), and the three quantitative tests (numbered 6 through 8) defined the second rotated factor (II'). While rotation has no effect upon the correlations between the variables, it does change the loadings (correlations) of the variables with the factors. For example, variable 7 now correlates in excess of .6 with factor II', and slightly negatively with factor I'.

one or more weighted composites of the DVs that maximize the differences between the levels of the IVs. It is these composite scores, called discriminant function scores, that are tested for significance. If two or more discriminant functions are formed, each discriminant function is independent of the discriminant functions already formed.

MANOVA has a number of advantages when compared with conducting separate ANOVAs on each dependent variable. First, MANOVA provides better control over Type I error. Subsequent statistical tests (e.g., ANOVAs) are only conducted if MANOVA indicates that at least one independent variable produces an effect on some linear combination of the dependent variables. (This rule is relaxed when a priori predictions are advanced.) Second, MANOVA may detect differences—when a weak effect is distributed over each of a number of correlated dependent variables—that would not be found if a separate ANOVA was conducted on each dependent variable. Thus, in some circumstances, MANOVA may be a more powerful method of analysis than are separate ANOVAs.

Other Statistical Techniques

A number of other, newer forms of analysis are available to developmental researchers. Two of these—structural equation modeling and meta-analysis—are sufficiently common and important to deserve mention.

Structural Equation Modeling

Structural equation modeling (SEM, structural modeling, linear structural equations, or covariance structural modeling) is a multiple regression-like statistical methodology for testing causal models. In contrast to more typical descriptive interpretations of, say, the regression coefficients in a multiple regression analysis, SEM hypothesizes that the coefficients indicate the rate with which the independent variables cause changes in the dependent variable. Structural equation modeling is perhaps most closely associated with the computer program, LISREL, developed by Joreskog and his associates (e.g., Joreskog & Sorbom, 1983) for estimating the parameters for structural models (LISREL is an acronym for *li*near *str*uctural *rel*ations). However, other approaches to structural model testing are available (e.g., Bentler, 1980; Heise, 1975; Kenny, 1979).

Structural modeling is particularly attractive to developmentalists. The reasons for this popularity are easily understood. The technique is well adapted for use with nonexperimental data, and it makes its strongest case with multiple wave longitudinal data—the kind of data that is traditionally associated with developmental investigations. In fact, manuscripts using, as well as misusing, structural modeling have increased at such a dramatic rate that a prominent developmental journal, *Child Development,* devoted much of an entire issue "to illuminate the nature and possible applications of this statistical technique to developmental data" (Bronson, 1987, p. 1).

Structural modeling employs a somewhat different vocabulary than do more traditional forms of design and analysis. In SEM, the variable set is divided into two classes, *exogenous* variables and *endogenous* variables. Exogenous variables are those variables that are hypothesized to produce changes in other (endogenous) variables in the model, but the causes for the exogenous variables themselves are not included in the model. Endogenous variables, in contrast, are those variables that are presumably changed as a result of other variables in the model. Thus, exogenous variables are always independent variables, whereas endogenous variables are dependent variables, but also can serve as independent variables. A variable serving both independent and dependent variable status is sometimes referred to as an intervening variable.

Variables included in some structural models also may be classified as *measured variables* or as *latent variables*. Measured variables, as the name suggests, are variables that are directly assessed; latent variables are merely estimated — usually by more than one measured variable. As this vocabulary exercise suggests, a structural model (the multiple regressionlike part of structural modeling) is often joined with a measurement model (the factor analytic-like part of SEM). When these two models are joined, as in LISREL, a good part of the Greek, and parts of the English alphabet, are required in order to symbolize the components of the model and their interconnecting equations. Fortunately, models typically are expressed pictorially, in the form of path diagrams, in addition to being expressed as a series of equations.

A path diagram illustrating the structural relations among four variables is displayed in Panel A of Fig. 2.10. In path diagrams such as this one, exogenous variables are placed on the far left of the diagram, intervening variables in the middle, and other endogenous variables at the far right. Once the data have been obtained, the path coefficients (correlations and regression coefficients) often are placed on the arrows, and the values of R^2s (the proportion of explained endogenous variable variance) are included in the circles. Panel B of Fig. 2.10 illustrates the measurement submodel for the Panel A latent variable of child social skills. This latent variable is indexed with three measurement operations, independent observations of the child, teacher ratings, and peer sociometrics.

Each variable in path diagrams that is touched by an arrowhead is included as the dependent variable in a structural equation. Each variable attached to the dependent variable by the end of an arrow is included on the right-hand side of the same structural equation as an independent variable. For example, in the rudimentary model described in Fig. 2.10, child social skills would be expressed as a function of child IQ and parental socioeconomic status (SES) and social skills (Panel A), whereas the observational measure of social skill would comprise the dependent variable in an equation including the latent variable of child social skill and error (Panel B).

SEM testing requires a number of reasonably complicated steps or phases. The first step involves formulation of the structural model, in which the hypothesized causal relations between sets of variables are formulated. James, Mulaik, and Brett (1982) indicate that this step involves some seven substeps, including provision of a theoretical rationale for the causal

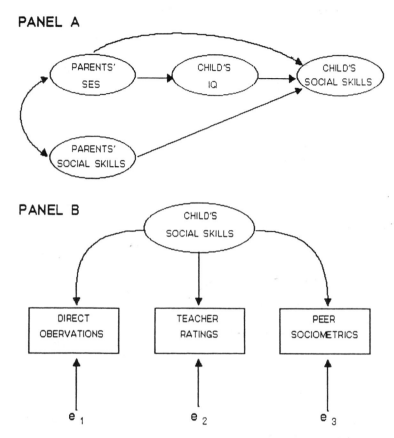

PANEL A

PANEL B

FIG. 2.10. Path diagrams. The diagram in Panel A illustrates the structural relations between the exogenous variables of parental SES and social skills, and the endogenous variables of child's IQ (an intervening variable) and social skills. Disturbance components are not included. The diagram in Panel B illustrates a measurement model for the latent variable, child's social skills.

hypotheses and specification of causal order and direction. The second step involves operationalization of the variables and gathering data relevant to the test of the model. Because causes require time to produce their effects, longitudinal data involving a time lag suitable for capturing the causal connections stipulated in the model typically are required. After the data have been gathered—and structural modeling requires substantial data, as do all multivariate statistical techniques—they are summarized in a form appropriate for testing the goodness of fit of the model. This form typically requires the calculation of the variances and covariances between the variables included in the model. These variances and covariances are then operated on, often with rather complex statistical programs such as LISREL, to produce estimates of the model parameters and tests of statistical significance. One or more of these tests of significance are conducted on the model as a whole (Anderson, 1987). A statistically nonsignificant (typically, chi-square) test indicates that the model adequately fits the data, whereas a statistically significant test suggests that the model requires revision — that significant amounts of variability in the data are not accounted for by the model. Statistical tests also are conducted on the individual model components, such as the regression weights relating putative effects to their causes and indicators to their latent variables. For these statistical tests of predicted relations, a nonsignificant (typically an $F-$) test indicates that the subpart of the model tested has been disconfirmed — that the expected relation is not reliably different from zero.

It is important to recognize the nature of the causal inferences that can be drawn from confirmation of a structural model. As anyone who has survived an elementary course in statistics has repeatedly heard, correlation does not prove causation. (Nor, it might be added, does any other statistic.) It is true, however, that causation implies correlation (Mulaik, 1987). Thus, finding that the predicted correlations between the variables included in the model fit the data increases the credibility of the causal model and the theory on which it was based. This increased credibility resulting from model confirmation assumes, of course, that the model was potentially disconfirmable by the data gathered (Popper, 1962).

Following testing of the model to determine whether it can be confirmed, or must be disconfirmed, further exploratory analyses may be conducted on the model. These analyses are performed in order to assess how the model might be revised to better fit the empirical results. The revised model produced as a result of this exploratory work requires additional empirical testing with a fresh sample of data — as does all exploratory model building, no matter which statistical technique provided the means of exploration — in order to determine whether it will pass a reasonable test of disconfirmation.

Structural equation modeling is a powerful approach for the analysis of nonexperimental data, but the power comes with some cost. The model requires a careful balance of variables to subjects (not more than [$N/10$] − 2 variables, where N is the number of subjects), multiple measures or indicators for its latent variables, appropriate lags between the waves of the longitudinal data that are gathered, and assurance that certain statistical assumptions, including that of linear relations among the variables, are upheld (Biddle & Marlin, 1987; Martin, 1987; Tanaka, 1987).

Very readable accounts of structural modeling can be found in the special issue of *Child Development* (Bronson, 1987) devoted to that topic, in Bentler (1980), and in the monographs by Dwyer (1983), Heise (1975),

James et al. (1982), and Kenny (1979). More technical presentations are available in Joreskog and Sorbom (1981) and in Long (1983).

Meta-Analysis

Meta-Analysis is a systematic, quantitative method of summarizing the results of studies composing a research literature (Strube & Hartmann, 1983). Traditional narrative reviews of the literature have been criticized for their subjectivity, imprecision, and neglect of important information contained in primary studies (Jackson, 1980). These concerns, coupled with the relative explosion of scientific information, suggest the need for better methods of summarizing research literatures.

Meta-analytic techniques serve a variety of functions involved in reviewing a research literature. From the very beginning of operationalizing the review, the techniques include methods for systematically collecting the studies composing the literature to ensure that the raw data for the analysis will not be biased (e.g., Hunter, Schmidt, & Jackson, 1982, chap. 7). The heart of meta-analysis, however, contains the statistical methods for summarizing the results of the primary studies composing the literature. Foremost among these statistical methods are techniques for combining probabilities across studies (Rosenthal, 1980b). While a number of probability-combining techniques are available, they all have as their principal purpose determining whether the set of results composing a literature could have risen by chance. The combination of effect sizes represents another major approach to summarizing results across studies. The methods of determining average effect size assist the reviewer in determining the importance or strength of effect of the findings in a literature. Although a number of effect size indicators are available for accomplishing this goal, the correlation coefficient and Cohen's d statistic, a standard score variant, are most commonly used for this purpose (Smith, Glass, & Miller, 1980).

Beyond the computation of a combined probability and of an average effect size, meta-analysis also provides methods of determining the stability of results. Stability is often assessed using Rosenthal's (1979) fail-safe method. This method estimates the number of unpublished studies with zero effect size that would have to be filed away in the desks of investigators in order to wash out the results of the available studies included in the review.

Finally, because the probability values and effect sizes of the individual studies composing a literature are likely to vary substantially, a number of procedures and strategies have been proposed for identifying those factors associated with variation in outcome across studies. Potential factors include any number of primary study characteristics that might be coded during the review such as the nature of the sample of subjects studied, the methods of operationalizing independent and dependent variables, as well as how adequately validity threats were handled in the study. These factors are then treated as IVs (the p-values and effect sizes serve as DVs) in analyses using regression or ANOVA techniques, or methods of analysis especially developed for meta-analysis (Hedges & Olkin, 1985).

Meta-analytic procedures themselves have been reviewed (Bangert-Drowns, 1986) — although, perhaps ironically, using traditional rather than meta-analytic techniques. Understandable, technical presentations of meta-analysis are given in Cooper (1989); Glass, McGaw, and Smith (1981); Hunter et al. (1982); and Rosenthal (1980).

Interpreting Statistics

The statement regarding probability associated with each application of an inferential statistical test, the "p is less than" statement, has a clear but often misunderstood meaning. Consider a two-group experiment in which $n_1 = n_2 = 20$, the difference between group means is 5 points, $t(38) = 2.03$, and $p = .05$. Which of the following conclusions can appropriately be made based on this statement?

1. The relation between the DV and the IV is large or important.
2. The probability of this result being replicated is .05.
3. The probability is .95 that the difference between the two population means is 5.
4. The probability is .05 that the difference between the two population means is 0.
5. If the experiment is run again and a nonsignificant outcome is obtained ($p > .05$), this necessarily means that the two studies are inconsistent.

If you endorsed any of these alternatives you are not interpreting the results of significance tests correctly (see Huitema, 1986). However, you are in good company, as even statisticians frequently err in interpreting the probability values from experiments (Tversky & Kahneman, 1971). In fact, none of the alternative interpretations is even approximately correct. The correct interpretation should read as follows: If a two-group experiment with $n_1 = n_2 = 20$ is conducted, and if the true difference between the population means is 0, a sample difference of at least 5 points would occur no more than 5 times in 100 ($p = .05$).

Let us briefly consider each of the alternatives to determine why they are incorrect.

Perhaps alternative 1 represents the most serious misinterpretation of significance tests. Probability values indicate neither effect size nor importance. Effect size is appropriately indexed by the correlation between IVs and DVs, or some variant of the standardized difference statistic *(d)* previously discussed, or a measure of overlap between the two distributions (Cohen, 1977). These effect size indicators are a function of the difference between means in comparison to some measure of within-group variability, while probability values are a function of effect size and sample size. Thus, given the same value of *d* or *r* in two studies differing only in sample size, the study with the larger sample size will be associated with a smaller probability value. Importance is a concept even more elusive, or at any rate more difficult, to quantify. Importance depends not only on effect size, but possibly also on the effect sizes produced by competing variables, on substantive theory concerning the variable, and on the measurement theory associated with the operationalization of the variable (Mitchell & Hartmann, 1981; O'Grady, 1982).

Alternative 2 is substantially incorrect. The probability of precisely replicating the results of the first study is extremely small. The probability of replicating the study in the sense of rejecting the null hypothesis at a similar level of significance depends on the design of the subsequent study and the true difference between the population means (see Cohen, 1977). In general, the larger the difference between the two population means, the better the design of the second study, and the larger that study's sample size, the greater the probability of rejecting the null hypothesis in that study.

Alternative 3 specifies the probability of a particular difference between the two population means. That interpretation is blatantly incorrect. The difference between two population means is a specific value; the value does not define a probability distribution. Our best (and only) estimate of the difference between the two population means is 5 points, and a particular probability cannot readily be associated with the correctness of that estimate.

Alternative 4, which stated that the probability is .05 of the difference between the two populations being 0, perhaps sounds like it may be the closest of the lot to a correct interpretation to the original finding. This interpretation has no meaning in the current problem, however. Furthermore, although the difference may be zero, it is extremely unlikely to be exactly that value. It is true that a confidence interval can be established about the obtained difference, say the .95 confidence limit. Over the long run, such intervals would include the true mean difference 95% of the time. But that is certainly not the equivalent of stating that the probability is .05 of the true difference being exactly 0.

Alternative 5 — that repetition of the experiment with a $p > .05$ outcome necessarily means that the two studies are inconsistent — is one of those incorrect interpretations to which even trained statisticians fall prey. If the experiment is run a second time, the probability of rejecting the null hypothesis (power) in the second study can be determined with some precision once the characteristics (e.g., sample size, reliability of the dependent measure, and potency of the IV) are determined. If the characteristics are poorly chosen, it can be expected that the null hypothesis will not be rejected. That is, failure to reject the null hypothesis in the second study is entirely consistent with rejection of the null hypothesis in the first study. If the difference found in the first study is exactly equal to the true population difference, and if the second study is conducted as an exact or operational replication (Lykken, 1968), the probability of rejecting the null hypothesis, as in the first study, is exactly .50!

ETHICS

Ethics, that field involving the study of right and wrong conduct, seems at first glance to have little relevance to a chapter on the technical aspects of research. But ethics is related to the conduct of research in very much the same way as are the various aspects of methodology and analysis previously discussed. Every investigator must make a variety of ethically based decisions during the course of developmental investigation. And these decisions interact with, and determine, the methodology and other technical aspects of the research.

Perhaps the most general ethical issue that every investigation must ask is: Should this research be conducted, given its likely contributions in comparison to the risk, discomfort, and inconvenience that would be inflicted on its participants? This question makes clear the conflict that potentially exists between two sets of rights: the rights of the investigator to free scientific inquiry, and those of the research participants to privacy and protection from harm.

In addition to this overarching ethical question, the investigator must confront numerous other ethical concerns: Are participants told about the research in a manner that is understandable to them? Are the incentives promised for participation likely to be coercive? Are research assistants respecting the subjects' confidentiality? Are subjects leaving the study feeling as good about themselves as before they began participation? Will the participants' confidence in research be maintained if deception is used? Have the data supporting the hypothesis been as carefully scrutinized for atypical respondents as have the data not supporting the hypothesis? Have the intellectual contributors to the study been appropriately cited? Have research collaborators and assistants been appropriately recognized in coauthorships, footnotes, and the like?

In this section, the history of ethics in research is briefly described, and a number of cause celebres that have intensified public and scientific concern with ethics are highlighted. Next, current procedures for protecting human subjects — and the principles on which these procedures are based — are discussed. Special ethical problems associated with using children as subjects are noted, and the ethical principles for the conduct of research with children promulgated by the Society for Research in Child Development (SRCD) are described. The multilayered safeguarding of children's rights as research subjects is illustrated with the procedures followed in the author's ongoing research program with children. Finally, a number of other ethical issues involved in research, including plagiarism and fraud, are noted.

A Brief Historical Sketch

Until approximately the mid-20th century, the ethics of research were largely left up to the consciences of individual investigators, perhaps aided by the informal and unsystematic opinions of colleagues. However, a number of events sent shockwaves through government and scientific enterprises that suggested the then-current methods were inadequate. Certainly foremost among those events were the medical research practices of German investigators during World War II, practices that were so shocking that some of the investigators were tried by the Nuremberg Military Tribunal. To provide a set of guidelines for the Tribunal, a code was formulated regarding the conduct of research with human subjects that came to be called the Nuremberg Code (Beecher, 1970). It was from this code that numerous sets of ethical guidelines were spawned by professional organizations and federal research funding agencies, such as the National Institutes of Health (NIH).

The need for greater ethical sensitivity was further emphasized by a number of cause celebres of the 1970s. Particularly notable among these were the notorious Tuskegee Syphilis Study, and the infamous fraud case involving Sir Cyril Burt, the dean of British Psychology. The Tuskegee Syphilis Study involved long-term monitoring of the consequences of *untreated* syphilis from the 1930s until the 1970s. In this study, the subjects, largely poor, rural Blacks living in the south, were systematically denied treatment for their life-threatening infections, even though effective antibiotic treatments were widely available for decades before the study was terminated (Jones, 1981). Here, a series of ethical principles were violated by ostensibly well-meaning scientists, including infliction of pain on subjects in excess of what the research could expect to contribute, failure of informed consent, and the concomitant use of deception.

The Cyril Burt scandal of the mid 1970s involved a quite different ethical concern: fraud in science. Burt was a highly influential psychologist in England — in fact, a luminary of British Psychology. He was a strong proponent of the importance of genetics to the development of IQ, and his studies of identical twins reared apart—a crucial contribution to the research literature in this area—had tremendous influences on beliefs about racial differences in IQ and on educational practices in Britain. Unfortunately, careful analysis of Burt's work following his death in 1971 indicates that he manufactured at least some of the twin data, and attributed false reports to others (Hearnshaw, 1979). Thus, Burt violated the unspoken pact that members of the scientific community have with each other—to report truthfully their observations (Dooley, 1990).

These, and other violations of ethics in social science research (see, e.g., Ad Hoc Committee on Ethical Standards in Psychological Research, 1973) spurred governmental agencies, such as NIH, as well as professional societies, such as the American Psychological Association (APA) and the SRCD, to generate ethical guidelines that now effectively govern most research involving human subjects in the United States (e.g., APA, 1982, 1987; Report from the Committee for Ethical Conduct in Child Development Research, 1990). For fuller accounts of the history of these guidelines, see Cooke (1982) and Reingold (1982). In addition, all universities and other research centers who accept federal research funding now are mandated to have institutional review boards (IRBs), that routinely monitor the proposals for all research engaged in by institutional members. The IRBs reflect one of the basic principles of research ethics: the principle of *independent review*. The notion here being that individual investigators are too involved in their own proposals to render a unbiased ethical judgments about the interests of their subjects, and require the opinion of a disinterested panel of experts.

IRBs typically solicit information from the investigator regarding the following ethically related topics (Miller, 1987, p. 274): What are the risks to the subjects from participation in the research? What are the benefits of the research? How will subjects be recruited, and what incentives will be offered for their participation? Will it be clear to the subjects that participation is voluntary, and that they can withdraw from participation at any time without penalty? How will subjects be debriefed regarding any deception in the study? How will confidentiality of responding be ensured? These topics have as their basis a set of principles guiding research with human subjects.

Principles Guiding Research Practices With Human Subjects

Ethical research practices with humans are guided by universal humanitarian principles of respect for the individual. These principles involve a number of rights, including the following: the right of informed consent prior to participating in the research, the right of freedom from pain as a result of participation in the research, and the right to confidentiality of the information obtained by means of the research.

Informed Consent

Participation in research must be voluntary, and the potential subjects must be informed of the nature of their participation.[14] Thus, subjects must understand the nature of their involvement in research, and they must be capable of providing consent. The former implies that the study is described in a manner understandable to the subject; the latter that the subject is free to agree or to refuse to participate.

The right of potential subjects to be informed of the research procedures and the expected consequences of these procedures for the subject often is violated, both inadvertently and intentionally. For example, the study may be described in a manner that unintentionally limits the understanding of potential subjects through the use of complex instructions and technical vocabulary (Tannenbaum & Cooke, 1977). At other times, it is not the skill, knowledge, and sensitivity of the investigator that limits subjects' understanding, but rather the nature of the research question. Some studies require that the subjects not be totally informed of either the research procedures or of the study's purpose, lest that knowledge affect their responses and perhaps limit the generalizability of the result to settings in which subjects are aware of the details of being investigated. This use of deception has a lengthy, and controversial history, particularly in social psychological research (cf. Baumrind, 1985; Cooper, 1976; Kelman, 1967). The consensus of opinion now seems to be that research questions should attempt to be conducted without the use of deception; if deception is required—and meets the approval of the IRB—the investigator assumes special obligations that the deception does not harm the subject. Thus, the investigator must be particularly sensitive to any untoward reactions from the subject, and must use debriefing procedures in a thorough and timely manner.

Investigators must also be certain that the subject is able to provide voluntary consent. Consent may not be voluntary when power differences exist between subject and experimenter or when the investigator has other control over the subject's life or well-being, as would be the case when the investigator is also the subject's instructor. Voluntary consent may also be

---

[14]An exception to this occurs with certain kinds of observational research conducted in contexts such as supermarkets and playgrounds. Generally, subject consent need not be obtained if the behaviors studied are naturally occurring ones that are unaffected by the decision to study them; the behaviors are innocuous and are neither revealing nor embarrassing; and the subjects are anonymous and certain to remain so (e.g., Miller, 1987, p. 275).

in question if excessive incentives are offered for research participation, and, of course, in the case of children (which is addressed subsequently) and other subjects who are not legally able to provide consent. Voluntary consent also implies that the subject may withdraw from participation at any time during the study without penalty.

Freedom from Harm

Subjects are entitled to the assurance that they will not be harmed as a result of their research participation. Harm, particularly psychological harm, may be difficult to assess or even to anticipate. Subjects may be upset by memories or fears that are idiosyncratically instigated by an investigation conducted by the most conscientious of investigators involving the most innocuous of topics. In those cases, the investigator must be prepared to take appropriate action to counter the unanticipated effects of the investigation, including the possibility of referral for counseling.

In some cases, the investigator may believe that although some discomfort is likely to be experienced by the subject, the discomfort is small in comparison to the expected scientific and other human advances that can be expected as a result of the research. Investigators may not be in the best of circumstances to make such decisions, however, and require the advice of potential subjects, colleagues, and the disinterested opinion of a local IRB panel. When it is deemed that subjects may be harmed, but that the benefits of the research are clearly likely to exceed the harm experienced by subjects, potential subjects must be clearly informed of the danger they face prior to being asked to provide their consent.

Confidentiality

Subjects have a right to privacy, and can expect that their reactions in studies will not come back to haunt them. Thus, for example, investigators must ensure that neither they nor their assistants will discuss responses to the research protocol in a manner that subjects' names are associated with their reactions. It is now common practice that investigators help ensure confidentiality by identifying research records by number only. If it is important to keep a record of subjects' names, the names are separated from the records, and the copy of the master list of names and numbers is kept in a locked cabinet. Subjects may, however, agree to having their privacy invaded—for example, by agreeing to having a best friend report on some aspect of their behavior to the investigator. Such cases obviously require informed consent by the subject.

At times, an investigator must violate confidentiality, for example, when child abuse is disclosed during the course of the investigation. If this or other information may require the violation of confidence, subjects must be apprised of this risk when they are asked to provide informed consent. The implementation of this, and the other rights described earlier, may require certain modification when applied to children as subjects.

Protection of Child Subjects

Children are common subjects in developmental research, and because of their legal status as minors, their incompletely developed cognitive capacities, and their limited experiences may present special ethical problems, particularly regarding informed consent. Based on these considerations, the Society for Research in Child Development promulgated a set of principles regarding the conduct of research with children. The 14 principles noted here are those formulated in the society's ethical standards (Report from the Committee for Ethical Conduct in Child Development Research, 1990); the annotations are paraphrased from the standards as well as interpretations of them by the author.

SRCD Principles

Principle 1: Nonharmful Procedures.   As in the case of adult subjects, the investigator should not use research procedures that may harm the child, and is obligated to use the least stressful research operation whenever possible. If stress is introduced to child subjects, the anticipated benefits of the study must clearly exceed any risk to them. If a study is carried out so negligently that nothing can be learned from the results, there is no justification for putting subjects though any unpleasant experiences (Aronson, Ellsworth, Carlsmith, & Gonzales, 1990). Whenever the investigator is in doubt of the harmful properties of his or her procedures, consultation should be sought from others. When harmful procedures are proposed, careful deliberation by an IRB should be sought.

Principle 2: Informed Consent.   Information should be given in a manner appropriate to the child's developmental level, and consent should be obtained for children 7 years of age and older (National Commission for the Protection of Human Subjects, 1977). For younger children, if possible, the child's assent should be sought. "Assent means that the child shows some form of agreement to participate without necessarily comprehending the full significance of the research necessary to give informed consent" (Report from the Committee for Ethical Conduct in Child Development Research, 1990, p. 6).

Investigators working with toddlers and preschool children should make efforts to at least tell the children what will be done, where it will be done, who will be involved, how long their participation will last, whether other children have participated and how they reacted to the research, whether an incentive will be offered, and that they can say "yes" or "no" regarding participation (Miller, 1987). Investigators working with infants and small children should take special effort to explain the research procedures to parents, and to be especially sensitive to any indicators of discomfort by their young subjects.

Principle 3: Parental Consent.   Informed consent should be obtained in writing from parents or those who act in loco parentis, such as teachers or camp counselors. Not only should the right of parents and others to refuse be recognized, but they should also be apprised of their right to withdraw permission at any time without penalty.

Principle 4: Additional Consent.   The same rights mentioned above for parents should also be afforded to other caregivers, such as teachers, whose interaction with the child is the subject of study.

Principle 5: Incentives.   Incentives to participate must be fair and must not unduly exceed the range of incentives that the child normally experiences.

Principle 6: Deception.   Although some psychologists take the position that deception is never justified with children (e.g., Ferguson, 1978), this is not a generally accepted position. If deception is used, investigators should satisfy their colleagues that such procedures are warranted. If there is reason to believe that subjects might be harmed by deception, they should be apprised of the need for deception in a sensitive and developmentally appropriate manner. Debriefing, which is so critical in research with adults and older children and adolescents, may with young children largely involve providing the children with good feelings as a result of their research participation (Smith, 1967).

Principle 7: Anonymity.   Permission should be obtained from responsible individuals if institutional records are to be used, and precautions taken that anonymity of the information contained in these records be preserved.

Principle 8: Mutual Responsibilities.   The responsibilities of all participants in the research enterprise—children, parents, teachers, administrators, and research assistants—should be made clear at the inception of the study, and all promises should be honored.

Principle 9: Jeopardy.   If information that jeopardizes a child's well-being should become available during the conduct of a study, the investigator has a responsibility to discuss the information with the parents and with experts in the field who may arrange the necessary assistance for the child.

Principle 10: Unforeseen Consequences. If research procedures result in unforeseen negative consequences for child subjects, the investigator should take immediate action to modify the untoward effects, and the procedures should be modified for subsequent subjects. If, for example, the procedures instigate negative affect in the child, procedures to reinstate positive feelings should immediately be instituted.

Principle 11: Confidentiality. Procedures should be placed into effect to ensure the confidentiality of subjects' responses. When a possibility exists that others may gain access to research responses, this possibility, together with the plans for protecting confidentiality, should be explained to the participants as part of the procedure of obtaining informed consent.

Principle 12: Informing Participants. The investigator recognizes a duty to inform the subjects of any misunderstandings, and to report general findings to them in terms appropriate to their understanding. If information must be withheld, efforts should be made so that the participants are not damaged by the withheld information.

Principle 13: Reporting Results. Because the investigator's comments may carry undue weight, caution should be exercised in reporting results, making evaluative statements, or giving advice to parents, teachers, and the like.

Principle 14: Implications of Findings. Investigators should be particularly mindful of the social, political, and human implications of their research.
It is important to recognize that these principles apply not only to the principle investigator, but that all assistant and technical personnel incur similar ethical obligations to the research participants.

Illustration of Ethical Safeguards for Child Subjects

In order to illustrate the multilayers of ethical precautions taken in research with children, the author describes the general procedures used in his ongoing research on the peer interactions of young grammar school children.

1. During the development of a research proposal, extensive discussions involving substance, methodology, and ethical implications are undertaken

by the investigator with members of his research group, which includes collaborators, senior research assistants, undergraduate assistants, and the like.

2. Before the study proposal is sent to granting agencies, a description of the study, with particular attention to ethically sensitive issues, is forwarded through the departmental chairman's office to the local IRB. The IRB may send the proposal out for review to local experts, or may act on the proposal without additional external review.

3. If the IRB is satisfied that ethical and other research issues have been adequately addressed, the proposal often goes to a funding agency. The funding agency, such as the National Institute of Mental Health, funnels the proposal to one of its institutional review groups (IRGs). The IRG may seek additional external reviews, or may operate on the proposal using agency personnel and its standing peer review committee.

4. At the same time that the proposal is routed to the funding agency, it also goes to the school board office responsible for overseeing research in the public schools. The director of research in the schools and his or her administrative staff make their independent assessment of the proposal.

5. If the school district administrators find the research acceptable, contact is made with potentially cooperative school principles, who also have veto authority over the proposal.

6. Following approval of the study by the school principal, relevant teachers are contacted, and their advice, permission, and approval is sought.

7. If permission and approval is forthcoming from individual teachers, the children are told of the research, and asked for their consent.

8. If the children's consent is obtained, forms that explain the research and seek permission are sent to parents or guardians, and only those children whose parents or guardians explicitly approve of the research are candidates for participation.

9. Finally, children are reminded immediately prior to their participation that they may withdraw from the study at any time without repercussions.

These layers of protection should ensure that the rights of children are respected during their participation. Other ethical issues involved with the conduct of research, however, are not as thoroughly protected or as open to scrutiny.

Other Ethical Issues

As the introduction to this section indicated, not all ethical issues concerned with the conduct of research involve the relations between investigator and subject. Investigators' relations with other researchers, funding agencies, and various special interest groups also involve ethical issues, concerns, and potential conflicts (Dooley, 1990). These may include plagiarism—the failure to appropriately credit the contributions of others—ranging from "stealing" the studies and research ideas of colleagues and assistants to lesser ethical indiscretions involving the order of authorships and the inclusion of assistants in acknowledgments. Other ethical violations may include fraud or other forms of scientific embezzlement, as already illustrated in the case of Sir Cyril Burt; other cases are described in Mahoney (1976) and in Broad and Wade (1982). Still other cases encompass potential conflict of interest, as when an investigator is hired by a drug or cigarette company to investigate the benefits of the company's products. Although clear guidelines are provided for action in these and other related situations, many fewer safeguards are available—perhaps because breaches of ethics in these areas are less likely to produce the shocking moral tragedies of those involving human subjects and perhaps because the relevant behaviors are less accessible to public scrutiny. Whatever the case, science is dependent on each individual investigator's conscience to move him or her in the direction of ethically correct behavior in these instances.

Final Comments

The advancement of science depends on the quality of substantive questions asked by investigators, and by the adequacy of the technical means they employ to answer these questions. This chapter has focused on these technical sides of research, including design, measurement, and analysis, as well as ethics. Readers should not expect to be qualified to meet the challenges represented by these technical aspects of the research armamentarium as a result of studying this chapter. However, they should have increased appreciation for these aspects of research, understand the major issues with which they are associated, and find themselves in a better position to secure the education necessary to acquire the expertise required to become sophisticated consumers and producers of developmental research.

ACKNOWLEDGMENTS

I thank the following individuals for their critical comments on an earlier draft of this chapter: Craig Abbott, Melissa Alderfer, Cacie Cheuvront, Louise Ewing, Steve Palmer, Mike Robbins, Suzanne Tyndall, and Cindy White. Remaining confusion and error can be attributed to my age-induced rigidities.

REFERENCES

Achenbach, T. M. (1978). *Research in developmental psychology: Concepts, strategies, methods.* New York: Free Press.

Achenbach, T. M., & Edelbrock, C. S. (1981). Behavioral problems and competencies reported by parents of normal and disturbed children aged four through sixteen. *Monographs of the Society for Research in Child Development, 46* (Whole No. 188).

Ad Hoc Committee on Ethical Standards in Psychological Research. (1973). *Ethical principles in the conduct of research with human participants.* Washington, DC: American Psychological Association.

Adams, J. (1978). Sequential strategies and the separation of age, cohort, and time-of-measurement contributions to developmental data. *Psychological Bulletin, 85,* 1309–1316.

Ainsworth, M. D. S., Blehar, M. C., Waters, E., & Wall, S. (1978). *Patterns of attachment.* Hillsdale, NJ: Lawrence Erlbaum Associates.

Allison, P. D., & Liker, J. K. (1982). Analyzing sequential categorical data on dyadic interaction: A comment on Gottman. *Psychological Bulletin, 91,* 393–403.

Allport, G. W. (1937). *Personality: A psychological interpretation.* New York: Henry Holt.

Altmann, J. (1974). Observational study of behavior: Sampling methods. *Behaviour, 49,* 227–267.

American Psychological Association. (1982). *Ethical principles in the conduct of research with human participants.* Washington, DC: Author.

American Psychological Association. (1985). *Standards for educational and psychological tests.* Washington, DC: Author.

American Psychological Association. (1987). *Casebook on ethical principles of psychologists.* Washington, DC: Author.

Anastasi, A. (1978). *Psychological testing* (4th ed.). New York: Macmillan.

Anastasi, A. (1988). *Psychological testing* (6th ed.). New York: Macmillan.

Anderson, J. G. (1987). Structural equation models in the social and behavioral sciences: Model building. *Child Development, 58,* 49–64.

Anderson, L. R., & Anger, J. W. (1978). Analysis of variance in small group research. *Personality and Social Psychology Bulletin, 4,* 341–345.

Appelbaum, M. I., & Cramer, E. M. (1974). Some problems in the nonorthogonal analysis of variance. *Psychological Bulletin, 81,* 335–343.

Appelbaum, M. I., & McCall, R. B. (1983). Design and analysis in developmental psychology. In P. H. Mussen (Ed.), *Handbook of child psychology: Vol. I. History, theory, and methods* (4th ed., pp. 415–476). New York: Wiley.

Aronson, E., Ellsworth, P. C., Carlsmith, J. M., & Gonzales, M. H. (1990). *Methods of research in social psychology* (2nd ed.). New York: McGraw-Hill.

Arrington, R. E. (1943). Time-sampling in studies of social behavior: A critical review of techniques and results with research suggestions. *Psychological Bulletin, 40,* 81–124.

Ary, D. (1984). Mathematical explanation of error in duration recording using partial interval, whole interval, and momentary time sampling. *Behavioral Assessment, 6,* 221–228.

Ary, D., & Suen, H. K. (1983). The use of momentary time sampling to assess both frequency and duration of behavior. *Journal of Behavioral Assessment, 5,* 143–150.

Baer, D. M. (1977). Reviewer's comment: Just because it's reliable doesn't mean that you can use it. *Journal of Applied Behavior Analysis, 10,* 117–119.

Baer, D. M. (1986). In application, frequency is not the only estimate of the probability of behavior units. In T. Thompson, & M. Zeiler (Eds.), *Analysis and integration of behavioral units* (pp. 117–136). Hillsdale, NJ: Lawrence Erlbaum Associates.

Bakeman, F., & Gottman, J. M. (1986). *Observing interaction: An introduction to sequential analysis.* Cambridge: Cambridge University Press.

Bandura, A. (1977). Self-efficacy: Toward a unifying theory of behavioral change. *Psychological Review, 84,* 191–215.

Bangert-Drowns, R. L. (1986). Review of developments in meta-analytic method. *Psychological Bulletin, 99,* 388–399.

Barber, T. X. (1976). *Pitfalls in human research: Ten pivotal points.* New York: Pergamon.

Barker, R. G., & Wright, H. F. (1951). *One boy's day: A specimen record of behavior.* New York: Harper & Row.

Barlow, D. H., & Hersen, M. (1984). *Single case experimental designs: Strategies for studying behavior change* (2nd ed.). New York: Pergamon Press.

Barrios, B., & Hartmann, D. P. (1988). Fears and anxieties. In E. J. Mash & L. G. Terdal (Eds.), *Behavioral assessment of childhood disorders* (2nd ed., pp. 196–262). New York: Guilford.

Baumrind, D. (1985). Research using intentional deception: Ethical issues revisited. *American Psychologist, 40,* 165–174.

Beecher, H. K. (1970). *Research and the individual: Human studies.* Boston: Little, Brown.

Bell, R. Q. (1968). A reinterpretation of the direction of effects of socialization. *Psychological Review, 75,* 81–95.

Bentler, P. M. (1980). Multivariate analysis with latent variables: Causal modeling. *Annual Review of Psychology, 31,* 419–456.

Berk, R. A. (1979). Generalizability of behavioral observations: A clarification of interobserver agreement and interobserver reliability. *American Journal of Mental Deficiency, 83,* 460–472.

Biddle, B. J., & Marlin, M. M. (1987). Causality, confirmation, credulity, and structural equation modeling. *Child Development, 58,* 4–17.

Bijou, S. W., & Baer, D. M. (1960). The laboratory-experimental study of child behavior. In P. H. Mussen (Ed.), *Handbook of research methods in child development* (pp. 140–197). New York: Wiley.

Bishop, Y. M. M., & Holland, P. W. (1975). *Discrete multivariate analysis: Theory and practice.* Cambridge, MA: MIT Press.

Boehm, A. E., & Weinberg, R. A. (1977). *The classroom observer: A guide for developing observation skills.* New York: Teachers College Press.

Boice, R. (1983). Observational skills. *Psychological Bulletin, 93,* 3–29.

Braybrooke, D. (1987). *Philosophy of the social sciences.* Englewood Cliffs, NJ: Prentice-Hall.

Broad, W. J., & Wade, N. (1982). *Betrayers of the truth.* New York: Simon & Schuster.

Bronfenbrenner, U. (1977). Toward an experimental ecology of human development. *American Psychologist, 32,* 513–531.

Bronfenbrenner, U. (1979). *The ecology of human development.* Cambridge, MA: Harvard University Press.

Bronson, W. C. (1987). Special section on structural equation modeling: Introduction. Forward. *Child Development, 58,* 1.

Brunswik, E. (1953). *The conceptual framework of psychology.* Chicago: University of Chicago Press.

Cairns, R. B. (Ed.). (1979). *The analysis of social interactions: Methods, issues, and illustrations.* Hillsdale, NJ: Lawrence Erlbaum Associates.

Cairns, R. B. (1983). Sociometry, psychometry, and social structure: A commentary on six recent studies of popular, rejected, and neglected children. *Merrill-Palmer Quarterly, 29,* 429–438.

Campbell, D. T. (1958). Systematic error on the part of human links in communication systems. *Information and Control, 1,* 297–312.

Campbell, D. T., & Fiske, D. W. (1959). Convergent and discriminant validation by the multitrait–multimethod matrix. *Psychological Bulletin, 56,* 81–105.

Campbell, D. T., & Stanley, J. C. (1963). *Experimental and quasi-experimental designs for research.* Chicago: Rand McNally.

Carlsmith, J. M., Ellsworth, P. C., & Aronson, E. (1976). *Methods of research in social psychology.* Reading, MA: Addison-Wesley.

Cattell, R. B. (1944). Psychological measurement: Normative, ipsative, interactive. *Psychological Review, 51,* 292–303.

Cattell, R. B. (1946). *The description and measurement of personality.* New York: World Book.

Cattell, R. B. (1957). *Personality and motivation structure and measurement.* New York: Harcourt, Brace & Jovanovich.

Cohen, J. (1960). A coefficient of agreement for nominal scales. *Educational and Psychological Measurement, 20,* 37–46.

Cohen, J. (1968). Multiple regression as a general data-analytic system. *Psychological Bulletin, 70,* 426–443.

Cohen, J. (1977). *Statistical power analysis for the behavioral sciences* (2nd ed.). New York: Academic Press.

Cohen, J., & Cohen, P. (1975). *Applied multiple/correlation analysis for the behavioral sciences.* Hillsdale, NJ: Lawrence Erlbaum Associates.

Comrey, A. L. (1978). Common methodological problems in factor analytic studies. *Journal of Consulting and Clinical Psychology, 46,* 648–659.

Cone, J. D. (1979). Confounded comparisons in triple response mode assessment. *Behavioral Assessment, 1,* 85–95.

Cone, J. D. (1981). Psychometric consideration. In M. Hersen & A. S. Bellack (Eds.), *Behavioral assessment* (2nd ed., pp. 38–68). New York: Pergamon.

Cone, J. D., & Foster, S. L. (1982). Direct observation in clinical psychology. In J. N. Butcher & P. C. Kendall (Eds.), *Handbook of research methods in clinical psychology* (pp. 311–354). New York: Wiley.

Conover, W. J. (1971). *Practical nonparametric statistics.* New York: Wiley.

Cook, T. D., & Campbell, D. T. (1979). *Quasi-experimentation: Design and analysis issues for field settings.* Chicago: Rand McNally.

Cooke, R. A. (1982). The ethics and regulation of research involving children. In B. B. Wolman (Ed.), *Handbook of developmental psychology* (pp. 149–172). Englewood Cliffs, NJ: Prentice-Hall.

Cooper, H. M. (1989). *Integrating research: A guide for literature reviews.* Newbury Park, CA: Sage.

Cooper, J. (1976). Deception and role playing: On telling the good guys from the bad guys. *American Psychologist, 31,* 605–610.

Costa, P. T., Jr., & McCrae, R. R. (1982). An approach to the contributions of aging, period, and cohort effects. *Psychological Bulletin, 92,* 238–250.

Crocker, L., & Algina, A. (1986). *Introduction to classical & modern test theory.* New York: Holt, Rinehart & Winston.

Cronbach, L. J. (1957). The two disciplines of scientific psychology. *American Psychologist, 12,* 671–684.

Cronbach, L. J. (1970). *Essentials of psychological testing* (3rd. ed.). New York: Harper & Row.

Cronbach, L. J. (1984). *Essentials of psychological testing* (4th ed.). New York: Harper & Row.

Cronbach, L. J., & Furby, L. (1970). How should we measure change—or should we. *Psychological Bulletin, 74,* 68–80. (Also see Errata, ibid., 1970, *74,* 218.)

Cronbach, L. J., Gleser, G. C., Nanda, H., & Rajaratnam, N. (1972). *The dependability of behavioral measurements.* New York: Wiley.

Cronbach, L. J., & Meehl, P. E. (1955). Construct validity in psychological tests. *Psychological Bulletin, 52,* 281–302.

Delucchi, K. L. (1983). The use and misuse of chi-square: Lewis and Burke revisited. *Psychological Bulletin, 94,* 166–176.

Dixon, W. J., Brown, M. B., Engelman, L., Frane, J. W., Hill, M. A., Jennrich, R. I., & Toporek, J. D. (1985). *BMDP statistical software: 1985 printing.* Berkeley, CA: University of California Press.

Dooley, D. (1990). *Social research methods* (2nd ed.). Englewood Cliffs, NJ: Prentice-Hall.

Dwyer, J. H. (1983). *Statistical models for the social and behavioral sciences.* New York: Oxford University Press.

Ekman, P. (1972). Universals and cultural differences in facial expressions of emotions. *Nebraska Symposium on Motivation, 19,* 207–283.

Epstein, S., & Brady, E. J. (1985). The person–situation debate in historical and current perspective. *Psychological Bulletin, 98,* 513–537.

Ferguson, L. R. (1978). The competence and freedom of children to make choices regarding participation in research: A statement. *Journal of Social Issues, 34,* 114–121.

Fienberg, S. E. (1980). *The analysis of cross-classified categorical data* (2nd ed.). Cambridge, MA: MIT Press.

Flavell, J. H., & Wohlwill, J. F. (1969). Formal and functional aspects of cognitive development. In D. Elkin & J. H. Flavell (Eds.), *Studies in cognitive development: Essays in honor of Jean Piaget* (pp. 67–120). New York: Oxford University Press.

Fleiss, J. L. (1973). *Statistical methods for rates and proportions.* New York: Wiley.

Fleiss, J. L. (1975). Measuring agreement between two judges on the presence or absence of a trait. *Biometrics, 31,* 651–659.

Fleiss, J. L. (1981). *Statistical methods for rates and proportions* (2nd ed.). New York: Wiley.

Furby, L. (1973). Interpreting regression toward the mean in developmental research. *Developmental Psychology, 8,* 172–179.

Games, P. A. (1971). Multiple comparisons of means. *American Educational Research Journal, 8,* 531–565.

Gardner, W., & Hartmann, D. P. (1984). On Markov dependence in the analysis of social interaction. *Behavioral Assessment, 6,* 229–236.

Gardner, W., Hartmann, D. P., & Mitchell, C. (1982). The effects of serial dependency on the use of χ^2 for analyzing sequential data. *Behavioral Assessment, 4,* 75–82.

Geisser, S., & Greenhouse, S. W. (1958). An extension of Box's results on the use of the *F* distribution in multivariate analysis. *Annals of Mathematical Statistics, 29,* 885–891.

Gelfand, D. M., & Hartmann, D. P. (1984). *Child behavior analysis and therapy* (2nd ed.). New York: Pergamon.

Gewirtz, J. L. (1969). Mechanisms of social learning: Some roles of stimulation and behavior in early human development. In D. A. Goslin (Ed.), *Handbook of socialization theory and research* (pp. 57–212). Chicago: Rand McNally.

Glass, G. V., McGaw, B., & Smith, M. L. (1981). *Meta-analysis in social research.* Beverly Hills, CA: Sage.

Glass, G. V., Peckham, P. D., & Sanders, J. R. (1972). Consequences of failure to meet assumptions underlying the analysis of variance and covariance. *Review of Education Research, 42,* 237–288.

Goetz, E. M., & Baer, D. M. (1973). Social control of form diversity and the emergence of new forms in children's blockbuilding. *Journal of Applied Behavior Analysis, 6,* 123–128.

Goodenough, F. L. (1949). *Mental testing.* New York: Rinehart.

Goodwin, WA. L., & Driscoll, L. A. (1980). *Handbook for measurement and evaluation in early childhood education.* San Francisco: Jossey-Bass.

Gorsuch, R. L. (1974). *Factor analysis.* Philadelphia: Saunders.

Gorsuch, R. L. (1983). *Factor analysis* (2nd ed.). Hillsdale, NJ: Lawrence Erlbaum Associates.

Gottman, J. M., & Roy, A. (1989). *Sequential analysis: A guide for behavioral research.* New York: Cambridge University Press.

Guilford, J. P. (1954). *Psychometric methods* (2nd ed.). New York: McGraw-Hill.

Guilford, J. P. (1965). *Fundamental statistics in psychology and education.* New York: McGraw-Hill.

Harris, C. W. (Ed.). (1963). *Problems in measuring change.* Madison, WI: University of Wisconsin Press.

Hartmann, D. P. (1977). Considerations in the choice of interobserver reliability estimates. *Journal of Applied Behavior Analysis, 10,* 103–116.

Hartmann, D. P. (1982a). Assessing the dependability of observational data. In D. P. Hartmann (Ed.), *Using observers to study behavior: New directions for methodology of social and behavioral science* (pp. 51–65). San Francisco: Jossey-Bass.

Hartmann, D. P. (Ed.). (1982b). *Using observers to study behavior: New directions for methodology of social and behavioral science.* San Francisco: Jossey-Bass.

Hartmann, D. P. (1984). Assessment strategies. In D. Barlow & M. Hersen (Eds.), *Single case experimental designs: Strategies for studying behavior change* (2nd ed., pp. 107–139). New York: Pergamon Press.

Hartmann, D. P., Roper, B. L., & Bradford, D. C. (1979). Some relationships between behavioral and traditional assessment. *Journal of Behavioral Assessment, 1,* 3–21.

Hartmann, D. P., & Wood, D. D. (1982). Observation methods. In A. S. Bellack, M. Hersen, & A. E. Kazdin (Eds.), *International handbook of behavior modification and therapy* (pp. 109–138). New York: Plenum.

Hartmann, D. P., & Wood, D. D. (1990). Observational methods. In A. S. Bellack, M. Hersen, & A. E. Kazdin (Eds.), *International handbook of behavior modification and therapy* (2nd ed., pp. 107–138). New York: Plenum.

Hawkins, R. P. (1982). Developing a behavior code. In D. P. Hartmann (Ed.), *Using observers to study behavior: New directions for methodology of social and behavioral science* (pp. 21–35). San Francisco: Jossey-Bass.

Haynes, S. N. (1978). *Principles of behavioral assessment.* New York: Gardner.

Hearnshaw, L. S. (1979). *Cyril Burt: Psychologist.* London: Hodder & Stoughton.

Hedges, L. V., & Olkin, I. (1985). *Statistical methods for meta-analysis.* New York: Academic Press.

Heise, D. R. (1975). *Causal analysis.* New York: Wiley.

Hersen, M., & Barlow, D. H. (Eds.). (1984). *Single case experimental designs: Strategies for studying behavior change* (2nd ed.). New York: Pergamon.

Hertzog, H. F., & Nesselroade, J. R. (1987). Beyond autoregressive models: Some implications of the trait–state distinction for the structural modeling of developmental change. *Child Development, 58,* 93–109.

Hicks, L. E. (1970). Some properties of ipsative, normative, and forced-choice normative measures. *Psychological Bulletin, 74,* 167–184.

Hill, M. (1981). Using P1D to identify and list cases containing special or unacceptable values. In W. J. Dixon et al. (Eds.), *BMDP statistical software, 1981 edition* (pp. 704–705). Los Angeles: University of California Press.

Hofstaetter, P. R. (1954). The changing composition of intelligence: A study of the *t*-technique. *Journal of Genetic Psychology, 85,* 159–164.

Hollander, M., & Wolfe, D. A. (1973). *Nonparametric statistical methods.* New York: Wiley.

House, A. E., House, B. J., & Campbell, M. B. (1981). Measures of interobserver agreement: Calculation formulas and distribution effects. *Journal of Behavioral Assessment, 3,* 37–57.

Huck, S. W., & Sandler, H. M. (1979). *Rival hypotheses: Alternative interpretations of data based conclusions.* New York: Harper & Row.

Huitema, B. E. (1980). *The analysis of covariance and alternatives.* New York: Wiley.

Huitema, B. E. (1986). Statistical analysis and single-subject designs. In A. Poling & R. W. Fuqua (Eds.), *Research methods in applied behavior analysis: Issues and advances.* New York: Plenum.

Hunt, J. M. (1961). *Intelligence and experience.* New York: Ronald Press.

Hunter, J. E., Schmidt, F. L., & Jackson, G. B. (1982). *Meta-analysis: Cumulating research findings across studies.* Beverly Hills, CA: Sage.

Hutt, S. J., & Hutt, C. (1970). *Direct observation and measurement of behavior.* Springfield, IL: Charles C. Thomas.

Iwata, B. A., etc. (Eds.). (1989). *Methodological and conceptual issues in applied behavior analysis: 1968-1988.* Lawrence, KS: Journal of Applied Behavior Analysis.

Jackson, G. B. (1980). Methods for integrative reviews. *Review of Educational Research, 50,* 438–460.

James, L. R., Mulaik, S. A., & Brett, J. M. (1982). *Causal analysis: Assumptions, models, and data.* Beverly Hills, CA: Sage.

Johnston, J. M., & Pennypacker, H. S. (1980). *Strategies and tactics of human behavioral research.* Hillsdale, NJ: Lawrence Erlbaum Associates.

Jones, H. E. (1954). The environment and mental development. In L. Carmichaael (Ed.), *Handbook of child psychology* (pp. 631–696). New York: Wiley.

Jones, J. H. (1981). *Bad blood: The Tuskegee syphilis experiment.* New York: Free Press.

Joreskog, K. G., & Sorbom, D. (1983). *Lisrel V and Lisrel VI: Analysis of linear structural relationships by maximum likelihood and least squares methods* (2nd ed.). Upsala, Sweden: University of Upsala, Department of Statistics.

Jung, J. (1971). *The experimenter's dilemma.* New York: Harper & Row.

Kahneman, D. (1965). Control of spurious association and the reliability of the controlled variable. *Psychological Bulletin, 64,* 326–329.

Kazdin, A. E. (1979). Situational specificity: The two-edged sword of behavioral assessment. *Behavioral Assessment, 1,* 57–75.

Kazdin, A. E. (1980). *Research design in clinical psychology.* New York: Harper & Row.

Kazdin, A. E. (1982). *Single-case research designs: Methods for clinical and applied settings.* New York: Oxford University Press.

Kelman, H. C. (1967). Human use of subjects: The problem of deception in social psychological experiments. *Psychological Bulletin, 67,* 1–11.

Kelly, M. B. (1977). A review of the observational data-collection and reliability procedures reported in *The Journal of Applied Behavior Analysis. Journal of Applied Behavior Analysis, 10,* 97–101.

Kenny, D. A. (1979). *Correlation and causality.* New York: Wiley.

Kenny, D. A., & Judd, C. M. (1986). Consequences of violating the independence assumption in analysis of variance. *Psychological Bulletin, 99,* 422–431.

Kerlinger, F. N. (1986). *Foundations of behavioral research* (3rd ed.). New York: Holt, Rinehart & Winston.

Kirk, R. E. (1982). *Experimental design: Procedures for the behavioral sciences* (2nd ed.). Monterey, CA: Brooks-Cole.

Kleinbaum, D. G., & Kupper, L. L. (1978). *Applied regression analysis and other multivariable methods.* North Scituate, MA: Duxbury.

Knoke, D., & Burke, P. J. (1980). *Log-linear models.* Beverly Hills, CA: Sage.

Kraemer, H. C., & Jacklin, C. N. (1979). Statistical analysis of dyadic social behavior. *Psychological Bulletin, 86,* 217–224.

Kuhn, T. S. (1970). *The structure of scientific revolutions* (2nd ed.). Chicago: University of Chicago Press.

Labouvie, E. W. (1982). The concept of change and regression toward the mean. *Psychological Bulletin, 92,* 251–257.

Labouvie, E. W., Bartsch, T. W., Nesselroade, J. R., & Baltes, P. B. (1974). On the internal and external validity of simple longitudinal designs. *Child Development, 45,* 282–290.

Lamb, M. E., Suomi, S. J., & Stephenson, G. R. (Eds.). (1979). *Social interaction analysis: Methodological issues.* Madison, WI: University of Wisconsin Press.

Landis, J. R., & Koch, G. G. (1979). The analysis of categorical data in longitudinal studies of development. In J. R. Nesselroade & P. B. Baltes (Eds.), *Longitudinal research in the study of behavior and development* (pp. 233–261). New York: Academic Press.

Lang, P. J. (1968). Fear reduction and fear behavior: Problems in treating a construct. In J. M. Shlien (Ed.), *Research in psychotherapy* (Vol. 3, pp. 90–103). Washington, DC: American Psychological Association.

Larzelere, R. E., & Mulaik, S. A. (1977). Single-sample tests for many correlations. *Psychological Bulletin, 84,* 557–569.

Lewis, D., & Burke, C. J. (1949). The use and misuse of the chi-square test. *Psychological Bulletin, 46,* 433–489.

Lewis, D., & Burke, C. J. (1950). Further discussion of the use and misuse of the chi-square test. *Psychological Bulletin, 47,* 347–355.

Long, J. S. (1983). *Covariance structure models: An introduction to LISREL.* Beverly Hills, CA: Sage.

Lykken, D. T. (1968). Statistical significance in psychological research. *Psychological Bulletin, 70,* 151–159.

Mahoney, M. J. (1976). *Scientist as subject: The psychological imperative.* Cambridge, MA: Ballinger.

Marascuilo, L. A., & Levin, J. R. (1983). *Multivariate statistics in the social sciences: A researcher's guide.* Monterey, CA: Brooks-Cole.

Martin, J. A. (1987). Structural equation modeling: A guide for the perplexed. *Child Development, 58,* 33–37.

McCall, R. B. (1977). Challenges to a science of developmental psychology. *Child Development, 48,* 333–344.

McDonald, R. P. (1985). *Factor analysis and related methods.* Hillsdale, NJ: Lawrence Erlbaum Associates.

McGuire, W. J. (1969). Suspiciousness of experimenter's intent. In R. Rosenthal & R. L. Rosnow (Eds.), *Artifact in behavioral research* (pp. 13–57). New York: Academic Press.

McNemar, Q. (1969). *Psychological statistics* (4th ed.). New York: Wiley.

Meehl, P. E. (1970). Nuisance variables and the ex post facto design. In M. Radner & S. Winokur (Eds.), *Minnesota studies in the philosophy of science, Vol. 4: Analyses of theories and methods of physics and psychology.* Minneapolis: University of Minnesota Press.

Meehl, P. E. (1978). Theoretical risks and tabular asterisks: Sir Karl, Sir Ronald, and the slow progress of soft psychology. *Journal of Consulting and Clinical Psychology, 46,* 806–834.

Mendinnus, G. R. (1976). *Child study and observation guide.* New York: Wiley.

Messick, S. (1983). Assessment of children. In P. Mussen (Ed.), *Handbook of child psychology: Vol. 1. History, theory, and methods* (4th ed., pp. 477–526). New York: Wiley.

Mickey, M. R. (1981). Detecting outliers with stepwise regression (P2R). In W. J. Dixon et al. (Eds.), *BMDP statistical software, 1981 edition* (p. 698). Los Angeles: University of California Press.

Miller, S. A. (1987). *Developmental research methods.* Englewoods Cliffs, NJ: Prentice-Hall.

Mischel, W., & Peake, P. K. (1983). Analyzing the construction of consistency in personality. In M. M. Page (Ed.), *Personality—Current theory & research: 1982 Nebraska symposium on motivation* (pp. 233–262). Lincoln, NE: University of Nebraska Press.

Mitchell, C., & Hartmann, D. P. (1981). A cautionary note on the use of omega squared to evaluate the effectiveness of behavioral treatments. *Behavioral Assessment, 3,* 93–100.

Mitchell, S. K. (1979). Interobserver agreement, reliability, and generalizability of data collected in observational studies. *Psychological Bulletin, 86,* 376–390.

Morrison, D. E., & Henkel, R. E. (Eds.). (1970). *The significance test controversy.* Chicago: Aldine.

Mulaik, S. A. (1987). Toward a conception of causality applicable to experimentation and causal modeling. *Child Development, 58,* 18–32.

Mussen, P. H. (Ed.). (1960). *Handbook of research methods in child development.* New York: Wiley.

National Commission for the Protection of Human Subjects. (1977). *Report and recommendations: Research involving children.* Washington, DC: U.S. Government Printing Office.

Nay, W. R. (1979). *Multimethod clinical assessment.* New York: Gardner.

Neale, J. M., & Liebert, R. M. (1980). *Science and behavior: An introduction to methods of research* (2nd ed.). Englewood Cliffs, NJ: Prentice-Hall.

Neher, A. (1967). Probability pyramiding, research error and the need for independent replication. *The Psychological Record, 17,* 257–262.

Nunnally, J. C. (1978). *Psychometric theory* (2nd ed.). New York: McGraw-Hill.

O'Grady, K. E. (1982). Measures of explained variance: Cautions and limitations. *Psychological Bulletin, 92,* 766–777.

Overall, J. E., & Woodward, J. A. (1977). Nonrandom assignment and the analysis of covariance. *Psychological Bulletin, 84,* 588–594.

Overton, W. F., & Newman, J. L. (1982). Cognitive development: A competence/utilization approach. In T. Field, A. Houston, H. Quay, L. Troll, & G. Finley (Eds.), *Review of human development* (pp. 217–241). New York: Wiley.

Ozer, D. J. (1985). Correlation and the coefficient of determination. *Psychological Bulletin, 97,* 307–315.

Parsonson, B. S., & Baer, D. M. (1978). The analysis and presentation of graphic data. In T. R. Kratochwill (Ed.), *Single subject research: Strategies for evaluating change* (pp. 101–165). New York: Academic Press.

Parten, M. B. (1932). Social participation among preschool children. *Journal of Abnormal Psychology, 27,* 243–269.

Patterson, G. R. (1982). *A social learning approach, Vol. 3: Coercive family process.* Eugene, OR: Castalia.

Pedhazur, E. J., & Pedhazur-Schmelkin, L. P. (1991). *Measurement, design, and analysis: An integrated approach.* Hillsdale, NJ: Lawrence Erlbaum Associates.

Popper, K. (1959). *The logic of scientific discovery.* New York: Basic.

Popper, K. R. (1962). *Conjectures and refutations.* New York: Basic.

Reid, J. B. (1970). Reliability assessment of observation data: A possible methodological problem. *Child Development, 41,* 1143–1150.

Reid, J. B. (1982). Observer training in naturalistic research. In D. P. Hartmann (Ed.), *Using observers to study behavior: New directions for methodology of social and behavioral science* (pp. 37–50). San Francisco: Jossey-Bass.

Reid, J. B., Baldwin, D. V., Patterson, G. R., & Dishion, T. J. (1988). Observations in the assessment of childhood disorders. In M. Rutter, A. H. Tuma, & I. Lann (Eds.), *Assessment and diagnosis in child psychopathology* (pp. 156–195). New York: Guilford.

Reingold, H. L. (1982). Ethics as an integral part of research in child development. In R. Vasta (Ed.), *Strategies and techniques of child study* (pp. 305–325). New York: Academic Press.

Report from the Committee for Ethical Conduct in Child Development Research. (1990, Winter). SRCD ethical standards for research with children. *SRCD Newsletter,* 5–7.

Rogosa, D. (1988). Myths about longitudinal research. In K. W. Schaie, R. T. Campbell, W. Meredith, & S. C. Rawlings (Eds.), *Methodological issues in aging research* (pp. 171–209). New York: Springer.

Rogosa, D., Brandt, D., & Zimowski, M. (1982). A growth curve approach to the measurement of change. *Psychological Bulletin, 92,* 726–748.

Rosenthal, R. (1979). The "file-drawer problem" and tolerance for null results. *Psychological Bulletin, 85,* 185–193.

Rosenthal, R. (Ed.). (1980a). *Quantitative assessment of research domains.* San Francisco: Jossey-Bass.

Rosenthal, R. (1980b). Summarizing significance levels. In R. Rosenthal (Ed.), *Quantitative assessment of research domains* (pp. 33–46). San Francisco: Jossey-Bass.

Rosenthal, R., & Rosnow, R. L. (Ed.). (1969). *Artifact in behavioral research.* New York: Academic Press.

Rosenthal, R., & Rosnow, R. (1985). *Contrast analysis: Focused comparisons in the analysis of variance.* New York: Cambridge University Press.

Rummel, R. J. (1967). Understanding factor analysis. *The Journal of Conflict Resolution, 11,* 444–480.

Sackett, G. P. (1978a). Measurement in observational research. In G. P. Sackett (Ed.), *Observing behavior. Vol. 2: Data collection and analysis methods* (pp. 25–43). Baltimore: University Park Press.

Sackett, G. P. (Ed.). (1978b). *Observing behavior. Vol. 2: Data collection and analysis methods.* Baltimore: University Park Press.

SAS Institute Inc. (1985). *SAS^R user's guide: Statistics* (5th ed.). Cary, NC: Author.

Schaie, K. W. (1965). A general model for the study of developmental problems. *Psychological Bulletin, 64,* 92–107.

Scheffé, H. (1959). *The analysis of variance.* New York: Wiley.

Siegel, S. (1956). *Nonparametric statistics for the behavioral sciences.* New York: McGraw-Hill.

Simpson, M. J. A. (1979). Problems of recording behavioral data by keyboard. In M. E. Lamb, S. J. Suomi, & G. R. Stephenson (Eds.), *Social interaction analysis: Methodological issues* (pp. 137–156). Madison, WI: University of Wisconsin Press.

Skinner, B. F. (1971). *Beyond freedom and dignity.* New York: Knopf.

Smith, M. B. (1967). Conflicting values affecting behavioral research with children. *American Psychologist, 22,* 377–382.

Smith, M. L., Glass, G. V., & Miller, T. I. (1980). *The benefits of psychotherapy.* Baltimore: Johns Hopkins University Press.

SPSS Inc. (1986). *SPSS^x user's guide* (2nd ed.). Chicago: Author.

Steiger, J. H. (1980). Tests for comparing elements of a correlation matrix. *Psychological Bulletin, 87,* 245–251.

Steiger, J. H., & Ward, L. M. (1987). Factor analysis and the coefficient of determination. *Psychological Bulletin, 101,* 471–474.

Stevens, S. S. (1968). Measurement, statistics, and the schemapiric view. *Science, 161,* 849–856.

Strube, M. J., & Hartmann, D. P. (1983). Meta-analysis: Techniques, applications, and functions. *Journal of Consulting and Clinical Psychology, 1983, 51,* 14–27.

Suen, H. K., & Ary, D. (1986). A post hoc correction procedure for systematic errors in time sampling duration estimates. *Journal of Psychopathology and Behavioral Assessment, 8,* 31–38.

Suen, H. K., & Ary, D. (1989). *Analyzing quantitative behavioral observation data.* Hillsdale, NJ: Lawrence Erlbaum Associates.

Tabachnick, B. G., & Fidell, L. S. (1989). *Using multivariate statistics* (2nd ed.). New York: Harper & Row.

Tanaka, J. S. (1987). "How big is big enough?": Sample size and goodness of fit in structural equation models with latent variables. *Child Development, 58,* 134–146.

Tannenbaum, A. S., & Cooke, R. A. (1977). Research involving children. In National Commission for the Protection of Human Subjects in Biomedical and Behavioral Research (Eds.), *Appendix to report and recommendations on research involving children* (pp. 1–129). Washington, DC: U.S. Government Printing Office.

Taplin, P. S., & Reid, J. B. (1973). Effects of instructional set and experimental influences on observer reliability. *Child Development, 44,* 547–554.

Thompson, B. (1984). *Canonical correlation analysis: Uses and interpretation.* Beverly Hills, CA: Sage.

Tukey, J. W. (1977). *Exploratory data analysis.* Reading, MA: Addison-Wesley.

Tversky, A., & Kahneman, D. (1971). Belief in the law of small numbers. *Psychological Bulletin, 76,* 105–110.

Vasta, R. (Ed.). (1982). *Strategies and techniques of child study.* New York: Academic Press.

Wasik, B. H. (1984). Clinical applications of direct behavioral observation: A look at the past and the future. In B. B. Lahey & A. E. Kazdin (Eds.), *Advances in clinical child psychology* (Vol. 7, pp. 153–193). New York: Plenum.

Webber, S. J., & Cook, T. D. (1972). Subject effects in laboratory research: An examination of subject roles, demand characteristics, and valid inference. *Psychological Bulletin, 77,* 273–295.

Weick, K. E. (1968). Systematic observational methods. In G. Lindzey & E. Aronson (Eds.), *The handbook of social psychology* (Vol. 2, 2nd. ed., pp. 357–451). Menlo Park, CA: Addison-Wesley.

West, S. (Ed.). (1983). Personality and prediction: Nomothetic and idiographic approaches. *Journal of Personality, 51,* (whole No. 3).

Wiggins, J. S. (1973). *Personality and prediction: Principles of personality assessment.* Reading, MA: Addison-Wesley.

Wright, H. F. (1960). Observational child study. In P. Mussen (Ed.), *Handbook of research methods in child development* (pp. 71–139). New York: Wiley.

Wright, H. F. (1967). *Recording and analyzing child behavior.* New York: Harper & Row.

Wohlwill, J. F. (1970). The age variable in psychological research. *Psychological Review, 77,* 49–64.

Yarrow, M. R., & Waxler, C. Z. (1979). Observing interaction: A confrontation with methodology. In R. B. Cairns (Ed.), *The analysis of social interactions: Methods, issues, and illustrations* (pp. 37–65). Hillsdale, NJ: Lawrence Erlbaum Associates.

II   PERCEPTUAL AND COGNITIVE DEVELOPMENT

In the four chapters that comprise this section, the focus shifts from foundations and methods to the substance of developmental research. In Chapter 3, Marc Bornstein reviews the controversies and issues that continue to make the study of perceptual development central to understanding psychological functioning. More than any other aspect of psychology, perceptual development has long been the forum for debates between nativists and empiricists—the fundamental battle that began with philosophical assertion and continues to this day as a driving force behind research on perceptual development, particularly in infancy. Now, however, sophisticated techniques have supplemented, if not supplanted, introspection and speculation, enabling researchers to address questions concerning the origins of perception empirically.

In Chapter 4, Deanna Kuhn moves from the registration and initial evaluation of sensory information to its interpretation. Kuhn summarizes a succession of attempts to explain the transformation of information into understanding, with an emphasis on Piagetian and neo-Piagetian approaches. Such theories place emphasis on developmental changes in the modes of understanding reality, rather than on the gradual accretion of information. From this perspective, individuals are seen as active interpreters of their experiences. From time to time, failures to incorporate new experiences prompt reorganizations in the individual's perspective in order to render new experiences explicable and consistent with his or her interpretive framework.

There are today alternative perspectives on cognitive development, and in Chapter 5 David Klahr discusses information-processing approaches to the development of mental functioning. Students of intelligence have traditionally emphasized psychometric issues of measurement, but in recent years information-processing specialists have attempted to explain cognitive functioning and development and individual stability by creating analogies with computerized systems for information acquisition and interpretation. Klahr overviews the origins, arguments, structure, and goals of this viewpoint on the nature of mental representation.

In Chapter 6, the last of this section, Peter and Jill de Villiers discuss the acquisition of language. Of all the hurdles faced by the young child, cracking the linguistic code is perhaps the most impressive in the eyes of parents and other observers. One cannot help but marvel at the speed with which preverbal infants learn not only how to articulate meaningful statements, but also to understand the speech of others. Because language is purely symbolic, furthermore, its acquisition serves as the basis for advanced and abstract problem solving and cognition. The de Villierses review and integrate modern developmental research on significant issues in production and comprehension of semantics and syntax.

3 Perception Across the Life Span

Marc H. Bornstein
National Institute of Child Health and Human Development

> . . . *all that a mammal does is fundamentally dependent on perception, past or present.*
>
> —D. O. Hebb (1953, p. 44)

INTRODUCTION

Perception begins our experience and interpretation of the world, and so is crucial to understanding the growth of thought as well as most other aspects of development. The input, translation, and encoding of sensory information in perception is requisite to cognition and action. For this reason, philosophers, psychologists, physiologists, and physicists have been strongly motivated to study perception and especially its development. Even very young children recognize that perception is fundamental for understanding (Pillow, 1989): Children as young as 3 years of age attribute knowledge about an object only to individuals who have viewed the object—themselves or someone else or even a puppet—and not to people who have not viewed the object.

Our everyday experiences provoke many challenging questions about perception. How accurate are our perceptions of properties, objects, and events in the world? How is a stable world perceived in the midst of continuous environmental and biological fluctuation? How are perceptual aspects of the world invested with meaning? How and why do perceptual qualities differ across modalities? How do we apprehend individual features of things as well as their synthesized whole?

155

Philosophy has provided major impetus to study perception: Epistemology questions the origins and nature of human knowledge. Extreme views on epistemology were proposed by *empiricists,* who asserted that all perceptual knowledge derives from the senses and grows by way of experience, and by *nativists,* who reasoned that some kinds of knowledge cannot possibly rely on experience and thus that human beings enter the world with a sensory apparatus equipped at the very least to order and organize rudimentary perceptual knowledge. These positions define the classic *nature–nurture* debate. This philosophical speculation focused attention especially on the early phases of perceptual development, as this is the period at which epistemologically meaningful issues related to the origins of knowledge can be most directly addressed. Thus, the study of perceptual development initially captured the philosopher's imagination as it promised to address questions about inborn knowledge versus knowledge that had to be acquired through experience. In this sense, studies of early perception constitute experimental tests of nativist and empiricist theories of knowledge.

Developmental studies of perception provide many and varied kinds of information, as for example, in normative data concerning the quality, limits, and capacities of the senses in early life. The sensory systems are brain matter and do not lie dormant until they are suddenly "switched on" at birth. Rather, they already function before birth. Determining how and approximately when they begin to function normally is important for several reasons. First, knowing about development of the sensory systems enlarges our understanding of the general relation between structure and function. Second, it is theoretically and practically important to learn how early brain development may be influenced by sensory stimulation. Preterm babies, born substantially before their expected due date, are exposed to environmental stimulation from which they would normally be shielded (Parmelee & Sigman, 1983). If the sensory systems are not functional at this stage, preterms would be "protected"; if the sensory systems are functional, however, then preterm babies may be adversely affected by the stimulating environment of the Neonatal Intensive Care Unit (Turkewitz & Kenny, 1985). Third, the infant is recognized today as "perceptually competent"; determining just how the senses function in infancy helps to specify the perceptual world of babies. If a substance tastes sweet to adults, they may suppose that it tastes that way to infants, too, and even that infants will like it; in fact, however, taste receptors for sweetness may not even be present in infants or, if present, may not function or signal the same perception to infants as to adults. Defining normative capacity in early life also permits developmental comparisons of mature versus immature perceptual function, and studies of perception in infancy provide baseline data against which the normal course of maturation and the effects of experience over time can be assessed.

All these reasons underpin the drive to study perceptual development, and given their nature it is not surprising that the study of perceptual development has focused most intensively on infancy. This chapter begins with a section considering philosophical foundations for studying perceptual development. The next section addresses theory and some central issues in perceptual development, namely status, origins, stability, and change in perceiving as well as the possible roles of experience. The main sections of the chapter then overview perceptual development in the context of a taxonomy of methodologies commonly employed to study it. A scheme of psychophysiological and behavioral methods is organized, first, to reflect different contemporary strategies of addressing major questions in perceptual development and, second, to underscore the fact that different perceptual methodologies require different degrees of inference. This discussion includes significant facts and principles of perceptual development in infancy, in childhood, and in old age.

The chapter focuses on perceptual development in early life,[1] reflecting the evolution of theory and the emphases of contemporary research. Two contrasting approaches to the assessment and analysis of perceptual systems compete. One approach is *top-down*. Because objects in the environment offer sight, touch, and sound information, our perception of them is invariably multimodal and coordinated across modalities, and so it is possible to discuss higher order or integrated aspects of perception and afterward move down to consider lower order sensory systems. This chapter follows an alternative traditional *bottom-up* approach in analyzing the components of perceptual structure and function. The bottom-up perspective has two advantages. First, it closely follows established scientific methods of analyzing individual aspects of a problem in approaching the nature of the problem as a whole. Second, it has a certain basis in reality, as sensory systems analyze the information array in the world, decompose it, and create separate cortical representations of separate dimensions of experience; in vision, for example, color, movement, orientation, depth, and more are separately represented (DeYoe & Van Essen, 1988; Living-

---

[1]The story of the ontogeny of perception begs the question of perceptual evolution. Organisms and their environments "co-construct" perceptual structure and function. In the terms of Levins and Lewontin (1985), in and through their interactions with the environment organisms determine which aspects of the ambient physical environment will constitute the effective environment, they alter the world external to them as they interact with it, and they transduce the physical signals that reach them (and so the significance of those signals depends on the structure of the organism), just as environments select sensory–motor capacities in animals and thereby constrain perceptual development and activity.

stone & Hubel, 1988; Sekuler & Blake, 1990). Top-down versus bottom-up views of perception have implications for theory as well as stimulus and design in perceptual research. In accordance with the history of developmental research in the perception field, this chapter also emphasizes the "higher" senses of sight and hearing, but includes some discussion about the "lower" senses — taste, smell, and touch — and how different sensory abilities interrelate and coordinate.

PHILOSOPHICAL UNDERPINNINGS

Among all of the different subject disciplines of developmental psychology, perception has historically been most intimately tied with nature–nurture questions. What do we know before we have any experience in the world? What knowledge depends on such experience? The two main outlooks are empiricist and nativist.

Empiricism

The extreme empiricist position is described in several steps: Empiricists asserted that there is no endowed knowledge at birth, that all knowledge comes through the senses, and that perceptual development proceeds through associative experience. In specific, empiricists argue that stimuli in the world naturally provoke bodily sensations that, occurring close together in space or in time, give rise to more global "ideas" and thereby begin to invest the perceptual world with meaning. It is through association, empiricism explains, that separate raw sensations aggregate into meaningful perceptions. The empiricist's view of the nature of the mind early in life has been fostered by two separate, if related, schools of thought. One derived from John Locke (1632–1704) who is reputed to have described the infant mind as a *tabula rasa:* Mental life begins with nothing, and understanding of the world depends wholly on the accretion of experiences. A slightly different empiricist view can be attributed to William James (1842–1910): The world of the infant is a "blooming, buzzing confusion" out of which the infant's experience helps to organize and create knowledge and order. According to empiricist beliefs, the naive infant does not share the perceptual world of an experienced adult. Empiricism is inherently developmental because, by whatever mechanism is postulated, children are thought to develop from perceptually naive to perceptually mature.

Nativism

The belief that humans begin life "empty headed" has been conceived by many to be both philosophically intolerable and logically indefensible.

Extreme nativists postulated that human beings are not "created" mindless, and that the knowledge that humans possess cannot be achieved by learning alone in so short a span of time as childhood. As a consequence, philosophers like René Descartes (1596–1650) and Immanuel Kant (1724–1804) conceived of human beings as endowed from birth with "ideas" or "categories" of knowledge that serve as the basis of perceptual functions. They postulated innate perceptual ideas, as for size, form, position, or motion, as well as more abstract conceptions, as for space and time. The nativist argument, contra the empiricist, holds that the mind naturally and from the beginning of life imposes order on sensory input, thereby transforming raw sensations into meaningful perceptions. According to the nativist account, the infant and adult share many perceptual capacities, and the two perceive the world in much the same way. For abilities that are congenital, nativism is not a developmental view; for abilities that mature, nativism is developmental in outlook.

Reflecting on these extreme nativist and empiricist opinions and the vigor with which they have been advanced, many authorities have observed that perceptual development stands as a central point of debate between nativists and empiricists on how the mind works. Indeed, in few other areas of psychology has the nativism–empiricism controversy been acknowledged as so meaningful or legitimate as in the study of perceptual development. We can examine one example of why in the question of how depth in space is perceived. This example is suitable for two reasons. First, perceiving depth is substantively crucial to determining the spatial layout of the environment, to recognizing objects, and to guiding motor activity. Second, answers to this question exemplify the typical historical course of perceptual study, originating with hotly contested philosophical debates between nativists and empiricists that spanned the 17th to 19th centuries and culminating with experimentation in infancy as well as contributions of animal physiology in the 20th century.

A Nativist-Empiricist Debate

How do human beings come to perceive depth in visual space?

The Phase of Philosophy. In *La Dioptrique* of 1638, Descartes offered a straightforward answer to this question that assumed the mind's intuitive grasp of basic mathematical relations. Descartes believed that human thought operated as a system driven by natural law; thus, the knowledge of depth is inborn. Descartes introspected: Our two eyes form the base of a triangle whose apex is the object under our gaze. When we look at a faraway object, our eyes are nearly parallel and the base angles of the triangle approach 90°, whereas when our eyes converge on a nearby object, the base angles are acute. The closer the object, the more acute the angles. Descartes (1824) concluded that distance is given by "an act of thinking which, being simple imagination [pure thought], does not entail [explicit] reasoning" (see pp. 59–66). We are all born with two eyes, and our eyes converge more for near than for far points of interest.

A counter explanation for depth perception (that actually built on that of Descartes) was put forward by the empiricist George Berkeley (1685–1753) in his 1709 *Essay Towards a New Theory of Vision*. Berkeley (1901) argued that humans do not deduce distance by "natural geometry."

> Since I am not conscious, that I make any such use of the Perception I have by the Turn of my Eyes. And for me to make those Judgments, and draw those Conclusions from it, without knowing that I do so, seems altogether incomprehensible. (sect. xix)

Rather, Berkeley argued that we come to know depth and distance through our experience. He reflected:

> . . . when an *Object* appears Faint and Small, which at a near Distance I have experienced to make a vigorous and large Appearance; I instantly conclude it to be far off. And this, 'tis evident, is the result of *Experience;* without which, from the Faintness and Littleness, I should not have infer'd any thing concerning the Distance of *Objects*. (sect. iii)

In essence Berkeley claimed that we associate the large apparent size of objects (their "vigorousness") with bringing our two eyes close together and the lesser cost of small arm movements when we reach for close-by objects, and we associate the small apparent size of objects (their "faintness") with the parallel position of the two eyes and the greater cost of large arm movements when we reach for faraway objects. Berkeley hypothesized that infants' consistent reaching in association with converging their eyes and the appearance of objects eventuate in a visual understanding of depth and distance.

Nativists in turn objected to this experiential argument on logic. In the *Critique of Pure Reason* of 1781, Kant asserted that the human mind does not rely on experience for meaning, but innately organizes sensations into meaningful perceptions. Kant (1924) argued that "Space is a necessary *a priori* idea":

> Space is not an empirical conception, which has been derived from external experiences. For I could not be conscious that certain of my sensations are relative to something outside of me, that is, to something in a different part of space from that in which I myself am. . . . No experience of the external relations of sensible things could yield the idea of space, because without the

consciousness of space there would be no external experience whatever. (see pp. 22–29)

Kant buttressed his theoretical argument with two compelling observations: One was that depth perception arises early in life and could not await extensive experience and learning. The second was that individuals with limited experience give evidence that they perceive depth. In support of this position, the philosopher Arthur Schopenhauer (1788–1860) invoked the case of Eva Lauk: Born without limbs and consequently restricted in her experience, Eva reportedly possessed normal intelligence and perceptions of space. (Eva could, of course, move about. Modern studies of profoundly handicapped infants, like thalidomide babies, demonstrate that the inability to locomote does not inhibit the development of normal perception and cognition; see, e.g., Décarie, 1969). Fueled thus, nativists concluded that (at least) some capacity to perceive depth must be inborn or directly given.

Immediately after Kant, however, the debate ensued with a defense of empiricism. In his classic 1866 *Handbook of Physiological Optics,* Hermann von Helmholtz (1821–1894) rebutted nativism with the logical and rational argument that "intuition theory is an unnecessary hypothesis." von Helmholtz (1925, Vol. III) asserted that it is uneconomical to assume mechanisms of innate perception especially when:

> It is not clear how the assumption of these original *"space sensations"* can help the explanation of our visual perceptions, when the adherents of this theory ultimately have to assume in by far the great majority of cases that these sensations must be overruled by the better understanding which we get by experience. In that case it would seem to me much easier and simpler to grasp, that all apperceptions of space were obtained simply by experience. (sect. 26)

After this blow by Helmholtz, the newly emerging school of Gestalt psychologists restored credibility to nativist views primarily through experimentation. At this time in scientific history, experimental investigation began to supplant pure philosophical speculation. In fact, psychology, which was also just beginning as a scientific discipline, was specifically organized to address such issues. Given the enormous and continuing significance attributed to these questions, and the power of an argument supported by the test of trial, it is hardly surprising to learn that an experimental psychology of perceptual development readily captured the imagination, efforts, and energy of subsequent generations of researchers.

Some Science.   Several lines of investigation exemplify how developmental researchers have addressed questions about the origins of depth perception. Each is valuable as no one alone provides definitive information, but taken together all converge to give a good idea how perceiving depth develops. The starting point for one is familiar:

> Human infants at the creeping and toddling stage are notoriously prone to falls from more or less high places. They must be kept from going over the brink by side panels on their cribs, gates on their stairways, and vigilance of adults. As their muscular coordination matures, they begin to avoid such accidents on their own. Common sense might suggest that the child learns to recognize falling-off places by experience—that is, by falling and hurting himself. But is experience really the teacher? Or is the ability to perceive and avoid a brink part of the child's original endowment?

Faced with this lingering conundrum, Gibson and Walk (1960, p. 64) attacked the question of depth perception in human infants with experimental investigation using a "visual cliff" apparatus. Babies were placed on a centerboard to one side of which was an illusory precipitous drop while the other side clearly continued the platform of the centerboard. In fact, however, a glass sheet provided firm support for the babies on *both* sides of the centerboard. Gibson and Walk found that a majority of infants between 6 and 14 months of age crawled across the shallow side of the apparatus from the centerboard when their mothers called them, and only a few crawled across the deep side. On this basis, Gibson and Walk concluded that depth perception must be present in infants as young as 6 months of age. However, the method used in these studies to assess depth perception is obviously limited by the capacity of infants to locomote, which they begin to do only in the second half of the first year of life. By this time the child may have plenty of experience with depth. To meet the challenge of this critique, Bertenthal and Campos (1990) monitored heart rate in precrawling babies suddenly exposed either to the deep or to the shallow drop of a visual cliff. When precrawling 4-month-olds are lowered over a height, their heart rate declines, reflecting interest; when older, mobile infants are suspended in the same way their facial expressions become increasingly negative (changing from frown to whimper to cry); concomitantly, their heart rates first decelerate from resting level and then accelerate during distress. These differences suggest that babies may perceive depth well before they begin to locomote. Of course, experiencing different depths may stimulate babies differently and thereby affect them differently without necessarily yielding a *perception* of depth.

Visual cliff experiments represent one way to explore the infant's capacity to perceive depth. In actuality, three types of stimulus information specify depth: binocular, static, and kinetic cues. First, as Descartes and Kant argued, by virtue of the fact that we human beings are *binocular* (have two eyes) we also have at least two bases for perceiving depth. The convergence angle of the two eyes and stereopsis (the disparity between the two slightly different images of the visual world the eyes receive) each provides some information about depth perception. Binocular convergence yields information only about close-up distances, but it appears to be a reliable source of information about depth by 5 months of age (Yonas & Owsley, 1987); and stereopsis may be a reliable depth cue for infants only 3 ½ months of age — interocular separation increases by 50% during postnatal development (Fox, Aslin, Shea, & Dumais, 1980; Held, Birch, & Gwiazda, 1980). Purely *static* monocular information is a second source of "seeing" depth as well. When normal conditions of viewing are degraded, a single eye looking at a nonmoving single point of observation may still perceive depth. Many such monocular cues to depth are known, as artists as far back as the Renaissance described ways to convince picture viewers of depth in a painting. One monocular static cue to depth is pictorial interposition, as when contours of a closer object overlap those of a more distant object. Seven-month-old babies show sensitivity to interposition cues, but 5-month-old babies do not (Granrud, Yonas, & Pettersen, 1984). Last, the world and the infant perceiving it are constantly in flux, and movement information from this continuously changing structure on the eye provides yet additional cues to depth. There are several such *kinetic* cues. When an object comes directly toward us on a "hit path," we normally move to avoid the impending collision. The infant's ability to plan a path of movement through environmental space implies depth perception. Yonas (1981) studied infant sensitivity to "looming." In the experimental situation he created, babies viewed a translucent screen onto which a silhouette of the three-dimensional object was cast. (This technique avoids babies actually being threatened with a solid object and cuing them with air changes that an actual approaching object might stir up.) Babies as young as 1 month of age consistently blinked to approaching objects. Another kinetic cue occurs when during movement closer surfaces are perceived to occlude more distant ones, that is accretion and deletion of texture: Sitting in the car, we see the telephone pole "move" in front of the more distant tree. Even 5-month-old babies appear to use kinetic information to perceive the layout of surfaces (Granrud, Yonas, Smith et al., 1984).

Other argumentation and data, such as behavioral or physiological sources of information provided by infrahuman animals, contribute to our understanding of the origins of depth perception. Animals offer special circumstances for research because they lend themselves to insights, experimentation, and manipulation often not possible or feasible with human beings. Such appeals have certain value, but they also run up against limits on generalizability. For example, a variety of species have been tested in the visual cliff, some of which, like chicks, move about on their own only a day after hatching. All show avoidance of the cliff, suggesting that depth perception may develop very early and independent of motor experience. Of course, it is still possible that depth perception is innate and congenital in some species but not in others, including human beings. For another example, it is possible with animals, but hardly with humans, to alter the conditions of their early perceptual environment (say, to render the newly developing organism monocular) in order to study perceptual capacity and adaptation. Finally, it is possible in animals, but not in humans, to examine substrates of perception in anatomy and brain function.

The general premise of the developmentalist's appeal to physiological data is that perceptions ought to have identifiable neural substrates; if substrates were found, they could contribute evidence to the nativist–empiricist argument. Continuing the example from depth perception: The fusion of two separate images such as are produced by the two eyes to yield a single image enhances depth perception. Single cells in the visual systems of cats and of monkeys are exquisitely sensitive to such fusion. Although these findings point to physiological bases of perception, developmentalists usually exercise caution about reductionism of this sort. Because such cells exist in other mature species does not mean that they exist in human beings; and because such cells exist at all, of course, does not mean that they signal "depth" in a perceptually meaningful way.

A Conclusion.   Although empirical studies clearly advance the understanding of perceptual function beyond philosophical debate, scientific investigation does not necessarily guarantee resolution. Experiments with human infants have demonstrated that babies are sensitive to binocular and kinetic information about depth by 3 to 5 months of age, but may not be sensitive to static information until about 7 months of age. It is important to point out, however, that infants younger than 3 months of age probably also perceive depth. Clear limits to understanding infant perception are placed on us by our methods of study, a topic to which we return shortly. Moreover, researchers on all sides of the issue are quick to point out that there can be no final triumph for nativism or for empiricism. *No matter how early in life depth perception can be demonstrated, the ability still rests on some experience, and no matter how late its emergence, it can never be proved that only experience has mattered.*

Looking back over this example, it is clear that theoretical, philosophical, and even theological differences of opinion about epistemology have burned like embers in the minds of thinkers for centuries, now and again igniting into flaming controversy over whether human ideas, abilities, and capacities are innately given or the products of worldly experience. Perhaps the sparks of speculation that flew in bygone days generated more heat than light. In modern times, science has added experimental, and especially behavioral evidence, to observations from animals and from physiology to fuel the ancient fires.

THEORIES AND ISSUES
IN PERCEPTUAL DEVELOPMENT

Theories

Perception's goals are to recover and represent properties of the external world to the organism. Theories of perceptual development need to be viewed from within the context of theories of perception. Some argue that meaningful perceptual structure exists in the environment independently of the way we perceive the world: "The world is real and this reality includes such things as structure. But the organism also interacts with reality to seek and select structure. Rarely, however, does the organism create structure. There is no need. Structure is everywhere to be found and the information processing organism need only look, find, and select" (Garner, 1974, p. 186). The developmental corollary of this view is that perceptual growth consists of the increasing sophistication of the perceiver to "pick up" relevant available information (e.g., E. J. Gibson, 1969, 1982; Gibson & Spelke, 1983; J. J. Gibson, 1979). These direct perception theories maintain that meanings of events in the world are "afforded" or automatically perceived in relations among higher order variables to which the sensory systems have specifically evolved; they are not constructed from individual sensations. Hence the difference between naive and sophisticated perceivers.

However, interpretations of the physical world are based on information in the world as well as the evolutionary and developmental history of the organism and whatever the contemporary neural, sensory, and cognitive constraints of the organism may be. This alternative view suggests that structure and information in the external environment are to a certain extent created through ongoing interactions between the organism and the environment (e.g., Hebb, 1949; Piaget, 1969). These constructivist theories may admit that a few rudimentary perceptual abilities—like the capacity to distinguish figure from ground—are inborn, but beyond these the bulk of perceptual development is based on action and experience. In seeing a form, we develop an internal representation of the form that is related to the movements of our eyes as well as to the activity of our brains. Interactive experiences thus promote perceptual organization and help to construct our understanding of the world, space, time, and so forth.

Status and Origins

Perhaps the first question the developmentalist of perception — or, for that matter, the sensory physiologist, neuroscientist, or cognitivist — wants to pose is what the current status of the perceptual *structure* or *function* of interest is in the organism under scrutiny. This is the proper and logical starting point. For many, the answer to this question is also the end point. Not so for the developmentalist, who will want to pose two additional questions: What are the origins of perceptual structure and function, and how does the development of perceptual structure and function unfold? In essence, nativism and empiricism constitute two major opinions about origins and assigning differential weights to the roles that experience and maturation play in development. Traditionally, theory and research in perceptual development are designed to evaluate when a structure or function emerges, the course of its development (i.e., whether and how it changes with age), and what factors influence that development.

The question of origins reduplicates in almost all spheres of perception. Do babies begin by differentiating parts of perceptual experiences, and later coalesce those parts into wholes? Or, do babies experience perceptual wholes, and later differentiate their parts? When we are by the ocean, we see waves, hear the surf pound, smell salt air, and these sensations go together to evoke an integrated experience. Seeing, hearing, and smelling are different percepts, however, even when they work in concert. In everyday life, there are many stimuli and events that may be specified in many modes, but about which the different modalities provide integrated and consonant information.

An engaging dispute currently occupies students of perceptual development concerning the origins of multimodal sensitivity, a dispute that contests whether sensations are initially integrated or initially differentiated. Integrationists propose that the newborn's senses are actually unified at birth — in that infants detect only invariant relations across modalities — and that perceptual development consists of the progressive differentiation of sources and features of environmental stimulation (Bower, 1977; E. J. Gibson, 1969). Some studies support this integrationist view, at least insofar as they show that newborns and very young infants respond in a similar fashion to, or treat as equivalent, visual and auditory or tactual stimuli. For example, adults match certain sounds and lights at relatively fixed loudness and brightness levels. Infants only 3 weeks old treat as equivalent loud and bright stimuli at just the intensity levels that adults choose in cross-modality matching (Lewkowicz & Turkewitz, 1980). Meltzoff and Borton (1979) were brought to an integrationist conclusion by their finding that infants in the first month of life can visually identify a shape they have only experienced tactually. The fact that infants match cross-modally in these ways certainly supports the integrationist position, but does not supply evidence that infants do not or could not distinguish among sensations—that they actually think that a sound and a light are the same.

An opposing school argues that the ability to coordinate information across the senses is not present at birth, but develops over the first years of life. The work of Rose, Gottfried, and Bridger (see Rose & Ruff, 1987) on the development of cross-modal transfer in infancy supports this view. They studied term and preterm infants on tasks that called for visual recognition of a shape that had been previously seen (intramodal recognition) or previously touched (intermodal recognition). Preterm 6-month-olds could perform neither the intramodal nor intermodal transfers successfully; preterm 12-month-olds and term 6-month-olds could perform the intramodal transfer, but still failed on the intermodal task; and only term 12-month-olds could pass both the intramodal and intermodal transfer tasks.

Development

Perception begins with the reception and transduction of physical information arriving at the sensory surface. Perceptual representations reflect the quality of this sensory transduction and information transmission. What, if anything, develops in perception? Differences in status over time raise the further question: Why has development occurred? It is as much the task of the perceptual developmentalist to explore processes underlying development as it is to unearth and describe status, origins, and development per se. Developmental changes in perception could be attributable to (a) neural, anatomical, or sensory maturation, (b) improvement in attention, (c) alteration in motivation or improved task performance, or (d) experience. Development could entail individuals becoming more or less acute sensory processors, and so their perceptual representations of sensory information could become more or less veridical. For example, developmental change in perceiving categories (see following) is marked by "tuning" (Bornstein, 1979), which refers to the broadening of categories and reciprocal sharpening of boundaries between them. Both speech and color perception in children give evidence of tuning of perceptual categories: Zlatin and Koenigsknecht (1975) found that the boundaries of speech categories sharpened between 2 and 6 years of age, and Raskin, Maital, and Bornstein (1983) found that boundaries of color categories sharpened between 3 and 4 years of age.

How is perception influenced in its development? Despite the fact that they are sometimes conceived as either–or contributors to developmental theories, nature and nurture interact. That is, perceptual development is usually provoked by maturation in the organism as well as by specific effects of perceptual experience. The potential ways in which the forces of nature and nurture could interact to influence the course of development can be conceptualized in a simple and comprehensive manner. Figure 3.1 shows different possible courses of development of a perceptual structure or function before the onset of experience, and the several possible ways experience may influence eventual perceptual outcome afterward. The onset of experience, and not birth, is used intentionally as a benchmark: The middle ear reaches maturity in structure by the sixth month after conception (Hecox, 1975); at about this time, fetuses respond to auditory stimuli behaviorally (Birnholz & Benacerraf, 1983), and it appears that babies still in the womb "overhear" parental conversations (DeCasper & Spence, 1986), even if acoustic transduction characteristics of the uterus, amniotic fluid, and abdominal wall of the mother alter human voice qualities for the fetus. Experience may consist of modification, enrichment, or deprivation.

How does experience (or the lack thereof) interact with maturation to affect the course of perceptual development? First, there is the possibility that a perceptual structure or function is undeveloped at the onset of experience, but can be induced by relevant experience; without such experience, the structure or function is presumed not to emerge. Second, a perceptual structure or function may develop partially before the onset of experience, after which experience could operate in one of three ways:

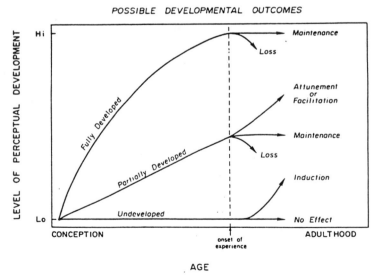

FIG. 3.1. Possible developmental outcomes given different levels of perceptual development before the onset of experience and different experiences afterward. (From Aslin, 1981. Copyright © Academic Press. Reprinted with permission.)

Relevant experience may facilitate further development of a structure or function or may attune that structure or function; experience may serve to maintain the structure or function at the partial level of development it attained before the onset of experience; or, without relevant experience the structure or function may be lost. (Of course, experience per se may not be altogether necessary where the perceptual structure or function would continue to mature as a reflection of the genetic blueprint.) Third, a perceptual structure or function may develop fully before the onset of experience, after which it requires experience only to be maintained; without relevant experience, the structure or function may be lost.

To flesh out this skeletal introduction to the ways nature and nurture interact in perceptual development, we can examine briefly a single perceptual domain in which these several possibilities have been documented. This domain is a narrow but important one in speech perception.

Sounds are essentially different sine-wave frequencies produced simultaneously, and speech is the complex array of different frequencies produced at different intensities over time. Languages abstract particular subsets from the universe of all possible speech sounds (phonetics), and invest some with meaning (phonemics). One dimension along which certain phonemes in many languages are distinguished is their voicing. Differences in voicing are perceived when a speaker produces different frequencies of sound waves at slightly different times. In voicing, a sound like /b/ (pronounced "ba") is produced by vibrating the vocal cords and producing higher frequencies before or at the time the lips are opened and low-frequency energy is released—/b/ is a voiced phoneme. By contrast, for sounds like /p/ (pronounced "pa") the vocal cords do not begin to vibrate higher frequencies until some time after the lips release lower frequencies. Thus, high-frequency components of a sound may precede low-frequency components, components may begin simultaneously, or high-frequency may follow low-frequency. The relative onset times of low and high frequencies cue phonemic perception. Physically, the relative onsets of low- and high-frequency components of a sound may vary continuously; however, adults perceive differences in voicing more or less categorically. That is, although we can distinguish among many differences in relative onset times of low- and high-frequency sounds, we classify some different sounds as similar while discriminating others. English distinguishes voiced and voiceless /b/-/p/. Of course, different people say /b/ and /p/ in different ways; yet adult listeners seldom misidentify these speech sounds, as they employ implicit category definitions to allot a given sound to the /b/ and /p/ categories. Cross-language research has revealed that adults in nearly all cultures hear only one, two, or three categories of voicing: prevoiced, voiced, and voiceless. Categorical perception means that across a nearly infinite spectrum of minute possibilities, only a small number of tokens are functionally distinguished; and they are distinguished by nearly all peoples despite wide language differences.

Many researchers speculate that phenomena so ubiquitous, consistent, circumscribed, and significant in human behavior as perceptual categories of speech sounds might have a biological foundation. To test this assumption, Eimas, Siqueland, Jusczyk, and Vigorito (1971) sought to discover whether preverbal human infants would perceive acoustic changes in voicing categorically; that is, in a manner parallel to adult phonemic perception. Using habituation, these investigators arranged to "ask" infants some simple same–different questions about their auditory perceptions. They found that 1- and 4-month-olds behaved as though they perceived speech sounds in the adultlike categorical manner: Babies distinguish /b/ from /p/, but not examples of two different /b/s. That is, babies categorize variations of sounds as either voiced or voiceless long before they use language or presumably have extensive experience in hearing language. This suggests that categorical perception is innate. Returning to Fig. 3.1, it would seem that categorical perception of phonemes closely fits the topmost developmental function.

However, the experiment does not conclusively rule out roles for experience in development. After all, the subjects were born into monolingual English-speaking families in which the voiced–voiceless distinction they discriminated is common, as in *baby* versus *papa*. It could be that categorical perception is partially developed at the onset of experience, and facilitated or attuned by the experience these babies had prior to the experiment. This is the middle course in Fig. 3.1. It could even be that categorical perception is undeveloped at the onset of experience, and that experience with the language, over several months of prenatal development (when fetuses hear) and 1 or 4 months of postnatal development (when they were tested), quickly induces sophisticated auditory perceptions.

Recall that surveys of the world's languages show that only three categories of voicing are common — prevoiced, voiced, and voiceless — but that not all languages use all categories. Eimas et al. (1971) had only tested an English category in their babies. Are all or only some of these categories universal among infants? That is, do infants from communities in which different patterns of voicing prevail in the adult language make the same categorical distinctions? Data indicating that infants everywhere possess some or all of the same categories, although the adults in their cultures do not, would go far toward classifying possible developmental courses of categorical perception of speech. Several researchers have attempted to address this question. Lasky, Syrdal-Lasky, and Klein (1975), for example, tested infants from Spanish-speaking (Guatemalan) monolingual families. Spanish was chosen because the voice–voiceless distinction is not quite the same as in English. Their 4- and 6-month-olds discriminated the English voice–voiceless sound contrast that is close to, but not the same as, the Spanish one. Likewise, Streeter (1976) found that Kenyan 2-month-olds from families that speak Kikuyu categorized the English voicing contrast that is not present in Kikuyu as well as a Kikuyu prevoiced–voiced contrast that is not present in English. Thus, the English voicing contrast might be inborn, experience with Spanish in growing up attunes a native perceptual discrimination, and experience with Kikuyu induces a new perceptual discrimination in babies only 2 months of age. Other types of perceptual change may be found in the speech perception literature as well (Werker, 1990). Infants from English-speaking households discriminate pairs of Hindi speech contrasts (not used in English) as well as do Hindi-speaking adults; however, English speakers 4 years of age and older do not. Further, 6-month-olds from English-speaking households discriminate pairs of Native Indian (Thompson) speech contrasts (not used in English) as well as do Indian (Thompson-speaking) adults, but this ability weakens over the first year: 6- to 8-month-olds perform the discrimination, 8- to 10-month-olds do so more poorly, and 10- to 12-month-olds are as poor at discriminating as are older children and adults. Spanish-speaking and Kikuyu-speaking adults perceive (although they do not use) the universal English voicing contrast, but they too perceive it only weakly. Sometime between infancy and maturity, therefore, a perceptual discrimination that is present at birth diminishes on account of lack of experience, although it is not wholly lost. Studies such as these underscore the diverse roles of experience in perceptual development.

The literature in categorical perception of speech phonemes has developed so as to illustrate almost fully the scheme depicted in Fig. 3.1. Related studies of infants and adults attest to the generality of these developmental principles of perceptual experience in nonspeech auditory domains as well as in visual perception (e.g., Atkinson & Braddick, 1989; Bornstein, 1979, 1985a, 1987; Lynch, Eilers, & Bornstein, 1992). Certain perceptions seem to be universal and developed at birth; they are maintained by experiences the child has, but may weaken without relevant experience. Other perceptions, present at birth, can be altered by experience. Still other perceptions can be induced during development through immersion in a particular perceptual environment.

As all human beings are believed to be endowed with roughly the same anatomy and physiology, it is reasonable to expect that most perceptual structures or functions are essentially universal and that all human beings begin life on much the same footing. Do varying rearing circumstances always influence perceptual development differently? As we have seen in the extended example from speech perception, some perceptions may be affected, others not. In many ways our perceptual systems appear to be unperturbed by normal (if large) variation in environmental stimulation.

There can be little doubt, however, that experience, or a lack thereof, plays an important role in maintaining, facilitating and attuning, and inducing perceptions in the growth of seeing, hearing, tasting, smelling, and touching. Perception is somewhat malleable to experience, and future research will determine the limits of that plasticity as well as which experiences are most influential. Overall, our physical and perceptual experiences seem to be sufficiently common so as to render perceptions more or less the same.

PERCEPTUAL DEVELOPMENT
IN INFANCY, CHILDHOOD, AND OLD AGE

Prolegomena

Research in perceptual development focuses on the related goals of describing the status of particular perceptual capacities, usually in infancy, and determining the origins and tracing the development (read: stability and continuity) of those capacities over time. Each of these concerns has engendered specific methodologies, which must all be understood clearly in order to grasp the nature, as well as the limits, of the contribution of research to our knowledge of perceptual development. Investigators of early perception have progressed so far as to understand that the basic sensory systems are functioning and providing infants from a very early age with highly sophisticated information. In this way, modern researchers have systematically and forever eradicated the view of the perceptually incompetent infant, and are now moving on to questions concerned with how information arriving at the different senses is processed into integrated and meaningful percepts.

The now well-known, exciting, and sometimes startling results of these kinds of observations of infants do not mean that newborn perceptual capacities are fully developed. Even if rudimentary function is present, qualitative sophistication is often still lacking. In some systems, technical problems limit access to our understanding of early perception; in others, it is clear that development simply has not yet occurred. Some perceptual development remains for the postinfancy period, and much of this development, as discussed later, is bound up with more comprehensive overarching developments in cognition.

In practice, the study of perceptual development is virtually, though not entirely, synonymous with studies of infancy. This is so for several reasons. First, as we have seen, perceptual study as a whole was given initial impetus by the nature–nurture debate. To study perception was to address this controversy, and so to study perception effectively was to do so near the beginning of life. Second, by the time human beings reach toddlerhood their basic perceptions of the world (although certainly not their interpretations) are (thought to be) reasonably mature. Thus, most of the action in perceptual development takes place during infancy. In the realm of vision, for example, infants still only in the first year of life discern patterns, depth, orientation, location, and movement, as well as color. As infants have been demonstrated to possess so advanced perceptual competencies, empirical and theoretical interest has turned to examine younger and younger age periods. Third, with older children, cognitive factors (including language mediation) play a role in perceptual performance, and so distinguishing perceptual processes per se from cognitive ones becomes problematic. The final reason that the study of perceptual development has been largely circumscribed to early life is that perceptual study in adulthood, while perennially popular, normally falls outside the province of *developmental* psychology; it belongs to a different area, namely to cognitive neuroscience, today's psychology of sensation and perception. Research on adults is normally excluded from studies of perceptual development with two important exceptions: One is when certain ontogenetic comparisons are called for, and the other is when studies of aging are undertaken.

Studies of perceptual development in infancy are especially challenging. There are two reasons for this: one phenomenological and the other methodological. We see the world—literally and figuratively—through adult eyes. Infants do not. They see the world through infant eyes. What looks like one thing to us may look quite different to a baby, and it would be a severe mistake to misattribute our perspective to the baby. As a consequence, perceptual research in infancy needs to be especially sensitive to the infant's point of view. To take a simple example, a visual stimulus may impress us as at one level of complexity but may be at quite another for a baby. We might see a 2 × 2 checkerboard as simpler than, say, a 24 × 24 checkerboard. However, when confronted with a 24 × 24 board, an infant may only look at one square or along one border. Consequently, the 2 × 2 and 24 × 24 boards might both be perceptually simple structures for the infant.

The early developmental focus of perceptual study also challenges research investigators methodologically. Perception is private. There is no way for one person to know what another's perceptions of *blue, D-minor, sour, fragrant,* or *hard* are like. Perceptual researchers are forced to rely on inferences from observers' reports or from their behaviors. From a developmental point of view, the study of perception from young adulthood through old age poses less difficulty in these respects because mature individuals can readily be instructed to report about or to behave in ways that communicate validly about their perceptions. In childhood and especially in infancy, however, the communication barrier throws up a fundamental impediment to perceptual study. Moreover, infants are motorically incompetent, subject to state fluctuations, and inherently unreliable. As a consequence, therefore, our knowledge of early perception must be inferred from reports and behaviors of varying, and usually impoverished, fidelity and credibility.

For these several reasons, research in early perception is intimately tied to actual methods of study, and so this section of the chapter is organized around the close connection between our knowledge of perceptual development and our methods for studying it. Critically, different methodologies available to the study of perceptual development vary in the power of *inference* they allow about the observer's perceptions. Some methods yield only weak inferences, whereas others yield stronger inferences. The concept of inference can best be defined with reference to an illustration. If we ascertain that a sound applied at the ear of an observer produces a regular pattern of electrical response in the brain, we can feel certain that some internal connections between the ear (the peripheral sensory system) and the brain (the central nervous system) are present. However, regularity of brain response tells us nothing, unfortunately, about how or even whether the observer actually perceives the sound; hence, inference about perception based on electrophysiological data is weak. (Even if two different stimuli gave rise to two distinctly different patterns of electrical activity in the brain, we still would not know whether the two stimuli were perceived, or whether they were perceived as different.) If, however, we were able to instruct or train the observer to respond behaviorally to a sound, or to respond in one way to one sound and in another way to another sound, our inference would be so strong that, barring artifact, we would possess incontrovertible evidence of perception. Note, however, that such methods allow us to get to the observer's discriminative capacities, but still fall short of allowing us access to the observer's *experience* of perception (Profitt & Bertenthal, 1990).

Two main response systems for the study of perception have been explored, *psychophysiological* and *behavioral,* and several different techniques within each system have been developed. Within behavioral systems, infants' perceptions have been studied using spontaneous (or unconditioned) activities as well as conditioned responses. For purposes of comparison, the methodologies reviewed in the following section are ordered along a hypothetical continuum roughly in terms of the strength of inference about the perception they permit.

Despite important differences among methodologies, virtually all techniques developed to study perception have been engineered to address a surprisingly small number of perceptual questions. One question has to do with whether an observer detects the presence of a stimulus—in the psychophysicist's terms, whether the stimulus passes above an *absolute threshold.* For perceptible stimuli, a second question has to do with whether an observer detects differences between them—whether the stimuli surpass a *difference threshold*. Physically nonidentical stimuli that are still not discriminated give evidence of *categorization*. Finally come the questions of how the stimulus is *perceived* and whether the stimulus is *meaningful*. Some investigators have elected to study naturally occurring, usually complex stimulation, whereas others have elected to study specially designed stimulus variation along isolated dimensions. Clearly, the scientific questions that motivate the research best dictate the nature of the stimulus as well as the methodology elected.

The next section of the chapter summarizes and illustrates some central principles and findings of early perceptual development. As we have indicated, to appreciate them it is important to view the data in different substantive domains of perception as embedded in the methodologies used to obtain them. In the sections after, some principles of perceptual development in childhood and old age are reviewed.

The Foundations of Perceiving and Psychophysiological Techniques

Investigations of perceptual development that have adopted psychophysiological techniques approach their subject of study via assessments of the central and autonomic nervous systems.

Central Nervous System. Research efforts related to perceptual development focused in the central nervous system (CNS) have been pitched at three general levels—neurological anatomy, single-cell and intercellular physiology, and gross cortical electrical activity. Questions asked at the level of anatomical investigation concern the structural ontogeny of the perceptual apparatus, with a view to defining its relation to function. A presumption of this research strategy is that structure (anatomy) is necessary for function (perception), and so understanding function is, in a sense, enriched by the knowledge of underlying structure. (On occasion, perceptual theorists turn this argument on its head and postulate the existence of structures based on observed functions; for example, the ability of newborns to discriminate shapes, orientations, and colors implies that some part or parts of the geniculo-striate pathway of brain function at birth; see Lewis, Maurer, & Brent, 1989; Slater, Morison, & Somers, 1988; Teller & Bornstein, 1986.) Note, however, that structure is necessary but not sufficient for function: Babies have legs but do not walk. Thus, insofar as inference about perception is concerned, evidence based on anatomical structure alone is very weak.

Nevertheless, understanding of anatomy can help to explain function. Like adults, infants orient toward or away from sound sources, thus showing auditory localization (Muir, 1985). But young babies should not be expected to be as good as adults at locating sounds in space on structural grounds: After all, they have smaller heads. The location of a sound in space depends on the fact that a sound coming, say, from the left reaches the left ear earlier than it does the right ear, even if only by a fraction of a second. Because the infant's ears are closer together than are those of the adult, this critical time difference is diminished, and presumably impairs the infant's capacity to localize a sound, especially when the sound does not come from an extreme lateral position (Clifton, Gwiazda, Bauer, Clarkson, & Held, 1988). In view of this handicap, it is especially remarkable how well (and quickly) babies locate sound sources in their environment; by 1 year of age, localization ability in infants is comparable to that in adults (Schneider, Bull, & Trehub, 1988).

The course of anatomical development of the sensory systems has received more than modest attention, leading to the conclusion that human beings are reasonably well prepared for perception once extrauterine life begins. By the midtrimester of prenatal life, the eye and the visual system (Bronson, 1974; Maurer, 1975), the ear and the auditory system (Hecox, 1975), the nose and the olfactory system (Tuchmann-Duplessis, Auroux, & Haegel, 1975), and the tongue and the gustatory system (Bradley & Stearn, 1967; Humphrey, 1978) are on their way to being structurally and functionally mature. In general, two principles of development appear to characterize sensory system development. Within systems, maturation tends to proceed centrally so that, for example, the eye differentiates structurally and reaches functional maturity before the visual cortex (e.g., Abramov et al., 1982; Conel, 1939–1959), and the electroretinogram matures before the cortical event-related potential (Barnet, Lodge, & Armington, 1965; Lodge, Armington, Barnet, Shanks, & Newcomb, 1969). Among systems, different senses tend to enter functional development in sequence (Gottlieb, 1983): vestibular, cutaneous, olfactory, auditory, and visual. Turkewitz and Kenny (1982, 1985) have persuasively argued the biopsychological advantages of this staggered program of development in terms of reduced mutual competition among systems for ambient stimulation, thus allowing for heightened sensory organization and integration.

The second level of psychophysiological investigation has focused narrowly on the development and specificity of individual neurons and interneuronal connectivity in different sensory systems. Neurophysiological recording reveals that individual cells code diverse specific characteristics of the environment. So-called "trigger features" of environmental stimulation to which individual neurons in the visual system, for example, have been found to be sensitive include wavelength of light, orientation of form, direction of object movement, and others (e.g., Livingstone & Hubel, 1988).

After cells are born, they grow, migrate, and associate with one another to form relatively stable interconnected patterns. Migrating cells appear to know their addresses, although it is not understood exactly how (Thoenen & Edgar, 1985). The process of myelination loosely correlates with the development of cellular function, and provides a general index of maturation (Conel, 1939–1959; Purpura, 1975; Yakovlev & Lecours, 1967), although function does not depend on myelination. With myelination, the velocity of intracellular neurotransmission more than triples, from a rate of less than 20 feet per second to more than 60 feet per second. Visual, auditory, and somesthetic cortex myelinate before birth, whereas higher brain centers that integrate information are not completely myelinated until puberty. Perhaps the two most important developments at the intercellular level involve biochemical neurotransmission and the restructuring of organization among neurons. In the first 2 years of life, interneural circuitry proceeds to the point at which there are up to 10,000 connections per cell. Moreover, the chaotic immature pattern of multiple intercellular connections is replaced by an efficient and streamlined system of information transmission (Bergström, 1969). A discrete stimulus that excites the immature system is likely to result in a diffuse tonic or global response. In the more developed state, interconnections are more orderly, and the same discrete stimulus produces a phasic response that is exact in time and parallel in space. Consider how younger and older babies respond to a loud clap. Early in life, such auditory stimulation elicits a gross reaction, a bodily shudder for example. Later, the same clap will lead to a discrete turn of the head. Central nervous system development at the intercellular level is characterized generally by such differentiation and growth of specificity (Purves & Lichtman, 1980).

Although this area of research is exciting and very provocative for the study of perceptual development, several questions render it of limited value, and indicate that findings in the area imported especially to explicate perceptual development need to be viewed with caution. For example, although single neurons show sensitivity to individual properties of environmental stimulation, their actual role (if any) in perception is largely undefined. Further, as virtually all studies of single units have been conducted in infrahuman species (usually in the cat or monkey), the direct relevance or applicability of single-unit studies to human perception is open to question. Finally, a very intriguing question for perceptual development is whether single units are innately sensitive to their trigger features; it could be that sensitivity grows or reflects experience.

The third level of research into CNS contributions to perception addresses perceptual development most directly in intact human beings, and derives from measures of overall electrical activity of the developing brain. The principal electrophysiological technique involved is the cortical evoked potential (CEP). The CEP arises from the complex sequence of electrical currents that are normally produced in the brain and can be derived from the electroencephalograph (EEG). When a stimulus is presented to the eye, for example, it gives rise to a characteristic waveform of activity in particular parts of the brain, and through computer averaging techniques this waveform can be isolated from the EEG as a whole. The CEP is also measurable before birth. Studies of the development of the CEP show that the waveform begins simply, is slower to start in response to a stimulus in infancy than in adulthood, but has a relatively stable amplitude across the life cycle. As is shown in the top panel of Fig. 3.2, the CEP for a visual stimulus can be detected in preterm babies (when it assumes a simple form), and it is already relatively complex at birth. The waveform remains variable up to about 3 years of age, however. As can be seen in the bottom panel of Fig. 3.2, the time between stimulus onset and the appearance of the major positive crest of the CEP shows an orderly decrease with age until it reaches adult values. The amplitude of the CEP (not shown in the figure) appears to follow a more complex course of development: It diminishes with age up to birth, then increases to about 3 years of age, then decreases again. It is important to note that these principles, although broad, are descriptive of normal infants viewing particular visual stimuli (Berg & Berg, 1987); variations among infants or among stimuli compromise these generalizations.

Autonomic Nervous System.   A second set of widely applied psychophysiological approaches to gaining information about perception early in life has developed through monitoring infants' autonomic nervous system (ANS) responses in perceptual tasks. Orienting reflexes, respiration, and heart rate are commonly measured, even with the youngest observers.

Among these several measures, heart rate has proved to be particularly useful in research on early perception because it is extremely sensitive to psychological state (Berntson & Boysen, 1990). It is also an important index of individual differences among infants (Fox & Fitzgerald, 1990; Porges, 1988, 1991). For example, heart rate can be used to infer whether an infant is simply staring blankly at a stimulus (heart rate is stable) or is attending to and (presumably) processing stimulus information (heart rate slows during periods of concentration). Heart rate does not depend on infant motor skills, such as reaching or crawling, and it reflects infant state, and thus can tell researchers whether the infant is about to become drowsy or fussy. One index of heart rate variability that is coming to serve infancy studies well is vagal tone. For example, Porges (1991) and Richards (1987) have focused on changes in heart rate variability as an index of sustained visual attention and reactivity to perceptually meaningful stimulation. Individual differences in baseline measures of vagal tone are associated with other indices of

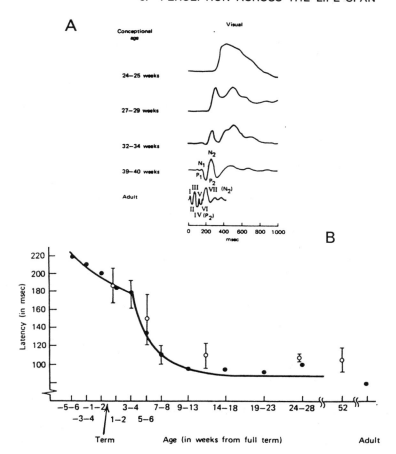

FIG. 3.2. Development of the form and latency of the cortical-evoked potential before and after term. A: Cortical responses evoked by visual stimuli in preterm infants, term newborns, and adults. (Derivations are bipolar: Oz–Pz for the visual response. Surface negatively in plotted upwards.) B: Latency (in msec) of the major positive component of the visual cortical-evoked response as a function of age (in weeks from term). (The solid and open dots represent data from two different experiments. The vertical lines passing through the open dots signify ± 1 SD for a group of 21 subjects.) (From Berg & Berg, 1987. Copyright © John Wiley and Sons. Reprinted with permission.)

sustained visual attention (Linnemeyer & Porges, 1986), and vagal tone increases developmentally between 3 and 13 months of age (Izard et al., 1991). Infants with highly variable heart rates are less visually distractible and also show higher levels of heart-rate deceleration in response to visual stimulation throughout the first year of life (Casey & Richards 1988;

Richards, 1987, 1989). In the same way, heart-rate variability declines when visual attention is sustained (Porges, 1991).

Overview. Our understanding of perception, its bases, and its development has been enhanced considerably by studies of the central and autonomic nervous systems. In immature organisms, psychophysiological indices are often valuable substitutes for behavioral ones as objective and sensitive measures of perception (although many factors other than those under experimental scrutiny can influence psychophysiological responses). The psychophysiological approach has also proved valuable for the light it sheds on atypical development. For example, the evoked potential has been used successfully to diagnose the etiology of deafness in infancy: If the infant does not respond to sound, the evoked potential can at least indicate whether or not brain pathways are intact.

Despite these several virtues, the contributions of psychophysiology to understanding perception proper are limited, and they require very high degrees of inference. As we argued earlier, that a cortex exists or that a stimulus presented to the sensory system creates an identifiable and even consistent pattern of cortical activity, does not guarantee that the stimulus registers in a perceptually meaningful way for the observer, whether infant or adult. Some ANS measures fare somewhat better in this regard, but they still do not provide convincing evidence of conscious perception as the body may respond in the absence of psychological awareness. Moreover, a basic principle of psychophysiology is that many factors influence such responses, and thus there is never an exact one-to-one correspondence between a physiological index and a psychological state. Access to conscious perceptual function is only achieved through behavioral report. Despite many virtues, the contributions of psychophysiology to our understanding of early perception are therefore circumscribed by the large degree of inference involved in interpreting physiological responses, and because many factors other than those of interest to researchers may influence psychophysiological responses. Behavioral techniques therefore constitute the second main class of approaches to perceptual development, and, from the point of view of understanding perception, they represent a profound improvement over psychophysiological ones.

Perception in Infancy and Behavioral Techniques

To assess perceptual life in infancy and early childhood, developmental psychologists have invented or adapted a wide variety of behavioral techniques. Prominent measures depend on natural responses and reactions, preferences, and learning. Again, this discussion is at least implicitly ordered according to the strength of inference different approaches yield about perception. Perception in infancy and early childhood can be illustrated with data from studies that use each of these strategies.

Sight and Corneal Reflection.   In the 1960s, Kessen, Haith, and Sala-patek (1970) argued that it ought to be possible to assess visual function at birth simply by "looking at infant looking." These investigators therefore photographed the reflection of a stimulus in the cornea of the baby's eye tracking eye movements. They assumed that perceiving is in some degree implied by the infant's fixating the stimulus — voluntary visual orienting so as to bring a stimulus into the line of visual regard — and that where a baby looks thus indicates visual selectivity and, hence, visual perception. Until their studies, basic questions such as whether or not newborn babies see were unanswered. In the three decades since their technique was introduced, many experimenters have advanced on the logic of their inquiry and its methodology, but the original findings are still among the most provocative and still demonstrate many basic principles. Eye scan patterns seem to indicate that infants from the first days of life consistently and actively orient to visual information in the environment, and such patterns indicate not just what babies look at, but how looking patterns develop and are distributed over different visual forms. Even in the first hours after birth, infants tend to look at the parts of stimuli that contain information (usually high-contrast features such as along the contours of figures) in lieu of scanning randomly about the background or over the central part of a figure, whether of faces or geometric forms (Hainline & Lemerise, 1982; Haith, 1980, 1991; Maurer, 1975, 1985).

Sight, Touch, Taste, and Smell in Preference and Natural Reaction.   In the 1960s as well, Fantz (1958, 1964) argued that if a baby looked preferentially at one stimulus over another in a paired-choice situation, irrespective of the spatial location of the two stimuli, that preference could be taken to indicate detection or discrimination. Today Fantz's argument is the bedrock of the most popular infant research techniques. Infants visually prefer and discriminate faces over nonfacial configurations of the same elements, some pattern organizations over others, and some colors over others; and they orient and attend preferentially and discriminatively to certain sights, sounds, and smells.

Studies of organized visual scanning indicate at a minimum *that* new-borns and young infants see something when they look at patterns, but do not reveal *how well* they see. In a study of visual acuity, Fantz, Ordy, and Udelf (1962) capitalized on the observation that infants prefer to look at heterogeneous over homogeneous patterns. They posted pairs of patterns for babies to look at, in which one member of the pair was always gray and the other a set of stripes that varied systematically in width. (The two stimuli always matched in overall brightness.) As pattern is consistently preferred, the stripe width that fails to evoke a preference for the baby is the one that marks the limit of the baby's ability to tell stripes from the solid gray. (At some point, stripe width can become so fine as to fade into homogeneity for all of us.) By this measure, acuity was found to improve steadily from infancy until reaching mature levels at about 5 years of age. Since this original study, techniques for measuring infant visual acuity have grown in sophistication, but the results agree tolerably well with these initial findings (Atkinson & Braddick, 1989; Banks & Danemiller, 1987; Brown & Yamamoto, 1986; Gwiazda, Bauer, & Held, 1989; Norcia & Tyler, 1985). Preferential looking and reaching have been used to investigate a wide variety of perceptual abilities in infancy, especially in pattern vision (Yonas & Granrud, 1985) and in color vision (Bornstein, 1981; Teller & Bornstein, 1986). Other sorts of preferences and natural reactions have been used to study perceptual development in other sensory systems as well.

We know from everyday experience that soothing pats can quiet a fussy infant, whereas the DPT shot invariably causes an infant distress. Newborns can clearly feel, but research has not progressed far in elucidating how acute infant tactile perception may be. The mouth is a highly developed tactile area early in life, and very young babies acquire information about objects when they mouth them. Infants as young as 1 month of age are influenced by which of two shapes to look at if one of the two matches a shape the babies just explored orally (Meltzoff & Borton, 1979). Sigmund Freud and Erik Erikson theorized that tactile sensitivity at the mouth was the psychic center of early infancy, and Piaget (e.g., 1954) brought the significance of manipulation to center stage when he proposed that such seemingly simple sensorimotor behaviors constitute the foundations of knowledge. Ruff (1984, 1989, 1990), who filmed 6-, 9-, and 12-month-olds looking and mouthing, found that mouthing decreased over the second half of the first year, whereas fingering and more precise forms of manipulation both increased (accompanying the further development of fine motor coordination). She also found that infants vary their exploratory activities to match the object being explored. When Ruff changed a stimulus on the infant (once the infant had the chance to explore the stimulus in some detail), the infant in turn changed patterns of tactual exploration so as to maximize information acquisition about the new stimulus: For example, infants respond to a change in shape by rotating the object more, and to a change in texture by fingering the object more, and in both cases they throw, push, and drop new objects less often than familiar ones.

Among the clearest demonstrations of natural preferences, and inferences made from preference, comes from Steiner and his colleagues (Steiner, 1977, 1979; Ganchrow & Steiner, 1984; Ganchrow, Steiner, &

Dahar, 1983; see, too, Rosenstein & Oster, 1988). Newborn babies, even those who have tasted nothing but amniotic fluid and smelled nothing but the delivery room, appear to discriminate among sensory qualities that signify different tastes and smells, and they prefer certain tastes and smells to others. Psychophysical evidence is compelling that four basic qualities together exhaust taste experience: sweet, salt, sour, and bitter (Cowart, 1981; Crook, 1987). Tastes are, as is well known, very powerful stimuli in learning: A single experience of nausea associated with a particular taste is sufficient to cause a permanent taste aversion (Garcia & Koelling, 1966). Steiner gave newborn infants sweet, sour, or bitter substances to taste, and he photographed their gustofacial reactions — all prior to the very first time any of the babies ate. Figure 3.3 shows the results. A sweet stimulus evoked an expression of satisfaction, often accompanied by a slight smile and sucking movements. A sour stimulus evoked lip-pursing, often accompanied or followed by wrinkling of the nose and blinking of the eyes. A bitter stimulus evoked an expression of dislike and disgust or rejection, often followed by spitting or even movements preparatory to vomiting. (These taste discriminations are organized at a primitive level of the brain, as they also appear in babies who have no cortex.) Further, babies discriminate within as well as between taste categories: Sweeter sucrose solutions elicit fewer and longer bursts of sucking separated by longer pauses than do less sweet solutions (Crook, 1987).

Steiner also documented neonates' nasofacial reactions to odors placed on cotton swabs held beneath the nose. Butter and banana odors elicit positive expressions; vanilla, either positive or indifferent expressions; a fishy odor, some rejection; and the odor of rotten eggs, unanimous rejection. Cernoch and Porter (1985; Porter, Bologh, & Malkin, 1988) systematically compared breast-fed with bottle-fed infants only 12 to 18 days of age for their olfactory recognition of mother, father, and stranger. Babies were photographed while exposed to pairs of gauze pads worn in the underarm area by an adult on the night previous to the baby test, and the duration of infant preferential orienting was recorded. Only breast-feeding infants oriented preferentially and exclusively to their own mother's scents, thereby giving evidence that they discriminate their mothers. (Infants did not recognize their fathers preferentially, nor did bottle-fed infants recognize their mothers.) This pattern of results suggests that, while they are breast-feeding, infants are exposed to and can learn unique olfactory signatures.

Demonstrable preferences evidence absolute and discriminative thresholds; unfortunately, the preference paradigm suffers from a major shortcoming. The failure to observe a preference is fundamentally ambiguous with respect to the observer's ability to detect or to discriminate stimuli. A

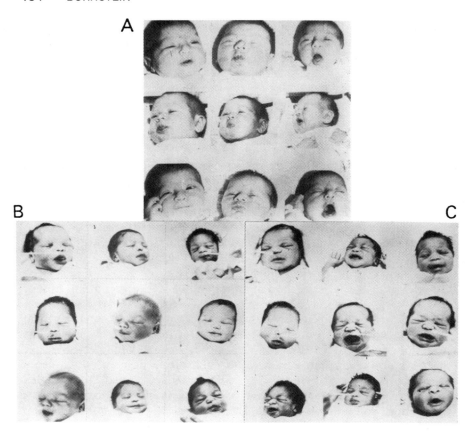

FIG. 3.3. Gustatory and olfactory sensitivity in newborn babies. (A) Infants' gustofacial response to the taste of sweet (left column), sour (middle column), and bitter (right column). Infants' nasofacial response to the smell of vanilla (B) and raw fish (C). (After Steiner, 1977.)

child in the laboratory may orient to mother and stranger equally, but still be able to smell them apart, and in certain circumstances unmistakably prefer one. This is a nontrivial methodological drawback, and for this reason many investigators have turned to paradigms that draw even more actively on definitive behavioral acts of infants and young children to study absolute and difference thresholds in perception. Among the most widely used such paradigms today are conditioned head rotation and habituation-recovery.

Hearing and Conditioned Head Rotation. Roughly speaking, physical development proceeds cephalocaudally (from the head downward) and proximodistally (from the center of the body outward); as a consequence, the eye, head, and neck are the most highly developed regions of the body structurally, and they function earliest in ontogenesis. Many of the procedures discussed thus far call on young children's looking or orienting or sucking for use in the analysis of perceptual function.

Another paradigm that successfully taps into infant perceptual development is conditioned head turning. In this form of conditioning, the reinforcement of a voluntarily controlled motor activity leads it to be repeated. In this situation, the baby sits on the mother's lap, otherwise unencumbered, and a loudspeaker stands to one side. When a sound (tone or speech syllable, for example) is played through the speaker and the baby responds by orienting to it, the baby is rewarded by activation of cartoons or a colorful mechanical toy located just above the speaker (Eilers, Wilson, & Moore, 1977). Using this procedure developmental psychoacousticians have charted the growth of basic sound perception capabilities in infants — the detection of sounds of different frequencies, discrimination among frequencies, and localization of sounds in space — as well as infants' responsiveness to complex sounds that specify speech.

On account of such methodological advances, therefore, our understanding of infant auditory perception has been augmented (Aslin, Pisoni, & Jusczyk, 1983; Colombo, 1986; Eilers & Oller, 1988; Morrongiello, 1990; Trehub & Schneider, 1985). How loud does a sound have to be for the infant to hear it? For adults, the amount of energy defining the auditory absolute threshold varies with the frequency of the sound: Both low and high frequencies (below or above 1,000 Hz) require more energy than middle frequencies. Several investigators have determined how the infant's threshold varies across the frequency spectrum. Virtually the entire frequency spectrum (from 200 to 19,000 Hz) in infants and children of various ages has been mapped and compared with that of adults (see Trehub & Schneider, 1985). Infant thresholds for noise (as opposed to pure tones) vary substantially with frequency; provocatively, they are higher than those of adults for low frequencies (200 Hz), approach adult levels for middle frequencies (1,000 Hz), and are again higher than those of adults at very high frequencies (10,000 Hz). Further, hearing at low and high frequencies nearly continuously improves during the first 20 years of life, with high frequency sensitivity maturing first (Schneider, Trehub, Morrongiello, & Thorpe, 1986; Trehub, Schneider, Morrongiello, & Thorpe, 1988, 1989). Changes in ear structure or nervous system maturation could account for increasing developmental sensitivity, and aging or noise exposure could account for sensitivity loss; see next section (Kryter, 1983).

Infants also clearly discriminate among sounds of different frequencies. Olsho and her coworkers (1982a, 1982b, 1984) first found that 5- to 8-month-old babies discriminate tones differing by only about 2% in frequency in the 1,000 to 3,000 Hz range (where adult frequency discrimination is about 1%), and they confirmed that infant thresholds were twice those of adults at low frequencies (250–1,000 Hz), whereas they were virtually the same as those of adults at high frequencies (3,000–8,000 Hz).

Earlier in this chapter, in illustrating the nature–nurture controversy, infants' perceptions of speech sounds were described. It would appear that by the middle of the first year infants discriminate most acoustic differences that signal phonologically relevant speech contrasts in language.

Seeing and Hearing Through Habituation-Recovery. The conditioned head rotation technique provides reasonably reliable data about infant perception because babies actively, voluntarily, and definitely respond and thereby directly "communicate" their perceptions to the experimenter. An equally demonstrative and reliable technique, and one that has been adopted widely in experimental studies of perception in the first years of life, is habituation-recovery (Bornstein, 1985b). This procedure has the advantage that it can and has used to investigate perception in every modality; for purposes of this exposition, vision serves as the main example.

In habituation, an infant is shown a stimulus, and the infant's visual attention to the stimulus is monitored. Typically, when placed in an otherwise homogeneous environment, an infant will orient and attend to a stimulus on its initial presentation. If the stimulus is available to the infant's view continuously, or if it is presented repeatedly, the infant's attention to the stimulus will wane. This decrement in attention, called habituation, presumably reflects two component processes: the infant's developing a mental representation of the stimulus, and the infant's continuing comparison of whatever stimulus is present with that internal model. If external stimulus and mental representation match and the infant knows the stimulus, there is little reason to continue to look; mismatches, however, appear to maintain or to evoke the infant's attention. A novel (and discriminable) stimulus, introduced after habituation to a familiar one in a test, typically reexcites infant attention to recover initial level of looking. Habituation to familiarity and recovery to novelty have proved to be most versatile and fruitful testing methods in infancy studies, permitting investigators the wherewithal to assess diverse aspects of early perception. In vision, developmental researchers have used habituation-recovery to address classic questions about the ontogeny of perception of form, orientation, location, movement, and color.

Consider first, form perception. The fact that an infant scans an angle of a triangle, and even resolves contour well, does not mean that the infant perceives the triangle (or even an angle of it) as a triangle. For some time, the problem of form perception proved remarkably resistant to solution because almost any discrimination between two forms (e.g., a triangle from a circle) could be explained as a discrimination on some simpler, featural basis (as between an angle and an arc) without whole form perception being implicated (Pipp & Haith, 1984). Using habituation-recovery techniques, Bertenthal, Campos, and Haith (1980) capitalized on the visual perception of so-called subjective contours, Bornstein (1982) evaluated infants' sensitivity to symmetry, and Slater (1989) studied shape constancy to assess whole form perception in infancy. These several lines of research (and others) provide converging evidence that babies still only in the first year of life can perceive form qua whole form.

Objects are specified not only by their form, but also by their coordination in space, that is by their orientation, location, and movement. Physical space extends outward from the central ego equally in all directions, yet perceived orientation is not uniform: For adults, vertical holds a higher psychological status than does horizontal, and horizontal is generally higher in status than oblique (Bornstein, 1982; Essock, 1980). We accept the statement that "5° is almost vertical" as somehow truer than the statement that "vertical is almost 5°." Vertical is the reference point for orientation (Rosch, 1975; Wertheimer, 1938). Studies of detection, discrimination, and preference using habituation-recovery suggest that this hierarchy among orientations exists in early life for artificial geometric forms as well as for more meaningful patterns like the human face, and for static as well as for dynamic forms (Bornstein, Ferdinandsen, & Gross, 1981; Hayes & Watson, 1981; Held, 1989; Leehey, Moskowitz-Cook, Brill, & Held, 1975; Watson, 1966). Young babies also seem able to discriminate orientation well, not only in telling vertical and horizontal apart. They can resolve finer differences involving only obliques (Atkinson, Hood, Wattam-Bell, Anker, & Tricklebank, 1988; Bornstein et al., 1981; Bornstein, Gross, & Wolfe, 1978; Ferdinandsen, & Bornstein, 1981; McKenzie & Day, 1971; Slater et al., 1988).

We know, from studies of the kind reviewed in the introductory section of this chapter, that young babies perceive depth in space. They can also locate stimuli in space reasonably well. Von Hofsten (1980, 1984; von Hofsten & Lindhagen, 1979) submitted babies' reaching for objects to longitudinal study, beginning at 4 months, when babies first make reliable contacts. Recording their following motions, goal-directed behaviors, and types of reaches to objects located at different distances and moving at different velocities, he found that infants as young as 4 ½ months of age will reach and contact an object, even if it is moving, and that their reaching is accomplished in a way that indicates sophisticated predictive targeting of object location.

Toddlers also are able to find their way in large-scale spaces almost as soon as they locomote. In anticipation of an event, infants in the second half of their first year incorrectly look in the same direction as was appropriate before they were moved to a different spot in the environment (Acredolo & Evans, 1980); that is, they give priority to subjective (egocentric) information in recalling spatial location. Toddlers in the second year of life rely on landmarks and possess an objective (allocentric) knowledge of coordinated perspectives of space. It could be that both egocentric and allocentric codes are available to babies at both ages, or that there is a major developmental change over the first year with regard to the child's understanding of spatial location. In this connection, some researchers have speculated that children's own beginning locomotion (crawling or walking) motivates their adopting the more mature, objective understanding of space (Benson & Užgiris, 1985; Bremner & Bryant, 1985). Pertinently, infants who crawl or have experience in a walker, versus those who do not, appear to extract form information efficiently (Campos, Bertenthal, & Benson, 1980) and to see depth (Campos, Svejda, Bertenthal, Benson, & Schmidt, 1981), and infants who crawl to a search location find hidden objects more frequently than infants who are carried to the search location (Benson & Užgiris, 1985).

Newborns are attracted by movement (Nelson & Horowitz, 1987). They prefer to look at moving stimuli even to identical stationary ones (Slater, Morison, Towne, & Rose, 1985), and they fixate dynamic patterns and faces longer than static ones (Kaufmann & Kaufmann, 1980), locking on to moving heads and blinking eyes (Samuels, 1985). Motion perception is cued by several types of information, including retinal image motion, retinal image displacement, and observer motion (Nelson & Horowitz, 1987). Even young infants show good sensitivity to relative motion (Dannemiller & Freedland, 1991), and they make compensatory head movements in response to static (Jouen, 1984) as well as dynamic visual displays (Butterworth, 1983). Habituation-recovery research shows that infant perception of motion is indeed quite acute. Ruff (1985) habituated babies to a series of objects, each one of which moved the same way (say, from side-to-side), and she then tested babies with a novel object moving in the familiar (side-to-side) motion and with a novel object moving in a novel way (say, from side-to-side and rotating). Infants in the first half-year discriminate side-to-side from side-to-side plus rotation, and by 5 months infants discriminate side-to-side from rotation alone, rotation from oscillation around the vertical, and left versus right rotation. Movement of objects is also important for it contributes information about position and shape (Kellman, 1984; Ruff, 1982). Perception of objects occurs naturally in the context of their movement, and from such perceptions observers appear to pick up information about movement as well as about objects (Butterworth, 1989). This information "pick-up" permits us to recognize the same object regardless of its motion *and* to recognize a particular movement regardless of the object that is moving (Gibson, 1979). On this account, object and movement perception are separate but closely intertwined.

Patterns and objects in the environment not only vary in terms of spatial dimensions that help specify, identify, and distinguish them, but these aspects of the environment are also perceived as having brightness and hue, or color. Indeed, color is an intellectually impressive and aesthetically attractive kind of information. Infants see colors, and seem to do so pretty well. Darwin (1877) speculated on his own children's seeing color in the 1870s, but real progress toward understanding the development of color vision only began in the 1970s. Studying color vision is particularly formidable technically (Bornstein, 1981; Teller & Bornstein, 1986): For example, hue and brightness, the two major components of color, covary so that whenever the color of a stimulus changes, both its hue and brightness are changing. In order to compare two stimuli on the basis of hue alone, therefore, it is necessary to match the two in brightness. With adults, this is relatively easy, as there exists a formula that relates the amount of change or difference in hue to the amount of change or difference in brightness; alternatively, adults can match colored stimuli for brightness directly. In babies, however, the precise relation between brightness and color was for a long time elusive, and babies cannot be asked to match brightnesses. The anatomy of the immature eye is also different enough to suggest some perceptual differences between infants and adults (e.g., Abramov et al., 1982). As a consequence, an understanding of early color vision begins with studies of the infant's perception of brightness, and, on the basis of proper brightness controls, proceeds to test discrimination, preference, and organization of hue.

Babies are nearly as acute as adults are when the task is to compare brightness differences between stimuli presented simultaneously, although they are much less acute if comparison stimuli are separated in space or time (Teller & Bornstein, 1986). Experiments comparing chromatic or spectral sensitivity using electrophysiological and behavioral techniques agree that, across a broad range of conditions and across most of the visible spectrum, infant sensitivity is reasonably similar to that of the adult. Thus, in studies in which the topic is hue discrimination per se, it is possible to adopt several different strategies to unconfound hue and brightness: to match colors in brightness by an adult standard in specific spectral regions in which infant and adult are known to correspond, to test discriminations displaced in time, or to vary brightness against hue systematically or unsystematically so that brightness is not an influential factor in discrimination. Peeples and Teller (1975) capitalized on the preference babies display for heterogeneity by showing 2- and 3-month-olds two screens, one white and the second white with either a white or a red bar stimulus projected onto it. They then systematically varied the brightness of the stimulus bar around the adult match to the brightness of the background screen. When the white bar was darker or brighter than the screen, it created the bar pattern that babies favored relative to the homogeneous white screen comparison; when the babies failed to show a preference, the investigators took the bar–screen brightness level to be the baby match point. Thus, just a shade of difference between the white bar and white screen engaged the babies to look: Babies' brightness sensitivity is acute. However, babies preferred the red bar–white screen combination at all brightness contrast levels, demonstrating that even when the red bar (must have) matched the white screen in brightness, babies still distinguished its hue.

"Color-blind" people are called so because they make identifiable color discrimination errors; they also confuse certain hues with white. Normal neonates only hours old and infants 3 months of age typically pass these discriminations (Adams, Maurer, & Davis, 1986; Bornstein, 1981; Hamer, Alexander, & Teller, 1982; Packer, Hartmann, & Teller, 1985; Varner, Cook, Schneck, McDonald & Teller, 1984). The development of color vision right after birth has not been studied so well, and is doubtlessly immature (Clavadetscher, Brown, Ankrum, & Teller, 1988). Yet infants 1 month and certainly 2 months of age and older are acknowledged to possess largely normal color vision based on their discrimination of color stimuli in the absence of brightness cues.

Adults perceive the color spectrum as organized qualitatively into categories of hue: We commonly distinguish blue when the wavelength of light falls around 450 nm, green around 530 nm, yellow around 580 nm, and red around 630 nm (although we recognize blends in between), and we tend to regard lights of wavelengths around 450 nm all as blue, even though we see them as different blues (see Fig. 3.4). It could be that the way that the visual system functions lends vision this organization, or it could be that children learn to organize the color world, perhaps when they acquire language. Bornstein, Kessen, and Weiskopf (1976) studied infants' categorization of color using a habituation-recovery strategy. They found that 4-month-olds who were habituated to a light of one color readily noticed when a light of a different color was shown on a test trial following habituation, even when the two lights were matched in brightness. These investigators then determined whether babies regard two different blues, for example, as more similar qualitatively than a blue and a green. Babies were habituated to 480 nm, a blue near the boundary between blue and green, and on test trials following habituation the babies were shown lights of 450 nm, 480 nm, and 510 nm, all matched for brightness. Thus, one test stimulus was the familiar hue, and the other two differed from the familiar hue by identical physical amounts; however, one new test light was blue (like the familiar stimulus), whereas the other was green. Babies shown the new blue stimulus treated it

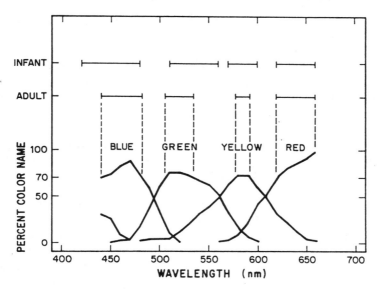

FIG. 3.4. Wavelength groupings (i.e., hue categories) for 4-month-old infants and for adults. Bottom: Percentage of color name use as a function of wavelength for the color names blue, green, yellow, and red (after Boynton & Gordon, 1965). The rising function at very short wavelengths is for red. Top: Summary results for hue categories for infants and adults. The infant summary is derived from Bornstein, Kessen, and Weiskopf (1976). The adult summary reflects a projection from the color-naming data at a psychophysical criterion of 70%. Infant and adult grouping patterns are highly similar, suggesting that by 4 months of age infants' hue categories are similar to those of adults.

and the familiar blue as the same, whereas they treated the green stimulus as different. Preverbal infants categorize the visible spectrum into relatively discrete basic hues of blue, green, yellow, and red, which are similar to those of adults (Fig. 3.4), even though infants, like adults, can discriminate among colors within a given category (Bornstein, 1981).

Perceptual Development in Childhood

Studies of perception in childhood are difficult and unique because considerations of perceptual development after infancy are often bound up in considerations of the development of cognition and language. Nonetheless, toddlers and preschoolers, after infants, are perhaps the next-most-studied ages in perceptual development. First, children in this age range are thought to undergo rapid growth in integrating perception with their conceptions and verbal descriptions of the world (Carey, 1982;

Johnston, 1985; Smith, 1989). Second, although children in this age range often serve as subjects of basic science perceptual study, more often they are engaged as subjects for applied reasons. For example, visual and auditory abilities (beyond verbal capacities) are persistently implicated in reading performance (e.g., Fisher, Bornstein, & Gross, 1985; Johnston, Anderson, Perrett, & Holligan, 1990; Kavale, 1982; Solan & Ficarra, 1990). A related applied topic is the perceptual developmentalist's perennial interest in children's artistic abilities, as in their representing depth, occlusion, and solidity in figures, size scaling, and the like (e.g., Enns & King, 1990; Ingram & Butterworth, 1989; Matsumura, 1989; Silk & Thomas, 1988), and their interest in perceptual substrates of children's musical skills, as in the development of tonal discrimination and rhythmic, melodic, and harmonic skills (e.g., Lynch et al., in press; Vera, 1989). A further practical side to the study of perceptual abilities is children's attention to and awareness of environmental dangers (e.g., Lis, Venuti, & de Zordo, 1990). Finally, of theoretical interest, as well as practical application, are studies of perceptually deprived infants and children and their modes of adaptation (e.g., Landau & Gleitman, 1985). How do blind children develop a sense of directional orientation, distance, and location? How do partially deaf children develop language skills?

As indicated, most applied investigators have been interested in perceptual development in childhood primarily to evaluate its relation to school performance. Thus, the significance of developmental questions of perception is brought home when children begin to learn how to read. For example, research shows that selective attention, visual integration of shape, and speed of visual information processing vary considerably among individuals, but all nevertheless generally increase over childhood, reaching whatever their adult asymptote will be around the onset of adolescence (e.g., Enns & Girgus, 1985, 1986; Nettlebeck & Wilson, 1985). Although sensory ability may mature by school age, therefore, more comprehensive perceptual functioning does not. Younger children are generally more distractible, less efficient, and slower than are older children.

Perceptual development in childhood is thought to involve increasing efficiency, as in the abstraction of invariants or constant stimulus features from the environmental array or the tuning of perceptual categories. Earlier we discussed category sharpening in speech perception and color vision. The Gibsons (E. J. Gibson, 1982; J. J. Gibson, 1979) asserted that perceptual life begins as diffuse, and through experience differentiates, becoming more selective and acute. They demonstrated increasing perceptual differentiation of form in children aged 6 to 11 years. Gibson and Gibson (1955) made successful identification of a form depend on the child's perceiving distinctive features. Adults initially score the highest number correct and reach 100% recognition after a relatively small number of stimulus exposures;

older children score fewer correct at first and also take longer than adults to reach perfect recognition; very young children score the fewest correct initially and never meet a learning criterion. In perception, we learn what to look for and what is distinctive versus what is irrelevant.

Methodological problems plague perceptual studies with children. First, children undergo frequent, even if shortlived, lapses of attention that can lead to errors and guessing (e.g., Wightman et al., 1989). Another problem is that, as mentioned, even the seemingly most straightforward studies of perceptual development appear to involve cognitive functioning. An example is Lee (1989). She undertook a series of studies asking 4- to 14-year-old children simply to copy line drawings of tables. Children's copying errors were found to relate to their knowledge that lines represent a table and not to difficulty in drawing the lines per se. Children made few errors when copying lines without knowledge of what they represented, but they made more errors when copying component parts of line drawings of a table. In other words, even in a simple copying task children's cognitive knowledge can interfere with their perception per se.

Language is the other domain inextricably entangled with perception. Some argue that perception precedes language developmentally and hence forms the basis on which language is built; others argue that perception depends on understanding the world, itself intimately involved with language categories and social interaction. Marks, Hammeal, and Bornstein (1987) investigated the development of cross-modal correspondences between perceptual dimensions of pitch and brightness, loudness and brightness, and pitch and size using purely perceptual as well as purely verbal stimuli in children aged 4 to 13 years. Children as young as 4 years of age easily make cross-modal matches between pitch and brightness and between loudness and brightness, and they do so in the perceptual realm earlier than they do in the verbal realm. Their consistent time lag points to a developmental priority of the perceptual over the language system.

Perceptual development after early childhood is often thought to reach a steady state until effects of aging obtain. In fact, studies of perception in childhood show developmental continuity in some spheres and developmental change in others. Bornstein and his coworkers observed continuity in one aspect of form perception. In studies of symmetry, Bornstein and Stiles-Davis (1984) found among 4- to 6-year-olds that vertical symmetry possesses the highest perceptual advantage (as in discrimination and memory), then horizontal, and then oblique, and Fisher and Bornstein (1982) also found vertical and horizontal to be special vis-à-vis oblique in adults. Likewise, Massaro and Burke (1991) found no developmental differences in rate of perceptual processing, but they did find differences in discrimination of auditory amplitude in 6 ½- to 8-year-olds versus college students.

Perception's importance to children—even older children in school—however underresearched, cannot be underestimated. Consider children's sometimes surprising level of comprehension and interpretation of drawings. Constable, Campbell, and Brown (1988) investigated secondary schoolers' understanding of biological illustrations in their textbooks. They found that the features of objects depicted, as well as the number and type of conventions used, posed significant difficulties even for adolescents.

Perception Among the Aged

Many structures and functions in the body deteriorate and die from a peak in early adulthood, although not all do (Birren & Schaie, 1990; Schneider & Rowe, 1990). Among the senses, however, perceptual deterioration is common and regular. Corso (1987) reviewed age changes in anatomy and physiology of the visual system: Many of its characteristics decline with age, as for example the size of the useful visual field, distance acuity, dynamic and static sensitivity, and depth perception (Fozard, 1990; Greene & Madden, 1987; Sekuler & Ball, 1986). Hearing thresholds change throughout adulthood, and in old age there is considerable loss at different frequencies. Less than 1% of individuals 17 to 20 years of age fail to discriminate odor qualities, whereas nearly 50% of individuals 65 to 88 years of age fail to do so, and, even among the half of elderly who discriminate odors, performance in odor identification is still worse than that of younger people (Schemper, Voss, & Cain, 1981).

Happily, deterioration is not a rule of aging. Taste and smell, which play important parts in enhancing the quality of life as well as in alerting us to danger, form a telling contrast. Taste receptor cells have relatively short life spans and are constantly replaced, whereas in the olfactory system receptive cells are neurons and decline with age. As a consequence, smell is subject to more loss in aging than is taste (Bartoshuk, Rifkin, Marks, & Bars, 1986; Bartoshuk & Weiffenbach, 1990; Weiffenbach, 1984). Schiffman (1977) found that, when blindfolded, elderly subjects could not identify foods as well as younger subjects. This effect could be isolated to olfaction rather than taste changes. Gilbert and Wysocki (1987) reported on the results of 26,200 randomly sampled responses from over 1.5 million readers of *National Geographic* magazine, who responded to a questionnaire insert to the September, 1986, issue that contained six "scratch and sniff" odorant samples. They found that the perceived intensity of odors, as well as the ability to identify odors, declines in the 50s and 60s, but that the ability to smell does not decline until the 70s. The ability to detect the six different odorants also declines at different rates with age.

If older individuals suffer relatively more than younger individuals from stimulus impoverishment, for many context, knowledge, and familiarity of information offset perceptual decrement and degradation of the information signal. In this way, meaning and survival are ensured.

When sensory and perceptual function are observed to decline in old age, the significant question turns on cause: Is organ impairment, nervous system degeneration, or reduction of psychological judgment involved? Some poor performance in old age seems clearly to reflect underlying physiological change. For example, conduction velocity of nerve fibers slows approximately 15% between 20 and 90 years of age, and simple reaction time to lights and sounds concomitantly lengthens 50% over the same period (Bromley, 1974). Similarly, in vision the lens of the eye grows like an onion over the course of the life span, adding layer upon layer. Each layer is pigmented, and so as the lens grows light must traverse more and more absorptive material before it reaches the retina to be effective in vision. As lens pigment selectively absorbs short-wavelength (blue) visible light, perception of blue systematically attenuates in old age (Pokorny, Smith, & Lutze, 1987; Weale, 1986). Attention continues to play an important role in perception in later life; among older adults, it is prerequisite to cognition and central to the continued success of many important kinds of behavior. Detailed studies of divided, switching, sustained, and selective attention have (with certain exceptions, as in more complex tasks) failed to support popular beliefs that older adults undergo a "global reduction in attentional resources" and that, in consequence, perceptual efficiency and cognitive processes are broadly compromised (see Salthouse, Rogan, & Prill, 1984; Somberg & Salthouse, 1982). Some performance declines in old age may reflect a combination of central nervous system or anatomical deterioration with adverse changes in judgment.

The question of cause leads to a caveat. Before ascribing differences in perceptual performance to aging, researchers need to take alternative factors into consideration, such as distractors, illumination levels, and context. In studying sensory and perceptual processes in the aged, investigators must always also show sensitivity to general effects of age per se versus effects of specific neural or sensory disorders.

Whatever their cause, changes in perception with aging are certain to have far-reaching consequences in function. In a comprehensive study of attention, intelligence, and search speed in adults 20 to 70 years of age, Stankov (1988) found that attentional factors explained age differences in fluid intelligence. Likewise, Schaie (1989, 1990) found significant age changes in several markers of perceptual speed in adults between 22 and 91 years of age, and he related these age differences to adult performance in a variety of other tasks, including verbal meaning, inductive reasoning, spatial orientation, number, and word fluency. Demographics reveal that there are today increasing numbers of older drivers as well as older workers.

A telling example of the practical implications of perceptual deterioration in aging is that drivers over age 60 need to be more than 75% closer to highway signs before correctly identifying them at night than drivers under age 25 (Sivak, Olson, & Pastalan, 1981), and perceptual impairment is a definite factor in vehicular accidents in older drivers (Owsley, Ball, Sloane, Roenker, & Bruni, 1991).

A survey of adults 18 to 100 years of age revealed that five dimensions of visual function become increasingly problematic in development: visual processing speed, light sensitivity, dynamic vision, near vision, and visual search (Kosnik, Winslow, Kline, Rasinski, & Sekuler, 1988). Johnson and Choy (1987) observed that 50 years is the average age at which these visual functions begin to change noticeably. But, Fozard (1990) has pointed out, many of these failings are subject to remediation.

This discussion of perceiving in old age, causes of change, and remediation offers an opportunity to reconsider the relative contributions of nature and nurture to perception, this time in a somewhat different light. Auditory sensitivity (as we learned earlier) is measured by assessing absolute thresholds for sounds of different frequencies. In aging, deterioration in auditory sensitivity is common: In essence, elderly people require more energy to hear certain frequencies than do younger people. As the top panel of Fig. 3.5 shows, among Americans hearing loss in aging is more pronounced at higher frequencies. One prominent and straightforward explanation for this finding has been that aging entails the natural and regular deterioration of anatomical and physiological mechanisms that subserve hearing. An alternative hypothesis is that exposure to noise over the course of the life span cumulates and deleteriously affects perception of high frequencies; it is the first cause of the physiological change. How can these nature and nurture explanations be weighed?

Additional data—first, from individuals in other cultures with other noise histories and, second, from individuals in our own society who have distinctive life histories of exposure to noise—help. As the bottom panel in Fig. 3.5 shows, older American women experience less hearing loss than older American men; and Sudanese Africans, who show no sex differences in hearing with age, sustain even less hearing deterioration than Americans of either sex. It could be, however unlikely, that sexes and races differ biologically in the integrity or susceptibility of their auditory apparatuses. However, contrary to the original biological hypothesis, gender and cultural data suggest that physiological aging alone is probably not the key factor in hearing loss. The data on elderly American men exposed to different amounts of noise over the course of their lifetimes lend further support to an experiential interpretation. Findings from this third research source—on the effects of noise history—strongly support the view that hearing loss in old age relates more to amount of exposure to noise and less to natural

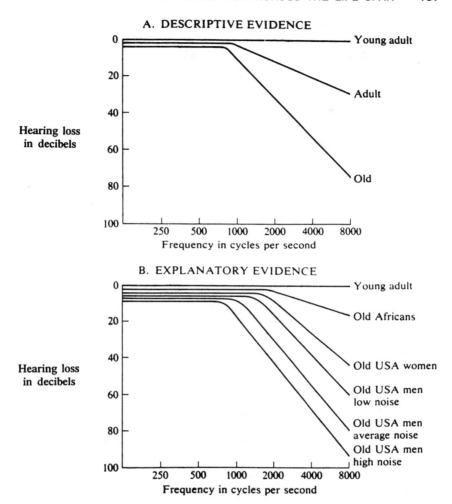

FIG. 3.5. Descriptive and explanatory evidence on auditory sensitivity in adulthood. (From Baltes, Reese, & Nesselroade, 1977. Copyright © Wadsworth Publishing Company. Reprinted with permission.)

physiological deterioration. The three research programs together supplement the original descriptive evidence with explanatory evidence and invest greater credence in a nurture explanation. Of course, the fact that noise history selectively affects high frequencies indicates that nature and nurture doubtlessly interact in development.

The influences of nature and nurture are always difficult to disentangle. Yet assessment of their differential contributions is critical to understanding the life-span ontogeny of perceptual processes. An especial virtue of developmental investigations derives from information they afford regarding prevention: Whereas the descriptive evidence alone strongly implicates physiological deterioration, the alleviation of which might best be achieved through specialized hearing aids for the elderly, the explanatory evidence, which derives from diverse biological and experiential comparisons in development, suggests more productive intervention strategies that would effectively prevent sensory deterioration and hearing loss in the first place.

SUMMARY AND CONCLUSIONS

Perception is among the oldest and most venerable fields in psychology and among the most closely tied to psychology's origins in philosophy. It is also among the most popular in developmental study. Studies of infancy constitute the bulk of research in perceptual development, and studies of perceptual development have, until recently perhaps, constituted the bulk of research in infancy for the many reasons outlined at the beginning of this chapter.

In recent years, many perceptual secrets of infants and young children — formidable and intractable as they once seemed — have been penetrated through a variety of ingenious procedural techniques. Research shows that even the very young of our own species perceive beyond simply sensing. But several traditional and important questions about perceptual development are still open, left unanswered even by the wealth of research amassed in the last decades. Moreover, many startling revelations that spring to mind even from our simplest introspections continue to spark curiosity about perceptual development. How do we develop from sensing patterns received and transduced at the surface of the body to perceiving objects and events in the real world as effortlessly as we do? How does a world that is constantly in flux come to be perceived as stable? As context is so influential in perception, how does selective attention to signal and figure develop in coordination with selective elimination of noise and ground? How do perceived objects come to be invested with meaning?

The development of perceptual capabilities should not be viewed as an isolated event. The study of perceptual development naturally spills over into studies of brain, motor, cognitive, language, and social development. Perception needs to be understood in terms of a systems model, that is, a unifying conception of different components (Thelen, 1989, 1990). Development in this perspective is dynamic in the sense that the organization of the system as a whole changes with maturity and the acquisition of new experiences. As one subsystem emerges, the change brings with it a host of new experiences influencing and being influenced by changes in related processes. Thus, change is not only dynamic but it is thoroughgoing, taking place at many levels in the system at the same time (Bertenthal & Campos, 1990).

The study of perception across the life span has widely acknowledged practical implications, in its relevance to social and emotional development and to medicine and education. Physical and social stimulations are perceptual stimulation, and many aspects of social development depend initially on perceptual capacity. Specific examples abound—from the neonate's perception and consequent ability to imitate facial expressions (Meltzoff & Moore, 1983), to the toddler's acceptance of photographs to mediate separation stress from parents (Passman & Longeway, 1982), to perceptual prerequisites for reading in the child (Gibson & Levin, 1975), to the role of attention and perceptual interpretation in defining normal personality (Achenbach, Chap. 11, this volume).

In the past, traditionalists have expressed reluctance at adding a developmental perspective to the formal study of sensation and perception—developmental psychology often being treated as a different field—and the experimental study of sensation and perception was confined largely to adults and to infrahuman animals. Today, research progress with infant, child, and aged populations demonstrates the broadly informative contribution of the developmental point of view. Knowledge of development is now regarded as essential by all enlightened students of sensation and perception.

Perceptual development could serve as a model of developmental studies, one as good as that of any field described in this text. It encompasses important questions of philosophy and methodology, and it confronts all of the overarching theoretical and empirical issues in developmental study. Some perceptual capacities are given congenitally—even, apparently, in the basic functioning of the sensory systems—whereas other perceptual capacities develop and change from infancy through maturity. This ontogenesis, in turn, has several possible sources: Development may be genetically motivated and transpire largely on the élan of maturational forces, or it may be experiential and in the main respond to the influences of the environment and of particular life events. At one time or another, each of these possibilities has been proposed as determinative. Modern studies have informed a modern view, however. Perceptual development doubtlessly reflects the complex transaction of these two principal forces. Through their systematic efforts at studying perception from infancy through maturity, developmentalists have determined that basic mechanisms in many cases help to impose perceptual structure, but that perceptual development is also determined and guided by a transaction of these structural endowments with experience. Thus, neither nativism nor empiricism holds sway over contemporary views of life-span perceptual development; rather, innate mechanisms and experience together codetermine how we first come—and continue—to perceive the world veridically.

ACKNOWLEDGMENTS

I thank B. Wright for assistance. Passages of this chapter also appear in Bornstein and Lamb (1992).

REFERENCES

Abramov, I., Gordon, J., Hendrickson, A., Hainline, L., Dobson, V., & LaBossiere, R. (1982). The retina of the newborn human infant. *Science, 217,* 265–267.

Acredolo, L. P., & Evans, D. (1980). Developmental changes in the effects of landmarks on infant spatial behavior. *Developmental Psychology, 16,* 312–318.

Adams, R. J., Maurer, D., & Davis, M. (1986). Newborns' discrimination of chromatic from achromatic stimuli. *Journal of Experimental Child Psychology, 41,* 267–281.

Aslin, R. N. (1981). Experiential influences and sensitive periods in perceptual development: A unified model. In R. N. Aslin, J. R. Alberts, & M. R. Peterson (Eds.), *Development of perception: Psychobiological perspectives. Vol. 2: The visual system.* New York: Academic Press.

Aslin, R. N., Pisoni, D. B., & Jusczyk, P. W. (1983). Auditory development and speech perception in infancy. In P. Mussen (Series Ed.) & M. M. Haith & J. J. Campos (Vol. Eds.), *Handbook of child psychology: Vol. 2. Infancy and the biology of development.* New York: Wiley.

Atkinson, J., & Braddick, O. (1989). Development of basic visual functions. In A. Slater & J. G. Bremner (Eds.), *Infant development.* Hillsdale, NJ: Lawrence Erlbaum Associates.

Atkinson, J., Hood, B., Wattam-Bell, J., Anker, S., & Tricklebank, J. (1988). Development of orientation discrimination in infancy. *Perception, 17,* 587–595.

Baltes, P. B., Reese, H. W., & Nesselroade, J. R. (1977). *Life-span developmental psychology: Introduction to research methods.* Monterey, CA: Brooks/Cole.

Banks, M. S., & Dannemiller, J. L. (1987). Infant visual psychophysics. In P. Salapatek & L. Cohen (Eds.), *Handbook of infant perception: From sensation to perception* (Vol. 1). New York: Academic Press.

Barnet, A. B., Lodge, A., & Armington, J. C. (1965). Electroretinogram in newborn human infants. *Science, 148,* 651–654.

Bartoshuk, L. M., Rifkin, B., Marks, L. E., & Bars, P. (1986). Taste and aging. *Journal of Gerontology, 41,* 51–57.

Bartoshuk, L. M., & Weiffenbach, J. M. (1990). Chemical senses and aging. In E. L. Schneider & J. W. Rowe (Eds.), *Handbook of the biology of aging.* San Diego, CA: Academic Press.

Benson, J. B., & Užgiris, I. C. (1985). Effect of self-initiated locomotion on infant search activity. *Developmental Psychology, 21,* 923–931.

Berg, W. K., & Berg, K. M. (1987). Psychophysiological development in infancy: State, startle, and attention. In J. D. Osofsky (Ed.), *Handbook of infant development* (2nd ed.). New York: Wiley.

Bergström, R. M. (1969). Electrical parameters of the brain during ontogeny. In R. J. Robinson (Ed.), *Brain and early behavior: Development in the fetus and infant.* New York: Academic Press.

Berkeley, G. (1901). *An essay towards a new theory of vision*. Oxford: Clarendon Press. (Original work published 1709)

Bertenthal, B. I., & Campos, J. J. (1990). A systems approach to the organizing effects of self-produced locomotion during infancy. In C. Rovee-Collier (Ed.), *Advances in infancy research* (Vol. 6). Norwood, NJ: Albex.

Bertenthal, B., Campos, J., & Haith, M. M. (1980). Development of visual organization: Perception of subjective contours. *Child Development, 51*, 1072–1080.

Berntson, G. G., & Boysen, S. T. (1990). Cardiac indices of cognition in infants, children, and chimpanzees. In C. Rovee-Collier & L. P. Lipsitt (Eds.), *Advances in infancy research* (Vol. 6). Norwood, NJ: Albex.

Birnholz, J. C., & Benacerraf, B. R. (1983). The development of human fetal hearing. *Science, 222*, 516–518.

Birren, J. E., & Schaie, K. W. (Eds.). (1990). *Handbook of the psychology of aging*. San Diego, CA: Academic Press.

Bornstein, M. H. (1979). Perceptual development: Stability and change in feature perception. In M. H. Bornstein & W. Kessen (Eds.), *Psychological development from infancy: Image to intention*. Hillsdale, NJ: Lawrence Erlbaum Associates.

Bornstein, M. H. (1981). Psychological studies of color perception in human infants: Habituation, discrimination and categorization, recognition, and conceptualization. In L. P. Lipsitt (Ed.), *Advances in infancy research* (Vol. 1). Norwood, NJ: Albex.

Bornstein, M. H. (1982). Perceptual anisotropies in infancy: Ontogenetic origins and implications of inequality in spatial vision. In H. W. Reese & L. P. Lipsitt (Eds.), *Advances in child development and behavior* (Vol. 16). New York: Academic Press.

Bornstein, M. H. (1985a). Infant into adult: Unity to diversity in the development of visual categorization. In J. Mehler & R. Fox (Eds.), *Neonate cognition: Beyond the blooming, buzzing confusion*. Hillsdale, NJ: Lawrence Erlbaum Associates.

Bornstein, M. H. (1985b). Habituation of attention as a measure of visual information processing in human infants: Summary, systematization, and synthesis. In G. Gottlieb & N. A. Krasnegor (Eds.), *Measurement of audition and vision in the first year of postnatal life: A methodological overview*. Norwood, NJ: Albex.

Bornstein, M. H. (1987). Perceptual categories in vision and in audition. In S. Harnad (Ed.), *Categorical perception*. New York: Cambridge University Press.

Bornstein, M. H., Ferdinandsen, K., & Gross, C. G. (1981). Perception of symmetry in infancy. *Developmental Psychology, 17*, 82–86.

Bornstein, M. H., Gross, J., & Wolf, J. (1978). Perceptual similarity of mirror images in infancy. *Cognition, 6*, 89–116.

Bornstein, M. H., Kessen, W., & Weiskopf, S. (1976). The categories of hue in infancy. *Science, 191*, 201–202.

Bornstein, M. H., & Lamb, M. E. (1992). *Development in infancy*. New York: McGraw-Hill.

Bornstein, M. H., & Stiles-Davis, J. (1984). Discrimination and memory for symmetry in young children. *Developmental Psychology, 20*, 639–649.

Bower, T. G. R. (1977). *A primer of infant development*. San Francisco: Freeman.

Boynton, R. M., & Gordon, J. (1965). Bezold–Brüke hue shift measured by color-naming technique. *Journal of the Optical Society of America, 55*, 78–86.

Bradley, R. M., & Stearn, I. B. (1967). The development of the human taste bud during the fetal period. *Journal of Anatomy, 101*, 743–752.

Bremner, J. G., & Bryant, P. E. (1985). Active movement and development of spatial abilities in infancy. In H. M. Wellman (Ed.), *Children's searching: The development of search skill and spatial representation*. Hillsdale, NJ: Lawrence Erlbaum Associates.

Bromley, D. B. (1974). *The psychology of human aging*. Harmondsworth, England: Penguin.

Bronson, G. W. (1974). The postnatal growth of visual capacity. *Child Development, 45,* 873–890.

Brown, A. M., & Yamamoto, M. (1986). Visual acuity in newborn and preterm infants measured with grating acuity cards. *American Journal of Ophthalmology, 102,* 245–253.

Butterworth, G. E. (1983). Structure of the mind in human infancy. In L. P. Lipsitt & C. Rovee-Collier (Eds.), *Advances in infancy research* (Vol. 2). Norwood, NJ: Ablex.

Butterworth, G. E. (1989). Events and encounters in infancy. In A. Slater & J. G. Bremner (Eds.), *Infant development.* Sussex, England: Lawrence Erlbaum Associates.

Campos, J. J., Bertenthal, B., & Benson, N. (1980). *Self-produced locomotion and the extraction of form invariance.* Paper presented at the meetings of International Conference on Infant Studies, New Haven, CT.

Campos, J. J., Svejda, M., Bertenthal, B., Benson, N., & Schmidt, D. (1981). *Self-produced locomotion and wariness of heights: New evidence from training studies.* Paper presented at the meeting of the Society for Research in Child Development, Boston, MA.

Carey, S. (1982). Semantic development: The state of the art. In G. Wanner & L. R. Gleitman (Eds.), *Language acquisition: The state of the art.* New York: Cambridge University Press.

Casey, B. J., & Richards, J. E. (1988). Sustained visual attention in young infants measured with an adapted version of the visual preference paradigm. *Child Development, 59,* 114–152.

Cernoch, J. M., & Porter, R. H. (1985). Recognition of maternal axillary odors by infants. *Child Development, 56,* 1593–1598.

Clavadetscher, J. E., Brown, A. M., Ankrum, C., & Teller, D. Y. (1988). Spectral sensitivity and chromatic discriminations in 3- and 7-week-old human infants. *Journal of the Optical Society of America, 5,* 2093–2105.

Clifton, R. K., Gwiazda, J., Bauer, J. A., Clarkson, M. G., & Held, R. M. (1988). Growth in head size during infancy: Implications for sound localization. *Developmental Psychology, 24,* 477–483.

Colombo, J. (1986). Recent studies in early auditory development. In G. J. Whitehurst (Ed.), *Annals of child development* (Vol. 3). Greenwich, CT: JAI Press.

Conel, J. L. (1939–1959). *The postnatal development of the human cerebral cortex* (Vols. 1–6). Cambridge, MA: Harvard University Press.

Constable, H., Campbell, B., & Brown, R. (1988). Sectional drawings from science textbooks: An experimental investigation into pupil's understanding. *British Journal of Educational Psychology, 58,* 89–102.

Corso, J. F. (1987). Sensory-perceptual processes and aging. *Annual Review of Gerontology and Geriatrics, 7,* 29–55.

Cowart, B. J. (1981). Development of taste perception in humans: Sensitivity and preference throughout the life span. *Psychological Bulletin, 90,* 43–73.

Crook, C. K. (1987). Taste and olfaction. In P. Salapatek & L. B. Cohen (Eds.), *Handbook of infant perception* (Vol. 1). New York: Academic Press.

Dannemiller, J. L., & Freedland, R. L. (1991). Detection of relative motion by human infants. *Developmental Psychology, 27,* 67–78.

Darwin, C. (1877). A biographical sketch of an infant. *Mind, 2,* 286–294.

Décarie, T. G. (1969). A study of the mental and emotional development of the thalidomide child. In B. M. Foss (Ed.), *Determinants of infant behavior* (Vol. 4). London: Methuen.

DeCasper, A. J., & Spence, M. J. (1986). Prenatal maternal speech influences newborns' perception of speech sounds. *Infant Behavior and Development, 9,* 133–150.

Descartes, R. (1824). La dioptrique (M. D. Boring, Trans.). In V. Coursin (Ed.), *Oeuvres de Descartes.* Paris: np. (Original work published 1638)

DeYoe, E. A., & Van Essen, D. C. (1988). Concurrent processing streams in monkey visual cortex. *Trends in Neuroscience, 11,* 219–226.

Eilers, R. E., & Oller, D. K. (1988). Precursors to speech: What is innate and what is acquired? *Annals of Child Development, 5,* 1–32.

Eilers, R. E., Wilson, W. R., & Moore, J. M. (1977). Developmental changes in speech discrimination in infants. *Journal of Speech and Hearing Research, 20,* 766–780.

Eimas, P. D., Siqueland, E. R., Jusczyk, P., & Vigorito, J. (1971). Speech perception in infants. *Science, 171,* 303–306.

Enns, J. T., & Girgus, J. S. (1985). Developmental changes in selective and integrative visual attention. *Journal of Experimental Child Psychology, 40,* 319–337.

Enns, J. T., & Girgus, J. S. (1986). A developmental study of shape integration over space and time. *Developmental Psychology, 22,* 491–499.

Enns, J. T., & King, K. A. (1990). Components of line-drawing interpretation: A developmental study. *Developmental Psychology, 26,* 469–479.

Essock, E. A. (1980). The oblique effect of stimulus identification considered with respect to two classes of oblique effects. *Perception, 9,* 37–46.

Fantz, R. L. (1958). Pattern vision in young infants. *Psychological Record, 8,* 43–47.

Fantz, R. L. (1964). Visual experience in infants: Decreased attention to familiar patterns relative to novel ones. *Science, 146,* 668–670.

Fantz, R. L., Ordy, J. M., & Udelf, M. S. (1962). Maturation of pattern vision in infants during the first six months. *Journal of Comparative and Physiological Psychology, 55,* 907–917.

Fisher, C. B., & Bornstein, M. H. (1982). Identification of symmetry: Effects of stimulus orientation and head position. *Perception and Psychophysics, 32,* 443–448.

Fisher, C. B., Bornstein, M. H., & Gross, G. G. (1985). Left–right coding skills related to beginning reading. *Journal of Developmental and Behavioral Pediatrics, 6,* 279–283.

Fisher, C. B., Ferdinandsen, K., & Bornstein, M. H. (1981). The role of symmetry in infant form perception. *Child Development, 52,* 457–462.

Fox, N. A., & Fitzgerald, H. E. (1990). Autonomic function in infancy. *Merrill-Palmer Quarterly, 36,* 27–52.

Fox, R., Aslin, R., Shea, S. L., & Dumais, S. (1980). Stereopsis in human infants. *Science, 207,* 323–324.

Fozard, J. L. (1990). Vision and hearing in aging. In J. E. Birren & K. W. Schaie (Eds.), *Handbook of the psychology of aging.* San Diego, CA: Academic Press.

Ganchrow, J. R., & Steiner, J. E. (1984). Classical conditioning in newborn humans 2–48 hours of age. *Infant Behavior and Development, 7,* 223–235.

Ganchrow, J. R., Steiner, J. E., & Daher, M. (1983). Neonatal facial expressions in response to different qualities and intensities of gustatory stimuli. *Infant Behavior and Development, 6,* 189–200.

Garcia, J., & Koelling, R. (1966). Relation of cue to consequence in avoidance learning. *Psychonomic Science, 4,* 123–124.

Garner, W. R. (1974). *The processing of information and structure.* Hillsdale, NJ: Lawrence Erlbaum Associates.

Gibson, E. J. (1969). *Principles of perceptual learning and development.* New York: Appleton, Century, Crofts.

Gibson, E. J. (1982). The concept of affordances in development: The renascence of functionalism. In W. A. Collins (Ed.), *The Minnesota symposia on child psychology* (Vol. 15). Hillsdale, NJ: Lawrence Erlbaum Associates.

Gibson, E. J., & Levin, H. (1975). *The psychology of reading.* Cambridge, MA: MIT Press.

Gibson, E. J., & Spelke, E. S. (1983). Development of perception. In P. H. Mussen (Ed.), *Handbook of child psychology* (Vol. 3). New York: Wiley.

Gibson, E. J., & Walk, R. D. (1960). The "visual cliff." *Scientific American, 202,* 64–71.

Gibson, J. J. (1979). *The ecological approach to visual perception.* Boston: Houghton Mifflin.

Gibson, J. J., & Gibson, E. J. (1955). Perceptual learning: Differentiation or enrichment? *Psychological Review, 62,* 32–41.

Gilbert, A. N., & Wysocki, C. J. (1987). The smell survey results. *National Geographic, 170,* 324–361.

Gottlieb, G. (1983). The psychobiological approach to developmental issues. In P. H. Mussen (Series Ed.) & M. M. Haith & J. J. Campos (Vol. Eds.), *Handbook of child psychology: Vol. 2. Infants and developmental psychobiology.* New York: Wiley.

Granrud, C. E., Yonas, A., & Pettersen, L. (1984). A comparison of monocular and binocular depth perception in 5- and 7-month-old infants. *Journal of Experimental Child Psychology, 38,* 19–32.

Granrud, C. E., Yonas, A., Smith, I. M., Arterberry, M. E., Glicksman, M. L., & Sorkness, A. C. (1984). Infants' sensitivity to accretion and deletion of texture and information for depth at an edge. *Child Development, 55,* 1630–1636.

Greene, H. A., & Madden, D. J. (1987). Adult age differences in visual acuity, stereopsis, and contrast sensitivity. *American Journal of Optometry and Physiological Optics, 64,* 749–753.

Gwiazda, J., Bauer, J., & Held, R. (1989). Binocular function in human infants: Correlation of stereoptic and fusion-rivalry discriminations. *Journal of Pediatric Ophthalmology and Strabismus, 26,* 128–132.

Hainline, L., & Lemerise, E. (1982). Infants' scanning of geometric forms varying in size. *Journal of Experimental Child Psychology, 32,* 235–256.

Haith, M. M. (1980). *Rules that babies look by.* Hillsdale, NJ: Lawrence Erlbaum Associates.

Haith, M. M. (1991). Gratuity, perception-action integration and future orientation in infant vision. In F. Kessel, M. Bornstein, & A. Sameroff (Eds.), *Contemporary constructions of the child.* Hillsdale, NJ: Lawrence Erlbaum Associates.

Hamer, R. D., Alexander, K., & Teller, D. Y. (1982). Rayleigh discriminations in young human infants. *Vision Research, 20,* 575–584.

Hayes, L. A., & Watson, J. S. (1981). Facial orientation of parents and elicited smiling by infants. *Infant Behavior and Development 4,* 333–340.

Hebb, D. O. (1949). *The organization of behavior: A neuropsychological theory.* New York: Wiley.

Hebb, D. O. (1953). Heredity and environment in mammalian behavior. *British Journal of Animal Behaviour, 1,* 43–47.

Hecox, K. (1975). Electrophysiological correlates of human auditory development. In L. B. Cohen & P. Salapatek (Eds.), *Infant perception: From sensation to cognition* (Vol. 2). New York: Academic Press.

Held, R. (1989). Perception and its neuronal mechanisms. *Cognition, 33,* 139–154.

Held, R., Birch, E., & Gwiazda, J. (1980). Stereoacuity in human infants. *Proceedings of the National Academy of Sciences of the U.S.A., 77,* 5572–5574.

von Helmholtz, H. (1925). *Handbook of physiological optics* (J. P. C. Southall, Trans.). New York: Optical Society of America. (Original work published 1866)

von Hofsten, C. (1980). Predictive reaching for moving objects by human infants. *Journal of Experimental Child Psychology, 30,* 369–382.

von Hofsten, C. (1984). Developmental changes in the organization of prereaching movements. *Developmental Psychology, 20,* 378–388.

von Hofsten, C., & Lindhagen, K. (1979). Observations on the development of reaching for moving objects. *Journal of Experimental Child Psychology, 28,* 158–173.

Humphrey, T. (1978). Function of the nervous system during prenatal life. In U. Stave (Ed.), *Perinatal physiology.* New York: Plenum.

Ingram, N., & Butterworth, G. (1989). The young child's representation of depth in drawing: Process and product. *Journal of Experimental Child Psychology, 47,* 356–369.

Izard, C. E., Porges, S. W., Simons, R. F., Haynes, O. M., Hyde, C., Parisi, M., & Cohen,

B. (1991). Infant cardiac activity: Developmental changes and relations with attachment. *Developmental Psychology, 27,* 432–439.

Johnson, M. A., & Choy, D. (1987). On the definition of age-related norms for visual function testing. *Applied Optics, 26,* 1449–1454.

Johnston, J. R. (1985). Cognitive prerequisites: Cross linguistic study of language acquisition. In D. Slobin (Ed.), *Universals of language acquisition: Theoretical issues* (Vol. 2). Hillsdale, NJ: Lawrence Erlbaum Associates.

Johnston, R. S., Anderson, M., Perrett, D. I., & Holligan, C. (1990). Perceptual dysfunction in poor readers: Evidence for visual and auditory segmentation problems in a sub-group of poor readers. *British Journal of Educational Psychology, 60,* 212–219.

Jouen, F. (1984). Visual-vestibular interactions in infancy. *Infant Behavior and Development, 7,* 135–145.

Kant, I. (1924). *Critique of pure reason* (F. M. Miller, Trans.). New York: Macmillan. (Originally work published 1781)

Kaufmann, R., & Kaufmann, F. (1980). The face schema in 3- and 4-month-old infants: The role of dynamic properties of the face. *Infant Behavior and Development, 3,* 331–339.

Kavale, K. (1982). Meta-analysis of the relationship between visual perceptual skills and reading achievement. *Journal of Learning Disabilities, 15,* 42–51.

Kellman, P. J. (1984). Perception of three-dimensional form by human infants. *Perception and Psychophysics, 36,* 353–358.

Kessen, W., Haith, M. M., & Salapatek, P. H. (1970). Human infancy: A bibliography and guide. In P. Mussen (Ed.), *Carmichael's manual of child psychology.* New York: Wiley.

Kosnik, W., Winslow, L., Kline, D., Rasinski, K., & Sekuler, R. (1988). Visual changes in daily life throughout adulthood. *Journal of Gerontology, 43,* 63–70.

Kryter, K. D. (1983). Presbycusis, sociocusis, and nosocusis. *Journal of the Acoustical Society of America, 73,* 1897–1917.

Landau, B., & Gleitman, L. R. (1985). *Language and experience.* Cambridge, MA: Harvard University Press.

Lasky, R. E., Syrdal-Lasky, A., & Klein, R. E. (1975). VOT discrimination by four- to six-and-a-half-month-old infants from Spanish environments. *Journal of Experimental Child Psychology, 20,* 215–225.

Lee, M. (1989). When is an object not an object? The effect of "meaning" upon the copying of line drawing. *British Journal of Psychology, 80,* 15–37.

Leehey, S. C., Moskowitz-Cook, A., Brill, S., & Held, R. (1975). Orientational anisotropy in infant vision. *Science, 190,* 900–901.

Levins, R., & Lewontin, R. (1985). *The dialectical biologist.* Cambridge, MA: Harvard University Press.

Lewis, T. L., Maurer, D., & Brent, H. P. (1989). Optokinetic nystagmus in normal and visually deprived children: Implications for cortical development. *Canadian Journal of Psychology, 43,* 121–140.

Lewkowicz, D. J., & Turkewitz, G. (1980). Cross-modal equivalence in early infancy: Auditory-visual intensity matching. *Developmental Psychology, 16,* 597–607.

Linnemeyer, S. A., & Porges, S. W. (1986). Recognition memory and cardiac vagal tone in 6-month-old infants. *Infant Behavior and Development, 9,* 43–56.

Lis, A., Venuti, P., & de Zordo, M. R. (1990). Representation and acquisition of the awareness of danger: A theoretical contribution. *Etá Evolutiva, 35,* 103–112.

Livingstone, M. S., & Hubel, D. H. (1988). Segregation of color, movement, and depth: Anatomy, physiology, and perception. *Science, 240,* 740–749.

Lodge, A., Armington, J. C., Barnet, A. B., Shanks, B. L., & Newcomb, C. N. (1969). Newborn electroretinograms and evoked electroencephalographic responses to orange and white light. *Child Development, 40,* 267–273.

Lynch, M. P., Eilers, R. E., & Bornstein, M. H. (1992). Speech, vision, and music perception: Windows on the ontogeny of mind. *Psychology and Music, 20,* 3–14.

Marks, L. E., Hammeal, R. J., & Bornstein, M. H. (1987). Perceiving similarity and comprehending metaphor. *Monographs of the Society for Research in Child Development, 52* (1, No. 215).

Massaro, D. W., & Burke, D. (1991). Perceptual development and auditory backward recognition masking. *Developmental Psychology, 27,* 85–96.

Matsumura, N. (1989). The representation of occlusion and solid figures in young children's drawings. *Japanese Journal of Educational Psychology, 37,* 225–233.

Maurer, D. (1975). Infant visual perception: Methods of study. In L. B. Cohen & P. Salapatek (Eds.), *Infant perception: From sensation to cognition* (Vol. 1). New York: Academic Press.

Maurer, D. (1985). Infants' perception of facedness. In T. Field & N. Fox (Eds.), *Social perception in infancy.* Norwood, NJ: Ablex.

McKenzie, B. E., & Day, R. H. (1971). Orientation discrimination in infants: A comparison of visual fixation and operant training methods. *Journal of Experimental Child Psychology, 2,* 366–375.

Meltzoff, A. N., & Borton, R. W. (1979). Intermodal matching by human neonates, *Nature, 282,* 403–404.

Meltzoff, A. N., & Moore, M. K. (1983). The origins of imitation in infancy: Paradigm, phenomena, and theories. In L. P. Lipsitt (Ed.), *Advances in infancy research* (Vol. 2). Norwood, NJ: Ablex.

Morrongiello, B. A. (1990). The study of individual differences in infants: Auditory processing measures. In J. Colombo & J. Fagen (Eds.), *Individual differences in infancy: Reliability, stability, prediction.* Hillsdale, NJ: Lawrence Erlbaum Associates.

Muir, D. (1985). The development of infants' auditory spatial sensitivity. In S. E. Trehub & B. Schneider (Eds.), *Auditory development in infancy.* New York: Plenum.

Nelson, C. A., & Horowitz, F. D. (1987). Visual motion perception in infancy: A review and synthesis. In P. Salapatek & L. Cohen (Eds.), *Handbook of infant perception: From perception to cognition* (Vol. 2). New York: Academic Press.

Nettlebeck, T., & Wilson, C. (1985). A cross-sequential analysis of developmental differences in speed of visual information processing. *Journal of Experimental Child Psychology, 40,* 1–22.

Norcia, A. M., & Tyler, C. W. (1985). Spatial frequency sweep VEP: Visual acuity during the first year of life. *Vision Research, 25,* 1399–1408.

Olsho, L. W. (1984). Infant frequency discrimination. *Infant Behavior and Development, 7,* 27–35.

Olsho, L. W., Schoon, C., Sakai, R., Turpin, R., & Sperduto, V. (1982a). Preliminary data on frequency discrimination. *Journal of the Acoustical Society of America, 71,* 509–511.

Olsho, L. W., Schoon, C., Sakai, R., Turpin, R., & Sperduto, V. (1982b). Auditory frequency discrimination in infancy. *Developmental Psychology, 18,* 721–726.

Owsley, C., Ball, K., Sloane, M. E., Roenker, D. L., & Bruni, J. R. (1991). Visual/cognitive correlates of vehicle accidents in older drivers. *Psychology and Aging, 6,* 403–415.

Packer, O., Hartmann, E. E., & Teller, D. Y. (1985). Infant color vision: The effect of test field size on Rayleigh discriminations. *Vision Research, 24,* 1247–1260.

Parmelee, A. H., & Sigman, M. D. (1983). Perinatal brain development and behavior. In P. H. Mussen (Series Ed.) & M. M. Haith & J. J. Campos (Vol. Eds.), *Handbook of child psychology: Vol. 2. Infancy and developmental psychophysiology.* New York: Wiley.

Passman, R. H., & Longeway, K. P. (1982). The role of vision in maternal attachment: Giving 2-year-olds a photograph of their mother during separation. *Developmental Psychology, 18,* 530–533.

Peeples, D. R., & Teller, D. Y. (1975). Color vision and brightness discrimination in two-month-old human infants. *Science, 189,* 1102–1103.

Piaget, J. (1954). *The construction of reality in the child.* New York: Basic Books. (Original work published 1937)

Piaget, J. (1969). *The mechanisms of perception* (G. N. Seagrim, Trans.). London: Routledge & Kegan Paul.

Pillow, B. H. (1989). Early understanding of perception as a source of knowledge. *Journal of Experimental Child Psychology, 47,* 116–129.

Pipp, S., & Haith, M. M. (1984). Infant visual responses to pattern: Which metric predicts best? *Journal of Experimental Child Psychology, 38,* 373–399.

Pokorny, J., Smith, V. C., & Lutze, M. (1987). Aging of the human lens. *Applied Optics, 26,* 1437–1440.

Porges, S. (1988). Neonatal vagal tone: Diagnostic and prognostic implications. In P. N. Vietze & H. G. Vaughn (Eds.), *Early identification of infants with developmental disabilities.* Philadelphia: Grune & Stratton.

Porges, S. (1991). Autonomic regulation and attention. In B. Campbell (Ed.), *The psychobiology of attention.* Hillsdale, NJ: Lawrence Erlbaum Associates.

Porter, R. H., Bologh, R. D., & Makin, J. W. (1988). Olfactory influences on mother-infant interactions. In C. Rovee-Collier & L. P. Lipsitt (Eds.), *Advances in infancy research* (Vol. 5). Norwood, NJ: Ablex.

Profitt, D. R., & Bertenthal, B. I. (1990). Converging operations revisited: Assessing what infants perceive using discrimination measures. *Perception and Psychophysics, 47,* 1–11.

Purpura, D. P. (1975). Morphogenesis of visual cortex in the preterm infant. In M. A. B. Brazier (Ed.), *Growth and development of the brain.* New York: Raven.

Purves, D., & Lichtman, J. W. (1980). Elimination of synapses in the developing nervous system. *Science, 210,* 153–157.

Raskin, L. A., Maital, S., & Bornstein, M. H. (1983). Perceptual categorization of color: A life-span study. *Psychological Research, 45,* 639–649.

Richards, J. E. (1987). Infant visual sustained attention and respiratory sinus arrhythmia. *Child Development, 58,* 488–496.

Richards, J. E. (1989). Development and stability in visual sustained attention in 14, 20, and 26 week old infants. *Psychophysiology, 26,* 422–430.

Rosch, E. (1975). Cognitive reference points. *Cognitive Psychology, 7,* 532–547.

Rose, S. A., & Ruff, H. A. (1987). Cross-modal transfer. In J. D. Osofsky (Ed.), *Handbook of infant development* (2nd ed.). New York: Wiley.

Rosenstein, C., & Oster, H. (1988). Differential facial responses to four basic tastes in newborns. *Child Development, 59,* 1555–1568.

Ruff, H. A. (1982). The role of manipulation in infants' responses to invariant properties of objects. *Developmental Psychology, 18,* 682–691.

Ruff, H. A. (1984). Infants' manipulative exploration of objects: Effects of age and object characteristics. *Developmental Psychology, 20,* 9–20.

Ruff, H. A. (1985). Detection of information specifying the motion of objects by 3- and 5-month-old infants. *Developmental Psychology, 21,* 295–305.

Ruff, H. A. (1989). The infant's use of visual and haptic information in the perception and recognition of objects. *Canadian Journal of Psychology, 43,* 302–319.

Ruff, H. A. (1990). Individual differences in sustained attention during infancy. In J. Colombo & J. Fagan (Eds.), *Individual differences in infancy: Reliability, stability, prediction.* Hillsdale, NJ: Lawrence Erlbaum Associates.

Salthouse, T. A., Rogan, J. D., & Prill, K. (1984). Division of attention: Age differences on a visually presented memory task. *Memory and Cognition, 12,* 613–620.

Samuels, C. A. (1985). Attention to eye contact opportunity and facial motion by three-month-old infants. *Journal of Experimental Child Psychology, 40,* 105–114.

Schaie, K. W. (1989). Perceptual speed in adulthood: Cross-sectional and longitudinal studies. *Psychology and Aging, 4,* 443–453.

Schaie, K. W. (1990). "Perceptual speed in adulthood: Cross-sectional and longitudinal studies": Correction. *Psychology and Aging, 5,* 171.

Schemper, T., Voss, S., & Cain, W. S. (1981). Odor identification in young and elderly persons: Sensory and cognitive limitations. *Journal of Gerontology, 36,* 452–466.

Schiffman, S. (1977). Food recognition by the elderly. *Journal of Gerontology, 32,* 586–592.

Schneider, B. A., Bull, D., & Trehub, S. E. (1988). Binaural unmasking in infants. *Journal of the Acoustical Society of America, 83,* 1124–1132.

Schneider, B. A., Trehub, S. E., Morrongiello, B. A., & Thorpe, L. A. (1986). Auditory sensitivity in preschool children. *Journal of the Acoustic Society of America, 79,* 447–452.

Schneider, E. L., & Rowe, J. W. (Eds.). (1990). *Handbook of the biology of aging.* San Diego, CA: Academic Press.

Sekuler, R., & Ball, K. (1986). Visual localization: Age and practice. *Journal of the Optical Society of America (Section A), 3,* 864–867.

Sekuler, R., & Blake, R. (1990). *Perception.* New York: McGraw-Hill.

Silk, A. M., & Thomas, G. V. (1988). The development of size scaling in children's figure drawings. *British Journal of Developmental Psychology, 6,* 285–299.

Sivak, M., Olson, P. L., & Pastalan, L. A. (1981). Effect of driver's age on nighttime legibility of highway signs. *Human Factors, 23,* 59–64.

Slater, A. M. (1989). Visual memory and perception in early infancy. In A. Slater & J. G. Bremner (Eds.), *Infant development,* Sussex England: Lawrence Erlbaum Associates.

Slater, A., Morrison, V., & Somers, M. (1988). Orientation discrimination and cortical function in the human newborn. *Perception, 17,* 597–602.

Slater, A., Morison, V., Town, C., & Rose, D. (1985). Movement perception and identity constancy in the new-born baby. *British Journal of Developmental Psychology, 3,* 211–220.

Smith, L. B. (1989). From global similarities to kinds of similarities: The construction of dimensions in development. In S. Vosniadow & A. Ortony (Eds.), *Similarity and analogy.* Cambridge, MA: Cambridge University Press.

Solan, H. A., & Ficarra, A. P. (1990). A study of perceptual and verbal skills of disabled readers in grades 4, 5 and 6. *Journal of the American Optometric Association, 61,* 628–634.

Somberg, B. L., & Salthouse, T. A. (1982). Divided attention abilities in young and old adults. *Journal of Experimental Psychology: Human Perception and Performance, 8,* 651–663.

Stankov, L. (1988). Aging, attention and intelligence. *Psychology and Aging, 3,* 59–74.

Steiner, J. E. (1977). Facial expressions of the neonate infant indicating the hedonics of food-related chemical stimuli. In J. M. Weiffenbach (Ed.), *Taste and development.* Bethesda, MD: Department of Health, Education, and Welfare.

Steiner, J. E. (1979). Human facial expressions in response to taste and smell stimulation. In H. Reese & L. Lipsitt (Eds.), *Advances in child development and behavior* (Vol. 13). New York: Academic Press.

Streeter, L. A. (1976). Language perception of 2-month-old infants shows effects of both innate mechanisms and experience. *Nature, 259,* 39–41.

Teller, D. Y., & Bornstein, M. H. (1986). Infant color vision and color perception. In P. Salapatek & L. B. Cohen (Eds.), *Handbook of infant perception.* New York: Academic Press.

Thelen, E. (1989). Self-organization in developmental processes: Can systems approaches work? In M. Gunnar & E. Thelen (Eds.), *Systems and development: The Minnesota symposia on child psychology* (Vol. 22). Hillsdale, NJ: Lawrence Erlbaum Associates.

Thelen, E. (1990). Dynamical systems and the generation of individual differences. In J.

Colombo & J. Fagen (Eds.), *Individual differences in infancy: Reliability, stability, prediction.* Hillsdale, NJ: Lawrence Erlbaum Associates.

Thoenen, H., & Edgar, D. (1985). Neurotropic factors. *Science, 229,* 238–242.

Trehub, S. E., & Schneider, B. (Eds.). (1985). *Auditory development in infancy.* New York: Plenum.

Trehub, S. E., Schneider, B. A., Morrongiello, B. A., & Thorpe, L. A. (1988). Auditory sensitivity in school-age children. *Journal of Experimental Child Psychology, 46,* 273–285.

Trehub, S. E., Schneider, B. A., Morrongiello, B. A., & Thorpe, L. A. (1989). Developmental changes in high-frequency sensitivity. *Audiology, 28,* 241–249.

Tuchmann-Duplessis, H., Auroux, M., & Haegel, P. (1975). *Illustrated human embryology* (Vol. 3). New York: Springer-Verlag.

Turkewitz, G., & Kenny, P. A. (1982). Limitations on input as a basis for neural organization and perceptual development: A preliminary theoretical statement. *Developmental Psychology, 15,* 357–368.

Turkewitz, G., & Kenny, P. A. (1985). The role of developmental limitations of sensory input on sensory/perceptual organization. *Journal of Developmental and Behavioral Pediatrics, 6,* 302–306.

Varner, D., Cook, J. E., Schneck, M. E., McDonald, M., & Teller, D. Y. (1984). Tritan discriminations by 1- and 2-month-old human infants. *Vision Research, 25,* 821–832.

Vera, A. (1989). The development of musical skills. *Infancia y Aprendizaje, 45,* 107–121.

Watson, J. S. (1966). Perception of object orientation in infants. *Merrill-Palmer Quarterly, 12,* 73–94.

Weale, R. A. (1986). Senescence and color vision. *Journal of Gerontology, 41,* 635–640.

Weiffenbach, J. M. (1984). Taste and smell perception in aging. *Gerontology, 3,* 137–146.

Werker, J. F. (1990). Cross-language speech perception: Developmental change does not involve loss. In H. Nusbaum & J. Goodman (Eds.), *The transition from speech sounds to spoken words: The development of speech perception.* Cambridge, MA: MIT Press.

Wertheimer, M. (1938). Numbers and numerical concepts in primitive peoples. In W. D. Ellis (Ed.), *A source book of gestalt psychology.* New York: Harcourt.

Wightman, F., Allen, P., Dolan, T., Kistler, D., and others (1989). Temporal resolution in children. *Child Development, 60,* 611–624.

Yakovlev, P. I., & Lecours, A. R. (1967). The myelogenetic cycles of regional maturation of the brain. In A. Minkowski (Ed.), *Regional development of the brain in early life.* Oxford: Blackwell Scientific Publishers.

Yonas, A. (1981). Infants' responses to optical information for collision. In R. N. Aslin, J. R. Alberts, & M. R. Peterson (Eds.), *Development of perception: Psychobiological perspectives* (Vol. 2). New York: Academic Press.

Yonas, A., & Granrud, C. E. (1985). Reaching as a measure of infants' spatial perception. In G. Gottlieb & N. A. Krasnegor (Eds.), *Measurement of audition and vision in the first year of postnatal life: A methodological overview.* Norwood, NJ: Ablex.

Yonas, A., & Owsley, C. (1987). Development of visual space perception. In P. Salapatek & L. B. Cohen (Eds.), *Handbook of infant perception* (Vol. 2). New York: Academic Press.

Zlatin, M. A., & Koenigsknecht, R. A. (1975). Development of the voicing contrast: Perception of stop consonants. *Journal of Speech and Hearing Research, 18,* 541–553.

4 Cognitive Development

Deanna Kuhn
Teachers College, Columbia University

INTRODUCTION

This chapter examines the succession of ways in which the study of cognitive development has been approached during its relatively brief history. The study of cognitive development has been shaped by an overlapping historical succession of conceptualizations of what it is that develops and the processes through which this development occurs. These successive conceptualizations have to a large degree dictated (a) the questions that are selected for investigation, (b) the methods by which investigation is conducted, and (c) how the products of this investigation are understood. They have thus provided a succession of "windows" through which cognitive development can be viewed.

A retrospective look through this succession of windows offers a rich picture of the complex phenomena and factors that are involved in the development of the mind, as well as an appreciation of the challenges and obstacles that are encountered in the effort to understand this development. What it does not provide is a single, integrated account of this development — the sort of overview of what develops and how that development occurs that a reader new to the field might hope to gain from this chapter. Yet, it is only through awareness of these windows themselves — of the conceptual and methodological frameworks that they embody — that one can gain any real insight into the phenomena they address.

One thing a reader new to the field will gain from this chapter is an appreciation of why the study of cognitive development has not yielded simple, straightforward answers to what would seem to be simple, straightforward, empirically researchable questions. For example, does memory capacity increase or remain constant with age? The reader should come to appreciate why such questions themselves, as well as their answers, turn out to be considerably more complex than they appear on the surface.

Although the reader new to the field may be disillusioned to learn that the field is not comprised of simple, easily answered research questions or an accumulated body of perspective-free facts, there is in fact considerable reason to be optimistic regarding the field's past and prospective progress. The field is in many ways at a turning point in its own development, with considerable promise for future progress. A number of longstanding polarities, controversies, and preoccupations that have detracted attention from the central questions crucial to an understanding of cognitive development have in recent years either been resolved, set aside, or recast, with the result that attention is now focused more directly on these key questions. Some might take the negative view that judging from the succession of windows through which it has proceeded, the field has done no more than repeat itself and thus in effect stand still. In this chapter, I suggest instead ways in which these windows are becoming larger and clearer as the perspectives they embody increase in explanatory power.

THE COORDINATION OF MIND AND REALITY: BASIC PERSPECTIVES

An explanation of cognitive development must, at a minimum, include answers to two basic questions: First, what is it that develops? Second, how does this development occur? The answer to the first question, at least, might appear obvious: The profound differences in the intellectual functions exhibited by the newborn infant and the mature adult are evident to the most casual observer. It is this development that is the obvious object of concern. In fact, however, different theoretical and methodological approaches to the study of cognitive development represent a wide variety of views as to what is developing, ranging from individual stimulus–response connections to discrete, context-linked skills, to a smaller set of more general cognitive functions, to a single broad system of cognitive operations that underlies all more specific intellectual abilities and behaviors.

The second question also harbors greater complexity than suggested on the surface. There is more to be explained than how it is that intellectual functioning, or mind, is transformed during the course of development, although formulating such an explanation is in itself a formidable challenge. The full question that must be addressed, rather, is how it is that mind comes to develop in the particular direction, or toward the particular end, that it does (rather than in a host of other possible directions) so as to become well-adapted to the external world of which the developing individual is a part. The two questions are of course not independent. The answer to the second question to a large degree shapes the answer to the first, although the reverse is less true. In the following discussion, then, we focus on answers to the second question, but note their implications with respect to the first.

Three broad answers to the second question have appeared and reappeared through the history of developmental psychology. All three have roots in classical philosophical traditions that predate psychology as a field of scientific study. Each of these perspectives can be classified in terms of which of these three answers it reflects. (See Dixon and Lerner, this volume, for further discussion of the history of these perspectives.)

The first answer, rooted in the philosophical tradition known as *rationalism,* is that mind and reality exist in preestablished coordination with one another. In other words, that the mind develops in the particular direction it does is predetermined, presumably through some form of genetic coding unique to the species. The second answer, whose roots lie in the philosophical tradition known as *empiricism,* is that the nature of reality is imposed on the mind from without during the course of development, and it is for this reason that mind and reality come to coordinate with one another. The third answer, rooted in the philosophical tradition of *interactionism,* is that mind is neither in preestablished coordination with reality nor molded by it from without; rather, through a lengthy series of interchanges between individual and environment, the coordination is gradually achieved.

Maturationism

The first of the three answers is reflected in the first theoretical perspective to have a major guiding influence on the study of child development by North American psychologists, the doctrine of *maturationism.*[1] Until the appearance of the work by Arnold Gesell, the major advocate of maturationism, studies of children's development had been conducted largely within the atheoretical "child study movement" that had flourished in the United States during the early part of the 20th century. It can be argued that the myriad of descriptive studies of children's knowledge and interests produced by the child study movement did not make a lasting contribution to our understanding precisely because these investigations were not guided by an overarching conceptual framework. Gesell's studies, in strong contrast, adhere clearly to a mold dictated by his theoretical view.

---

[1]The theories of James Baldwin, as we note later, had an influence largely confined to Europe, despite the fact that Baldwin was an American.

Gesell was struck by the regularity he observed in the emergence of various motor abilities during the first years of life, despite huge variability in environmental circumstances. These observations led him to the thesis that new skills emerge according to a regular sequence and timetable that are the product of a predetermined genetic code, similar, for example, to the code that governs appearance of secondary sexual characteristics at puberty. Maturation, Gesell proposed, is the internal regulatory mechanism that governs the emergence of all skills and abilities, cognitive as well as behavioral, that appear with advancing age. According to such a view, then, a sequence of discrete skills develops and the mechanism is one of predetermined unfolding.

Gesell and his coworkers engaged in meticulous cross-sectional and longitudinal observations of infants, enabling them to describe in precise detail the sequence and timetable on which early motor abilities appeared. Subsequent research of this sort in developmental psychology has been criticized as "merely descriptive," but one cannot lodge this criticism against Gesell's work, for there is a logical link between his research strategy and his theory: If the appearance of new behaviors is the product of an innate genetic code, the researcher's task is merely to provide a precise description of this unfolding; no further explanation is necessary.

An experimental methodology would seem to have no place in Gesell's work. One experiment Gesell performed, however, has become a classic. Gesell (1929) conducted the experiment for the purpose of demonstrating the secondary role of the environment, relative to the central role he believed to be played by the process of maturation. Quite unlike most modern experiments, Gesell's experiment had only two subjects, 11-month-old twin girls. At the onset of the experiment, neither twin exhibited any proficiency in the skill that was to be the focus of the experiment, stair-climbing. Gesell proceeded to subject one of the twins to daily training sessions on a specially constructed staircase, for a period of 6 weeks. At the end of this period, the trained twin was a proficient stair-climber, while the control (untrained) twin still showed no ability.

At this point, the experiment would appear to show exactly the opposite of what Gesell held, that is, it appears to show the acquisition of motor skills is highly susceptible to environmental influence. The experiment did not end at this point, however. Several weeks later, the control twin spontaneously began to exhibit some stair-climbing proficiency. At this point, Gesell instituted a 2-week period of training of the same type that had been administered to the experimental twin. At the end of this period, the control twin equalled her experimental twin in stair-climbing proficiency, and the two remained equivalent in proficiency from then on.

What Gesell wished to demonstrate by this experiment, of course, is that the environment, or "experience," plays at most a superficial, secondary role in temporarily accelerating the emergence of a skill that is destined by the maturational code to appear at a later time. While these results were initially accepted by some as evidence of the accuracy of Gesell's maturational doctrine, a major criticism of the experiment was subsequently raised. Did the experimental design adequately control for the effects of experience? The untrained twin continued to have experience of a variety of sorts, even if not specifically stair-climbing, during the period the experimental twin was being trained. Could this experience legitimately be ruled out as having contributed to the eventual appearance of the untrained twin's skill?

At first, the issue appeared to be a problem in research design. Were it feasible on ethical and technical grounds to restrict totally the experience of the control twin during the training period, then experience could be ruled out as a contributing factor. Ultimately, however, the problem was recognized as a logical, not a methodological, one. As long as an organism has life, it is undergoing some experience, by the very definition of what it is to be alive. Thus, a process of maturation can be observed only in the case of a living organism that is undergoing experience of some sort during the period of observation. It is, in turn, impossible to rule out this experience as having played a role in the emergence of new behaviors exhibited by the organism.

Following this and some other similar studies, there occurred a gradual recognition of the impossibility of eliminating experience as a contributing factor to development. As a result, interest in the maturational doctrine declined, and attention turned instead toward investigating how experience influences development. As we shall see, the idea that patterns of developmental change may be genetically coded has by no means been abandoned; yet few if any current developmental psychologists would categorize themselves as maturationists in the strict sense that Gesell represented. One modern-day theorist to whom the maturationist (or the more common term, *nativist*) view is often attributed is the linguist Chomsky. It is important to note, however, that Chomsky does not subscribe to a nativist doctrine in anything like the strong sense that Gesell did. Chomsky regards the capacity to acquire language as an innate capacity unique to the human organism (in contrast to Piaget, who regards the capacity for language as evolving out of sensorimotor activity during infancy). Chomsky (as well as Piaget), however, regards experience as an essential aspect of the process of language acquisition.

The pure doctrine of maturationism, then, is significant largely because of its historical influence, rather than as a guiding perspective in the present-day study of cognitive development. Rejection of the maturationist doctrine, it should be emphasized, however, does not imply rejection of underlying biological changes as critical to the emergence of new cognitive or behavioral skills. On the contrary, developments in the brain and nervous system that appear to be critical for behavioral development have become a topic of intense interest and research effort (Siegler, 1989b, 1991). Such physical developments, however, do not by themselves initiate related behavioral developments. At most, they are enabling conditions that make it possible for the behavioral developments to take place; the process of behavioral development itself remains to be explained.

Empiricism

Although Gesell's studies were theoretically motivated, his descriptions of developmental patterns were attended to more for their practical than their theoretical significance, as the field at this point, under the influence of the child study movement, was still very practically oriented. In fact, the series of books by Gesell and his coworkers describing developmental norms are still referred to today. It is probably accurate to say, then, that when the empiricist movement that had come to occupy the mainstream of academic psychology by the middle of the century embraced the field of child development, it was the first time that the field's research efforts became dominated by an overarching theoretical framework.

The empiricist view represented a striking counterinfluence following Gesell's maturationism. If developmental change does not arise from within the organism, then perhaps it is imposed from without by the environment. This solution represents the second of the three answers presented earlier: Mind and reality come to be coordinated with one another because reality imposes itself on and hence shapes the mind over the course of development. Mind, then, is in the beginning Locke's classic *tabula rasa,* or blank slate.

The name of B. F. Skinner is the one most closely identified with the empiricist doctrine of behaviorism. Skinner explored the full implications of the Law of Effect originally proposed by Thorndike at the turn of the century: Organisms tend to repeat those behaviors that have satisfying consequences and to eliminate those that do not. Thus, the behaviors an organism comes to exhibit are a function of their environmental consequences. The organism is thereby shaped by its environment.

Bijou and Baer are the two theorists most widely known for applying Skinner's doctrine to child development. The child, they have proposed, is best conceptualized as "a cluster of interrelated responses" (Bijou & Baer, 1961). Development, in turn, consists of the progressive shaping of these responses by the environment. Like Skinner, Bijou and Baer claimed as one of their most important tenets that the temptation of relying on unobservable internal constructs to explain behavior must be avoided. Only external, observable behaviors are the proper object of scientific study. The observable behaviors, in turn, are a function of observable external events. To speculate about processes internal to the individual only obscures the direct connection between external behavior and the external stimuli that control it.

One might wonder what relevance such a doctrine could have for the study of cognition and its development, as cognition almost by definition is a process internal to the individual. Bijou and Baer take the position, however, that cognition is nothing more than a particular class of behavior and as such is under the same environmental control as any other behavior. For example, consider what (mistakenly, according to Bijou and Baer) might be regarded as an internal concept that a young child has of, say, the concept *animal*. Bijou and Baer held that what this so-called "concept" actually consists of is a common behavioral response the child has learned to exhibit (as a function of external reinforcement) in the presence of objects or events that have a certain set of properties (e.g., movement, four legs, eyes, nose, mouth, perhaps fur or a tail). It is thus not fruitful to regard the concept as either inside the child's head or existing in nature. Rather, such conceptual behavior is under the control of the environmental agents that administer the appropriate reinforcement contingencies (i.e., signify approval if the child emits the response when the defining properties are present). It could well be a different set of properties (and hence a different conceptual behavior) that the agents chose to reinforce (see Bijou, 1976, Chaps. 3 & 4, for an elaboration of this view of concept development).

A few fundamental principles have governed research in cognitive development carried out within the empiricist framework; the most important are the principle of reductionism, the related principle of parsimony, and the principle of experimental control. *Reductionism* has been influential both as a theoretical principle and as a research strategy. As a theoretical principle, reductionism is the assertion that any complex behavior is, in fact, a constellation of very simple behaviors. As a research strategy, reductionism dictates that the smallest possible behavioral units that make up a complex behavior be isolated and investigated individually. Once the process governing each of these individual units is understood, explanations of more complex forms of behavior should follow.

The related principle of *parsimony* holds that an explanatory mechanism that accounts for the broadest range of phenomena is to be preferred over one that accounts for a narrower range of phenomena. In the case of behaviorist theory, this has meant that more complex explanations must be rejected if a behavior can be accounted for in terms of the simple mechanism of operant conditioning, that is, control by means of external reinforcement. Applied in the field of developmental psychology, the major implication is that developmental phenomena can (and should) be regarded as the accumulated effects of the operation of the simple conditioning (or learning) mechanism. In other words, development can be reduced to the simpler process of learning. Hence, there is no need to retain the more complex term.

The parsimony principle is also reflected in the assumption that the basic learning mechanism functions in an identical way throughout the individual's development. An implication of this assumption with respect to research strategy is that there is no need to compare individuals at different points in development. If a particular learning process is observed to operate at one age level, it is assumed that it will operate in the same way at any other age level. Thus, researchers studying cognitive development within an empiricist framework have tended to utilize a single age group in their studies. Rarely have they engaged in the cross-sectional and longitudinal age comparisons characteristic of most developmental research.

The principle of *experimental control* has led to the almost exclusive choice of an experimental laboratory method. Because the laboratory provides a controlled environment, the researcher can introduce the environmental variable believed to control a particular behavior in order to establish that it does, in fact, produce that behavior, with reasonable assurance that it is not some other (uncontrolled) variable that has actually produced the behavior, as might be the case in a natural setting.

A research program conducted within the empiricist framework that illustrates all of these principles is the laboratory study of paired-associate learning that was prevalent in the 1950s and 1960s. In a paired-associate learning experiment, a subject is exposed to pairs of nonsense syllables (e.g., PIF and LER) until the subject establishes a connection between the two members of the pair, such that on presentation of one syllable, the subject is able to recite the other. The choice of arbitrary (nonsensical) material to be learned is not itself arbitrary but rather is an important part of the research strategy, dictated by the objective of experimental control. Arbitrary associations between meaningless syllables will be completely, and therefore equally, new to all learners. Individual differences in past learning and reinforcement are thus controlled for.

Paired-associate learning experiments were conducted both with children and with adults as subjects. The purpose of these experiments, however, was not to compare the performance of different age groups. Rather, the large number of studies conducted were all devoted to identifying the variables (e.g., exposure time or distinctiveness of syllables) that affect the learning process; it was assumed that these variables would function in an identical way for all subjects at all ages.

The tremendous effort devoted to the study of paired-associate learning was justified on the assumption that it represents one of the simplest, most basic forms of learning and that understanding how it operates would provide a key to understanding the more complex and significant forms of learning that occur in schools and other natural settings. To critics who argue it would be preferable to devote research effort to studying these more complex forms of learning directly, proponents of the reductionist strategy counter the learning that occurs in natural contexts is simply too complex to be amenable to investigation. The reductionist strategy, they would claim, provides the only avenue to eventual understanding. The controversy between pro- and anti-reductionist positions continues through the present day, as will be illustrated later in examining the controversies that have arisen between advocates of constructivist and information-processing approaches.

The maturationist and empiricist perspectives that have been described in this section reflect two of the three answers to the basic question posed at the outset: How does the mind develop so as to become coordinated with the external world it inhabits? The answers that underlie these two perspectives are diametrically opposed. The maturationist answer is that this coordination is preestablished within the individual, whereas the empiricist answer is that this coordination is imposed on the individual from without by the external world. Let us turn now to the perspective that reflects the third of these answers.

PIAGET AND CONSTRUCTIVISM

Rediscovering the Child's Mind

Developmental psychology in North America was in many ways ripe for its "discovery" of Piaget in the 1950s. The Piagetian influence brought something that was new and that many would argue had been conspicuously absent in the study of the child's cognitive (as well as social) development: the "rediscovery of the child's mind," as one observer (Martin, 1959/1960) put it at the time. Some would go so far as to claim that the study of cognitive development began with Piaget; before Piaget, there existed a psychology of learning, not a psychology of development. Many of Piaget's ideas are evident in the work of the philosopher and psychologist, James Mark Baldwin (Wozniak, 1982), as well as Piaget's contemporary, Heinz Werner (1948). Yet it was Piaget who was to have the major influence on the study of cognitive development in North American psychology, even though his scholarly career had been underway in Europe for several decades before North American psychologists became interested in his work.

Piaget's descriptions of "childish" thought intrigued a wide audience of psychologists and educators. That young children believe that the amount of liquid changes when poured into a differently shaped container, that names are a part of the objects they represent, that the sun follows one around and thinks and feels as humans do, that one's own thoughts and dreams are material objects apparent to observers, to cite a few of the most well-known examples, were startling revelations to many who regarded themselves as knowledgeable about children. Such features of children's thought evidently had been "there to be seen" for centuries, but in most cases had never been noted before.

Yet Piaget himself found these observations of childish thought significant not so much for their own sake as for their implications regarding the mechanisms by means of which the mind develops. Consider, for example, the container of liquid portrayed in Fig. 4.1. If asked to draw the liquid as it would appear while the container is tilted at a 45-degree angle, young children tend not to represent the liquid by a line parallel to the true horizontal (left side of Fig. 4.1). Instead, they draw the line representing the liquid as parallel to the top and bottom of the container (right side of Fig. 4.1). No child has ever seen liquid in a container in this way. The child's drawing, therefore, cannot be a direct reflection of his or her experience with objects and events in the physical world. Instead, Piaget argued, it must be an intellectual construction—the child's understanding of what he or she sees.

Each observation of this sort was significant in Piaget's view as testimony to the fact that the child is engaged in an extended intellectual "meaning-making" endeavor. In other words, the child is attempting to construct an understanding of self, other, and the world of objects. Childish beliefs, such as nonconservation (e.g., of the true horizontal, following a perceptual alteration such as tilting of the container, or of quantity, following transfer to a differently shaped container), are significant for the reason that they cannot have been directly internalized from the external world. Nor is it

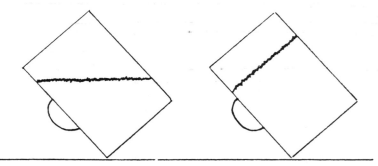

FIG. 4.1. When asked to draw a line indicating the level of liquid in a tilted container, young children typically draw the line parallel to the top and bottom of the container (right) rather than to the true horizontal (left).

plausible that such beliefs are innate and simply appear, uninfluenced by the child's experience in the world.

In discounting these opposing alternatives, Piaget proposed at least the general form of a third solution to the question posed earlier of how mind and reality come to be coordinated with one another. Through a process of organism–environment, or subject–object, interchanges, the child gradually constructs an understanding of both its own actions and the external world. The most important feature of this interchange is that it is bidirectional: The organism and the external world gradually come to "fit" one another — neither makes any radical or unilateral accommodations to the other. Each new childish belief that is discovered, that is, each new belief that directly reflects neither the external world nor the child's innate disposition, provides further evidence of the occurrence of some such bidirectional interchange and hence constructive process.

The Doctrine of Stages

It has been suggested that the single most central idea in Piaget's wide-ranging theorizing is that the intellectual effort to understand one's own actions and their relation to the world of objects, that is, the individual's extended meaning-making enterprise, motivates or energizes a constructive process directed toward progressively greater equilibrium between individual and environment. Thus, when Piaget's influence became prominent in North American psychology, one might have expected that it would be this constructive, meaning-making enterprise, or at the very least the "rediscovery of the child's mind" that Piaget would come to stand for.

Instead, it was the derivative doctrine of stages that Piaget's theory became identified with in North American developmental psychology. The individual's meaning-making effort, Piaget believed, was marked by a striving for coherence, with the result that the individual's ideas had a unity to them, even if the ideas were largely incorrect by external, or mature, standards. In other words, stated more formally, these ideas were reflections of a broad, unified cognitive system. From this system derived all of the more specific aspects of the individual's cognitive functioning.

Furthermore, it was this system as a whole that allegedly underwent developmental change. As a result of the interactive process directed toward adaptation, or greater equilibrium between organism and environment, the cognitive system underwent a series of major reorganizations, each reflecting an improved equilibrium, that is, mind and reality were better coordinated with one another than they had been previously. These newly and better organized mental structures, or stages, were held to appear in an invariant sequence universal to the human species, each new structure reflecting the most probable organization to emerge from the organism-environment interactions that characterized the preceding level. Each new structure represented a new set of principles or rules that governed the interaction between organism and environment. One reason the doctrine of stages may have become the focus of attention for North American developmental psychologists, then, is that it represented a challenge (and what looked like an empirically testable one) to prevailing empiricist theories, as it implied both the inevitability of the sequence of stages and their resistance to environmental influence.

Following from this structuralist theoretical perspective is an inductive research strategy aimed at inferring the nature of the underlying cognitive system by observing a varied sampling of intellectual behaviors and postulating a model of mental structure that might underlie them. Implied in this strategy is the view that any one of these individual behaviors cannot be fully understood and appreciated in isolation. It is only by understanding their relation to each other and to the underlying mental structure they reflect that their true nature can be appreciated.

Following from the theoretical claim that the cognitive system undergoes a series of major transformations is a developmental research strategy. The functional rules that describe interaction between organism and environment do not remain constant, as assumed from the empiricist perspective. Rather, these rules undergo transformation, as part of the transformation of the cognitive system as a whole. Each new structure is unique, and consequently the individual at each new stage of development must be studied as a unique organism, different from what it was earlier or what it will be at a later stage of development.

In Piaget's work these postulated structures are represented in the symbolic medium of formal logic, and each of the major structures—sensorimotor, preoperational, concrete operational, and formal operational—is regarded as a broad system of logical operations that mediates and hence unites a whole range of more specific intellectual behaviors and characteristics (Piaget, 1970). The most appropriate structure for us to examine as an example of Piagetian stage structures is the structure labeled *concrete operations,* alleged to emerge in the age range of 6 to 8 years, as it is the one that has received the most attention both in Piaget's own work and in subsequent research by others.

The central feature that defines the concrete operational thought structure and differentiates it from the earlier preoperational thought structure, Piaget claimed, is the reversibility of mental operations. Mental acts emanating from the preoperational thought structure are irreversible; they cannot be reversed and performed in the opposite direction. Thus, judging that A is smaller than B does not entail the identical judgment made from the reference point of B rather than A, that is, that B is larger than A. For this reason, the child conceptualizes phenomena in absolute rather than relative terms. For example, a young child who regards a ball as large is likely to find it difficult subsequently to regard this same ball as small, relative to another, larger ball.

The underlying irreversibility of preoperational thought, Piaget claimed, is what is responsible for many of the unique features of young children's thinking described in his investigations. Most central are the absence of operations reflecting the logic of relations, as just illustrated, and the logic of classes, that is, the ability to conceptualize elements as having multiple membership in a set of hierarchical classes (e.g., living things, human beings, men, fathers). It is this absence of class logic to which Piaget attributed one of his most widely cited examples of preoperational reasoning: A young child asked if there are more roses or more flowers in a set of four roses and three tulips is likely to reply more roses. Such a reply, Piaget claimed, reflects the child's inability to simultaneously (and hence reversibly) regard the roses as both a subclass and a part of the larger class (flowers). Hence, the child compares the subclass *roses* to its complement *tulips,* rather than to the class *flowers.*

The complete system of operations proposed by Piaget as the concrete operational thought structure is an integrated system of reversible operations of classification—the combining of elements into groups based on their equivalence—and relation—the linking of one element to another in an equivalence relation of symmetry (A is to B as B is to A, as in the case of two brothers) or in a difference relation of asymmetry (A is less than B and B is greater than A). The evolution of this structure was postulated by Piaget also to underlie the attainment of conservation: With concrete operations the child can mentally reverse the transformation (e.g., the pouring of the liquid from the original to a differently shaped container) and hence deduce that the quantity must remain invariant, despite its altered appearance. In addition, the irreversibility of thought prior to the evolution of the concrete operational structure was alleged to underlie all of the characteristics of young children's thinking that Piaget labeled as *egocentric:* inability to assume the perspective of another, attribution of one's own psychological characteristics to material objects (animism), and elevation of the products of one's own psyche (thoughts, dreams) to the status of real, material events visible to others (realism).

Summary: Constructivism and Empiricism

In summary, the constructivist perspective that has just been described and the empiricist perspective, described previously, historically have been the two major guiding theoretical influences leading up to the present-day study of cognitive development. The two perspectives differ from one another on a number of major dimensions. The constructivist views what it is that develops as the internal cognitive system as a whole, the central feature of which is the individual's meaning-making effort to understand his or her own actions and the external world. The empiricist views what it is that develops as independent units of external, observable behavior, each under the individual control of environmental variables.

With respect to how development occurs, the empiricist posits a *cumulative* process in which each new behavior unit is acquired independently through operation of the same basic mechanism of shaping by the environment. The constructivist posits a *bidirectional interaction* between individual and environment, leading to a series of major qualitative reorganizations in the cognitive system as a whole and reflecting progress in the individual's meaning-making enterprise.

The research strategy employed by the empiricist is a nondevelopmental experimental laboratory strategy devoted to examining the process through which an individual behavior is shaped by environmental contingencies. Empirical investigations are therefore devoted to detailed analysis of a single simple behavior. The research strategy employed by the constructivist is inductive, as well as developmental. The researcher samples a wide range of behaviors as a basis for hypothesizing the nature of the underlying cognitive system as a whole that is presumed to generate these behaviors. Cross-age comparisons are made as a basis for inferring changes that occur in the cognitive system.

It is probably because the two perspectives are so diametrically opposed that the study of cognitive development during the 1960s to a large extent became polarized into two camps, with a good deal of the research and theoretical writing during this period directed toward demonstrating the merits of one of the approaches and deficiencies of the other. Since then, serious weaknesses have become apparent in each of the approaches. As a result, at most a few theorists or researchers studying cognitive development today would classify themselves as adhering to either the empiricist or constructivist perspectives in their pure forms as they have been described here. In turn, several new perspectives have evolved and gained adherents; each of these new perspectives retains certain aspects of empiricism or constructivism, but none is in such polar opposition to another as were the original constructivist and empiricist perspectives that preceded them. Let us turn then to the weaknesses that became apparent in the empiricist and constructivist perspectives.

THE LIMITS OF EMPIRICISM

It has been suggested by some observers that researchers who conducted studies of children's learning and memory in the 1950s within the empiricist tradition that dominated at the time had no interest in childhood per se but rather used children as subjects of convenience to investigate the processes of learning that were the real focus of their interest. Whether this claim is justified or not, a sizeable accumulation of such research supported a conclusion that gained wide acceptance: The basic mechanisms of learning function in an identical way across species and across humans of different ages. A psychology of learning is therefore applicable to children and adequate to explain development.

The Study of Learning

Subsequent research has forced a modification of this basic conclusion. The most influential series of studies, by Kendler and Kendler, originated directly in the discrimination-learning paradigm prevalent at the time (see Kendler & Kendler, 1975, for an interesting historical review of their work).

An example of the stimuli and reinforcement contingencies used in the basic experimental paradigm is shown in the left column of Fig. 4.2. Reinforcement is always administered if the response is made in the presence of either of the two top stimuli (designated +) and is never administered if it is made in the presence of either of the bottom stimuli (designated −). This initial training phase of the experiment continues until the subject reaches a preestablished criterion of some number of errorless trials, that is, repeated presentations of the four stimuli during which the subject always makes the response in the presence of a reinforced (+)

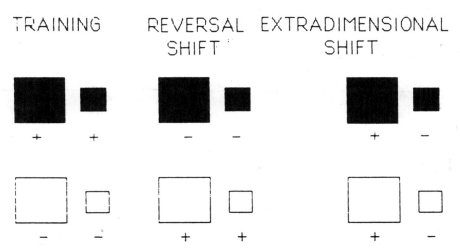

FIG. 4.2. An example of the stimuli and reinforcement contingencies used in the basic experimental paradigm.

stimulus and never in the presence of a nonreinforced ($-$) stimulus. This basic experimental paradigm was employed with diverse types of subjects, and so the response and reinforcer themselves might be anything from a lever press and a food pellet in the case of an animal to verbal responses and reinforcers in the case of a college student.

At this point the training phase of the procedure ends and the test phase begins. The stimuli remain unchanged during the test phase; only the reinforcement contingencies associated with them change. The contingencies are changed in one of two ways. One of the two ways (labeled *reversal shift*) is portrayed in the center column of Fig. 4.2. The other (labeled *extradimensional shift*) is portrayed in the right column of Fig. 4.2. The question of interest is how long it takes the subject to learn the new response so as to reattain the criterion of errorless responding—that is, to respond consistently in the presence of the $+$ stimuli and never in the presence of the $-$ stimuli. In particular, which of the two altered contingency patterns portrayed in Fig. 4.2 should result in more rapid learning, that is, more rapid reattainment of the criterion? Readers unacquainted with this research may wish to study Fig. 4.2 and make their own prediction before reading on.

Classical empiricist theories of learning yield a clear prediction. The response (or nonresponse) to each stimulus is regarded as an associative bond that is built up as a function of the reinforcement contingencies. When the shift to the test phase occurs, at least some of these bonds must be relearned. The number of such bonds that need to be relearned, however, depends on the type of shift. The reader can verify from Fig. 4.2 that in one case (extradimensional shift), only two bonds must be relearned; the other two remain unchanged. In the other case (reversal shift), in contrast, all four must be relearned. It can be predicted, therefore, that the former will be easier to master.

Kendler and Kendler compiled substantial evidence confirming this prediction in the case of animals and young human subjects (below about 6 years of age). Uncharacteristic of researchers studying learning, however, they also studied subjects at a range of different age levels, including adulthood. They discovered that older subjects performed contrary to the learning theory prediction: For them, the reversal shift was easier to relearn than the extradimensional shift.

The inability of traditional learning theory to account for the performance of older subjects in these experiments led the Kendlers to develop a new, modified theory that they termed *mediation* theory. What the older subject is learning in the training phase of the experiment, the Kendlers proposed, is not a set of discrete associations between stimuli and responses, but rather a covert (internal) mediational response. In the instance portrayed in Fig. 4.2, for example, a subject may, in effect, say to herself,

"Oh, it's the color that matters; the size has nothing to do with it." This covert response mediates, or controls, the overt responses (i.e., responding in the presence of the black stimuli and inhibiting response in the presence of the white stimuli). The Kendlers initially emphasized the verbal nature of these mediating responses; that is, it was verbal labels that could be applied to the stimuli (size, color; black, white), that older subjects had learned and verbalized to themselves during the experiment. Subsequently, however, the Kendlers broadened their theory somewhat to regard mediating responses as any covert symbolic responses the subject makes to common features of the stimuli.

If older subjects do indeed make mediational responses during the training phase, then the predicted relative difficulty of the two kinds of shifts changes. In the extradimensional shift, not only the overt responses but the covert mediating response must be relearned (e.g., size instead of color). In the reversal shift, only the overt responses must be relearned (e.g., respond to white, not black). Therefore, the reversal shift should be easier, exactly what the Kendlers found for subjects above the age of 5 or 6 years.

The Kendlers therefore proposed what was, in effect, a developmental theory of learning. The traditional model of formation of discrete stimulus–response bonds characterizes the learning of children until the age of 5 or 6 years. At about this age children develop mediational learning capacity, and at this point the mediational model becomes a more accurate description of the learning process. The historical significance of Kendlers' formulation of mediation theory is twofold. First, their theory represented a refutation of the behaviorist maxim that the basic learning process functions in an identical way across the life cycle. How an individual learns, the Kendlers' work indicates, depends on the individual's developmental level; as a result learning cannot be studied independent of development.

Second, mediation theory represented a departure from the behaviorist maxim that observable behavior is the only proper object of scientific study and that it is not fruitful to postulate unobservable internal constructs that mediate this observed behavior. The Kendlers' work indicated that speculating about internal processes was, in this case, the only route to an adequate conceptualization of the external behavior that was observed. By not doing so, one ran the risk of serious misinterpretation. In the shift experiments, the achievement of laboratory rats, 5-year-olds, and college students appears equivalent at the end of the training phase (although one group may require more trials to reach the criterion than another). Performance of the respective subject groups during the test phase, however, indicates that the learning that takes place during the training phase, although it appears equivalent in its external manifestations, is actually quite different across subject groups. A theory that makes reference to the processes underlying these seemingly equivalent observable performances seemed the only way to explain the differences in performance that the subsequent test phase revealed to be present. In other words, the Kendlers' work pointed to the importance of a distinction that would become fundamental in future work in cognitive psychology: the distinction between product (performance) and the process that generated it.

The Study of Memory

Some notable parallels exist between historical developments in the study of learning and historical developments in the study of memory, to which we now turn our attention.

Memory as Storage.   From the empiricist perspective that dominated psychology in the 1940s and 1950s, learning and memory were two sides of a single coin. Recall, as an example, the paired-associate paradigm discussed earlier. Learning refers to the process by which the associative bond (between the two nonsense syllables) is formed, memory to the retention or storage of that bond once it has been formed. Because the stimuli are meaningless to the subject (because the subject has no prior history of associations to them), they were considered as the ideal medium in which to study the basic processes of learning and retention in their pure form. By employing these elementary, neutral stimuli, basic properties of the human learning and memory apparatus might be identified. For example, how many exposures are required for an association to be formed and what is the organism's storage capacity for associations once formed? From such a perspective, the only role that development might play in the operation of memory processes is to increase the individual's storage capacity. Memory, then, could be regarded as a set of storage compartments that become larger with age.

Memory as Construction.   Memory became a popular research topic in the 1960s, and many laboratory studies were conducted with both children and adults as subjects. The findings from much of this research, however, were difficult to reconcile with the concept of memory as a storage of associations or development as the expansion of storage space. Consider, for example, memory for an arrangement of chess pieces on a chessboard after a subject studies the board and it is then removed. One might anticipate that studies of this nature would provide indices of the capacity of the human visual memory system. Such estimates, however, have been found to depend on the subject's familiarity with the stimulus material and the constraints imposed on the stimulus material to be remembered. In the chess example, a critical factor turns out to be whether the pieces are arranged on the board randomly or in a pattern conforming to the rules of chess. If the arrangement is random, chess experts and nonchess players show equal memory capacity; if the arrangement is legitimate, however, chess experts display greater memory capacity than nonchess players, even when the chess experts are children and the nonplayers adults (Chi, 1978). Other studies have shown exceptional memory capacity in very young children within domains in which they have a great deal of knowledge and experience (Chi & Ceci, 1987; Chi & Koeske, 1983). Thus, one cannot speak of any absolute memory capacity, even one that increases in an age-linked manner. It all depends on what it is that is being remembered, relative to the rememberer's existing cognitive system.

A great many other studies have suggested that, when processing a piece of information to be remembered, an individual does not store it in its intact form as an isolated unit. Instead, the individual assimilates the new information to a framework provided by the individual's existing knowledge, often altering or elaborating the new information in a way consistent with this existing knowledge base. In a series of studies, Paris and his coworkers asked children simple questions to assess their memory of short narratives. Even young children were willing to reply "yes" to a question such as "Did she use a broom?" when the story stated only, "She swept the kitchen floor" (Paris & Carter, 1973). Moreover, by the age of 9 years children were able to recall a sentence such as the preceding one from the cue "broom" as effectively as from the cue "swept" (Paris & Lindauer, 1976), even though one had been explicitly and the other only implicitly present.

It appears, then, that individuals integrate new material into a framework provided by their existing knowledge and draw on this existing knowledge to make inferences that go beyond what is explicitly presented. As a result, newly acquired material cannot be clearly separated from what is already known. Memory, then, is more aptly conceptualized as a process of construction, or reconstruction, than as a process of storage. As such, it cannot be strictly separated from broader processes of reasoning and comprehension; that is, from the individual's more general meaning-making activity.

Memory and Development.   If memory is part of the broader cognitive system, then developmental changes in this system ought to have implications for memory functions. That this is the case has been demonstrated in both a narrow and broad sense. In the narrow sense, level of comprehension of material to be remembered should affect how and how well it is remembered. A simple demonstration of this influence has been provided by studies of children's ability to draw an ordered set of sticks of graduated length after they have viewed it and it is then removed (Inhelder, 1969; Liben, 1977). Children who do not comprehend the logic of asymmetrical relations (as indicated by their inability to construct a seriated array from a set of randomly ordered sticks of different lengths) have been found less able to draw a seriated array from memory after viewing one (array 3 in Fig. 4.3); instead they report very different-looking configurations (arrays 1 & 2a-d in Fig. 4.3) as what they "remember" having seen.

In the broad sense, transformations of the cognitive system ought to affect the memory function itself. A wide range of studies has been conducted indicating such developmental changes. The bulk of these have centered around the utilization of strategies to enhance memory. Organization of material to be remembered into conceptual categories and rehearsal, for example, are both strategies that aid memory. Children below the age of Piaget's concrete operational stage show very little use of these or other strategies to aid memory (Bjorklund, 1990; Brown, Bransford, Ferrara, & Campione, 1983). For example, given a list of items to memorize containing foods, animals, toys, and items of clothing in a random order, older children and adults tend to recall the individual items within these superordinate categories; young children show no such organizational tendency in their recall. The absence of strategic devices in young children's performance on memory tasks is further substantiated by the finding that young children perform equivalently in a memory task whether they are

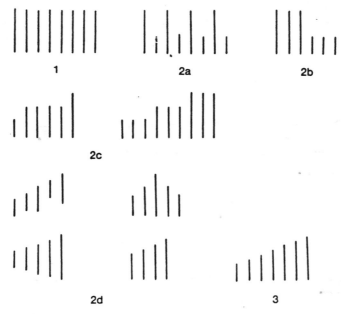

FIG. 4.3. Various arrays produced by subjects in Inhelder's studies of memory development in children (Inhelder, 1969).

instructed to try to remember the presented items or simply to look at them (Flavell, Beach, & Chinsky, 1966). Later we shall consider further what governs the development and utilization of memory strategies, as well as other kinds of cognitive strategies. The most important implication to note here is that, as the Kendlers' work demonstrated with respect to learning, memory functions cannot be studied without regard to the developmental status of the subject.

Summary: The Limits of Reductionism

We have traced the ways in which both the study of learning and the study of memory came to take on both a more cognitive and a more developmental cast. Neither learning nor memory can be studied profitably as a basic process that functions uniformly independent of what it is that is being learned or remembered and its relation to what the learner already knows. Given that this is the case, two implications for the study of the development of learning and memory follow, each of which has received considerable empirical support (Brown et al., 1983; Paris & Lindauer, 1982; Paris, Newman, & Jacobs, 1985; Schneider & Pressley, 1989; Siegler, 1991; Siegler & Klahr, 1982). Developmental change in the cognitive system influences learning and memory performance in the narrow sense that the level of comprehension of new material affects how and how well it is both learned initially and remembered. Developmental change in the cognitive system affects learning and memory in the broad sense of influencing the learning or memory function itself, that is, the strategies the individual utilizes in executing the task.

Perhaps the most telling indicator of the evolution that has been described is that in contrast to the 1950s and 1960s, few current psychologists classify their work as devoted exclusively to the study of learning or memory. Instead, they tend to classify themselves as cognitive psychologists, interested in the study of the cognitive system as a whole. In some ways the evolution described here might be interpreted as a failure on the part of the principle of reductionism. As described earlier, the principle of reductionism and the related principle of parsimony led to the invocation of a single basic mechanism to account for acquisition of new behavior, irrespective of the behavior, the organism, or the relation between the two. The research reviewed here indicates that this assumption is incorrect. As a research strategy, reductionism dictated that very simple behaviors be isolated and studied independently. Once the acquisition mechanism governing these very simple isolated behaviors was understood, understanding of more complex and significant forms of behavior would follow. It is fair to say that this promise has not been realized. It is now largely accepted that the search for a single content- and context-free acquisition mechanism will not be fruitful, and that mastery of new cognitive material cannot be investigated independent of the broader context of the meaning the subject attributes to the material and to the task.

The implications for methodological practice are substantial. In the case of the paired-associate research paradigm described earlier, strong critics (e.g., Riegel, 1978) have characterized the studies themselves, not just the task material, as nonsensical and bound to have failed on the grounds that the learning that is observed is of no meaning or relevance to the learner; that is, it occurs completely out of any context, and therefore cannot possibly provide insight into natural context-bound processes of learning. At a minimum, it has been established that context and meaning have a profound effect on performance (Paris et al., 1985), an issue we explore further later on. Thus, studying the acquisition of arbitrary (meaningless) material in artificial settings offers at best limited insight into the acquisition of meaningful material as it occurs in complex, meaning-rich contexts. This limitation has been particularly severe in the study of memory development, in which work has been confined largely to the laboratory study of memory for arbitrary stimuli (Brown & DeLoache, 1978; Brown et al., 1983; Schneider & Pressley, 1989). The last decade, however, has seen an increasing concern with the investigation of cognitive functions and their development in contexts that are meaningful to the individuals being studied, a trend we shall have more to say about later on.

Even a rejection of reductionism, and the resulting theoretical and methodological concepts of a context-free acquisition mechanism, however, does not force a total repudiation of the empiricist view. A few theorists, such as Bijou and Baer, have retained an orthodox behaviorist perspective. More common, however, are the neobehaviorist formulations proposed by the Kendlers and several others (Gagne, 1968; Gholson, 1980; Rosenthal & Zimmerman, 1978). Largely abandoned by the neo-behaviorists are the refusal to speculate about internal processes, reductionism in its radical form, and the nondevelopmental research strategy. Common to all of these neobehaviorist formulations, however, is endorsement of the empiricist solution to the question of mechanism: Mind is shaped from without by the unidirectional effects of the environment.

THE LIMITS OF CONSTRUCTIVISM

Empirical evidence incompatible with the theory brought into focus the limitations of orthodox behaviorism as an explanatory framework for cognitive development. During the 1960s and 1970s, American developmental psychologists conducted extensive research related to Piaget's work, much of it disconfirming predictions derived from Piagetian theory. One might have expected, then, that this work, in a similar way, would have brought into focus the limitations of constructivism as an explanatory framework for cognitive development. In this case, however, matters are more complex, for it was not constructivism to which researchers principally addressed their studies, but rather Piaget's doctrine of stages.

Stages

The most straightforward prediction derived from stage theory is that the various behaviors that are the alleged manifestations of the underlying stage structure ought to emerge in synchrony, as indicators of the emergence of the underlying structure. In the case of the various behaviors alleged to be manifestations of the concrete operational structure, a large number of studies were performed replicating Piaget's findings that these behaviors emerge in the age range of 6 to 8 years. Researchers then went on to investigate whether the behaviors appear synchronously within individual children at some point during this age period, an issue with respect to which Piaget himself had not reported empirical data. A substantial amount of data has now been collected, none of which has yielded strong evidence that concrete operational concepts, such as hierarchical classification, seriation, transitivity, conservation, and various forms of perspective-taking, emerge synchronously, even though they all appear during the same general age range (Gelman & Baillargeon, 1983; Halford, 1989).

In the face of such findings, many developmentalists came to Piaget's defense, objecting that Piagetian theory did not proclaim a precise synchrony (as reflected in Piaget's concept of *decalage*) but rather only emergence during a broader period of several years, by the end of which the various abilities had consolidated into the structured whole specified by the theory. Others objected to the studies showing lack of synchrony on methodological grounds: The set of tasks administered to a subject to assess the various concepts, they claimed, had not been equated with respect to their more superficial performance demands, having little to do with the concept itself. One assessment task, for example, may have been presented in a manner such that it made greater demands on the subject's verbal skills than did the other tasks, and for this reason display of the concept being assessed by this task was delayed relative to the concepts assessed by the other tasks.

This second objection, however, points to what is an even more fundamental problem for stage theory: Even slight and what one would expect to be insignificant modifications in task format can drastically alter the likelihood that subjects will exhibit the concept being assessed. For example, whether children will recognize the subclass as part of the class (class inclusion) in the example of roses and flowers given earlier is affected by the numerical ratio between the two. Thus, even within a single task or concept domain, whether the concept is judged to be present or absent depends to a considerable extent on particulars of the assessment procedure. The sizeable literature that accumulated on children's attainment of Piagetian concepts showed this to be the case for every one of the concepts investigated (Halford, 1989). Using one assessment procedure, for example, 30% of 6-year-olds might be assessed as having attained a particular concrete operational concept. Using a slightly different procedure, perhaps 70% of the same group of 6-year-olds would be assessed as having attained the concept. On what basis does one decide which procedure yields the "true" incidence of attainment?

These demonstrations of so-called task variance were particularly significant because they suggested that Piagetian assessment tasks were not pure measures of an underlying reasoning competency, in the way that Piaget's descriptions of them implied. Rather, a number of distinguishable skills appeared to be involved in successful performance on a task, many of which were not an integral part of the reasoning competency that was the focus of the assessment. Consider, for example, the concept of transitivity, alleged to be part of the concrete operational structure. Once the child's mental actions involving relational comparisons of the form A > B are organized into a reversible mental structure, such that A > B is recognized as entailing B < A, Piaget theorized, this reversibility should enable the child mentally to construct a seriated array, that is, A > B > C > D, as well as to derive additional order relations from those given. For example, given A > B and B > C, the child should be able to make the inference A > C. Because B is understood as participating in dual relations, in one as less than A and in another as greater than C, it can serve as the mediator linking A and C. Piaget referred to this inference as the inference of transitivity.

A number of subsequent studies of the transitivity inference, however, by Trabasso, Bryant, and others (Bryant & Trabasso, 1971; Trabasso, 1975) aimed to demonstrate that there is more involved in making an inference of transitivity than the inference itself. Each of the individual relations, that is, A > B and B > C, must first of all be attended to and encoded by the subject. Each relation must then, in some manner, be represented and retained in the subject's cognitive system. Failure with respect to any of these steps would be sufficient to prevent the inference from being made; for example, if the subject forgot one of the initial relations. The studies by Trabasso and Bryant endeavored to show that, if successful execution of these initial components were ensured (e.g., by exposing subjects to extended training with respect to the initial relations), children several years younger than the ages reported by Piaget showed successful performance on a transitivity task. Similar analyses of other concrete operational concepts have been proposed; for example, an analysis of the class inclusion concept by Trabasso et al. (1978).

In addition to suggesting that multiple skills enter into performance on a Piagetian reasoning task, the Trabasso and Bryant studies were examples of the numerous so-called training studies conducted in the 1960s and 1970s, which are examined in more detail later in a discussion of methods for studying developmental change. In these studies, attempts were made to induce a particular concept alleged to be part of the Piagetian stage structure by exposing children who had not yet attained the concept to some form of training in an experimental laboratory session. Whether the changes from pretest to posttest assessment that occurred in many of these studies were superficial or genuine became the topic of extended debate. At the very least, however, the studies demonstrated that with relatively minimal instruction children could be taught to display some of the behaviors characteristic of the stage structure they had not yet attained naturally, bringing into question the claim that such behaviors are integral parts of a structured whole.

All the forms of evidence described so far—evidence of asynchrony in emergence, of heterogeneous skills contributing to performance on assessment tasks, and of susceptibility of this performance to environmental influences—contributed to an increasing disenchantment with the Piagetian doctrine of stages during the 1970s. Positing a single, unified structure, the evolution of which is totally responsible for all of the more specific changes in intellectual functioning that occur over the course of development, appeared an oversimplification that did not fit with a growing body of research data. In a certain sense, stage doctrine in its strong form appeared to be a kind of reductionism of an opposite sort to that adopted by those working within the empiricist framework: Instead of the accumulation of large numbers of individually governed small behavioral units, development could be reduced to the evolution of a single, unitary, all-encompassing structure. For further discussion of the debate surrounding stage theory, the reader is referred to articles by Brainerd (1978), Flavell (1982), and Halford (1989), and an edited volume by Levin (1986).

The disenchantment with stage theory was further contributed to by the fact that Piaget's descriptions of the major stage structures such as concrete operations were not closely linked to the actual mental processes in which a subject might engage when responding to one of the typical assessment tasks. Rather, as was illustrated earlier, these structures were described in terms of formal logical models sufficiently abstract and removed from surface behavior that readers of Piaget's descriptions were left uncertain as to how such models might ever be validated as true portrayals of the individual's mental structure.

In the absence of satisfying answers to such questions, large numbers of developmental psychologists turned away from stage theory, in search of what they hoped would be more promising models of cognitive development. The problem came, however, in articulating what might replace stage theory. To conclude that the positing of a single unified structure as what develops is an over-simplification does not dictate the opposite extreme: that discrete competencies develop entirely independent of and unrelated to one another. The truth is almost certain to lie between these two extremes. The central theoretical and research challenge, then, becomes one of characterizing the interdependencies that exist between developments that occur within distinct domains. But note that the question being posed is no longer a question about the existence of stages but a question about developmental process: To what extent and in what manner do developmental changes that occur within domains interact with one another as they take place?

Following their disillusionment with stage theory, theorists and researchers in cognitive development were not in a particularly strong position at that point to formulate theoretical models or research hypotheses regarding developmental process. As we have observed, Piaget's views with respect to developmental process had received relatively little attention from American developmental psychologists, in favor of the derivative theory of stages. The tendency in many circles, then, was to discount Piaget's theory in its entirety in rejecting the stage doctrine. On the other hand, there was little enthusiasm following North American developmental psychology's absorption with Piaget to return to an empiricist conception of mechanism, which had become widely perceived as inadequate to deal with the complexity of human cognition and cognitive development. We turn shortly to a description of the directions in which the study of cognitive development did turn, following the disillusionment with Piaget's stage doctrine. First, however, it is important to say something more about constructivism, because, during the field's preoccupation with stage theory, a few developmentalists continued to focus their attention on questions of process, or mechanism, and therefore on an examination of the merits of Piaget's constructivist hypothesis.

Constructivism

Questions about structures, it has been suggested, are really questions about the process of construction of such structures, and it is understanding of the former that provides a key to conceptualizing the latter. It can be argued that the study of stages within North American developmental psychology came to the dead end it did because one cannot study structures apart from the constructive processes that give rise to them.

Piaget, however, portrayed the constructive process in somewhat the same manner as he did structures; that is, in a very general, abstract form, and to some extent this mode of characterization has given rise to a similar set of problems. The process Piaget described was one in which the individual's own actions on the external world generate feedback that leads to the modification of those actions and their reorganization into new interrelations with one another. In other words, individuals themselves produce their own development (Lerner, 1982; see also Dixon & Lerner, this volume). To many, this conception of developmental change seemed a welcome and desirable corrective to the empiricist view of the individual as the passive recipient of effects produced by the environment.

The effort of those who undertook to explore Piaget's constructivist model, either theoretically or empirically, however, led to articulation of two related weaknesses in Piaget's model. First, the actions generated by the individual's cognitive system that give rise to change are described by the model in such general abstract terms that it is not easy to draw on the model in conceptualizing the varieties of more specific, cognitively salient acts the individual engages in and their likely influence on cognitive development. For example, cross-cultural findings indicating that conservation of quantity developed more rapidly in cultures that emphasized certain kinds of experiences (Newman, Riel, & Martin, 1983) were not incongruent with Piaget's model, but the model offered no way of predicting the effects of such specific variations in experience.

The second limitation, related closely to the first, is that in emphasizing the role of the individual's own self-generated actions, the constructivist model neglects the social context in which these actions, and therefore cognitive development, necessarily occur. The constructive process, whatever its precise nature, does not take place in a vacuum. In the course of their everyday experiences, children encounter all sorts of implicit or explicit examples of the higher level concepts they themselves will acquire. That does not imply they internalize these examples to which they are exposed in any direct or automatic way. But it is equally unlikely that they systematically ignore them. Indeed, there is evidence to show children attend to external models of higher level concepts in a sustained and deliberate manner (Morrison & Kuhn, 1983). The objective, then, must be to understand the specific ways in which the individual's constructive activity utilizes these external data. Internal disequilibrium may be the force that energizes and propels cognitive development, as Piaget claimed (Acredolo & O'Connor, 1991; Piaget, 1977), but the contribution of external influences to this process needs to be recognized and understood (Boom, 1991).

Summary: Neoconstructivist Directions

The preceding discussion briefly traces the impact that Piaget's work has had on North American developmental psychology from its introduction in the 1950s to the present day. During this period, North American researchers collected data suggesting asynchrony in emergence of stage-related competencies, the contribution of heterogeneous skills to performance on assessment tasks, and susceptibility of this performance to environmental influence. All of these kinds of evidence contributed to a disillusionment with stage doctrine in its strong form—the doctrine that all of cognitive development can be accounted for by the evolution of a single, unitary structure. The lesser attention devoted to Piaget's more central constructivist hypothesis also revealed a set of serious problems and limitations, however, centering around the effects of specific forms of experience on the individual's cognitive development.

Faced with the limitations they perceived in Piaget's constructivist formulation, a number of developmentalists concerned with questions of process sought ways to modify or to expand on the Piagetian model, with the aim of making it more explicit and empirically testable, as well as to take into greater account the specific influence of the environmental context in which development takes place. Fischer (1980, Fischer & Farrar, 1988); for example, while maintaining many of the central features of Piaget's structuralism, has proposed a model in which new cognitive skills are at least initially wedded to the concrete contexts in which they are acquired; they are not the totally general, content-free acquisitions implied by Piaget's theory. Other neo-Piagetian theories have been proposed by Case (1985, 1988), Halford (1988, 1989), and Pascual-Leone (1970, 1988). Also, to a large extent in reaction to the neglect of social context in Piaget's constructivism, a renewed interest occurred in developmental theories originating within Soviet psychology, notably those of Luria (1976) and Vygotsky (1978). The Soviet perspective has had a substantial impact in recent years with respect to methodology as well as theory, as we see later. The attention of a large number of researchers in cognitive development, however, turned in another direction.

THE INFORMATION-PROCESSING APPROACH

Largely unknown to developmental psychologists in the 1960s, the information-processing approach was declared by Siegler in his 1983 review chapter to be "arguably the leading strategy for the study of cognitive development." In fact, as Klahr (1989, this volume) has noted, it has achieved such widespread allegiance that it has become unclear exactly what assumptions define the approach. Many researchers appear to have adopted the terminology of information processing without necessarily subscribing to any specific assumptions regarding the nature of cognition or its development, a fact that has led Klahr (1989, this volume) to contrast hard-core and soft-core information-processing approaches. In his chapter in this volume, Klahr details the assumptions and principles that distinguish hard-core and soft-core information-processing approaches to cognitive development and reviews research illustrating both approaches. In this section, in contrast, I undertake to put the information-processing approach to cognitive development into some historical perspective, relating it to theoretical perspectives and approaches that have preceded it and currently contrast to it.

The information-processing approach to the study of cognitive development is not as readily classifiable as have been the theoretical perspectives examined up to this point. The major reason is that it is by the admission of its own adherents not a comprehensive theory of development, or even of cognition, but rather an approach to the study of cognition and, to a lesser extent, its development. Thus, it does not take an explicit position on some of the questions a theory of cognitive development must address.

The Computer Metaphor

The origins of the information-processing approach are in cognitive rather than in developmental psychology. A major impetus for its development was the technological innovation of the modern electronic computer. At the heart of the approach is the concept that the human intellect may function as an information-processing system, of which a mechanical information-processing system, that is, the computer, is a fruitful model.[2] How did it happen that this approach very rapidly attracted the attention and enthusiasm of a large number of developmental psychologists? It is not difficult to trace the major reasons.

Recall our earlier example of the transitivity inference. Piaget attributed the child's ability at the level of concrete operations to infer A > C, given the information A > B and B > C, to the underlying thought structure acquiring the characteristic of reversibility: The operation A > B entailed the reverse operation B < A, and B could thus be regarded as simultaneously less than A and greater than C, thereby serving as the mediator linking A and C. This explanation in terms of underlying logical structure, however, does not identify the specific mental processes by which the child

---

[2]More precisely, as Klahr (1989, this volume) pointed out, it is in the computer *program*, or software, not the computer, that the parallel lies. Hence, of potential relevance to human cognition are the concepts and operations devised by computer scientists, rather than the structure and function of the computer itself.

produces a judgment of transitivity in a particular instance. And thus, critics of Piaget's structural approach complained that there was no way ever to prove or disprove the accuracy of such models as explanations of the child's behavior.

Moreover, researchers studying the transitivity inference identified a number of specific processes that must go into its correct performance, such as encoding and retention of the initial relations. From such work it is only a short step to the suggestion that performance of a cognitive task is made up entirely of the serial execution of a number of individual processes such as these. The computer-inspired information-processing model from cognitive psychology offered a formal model of just such a possibility, for it is by means of such serial execution of operations that the computer functions. The guiding assumption underlying the model is that human cognitive functioning is composed of a set of individual processes that operate sequentially and that are not necessarily governed by the same principles of operation. The information-processing approach focuses on these individual processes and the manner in which they operate individually and combine serially to produce the subject's performance.

What are these individual processes? The major source of influence in defining them has been the information-processing operations executed by a computer. Thus, it is assumed that information from the environment must be encoded and stored in symbolic representational form. Various processes then operate on the contents of this representation, manipulating and transforming it in ways that create new representations. These processes may be constrained by the fixed processing capacity of the system, and representations may be constrained by a fixed storage capacity. When processing is completed, output is generated in the form of a final performance, or solution to the problem.

As Klahr describes (this volume), some information-processing psychologists (those Klahr characterizes as adopting a hard-core approach) have taken the computer metaphor quite literally, undertaking to describe the cognitive operations generating a performance by means of a computer program that enables a computer to produce the performance. This approach has the attractive feature of containing a ready test of the model's sufficiency: Does the program successfully simulate performance? Klahr and Wallace (1976), for example, modeled performance of a number of the Piagetian concrete operational tasks using as the basic elements of their models a collection of condition–action links termed *productions*. In sharp contrast, however, to the study of condition–action (or stimulus–response) links by behaviorists of the 1950s, the work of information-processing psychologists like Klahr and Wallace was focused squarely on modeling those processes inside the black box that behaviorists sought to bypass. Every minute aspect of the process must be represented explicitly or the model will fail to meet the sufficiency criterion. The computer cannot make any decisions itself that the program has left unspecified.

Klahr and Wallace's models were criticized by some as substituting one formalism (i.e., Piaget's models employing symbolic logic) with another (i.e., a computer programming language), and, indeed, following Klahr and Wallace's pioneering effort only a few attempts to construct similar models appeared. More recently, however, more efforts in this vein have appeared, including self-modifying programs intended to simulate development (see Klahr, 1989, this volume, for examples).

A much larger group of researchers (whom Klahr characterizes as following a soft-core approach) endorse the general spirit of the information-processing approach without casting their models in the form of explicit computer simulations. It is interesting to note that many of these researchers have drawn on Piagetian tasks as the basis for their research, including tasks from Piaget's formal operational, as well as concrete operational, stage. Siegler (1976), for example, undertook to characterize a child's performance on a task by describing the "rule" to which that performance conforms. A test of the adequacy of the rule in characterizing the child's behavior is the extent to which it predicts performance over a variety of specific task items. The most widely cited example is Siegler's (1976) rule-based model of performance on Piaget's balance scale task. The subject is shown a balance scale on which weights are placed at various distances from the center, and the subject must predict whether one or the other (or neither) side of the scale will go down following the removal of a supporting block. Siegler showed that the performance of 5- and 6-year-old children on such problems conformed to what he termed Rule I, in which only the number of weights is considered: Predict that the side with more weights will go down; if the weights are equal, predict balance. Older children's performance conformed better to Rule II — identical to Rule I except that in the case of equal weights, predict the side with weights at a greater distance from the fulcrum will go down — or to Rule III, which includes processing of both weight and distance information but lacks a consistent rule for integrating them. Not until mid- to late-adolescence did a fully correct rule (Rule IV) begin to characterize some subjects' performance (consistent with Piaget's findings on this task). The major virtue of this kind of rule-based model of performance on a cognitive task is its explicit specification of the sequence of mental operations the individual allegedly performs to execute the task.

A different approach originated with Pascual-Leone (1970) and later Case (1978a, 1985). Their efforts clearly drew on an information-processing approach, but, in contrast to Siegler, these theorists saw their models as revisions of Piaget's theory, rather than as alternatives to it. At the heart of their work is what they term *task analysis* of the operations a subject would have to perform in order to execute a cognitive task. An example is their task analysis of Piaget's isolation of variables task. In one form of the task, Piaget asked children and adolescents to experiment with a set of rods that differed on several dimensions (e.g., length, thickness, material) to discover what determined their flexibility. Not until early adolescence, Piaget found, do subjects employ an isolation of variables strategy, that is, hold the level of all other variables constant while systematically varying the level of one variable to assess its effect. Piaget linked this development to emergence of the cognitive structure of formal operations.

Based on his task analysis, Case (1978b) argued that what the subject needs to perform this task is very simple:

> All the subject must do is to identify an object with an extreme position value on the dimension to be tested (e.g., a long stick), then identify an object with an extreme negative value (e.g. a short stick), and then check to see if there is any *other* difference between these two objects that might affect the result of interest (e.g., bending). (p. 199)

Portrayed more formally, the subject must execute the set of procedures shown in Table 4.1 (from Case, 1978b).

The virtues of the information-processing approach to analyzing performance on cognitive tasks are readily apparent, and it is easy to see why the approach was particularly attractive to those developmentalists who had become disillusioned with Piagetian stage theory. In contrast to Piagetian models of cognitive competence, which seemed vague, abstract, removed from specific behavior, and unverifiable, information-processing analyses offered explicit, precisely articulated models of the series of cognitive operations a subject actually executes in performing a cognitive task. Less readily apparent, however, were several of the strengths of the constructivist approach that one sacrificed in embracing the information-processing approach. The reason this loss was less apparent has to do with what we have already noted with respect to the way North American psychologists interpreted Piaget—that is, their focus on the doctrine of stages at the expense of the more fundamental concepts that define constructivism.

Reductionism Revisited

The constructivist and information-processing perspectives differ most fundamentally in two respects. One is the information-processing perspective's commitment to reductionism, in contrast to the constructivist perspective's explicit commitment to anti-reductionism, or holism. The other is the focus within the constructivist perspective on reflective aspects of

TABLE 4.1
Detailed Model for Control of Variables[a] (from Case, 1978)

Step or Operation	Specific Schemes	Symbol[b]
1. Identify the object with extreme positive value on the dimension to be tested (e.g., long).	(1) Operative scheme corresponding to the working definition of the positive pole of the dimension to be tested (e.g., for length, if the object sticks out the most, call it the longest).	ψ Dimension to be tested (+)
	(2)[c] Figurative scheme representing the array of the objects in the visual field.	ϕ Array
2. Identify the object with value at the other extreme of dimension to be tested.	(1) Operative scheme corresponding to the working definition of the other pole of dimension to be tested (e.g., for length, if the object is recessed the most, call it the shortest).	ψ Dimension to be tested (−)
	(2)[c] Figurative scheme representing the array of the objects in the visual field.	ϕ Array
3. Check to see if there is any difference between the two objects, other than the one to be tested.	(1) Figurative scheme representing the dimension to be tested.	ϕ Dimension to be tested.
	(2) Operative scheme representing the routine for scanning back and forth between the two objects and isolating any salient difference between them.	ψ Find difference
	(3) Figurative scheme representing object A.	ϕ Object A
	(4)[c] Figurative scheme representing object B.	ϕ Object B
4. If a difference is found recycle to Step 2.		
5. If no difference is found, conduct the test for property (i.e., see if object A > B on property of interest, e.g., bending).		

Note: Adapted from "Structures and Structures: Some Functional Limitations on the Course of Cognitive Growth" by R. Case, *Cognitive Psychology,* 1974, *6,* 544–573. Copyright 1974 by Academic Press. Reprinted by permission.

[a]Problem Question: Given a set of multidimensional objects with property X (e.g., bending), does dimension Y affect magnitude of X?

[b]ψ = operative scheme; ϕ = figurative scheme.

[c]Scheme activated by perceptual field. No M-power necessary.

Discuss cognition, in contrast to their de-emphasis within the information-processing perspective. Consider the issue of reductionism first.

The basic unit to which complex performance is to be reduced is now the internal information-processing operation, rather than an observable behavior. Yet, the dual respects in which the modern-day information-processing approach is committed to reductionism parallel the respects in which the behaviorist approach of the 1950s and 1960s was described earlier as reductionist. First, in a theoretical vein, molar behavior is assumed to be composed of a number of smaller individually controlled elements. Hence, ". . . a relatively small set of elementary processes suffices to produce the full generality of information processing" (Newell & Simon, 1972, p. 29). Second, in a methodological vein, the research strategy is to focus on a particular, well-specified task domain (such as our earlier example of paired-associate learning), which, once well understood, will permit generalization to broader (and more significant) domains of behavior. Constructivist theory and research strategy, of course, are notable, in contrast, as nonreductionistic—individual elements can be properly interpreted only in relation to the whole.

Methodologically, the result has been a series of exceptionally meticulous, detailed models of the procedures subjects are believed to employ in performing a particular task—models that in some sense serve as pioneering examples of the precision to which psychological models might aspire. One of the major criticisms, however, that has been leveled against these task analyses of specific cognitive tasks pertains to their verifiability. Although closer to observable performance than Piaget's logical models, task analyses by no means constitute a magical key that unlocks the secret of how a correct (or incorrect) performance is produced. How do we know that a particular task analysis is correct? Researchers might collect converging behavioral evidence, such as eye movement patterns or reaction times, that are in accordance with what would be predicted by a given task analysis (see Klahr, this volume, for some examples), but alternative hypotheses always remain possible. Indeed, researchers engaged in task analysis of cognitive tasks have tended to produce as many different analyses of a given task as there are analyzers of it. Empirical data have not as yet served in the role of disconfirming a task analysis that has been proposed.

 Another criticism of task analysis and the information-processing approach more generally has been that it limits itself to proposing models of performance on specific tasks and has not undertaken to integrate those models into a broader theory of human cognitive performance. Adherents of the information-processing approach, on the other hand, have defended this omission as a matter of appropriate sequence: Precise models of performance in very specific, restricted domains are alleged to be prerequisites for the formulation of broader, more comprehensive theories. Stated differently, the information-processing psychologist justifies, in the short term at least, sacrificing explanatory breadth for explanatory precision. Here again the parallel to the historically earlier reductionist research strategy adhered to by behaviorists is clear. And so the debate over reductionism continues, with the information-processing approach assuming the pro-reductionist role.

Theoretically, the concept promoted by the information-processing approach that multiple, largely independent processes are likely to be involved in performance of a cognitive task has contributed valuably to thinking about cognitive development, particularly as an antidote to the Piagetian stage doctrine examined earlier. But the problem, and the reductionism debate, arises in deciding whether it is justified to go on to maintain that the performance is nothing but the serial execution of a specified set of individual processes, or whether some higher order organizing entity must be invoked.

The Role of Reflection

This brings us to the second major way in which the constructivist and information-processing perspectives differ. Consider again Case's analysis of the isolation of variables strategy portrayed in Table 4.1. One can agree with Case that the sequence of strategies he specifies is not difficult to execute, and it is not surprising to learn that he was successful in teaching 8-year-olds to execute it (Case, 1974). But if not specifically directed to do so, how would an individual know that this set of strategies ought to be applied to such a problem? Without such knowledge, knowledge of how to execute the strategies is of limited value.

In comparison to knowledge of the first type—knowledge of how to execute strategies, which is to a considerable extent ascertainable from the surface features of performance—knowledge of this second type is subtle and complex (Kuhn, 1983). In order to select a strategy as the appropriate one to apply in solving a problem, the individual must understand the strategy, understand the problem, and understand how the strategy and problem intersect or map onto one another. In the case of the isolation of variables strategy represented in Table 4.1, such knowledge includes an understanding of (a) why the isolation or "all other things equal" method is the only means of achieving the task objective, (b) how and why each component of the strategy (such as ". . . check to see if there is any other difference between these two objects that might affect the result") constitutes an essential step in correct application, and (c) why any other strategy would not yield a correct solution. In other words, one must understand why to use the strategy, not just how to use it.

To be convinced of the importance of this second kind of knowledge, one need only note that it is this knowledge that will determine whether or not an individual utilizes the strategy when an appropriate occasion arises in other situations, in the absence of direct instruction. It is the absence of such knowledge that is responsible for the common failures of generalization following training interventions: The subject learns the strategy in the particular context in which it is taught but fails to apply it subsequently in other contexts in which it is equally appropriate. This problem of transfer of training, or more precisely failure of transfer, is one that has occupied psychologists from early (James, 1890) to modern time (Ferrara, Brown, & Campione, 1986).

Knowledge of one's own cognitive strategy as it applies to a task implies a reflection on the strategy that clearly differentiates it from execution of the strategy. The reader may recognize such a developing reflection on one's actions as at the heart of the constructivist account of cognitive development originating with Baldwin and Piaget. It is just such reflection that is difficult to incorporate into the information-processing model.

A slightly different aspect of this reflection on a strategy is implicated in another concept central to Piagetian theory, that of logical necessity. Consider once again the example of a transitivity inference. In the research by Trabasso and his colleagues described earlier, young children who did not show the transitivity concept were trained with respect to each of a set of individual relations, that is, A > B, B > C, C > D, D > E, using a set of sticks of graduated lengths. It was hypothesized that subjects encoded and represented the set of relations as a visual image, that is, A > B > C > D > E. If so, this would explain how a child was able to answer questions about the relation between nonadjacent elements, for example, A and C, correctly: The child could simply refer to the internal pictoral array that had been formed and produce the information A > C. These findings prompted an extended debate as to whether such children had indeed been shown to have mastered the concept of transitivity (Breslow, 1981), and Piagetians were quick to make the distinction between an empirical judgment of transitivity and a judgment of transitivity that had the characteristic of logical necessity. In other words, the child just indicated might read off her mental representation the fact that A > C, but it does not follow that she sees the relation A > C as an inevitable logical necessity following from the relations A > B and B > C, rather than as an empirical fact that happened to be true but could have been otherwise. The distinction is a difficult one to assess empirically, yet it is this logical necessity that was the heart of the matter for Piaget. Such concepts of logical necessity can only come about as a product of reflection on one's own mental actions—in this case the mental actions of relating A to B and B to C.

Why is it that those utilizing an information-processing approach have tended not to focus on the processes of reflection on one's own cognition? This neglect is most likely ascribable not to accident but to the fact that the information-processing perspective does not lend itself readily to the incorporation of this aspect of cognition, precisely because its underlying metaphor, the information-processing computer, does not, indeed cannot, reflect on what it is doing, at a level differentiated from the doing itself. Unlike humans, computers do not know what they are doing. The computer can contemplate or evaluate its own actions only in the limited sense represented by the programmer specifying the operations that will consti- tute such an evaluation, for example, a condition–action link directing that processing be terminated once a certain set of conditions is met, but, again, such evaluating operations are not at a level distinct from the processing operations themselves.

Toward a Developmental Information-Processing Model

There are both strengths and limitations of the information-processing approach to the study of cognitive development. The major strength is the explicitness and precision with which it attempts to model specific kinds of cognitive performances. In addition, the information-processing approach is responsible for the concept that such performance is composed of a set of sequentially operating individual processes. This specificity and precision, however, are tied closely to a significant limitation—the scant attention that has been paid to integrating specific models into a broader theory of cognition and, particularly, cognitive development.

The major limitation that has been focused on is the lack of attention to what we have referred to as reflective cognition. If the information-processing approach is not to restrict itself unduly in explaining cognitive development, it can be argued that it will eventually have to go beyond a literal model of the computer to incorporate the reflective, or evaluative, components of cognition and cognitive development. One simple indication of its need to do so is the frequent finding that subjects are able to execute all of the component strategies that a task analysis requires for performance and yet do not assemble those components to produce the performance. Something else appears necessary for success.

This something else involves the second of the two kinds of knowing contrasted earlier. It might be referred to as *metacognition,* that is, cognition about cognition, although this term has been employed in such broad and diverse ways that its usefulness as a scientific construct has been jeopardized (Forrest-Pressley, MacKinnon, & Waller, 1985). In its most general sense, the term metacognition has been used to refer to an executive function that selects, controls, and monitors the use of cognitive strategies,

Discuss but it is often left unclear as to whether this function entails conscious awareness. Theorists who address cognitive development from an information-processing perspective and who include metacognition in their theorizing (e.g., Sternberg, 1984; Sternberg & Powell, 1983) have tended to regard metacognitive processes as functioning in an unconscious, automatic manner. This approach to metacognition thus does not incorporate the reflective aspects of metacognition, that is, individuals' reflective awareness of the cognitive operations they perform. The earlier view expressed in Vygotsky's (1962) writing, in contrast, regards reflective awareness and deliberate control as the dual aspects of metacognition. The two can be regarded as describing the subjective (or phenomenological) and the objective (or behavioral) aspects of the same phenomenon: A person aware of his or her own mental acts is able to reflect on those acts as objects of cognition and is also able to access and apply them in a manner under their voluntary control.

Perhaps the strongest evidence for the critical role of reflective cognition is the fact that even theorists who have been the most explicit adherents to an information-processing perspective have eventually found it necessary to incorporate such constructs into their theorizing. Siegler, for example, initially proposed the rule-based model described earlier, in which performance is characterized by a developing sequence of rules that the individual uses to solve specific problems (Siegler, 1976). Subsequently, Siegler became concerned with the question of how an individual chooses which of a set of alternative rules or strategies to use in a particular situation. His initial efforts to address this question focused on nonreflective mechanisms, such as associative strength, to explain strategy choice (Siegler, 1986, 1988; Siegler & Shrager, 1984). In his words, "Rather than metacognition regulating cognition, cognitive representations and processes are assumed to be organized in such a way that they yield adaptive strategy choices without any direct governmental process" (Siegler, 1988). In more recent work, however, Siegler has turned increasingly to conscious awareness as a means of predicting both strategy usage and subsequent generalization to new situations. In summarizing their research on arithmetic strategies, for example, Siegler and Jenkins (1989) conclude, "the [other] clear influence on amount of generalization of the new strategy was whether the child seemed conscious of the strategy being used."

One final limitation of the information-processing approach, one that has only been alluded to until now, has been widely noted by both adherents and critics of the approach. Until recently, information-processing models of cognition have not included any explanation of how the human information-processing system changes. The capacity of the information-processing approach to explain change is obviously crucial if the approach is to be applicable to cognitive development. Why and how is the information-processing system modified over the course of development? However, the information-processing approach is in good company here, for it is the mechanism of change that has proved the most difficult and formidable problem for all theories of cognitive development. Like many other developmental theorists, information-processing theorists such as Klahr (Klahr, Langley, & Neches, 1987) and Siegler (Siegler & Crowley, 1991; Siegler & Jenkins, 1989) are increasingly turning their attention to the process of change. Let us turn, then, to the general question of mechanisms of developmental change.

MECHANISMS OF DEVELOPMENTAL CHANGE

Only two decades ago, it appeared as if the question of mechanism in cognitive development were a clear-cut one. There were only two possibilities; it seemed, moreover, that the data from a set of critical experiments would make it easy to choose between the two. Either the learning theorists were right, and the same basic processes of learning could account for development as well, or Piaget was right and a small number of reorganizations of the cognitive system as a whole, occurring only a few times during the course of the individual's development, were sufficient to account for all developmental change. To decide between these two alternatives, it was thought, one needed only to conduct some so-called "training" studies. In the training study, the investigator attempts to induce via simple learning mechanisms competencies held by Piaget to be manifestations of a global stage structure. If such studies were successful, the developmental process could be explained by simple learning mechanisms. If they were unsuccessful, Piaget's concept of global stage transformation would be implicated.

Remarkably, several hundred such training studies were carried out in the decade from the early 1960s to the early 1970s. Even more striking, almost all of these studies were devoted to inducing a single Piagetian competency, conservation of quantity. The one thing that can be concluded about these studies is that they did not clearly decide the issue, and the issue indeed is now recognized to be much more complex than just portrayed. Many of the studies showed significant changes in children's performance on conservation tasks following training of a variety of different kinds, ranging from telling the children the correct answer ("The amount doesn't change.") and rewarding them for making it, to more cognitively oriented attempts to get children to appreciate the logic that dictates the invariance. Exactly what these results implied about how and why children shift during the natural course of development from believing that quantity varies with perceptual rearrangement to believing that it is invariant, however, is far from clear.

In one of the most widely cited conservation training studies, often praised as a model of elegant experimental design, Gelman (1969) claimed that young children fail to conserve because they do not attend to the relevant attribute, for example, the number of elements rather than the length of the row in the case of number conservation. She demonstrated that by reinforcing children over many trials for choosing as same (as a standard) the row with the same number of items but different length (rather than the row of the same length but a different number of items), many children could be induced to respond correctly in the standard conservation task, that is, to respond that the number of items in two rows remained the same after one of them was spread out so as to be of greater length than the other. In the terms used by Gelman, she taught such children to discriminate to which of two possibilities (spatial magnitude or number) the term "same" refers. Gelman, however, quite pointedly did not go on to draw from her findings the conclusion that natural attainment of the conservation concept involves nothing but (i.e., is reducible to) simple processes of discrimination learning and reinforcement. Nor have the many others who have cited her study seemed prepared to draw such a conclusion.

Exactly what conclusions are to be drawn from such studies, then, is far from clear. Much of the uncertainty can be traced to two major sources of ambiguity surrounding experiments that have utilized the training study methodology. First, many observers questioned the authenticity of the experimentally induced attainments: Had the child merely acquired the surface behaviors indicative of an understanding of conservation or had some genuine change in understanding, that is, cognitive reorganization, taken place? Although much debate ensued, the matter was largely unresolvable inasmuch as opinion differed widely as to what conservation attainment in fact consists of: Is some underlying cognitive reorganization involved or is it merely the acquisition of a simple empirical fact or rule (quantity doesn't change through perceptual rearrangement)? In other words, what is it that is developing?

Even if these fundamental issues were agreed, however, and the experimentally induced change were accepted as genuine, a second and even more fundamental and troubling issue remains with respect to the method itself: the issue of can versus does. If a particular treatment is sufficient to produce a behavior in an experimental laboratory situation, it does not follow that the salient features of such a treatment are always, or ever, involved in the emergence of that behavior during the natural course of development. It is this second issue that is probably most responsible for the disillusionment that developed with the training study as a tool for investigating mechanisms of developmental change. Perhaps the most striking testimony to its limitations is the fact that despite the 200 or more training studies of conservation that were conducted, there continued to exist a remarkably wide variety of theories regarding the process by which conservation is attained (Acredolo, 1981; Anderson & Cuneo, 1978; Brainerd, 1979; Pinard, 1981; Shultz, Dover, & Amsel, 1979; Siegler, 1981). Thus, the vast conservation training study literature has not significantly constrained our theories of the developmental process that underlies the attainment of conservation.

Multiple Dimensions and Mechanisms of Change

Along with abandoning the idea of training studies as providing a critical test of empiricist versus constructivist explanations of change came a gradual abandonment of the idea that either could provide a comprehensive theoretical account of developmental change in cognitive functioning. One reason is that, following in part from work done within the information-processing approach, a considerably more complex picture of what it is that is developing has emerged—a "what" that encompasses a diverse set of competencies, rather than only a single entity. As a result, it is likely to require a more complex process, or set of processes, to explain that development. A range of possibilities exists with respect to what it is that may develop, including basic processing capacity, processing efficiency, processes of encoding and representation, knowledge, strategies, and metacognitive processes of strategy selection and regulation. Developmental changes in each of these conceivably could be governed by different mechanisms; moreover, changes in some (e.g., processing capacity) might be invoked to account for changes in others (e.g., strategy usage).

Processing Capacity.   A possibility that is very attractive because of its simplicity is that the change responsible for most if not all advances in cognitive functioning with age is an increase in basic processing capacity, presumably as the result of neurological development. Thus, this alternative attributes cognitive development most directly to an underlying biological process of maturation, at least as a necessary, if not sufficient, factor to account for developmental change. Pascual-Leone (1970) and Case (1985) have advanced respective versions of a neo-Piagetian theory of cognitive development founded on the assumption of age-linked increase in absolute processing capacity. The fact that performance increases with age on tests of basic processing such as digit span appears to support such a view. A 3-year-old can repeat an average of only three digits, whereas a 10-year-old can repeat an average of six digits.

That such improvements in performance are attributable to increases in processing capacity, however, is extremely difficult, if not impossible, to prove as a number of hard-to-discount alternative explanations exist. In the instance of digit span, for example, the older child may be employing some strategic device, such as rehearsal or chunking, that the younger child is not. In other words, it is difficult to prove that children of the two ages are executing the task in exactly the same way, the only difference being that the older children have a quantitatively greater capacity. Furthermore, as discussed earlier, capacity is highly influenced by familiarity with the material: If the domain is one in which a particular child is highly experienced (e.g., chess boards), that child's recall performance may exceed that of much older children less familiar with the domain. Similarly, Case and his colleagues demonstrated that the capacity of an adult drops to that of a 6-year-old if the adult is required to execute a digit memory task using a newly learned set of digit symbols (Case, Kurland, & Goldberg, 1982).

Processing Efficiency. Case (1985, 1988) argued, in opposition to Pascual-Leone, that improvements with age in performance on tests such as digit span only appear to be the result of an absolute capacity increase. Actually, he claimed, improved performance is ascribable to an increase in the efficiency with which basic operations, such as encoding, are executed; accordingly, less capacity is required for their execution. This leaves the individual with a greater remaining functional capacity for holding the products of those operations in memory, even though total capacity remains unchanged. In support of his view, Case cited recent evidence that performance on measures of basic operations, for example, counting an array of objects, becomes faster and more efficient with age, making plausible his view that such increases in efficiency are at least in part responsible for increases in functional capacity and hence in performance on processing tests such as digit span. Whether the fundamental change is one of processing efficiency, as Case claimed, or of total processing capacity, as Pascual-Leone claimed, both argue that such change itself is a function of underlying neurological development, although Case raised the possibility that experience of a very broad, general sort may also contribute to increased efficiency.

An issue even more crucial to debate, however, is the extent to which age-related increases in processing capability (whether absolute or only functional) explain all of cognitive development, as both Case and Pascual-Leone's theories imply. Cognitive functioning changes developmentally in many respects, in addition to improvement in basic processing capability. Children acquire new, qualitatively different strategies they did not have previously, they integrate existing strategies in new ways, they encode new and different kinds of information and represent it in new and different ways, and they develop new forms of executive, or metacognitive, control over their cognitive functioning. Most developmentalists today would agree with the view that increases in basic processing efficiency and/or capacity are implicated at most as necessary conditions for many of these other kinds of changes. They fall far short of being by themselves sufficient to explain how these changes come about. Let us turn then to these other kinds of changes and the mechanisms that may underlie them.

Encoding and Representation.   Another factor that undergoes developmental change, and might account for improvements in performance on many kinds of cognitive tasks, is improved encoding and representation of information essential to successful execution of the task. No matter how efficiently they are developed, operations cannot be performed on material that has not been attended to, encoded, and in some manner represented within the cognitive system. Siegler and Klahr (1982) demonstrate this point nicely in the case of the balance beam task described earlier: At a certain level children do not encode information about fulcrum, as evidenced by their ability to reproduce weight but not distance information in tests of recall. The encoding of distance information is an obvious prerequisite to the execution of the more advanced strategies in which distance is taken into account. Their work does not prove, however, that it is a change in encoding behavior that causes the change in strategy. Conceivably, the causal relation is the reverse: The child's intent to use a new strategy leads the child to encode new kinds of information.

As important as learning what to encode is learning what not to encode. Selective attention to what is most relevant in a situation, ignoring irrelevant information, is another important factor that has been shown to undergo developmental change (Bjorklund & Harnishfeger, 1990; Miller, 1990), and it, too, may play a role in improved performance with age on many kinds of tasks.

Knowledge.   Still another factor that clearly undergoes developmental change is the knowledge the child possesses within specific content domains. The growth of domain-specific knowledge was long ignored by developmental researchers as incidental to, or a byproduct of, what were presumed to be more fundamental changes in modes of cognitive processing and strategy use. Yet, older children have acquired a much larger knowledge base than have younger children, with respect to virtually any content domain in which we might examine their cognitive functioning. Is it not likely that these variations in knowledge play a role in the differences in performance observed across age groups?

Keil (1984) has argued that the acquisition of domain-specific knowledge in fact plays the major role in developmental change, and more general changes in process or strategy play a lesser role. In research on ability to understand metaphors Keil (1986), for example, noted that very young children are able to understand metaphorical relations between certain domains (e.g., animal terms and automobiles, as in "The car is thirsty"), but relations between other domains are comprehended only at a much later age (e.g., human food consumption and reading, as in "She gobbled up the book"). Based on such evidence, Keil argued that what is most significant developmentally is not the ability to understand metaphor, that is, the juxtaposition of semantic fields, itself, but the gradual extension of this ability to new semantic fields, in a sequence that Keil argued is predictable from an analysis of the structure of those fields. (See related research on the development of metaphor comprehension by Marks, Hammeal, & Bornstein, 1987.)

Consistent with his emphasis on domain-specific knowledge, Keil (1984) advocated a research approach in which the investigator focuses attention on the structure of the knowledge that is acquired, and from this analysis makes inferences about how transitions occur within the specific content domain, rather than searching for general mechanisms of change. Others who express a similar view are Carey (1985), Chi and Ceci (1987), and Glaser (1984). Critics of the domain-specific view, such as Sternberg (1984, 1985, 1989), claim that in their zeal to correct what they see as the neglect of domain-specific knowledge and overemphasis on general strategies in prior work, proponents of the domain-specific view are guilty of the reverse overemphasis. What produces variations in the knowledge base individuals have acquired, or, to put the question in its most fundamental form, what are the processes through which knowledge is acquired? This question leads inevitably to a consideration of strategy.

Strategy Execution. How does an individual come to use new or modified strategies in performing a cognitive task? Constructivist accounts traditionally have emphasized the role of self-regulatory mechanisms within the individual: The individual gradually constructs a more adequate, comprehensive, and better equilibrated set of cognitive operations to be applied to the external world. But, as noted, such accounts have tended to minimize the role of the external environment. Within some versions of the constructivist account, exposure to material reflecting the higher level structure toward which the individual is developing is a necessary condition for change, while others theorizing within the constructivist framework hold to the more radical position (reflected in Piaget's writings) that the individual literally constructs anew each more advanced mode of cognitive functioning based on the discrepant feedback produced by actions executed at the existing level. According to this formulation, then, simply the functioning of the cognitive system leads to its modification, a view endorsed by theorists operating from such disparate frameworks as Piaget (1971, 1977) and Klahr (Klahr et al., 1987).

This stronger version of constructivism ignores the fact that models of the more advanced concepts or strategies the individual will acquire are often prevalent in the individual's environment, as emphasized by the Soviet theories of Luria and Vygotsky mentioned earlier. Case's (1978b) work on the isolation of variables strategy suggests that an individual can be taught to execute this strategy through social facilitation, at least in a laboratory context. The role of social influence in its acquisition in natural contexts is another question. But the role of both these processes (individual construction and social facilitation) must be considered in positing an explanation of how an individual masters execution of a new strategy. Even though external models are not directly or automatically internalized, it is most unlikely that they are systematically ignored.

Strategy Selection and Regulation.   With respect to one final factor, the individual's metacognitive decision to utilize particular strategies, the power of social facilitation is less clear. An individual might be instructed successfully in exactly how to execute a particular strategy and even be instructed regarding the conditions under which it is appropriate to apply the strategy, provided these conditions can be well specified. But whether the individual will choose to use the strategy in contexts that are not identical to the instructed one is more problematic. For example, children might be taught to use rehearsal to facilitate memory and yet not employ the strategy in their own activities, a finding that has, in fact, been reported by Paris and Lindauer (1982). As suggested earlier, whether a strategy is selected in noninstructed, natural contexts is likely to depend on metacognitive understanding of the strategy itself. A growing body of research suggests that it is this understanding that predicts whether or not the strategy will be adopted outside of the instructional context (Schneider & Pressley, 1989).

Interaction of Dimensions.   For many years, some of the dimensions of development that have been outlined here, such as content knowledge and encoding, were simply overlooked. Once these various dimensions achieved recognition, the tendency emerged to treat them in either-or fashion — it was either processing capacity or strategies or knowledge that explained cognitive development. The strategy versus knowledge debate has been particularly divisive, as both of these dimensions clearly show developmental change and cannot be ignored. The most recent indications are that this debate is coming to a close, with the recognition that the issue is not one of either-or (Sternberg, 1989). The development of new strategies does not imply a constant knowledge base. Conversely, the development of knowledge within content domains does not preclude the possibility of cross-domain strategic developments in the way in which knowledge is acquired and processed (Kuhn, 1989a). Moreover, there is increasing evidence of ways in which the dimensions of development outlined here interact with one another. The nature and organization of content knowledge affects the application of strategies to this knowledge (Schneider & Pressley, 1989; Siegler, 1989a). The familiarity of content has been shown to affect its ease of encoding (Harris, Durso, Mergler, & Jones, 1990). And, as noted above, metacognitive understanding governs the use of strategies (Schneider & Pressley, 1989).

New Approaches to Studying Change

Two major factors have limited progress in understanding the mechanisms of developmental change. One is uncertainty regarding the appropriate research method. The other is the scarcity of specific hypotheses amenable to empirical investigation. Piaget's (1977) theory of equilibration as the mechanism of change is cast in very abstract, general terms not readily translated into empirically testable hypotheses. Information-processing computer simulations—self-modifying production systems (Klahr et al., 1987)—are impressive in their level of detail and precision, but likewise far removed from human behavior and development. It has not been clear exactly how one would proceed to test the hypothesis that human mechanisms of change resemble the artificial ones.

On the positive side is the fact that we now have a considerably more sophisticated conception of what it is that is developing and, as a result, of the mechanism, or more likely mechanisms, that will be necessary to account for this development. Also on the positive side is the fact that in recent years, after being diverted by a number of subsidiary issues, such as the existence of stages, current developmentalists of virtually every theoretical orientation have identified a better understanding of the process of change as their primary objective, and a great many of them have begun to focus their research efforts on investigating the mechanisms of developmental change. In particular, researchers have begun to explore use of new microgenetic methods as means of obtaining detailed observations of the process as it occurs. These methods differ markedly from the training study methodology discussed earlier in that the focus is on the change process itself, rather than pretest and post-test performance, the approach is observational, rather than hypothesis-testing, and the observation is extended over time, as subjects engage in repeated encounters with the task.

Microgenetic methods show promise in affording insight into the change process, though they do not fit into traditional methodological categories (Siegler & Crowley, 1991). Klahr (this volume) described Siegler and Jenkins's (1989) use of a microgenetic method in studying young children's elementary arithmetic strategies. The microgenetic research my coworkers and I have conducted (Kuhn, Amsel, & O'Loughlin, 1988; Kuhn & Phelps, 1982; Schauble, 1990) has been devoted to causal or scientific reasoning—

a notable contrast to the domain studied by Siegler and Jenkins. In the earliest study (Kuhn & Phelps, 1982), preadolescent subjects were asked to experiment with chemical mixtures in order to determine which element(s) were responsible for making the mixture turn cloudy in one case or red in another. In later studies, we have asked subjects to determine which features of a set of sports balls affect a player's serve and which features of a set of race cars influence the cars' speed (Kuhn, Schauble, & Garcia-Mila, in press). In contrast to elementary arithmetic, scientific reasoning is complex and rarely the subject of explicit instruction in school. People presumably acquire the ability to make causal inferences and to reason scientifically in some broad, inductive manner, as the result of very general kinds of experience. The fact that microgenetic methods yield similar conclusions across two such different domains as ours and Siegler's is testimony, perhaps, to their power and versatility.

Most subjects' progress, we found, occurred only very gradually and involved prolonged use of both less and more advanced strategies in conjunction with one another. This fundamental finding regarding the change process has in fact been observed by all researchers who have investigated change microgenetically (Brown & Campione, 1990; Karmiloff-Smith, 1984, 1988; Kuhn et al., in press; Metz, 1985; Paris, Newman, & McVey, 1982; Schauble, 1990; Siegler & Crowley, 1991). During the prolonged period of gradual change, Kuhn and Phelps (1982) proposed, the subject is gaining metacognitive understanding of which strategies are effective and why, as well as gaining practice in execution of the more advanced strategies. Their observations also pointed to an aspect of the change process that has been largely ignored. The most formidable problem for subjects appears to be not the acquisition and consolidation of new strategies but rather the ability to abandon old, less adequate strategies—a reversal of the way in which we typically think about development. The microgenetic method, then, promises to offer new insights into the most central question in the study of cognitive development—that of how change takes place.

COGNITIVE DEVELOPMENT IN CONTEXT

The evolution from the training study to the microgenetic study as methods for studying mechanisms of change arose out of a recognition of the need to study processes of development in a form as similar as possible to the form in which these processes occur naturally. In a similar way, the field of cognitive development more broadly has in the last few years moved in a direction that reflects this concern.

In part this movement reflects a reaction to the shortcomings that have been perceived in theories and methods that have not concerned themselves with context, shortcomings that we have noted in the preceding sections of this chapter—the futility of the search for context-free processes of learning and memory, the vulnerability of assessments of Piagetian stage level to task effects, the indifference of constructivist accounts of development to children's specific experiences, and the task-boundedness of information-processing models of cognitive performance. In a more positive vein, however, the increasing attention given to context is attributable as well to the influence of two disparate schools of thought and research, one focused on the relation of culture and cognition and the other on cognitive development across the life span. Though the two can be regarded as possessing common roots in the philosophical school of contextualism (Dixon & Lerner, this volume), they are both relatively new to developmental psychology and thus far have existed largely independent of one another.

Culture and Cognition

Populations containing large numbers of unschooled children, adolescents, and adults seemed to provide an ideal means for investigating the effects of schooling on cognitive development. A number of large-scale cross-cultural studies of cognition that were undertaken had as their major purpose the identification of these effects. These studies, however, turned out to be much less decisive than had been hoped. Sharp, Cole, and Lave (1979) reported the inferior performance of unschooled subjects from a non-Western culture on a wide range of cognitive tasks. These authors, however, were quick to realize the limited interpretability of their findings. The kinds of tasks administered to their unschooled subjects were by and large identical or related to the kinds of tasks and activities that schooled individuals engage in at school (activities such as categorization and memorization). Little could be inferred on the basis of such findings, then, beyond the conclusion that experience in performing school-related skills enhances the performance of those skills. The nature of cognition among unschooled individuals remained an embarrassingly open question.

Exactly the same dilemma was recognized as applying within as well as across cultures. A Soviet study by Istomina (1977), for example, has been widely cited as demonstrating the critical importance of assessing cognitive performance in contexts that are familiar and meaningful to the subjects being assessed. In Istomina's study, preschoolers asked to memorize a list of items on the average remembered only half as many items as they remembered when asked to retrieve the same set of items from a make-believe grocery store. Istomina's study subsequently has been criticized as reflecting an oversimplified conception of the role of context and perhaps itself only replicable under a limited range of cultural and contextual conditions (Weissberg & Paris, 1986). A number of different contextual and motivational features of the two conditions no doubt influence subjects' performance in each of these conditions. The important point remains, however, that cognition and cognitive development must be examined in the context of cognitive activities that are meaningful and salient in the lives of the individuals being investigated, if valid conclusions are to be drawn. The appropriate unit of investigation, it has been suggested, should become cultural (and subcultural) practices, not psychological tests and experiments (Cole, 1988, this volume; Laboratory of Comparative Human Cognition, 1983).

Researchers working within this contextualist perspective have been attracted to the theories of the Soviet psychologists Vygotsky (1962, 1978) and Luria (1976) because of their emphasis on the effects of the culture on the individual. It is the child's first social relations, and, in particular, the resulting exposure to a language system, that give rise to mental development, according to the Soviet view. The mode of such transmission is social interaction: What starts out as interpersonal regulation—for example, a mother guiding her child in performing a task the child is unable to do alone—gradually becomes intrapersonal regulation: The child becomes capable of regulating her own actions to produce the performance, without external guidance. Wertsch (1979) has conducted interesting observational studies of this process as it occurs during the course of an adult assisting a child in a task, as have other investigators working within this perspective (Rogoff, 1990; Saxe, 1991). Adult-child relationships, however, are only one type of social relation in which children participate. Equally interesting are studies of cognitive change that occurs in the context of children's peer relations (Damon, 1990, this volume).

The influence of the Soviet perspective has been an important one, as it balances Piaget's emphasis on the role of individuals in producing their own development. In emphasizing the external influences stemming from social interaction, however, the Soviet view neglects the complementary part of the individual–environment interaction, that is, the role of the individual. Little attention is given to how children attribute meaning to the social interactions they are involved in and how this attributed meaning mediates the process by which society affects mind. Descriptions of the shift from interpersonal to intrapersonal regulation in parent–child interaction provide an insightful conceptualization of how parents structure their behavior in efforts to aid the child but less insight into the cognitive processes that enable the child to make use of the adult's input.

Cognitive Development in Life-Span Perspective

The situation confronting the researcher interested in cognitive development during the 80% of the life span that remains following childhood is in many ways similar to that of the cross-cultural researcher. For a number of converging reasons, studies of cognitive development traditionally have stopped at roughly the point in the life cycle at which both biological maturation and universal schooling cease. For most individuals beyond this point, school-related tasks are no longer a significant part of their everyday activities, yet such tasks are the only tools researchers have to assess their cognitive functioning. In contrast to the study of child development, studies of adult cognition and cognitive development lack the advantage of a meaningful anchor in either biology or the cultural universal of schooling. Nor is there any other readily apparent anchor or unifying concept with respect to the intellectual life of adults that could serve as a point of departure for such studies.

Developmentalists who first undertook to study the course of cognitive functioning across the life span understandably did not wish to add the burden of new, unvalidated measures to the already considerable set of methodological challenges they faced. As a result, the bulk of our present knowledge about cognitive development in adulthood is based on adult performance on the measures of cognitive functioning that have received the most extensive examination by psychologists, those associated with the psychometric assessment of intelligence. These also, of course, happen to be measures whose origins lie in the prediction of school performance. Some of the findings from these developmental studies have led to increasing uneasiness about the measures themselves.

Life-span developmental psychology (Baltes, 1987; Baltes, Reese, & Lipsitt, 1980; Dixon, Kramer, & Baltes, 1985; Dixon & Lerner, this volume) undertook as one of its initial missions the seemingly straightforward task of assessing whether, during the course of adulthood, normative age-related changes in intellectual performance occur that are not attributable to sampling, testing, or historical (cohort) factors. Not only does this seemingly fundamental question remain unanswered but most life-span developmental psychologists have come to the view that it is not the right question to ask (Dixon & Baltes, 1986). Several consistent findings from the life-span study of performance on psychometric tasks have led to this conclusion. The major one is the finding of substantial effects of cohort. In other words, the accumulated historical experience common to members of a particular cohort makes cohort membership an equally or more powerful predictor of performance than is the predictor of chronological age. These results have led theorists in the life-span movement to postulate a model that includes several sources of influence on life-span development— age-graded influences, history-graded influences (unique to cohorts), and non-normative influences (unique to individuals).

A second major finding has been that of substantial plasticity in the performance of adults, especially older adults, on psychometric tasks.

Simple practice over an interval of time is often sufficient to improve the performance of older adults dramatically (Blieszner, Willis, & Baltes, 1981; Schaie & Willis, 1986). This finding has led to serious questioning of the validity of these measures in providing accurate or meaningful assessments of normative intellectual functioning across the adult years of the life span. Specifically, psychometric assessment measures have been criticized as youth-centered (Baltes & Willis, 1979; Schaie, 1978), that is, developed for the purpose of measuring intelligence in the early part of the life cycle and subsequently simply applied to the testing of intellectual functioning in older persons, regardless of their appropriateness for those age groups.

These two major findings from life-span research on intellectual functioning have led to two related developments in the life-span research program. One is a recognition of the need to base assessment instruments for adult populations on the kinds of intellectual tasks that are salient in adult life (Baltes, 1987; Willis & Schaie, 1986). In reality we have very little knowledge of the cognitive activities that are part of the everyday lives of the majority of adults who do not pursue scholarly careers. What are these activities and how well or poorly do average adults carry them out? Without such an "ecology of adulthood cognition," we do not have the knowledge that would allow us to evaluate the appropriateness of traditional laboratory tasks in the assessment of adult cognition across the life span.

The second development is a shift away from questions of normative, age-graded intellectual functioning toward questions of range, modifiability, plasticity, and process with respect to intellectual functioning during the adult years (Baltes, 1987; Dixon & Baltes, 1986). This shift reflects an acknowledgment of the substantial role of specific experiential factors (in contrast to inevitable biologically governed aging) in intellectual functioning during the adult years. It is also closely linked to the shift toward more ecologically relevant measures. If specific experiences particular to individuals are accorded a major role, it becomes more essential than ever to attempt to assess their impact with respect to specific intellectual activities and functions that are significant in these individuals' lives.

Other psychologists not associated with the life-span group turned initially to Piaget—in particular to his stage of formal operations—as the most promising gateway to the study of adult cognitive development. Formal operations held the promise of a qualitative rather than quantitative approach to the assessment of cognitive functioning, and the reasoning strategies described by Inhelder and Piaget (1958) as reflecting formal operations appeared to possess the broad generality that made it likely they would be successful in characterizing an individual's reasoning across a wide range of everyday contexts. Moreover, all of the available data pointed to the conclusion that the stage of formal operations, unlike the earlier Piagetian stages, is not attained universally. This finding suggested both that significant variability in the use of formal operational reasoning exists within adult populations and that a developmental perspective may be useful in understanding adult cognition. It seemed a simple matter to remedy the problem that Inhelder and Piaget's assessment tasks were drawn largely from the domain of physics, unfamiliar to most adolescents and adults. Familiar, everyday content could easily be substituted without altering the more general form of the problems posed to subjects.

It soon became apparent, however, that the problem was a deeper one that would not be solved simply by recasting Piaget's tasks into everyday content (Kuhn, Pennington, & Leadbeater, 1983). Doing so still leaves painfully open the question of the extent to which the form of reasoning subjects are asked to engage in (irrespective of the content) is anything like forms of reasoning they normally have occasion to engage in. To the extent this question remains unresolved, so does the significance of subjects' proficient or inferior performance. Thus we remain unable to say whether poor performance on such tasks reflects important deficits in adult reasoning or the inappropriateness of the measures in reflecting the cognitive competence that subjects possess.

A case can be made for the value of a developmental framework in investigating the ecology of adult cognition. Some of the recent work examining adult cognitive functioning in ecologically valid tasks has been undertaken within an explicitly developmental framework (Kuhn, 1991; Perlmutter, Kaplan, & Nyquist, 1990; Smith, Dixon, & Baltes, 1989), but the majority has not (Sternberg & Wagner, 1986). If a major goal is to understand the range, the modifiability, the plasticity of adult cognitive functioning, a developmental framework may be, if not essential, at least extremely illuminating: In what directions and toward what ends does adults' cognitive functioning develop? The age relations in youthful samples can serve as a basis for ordering response patterns into an ordinal hierarchy of developmental levels. Often, a second criterion for such ordinal ranking exists: the adequacy, power, or validity of the reasoning reflected by different response patterns, on logical or rational grounds. To the extent the two orderings match, they reinforce one another in a bootstrapping fashion, even though neither one alone nor even both together prove the accuracy or the validity of the ordering. A third is longitudinal data indicating sequential order of attainment. A fourth form of evidence is the predictive power of the ordered levels, that is, the extent to which knowledge of an individual's position in the ordering can predict performance in some external criterion domain—in the way, for example, that aptitude test scores predict school performance.

To the extent a particular sequential ordering receives validation by any combination of these means, it then can serve as a framework through which performance variability in adult samples (which typically is not age-linked to any appreciable extent) can be conceptualized. In other words, administering the same set of measures to a combination of youthful and mature samples of subjects provides a framework for interpreting the performance of the latter. To be sure, such an approach provides not a set of answers with respect to understanding adult cognition but rather a set of questions — an investigative framework — from which the cognitive functioning of adults can be examined.

PAST PROGRESS AND FUTURE DIRECTIONS

In this chapter I have undertaken to describe how the study of cognitive development has been conceived and conducted in North American psychology over a period of almost half a century, culminating in the current emphasis on studying cognitive development and the mechanisms underlying it in ways that are sensitive to the contexts in which this development occurs and their effects on the developmental process. How might we summarize the progress that the evolution we have described reflects?

Evolution in Theory

One way to summarize this evolution is as the successive rejection of a series of explanatory mechanisms on the grounds that they are too simple to explain what a theory of cognitive development must account for — in other words as too simple to answer the question posed at the outset as underlying the study of cognitive development: How do mind and reality come to be coordinated with one another?

A biologically governed unfolding of developmental forms without regard to environmental influence is no longer taken seriously as a model of psychological development. The more recent hypothesis of a biologically governed, quantitatively increasing processing capacity similarly has been criticized as inadequate by itself to explain how and why cognition develops. Similarly rejected as too simple to account for the complexity of cognitive functioning and its development are explanatory mechanisms that bypass the internal functioning that takes place within the organism. Influences of external variables on the developmental process are now widely accepted as mediated by characteristics internal to the individual. Likewise rejected are simple acquisition mechanisms purported to function in an identical manner irrespective of the material being acquired and its relation to what is already known by the acquirer and to the capabilities of his or her cognitive system. Put another way, it is now widely accepted that mechanisms of learning or retention do not function independently of the individual's intellect as a whole.

Although the individual's intelligence, or active structuring of experience, is thus recognized, there also has been criticism and widespread rejection of explanatory mechanisms that attribute cognitive development to the progressive restructuring of this intelligence as an activity of the individual that takes place isolated from social contexts that might influence it. Individuals develop in a social context of other individuals, and the interdependence of cognitive and social processes must therefore be acknowledged and investigated.

Along with this evolution in concepts of developmental process there has occurred an evolution in concepts of what it is that is developing. The concept of isolated competencies that accumulate independently has been rejected as ignoring the crucial organizational features of behavior and knowledge. But likewise largely rejected has been the concept of a single structured whole that develops as an integrated entity and mediates all more specific components of cognitive functioning. A major contribution of the information-processing approach has been to highlight the fact that there exist a number of distinct cognitive functions, each of which may undergo developmental change. A unique contribution of the constructivist perspective, on the other hand, and one difficult for the information-processing approach to encompass, is its focus on the reflective aspects of cognition and its development—and the meaning-making endeavor of which such reflection is a part.

The preceding summary conversely serves to prescribe the features a fully satisfactory explanatory account of cognitive development would need to possess.

1. It would need to refer to mental processes that take place within the organism, including those aspects of such processes referred to as reflective, or metacognitive;
2. It would need to characterize development as a gradual coordination of individual mind and external physical and social reality, in which neither internal nor external forces predominate over the other;
3. It would need to address the social contexts in which development occurs and the ways in which those contexts relate to individual development;
4. It would need to account for context specificity of cognitive attainments as well as transsituational commonalities in cognitive functioning and development; and
5. It would need to specify mechanisms by means of which developmental change occurs.

During the next several decades, theories that are proposed to account for cognitive development are likely to possess at least the preceding characteristics, as well as others not yet clear. That this is so serves as an indication that the field has progressed, despite the absence of an accumulation of the hard facts a reader of this chapter might have anticipated. The specific directions in which theorizing will evolve are hard to predict. The emergence of new metaphors for cognition and cognitive development may have a major influence on these directions. The new parallel distributed processing (PDP) approach in cognitive psychology (Rumelhart, McClelland & the PDP Research Group, 1986), for example, suggests the neurological structure of the brain, rather than the information processing of a computer, as a guiding metaphor for mental activity (Bjorklund & Har- nishfeger, 1990). One direction that can be predicted is toward theories that are increasingly contextual and holistic, taking into account the complexity of the contexts in which people act and the complexity of their thinking as a whole. As we noted at the beginning of this chapter, simple questions very often become complex ones. The most recent work on the development of concept knowledge, for example, makes clear that we cannot understand how a child comes to attribute meaning to even simple concepts like *food* or *brother* except in the context of the broader theories children construct in the course of their meaning-making effort (Keil, 1989; Markman, 1989).

Evolution in Method

Not surprisingly, as the field of cognitive development has evolved in its theoretical sophistication, so has it evolved with respect to its methods, and this latter evolution also gives reason for optimism regarding the field's future. Just a decade or two ago, researchers in the field of cognitive development, with some justification, could be portrayed as preoccupied with a narrow range of cognitive phenomena investigated in experimental laboratory contexts, where both phenomenon and context were of uncertain relevance to children's cognitive functioning and development in natural settings. Meanwhile, crucial practical decisions as to how children might be reared and educated so as to maximize their cognitive potential and their productivity and fulfillment as adults were left to others outside the academic enterprise.

Today, these characterizations of the field of cognitive development are much less accurate than they were. As we have indicated, recognition has grown that context and meaning have a profound effect on performance, and increasingly researchers are undertaking to examine cognitive func- tioning within the natural contexts of meaningful activities that children engage in—in school as well as in nonschool environments. Cognitive abilities such as reading are currently of great interest to cognitive and developmental psychologists to a large extent because of, rather than despite, their practical importance. The study of cognitive development in contexts not clearly linked to contexts in which that cognitive development occurs naturally seriously constrains the insight such study can yield. There are signs that developmentalists are beginning to take this admonition seriously and that the academic study of cognitive development in the future will not be as divorced from practical or applied concerns as it has been (Kuhn, 1989b).

This issue of ecological validity has been highlighted even further by another trend of the last decade: The study of cognitive development is no longer limited to an exclusive focus on the childhood years. There are indications that it may be fruitful to conceptualize cognitive functioning in adulthood, and particularly the substantial individual variation in cognitive functioning among adults, from a developmental perspective. Parallel to what has been recognized to be the case in cross-cultural work, however, it has become apparent that it will be essential to study cognitive functioning beyond the childhood years in contexts that are meaningful and salient to the individuals studied, if our interpretations are to be valid.

This expansion of the traditional child-focused study of cognitive development to encompass the latter 80% of the life span promises benefits not only for our understanding of adult cognition but for our understanding of cognition and cognitive development during childhood as well. The process of cognitive development during childhood can be fully appreciated only to the extent that we understand the end points toward which it is evolving. The study of cognitive development as a process that takes place throughout life, then, will most likely enrich the conceptual perspectives that over the next several decades will succeed those that have been described in this chapter.

REFERENCES

Acredolo, C. (1981). Acquisition of conservation: A clarification of Piagetian terminology, some recent findings, and an alternative formulation. *Human Development, 24,* 120–137.

Acredolo, C., & O'Connor, J. (1991). On the difficulty of detecting cognitive uncertainty. *Human Development, 34,* 204–223.

Anderson, N., & Cuneo, D. (1978). The height and width rule in children's judgements of quantity. *Journal of Experimental Psychology: General, 107,* 335–378.

Baltes, P. (1987). Theoretical propositions of life-span developmental psychology: On the dynamics between growth and decline. *Developmental Psychology, 23,* 611–626.

Baltes, P., Reese, H., & Lipsitt, L. (1980). Life-span developmental psychology. *Annual Review of Psychology, 31,* 65–110.

Baltes, P. B., & Willis, S. L. (1979). The critical importance of appropriate methodology in the study of aging: The sample case of psychometric intelligence. In F. Hoffmeister & C. Muller (Eds.), *Brain function in old age.* Heidelberg: Springer.

Bijou, S. (1976). *Child development: The basic stage of early childhood.* Englewood Cliffs, NJ: Prentice-Hall.

Bijou, S., & Baer, D. (1961). *Child development: A systematic and empirical theory.* New York: Appleton-Century-Crofts.

Bjorklund, D. (Ed.). (1990). *Children's strategies: Contemporary views of cognitive development.* Hillsdale, NJ: Lawrence Erlbaum Associates.

Bjorklund, D., & Harnishfeger, K. (1990). The resources construct in cognitive development: Diverse sources of evidence and a theory of inefficient inhibition. *Developmental Review, 10,* 48–71.

Blieszner, R., Willis, S., & Baltes, P. (1981). Training research in aging on the fluid ability of inductive reasoning. *Journal of Applied Developmental Psychology, 2,* 247–266.

Boom, J. (1991). Collective development and the learning paradox. *Human Development, 34,* 273–287.

Brainerd, C. (1978). The stage question in cognitive-developmental theory. *Behavioral and Brain Sciences, 1,* 173–213.

Brainerd, C. (1979). Markovian interpretations of conservation learning. *Psychological Review, 86,* 181–213.

Breslow, L. (1981). Reevaluation of the literature on the development of transitive inferences. *Psychological Bulletin, 89,* 325–351.

Brown, A., Bransford, J., Ferrara, R., & Campione, J. (1983). Learning, remembering, and understanding. In P. Mussen (Ed.), *Carmichael's manual of child psychology* (4th ed.). New York: Wiley.

Brown, A., & Campione, J. (1990). Communities of learning and thinking, or a context by any other name. In D. Kuhn (Ed.) *Developmental perspectives on teaching and learning thinking skills. Contributions to human development* (Vol. 21). Basel: Karger.

Brown, A., & DeLoache, J. (1978). Skills, plans, and self-regulation. In R. Siegler (Ed.), *Children's thinking: What develops?* Hillsdale, NJ: Lawrence Erlbaum Associates.

Bryant, P., & Trabasso, T. (1971). Transitive inferences and memory in young children. *Nature, 232,* 456–458.

Carey, S. (1985). Are children fundamentally different kinds of thinkers and learners than adults? In S. Chipman, J. Segal, & G. R. Glaser (Eds.), *Thinking and learning skills* (Vol. 2). Hillsdale, NJ: Lawrence Erlbaum Associates.

Case, R. (1974). Structures and strictures: Some functional limitations on the course of cognitive growth. *Cognitive Psychology, 6,* 544–573.

Case, R. (1978a). Intellectual development from birth to adulthood: A neo-Piagetian interpretation. In R. Siegler (Ed.), *Children's thinking: What develops?* Hillsdale, NJ: Lawrence Erlbaum Associates.

Case, R. (1978b). Piaget and beyond: Toward a developmentally based theory and technology of instruction. In R. Glaser (Ed.), *Advances in instructional psychology* (Vol. 1). Hillsdale, NJ: Lawrence Erlbaum Associates.

Case, R. (1985). *Intellectual development: Birth to adulthood.* New York: Academic Press.

Case, R. (1988). The structure and process of intellectual development. In A. Demetriou (Ed.), *The neo-Piagetian theories of cognitive development: Toward an integration.* North-Holland: Elsevier.

Case, R., Kurland, D., & Goldberg, J. (1982). Operational efficiency and the growth of short-term memory span. *Journal of Experimental Child Psychology, 33,* 386–404.

Chi, M. (1978). Knowledge structures and memory development. In R. Siegler (Ed.), *Children's thinking: What develops?* Hillsdale, NJ: Lawrence Erlbaum Associates.

Chi, M., & Ceci, S. (1987). Content knowledge: Its representation and restructuring in memory development. In H. Reese (Ed.), *Advances in child development and behavior* (Vol. 20). Orlando, FL: Academic Press.

Chi, M., & Koeske, R. (1983). Network representation of a child's dinosaur knowledge. *Developmental Psychology, 19,* 29–39.

Cole, M. (1988). Cross-cultural research in the sociohistorical tradition. *Human Development, 31,* 137–157.

Damon, W. (1990). Social relations and children's thinking skills. In D. Kuhn (Ed.), *Developmental perspectives on teaching and learning thinking skills. Contributions to human development* (Vol. 21). Basel: Karger.

Dixon, R., & Baltes, P. (1986). Toward life-span research on the functions and pragmatics of intelligence. In R. Sternberg & R. Wagner (Eds.), *Practical intelligence: Nature and origins of competence in the everyday world.* New York: Cambridge University Press.

Dixon, R., Kramer, D., & Baltes, P. (1985). Intelligence: A life-span developmental perspective. In B. Wolman (Ed.), *Handbook of intelligence: Theories, measurements, and applications.* New York: Wiley.

Ferrara, R., Brown, A., & Campione, J. (1986). Children's learning and transfer of inductive reasoning rules: Studies of proximal development. *Child Development, 57,* 1087–1099.

Fischer, K. (1980). A theory of cognitive development: The control and construction of hierarchies of skills. *Psychological Review, 87,* 477–531.

Fischer, K., & Farrar, M. (1988). Generalizations about generalization: How a theory of skill development explains both generality and specificity. In A. Demetriou (Ed.), *The neo-Piagetian theories of cognitive development: Toward an integration.* North-Holland: Elsevier.

Flavell, J. (1982). On cognitive development. *Child Development, 53,* 1–10.

Flavell, J., Beach, D., & Chinsky, J. (1966). Spontaneous verbal rehearsal in a memory task as a function of age. *Child Development, 37,* 283–299.

Forrest-Pressley, D., MacKinnon, G., & Waller, T. G. (1985). *Metacognition, cognition, and human performance.* Orlando, FL: Academic Press.

Gagne, R. (1968). Contributions of learning to human development. *Psychological Review, 75,* 177–191.

Gelman, R. (1969). Conservation acquisition: A problem of learning to attend to relevant attributes. *Journal of Experimental Child Psychology, 7,* 167–187.

Gelman, R., & Baillargeon. (1983). A review of some Piagetian concepts. In P. H. Mussen (Series Ed.) & J. Flavell & E. Markman (Vol. Eds.), *Handbook of child psychology: Vol. 3. Cognitive development.* New York: Wiley.

Gesell, A. (1929). Maturation and infant behavior pattern. *Psychological Review, 36,* 307–319.

Gholson, B. (1980). *The cognitive-developmental basis of human learning: Studies in hypothesis testing.* New York: Academic Press.

Glaser, R. (1984). Education and thinking. *American Psychologist, 39,* 93–104.

Halford, G. (1988). A structure-mapping approach to cognitive development. In A. Demetriou (Ed.), *The neo-Piagetian theories of cognitive development: Toward an integration.* North-Holland: Elsevier.

Halford, G. (1989). Reflections on 25 years of Piagetian cognitive developmental psychology, 1963–1988. *Human Development, 32,* 325–387.

Harris, J., Durso, F., Mergler, N., & Jones, S. (1990). Knowledge base influences on judgments of frequency of occurrence. *Cognitive Development, 5,* 223–233.

Inhelder, B. (1969). Memory and intelligence in the child. In D. Elkind & J. Flavell (Eds.), *Studies in cognitive development.* London: Oxford University Press.

Inhelder, B., & Piaget, J. (1958). *The growth of logical thinking from childhood to adolescence.* New York: Basic.

Istomina, Z. (1977). The development of voluntary memory in preschool-age children. In M. Cole (Ed.), *Soviet developmental psychology.* White Plains, NY: Sharpe.

James, W. (1890). *The principles of psychology* (Vol. 1). New York: Dover.

Karmiloff-Smith, A. (1984). Children's problem solving. In A. Brown & B. Rogoff (Eds.), *Advances in developmental psychology* (Vol. 3). Hillsdale, NJ: Lawrence Erlbaum Associates.

Karmiloff-Smith, A. (1988). The child is a theoretician, not an inductivist. *Mind and Language, 3,* 1–13.

Keil, F. (1984). Mechanisms in cognitive development and the structure of knowledge. In R. Sternberg (Ed.), *Mechanisms of cognitive development.* New York: Freeman.

Keil, F. (1986). Conceptual domains and the acquisition of metaphor. *Cognitive Development, 1,* 73–96.

Keil, F. (1989). *Concepts, kinds, and cognitive development.* Cambridge, MA: Bradford/MIT Press.

Kendler, H., & Kendler, T. (1975). From discrimination learning to cognitive development: A neobehavioristic odyssey. In W. K. Estes (Ed.), *Handbook of learning and cognitive processes* (Vol. 1). Hillsdale, NJ: Lawrence Erlbaum Associates.

Klahr, D. (1989). Information-processing approaches. In R. Vasta (Ed.), *Annals of child development: Vol. 6. Six theories of child development.* Greenwich, CT: JAI Press.

Klahr, D., Langley, P., & Neches, R. (1987). *Production system models of learning and development.* Cambridge, MA: MIT Press.

Klahr, D., & Wallace, J. (1976). *Cognitive development: An information-processing view.* Hillsdale, NJ: Lawrence Erlbaum Associates.

Kuhn, D. (1983). On the dual executive and its significance in the development of developmental psychology. In D. Kuhn & J. Meacham (Eds.), *On the development of developmental psychology.* Basel: Karger.

Kuhn, D. (1989a). Children and adults as intuitive scientists. *Psychological Review, 96,* 674–689.

Kuhn, D. (1989b). Making cognitive development research relevant to education. In W. Damon (Ed.), *Child development today and tomorrow.* San Francisco: Jossey-Bass.

Kuhn, D. (1991). *The skills of argument.* New York: Cambridge University Press.

Kuhn, D., Amsel, E., & O'Loughlin, M. (1988). *The development of scientific thinking skills.* Orlando, FL: Academic Press.

Kuhn, D., Pennington, N., & Leadbeater, B. (1983). Adult thinking in developmental perspective. In P. Baltes & O. Brim (Eds.), *Life-span development and behavior* (Vol. 5). New York: Academic Press.

Kuhn, D., & Phelps, E. (1982). The development of problem-solving strategies. In H. Reese (Ed.), *Advances in child development and behavior* (Vol. 17). New York: Academic Press.

Kuhn, D., Schauble, L., & Garcia-Mila, M. (in press). Cross-domain development of scientific reasoning. *Cognition and Instruction.*

Laboratory of Comparative Human Cognition. (1983). Culture and cognitive development. In P. Mussen (Ed.), *Carmichael's manual of child psychology* (4th ed.). New York: Wiley.

Lerner, R. (1982). Children and adolescents as producers of their own development. *Developmental Review, 2,* 342–370.

Levin, I. (1986). *Stage and structure: Reopening the debate.* Norwood, NJ: Ablex.

Liben, L. (1977). Memory in the context of cognitive development: The Piagetian approach. In R. Kail & J. Hagen (Eds.), *Perspectives on the development of memory and cognition.* Hillsdale, NJ: Lawrence Erlbaum Associates.

Luria, A. (1976). *Cognitive development: Its cultural and social foundations.* Cambridge, MA: Harvard University Press.

Markman, E. (1989). *Categorization and naming in children: Problems of induction.* Cambridge, MA: Bradford/MIT Press.

Marks, L., Hammeal, R., & Bornstein, M. (1987). Perceiving similarity and comprehending metaphor. *Monograph of the Society for Research in Child Development, 52* (Serial No. 215).

Martin, W. (1959/1960). Rediscovering the mind of the child. *Merrill-Palmer Quarterly, 6,* 67–76.

Metz, K. (1985). The development of children's problem solving in a gears task: A problem space perspective. *Cognitive Science, 9,* 431-471.

Miller, P. (1990). The development of strategies of selective attention. In D. Bjorklund (Ed.), *Children's strategies: Contemporary views of cognitive development* Hillsdale, NJ: Lawrence Erlbaum Associates.

Morrison, H., & Kuhn, D. (1983). Cognitive aspects of preschoolers' peer imitation in a play situation. *Child Development, 54,* 1041-1053.

Newell, A., & Simon, H. (1972). *Human problem solving.* Englewood Cliffs, NJ: Prentice-Hall.

Newman, D., Riel, M., & Martin, L. (1983). Cultural practices and Piagetian theory: The impact of a cross-cultural research program. In D. Kuhn & J. Meacham (Eds.), *On the development of developmental psychology.* Basel: Karger.

Paris, S., & Carter, A. (1973). Semantic and constructive aspects of sentence memory in children. *Developmental Psychology, 2,* 109-113.

Paris, S., & Lindauer, B. (1976). The role of inference in children's comprehension and memory for sentences. *Cognitive Psychology, 8,* 217-227.

Paris, S., & Lindauer, B. (1982). The development of cognitive skills during childhood. In B. Wolman (Ed.), *Handbook of developmental psychology.* Englewood Cliffs, NJ: Prentice-Hall.

Paris, S., Newman, D., & Jacobs, J. (1985). Social contexts and functions of children's remembering. In C. Brainerd & M. Pressley (Eds.), *The cognitive side of memory development.* New York: Springer-Verlag.

Paris, S., Newman, R., & McVey, K. (1982). Learning the functional significance of mnemonic actions: A microgenetic study of strategy acquisition. *Journal of Experimental Child Psychology, 34,* 490-509.

Pascual-Leone, J. (1970). A mathematical model for transition in Piaget's developmental stages. *Acta Psychologica, 32,* 301-345.

Pascual-Leone, J. (1988). Organismic processes for neo-Piagetian theories: A dialectical causal account of cognitive development. In A. Demetriou (Ed.), *The neo-Piagetian theories of cognitive development: Toward an integration.* North-Holland: Elsevier.

Perlmutter, M., Kaplan, M., & Nyquist, L. (1990). Development of adaptive competence in adulthood. *Human Development, 33,* 185-197.

Piaget, J. (1970). Piaget's theory. In P. Mussen (Ed.), *Carmichael's manual of child psychology* (3rd ed.). New York: Wiley.

Piaget, J. (1971). *Biology and knowledge.* Chicago: University of Chicago Press.

Piaget, J. (1977). *The development of thought: Equilibration of cognitive structures* (A. Rosin, Trans.). New York: Viking.

Pinard, A. (1981). *The conservation of conservation: The child's acquisition of a fundamental concept.* Chicago: University of Chicago Press.

Riegel, K. (1978). *Psychology mon amour: A countertext.* Boston: Houghton Mifflin.

Rogoff, B. (1990). *Apprenticeship in thinking: Cognitive development in social context.* New York: Oxford University Press.

Rosenthal, T., & Zimmerman, B. (1978). *Social learning and cognition.* New York: Academic Press.

Rumelhart, D., McClelland, J., & the PDP Research Group. (1986). *Parallel distributed processing: Explorations in the microstructure of cognition: Vol. 1. Foundations.* Cambridge, MA: MIT Press.

Saxe, G. (1991). *Culture and cognitive development: Studies in mathematical understanding.* Hillsdale, NJ: Lawrence Erlbaum Associates.

Schaie, K. W. (1978). External validity in the assessment of intellectual performance in adulthood. *Journal of Geronotology, 33,* 695-701.

Schaie, K. W., & Willis, S. (1986). Can decline in adult intellectual functioning be reversed? *Developmental Psychology, 22,* 223-232.

Schauble, L. (1990). Belief revision in children: The role of prior knowledge and strategies for generating evidence. *Journal of Experimental Child Psychology, 49,* 31–57.

Schneider, W., & Pressley, M. (1989). *Memory development between 2 and 20.* New York: Springer-Verlag.

Sharp, D. Cole, M., & Lave, J. (1979). Education and cognitive development: The evidence from experimental research. *Monographs of the Society for Research in Child Development, 44* (Serial No. 178).

Shultz, T., Dover, A., & Amsel, E. (1979). The logical and empirical bases of conservation judgments. *Cognition, 7,* 99–123.

Siegler, R. (1976). Three aspects of cognitive development. *Cognitive Psychology, 4,* 481–520.

Siegler, R. (1981). Developmental sequences within and between concepts. *Monographs of the Society for Research in Child Development, 46* (Serial No. 189).

Siegler, R. (1983). Information processing approaches to development. In P. Mussen (Ed.), *Carmichael's manual of child psychology* (4th ed.). New York: Wiley.

Siegler, R. (1986). Unities in strategy choice across domains. In M. Perlmutter (Ed.), *Minnesota Symposium on Child Psychology* (Vol. 21). Minneapolis: University of Minnesota Press.

Siegler, R. (1988). Strategy choice procedures and the development of multiplication skill. *Journal of Experimental Psychology: General, 117,* 258–275.

Siegler, R. (1989a). How domain-general and domain-specific knowledge interact to produce strategy choices. *Merrill-Palmer Quarterly, 35,* 1–26.

Siegler, R. (1989b). Mechanisms of cognitive development. *Annual Review of Psychology.* Palo Alto, CA: Annual Reviews.

Siegler, R. (1991). *Children's thinking.* Englewood Cliffs, NJ: Prentice-Hall.

Siegler, R., & Crowley, K. (1991). The microgenetic method: A direct means for studying cognitive development. *American Psychologist, 46*(6), 606–620.

Siegler, R., & Jenkins, E. (1989). *How children discover new strategies.* Hillsdale, NJ: Lawrence Erlbaum Associates.

Siegler, R., & Klahr, D. (1982). When do children learn? The relationship between existing knowledge and the acquisition of new knowledge. In R. Glaser (Ed.), *Advances in instructional psychology* (Vol. 2). Hillsdale, NJ: Lawrence Erlbaum Associates.

Siegler, R., & Shrager, J. (1984). A model of strategy choice. In C. Sophian (Ed.), *Origins of cognitive skills.* Hillsdale, NJ: Lawrence Erlbaum Associates.

Smith, J., Dixon, R., & Baltes, P. (1989). Expertise in life-planning: A new approach to investigating aspects of wisdom. In M. Commons, J. Sinnott, F. Richards, & C. Armon (Eds.), *Adult development: Vol. 1. Comparisons and applications of developmental models.* New York: Praeger.

Sternberg, R. (Ed.). (1984). *Mechanisms of cognitive development.* New York: Freeman.

Sternberg, R. (1989). Domain-generality versus domain-specificity: The life and impending death of a false dichotomy. *Merrill-Palmer Quarterly. 35,* 115–130.

Sternberg, R., & Powell, J. (1983). The development of intelligence. In P. Mussen (Ed.), *Carmichael's manual of child psychology* (4th ed.). New York: Wiley.

Sternberg, R., & Wagner, R. (Eds.). (1986). *Practical intelligence: Nature and origins of competence in the everyday world.* New York: Cambridge University Press.

Trabasso, T. (1975). Representation, memory, and reasoning: How do we make transitive inferences? In A. D. Pick (Ed.), *Minnesota Symposia on Child Psychology* (Vol. 9). Minneapolis: University of Minnesota Press.

Trabasso, T., Isen, A., Dolecki, P., McLanahan, A., Riley, C., & Tucker, T. (1978). How do children solve class-inclusion problems? In R. Siegler (Ed.), *Children's thinking: What develops?* Hillsdale, NJ: Lawrence Erlbaum Associates.

Vygotsky, L. (1962). *Thought and language.* Cambridge, MA: MIT Press.

Vygotsky, L. (1978). *Mind in society: The development of higher psychological processes.*

Cambridge, MA: Harvard University Press.

Weissberg, J., & Paris, S. (1986). Young children's remembering in different contexts: A reinterpretation of Istomina's study. *Child Development, 57,* 1123–1129.

Werner, H. (1948). *Comparative psychology of mental development.* New York: International Universities Press.

Wertsch, J. (1979). From social interaction to higher psychological processes. *Human Development, 22,* 1–22.

Willis, S., & Schaie, K. W. (1986). Practical intelligence in later adulthood. In R. Sternberg & R. Wagner (Eds.), *Practical intelligence: Nature and origins of competence in the everyday world.* New York: Cambridge University Press.

Wozniak, R. (1982). Metaphysics and science, reason and reality: The intellectual origins of genetic epistemology. In J. Broughton & D. J. Freeman-Moir (Eds.), *The cognitive-developmental psychology of James Mark Baldwin: Current theory and research in genetic epistemology.* Norwood, NJ: Ablex.

5 Information-Processing Approaches to Cognitive Development

David Klahr
Carnegie Mellon University

INTRODUCTION

Few psychologists would disagree with the claim that cognition involves the processing of information or that cognitive development involves changes in the content, structure, and processing of information. Indeed, since the 1970s, most of what has been discovered about children's thinking deals, in one way or another, with how they process information. However, if you asked different developmental psychologists to identify examples of information-processing approaches to cognitive development, you would probably find some interesting and important differences in their responses. Some might include the Piagetian and neo-Piagetian research that focuses on structures and structural changes. Others would limit the information-processing label to research that uses computer simulation to model developmental phenomena. Still others might point to the distinction between "classic" symbol-oriented information-processing theories (Newell & Simon, 1972) and more recent connectionist approaches (Bechtel & Abrahamsen 1991; Rumelhart & McClelland, 1986) to computational modeling of cognitive changes, arguing that only the latter are really suitable for modeling developmental processes (McClelland, 1989).

The nearly universal acceptance of the term *information processing,* when combined with diverse interpretations of its meaning, can conspire to bewilder and perplex the student of cognitive development. Which research paradigms exemplify information processing approaches? What are their merits? What have we learned about cognitive development from them? The goals of this chapter are twofold: (a) to describe the characteristic features of information-processing approaches to cognitive development, and (b) to illustrate what we have learned about children's cognitive development from the research characterized by different combinations of these features.

Defining "Information-Processing Approaches" to Cognitive Development

In psychology, as in all other scientific fields, research is carried out within the constraints of a set of basic theoretical assumptions and according to widely accepted methodological practices. Because they determine what questions will be asked and how they will be answered, these assumptions and practices can profoundly affect our understanding of cognition and its development. Information-processing approaches to cognitive development have their own characteristic set of theoretical assumptions and methodological practices. In this chapter, I attempt to reduce these to a manageable few: They are listed in Table 5.1. I organized this chapter around the list of assumptions and practices presented in Table 5.1. For each of the entries listed, I describe several studies, models, or findings that exemplify that entry. Although any particular example represents a combination of features listed in Table 5.1, I have attempted to locate them where they best illustrate the item being discussed.

The assumptions (A1, A2, and A3) and the practices associated with them (P1–P4) vary along what I have called a *soft-core* to *hard-core* continuum (Klahr, 1989). For example, some of the studies described in this chapter, while accepting assumptions A1 to A3, are not at all specific about any of

TABLE 5.1
Assumptions and Practices of Information-Processing Approaches to the
Study of Cognitive Development

Theoretical Assumptions

A1: Children's mental activity involves processes that manipulate symbols and symbol structures.

A2: These symbolic processes operate within an information-processing system having identifiable properties, constraints, and consequences.

A3: Cognitive development occurs via self-modification of the information-processing system.

Methodological Practices

P1: Use of highly detailed analyses of the environment facing the child on specific tasks.

P2: Use of formal notational schemes for expressing complex, dynamic systems.

P3: Measuring the time-course of cognitive processing over both relatively short durations (chronometric analysis) and medium durations (microgenetic studies).

P4: Use of high-density data from error patterns and protocols to induce and test complex models.

them, while other studies include computer-simulation models of how children accomplish some tasks. The former would be soft-core examples, and the latter would be hard core. With respect to the methodological practices, the soft end of P2 would involve the use of flow-charts and diagrams to describe a model of children's thinking, whereas the hard end would involve a computational model. In addition to varying along the hardness continuum, different examples vary with respect to how many of the assumptions and practices they reflect. Rather than treating these descriptors as a set of defining properties, they should be interpreted as likely properties of typical examples. That is, the information-processing notion itself is better expressed in terms of family resemblance than as an idea having clear defining properties. Before visiting the members of this family, it may be useful to explore a bit of its genealogy.

Origins

In the early 1970s, Roger Brown reviewed the previous two decades in an attempt to identify the forces that revitalized research in cognitive development in the late 1950s. One of them was the creation of computer simulation models of cognitive processes in adults. As Brown (1970) said:

> Since machines—hardware—could accomplish information processing of great complexity, it was obviously perfectly scientific and objective to attribute such processing to the human brain. Why limit the mind to association by contiguity and reinforcement when the computer, admittedly a lesser mechanism, could do so much more? Computers freed psychologists to invent mental processes as complex as they liked. (pp. ix–x)

The other force identified by Brown was America's discovery of Jean Piaget:

> computer simulation, psycholinguistics, curriculum reform, and mathematical models altered our notions of the scientific enterprise in such a way to cause us to see Piaget as a very modern psychologist. To see that he was, in fact, the great psychologist of cognitive development. (p. x)

Ten years prior to Brown's acknowledgment of the relevance and impact of computational models to the topics first addressed by Piaget, Herbert Simon (1962) had suggested the general form of an information-processing approach to cognitive development:

> If we can construct an information-processing system with rules of behavior that lead it to behave like the dynamic system we are trying to describe, then this system is a theory of the child at one stage of the development. Having

described a particular stage by a program, we would then face the task of discovering what additional information-processing mechanisms are needed to simulate developmental change—the transition from one stage to the next. That is, we would need to discover how the system could modify its own structure. Thus, the theory would have two parts—a program to describe performance at a particular stage and a learning program governing the transitions from stage to stage. (pp. 154–155)

Simon's suggestion contained two ideas that departed radically from the then prevailing views in developmental psychology.[1] The first idea was that theories about thinking could be stated as computer programs. These "computational models of thought," as they came to be called, have one important property that distinguishes them from all other types of theoretical statements: They independently execute the mental processes they represent. That is, rather than leaving it to the reader to interpret a verbal statement about what is involved in an analogical mapping or a memory search or a match between two symbols, computational models actually do the mapping, searching, and matching so that the complex implications of multiple processes can be unambiguously derived. The second idea in Simon's suggestion followed from the first: If different states of cognitive development could be described as programs, then the developmental process itself could also be described as a program that took the earlier program and transformed it into the later one. Such a program would have the capacity to alter and extend its own processes and structures. That is, it would be a computational model possessing some of the same self-modification capacities as the child's developing mind.

Today, the soft-core versions of Simon's two ideas form the cornerstone of a very large proportion of the research on both adult cognition and cognitive development. There is no question that in the field of adult cognition, information-processing approaches have had an enormous impact on both theory and methodology (Lachman, Lachman, & Butterfield, 1979; Palmer & Kimchi, 1986). One reason that the idea of thinking as information processing is so widespread is that it is highly nonspecific. As we shall see, different investigators draw quite different implications from this general notion. However, the hard-core version of A1 to A3—the "theory is the program" view expressed by Simon—has yet to become the dominant view in developmental psychology. Even among the many developmentalists who accept assumptions A1 to A3, there are relatively few who can point to examples in their own work of hard-core implemen-

---

[1] It is easy to forget just where the field was in the early 1960s. Note that the Kendlers' famous work on reversal shift, which challenged the prevailing notions of S–R learning by suggesting that an internal mediator played a role in concept acquisition, was published in the same year as Simon's (Kendler & Kendler, 1962).

tations of information-processing theories. Nevertheless, there is a general trend in the field toward "hardening the core," and throughout this chapter I refer to examples of the trend.

CHILDREN'S MENTAL ACTIVITY INVOLVES PROCESSES THAT MANIPULATE SYMBOLS AND SYMBOL STRUCTURES

The first of the assumptions listed in Table 5.1 is the most pervasive and, correspondingly, the most diffusely defined. In this section I illustrate the different meanings that assumption A1 has taken in the developmental literature. The examples will also describe some important findings about children's information processing. This is the pattern followed throughout the rest of the chapter: Specific examples illustrate the main features listed in Table 5.1, and describe a bit of what we know about how children think.

Symbolization in the most diffuse sense addresses the power of the child's representational capacity, without any concern with, or commitment to, how that capacity might be supported in a physical system. Examples include Piagetian accounts of "symbolic play" or imagery (Piaget, 1951). As information-processing accounts move along the soft to hard dimension, they use terms such as *symbol* and *symbol-structure* in ways that are both more mechanistic and more microscopic.

Newell (1980) defined the hard-core information-processing view of the role of symbols, symbol structures, and symbol manipulation in cognition. He defined a physical symbol system as one that:

> is capable of having and manipulating symbols, yet is also realizable within our physical universe . . . [This concept] has emerged from our growing experience and analysis of the computer and how to program it to perform intellectual and perceptual tasks. The notion of symbol that it defines is internal to this concept of a system. Thus, it is a hypothesis that these symbols are in fact the same symbols that we humans have and use everyday of our lives. Stated another way, the hypothesis is that humans are instances of physical symbol systems, and by virtue of this, mind enters into the physical universe. (p. 136)

The fundamental property of a symbol is that it can designate[2] something else (represented as a symbol structure). Such symbols comprise the elementary units in any representation of knowledge including sensory-motor knowledge or linguistic structures. Philosophical distinctions be-

---

[2]As Newell noted, many terms similar to designate could be used here: refer, denote, name, stand for, mean, etc.

tween dense and articulated symbols (Goodman, 1968) or personal and consensual symbols (Kolers & Smythe, 1984) emphasize the likelihood of idiosyncratic symbol structures for specific individuals, and the difference between internal symbol structures and their external referents. However, they are entirely consistent with Newell's Physical Symbol System hypothesis.

Are Preschoolers Presymbolic?

These terminological distinctions become important when one asks questions about the developmental course of symbolic capacity, because unless one is specific about the sense in which symbolic is intended, one will find inconsistent and contradictory results in the literature. A very clear distinction is made by DeLoache (1987) in her investigations of preschoolers' ability to use one thing to represent another.

DeLoache investigated this question by presenting children with a scale model of a full-sized room, and then determining the extent to which children understood the correspondences between the two. In one series of studies, children were familiarized with a room filled with assorted furniture, and they watched while a toy was hidden. Then they were shown a scale model of the room, and asked to find a miniature version of the toy. They were instructed that the miniature toy was in the "same place" in the model as the full-sized one was in the full-sized room, and they were instructed to try to find it. Following the retrieval from the model, the children were asked to find the original item. (This was done as a memory check to make sure that children had not forgotten where the toy was originally hidden.) For some children the role of the model and the full-size room was as just described, and for others it was reversed. Two age groups were used: a 2.5-year-old group and a 3-year-old group.

The results were dramatic. The older group found the toy on about 80% of the trials, while the younger group found it on less than 20%. Both groups could remember the original hiding place on about 80% of the trials, so faulty memory cannot explain the results. Nor was there any effect for whether the room or the model was used for the original hiding (with the model or room, respectively used as the retrieval location). In a second experiment, DeLoache used a photograph of the room, instead of the actual room, to indicate where the object was hidden. With this change, 2.5-year-old children were able to perform at nearly the same level as the 3-year-olds in the first experiment. DeLoache notes that this outcome is "directly contrary to the standard view of the efficacy of pictures versus real objects" (p. 1557).

Taken as a whole, DeLoache's results demonstrate an abrupt improvement between 30 and 36 months in children's ability to understand the symbolic relations between a model of a room and the real room. DeLoache summarizes this as a milestone in "the realization that an object can be understood both as a thing itself and as a symbol of something else" (DeLoache, 1987, p. 1556), and she notes that the younger children fail "to think about a symbolic object both as an object and as a symbol" (p. 1557). Thus, at the global (or conventional) level, DeLoache's results suggest that the 2.5-year-old children are presymbolic (at least on this task.) But it is clear that if one were to formulate detailed models of both the younger and older children's knowledge about this task, one would, in both cases, postulate systems that had the ability to process symbols at the microscopic level defined above. Thus, even in an ingenious research program—such as DeLoache's—directed at discovering rapid changes in the "symbolic functioning of very young children," the assumption of underlying symbol-processing capacity remains.

Knowledge Structures as Symbol Structures

Assumptions about the centrality of symbol structures are implicit in the "knowledge is power" approach to cognitive development. The general goal of this line of work is to demonstrate that much of the advantage adults have over children derives from their more extensive knowledge base in specific domains, rather than from more powerful general processes. But as Chi and Ceci (1987) comment, "saying that young children have less knowledge than older children or adults borders on triviality. The sheer quantity of knowledge, although important, is not nearly as important as how that knowledge is structured" (p. 115). Chi's studies (1976, 1977, 1978) provide convincing evidence for the influence of both more and better structured knowledge. In all of these investigations, Chi found that children who have more richly connected, domain-specific, knowledge than adults (e.g., children who have more knowledge than their adult counterparts about chess or dinosaurs or classmates' faces) outperform their adult counterparts on a range of tasks in which access to that knowledge is a determining factor in performance.

For example, in one study Chi (1978) examined the differences between adults and 10-year-olds on two tasks: a conventional digit span task and memory for chess positions. The children were all experienced chess players, and on a standard chess task, they performed slightly better than did the adults, who were novice chess players. The digit span task, presented to both groups, yielded the standard result: Adults' spans are greater than children's. The criterion chess task was memory for the location of pieces from various mid-game positions. Here, the children outperformed the adults. This general effect has been replicated many times, with a wide range of materials (Barrett, 1978; Lindberg, 1980).

In all of these, and related, studies, the major explanatory variable is access to symbolic structures (chunks, semantic nets, etc.) that support the superior performance of the children. Although, as Chi and Ceci (1987) argue, there exists "a lack of consensus on precisely what *structure* means" (p. 129), just about every definition includes the ability for one part of the structure to be connected to (or provide access to, or evoke, or derive inferences or generalizations from) some other part of the structure. And underlying any of these interpretations are just the kind of symbol structures described in Newell's concept of physical symbol systems.

SYMBOLIC PROCESSES OPERATE WITHIN AN INFORMATION-PROCESSING SYSTEM HAVING IDENTIFIABLE PROPERTIES, CONSTRAINTS, AND CONSEQUENCES

Developmentalists interested in a variety of cognitive processes have generally adopted the view of the adult information-processing system that emerged in the late 1960s and early 1970s (Atkinson & Shiffrin, 1968; Craik & Lockhart, 1972; Norman, Rumelhart, & the LNR Research Group, 1975). However, as in all other aspects of information processing, there is a wide range of interpretations and applications of the general idea of information processing that vary along the hard to soft dimension. In this section, I begin with a general description of a widely accepted view of the human information-processing system. Then I go on to describe some specific hard-core computational models. Following that I discuss some soft-core examples of information-processing systems.

The Organization of the Human Information-Processing System

The standard description of the human information-processing system includes several sensory buffers (e.g., "iconic" memory, an "acoustic buffer"), a limited capacity short-term memory (STM), and an unlimited, content-addressable long-term memory). This characterization is unabashedly derived from, and analogous to, the gross functional features of computer architectures. Nevertheless, as I argue later in this chapter, this does not imply that information-processing psychologists believe that the brain is structurally organized like a computer.

Newell (1972, 1973, 1981) originated the idea of a *cognitive architecture* of the mind. The idea has gone through successive elaborations, one of which is described in Card, Moran, and Newell's (1983) proposal for what they called the Model Human Processor (MHP). This is a model of the human information-processing system that includes not only the gross organization of the different information stores and their connections, but also estimates of processing rates and capacities. MHP was designed to facilitate predictions about human behavior in a variety of situations involving interactions between humans and computers. It was based on a vast amount of empirical data on human performance in perceptual, auditory, motor, and simple cognitive tasks.

Their model is illustrated in Fig. 5.1a and 5.1b. It includes a long-term memory, a working memory, two perceptual stores for visual and auditory information, and three subsystems for cognitive, motor, and perceptual processing. For each of these stores, there are associated estimates of storage capacity, decay times, cycle times, and the type of code as well as connectivity to the rest of the system.

> The perceptual system consists of sensors and associated buffer memories, the most important buffer memories being a Visual Image Store and an Auditory Image Store to hold the output of the sensory system while it is being symbolically coded. The cognitive system receives symbolically coded information from the sensory image stores in its Working Memory and uses previously stored information in Long-Term Memory to make decisions about how to respond. The motor system carries out the response. As an approximation, the information processing of the human will be described as if there were a separate processor for each subsystem: a Perceptual Processor, a Cognitive Processor, and a Motor Processor. For some tasks (pressing a key in response to a light) the human must behave as a serial processor. For other tasks (typing, reading, simultaneous translation) integrated, parallel operation of the three subsystems is possible, in the manner of three pipelined processors: information flows continuously from input to output with a characteristically short time lag showing that all three processors are working simultaneously.
>
> The memories and processors are described by a few parameters. The most important parameters of a memory are μ, the storage capacity in items, δ, the decay time of an item, and $\varkappa$, the main code type (physical, acoustic, visual, semantic). The most important parameter of a processor is τ, the cycle time. (Card et al., 1983, pp. 24–25)

Although the MHP was formulated to account for the perceptual and motor behavior of adults interacting with computers, it is a good example of the more general attempt to formulate a cognitive architecture of the mind. More specifically, it is a very successful integration of a general information-processing orientation with the constraints provided by a massive amount of experimental data on human performance. To date, no one has proposed a "kiddie" version of MHP, although some attempts have

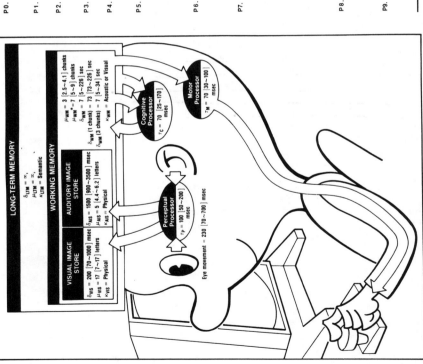

(a)

LONG-TERM MEMORY

$\delta_{LTM} = \infty$,
$\mu_{LTM} = \infty$,
$\kappa_{LTM} = $ Semantic

WORKING MEMORY

VISUAL IMAGE STORE

$\delta_{VIS} = 200\ [70\sim1000]$ msec
$\mu_{VIS} = 17\ [7\sim17]$ letters
$\kappa_{VIS} = $ Physical

AUDITORY IMAGE STORE

$\delta_{AIS} = 1500\ [900\sim3500]$ msec
$\mu_{AIS} = 5\ [4.4\sim6.2]$ letters
$\kappa_{AIS} = $ Physical

$\mu_{WM} = 3\ [2.5\sim4.1]$ chunks
$\mu^*_{WM} = 7\ [5\sim9]$ chunks
$\delta_{WM} = 7\ [5\sim226]$ sec
δ_{WM} (1 chunk) $= 73\ [73\sim226]$ sec
δ_{WM} (3 chunks) $= 7\ [5\sim34]$ sec
$\kappa_{WM} = $ Acoustic or Visual

Perceptual Processor
$\tau_P = 100\ [50\sim200]$ msec

Cognitive Processor
$\tau_C = 70\ [25\sim170]$ msec

Motor Processor
$\tau_M = 70\ [30\sim100]$ msec

Eye movement $= 230\ [70\sim700]$ msec

P0. *Recognize-Act Cycle of the Cognitive Processor.* On each cycle of the Cognitive Processor, the contents of Working Memory initiate actions associatively linked to them in Long-Term Memory; these actions in turn modify the contents of Working Memory.

P1. *Variable Perceptual Processor Rate Principle.* The Perceptual Processor cycle time τ_P varies inversely with stimulus intensity.

P2. *Encoding Specificity Principle.* Specific encoding operations performed on what is perceived determine what is stored, and what is stored determines what retrieval cues are effective in providing access to what is stored.

P3. *Discrimination Principle.* The difficulty of memory retrieval is determined by the candidates that exist in the memory, relative to the retrieval clues.

P4. *Variable Cognitive Processor Rate Principle.* The Cognitive Processor cycle time τ_C is shorter when greater effort is induced by increased task demands or information loads; it also diminishes with practice.

P5. *Fitt's Law.* The time T_{pos} to move the hand to a target of size S which lies a distance D away is given by:

$$T_{pos} = I_M \log_2 (D/S + .5),$$

where $I_M = 100\ [70\sim120]$ msec./bit.

P6. *Power Law of Practice.* The time T_n to perform a task on the nth trial follows a power law:

$$T_n = T_1 n^{-\alpha},$$

where $\alpha = .4\ [.2 - .6]$.

P7. *Uncertainty Principle.* Decision time T increases with uncertainty about the judgement or decision to be made:

$$T = I_C H,$$

where H is the information-theoretic entropy of the decision and $I_C = 150(0 \sim 157)$ msec./bit. For n equally probable alternatives (called Hick's Law),

$$H = \log_2 (n + 1).$$

For n alternatives with different probabilities, p_i, of occurrence,

$$H = \sum_i p_i \log_2 (1/p_i + 1).$$

P8. *Rationality Principle.* A person acts so as to attain his goals through rational action, given the structure of the task and his inputs of information and bounded by limitations on his knowledge and processing ability:

Goals + Task + Operators + Inputs + Knowledge + Process-limits → Behavior

P9. *Problem Space Principle.* The rational activity in which people engage to solve a problem can be described in terms of (1) a set of states of knowledge, (2) operators for changing one state into another, (3) constraints on applying operators, and (4) control knowledge for deciding which operator to apply next.

(b)

FIG. 5.1. (a) The Model Human Processor—memories and processors. Sensory information flows into Working Memory through the Perceptual Processor. Working memory consists of activated chunks in Long-Term Memory. The basic principle of operation of the Model Human Processor is the *Recognize-Act Cycle of the Cognitive Processor* (P0 in Fig. 5.1b). The Motor Processor is set in motion through activation of chunks in Working Memory been made to chart the developmental course of some of its parameters. (See the description of Kail's work in a later section.)

Production Systems

Cognition has both a serial and a parallel aspect to it. At both the underlying neural level, where massively parallel computations are occurring, and at the perceptual–cognitive interface, where the sense organs encode the external world for further processing by higher order mental processes, there must be a high degree of parallelism. On the other hand, both rational thought and motor acts from speech to locomotion require a certain degree of seriality. These considerations led Newell and Simon (1972) to propose a formalization of high-order mental processes in terms of condition-action rules called productions. Newell (1973) implemented this idea as a programming language, called PSG,[3] for creating computational models as running production systems.

Production systems are a class of computer-simulation models stated in terms of condition–action rules. A production system consists of two interacting data structures: (a) A *working memory* consisting of a collection of symbol structures called working memory *elements;* (b) A *production memory* consisting of condition–action rules called *productions,* the conditions of which describe configurations of working memory elements and the actions of which specify modifications to the contents of working memory. Production memory and working memory are related through the *recognize–act* cycle, which is comprised of three distinct processes:

1. The *match* process finds productions the conditions of which match against the current state of working memory. The same rule may match against working memory in different ways, and each such mapping is called an *instantiation.* When a particular production is instantiated, we say that its conditions have been satisfied. In addition to the possibility of a single production being satisfied by several distinct instantiations, several different productions may be satisfied at once. Both of these situations lead to conflict.
2. The *conflict resolution* process selects one or more of the instantiated productions for applications.

---

[3]PSG is an acronym for "Production System, version G." Although this was the first publically distributed general-purpose system for running production systems on computers, the "version G" implies that Newell had deemed its six precursor versions unsuitable for public consumption. For a brief account of the genealogy of production system languages see Neches, Langley, and Klahr (1987).

3. The *act* process applies the instantiated actions of the selected rules. Actions can include the modification of the contents of working memory, as well as external perceptual–motor acts.

Production systems can be thought of as complex, dynamic stimulus–response pairs in which both the S and the R involve symbolic structures. They provide both a parallel associative recognition memory, on the condition side, and a serial response on the action side. The basic recognize–act process operates in cycles, with one or more rules being selected and applied, the new contents of working memory leading another set of rules to be applied, and so forth.

Both Newell's PSG, and Anderson's (1983) ACT*, which combined production systems with semantic nets, provided computational languages for formulating cognitive models. More important, these systems were theoretical extensions of the standard model into some very specific proposals about how the human cognitive architecture is structured. These proposals took the form of a type of computational architecture—the production system—and production systems have since been used to model several aspects of cognitive development.

Production-System Models of Children's Performance

For developmentalists, one of the most valuable features of production systems is their potential to model the change process itself: their potential for self-modification. Later in this chapter, I explain why self-modification is such an important and powerful feature of hard-core information-processing models, and I describe some approaches that exploit this self-modification capacity. But first, I describe production-system models of children's performance at specific levels of development. These models, even though cast only as models of different performance levels, rather than as models of transition processes, serve useful functions.

In this section I describe four different ways in which *non* self-modifying production systems have been used to model children's performance. The first example illustrates how production systems can be matched to chronometric data to produce some estimates of the duration of elementary components of the recognize–act cycle. The second example illustrates one of the most valuable features of production systems for modeling cognitive development: the ease with which different performance levels can be represented by a family of models having different production sets. The third example focuses on how production systems can include encoding and performance productions in the same general format, and the final example illustrates a kind of vertical integration in a production-system model that represents several levels of knowledge from general principles down to specific encoding rules.

Quantification: Matching Production Firings to Chronometric Data. Production-system models of thinking were initially developed to account for the verbal protocols generated by subjects working on puzzles requiring several minutes to solve (Newell, 1966). However, a much finer temporal grain of analysis was used in the first production-system models that actually ran as computer simulations. Newell (1973) introduced PSG in the context of the Sternberg memory-scanning paradigm (described later in this chapter). The same volume (Chase, 1973) included a description of a model, written in PSG, of elementary processes for quantification: subitizing, counting, and adding (Klahr, 1973). Both of these models were atypical of most subsequent production-system models in that they attempted to account for chronometric data in terms of the dynamic properties of the production-system execution cycle. That is, they estimated the duration of specific microprocesses within the recognize–act cycle (such as the time to do a match, or the time to execute an action) by relating the number of such microprocess executions to the reaction-time data.

Although neither of these early models dealt with developmental data, the model of elementary quantification processes was subsequently elaborated into one that did deal with the differences in subitizing rates between children and adults (Klahr & Wallace, 1976, Chapter 3 & 8). The elaboration included two distinct working memories: one corresponding to the traditional short-term memory, and the other corresponding to an iconic store. Accordingly, the condition elements in productions could refer to either of these information sources, and the time parameters associated with matches in the two stores differed.

By attempting to constrain the model-building process with the chronometric data from very different domains, both Newell's model and Klahr and Wallace's model converged on a gross estimate of the time duration for the basic production-system cycle time of between 10 and 100 ms. While this may seem to be a fairly loose parameter estimate, it is important to note that it is not 1 ms, nor is it 1000 ms. That is, if the production cycle is constrained, even within these broad limits, then one can evaluate the plausibility of particular production systems in terms of whether they exhibit — within an order of magnitude — the same absolute as well as relative temporal patterns as do the humans they are modeling.

Production Systems for Different Levels of Performance.   Another use of production systems by developmentalists has been the sequence-of-models approach. The goal here is to produce a sequence of production-system models for a specific task such that each model represents a different level of performance. Once it has been demonstrated that the models can indeed produce the appropriate behavior at each level of performance, then one can examine the differences between successive models in order to infer what a transition mechanism would have to accomplish.

Baylor and Gascon (1974) did this type of analysis in their investigation of developmental differences in children's ability to do weight seriation. They presented children between the ages of 6 and 12 years old with a task in which the goal was to create an ordered series of identically appearing objects having different weights. Children could make pair-wise comparisons of the objects by using a balance scale, but they could not get an absolute measurement of an object's weight. Baylor and Gascon observed children's behavior as they weighed different pairs of objects and attempted to arrange them according to weight. From the sequence of children's pair-wise comparisons, Baylor and Gascon inferred a set of increasingly effective strategies. Each strategy was formulated as a production system having different collections of elementary components. Each of these production systems was implemented as a running computer program and the program's sequence of comparisons and the final outcome provided a good fit to individual children's sequences of object manipulations.

Klahr and Siegler (1978) used production systems in a different way: to take a soft-core information-processing model—one that had already shown an excellent fit to the children's performance—and extend it to a production-system format so as to get a better idea of its demands on short-term memory and its dynamic properties. Siegler had previously proposed an elegant analysis of rule sequences characterizing how children (from 3 years old to 17 years old) make predictions in several domains (Siegler, 1976, 1981), and the sequences were formulated as a series of increasingly elaborated binary decision trees. By recasting the rules as production systems, Klahr and Siegler were able to make a more precise characterization of what develops than was afforded by just the decision-tree representation. The following quotation from Klahr and Siegler (1978) conveys the level of detail that was facilitated by the production-system formulation.

> We can compare the four models [production system versions of Siegler's four "rule models"] at a finer level of analysis by looking at the implicit requirements for encoding and comparing the important qualities in the environment. Model I tests for sameness or difference in weight. Thus, it requires an encoding process that either directly encodes relative weight, or encodes an absolute amount of each and then inputs those representations into a comparison process. Whatever the form of the comparison process, it must be able to produce not only a same-or-different symbol, but if there is a difference, it must be able to keep track of which side is greater. Model II requires the additional capacity to make these decisions about distance as well

as weight. This might constitute a completely separate encoding and comparison system for distance representations, or it might be the same system except for the interface with the environment.

Model III needs no additional operators at this level. Thus, it differs from Model II only in the way it utilizes information that is already accessible to Model II. Model IV requires a much more powerful set of quantitative operators than any of the preceding models. In order to determine relative torque, it must first determine the absolute torque on each side of the scale, and this in turn requires exact numerical representation of weight and distance. In addition, the torque computation would require access to the necessary arithmetic production systems to actually do the sum of products calculations. (p. 80)

Representing the Immediate Task Context. One advantage of a production-system formulation is that it facilitates the extension of a basic model of the logical properties of a task to include the processing of verbal instructions, encoding of the stimulus, keeping track of where the child is in the overall task, and so on. For example, in their analysis of individual subject protocols on the balance scale, Klahr and Siegler proposed some models to account for some children's idiosyncratic—but consistent— response patterns. One of these models included not only the basic productions for a variant of one of Siegler's four models for balance scale predictions, but also a lot of other knowledge about the task context:

The model represents, in addition to the child's knowledge about how the balance scale operates, her knowledge about the immediate experimental context in which she is functioning. The trial-by-trial cycle during the training phase comprises (1) observation of the static display, (2) prediction of the outcome, (3) observation of the outcome, (4) comparison of the outcome with the prediction, and (5) revision if necessary of the criterion. . . . This model utilizes, in one way or another, representation of knowledge about when and how to encode the environment, which side has *more* weight or distance, which side has a *big* weight or distance, what the current criterion value is, what the scale is expected to do, what the scale actually did, whether the prediction is yet to be made or has been made, and whether it is correct or incorrect. (Klahr & Siegler, 1978, p. 89)

This kind of model raises two issues that might otherwise escape notice. First, what kinds of knowledge are necessary to generate these different encodings? It has long been known that surface variations in tasks can cause wide variation in children's performance—even on the tasks purported to index developmental level, such as class inclusion (Klahr & Wallace, 1972). Production-system formulations avoid the arbitrary dichotomy between performance demands and the so-called logical properties of a task, and force an unambiguous specification of all the processing necessary to complete the task. Second, how much of the encoded knowledge (i.e., the contents of working memory) must be available at any one moment? That is, in order to do the task, how much working memory capacity is required? Case (1986) addresses this issue informally in his proposed procedures for quantifying tasks in terms of their demands on the Short-Term Storage Space (STSS). However, without a clear and principled specification of the grain-size and computational power of the routines that use the contents of STSS, it is difficult to apply his demand-estimating procedure to a new domain.

Multiple-Level Production Systems: From General Rules to Detailed Encodings. Klahr and Wallace (1976) describe a model of children's performance on Piaget's conservation of quantity task. Their model contains productions dealing with several different levels of knowledge. At the highest level are productions that represent general conservation rules, such as "If you know about an initial quantitative relation, and a transformation, then you know something about the resultant quantitative relation." (See Klahr & Wallace, 1973, for an elucidation of these conservation rules.) At the next level are productions representing pragmatic rules, such as "If you want to compare two quantities, and you don't know about any prior comparisons, then quantify each of them." At an even lower level are rules that determine which of several quantification processes will actually be used to encode the external display (e.g., subitizing, counting, or estimation). Finally, at the lowest level, are productions for carrying out the quantification process. These are the same productions that comprised the systems described earlier in our discussion about matching production systems to chronometric data.

Although I have described this system as if there were a hierarchy of productions, there is only the flat structure of a collection of productions. Each production simply checks for its conditions. If it fires, then it deposits its results in working memory. The hierarchy emerges from the specific condition elements in each production, which ensure that productions only fire when the current context is relevant.

Nontransition Models: A Summary. These four instances by no means exhaust the set of computer simulations of children's thinking processes. Rabinowitz, Grant, and Dingley (1987) summarize over a score of other computer simulation models relevant to cognitive development, including those that use non-production-system architectures, and including both state and transition models. The production-system models include work on seriation (Baylor, Gascon, Lemoyne, & Pother, 1973; Young, 1976) and subtraction (Young & O'shea, 1981). Computer simulations based on schema architectures have been proposed in the area of arithmetic (Greeno, Riley, & Gelman, 1984; Kintsch & Greeno, 1985; Riley, Greeno, & Heller, 1983) and language acquisition (Hill, 1983). Task-specific architectures have been used to model children's performance on addition (Ashcraft, 1987; Siegler, 1988), subtraction (Brown & VanLehn, 1982), and series completion (Klahr & Wallace, 1970a). As Rabinowitz and colleagues observe, only a handful of these models include self-modifying mechanisms. Nevertheless, the underlying assumption in all of the computer simulations is that by clarifying the nature of children's thought at any particular level of development, the requirements of a transition theory become better defined.

Other Computational Models[4]

Production systems are not the only kind of computational model used to model children's thinking. In some cases, the researcher is not conforming to any particular theoretical assumptions about cognitive architectures, but still has a theory that is sufficiently complex that only a computational model will enable him or her to derive predictions from it. In such cases the researcher simply chooses to focus on the main data structures and computational processes, and employs an atheoretical computational architecture in which to formulate and run the model.

Siegler and Shrager (1984) proposed such a model to account for an unusually rich data set based on 4- and 5-year-old children's performance on simple addition problems (with sums less than 10). The model, shown in Fig. 5.2, is based on two basic ideas: (a) Children will retrieve answers from memory to problems that they are very certain about, and they will use other strategies (such as counting on their fingers) when they are not so sure; (b) Each possible problem (m + n) has a distribution of possible responses associated with it (see Fig. 5.2a). Some problems (e.g., 1 + 2) have very sharply peaked distributions, so that a single answer (3), is strongly associated with the problem. Other problems have distributions of possible answers that are bimodal (e.g., both 5 and 7 are likely to be retrieved in response to the problem 3 + 4), or relatively flat (e.g., 5 + 3), so that several answers are weakly associated with the problem. Siegler and Shrager elaborated these rather general and intuitive notions into a computational model that both acquired the distributions of associations with

---

[4]The computational models described in this chapter are all variants of the symbol-oriented approach to cognition, in contrast to the connectionist (or parallel distributed processing — PDP — approach). In the penultimate section on "Constraints and Limitations," I discuss some of the potential contributions of connectionist approaches to information processing in children.

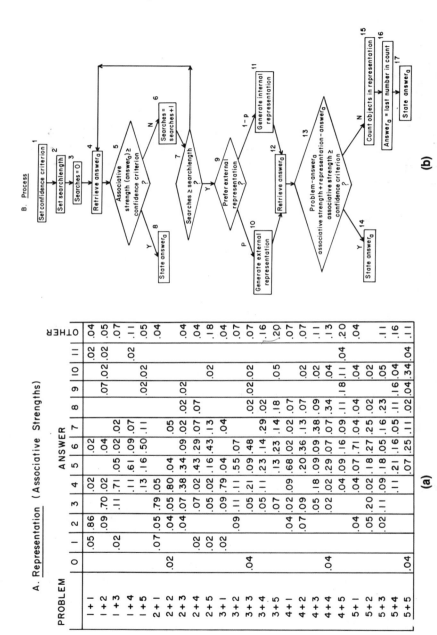

B. Process

A. Representation (Associative Strengths)

(a)

(b)

FIG. 5.2. (a) Associative strengths for the strategy choice model. Rows correspond to problems of the form $m + n$, columns refer to possible answers to problems, and table entries show the associative strength between a given problem and answer. (b) Flow chart for the strategy choice model. "$answer_a$" refers to whichever answer is retrieved on the particular retrieval effort; "problem-$answer_a$ associative strength" refers to the association between the elaborated representation and the retrieved answer (from Siegler & Shrager 1984).

training, and responded to problem probes according to the current distributions.

The model first attempts a direct retrieval. If the associative strength is not sufficiently high, it goes on to the later stages in which some additional representation (such as putting up fingers, or imaging the sets) is used. The model is very successful at accounting for some otherwise puzzling relations among several measures, including proportion of overt strategy use, error rates, and mean solution times. Figure 5.2 depicts the model as a flow-chart. Its computational implementation was written in a programming language that was simply a straightforward conversion of the flow chart. That is, the computational model was not constrained by any issues of working memory, a recognize–act cycle, or the structure of semantic memory.

Implicit Architectures

Soft-core information-processing approaches are not very explicit about the structures or processes that are involved in thinking and development. Case's (1985, 1986) theory of cognitive development illustrates the use of what I call *implicit architectures*. Case postulated *figurative schemes, state representations, problem representations, goals, executive control structures,* and *strategies* in order to account for performance at specific levels of development, and *search, evaluation, retagging,* and *consolidation* to account for development from one performance level to the next. More recently, he has suggested that children can overcome the limitations of short-term memory by acquiring "central conceptual structures" (Case & Griffin, 1990).

Although Case made no explicit reference to symbol structures, his central theoretical construct—what he called Short-Term Storage Space (STSS)—implies that what occupies this space are symbols and symbol structures. Furthermore, the STSS construct assumes that a limited-capacity bottleneck in both storage capacity and computational power accounts for the characteristic differences that many theorists associate with distinct stages of cognitive development. In summary, Case's theoretical constructs appear to require the further assumption of a limited capacity computational architecture that funnels its computational results through the STSS.

Typical of soft-core approaches to information processing in children are models that focus on the structure of thought, without explicit attention to the nature of a computational system that could support that abstract structure. Such approaches, best exemplified by Piaget, have been recently refined and extended by such theorists as Halford (1975) and Fischer (1980). For example, Fischer's skill theory is cast entirely in terms of abstract structures with scant attention to processes. The transition processes that he does discuss — substitution, focusing, compounding, differentiation, and intercoordination — are presented in terms of their global characteristics, and are not constrained by any explicit architecture.

COGNITIVE DEVELOPMENT OCCURS VIA SELF-MODIFICATION OF THE INFORMATION-PROCESSING SYSTEM

Regardless of its location on the hard-soft dimension, every information-processing approach is predicated on the assumption that cognitive development can be characterized as self-modification. This includes accounts ranging from Piaget's original assertions about assimilation, accommodation, and the active construction of the environment, to proposals for various kinds of structural reorganizations (e.g., Case, 1986; Fischer, 1980; Halford, 1970; Kuhn, this volume), to interaction between performance and learning (Siegler, 1987), to explicit mechanisms for self-modifying computer models (Klahr, Langely, & Neches, 1987; Simon, Newell, & Klahr, 1991). This emphasis on self-modification does not deny the importance of external influences such as direct instruction, modeling, and the social context of learning and development. However, it underscores the fact that whatever the external context, the information-processing system itself must ultimately encode, store, index, and process that context. Here too, soft-core approaches tend to leave this somewhat vague and implicit, whereas hard-core approaches make specific proposals about some or all of these processes. However, all information-processing approaches to development acknowledge the fundamental importance of the capacity for self-modification.

Hard-Core Approaches to Self-Modification

In discussing self-modification, I do not make a distinction between learning and development. Instead, I use the more neutral term *change*. (See Klahr, 1989, for a discussion of whether self-modifying production systems are best thought of as models of learning or of development.) It will be understood that change is imposed by the system's own information-processing mechanisms (hence *self-modification*). *Learning* is usually defined as "the improvement of performance over time," but such monotonicity is not assumed here. Indeed, in many areas of development, the measured trajectory is U-shaped, rather than monotone (Strauss, 1982), and a theory of change must ultimately account for these cases.

Many general principles for change have been proposed in the developmental literature. These include: equilibration, encoding, efficiency, redundancy elimination, search reduction, self-regulation, consistency detection, and so on. However, they are not computational mechanisms. That is, they do not include a specification of how information is encoded, stored, accessed, and modified. It is one thing to assert that the cognitive system seeks to avoid unnecessary processing; it is quite another to formulate a computational model that actually does so.

Adoption of a production system architecture allows one to pose focused questions about how broad principles might be implemented as specific mechanisms. One way to do this is to assume the role of a designer of a self-modifying production system, and consider the issues that must be resolved in order to produce a theory of self-modification based on the production-system architecture. The two primary questions are:

1. What are the basic change mechanisms that lead to new productions? Examples are generalization, discrimination, composition, proceduralization, and strengthening.
2. What are the conditions under which these change mechanisms are evoked: when an error is noted, when a rule is applied, when a goal is achieved, or when a pattern is detected?

The recognize–act cycle offers three points at which change can have an effect: A production system's repertoire of behaviors can be changed by affecting the outcome of (a) production matching, (b) conflict resolution, and (c) production application. Each of these is discussed in detail in Neches, Langley, and Klahr (1987), and they are summarized here.

1. Change during the match. The most commonly used technique for altering the set of applicable productions found by the matching process is to add new productions to the set. One way to generate the new productions is to modify the conditions of existing rules. Anderson, Kline, and Beasley (1978) were the first to modify production system models of human learning via *generalization* and *discrimination*. The first mechanism creates a new rule (or modifies an existing one) so that it is more general than an existing rule, while retaining the same actions. The second mechanism—discrimination—creates a new rule (or modifies an existing one) so that it is less general than an existing rule, while still retaining the same actions. The two mechanisms lead to opposite results, although in most models they are not inverses in terms of the conditions under which they are evoked.

2. Change during conflict resolution. Once a set of matching rule instantiations has been found, a production-system architecture still must make some determination about which instantiation(s) in that set will be executed. Thus, conflict resolution offers another decision point in the

recognize–act cycle where the behavior of the system can be affected.

The knowledge represented in a new production is essentially a hypothesis about the correctness of that production. A self-modifying system must maintain a balance between the need for feedback obtained by trying new productions and the need for stable performance obtained by relying on those productions that have proven themselves successful. This means that the system must distinguish between rule *applicability* and rule *desirability*, and be able to alter its selections as it discovers more about desirability. Production systems have embodied a number of schemes for performing conflict resolution, ranging from simple fixed orderings on the rules, to various forms of weights or strengths, to complex schemes that are not uniform across the entire set of productions, to no resolution at all.

3. Changing conditions and actions. Various change mechanisms have been proposed that lead to rules with new conditions and actions. *Composition* was originally proposed by Lewis (1978) to account for speedup as the result of practice. This method combines two or more rules into a new rule with the conditions and actions of the component rules. However, conditions that are guaranteed to be met by one of the actions are not included. For instance, composition of the two rules: AB → CD and DE → F would produce the rule ABE → CDF.

Another mechanism for creating new rules is *proceduralization* (Neves & Anderson, 1981). This involves constructing a very specific version of some general rule, based on some instantiation of the rule that has been applied. This method can be viewed as a form of discrimination learning because it generates more specific variants of an existing rule. However, the conditions for application tend to be quite different, and the use to which these methods have been put have quite different flavors. For instance, discrimination has been used almost exclusively to account for reducing search or eliminating errors, whereas proceduralization has been used to account for speedup effects and automatization.

A basic mechanism for change via chunking was initially proposed by Rosenbloom and Newell (1982, 1987) and first used to explain the power law of practice (the time to perform a task decreases as a power-law function of the number of times the task has been performed). The learning curves produced by their model are quite similar to those observed in a broad range of learning tasks. The chunking mechanism and the production-system architecture to support it has evolved into a major theoretical statement about the nature of the human cognitive system. The system (called Soar) represents the most fully elaborated candidate for a complete cognitive theory—a "unified theory of cognition" as Newell (1990) calls it. It would require a substantial extension of the present chapter to give a comprehensive overview of Soar. However, because the Soar architecture has been used in a recently developed theory of conservation acquisition to be described later, I briefly summarize its main features here.

The Soar architecture is based on formulating all goal-oriented behavior as search in problem spaces. A problem space consists of a set of states and a set of operators that move between states. A goal is formulated as the task of reaching one of a desired set of states from a specified initial state. Under conditions of perfect knowledge, satisfying a goal involves starting at the initial state and applying a sequence of operators that result in a desired state being generated. Knowledge is represented as productions. When knowledge is not perfect, the system may not know how to proceed. For example, it may not know which of a set of operators should be applied to the current state. When such an impasse occurs, Soar automatically generates a subgoal to resolve the impasse. These subgoals are themselves processed in additional problem spaces, possibly leading to further impasses. The overall structure is one of a hierarchy of goals, with an associated hierarchy of problem spaces. When a goal is terminated, the problem solving that occurred within the goal is summarized in new productions called chunks. If a situation similar to the one that created the chunk ever occurs again, the chunk fires to prevent any impasse, leading to more efficient problem solving.

Soar contains one assumption that is both parsimonious and radical. It is that all change is produced by a single mechanism: chunking. The chunking mechanism forms productions out of the elements that led to the most recent goal achievement. What was at first a search through a hierarchy of subgoals becomes, after chunking, a single production that eliminates any future search under the same conditions. Chunking is built into the Soar architecture as an integral part of the production cycle. It is in continual operation during performance—there is no place at which the performance productions are suspended so that a set of chunking productions can fire. Chunking occurs at all levels of sub-goaling, and in all problem spaces. (Soar operates entirely through search in problem spaces: Spaces for encoding the environment, for applying operators, for selecting operators, etc.) Chunking reduces processing by extending the knowledge base of the system.

Simon et al. (1991) used Soar as the theoretical context in which to formulate a computation model of how children acquire number conservation. Their model, called Q-Soar, simulates a training study (Gelman, 1982) in which 3- and 4-year-old children were given a brief training session that was sufficient to move them from the classical nonconserving behavior to the ability to conserve small and large numbers. Q-Soar is designed to satisfy several desirable features of computational models of cognitive development: (a) It is based on a principled cognitive architecture (in this case Newell's Soar theory of cognition); (b) It is constrained by general regularities in the large empirical literature on number conservation; (c) It generates the same behavior as do the children in the specific training study being modeled. That is, it starts out by being unable to pass number conservation tasks, and then, based on the chunks that it forms during the training study, it is able to pass post-tests that include both small and large number conservation tests.

> Q-SOAR's design presumes that young children acquire number conservation knowledge by measurement and comparison of values to determine the effects of transformations on small collections of discrete objects. Having been shown a transformation to a set of objects, the child first categorizes the transformation and then initiates a conservation judgment about the transformation's effect. Ideally, categorization will identify the observed transformation as an instance of a larger class, with effects that are known to be associated (through chunking) with this class. If not, then pre- and post-transformation values created by measurement processes are compared to determine the effect of the transformation. The learning over this processing creates new knowledge about this kind of transformation, which will become available on future occurrences in similar contexts. Now the transformation's effects can be stated without the need for any empirical processing. In other words, the necessity of the effects is recognized. (Simon et al., 1991, p. 438)

Are Other Mechanisms Necessary?   Although these processes—generalizations, discrimination, composition, proceduralization, and chunking—may be necessary components of a computational change theory, they may not be sufficient. It is not yet clear whether they could account for the observed differences between the strategies employed by experts and novices (Hunter, 1968; Larkin, 1981; Lewis, 1981; Simon & Simon, 1978). The reorganization necessary to get from novice to expert level may involve much more than refinements in the rules governing when suboperations are performed. Such refinements could presumably be produced by generalization and discrimination mechanisms. However, producing a new procedure requires the introduction of new operations. Those new operations may require the introduction of novel elements or goals—something that generalization, discrimination, and composition and chunking are not clearly able to do.

There are only two simulation studies in which change sequences, and the intermediate procedures produced within them, have been directly observed. Fortunately, a similar picture emerges from both studies. Anzai and Simon (1979) examined a subject solving and re-solving a five-disk Tower of Hanoi puzzle.[5] They found a number of changes in procedure that seemed

---

[5]This puzzle—widely used in psychological studies of problem solving—consists of a "pyramid" of N disks stacked on one of three pegs. The disks are graduated in size, with the

to require more than the processes listed previously. These included eliminating moves that produced returns to previously visited problem states, establishing subgoals to perform actions that eliminated barriers to desired actions, and transforming partially specified goals (e.g., moving a disk off a peg) into fully specified goals (e.g., moving the disk from the peg to a specific other peg).

Neches (1981) traced procedure development in the command sequences issued by expert users of a computer graphics editing system. He found a number of changes that involved reordering operations and replanning procedure segments on the basis of efficiency considerations. Subjects were able to evaluate their own efficiency at accomplishing goals and to invent new procedures to reach the same goals more efficiently. Based on these studies, as well as his observations of children "inventing" a novel and efficient strategy for doing simple addition, Neches (1987) created a self-modifying production system called HPM (for Heuristic Procedure Modification). Although these studies just cited deal with adult subjects, the self-modifying processes used by the adults are very likely to be some of the same ones involved in developmental changes.

Metacognition and Information-Processing Approaches

The important point in these examples is that change appears to involve reasoning on the basis of knowledge about the structure of procedures in general, and the semantics of a given procedure in particular. In each example, procedures were modified through the construction of novel elements rather than through simple deletions, additions, or combinations of existing elements.

Beyond the hard-core approaches, this kind of self-analysis of procedures and their byproducts is usually treated as an issue of "metacognition." As Kuhn (this volume) points out, hard-core information-processing approaches have not had a lot to say about metacognition, or reflection, or consciousness, at least not directly. However, HPM is one clear instantiation of the notion, and it is also captured to some extent the way that Soar forms chunks out of the goal trace and local context for satisfied subgoals.

Perhaps the most elaborate consideration of metacognitive processing appears in the "time line processing" sketched by Wallace, Klahr, and Bluff

---

largest disk on the bottom of the stack. The goal is to move the stack from the initial peg to a goal peg, subject to two constraints: (a) only one disk can be moved at a time; (b) a larger disk can never be placed on a smaller disk. The minimum number of moves required to move the N-disk stack from one peg to another is $2^N - 1$. Thus a 5-disk problem requires a minimum of 31 moves. A three-disk version, adapted for use with preschoolers by Klahr and Robinson (1981) is described later in this chapter.

(1987). Wallace et al. described a plan for a self-modifying production system called BAIRN (a Scottish term for child) in which a continuous record of the initial and final conditions of production firings is kept in a time line that provides a sequential record of processing activity. BAIRN learns about the world by processing the information in the time line.

> At first, this information is very primitive, being based [on] only the results of BAIRN's innate endowment of primitive perceptual and motor nodes. As . . . [BAIRN's knowledge of the world] gets more elaborated, so does the information available for processing the time line, as richer and more powerful nodes are added to long-term memory. (Wallace et al., 1987, pp. 360–361)

The general idea in systems like BAIRN, Soar, or HPM is to include mechanisms that enable the system to improve its performance by accessing information about the context and effectiveness of its earlier performance. These mechanisms allow the systems to exhibit the type of behavior that, when seen in humans, is classified as metacognitive.

To the best of my knowledge, only one developmentalist has made the explicit mapping between an information-processing model and metacognition. Siegler's (1989) model of children's strategy choice in multiplication exhibits the emergent property of a rational choice of an efficient and effective strategy. In that model, strategy choices about whether to retrieve the answer to a problem from memory or to calculate the result are made without any rational calculation of the advantages and disadvantages of each strategy. One of the most important features of Siegler's model is that:

> it indicates in detail how a self-regulatory process could operate. The need for self-regulatory processes — executive processes, metacomponents, autonomous regulation, and so on has been persuasively argued previously, but the way in which they accomplish their function has not been clearly elaborated. The present mechanism both resembles and differs from previous suggestions. The mechanism resembles Piagetian and Vygotskian suggestions in that the child's own activity determines future strategy choices. It differs from these and numerous other approaches, however, in that the self-regulation does not depend on reflection or on any other separate governmental process. Instead, it is part and parcel of the system's basic retrieval mechanism. (Siegler, 1988, p. 272)

Summary: Production Systems as Frameworks for Cognitive Developmental Theory

In this section I provide a brief overview of issues that arise in applying production-system architectures to the areas of learning and development.

The framework rests on three fundamental premises of the hard-core approach:

1. The structure of production-system architectures provides insight into the nature of the human information-processing system architecture. This premise derives from observations about similarities in terms of both structural organization and behavioral properties. Structurally, production systems provide a plausible characterization of the relations between long-term memory and working memory, and about the interaction between procedural and declarative knowledge. Behaviorally, strong analogies can be seen between humans and production systems with respect to their abilities to mix goal-driven and event-driven processes, and with their tendency to process information in parallel at the recognition level and serially at higher cognitive levels.

2. Change is a fundamental aspect of intelligence; we cannot say that we fully understand cognition until we have a model that accounts for its development. The first 20 years of information-processing psychology devoted scant attention to the problems of how to represent change processes, other than to place them on an agenda for future work. Indeed, almost all of the information-processing approaches to developmental issues followed the two-step strategy outlined in the Simon quotation that opened this chapter: First, construct the performance model, and then follow it with a change model that operates on the performance model. In recent years, as researchers have finally started to work seriously on the change process, they have begun to formulate models that inextricably link performance and change. Self-modifying production systems are one such example of this linkage.

3. All information-processing system architectures, whether human or artificial, must obey certain constraints in order to facilitate change. It is these constraints that give rise to the seemingly complex particulars of individual production-system architectures. Thus, following from our second premise, an understanding of production-system models of change is a step toward understanding the nature of human development and learning.

The Computer's Role in Simulation Models

Given the centrality of computer simulation to hard-core information processing, it may be useful to address a few common misunderstandings about the role of the computer in psychological theory. First of all, it is important to distinguish between the theoretical content of a program that runs on a computer and the psychological relevance of the computer itself. Hard-core information-processing theories are sufficiently complex that it is necessary to run them on a computer in order to explore their implications. However, this does not imply that the theory bears any resemblance to the computer on which it runs. Meteorologists who run computer simulations of hurricanes do not believe that the atmosphere works like a computer. Furthermore, the same theory could be implemented on computers having radically different underlying architectures and mechanisms. Failure to make the distinction between theory and computer leads to the common misconception that information-processing approaches can be arranged along a dimension of "how seriously they take the computer as a model" (Miller, 1983, p. 250). It would be counterproductive to take the computer at all seriously as a model for cognitive development, because the underlying computer does not undergo the necessary self-modification.

The first computer simulations of developmental phenomena were intended to explain distinct performance levels along a developmental trajectory. These early models did not contain any self-modification mechanisms. Instead, they were intended to explicate the complex requirements for a self-modifying system (an explication entirely absent from Genevan accounts of equilibration). Critics of these early simulation models (Beilin, 1983; Brown, 1982) faulted them for their lack of attention to issues of transition and change. However, the critics failed to appreciate the principal virtue of computational models of distinct developmental levels: that they sharpened the question of self-modification in a way that is simply unattainable in more traditional verbal formulations of developmental theories. In the past few years, several self-modifying systems have been created. These systems—some of which were described in the previous section—exhibit the same performance that, when observed in humans, has been labeled as either learning or development.

A similar misunderstanding of the role of the computer in hard-core information-processing models may have lead to Brown's (1982) widely quoted (but misdirected) criticism that "A system that cannot grow, or show adaptive modification to a changing environment, is a strange metaphor for human thought processes which are constantly changing over the life span of an individual" (p. 100). I agree, but as evidenced by the systems described earlier, the criticism does not apply here: we have some hard-core information-processing approaches that propose very explicit mechanisms for "adaptive modification to a changing environment."

The hard-core information-processing approaches are serious, not about the similarity between humans and computers, but rather about the extent to which intelligent behavior—and its development—can be accounted for by a symbol-processing device that is manifested in the physical world. The strong postulate for hard-core information-processing is that both computers and humans are members of the class of "physical symbol systems" (Newell, 1980), and that some of the theoretical constructs and insights that have come out of computer science are relevant for cognitive developmental theory. One such insight is what Palmer and Kimchi (1986) call the *recursive decomposition* assumption: Any nonprimitive process can be specified more fully at a lower level by decomposing it into a set of subcomponents and specifying the temporal and informational flows among the subcomponents. This is a good example of how abstract ideas from computer science have contributed to hard-core information processing: "It is one of the foundation stones of computer science that a relatively small set of elementary processes suffices to produce the full generality of information processing" (Newell & Simon, 1972, p. 29). An important consequence of decomposition is that

> . . . the resulting component operations are not only quantitatively simpler than the initial one, but *qualitatively different* from it. . . . Thus we see that higher level information-processing descriptions sometimes contain *emergent properties* that lower level descriptions do not. It is the *organization* of the system specified by the flow relations among the lower level components that gives rise to these properties. (Palmer & Kimchi, 1986, pp. 52–53)

The importance of emergent properties cannot be overemphasized, for it provides the only route to explaining how intelligence — be it in humans or machines — can be exhibited by systems comprised of unintelligent underlying components — be they synapses or silicon. Even if one defines underlying components at a much higher level — such as production systems or networks of activated nodes, emergent properties still emerge, for that is the nature of complex systems.

The emergent property notion provides the key to my belief that hard-core information-processing approaches provide a general framework, particular concepts, and formal languages that make possible the formulation of powerful theories of cognitive development. The fundamental challenge is to account for the emergence of intelligence. Intelligence must develop from the innate kernel. The intelligence in the kernel, and in its self-modification processes, will be an emergent property of the *organization* of elementary (unintelligent) mechanisms for performance, learning, and development. Thus, the issue is not "sacrificing explanatory breadth for explanatory precision" (Kuhn, this volume), but rather achieving explanatory breadth on the basis of the emergent properties revealed by explanatory precision.

USING HIGHLY DETAILED ANALYSES
OF THE ENVIRONMENT FACING THE CHILD
ON SPECIFIC TASKS

The realization that investigation of psychological processes presupposes a highly developed, abstract analysis of the task and available constraints has perhaps been the major advance in psychology in the last several decades. (Kellman, 1988, p. 268)

Kellman's observation echoes Simon's (1969, Chap. 2) well-known parable of the ant, whose complex path toward a goal was characterized as a set of simple mechanisms encountering a complex and irregular environment. Simon's claim was that, in the human as well as in the ant, much of the apparent complexity of behavior is a function of the complexity of the environment rather than of the cognitive system. This insight is particularly important for developmentalists, for it demands that our explanations for changes in behavior include an account of changes in both the organism and the environment in which it is embedded.

All of the methodological practices to be described in the remainder of this chapter start with a careful task analysis. Both chronometric techniques and error analysis require at least a rudimentary analysis of the task environment. In addition, there are some information-processing approaches in which complex and detailed task analysis plays a central role, even when neither error analysis nor chronometrics are used. In a sense, these approaches consist of nothing but task analysis. While such work is typically preliminary to further work in either error analysis or computer simulation (or both), it is often useful for its own sake, as it clarifies the nature of the tasks facing children.

Klahr and Wallace's (1970b) task analysis of class inclusion is an early example of such a formal characterization of an important developmental task. Their goal was to illustrate how a common "Piagetian experimental task" (i.e., the full set of test items that are typically given when assessing class inclusion competence, including finding some objects, finding all objects, comparing subsets of objects, etc.) involved the coordination of several more basic information processes. They proposed a network of interrelated processes—similar to Gagne's (1968) learning hierarchies—in which some processes had common subcomponents, while others were relatively independent. Klahr and Wallace's analysis enabled them to explain how surface variations in a task could invoke different processes, that, in turn, would have profound effects on performance, even though the underlying formal logic of the task remained invariant.

In the area of children's counting, Greeno, Riley, and Gelman (1984) formulated a model for characterizing children's competence. Their model is much more complex than the early Klahr and Wallace analysis of classification, but it is fundamentally similar with respect to being a formal task analysis whose primary goal is to elucidate the relations among a set of underlying components.

Klahr and Carver (1988) used a formal task analysis to design an instructional unit to teach elementary school children how to debug computer programs. The unit was designed to be inserted in the normal curriculum for teaching a graphics programming language. Children tend to write programs that are "buggy," that is, programs in which the desired picture does not match the picture drawn by the child's program. Children typically fail to acquire very effective procedures for debugging programs, so Klahr and Carver attempted to teach the necessary skills explicitly. First they analyzed the components of debugging into four distinct phases.

1. Bug identification—the child generates a description of the discrepancy between the program plan (e.g., what the desired picture should look like) and the program output (e.g., what the program actually drew). Based on the discrepancy description, propose specific types of bugs that might be responsible for the discrepancy.

2. Program representation—the child articulates the structure of the program in order to investigate the probable location of the buggy command in the program listing.

3. Bug location—the child uses the cues gathered in the first two phases to examine the program in order to locate the alleged bug.

4. Bug correction—the child examines the program plan to determine the appropriate correction, replaces the bug with the correction in the program, and then reevaluates the program.

Based on the formal task analysis, Klahr and Carver then created a production system model that could actually do the debugging, and they used the productions in the model to specify a set of cognitive objectives for insertion in a programming curriculum (Carver, 1986). In addition to the instructional elements, their debugging model provided a framework for assessment of debugging skills, for creation of transfer tasks, and for evaluation of transfer. Thus, the entire instructional intervention (which was very successful in teaching debugging skills) was based on the initial task analysis.

USING FORMAL NOTATIONAL SCHEMES
FOR EXPRESSING COMPLEX,
DYNAMIC SYSTEMS

The use of computer-simulation languages is the sine qua non of hard-core information processing. Nevertheless, there are several lesser degrees of formalization that mark the soft-core methods, including such devices as scripts, frames, flow charts, tree diagrams, and pseudo-programming languages. The attractive property of any of these formal notations is that they tend to render explicit what may have only been implicit, and they frequently eliminate buried inconsistencies. That is, compared to verbal statements of theoretical concepts and mechanisms, each of these notations offers increased precision and decreased ambiguity.

Flow charts are perhaps the most common type of formal notation used by information-processing psychologists. For example, Sternberg and Rifkin (1979) used a single flow chart to represent four distinct models of analogical reasoning. Their depiction clearly indicates how the models are related and what parameters are associated with each component of each model.

Another type of formal notation commonly used in research on children's comprehension of stories is the *story grammar* (Mandler & Johnson, 1977; Stein & Glenn, 1979). Nelson has analyzed children's event representations in terms of *scripts* (Nelson & Gruendel, 1981). Mandler (1983) provides a comprehensive summary of how these kinds of representations have been used in developmental theory. In both areas, the underlying theoretical construct is the *schema:* an organized knowledge structure containing both fixed and variable components. The fixed components bear relations that are characteristic of the general properties of the situation represented by the schema, and the variable components represent the specific instance that is currently being processed. For example, a story grammar would have components for the main protagonist, the goal or intent of the protagonist, an obstacle or threat to the achievement of the goal, and the resolution of the threat. For event representations, children appear to have scripts for common activities such as going to a restaurant, in which the fixed components include driving, parking, ordering, eating, and paying, and the variable components might include the order in which the events occur (e.g., pay before or after eating), the particular things ordered, the seating arrangement, and so on.

As with any other of the constructs used in information-processing approaches, the schema construct can be used in a variety of ways, and with varying degrees of ambiguity (Mackworth, 1987). However, it is possible to be quite specific about what one means by the term. For example, Hill and Arbib (1984) attempted to clarify some of the different senses in which the term *schema* has been used, and they go on to describe a schema-based computational model of language acquisition.

Given this range of notational options for describing information-processing theories, what criteria should be used in choosing among them? This issue is discussed at length by Klahr and Siegler (1978). They suggest that the following four criteria be used in choosing a representation:

1. Is the representation sufficient to account for behavior? Does it have a clear mapping onto the empirical base for which it is supposed to account?

2. Is the representation amenable to multiple-level analyses? Is it easy to aggregate and disaggregate the grain of explanation? That is, can one easily go from a characterization of the average behavior of a group of children to more specific models that capture individual performance? For the design of well-controlled experiments or curriculum design, the representation will have to be stated in terms of averages across many subjects; it must be a modal form. For detailed study of individual strategies and component processes, it must be capable of disaggregation without drastic revision.

3. Is the representation consistent with well-established processing constraints?

4. Does the representation have "developmental tractability" (Klahr & Wallace, 1970a)? That is, does it allow the theorist to state both early and later forms of competence and provide an easy interpretation of each model as both a precursor and successor of other models in a developmental sequence?

What about mathematical models of developmental phenomena? Should they be included in the set of formal notational schemes that signal soft-core information processing? The situation is not straightforward. On the one hand, mathematical modeling certainly meets the criteria of formalization and precision. Indeed, the following argument for mathematical models could equally well be made for computational models.

> It is precisely because the phenomena are so complex that we must have mathematics. Even in relatively simple (one might suppose) areas of psychology, a reader of the literature can easily be led down the primrose path through verbal argument. The logic seems impeccable. However, when the psychological principles on which the theory is based are put into mathematical form, the stated predictions may fail to follow at all. Moreover, just as in other sciences, the predictions are often rendered more testable by being derived as mathematical propositions or theorems. (Townsend & Kadlec, 1990, p. 227)

Nevertheless, most of the developmentally relevant mathematical modeling has focused on perception, rather than cognition. Those models that have addressed higher order cognitive developmental issues have characterized information processing at a very abstract level: in terms of states and transition probabilities, rather than in terms of structural organization and processes that operate on that structure (e.g., Brainerd's, 1987, Markov models of memory processes). As Gregg and Simon (1967) demonstrated very clearly with respect to stochastic models of concept learning, most of the interesting psychological assumptions in such models are buried in the text surrounding the mathematics. They point out that "the accurate predictions of fine-grain statistics that have been achieved with [stochastic theories] must be interpreted as validations of the laws of probability rather than of the psychological assumptions of the theories" (p. 275).

To cite a specific example of this general problem from the developmental literature, Wilkinson and Haines (1987) used Markov learning models to propose some novel answers to the important question of how children assemble simple component skills into reliable strategies. However, they couched their analysis in terms of the probabilities of moving between abstract states, while their discussion in the text was rife with undefined processes whereby the child "discovers," "adopts," "retains," "invokes," "moves," "prefers," "abandons," or "reverts." As is often the case in the use of mathematical models, the formalism of the mathematics obscures the informality of the underlying theory. Perhaps this is the reason why mathematical modeling has not played a central role in information-processing approaches to cognitive development.

MEASURING THE TIME-COURSE OF COGNITIVE PROCESSING

Many information-processing psychology studies of children's thinking ask questions about the rates at which different mental processes occur. When the mental processes of interest have durations of seconds or fractions of seconds, the methodology associated with their analysis is called *chronometric analysis*. The focus in these studies is on how a specific mental algorithm or strategy is organized and executed. When the focus shifts from how these strategies work to where they came from in the first place, it becomes necessary to study children's performance repeatedly over several days or weeks or perhaps months, seeking characteristic patterns that signal changes in the organization and content of underlying processes. Medium-duration studies of this type are called *microgenetic studies*. In the next two sections I describe each kind of methodology.

Chronometric Analysis

Chronometric analysis is based on three assumptions. First, there is a set of distinct, separable processes that underlie the behavior under investigation. Second, the particular process of interest can be isolated, via a task analysis, such that experimental manipulations can systematically induce the system to increase or decrease the number of executions of the focal process. The third assumption is that the experimental manipulations affect *only* the number of executions of the focal process, and nothing else about that process or the total set of processes in which it is embedded. (For a thorough discussion of the history and methodology of chronometric studies, primarily with adults, see Chase, 1978.)

Chronometric analysis can be used at several levels of aggregation. At the smallest grain sizes, it is used to obtain estimates of the mean time to execute underlying processes. At larger grain sizes, it is used to determine the overall organization of a cognitive process comprised of smaller components. In the following descriptions, I start with examples of the finer grained use of chronometric analysis. Then I describe a few examples of chronometrics at a more aggregate level.

Memory Scanning.   The use of chronometric methods with children is exemplified by Keating and Bobbit's (1978) extension of Sternberg's (1966) memory-scanning paradigm. The question of interest here is how people search their short-term memory. The basic procedure is to present subjects with a set of several digits, followed by a *probe* digit. The subject's task is to decide whether the probe digit was in the original set. The main independent variable is the size of the original set. Reaction time is measured from the onset of the probe until the subject responds. In addition to the general assumptions listed above, the paradigm assumes that the items in the set are stored in some kind of passive buffer, and that there is an active process that sequentially compares the probe with each of the items stored in the buffer. The empirical question is how long each comparison (and move to the next item) takes. Sternberg had discovered that when adults were attempting to decide whether a probe item was a member of a previously stored list, they could compare the probe item to the list items at the rate of approximately 20 items per sec (or 50 msec per item). Furthermore, adults appear to use an exhaustive search: They go through the entire list regardless of whether or not a match is found along the way. Keating and Bobbit found that 9-year-olds took almost twice as long per item as 17-year-olds.

Other Basic Cognitive Processes.   Such age differences in processing rates are found in almost all chronometric studies. Indeed, as Kail (1991b) noted in his review of 72 studies comparing processing speed in children and adults: "Age differences in performance on speeded tasks are large and remarkably consistent" (p. 490). Kail (1988) suggested the following explanation for these differences:

One hypothesis is that age differences in processing time reflects changes that are specific to particular processes, tasks, or domains. For example, age differences in processing speed may reflect the developmental acquisition of more efficient strategies for task solution. . . . A second hypothesis is that age differences in processing speed are due to more general developmental change. For example, in information-processing theories, performance on many cognitive tasks requires processing resources or attention. . . . increasing resources typically increases speed of processing, even when all other factors are held constant. Therefore, age-related increases in the amount of processing resources could produce age-related increases in processing speed. (pp. 339–340)

Kail (1988) reasoned that one could distinguish between the two hypotheses by examining the general shape of the functions that plot age versus processing speed for a variety of tasks. "Specifically, if some central mechanism changes monotonically with age, and if the function that relates decreases in processing time to changes in this central mechanism has the same form for two or more processes, the form of the growth function should be the same for those processes" (p. 340). His work represents an elegant example of the extent to which chronometric analysis can illuminate important developmental questions.

For each of the 15 ages from 8 years to 22 years (e.g., 8-year-olds, 9-year-olds, and so forth), Kail estimated the processing rate for five different tasks that involve very basic mental processes. For each task, Kail arranged the stimulus materials so that the process in question had to be executed repeatedly as a function of the stimulus. This enabled him to estimate the duration of the underlying focal process. The five tasks, and the resulting rates were:

1. Visual search. The stimuli were the digits 1 to 9. First a single digit — the *study digit* — appeared on a computer screen. Then, after a short delay, a set of one to five digits appeared. This was the *probe set*. The subject's task was to signal, as fast as possible, whether or not the probe set contained the study digit. Note that in this task the subject had to match a digit from memory (the study digit) with each of the digits in an external display. The processing time per item ranged from about 80 msec for the 8-year-olds to about 25 msec for the adults. (See Fig. 5.3 for the results from this and the other four Kail tasks.)

2. Memory search. Here Kail used the standard Sternberg (1966) memory scanning paradigm described earlier, with the same kind of materials as in the Visual Search task. For this task, each trial started with the subject learning a set of digits (set size 1, 3, or 5). Once the initial set had been studied, a probe digit was presented, and the subject had to indicate if the probe was a member of the study set. Here, the single digit in the external display had to be matched against a mental representation of the study set. The processing time per item ranged from about 150 msec for the 8-year-olds to about 50 msec for the adults.

3. Mental rotation. In this task, subjects were presented with a pair of letters in any of six different orientations, and they had to decide whether the letters were identical or mirror images. At all ages, reaction time increased with increasing orientation, and the slope of the reaction time versus orientation function decreased with age. Mean slopes were 4.5 msec/degree for children, 3.3 for adolescents, and 3.0 for adults.

4. Name retrieval (reported originally in Kail, 1986). The purpose of this task was to estimate the time necessary to retrieve the name of something, given a picture of it. Stimuli were pairs of pictures of common objects in two formats (e.g., an open umbrella or a closed umbrella, a peeled or an unpeeled banana). These pictures were combined into three different kinds of pairings: (a) pairs that were identical physically and in name (e.g., a pair of open umbrellas); (b) pairs that were identical in name only (e.g., an open and a closed umbrella); and (c) pairs that were different both physically and in name (e.g., an umbrella and a banana). Subjects were presented with a series of these different pairs, and given two types of instruction. In one condition, the subjects had to decide whether the pairs of objects had the same name, and in the other they had to decide if they were physically identical. By subtracting the response times on those trials that required the subjects to retrieve the name of the object from the response times on those trials that required only a physical match, Kail was able to estimate the mean name retrieval time for each of the age groups studied. It ranged from approximately 300 msec for the youngest children to about 150 msec for adults.

5. Mental addition. Subjects were presented with problems of the form $m + n = k$, where $1 \le m, n \le 9$. Problems with $n = m$ were not used. For half the problems the sum was correct and for the other half it was incorrect. Subjects responded by pressing either of two response buttons. Kail based his analysis of subject's response times on Ashcraft's (1987) associative retrieval model in which solution of these problems involves entering an arithmetic network at nodes corresponding to m and n, then searching for the intersection at which is stored the sum. The model assumes that memory search time increases as a function of the square of the sum, and that overall response time is a function of whether the equation $m + n = k$ is true or false. Accordingly, Kail estimated the memory search rate by using multiple regression to fit the median RTs at each age to the function

$$RT = B(m + n)^2 + t + k$$

where B is the memory search rate, and t is the additional amount of time to respond "false." Memory search rates ranged from approximately 7.5 sec per squared increment for the 8- and 9-year-olds to less than 3 sec for the adults.

Having determined the processing time per item for each age group on each of the five tasks, Kail then determined the relations between processing time and age for each task. Not surprisingly, for all of the tasks, there was a decrease in processing time with age. But more important, the best-fitting function for processing time versus age was an exponential decay function that could be fit by a single decay parameter (see Fig. 5.3). Furthermore, these exponential decay curves are found in speeded perceptual-motor tasks (Kail, 1991a), as well as the cognitive tasks described here. Kail interpreted these results by positing an increasing amount of common, nonspecific processing resources that become available to children as they develop: "Common growth functions are found because the increased resources yield a constant increment in speeded performance across tasks" (p. 362).

Kail's work represents an interesting mix of the hard-soft dimensions that I have been using to characterize the field. With respect to experimental methodology, it is about as hard as it can get. The experiments are very clean and the analysis is deeply quantitative. However, with respect to theoretical assumptions, it is at the soft end of the spectrum: It posits no clear mechanism through which the vague construct of "processing resources" might be realized. Nevertheless, these results provide an important empirical constraint for such models.

In addition to the three standard assumptions—listed earlier in this section—underlying chronometric analysis, Kail's approach is based on a fourth: that the organization of the strategy for accomplishing a task remains constant across ages, and only the speed of processing changes. That is, Kail assumed that children's processes for memory scanning were organized in the same way as adults'. Then he proceeded to estimate some of the critical parameters of these processes and to chart their developmental course. However, in many cases, rather than presuming that the organization is known and age-invariant, the researcher's goal is to determine just what that organization is at different ages or skill levels. Chronometric analysis can be applied to this situation at a somewhat coarser grain size. The focus is not so much on individual processing rates as on the overall temporal pattern of responses generated by different cognitive strategies. The next three examples illustrate this kind of coarser grained use of chronometric analysis.

Mental Arithmetic.   One of the best-known studies using chronometric analysis with children was Groen and Parkman's (1972) analysis of how first graders solved simple addition problems. Groen and Parkman proposed several alternative models of how these children might add two single digit numbers to produce their sum. One plausible model would be for the child to represent the first argument, then the second argument, and then *count out* the sum. The actual representation could be external (on fingers or

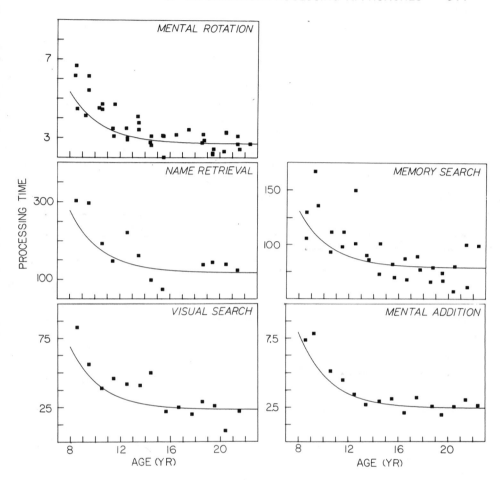

FIG. 5.3. Developmental functions for rates of mental rotation (data from Kail, 1988, Experiment 2 and from Kail, 1986, Experiments 1 and 2), name retrieval (from Kail, 1986, Experiment 1), memory search (from Kail, 1988, Experiments 1 and 2), visual search (from Kail, 1988, Experiment 1), and mental addition (from Kail, 1988, Experiment 2). Rate of mental rotation is estimated by the slope of the function relating response time to the orientation of the stimulus. Name retrieval is estimated by the difference between times for name and physical matching. Visual search is estimated by the slope of the function relating response time to the size of the search set. Memory search is estimated by the slope of the function relating response time to the size of the study set. Retrieval of sums on the mental addition task is estimated from the slope of the function relating response time to the sum squared. The solid line depicts values derived from the best-fitting 11-parameter exponential function (i.e., one in which the decay parameter, c, is the same for all five processes; from Kail, 1988).

counting blocks) or internal. In either case, the expected time to compute the sum would be proportional to the sum of the two numbers. Another strategy might be to *count on* from the first number: start with the first, and count as many steps as the second. A child following this strategy on the problem 3 + 5, would, in effect, say to herself "3 + 5; that's 3, 4, 5, 6, 7, 8 — the answer is 8." Response times for this strategy would be proportional to the value of the second number in the pair of addends. Yet another strategy is the *min model*. This is like counting on, except that the child always starts counting from the larger of the two arguments, thereby minimizing the number of steps (e.g., for both 3 + 5, and 5 + 3, the child would start with the 5, and increment it 3 times). Times for this strategy are proportional to the minimum of the two arguments.

Reasoning in this way, Groen and Parkman predicted a pattern of reaction times as a function of several relations among the two addends (sum, difference, min, max). Based on their analysis of mean reaction times across subjects and trials, Groen and Parkman concluded that the min model provided the best fit to their data. (Even at the time, there were some exceptions to this general result, and further analysis by Siegler & Jenkins, 1989 — described later — revealed a much more complex picture. Nevertheless, the initial Groen and Parkman work still stands as a pioneering effort in chronometric analysis of children's performance.)

Transitive Reasoning. "Bill is taller than Sue and shorter than Sally. Is Sally shorter than Sue?" How do children solve this kind of transitive inference problem? Ever since Burt (1919) first explored children's developing ability to deal with transitive relations, developmentalists have been interested in this question. One specific question that arises in this context is how the individual premises (X is taller than Y) are stored and accessed. There are two distinct possibilities. One alternative is that children construct an integrated representation of the individual items as the pairwise relations are presented. Then, when a probe is presented, they *read off* the relative sizes of the probe items from the integrated display. Another alternative is that children store the individual pairs, and at probe time they link them together to produce the answer.

Trabasso and his colleagues used chronometric analysis to decide the issue (Trabasso, 1975; Trabasso, Riley, & Wilson, 1975). They reasoned that if children use an integrated representation, then their response times should show the same pattern for the internally stored representation as for an external visual display of the same ordered set of objects. In particular, the pattern should exhibit the familiar *symbolic distance* effect, in which it takes less time to determine the ordering for two widely separated objects, than to decide the ordering for two adjacent items. On the other hand, if children are connecting the premises at probe time, then the closer objects should take less time to resolve (because there are fewer connections to make). Trabasso and his colleagues investigated this problem by using six-term problems (the example given at the opening of the previous paragraph was a three-term problem). They presented children with repeated exposure to all adjacent pairs (i.e., AB, BC, CD, DE, EF), in both orders (e.g., A is larger than B; B is smaller than A), appropriately randomized, until they met a learning criterion for each adjacent pair. Then they presented probe questions about all possible pairs and measured response times. The probes included pairs of items (in both orders; i.e., both BF and FB) that were zero inferential steps apart (i.e., the adjacent pairs used in the training lists, such as BC), pairs that were one inferential step apart (e.g., BD), and pairs that were two inferential steps apart (e.g., EB). The subjects included a group of 6-year-olds, a group of 9-year-olds, and a group of adults.

The resulting reaction time patterns were (with minor exceptions) very consistent: Reaction time was inversely related to the number of inferential steps. That is, pairs that were very far apart produced faster responses than the adjacent pairs on which subjects had been trained. This was true at all ages (as expected, older subjects were faster than younger subjects), and for all display conditions (verbally presented pairs, visually presented pairs, and an integrated visual display of all objects.) By using this kind of chronometric analysis in a series of related studies with a variety of subject populations, Trabasso (1975) was able to make some very strong statements about an important mnemonic skill:

> Our analysis suggests that children ranging in age from 4 to 10 years-of-age, mentally retarded adolescents and college students use similar strategies of constructing linear orders from pairwise, ordered information, store this representation in memory and use it to make comparative relations on all members in the array. . . . In short, we believe that we have provided a mechanism for information integration and inference-making that cuts across a variety of situations and tasks. (pp. 167–168)

Elementary Quantification: Subitizing and Counting. Our final example represents a mix of the two kinds of chronometric analysis described here. In this case, the goals of the research are twofold: (a) to determine whether or not children and adults use the same general strategies and (b) to estimate the rates of the components of those strategies. Chi and Klahr (1975) addressed the question of how kindergarten children and adults quantify (i.e., generate an internal quantitative symbol for) displays of discrete objects. One quantification strategy might be simply to count each object. The processing time for counting should be a linear function of the number of objects being counted. On the other hand, the earliest conceptions of the "span of apprehension" (Jevons, 1871) assumed that there was some number, *N,* of discrete objects that the mind could immediately perceive, apprehend, or recognize. Such a process—later called *subitizing* (Jensen, Reese, & Reese, 1950)—would produce a flat slope of reaction time versus *N*. In addition to assessing these two positions, Chi and Klahr addressed the developmental question of how the two processes differed in children and adults.

Subjects were presented with randomly arranged displays of *N* dots and asked to say as rapidly as possible how many there were in the display. The range of *N* was from 1 to 10 for adult subjects and from 1 to 8 for the children. Reaction times were measured from the onset of the display to the beginning of the verbal response. The results are shown in Fig. 5.4. For both the adults and the children, the mean reaction times were best fit by a two-segment linear regression analysis with a break point between $N = 3$ and $N = 4$. For $N \leq 3$—the subitizing range—the slope of the adult function is about 50 msec per dot, whereas for the children it is nearly 4 times as great. For $N \in 4$—the counting range—the slope is about 300 msec for adults and about 1 sec for children. Error rates were nearly zero for $N \leq 4$ for both children and adults. Beyond that range, they abruptly increased to about 25% for children, and about 5% for adults. Based on the characteristic pattern of results (both RTs and errors) and the specific parameter estimates for rates and ranges, Chi and Klahr (1975, p. 438) concluded that in both adults and young children, there appear to be two

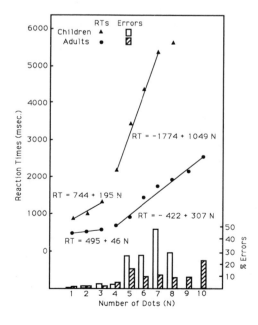

FIG. 5.4. Mean reaction times and error rates for children and adults as a function of the number of dots in the display (from Chi & Klahr, 1975).

distinct quantification processes. One process, operating almost errorlessly on the range below $N = 4$ is 5 to 6 times as rapid as the other, which operates on the range above $N = 3$.

Microgenetic Studies

In the context of chronometric studies, the phrase "time course of cognitive processing" implies brief tasks with components identified at the level of fractions of a second. But the phrase can also refer to the much longer intervals (weeks, months, or years) over which cognitive change occurs. The most common way to investigate change is to design cross-sectional studies in which the same task is presented to groups of subjects at different ages (e.g., Kail's studies described earlier). Somewhat less common are longitudinal studies in which the same group of subjects is assessed repeatedly over an extended time period. Typically, the observation points in longitudinal studies are months or years apart and the measurements are relatively crude when compared to chronometric tasks. However, an interest in the more detailed aspects of changes in children's information processing has led to an approach called the *microgenetic method* that is particularly well suited to detecting changes in children's strategies.

> Three key properties define the microgenetic approach: (a) Observations span the entire period from the beginning of the change of interest to the time at which it reaches a relatively stable state; (b) The density of observations is high relative to the rate of change of the phenomenon; (c) Observed behavior is subjected to intensive trial-by-trial analysis, with the goal of inferring the processes that give rise to both quantitative and qualitative aspects of change. (Siegler & Crowley, 1991, p. 606)

Siegler and Crowley summarize the history and current status of microgenetic studies, and then provide a detailed account of one study that exemplifies the microgenetic method. Siegler and Jenkins (1989) focused on how children discovered the min strategy for addition (described earlier). They followed eight 4- and 5-year-old children over an 11-week period. At the start of the period all of the children were proficient at simple addition (problems with addends 1–5 inclusive), and their most common addition strategy was to count from 1. Children received seven problems in each of approximately three sessions per week during the 11-week period. In order to determine what strategy a child used on each problem, Siegler and Jenkins used a variety of methods such as observing their behavior (counting on fingers, and so forth) and measuring speed and accuracy. However, their primary method involved simply asking children how they solved each problem. The following example is taken from a trial on which a 5-year-old first used the min strategy (Siegler & Crowley, 1991, p. 613):

E: How much is 2 + 5?
S: 2 + 5 — (whispers), 6, 7 — it's 7.
E: How did you know that?
S: (excitedly) Never counted!
E: You didn't count?
S: Just said it — I just said after 6 something — 7, 6 — 7.

The rich data set produced by this high-density measurement technique yielded a correspondingly rich portrait of developmental change. At the most aggregate level, children improved from about 75% correct to nearly perfect performance over the 11 weeks. More interesting than just the outcome of each trial was the pattern of strategies used to produce those outcomes. Overall, children used half a dozen different strategies, and, more important, this variability was true not only for the group, but for individual children. Furthermore, the study provided clear data on the discovery of new strategies, on the precursors of strategy discovery, and on the subsequent consequences of strategy discovery. Based on their own work and that of others, Siegler and Crowley (1991) conclude that

> . . . microgenetic experiments have yielded closely parallel results across quite diverse changes. One such finding involves the halting and uneven use of newly acquired competencies. Even after children discover sophisticated scientific experimentation strategies, they often continue to use less sophisticated ones as well (Kuhn, Amsel, & O'Loughlin, 1988; Kuhn & Phelps, 1982; Schauble, 1990). When they discover a new problem solving method with the help of their mothers, they may later fall back on shared control rather than continuing to exert sole responsibility for its execution (Wertsch & Hickmann, 1987). New concepts about the workings of gears are applied in a similarly sporadic fashion (Metz, 1985), as are new strategies for adding numbers (Siegler & Jenkins, 1989). (p. 618)

Another common finding of microgenetic studies is that innovations occur following successes as well as failures. Discoveries have been found to follow successes, rather than impasses or errors, in many children's map drawing and language use (Karmiloff-Smith, 1984), arithmetic (Siegler & Jenkins, 1989), pictorial representations (Inhelder et al., 1976), and scientific experimentation strategies (Kuhn, Amsel, & O'Loughlin, 1988; Kuhn & Phelps, 1982; Schauble, 1990). These findings point to the importance of observing in a variety of domains the frequency and types of variation produced without apparent external motivation.

USING HIGH-DENSITY DATA FROM ERROR
PATTERNS AND PROTOCOLS TO INDUCE
AND TEST COMPLEX MODELS

Pass/fail data provide only the crudest form of information about underlying processes. Nevertheless, most of the empirical research in cognitive development is reported in terms of percentage of correct answers. Another characteristic of the information-processing approach is the premise that much more can be extracted from an appropriate record of children's performance. The basic assumption is that, given the goal of understanding the processing underlying children's performance, we should use all the means at our disposal to get a glimpse of those processes as they are occurring, and not just when they produce their final output. Verbal protocols, eye movements, and error patterns (as well as chronometric methods, mentioned earlier) all provide this kind of high-density data. Examples of some of these methods have already been provided in previous sections, but here we look at them in more detail.

The view that detailed error analysis provides a powerful window into the child's mental processes is neither novel nor radical. Piaget's pioneering analysis (Piaget, 1928, 1929) of children's characteristic errors and misconceptions in a wide variety of domains made him, in effect, a founding member of the soft-core information-processing club. He was probably the first to demonstrate that children's errors could reveal as much, or more, about their thought processes as their successes, and a substantial proportion of his writing is devoted to informal inferences about the underlying knowledge structures that generate children's misconceptions in many domains (see Kuhn, this volume). Siegler (1981) put the issue this way:

> Many of Piaget's most important insights were derived from examining children's erroneous statements; these frequently revealed the type of changes in reasoning that occur with age. Yet in our efforts to make knowledge-assessment techniques more reliable and more applicable to very young children, we have moved away from this emphasis on erroneous reasoning and also away from detailed analyses of individual children's reasoning. . . . The result may have been a loss of valuable information about the acquisition process. . . . [My] hypothesis is that we might be able to increase considerably our understanding of cognitive growth by devoting more attention to individual children's early, error-prone reasoning. (p. 3)

Analysis of Error Patterns

The basic assumption in error-analytic methodologies is that children's knowledge can be represented as a set of stable procedures that, when probed with an appropriate set of problems, will generate a characteristic profile of responses (including specific types of errors). Application of this idea to children's performance reached perhaps its most elegant form in the computer simulation models of children's subtraction errors by Brown and his colleagues (Brown & Burton, 1978; Brown & VanLehn, 1982). Brown and his colleagues demonstrated that a wide variety of children's subtraction errors could be accounted for by a set of "bugs" in their calculation procedures. For example, two of the most frequent bugs discovered by Brown and Burton were:

BORROW FROM ZERO:

When borrowing from a column whose top digit is 0,	103
the student writes 9, but does not continue borrowing	− 45
from the column to the left of the zero.	158

SMALLER FROM LARGER:

The student subtracts the smaller digit in a column from	254
the larger regardless of which one is on top.	− 118
	144

These and dozens of more subtle and complex bugs were inferred from the analysis of thousands of subtraction test items from 1,300 children. The key to the analysis was the creation of a network of subprocedures that comprise the total knowledge required to solve subtraction problems. This procedural network was then examined for possible points of failure, to explain the patterns of erroneous answers.

Another highly productive research program based on the analysis of error patterns is Siegler's well-known *rule assessment* methodology (Siegler, 1976, 1981). The basic idea in this and other developmentally oriented error-analysis work (e.g., Baylor & Gascon, 1974; Klahr & Robinson, 1981; Young, 1976) is that, at any point in the development of children's knowledge about a domain, their responses are based on what they know at that point, rather than on what they don't know. In order to characterize that (imperfect) knowledge, the theorist attempts to formulate a model of partial knowledge that can generate the full set of responses — both correct and incorrect — in the same pattern as did the child. The model thus becomes a theory of the child's knowledge about the domain at that point in her development.

Fay and Mayer (1987) applied this kind of error analysis to the domain of spatial reference. They were attempting to teach children (from 9 to 13 years old) how to write programs in Logo, a programming language in which children write commands for a "turtle" that draws lines on the computer screen. Logo includes commands that can move the turtle forward or backward (FD or BK) a specified number of units, and that can rotate the turtle to the left or right (LT or RT) a specified number of degrees. For example, to draw a square box 5 units on a side, the child might write the following program:

FD 5 RT 90 FD 5 RT 90 FD 5 RT 90 FD 5 RT 90.

During the execution of this program, the turtle would be in four different orientations, and the RT command would be interpreted relative to the turtle's current orientation, rather than absolutely.

The distinction between relative and absolute orientation is difficult for children of this age, and so Fay and Mayer used the Logo context to study children's naive conceptions about spatial reference. They examined how children interpreted Logo commands to move and turn from various initial orientations. Children were presented with problems that varied in initial orientation of the turtle, the type of command (move or turn), and the value of the argument (how far to move or turn). Their task was to predict the final orientation of the turtle, given its initial orientation and command.

Fay and Mayer first constructed an ideal model, comprised of about a dozen elementary operations. Then, based on the general characteristics of children's errors, they proposed six types of misconceptions (e.g., that a right-turn command actually slides the turtle to the right) and formulated models for the microstructure of each misconception, in terms of degenerate versions of relevant parts of the ideal model. For the subjects to which these degenerate models were applied, Fay and Mayer were able to account for nearly every one of the (mostly) incorrect responses to the 24 items in their test battery.

Error-analyses of this type are not only useful for cognitive developmental theory, but they also have pedagogical implications. The potential for facilitating remedial instruction is what originally motivated the Brown and Burton work on children's subtraction bugs, and it continues to be a valuable by-product of detailed error-analysis research:

> . . . novice Logo programmers appear to enter the Logo environment with individual confusions and misconceptions that they apply fairly consistently during instruction. Diagnosis of the specific confusions—such as a misunderstanding of what left and right mean or a misunderstanding of what degrees of rotation means—provides a more detailed and potentially useful evaluation of students' knowledge than the traditional global measurement of percentage correct. A cognitive diagnosis . . . provides information concerning *what* a student knows rather than a traditional measurement of *how much* a student can do. (Fay & Mayer, 1987, p. 265)

I believe that this kind of work illustrates the basic premise of this aspect of information-processing approaches: Careful and creative analysis of complex error patterns can provide an extremely informative window into the child's mental processes.

Analysis of Protocols

Protocol analysis is another form of high-density data that is often associated with information-processing approaches. The basic idea here is that, in addition to final responses on tasks, the subject can generate external indications of intermediate states, and that this pattern of intermediate indicators (the protocol) can be highly informative about the underlying processes that generated the final response. Included here are not only children's verbal protocols, such as the Siegler and Jenkins data described earlier, but also sequences of eye movements (Haith, 1980; Vurpillot, 1968) and other motor responses, such as reaching (Granrud, Haake, & Yonas, 1985). The classic verbal protocol analyses with adults are reported in Newell and Simon (1972), and a theoretical and methodological discussion of protocol analysis is offered in Ericsson and Simon (1984).

A common misconception about the verbal protocol analysis methodology is that it requires subjects to give an introspective account of their own behavior, and therefore is unreliable and unacceptably subjective (Nisbett & Wilson, 1977). Clearly, this would be a fatal flaw in the methodology, especially if it is to be used with children. But the criticism is unfounded. As Anderson (1987) summarized the issue:

> Many of these unjustified criticisms of protocols stem from the belief that they are taken as sources of psychological theory rather than as sources of data about states of the mind. For the latter, one need not require that the subject accurately interpret his mental states, but only that the theorist be able to specify some mapping between his reports and states of the theory. (p. 472)

In adult information-processing psychology, protocol analysis is a widespread method, but it is only infrequently used in more than a casual fashion by current cognitive developmentalists. This is very surprising, when one considers the fact that Piaget was the most prolific collector and analyzer of verbal protocols in the history of psychology.

Klahr and Robinson (1981) used a combination of motor and verbal protocol analysis and error analysis to explore preschool children's problem-solving and planning skills. They used a variant of the Tower of Hanoi puzzle (described earlier) in which both the initial state and the goal state were physically displayed (see Fig. 5.5). Children were presented with partially completed three-disk (actually, "three-can") problems requiring from two to seven moves to solution, and they were instructed to describe

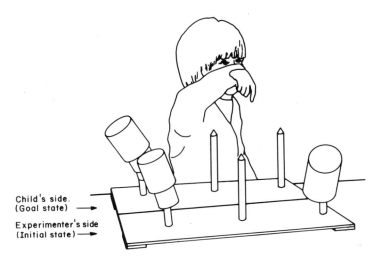

Child's side.
(Goal state)   →

Experimenter's side
(Initial state) →

FIG. 5.5.   Children's version of the Tower of Hanoi puzzle. The cans and pegs on the child's side of the table represent the goal state, and the can's and pegs on the opposite side represent the initial state. The child's task is to describe the full sequence of legal moves that will transform the initial state into the goal state. The problem depicted here can be solved in one move (from Klahr & Robinson, 1981).

the full sequence of moves that would change the initial state so that it matched the goal state. Children were videotaped as they described — verbally and by pointing — what sequence of moves they would use to solve the problem, but the cans were never actually moved. The protocols enabled Klahr and Robinson to infer the children's internal representation of the location of each can, and the processes whereby children made moves. They then constructed several alternative models of children's strategies, and used the error-analysis technique described earlier to identify each child's response pattern with a specific strategy. Note that nowhere were the children asked to reflect on their own mental processes, or to give a report on what strategies they were using while solving the problems.

The information extracted from the protocols in the Klahr and Robinson study consisted of a planned sequence of well-defined moves of discrete objects. This level of mapping from the protocol to hypothesized representations and processes is characteristic of the kind of protocol analyses presented in Newell and Simon's (1972) seminal work. A "richer" use of protocols, similar to some of the later examples in Ericsson and Simon (1984), provides the basis of recent investigations of children's strategies for scientific reasoning (Dunbar & Klahr; 1989; Kuhn, 1989; Schauble, 1990). Klahr, Fay, and Dunbar (1991) used verbal protocols as the primary data source in their study of experimentation strategies. Children (aged 8 to 11 years old) and adults were presented with a programmable robot, taught about most of its operating characteristics, and then asked to discover how some additional feature worked. They were asked to talk aloud as they generated hypotheses, ran experiments (i.e., wrote programs for the robot and ran them), and made predictions, observations, and evaluations. These verbal protocols were then analyzed in terms of different classes of hypotheses, the conditions under which experiments were run, how observed results were assessed, and so on. Based on this analysis, Klahr and his colleagues were able to characterize some of the differences in scientific reasoning skills between children and adults. In particular, they demonstrated that younger children have very poor general heuristics for designing experiments and evaluating their outcomes.

CONSTRAINTS AND LIMITATIONS

For all of its pervasiveness, the information-processing approach to cognitive development has several constraints and limitations. In her discussion of the limitations of information-processing approaches, Kuhn (this volume) addresses some of these issues. Here, I offer a somewhat different perspective. The extent to which these limitations and constraints are temporary or fundamental and permanent remains to be seen.

Populations

To date, hard-core information-processing approaches to cognitive development have been focused primarily on normal children over 2 years old. Those approaches that have dealt with younger, older or special populations have tended to be of the soft-core variety: for example, Davidson's (1986) study of gifted children, Hoyer and Familant's (1987) and Madden's (1987) studies of elderly subjects, and Geary, Widaman, Little, and Cormier's (1987) and Spitz and Borys' (1984) investigations of learning disabled and retarded subjects. In the case of special populations, issues are usually framed by the theoretical or empirical results emerging from studies of normal populations, and the question of interest is the qualitative or quantitative difference in a particular information-processing construct. For example, Spitz and Borys (1984) investigated the differences in search processes between normal and retarded adults on the classic Tower of Hanoi puzzle. Interesting work using information-processing concepts and techniques has also been done with non-human species. For example, Arbib (1987) proposed a series of models of visually guided behavior in frogs that utilize the schema notion described earlier. His work has many of the information-processing features discussed in this chapter, including formal representations and computer simulation. None of these populations, however, has been the subject of as much information-processing research as have typical children.

Topics

The developmental topics studied within this approach range from higher cognitive processes, such as problem solving (Resnick & Glaser, 1976) and scientific reasoning (Dunbar & Klahr, 1989; Kuhn & Phelps, 1982), to more basic processes, such as attention and memory (Chi, 1981; Kail, 1984). Because the focus of this chapter is cognitive development, I have drawn the conventional — and arbitrary — boundary that precludes an extensive discussion of perceptual–motor or language development. Nevertheless, I would be hard pressed to present a principled argument for excluding either of these areas from mainstream information processing, for in both of them one can find many examples of the approach (MacWhinney, 1987b; Yonas, 1988). MacWhinney's (1987a) edited volume on mechanisms of language acquisition contains an array of information-processing approaches that run the gamut from soft- to hard-core features. In the area of perceptual development, Marr's (1982) seminal work, which advocates computational models as the proper approach to constructing theories of vision, is increasingly influential. Indeed, Banks (1988), in presenting his own computational model of contrast constancy, argued that perceptual development is a more promising area in which to construct computational models than cognitive or social development, because there are more constraints that can be brought to bear to limit the proliferation of untested (and untestable) assumptions.

Change and Stability

Throughout this chapter I have offered examples of how information-processing approaches can account for cognitive changes. But stability is also an important feature of development and the topic has received extensive attention from developmentalists (Bornstein & Krasnegor, 1989). Developmentalists' interest in stability is primarily based on psychometric approaches. That is, it deals with relative constancy with respect to measures that compare one person to another. These approaches do not study the absence of change, but rather the lack of change in the rank order of individuals in a group on some measure. For example, consider the question of whether IQ scores are stable over time. IQ is a relative measure. The test is designed to order individuals from high to low, and any stability that is found in such scores means that if Sue scored higher than Sam at age 2, she continued to do so at age 4 (or 10 or 20). There is no question that both Sue and Sam have undergone substantial change in knowledge, skills, LTM structures, basic processes, and so forth. (Indeed, Kail's work, cited earlier, suggests that even at the level of elementary information processes, both Sue and Sam must have improved proportionally.)

The interesting question is why all of these changes in various aspects of the information-processing system have not changed the relative standing of Sue and Sam. To the best of my knowledge, the information-processing approaches that have addressed this question have either (a) been of the soft-core variety, or (b) focused on stability in infancy and early childhood (Bornstein, 1989; Colombo, Mitchell, O'Brien, & Horowitz, 1987; Fagan & Singer, 1983). A promising area for future research would be the application of microgenetic and chronometric techniques to individual differences and questions of change and stability.

Nonsymbolic Computational Architectures

One of the justifications given earlier for excluding perceptual, motor, and language development from this chapter was its focus on higher cognitive processes in children of school age and above. Another reason is that this chapter has focused on symbolically oriented information-processing approaches, to the exclusion of the newer connectionist framework. Advocates of this approach to computational models of cognition argue that information-processing approaches of the symbolic variety are inherently inadequate to account for the important phenomena in language acquisition and perceptual-motor behavior. The gist of the argument is that, given the highly parallel and "presymbolic" nature of these areas, it is doubtful that highly serial symbol-oriented information-processing models will ever be able to provide plausible accounts of development in these areas.

Indeed, this purported weakness is, according to some connectionists (McClelland, 1989; Rumelhart & McClelland, 1986), the Achilles heel of the symbolic approach to computational modeling. Furthermore, from a developmental perspective, the situation is particularly troublesome, for if we are to model a system from its neonatal origins, then we will have to invent new ways to model the interface between perceptual–motor systems and central cognition, particularly at the outset, when they provide the basis for all subsequent cognition.

Connectionism's advocates have suggested several very important and exciting possibilities, including the possibility that connectionist approaches may be particularly well suited for modeling biological changes underlying cognitive development. To date, the most interesting work has been in the area of language acquisition (MacWhinney, Leinbach, Taraban, & McDonald, 1989; Plunkett & Marchman, 1991), although there are a few connectionist models of higher order cognitive transitions, such as McClelland and

Jenkins' (1991) simulation of rule acquisition on Siegler's balance scale task. Many other connectionist models are summarized by Bechtel and Abrahamsen (1991). Included in their set of potential contributions are (a) a new interpretation of the distinction between maturation and learning, (b) a computational instantiation of the distinction between accommodation and assimilation, (c) an account of context effects (in which minor task variations have large effects on preschoolers' performance [Gelman, 1978]), and (d) explanations of many of the phenomena and anomalies associated with stages and transitions.

At present, there are not enough connectionist models of developmental phenomena to decide the extent to which they will replace, augment, or be absorbed by the symbolic variety of information-processing models described in this chapter. Nevertheless, both the broad-gauged connectionist criticisms of symbol-oriented approaches to cognition and the potential connectionist contributions to computational models of cognitive development warrant careful consideration.

CONCLUSIONS

Rather than attempt to summarize a chapter that is already a summary of ongoing research, in this concluding section I (a) reiterate the case for computational models of developmental phenomena, and (b) speculate about the future of information-processing approaches to cognitive development.

Why Bother?

Why should someone interested in theories of cognitive development be concerned about computational models of the sort discussed earlier? The primary justification for focusing on such systems is the claim that self-modification is the central question for cognitive developmental theory. It appears to me that in order to make theoretical advances, we will have to formulate computational models at least as complex as the systems described here.

Kuhn (Chap. 4, this volume) criticizes the information-processing approach for being insufficiently attentive to the issue of self-modification. As noted earlier, she is not alone in this regard, but there is some irony in the current situation. Although it is not difficult to find developmentalists who fault hard-core treatments of transition and change, it is even easier to find criticisms of the entire field of developmental psychology for its inability to deal adequately with these central topics.

I have asked some of my developmental friends where the issue stands on transitional mechanisms. Mostly, they say that developmental psychologists don't have good answers. Moreover, they haven't had the answer for so long now that they don't very often ask the question anymore — not daily, in terms of their research. (Newell, 1990, p. 462)

Is this too harsh a judgment? Perhaps we can dismiss it as based on hearsay, for Newell himself is not a developmental psychologist. But it is harder to dismiss the following assessment from John Flavell (1984):

... serious theorizing about basic mechanisms of cognitive growth has actually never been a popular pastime. . . . It is rare indeed to encounter a substantive treatment of the problem in the annual flood of articles, chapters, and books on cognitive development. The reason is not hard to find: Good theorizing about mechanisms is very, very hard to do. (p. 189)

Even more critical is the following observation on the state of theory in perceptual development from one of the area's major contributors in recent years:

Put simply, our models of developmental mechanisms are disappointingly vague. This observation is rather embarrassing because the aspect of perceptual developmental psychology that should set it apart from the rest of perceptual psychology is the explanation of how development occurs, and such an explanation is precisely what is lacking. (Banks, 1987, p. 342)

It is difficult to deny either Newell's or Bank's assertions that we don't have good answers, or Flavell's assessment of the difficulty of the question. However, I believe that it is no longer being avoided: Many developmentalists have been at least asking the right questions recently. In the past few years we have seen Sternberg's (1984) edited volume *Mechanisms of Cognitive Development,* MacWhinney's (1987b) edited volume *Mechanisms of Language Acquisition,* and Siegler's (1989) *Annual Review* chapter devoted to transition mechanisms. So the question is being asked.

Furthermore, the trend is in the direction of hardening the core. Only a few of the chapters in the 1984 Sternberg volume specify mechanisms any more precisely than at the flow-chart level, and most of the proposed mechanisms are at the soft end of the information-processing spectrum. However, only 3 years later, Klahr et al.'s (1987) *Production System Models of Learning and Development* included several chapters that described running programs, and within 5 years, Siegler (1989), in characterizing several general categories for transition mechanisms (neural mechanisms, associative competition, encoding, analogy, and strategy choice), cited computationally based exemplars for all but the neural mechanisms (e.g., Bakker & Halford, 1988; Falkenhainer, Forbus, & Gentner, 1986; Holland, 1986; MacWhinney, 1987a; Rumelhart & McClelland, 1986; Siegler, 1988).

A clear advantage of such computational models is that they force difficult questions into the foreground, where they can be neither sidetracked by the wealth of experimental results, nor obscured by vague characterizations of the various essences of cognitive development. The relative lack of progress in theory development—noted by Banks, Flavell, and Newell—is a consequence of the fact that, until recently, most developmental psychologists have avoided moving to computationally based theories, attempting instead to attack the profoundly difficult question of self-modification with inadequate tools. Mastery of the new tools for computational modeling is not easy. Nevertheless it appears to be a necessary condition for advancing our understanding of cognitive development. As Flavell and Wohlwill (1969) noted more than 20 years ago: "Simple models will just not do for human cognition" (p. 74).

The Future of the Hard-Core Approach

That brings me to my second concluding topic: the education of future cognitive developmentalists. The conceptual and technical skills necessary for computational modeling require training of a different sort than one finds in most graduate programs today. However, I see the current situation as analogous to earlier challenges to the technical content of graduate training. When other kinds of computational technology that are now in common use—such as statistical packages, or scaling procedures—were first being applied to psychological topics, journal articles invariably included several pages of description about the technique itself. Writers of those early articles correctly assumed that their readers needed such background information before the psychological issue of interest could be addressed. Today, writers of papers using analysis of variance, or multidimensional scaling, or path analysis simply assume that their readers have had several courses in graduate school, learning the fundamentals.

Similarly, in the early years of computer simulation, the necessary resources of large main frame computers were limited to very few research centers, and exposure to computational modeling was inaccessible to most developmentalists. Even today, few developmental psychologists have had any training with computational models, and only a handful of computational modelers have a primary interest in cognitive development. Nevertheless, the intersection of these two areas of research is growing. (The 1991 meeting of the Society for Research in Child Development included two hard-core symposia, one entitled "Connectionist Models and Child Development" and the other "Computational Models of Cognitive Transition

Mechanisms.") Moreover, with the increasing availability of powerful work-stations, the proliferation of computer networks for dissemination of computational models, and the increasing number of published reports on various kinds of computationally based cognitive architectures, the appropriate technology and support structures are becoming widely accessible. This accessibility will make it possible to include simulation methodology as a standard part of graduate training.

My hope is that, over the next few decades, we will begin to see many papers about cognitive development couched in terms of extensions to systems like Soar, or ACT*, or some other well-known (by then) cognitive architecture, or some future connectionist model. Just as current writers need not explain the conceptual foundations of an analysis of variance, so future writers will deem it unnecessary to include tutorials on computational models in their papers. Once we are fully armed with such powerful tools, progress on our most difficult problems will be inevitable. We will no longer talk of approaches to our problems, but rather, of proposals for their solutions.

ACKNOWLEDGMENTS

This chapter is an adaptation and extension of an earlier characterization of hard-core and soft-core approaches (Klahr, 1989) and includes some issues originally treated in Neches, Langley, and Klahr (1987). Preparation of the chapter was supported in part by a grant from the A. W. Mellon Foundation. Very helpful comments and suggestions for improvements in an earlier draft came from Robert Siegler, Leona Schauble, and David Penner. Becky Duxbury provided excellent secretarial support throughout the project.

REFERENCES

Anderson, J. R. (1983). *The architecture of cognition*. Cambridge, MA: Harvard University Press.

Anderson, J. R. (1987). Skill acquisition: Compilation of weak-method problem solutions. *Psychological Review, 94*, 192–210.

Anderson, J. R., Kline, P. J., & Beasley, C. M., Jr. (1978). *A general learning theory and its application to schema abstraction* (Tech. Rep. 78-2). Pittsburgh, PA: Carnegie Mellon University, Department of Psychology.

Anzai, Y., & Simon, H. A. (1979). The theory of learning by doing. *Psychological Review, 86*, 124–140.

Arbib, M. A. (1987). Levels of modeling of mechanisms of visually guided behavior. *Behavioral and Brain Sciences, 10*, 407–465.

Ashcraft, M. H. (1987). Children's knowledge of simple arithmetic: A developmental model and simulation. In J. Bisanz, C. J. Brainerd, & R. Kail (Eds.), *Formal methods in developmental psychology: Progress in cognitive development research* (pp. 302–338). New York: Springer-Verlag.

Atkinson, R. C., & Shiffrin, R. M. (1968). Human memory: A proposed system and its control processes. In K. W. Spence & J. T. Spence (Eds.), *The psychology of learning and motivation* (pp. 90–195). New York: Academic Press.

Bakker, P. E., & Halford, G. S. (1988). *A basic computational theory of structure-mapping in analogy and transitive inference* (Tech. Rep.). St. Lucia, Australia: University of Queensland, Centre for Human Information Processing and Problem Solving.

Banks, M. S. (1987). Mechanisms of visual development: An example of computational models. In J. Bisanz, C. J. Brainerd, & R. Kail (Eds.), *Formal methods in developmental psychology: Progress in cognitive development research* (pp. 339–371). New York: Springer-Verlag.

Banks, M. S. (1988). Visual recalibration and the development of contrast and optical flow perception. In A. Yonas (Ed.), *Perceptual development in infancy* (pp. 145–196). Hillsdale, NJ: Lawrence Erlbaum Associates.

Barrett, T. R. (1978, November). *Aging and memory: Declining or differences*. Paper presented at the meeting of the Psychonomic Society, San Antonio, TX.

Baylor, G. W., & Gascon, J. (1974). An information processing theory of aspects of the development of weight seriation in children. *Cognitive Psychology, 6,* 1–40.

Baylor, G. W., Gascon, J., Lemoyne, G., & Pother, N. (1973). An information processing model of some seriation tasks. *Canadian Psychologist, 14,* 167–196.

Bechtel, W. & Abrahamsen, A. (1991). *Connectionism and the mind*. Cambridge, MA: Basil Blackwell.

Beilin, H. (1983). The new functionalism and Piaget's program. In E. K. Scholnick (Ed.), *New trends in conceptual representation: Challenges to Piaget's theory?* (pp. 3–40). Hillsdale, NJ: Lawrence Erlbaum Associates.

Bornstein, M. H. (1989). Stability in early mental development: From attention and information processing in infancy to language and cognition in childhood. In M. H. Bornstein & N. A. Krasnegor (Eds.), *Stability and continuity in mental development: Behavioral and biological perspectives* (pp. 147–170). Hillsdale, NJ: Lawrence Erlbaum Associates.

Bornstein, M. H., & Krasnegor, N. A. (Eds.). (1989). *Stability and continuity in mental development: Behavioral and biological perspectives*. Hillsdale, NJ: Lawrence Erlbaum Associates.

Brainerd, C. J. (1987). Structural measurement theory and cognitive development. In J. Bisanz, C. J. Brainerd, & R. Kail (Eds.), *Formal methods in developmental psychology: Progress in cognitive development research* (pp. 1–37). New York: Springer-Verlag.

Brown, A. L. (1982). Learning and development: The problem of compatibility, access and induction. *Human Development, 25,* 89–115.

Brown, J. S., & Burton, R. R. (1978). Diagnostic models for procedural bugs in basic mathematical skills. *Cognitive Science, 2,* 155–192.

Brown, J. S., & VanLehn, K. (1982). Towards a generative theory of 'bugs'. In T. Romberg, T. Carpenter, & J. Moser (Eds.), *Addition and subtraction: A developmental perspective* (pp. 117–135). Hillsdale, NJ: Lawrence Erlbaum Associates.

Brown, R. (1970). Introduction. In Society for Research in Child Development (Ed.), *Cognitive development in children* (pp. ix–xii). Chicago: University of Chicago Press.

Burt, C. (1919). The development of reasoning in school children. *Journal of Experimental Pedagogy, 5,* 68–77.

Card, S., Moran, T. P., & Newell, A. (1983) *The psychology of human-computer interaction*. Hillsdale, NJ: Lawrence Erlbaum Associates.

Carver, S. M. (1986). *Transfer of LOGO debugging skill: Analysis, instruction and assessment*. Unpublished doctoral dissertation, Carnegie Mellon University, Pittsburgh, PA.

Case, R. (1985). *Intellectual development: Birth to adulthood*. New York: Academic Press.

Case, R. (1986). The new stage theories in intellectual development: Why we need them; what they assert. In M. Perlmutter (Ed.), *Perspectives for intellectual development* (pp. 57–91). Hillsdale, NJ: Lawrence Erlbaum Associates.

Case, R., & Griffin, S. (1990). Child cognitive development: The role of central conceptual structures in the development of scientific and social thought. In C. A. Hauert (Ed.), *Developmental psychology: Cognitive, perceptuo-motor and neuropsychological perspectives* (pp. 193–230). Amsterdam: North Holland.

Chase, W. G. (Ed.). (1973). *Visual information processing.* New York: Academic Press.

Chase, W. G. (1978). Elementary information processes. In W. K. Estes (Ed.), *Handbook of learning and cognitive processes* (Vol. 5, pp. 19–90). Hillsdale, NJ: Lawrence Erlbaum Associates.

Chi, M. T. H. (1976). Short-term memory limitations in children: Capacity or processing deficits? *Memory and Cognition, 4,* 559–572.

Chi, M. T. H. (1977). Age differences in memory span. *Journal of Experimental Child Psychology, 23,* 266–281.

Chi, M. T. H. (1978). Knowledge structures and memory development. In R. Siegler (Ed.), *Children's thinking: What develops?* (pp. 73–96). Hillsdale, NJ: Lawrence Erlbaum Associates.

Chi, M. T. H. (1981). Knowledge development and memory performance. In M. Friedman, J. P. Das, & N. O'Connor (Eds.), *Intelligence and learning* (pp. 221–229). New York: Plenum.

Chi, M. T. H., & Ceci, S. J. (1987). Content knowledge: Its role, representation, and restructuring in memory development. *Advances in Child Development and Behavior, 20,* 91–141.

Chi, M. T. H., & Klahr, D. (1975). Span and rate of apprehension in children and adults. *Journal of Experimental Child Psychology, 19,* 434–439.

Colombo, J., Mitchell, D. W., O'Brien, M., & Horowitz, F. D. (1987). The stability of visual habituation during the first year of life. *Child Development, 58,* 474–487.

Craik, F. I. M., & Lockhart, R. S. (1972). Levels of processing: A framework for memory research. *Journal of Verbal Learning and Verbal Behavior, 11,* 671–684.

Davidson, J. E. (1986). The role of insight in giftedness. In R. J. Sternberg & J. E. Davidson (Eds.), *Conceptions of giftedness* (pp. 201–222). New York: Cambridge University Press.

DeLoache, J. S. (1987). Rapid change in the symbolic functioning of very young children. *Science, 238,* 1556–1557.

Dunbar, K., & Klahr, D. (1989). Developmental differences in scientific discovery strategies. In D. Klahr & K. Kotovsky (Eds.), *Complex information processing: The impact of Herbert A. Simon* (pp. 109–143). Hillsdale, NJ: Lawrence Erlbaum Associates.

Ericsson, A. & Simon, H. A. (1984). *Protocol analysis: Verbal reports as data.* Cambridge, MA: MIT Press.

Fagan, J. F., & Singer, L. T. (1983). Infant recognition memory as a measure of intelligence. In L. P. Lipsitt (Ed.), *Advances in infancy research* (Vol. 2, pp. 31–78). Norwood, NJ: Ablex.

Falkenhainer, B., Forbus, K. D., & Gentner, D. (1986). The structure-mapping engine. In 5th *Proceedings of the American Association for Artificial Intelligence* (pp. 272–277). Philadelphia: American Association for Artificial Intelligence.

Fay, A. L., & Mayer, R. E. (1987). Children's naive conceptions and confusions about LOGO graphics commands. *Journal of Educational Psychology, 79*(3), 254–268.

Fischer, K. W. (1980). A theory of cognitive development: The control and construction of hierarchies of skills. *Psychological Review, 87,* 477–531.

Flavell, J. H. (1984). Discussion. In R. J. Sternberg (Ed.), *Mechanisms of cognitive development* (pp. 187–210). New York: Freeman.

Flavell, J. H., & Wohlwill, J. F. (1969). Formal and functional aspects of cognitive development. In D. Elkind & J. H. Flavell (Eds.), *Studies in cognitive development* (pp. 67–120). New York: Oxford University Press.

Geary, D. C., Widaman, K. F., Little, T. D., & Cormier, P. (1987). Cognitive addition: Comparison of learning disabled and academically normal elementary school children. *Cognitive Development, 2*(3), 249–270.

Gelman, R. (1978). Cognitive development. *Annual Review of Psychology, 29,* 297–332.

Gelman, R. (1982). Accessing one-to-one correspondence: Still another paper about conservation. *British Journal of Psychology, 73,* 209–220.

Goodman, N. (1968). *Languages of art.* Indianapolis: Bobbs-Merrill.

Granrud, C. E., Haake, R. J., & Yonas, A. (1985). Infants' sensitivity to familiar size: The effect of memory on spatial perception. *Perception and Psychophysics, 37,* 459–466.

Gagné, R. M. (1968). Learning hierarchies. *Educational Psychology, 6,* 1–9.

Greeno, J. G., Riley, M. S., & Gelman, R. (1984). Conceptual competence and children's counting. *Cognitive Psychology, 16*(1), 94–143.

Gregg, L. W., & Simon, H. A. (1967). Process models and stochastic theories of simple concept formation. *Journal of Mathematical Psychology, 4,* 246–276.

Groen, G. J., & Parkman, J. M. (1972). A chronometric analysis of simple addition. *Psychological Review, 79,* 329–343.

Haith, M. M. (1980). *Rules that infants look by.* Hillsdale, NJ: Lawrence Erlbaum Associates.

Halford, G. S. (1970). A theory of the acquisition of conservation. *Psychological Review, 77,* 302–316.

Halford, G. S. (1975). Children's ability to interpret transformations of a quantity, I: An operational system for judging combinations of transformations. *Canadian Journal of Psychology, 29,* 124–141.

Hill, J. C. (1983). A computational model of language acquisition in the two-year-old. *Cognition and Brain Theory, 6,* 287–317.

Hill, J. C., & Arbib, M. A. (1984). Schemas, computation, and language acquisition. *Human Development, 27,* 282–296.

Holland, J. H. (1986). Escaping brittleness: The possibilities of general purpose machine learning algorithms applied to parallel rule-based systems. In R. S. Michalski, J. G. Carbonell, & T. M. Mitchell (Eds.), *Machine learning: An artificial intelligence approach* (pp. 593–624). Los Altos, CA: Morgan-Kaufmann.

Hoyer, W. J., & Familant, M. E. (1987). Adult age differences in the rate of processing expectancy information. *Cognitive Development, 2*(1), 59–70.

Hunter, I. M. L. (1968). Mental calculation. In P. C. Wason & P. N. Johnson-Laird (Eds.), *Thinking and reasoning* (pp. 341–351). Baltimore, MD: Penguin.

Inhelder, B., Ackerman-Vallado, E., Blanchet, A., Karmiloff-Smith, A., Kilcher-Hagedorn, H., Montagero, J., & Robert, M. (1976). The process of invention in cognitive development: A report of research in progress. *Archives de Psychologie, 171,* 57–72.

Jensen, E. M., Reese, E. P., & Reese, T. W. (1950). The subitizing and counting of visually presented fields of dots. *Journal of Psychology, 30,* 363–392.

Jevons, W. S. (1871). The power of numerical discrimination. *Nature, 3,* 281–282.

Kail, R. (1984). *The development of memory in children* (2nd ed.). New York: Freeman.

Kail, R. (1986). Sources of age differences in speed of processing. *Child Development, 57,* 969–987.

Kail, R. (1988). Developmental functions for speeds of cognitive processes. *Journal of Experimental Child Psychology, 45,* 339–364.

Kail, R. (1991a). Processing time declines exponentially during childhood and adolescence. *Developmental Psychology, 27,* 259–266.

Kail, R. (1991b). Developmental change in speed of processing during childhood and adolescence. *Psychological Bulletin, 109,* 490–501.

Karmiloff-Smith, A. (1984). Children's problem solving. In M. Lamb, A. Brown, & B. Rogoff (Eds.), *Advances in developmental psychology* (pp. 33-99). Hillsdale, NJ: Lawrence Erlbaum Associates.

Keating, D. P., & Bobbitt, B. L. (1978). Individual and developmental differences in cognitive processing components of mental ability. *Child Development, 49,* 155-167.

Kellman, P. H. (1988). Theories of perception and research in perceptual development. In A. Yonas (Ed.), *Perceptual development in infancy* (pp. 267-282). Hillsdale, NJ: Lawrence Erlbaum Associates.

Kendler, H. H., & Kendler, T. S. (1962). Vertical and horizontal processes in problem solving. *Psychological Review, 69,* 1-16.

Kintsch, W., & Greeno, J. G. (1985). Understanding and solving word arithmetic problems. *Psychological Review, 92,* 109-129.

Klahr, D. (1973). A production system for counting, subitizing, and adding. In W. G. Chase (Ed.), *Visual information processing* (pp. 3-34). New York: Academic Press.

Klahr, D. (1989). Information processing approaches. In R. Vasta (Ed.), *Annals of child development* (pp. 131-185). Greenwich, CT: JAI Press.

Klahr, D., & Carver, S. M. (1988). Cognitive objectives in a LOGO debugging curriculum: Instruction, learning, and transfer. *Cognitive Psychology, 20,* 362-404.

Klahr, D., Fay, A. L., & Dunbar, K. (1991). *Heuristics for scientific experimentation: A developmental study.* Working Paper, Carnegie Mellon University.

Klahr, D., Langley, P., & Neches, R. (Eds.). (1987). *Production systems models of learning and development.* Cambridge, MA: MIT Press.

Klahr, D., & Robinson, M. (1981). Formal assessment of problem solving and planning processes in preschool children. *Cognitive Psychology, 13,* 113-148.

Klahr, D., & Siegler, R. S. (1978). The representation of children's knowledge. In H. W. Reese & L. P. Lipsitt (Eds.), *Advances in child development and behavior* (Vol. 12, pp. 61-116). New York: Academic Press.

Klahr, D., & Wallace, J. G. (1970a). The development of serial completion strategies: An information processing analysis. *British Journal of Psychology, 61,* 243-257.

Klahr, D., & Wallace, J. G. (1970b). An information processing analysis of some Piagetian experimental tasks. *Cognitive Psychology, 1,* 358-387.

Klahr, D., & Wallace, J. G. (1972). Class inclusion processes. In S. Farnham-Diggory (Ed.), *Information processing in children* (pp. 144-181). New York: Academic Press.

Klahr, D., & Wallace, J. G. (1973). The role of quantification operators in the development of conservation of quantity. *Cognitive Psychology, 4,* 301-327.

Klahr, D., & Wallace, J. G. (1976). *Cognitive development: An information processing view.* Hillsdale, NJ: Lawrence Erlbaum Associates.

Kolers, P. A., & Smythe, W. E. (1984). Symbol manipulation: Alternatives to the computational view of mind. *Journal of Verbal Learning and Verbal Behavior, 23,* 289-314.

Kuhn, D. (1989). Children and adults as intuitive scientists. *Psychological Review, 96,* 674-689.

Kuhn, D., Amsel, E., & O'Loughlin, M. (1988). *The development of scientific reasoning skills.* Orlando, FL: Academic Press.

Kuhn, D., & Phelps, E. (1982). The development of problem solving strategies. In H. W. Reese (Ed.), *Advances in child development and behavior* (pp. 2-44). New York: Academic Press.

Lachman, R., Lachman, J., & Butterfield, E. C. (1979). *Cognitive psychology and information processing: An introduction.* Hillsdale, NJ: Lawrence Erlbaum Associates.

Larkin, J. H. (1981). Enriching formal knowledge: A model for learning to solve textbook physics problems. In J. R. Anderson (Ed.), *Cognitive skills and their acquisition* (pp. 311-334). Hillsdale, NJ: Lawrence Erlbaum Associates.

Lewis, C. H. (1978). *Production system models of practice effects.* Unpublished doctoral dissertation, University of Michigan, Ann Arbor.

Lewis, C. (1981). Skill in algebra. In J. R. Anderson (Ed.), *Cognitive skills and their acquisition* (pp. 85–110). Hillsdale, NJ: Lawrence Erlbaum Associates.

Lindberg, M. A. (1980). Is knowledge base development a necessary and sufficient condition for memory development? *Journal of Experimental Child Psychology, 30,* 401–410.

Mackworth, A. K. (1987). What is the schema for a schema? *Behavioral and Brain Sciences, 10*(3), 443–444.

MacWhinney, B. J. (1987a). Competition and cooperation in language processing. In R. Tomlin (Ed.), *Proceedings of the Pacific Conference on Linguistics.* Eugene, OR: University of Oregon Press.

MacWhinney, B. J. (Ed.). (1987b). *Mechanisms of language acquisition.* Hillsdale, NJ: Lawrence Erlbaum Associates.

MacWhinney, B., Leinbach, J., Taraban, R., & McDonald, J. (1989). Language learning: Cues or rules? *Journal of Memory and Language, 28,* 255–277.

Madden, D. J. (1987). Aging, attention, and the use of meaning during visual search. *Cognitive Development, 2,* 201–216.

Mandler, J. M. (1983). Representation. In P. H. Mussen (Ed.), *Cognitive development: Vol. III. Handbook of child psychology* (pp. 420–494). New York: Wiley.

Mandler, J. M., & Johnson, N. S. (1977). Remembrance of things parsed: Story structure and recall. *Cognitive Psychology, 9,* 111–151.

Marr, D. (1982). *Vision: A computational investigation into the human representation and processing of visual information.* San Francisco: Freeman.

McClelland, J. L. (1989). Parallel distributed processing: Implications for cognition and development. In R. G. M. Morris (Ed.), *Parallel distributed processing: Implications for psychology and neurobiology* (pp. 8–45). Oxford: Clarendon Press.

McClelland, J. L., & Jenkins, E. (1991). Nature, nurture, and connections: Implications of connectionist models for cognitive development. In K. VanLehn (Ed.), *Architectures for intelligence* (pp. 41–73). Hillsdale, NJ: Lawrence Erlbaum Associates.

Metz, K. E. (1985). The development of children's problem solving in a gears task: A problem space perspective. *Cognitive Science, 9,* 431–471.

Miller, P. H. (1983). *Theories of developmental psychology.* San Francisco: Freeman.

Neches, R. (1981). *Models of heuristic procedure modification.* Unpublished doctoral dissertation, Department of Psychology, Carnegie Mellon University.

Neches, R. (1987). Learning through incremental refinement of procedures. In D. Klahr, P. Langley & R. Neches (Eds.), *Production system models of learning and development* (pp. 163–220). Cambridge, MA: MIT Press.

Neches, R., Langley, P., & Klahr, D. (1987). Learning, development and production systems. In D. Klahr, P. Langley, & R. Neches (Eds.), *Production system models of learning and development* (pp. 1–53). Cambridge, MA: MIT Press.

Nelson, K., & Gruendel, J. M. (1981). Generalized event representations: Basic building blocks of cognitive development. In M. E. Lamb & A. L. Brown (Eds.), *Advances in developmental psychology* (Vol. 1, pp. 131–158). Hillsdale, NJ: Lawrence Erlbaum Associates.

Neves, D., & Anderson, J. R. (1981). Knowledge compilation: Mechanisms for the automatization of cognitive skills. In J. R. Anderson (Ed.), *Cognitive skills and their acquisition* (pp. 57–84). Hillsdale, NJ: Lawrence Erlbaum Associates.

Newell, A. (1966). On the representation of problems. *Computer science research review,* 18–33. Computer Science Department, Carnegie Institute of Technology.

Newell, A. (1972). A note on process-structure distinctions in developmental psychology. In S. Farnham-Diggory (Ed.), *Information processing in children* (pp. 126–143). New York: Academic Press.

Newell, A. (1973). Production systems: Models of control structures. In W. G. Chase (Ed.), *Visual information processing* (pp. 463–526). New York: Academic Press.

Newell, A. (1980). Physical symbol systems. *Cognitive Science, 4,* 135–183.

Newell, A. (1981). Reasoning problem solving and decision processes: The problem space as a fundamental category. In R. Nickerson (Ed.), *Attention and performance* (Vol. 8, pp. 693-718). Hillsdale, NJ: Lawrence Erlbaum Associates.

Newell, A. (1990). *Unified theories of cognition*. Cambridge, MA: Harvard University Press.

Newell, A., & Simon, H. A. (1972). *Human problem solving*. Englewood Cliffs, NJ: Prentice-Hall.

Nisbett, R. E., & Wilson, T. D. (1977). Telling more than we can know: Verbal reports on mental processes. *Psychological Review, 84,* 231-259.

Norman, D. A., Rumelhart, D. E., & the LNR Research Group. (1975). *Explorations in cognition*. San Francisco: Freeman.

Palmer, S. E., & Kimchi, R. (1986). The information processing approach to cognition. In T. J. Knapp & L. C. Robertson (Eds.), *Approaches to cognition: Contrasts and controversies* (pp. 37-77). Hillsdale, NJ: Lawrence Erlbaum Associates.

Piaget, J. (1928). *Judgement and reasoning in the child*. New York: Harcourt, Brace.

Piaget, J. (1929). *The child's conception of the world*. New York: Harcourt, Brace.

Piaget, J. (1951). *Play, dreams, and imitation in childhood*. New York: Norton.

Plunkett, K., & Marchman, V. (1991). U-shaped learning and frequency effects in a back-propagation network: Implications for language acquisition. *Cognition, 38,* 1-60.

Rabinowitz, F. M., Grant, M. J., & Dingley, H. L. (1987). Computer simulation, cognition, and development: An introduction. In J. Bisanz, C. J. Brainerd, & R. Kail (Eds.), *Formal methods in developmental psychology: Progress in cognitive development research* (pp. 263-301). New York: Springer-Verlag.

Resnick, L. B., & Glaser, R. (1976). Problem solving and intelligence. In L. B. Resnick (Ed.), *The nature of intelligence* (pp. 205-230). Hillsdale, NJ: Lawrence Erlbaum Associates.

Riley, M. S., Greeno, J. G., & Heller, J. I. (1983). Development of children's problem-solving ability in arithmetic. In H. P. Ginsburg (Ed.), *The development of mathematical thinking* (pp. 153-200). New York: Academic Press.

Rosenbloom, P. S., & Newell, A. (1982). Learning by chunking: Summary of a task and a model. In *Proceedings of the Second National Conference on Artificial Intelligence* (pp. 255-257). Los Altos, CA: Morgan-Kaufmann.

Rosenbloom, P. S., & Newell, A. (1987). Learning by chunking: A production system model of practice. In D. Klahr, P. Langley, & R. Neches (Eds.), *Production system models of learning and development* (pp. 221-286). Cambridge, MA: MIT Press.

Rumelhart, D. E., & McClelland, J. L. (1986). *Parallel distributed processing: Explorations in the microstructure of cognition*. Cambridge, MA: MIT Press.

Schauble, L. (1990). Belief revision in children: The role of prior knowledge and strategies for generating evidence. *Journal of Experimental Child Psychology, 49,* 31-57.

Siegler, R. S. (1976). Three aspects of cognitive development. *Cognitive Psychology, 8*(4), 481-520.

Siegler, R. S. (1981). Developmental sequences within and between concepts. *Monographs of the Society for Research in Child Development, 46* (Whole No. 189).

Siegler, R. S. (1987). The perils of averaging data over strategies: An example from children's addition. *Journal of Experimental Psychology: General, 116,* 250-264.

Siegler, R. S. (1988). Strategy choice procedures and the development of multiplication skill *Journal of Experimental Psychology: General, 117,* 258-275.

Siegler, R. S. (1989). Mechanisms of cognitive development. *Annual Review of Psychology, 117,* 258-275.

Siegler, R. S., & Crowley, K. (1991). The microgenetic method: A direct means for studying cognitive development. *American Psychologist, 46,* 606-620.

Siegler, R. S., & Jenkins, E. (1989). *How children discover new strategies*. Hillsdale, NJ: Lawrence Erlbaum Associates.

Siegler, R. S., & Shrager, J. (1984). Strategy choices in addition and subtraction: How do children know what to do? In C. Sophian (Ed.), *Origins of cognitive skills* (pp. 229–293). Hillsdale, NJ: Lawrence Erlbaum Associates.

Simon, D. P., & Simon, H. A. (1978). Individual differences in solving physics problems. In R. Siegler (Ed.), *Children's thinking: What develops?* (pp. 325–348). Hillsdale, NJ: Lawrence Erlbaum Associates.

Simon, H. A. (1962). An information processing theory of intellectual development. *Monographs of the Society for Research in Child Development, 27,* (2, Serial No. 82).

Simon, H. A. (1969). *The sciences of the artificial.* Cambridge, MA: MIT Press.

Simon, T., Newell, A., & Klahr, D. (1991). A computational account of children's learning about number conservation. In D. Fisher & M. Pazzani (Eds.), *Concept formation: Knowledge and experience in unsupervised learning* (pp. 423–462). Palo Alto, CA: Morgan-Kauffman.

Spitz, H. H., & Borys, S. V. (1984). Depth of search: How far can the retarded search through an internally represented problem space? In P. H. Brooks, R. Sperber, & C. McCauley (Eds.), *Learning and cognition in the mentally retarded* (pp. 333–358). Hillsdale, NJ: Lawrence Erlbaum Associates.

Stein, N. L., & Glenn, C. G. (1979). An analysis of story comprehension in elementary school children. In R. O. Freedle (Ed.), *New directions in discourse processing,* (Vol. 2., pp. 53–120). Norwood, NJ: Ablex.

Sternberg, R. J. (Ed.). (1984). *Mechanisms of cognitive development.* New York: Freeman.

Sternberg, R. J., & Rifkin, B. (1979). The development of analogical reasoning processes. *Journal of Experimental Child Psychology, 27,* 195–232.

Sternberg, S. (1966). High speed scanning in human memory. *Science, 153,* 652–654.

Strauss, S. (Ed.). (1982). *U-shaped behavioral growth.* New York: Academic Press.

Townsend, J. T., & Kadlec, H. (1990). Psychology and mathematics. In R. E. Mickens (Ed.)., *Mathematics and science* (pp. 223–249). Singapore: World Scientific Publishing.

Trabasso, T. (1975). Representation, memory and reasoning: How do we make transitive inferences? In A. D. Pick (Ed.), *Minnesota symposia on child psychology.* (Vol. 9., pp. 135–172). Minneapolis: University of Minnesota Press.

Trabasso, T., Riley, C. A., & Wilson, E. G. (1975). The representation of linear order and spatial strategies in reasoning: A developmental study. In R. J. Falmagne (Ed.), *Reasoning: Representation and process* (pp. 201–230). Hillsdale, NJ: Lawrence Erlbaum Associates.

Vurpillot, E. (1968). The development of scanning strategies and their relation to visual differentiation. *Journal of Experimental Child Psychology, 6,* 632–650.

Wallace, J. G., Klahr, D., & Bluff, K. (1987). A self-modifying production system of cognitive development. In D. Klahr, P. Langley, & R. Neches (Eds.), *Production system models of learning and development* (pp. 356–435). Cambridge, MA: MIT Press.

Wertsch, J. V., & Hickmann, M. (1987). Problem solving in social interaction: A microgenetic analysis. In M. Hickmann (Ed.), *Social and functional approaches to language and thought* (pp. 251–266). New York: Academic Press.

Wilkinson, A. C., & Haines, B. A. (1987). Learning a cognitive skill and its components. In J. Bisanz, C. J. Brainerd, & R. Kail (Eds.), *Formal methods in developmental psychology: Progress in cognitive development research* (pp. 86–114). New York: Springer-Verlag.

Yonas, A. (Ed.). (1988). *Perceptual development in infancy.* Hillsdale, NJ: Lawrence Erlbaum Associates.

Young, R. M. (1976). *Seriation by children: An artificial intelligence analysis of a Piagetian task.* Basel: Birkhauser.

Young, R. M., & O'Shea, T. (1981). Errors in children's subtraction. *Cognitive Science, 5,* 153–177.

6 Language Development

Peter A. de Villiers
Jill G. de Villiers
Smith College

INTRODUCTION

The fundamental questions in the field of language development revolve around issues that echo the past 400 years of philosophy of mind. What are the concepts that furnish the child's mind at the beginning of language development? Where do these concepts arise, and are they linguistic or more generally cognitive? Does the child build a lexicon or grammar through induction from particulars to general rules? What principles guide or constrain this process?

There are further questions that occur to a developmental psychologist: Is a child different from an adult in the learning of language? Does maturation play a role? Does cognitive or social development offer any constraint on this process? How does the social-interaction context of acquisition affect its course?

In this chapter, we isolate certain areas of debate that crystallize these issues, in full recognition that we are being highly selective within the vast literature on language development. We have chosen to limit the material covered to major issues in the domains of semantics (lexical development) and syntax (grammatical development). Psycholinguistics is a difficult area, drawing as it does on the very different empirical traditions of psychology and linguistics. We can provide only a glimpse of the important work in modern linguistics that stimulates many studies in child language, but it is important to realize that such background is an essential ingredient for serious work in this area.

Discuss

Consider for a moment the nature of the task facing the infant in acquiring a language. All around is talk, and action, and stimulation by the world and social beings. From that stream of stimulation the child must "discover" words, must "recognize" their social and cognitive significance, must "attach meaning" to them, and must begin to participate in "using them" in acts of reference and discourse. But words do not come detached from sentences, and the ways in which words combine into sentences vary with the language. Children have to "parse" the stream of speech into its component parts—words, inflectional morphemes, phrases, clauses, sentences—and "derive" the rules for their construction. Beyond that they must "use the rules" of the language to create new meanings using new structures, and "understand the conditions of their use." The quotation marks in this paragraph emphasize our ignorance about all of the processes they highlight.

The areas of lexical and grammatical development share certain common problem areas, and certain styles of solution, that we emphasize throughout. The central problem in each area is that of induction, sometimes called *Plato's Problem.* How is it that human beings, on the basic of particularistic and limited experience, come to know as much as they do? For Plato, the solution was to be found in the memory of prior existence. For some contemporary theorists of child language acquisition, Plato's solution is not too wide of the mark. They would argue that the problem of induction is insoluble unless children are equipped with some way to restrict the vast number of hypotheses that are compatible with the limited linguistic data to which they are exposed. For others, the solution is to be found in the environmental support that the world provides: for example, in the way that caregivers prestructure and order the input. For still a third group, an intermediate position seems possible: Children's cognitive capacities are rich enough to make order from the chaos of stimulation, at least with the aid of attentive caregivers.

The parallel styles of solution are to be found throughout, and we highlight them again at the end of the chapter. However, another similarity in the domains of semantic development and grammar deserves commentary. In both, it is striking that the notion of a preexistent, constrained hypothesis space is most compelling for the more complex developments. It is common for attacks on this position to be launched from investigators who study simpler domains: first words or first sentences. But any adequate theory of language acquisition must account for the errors that children do not make as well as the characteristic errors they do make in mastering the abstract and complex semantic and syntactic system of their native language. It is important that we not do what Gleitman (1981) described as "account for *the cat is on the mat* and then cross one's fingers" (p. 104).

LEXICAL DEVELOPMENT

Issues

Several key issues dominate current work on lexical development. They are discussed here.

What Is the Role of Children's Conceptual Development in Their Semantic Development?   This question takes several forms in the literature. First, are there prerequisites in cognitive development that precede particular stages or transitions in lexical development? The strongest form of this notion comes from research and theories in the Piagetian tradition that suggest particular cognitive masteries in the sensorimotor stages of development — such as the concept of permanent objects — constrain the onset of symbolic word use.

Second, when children learn words, are the nonlinguistic concepts they denote established before the lexical development takes place, such that word meanings are simply mapped onto nonlinguistic categories already represented in the children's memory? For example, when children learn the words "in" and "on," are the concepts of containment and support already understood in a nonlinguistic way, so that they simply have to learn which word refers to which concept? Or, does children's exposure to the adult language around them serve to shape their nonlinguistic categorization of objects and events? The way words in a particular language group or contrast different features of the world may draw children's attention to conceptual or perceptual similarities and distinctions that they had not noted before.

Of course, the interaction between lexical and cognitive development may be more complex and reciprocal in nature, with the two developmental processes influencing each other in different ways for different aspects of semantics or cognition.

What Is the Role of the Input in Lexical Development?   Again this general question takes several forms. For example, how does the nature of parental language in the early stages of development contribute to the pattern of word acquisition: in the kinds of words that children initially acquire, the rate at which they learn them, and in the way they use them? This issue includes the frequency of different types of words in parents' speech to children, how parents' naming practices relate to children's ongoing actions, and the kinds of feedback parents give when children misuse words.

In a different sense, syntactic information in the input language can provide clues that help children constrain the hypotheses they entertain as to the possible meanings of new words they hear. For example, syntactic usage distinguishes common from proper nouns ("*the* dog" vs. "Rover"), and mass from count nouns ("*some* jelly" vs. "*a few* cookies").

What Biases or Constraining Principles Does the Child Bring to the Task of Acquiring the Lexicon of the Language Community? This question acquires particular importance in the light of the uncertainty inherent in inducing a meaning for a new word on the basis of hearing it used in context. If an adult says the word "rabbit" in the presence of the child and a rabbit is hopping by, how does the child decide that the word refers to the rabbit itself and not to its ears or its furriness, nor to the action of hopping or the configuration of a rabbitlike creature hopping? Yet lexical development proceeds remarkably rapidly and smoothly with rare direct instruction in word meanings, few dramatic misunderstandings on the part of the child, and little direct feedback about the correctness of the meanings the child assumes. How does the child constrain the many hypotheses that could be entertained when a new word is encountered in any particular linguistic and nonlinguistic context? Several researchers have proposed that children follow a set of principles that limit the meanings they consider when they hear a new word.

These issues recur in several areas and stages of semantic development, and they shape our selection of topics and empirical studies in this chapter. But first, it helps to get a general overview of the course of lexical acquisition in the preschool years.

A Brief Characterization of Major Periods of Acquisition

Over the past 15 years most research and theory on lexical development has focused on the following three periods.

The First Words (10–18 Months): Learning What Words Do. When children are only producing a small number of words (typically 10 to 30), those words tend to be tied to social, pragmatic purposes and limited in their use to the particular referential or action situations in which they were first or most frequently heard. Nelson (1985) suggested that during this time the child is learning what words do: first their social functions and effects on others, and later their referential function as labels.

The Later One-Word Period and Transition to Simple Sentences (18–30 Months): Learning What Particular Words Denote. Toward the end of the second year, there is often a rapid increase in word learning, characterized by some authors as a *naming explosion.* Words are generalized across many different contexts (sometimes inappropriately) and used freely to refer to the many things and activities that toddlers find interesting and important: people, pets, toys, food, salient actions in games and social routines, bodily functions, and so on. For many children, this spurt in vocabulary is focused on names for things rather than words for properties, actions, and social regulation, although this seems to vary with the nature of the caregiver–child interaction and the culture. The major focus of development during this time seems to be working out the *referential extension* of words, that is, the set of objects and events to which a particular word correctly applies—what linguists like Lyons (1981) have called a word's *denotative* meaning. A striking phenomenon during this period is the young child's overextension of words to refer to new objects and actions. The attention of parents and linguists alike is captured when all men become "daddy" and all animals are "doggie."

The Preschool Years (30 Months–5 Years): Learning the Meaning Relations Among Words.   The meanings of words in the lexicon of any language are related to each other in a variety of ways. In *semantic fields* (such as kinship relationships among people, size relations between objects, or relative position in space), words that refer to a particular domain of meaning are organized by similarity and opposition along semantic dimensions. In *taxonomic hierarchies* (such as living things, animals, mammals, dogs, and chihuahuas), words are organized at different levels of generality in subordinate–superordinate relations. A major characteristic of vocabulary development in the preschool and early school years is the child's increasing understanding of the *sense relations* (Lyons, 1981) between words in these groupings or networks—what Aitchison (1987) called "cobwebs" of meaning. The discovery of similarities and differences in the meanings of related words sometimes leads to apparent reorganizations in the child's lexicon and late emerging errors in her understanding and use of those words following a previous period of appropriate usage (Bowerman, 1982).

Another important phenomenon during this period of language development is the rapidity with which children are able to make at least partial mappings of the meanings of previously unknown words on encountering them once or twice in context in the adult input. This *fast mapping* of meaning is an essential component of the astounding rate of vocabulary growth during childhood (as many as 5 to 10 words per day).

Sources of Data

Before we turn to a more detailed consideration of each of these periods of development and the theoretical issues that they raise, let us briefly look at the range of methods available to the researcher investigating these topics. How do we gather the data from which to describe and account for the patterns and stages in children's learning of words?

Diary Studies. Much of the data on the earlier stages of vocabulary development come from diary studies of single or small numbers of children in which parents (often the researchers themselves) systematically recorded all the usages of words by the child (for examples see Bloom, 1973; Dromi, 1987; Leopold, 1939–1949). The best of these have detailed notes of linguistic and nonlinguistic context, and record multiple uses of particular words (preferably all of the child's words that were observed) over a period of months or more, so that changes in the pattern of usage of a particular word can be traced as the child's lexicon grows. The best diary studies also note lexical aspects of the parent-to-child input at different points in time (for a model single-subject case study of this sort see Dromi, 1987)

Several recent studies have asked parents (mothers) to keep a diary of the words used by their children over the period of the study (usually from 6 weeks to 6 months), noting situations in which the words were used, and any noted changes in usage over time. Some supplemented these diaries with parental interviews in which the mothers completed a vocabulary checklist on their children containing common words reported from previous studies (Bates, Bretherton, & Snyder, 1988; Reznick & Goldsmith, 1989). This is obviously a much easier procedure for a researcher to employ than repeated observation of the children in controlled testing situations. It has the inherent danger of exaggeration on the part of the parent of the language skills of their offspring, but in the case of well-instructed parents it has proved a fairly reliable index of development when checked against other more objective recording techniques (Dale, Bates, Reznick, & Morisset, 1990).

Recorded Samples. Transcribed recordings, audio or video, of toddlers' spontaneous speech either longitudinally at periods about 2 to 6 weeks apart, or cross-sectionally across different ages, have typically been used to supplement diary data. These recordings, especially if they are audio alone, must be supplemented by considerable information about the nonlinguistic social and referential context in which the recorded verbal interactions took place.

Comprehension Testing. Controlled testing of the comprehension of words, usually in a picture or object identification format, is also a frequent technique. In interpreting children's choices in such paradigms, consideration must be taken of any nonlinguistic strategies they may adopt in responding to the researcher's questions (de Villiers & de Villiers, 1982). Here, too, the best information comes from longitudinal testing, although it is rare for such data to be collected.

Some recent studies have used preferential looking paradigms in which longer fixation times to a picture, object, or video that matches a spoken word or sentence rather than being unrelated to it are taken as evidence of the comprehension of words (Golinkoff, Hirsch-Pasek, Cauley, & Gordon, 1987). This procedure allows testing of comprehension in younger toddlers than do procedures in which the child has to point to or act on an object or picture.

Interviews. In studies of later development in 3- to 5-year-olds, several researchers have adapted the classic Piagetian interview technique in which the child is asked to give a meaning for the word being studied and then the basis for that response is probed by a series of questions. While in the case of 2-year-olds few discriminating answers are given to requests for judgments like "Is blue a color?", in older children the interview can provide informative data, especially when data on the children's use of the words in spontaneous speech are open to several interpretations (Anglin, 1986).

Teaching New Words. A final technique that is particularly apt for developing and testing theories about the *process* by which words are acquired is to attempt to teach children a new word, either by ostensive labeling ("This is a _____"), or by simply embedding the unknown word in language addressed to the child in particular contexts. Experiments vary as to whether the unknown word is a real word in the language or a nonsense word (the literature is now replete with "zivs" and "feps" and "daxes"), and whether or not the child already has a more familiar name for the referent. The best training studies examine children's generalization of the new word to novel exemplars in both comprehension and production.

For much of the research on lexical development, a major problem of interpretation arises when the empirical data consist of observed *extensions of the word* in production and comprehension, but the theoretical accounts are couched in terms of differences and changes in children's underlying *meaning representations,* which are not directly observable. Hence multiple, converging measures on the same children would seem to be the best methodology (Anglin, 1986; de Villiers & de Villiers, 1982). Different methods have different strengths and weaknesses, and complementary sources of information provide a more complete picture of children's changing knowledge of word meaning.

We turn now to a more detailed characterization of the pattern of semantic development in each of the major stages just outlined.

PATTERNS AND DETERMINANTS
OF EARLY DEVELOPMENT

What words do children learn first and how do they use them?

Context-Bound Early Use

Most studies report that the first recognizable words—productions that have consistent phonological form related to adult words, and an interpretable usage—emerge around the end of the first year and into the middle of the second year. These are frequently preceded by proto-words, consistent vocalizations that are idiosyncratic to particular children and bear no clear relationship to adult forms (Griffiths, 1987; Nelson, 1985).

Several studies report that word learning over the first few months (the first 10 to 30 words) is slow and somewhat erratic, with some words disappearing after short periods of use (Bloom, 1973; Leopold, 1939), and many words being closely tied in their usage to restricted actional and interactional contexts and not generalizing across situations (Barrett, 1986; Bates, Benigni, Bretherton, Camaioni, & Volterra, 1979; Bloom, 1973; Dromi, 1987). For example, Bloom (1973) noted that her daughter, Allison, produced the word "car" at the age of 9 months, but initially used it only when she was looking down on a moving car from the living room window. At this time Allison did not use the word "car" when she saw stationary cars in other circumstances, while she was riding in a car, nor while looking at pictures of cars.

Of the first 10 words for each of four children from the ages of 10 to 24 months, Harris, Barrett, Jones, and Brookes (1988) found that between 30% and 80% were initially context-bound. In these cases, the child seems to have identified a single, global event as the appropriate context in which to use the word. Nelson (1985) suggested that the word is an integral part of the child's holistic representation of the event and does not yet refer to any separable action or object concept. However, after a relatively short period of time, rarely more than a few weeks, the contexts of use of these early words expand as the child generalizes to a variety of situations.

The Naming Explosion

For many children there then seems to be an accelerated burst of word acquisition for a period of a few months in the latter part of the second year (Benedict, 1979; Bloom, 1973; Dromi, 1987; McShane, 1980). In this period the acquisition of names for objects seems to dominate lexical development, and several words may be learned together as contrasting sets, such as names for foodstuffs, animals, and body parts (Dromi, 1987).

Various accounts of the vocabulary spurt have been offered. Nelson (1985) proposed that a major task for the child in the earliest stages of language development is finding out what words do pragmatically and referentially. The beginning of the vocabulary spurt may correspond to the child's discovery that words can function as labels that refer to objects and events. Some authors characterize this as a sudden linguistic insight — an "aha" experience (Dore, 1978; McShane, 1980; see a dramatic case study description of this by Kamhi, 1986). However, we should be cautious about overstating the discontinuity between this stage and the earlier period in which words are being learned more slowly and seem to be situation-bound. Harris et al. (1988) note that several of the earliest words they found in toddlers' vocabularies were used referentially and productively from the first; and Goldfield and Reznick (1990) did not observe any marked naming explosion in about one third of the toddlers they studied. Instead, these subjects' acquisition of words seemed to proceed at a more measured pace and with an even distribution across word types. Other researchers suggest that the vocabulary spurt is more closely tied to cognitive developments in this period, particularly the emergence of object and event categorization skills (Gopnik & Meltzoff, 1986), or to the kinds of linguistic interaction engaged in by the children and their parents (Goldfield & Reznick, 1990).

Types of Words

The early vocabulary of Western middle-class children (the first 200 words or so) tends to be dominated by *labels for objects* (Benedict, 1979; E. Clark, 1983; Griffiths, 1987; Rescorla, 1980). Important people like Mommy, Daddy, Granny, and the family dog; body parts and articles of clothing; things to eat and drink; and animals learned from picture books; these are frequently the focus of young children's activity and communicative interaction in that social group and tend to be among the first things labeled. Thus, many theoretical accounts of the meanings underlying children's early words have concentrated on object words (Anglin, 1977; E. Clark, 1973; Kuczaj, 1986).

However, several different types of words, defined by their use or function in conversation, also appear in the earliest stages (Gopnik, 1988). Besides names, the child's first 30 to 50 words typically include *social words;* words that are consistently used to fulfill some particular social function or speech act such as requesting objects or actions, or as part of a social ritual of greeting or leave-taking. This includes words like "dere" or "dat" to draw the parents' attention to an object or to request an object, "no" to reject actions, and "bye bye" to take leave of people. These words frequently emerge out of routinized social interactions, and are often related to prior vocalization–gesture sequences (Bruner, 1983; Carter, 1978).

A little later in development, the child begins to use *relational words*. Some of these seem to encode success ("there" said when the child has succeeded in some action), or failure ("uhoh," "oh dear," or even a heartfelt "oh bugger" when something goes wrong) in the actions the child is attempting. Others concern the recurrence ("more" or "another"), disappearance ("gone" or "allgone"), direction of movement ("down," "up," "in," or "out"), or location of objects ("there"). Gopnik (1982, Gopnik & Meltzoff, 1986) suggested that relational terms first encode aspects of the child's plans. Children in this stage are most likely to use words like "gone" when they themselves have made an object disappear, or "down" when they make an object move in that direction. Only later do they use the same words to encode other people's actions in this way, or to refer to the static relationships of objects.

Several writers have suggested that there is a transition from a more socially determined use of early vocabulary to a more decontextualized or cognitively determined usage around the middle of the second year (Gopnik, 1988; Griffiths, 1987; McShane, 1980). Halliday (1975) referred to this as a shift from the *pragmatic* to the *mathetic* functions of language being dominant for the child: that is, a shift from preoccupation with the communicative aspects of language to the use of language to organize and categorize experience.

The Role of the Social-Interactional Setting

How does early word learning relate to the nature of the interaction between children and their primary caregivers? Vygotsky (1962) argued that symbol formation and symbolic thought first take form for children in social interaction. For the child, socially derived symbols, such as words, as well as their manipulation, are first constituted in the joint activity of the child and caregiver, and are only later gradually internalized. Thus, both cognitive and language development are essentially embedded in a social interaction in which the child is viewed as a novice performer who is apprenticed to an expert performer, the caregiver. This social-interactional view of language acquisition has been taken up by several recent theorists and led to an increased focus on the context of early language development and the nature of the parental language in that interaction (Adams & Bullock, 1986; Bruner, 1983; Wells, 1981).

For example, Bruner and his coworkers (Bruner, 1983) have stressed the social-communicative interaction between the caregiver and child as a "support system" for early language acquisition, especially for lexical and conversational aspects. At least in Western middle-class families, caregiver and child engage in a variety of interactional routines that serve to "scaffold" the child's early language by providing a predictable referential and social context that makes the meaning of both the child and the caregiver's language immediately apparent in those contexts. In repetitive games like build-and-bash (building and then knocking down towers of blocks or other objects) or peek-a-boo, in picture-book reading routines, and in reciprocal naming games of "What's that?", familiar interactional frames are created into which simple words and phrases are slotted, first by the caregiver and then by the child (Ninio, 1980; Ninio & Bruner, 1978; Ratner & Bruner, 1978).

Central to these routines is the establishment of joint attention between child and caregiver through which the toddler can establish the intended referents of the caregiver's language. Recent empirical studies have strongly implicated the establishment and use of joint attention in the lexical development of the child. There is typically a close correspondence between mothers' speech to their toddlers between the ages of 6 and 18 months and the objects and activities that are the focus of the child's attention during the interactions. Indeed, during this period mothers mostly take their cue about what would be an appropriate topic of conversation from their child's behavior. The vast majority of mothers' utterances during free play refer to the object that is the current focus of the child. Directives to shape the child's attention (e.g., "Look, a bunny") and actions (e.g., "Kiss the bunny") are generally timed to coincide with points in the interaction when the child is already looking at or touching the relevant object rather than when their attention is engaged elsewhere (Bridges, 1986; Harris, Jones, & Grant, 1984; Schaffer, Hepburn, & Collis, 1983).

Within these periods of joint attentional focus (e.g., joint play with an object) mother–child dyads speak more and engage in longer turn-taking conversations on each topic than they do at other times when the communication is more one way. Furthermore, Tomasello and Farrar (1986a) demonstrated that within clearly defined episodes of joint attention to an object or activity, the more mothers provided labels for the objects on which their children were focused, the larger the child's vocabulary was likely to be, and the more object words they learned at 15 and 21 months. Frequent use of object names to redirect the child's attention and behavior away from the objects with which they were interacting was negatively correlated with vocabulary size. The same measures of the mothers' referential language outside joint attentional episodes did not correlate with either the size or composition of the children's vocabulary.

Individual Differences

Nelson (1973) highlighted *individual differences* in the content of early vocabularies of children and the ways in which they use those words. She distinguished between a *referential* and an *expressive* language style on the basis of the distribution of different types of words in the first 50 words learned. Referential children used predominantly content words, especially object names, to label their world; whereas expressive children used their words more to regulate their social interaction with adults, and so had fewer object names relative to social words. Other researchers have subsequently reported that children who adopt a referential style and focus on learning names for things appear more likely to show a spurt in lexical acquisition in the latter part of the second year, as many of the words acquired during the accelerated periods of vocabulary growth are object names (Goldfield & Reznick, 1990).

Several factors could determine such individual differences. Input that emphasizes nouns and the naming function of language may interact with cognitive changes in the child's understanding of categorization, and thus the characteristic verbal interaction of the parents with the child may be a contributing factor. Della Corte, Benedict, and Klein (1983) actually found few differences between the speech of mothers of referential and expressive children across three different caretaking situations: bathing, diapering, and dressing. However, the mothers of the most referential children used language relatively less frequently to control and direct their offspring's behavior, and more frequently to comment on aspects of the environment and ongoing activities. Across all of the children in the study, the percentage of nominal words in their vocabularies was positively related to their mother's descriptive use of language and inversely related to their directive use. Thus, the extent to which the primary caregiver adopts the role of commentator versus director in relation to the toddler's actions and activities may influence both the rate and character of early lexical development (Bridges, 1986; Goldfield, 1987; Tomasello & Farrar, 1986a).

However, the direction of effect between mothers' interactive style and children's preferences and capabilities may be a reciprocal one. In a longitudinal study of the interrelations among play, language, and cognitive development from 9 to 24 months, Rosenblatt (1977) reported that toddlers whose vocabularies at 50 words contained mainly object names were more toy-oriented and investigative of objects from the beginning. Bridges (1986) suggested that the close visual and manipulative exploration of objects in many children's spontaneous play is interpreted by Western middle-class parents as indicating that the child has a special interest in objects at this stage of development. Parents' descriptive commentaries that accompany the activities of these children are therefore more likely to emphasize the objects that are the focus of behavior.

Several caveats are necessary in interpreting these and other studies of mother–child interaction and child acquisitional style differences, however. First, the referential–expressive dimension is a continuous one and significant numbers of children do not adopt a predominantly object-name learning approach in early acquisition (Goldfield & Resnick, 1990; Hampson, 1989). In fact, some writers have argued that too few children acquire an extreme enough distribution of nominals versus other words for this to count as a distinct "style" (Goldfield & Snow, 1989).

Second, almost all of the research in this tradition to date has been limited to toddlers and parents from the middle- and upper middle-classes of industrialized Western societies. Such cross-cultural and cross-linguistic studies of caregiver–child verbal interaction as do exist suggest that the dominant pattern of object-labeling reported for referential children and their parents may be confined to a small part of the broad sweep of language-learning situations to which children around the world are exposed (Lieven & Pine, 1990; Ochs & Schieffelin, 1984). Gopnik and Choi (1987) suggest that object names form a much smaller percentage of the input to Korean children; and Heath (1983) and Ochs (1988) similarly report that children in the cultural groups that they studied rely far more on rote learning of short phrases than on isolated nouns in their early language acquisition. In general, then, the kinds of language interaction in which toddlers and their caregivers engage may affect the pattern as well as the rate of early lexical development, but we need far more cross-cultural work in this area.

The Conceptual Level of Early Words

As we have said, for many children early vocabulary is dominated by words for objects, yet objects can be named at different levels of generality. Thus a rose can be called "Peace," or a "rose," a "flower," a "plant," a "living thing," or an "entity." Children initially learn names for objects at an intermediate level of generality ("flower" in the above example), at what Rosch, Mervis, Gray, Johnson, and Boyes-Braem (1976) have called the *basic object level,* and only later acquire more specific names ("rose") or general superordinate labels ("plants"); (Anglin, 1977; Brown, 1958; Mervis, 1984).

At the basic object level, categories have both the coherence and differentiation appropriate for the behavioral and communication needs of the child. Rosch and colleagues (1976) noted that objects in a basic level category share many perceptual and functional features, yet their properties do not overlap too much with members of related semantic categories. Hence children more readily learn basic object categories than either superordinate or subordinate categories (Mervis & Crisafi, 1982).

There is a large functional component to this notion of the optimal level of object labels for the child. Average toddlers have no need to distinguish between "roses" and "tulips"; they need to know that "flowers" are those objects that are to be smelled and admired, but not usually picked (except by adults), and certainly not trampled or eaten. "Plants," on the other hand, is too general a term, and leads to behavioral contradictions for the child. Some plants, such as lettuce and cabbage, are required eating, while others like grass are perfect for trampling and rolling on (Brown, 1958; de Villiers & de Villiers, 1979).

Thus, the explanation for children's initial acquisition of basic-level terms could be both cognitive and functional, as it is at that level that forms and functions are most closely correlated. Of course, because children do not possess all of the adult knowledge of the appropriate functions of objects in their culture nor of the correlated attributes that those objects share, child basic categories will frequently differ somewhat from adult basic object-level categories (Mervis, 1984).

Parental Naming and Basic Object-Level Words

There is considerable evidence that parental naming practices also contribute to the child's acquisition of semantic categories associated with basic object terms. In a classic paper on categorization and naming, Brown (1958) hypothesized that parents name objects at the level of specificity at which those objects require the same actions from the child. At times these functional considerations overrule perceptual similarities, as when parents call all types of money "money" rather than distinguishing between coins and bills. Later on, when the child becomes capable of buying, selling, and saving, the parental use of words in this domain becomes more differentiated.

Brown's speculation was taken up and confirmed by several studies that recorded mothers' naming practices in naturalistic interactions with toddlers, or asked parents to name pictured objects for either adult or child audiences. In book-reading or play with their toddlers, mothers' references to objects are predominantly at the basic object level, and adults overwhelmingly label pictures for young children at the same basic level. Thus, they talk about "dogs" and "cats" rather than "animals" or "collies"; and "chairs" and "tables" rather than "furniture" or "Windsor chairs" (for a review see Adams & Bullock, 1986).

Nevertheless, the parental input is not devoid of superordinate labels nor of more specific subordinate terms. The likelihood that parents will use a superordinate term or a subordinate name for an object depends on the referential and interactional context as well as the age and level of conceptual development of the child. For example, subordinate labels are more likely to be used for atypical exemplars of basic categories (a penguin is more likely to be called a "penguin" than a "bird"; a tiger is a "tiger" rather than a "cat"), especially if the atypical objects are contrasted with other more prototypical members of that category (e.g., a picture of a tiger in a set of domestic cats).

In contrast, superordinate terms are most likely to be used when parents are referring to a group of objects, especially in familiar routines like dressing or mealtimes ("Let's get your *clothes* on," or "Don't play with your *food*"), or when a single behavioral response is desired toward the whole group ("Put your *toys* away," or "Don't jump on the *furniture*"); (Adams & Bullock, 1986; Callanan, 1985; Lucariello & Nelson, 1986; Wales, Colman, & Pattison, 1983). When parents produce superordinate labels, they also frequently link them in an utterance or two with the basic-level name for the object. A common format for this is a class inclusion statement: "A bus is a vehicle," or "A koala bear is a kind of animal" (Adams & Bullock, 1986; Shipley, Kuhn, & Madden, 1983).

Thus the overwhelming tendency of parents to name single objects at the basic object level, together with the manner in which superordinate-level labels are introduced, likely contribute to the acquisition of words at different levels of abstraction: basic object level terms first and only later superordinate labels and the specific names of subordinate categories.

EXTENSIONAL USAGE OF EARLY WORDS

How are the children's early words extended and generalized to new objects? Toddlers' use of the words in their vocabularies differs from the normal adult usage of those words in several characteristic ways.

Overextensions. One of the most prominent properties of young children's use of words is overextension; that is, a word is used to label a broader set of objects or actions than it is usually applied to by adults. This feature of their own children's speech has caught the attention of linguists since the turn of the century. For example, Chamberlain and Chamberlain (1904) recount their child's use of "mooi" to refer first to the moon, but progressively thereafter to label cakes, round marks on the window, round shapes in books, tooling on leather book covers, round postmarks on envelopes, and the letter O. This overextension seems to be determined quite straightforwardly, by perceived similarity in shape, and many similar overextensions on the basis of perceptual similarities have been recorded (see E. Clark, 1973, for an extensive list taken from diary studies).

But young children's overextended use of their early words can be far more complex, as demonstrated by some of our observations of our son, Nicholas. At the age of 15 months, Nicholas had divided the animal kingdom into four species: "Nunu"[1] (dogs and other small animals), "moo" (cows, horses, and other large animals), "du" (ducks and other birds), and

---

[1]The name of our hairy sheepdog—a Zulu word from the childhood of one of the authors meaning roughly "little wild beast."

"turtle" (a wind-up toy turtle that swam in his bath). In typical fashion, "turtle" was soon generalized from the original toy to other objects that shared perceptual and functional properties with it. So within days of its first production, "turtle" was used to refer to other toy turtles, including one with wheels, to a real turtle, and to pictured turtles. But other objects were also called "turtle": several toys that shared his bath, including a plastic walrus and a wind-up frog; a multicolored corncob in a photograph; and a pinecone with a stem that stuck out like a turtle's head. Finally, when he was 17 months old Nicholas was riding along in his car seat wearing an old all-in-one pajama suit. The suit was much worn and frayed at the feet, and Nicholas's big toe stuck out through a hole. To our great amusement he suddenly lifted his foot in the air and said with delight: "Turtle!"

These examples illustrate the variety of similarities that provide the child with a basis for overextended use: one or more common perceptual features, a shared function, a complex of attributes and associations that link the referents (with no single feature or set of features shared by all exemplars), or even a seemingly metaphorical or pragmatic function (a desire to draw the parents' attention to a general similarity across very different domains of objects). Next we discuss the implications of these different types of overextension for theories of the child's representation of the meanings of words.

Underextensions.   The opposite of overextended use occurs when the child does not generalize a word's usage broadly enough and does not apply the term to some objects or situations for which an adult would use the word. Barrett (1986), for example, described his son Adam's use of the word "duck" (usually pronounced "dut") between the ages of 12 and 20 months. At first the word was only uttered while Adam was hitting one of his three toy yellow ducks off the edge of the bath (see previously for discussion of event-bound initial word usage). But after a couple of weeks it was used to refer to his toy ducks in several situations. At this point, the word was used referentially in the sense of being dissociated from a single event representation, but it was still underextended in comparison with normal adult extension for "duck." Some 5 months later, Adam overextended "duck" to refer to several different water birds and a picture of a quail.

Overlaps.   In some cases, the child may apply a word in a way that overlaps, but is not the same as, its referential usage for adults. In this case, both overextension and underextension errors occur. The child uses the word for some referents that are outside the referential meaning of the word for an adult, yet at the same time does not apply it to some referents that are within normal adult usage. An example of overlapping extension would be the case of a child who used the word "dog" to refer to small dogs and other small hairy animals (e.g., cats, goats, etc.), but called very large dogs (e.g., Irish wolfhounds) and other large hairy animals (e.g., ponies, horses, and cows) "horses" (E. Clark, 1983).

Mismatches. In rare cases the child seems to have got it all wrong and uses a word only for a set of situations that are quite unlike the adult referential use of the word. We observed one such mismatch in our daughter Charlotte while we were spending a bucolic sabbatical semester in a cottage in rural Devon. One of us had drawn Charlotte's attention to one sheep in the herd behind the cottage with the words: "Ah shame, there's one with a limp." The next day she used the new word herself (pronouncing it "mimp"), only she used it to refer to a particularly sheeplike facial expression that she put on. Such mismatches are short-lived in children's production and almost always elicit a correction from the parents, in our case an elaborate pantomime of hobbling about.

Correct Use. Finally, it is sometimes impossible to detect any difference between the child's extensional meaning for a word and the adult usage (Dromi, 1987). Of course, given the limited range of referential situations that are usually sampled in any one study, even in a detailed longitudinal diary, it is not possible to conclude that the child's usage would always be the same as the adults' across the entire extension of that term in the language.

Changing Patterns of Extension

Does each of these patterns of extension co-occur from the beginning of word learning, or are they developmentally related? As we noted earlier, many of the earliest words seem to be tied to whole situations or action representations, and so are only used in very limited contexts. Underextension of words thus seems to be more frequent in the earliest stages of development. In contrast, overextensions and overlaps become more frequent at the point at which the child is acquiring new words quite rapidly and trying to determine their appropriate referential use relative to other words he or she knows. However, it should be noted that underextension is again a dominant pattern of referential use later in development, when the child begins to acquire superordinate category labels, such as "animal," "plant," or "living thing." In the acquisition of superordinate terms children tend to limit their usage initially to typical exemplars, such as calling only mammals "animals" (Anglin, 1977).

In one of the few studies that measured both comprehension and production of over- and underextended words in a longitudinal fashion,

Kuczaj (1986) found that words never changed from being overextended to underextended by the same child. The most common patterns of development over a 6-month interval were transitions from underextension to overlap or overextension; from overlap to overextension; and from either underextension, overextension, or overlap to correct usage. Dromi (1987) followed her daughter Keren's production of all the words in her vocabulary in a remarkably detailed longitudinal diary study of the one-word period. Tracing the extension of particular words in Keren's speech on a week-by-week basis, Dromi observed all sorts of sequences of changes in extension, but here, too, underextensions tended to dominate early and overextensions later in this period of development.

THEORIES OF EARLY WORD MEANING

Three contrasting accounts of early lexical development dominated research from early in the 1970s through the middle of the 1980s. These are the *semantic feature hypothesis* (E. Clark, 1973), the *functional core model* (Nelson, 1974), and various versions of *prototype theory* (Anglin, 1977; Barrett, 1982; Bowerman, 1978; Greenberg & Kuczaj, 1982; Griffiths, 1976). Each of these theories was originally proposed to account for the patterns of extension of words (mostly object names) in the first 2 years, and each does so in terms of hypotheses about the nature of children's semantic representations of words. Developmental changes in meaning representations were postulated to account for changes in word usage observed in the course of lexical acquisition.

Semantic Feature Hypothesis

E. Clark (1973) adopted the notion of componential meaning from lexical semantics, the suggestion that for adults the meaning of any word is composed of more primary semantic concepts that distinguish the word from other words of similar meaning (Bierwisch, 1970). Thus, among the semantic features in the representation of "boy" would be [male], [nonadult], and [human]; in contrast with "girl" which would contain [female], [nonadult], and [human]. Several of these semantic features distinguish the meanings of many different words. The features [male] versus [female] characterize the difference between "man" and "woman," "husband" and "wife," "gander" and "goose," and "bull" and "cow," among others.

Applying this notion to early lexical development, Clark's semantic feature hypothesis maintains that when children first acquire words they do not know their full meaning for adults. Instead, they identify the meaning of a word with only some subset of the semantic features in its meaning for adults. Children will therefore make errors of extension because they will use only one or two properties of an object or action as critical for the application of a word. For example, if children extract only the feature [four-legged] from all of the instances of dogs that have been labeled for them as "doggie," they might overextend "doggie" to all other four-legged animals.

In addition to the acquisition of new words, semantic development according to this theory takes the form of children refining their meaning representations for known words by adding missing semantic features to distinguish one word meaning from another. So when children who over-extend "doggie" to other animals come to learn the words "cow" and "kitty," they might add such properties as [barks], [licks], and [wags tail] to [four-legged] as the defining features of "doggie." In turn, they might specify "kitty" as [has whiskers] and [meows], and represent "cow" as [moos], [has an udder], and [relatively large]. Children need not know the names for any of these properties; they need only to identify them perceptually.

From her examination of overextensions reported in early diary studies of children's lexical development, Clark added two further hypotheses to her theory. First, she proposed that the features initially taken as defining of the use of object names would overwhelmingly be perceptual properties like shape, texture, movement, sound, and so on. And second, she suggested that the initial features internalized by the child would be the more general ones that distinguish among broad object classes. Thus the direction of development would be from word meanings that were initially too general to ones that were more and more specific, and systematic overextension rather than underextension would characterize early word use.

Functional Core Model

In contrast to the semantic feature hypothesis, the functional core model of Nelson (1974) stressed the role of action schemas in the child's knowledge of objects during the sensorimotor period (Piaget, 1952). Nelson suggested that object concepts would first be tied to the specific activities in which the child acted on them. Only later in the second year as action schemas became more decontextualized would the child analyze the features common to objects participating in those events. At this point in development, Nelson argued, a hierarchy of attributes begins to be organized, with functional properties (things that the objects did or could be done with them) at the core and perceptual attributes at the periphery of the conceptual represen-tation. Perceptual characteristics might be used as guides to the likely functional properties of objects, but the latter were more centrally defining of category membership.

Nelson's model of semantic development therefore suggested that initial uses of object names would be restricted to a particular referent, often in highly specific situations, and only later be extended in broader application. In addition, categorical overextensions when they began to emerge could be based on both functional and perceptual similarities, although the former were emphasized in Nelson's experimental work (Nelson, 1974).

Comparison of the Two Theories

Much of the empirical work directed toward evaluating these two theories in the 1970s focused on the predictions made about overextensions. The following are the most relevant findings:

1. Several investigators reported both perceptually and functionally based overextensions (Anglin, 1977; Bowerman, 1978). Functionally based overextensions contradict any strong application of Clark's hypothesis about the dominance of perceptual features. However, children's frequent use of perceptual similarity as a basis for word extension even when the objects have dissimilar functions, also counts against the functional core model unless perceptual similarities are given greater weight in the underlying meanings of words.

2. Initial use of words tends to be restricted and context-bound, and even later on, underextensions are about as frequent as overextensions (Anglin, 1977; Dromi, 1987; Kuczaj, 1986). This is more in keeping with Nelson's model of the course of development than it is with Clark's account. The relative infrequency of overextensions themselves (rarely more than 30% of a child's object words and often much less) also questions the central notion of incomplete meaning representations in the semantic feature hypothesis.

3. Some studies observed overextensions only in production and not in comprehension (Fremgen & Fay, 1980; Thompson & Chapman, 1977). More recent studies have revealed overextensions in comprehension when more sensitive testing procedures are used, but it still appears that overextensions are more likely to occur in production than in comprehension (Kuczaj, 1986). Neither theory as originally stated predicts any such asymmetry, although each can be salvaged in a somewhat modified form. For example, it could be claimed that production is influenced by other factors (e.g., memory or communication strategies) that are not part of the child's meaning representation of the words. In essence, some data from overextensions can be discounted by suggesting that they do not arise from the child's representations of meaning but from pragmatic communication strategies (see also under no. 4).

4. Many overextensions in children's early word use do not seem based on one or even a few perceptual or functional features that are common to all of the objects and events labeled by the word. Rather, these overexten-

sions seem more *complexive* in nature, with the similarities between referents shifting from one feature to another in different uses of the word (Bowerman, 1978). For example, a child might use "doggie" initially to refer to dogs but extend it to other four-legged animals such as horses and cows, to other furry things such as a woolly blanket, and to other creatures that move by themselves such as beetles or spiders.

Complexive overextensions appear incompatible with a model of word meanings as sets of necessary and sufficient features as is assumed by both E. Clark (1973) and Nelson (1974). However, both the general semantic feature hypothesis (stripped of its ancilliary hypotheses of perceptual and general features first) and the functional core model (including perceptual features in the concepts underlying early word meanings) can be, and were, defended against these data by distinguishing between different types of overextensions: "pure" or "categorical" extensions and other overextensions that are motivated by pragmatic, conversational factors. The latter might include attempts to draw an adult's attention to an object or action for which the child has no appropriate label, the use of a term in uncertain conditions in order to get adult feedback (Clark & Clark, 1977), or to point out similarities or analogies between referents (perhaps the beginnings of metaphorical reference?) (de Villiers & de Villiers, 1979; Nelson, Rescorla, Gruendel, & Benedict, 1978; Rescorla, 1980). Nevertheless, it has proved difficult to specify criteria for determining which overextensions directly reflect the child's underlying meaning representations and which do not. Word extension data are at best an uncertain measure of word meanings for the child. However, the cumulative weight of the empirical findings outlined above led to a third account of young children's patterns of word extension.

Prototype Theories

Noting the similarity between complexive overextensions and prototype models of the organization of concepts (Rosch, 1978; Rosch & Mervis, 1975), several authors proposed that children's meanings for their words were mental representations of prototypical exemplars (Anglin, 1977; Barrett, 1982; Bowerman, 1978; Greenberg & Kuczaj, 1982; Griffiths, 1976). On the basis of experience with the exemplars first or most frequently labeled by the parents, the young child initially internalizes a representation of a prototypical referent for the word. At the beginning, the word might only be applied to the particular prototypical exemplar or to referents that closely resemble it in a holistic perceptual or functional way, which would usually lead to underextension. But subsequently the child abstracts some of the more specific perceptual and functional attributes of the prototypical exemplar (or exemplars) and stores them as part of the meaning representation for the word. At this point, the word is more broadly extended to any referents that share one or more features with the prototype, and so overextensions become more common.

Particular prototype theories share these general features (a prototypical prototype theory?), but they differ in their characterization of the initial prototypes: a mental "videotape recording" of one or more episode involving the prototypical object–referent (Griffiths, 1976); individual experiences with particular exemplars (Greenberg & Kuczaj, 1982); or a decontextualized representation of the prototypical referent (Barrett, 1986). For all of them, however, as the child extends a word to new exemplars the meaning representation of the word broadens, becomes independent of particular exemplars, and is based on clusters of correlated perceptual and functional features (as postulated for adult word meanings by Rosch & Mervis, 1975).

Evaluation of the Theories

Each of the models, and their more recent descendants, has several attractive features. Semantic feature models make contact with linguistic theories of the composition of meaning representations and their basis in the perception and conceptual development of the child (Miller & Johnson-Laird, 1976). They also stress the process of semantic contrast between words, a process that may be basic to the development of word meanings across the entire period of lexical development. As such, semantic feature analyses of words in domains of meaning like dimensional adjectives, spatial prepositions, and verbs of possession have proved valuable accounts of the normal pattern of acquisition of those words in preschoolers.

Nelson's (1985) refinements of her functional core model based on script notions of event representation (Schank & Abelson, 1977) provide an interesting account of the shift from situation-bound to decontextualized word usage, as well as stressing the contribution of both the conceptual development of the child and the social–communicative interaction between parent and child in lexical development. Most recently, Nelson (1988b) has extended her theory to give a description of the acquisition of superordinate relations between words in later development that also stresses the child's event knowledge.

And the various prototype models build on what is arguably the most influential recent account of the nature of concept representations in both adults and children. This account not only relates to the extension patterns in early word use but also explains the priority of naming at the basic object level in terms of the interdependence between perceptual and functional features at this level and the maximization of category similarity and distinctiveness (Mervis, 1984). Many prototype models also incorporate notions of semantic features, while denying that any small set of these features is criterial or necessary and sufficient for an object's membership in a semantic category. In this way, refinements in the models have made them much more similar to each other.

CONCEPTUAL DEVELOPMENT
AND LEXICAL ACQUISITION

What constraints does the child's conceptual development place on the course and structure of early lexical development? Extensive research on infant development in the 1st year of life converges on the view that young children come to the task of acquiring the words and meanings of their native language with considerable factual and conceptual knowledge about their physical and social world. For example, infants seem to perceive a world of objects that are unitary, bounded, and persist over time. By 6 months of age they can discriminate among a wide variety of perceptual properties of those objects: such as their size, color, rigidity, movement, and position relative to other objects or to the child herself (see, e.g., Bornstein, Chap. 3, this volume; Gibson & Spelke, 1983; Spelke, 1985). Furthermore, before they are 9 months old infants can detect perceptual similarities among instances of basic object categories like birds and distinguish them from other animals (Colombo, O'Brien, Mitchell, Roberts, & Horowitz, 1987). Most developmental psycholinguists believe that these early nonlinguistic representations of the world (and the perceptual and conceptual expectations that derive from them) both contribute to and constrain the semantic development of the child. However, the specific relation between the pattern of emergence of early words and cognitive development has proved difficult to pin down.

Sensorimotor Development and Early Words

On a strict interpretation of the classical Piagetian view of sensorimotor development, words should not be used referentially and productively until the emergence of *symbolic representation* in Stage 6 of the sensorimotor period (Sinclair, 1970). Thus, both Bloom (1973) and Brown (1973) suggested that attainment of the concept of permanent objects should be a cognitive prerequisite for linguistic reference to objects.

This all seems very logical, but demonstrating such a relation in empirical studies has been troublesome. Most studies have given toddlers a set of Piagetian cognitive tasks believed to be diagnostic of different stages of sensorimotor development, and then examined the relation between the children's solutions to those nonlinguistic puzzles and measures of their comprehension and/or production of language. Contrary to the Piagetian prediction, children do use some words productively before they solve Stage 6 cognitive problems. General levels of object permanence are only weakly correlated, if at all, with the number of object words in a child's early vocabulary (Bates et al., 1979; Gopnik & Meltzoff, 1986). One of the problems seems to be methodological: Significant relations between measures of cognitive stage and language acquisition come and go as tasks and task interpretations vary (Bloom, Lifter, & Broughton, 1985; Corrigan, 1979).

More recent studies have therefore moved away from general characterizations of cognitive and semantic development and looked for relations between much more specific cognitive achievements and the emergence of particular types of lexical items in children's comprehension and production. For instance, words like "gone" and "away" that encode disappearances or nonexistence of objects emerge in children's productive vocabulary at the same time as they are able to solve Piagetian serial invisible displacement tasks (Gopnik & Meltzoff, 1987a; Tomasello & Farrar, 1984, 1986b). These word meanings and the solution of the cognitive tasks both require that the child be able to conceive of an object existing at a location without actually perceiving it at that location—the late Stage 6 conception of object permanence. Thus the emergence of expressions of disappearance is more closely related to mastery of late Stage 6 object permanence than it is to other cognitive developments in Stage 6, such as solving Piagetian means–ends problems. In contrast, the production of relational words such as "there" or "uh-oh" to encode the success or failure of planned actions is related more to the solution of means–ends tasks that require the child to compare and reflect on possible plans but less related to object permanence (Gopnik & Meltzoff, 1987a).

Similar dependencies between particular lexical developments and particular cognitive understandings have been proposed by Smith and Sachs (1990) for growth in the comprehension of action words around 15 to 18 months of age, and by Nelson (1985) and Gopnik and Meltzoff (1987b) for the rapid spurt in the acquisition of object names around the age of 18 months in many children.

Spatial Words and Spatial Cognition

The discrimination and categorization of spatial relations is often taken as the quintessential domain in which concepts are mastered first in nonlinguistic cognition and then mapped onto words or other morphemes. Thus, H. Clark (1973) stated that the child "acquires English spatial expressions by learning how to apply them to his prior knowledge about space" (p. 62).

Indeed, across a number of languages a consistent order of acquisition is found for comprehension and production of prepositions that express spatial notions: "in" < "on" < "under" < "beside" < "between" < "in front of/behind" (Halpern, Corrigan, & Aviezer, 1983; Johnston & Slobin, 1979). This pattern corresponds closely to the order of emergence of these concepts in cognitive development (Piaget & Inhelder, 1967). Inherent containment and support notions (in, on) are labeled first, then proximity relations (beside, between), and finally prospective deictic relationships (in front of, behind). The usage of "in front of" and "behind" that refers to the inherent front of an object (e.g., "in front of the horse") is understood before the deictic usage that locates an object relative to the speaker (or listener) and the reference object (e.g., "in front of the wall") and so requires consideration of perspective (Johnston, 1985).

These findings suggest the priority of conceptual categorizations and distinctions over linguistic usage, but Bowerman (1989) argued cogently that in the spatial domain (as well as in several others) languages do not divide up the conceptual space in the same way, so there must be a central role for the input. Take the case of the most basic spatial relations of "in" and "on." As we have seen, the crucial distinction for English and several other languages is "containment" versus "support." Thus, in English all six spatial relations depicted in Fig. 6.1 are appropriately referred to by the preposition "on" because there is some general sort of support relation between the objects. In German, however, three different prepositions ("auf," "an," and "um") encode subsets of the same six relations, and they are distinguished by whether the contact point between the objects involves a relatively horizontal surface (table, shoulder = "auf"), a nonhorizontal surface (wall, twig, leg = "an"), or a relation of encirclement (napkin = "um"). Dutch, on the other hand, cares about what type of attachment there is between the objects rather than whether the supporting surface is horizontal or not. Thus, "picture on wall" and "leaves on twig" are "aan," because there is one or more fixed, punctate attachment points; but with a flattish object attached over its entire base like the Band-Aid on the leg, it becomes "op," even though the supporting surface is typically vertical like the wall.

Up to this point, the argument is based on logic: If there are cross-linguistic differences in semantic classification, then semantic development cannot simply be the mapping of forms onto previously established nonlinguistic concepts. But Bowerman also calls for research into how children learn language-dependent semantic categorizations. It could plausibly be argued that children will learn semantic distinctions that relate more closely to cognitively salient ways of categorizing the world at a much

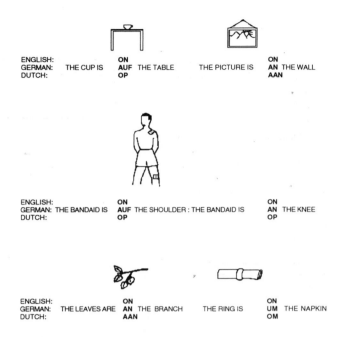

ENGLISH: ON   ON
GERMAN: THE CUP IS   AUF   THE TABLE   THE PICTURE IS   AN   THE WALL
DUTCH: OP   AAN

ENGLISH: ON   ON
GERMAN: THE BANDAID IS   AUF THE SHOULDER : THE BANDAID IS   AN   THE KNEE
DUTCH: OP   OP

ENGLISH: ON   ON
GERMAN: THE LEAVES ARE   AN   THE BRANCH   THE RING IS   UM   THE NAPKIN
DUTCH: AAN   OM

FIG. 6.1.   Different uses of prepositions in English, German, and Dutch.

earlier stage of language development than the more language-specific
distinctions (Slobin, 1985). Hence, children acquiring a language that
divides up spatial relations in a language-specific way should acquire the
forms that encode those distinctions at a later age or stage of language
development than children acquiring a language that makes conceptually
given categorizations (provided that the forms in the two languages are of
similar syntactic complexity). Furthermore, use of locative forms (whatever
their more specific meaning in the adult language) may first mark more
conceptually given, language-general distinctions like support and containment before their language-specific meanings are learned.

Bowerman (1989) examined these predictions in young children acquiring
English and Korean. "In," "on," "out," and "off" are among the earliest
relational words used by English-speaking toddlers, often with the initial
meaning of "put in/on" and "take out/off" before they encode static spatial
relations, and several authors have suggested that they map directly onto
relational concepts formed toward the end of the sensorimotor period
(Bloom, 1973; McCune-Nicolich, 1981). However, these action relations are
categorized quite differently by English and Korean (see Fig. 6.2). In
English "put in" and "put on" encode containment versus various sorts of
supporting relations, while "put together" seems reserved for cases in which

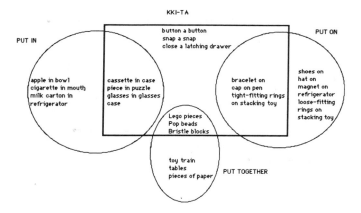

FIG. 6.2. How Korean and English locative terms divide up spatial relations.

objects of roughly similar size move into contact or close proximity. In contrast, two Korean verbs, "kki-ta" and "ppay-ta," carve up roughly the same semantic domain along an orthogonal dimension, tightness of fit. "Kki-ta" encodes the action of bringing objects into a relation of "tight fit or attachment"; "ppay-ta" encodes taking them out of it regardless of the topological or geometrical relations between them. Thus, "kki-ta" classes together a number of "in," "on," and "together" relations and also includes some situations that English does not lexicalize with any of these particles (such as closing a latching drawer). Different verbs are used in Korean for the various "loosely fitting" spatial relations that cut across the same semantic domain.

At less than 2 years of age, Korean children have a clear understanding of the critical role of tight fit or attachment in the meaning of "kki-ta" and "ppay-ta." They freely apply these words across all the geometrical relations contrasted by "in," "on," and "together" in English; but they do not extend them to any loose-fit or no-attachment situations like putting on loose-fitting clothing or placing small objects in large boxes or paper bags. There is no apparent stage at which the Korean children think that their language marks the postulated cognitively basic concepts of containment or support, and so on (Bowerman, 1989).

To summarize, the relation between cognitive structures and lexical representations is undoubtedly more complex than simply mapping words in the input directly onto nonlinguistically constructed concepts. Clearly, the categorizations and distinctions between objects, events, and relations that are lexically encoded in a language must be perceptually and conceptually accessible to young children, and some conceptual distinctions or principles of categorization may be more natural than others, and so easier or earlier acquired in lexical development (Jackendoff, 1983; Rosch et al., 1976; Slobin, 1973, 1985). But the more psycholinguists carry out cross-linguistic studies of semantic development, the more we learn about both broadly universal semantic categorizations and language-specific semantic organizations. Most developmental psycholinguists therefore hold to an interactionist position in which there is a reciprocal relation between language and cognition in semantic development, although they may emphasize the contribution of each of these factors to differing degrees in particular lexical domains.

LEXICAL DEVELOPMENT
IN THE PRESCHOOL YEARS

The early stages of lexical development appear dominated by acquisition of the denotation of words—discovering the categories of objects, and to a lesser extent, the actions and relations to which words are appropriately applied. Two-year-olds have little or no understanding of the different sense relations between words: Their names for objects seem to be organized almost exclusively in terms of contrasting extensions between basic level terms. Superordinate and subordinate names are extremely rare in early lexicons, and when they appear they are not usually used in hierarchical relations to known basic level words (E. Clark, 1983; Griffiths, 1987).

In the adult lexicon, however, there is an elaborate set of sense relations among words: hierarchical class-inclusion relations ("collie," "dog," "mammal," "animal," "living thing"); collection/grouping relations ("trees," "forest"); referential synonymy ("anger" and "ire," or "chase" and "pursue"); and semantic opposition ("high" versus "low," or "deep" versus "shallow"), for example. Appreciation of these relations and the organization of words into networks of meaning is a major aspect of later semantic development beginning in the third year and continuing through the school years.

Thus, in sets of words that are hierarchically related, such as animals, clothing, birds, or furniture, lexical development takes place in both a horizontal and vertical direction. The child acquires more labels for exemplars at the basic object level of abstraction (e.g., the names of more unfamiliar and atypical animals), while concurrently learning that all of those objects are included in the higher-order class and can be called by the same label at that level (e.g., "animal"). Similarly, more specific subordinate level names ("collie," "rattlesnake," "Siamese cat") are acquired when needed to differentiate among exemplars within basic level categories.

Development of Sense Relations in Semantic Fields

Much research on later lexical development has therefore explored the emergence of children's understanding of sense relations among words in semantic hierarchies (Anglin, 1977), or in semantic fields in which sets of words relate to each other along various dimensions of meaning. Some of these are: kinship terms (Benson & Anglin, 1987; Haviland & Clark, 1974); dimensional adjectives (Carey, 1978; Richards, 1979); verbs of possession and transfer of possession (Gentner, 1975); and spatial/locative adjectives (E. Clark, 1977; Johnston & Slobin, 1979).

Several factors combine to determine the order of acquisition of terms within each of these domains, as well as the characteristic errors that children make in production and comprehension. These include the frequency of the terms in the input (Carey, 1978); the children's experiential familiarity with the terms and their referents (Benson & Anglin, 1987; Carey, 1982); the communicative salience of the terms, that is, the likelihood of needing to talk about that particular notion (Johnston, 1985); the use of certain nonlinguistic comprehension strategies (E. Clark, 1977; Richards, 1979); and semantic complexity as measured by the number of meaning dimensions needed to specify each term's meaning (E. Clark, 1979; Gentner, 1975).

Reorganizations in the preschoolers' lexicon as they discover similarities in the meaning and syntactic usage of words can now lead to errors on words that earlier were used correctly. For example, when they were between 3 and 4 years old, Bowerman's two daughters occasionally substituted "make" for "let" and "let" for "make," as in:

Christy (3;6 years): I don't want to go to bed. Don't let me go to bed.
Eva (3;9):   Make me watch it! (Begging to watch a TV program)

In English both "make" and "let" refer to causation of actions, but causation in different senses: "make" when the causer is directly active in producing the event; "let" when the causer simply refrains from doing something to prevent the event (permissive causation). Bowerman's daughters respected this distinction when they first learned these verbs. But as they began to organize their knowledge of verbs of causation, the similarities in meaning and syntactic usage led to characteristic errors like the "make"–"let" confusion and the use of noncausative verbs as if they were causatives (Bowerman, 1982):

Christy (3;1): I'm singing him (= making him sing); (pulling on a string that is used to make a cow music box play).

Eva (3;7):   I'm gonna put the washrag in and disappear something under the washrag (= make something disappear).

PROCESSES AND CONSTRAINTS
ON LEXICAL ACQUISITION

Descriptive research on preschoolers' mastery of word relations in semantic domains continues to emerge at a steady rate in publications on language development, but two issues concerning the process of vocabulary acquisition from age 2 years on dominated most of the theoretical work through the 1980s. Both of these issues concern the way in which preschoolers map out the meanings of novel lexical items encountered in the input.

Fast Mapping of Word Meanings

Children's vocabulary growth through the preschool years is remarkable, on the order of five to ten new words learned per day (Templin, 1957). Yet beyond the age of 2 or 3 years, extensive tutoring in word meanings by the use of ostensive definitions and direct instruction in "What's that?" games is rather infrequent in parent–child interaction. How then does the child do it? Carey (1978) suggested that young children can make a *fast-mapping* of at least a partial meaning for novel words that they encounter in the input on the basis of only one or two exposures to the word in context.

Carey and Bartlett (1978) were the first to investigate the process of fast mapping. They introduced a new color term, "chromium," to 3-year-olds in a naturalistic classroom setting. They believed that fast mapping would be most likely to occur when a new word was introduced in clear linguistic contrast to a familiar word, and when the words came from a well-structured semantic domain in which the children already knew a few related words. Indeed, after being told to bring the teacher "the *chromium* tray, not the blue one, the *chromium* one," several of the children later showed that they knew at least that the word "chromium" referred to the dimension of color, and in a few cases, they even knew the general type of olive green color that it designated in the experiment. On the other hand, almost half of the children apparently learned nothing about the new word, suggesting that fast mapping was not a particularly robust phenomenon at this age. However, a number of subsequent experiments have confirmed and extended Carey and Bartlett's demonstration of fast mapping. For example, 3- and 4-year-olds readily acquire a nonsense name for a new animal despite only one introduction to that word, in contrast with the names of familiar farm animals (Dockrell & Campbell, 1986). Rice (1990) established that fast mapping meanings for unknown words in the narrative of a video did not depend on tutoring or any explicit contrast in either the nonlinguistic or the linguistic context. However, words referring to objects or to attributes of objects shown in the video were more easily acquired than words referring to actions or affective states.[2]

Other studies have shown that children's fast mapping of explicit linguistic contrasts in the input varies with the attribute dimension to which the word applies. For example, Dockrell and Campbell (1986) introduced a nonsense adjective, "gombe," to 3- to 4-year-olds in the context of asking them to manipulate three wooden blocks that varied in shape and color. To one group they said: "Pass me the *gombe* block, not the round one or the square one, but the *gombe* one." The other group was asked to "Pass me the *gombe* block, not the red one or the green one, but the *gombe* one." All six children who heard the new word contrasted with known shapes later comprehended "gombe" as a shape word and took it to denote hexagonal, the shape of the block that was picked out by the utterance introducing the word. On the other hand, only one of seven children who heard the color-term contrast identified "gombe" as a color word; five of them thought that it referred to the hexagonal shape that also distinguished that block from the other two.

In the most comprehensive study to date, Xu (1991) found that children of this age have a stable hierarchy of preferences for what a new word might mean. First they assume that a new word refers to the novel object itself (see the taxonomic-category constraint discussed later). If they already have a name for the object, they interpret the new word as applying to an unusual part of the object rather than several other unusual properties. If they have labels for the object and its parts, they assume the word refers to unusual texture or shape; and, if object, part, and texture are familiar, they pick unusual shape rather than color as the denotation of the word. In keeping with previous studies (Au & Markman, 1987), when only the color of the object was unusual, the children did not map the novel word onto that attribute. Young children's preference hierarchy in fast mapping meanings onto novel words for objects and attributes is therefore:

whole object < part < texture/shape < color

The results for color are surprising, given the well-established preference in many nonlinguistic categorization tasks for younger preschoolers to sort and group objects by color similarity rather than form similarity (Melkman, Koriat, & Pardoe, 1976; Suchman & Trabasso, 1966). But several factors may contribute to the difficulty of mapping novel labels onto the dimension of color, even though color is perceptually salient to young children. Soja

---

[2]The difficulty in depicting actions and affective states in the static pictures used to test comprehension may have contributed to this finding.

(1986) suggested that children initially lexicalize only functionally relevant properties, and color tells us little about the functions or other properties of artifactual objects; thus, color words are acquired relatively late when compared with other dimensional terms (Bartlett, 1977). In addition, the categories named by colors do not have sharp boundaries and so children can readily stretch the meaning of known color words to refer to an object of unfamiliar color. Ironically, then, the first study to investigate fast mapping (Carey & Bartlett, 1978) also used the most difficult dimension for which to demonstrate it, color.[3]

Indeterminacy of Reference and the Problem of Induction

The remarkable speed and accuracy of fast mapping for object and attribute words represent a puzzle for developmental psycholinguists. Several writers have pointed out that on hearing a word uttered for the first time in a particular linguistic and nonlinguistic context, the child faces a major problem in inducing an appropriate meaning for the word. For any particular referential context there will be many hypotheses about the new word's meaning that will fit the situation. To illustrate the problem, authors often invoke a philosophical puzzle termed by Quine (1960): the problem of the *indeterminacy of translation*. Suppose a linguist studying the language of an alien society observes a native speaker say "gavagai," as a rabbit runs past. How can the linguist be sure that "gavagai" means "rabbit"? Solely on the basis of the relation between the utterance and the context, "gavagai" could refer to the rabbit or its action ("running"); to a property or part of the rabbit ("furry" or "ears"); to various thematic relations between the rabbit and its actions and surroundings ("rabbit running" or "rabbit in grass"); or to a concept as exotic as "all and sundry undetached parts of rabbits" (Quine, 1960, pp. 51–52). Even if we limit the referential possibilities to the rabbit itself, without more explanation it is not clear whether the label applies at the basic object level ("rabbit"), at a more subordinate level ("angora"), or at a superordinate level ("animal").

 In discussing the indeterminacy of translation, Quine was concerned with the philosophical problem of the correspondence between individual private worlds and the theory-laden (and, hence, language system dependent) nature of sentence meaning. But psycholinguists studying lexical development have noted that the problem for the young child in fast mapping an appropriate meaning onto a word in the input is similar to the "gavagai" problem. In this process the child must segment the stream of speech into words and other syntactic units, identify which words are unfamiliar, match

---

[3]See Landau and Gleitman (1985) and Bornstein (1985) for an extensive discussion of why color terms may be difficult for children to acquire as dimensional labels.

up those words with possible referents, compare that mapping with known lexical items and their represented meanings, perhaps refine the new mapping on that basis, and then store the new word–referent mapping in semantic memory (Rice, 1990). The crucial problem is in limiting the possible hypotheses available from the linguistic and nonlinguistic context. Proposed solutions to the problem take two major forms.

Appeal to Principles and Constraints

One way to solve the meaning induction problem is to invoke principles or constraints that guide the child's choices of hypotheses, and several authors have proposed such principles.

Contrast and Conventionality.   The most general of these proposals is the *principle of contrast,* described by E. Clark (1983, 1988, 1990) as a basic principle of lexical organization and development for both adults and children. Clark noted that all words in a given language arguably contrast in meaning in one or more of several ways: in reference at a given level of abstraction ("dog" vs. "cat"); in taxonomic level in a semantic hierarchy ("dog" vs. "collie"); in sociolinguistic register, such as formality ("policeman" vs. "cop") or social class ("toilet" vs. "lavatory"); and so on. Some of these contrasts are substantial and seem to be based on the concepts for which the words stand: so the contextual distributions of these word seldom overlap. Others are much more subtle and seem to be based on pragmatic or social factors: the usage of these words may overlap in all but a few critical contexts. Thus "policeman" and "cop" have the same denotative meaning, but they vary in the social context of the speech in which they are found.

E. Clark argued that without any guiding principles, children working out the meaning of a new word would have to go through the exhaustive process of comparing its linguistic and nonlinguistic contexts of use with those of all of the words they know. In such a process children might never get enough evidence to reject the possibility that two words always mean the same, because they would have to encounter just those contexts that do differentiate their meanings. Instead of this word-by-word comparison process, Clark proposed that young children from the earliest stages of lexical acquisition assume both the principle of contrast, "every two forms in a language contrast in meaning," and the *principle of conventionality,* "for certain meanings there is a conventional form that speakers expect to be used in the language community." If speakers do not use the conventional form expected in the context, that is, the word familiar to us, we assume they must have some contrasting meaning in mind.[4]

---

[4]Clark and Clark (1979) noted that this is very similar to some of the conversational axioms that Grice (1975) proposed must hold for successful communication to take place between a speaker and listener — the *cooperative principle.*

Clark's principles do not eliminate the process of comparisons between possible word meanings, nor even limit it much. She must add the notion that children use the immediate context of the new word to determine its general semantic field and so constrain the known words to which it will be contrasted. This will certainly reduce the number of hypotheses that children might entertain, particularly as their vocabulary grows in size and organization, although it does not mean that word learning will be errorless.

The principle of contrast is a rather general constraint on word learning and difficult to test empirically (see Gathercole, 1987, 1989), as it applies to subtle underlying meaning contrasts rather than observed word extensions, and also allows for considerable overlap in word meanings (E. Clark, 1988). Thus, even apparent interchangeable use of different words for the same referent in some contexts (Chapman & Mervis, 1989; Gathercole, 1987) is not direct evidence against children's application of the principle of contrast, since as long as there is any context in which the words are used differently, some contrast holds (E. Clark, 1988).

Mutual Exclusivity. A far stronger assumption of meaning contrast is suggested by the constraint of *mutual exclusivity* (Markman, 1989), which proposes that young children assume that each object has only one label, and each label can refer to only one category of objects. Thus, when children hear a new word in the input they should look around for a referent for which they do not already have a label.[5] As the child's vocabulary grows, this constraint would certainly limit the hypotheses that would be entertained when the child engaged in fast mapping a meaning onto a new word. It would be particularly useful at the basic object level, where categories of objects do, in fact, contrast and rarely overlap (Rosch et al., 1976).

In fact, a number of anecdotal reports note the reluctance of 2- and 3-year-olds to accept a superordinate name for an object for which they already have a basic level label: The literature is replete with examples of children saying: "That's not an animal. It's a dog," or words to that effect. Macnamara (1982) reported that this resistance to applying superordinate terms to individual basic level objects is found even when the children can be shown to understand hierarchical relations in other conceptual domains.

Markman (1989; see also Markman & Wachtel, 1988) used the notion of mutual exclusivity to explain why children have more difficulty interpreting class-inclusion relations between category terms (a collie is a dog and also an animal), than part–whole relations in collections (individual trees are part of a forest, but each tree is not a forest). Callanan and Markman (1982)

---

[5]Carey (1978) proposed a similar strategy in which any odd name heard by the child would be interpreted as referring to an unfamiliar, unnamed object, property, or event.

found that 2- and 3-year-olds will often agree that the set of playthings in front of them are "toys," but at the same time they deny that a single object like a doll is a "toy." When asked to show the experimenter "a toy," these children typically point out several objects rather than one. Markman and Wachtel (1988) interpreted this behavior as showing that the children are "preserving mutual exclusivity by distorting class inclusion into a collection structure" (p. 123).

Finally, as we described in the section on fast mapping, many experiments in which young children heard an object labeled with a new word showed that their interpretation of the meaning of the novel word depended on whether they already had a label for the object. A new word was treated as a name for a previously unknown object rather than as a second name for the familiar object. However, if the child already had a name for the object, the novel word was assumed to refer to some property of the object, or to be a subordinate label or proper name (Markman & Wachtel, 1988; Taylor & Gelman, 1989; Xu, 1991).

Taxonomic and Whole-Object Constraints.   This brings us to two more assumptions that preschoolers seem to make about new words (especially nouns) that they encounter in a naming situation: (a) New labels refer to whole objects rather than parts or properties, the *whole-object constraint;* and (b) they refer to objects of the same type, that is, nouns refer to categorical relations among objects, the *taxonomic constraint* (Markman, 1989).

Much of the research described above attests to the whole-object bias in the meanings children assign to unknown words, but what about the taxonomic assumption? Markman (1989) pointed out that children have extensive knowledge of thematic relations between objects, including their spatial or causal relations, and their frequent association in events (e.g., dog–bones, cow–barn). Indeed, young children frequently sort or organize objects in a thematic fashion, such as putting together the things that are typically associated in actions or in space and time (such as a cup and a spoon, or a baby and its bottle; Bruner, Olver, & Greenfield, 1966). However, single words, especially nouns, very rarely categorize objects together on the basis of thematic relations. Instead, nouns serve to group things of the same type together in category relations.

Several studies have shown that young children readily group objects in thematic ways when they are told simply to "find another one like this one" or "put together the ones that go together." But when they are given a noun label as the organizer, whether it is a familiar one ("find another *animal*") or a novel one ("find another *fep*"), they do not consider thematic relations as a possible basis for word meanings. Instead, they choose on the basis of categorical (taxonomic) relations. The use of the noun seems to highlight the categorical relations between objects, rather than their properties (Markman, 1989; Waxman & Gelman, 1986; Waxman & Kosowski, 1990).

Some Questions About Constraints

The constraints or biases described here serve to limit and prioritize the initial hypotheses children entertain about word meanings, but they also raise a number of questions.

The Constraints Work Very Well for Nouns, But What About Other Form Classes? Markman and Wachtel (1988) suggested that the taxonomic assumption, that words refer to object categories, supplies the young child with a first hypothesis about the referent for any new word. But in the case of words other than nouns, for example, words referring to actions or properties of objects, could the taxonomic constraint lead them astray? Markman and Wachtel argued that the two constraints, the taxonomic constraint and the mutual exclusivity assumption, work together to help the child learn words for properties and parts of objects as well as new names for the whole object. If the child already has a name for the object, the assumption of mutual exclusivity leads to a rejection of the hypothesis that a new word is another possible object label. Then the child is more likely to analyze the apparent referent object for some other attribute in order to find a meaning for the unknown word. Terms for properties of objects like shape, texture, and color should therefore be learned easiest if applied to familiar objects for which the child already has a name.

What Is the Nature of the Constraint in Each Case: Specific to Semantic Development, Pragmatic, or Based on Some More General Cognitive Factor? E. Clark (1988, 1990) argued that the principles of contrast and conventionality are pragmatic conventions about the use of language that are related to conversational principles required for communication to take place (Grice, 1975). The child discovers them in language acquisition as soon as she understands interpersonal intentions in communication, namely, "that people do things intentionally, and they always have a reason for choosing one word, x, on a particular occasion, rather than another, y. From this it would follow that x would not be equivalent to y, and so must contrast with it in some way" (E. Clark & H. Clark, 1979, p. 800). As general pragmatic principles, they apply not only to lexical development but also to morphological and syntactic domains of language (E. Clark, 1990).

The taxonomic constraint, that nouns mark category relations, may be narrowly specified as a linguistic constraint applying to word meanings, but it may also be based on the general cognitive principles that underlie the categorization of objects (Rosch et al., 1976). Mutual exclusivity can also be linguistically specified as one aspect of a general assumption of one-to-one mappings between forms and meanings that young children appear to apply to the task of language acquisition in each of the domains of syntax, morphology, and semantics (Markman, 1989; Pinker, 1984; Slobin, 1973, 1985). On the other hand, Flavell (1989) related it to a basic cognitive assumption made by children that objects have only one identity and so cannot be represented in more than one way, which may account for young children's well-documented difficulties in appreciating multiple perceptual or conceptual perspectives as well as their initial failure to understand the appearance–reality distinction.

In What Sense Are the Principles "Constraints" on the Child's Lexical Development? Nelson (1988a, 1990) took issue with the use of the term *constraint* rather than preference, bias, or strategy, because she regarded the connotations of that term to be too strong in suggesting an effect on children's mapping hypotheses that is "all or none." In the word-learning experiments, children's choices characteristically show only about a 70% preference for the referent predicted by the constraining principles. However, the theoretical notions of principles or constraints are postulated as processes underlying the observed biases and preferences in behavior (Behrend, 1990), part of a more comprehensive theoretical account of the determinants of semantic development.

Clearly, the lexicons of most languages violate the notion of mutual exclusivity, and many nouns, not to mention other words, do not refer to taxonomic categorizations of objects. Thus, in the course of acquisition these principles must be overcome if the child is to acquire the full adult lexicon. Like the assumption of one-to-one mapping (Slobin, 1973) and the uniqueness principle (Pinker, 1984), they are seen as heuristics that are necessary for reducing the problem of induction in the absence of sufficient systematic feedback. But they are dropped when sufficient or explicit evidence in the input indicates that they do not hold for some form-meaning relation (Markman, 1989).

Are the Principles Innate Aspects of the Language Acquisition Device, or Are They Derived From Experience With Language? Clearly the gavagai problem is at its most acute in early acquisition when the child has few words with which to contrast new vocabulary in the input, and a limited understanding of syntactic clues to meaning. E. Clark (1990) suggested that the principles of contrast and conventionality are necessary features of communication, so they are discovered by children as soon as they have a rudimentary understanding of communicative intent: They are not strictly learned from success or failure of communication, but are part of the assumptions that communicators make. This does not seem to us to be an empirically testable position, but can only be evaluated in the context of a more general theory of language development.

In the case of the more specific mutual exclusivity and taxonomic constraints, it has proved difficult to show that they apply much before the child is 2 or 3 years of age. A few studies suggest that mutual exclusivity is initially not applied and early words are often used with overlapping meanings (see Chapman & Mervis, 1989; Merriman & Bowman, 1989). In the novel-word learning experiments, these principles seem to be most strongly applied from age 3 years on. Assumptions of mutual exclusivity as well as the taxonomic and whole-object constraints may derive from developing nonlinguistic categorization of objects (Gopnik & Meltzoff, 1986; Mervis, 1984), or from specific aspects of the input, such as parents' overwhelming use of contrasting basic object terms that refer to whole objects (Ninio, 1980).

Syntactic Bootstrapping

Gleitman and several coworkers (Gleitman, 1990; Gleitman, Gleitman, Landau, & Wanner, 1987; Landau & Gleitman, 1985) have addressed the Quinean problem from a different perspective for the acquisition of verbs. They argued that despite the powerful perceptual and conceptual abilities that the young child brings to the process of mapping meanings onto words, these cognitive processes still produce too many hypotheses about that mapping. As Gleitman (1990) pointed out, "there are always many highly salient, linguistically sanctioned, interpretations of a single action scene" (p. 15). For example, in many verb pairs in English, the individual words in the pair allude to the same type of event: Every case of "chasing" is also a case of "fleeing," every case of "giving" is also one of "getting," and so on. These verbs describe the event from different perspectives that are not given by the events themselves, and thus, their meanings cannot be extracted solely by observing the events when the verb is uttered. Similarly, verbs, like nouns, can describe events at a different level of specificity. Take the set of perception verbs: "perceive," "see," "look," "notice," and so on. Here, again, any event that satisfies the referential conditions for one of these words is also compatible with any other. There are no cases of "seeing" without "looking," or of "seeing" without "perceiving." And, finally, some verbs like "think" and "know" do not refer to events that are observable at all. Yet despite these problems, Landau and Gleitman (1985) demonstrated that not only do normally sighted children acquire appropriate meaning distinctions and categorizations for these verbs, so can blind children without visual access to the scenes to which the words refer. Although the blind child they studied applied visual perception words to her sense of touch, she distinguished between "touch" and "look," and between "look" and "see." "Look" referred to active or exploratory perception with the hands, while "see" was the static achievement of perception.

The solution that Gleitman and colleagues propose builds on the notion that there is a strong correlation between verb syntax and verb meaning across different languages (Fisher, Gleitman, & Gleitman, 1991; Jackendorf, 1983). They suggest that as soon as children are able to parse utterances into syntactic units (Gleitman & Wanner, 1982), they use evidence about the sentence structure frames in which verbs can and cannot appear to distinguish between their meanings. They call this process *syntactic bootstrapping*. The syntactic clues to meaning include such features as the number of argument noun phrases required by a verb; "see" requires only two (observer and object), but "give" usually requires three (giver, receiver, and object). Another is whether the verb can appear in either transitive or intransitive sentence frames, or the type of locative prepositions that can appear with it. Landau and Gleitman showed that a variety of these syntactic clues to the distinctions in meaning between perception verbs were available to the blind child in her mother's speech.

In a recent experiment using visual preference as a measure of children's matching of spoken nonsense verbs to filmed events, Naigles (1990) demonstrated that children as young as 2 years of age are able to use a verb's appearance in a transitive or intransitive frame to determine whether the word refers to a causative or noncausative action. So if they heard the word "gorp" in a transitive utterance:

The duck is gorping the bunny.

they selectively looked at a video of a duck forcing a rabbit[6] into an odd bending position, as opposed to the same duck and rabbit together making arm gestures, but not acting on each other. In contrast, if they heard:

The duck and the bunny are gorping.

they chose to look more at the noncausative action of the pantomime characters acting in concert.

Syntactic information is thus a powerful constraint on the process of inducing meanings for new words in the input, but the extent to which it is used with other form classes of words in fast mapping has yet to be established.

Fast Mapping and Lexical Development — Conclusion

A major problem for theories of lexical acquisition is to account for the rapid acquisition of word meanings. Each of the above solutions has some

---

[6]Actually people dressed up in appropriate costumes.

merit and may be true for different periods of development and for different types of words. Hence, theories that place great weight on the social–interactional setting and the negotiation of meaning between caregiver and child seem best to capture the period of earliest word learning. Specific constraints on possible word meanings may drive the child's rapid acquisition of names for objects and their properties at a later stage in development. These principles may reflect innate assumptions about the nature of languages, but may also be derived from the patterns of naming present in the input or from the child's cognitive development during this period. Fast mapping may apply best in the case of nouns and words for physical attributes. In the case of verbs and other relational words where meaning representations may be less concrete and more dependent on semantic and syntactic relations between words, the use of clues from the syntactic frames in which such words appear may be paramount. In all of this research there is a need for the kind of cross-linguistic comparison of acquisition that has proven so informative in extending theories of syntactic development and notions of linguistic constraints on syntax acquisition (see next section).

GRAMMATICAL DEVELOPMENT

Issues

In the area of grammatical development the recurring issues parallel some of those in lexical development, although they take a slightly different form. These issues are:

1. *Are Early Grammars Continuous or Discontinuous With Adult Grammars?* When children begin using sentences, they are only 1 or 2 years old, a stage at which intellectual capacity is quite limited compared to an adult. Does the child initially develop a kind of communication system that is based on less abstract, more concrete, principles than adult grammars?

2. *What Contribution to the Acquisition of Grammar Is Made by the Child's General Cognitive Development?* This issue takes different forms. First, does the grammar simply map onto existing prelinguistic concepts of event structures? Just as in the lexical domain, in answering this question one must consider the uniformity or lack of uniformity across languages in the concepts underlying grammatical forms. Second, is syntax learning special, or does it call on more general cognitive processes such as simple rote memory, or hypothesis formation?

3. *What Is the Role of the Input in Acquiring the Grammar?* The child has to learn how to say what adults can say, and modeling seems to be a reasonable learning procedure to invoke to explain that process. But the child also has to learn not to say what can't be said in the language, and therein lies the rub. As we shall see, the evidence that children encounter systematic *negative evidence,* that is, corrective feedback for errors, is very weak.

4. *What Special Biases or Constraints Does the Child Bring to the Process of Grammar Acquisition?* Perhaps more so than in semantic development, researchers have argued that the child comes prepared for grammar, with existing hypotheses about the forms that human grammars should take. Chomsky (1965, 1986b) and many others (e.g., Lightfoot, 1982; Wexler & Culicover, 1980) have argued that the child comes equipped with a knowledge of Universal Grammar (UG), a set of principles and parameters that define the possible structures of human grammars.

Each of these issues recur in the particular areas of grammatical development that we discuss in the next section.

Conflicting Paradigms in the Study of Grammatical Development

There are, in fact, two broad competing paradigms in the field, in the sense of Kuhn (1962). Atkinson (1983) has characterized the two paradigms as the SHARPS and the FLATS.[7] The SHARPS have their roots in linguistic theory, particularly the generative grammar of Chomsky. They hold a set of assumptions about language such that it is a specialized module in the human mind, not shared by any other creatures; that language acquisition is only possible because every human being has a prewired set of assumptions about UG; that children's grammars conform to the nature of human grammars in general; that input is necessary only to "trigger" children's preexisting grammatical knowledge; and that syntax development is not dependent in any significant way on the child's cognitive or social development.

The FLATS, on the other hand, have their roots in psychology, and particularly developmental psychology: Theorists like Piaget, Vygotsky, and Bruner are their inspiration. Among their assumptions lies a belief that the child's social and cognitive development in the first 2 years is the

---

[7]Atkinson invented the acronym FLATS for First Language Acquisition Theorists. SHARPS are simply their opposites. Which may already demonstrate a bias—which would you rather be?

fundamental basis for language learning; that language learning is another cognitive skill, albeit the most complex, that the child must acquire; that parents and other caregivers provide significant environmental support for this learning by tailoring the input and feedback provided to the child; that children's early sentences are grammatically less abstract and more semantically based; and that induction from particular sentences to general rules is the fundamental mechanism of learning.

Understanding the foundations of the two paradigms will go a long way toward clarifying why there is so much dispute in the research arena.

A Brief Overview of Major Periods of Acquisition

We begin with a very broad characterization of grammatical development in English-speaking children. Following that, we consider particular developments in more detail, and emphasize their theoretical consequences.

First Sentences (18–27 Months of Age).   Around age 2, most children begin to combine words into simple sentences that typically preserve the order of English but lack many of the little grammatical words:

Give juice.
Mommy drop.
Read book.

At this stage there is no tense marking, little use of articles, no special syntax for questions, which are marked by rising intonation:

Mommy read?

and often preposed negatives:

No Mommy read.

Despite the lack of grammatical form, however, the functions and meanings conveyed seem diverse, in that adults in interaction with the child "read into" their utterances quite complex meanings, references to the past, and distinct communicative intentions that seem justified by the child's behavior and the context.

Grammar Explosion (27–36 months).   Rather like the vocabulary explosion in the second year, sometime in the third year there is a grammatical flowering. The missing function words and inflections make their first appearance, although it is many months (sometimes even years) before they consistently appear in every context in which an adult would use them. The child begins to use auxiliary and modal verbs:

Mommy can read.
I will do it.

and to invert them for questions:

Can you do it?

and negate them:

I don't like that.

Tense appears, and overgeneralizes to irregular verbs:

You liked my picture.
I catched it!

Pronouns appear, and articles, as well as the first complex phrases:

The teddy and the doll are gonna play.

Complex Sentences (30–48 Months).   Shortly after the sprouting of the missing "little words," children begin to attempt constructions that drive nonlinguists to their descriptive grammar books. They combine sentences:

I didn't catch it but Teddy did!
After I clean my teeth can I have a story?

and they embed phrases in relative clauses:

I'm gonna sit on the one you're sitting on.

They ask and answer complex questions:

Where did you say you put my doll?
Those are punk rockers, aren't they?

and they sometimes use verbs in ways that seem creative to the listener:

Now you jump me off here!

Much of the remaining progress in grammar is made as children encounter exceptions and master them: straightening out overgeneralizations of irregular verbs; discovering rarer spoken forms such as the passive:

The dog got bitten by the cat.

and the cleft:

It was the man that the dog bit.

as well as verbs with exceptional properties:

John promised Mary to mow the lawn.

This means John, not Mary, mowed the lawn (unless Mary is some kind of slave to be lent out).

Considering the complexity of the syntax that children master, grammatical development is remarkably rapid. But as we see later, it is not error-free, although sometimes it takes an experimental task to elicit the interesting mistakes that children make and adults resist. Having sketched the course of acquisition in this very broad way, consider the methodology of the research before looking at each stage in more depth.

Methods of Study

The methodology for the study of grammatical development has become increasingly varied and inventive since the early days of transcript collection.

Conversational Samples.   Naturalistic data from transcripts of parents interacting with their children still form the bulk of evidence. It is usual to collect data with the parents because children may speak more freely to them, and the parents' speech may also be of interest for studying characteristics of the input. Twenty years ago audio recordings were the norm, now it is more likely to be videotape because of the extra contextual information that it provides. A major breakthrough in the availability of evidence from naturalistic data has come from the CHILDES project headed by MacWhinney and Snow (1985), who have overseen an effort to computerize (and partially standardize) most of the major sets of transcripts collected on English and several other languages.

Naturalistic data cannot always supply needed evidence, however. In particular, it may not be clear that a child has "analyzed" what is being said; the child may be producing an unanalyzed whole (R. Clark, 1974).

Furthermore, there may be omissions of rare types of sentences — passives, or some kinds of relative clauses, for example. Is that an artifact of sampling or does the child not know the construction in question? Finally, interpretations of sentences are hard to figure out from a naturalistic transcript; in part, because parents seem reluctant to ask the child just those questions that would settle important linguistic disputes! For all these reasons, naturalistic data are frequently supplemented by experiments.

Elicited Production.   Elicited production studies have become increasingly popular in the last 10 years, and Crain (in press), among others, has used them with great success. The principle is to arrange the situation so as to make the child produce a sentence that would otherwise be too rare to study; for example, subject-modifying relative clauses:

The man who rode the horse ate the cheese.

(see de Villiers, 1988; Tager-Flusberg, 1982) or complex coordinations:

The boy held a kite and the girl, a balloon.

(Tager-Flusberg, de Villiers, & Hakuta, 1982).
This research has also led to more careful consideration of the pragmatic circumstances of comprehension tests (Grimshaw & Rosen, 1990; Hamburger & Crain, 1982).

Comprehension Tests.   In simple comprehension tests, the task has usually been for the child to act out with toys what the experimenter (or better still, a puppet) says, or to point to a picture that represents it. In more elaborate techniques, and with slightly older subjects, the child may listen to a brief story illustrated by a sequence of pictures, and then be asked a question about it (de Villiers, Roeper, & Vainikka, 1990).

Teaching New Grammatical Rules.   Finally, the advantages of *teaching* studies, in the study of syntax as in semantics, should be mentioned. Some investigators have tried deliberately teaching (via modeling) some aspect of grammar and then watching the generalizations that the child goes on to make (de Villiers, 1980; Pinker, Lebeaux, & Frost, 1987). In this way the biases and assumptions that the child brings to the learning can be studied in a situation in which input has been more carefully controlled.

FIRST SENTENCES

Most toddlers produce their first two-word sentence at 18 to 24 months of age, usually once they have acquired between 50 and 100 words. Before their first sentences, they achieve the effect of complex expressions by stringing together their simple words (Bloom, 1973):

Book.
Mine.
Read.

but then their first sentence puts these under a single intonational envelope, with no pause (Branigan, 1976). Early sentences are not profound, but they represent a major advance in the expression of meaning.

However, the appropriate characterization of this first stage of grammatical development is in considerable dispute. Some researchers have pointed out the continuity between the first sentences and the earlier cognitive and social achievements in the sensorimotor period. Others have claimed the two-word period as the point at which the true and abstract nature of language can be discerned, emphasizing the continuity with adult language. Hence we must consider the first sentences from a variety of theoretical perspectives.

Telegraphic Speech

A long-held view of young children's speech is that it is *telegraphic*; that is, some words are more likely to appear than others (Brown, 1973). These are content words, primarily the nouns and verbs necessary in the situation. Words and morphemes that have grammatical functions, but do not themselves make reference, such as articles, prepositions, auxiliary verbs, and inflections attached to nouns and verbs, do not occur as often. What underlies this selective production? Notice that the very properties that make content words more necessary in speech also make them more salient for the language learner: They have relatively concrete meanings and usually attract sentence stress, whereas function words do not. Finally, content words can sometimes occur alone as elliptical answers to questions:

Who did you see?
Mom.
How are you going to get there?
Walk.

It is rare, indeed, for the answer to a question to be "the" or "in" (unless it is in English class). Hence the telegraphic nature of early child speech is usually given a functional explanation, but its true character is still debated. For instance, does the child really reduce an equivalent adult sentence, as we do when writing a telegram? Are the little grammatical words, the so-called closed class items, deleted in production from a full underlying sentence representation, or never present?

Most important, it is now being recognized that there may be (on this dimension) two kinds of languages in the world: languages like English and French, that emphasize word order but have relatively impoverished inflection, and languages like Turkish and Russian that have rich inflection but more variable word order (see Slobin, 1985). The child exposed to an inflectionally rich language cannot easily be characterized as speaking telegraphically; the child does not strip the forms to their root words but has inflections from the start. Focusing on English may have misled us about acquisition in general.

Word Order in Early Sentences

Consider the basic data: Children learning English produce two-word utterances that seem to conform to adult orders, in that they say:

Daddy eat.

rather than:

Eat Daddy.

and:

My chair.

rather than:

Chair my.

at least with greater probability in the right direction. For many of these utterances there is no immediate model from the adult conversation, so the child must have developed some ordering rules that allow him to construct these utterances. This is especially clear when the child creates sentences that the adult never said at all, such as:

My softy.

or:

Teddy eat.

Clearly these must have been made by analogy with other forms. But what is the analogy based on? The question is, how does the child know that "Teddy," "dolly," "Daddy," "Mommy," and "you" all fall into the same category, namely, a word you can put before the word "eat"? Braine (1963) made a plausible proposal based on his studies of the two-word stage in three children. He argued that children create a grammar not at all like the adults', but based on learning the position of certain key words, called *pivots,* and that by learning the position of a few high-frequency words, the child could begin to construct a grammar for simple sentences. Unfortunately, this grammar would not resemble adult grammar at all, in fact, there is no simple way to make a transition from a pivot grammar to the proposals of linguists about adult grammar. Why, it was argued, would the child start down such a false path? Furthermore, empirical evidence soon mounted to show the inadequacy of Braine's proposal even as a self-contained description of the two-word stage (Bowerman, 1973).

Yet the strongest criticism was not just on empirical grounds: Bloom (1970) argued that children have a richer representation of the sentence *meaning* than is carried by the two-word structure alone. She presented evidence that children at the two-word stage produce structural homonyms: two-word sentences identical in form but with different meanings. For example, her daughter produced the sentence:

Mommy sock.

on two occasions, once when the mother was putting the daughter's sock on the daughter, and once when the daughter found her mother's stocking. Given the context, it seems hard to resist the interpretations:

Mommy is putting on my sock on me.

versus:

Here is Mommy's sock.

Bloom proposed that the entire proposition was present in some form in the child's mind, but that production constraints forced her to reduce it to two words. She presented compelling examples of children expressing a complex proposition over several utterances, again suggesting that there was a production limit rather than a thought limit.

But what is the nature of the more complex, mental representation that gets reduced? For Bloom in 1970, it was a full adultlike grammar. In making this claim, she opened the door to a new form of analysis of child language: explicitly taking into account not just the arrangements of words but how they were interpreted in context.

The Role of Meaning

The child is at some fundamental level learning to mean, not just to say word combinations. That is, the child has a proposition in mind, and needs to find the conventional way to express it. However, the very productivity and freedom of language has the consequence of great indeterminacy for the language learning child, for any given scene may be described in a multitude of different ways. Despite these cautions, it is now a general assumption among theorists of language acquisition that the child entering the sentence-making stage has the ability to read the situational context in the same or equivalent terms as the adult speakers around him. In addition, the child knows a substantial vocabulary before beginning to put words together, generally about 50 words but sometimes as high as 500. Given these two abilities, the child can then map the meaning onto the utterances heard from others, providing a bootstrap into the grammar of the language.

Further evidence that the child at the two-word stage is concerned with the expression of meaning relations comes from the cross-linguistic study of children. Brown (1973) surveyed all the most fully reported studies on early child language, which included languages as remotely related as French, Samoan, Luo (spoken in Kenya), German, Finnish, and Cakchiquel (a Mayan language spoken in Guatemala). The children learning each of these languages expressed only a narrow range of the possible meanings that the adult language could express. Table 6.1 gives examples of the semantic relations expressed in various languages.

Debate has raged over how significant this finding of universal semantic relations is for the study of grammatical development. On the one hand, a grammar based on how to map propositions onto elementary word combinations seems like a sensible starting point, given the child's communicative needs, and one that is continuous with the cognitive developments of that period of life (de Villiers & de Villiers, 1985). On the other hand, that approach delays the larger problem of how the child builds a grammar that resembles the adult's, for a semantics-based grammar is not favored as an approach to adult language. For true linguistic competence, the child needs to build a theory out of the right components: subjects, objects, noun phrases and verb phrases, and the rest. These abstract categories do not translate easily into semantic relations, if at all. The alternative interpretation of the findings about early sentences is that children all over the world are constrained by cognitive development and by interests to talk about the same things, but that their doing so should not be interpreted to mean that

TABLE 6.1
The Early Expression of Common Meaning Relations

Semantic Relation	English	Russian	German	Samoan
agent– action	teddy fall	mama prua (Mama walk)	Puppe kommt (doll comes)	pa'u pepe (fall doll)
action– object	hit ball	day chasy (give watch)	Tur aufmachen (door open)	tapale 'oe (hit you)
entity– location	there car	Tosya tam (Tosya there)	Buch da (book there)	Keith lea (Keith there)
possessor– possession	mama dress	pup moya (navel my)	mein Ball (my ball)	lol a'u (candy my)
entity– attribute	big truck	papa bol'shoy (papa big)	Milch heiss (milk hot)	fa'ali'i pepe (headstrong baby)
rejection– action	no wash	vody net (water no)	nicht blasen (not blow)	le 'ai (not eat)

they have grammars based on semantic relations (Pinker, 1984; Valian, 1986).

Finally, there is strong empirical evidence against the notion that semantics provides the basis for sentence construction at the two-word stage. Bloom (1990) pointed out that children never say sentences such as:

Big he.
Hot it.

in which the adjective precedes the pronoun, even though their speech contains many examples of that construction when the nominal is a full noun phrase:

Big dogs.
Hot coffee.

Instead, with pronouns they use nominal–adjective structure:

He big.
It hot.

Yet pronouns and nominals refer to the same semantic categories, thus showing that children at this stage have a sensitivity to formal parts of speech, not just meaning (see also Maratsos & Chalkley, 1980).

Abstract Grammatical Categories

Gleitman and Wanner (1982) discussed the two opposing positions on early grammar in terms of a biological metaphor. Either children are just like adults from the beginning, only smaller and less experienced, or they undergo a kind of metamorphosis during development, rather like frogs develop from frogspawn to tadpoles to frogs. In the study of early grammar, these are the two choices. Either children's grammars are just like those of adults, that is, based on the same principles and abstract categories but somehow less complete, or they begin as something quite different, say lexically or semantically based grammars, and then undergo a radical restructuring during development so they end up like adult grammars.

So, the semantic analysis of children's early sentences offers fascinating data on the meanings children express at that age. It is less clear that these semantic notions are the components out of which children's early grammars are constructed (Levy, 1983). Pinker (1987) argued that the child might gain a foothold into a more abstract analysis by knowing:

1. the meaning of the individual words,
2. the conceptual structure of the event, namely that "dog" is the agent; "bit" is the action.

Notice that the semantic grammar approach would stop right here. Pinker speculates that the child goes further, in making the following hypothesis:

3. agents are usually subjects.

This assumption comes from built-in notions about grammar, not from regularities gleaned from experience; It is a rationalist assumption. Knowing that, the child can now construct a partial phrase structure for the sentence. If the child makes a further pair of hypotheses:

4. actions are usually verbs,
5. things are usually nouns

the entire phrase structure of the sentence is fixed. Semantic notions then become vital bootstraps for the learning of grammar, not peculiar grammatical cul-de-sacs on the way to adult competence. Of course, there is a cost: the postulation of some innate assumptions that many will find hard to swallow. In addition, controversy rages over whether these generalizations hold over the world's languages.

Universal Grammar and Parameter Setting

There is an alternative approach to early sentences that makes more radical assumptions about the language-learning capacity of the human child. In this view, the child comes equipped with universal grammar (UG), a knowledge of the universal forms that grammars take, and acquiring the language is a matter of setting parametric switches that distinguish, say, Zulu from Japanese, or German from English. This position follows Chomsky (1986b) in arguing that underlying language structure is universally the same, with the superficial variations among languages being represented as variations along a set of parameters: for example, word order within phrases, optionality of subject pronouns, and so forth.

A basic assumption under this view is that the child's search for grammar is constrained by UG, and hence among a restricted set of hypotheses. On this view, there are no wild grammars—each stage of the child's development represents a sensible, possible human language, although it might not yet be English, or whatever the target is.

Consider a provocative account by Radford (1988), which reinterprets the telegraphic nature of English grammar at the beginning stages. In Radford's account, the first sentences that children produce are like small clauses, a shrunken type of embedded clause found in adult grammar. The difference is that adult small clauses are always embedded in a sentence:

> Let [that one go round].
> I consider [Paula a good girl].
> I found [Wayne in the bedroom].

but children's are not:

> That one go round.
> Paula a good girl.
> Wayne in the bedroom.

(children's utterances from Radford, 1988).

How does the structure of small clauses differ from full adult grammar? Radford argues that the small clause is a sentence stripped of all but two major lexical categories:

$$S \rightarrow NP, XP$$

where NP is a noun phrase ("Paula," "Wayne," "that one"), and XP is any other type of lexical phrase: a Verb Phrase (VP; "go round"), a Prepositional Phrase (PP; "in the bedroom"), an Adjectival Phrase (AdjP; "very nice"), or another Noun Phrase (NP; "a good girl"). All of these phrases are "headed" by content words: verbs, nouns, adjectives, prepositions.

But for a sentence in adult English, contemporary linguistic accounts include not only lexically headed phrases such as NP, VP, AdjP, but also phrases headed by functional components, I (for inflection) and C (for complementizer). These functional components do not have content words as the heads of their phrases and have less to do with meaning than with grammatical function. Hence, the structure of a full sentence in English looks something like Fig. 6.3a in contemporary syntax, whereas the child's first structures resemble Fig. 6.3b. Radford's claim is that children's grammars lack *functional categories* at the start, and their earliest sentences are constructed entirely of *lexical-thematic categories*, such as noun phrases and verb phrases. This is a claim for which others have also

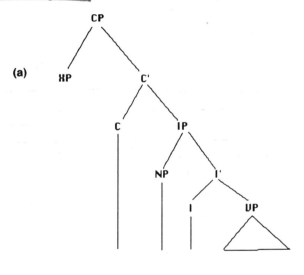

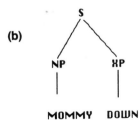

FIG. 6.3. Phrase structure grammar for adult and child clauses. (a) The adult phrase structure. (b) The small clause.

argued (Lebeaux, 1988; Platzack, in press) and disputed (Hyams, in press; Weissenborn, 1990).

How do these facts bear on the choice of model of grammatical development mentioned earlier? Syntactic theory is not sufficiently advanced to be able to state with certainty that all languages have functional categories (see Fukui & Speas, 1985), but it is at the moment a working assumption that they do. If so, then don't children's first grammars reflect a wild grammatical option? On one view they do, and such a stage might be maturationally determined; that is, it might reflect the child's state of immaturity at the earliest stages of grammatical learning, soon to be replaced (see e.g., Borer & Wexler, 1987). Radford's data are in fact all from children less than 2 ½ years old. An interesting implication of the maturational claim is that a second language learner, with a mature brain, should never go through a small clause stage of grammar. Some data in fact point in that direction (Hakuta, 1974).

Summary

Children's first sentences may appear simple, but attempts to capture the grammar underlying them have generated radically different descriptions and theories: from lean descriptions based on types of words present or absent and their ordering in the sentences; to semantic notions and their expression; to abstract grammatical notions such as subject and object. Evaluation of these different approaches depends less on how well they describe the form of early sentences — they all do that well — but more on the explanatory power of the theories that underlie them.

CROSS-LINGUISTIC VARIATION

In studying language acquisition across languages, researchers ask whether there are universal biases that children share, and then debate whether the children's preferences are cognitive or linguistic in origin. In this section we first describe Slobin's approach to these questions, and then we turn to three areas in which cross-linguistic study has provided crucial information for understanding the nature of grammatical development: the acquisition of word order rules; the providing or dropping of subjects in sentences; and the acquisition of the passive voice.

Basic Child Grammar

Slobin (1973, 1985) has undertaken a program of cross-linguistic research designed to test whether children bring biases and assumptions to the task of language acquisition. Slobin's work is motivated by consideration of the diversity of linguistic encodings across languages, and the problem children face in mapping their conceptual schemes onto this diversity of forms.

In 1985, Slobin undertook an ambitious multivolume survey of cross-linguistic work on language acquisition, and assessed the evidence and revised the formulation of several *operating principles* he first introduced in 1973. For example:

> QP (ATTENTION): ENDS OF UNITS — Pay attention to the last syllable of an extracted speech unit. Store it separately and also in relation to the unit with which it occurs.

Children learning different languages seem to prefer postpositions — markers that come after the content words — to prepositions, and more easily learn inflections that occur on the ends of words.

> OP (STORAGE): FUNCTOR CLASSES — Store together all functors (grammatical morphemes) that co-occur with members of an established word class and try to map each functor onto a distinct notion.

When this fails, children use a single functor to express a range of meanings that are treated distinctly in the adult language. For instance, children learning German may use a single article for all three genders; Turkish children may use one past tense form instead of the two that occur in the adult language, ignoring the distinction as to whether the event was witnessed or not.

> OP (MAPPING): UNIFUNCTIONALITY — If you discover that a linguistic form expresses two closely related but distinguishable notions, use available means in your language to mark the two notions distinctly.

For instance, Karmiloff-Smith (1979) found that French children resist the use of "un/une" to mean both the indefinite article and the number one, instead distinguishing these meanings by saying "une voiture" (a car) and "une de voiture" (one car).

> OP (POSITION): FIXED WORD ORDER — If you have determined that word order expresses basic semantic relations in your language, keep the order of morphemes in a clause constant.

As an example, Slobin cited Radulović (1975), whose Serbo-Croatian subjects used rigid word order to express semantic relations even after the acquisition of the morphological inflections that marked those notions.

The operating principles are meant to define jointly universal child preferences in such a way that children everywhere might be said to be constructing a "Basic Child Grammar," an ideal form of human language, which might differ in significant ways from the target language to which they are exposed. It might include meaning distinctions that frequently figure in the semantic systems of human languages, those that Slobin has referred to as *grammaticizable notions*, such as agency, animacy, force, cause, reality status, locative relations of figure-ground, and so forth (Talmy, 1983). As evidence for the universality of the prepared semantic space in the domain of locative terms, Johnston and Slobin (1979) found a common order of development of locative notions in English, Italian, Serbo-Croatian, and Turkish. Others are less impressed by the evidence for conceptual preparedness, however, preferring to argue that the child has multiple schemes available and is guided early by the formal markings in the language input (see Bowerman, 1985, 1989).

The process oriented operating principles have a rather ill-defined status: They are not just cognitive principles, because they refer to rather specific linguistic entities, but neither are they theoretically motivated within linguistics. Bowerman (1985) makes an appeal for a theoretical integration to shore up the principles, and a more systematic assessment of their consequences (Smoczyńska, 1985). It is likely that the notion of Basic Child Grammar will be an important perspective on the process of language acquisition for some time to come.

Word Order

Speculation about the preferred word order for languages is rampant, with most writers converging on the notion that subject-verb-object (SVO) order is the most "natural" (e.g., Bickerton, 1981). Evidence suggests instead that children are attentive to the structural possibilities that their language provides and that they establish that word order early in their own speech. Berwick (1986) argued that one of the first aspects of grammar a child must learn is the major direction of heads in a phrase: Does the verb in a verb phrase appear at the left or the right of the phrase, for instance? Japanese has the opposite head direction to English, so its verb, for instance, appears at the right of the phrase:

The child lifted up the cat that chased the rat.
Nezumi o oikaketa neko o kodomo ga dakiageta.
Rat chased cat child lifted up.

In setting the head direction, the child will establish the basic word order of the language.

From the start, English-speaking children combine their single words into two-word strings that usually preserve the common word order of their parents' sentences. At the same time, comprehension tests (de Villiers & de Villiers, 1973b) show that the child can distinguish between sentences that contrast in word order and hence meaning:

The dog licks the cat.
The cat licks the dog.

Researchers using innovative techniques with preverbal infants (Golinkoff, Hirsch-Pasek, Cauley, & Gordon, 1987) have suggested that even before they learn to talk, infants understand basic word order contrasts. They presented infants a choice to look at two brief movies along with spoken sentences, and observed to which movie the infants attended. The 1- to 2-year-olds preferred to look at the movie of the event that was congruent with the spoken sentence, where the only contrast was in word order. So when hearing "Find Big Bird tickling Cookie Monster," toddlers preferred to look at a film of Big Bird tickling Cookie Monster than at a film with the roles reversed.

Examples from German and French also suggest that young children are sensitive to particular word order possibilities in the early stages. Children learning German position the verb correctly in the second position of the sentence from a surprisingly early age:

Ivar (2;4):   Kaputt is der.
                 (Broken is it)
Caroline (2;4): Da fahrt die Caroline.
                 (There goes the Caroline)

(data from Meisel & Muller, 1990).

This is usually interpreted to mean that the verb has moved to the second position, because the underlying word order of German (seen in embedded clauses) is subject–object–verb (SOV; e.g., Weissenborn, 1990). French, on the other hand, allows more postverbal subjects than English, for instance:

Il est là, le garçon.
(He is there, the boy)

Pierce (1989) reported that French children begin with postverbal subjects predominating

Daniel (1;8):   Pleure pas garçon.
                 (Cries not boy).

Nathalie (2;0):   Mets le manteau maman.
                   (Puts on the coat mommy).

Pierce argued that French children's grammars begin with the subject generated post-verbally, and later it moves into the preverbal position. Clearly, French and German children are responding to patterns provided by their own language at an early stage. In other languages that have less use of word order, however, the evidence is more mixed. Slobin (1973) argued that children have certain preferences for how a language should be, and among those preferences is a reliance on word order to signal meaning contrasts. However cross-linguistic evidence modulates this strong claim, suggesting instead that the preference for order appears when the target language contains unclear morphological indications of basic semantic relations (Slobin, 1985).

Subject Dropping

Consider the following sentences from the two- and three-word stage:

Read bear book.
Want go get it.
Ride truck.

(Bloom, Lightbown, & Hood, 1975).
    What is odd about these sentences is that they have no subjects, yet they are not intended as imperatives. English sentences are supposed to have subjects; in fact, even when there isn't really a meaning for a subject element, English supplies one:

It is raining.

What is "it"? The "it" in such sentences is called an *existential* to distinguish it from the pronoun "it" that refers to something. So English insists on the expression of a subject even when it makes no semantic contribution to the sentence. However, it is perfectly fine in Spanish to say:

Llueve.
(Raining)

In fact, Italian and Spanish optionally omit their subject pronouns. The world's languages divide into those that obligatorily require a subject pronoun, like English and French, and those that can drop it, like Italian, Spanish, and Sesotho (a Bantu language of southern Africa). So one of the syntactic parameters that characterizes the different languages of the world is the parameter of *prodrop*. Italian and Spanish are prodrop languages, but English is a non-prodrop language.

Hyams (1986) claimed that children begin language learning everywhere with the assumption that their language is prodrop, which accounts for their odd sentences in English. This is an example of the no wild grammars hypothesis, and it also entails an idea that children everywhere may start out with the same ideas about grammars (Lebeaux, 1988; Slobin, 1973, 1985). If we accept Hyams' analysis, how could English children recover from their mistake of dropping the subject in early sentences? What evidence would allow them to reset the parameter to non-prodrop? Even in Italian, subject pronouns appear some of the time. So one can't claim that simply hearing them in adult speech would reset the parameter, because then Italian kids would switch to English! Hyams proposes that the presence of expletive pronouns as in:

It's raining.

may provide the necessary evidence, because expletive pronouns, empty of content, typically occur only in languages that require a subject pronoun. Thus expletives might be the trigger to reset the parameter for English children. The proposal is not without difficulties (Valian, 1990), as the correlation between the presence of expletives and non-prodrop in language is apparently not perfect.

Several have argued there is some other explanation for children's dropping of subjects in English. For instance, maybe they drop what is not semantically necessary, regardless of its sentence role. Yet object deletion is not as prevalent, even where the object would be understood (Bloom, 1990; Bloom, Miller, & Hood, 1975; Hyams, 1986). Perhaps children have a limit on production that forces them to omit subjects? This argument is made most cogently by Bloom (1990), who presents evidence that children's subjectless sentences differ from those in which there are expressed subjects in several ways. He concluded with the opposite claim to that of Hyams: namely, that the default setting of the parameter should be non-prodrop, and that English children's dropping of the subject is not a function of grammar so much as performance limitations.

Future research is needed to understand how these claims can be reconciled: subject pronoun dropping is clearly different for Italian and English children (Valian, 1990), suggesting an early sensitivity to the potential of the languages. But if English children drop subjects for performance reasons (Bloom, 1990), it is hard to pinpoint the moment of discovery that English is a non-prodrop language.

Passive Sentences

As a final example of language variation, consider the differences between children learning the passive voice in English versus Sesotho. The passive construction has formed the basis for a good deal of empirical study in language acquisition, and the late acquisition of the passive in English in both production (Horgan, 1978) and comprehension (Bever, 1970; de Villiers & de Villiers, 1973b; Maratsos, 1974) has fueled a great deal of theoretical speculation. The English passive involves a deformation of the basic SVO structure:

The boy was chased by the bull.

and young children go through a stage of systematically misinterpreting it as an active sentence, apparently insensitive to the special passive morphology "was V + participle by."

The passive represents another case of the debate over semantic versus syntactically based rules, as it was noticed by several investigators that the passive was learned first (understood first) with reference to action verbs, and only later with respect to nonaction verbs (e.g., verbs of mental activity) (de Villiers, 1980; Maratsos, Fox, Becker, & Chalkley, 1985; Pinker, Lebeaux, & Frost, 1987). This suggested that the child's rule might not be abstract at first, but may be restricted to some thematic subclass of verbs (but see Gordon & Chafetz, 1989, for another interpretation).

It has also been claimed that children's first passives are restricted syntactically. Borer and Wexler (1987) argue that early passives are not formed by movement of a noun phrase into the initial position in the sentence but are generated directly in some simpler fashion akin to an adjectival construction. The child may make a passive such as:

My car was broken.

analogous to:

My car was green.

However, these proposals for English — that children have difficulty with the passive because it is a deformation; that their representation of the rule is less than abstract; and that it may not involve movement rules — are all called into question by data Demuth (1990) collected on Sesotho-speaking children. Here are some examples:

Keneoue (2;8):   o-tla-hlaj-uw-a ke tshelo.
                   (you'll be stabbed by a thorn)
Hlobohang (2;9):   o-le-f-uo-e lena ke nkono Mamokoena.
                   (you were given it by grandmother M.)

Apparently passives appear among the early utterances in Sesotho: Children less than 3 years old have no difficulty with the change in word order, and they mark the full abstract and semantic range for which the adult language uses the passive voice. Why should this difference occur? Demuth offers the proposal that the passive is much more frequent in everyday discourse in Sesotho than in English. In particular, one can only question the subject in Sesotho by passivizing. One cannot say:

Who asked you?

but only the equivalent of:

Whom were you asked by?

Hence, children in Sesotho are exposed to many more passives in greater variety.

In each of these examples — word order, subject pronouns, and passives — the form that the language takes sets some constraints on the speed and course of acquisition, even though there may also be important constraints of maturation and child preference to be isolated, too.

LEARNABILITY

Language acquisition research has as one of its major goals an understanding of how language could be learned. Chomsky (1959) made a devastating attack on learning theories in psychology in a review of B. F. Skinner's 1957 book, *Verbal Behavior*. In 1967, Gold demonstrated mathematically that a human language could not be learned in a finite time by a learning machine equipped with only general learning mechanisms, unless corrective feedback were available. As discussed in the following section, corrective feedback of the appropriate sort does not seem to be present for the human child (Brown & Hanlon, 1970). In 1980, Wexler and Culicover proved that a human language was learnable, provided the learner was equipped with substantial preexisting knowledge of linguistic universals. As might be predicted, these findings have not been comfortably assimilated into the mainstream of American psychology. In the following sections we provide some illustrations of contemporary work that considers the ques-

tion of the "learnability" of various features of language. The first—
connectionism—represents an attempt to revitalize learning theory as a
contestant within a framework provided by computer modeling. The
remaining examples describe the nature of the learning problem that faces
the child, and raise problems for pure learning-based accounts.

Connectionism or Rules

After the basic phrase structure and word order are acquired, what does the
child learn next? Brown (1973) argued that the inflectional morphology
came next—tense marking, articles, plural, and possessive markings—all
the subtle modulations of basic sentence meaning that are omitted in the
English-speaking child's first sentences. For English, Brown showed that 14
morphemes that carry these modulations of meaning are mastered gradually
in children's speech in a virtually invariant order determined by relative
semantic and grammatical complexity (see de Villiers & de Villiers, 1973a,
1985, for a fuller review).

But what is the nature of the learning that is taking place? The original
arguments that the child learns generative grammatical rules are:

1. The child goes beyond the examples heard to produce novel uses: to
   do so involves extracting and generalizing the rules.
2. The child applies the rule to cases in which the language has an
   exception (e.g., saying "foots" or "runned").
3. The child can apply the rule to nonsense words (e.g., "There are two
   wugs" or "the man *bodded* yesterday") (Berko, 1958).

The notion of *rule-learning* is usually contrasted with learning words or
phrases *by rote,* as individual chunks of speech stored in memory. Yet there
are more subtle alternatives than rule versus rote learning. For instance, the
child could learn to produce forms by analogy (MacWhinney, 1978), by
which is meant that full analysis and representation of the rule are not
needed, rather the child operates by similarity among exemplars: if "wad-
wadded," why not "bod-bodded"?

More recently, there has been a frontal attack on the whole notion of
rules and mental representations by researchers in artificial intelligence
working on parallel distributed processing models, an approach known as
connectionism. In one of the first models, Rumelhart and McClelland
(1987) modeled the learning of the past tense morphology of English, basing
their model on data from children summarized by Bybee and Slobin (1982).
Their model was hailed as successfully capturing several aspects of children's acquisition of past tense morphology in English. For example,
children often produce correct irregular forms of the past tense at an early

age: "went" or "caught." Then they make mistakes at a later time when they overgeneralize the regular tense ending: "goed," "catched." Finally, they straighten out the exceptions. Rumelhart and McClelland's model did precisely that, and, furthermore, its overgeneralizations were more common for verbs with certain phonological properties than with others, just like children's (Bybee & Slobin, 1982). For example, learners are more prone to produce an overgeneralization if the verb root in question does not end in a dental phoneme such as [t] or [d]. So "knowed" and "seed" are more likely than "bited" or "spended."

The controversial aspect of the result was that the model contained no explicit formulation of a rule at all, yet most accounts of children's past tense learning have assumed implicit knowledge of a rule that was represented mentally in an explicit form. In the connectionist model, the system learned by simply associating examples of verbs in the past tense and the root forms. It contained only neuron-type units that stood for phonetic representations of the stem, another set of units that stood for phonetic representations of the root, and an array of associative connections between the two sets of units that were modified in strength by learning.

However, Pinker and Prince (1988) were not long in attacking the connectionist model on several grounds, and defending the classical theory in which rules are indispensable. In particular, they argue that the connectionist model does not solve the problems of induction, because it essentially begs all the important questions, leaving unspecified how the child would recognize the stem of the verb (provided to the model), as well as how to represent the elements phonetically. For instance, to get the rules straight involves representing the root form as either derived from a verb (e.g., "come" → "become" or "overcome," but not "succumb") or a noun ("brake," "fly" in baseball, "ring" as in encircle). Notice that all noun-derived forms are regular in past tense morphology—"braked," "flied," "ringed"—despite their verb homonyms, which are irregular—"broke," "flew," "rang." Empirical research on the past tense in English points up many similar problems for the connectionist model (Marcus et al., 1991). Nevertheless, other researchers are enthusiastic about the potential for modeling morphological acquisition, particularly in languages with rich morphological paradigms, like German or Hungarian (MacWhinney, 1991).

Generalization and Negative Evidence

To find out about children's grammars we often need to ask what appears to be a paradoxical question: That is, how does a child know what can't be said? This question is considered in this and the next two sections.

Discussing this question also provides an opportunity to consider the influence of the input in the acquisition of syntax.

Consider the difficulties that a child encounters in learning the behavior of verbs. In English, for instance, there is a variety of verbal paradigms — the present progressive, the passive, the double dative, the causative, and so forth — but not all verbs enter these paradigms. In the present progressive one can say:

I am sitting.

but not:

*[8]I am knowing that.

In the passive, one can't say:

*100 lbs is weighed by John.
(in the sense that 100 lbs is his own weight)

In the double dative, the alternation with the regular dative is fine for some verbs:

The tycoon gave the books to the library.
The tycoon gave the library the books.

but not for others. For example:

The tycoon donated the books to the library.

is correct, but not:

*The tycoon donated the library the books.

How does a child learning English come to avoid such pitfalls? There are several classes of solution to what has become known as Baker's paradox, after the linguist who raised it (Baker, 1979). Pinker (1989b) spelled out the options as:

1. The child could act conservatively. That is, the child may not produce a form until it is heard from an adult. If the child waits before generalizing, these mistakes won't occur.

---

[8]The convention in linguistics is that an asterisk (*) indicates the form is ungrammatical.

2. The child could receive negative feedback from adults for a mistaken generalization. In this way the mistakes will be weeded out of the child's grammar.
3. Some principled difference could exist between classes of verbs that would exclude certain generalizations. Once the child acquires that principle, the mistakes would not appear.

Bowerman (1974, 1982) and Pinker (1989b) have striking evidence of nonconservatism in children's use of verbs. In Bowerman's (1974) spontaneous speech data she observed scores of generalizations of verbs, especially into inappropriate causative forms:

Christy (2;3):   I come it closer so it won't fall.
                 (child pulls a bowl closer to herself as she sits at the kitchen table)
Christy (3;7):   I want to stay this rubber band on.
                 (child looking at herself in mirror, she has a pony tail held with a rubber band)

E. Clark (1982) presented many examples of creative denominal verb uses by young children:

S (2;7):   I broomed her.
           (child hit his sister with a broom)

Children do not seem to be taking a wait-and-see approach!

In experimental tasks, Pinker (1989b) and his associates cleverly taught children new verbs in certain constructions, and then listened for overgeneralizations. In all cases, the experimentation involved discovering the right *felicity conditions* for encouraging use of certain verb constructions, and then seeing if the child could use the new verb in the novel form. For instance, having heard a new verb "to pilk" in the context of "the bear is pilking the horse" the child would be asked a question that focused attention on the thing affected, a natural condition for the passive voice to be used. For instance, the adult might ask:

What's happening to the horse?

Even 4-year-old children were quite likely (44% of trials) to reply with the new verb in the passive voice:

He's getting pilked by the bear.

Pinker's conclusion is that children's conservatism is not the solution to the paradox.

Consider the second class of solution, namely, negative feedback. In the most straightforward interpretation of this claim, one might expect adults correcting misuses of verbs. However, the literature reaches (unusual) consensus that correction of grammatical mistakes is vanishingly rare in the preschool years (Brown & Hanlon, 1970; Hirsch-Pasek, Treiman, & Schneiderman, 1984). Instead, the search has been for indirect negative evidence of various sorts. For example, parents and others often gloss their children' speech:

Child: He want milk.
Parent: Oh, he wants some milk?

thus expanding a telegraphic utterance into a more nearly adult form. In addition, parents make requests for clarification:

What did you say?

and they also repeat the child's utterances:

Child: Big dropped.
Parent: Big dropped?

Could it be the case that this negative feedback is differentially applied to the child's ungrammatical utterances? If so, the child might be able to recognize the deviance and make a revision in her grammar. Several studies have argued that the parent's feedback is differential: Hirsch-Pasek and colleagues (1984) found 20% of ungrammatical utterances were repeated (includes both verbatim repetition and glossing) by the parents, but only 12% of grammatical utterances. Demetras, Post, and Snow (1986) found statistical differences on well-formedness for three of eight feedback measures, but did not distinguish between phonological and grammatical ill-formedness. Bohannon and Stanowicz (1988) found glossing more common for ungrammatical utterances, and exact repetition for grammatical utterances. Hence at a statistical level, parents do respond differently to their children's deviant utterances. However, Marcus (1991) demonstrated that these effects may be artifactual, because the parental response was not coded independently of what the child said. For example, it is a basic assumption (and finding, Snow, 1972) that parents speak grammatically most of the time. When their children say something ungrammatical, such as:

Him drop truck

the parents' well-formed response repeating the content:

He dropped the truck

would be coded as an expansion. The same parental utterance following the equivalent well-formed child utterance would be coded as a repetition. The finding of differential feedback would then follow inevitably (and spuriously) from that coding scheme (see also Valian, in press). Furthermore, considered realistically, the feedback may not be a plausible candidate for teaching grammar (Gordon, 1990; Marcus, 1991; Pinker, 1989b; but see also Bohannon, MacWhinney, & Snow, 1990).

The third possibility is that there exists a principled difference between the class of verbs that enters a construction and the class of verbs that does not. The solution requires several ingredients: Linguistics must supply a criterion by which the verbs differ; children must be shown to be sensitive to that distinction; and its learnability must be established. After all, it would be embarrassing to substitute an even worse learnability problem for the one this is designed to solve! Research is proceeding on all these levels (e.g., Mazurkewich & White, 1984), and Pinker (1989a, 1989b) described some ways in which the verbs that enter the double dative differ from those that do not, and how the child could use that information to arrive at the correct grammar.

Structure Dependence

It is a commonplace of linguistic theory that languages are deeply similar in ways that have only just begun to be uncovered. All languages seem to make use of the same small inventory of formal categories for the construction of sentences: noun phrases, verb phrases, adjectives, and the like. By looking very carefully at the linguistic knowledge that young children have, we can compare their knowledge of the language with that of adults, and see to what extent their assumptions depart from ours. If language learning is by slow accretion of particular knowledge, any sample of 3-year-olds should show a rich diversity of variants of English depending on their individual experience. (This does not refer to variations in vocabulary: These obviously depend on experience and are thus widely observed.) In much of the current work on language development, linguists and psychologists are exploring whether 3-year-olds have similar grammars, at a fundamental level, to those of adults.

One of the basic features of the world's languages is that grammatical rules are *structure dependent*. This means that rules refer to units that are parts of syntactic structure (i.e., defined by their role in the syntax of the sentence) rather than to units that are nonstructural. For instance, a naive guess at how to formulate a question in English might be "Invert the order of the first two words":

John can sing. → Can John sing?
Play is fun. → Is play fun?

But obviously such a structure-independent rule would fail:

The boy must go. → *Boy the must go?

A rule that referred not to word position, but to particular types of words, such as "Put the first word like 'can,' 'may,' or 'is' in the front," would also fail:

The little boy who can swim rescued the dog.
*Can the little boy who swim rescued the dog?

(see Chomsky, 1986c). Instead, the question formation rule in English, like all linguistic rules, must refer to grammatical structures in its proper formulation: It is the auxiliary verb in the head of IP (Inflection Phrase; see, e.g., Fig. 6.3a) that moves in front of the subject. If the child comes equipped with this generalization about structure dependence, it is claimed that many false hypotheses could be ignored, many false paths not taken. In other words, the child must know "Don't waste your time on structure-independent rules!"

Is there any evidence for this? Crain and Nakayama (1987) provide an experimental demonstration that children will not adopt a structure-independent solution for precisely the case described above, namely, yes–no questions. They invented a game with the child in which a puppet presented a sentence and then the child had to convert it into a question. Despite the opportunity for misanalyses of the kind above, no child produced questions that violated structure-dependence. Given a sentence such as:

The man who is coming is tall.

the 3-year-olds invariably[9] produced forms such as:

Is the man who is coming tall?

---

[9]Although there were errors of the sort that involved a "copy" of the auxiliary: Is the man who is coming is tall?

and not:

*Is the man who coming is tall?

In the next section we discuss examples of one final problem for language acquisition: Not only does the child have to learn what can't be said, but also how things can't be interpreted.

Long Distance Movement

Consider the nature of "wh" questions in English: who, what, why, when, and the like. The wh word moves from a location in the sentence to a position in front of the sentence, actually in the CP (see Fig. 6.3a again). So each of the following questions has a "trace" (t) left behind:

Whom did she see **t** at the party?
Where did he think he was going **t**?
How did the girl ride **t** her bike?

Yet there are restrictions on wh movement, some of them the most well-studied aspects of modern generative grammar (Chomsky, 1986a; Rizzi, 1990). For example, one cannot question an element in a relative clause:

She spoke to the man who brought the van.
*$What_i$ did she speak to the man who brought t_i?

This does not seem to be due to any kind of communication principle forbidding one to ask about obscure things, although that is the first guess that most people have. For instance, an equivalent echo question presents no difficulty:

She spoke to the man who brought **what?**

Instead, it is the syntactic wh movement that is blocked.

de Villiers and colleagues (1990) looked at whether young children share adults' intuitions about the constraints on wh movement. They employed ambiguous questions that permitted the children a choice between a grammatical and an ungrammatical interpretation, to see if they would systematically resist the latter. For example, take the following short story and associated pictures in Fig. 6.4:

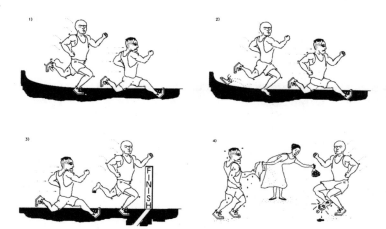

FIG. 6.4.   Pictures to accompany question "When did he say he hurt himself?"

The man was in a race, but his shoe came loose. He kicked it off and ran with only one shoe. He won, but his foot was very sore. After the race he said to the woman, "Please can I have some ice for my foot? I hurt it on the track when I was running."

Now comes the question.

(1) When did the man say he hurt his foot?

You might find yourself hesitating, but if you didn't, look back at the question again. There are two possible answers: either to when he said it, or to when he hurt his foot. The two interpretations can be represented by showing the trace in two alternative positions.

(1a) **When** did the man say t [he hurt his foot]
(1b) **When** did the man say [he hurt t his foot].

(1a) is called a *short distance* movement, because the wh word moves within the first clause. (1b) on the other hand involves a *long distance* movement because the wh word moves from the lower, or embedded, clause (marked with the square bracket). Children 3 years of age also allow both answers, showing that their grammars allow long distance as well as short distance movement. But now consider a subtle variant:

(2) When did the man say how he hurt his foot?

Those who answered "when he was running" before, the long distance answer, should find that answer awkward now. Suddenly, the ambiguity is gone, and only one answer seems right: "After the race." This array of facts has been known for several years about the adult language (Chomsky, 1986a), but do children see the subtle difference? In fact, only rarely do 3-year-old children answer "when he was running" to (2). They seem to know already the constraint that question words may not move over another question word: A constraint that reflects abstract principles of UG. Recent studies have explored children's knowledge of this constraint in German, French, (Weissenborn, Roeper, & de Villiers, 1991), Spanish (Perez-Leroux, 1991), and Greek (Leftheri, 1991) and have found strikingly similar results from young children exposed to the translations of (1) and (2).

For a learning theory account of this phenomenon to work, the 2-year-old would have to be equipped with the ability to sift through evidence of extraordinary subtlety to arrive at the appropriate generalization (see Rizzi, 1990, for one account in linguistic theory). Suppose it could be done (unconsciously, of course): The problem that then arises is the rarity of such sentences in the input. In hundreds of hours of recorded conversations between several young children and their caregivers, we have found a couple of dozen examples, and of course never the closely contrasting pairs described above. That is, the chance that a child would hear (1) twice, with one person answering it in two different ways, and then hear (2), is highly improbable. Given that each situation will be unique, and that the child will be lucky to hear half a dozen such sentences before the age of 3 years, it does not seem plausible that these contrasts are learned. Instead, it is argued, the child does not independently induce the rules, but is in possession of considerable preexisting knowledge about the principles of UG that define the form that rules can take.

CONCLUSION

What learning mechanisms in the child permit the acquisition of language in so short a time? We discussed Plato's Problem at the beginning of this chapter, and we have seen it manifest in several areas. For example, in learning the meaning of words, the lexical disparities among different languages mean that opportunities for observing language used in context by competent adults is of supreme importance. Adult caregivers in this culture at least seem to make adjustments for the child's level of knowledge in the way they converse about the world. Nevertheless, it is becoming clear that the child brings biases and constraints to the task of word learning.

The acquisition of the first sentences seems likewise to depend on discourse with a competent speaker of the language, because again, languages are not all alike. The raw data children receive is from conversations in context with competent speakers, whose communicative goals do not usually include explicit teaching of the language. Parents engage in virtually no language teaching, although their speech provides the necessary evidence for the child to determine the form that the particular language takes. Here, too, researchers invoke innate biases and principles to explain why the child's errors and hypotheses lie within a narrow set of options.

In both word learning and the early sentences, there is controversy over the basis for the constraints and biases that are invoked. Are they specifically linguistic, or do they derive from more general cognitive or communicative principles? In acquiring the rich and idiosyncratic inflectional morphology of a language, general-purpose connectionist learning procedures may yet provide a rival account to that of rule-learning. It is in complex domains of syntax that an appeal to specifically linguistic principles and constraints seems especially necessary, because there it is much less plausible that the path chosen is cognitively determined, or derived from parental influence.

One might ask about a compromise: Could different areas of language development not be more appropriately considered through different paradigms? Such a reasonable proposal ignores the role that rival theories play in providing the fuel for the scientific endeavor. Cross-linguistic and cross-cultural work is likely to be increasingly important in the future to test the generality of the claims made by each of the theories.

REFERENCES

Adams, A., & Bullock, D. (1986). Apprenticeship in word use: Social convergence processes in learning categorically related nouns. In S. Kuczaj & M. Barrett (Eds.), *The development of word meaning*. New York: Springer.

Aitchison, J. (1987). *Words in the mind: An introduction to the mental lexicon*. Oxford: Basil Blackwell.

Anglin, J. (1977). *Word, object, and conceptual development*. New York: Norton.

Anglin, J. (1986). Semantic and conceptual knowledge underlying the child's words. In S. Kuczaj & M. Barrett (Eds.), *The development of word meaning*. New York: Springer.

Atkinson, M. (1983). FLATS and SHARPS: The role of the child in language acquisition. In J. Durand (Ed.), *A festshcrift for Peter Wexler: University of Essex Department of Language and Linguistics Occasional Papers, 27.*

Au, T., & Markman, E. (1987). Acquiring word meanings via linguistic contrast. *Cognitive Development, 2,* 217–236.

Baker, C. (1979). Syntactic theory and the projection problem. *Linguistic Inquiry, 10,* 533–581.

Barrett, M. (1982). The early acquisition and development of the meaning of action-related words. In T. Seiler & W. Wannemaker (Eds.), *Concept development and the development of word meaning*. Berlin: Springer.

Barrett, M. (1986). Early semantic representations and early word-usage. In S. Kuczaj & M. Barrett (Eds.), *The development of word meaning*. New York: Springer.

Bartlett, E. (1977). The acquisition of the meaning of color terms: A study of lexical development. In P. Smith & R. Campbell (Eds.), *Proceedings of the Stirling Conference on the psychology of language*. New York: Plenum.

Bates, E., Benigni, L., Bretherton, I., Camaioni, L., & Volterra, V. (1979). *The emergence of symbols: Cognition and communication in infancy*. New York: Academic Press.

Bates, E., Bretherton, I., & Snyder, L. (1988). *From first words to grammar: Individual differences and dissociable mechanisms*. New York: Cambridge University Press.

Behrend, D. (1990). Constraints and development: A reply to Nelson (1988). *Cognitive Development, 5,* 313-330.

Benedict, H. (1979). Early lexical development: Comprehension and production. *Journal of Child Language, 6,* 183-200.

Benson, N., & Anglin, J. (1987). The child's knowledge of English kin terms. *First Language, 7,* 41-66.

Berko, J. (1958). The child's learning of English morphology. *Word, 14,* 150-177.

Berwick, R. (1986). *The acquisition of syntactic knowledge*. Cambridge, MA: MIT press.

Bever, T. (1970). The cognitive basis for linguistic structures. In J. Hayes (Ed.), *Cognition and the development of language*. New York: Wiley.

Bickerton, D. (1981). *The roots of language*. Ann Arbor, MI: Karoma Press.

Bierwisch, M. (1970). Semantics. In J. Lyons (Ed.), *New horizons in linguistics*. Baltimore, MD: Penguin Books.

Bloom, L. (1970). *Language development: Form and function in emerging grammars*. Cambridge, MA: MIT Press.

Bloom, L. (1973). *One word at a time: The use of single word utterances before syntax*. The Hague: Mouton.

Bloom, L., Lifter, K., & Broughton, J. (1985). The convergence of early cognition and language in the second year of life: Problems in conceptualization and measurement. In M. Barrett (Ed.), *Children's single-word speech*. New York: Wiley.

Bloom, L., Lightbown, P., & Hood, L. (1975). Structure and variation in child language. *Monographs of the Society for Research in Child Development, 40.*

Bloom, L., Miller, P., & Hood, L. (1975). Variation and reduction as aspects of competence in language development. In A. Pick (Ed.), *Minnesota symposium on child psychology* (Vol. 9). Minneapolis: University of Minnesota Press.

Bloom, P. (1990). Syntactic distinctions in child language. *Journal of Child Language, 17,* 343-355.

Bohannon, J. N., MacWhinney, B., & Snow, C. (1990). No negative evidence revisited: Beyond learnability or who has to prove what to whom. *Developmental Psychology, 26,* 221-226.

Bohannon, J. N., & Stanowicz, L. (1988). The issue of negative evidence: Adult responses to children's language. *Developmental Psychology, 24,* 684-689.

Borer, H., & Wexler, K. (1987). The maturation of syntax. In T. Roeper & E. Williams (Eds.), *Parameter setting*. Dordrecht: D. Reidel.

Bornstein, M. (1985). On the development of color naming in young children: Data and theory. *Brain and Language, 26,* 72-93.

Bowerman, M. (1973). Structural relationships in children's utterances: Syntactic or semantic? In T. E. Moore (Ed.), *Cognitive development and the acquisition of language*. New York: Academic Press.

Bowerman, M. (1974). Learning the structure of causative verbs: A study in the relationship of cognitive, semantic and syntactic development. *Papers and Reports on Child Language Development*. Stanford University, Stanford, CA.

Bowerman, M. (1978). The acquisition of word meaning: An investigation of some current conflicts. In N. Waterson & C. Snow (Eds.), *The development of communication.* New York: Wiley.

Bowerman, M. (1982). Reorganizational processes in lexical and syntactic development. In E. Wanner & L. Gleitman (Eds.), *Language acquisition: The state of the art.* New York: Cambridge University Press.

Bowerman, M. (1985). What shapes children's grammars? In D. Slobin (Ed.), *The cross-linguistic study of language acquisition. Volume 2: Theoretical issues.* Hillsdale, NJ: Lawrence Erlbaum Associates.

Bowerman, M. (1989). Learning a semantic system: What role do cognitive predispositions play? In M. Rice & R. Schiefelbusch (Eds.), *The teachability of language.* Baltimore, MD: Brookes.

Braine, M. (1963). On learning the grammatical order of words. *Psychological Review, 70,* 323–348.

Branigan, G. (1976). *Sequences of single words as structured units.* Paper presented at the eighth annual Child Language Research Forum, Stanford University, Stanford, CA.

Bridges, A. (1986). Actions and things: What adults talk about to 1-year-olds. In S. Kuczaj & M. Barrett (Eds.), *The development of word meaning.* New York: Springer.

Brown, R. (1958). How shall a thing be called? *Psychological Review, 65,* 14–21.

Brown, R. (1973). *A first language: The early stages.* Cambridge, MA: Harvard University Press.

Brown, R., & Hanlon, C. (1970). Derivational complexity and the order of acquisition in child speech. In J. Hayes (Ed.), *Cognition and the development of language.* New York: Wiley.

Bruner, J. (1983). *Child's talk: Learning to use language.* Oxford: Oxford University Press.

Bruner, J., Olver, R., & Greenfield, R. (1966). *Studies in cognitive growth.* New York: Wiley.

Bybee, J., & Slobin, D. (1982). Rules and schemas in the development and use of the English past tense. *Language, 58,* 265–289.

Callanan, M. (1985). How parents label objects for young children: The role of input in the acquisition of category hierarchies. *Child Development, 56,* 508–523.

Callanan, M., & Markman, E. (1982). Principles of organization in young children's natural language hierarchies. *Child Development, 53,* 1093–1101.

Carey, S. (1978). The child as word learner. In M. Halle, J. Bresnan, & G. Miller (Eds.), *Linguistic theory and psychological reality.* Cambridge, MA: MIT Press.

Carey, S. (1982). Semantic development: The state of the art. In E. Wanner & L. Gleitman (Eds.), *Language acquisition: The state of the art.* New York: Cambridge University Press.

Carey, S., & Bartlett, E. (1978). Acquiring a single new word. *Papers and Reports on Child Language Development, 15,* 17–29.

Carter, A. (1978). From sensorimotor vocalizations to words: A case study of the evolution of attention-directing communication in the second year. In A. Lock (Ed.), *Action, gesture, and symbol: The emergence of language.* New York: Academic Press.

Chamberlain, A., & Chamberlain, J. (1904). Studies of a child. *Pedagogical Seminary, 11,* 264–291.

Chapman, K., & Mervis, C. (1989). Patterns of object name extension in production. *Journal of Child Language, 16,* 561–571.

Chomsky, N. (1959). A review of B. F. Skinner's *Verbal Behavior. Language, 35,* 26–58.

Chomsky, N. (1965). *Aspects of the theory of syntax.* Cambridge, MA: MIT Press.

Chomsky, N. (1986a). *Barriers.* Cambridge, MA: MIT Press.

Chomsky, N. (1986b). *Knowledge of language: Its nature, origin and use.* New York: Praeger.

Chomsky, N. (1986c). *Language and problems of knowledge.* Cambridge, MA: MIT Press.

Clark, E. (1973). What's in a word? On the child's acquisition of semantics in his first language. In T. E. Moore (Ed.), *Cognitive development and the acquisition of language.* New York: Academic Press.

Clark, E. (1977). Strategies and the mapping problem in first language acquisition. In J. Macnamara (Ed.), *Language learning and thought*. New York: Academic Press.

Clark, E. (1979). Building a vocabulary: Words for objects, actions, and relations. In P. Fletcher & M. Garman (Eds.), *Language acquisition* (1st ed.). New York: Cambridge University Press.

Clark, E. (1982). The young word maker: A case study of innovation in the child's lexicon. In E. Wanner & L. Gleitman (Eds.), *Language acquisition: The state of the art*. New York: Cambridge University Press.

Clark, E. (1983). Meanings and concepts. In J. Flavell & E. Markman (Eds.), *Handbook of child psychology. Vol. 3: Cognitive development*. New York: Wiley.

Clark, E. (1988). On the logic of contrast. *Journal of Child Language, 15,* 317–335.

Clark, E. (1990). On the pragmatics of contrast. *Journal of Child Language, 17,* 417–431.

Clark, E., & Clark, H. (1979). When nouns surface as verbs. *Language, 55,* 767–811.

Clark, H. (1973). Space, time, semantics, and the child. In T. E. Moore (Ed.), *Cognitive development and the acquisition of language*. New York: Academic Press.

Clark, H., & Clark, E. (1977). *Psychology and language*. New York: Harcourt Brace Jovanovich.

Clark, R. (1974). Performing without competence. *Journal of Child Language, 1,* 1–10.

Colombo, J., O'Brien, M., Mitchell, D. W., Roberts, K., & Horowitz, F. (1987). A lower boundary for category formation in preverbal infants. *Journal of Child Language, 14,* 383–385.

Corrigan, R. (1979). Cognitive correlates of language. *Child Development, 50,* 617–631.

Crain, S. (in press). Language acquisition in the absence of experience. *Behavioral and Brain Sciences*.

Crain, S., & Nakayama, M. (1987). Structure dependence in grammar formation. *Language, 63,* 522–543.

Dale, P., Bates, E., Reznick, J. S., & Morisset, C. (1989). The validity of a parent report instrument of child language at twenty months. *Journal of Child Language, 16,* 239–249.

de Villiers, J. (1980). The process of rule-learning in child speech—A new look. In K. Nelson (Ed.), *Child language* (Vol. 2). New York: Gardner.

de Villiers, J., & de Villiers, P. A. (1973a). A cross sectional study of the acquisition of grammatical morphemes in child speech. *Journal of Psycholinguistic Research, 2,* 267–278.

de Villiers, J., & de Villiers, P. (1973b). Development of the use of word order in comprehension. *Journal of Psycholinguistic Research, 2,* 331–341.

de Villiers, J., & de Villiers, P. (1982). Language development. In R. Vasta (Ed.), *Strategies and techniques of child study*. New York: Academic Press.

de Villiers, J., & de Villiers, P. (1985). The acquisition of English. In D. I. Slobin (Ed.), *Cross-linguistic studies of language acquisition*. Hillsdale, NJ: Lawrence Erlbaum Associates.

de Villiers, J., Roeper, T., & Vainikka, A. (1990). The acquisition of long distance rules. In L. Frazier & J. de Villiers (Ed.), *Language processing and acquisition*. Dordrecht: Kluwer.

de Villiers, P. (1988). Assessing English syntax in hearing-impaired children: Eliciting production in pragmatically-motivated situations. In R. Kretschmer & L. Kretschmer (Eds.), *Communication assessment of hearing impaired children: From conversation to classroom. Journal of the Academy of Rehabilitative Audiology: Monograph Supplement,* 21.

de Villiers, P., & de Villiers, J. (1979). *Early language*. Cambridge, MA: Harvard University Press.

Della Corte, M., Benedict, H., & Klein, D. (1983). The relationship of pragmatic dimensions of mothers' speech to the referential–expressive distinction. *Journal of Child Language, 10,* 35–43.

Demetras, M., Post, K., & Snow, C. (1986). Feedback to first language learners: The role of repetition and clarification questions. *Journal of Child Language, 13,* 275–292.

Demuth, K. (1990). Maturation and the acquisition of the Sesotho passive. *Language, 65.1,* 56–81.

Dockrell, J., & Campbell, R. (1986). Lexical acquisition strategies in the preschool child. In S. Kuczaj & M. Barrett (Eds.), *The development of word meaning.* New York: Springer.

Dore, J. (1978). Conditions for the acquisition of speech acts. In I. Markova (Ed.), *The social context of language.* New York: Wiley.

Dromi, E. (1987). *Early lexical development.* New York: Cambridge University Press.

Fisher, C., Gleirman, H., & Gleirman, L. (1991). On the semantic content of subcategorization frames. *Cognitive Psychology, 23,* 331–392.

Flavell, J. (1989). The development of children's knowledge about the mind: From cognitive connections to mental representations. In J. Astington, P. Harris, & D. Olson (Eds.), *Developing theories of mind.* New York: Cambridge University Press.

Fremgen, A., & Fay, D. (1980). Overextensions in production and comprehension: A methodological clarification. *Journal of Child Language, 7,* 205–211.

Fukui, N., & Speas, M. (1985). Specifier and projection. *MIT working papers in Linguistics,* Vol 8.

Gathercole, V. (1987). The contrastive hypothesis for the acquisition of word meanings: A reconsideration of the theory. *Journal of Child Language, 15,* 317–335.

Gathercole, V. (1989). Contrast: A semantic constraint. *Journal of Child Language, 16,* 685–702.

Gentner, D. (1975). Evidence for the psychological reality of semantic components: The verbs of possession. In D. Norman, D. Rumelhart, & the LNR Research Group (Eds.), *Explorations in cognition.* San Francisco: Freeman.

Gibson, E., & Spelke, E. (1983). The development of perception. In J. Flavell & E. Markman (Eds.), *Handbook of child psychology. Vol. 3: Cognitive development.* New York: Wiley.

Gleitman, L. (1981). Maturational determinants of language growth. *Cognition, 10,* 103–114.

Gleitman, L. (1990). The structural sources of verb meanings. *Language Acquisition, 1,* 3–55.

Gleitman, L., Gleitman, H., Landau, B., & Wanner, E. (1987). Where learning begins: Initial representations for language learning. In E. Newmayer (Ed.), *The Cambridge linguistic survey* (Vol. 2). New York: Cambridge University Press.

Gleitman, L., & Wanner, E. (1982). Language acquisition: The state of the state of the art. In E. Wanner & L. Gleitman (Eds.), *Language acquisition: The state of the art.* New York: Cambridge University Press.

Gold, E. (1967). Language identification in the limit. *Information and Control, 10,* 447–474.

Goldfield, B. (1987). The contributions of child and caregiver to referential and expressive language. *Applied Psycholinguistics, 8,* 267–280.

Goldfield, B., & Reznick, J. S. (1990). Early lexical acquisition: Rate, content, and the vocabulary spurt. *Journal of Child Language, 17,* 171–183.

Goldfield, B., & Snow, C. (1989). Individual differences in language acquisition. In J. Berko Gleason (Ed.), *The development of language* (2nd ed.). Columbus, OH: Merrill.

Golinkoff, R., Hirsch-Pasek, K., Cauley, K., & Gordon, L. (1987). The eyes have it: Lexical and syntactic comprehension in a new paradigm. *Journal of Child Language, 14,* 23–45.

Gopnik, A. (1982). Words and plans: Early language and the development of intelligent action. *Journal of Child Language, 9,* 303–318.

Gopnik, A. (1988). Three types of early words. *First Language, 8,* 49–70.

Gopnik, A., & Choi, S. (1987). *Do linguistic differences lead to cognitive differences: A cross-linguistic study of semantic and cognitive development.* Paper presented at the Boston University Child Language Conference, Boston University, Boston, MA.

Gopnik, A., & Meltzoff, A. (1986). Words, plans, things, and locations. In S. Kuczaj & M. Barrett (Eds.), *The development of word meaning*. New York: Springer.

Gopnik, A., & Meltzoff, A. (1987a). Language and thought in the young child: Early semantic developments and their relationship to object permanence, means–ends understanding and categorization. In K. Nelson & A. van Kleeck (Eds.), *Children's language* (Vol. 6). Hillsdale, NJ: Lawrence Erlbaum Associates.

Gopnik, A., & Meltzoff, A. (1987b). The development of categorization in the second year and its relation to other cognitive and linguistic developments. *Child Development, 58,* 1523–1531.

Gordon, P. (1990). Learnability and feedback. *Developmental Psychology, 26,* 215–218.

Gordon, P., & Chafetz, J. (1989). *Verb-based versus class-based accounts of actionality effects in children's comprehension of passives*. Unpublished manuscript, University of Pittsburgh, Pittsburgh, PA.

Greenberg, J., & Kuczaj, S. (1982). Towards a theory of substantive word-meaning acquisition. In S. Kuczaj (Ed.), *Language development: syntax and semantics* (Vol. 1). Hillsdale, NJ: Lawrence Erlbaum Associates.

Grice, H. (1975). Logic and conversation. In P. Cole & J. Morgan (Eds.), *Syntax and semantics. Vol. 3: Speech acts*. New York: Academic Press.

Griffiths, P. (1976). *The ontogenetic development of lexical reference*. Unpublished doctoral dissertation, Edinburgh University, Edinburgh.

Griffiths, P. (1987). Early vocabulary. In P. Fletcher & M. Garman (Eds.), *Language acquisition* (2nd ed.). New York: Cambridge University Press.

Grimshaw, J., & Rosen, S. (1990). Obeying the binding theory. In L. Frazier & J. de Villiers (Eds.), *Language processing and language acquisition*. Dordrecht: Kluwer.

Hakuta, K. (1974). Prefabricated patterns and the emergence of structure in second language acquisition. *Language Learning, 24,* 287–297.

Halliday, M. (1975). *Learning how to mean: Explorations in the development of language*. London: Edwin Arnold.

Halpern, E., Corrigan, R., & Aviezer, O. (1983). In, on and under: Examining the relationships between cognitive and language skills. *International Journal of Behavioral Development, 6,* 153–166.

Hamburger, H., & Crain, S. (1982). Relative acquisition. In S. Kuczaj (Ed.), *Language Development* (Vol. 2). Hillsdale, NJ: Lawrence Erlbaum Associates.

Hampson, J. (1989). *Elements of style: Maternal and child contributions to the expressive and referential styles of language acquisition*. Unpublished doctoral dissertation, City University of New York, New York.

Harris, M., Barrett, M., Jones, D., & Brookes, S. (1988). Linguistic input and early word meaning. *Journal of Child Language, 15,* 77–94.

Harris, M., Jones, D., & Grant, J. (1984). The social–interactional context of maternal speech to infants: An explanation for the event-bound nature of early word use? *First Language, 5,* 89–100.

Haviland, S., & Clark, E. (1974). "This man's father is my father's son": A study of the acquisition of English kin terms. *Journal of Child Language, 1,* 23–47.

Heath, S. (1983). *Ways with words*. New York: Cambridge University Press.

Hirsch-Pasek, K., Treiman, R., & Schneiderman, M. (1984). Brown and Hanlon revisited: Mother's sensitivity to ungrammatical forms. *Journal of Child Language, 11,* 81–88.

Horgan, D. (1978). The development of the full passive. *Journal of Child Language, 5,* 65–78.

Hyams, N. (1986). *Language acquisition and theory of parameters*. Dordrecht: D. Reidel.

Hyams, N. (in press). The genesis of functional categories. In J. Meisel (Ed.), *The acquisition of verb placement: functional categories and V2 phenomena in language development*.

Dordrecht: Kluwer.

Jackendoff, R. (1983). *Semantics and cognition.* Cambridge, MA: MIT Press.

Johnston, J. (1985). Cognitive prerequisites: The evidence from children learning English. In D. Slobin (Ed.), *The cross-linguistic study of language acquisition. Vol. 2: Theoretical issues.* Hillsdale, NJ: Lawrence Erlbaum Associates.

Johnston, J., & Slobin, D. (1979). The development of locative expressions in English, Italian, Serbo-Croatian, and Turkish. *Journal of Child Language, 6,* 529–545.

Kamhi, A. (1986). The elusive first word: The importance of the naming insight for the development of referential speech. *Journal of Child Language, 13,* 155–161.

Karmiloff-Smith, A. (1979). *A functional approach to child language.* Cambridge: Cambridge University Press.

Kuczaj, S. (1986). Thoughts on the intensional basis of early object word extension: Evidence from comprehension and production. In S. Kuczaj & M. Barrett (Eds.), *The development of word meaning.* New York: Springer.

Kuhn, T. (1962). *The structure of scientific revolutions.* Chicago: University of Chicago Press.

Landau, B., & Gleitman, L. (1985). *Language and experience: Evidence from the blind child.* Cambridge, MA: Harvard University Press.

Lebeaux, D. (1988). *Language acquisition and the form of the grammar.* Unpublished doctoral dissertation, University of Massachusetts, Amherst, MA.

Leftheri, K. (1991). *Learning to interpret wh-movement in modern Greek.* Senior honors thesis, Smith College, Northampton, MA.

Leopold, W. (1939–1949). *Speech development of a bilingual child: A linguist's record* (Vol. 1–4). Evanston, IL: Northwestern University Press.

Levy, Y. (1983). Lr's frogs all the way down. *Cognition 15,* 75–93.

Lieven, E., & Pine, J. (1990). Review of Bates, Bretherton, and Snyder: *From first words to grammar. Journal of Child Language, 17,* 495–501.

Lightfoot, D. (1982). *The language lottery: Toward a biology of grammars.* Cambridge, MA: MIT Press.

Lucariello, J., & Nelson, K. (1986). Context effects on lexical specificity in maternal and child discourse. *Journal of Child Language, 13,* 507–522.

Lyons, J. (1981). *Language and linguistics.* New York: Cambridge University Press.

Macnamara, J. (1982). *Names for things.* Cambridge, MA: MIT Press.

MacWhinney, B. (1978). The acquisition of morphophonology. *Monographs of the Society for Research in Child Development, 42,* 1–122.

MacWhinney, B. (1991). Connectionism as a framework for language acquisition. In J. Miller (Ed.), *Research on child language disorders.* Austin, TX: Pro-ed.

MacWhinney, B., & Snow, C. (1985). The child language data exchange system. *Journal of Child Language, 12,* 271–295.

Maratsos, M. (1974). Children who get worse at understanding the passive: A replication of Bever. *Journal of Psycholinguistic Research, 3,* 65–74.

Maratsos, M., & Chalkley, M. (1980). The internal language of children's syntax: The ontogenesis and representation of syntactic categories. In K. Nelson (Ed.), *Children's language* (Vol. 2). New York: Gardner.

Maratsos, M., Fox, D., Becker, J., & Chalkley, M. (1985). Semantic restrictions on children's passives. *Cognition, 19,* 167–191.

Marcus, G. (1991) *Negative evidence.* Unpublished manuscript, MIT, Cambridge, MA.

Marcus, G., Ullman, M., Pinker, S., Hollander, M., Rosen, T. J., & Xu, F. (1991). *Overregularization* (Working papers in Cognitive Science). Cambridge, MA: MIT.

Markman, E. (1989). *Categorization and naming in children.* Cambridge, MA: MIT Press.

Markman, E., & Wachtel, G. F. (1988). Children's use of mutual exclusivity to constrain the meanings of words. *Cognitive Psychology, 20,* 121–157.

Mazurkewich, I., & White, L. (1984). The acquisition of the dative alternation: Unlearning overgeneralizations. *Cognition, 16,* 261–283.

McCune-Nicolich, L. (1981). The cognitive bases of relational words in the single word period. *Journal of Child Language, 8,* 15–34.

McShane, J. (1980). *Learning to talk.* New York: Cambridge University Press.

Meisel, J., & Muller, N. (1990, October). *On the position of finiteness in early child grammar: Evidence from simultaneous acquisition of two first languages: French and German.* Paper presented at the Boston University Conference on Language Development, Boston, MA.

Melkman, R., Koriat, A., & Pardoe, K. (1976). Preferences for color and form in preschoolers related to color and form differentiation. *Child Development, 47,* 1045–1050.

Merriman, W., & Bowman, L. (1989). The mutual exclusivity bias in children's word learning. *Monographs of the Society for Research in Child Development, 54,* 3–4, #220.

Mervis, C. (1984). Early lexical development: The contributions of mother and child. In C. Sophian (Ed.), *Origins of cognitive skills.* Hillsdale, NJ: Lawrence Erlbaum Associates.

Mervis, C., & Crisafi, M. (1982). Order of acquisition of subordinate-, basic-, and superordinate-level categories. *Child Development, 53,* 267–273.

Miller, G., & Johnson-Laird, P. (1976). *Language and perception.* Cambridge, MA: Harvard University Press.

Naigles, L. (1990). Children use syntax to learn verb meanings. *Journal of Child Language, 17,* 357–374.

Nelson, K. (1973). Structure and strategy in learning to talk. *Monographs of the Society for Research in Child Development, 38,* (1–2)#149.

Nelson, K. (1974). Concept, word and sentence: Interrelations in acquisition and development. *Psychological Review, 81,* 267–285.

Nelson, K. (1985). *Making sense: The acquisition of shared meaning.* New York: Academic Press.

Nelson, K. (1988a). Constraints on word learning? *Cognitive Development, 3,* 221–246.

Nelson, K. (1988b). Where do taxonomic categories come from? *Human Development, 31,* 3–10.

Nelson, K. (1990). Comments on Behrend's "constraints and development." *Cognitive Development, 5,* 331–339.

Nelson, K., Rescorla, L., Gruendel, J., & Benedict, H. (1978). Early lexicons: What do they mean? *Child Development, 49,* 960–968.

Ninio, A. (1980). Ostensive definition in vocabulary teaching. *Journal of Child Language, 7,* 565–574.

Ninio, A., & Bruner, J. (1978). The achievement and antecedents of labelling. *Journal of Child Language, 5,* 1–15.

Ochs, E. (1988). *Culture and language acquisition: Acquiring communicative competence in a Western Samoan village.* New York: Cambridge University Press.

Ochs, E., & Schieffelin, B. (1984). Language acquisition and socialization: Three developmental stories and their implications. In R. Shweder & R. LeVine (Eds.), *Culture theory: Essays on mind, self, and emotion.* New York: Cambridge University Press.

Perez-Leroux, A. (1991). The acquisition of wh-movement in Caribbean Spanish. In T. Maxfield, & B. Plunkett (1991). *The acquisition of Wh.* University of Massachusetts Occasional papers in Linguistics, G.S.L.A., Amherst, MA.

Piaget, J. (1952). *The origins of intelligence in the child.* New York: Norton.

Piaget, J., & Inhelder, B. (1967). *The child's conception of space.* New York: Norton.

Pierce, A. (1989). *On the emergence of syntax: A cross-linguistic study.* Unpublished doctoral dissertation, MIT, Cambridge, MA.

Pinker, S. (1984). *Language learnability and language development.* Cambridge, MA: Harvard University Press.

Pinker, S. (1987). The bootstrapping problem in language acquisition. In B. MacWhinney (Ed.), *Mechanisms of language acquisition*. Hillsdale, NJ: Lawrence Erlbaum Associates.

Pinker, S. (1989a). *Learnability and cognition: The acquisition of argument structure.* Cambridge, MA: MIT Press.

Pinker, S. (1989b). Resolving a learnability paradox in the acquisition of the verb lexicon. In M. Rice & R. Schiefelbusch (Eds.), *The teachability of language*. Baltimore: Paul Brookes.

Pinker, S., Lebeaux, D., & Frost, L. (1987). Productivity and constraints in the acquisition of the passive. *Cognition, 26,* 195-267.

Pinker, S., & Prince, A. (1988). On language and connectionism: Analysis of a parallel distributed processing model of language acquisition. *Cognition, 28,* 73-193.

Platzack, C. (in press). Word order and the finite verb in early Swedish. In J. Meisel (Ed.), *The acquisition of verb placement: Functional categories and V2 phenomena in language development.* Dordrecht: Kluwer.

Quine, W. (1960). *Word and object.* Cambridge, MA: MIT Press.

Radford, A. (1988). Small children's small clauses. *Transactions of the Philological Society, 86,* 1-46.

Radulović, L. (1975). *Acquisition of language: Studies of Dubrovnik children.* Unpublished doctoral dissertation, University of California, Berkeley.

Ratner, N., & Bruner, J. (1978). Games, social exchange, and the acquisition of language. *Journal of Child Language, 5,* 391-402.

Rescorla, L. (1980). Overextensions in early language development. *Journal of Child Language, 7,* 321-335.

Reznick, J. S., & Goldsmith, L. (1989). A multiple form word production checklist. *Journal of Child Language, 16,* 91-100.

Rice, M. (1990). Preschoolers QUIL: Quick incidental learning of words. In G. ContiRamsden & C. Snow (Eds.), *Children's language* (Vol. 7). Hillsdale, NJ: Lawrence Erlbaum Associates.

Richards, M. M. (1979). Sorting out what's in a word from what's not: Evaluating Clark's semantic feature acquisition theory. *Journal of Experimental Child Psychology, 27,* 1-47.

Rizzi, L. (1990). *Relativized minimality.* Cambridge, MA: MIT Press.

Rosch, E. (1978). Principles of categorization. In E. Rosch & B. Lloyd (Eds.), *Cognition and categorization.* Hillsdale, NJ: Lawrence Erlbaum Associates.

Rosch, E., & Mervis, C. (1975). Family resemblance: Studies in the internal structure of categories. *Cognitive Psychology, 7,* 573-605.

Rosch, E., Mervis, C., Gray, W., Johnson, D., & Boyes-Braem, P. (1976). Basic objects in natural categories. *Cognitive Psychology, 8,* 382-439.

Rosenblatt, D. (1977). Developmental trends in infant play. In B. Tizard & D. Harvey (Eds.), *The biology of play.* London: Heinemann Medical Publications.

Rumelhart, D., & McClelland, J. (1987). Learning the past tense of English verbs: Implicit rules or parallel distributed processing? In B. MacWhinney (Ed.), *Mechanisms of language acquisition.* Hillsdale, NJ: Lawrence Erlbaum Associates.

Schaffer, H., Hepburn, A., & Collis, G. (1983). Verbal and non-verbal aspects of mothers' directives. *Journal of Child Language, 10,* 337-355.

Schank, R. C., & Abelson, R. P. (1977). *Scripts, plans, goals and understanding.* Hillsdale, NJ: Lawrence Erlbaum Associates.

Shipley, E., Kuhn, I., & Madden, E. C. (1983). Mothers' use of superordinate category terms. *Journal of Child Language, 10,* 571-588.

Sinclair, H. (1970). The transition from sensorimotor to symbolic activity. *Interchange, 1,* 119-126.

Skinner, B. F. (1957). *Verbal behavior.* New York: Appleton-Century-Crofts.

Slobin, D. (1973). Cognitive prerequisites for the development of grammar. In C. A. Ferguson

& D. Slobin (Eds.), *Studies of child language development*. New York: Holt, Rinehart & Winston.

Slobin, D. (1985). Cross-linguistic evidence for the language-making capacity. In D. Slobin (Ed.), *The cross-linguistic study of language acquisition. Volume 2: Theoretical issues*. Hillsdale, NJ: Lawrence Erlbaum Associates.

Smith, C., & Sachs, J. (1990). Cognition and the verb lexicon in early lexical development. *Applied Psycholinguistics, 11*, 409–424.

Smoczyńska, M. (1985). The acquisition of Polish. In D. Slobin (Ed.), *The cross-linguistic study of language acquisition. Volume 2: Theoretical issues*. Hillsdale, NJ: Lawrence Erlbaum Associates.

Snow, C. E. (1972). Mother's speech to children learning language. *Child Development, 43*, 549–565.

Soja, N. (1986). Color word acquisition: Conceptual or linguistic challenge? *Papers and Reports on Child Language Development, 25*, 104–113.

Spelke, E. (1985). Perception of unity, persistence, and identity: Thoughts on infants' conceptions of objects. In J. Mehler & R. Fox (Ed.), *Neonate cognition*. Hillsdale, NJ: Lawrence Erlbaum Associates.

Suchman, R., & Trabasso, T. (1966). Color and form preference in young children. *Journal of Experimental Child Psychology, 37*, 439–451.

Tager-Flusberg, H. (1982). The development of relative clauses in child speech. *Papers and Reports on Child Language Development* (Stanford University), 21.

Tager-Flusberg, H., de Villiers, J., & Hakuta, K. (1982). The development of coordination. In S. A. Kuczaj (Ed.), *Language development: Syntax and semantics*. Hillsdale, NJ: Lawrence Erlbaum Associates.

Talmy, L. (1983). How language structures space. In H. Pick & L. Acredolo (Eds.), *Spatial orientation: Theory research and application*. New York: Plenum.

Taylor, M., & Gelman, S. (1989). Incorporating new words into the lexicon: Preliminary evidence for language hierarchies in two-year-old children. *Child Development, 60*, 625–636.

Templin, M. (1957). *Certain language skills in children*. Minneapolis: University of Minnesota Press.

Thompson, J., & Chapman, R. (1977). Who is "daddy"? The status of two-year-old's overextended words in use and comprehension. *Journal of Child Language, 4*, 359–375.

Tomasello, M., & Farrar, J. (1984). Cognitive bases of lexical development: Object permanence and relational words. *Journal of Child Language, 11*, 477–493.

Tomasello, M., & Farrar, M. (1986a). Joint attention and early language. *Child Development, 57*, 1454–1463.

Tomasello, M., & Farrar, J. (1986b). Object permanence and relational words: A lexical training study. *Journal of Child Language, 13*, 495–505.

Valian, V. (1986). Syntactic categories in the speech of young children. *Developmental Psychology, 22*, 562–579.

Valian, V. (1990). Logical and psychological constraints on the acquisition of syntax. In L. Frazier & J. de Villiers (Eds.), *Language processing and language acquisition*. Dordrecht: Kluwer.

Valian, V. (in press). *Parental replies: Linguistic status and didactic role*. Cambridge, MA: MIT Press.

Vygotsky, L. (1962). *Thought and language*. Cambridge, MA: MIT Press.

Wales, R., Colman, M., & Pattison, P. (1983). How a thing is called — A study of mothers' and children's naming. *Journal of Experimental Child Psychology, 36*, 1–17.

Waxman, S., & Gelman, R. (1986). Preschoolers use of superordinate relations in classification and language. *Cognitive Development, 1*, 139–156.

Waxman, S., & Kosowski, T. (1990). Nouns mark category relations: Toddlers' and pre-schoolers' word-learning biases. *Child Development, 61,* 1461–1473.

Weissenborn, J. (1990, July 15–21). *Functional categories and verb movement in early German.* Paper presented at the fifth International Congress for the Study of Child Language, Budapest.

Weissenborn, J., Roeper, T., & de Villiers, J. (1991). The acquisition of wh-movement in German and French. In T. Maxfield & B. Plunkett. *The acquisition of Wh.* University of Massachusetts Occasional papers in Linguistics, G.S.L.A., Amherst, MA.

Wells, G. (1981). *Learning through interaction: The study of language development.* New York: Cambridge University Press.

Wexler, K., & Culicover, P. (1980). *Formal models of language acquisition.* Cambridge, MA: MIT Press.

Xu, F. (1991). *A hierarchy of preferences in fast mapping of word meaning.* Senior honors thesis. Smith College, Northampton, MA.

III SOCIAL AND PERSONALITY DEVELOPMENT

Language permits abstract thought; it also allows interpersonal communication, a primary medium for the social interaction that lies at the base of social and personality development. Chapters in this section examine social and personality development in the context of the various relationships and situations in which developing individuals function and by which they are shaped. Chapter 7 focuses on the development of an understanding of self. As William Damon and Daniel Hart show, the sense of self is closely integrated with individuals' conceptions of their social relationships and of their moral responsibilities and judgments. Therefore, self-understanding, social interaction, and morality are closely intertwined in the course of early psychological development. Consequently, one must understand developing conceptions of self in order to understand the processes of social and personality development.

As Damon and Hart make clear, however, the understanding of self emerges in social contexts. One primary social context for developing individuals is represented by the family. In Chapter 8, Michael Lamb, Robert Ketterlinus, and Maria Fracasso recount the development of social relationships within the family over the first 15 to 20 years of life. They describe normative developmental progressions in the emergence of these relationships as well as the factors that account for individual differences among relationships, creating some that foster healthy adjustment and development and others that subvert developmental processes and lead to the emergence of behavioral pathology.

In Chapter 9, Kenneth Rubin and Robert Coplan shift focus to relationships established by children outside the family, notably with peers. As Rubin and Coplan point out, relationships with peers play a central and formative role in children's development. These authors document that, with increasing age, peers occupy a growing proportion of children's social experiences, providing an increasingly important context within which children manifest their distinctive social and personality styles and by which these styles are modified and honed.

For most children, peer relationships are increasingly organized within an institutional context — the school. Like other social institutions, the school serves as an environment in which children are expected to perform and by which their tendencies, preferences, and abilities are shaped. School is, as Deborah Stipek shows in Chapter 10, a pervasive and powerful developmental ecology. Although psychologists have often viewed the family as the primary context within which children are reared, the authors of Chapters 9 and 10 make it clear that children are profoundly influenced by relationships and experiences within and outside the family.

7 Self-Understanding and Its Role in Social and Moral Development

William Damon
Brown University

Daniel Hart
Rutgers University

INTRODUCTION

In most textbooks, self-concept, social cognition, and morality are discussed in separate chapters and treated as distinct topics of study (see, e.g., Mussen, 1983). This may serve certain organizational purposes, but it does not accurately reflect the psychological makeup of the developing child. Throughout all phases of life, the conceptual and behavioral systems of self, social, and moral understanding interpenetrate with one another. Children cannot know themselves without some sense of the other. Nor can they forge their self-identities without an awareness of their own values. Moreover, at all developmental periods, social activities derive from — and in turn shape — judgments about the self, others, and morality. In these and many other ways, self-understanding, social interaction, and morality are intertwined in a developing psychological system that grows and changes throughout the life span.

In the field of developmental psychology, the past two decades have seen a wave of studies chronicling the development of self, social, and moral understanding. In the 1960s and 1970s, during the extended period of excitement about the ideas of Piaget, there was interest in discovering whether Piagetian conclusions about cognitive growth validly could be applied to children's understanding of themselves and the social events that they experience. The early developmental studies of self-conception, role-taking, and person perception all were attempts to see whether ontogenetic changes in these interpersonal areas could be described by stagelike models à la Piaget (Feffer & Gourevitch, 1960; Flavell, 1968; Livesley & Bromley,

1973; Mullener & Laird, 1971). Kohlberg's appropriation of Piaget's clinical-interview approach to moral judgment, resulting in the renowned six-stage "cognitive-developmental" model, provided an energetic line of support for this research direction (Kohlberg, 1963).

Recently, more finely tuned developmental descriptions of how self and social concepts change with age have been formulated, and these have led to examinations of the dynamic relations among all the systems of conception and conduct that are implicated in the self's transactions with others (Damon & Hart, 1988; Ruble & Higgins, 1986). Some researchers have brought notions like context, communication, and social influence into the mix (Butterworth & Light, 1982; Dunn, 1988; Higgins, Ruble, & Hartup, 1983; Rogoff, 1990). Methods for studying self and social concepts have become increasingly contextualized, bolstering tried-and-true interview procedures with observational and narrative approaches (Miller & Sperry, 1987; Stigler, Shweder, & Herdt, 1990). As one consequence of these conceptual and methodological advances, our view of self and social cognition has become expanded and enriched. As another, it has become possible to understand more fully how self and social conceptions contribute to a person's behavioral choices in real-life settings.

This chapter discusses what is known about the development of self-understanding, social interaction, and morality during the course of development. We discuss some of the prominent ways in which these conceptual systems inform and support one another's growth. For example, we point to some fundamental conceptual links between self and social and moral understanding, such as the ways in which all rely on basic ideas about the nature of people. We also discuss how the notions of self and self-interest sometimes contribute to and sometimes collide with the notions of responsibility toward others, presenting in some cases an incentive for, and in other cases an obstacle to, people's implementation of their social and moral beliefs.

This last concern takes us into the area of morality and its relation with self-development. It has long been clear from abundant evidence that one's moral perspective is an important part of one's self-conception, especially during the adolescent years and beyond. What is also becoming clear from more recent study is that the nature of one's total self-conception heavily influences one's commitment to moral concerns. People with essentially similar moral beliefs may differ dramatically in how important they consider these beliefs to be in their own lives. In this sense, one's self-definition can determine the role of morality in one's life.

Our final focus in this chapter, therefore, is moral values: how people acquire them, how they contribute to one's sense of self, and how they interact with self-understanding to influence interpersonal behavior. In considering this final complex issue, we examine two specific areas of interpersonal behavior that have attracted a good deal of research in developmental psychology: altruism and youth violence. We examine these particular topics not only for their intrinsic interest but also because they illustrate how self-understanding acts as a mediator between values and conduct in social life.

SELF-UNDERSTANDING
AND ITS DEVELOPMENT

Understanding the Self as a Person

The self, first and foremost, is a person among all the world of persons. One's conception of people, therefore, bears directly on one's conception of self. We argue that knowing the self entails far more than just knowing about people generally; but person knowledge is certainly one core element in self-understanding. Many philosophers and psychologists, in fact, have based their studies of self-concept on an assumption of essential similarity between an individual's understanding of self and the individual's understanding of others. This similarity postulate was originally presented in developmental psychology by James Mark Baldwin (1902). Baldwin offered this example of the intimate connections between an understanding of self and others:

> Last year I thought of my friend W as a man who had great skill on the bicycle and who wrote readily on the typewriter. . . . But now, this year, I have learned to do both these things. I have taken the elements formerly recognized in W's personality, and by imitative learning brought them over to myself. I now think of myself as one who rides a "wheel" and writes on a "machine." (p. 16)

Baldwin concluded that what a person thinks of "another is—not stands for, or represents, or anything else than is—his thought of himself, until he adds to it a further interpretation; the further interpretation is in turn, first himself, then is—again nothing short of this is—his thought of the other" (p. 89). This argument (and similar ones, e.g., Mead, 1934) has led many researchers to conclude that one can know what the individual thinks about the self if one knows what the individual thinks about others. In the following sections, we briefly review developmental research following from this assumption.

Infancy

The neonate is born without many of the skills that are necessary for adult social interaction. Language can neither be understood nor produced;

gross motor development does not permit the signaling messages nor the obvious orienting of one's body as a response to another's communication; intentional control of facial muscles has yet to develop. These significant limitations on early abilities contribute to the difficulties in assessing the infant's understanding of self or others. Yet several lines of investigation have yielded valuable insights concerning infants' understanding of others, and, by inference, self. The first of these has traced the infant's abilities to recognize the facial expressions of others.

Facial expressions are an important channel of communication, and perhaps especially so for the infant, who cannot make full use of language. Since the 1970s, researchers, aided by new technologies in film and videotape, have succeeded in uncovering neonate's abilities to make use of facial expressions as a mode of communication. It now appears that infants are sensitive to the facial expressions of others in the first few months of life. This suggests that infants may have some understanding of their own emotional lives as well.

One early study purporting to demonstrate the existence of this ability in infants was conducted by Meltzoff and Moore (1977). Meltzoff and his colleagues posed four different facial expressions to 2-week-old infants. The infants' reactions to each of the four posed expressions were video-taped, and then coded for the type of facial expression exhibited by the infant (the raters were unaware of the expressions posed by the experiment-ers). The analyses indicated that the infants appeared to imitate the facial expressions of the experimenters, which suggests that infants must be able to identify the expressions of others. Although the facial expressions posed by Meltzoff and Moore were not typical of particular emotions, and although some of Meltzoff and Moore's interpretations of data have been challenged, later studies using the same methodology but with facial expressions of happy, sad, and surprise have replicated the basic findings (Field et al., 1982). Together, these studies suggest that infants shortly following birth are able to abstract some information about others through the interpretation of facial expressions. Meltzoff (1990) suggested that the experience of imitating and interpreting the facial expressions of others infuses the infant's understanding of its own subjective states with new meaning, and provides a core on which an elaborated sense of self can be built.

Although neonates are sensitive to the expressions of others in the weeks following birth, they cannot make full use of the information latent in facial expressions. In part, this is a consequence of physical limitations; neonates have poorly developed vision that prohibits fine discriminations, and do not scan faces so as to inspect the mouth and eyes of others (see Nelson, 1987, for an excellent review). Neonates also lack a concept or schema for faces (Fagan, 1979), which limits their ability to integrate images of different facial features into coherent wholes. Both limitations disappear quickly. The rapid maturation of the visual system and a growing familiarity with faces permits the developing infant to become increasingly able to make use of information about facial expressions. By the age of 5 to 6 months, infants are able to classify facial expressions as "happy" or "fearful," which permits them to relate the current expression of the person with whom they are interacting to past experiences (Nelson, 1987).

Between 6 and 18 months of age, infants demonstrate an ability to use the facial expressions of others as guides to their own behavior; this is the social referencing phenomenon. In one well-designed study, Sorce, Emde, Campos, and Klinnert (1985) demonstrated the ability of infants to make use of facial expressions of their mothers. Infants were placed on the shallow end of a visual cliff, with mothers standing at the other, deep end. As infants approached the apparent drop off, mothers posed either positive emotions (happy, interested) or negative emotions (fear, sadness, anger). The results indicated that most infants would cross the deep end if their mothers were posing the positive emotions, but would withdraw from the cliff if their mothers were exhibiting the negative ones. These findings demonstrate that infants, by the age of 12 months, make use of their mothers' expressions as guides to their own behavior. Emde and Buchsbaum (1990) have claimed that social referencing "has an important adaptive function in facilitating self-development—that is, in promoting, sustaining, and enlarging working models of the three dynamic aspects of the self system: (a) the experience of self, (b) the experience of the other (e.g., the attachment figure), and (c) the experience of self with other, or *we*" (p. 47). This hypothesis accords infants a large store of information concerning subjective states at an early age.

Other studies with infants reveal their sensitivity to a variety of person characteristics. Infants distinguish among the individuals with whom they interact on the basis of gender, age, and familiarity (Lewis & Brooks-Gunn, 1979), and can detect when the appearance of familiar others has been altered (Pipp, Fischer, & Jennings, 1987). There is evidence to indicate that infants are sensitive to the typical dispositions of others as well; Tronick (1989) reported that infants of depressed mothers behave differently with them than do infants of nondepressed mothers. These findings indicate that infants are aware of differences among individuals at a young age, distinctions that they may be able to apply to the self as well (Butterworth, 1990).

Childhood and Adolescence

A great deal of research was done in the 1960s and 1970s on children's and adolescents' understanding of people. Much of the research utilized free-description tasks, in which children were asked to describe a variety of people (parents, friends, siblings, people they did and did not like, and so on). For instance, Livesly and Bromley (1973) elicited this description of a peer from a 9-year-old:

> He smells very much and is very nasty. He has no sense of humor and is very dull. He is always fighting and he is cruel. He does silly things and is very stupid. He has brown hair and cruel eyes. He is sulky and 11 years old and has lots of sisters. I think he is the most horrible boy in the class. He has a croaky voice and always chews his pencil and picks his teeth and I think he is disgusting. (p. 217)

These sorts of descriptions are parsed into small units (e.g., "nasty"), and then assigned to different categories, such as age, physical appearance, personality characteristics, and so on. Generally, the results from these sorts of studies (e.g., Peevers & Secord, 1973) confirm Livesly and Bromley's findings that with increasing age there is movement away from a reliance on peripheral characteristics (gender, appearance, behavior) to central characteristics (personality, attitudes).

Two important qualifications to this general shift have emerged from recent research. Barenboim (1981) demonstrated that there is more to the development of person understanding than the movement from peripheral to central characteristics. In his interviews with children between the ages of 6 and 11 years, Barenboim found that between the ages of 6 and 8 years there was an increase in the use of behavioral comparisons in describing other people (e.g., "he's a good kickball player"). These types of characteristics are less salient in the descriptions of others offered by children between the ages of 10 and 11 years, who use instead psychological comparisons (e.g., "she's the smartest kid in our class"). Barenboim argued that these findings suggest that there is a sequence from behavioral ("peripheral" in Livesley & Bromley's terms) descriptions, to behavioral comparisons, to psychological (or "central") descriptions, to psychological comparisons. Although these trends need to be confirmed in replication studies, Barenboim's findings suggest that the development of person perception is more complicated than merely a shift from peripheral to central.

A second qualification is that the meaning of psychological or central descriptions changes with development. For instance, "smart" has different implications for understanding self and other among children than it does among adolescents and adults. Rholes and Ruble (1984) found that as children get older, they increasingly believe that an observation of another person's behavior in one setting is a good predictor of that person's behavior in another context. Children between the ages of 5 and 10 years viewed videotaped excerpts of behavior in which child actors portrayed desirable and undesirable personality traits and behaviors (e.g., generous, athletic, stingy, poor problem solving). After watching the vignettes, the children were asked to make predictions about the behavior of the characters they had observed in videotapes. The older children were more likely than the younger children to expect the characters to behave in ways consistent with their actions in the vignette: For instance, characters who exhibited generosity were expected to continue doing so, while stingy characters were predicted to be stingy in other settings. These findings indicate that, for the older children, personality and ability characteristics are stable features of the self or another that motivate and guide behavior in diverse settings. Apparently, younger children are less likely to deduce stable personality and ability characteristics from their observations of persons.

Summary. The research on understanding people in general suggests some age-related constraints on the development of self-understanding. Infants are mainly aware of discrete emotions, patterns of social interactions, and physical characteristics of people. From childhood through adolescence, there is a gradual shift from focus on physical and behavioral attributes to a focus on psychological and personality attributes. How such attributes are understood changes with age as well: Older children are more likely than younger children to use personal characteristics comparatively and to link psychological traits with their behavioral implications.

Understanding the Self as a Unique Social Concept

Although much can be inferred about the understanding of self from the study of how people generally are understood, the two always remain partially independent conceptual systems. This is because the two differ in the types of information on which they are based and in the functions they serve. These issues have been explored by Neisser (1988) and Hart and Damon (1985). According to Neisser's view, one's sense of self is based (in part) on a variety of perceptual experiences that are not shared with one's sense of the other. Neisser pointed out that movement through the world reveals two classes of objects: those that move with the individual's point of observation, and those that do not. Those that move in coordination with the point of observation are considered part of the self, with all others seen as belonging to the nonself-class of objects. For instance, one's hand is considered to be part of oneself because it always occupies approximately the same position in the perceptual field, no matter where one goes. A favorite chair may not be considered a part of the self, because it is not always present in the perceptual field, and when it is, it may occupy varying locations. Neisser's point is that the self is perceptually distinct from all other concepts.

Hart and Damon (1985) argued that there are other reasons to suspect that an understanding of self is distinct from an understanding of others. In particular, one has a great deal more information about one's own behavior than one has about another's actions. One knows the intentions that precede and the emotions that accompany the self's actions, but the intentions and emotions of others must be inferred on the basis of their actions, a process that is prone to error. Similarly, one's own action can be viewed within a stream of behavior that extends over great lengths of time. Rarely does the observer have much information about the history of another person's action. The consequence is that the sorts of inferences one makes about the self may be very different from the inferences one makes about others. For instance, an adolescent refusing to eat meat may view it as reflecting a commitment to animal rights, whereas others might see it as identification with a famous vegetarian entertainer.

Hart and Damon have also argued that an understanding of self serves a role different from that played by an understanding of others. An understanding of self is the cognitive base for the sense of identity (Damon & Hart, 1988), and integrates the self's continuity over time, distinctness from others, and self-control, experiences that are central to selfhood (and that we discuss later) but that are not usually included in our conceptions of others (Hart & Damon, 1986). Furthermore, one's conception of another is usually shaped by a need to inform one's interactions with that specific person; in contrast, one's conception of self need not be directed toward guiding one's interactions with any particular person. For all these reasons, self-understanding and person perception require separate investigations.

There is general agreement among self-understanding researchers that the distinctions proposed by William James (1892/1961) are useful for organizing the types of thoughts and beliefs that one might have about oneself. According to James, the experience of self is composed of two basic types: the self-as-subject, or the "I," and the self-as-object, or the "Me." The self-as-subject facet encompasses the subjective, volitional elements of the self. Within James' framework, the self-as-subject is the vantage from which one reflects on the self. As we have suggested elsewhere (Damon & Hart, 1988), the self-as-subject can be distilled into three types of experiences that lend themselves to empirical investigation: self-continuity, the sense that the self is continuous over time and context; distinctness, the perception of one's own uniqueness in respect to others; and agency, the experience of one's control over life events.

The self-as-object includes within it a wide variety of attributes and qualities that an individual uses to define the self. James described three basic types of characteristics: physical (appearance, possessions), social

Self vs. Soul.
vs Mind
vs Identity
vs Consciousness

7. SELF-UNDERSTANDING   429

(roles, social–personality traits), and psychological (beliefs, cognitive states). To this list, we have added a fourth, the active characteristics (the self's activities and capabilities), because a previous literature review suggested that the active qualities of self are quite important to children (Damon & Hart, 1982). These distinctions among the different facets of self-understanding serve to organize the review of studies on infancy, childhood, and adolescence that follow.

Infancy

It is difficult to ascertain what infants think about themselves, because infants are restricted in the information they can provide about their own thoughts. In fact, only one technique has gained acceptance by researchers as a tool through which the infant's self-concept can be studied. This technique is the *mirror and rouge task,* which was independently developed by Gallup (1977) in his work with primates and Amsterdam (1972) on work with infants. In Amsterdam's study, the infant's nose was surreptitiously marked with rouge, and then the infant was seated in front of a mirror, with the behaviors recorded by the experimenter. If the infant touched its own nose (mark-directed behavior) in an effort to remove the rouge, Amsterdam inferred that the infant "associates his own face with the face in the mirror" (1972, p. 304). This demonstrates that the infant has some knowledge of its physical characteristics, one facet of the self-as-object. Furthermore, it is a demonstration that infants are aware they are continuous over time, because mark-directed behavior is occasioned by the realization that the face looks different than it has in the past. Amsterdam found that infants rarely demonstrated mark-directed behavior before 20 months of age. Amsterdam's basic findings have been replicated many times (e.g., Bertenthal & Fischer, 1978; Johnson, 1983; Lewis & Brooks-Gunn, 1979), with most investigators finding mark-directed behavior emerging between 17 to 24 months of age.

Other techniques have been used to explore infant self-understanding, but it should be noted that these tasks have not gained the wide acceptance of the mirror-and-rouge task as an index of the infant's sense of self. Lewis and Brooks-Gunn (1979) made use of videotape technology to present infants with three types of images: (a) live images of themselves, in which case the image mirrored exactly, or contingently with, the behavior of the self; (b) a prerecorded image of the self made 1 week earlier in the same setting (the physical appearance is the same, but the behavior is noncontingent); and (c) a prerecorded image of another baby. The researchers found that infants as young as 9 months of age were able to distinguish between the live images (a) and the other two types (b and c). Accordingly, they argue that infants are able to distinguish between self and other (an awareness of the self-as-subject's distinctness) on the basis of contingency sometime in the 1st year of life. Although this conclusion is reasonable in light of their results, it is also clear that the differentiation between contingent and noncontingent images can be made on the basis of other clues as well. For instance, it is well known that infants are capable of intermodal perception, which means that they are capable of coordinating perceptions from different senses (e.g., Spelke, 1979). Even young infants prefer visual images that correspond with perceptions from another sense: A visual image that moves in conjunction with the beating of a drum will be preferred to an image that is not in phase with the rhythm. Perhaps, then, the phenomenon observed in the videotape studies in which the contingent image is preferred is an example of intermodal perception, with the image of self preferred because its activity level corresponds most closely to that of the self, with the noncontingent images either too active or too inactive. If this is the basis of the distinction, then there is little reason to hypothesize that it represents a cleavage between self and other; instead, it suggests only an ability for intermodal perception. The plausibility of alternative explanations for this phenomenon is one reason why it is not widely accepted as a marker of self-understanding.

Jerome Kagan (1981) has offered intriguing evidence that infants may develop knowledge of the self's capabilities at approximately the same age as they develop mark-directed behavior. Infants of varying ages observed an experimenter use several different toys to model a variety of simple and complex sequences of behaviors. Following each modeled sequence, the experimenter placed the toys in front of the infant, and encouraged the infant to perform the sequence. Kagan reported a strange reaction among infants between the ages of 23 and 25 months: They would imitate the simple sequences, but cry when asked to replicate the complicated ones. The crying, Kagan asserted, resulted from the infant's awareness that he or she was incapable of performing the requested action, which in turn produced distress. Crying was not evident in younger infants because they lack the awareness of their own capabilities, and older infants are better able to handle the distress and consequently do not cry either. This chain of inferences — crying is an index of distress resulting from the recognition of the self's inability to imitate when expected to do so, evident only in a small age range of infants for several reasons — is plausible, but complex and in need of replication.

In summary, infant research has demonstrated that the distinctness facet of self-understanding may be detected in the middle of the 1st year of life. Between 18 and 24 months of age, infants develop knowledge of their own physical and active characteristics and are aware that their appearance is stable and continuous over time. Note that none of the studies described above report evidence concerning infants' understanding of their own emotional characteristics; although the research on social referencing suggests that infants may be aware of their own emotional states (an inference based on their evident concern with the emotions of others), compelling observational or experimental data have yet to be collected.

Childhood and Adolescence

Damon and Hart (1988) have written that self-understanding in childhood and adolescence is characterized by developmental transformations that cut across the divisions in the self-as-object and the self-as-subject. Their initial review of the psychological literature revealed that there was evidence for developmental transformations in the understanding of each of the facets of self-understanding described by James, although additional research was needed to clarify the nature of these trends (Damon & Hart, 1982). The review also suggested that much of the research on self-understanding was hampered by a failure to distinguish adequately between the attributes a child or adolescent ascribes to the self and an understanding of them. All too often, researchers simply asked children and adolescents to list characteristics that describe the self. These lists were then analyzed for the presence or absence of particular categories of characteristics. For instance, because children often described themselves in terms of their appearance, their self-understanding was characterized as "physicalistic." The same procedure revealed that adolescents' offered many characteristics that seemed to refer to cognitive or personality traits, which led to the characterization of their self-understanding as "psychological" (Montemayor & Eisen, 1977).

But such a depiction of self-understanding development as proceeding in a straight line from physical to psychological is misleading. Even young children have an understanding of the psychological qualities of self (Eder, 1989); and young children can make use of psychological characteristics in their discussions about people (Bretherton, McNew, & Beeghly-Smith, 1981). Moreover, only researchers without teenagers at home could presume that adolescents are not concerned with their own physical appearance. The conclusion must be that it is the child's understanding of these qualities, and not the child's simple use of them, that shows the most predictable developmental transformations—an interpretation consonant with the findings of Rholes and Ruble (1984) mentioned earlier. Damon and Hart, therefore, rely heavily on clinical interviews, which permit a full assessment of the individual's understanding of the various features of self. A variety of cross-sectional (Hart & Damon, 1986), longitudinal (Damon & Hart, 1986; Hart, Maloney, & Damon, 1987), cross-cultural (Hart &

Edelstein, in press; Hart, Lucca-Irizarry, & Damon, 1986), and clinical studies (Levitt & Hart, in press) resulted in the formulation of the model graphically depicted in Fig. 7.1.

The model incorporates the basic distinctions proposed by James, discussed earlier. The front face of the model corresponds to the self-as-object, or the "me," and has four columns, one each for the physical, active, social, and psychological qualities or selves. The side face of the model represents the self-as-object, with three columns there for continuity, distinctness, and agency, which in the earlier discussion were described as the facets of the self-as-subject amenable to empirical investigation.

Developmental change occurs principally along the vertical dimension, with four discrete developmental levels depicted. This results in a model with 28 distinct boxes, each representing the intersection of a facet of self-understanding (e.g., the physical self) and a developmental level (e.g., Categorical Identifications). This organization reflects our beliefs (a) that each of these intersections of a facet of self-understanding and a developmental level is somewhat unique, and requires its own description and (b) there are important commonalities within columns (the same experiences of self) and rows (developmental levels). In the paragraphs that follow, the developmental levels are described. The nature of the levels is clarified through examples of interview responses that might be offered for each of them.

 At the first developmental level, Categorical Identifications, the self is understood to be a collection of separate categorical identifications. The child sees each one of these categorical identifications as defining the self, and there is little expressed organization among them. When asked to describe the self, for instance, the child might offer a variety of self-as-object characteristics such as "I have blue eyes" (physical self), "I play baseball" (active self), "I have two sisters" (social self), and "I'm happy." Each of these features is seen to be revealing of the self, and independent of each of the others; interviewer requests to explain the interrelationships of the features are often met with expressions suggesting that children consider the task alien and unimportant to their own views of self. The self's continuity, distinctness, and agency are experienced in similar ways: "How do you know you are still the same person that you were in the past?" "I'll always have blue eyes" (continuity); "What makes you different from everyone you know?" "No one else has red hair like mine" (distinctness); "How did you get to be the way you are?" "I just grew" (agency).

 The next level, Comparative Assessments, which is characteristic of school-age children, reflects a new organizational principle—comparison with others, in self-understanding. The various characteristics of self draw their value through comparisons between the performances and capabilities of self with those of others. When asked to describe the self, the child at

Developmental Level

The Self-As-Object

Developmental Level		Physical Self	Active Self	Social Self	Psychological Self
4. Late Adolescence	Systematic Beliefs and Plans	Physical Attributes Reflecting Volitional Choices, or Personal and Moral Standards	Active Attributes That Reflect Choices, Personal or Moral Standards	Moral or Personal Choices Concerning Social Relations or Social-Personality Characteristics	Belief Systems, Personal Philosophy, Self's Own Thought Processes
3. Early Adolescence	Inter-personal Implications	Physical Attributes That Influence Social Appeal and Social Interactions	Active Attributes That Influence Social Appeal & Social Interactions	Social-Personality Characteristics	Social Sensitivity, Communicative Competence, & Other Psychologically Related Social Skills
2. Middle & Late Childhood	Comparative Assessments	Capability - Related Physical Attributes	Abilities Relative to Others, Self or Normative Standards	Abilities or Acts Considered in Light of Others' Reactions	Knowledge, Cognitive Abilities, or Ability-Related Emotions
1. Early Childhood	Categorical Identifications	Bodily Properties or Material Possessions	Typical Behavior	Fact of Membership in Particular Social Relations or Groups	Momentary Moods, Feelings, Preferences & Aversions
General Organizing Principle		Physical Self	Active Self	Social Self	Psychological Self

The Self-As-Subject

Developmental Level	Continuity	Distinctness	Agency
4. Late Adolescence	Relations Between Past, Present, and Future Selves	Unique Subjective Experiences Interpretations of Events	Personal and Moral Evaluations Influence Self
3. Early Adolescence	Ongoing of Recognition Self by Others	Unique of Combination and Psychological Attributes Physical Attributes	Communication and Reciprocal Interaction Influence Self
2. Middle & Late Childhood	Permanent and Core Capabilities Active Capabilities and Characteristics	Comparisons Self Between Self and Other Along Dimensions Isolated Dimensions	Efforts, Wishes, Talents and Influence Self
1. Early Childhood	Categorical Identifications	Categorical Identifications	Externalizable Uncontrollable Factors Determine Self

FIG. 7.1. Developmental model of self-understanding (from Damm & Hart, 1988).

Level 2 offers self-as-object descriptions such as these: "What are you like?" "I'm bigger than most kids, which is important because I can run faster than them." Comparisons of the self to other allow the child to defend the self's continuity and distinctness from others on the basis of permanent, personal characteristics, "I've always been good at baseball, I'll always be good at baseball" or "no one in my class kicks home runs like I do." The self's agency is seen as deriving from personal effort and willpower "How did you get to be like you are now?" "I tried really, really hard."

 Early adolescence brings with it a new organizing principle for self-understanding, Interpersonal Implications. The organizing theme here is the importance of a particular feature of self for interacting with others. At Level 3, the meaning of a feature of self is determined by its role in determining how one gets along in the social world. A request for self-description elicits self-as-object descriptions such as "I'm tall, and boys don't like tall girls" or "I'm friendly, so people like me." The importance of the social context extends to the understanding of the self-as-subject as well. The young adolescent asserts that formation of the self occurs within a communicative context "I got to be the person I am by learning from my parents, I even learned from my friends, just listening to 'em and talking to 'em." The continuity of the self depends on a stable social network ("no matter how much I change, my friends and family always know its me"), and one's distinctness from others in the network derives from a unique combination of qualities ("some people have some of the same things as me, but nobody has exactly the same interests, friends, and body").

 At the highest level, Systematic Beliefs and Plans, the various features of self are organized by a personal philosophy or patterning of beliefs. For an older adolescent, for instance, "honest" may be an important feature of the self-as-object because "I don't think anything is more important to my personal value system than being an honest person, both to myself and to others." The agency of the self is seen as deriving fundamentally from one's personal or moral evaluations of others. The continuity of self is established not by the stability of any feature of the self, but instead by the recognition of the evolution of the current self out of earlier ones ("well, nothing about me always stays the same, but I am always kind of like I was a while ago, and there is always some connection"). The individuality of the self resides in its unique interpretations and subject experiences of the world ("nobody else sees things or feels the same way about things as I do").

Because the results of the various studies using the model are complex, only an overview can be provided here. First, there is evidence for the interrelatedness of development across the various facets of self-understanding, at least for nonclinical samples (Hart & Damon, 1986). Second, there are clear age trends for the developmental levels, with longitudinal trends suggesting that people move from one level to the next higher one, with no regression to lower levels (Damon & Hart, 1986; Hart, Maloney et al., 1987). Third, there is some evidence for a gradual shift in the salience of the different selves (physical, active, social, psychological) composing the self-as-object. The physical and active selves are generally more salient for children than for adolescents, with the social and psychological selves more salient for the latter than the former (Hart, 1988; Hart & Damon, 1986). This set of findings is congruent with the research on the understanding of persons revealed earlier. However, shifts of salience in the different selves of the self-as-object are influenced by culture and social class to a greater degree than are developmental levels (Hart et al., 1986; Hart & Edelstein, in press). Fourth, developmental lags in specific facets of self-understanding may be clinically informative; for instance, the immaturity of anorexic adolescents' understanding of agency (Levitt & Hart, in press) can be used to guide clinical practice (Schorin & Hart, 1988).

Rather than focus on broad patterns of self-understanding development, other researchers have attempted to elucidate children's understanding in more circumscribed domains. One of the most productive of these lines of study has concerned children's understanding of themselves as learners. Carol Dweck and her colleagues (Dweck & Bempechat, 1983) have argued that children's achievement in school depends not only on their academic ability, but also on their inferences about themselves. According to Dweck, children offer one of two basic views of the self as a learner: (a) an incremental theory, according to which the self's intelligence is always increasing as one acquires new skills, and therefore one is capable of mastering very difficult problems if enough energy and time is invested, and (b) an entity theory, from which follows the notion that intelligence is a stable trait that one possesses to a certain extent, and therefore one is either capable or incapable of solving a difficult problem. The two perspectives on the self-as-learner lead to different motivational patterns. The incremental theorists prefer tasks that are difficult but result in the acquisition of new skills, while the entity theorists prefer tasks that can be solved without errors, and thereby confirm their competence.

Although there are connections between Dweck's description of the theories of the self-as-learner that children may hold and Damon and Hart's account of the agency component of the self-as-subject, the two differ in an important way. Dweck's model is intended to capture enduring facets of children's views of themselves, and thus is most similar to the individual differences orientation of personality research, while Damon and Hart's description of agency is more developmental in orientation. The two approaches point to complementary features of self-concept: As research has shown, there are both predictable change and personal stability in children's and adolescents' understanding of themselves.

Discuss adult devel - issues?
Reciprocal Socializer

Adulthood

There is much less empirical research on the understanding of self in late adolescence and adulthood, although there are a number of provocative theories (see Hart, in press, for a review of these studies and theories). Perhaps the most influential of these has been proposed by Levinson (1978). Levinson's perspective is that the understanding of self changes as a consequence of broad transformations in the structure of one's life. According to Levinson, there are four major eras in the life span: infancy through adolescence (birth to age 22 years), early adulthood (17–45 years), middle adulthood (40–65 years), and late adulthood (60 years to death). The transitions from one era to the next, the periods during which the eras overlap (17–22, 40–45, 60–65), are particularly stressful and problematic for the individual. During these transitions, major reorganizations in a person's life occur, which result in dramatic reformulations of the understanding of self.

Within each era, there are transitions as well, and there are also stressful periods of reorganization, but of lesser magnitude than of those occurring between eras. For the period of life for which his theory is most relevant, late adolescence through early adulthood, Levinson has proposed alternating periods of stability and change. In late adolescence, according to Levinson, the individual enters the early adult transition, which occurs between ages 17 and 22. This transition is the tumultuous period intervening between the relative stability of adolescence and early adulthood. Two tasks must be accomplished during this transition, according to Levinson: (a) The *Discuss* world of childhood must be left behind, and (b) a preliminary basis for life in the world of adulthood must be formed.

The first task requires that the adolescent terminate or radically revise relationships from the childhood and adolescent years. This task is seen most clearly in relationships to parents; the fledgling adult must renegotiate the expectations that his parents have for him, and must develop some understanding of the self's independence from them as well. Although it is most evident in the context of parent–child relationships, the same task must occur in relationships with other authority figures and childhood friends. The second task, the construction of a preliminary basis for life in adulthood, takes several forms. Attending college, military service, and apprenticeships are all first steps toward beginning a life in adulthood.

The early adult transition is followed by the Entering the Adult World phase, which is characterized by relative stability. The young adult works on both exploring the opportunities offered by the adult world and defining him or herself as an adult with specific goals. It is here in this stage of life that the individual forms what Levinson called The Dream. The Dream is the vision of the self in the future as it will be under ideal circumstances; it is The Dream that animates a person's life and gives it meaning. The Dream organizes and guides the choices that give rise to a person's life structure, which is the configuration of self-selected occupations, relationships, values, and activities that define a person's life.

The calm of the Entering the Adult World phase ends in the tumult of the Age 30 Transition, which occurs between ages 28 and 33. Entry into this transition is brought on by a person's recognition that the life structure he or she built during his or her 20s is no longer satisfactory; the choices and decisions during this early phase of life were based on an inadequate understanding of both the self and the adult world. Consequently, the life structure must be revised, and better choices must be made. This transition is marked by a sense of urgency, Levinson claimed, because there is the recognition that one is no longer an adolescent; there is considerable pressure to enter fully the world of adulthood.

Emerging from the Age 30 Transition, the person seeks to establish a secure niche in the world of adulthood. He or she seeks acknowledgment of his or her status as an adult; wants a good job; wants to establish roots in a particular community; desires security and stability in life. Levinson argues that this set of desires is superceded to an extent in the later 30s by a desire to demonstrate special competencies, to "climb the ladder of success." The person still believes that it will be possible to realize fully his hopes and aspirations constituting The Dream, and works hard to do so.

The mid-life transition, which stands between Early and Middle Adulthood, is a period of significant reorganization in the life structure and considerable stress. One of the most important changes, Levinson asserted, is that The Dream is deflated. The person recognizes that those facets of The Dream that were realized in life are not as satisfying as expected. Moreover, for most people, there is an awareness that most of the goals constituting The Dream will never be accomplished: Only a very few of the people who dream of becoming senators, or chief executive officers, or supreme court justices find that their dreams come true, and this recognition occurs to them as they enter their 40s.

To test his theory, Levinson relied on a single study in which 40 middle-aged men (10 biologists, 10 novelists, 10 hourly workers, 10 business executives) were intensively studied. Each man was interviewed in depth about his life and how it had changed since adolescence. These interviews permitted the investigative team to construct biographies for each of the men. The analysis of the biographies indicated that the periods of stability and change outlined above occurred for all the men in the study. Furthermore, Levinson found that the transitions were closely linked to age; for instance, the age 30 transition, marked by instability and revision in the life structure, occurred between ages 28 and 33 — not between 25 and 28, or 33 and 36 — for all of the men. The robustness of these findings across the men in the study, who differ significantly in social class and educational backgrounds as well as in the occupations they held at the time of their participation, led Levinson to conclude that the patterns he described constitute a universal sequence that can be found in men in all cultures.

Levinson's theory has yet to derive much support from empirical research. On the one hand, Levinson's own data seem to provide strong support for his claims; he finds the transformations and age-linkages specified by his theory. Even sympathetic critics, however, have noted that his research is problematic in a variety of aspects:

1. The sample does not even approximate a representative sample of American men; few researchers would agree that a description of development derived from such a group would be characteristic of men in the United States, much less of men in other cultures. The omission of women from the study, of course, leaves unanswered the relevance of the theory for one half the population.

2. The biographies are written by Levinson and his colleagues, and therefore the construction of the biographies may be influenced by theory, and consequently cannot be used to confirm it.

3. The biographies are based on the men's recollections about their lives in their 20s and 30s, and there is substantial evidence that remembering one's life at a later date can be significantly different from one's experience of it at the time (Vaillant, 1977).

Independent researchers have found some evidence of change in the understanding of self in late adolescence and adulthood. From the results of their cross-sectional study of adolescents and adults, Lowenthal, Thurnher, and Chiriboga (1985) inferred that the ideal selves of older adolescents are oriented toward achievement and productivity, concerns that become more focused in early adulthood when career roles are ascendant. Other researchers, while acknowledging that career roles are important to young people, point out that family roles continue to be prominent sources of self-satisfaction (Veroff, Douvan, & Kulka, 1981). Together, these findings suggest that the ideal self during adolescence and early adulthood is constituted, in part, of both career and family-role aspirations.

Yet not all of the research on late adolescence and adulthood yields results that are congruent with those of Levinson. In studies in which subjects' occupational interests (one important facet of the ideal self) are elicited through their endorsement of various jobs as either desirable or undesirable, there is considerable stability of individual differences over intervals of 1 to 10 years during late adolescence and early adulthood (Holland, 1973). The stability of individual differences seems to increase with age, so that over a 5-year span of time one can expect the young adult to have changed less in occupational interests and aspirations than an adolescent (Strong, 1943). Studies by Costa and McCrae (Costa et al., 1986) find little evidence of age-related shifts in negative emotions, occupational and family dissatisfaction, or the sense of inner turmoil. This is contrary to the expectation that these variables ought to be related to the phases and transitions posited in Levinson's model. For instance, one would predict that all three (negative emotions, dissatisfaction, inner turmoil) would be high during the Age 30 Transition, and low in the relative calm of the next phase. Yet this hypothesis and similar ones were not confirmed.

In summary, the extent to which an understanding of self evolves in adulthood has yet to be answered fully. There is some evidence that early adulthood brings with it a focus on career and occupational development. Further, research from the related domain of occupational aspirations suggests that the rate of change in the ideal self, one type of self-understanding, declines from adolescence through adulthood.

SELF-UNDERSTANDING AND SOCIAL COGNITION

To this point, we have described the development of self-understanding and have argued that it constitutes a partially unique domain of social understanding. In this section, the relation of self-understanding to several other domains of social reasoning is examined. As one of the central constructions of social understanding, the understanding of self interpenetrates the individual's interpretation of social interactions, moral transgressions, and social institutions. Indeed, the developing sophistication in social cognition over time is, in part, the result of an increasingly effective deployment of an understanding of self as a template for understanding.

Infancy

The significant limitations on early abilities contributed to an underestimation of the infant's social qualities, which was reified in a construct called infant egocentrism or profound egocentrism. The idea underlying this construct is that infants for the first year and a half of life are incapable of genuine social interaction because they are presumed to be insensitive to the peculiarities of the perspectives of others; instead, infants are thought to project onto others without any modification their own emotions, thoughts, and desires. Consequently, infants are thought to be locked in to their own autistic worlds, and therefore unable to demonstrate any of the features of genuine social interaction that were discussed in the introduction (see

Damon, 1983; Hart, Kohlberg, & Wertsch, 1987 for further discussions of profound egocentrism).

The evidence against profound egocentrism is now overwhelming; clearly, infants do not always inappropriately project onto others their own thoughts and feelings. For instance, there is quite a bit of research on the intricate interactions that occur between infant and mother as they work to initiate and to maintain intersubjectivity, which is the understanding that emerges between the infant and mother through coordinated activity. The development of intersubjectivity (and social referencing, which was discussed earlier) has a variety of practical implications that cannot be explored in this chapter; here we discuss only the emergence of these skills, their development, and their relationships to self-knowledge.

A wave of studies since the 1970s has provided impressive testimony to the infant's ability to coordinate its attention and action with that of another. For instance, research with young infants has demonstrated that they are aware when intersubjectivity is present and when it is not. Murray and Trevarthen (1985) conducted a study with particularly compelling results. The researchers had 2- to 4-month-old infants interact with their mothers via closed circuit TV for 2 minutes. During the first minute of interaction, infants viewed live images of their mothers. For the most part, the infants reacted with interest and pleasure to the images they viewed. During the second minute, the infants watched videotape recordings of the first minute; in other words, the infants saw the exact same images as they had previously viewed. However, the infants exhibited signs of distress in viewing the recording. Murray and Trevarthen argue that the distress arises from the infants' recognition that the recorded images of their mothers are not synchronized with their own. This suggests that the infants are (a) aware of their own actions (a form of the contingency self-awareness, an awareness of the self's distinctness, discussed previously), and (b) sensitive to the presence or absence of coordination of the caretakers' actions.

Childhood and Adolescence

Social cognitive investigations take a different direction in childhood. Infancy studies tend toward demonstrating that infants are aware of themselves and sensitive to social interaction; the research concerning childhood is more often directed at identifying the social cues and features of self to which children at different ages attend and to their understanding of these cues and their implications for behavior. This task is made easier by children's ability to respond to interview questions that elicit their understanding of social situations and social behavior. Of course, verbal measures cannot provide a complete picture of children's abilities (Berscheid, 1985), but they can provide access to some of the thoughts and experiences that are not easily elicited through any other measure, and consequently are invaluable for many purposes.

There are a variety of ways of parsing the social world, and investigators have yet to reach consensus on the ways children and adolescents do so. However, one frequently accepted division is between horizontal and vertical relationships (Hartup, 1989). Horizontal relationships exist between two people of equal, or nearly equal, status, and most often characterize friendships and relationships among peers. Vertical relationships are those between people who differ significantly in status and power, and frequently map onto the parent–child relationship. We discuss the relevance of self-understanding for each of these types of relationship in turn.

Horizontal Relationships.   There have been a variety of studies that have investigated children's and adolescents' understanding of relationships with their peers, with most of them focusing on friendship (for reviews, see Berndt, 1989; Damon, 1983; Selman & Schultz, 1990; Shantz, 1983). In large part, these studies have elicited children's understanding of relationships through questionnaires or interviews, using questions such as: "What is a friend?" "How do you make friends?" "How can you tell if someone is your friend?" "What makes someone a good friend?" "What makes people stop being friends?"

Responses to these questions have been coded in a variety of ways, with some investigators assigning responses to developmental stages (e.g., Selman, 1980), and others preferring to analyze responses with content-coding schemes (e.g., Berndt, 1985). Although the methodologies differ, the different studies (Berndt, 1985; Bigelow, 1977; Selman, 1980; Youniss, 1980; see Shantz, 1983, for a thorough review) converge on some general developmental trends. For young children, friendship depends on physical proximity and the resulting association. The young child believes the formation and termination of friendships occurs frequently, as one meets new peers; at nursery schools, one can overhear one child ask another "Do you want to be my friend?", with only an affirmative response necessary for the relationship to be established.

As children grow older, their conceptions of friendship begin to include a temporal dimension. A friend is someone with whom one shares a history of interaction and association. Friends are thought to exchange favors, to help each other, and to refrain from hurting each other through aggression. In late childhood and early adolescence, the essential criteria for friendship are loyalty and intimacy. Friends are seen as sharing secrets, maintaining confidences, and remaining faithful to one another; without these qualities, older children and adolescents believe that friendship is not possible.

Developmental trends in self-understanding do not explain the transformations in friendship reasoning, but they do complement them. For instance, the distress that adolescents experience when their relationships with peers are threatened or terminated can be partially understood in terms of their focus on intimacy and commitment as constituent elements in friendship. This view of friendship means that a friend cannot be easily or quickly replaced, and therefore a friend is particularly valuable. Yet the depth of despair and constant rumination that follows from ruptures in adolescent peer relationships cannot be fully explained by the developmental form of friendship reasoning (adults, for instance, also are oriented toward intimacy and commitment in friendship, but typically are not threatened to the same extent by the loss of a relationship). If the observer knows, however, that the young adolescent understands the self in terms of its interpersonal implications (Level 3 in the model) — where the very nature of the self derives from its influence and connection to the immediate social context — then the adolescent's efforts to preserve interpersonal relationships can be understood as efforts to protect the core features of the self. For the adolescent, then, friendships are not merely a form of relationship but also are part of the context within which the self takes meaning. This richer understanding is only possible through augmenting accounts of friendship reasoning with a developmental perspective on self-understanding.

Vertical Relationships.   Relatively little research has considered children's and adolescents' understanding of vertical relationships, which are characterized by disparity in power between the self and other, and usually involve issues of authority as well. The most important vertical or authority relationship in the child's life is with the parents. Damon (1977, 1980) investigated the development of children's understanding of authority relationships by posing hypothetical dilemmas to them such as stories about parents asking children to do chores. The stories are followed by questions that elicit children's understanding of the legitimacy of the parent's authority and the rationale for complying with the authority's wishes.

Analyses of responses to these sorts of questions have led to the formulation of developmental levels of authority understanding (Damon, 1977; Maccoby, 1980). At the first level, children fail to distinguish between their own desires and those of the authority; a mother would not ask a child to do something the child did not want to do. At the second level, the child distinguishes between the self's desires and those of the authority, and follows the dictates of the latter in order to avoid punishment. Children whose understanding is characteristic of the third level believe that the authority's great strength, size, and power legitimize his or her commands. The understanding of authority at the fourth level continues to emphasize the special nature of the authority, but the focus is on the authority's greater knowledge and skills. At the fifth level, the authority relationship is seen to be constituted of two persons, both of whom have rights; the authority generally should be followed, but only if those commands do not violate the legitimate boundaries of the relationship. At the sixth level, children believe that the authority relationship is constituted of two fundamentally equal individuals; one person is in the position of authority only in contexts in which that person has special expertise and knowledge.

The development of self-understanding very likely plays a part in the development of authority reasoning. Consider the last level of authority reasoning, at which children believe that the authority relationship is situationally dependent, and derives from one person's special expertise. This form of reasoning arises at the same time that children are beginning to think of themselves in terms of comparative assessments (Level 2 in the model). The process of constantly viewing themselves in terms of their abilities relative to those of others results in children's awareness that in some domains they are more able than many people, including their parents. This new self-perspective permits them to assert that in some situations, they should personally exercise authority.

The issue of authority is both a social and a moral one. Indeed, understanding authority is crucial to developing a sense of morality. This leads us to the final section of this chapter, where we consider moral development and its links to self and social understanding.

THE SELF AND MORALITY

As we discussed in the section on self-understanding, a person's moral beliefs often become an important part of the person's self-identity, especially during the adolescent years and beyond. Adolescents understand themselves primarily in terms of their interpersonal relations (Fig. 7.1, Level 3) or ideological belief systems (Fig. 7.1, Level 4). Both interpersonal relations and belief systems are closely linked to moral values and ideas. Teenagers who consider themselves to be kind, generous, fair, caring, honest—all of which are interpersonal notions commonly expressed during self interviews with adolescents (Damon & Hart, 1988)—are defining themselves in terms of their moral values. Likewise, a teenager who says that she is the kind of person who is dedicated to social justice or environmental preservation—both of which are ideological notions of the sort often expressed during late adolescence—are centering their senses of self on their moral belief systems. From studies of adult self-development, there is every reason to believe that interpersonal and ideological moral notions become increasingly important pillars of self-definition for many people (Erikson, 1980; Levinson, 1978; Loevinger, 1976; Perry, 1968; Vaillant, 1977).

Moral/personal self.

Still, not all people link morality to self in the same way. The develop-ment of self can take many paths, and people vary widely in the extent to which they look to their moral convictions in defining their personal identities. For some, moral values are central to their self-understanding as early as childhood; for others, morality may always remain peripheral to who they think they are (Damon, 1984; Damon & Hart, 1988).

Discuss
Naturally, such a difference can be expected to affect the extent to which people take moral concerns seriously and translate their values into action. Studies of people who show high levels of active moral commitment during their lives have found that such people make little distinction between their moral and personal selves (Colby & Damon, 1992; Oliner & Oliner, 1988). They identify themselves very closely with their moral goals and believe that if they were to forsake such goals they would not remain the same. This stands in sharp contrast to those for whom moral concerns are compart-mentalized, isolated from other primary self concerns such as material well-being, physical attractiveness, career success, or social status. As one reviewer of the literature on moral judgment–conduct relations has con-cluded: "Being moral, being a good person, being fair and just in a general sense, may be, but need not be, a part of an individual's essential self" (Blasi, 1984, p. 72). Studies have shown that the manner in which a person integrates moral and self concerns is at least as important in determining the person's moral conduct as the nature of the person's moral judgment (Blasi, 1983; Blasi & Oresick, 1986).

Davidson and Youniss (1991) proposed a model of moral judgment and behavior that hinges on the individual's mode of self-understanding. In this model, Davidson and Youniss distinguish between an individual's primary identity, represented by the kind of self-understanding discussed earlier in this chapter, and an individual's autonomous identity, represented by nonreflective social behavior practiced in real-life situations. Moral devel-opment, they propose, "is the primary identity's acquisition of facility in entering, or opening up to, and eventually becoming explicitly aware of, the autonomous identity" (Davidson & Youniss, 1991, p. 25). In other words, development results in stronger and more functional connections between self-understanding and spontaneous moral behavior. As a person becomes increasingly able to combine self-reflection with the kinds of nonmediated moral thought and action that one engages in during daily social life, the person becomes better able to effectively carry out moral goals and commitments.

The relation between self and morality has been treated differently by developmental psychologists from various theoretical orientations. In many ways, the theoretical differences derive from more fundamental disagree-ments about how morality is best defined. All agree that self and morality are both distinct from, and yet overlap with, one another. In some ways, morality represents the abnegation of one's self-interest in favor of the welfare of others. In other ways, morality clearly represents the best way to achieve one's enlightened self interest. All theorists recognize, therefore, that self and morality must be codefined in relation to each other. But definitional issues go beyond this tenet. In the following section we consider these issues and their implications for developmental psychology.

The Definitional Issue: What Is Morality?

Like laypeople, social scientists often use the term *morality* in different ways. Often, disagreements among psychologists about how morality develops are rooted in such definitional differences. In developmental psychology, there have been three primary definitions for morality, each reflecting a certain philosophical tradition and leading to a focus on particular sorts of human behavior. Naturally, many researchers trying to capture the full complexity of moral development blend these definitions in various ways; but even the more comprehensive approaches tend to emphasize one or the other primary conceptualization.

Morality as Respect for Social Rules. Piaget (1932/1965) borrowed from Durkheim (1925/1961) in defining morality as a "respect for social rules." For the sociologist Durkheim, moral values reside in society, the existence and moral legitimacy of which transcend any individual's sole judgment. Social regulation, from this perspective, becomes the primary instrument for moral communication within and between the generations: The child is "moralized" by learning to follow the rules. Piaget accepted Durkheim's position as a starting point, but added his own psychological twist. Piaget maintained that respect for social rules must develop within the individual, along with an understanding of the purpose and function of rules. Through universal developmental processes, Piaget wrote, all children *construct* their own understanding of social rules. Moreover, the more advanced forms of childhood understanding (see following) include other fundamental moral concepts like justice, cooperation, and consensual contract. The original French subtitle of Piaget's moral judgment book was *The Child Invents the Social Contract.*

Other researchers with less of a constructivist orientation than Piaget also have centered their attention on the child's rule-following behavior. The social learning tradition generally conceptualized child morality as conformity to the norms of adult behavior (Bandura, 1977; Sears, Maccoby, & Levin, 1957; Sears, Rau, & Alpert, 1965). Obedience to rules and authority served as the criteria for morality in most social learning experiments. Immoral behavior was operationalized as yielding to the temptation of ignoring a rule. Personality theorists who have designed psychological inventories to test for moral character have taken a similar tack (Hogan, 1975). More recently, cultural psychologists have approached children's morality with the same societal orientation (Shweder, Mahapatra, & Miller, 1987). Moral concepts are conceptualized as representations of a society's traditional norms and practices; and moral breaches are seen as the violation of implicit or explicit cultural codes (LeVine & White, 1986; Much & Shweder, 1978; Whiting & Edwards, 1988).

Morality as Justice.   A large share of contemporary research on moral development stems from Kohlberg's theory and methods — an approach that is firmly grounded in a view of morality as justice (Colby, Gibbs, Kohlberg, & Lieberman, 1983; Colby & Kohlberg, 1987; Kohlberg, 1986; Rest, 1983). In his influential approach, Kohlberg consciously drew from philosophical tradition that has been dominant in Western academic, political, and legal theory since the days of the Enlightenment (Rawls, 1971).

Defining morality as a "justice structure," as Kohlberg (1971) did, implies that the ultimate end of all moral acts, prescriptions, and sanctions must be to ensure fairness to the individual. When individual claims conflict (as they inevitably will in any society), impartial procedures must be administered to resolve the conflict in a manner respectful of all individuals' rights. When a social rule or law operates in contradiction to the rights of individuals — even if the individuals constitute only a minority of the society — the rule is morally illegitimate and must be changed. Such a conclusion would not necessarily follow from a societally oriented, Durkheimian perspective. Conceptualizing morality as justice means emphasizing human conditions such as equality, liberty, reciprocity, and the respect for life. The rights of all people to such conditions are considered universal. Morally, these take priority over any particular sets of social norms, rules, or conventions (Turiel, 1983).

Morality as Care.   World religions long have preached the moral imperative of care. In Christianity, for example, care-oriented virtues such as benevolence, charity, and mercy always have been considered supreme, superceding even justice and obedience in the eyes of God. Despite such long-standing theological influence, care has not weighed heavily in psychological considerations of human morality. Some contemporary social scientists, reacting against this trend, have worried that the caring virtues have been systematically overlooked by our theories and measures (Bakan, 1966; Mussen & Eisenberg-Berg, 1977).

The strongest critique along these lines has come from one stream of feminist thought (Belenky et al., 1988; Chodorow, 1977; Gilligan, 1982). According to these researchers, there is an empirical association between women's development and a caring orientation. Some — like Chodorow and

Gilligan — suggest that there is a deep-seated psychological reason behind this empirical link. The link, they argue, stems from the differing ways in which girls and boys establish a sense of self. Girls, these theorists reason, build their early identities connecting themselves to the mother (usually the primary caregiver), whereas boys identify themselves by separating from their opposite-sex mothers. In the process, girls acquire an orientation toward connection and care, whereas boys acquire an orientation toward separation, individual rights, and the need to protect such rights through rules and codes of justice. Thus, in this line of theoretical speculation, the formation of self-identity shapes moral orientation along gender lines.

Feminist theorists such as Gilligan argue that social science has neglected women — and by implication, the morality of care — by tending to conduct research studies with all-male samples. This is, in fact, the case with Kohlberg's landmark longitudinal investigation, but it is less true of more recent empirical work (Damon, 1988). The more recent work had shed doubts on claims that the sexes are divided either in their processes of self-formation or in their moral orientations (Damon, 1988; Mednick, 1989; Walker, 1984). The purported link between female self-development and caring will remain uncertain until more definitive evidence is available. But whatever its relation to gender may turn out to be, there is no question that caring has greater importance in the moral scheme of things than social science has recognized until very recently.

Origins of Moral Awareness

Following the tripartite distinction introduced above, the child's earliest notions of rules, justice, and care all appear during the first years of life. In a moral sense, the very young child's rule awareness is probably the most limited of the three, as it is not yet social and not yet imbued with a sense of obligation (Piaget, 1951). During infancy and toddlerhood, children invent repetitive patterns of playful behavior that become developmental precursors to games with social rules. For example, a toddler might pull a toy horse around the house in a circular pattern, even involving a friend in the game; but there will be no expectation or sanction attached to maintaining or breaking the pattern from one occasion to the next. Young children also observe regularities in their social environment, ranging from dress codes to modes of conduct. They also will follow the directions of adults who enforce such regularities on the child's own behavior. But there is not yet respect for the rules per se, nor any internalized sense that one should follow them.

Justice is a large-scale word in human affairs; yet even on the modest scale of infant and toddler behavior, it has its behavioral manifestations. Infants and toddlers share objects with playmates, divide desirable foods, and learn to take turns with swings and bikes (Buhler, 1933; Mueller, 1989; Mueller & Vandell, 1977). The social symmetry of sharing, and the social reciprocity of turn-taking, are developmental precursors to the child's emerging sense of distributive justice (i.e., the attempt to dispense goods fairly). Because of the children's active early sharing experiences in social play, the sense of distributive justice probably develops before the sense of retributive justice (the attempt to punish or penalize fairly; see Damon, 1977, 1988). As with the very young child's first intimations of social regulation, the earliest notions of distributive justice are not yet accompanied by an internalized sense of obligation. Nor do very young children use key principles like equality or reciprocity in any systematic way, beyond the occasional act of sharing or turn-taking. But the groundwork for justice has been prepared by the child's playful peer encounters in the first years of life.

Of all the child's early moral sensibilities, care seems to be the one most directly supported by natural proclivities. There is a substantial body of evidence suggesting that children are born with social and emotional orientations that predispose them toward caring for others (Campos, Campos, & Barrett, 1989; Eisenberg, 1989; Hoffman, 1981). The first and most enduring of these is the capacity to respond empathically to another's joy or distress. Signs of this have been detected almost at birth, in the "contagious" crying of infants who hear one another's cries (Sagi & Hoffman, 1976). Observations of early social behavior are rich with accounts of infants and toddlers comforting others by offering their teddy bear or security blanket (Hoffman, 1984). These early acts of charity, clearly well-intentioned, may not always be appropriate—as when the other in need is beyond the age when a security blanket would produce much emotional relief.

Childhood Morality

During childhood, norms and standards take on a general importance beyond their momentary significance for the child's idiosyncratic social impulses. The child acquires a sense of objective responsibility to follow the rules, play fair, and act in a caring way toward others. Along with this sense of responsibility come new insights about rules, authority, justice, truth, and a host of other moral concepts.

One of the watershed moral events of childhood is the transformation of playful regularities into collective rules, usually through media such as organized games, household family injunctions, and school codes. Collective rules are shared and enforced; they are not subject to individual discretion or whim. Submitting to collective rules is a key socializing experience for a young child, heightening the child's awareness of the rights of others and the obligations of the self. When children first realize the importance of following rules, they often do so with an exaggerated compulsion to obey the strict letter of the law (Piaget, 1932/1965). They imagine that rules are sacrosanct, immutable, and breakable only at grave peril. Ironically, during this early- to mid-childhood period, children are notably erratic in their actual rule-following behavior, perhaps because their mental representations are so out of touch with their own behavioral capabilities and inclinations (Damon, 1988). A few years later, children develop a more balanced understanding of rules as consensual agreements between people who are free collectively to modify the rules if they so choose (Piaget, 1932/1965). Rule-following, then, becomes more uniform and more predictable.

Psychologists have distinguished between two kinds of rules that children encounter in their social environments: moral rules and conventional rules (Turiel, 1983). A social convention can be any standard that is commonly upheld in any society. Conventions differ across the world. In our society, it is conventional for men to wear pants and to open doors for women; in other societies, men may wear robes and walk several steps ahead of women. Conventional rules, such as dress codes in schools, enforce the social conventions of a particular society. Moral rules, on the other hand, enforce moral concerns — such as preventing harm or ensuring justice. Laws against stealing, killing, or fraudulent behavior are examples of moral rules because they protect some fundamental rights of other people. Children at a very early age distinguish between conventional and moral rules, recognizing that moral rules are more important. Whereas conventional rules are more frequently encountered while growing up, it is a child's exposure to moral rules that has the greatest impact on the child's moral development (Turiel, Killen, & Helwig, 1987).

In a child's life, social rules are manifestations of adult authority. The importance of respecting authority for a child's moral development has been noted by every psychologist who has written about how children acquire values (e.g., Baumrind, 1989; Freud, 1921; Kohlberg, 1969; Piaget, 1932/1965; Sears et al., 1965). In fact, the significance of authority in childhood is so apparent that some have described this period as an age at which morality consists primarily of obedience to power (Hogan, 1975; Kohlberg, 1963, 1986). But others have countered that children also work out some basic moral concepts in the course of social relations that have little to do with authority (Damon, 1977, 1983; Youniss, 1980). Notions of sharing, fairness, and cooperation, for example, often develop during peer interactions that are separate from the child's commerce with parents or teachers. Also, as we have discussed earlier, children's conceptions of authority develop in the direction of understanding that authority itself can be a consensual and mutually valuable relation between equals.

Observations of children's rich social interactions with peers have led many contemporary developmental psychologists to the hypothesis that young children live simultaneously in two moral worlds rather than in one (Damon, 1988; Hartup, 1989; Youniss, 1980). At the same time as children are learning rules and other prescriptions from the authority figures in their lives, they are forging ideas about equality, social reciprocity, and fairness in their play with friends (Selman, 1990). Comprehensive developmental analyses of children's moral conceptions bears out this hypothesis. Youniss (1980), for example, reports that children highly value cooperation with both peers and adults; but with peers they interpret cooperation as reciprocal exchange, whereas with adults they interpret it as simple obedience. Damon (1980) found that the same children who adamantly state they always obey their parents without question also will state that they would be fair to a friend even if their parents told them not to be. Damon (1977, 1980, 1988) has described sequences of authority and justice conceptions that proceed on separate tracks during the childhood years. While children are learning about the properties that legitimize power and leadership (ranging from size and strength to competence and good will), they also are learning about the demands of justice (such as equality, compromise, and compensation). Although these two conceptual systems may inform each other from time to time, in early childhood they focus on quite separate concerns. It is only later, when adolescents reformulate their views of authority, that the two systems become integrated. From all the evidence we now have, therefore, it is no longer plausible to claim, as Kohlberg and others have done, that the child's understanding of justice and morality derive developmentally from an initial orientation toward adult authority.

The other key moral dimension of childhood, beyond authority and justice, is the humanitarian concern of care. Although infants and toddlers are capable of responding empathicly to another's pain, they rarely are able to do anything effective about it. Children, in contrast, are able genuinely to help other people. Studies of children's prosocial behavior have shown that children can be generous donors to good causes, eager helpers of those in need, and quick responders to others' cries of distress (Eisenberg, 1989; Eisenberg & Miller, 1987; Staub, 1978). Moreover, their greater role-taking capacities enable them to understand better the nature of another's problem and to tailor their actions accordingly (Hoffman, 1984). This greatly increases the effectiveness of children's caring behavior.

During childhood, caring concerns are focused mostly on friends, relatives, and others with whom the child comes in immediate contact. By the end of this period, however, many children have expanded these concerns into a more general sense of altruism (Hoffman, 1984). They begin to feel that they should take some responsibility for human need wherever it is found, whether in their immediate environment or not. Children then may become concerned about such (to them) distant issues as hunger in a foreign land or sickness among the disadvantaged elderly.

The child's cultural context has a direct impact not only on the child's values but also on how these values change with age. Cross-cultural studies of children's moral beliefs have revealed that children in many traditional societies place a higher value on care and service than do children in contemporary Western societies (Whiting & Edwards, 1988). Very likely this is due to the practice of giving children important responsibilities at an early age: Children in traditional societies often are expected to take charge of their younger siblings, help care for their older relatives, and so on. In general, agrarian cultures transmit to younger generations a sense of interdependence between people, in contrast to the abiding belief in the self's autonomy that often accompanies socialization in industrial cultures (LeVine & White, 1986). A fundamental belief in human interdependence strongly supports the growth of an orientation toward care and again demonstrates the developmental links between one's sense of self and one's moral perspective.

In a study comparing Hindu–Brahmin culture in India with the culture of an American middle-class community, Shweder and his colleagues found dramatic differences in how children in the two cultures view their moral commitments (Shweder et al., 1987). The Hindu–Brahmin children placed a high priority on matters of social and religious convention, such as eating codes. (The worst infraction that they could imagine was "The day after his father's death, the eldest son had a haircut and ate chicken.") The American children, in contrast, were more attuned to concerns about violence, harm, fairness, and trust. Shweder attributes the difference to the two cultures' opposing world views on the meaning of traditional rules. In the Hindu–Brahmin culture that Shweder studied, all rules are considered to be part of the natural religious order, found rather than founded by people. Consequently, the rules themselves take on a transcendent moral meaning unknown to children from a Western culture.

Adolescent Morality

Despite popular myths about the yawning gap between peer and adult culture during adolescence, in actuality the two social worlds of the child come closer together during the teenage years. Excluding matters of style—such as music preference and clothing fashion—most adolescents share their parents's core values (Brittain, 1969; Damon, 1988). Adolescents normally continue looking to their parents for moral guidance well past the childhood years (Youniss & Smollar, 1985). Studies of well-functioning communities have found that there generally is good consensus about basic values among all the peers and adults in an adolescent's life (Ianni, 1989). Only in cases of individual or community breakdown is there serious disharmony between the adolescent's peer and adult cultures (Ianni, 1989).

One reason for the increasing convergence of peer and adult worlds is that adolescents begin feeling greater equality with adults (Youniss & Smollar, 1985). Because adolescents no longer see adults solely through the filters of power, affiliation, and obedience, they bring the standards that they have established in their peer relations to their adult ones. They expect mutual respect, even within the confines of the parent–child relationship. This, of course, often leads to the turmoil commonly associated with teenage behavior. But it also leads to a constructive reconceiving of the parent–child relationship. In the process, a new and deeper understanding of authority is gained. The adolescent understands that authority, when legitimized by qualities such as greater knowledge or wisdom, can serve both the leader and the follower (Damon, 1988). Such insights not only make adolescents better partners in a cooperative relation with adults but also can prepare them to assume authority when it becomes appropriate for them to do so.

As adolescents reformulate their views about authority, they also begin to understand social rules in a new way. Their emerging sense of equal social status and their increasing intellectual capacities enable adolescents to imagine themselves as rule creators in addition to rule followers. One manifestation of this is a fascination with the process of inventing formal rule systems (Piaget, 1932/1965). Another is a utopian perspective that questions all imperfections of the existing social order (Adelson & O'Neil, 1966). Many adolescents believe that it should be possible to fashion societal rules and policies with an absolute moral purity and they make their own ideological choices accordingly. This can be a time of political and moral fervor, untempered by an awareness of the constraints that social reality inevitably places on utopian dreams (Inhelder & Piaget, 1958). Unfortunately, for adolescents in severely disadvantaged circumstances, it also can be a time of growing hopelessness and cynicism about the social system. These young people have difficulty imagining a promising future place for themselves in the society that they have observed.

The adolescent's greater understanding of social rules and their societal importance transforms his or her moral perspective in fundamental ways. As we noted earlier, there are serious questions about whether Kohlberg's authoritarian Stage 1 *punishment and obedience orientation* is a good characterization of childhood morality; but the next four stages in Kohlberg's system do seem to describe moral changes in adolescence and beyond. At the beginning of adolescence, moral judgment normally is characterized by what Kohlberg called a Stage 2 *concrete individualistic perspective* (Kohlberg, 1986). Justice is seen as an exchange system that mediates between the clash of individual interests; and the result is a primitive moral reciprocity that advocates payback for favors or blows (as in "you scratch my back and I'll scratch yours" or "an eye for an eye, a tooth for a tooth"). By mid-adolescence, according to Kohlberg, many teenagers begin expressing a Stage 3 *social–relational perspective*. This is a more ideal form of reciprocity than the concrete tit-for-tat of Stage 2, because it represents a genuine attempt to share the other's concerns and feelings. Morality means treating others well in the course of interpersonal relations and garnering from one's good behavior a well-earned positive social reputation.

The key transformation in middle to late adolescence occurs when the adolescent begins to take a Stage 4 *member-of-society* perspective (Kohlberg, 1986). Rather than simply considering individuals or relations, the adolescent now views the social system as the primary unit of moral evaluation. Morality is seen as a means of maintaining the social order, and especially its basic laws and rules. Justice now becomes a means of carefully regulating the relations between individuals and the society-at-large. The best way to do so is to impartially enforce the law for everyone. After adolescence, according to Kohlberg and his followers, some people develop a Stage 5 *prior-to-society* perspective (Kohlberg, 1986). Social rules continue to be respected, but any particular regulation may be held up to question if it conflicts with universal principles of justice such as equality and human rights.

Kohlberg derived his stage sequence from a longitudinal sample of adolescent boys followed over a 20-year period (Colby et al., 1983; Kohlberg, 1963). As we noted earlier, some have suggested that, partly for this reason, Kohlberg's analysis may be biased against women (Gilligan, 1982). Studies of mixed-sex samples, however, have revealed no such systematic bias, particularly when the educational levels of subjects have been controlled (Walker, 1984).

But there still remains the question of whether Kohlberg's measure is comprehensive enough to capture all the moral concerns expressed by both females and males during the course of their development. As stated, Kohlberg intentionally focused his view on morality as justice. Recent studies of adolescent girls suggest that young girls tend to interpret moral dilemmas as problems of caring rather than of justice (Gilligan, Hamner, & Lyons, 1990). Rather than trying to resolve conflicts over individual rights, the female subjects looked for ways that people in the dilemma could take responsibility for one another's welfare. Unfortunately, these recent studies have not included comparison samples of boys, so it impossible to determine whether this finding indicates a sex difference or a general, although previously untapped, dimension of adolescent moral development. Whichever proves to be the case, the finding suggests that new elements would need to be added to the Kohlberg instrument if it is to become fully sensitive to the caring as well as the justice side of adolescent morality—and, by implication, to the interpersonally connected as well as to the individualistic aspects of the developing self.

Self, Values, and Youth Conduct

Philosophers and social theorists have explored the link between understanding and conduct for centuries. The link clearly is a complex one. Despite the common-sense intuitions of parents and teachers, research has found self-concept to be a weak predictor of children's behavioral adjustment at home or in school (Wylie, 1979). Empirical studies have found only sporadic associations between individuals' moral judgment and their social conduct (Blasi, 1983). People with similar modes of moral judgment have been observed to act quite differently in social settings. Conversely, people with disparate values may act similarly when faced with a real-life moral problem (Kohlberg & Candee, 1985). Rather than revealing direct links between judgment and conduct, the empirical relations that have been found tend to be mediated through personality systems like self-identity or through social–contextual factors like the "moral atmosphere" of the setting (Blasi, 1983; Kohlberg & Higgins, 1987; Rest, 1985).

Although the problem is far from resolved, developmental psychology has made some important contributions in defining the nature of this mediation process. Developmental theory and research have generated a number of principles underlying the judgment–conduct relationship during childhood and adolescence. These principles are helpful in understanding the critical real-life social concerns of youth today. Such concerns include prosocial engagements, such as altruism and community service, as well as anti-social ones, such as destructive risk-taking and violence.

Self-Identity as a Mediator. As noted, people who may agree with one another on general moral issues often act in divergent ways when it comes to their own live choices. One reason for this is that morality does not occupy the same position in all people's self-understanding. For some people, morality is a central part of how they define themselves, whereas for others it is much more peripheral. Differences between the centrality of morality to an individual's self-concept may be detected as early as adolescence. In one longitudinal study of self-understanding development, a small proportion of subjects held their moral beliefs to be central to their self-identities and maintained this conviction over the 4-year course of the study (Damon, 1984; Damon & Hart, 1988). The majority of subjects, in contrast, generally segregated their moral concerns from their self concerns and showed little change in this dimension even by the time of late adolescence.

There are both theoretical and empirical reasons to believe that the centrality of morality to self may be the single most powerful determiner of concordance between moral judgment and conduct (Blasi, 1984; Blasi & Oresick, 1986; Colby & Damon, 1992; Davidson & Youniss, 1991). People whose self-concept is organized around their moral beliefs are highly likely to translate those beliefs into action consistently throughout their lives (Caspi, Bem, & Elder, 1989). Such people tend to sustain a far higher level of moral commitment in their actual conduct than those who may reason well about morality but who consider it to be less pivotal for who they are. In their own verbal reports, such people often maintain that they have no choice but to actively pursue their moral commitments, as their most fundamental life goals are determined by their moral convictions. They demonstrate what has been termed a "uniting of self and morality" (Colby & Damon, 1992).

Bicausal Relations Between Judgment and Conduct.   In his pioneering study of children's marble games, Piaget introduced the counter-intuitive notion that real-life conduct may have developmental priority over moral reasoning (Piaget, 1965). Piaget's finding was that children act out conceptions of rules some years before they are able to explain them verbally. Kohlberg's research program was based on the opposite assumption that a child's moral judgment ultimately determines the child's conduct (Rest, 1983). Research findings have not favored either view, but rather have pointed to bicausal relations between judgment and conduct all through the course of development. For example, it is clear that a person's moral values influence the person's choice of a line of work; but it has also been found that certain work experiences, such as those that bring one in contact with the needy, can facilitate the growth on moral judgment (Kohlberg & Higgins, 1987). Similarly, highly moral people select colleagues and friends who share their values; but these group associations often trigger further moral growth by confronting these highly moral people with unanticipated moral problems (Colby & Damon, 1992). Again, one mediator is the individual's sense of self, because people who think of themselves primarily as moral agents are those most likely to seek social experiences that stimulate their further moral growth (Caspi, Bem, & Elder, 1989).

The Role of Developmental and Nondevelopmental Dimensions of Judgment.   In the case of anti-social behavior during youth, a special kind of maladaptive judgment often comes into play: social-cognitive distortions of others' acts and intentions. The young offender frequently attributes hostile motives to others even when they clearly do not exist (Dodge, 1985).

For example, such a child may believe that a peer has bumped into him on purpose when the other child simply was innocently brushing past him in the hallway. This kind of "hostile attribution bias" can lead a child into persistent forms of "reactive" violence (Dodge, 1989). It can also become a self-fulling prophecy, creating the very social response in others that one defensively fears (Dodge & Frame, 1982). This, in turn, confirms the violent child's suspicions, creating an "interactional continuity" that sustains the behavior in perpetuity (Caspi, Bem, & Elder, 1989). For this reason, the cycle of youthful violence becomes increasingly hard to break as the young person grows older.

Aggressive youth often devalue the feelings of others. They express little regret about causing suffering and believe that aggression is a legitimate means of getting their way (Guerra & Slaby, 1990; Slaby & Guerra, 1989). Most of all, they value control over others, placing this goal well above the more normal adolescent goal of maintaining positive relations with others (Boldizar, Perry, & Perry, 1989). They also tend to value material gain and discount the fear of punishment or condemnation.

Dodge's work has shed light on how maladaptive social-cognitive processes become translated into aggressive behavior in the peer group (Dodge, 1985). In Dodge's information-processing model, children's aggressive behavior is seen to be the outcome of a sequence of steps: (a) encoding, (b) interpretation, (c) response search, (d) response decision, (e) enactment, and (f) monitoring. Encoding refers to the cues to which the child attends in a social context. Imagine a child who has just been punched by another on the school playground. If the child focuses on the pain, or the social humiliation accompanying being hit, an aggressive response may not be forthcoming. However, if the child attends to the person doing the punching, it may increase the likelihood that the child will respond in kind.

At the second, interpretation step, the child must abstract the meaning of information obtained in Step 1. Dodge (1985) has demonstrated that hyperaggressive children are more likely than normal children to interpret the behaviors of others that result in injury to self as intentional in origin, even when the evidence for intentionality is ambiguous. Having settled on an interpretation, the child searches for an appropriate response: Should one respond with physical aggression? verbal aggression? tell an authority? Children lacking a range of adequate, nonaggressive responses are more likely to be overly aggressive than those with a wider range of options.

Next, the child must select a response, enact it, and then monitor its success. Here, too, differences emerge between overly aggressive and normal children. Highly aggressive children, in monitoring the success of an aggressive response, are likely to believe that the action was effective in achieving a goal (Perry, Perry, & Rasmussen, 1986). Furthermore, aggressive children have different value criteria for evaluating the success of an aggressive response than do normal children (Boldizar et al., 1989); aggressive children care less about the emotional pain that aggression toward others causes, and value more the sense of control over another that arises from aggression.

Gibbs (1987) has proposed that developmental factors, such as moral judgment stage, combine with nondevelopmental ones, such as social-cognitive distortion, to predispose certain youth toward violence. The egocentrism and instrumental hedonism of primitive moral reasoning constrain the young offender's ability to take the role of the victim. Moreover, the young offender has developed little appreciation of authority, the law, and other social rules. When social-cognitive distortions such as hostile attribution bias and externalization of blame are added to this moral immaturity, and when the self's main values are material and controlling in nature, the preconditions for violent conduct are set. As a means of remediating such explosive psychological processes, Gibbs and others have designed integrated programs to instruct young offenders in prosocial values, train them in empathic responding and role-taking skills, and build their self-esteem, and help them develop more veridical views of self and other (Gibbs, 1987; Guerra & Slaby, 1990). In this way, advances in children's social skills can facilitate developments both in their social cognition and in their self-understanding.

CONCLUSIONS

Because of a burgeoning of research on children's social, self, and moral concepts since the 1970s, we now have a fairly good picture of how these concepts develop in the period from infancy through adolescence. We know that infants early in life have some social awareness, some sense of their own distinctness and continuity, and some empathic feelings for others. From these foundations develop a complex of insights and beliefs about other people, the self, and the relations between them. These insights and beliefs shape children's values, which, in turn, influence children's interpersonal behavior. At the same time, the social relations that children experience, and the social communications that children receive from parents, peers, and other participants in their culture, bear a direct influence on the social, self, and moral conceptions that children are forming.

One of the most important outcomes of the recent intensive study in this area has been the realization that not all social and self conceptions develop in the same way. There are critical differences, for example, in how children understand the self versus how they understand other people. Many early social and moral conceptions bear little similarity to one another. Nor do they match general Piagetian or Kohlbergian stages. On the other hand, there clearly are interconnections among the complex of social skills and ideas that children develop. Children use their perspective-taking abilities all across the social domain; notions of authority and friendship play key parts in moral as well as social understanding; and fundamental distinctions, such as between moral and conventional events or between the physical and psychological aspects of individuals, help children organize many diverse areas of their social worlds and self identities.

A full account of social and self understanding must capture the interpenetration of many distinct cognitive and behavioral systems. In this chapter, we have discussed how social processes such as intersubjectivity, communication, and peer group formation contribute to the forging of children's social, self, and moral beliefs. Recent research has shown how, in areas as divergent as altruism and violence, social conceptions and moral values become directly translated into persistent patterns of conduct. Through it all, the understanding of self acts as a central mediator. Self-understanding determines the role of morality in one's life and, consequently, the extent to which one's moral values will determine one's everyday conduct.

REFERENCES

Adelson, J., & O'Neil, R. (1966). Growth of political ideas in adolescence: The sense of community. *Journal of Personality and Social Psychology 4*, 295–306.

Amsterdam, B. (1972). Mirror image reactions before age two. *Developmental Psychobiology, 5*, 297–305.

Bakan, D. (1966). *The duality of human existence*. Boston: Beacon Press.

Baldwin, J. M. (1902). *Social and ethical interpretations in mental life*. New York: Wiley.

Bandura, A. (1977). *Social learning theory*. Englewood Cliffs, NJ: Prentice-Hall.

Barenboim, C. (1981). The development of person perception in childhood and adolescence from behavioral consequences to psychological constructs to psychological comparisons. *Child Development, 52*, 129–144.

Baumrind, D. (1989). Rearing competent children. In W. Damon (Ed.), *Child development today and tomorrow*. San Francisco: Jossey-Bass.

Belenky, M., Clinchy, B. M. V., Goldberger, N. R., & Tarule, J. M. (1988). *Women's ways of knowing*. New York: Basic.

Berndt, T. (1985). Children's comments about their friendships. In M. Perlmutter (Ed.), *Cognitive perspectives on children's social and behavioral development: Minnesota Symposia on Child Development* (Vol. 18, pp. 189–212). Hillsdale, NJ: Lawrence Erlbaum Associates.

Berndt, T. (1989). Friendships in childhood and adolescence. In W. Damon (Ed.), *Child development today and tomorrow*. San Francisco: Jossey-Bass.

Berscheid, E. (1985). Comment on Berndt: Children's comments about their friendships. In M. Perlmutter (Ed.), *Cognitive perspectives on children's social and behavioral development:*

Minnesota Symposia on Child Development (Vol. 18, pp. 213–218). Hillsdale, NJ: Lawrence Erlbaum Associates.

Bertenthal, B., & Fischer, K. (1978). Development of self-recognition in the infant. *Developmental Psychology, 14,* 44–50.

Bigelow, B. J. (1977). Children's friendship expectations: A cognitive developmental study. *Child Development, 48,* 246–253.

Blasi, A. (1980). Bridging moral cognition and moral action: A critical review of the literature. *Psychological Bulletin, 88,* 593–637.

Blasi, A. (1983). Moral cognition and moral action: A theoretical perspective. *Developmental Review, 3,* 178–210.

Blasi, A. (1984). Moral identity: Its role in moral functioning. In W. Kurtines & J. Gewirtz (Eds.), *Morality, moral behavior, and moral development.* New York: Wiley.

Blasi, A., & Oresick, R. (1986). Emotions and cognitions in self-inconsistency. In D. Bearison & H. Zimiles (Eds.), *Thought and emotion: Developmental perspectives.* Hillsdale, NJ: Lawrence Erlbaum Associates.

Boldizar, J., Perry, D., & Perry, L. (1989). Outcome values and aggression. *Child Development, 60,* 571–579.

Bretherton, I., McNew, S., & Beeghly-Smith, M. (1981). Early person knowledge as expressed in gestural and verbal communication: When do infants acquire a "Theory of Mind"? In M. Lamb & L. Sherrod (Eds.), *Infant social cognition: Empirical and theoretical considerations* (pp. 333–373). Hillsdale, NJ: Lawrence Erlbaum Associates.

Brittain, C. (1969). A comparison of rural and urban adolescents with respect to peer versus parent compliance. *Adolescence, 13,* 59–68.

Buhler, C. (1933). The social behavior of children. In C. A. Murchison (Ed.), *A handbook of child psychology.* Worcester, MA: Clark University Press.

Butterworth, G. (1990). Self-perception in infancy. In D. Cicchetti & M. Beeghly (Eds.), *The self in transition: Infancy to adulthood* (pp. 119–138). Chicago: University of Chicago Press.

Butterworth, G., & Light, P. (Eds.). (1982). *Social cognition: Studies of the development of understanding.* Chicago: University of Chicago Press.

Campos, J. J., Campos, R., & Barrett, K. (1989). Emergent themes in the study of emotional development. *Developmental Psychology, 25,* 8–32.

Caspi, A., Bem, D., & Elder, G. (1989). Continuities and consequences of interactional styles across the life course. *Journal of Personality, 57*(2), 376–406.

Caspi, A., Elder, G., & Bem, D. (1987). Moving against the world: Life course patterns of explosive children. *Developmental Psychology, 23,* 308–313.

Chodorow, N. (1978). *The reproduction of mothering.* Berkeley: University of California Press.

Colby, A., & Damon, W. (1992). *Pathways to commitment: Moral leaders in our time.* New York: The Free Press.

Colby, A., Gibbs, J., Kohlberg, L., & Lieberman, M. (1983). A longitudinal study of moral development. *Monographs of the Society for Research in Child Development.* Chicago: University of Chicago Press.

Colby, A., & Kohlberg, L. (1987). *The measurement of moral judgment.* Cambridge: Cambridge University Press.

Costa, P. T., McCrae, R., Zonderman, A., Barbano, H., Lebowitz, B., & Larsen, D. (1986). Cross-sectional studies of personality in a national sample: 2. Stability in neuroticism, extraversion, and openness. *Psychology and Aging, 1,* 144–149.

Damon, W. (1977). *The social world of the child.* San Francisco: Jossey-Bass.

Damon, W. (1980). Patterns of change in children's social reasoning: A two-year longitudinal study. *Child Development, 53,* 831–857.

Damon, W. (1983). *Social and personality development.* New York: Norton.

Damon, W. (1984). Self-understanding and moral development from childhood to adolescence. In W. Kurtines & J. Gewirtz (Eds.), *Morality, moral behavior, and moral development.* New York: Wiley.

Damon, W. (1988). *The moral child.* New York: Free Press.

Damon, W., & Hart, D. (1982). The development of self-understanding from infancy through adolescence. *Child Development, 52,* 841–864.

Damon, W., & Hart, D. (1986). Stability and change in children's self-understanding. *Social Cognition, 4,* 102–118.

Damon, W., & Hart, D. (1988). *Self-understanding in childhood and adolescence.* New York: Cambridge University Press.

Davidson, P., & Youniss, J. (1991). Which comes first: Morality or identity? In W. Kurtines & J. Gewirtz (Eds.), *Handbook of moral behavior and development.* Hillsdale, NJ: Lawrence Erlbaum Associates.

Dodge, K. (1985). A social information processing model of social competence in children. In M. Perlmutter (Ed.), *Cognitive perspectives on children's social and behavioral development: Minnesota Symposia on Child Development* (Vol. 18, pp. 77–126). Hillsdale, NJ: Lawrence Erlbaum Associates.

Dodge, K. A., & Frame, C. L. (1982). Social cognitive biases and deficits in aggressive boys. *Child Development, 53,* 620–635.

Dunn, J. (1988). *The development of social understanding.* Cambridge, MA: Harvard University Press.

Durkheim, E. (1961). *Moral education: A study in the theory and application of the sociology of education.* New York: Free Press. (Original work published 1925)

Dweck, C., & Bempechat, J. (1983). Children's theories of intelligence: Consequences for learning. In S. Paris, G. Olsen, & H. Stevenson (Eds.), *Learning and motivation in the classroom* (pp. 239–256). New York: Academic Press.

Eisenberg, N. (1989). Empathy and sympathy. In W. Damon (Ed.), *Child development today and tomorrow.* San Francisco: Jossey-Bass.

Eisenberg, N., & Miller, P. A. (1987). The relation of empathy to prosocial and related behaviors. *Psychological Bulletin, 94,* 100–131.

Eder, R. (1989). The emergent personologist: The structure and content of 3 ½-, 5 ½-, and 7 ½-year-olds' concepts of themselves and other persons. *Child Development, 60,* 841–864.

Emde, R., & Buchsbaum, H. (1990). "Didn't you hear my mommy?": Autonomy with connectedness in moral self emergence. In D. Cicchetti & M. Beeghly (Eds.), *The self in transition: Infancy to adulthood* (pp. 35–60). Chicago: University of Chicago Press.

Erikson, E. (1980). *Identity and the life cycle.* New York: Norton.

Fagan, J. (1979). The origins of facial pattern recognition. In M. Bornstein & W. Kessen (Eds.), *Psychological development from infancy: Image to intention* (pp. 83–113). Hillsdale, NJ: Lawrence Erlbaum Associates.

Feffer, M., & Gourevitch, V. (1960). Cognitive aspects of role-taking in children. *Journal of Personality, 28,* 383–396.

Field, T., Woodson, R., Greenberg, R., & Cohen, C. (1982). Discrimination and imitation of facial expressions by neonates. *Science, 218,* 179–181.

Flavell, J., (1968). *The development of role-taking and communication skills in children.* New York: Wiley.

Freud, S. (1921). *The ego and the id.* New York: Norton.

Gallup, G. (1977). Self-recognition in primates: A comparative approach to the bidirectional properties of consciousness. *American Psychologist, 32,* 329–338.

Gibbs, J. C. (1987). Social processes in delinquency: The need to facilitate empathy as well as sociomoral reasoning. In W. Kurtines & J. Gewirtz (Eds.), *Moral development through social interaction* (pp. 301–321). New York: Wiley.

Gilligan, C. (1982). *In a different voice*. Cambridge, MA: Harvard University Press.

Gilligan, C., Hamner, T., & Lyons, N. (1990). *Making connections*. Cambridge: Harvard University Press.

Guerra, N. G., & Slaby, R. G. (1990). Cognitive mediators of aggression in adolescent offenders: 2. Intervention. *Developmental psychology, 26,* 269–277.

Hart, D. (1988). A philosophical dilemma approach to adolescent identity. *Merrill-Palmer Quarterly, 34,* 105–114.

Hart, D. (in press). *Becoming men: The development of aspirations, values and adaptational styles*. New York: Plenum.

Hart, D., & Damon, W. (1985). Contrasts between the understanding of self and an understanding of others. In R. Leahy (Ed.), *The development of self* (pp. 151–178). New York: Academic Press.

Hart, D., & Damon, W. (1986). Developmental trends in self-understanding. *Social Cognition, 4,* 388–407.

Hart, D., & Edelstein, D. (in press). The relationship of self-understanding to community type, social class, and teacher-rated intellectual and social competence. *Journal of Cross-Cultural Psychology*.

Hart, D., Kohlberg, L., & Wertsch, J. (1987). The developmental social self-theories of James Mark Baldwin and George Herbert Mead. In L. Kohlberg & R. Devries (Eds.), *Child psychology and childhood education: A structural developmental view* (pp. 223–258). New York: Longman.

Hart, D., Lucca-Irizarry, N., & Damon, W. (1986). The development of self-understanding in Puerto Rico and the United States. *Journal of Early Adolescence, 8,* 388–407.

Hart, D., Maloney, J., & Damon, W. (1987). The meaning and development of personal identity. In T. Honess & K. Yardley (Eds.), *Self and identity* (pp. 121–133). London: Routledge & Kegan Paul.

Hartup, W. (1989). Social relationships and their developmental significance. *American Psychologist, 44,* 120–126.

Higgins, E. T., Ruble, D., & Hartup, W. W. (Eds.). (1983). *Social cognition and social development: A sociocultural perspective*. New York: Cambridge University Press.

Hoffman, M. (1981). Is altruism part of human nature? *Journal of Personality and Social Psychology, 40,* 121–137.

Hoffman, M. L. (1984). Interaction of affect and cognition on empathy. In C. E. Izard, J. Kagan, & R. B. Zajonc (Eds.), *Emotions, cognition, and behavior*. Cambridge: Cambridge University Press.

Hogan, R. (1975). Moral development and personality. In D. J. DePalma & J. M. Foley (Eds.), *Moral development: Current theory and research*. Hillsdale, NJ: Lawrence Erlbaum Associates.

Holland, J. (1973). *Making vocational choices: A theory of careers*. Englewood Cliffs, NJ: Prentice-Hall.

Ianni, F. (1989). *The structure of experience*. New York: Free Press.

Inhelder, B., & Piaget, J. (1958). *The growth of logical thinking from childhood to adolescence*. New York: Basic.

James, W. (1961). *Psychology: The briefer course*. New York: Harper & Row. (Original work published 1892)

Johnson, D. (1983). Self-recognition in infants. *Infant Behavior and Development, 6,* 211–222.

Kagan, J. (1981). *The second year of life*. Cambridge: Harvard University Press.

Kagan, J. (1984). *The nature of the child*. New York: Basic Books.

Kohlberg, L. (1963). The development of children's orientations toward a moral order: I.

Sequence in the development of human thought. *Vita Human, 6,* 11–33.

Kohlberg, L. (1969). Stage and sequence: The cognitive developmental approach to socialization. In D. A. Goslin (Ed.), *Handbook of socialization theory and research.* Chicago: Rand McNally.

Kohlberg, L. (1971). From is to ought: How to commit the naturalist fallacy and get away with it in the study of moral development. In T. Mischel (Ed.), *Cognitive development and epistemology.* New York: Academic Press.

Kohlberg, L. (1986). *The psychology of moral development.* New York: Harper & Row.

Kohlberg, L., & Candee, D. (1985) The relationship of moral judgment to moral action. In W. Kurtines & J. Gewirtz (Eds.), *Morality, moral behavior, and moral development.* New York: Wiley.

Kohlberg, L., & Higgins, A. (1987). School democracy and social interaction. In W. Kurtines & J. Gewirtz (Eds.), *Moral development through social interaction* (pp. 102–131). New York: Wiley.

LeVine, R., & White, M. (1986). *Human conditions: The cultural basis of educational developments.* London: Routledge & Kegan Paul.

Levinson, D. (1978) *Seasons of a man's life.* New York: Knopf.

Levitt, M., & Hart, D. (in press). Development of self-understanding in anorectic and non-anorectic adolescent females. *Journal of Applied Developmental Psychology.*

Lewis, M., & Brooks-Gunn, J. (1979). *Social cognition and the acquisition of self.* New York: Plenum.

Livesley, W., & Bromley, D. (1973). *Person perception in childhood and adolescence.* New York: Wiley.

Loevinger, J. (1976). *Ego development: Conceptions and theories.* San Francisco: Jossey-Bass.

Lowenthal, M. F., Thurner, M., & Chiriboga, D. (1985). *Four stages of life.* San Francisco: Jossey-Bass.

Maccoby, E. (1980). *Social development: Psychological growth and the parent child relationship.* New York: Harcourt Brace Jovanovich.

Mead, G. H. (1934). *Mind, self, and society.* Chicago: University of Chicago Press.

Mednick, M. (1989). Stop the bandwagon, I want to get off: Feminist dogma and psychological research. *American psychologist, 44,* 1114–1132.

Meltzoff, A. (1990). Foundations for developing a concept of self: The role of imitation in relating self to other, and the value of social mirroring, social modeling, and self-practice in infancy. In D. Cicchetti & M. Beeghly (Eds.), *The self in transition: Infancy to adulthood* (pp. 139–164). Chicago: University of Chicago Press.

Meltzoff, A., & Moore, M. (1977). Imitation of facial and manual gestures by human neonates. *Science, 198,* 75–78.

Miller, P., & Sperry, L. (1987). The socialization of anger and aggression. *Merrill-Palmer Quarterly, 33,* 1–31.

Montemayor, R., & Eisen, M. (1977). The development of self-conceptions from childhood to adolescence. *Developmental Psychology, 13,* 314–319.

Much, N., & Shweder, R. (1978). Speaking of rules: The analysis of culture in breach. *New directions for child development, 2,* 19–39.

Mueller, N. (1989). Toddler's peer relations. In W. Damon (Ed.), *Child development today and tomorrow.* San Francisco: Jossey-Bass.

Mueller, N., & Vandell, D. (1977). Infant–infant interaction. In J. Osovsky (Ed.), *Handbook of infancy.* New York: Wiley.

Mullener, N., & Laird, J. (1971). Some developmental changes in the organization of self-evaluations. *Developmental Psychology, 5,* 233–236.

Murray, L., & Trevarthen, C. (1985). Emotional regulation of interactions between two-month-olds and their mothers. In T. Field & N. Fox (Eds.), *Social perception in infants.* Norwood, NJ: Ablex.

Mussen, P. (Ed.). (1983). *Handbook of child psychology.* New York: Wiley.

Mussen, P., & Eisenberg-Berg, N. (1977). *Roots of caring, sharing, and helping.* San Francisco: Freeman.

Neisser, U. (1988). Five kinds of self-knowledge. *Philosophical Psychology, 1,* 35–59.

Nelson, C. (1987). The recognition of facial expressions in the first two years of life: Mechanisms of development. *Child Development, 58,* 889–909.

Oliner, S., & Oliner, P. (1988). *The altruistic personality.* New York: Free Press.

Peevers, B., & Secord, P. (1973). Developmental changes in attributions of descriptive concepts to persons. *Journal of Personality and Social Psychology, 26,* 120–128.

Perry, D., Perry, L., & Rasmussen, P. (1986). Cognitive social learning mediators of aggression. *Child Development, 57,* 700–711.

Perry, W. B. (1968). *Forms of intellectual and ethical development in the college years.* New York: Holt, Rinehart & Winston.

Piaget, J. (1951). *Play, dreams, and imitation in childhood.* New York: Norton.

Piaget, J. (1965). *The moral judgment of the child.* New York: Free Press. (Original work published 1932)

Pipp, S., Fischer, K., & Jennings, S. (1987). Acquisition of self and mother knowledge in infancy. *Developmental Psychology, 23,* 86–96.

Rawls, J. (1971). *A theory of justice.* Cambridge, MA: Harvard University Press.

Rest, J. (1983). Morality. In P. H. Mussen (Series Ed.) & E. M. Hetherington (Vol. Ed.), *Handbook of child psychology: Vol. 4. Socialization, personality, and social development.* New York: Wiley.

Rest, J. (1985). The major components of morality. In W. Kurtines & J. Gewirtz (Eds.), *Morality, moral behavior, and moral development* (pp. 24–41). New York: Wiley.

Rholes, W., & Ruble, D. (1984). Children's understanding of dispositional characteristics of others. *Child Development, 55,* 550–560.

Rogoff, B. (1990). *Apprenticeship in thinking.* New York: Oxford University Press.

Ruble, D., & Higgins, E. T. (Eds). (1986). Developmental perspectives on social-cognitive theories [Special Issue]. *Social Cognition, 4,* 97–261.

Sagi, A., & Hoffman, M. L. (1976). Empathic distress in newborns. *Developmental psychology, 12,* 175–176.

Schorin, M., & Hart, D. (1988). Psychotherapeutic implications of the development of self-understanding. In S. Shirk (Ed.), *Cognitive development and child psychotherapy* (pp. 161–186). New York: Plenum.

Sears, R., Maccoby, E. E., & Levin, H. (1957). *Patterns of child rearing.* Evanston, IL: Row Peterson.

Sears, R., Rau, L., & Alpert, R. (1965). *Identification and child rearing.* Stanford, CA: Stanford University Press.

Selman, R. (1980). *The growth of interpersonal understanding.* New York: Academic Press.

Selman, R., & Schultz, L. (1990). *Making a friend in youth: Developmental theory and pair therapy.* Chicago: University of Chicago Press.

Shantz, C. (1983). Social cognition. In P. H. Mussen, J. H. Flavell, & E. M. Markman (Eds.), *Handbook of child psychology: Vol. 3. Cognitive development* (pp. 495–555). New York: Wiley.

Shweder, R., Mahapatra, M., & Miller, J. (1987). Culture and moral development. In J. Kagan & S. Lamb (Eds.), *The emergence of morality in young children.* Chicago: University of Chicago Press.

Slaby, R. G., & Guerra, N. G. (1989). Cognitive mediators of aggression in adolescent offenders: 1. Assessment. *Developmental psychology, 24,* 580–588.

Sorce, J., Emde, R., Campos, J. J., & Klinnert, M. (1985). Maternal emotional signaling: Its effects on the visual cliff behavior of 1-year-olds. *Developmental Psychology, 21,* 195–200.

Spelke, E. (1979). Perceiving bimodally specified events in infancy. *Developmental Psychology, 15,* 626–646.

Staub, E. (1978). *Positive social behavior and morality.* New York: Academic Press.

Stigler, J., Shweder, R., & Herdt, R. (Eds.). (1990). *Cultural psychology.* New York: Cambridge University Press.

Strong, E. K. (1943). *Vocational interests of men and women.* Stanford, CA: Stanford University Press.

Tronick, E. (1989). Emotions and emotional communication. *American Psychologist, 44,* 112–119.

Turiel, E. (1983). *The development of social knowledge.* New York: Cambridge University Press.

Turiel, E., Killen, M., & Helwig, C. C. (1987). Morality: Its structure, functions, and vagaries. In J. Kagan & S. Lamb (Eds.), *The emergence of moral concepts in young children* (pp. 155–244). Chicago: University of Chicago Press.

Vaillant, G. (1977). *Adaptation to life.* Boston: Little, Brown.

Veroff, J., Douvan, E., & Kulka, R. (1981). *The inner American: A self-portrait from 1957 to 1976.* New York: Basic.

Walker, L. (1984). Sex differences in the development of moral reasoning: A critical review. *Child Development, 29,* 113–124.

Whiting, B. B., & Edwards, C. (1988). *Children of different worlds.* Cambridge, MA: Harvard University Press.

Wylie, R. (1979). *The self-concept: Theory and research on selected topics* (Vol. 2). Lincoln, NE: University of Nebraska Press.

Youniss, J. (1980). *Parents and peers in social development: A Sullivan–Piaget perspective.* Chicago: University of Chicago Press.

Youniss, J., & Smollar, J. (1985). *Adolescent relations with mothers, friends, and fathers.* Chicago: University of Chicago Press.

8 Parent–Child Relationships

Michael E. Lamb
Robert D. Ketterlinus
Maria P. Fracasso
National Institute of Child Health and Human Development

INTRODUCTION

Since the emergence of psychology as a distinct discipline around the turn of the present century, all accounts of socialization and personality development have emphasized the crucial importance of parent–child relationships. In large part, this emphasis can be attributed to Freud's seminal conceptualization of the processes involved in personality development. Two aspects of his psychoanalytic theory are especially important: his emphasis on the crucial formative role of early experiences, and his description of the complex ways in which children's experiences, memories, and fantasies in early life have enduring influences on their subsequent personalities. Much of psychoanalysis involved a portrayal of the ways in which early experiences, transformed in memory by various defense mechanisms, provide a set of psychic orientations and perceptions that guide the psychological and behavioral functioning of adults. Based on his clinical work, Freud concluded that individuals come to understand the intimate links between their unconscious motivations, on the one hand, and the memories and fantasies of their early childhood, on the other, only through psychoanalytic therapy.

In his earliest writings, Freud was concerned primarily with experiences during what he called the phallic phase of development, the period between 4 and 8 years of age when unconscious and/or ill-understood sexual attractions toward the parents shaped the child's relationships with them. Gradually, however, Freud came to place increasing emphasis on events that occurred earlier in the child's life, so that in his final work, published after his death in 1939, Freud announced the dramatic and often-cited conclusion that the relationships between infants and their mothers served as prototypes for all later intimate relationships. In doing so, Freud emphasized not only the formative importance of parent–child relationships but also the ways in which their roots were laid in the earliest months of life. Much later, Freud's daughter, Anna, also a psychoanalyst, applied her father's theories about the importance of early parent–child relationships in her own work with disturbed adolescents.

In this chapter, we review the current conceptualization of parent–child relationships, summarizing research that describes the nature and impact of these relationships. In the first section we discuss normative developmental issues. We begin by describing the patterns of interaction that characterize infant–mother and infant–father relationships, discussing the processes by which infants become attached to their parents. Next, we discuss the nature of relationships between preschool and elementary school children and their parents. Finally, we describe the relationships between parents and their adolescent children, as well as the mechanisms by which these relationships are gradually transformed.

In the second section, we turn our attention from normative issues to the factors that distinguish individual parent–child relationships from one another. We focus particularly on the factors that appear to influence the adequacy or quality of the relationships established between parents and their children, as well as the implications of individual differences in the quality of parent–child relationships for subsequent child development.

Finally, in an attempt to underscore the limitations of our current knowledge and the dangers of overgeneralization, we devote the third section to a discussion of factors — parent and child gender, sociocultural and socioeconomic variations, divorce and single parenthood, and family violence — that affect the development and quality of parent–child relationships.

NORMATIVE DEVELOPMENTAL ISSUES

Infancy

The development of attachment relationships between children and parents constitutes one of the most important aspects of human social and emotional development. Although most major theories of socioemotional development have contributed to our understanding of parent–child attachment, the most popular explanation of the processes involved was provided by John Bowlby (1969). Bowlby, a psychoanalyst who was much impressed by ethological theories explaining the emotional communication between nonhuman infants and their parents, emphasized the infant's innate capacity to emit signals to which adults are biologically predisposed to respond. He began with the assumption that survival in the "environment of evolutionary adaptedness" (p. 50) depended on the infant's ability to maintain proximity to protective adults. Unlike the young of many other species, however, human infants cannot maintain proximity to adults on their own because they are not ambulatory and cannot cling to adults. Instead, human infants rely on signals (like cries and smiles) to entice adults to approach them, and their signals are effective because human adults are predisposed to respond to them. One crucial aspect of this process, called *attachment formation,* is that infants come to focus their bids for attention on a small number of familiar individuals. This focalization represents one aspect of the process of attachment formation which, Bowlby (1969) proposed, involves four phases: *indiscriminate social responsiveness* (first and second months); *discriminating sociability* (2 to 7 months); *maintenance of proximity to a discriminated figure* (Month 7 through the second year); *goal-corrected partnerships* (from Year 3 on). The first three phases are discussed next, and the fourth is discussed in the subsection on preschool children.

Phase 1: Indiscriminate Social Responsiveness. This phase is marked by the development of a repertoire of signals, of which the cry is most effective. Infant cries have a markedly arousing effect on those who hear them because adults are highly motivated to relieve the cause of a baby's distress (Frodi, Lamb, Leavitt, & Donovan, 1978; Murray, 1979), often by picking up and holding the distressed infant (Bell & Ainsworth, 1972; Korner & Thoman, 1970, 1972).

Crying is the first example of a class of behaviors labeled *attachment behaviors* by Bowlby. The defining characteristic of these behaviors is that they provide comfort and security by bringing the baby close to a protective adult. Smiling is another signal that powerfully affects adult behavior; it enters the baby's repertoire in the second month of life. However, smiles encourage adults to stay near the baby in order to prolong rewarding interactions, whereas cries encourage adults to approach in order to terminate signals that they find aversive (Ambrose, 1969; Frodi et al., 1978).

Newborns experience marked, sudden, unpredictable changes in state (levels of arousal and distress) and cannot coordinate their movements well (Thoman, 1990). Behavior becomes increasingly organized over time as neural control mechanisms develop and parental responsiveness reinforces the child's capacities (Emde & Robinson, 1979). During the first 2 months, caretakers have a major impact on the baby's state of arousal. For example, by picking up distressed infants, parents both soothe them and put them into states of alertness (Korner & Thoman, 1966, 1972). Because infants can thus feel, smell, hear, and see caretakers who are in close proximity, babies learn to associate the presence of their caretakers with alertness and the relief of distress (Lamb, 1981a; Lamb & Malkin, 1986).

Distress–relief sequences are not the only contexts in which infants interact with their parents, of course. Parents attempt to capture and maintain their infants' attention in the course of face-to-face play by moving their heads, exaggerating their facial expressions, modulating their vocal intonation, and employing a variety of temporally patterned tactile and visual behaviors (Koester, Papousek, & Papousek, 1989; Papousek & Papousek, 1989, 1991). In addition, various caretaking routines, including feeding, provide the context for social interaction. Stevenson, Roach, verHoeve, and Leavitt (1990) and Kaye (1982), for example, described elegant patterns of reciprocal interaction between mothers and infants during feeding, at which time mothers only vocalize when infants are not sucking. As babies become more vocal, furthermore, mothers act as if the baby is taking turns in conversations, pausing as long as in adult conversations, and listening for an imagined response before they respond (Stern, 1977). This systematic turn-taking alerts the infant to the basic principle of reciprocity, although as Tronick (1989) has cautioned, coordinated reciprocal interaction is not typical, and occurs quite infrequently.

Frequent interactions between caretakers and alert infants may facilitate the ability to recognize specific individuals (Lamb, 1981c). Bowlby suggested that this ability marked the transition to the second phase of attachment development, but recent studies show that infants are able to recognize their parents much earlier than Bowlby believed. For example, young infants appear able to distinguish and prefer their own mother's voice and smell from those of other mothers within the first 2 weeks of life (Cernoch & Porter, 1985; DeCasper & Fifer, 1980; Macfarlane, 1975, 1977).

Phase 2: Discriminating Sociability (2 to 7 months). Presumably because they have been associated with pleasurable experiences and the relief of distress, familiar people like parents become the people with whom the baby prefers to interact. Initially, these preferences are evident in fairly subtle ways—certain people are better able than others to soothe the baby or to elicit broad smiles and coos, for example. Parents feel enormously rewarded by this change in the baby's behavior, however, because it signifies the first obvious appreciation of their devoted efforts.

During this phase, behavior becomes increasingly coordinated, levels of arousal come to vary less, less distress is experienced, more time is spent in alert states, and interactions with adults increasingly involve play (Emde & Robinson, 1979). Although face-to-face games with parents initially appear in the first phase, they are most common, at least in Western cultures, between 3 and 6 months of age (Adamson & Bakeman, 1984; Keller,

Scholmerich, & Eibl-Eibesfeldt, 1989; Tronick, 1989). Early mother–infant face-to-face interactions often have a conversation-like pattern in which each partner appears to be responsive to the other, either by imitating or emitting a different social bid (Cohn & Tronick, 1988). Although adults assume the major responsibility for keeping interactions going (Kaye, 1979, 1982), babies are not simply passive partners in face-to-face games. For example, 2- to 3-month-olds sometimes withdraw when their mothers fail to respond normally (Cohn & Tronick, 1983; Lamb, Morrison, & Malkin, 1987). The infant's behavior in this context appears to reflect disappointment or puzzlement over the adult's failure to behave appropriately, suggesting that infants are beginning to comprehend the rules of social interaction. Because well-coordinated reciprocity is quite rare, however, these rules are learned slowly, but babies do appear to learn three things from repeated experiences of distress-relief and face-to-face play. First, they learn the rule of *reciprocity* — during social interactions, partners take turns acting and reacting. Second, babies learn *effectance*, realizing that they can affect the behavior of others in a consistent and predictable fashion. Third, babies learn *trust*, because their parents can be counted on to respond when signaled. These lessons signify major transitions in the development of coherent views of the self, of significant others, and of the social world. The degree to which babies feel confident in their predictions regarding the behavior of others — that is, the degree to which they trust or have faith in the reliability of specific people — may influence the security of their attachment relationships, a topic to which we return later.

Phase 3: Attachments (7 to 24 months).   By 6 or 7 months of age, infants have made great progress in all domains of development. Exploiting their newly acquired mobility, infants begin to take responsibility for attaining proximity to their caretakers instead of waiting for parents to respond to infant signals. Because they now understand and respect the rule of reciprocity, intentional social behavior becomes possible. Infants thus play an increasingly active role in interactions with their attachment figures, and initiate an increasing proportion of their social interactions (Green, Gustafson, & West, 1980; Lamb, 1981a, 1981c). One sign of this new social sophistication is that 7-month-olds begin to protest more reliably when their parents leave, although they can tolerate a growing distance from attachment figures as they grow older (Anderson, 1972; Rheingold & Eckerman, 1970), and become increasingly adept at interacting with peers and unfamiliar adults. Wariness of strange adults also becomes more prominent around this time (Sroufe, 1977).

According to Bowlby (1969) and Ainsworth (1979), infants become attached to those people who have been associated over time with consistent, predictable, and appropriate responses to the baby's signals and to their basic needs. The quality of interaction is also important, however, as underscored by evidence indicating that babies may become attached to both of their parents at about the same time, even though they spend much less time with their fathers than with their mothers (Lamb, 1977a, 1977c, 1981b; Lamb, Pleck, Charnov, & Levine, 1987). Obviously, there must be a minimal amount of time that individuals regularly interact with infants if attachments are to form, but, unfortunately, we do not know what this minimum level is or how it varies depending on the style or quality of interaction.

Although most babies do become attached to their fathers at around 7 months of age—the same age at which they form attachments to their mothers—the evidence suggests that mothers are the primary or preferred attachment figures of young infants, who seek out their mothers when under stress (Lamb, 1976a, 1976c). From shortly after birth, mothers and fathers offer their infants different types of experiences. During face-to-face play, fathers provide more unpredictable, less rhythmic, and more exciting (rather than calming) physical and vocal stimulation to their infants than mothers do (Yogman, 1982), and in naturalistic settings, mothers emphasize instructional play while fathers specialize in functional play (Pedersen, 1980; Stevenson, Leavitt, Thompson, & Roach, 1988). In Western as well as in some non-Western societies, furthermore, mothers hold their babies most often for caretaking purposes, whereas fathers hold their babies most often to play with them (Lamb, 1976b, 1977c; Roopnarine, Taluker, Jain, Joshi, & Srivastavi, 1990). It is not surprising, therefore, that children learn to expect playful, stimulating interactions with their fathers, and thus come to prefer playing with them (Clarke-Stewart, 1980; Lamb, 1977a, 1977c; Lynn & Cross, 1974).

In both traditional (role-sharing) and nontraditional (role-sharing or role-reversing) Swedish families (Lamb, Frodi, Frodi, & Hwang, 1982; Lamb, Frodi, Hwang, Frodi, & Stenberg, 1982), as well as traditional American families (Belsky, Gilstrap, & Rovine, 1984), parental gender appears to have a much more powerful influence than does parental role on styles of parental behavior, in that fathers and mothers tend to behave in characteristic ways. In these studies, mothers were more likely to kiss, hug, talk to, smile at, tend, or hold their infants than fathers were, regardless of their degree of involvement in caretaking. These findings contrast with those reported earlier by Field (1978) and we do not yet know the extent to which differences between maternal and paternal styles are determined by biological gender as opposed to sex-role socialization.

Summary.   Because human infants have such limited behavioral capacities at birth, social relationships with caretakers are critical to their survival, and the relationships with parents constitute a foundation for later social relationships. John Bowlby's influential theory of attachment, combining elements of psychoanalytic, cybernetic, and ethological theory, describes four phases in the development of parent–infant relationships. Infants employ a repertoire of signals (such as crying and smiling) to promote proximity to and interaction with caretakers, and as they come to recognize their parents, infants come to engage in increasingly complex interactions, from which they learn the principles of reciprocity, effectance, and trust. Infancy is characterized by the onset of language, increasingly intentional behavior, a widening social world and crystallization of parent–child attachments. In the fourth phase, which is more fully described in the next subsection, relationships between parents and children are increasingly characterized by reciprocity and trust, are more goal-directed than in previous phases, and function to facilitate children's gender-role socialization.

The Preschool Child

The years between infancy and the entry into formal educational settings are marked by dramatic developmental changes. Objects-relations theorists emphasized the process of separation-individuation by which toddlers experience an increasing desire for self-determination and a growing realization of individuality (Mahler, Pine, & Bergman, 1975). Maccoby (1984) later described seven areas of change—including physical and locomotor growth, language, impulse control, social–cognitive understanding, conception of the self, cognitive executive processes, and the desire for autonomy—that have significant effects on the nature and quality of parent–child relationships. Around their second birthday, children begin to develop a sense of autonomy and to assert control (sphincter control, saying "no"), even though they continue to require guidance and support from their parents. During the third and fourth years, growing cognitive–representational abilities facilitate increasingly complex and planful behavioral sequences. Linguistic sophistication permits children to communicate effectively and to exercise newly developed skills such as perspective-taking and self–other differentiation (Marvin, 1977; Marvin & Greenberg, 1982). By age 5, children have acquired an impressive array of social skills, engaging in fantasy-based role play and peer interactions involving clearly defined rules and expectations (Garvey & Hogan, 1973; Mueller & Lucas, 1975; Youniss, 1980). With the expansion of the child's world beyond home and family, children are challenged by new opportunities to explore and master their environment, to become more self-reliant, and to form new relationships with peers.

The transition from infancy to early childhood brings a dramatic change in the roles assumed by agents of socialization as parents recognize that physical, mental, and language development make new behavioral capacities possible and facilitate the comprehension of more complex parental instructions. Toward the end of the second year of life, for example, parents increase their efforts to shape their children's social lives by assuming an increasingly directive role, encouraging their children to behave in appropriate ways and discouraging them from inappropriate and socially proscribed behavior. Phase 4 in the development of attachment, *the goal-corrected partnership,* sees the emergence of joint planning between parent and child. Children become less egocentric, and thus come to take their parents' feelings, motives and plans into account, accommodating their parents' plans so as to achieve mutually acceptable compromises. These partnership skills may lay the foundation for negotiation in a variety of later relationships (Marvin, 1977; Marvin & Greenberg, 1982).

This phase of development is also marked by the onset of the ability to represent objects and actions symbolically and to communicate verbally. By the time the average 5- to 6-year-old enters school, he or she has an implicit understanding of most grammatical rules and has a vocabulary of several thousand words. One major implication of these developments is that parents of preschoolers, unlike parents of infants, do not have to rely on concrete rewards and punishments to shape their children's behavior. Instead, they may employ verbal rewards (encouragement, praise), demands (commands), and punishment (criticism, threats), and this increases the range of behaviors and inclinations that they can modify. For example, parents can encourage their children to engage in novel behavior, whereas they were previously limited to reinforcing or punishing behavior their children had already performed.

The ability to conceptualize symbolically facilitates another important process — observational learning. Social-learning theorists like Bandura (1969, 1977) argue that a large proportion of the behavior patterns people learn are acquired simply by observing other people. For a model's behavior to enter the observer's behavioral repertoire, however, the observer must be able to store it in memory and then recall it for subsequent performance.

Despite these important developments, children's understanding of the physical and social world remains quite immature (Piaget, 1932/1965), and the tendency to think egocentrically may have an important influence on children's sociopersonality development (Shantz, 1975). Young children implicitly assume that others perceive the social world the same way that they do. One implication is that children under about 7 years of age are deficient in the ability to empathize — the capacity to place themselves in the position of others and to infer how the others must feel (Flavell, 1963). There are, consequently, restrictions on children's abilities to assume the roles of others. In addition, the immaturity of social cognition among preschoolers imposes restraints on their interaction skills and, presumably, on the extent to which they can benefit from complex (e.g., observational) learning experiences.

In their formulations about early childhood, most theorists and researchers have concerned themselves primarily with attempts by parents to socialize their children. Behaviors that are acceptable for infants are considered inappropriate for preschoolers, who both seek and are pressured toward independence and assertiveness. Parental sensitivity and nurturance are increasingly challenged by the need to set appropriate limits while accommodating a growing sense of independence and autonomy. Most parents want their children to be independent and socially competent, but there is considerable disagreement about how these results are best achieved. Some theorists believe that social competence is a product of "self-actualization"; they assume that it will develop without any explicit efforts on the part of parents. Most parents and specialists, however, believe that parents must assume a directive role, allowing the child to express emotions fully, making important norms salient, and setting appropriate limits when necessary (Greenberg & Speltz, 1988).

Summary.   During the preschool years, children experience a myriad of developmental changes that have implications for the development of personality and parent–child relationships. During the preschool period the child's social world expands considerably. Interactions with peers and exposure to extrafamilial agents such as the media open new pathways of influence, but relationships with parents remain formatively crucial. Parents of preschoolers must adjust their parenting styles to accommodate their children's egocentrism and the genesis of their strivings for individuality and autonomy. According to Bowlby, this redefinition of parent–child relationships demands the joint construction of "goal-corrected partnerships."

The School-Aged Child

Few researchers have focused on the relationship between parents and children between 6 and 12 years of age. Most research on socialization during this phase has been concerned with the influences of peers, teachers, and educational institutions on children's adjustment. Those researchers who have examined parent–child relationships during the elementary school years have largely focused on parents' influence on achievement and achievement motivation, or on the competition between parents and peers, rather than on the association between the quality of parent–child relationships and aspects of children's socioemotional development. There is some evidence, however, that parents remain influential and affectively salient throughout this period and into adolescence.

Interactions with parents allow children to practice, rehearse, and refine skills that later facilitate interactions with peers (MacDonald & Parke, 1984; Youniss, 1980). Furthermore, by the end of middle childhood, most children rate alliances with parents as more enduring and reliable than those formed with people outside the family (Buhrmester & Furman, 1990; Furman & Buhrmester, 1985).

Due in part to advances in children's cognitive skills and abilities, school-aged children need less, and more subtle, monitoring and exert more self-control than younger children. Parental monitoring is still valuable, however Crouter, MacDermid, McHale, and Perry-Jenkins (1990) found that less well-monitored boys received lower grades than children whose parents monitored them more closely. Parents must therefore be sensitive to the changing needs of growing children, and should gradually increase their involvement in such family decisions as the allocation of responsibilities and household chores (Goodnow, 1985, 1988).

Parents adjust their demands during middle childhood in accordance with the expectation that by the time children reach adolescence they should approach adult standards of behavior. Compared with parents of younger children, for example, parents of school-aged children are less inclined to use physical coercion with their children and are more apt to appeal to their self-esteem or to their sense of humor, and seek to arouse their guilt (Maccoby, 1984). Verbal mediation of control replaces physical control and this transition affects children's behavior: When mothers rely on reasoning and suggestions, children tend to negotiate, whereas when mothers use direct maternal strategies, children tend to be defiant (Kuczynski, Kochanska, Radke-Yarrow, & Girnius-Brown, 1987).

During this phase, there are also changes in the manner in which children interact with their parents. School-aged children do not express anger toward their parents as openly and as often as they did when they were younger (Goodenough, 1931), and they are less likely to whine, yell, and hit (Patterson, 1982). In part, this is because parents of school-aged children are less concerned with promoting autonomy and establishing daily routines and more concerned with children's industriousness and achievement. Parents worry about the extent to which they should become involved in their children's school work, whether they should require children to do chores, what standards of performance they should demand, and the extent to which they should monitor their children's social life (Maccoby, 1984). Anticipatory guidance of the child, monitoring of the child's activities, expressions of affection, and parental teaching during this phase all serve to prevent behavior problems (Holden, 1985; Kuczynski, 1984; Maccoby, 1984).

According to Maccoby (1984), children are best adjusted when their parents foster *co-regulation:* cooperation and shared responsibility. Advances in cognitive development enable children to understand the legitimacy of parental authority (Damon, 1983). Based on new methods of monitoring, guiding, and supporting their children, adults use time together to reinforce children's understanding of moral standards, although there is more concern with equity and fairness in the parent–child relationship during middle childhood than there was earlier. Consequently, effective socialization increasingly involves monitoring children rather than directing them (Hetherington, 1988; Patterson & Dishion, 1988).

According to Sigmund Freud, the superego begins to become dominant in middle childhood and as a result children become preoccupied with mastering adult standards of behavior. Children thus want to meet their parents' expectations and feel distressed when they fail, although they may blame the distress on the parents or themselves. This ambiguity may mark the beginning of the intra- and interpersonal conflict that becomes prominent during adolescence (A. Freud, 1958).

Summary. Unfortunately, much less research has been conducted on parent–child relationships in the school-age period than in other developmental epochs. There is no evidence that parental influences become less significant, however. Instead, parent–child relationships continue to be recalibrated and redefined as parents become increasingly involved in monitoring, anticipatory guidance, and emotional support. Parents continue to promote emotional stability by serving as secure bases, despite the fact that their children begin to shield their emotional lives from their parents' view. Conflicts over behavioral control are replaced by a concern with achievement and industriousness, with an explicit focus on helping children make the transition to adult roles. Both parents and children play important roles in the redefinition of their relationships. According to Freud, the ascendance to prominence of the superego sets the stage for heightened interpersonal and intrapsychic conflict that continues into adolescence. As discussed next, however, recent research casts doubt on the psychoanalytic depiction of adolescence as a period of significant conflict.

Prepuberty and Adolescence

Parent–child relationships were little studied in the elementary school years in part because psychoanalysts described a period of latency following the Oedipal phase and before the emergence of genital sexuality. According to psychoanalysts, sexually charged relationships with parents become too difficult for children to handle and, as a result, behavioral manifestations of emotional attachment are suppressed.

These observations laid the ground work for recent research on qualitative and functional transformations in parent–child relationships from the prepubertal through the adolescent periods (Collins, 1990; Hauser et al.,

1987; Hill, 1988; Steinberg, 1981; Youniss & Smollar, 1985). Children shift their dependence first to same-sex and then to opposite-sex peers, and continue the processes of self-differentiation and individuation that become the major themes of development in adolescence (Coleman, 1977). The biological changes associated with puberty also foster change and promote distance between parents and children (Collins, 1990; Hill & Holmbeck, 1987; Steinberg, 1988, 1990). Among both human and nonhuman primates, the parent–child relationship is increasingly marked by self-assertion, distance, and conflict as children grow older. These developments are associated with both age and the rate of maturation. For example, Steinberg (1987) found that early maturing sons and daughters reported more conflict with their mothers than later maturing children, although these processes may take a different form and have different meaning in mother–child and father–child relationships (Collins & Russell, in press). Adolescents believe that their mothers know them better than their fathers do, and although they care about both mothers and fathers, daughters are more likely than sons to differ with parents regarding the degree of closeness (Youniss & Ketterlinus, 1987). In addition, girls who have recently experienced menarche perceive higher levels of parental control than do either pre- or postmenarchial girls (Hill, Holmbeck, Marlow, Green, & Lynch, 1985). In general, however, researchers have not been able to distinguish the effects of puberty from the effects of other age-related changes such as the transition from elementary to junior high or from junior high to high school (Collins & Russell, in press; Simmons & Blyth, 1987). Whatever their relative importance, the biological, social, and cognitive changes of puberty all make early adolescence a critical transitional period (Hamburg, 1985) during which children are expected to begin to consolidate their knowledge of the norms and roles of adult society and, at least in Western industrialized societies, to become emotionally and economically independent of their parents.

The nature of parent–adolescent relationships has been of interest to psychologists since the publication of G. Stanley Hall's classic work, *Adolescence,* in 1904. Like Freud, Hall saw adolescence as a period of *sturm und drang*—storm and stress—with vacillating mood swings that both men attributed to potent and uncontrollable physiological factors associated with puberty; Hall further argued that parents were responsible for channeling their children's disorganized energies in socially acceptable directions.

Until the mid-1970s, adolescence was viewed as a period during which parental influence was gradually usurped by the influence of the peer group as a result of intergenerational conflict over values, norms, and behavior (Coleman, 1961). Research on parent–adolescent relationships was largely influenced by psychoanalysts such as Anna Freud (1958) who believed that the biological changes associated with puberty caused emotional distress, which in turn led to rebelliousness and family conflict in the context of a second Oedipal constellation (see also Blos, 1979; Josselson, 1980; Sebald, 1977). These normative processes allegedly drove an emotional wedge between adolescents and their parents and this, in turn, was believed to facilitate the successful transition from childhood to adulthood. In fact, Anna Freud thought that adolescents who had close respectful relationships with their parents were probably at greatest risk for later psychopathology, a hypothesis that has not been supported empirically (Offer & Offer, 1975; Steinberg, 1990).

Perhaps the greatest legacy of the psychanalytic view is the notion that adolescence is typically characterized by conflict and turmoil rather than by closeness and harmony (Steinberg, 1990). Despite its popularity (e.g., Hayman, 1986) this belief remains unsubstantiated. Instead, adolescence appears to be a period during which most children make the transition to adulthood without significant ego instability (Douvan & Adelson, 1966). Large-scale surveys show that the vast majority of adolescents continue to rely on their parents for advice, support, and emotional intimacy (Maccoby & Martin, 1983; Noller & Callan, 1986; Offer, Ostrov, & Howard, 1981), suggesting that parent–adolescent relationships are marked by increasing interdependence and mutuality rather than by detachment and conflict. In one study of 2,800 adolescents, 12 to 15 years old, most of the study participants named parents and siblings as significant others, although a majority also listed at least one member of the extended family and one unrelated adult as important influences on their lives (Blyth, Hill, & Thiel, 1982).

Researchers have also studied the supposed transition from parental to peer influence intensively, often by asking adolescents to choose between two solutions to hypothetical interpersonal or behavioral dilemmas, one favored by parents and the other favored by peers. Much of this research suggests that adolescents conform differently to parental or peer standards depending on the content of the dilemma (Emmerich, 1978; Larson, 1972). For example, Brittain (1963) found that adolescent girls were more likely to choose peer-favored solutions when the dilemmas involved personal taste, but were more likely to choose parent-preferred solutions when the dilemma involved educational or occupational choices. Some researchers have reported that the adherence to peer influences follows a curvilinear age trend (Berndt, 1979; Curtis, 1975; Ketterlinus, 1987), although adolescents do not at any age routinely reject parental values in favor of peer values. Instead, peers and parents play complementary rather than competing roles in socialization (Lamb & Urberg, 1978; Youniss, 1980).

Although parent–adolescent relationships are not typically characterized by conflict and turmoil, there is a significant amount of minor but persistent conflict between parents and adolescents (Coleman, 1974, 1977; Douvan & Adelson, 1966; Hill & Holmbeck, 1987; Kandel & Lesser, 1972; Montemayor, 1983; Rutter, Graham, Chadwick, & Yule, 1976; Steinberg, 1981), which reaches a peak in mid-adolescence and then declines (Offer et al., 1981; Steinberg, 1981). It has been estimated that families with adolescent children on average argue approximately twice a week (Montemayor, 1983), but this bickering or quarreling over everyday issues is rarely severe enough to interfere with the development of healthy parent–adolescent relationships. Steinberg (1990) has estimated that conflict severe enough to yield a drastic deterioration in the quality of family relationships occurs in only about 5% to 10% of families. The types of issues that are the focus of family arguments change little from preadolescence through late adolescence (Smetana, 1989), although disputes over household responsibilities become more frequent in late adolescence, whereas disputes about academic performance peak in early adolescence with the transition to junior high school (Hamburg, 1985).

In general, parent–adolescent conflict involves bickering and quarreling about everyday issues (schoolwork, chores, quarrels with siblings, personal hygiene and grooming, activities, friends, and mundane disobedience) rather than overt confrontation over issues such as religion, politics, and career choices (Acock & Bengtson, 1978; Youniss & Smollar, 1985). Preadolescents and adolescents seldom dispute parents' authority to make rules although they do argue that parents should not impose such rules unilaterally, and should not have such low expectations of their abilities to comply (Damon, 1977; Hunter, 1984). Perhaps, therefore, family conflicts facilitate communication and adolescent autonomy by promoting open discussions of the parents' reasons and adolescents' protests over their parents' unilateral authority and demands (Youniss, 1988; Youniss & Smollar, 1985). The fact that children contest the basis of their parents' authority also suggests that parent–adolescent conflict may be interpreted differently by parents and children. Parents are more likely to offer conventional interpretations of conflict, whereas adolescents are more likely to interpret conflict in terms of personal jurisdiction (Smetana, 1983, 1988a, 1988b, 1989, in press); Youniss and Smollar (1985) likewise found that adolescents are concerned primarily with interpersonal and psychological issues.

Summary. The preadolescent period marks the beginning of the biological changes associated with puberty that parallel transformations in the quality and meaning of parent–child relationships. Self-differentiation and individuation are linked to children's growing sexuality, and initiate distance and conflict in the relationship. Unfortunately, researchers studying the transformations of relationships during this period have not yet successfully disentangled the effects of puberty and children's responses to their role transitions.

During adolescence, children are expected to consolidate and apply their knowledge about the roles and rules of adult society, to begin to achieve emotional and economic independence from parents, and to complete the biological and physical changes that began in the preadolescent period. Psychoanalysts such as Anna Freud believe that intrapsychic forces associated with a second Oedipal event, interacting with the biological changes associated with pubertal development, disrupt emotional functioning, thereby producing adolescent rebelliousness and intrafamilial strife. This view has been challenged by the results of large-scale surveys showing no widespread psychopathology among adolescents, with only about 5% to 10% of families experiencing a dramatic decline in the quality of parent–child relationships during adolescence. Contrary to the psychoanalytic view, furthermore, adolescents do not become disengaged from their parents; instead the parent–child relationship is qualitatively and functionally transformed. Some researchers have hypothesized that adolescents increasingly distance themselves from their parents, with the result that the parent–offspring relationship is increasingly marked by self-assertion and conflict over family decisions. Other researchers have suggested that parent–child relationships characterized by unilateral authority become parent–adolescent relationships marked by cooperative negotiations (mutuality), emotional closeness, and continuing parental support and influence.

INDIVIDUAL DIFFERENCES AND THEIR IMPLICATIONS

In this section, we switch focus from an analysis of normative developmental changes to a review of research concerned with the various dimensions along which parent–child relationships may vary. Our main concern is with understanding the basis of these individual differences and their implications for the quality of children's adjustment. In much of the section, therefore, we discuss research on psychological and sociological differences among parents. However, because an important dimension of individual differences may be the goodness-of-fit between the temperaments of individual children and the contexts in which they live, we first discuss temperament and its likely effects on the parent–child relationships on which we then focus.

Temperament

Interest in endogenous temperamental differences among individuals has waxed and waned throughout the history of developmental psychology.

Research on individual differences in temperament was stimulated in the late 1950s by Thomas and Chess (1977), who reacted against the widespread tendency to attribute children's maladjustment to poor parenting (particularly poor mothering), a legacy of the psychoanalytic thinking that remained prominent in clinical circles. Believing that the tendency to blame mothers for their children's ills had gone too far, Thomas and Chess undertook the New York Longitudinal Study (NYLS), in which they attempted to demonstrate that biologically based differences in temperament play a major role in children's adjustment.

Following extensive interviews with parents, Thomas and Chess described four basic temperamental styles. First, there are children whose temperament is *easy*. These children are adaptable, persistent, flexible, and of generally positive mood. Second, there are children who are *slow-to-warm-up*. These children are basically flexible and have positive moods, but take a while to adjust to changing circumstances. A third group comprises children who have *difficult* temperaments; these children are irritable, react adversely to changes in routines, and have unpredictable endogenous rhythms. The remaining children were deemed to have *average* temperaments.

In the course of the NYLS, which still continues, Thomas and Chess concluded that the major determinant of children's adjustment was the goodness-of-fit between their temperaments and the environments in which they were raised. One important characteristic of this environment is the parents' temperament. For example, slow-to-warm-up children are more likely to experience developmental problems if their parents cannot accommodate their children's style and insist on rapid adaptation. Conversely, children with difficult temperaments may avoid maladjustment if their parents adjust their own behavior and expectations to accommodate their children's temperament and behavior.

The goodness-of-fit remains important from infancy through adulthood (J. Lerner, 1984; Lerner & Lerner, 1983; Nitz, Lerner, Lerner, & Talwar, 1988), although Lerner and his colleagues have reported that an emphasis on temperament alone may often explain as much of the variance in children's development as a model that emphasizes both temperament and context (Lerner et al., 1986). In either case, endogenous characteristics may influence the quality of parent–child relationships and the course of children's development.

Consequently, researchers have begun to focus on the reciprocal processes of influence that characterize parent–infant relationships. For example, Sroufe (1985) has argued that differences in infant characteristics, such as irritability, sociability, and pleasurable responses to close physical contact, can affect children's behavior by altering the nature of the mother–infant interaction and, thus, indirectly affecting behavior in the

Strange Situation (see following). For example, infants who are less social may be considered temperamentally inhibited, may interact less with their mothers, and may thus become less securely attached, although a sensitive parent may adjust to the individual characteristics of the infant and thus abort these processes. Although sensitive parents may need to behave differently to accommodate infants who are and are not susceptible to distress, sensitively responsive parents compensate for their children's dispositions and find ways to meet their infants' basic needs.

Individual Differences in Infant-Parent Attachments

Researchers inspired by the ethological–adaptational theorists have made extensive efforts to explore the origins, characteristics, and consequences of individual differences in infant–parent attachment (e.g., Ainsworth, Blehar, Waters, & Wall, 1978; Lamb, Thompson, Gardner, & Charnov, 1985; Lamb, Thompson, Gardner, Charnov, & Estes, 1984). Instead of focusing on discrete behaviors, these researchers have concentrated on the patterned organization of attachment behavior. Individual differences in attachment behavior are usually assessed using a procedure called the *Strange Situation* (Ainsworth & Wittig, 1969; Ainsworth et al., 1978). This procedure is designed to subject 10- to 24-month-old infants to gradually increasing amounts of stress induced by the strange setting, the entrance of an unfamiliar female, and two brief separations from the parent. According to Ainsworth, stress should increase the infant's desire for proximity to and/or contact with the parent or attachment figure, thus leading to the intensification of attachment behaviors (e.g., crying, approaching, and clinging) that help infants to attain or maintain proximity or contact. As stress increases, infants should reduce their exploration and affiliation (e.g., with strangers) and increasingly organize their behavior around their parents. In particular, they should exhibit distress when separated from their parents, attempt to search for them, and greet them with bids for renewed interaction either in the form of proximity or contact-seeking or by smiling, vocalizing, and showing toys.

When American infants and parents are observed in the Strange Situation, about 65% to 70% behave in the pattern just described, which is termed the secure (or B) pattern because the infant seems to gain security and comfort from the parent to whom it turns in times of stress or alarm. The remainder display one of two types of insecure reactions. Typically, 20% to 25% behave in an avoidant (A) fashion—turning away from rather than toward the adult, especially on reunion, when one would expect proximity-seeking behaviors to be most intense. Another group, the resistant or C group, comprising 10% to 15% of most samples, consists of infants who are unable to use parents as a base for exploration even in the preseparation episodes. These infants behave in an ambivalent fashion on reunion, both seeking contact and angrily rejecting it when offered.

Ainsworth has argued that the A, B, and C patterns of attachment behavior in the Strange Situation reflect individual differences in attachment security, and she has developed hypotheses concerning the ontogeny of these individual differences. According to Ainsworth, infants learn about people from their interactions with them. When parents respond promptly and appropriately, infants develop confidence in their own effectance (ability to act on the environment successfully), and learn that parents will reliably respond to their needs in predictable ways. Adults differ in their sensitivity to infant signals and cues, however, and thus infants should differ in the extent to which they have confidence in their own effectance and in the reliability and predictability of others (Lamb, 1981a, 1981c). Ainsworth hypothesized that sensitively responsive parents, those who provide appropriate responses to their infants' vocal and distress requests, should have babies who behave in the B-type pattern, whereas A- and C-type behaviors would be exhibited by children of insensitively responsive parents (Ainsworth, Bell, & Stayton, 1974).

Subsequent to Ainsworth's groundbreaking research, many other researchers have attempted to replicate her results in their own longitudinal studies (e.g., Bates, Maslin, & Frankel, 1985; Belsky, Rovine, & Taylor, 1984; Egeland & Farber, 1984; Erickson, Sroufe, & Egeland, 1985; Grossmann, Grossmann, Spangler, Suess, & Unzner, 1985; Miyake, Chen, & Campos, 1985; Sagi et al., 1985). After reviewing the results of these studies, Lamb and colleagues (1985) concluded that, at least when studies were conducted in the United States, nurturant, attentive, nonrestrictive parental care was associated with Type B behavior in the Strange Situation. More recent studies have also noted positive relationships between maternal responsivity and Type B behavior in the Strange Situation (Bohlin, Hagekull, Germer, Andersson, & Lindberg, 1989; Frankel & Bates, 1990; Isabella & Belsky, 1990; Isabella, Belsky, & von Eye, 1989; Lewis & Feiring, 1989; Schaefer, 1989; Smith & Pederson, 1988), whereas mothers of infants who exhibit Type A or Type C behavior in the Strange Situation manifest less socially desirable patterns of behavior, including over or understimulation, noncontingent responding, or rejection. Unfortunately, there is too much variability in the results both within and across these studies to identify precisely what aspects of parental behavior are most formatively important. For example, some studies identify warmth but not sensitivity, some level of stimulation, some patterning of stimulation but not warmth or amount of stimulation, and so forth.

The notion that Strange Situation behavior reflects the quality of parent–child relationships was initially supported by research showing remarkable stability over time in patterns of infant behavior (Connell, 1976;

Waters, 1978). For example, Waters (1978) reported that 48 out of 50 infants obtained the same classification at 12 and 18 months of age. However, test–retest reliability is not always as high. Vaughn, Egeland, Sroufe, and Waters (1979), for example, found that about 40% of the infants from economically disadvantaged families changed attachment classifications between 12 and 18 months of age, and, in another study, Thompson, Lamb, and Estes (1982) reported that attachment classifications were quite unstable in a middle-class sample. As major changes in family circumstances or caretaking arrangements accounted for changes in Strange Situation behavior in both studies, these results suggest that changes in the amount of stress experienced by mothers may have affected their sensitivity to infant cues (Thompson & Lamb, 1986). More recently, Easterbrooks and Goldberg (1990) have reported that changes in maternal work patterns that involve changes in the amount of interaction with mothers and other caretakers were associated with changes in Strange Situation behavior, and that stable childcare arrangements promoted greater ego resiliency among kindergartners who were securely attached to their mothers in infancy. In addition, changes in caretaking arrangements had an adverse effect on children who had been securely attached but had a positive effect on children who had been insecurely attached. It is interesting that the least adaptive behavior was manifested by those children who remained in stable care environments and had been insecurely attached to their mothers.

Developmental psychologists are also interested in attachment classifications because they are believed to predict aspects of children's future behavior. For example, Type B infants appear to be more cooperatively playful and more sociable when interacting with both their mothers and friendly adult strangers than Type A or Type C infants (Main, 1983; Main & Weston, 1981; Roggman, 1987; Thompson & Lamb, 1983; Zaslow, Rabinovich, Suwalsky, & Klein, 1988). Furthermore, Strange Situation behavior is associated with the frequency and quality of interactions with peers such that Type B infants engage in more frequent and more mature forms of interaction with their peers, share more, and are better able to initiate and maintain interactions (Easterbrooks & Lamb, 1979; Pastor, 1981; Sroufe, 1983; Waters, Wippman, & Sroufe, 1979). Several researchers have not replicated these results, however, suggesting that the relation between attachment classification and peer competence is neither direct nor powerful (Jacobson & Wille, 1984, 1986; Jacobson, Wille, Tianen, & Aytch, 1983). Other researchers have reported that when kindergarten-aged children are placed in cognitively challenging situations, those who were classified as Type B in infancy persisted longer and more enthusiastically than did those who were classified as Type A or Type C in infancy (Arend, Gove, & Sroufe, 1979; Matas, Arend, & Sroufe, 1978; Sroufe, 1983). In addition, Type B infants were more compliant, exhibited more self-control, and appeared to be more focused on the task and tried to perform better than either Type A or Type C infants (Bates et al., 1985; Buss & van IJzendoorn, 1988; Frankel & Bates, 1990; Londerville & Main, 1981). Finally, Type B infants appear more socially competent and independent in preschool (Sroufe, 1983; Sroufe, Schork, Motti, Lawroski, & LaFreniere, 1984), they show fewer behavior problems (Bates et al., 1985; Erikson et al., 1985; Lewis, Feiring, McGuffog, & Jaskir, 1984), and they appear to be more emotionally resilient when stressed or challenged in a variety of situations (Block & Block, 1980). Children who were securely attached to both parents may be more trusting and open with strangers by the time they reach kindergarten and first grade (Weston & Richardson, 1985).

The long-term predictive validity of the Strange Situation procedure is far from perfect, however. In fact, the relation between Strange Situation behavior in infancy and subsequent child behavior is found only when there is stability in caretaking arrangements, family circumstances, and patterns of parent–child interaction (Lamb, Thompson et al., 1984, 1985). This raises a question: Are predictions over time attributable to individual differences in the quality of early parent–child interaction, or is stability in the quality of parent–child interaction more important? Unfortunately, this question has not received much attention, so no definitive conclusion is possible.

Internal Working Models.   Although most of the research on parent–child attachments has concentrated on relationships between parents and their infants, developmentalists have recently sought to examine the nature and function of parent–toddler and parent–adolescent attachment relationships on the assumption that parent–child relationships continue to develop and change in ways that require continued coordination and integration as individuals adapt to their changing environments (see Collins & Russell, in press; Greenberg, Cicchetti, & Cummings, 1990; Sroufe, 1988). In much of this research it has been assumed that, in the course of early interactions, infants and young children construct internal working models of relationships that guide their behavior in later relationships (Bowlby, 1973; Bretherton, 1985, 1990; Main, Kaplan, & Cassidy, 1985). Bowlby (1973) suggested that although internal working models continue to be formed during and after early childhood, maintaining continuity in individual developmental pathways, there exists wide variation across individuals in the degree to which working models reflect the individual's own experiences, as well as their cognitive, linguistic, and behavioral skills.

Internal working models represent children's conceptions of attachment figures as reflected in their interactions and in the feedback they receive from their parents. Working models influence overt demonstrations of attachment behavior as children grow older, but attachment behavior becomes more subtle with age because older children are more capable of evaluating the intentions, motives, and behaviors of attachment figures (Bretherton, 1985).

Researchers have recently begun to examine the relation between individual differences in the working models of the self and parent and qualitative differences in the behavior manifest in contexts like the Strange Situation. Main et al. (1985) suggested that emotional openness in discussing imagined parent–child separations and conversations with parents reflected aspects of children's mental representations of their relationship with their parents. Specifically, those children who were securely attached at 12 months were coherent, elaborate, emotionally open, and coped constructively at 6 years of age, whereas those children who were insecurely attached at 12 months, produced sad responses, were completely silent, or provided irrational or bizarre reactions. Slough (1988) reported similar results. Using a story completion task, furthermore, Cassidy (1988) found that children who behaved securely on reunion with their mothers represented themselves positively in an interview and were better able to acknowledge less-than-perfect aspects of the self than children who behaved insecurely. Main and her colleagues have also developed the adult attachment interview (AAI) to assess adults' ability to integrate early memories of their relationships with parents into overarching working models of relationships. According to Main, these working models fall into one of three categories: *secure* (respondents who appear free to evaluate their early attachment relationships), *dismissive* of their attachment relationships, or *preoccupied* with their attachment relationships. Kobak and Sceery (1988) subsequently studied the affective and representational correlates of these three attachment patterns in late adolescence. Adolescents in the secure group were rated as more ego resilient, less anxious, and less hostile by their peers. They also reported little distress and high levels of social support, whereas adolescents in the dismissing group were rated low on ego resilience and high on hostility by their peers, and reported more distant relationships with others. Compared to these two groups, adolescents in the preoccupied group were viewed as less ego resilient and more anxious by their peers, and they reported higher levels of personal distress and family support than those in the dismissing group. Steinberg (1990) hypothesized that securely attached adolescents may be more likely than dismissed or preoccupied adolescents to renegotiate healthy relationships with their parents successfully. Hypotheses of this sort are likely to play a major role in research on parent–adolescent relationships in the future.

Summary.   These studies on the association between individual internal working models and parent–child relationships clearly demonstrate that secure children, adolescents, and adults see attachment figures as well as the self as primarily good, but not perfect; are able to communicate with ease; and tend to be flexible in interpersonal conduct, to express empathy for others, and to discuss attachment relationships coherently without idealizing them.

Closeness and Conflict

Although most adolescents report generally positive, close, and conflict-free relationships with both of their parents (Collins & Russell, in press; Youniss & Ketterlinus, 1987), individual differences may be important. Compared with adolescents who are not close to their parents, for example, adolescents who report close relationships seem more competent and better adjusted than their peers (Maccoby & Martin, 1983; Steinberg & Silverberg, 1986) and are less likely than their peers to exhibit problem behaviors (Barnes, 1984; Hirschi, 1969; Jessor & Jessor, 1977).

Three factors appear to influence the intensity of parent–adolescent conflict: parental characteristics, adolescent characteristics, and family system characteristics. Conflict is heightened when parents have trouble learning how to relate to and manage their adolescent children (Burr, Reige, Day, & Constantine, 1979; Montemayor, 1982a). Thus, adolescents who report high levels of conflict say that their parents do not understand them, often scold or nag them, use harsh and restrictive disciplinary techniques, and abuse them (Duncan, 1978; Libbey & Bybee, 1979; Nye, 1958; Straus, Gelles, & Steinmetz, 1980). Conflict is also related to a wide range of adolescent characteristics including low self-esteem (Bachman, 1970), school failure (Bachman, Green, & Wirtanen, 1971), psychiatric disorder (Rutter et al., 1976), and illicit drug use (Kandel, Kessler, & Marguiles, 1978), but not the degree to which adolescents spend time alone rather than with peers (Montemayer, 1982b). Furthermore, family conflict may be greater between firstborns and their parents than between later-borns and their parents (Hill, 1988), as well as within families experiencing such stresses, as those associated with parental separation, divorce, and remarriage (Furstenberg, 1990; Montemayor, 1986; Steinberg, 1990). The mechanisms are not clear, however (Furstenberg, 1990; Uhlenberg & Eggebeen, 1986; Youniss, 1988).

The affective cohesiveness of the family is also associated with the level of conflict. Collins (1990) found that heightened conflict occurs when parents' and adolescents' expectations are highly discordant and there is little emotional closeness between parents and children (Youniss & Smollar, 1985). Finally, intense parent–adolescent conflict has been related to parents' mid-life identity crises (particularly among women) and decreased sense of well-being (Silverberg & Steinberg, 1987).

Summary. Because attempts to develop models of parent–child and parent–adolescent attachment relationships are relatively new, it is difficult to evaluate their success in describing and explaining individual differences in the nature and quality of parent–child and parent–adolescent relationships. Much of the research on internal working models is problematic because of the reliance on retrospective accounts of early relationships, and because validating external correlates are seldom assessed. Research on the affective components of parent–adolescent relationships has had a much longer history and a greater impact, although operational definitions of closeness and affection remain elusive. Most common is research on parent–adolescent conflict, which suggests that individual differences in parent–adolescent conflict may be related to characteristics of both individuals and family systems. Because all of the available evidence is correlational, however, questions of causality cannot be addressed adequately.

Parental Disciplinary Styles

Over the last three decades, Diana Baumrind and her colleagues have conducted research aimed at determining whether or not specific child-rearing patterns are associated with particular child outcomes (Baumrind, 1967, 1971, 1973, 1975, 1991; Baumrind & Black, 1967; Lamb & Baumrind, 1978). Baumrind's goal was to extend the work of those researchers who concluded that parents could extinguish their children's undesirable behavior through punitive discipline (e.g., Aronfreed, 1968; Parke, 1975; Patterson, 1975) by attempting to determine whether or not parents' disciplinary styles have a discernible impact not only on their children's current behavior, but also on future behavior in a variety of settings. Her initial assumption was that most parents, regardless of their parenting ideology, desire socially or instrumentally competent children—that is, children who are self-assertive, friendly with peers, and unintrusive with adults—and that the "best" parenting style would produce such children. Baumrind further hypothesized that individual differences among children could best be accounted for by differences in patterns of parental behavior, rather than by variations in the children's innate temperament or personality.

Baumrind assessed patterns of parental behavior using lengthy interviews, standardized test instruments, and observations of parent–child interactions at home. Preschool-aged children were observed in nursery schools, and reports of their behavior and personality styles were obtained from teachers and parents. Baumrind and her colleagues distinguished four patterns of parenting, which they labeled *authoritarian, authoritative, permissive,* and *nonconformist.* According to Baumrind, "the Authoritarian parent values obedience as a virtue and favors punitive forceful measures to curb self-will . . . [the parent believes] that the child should accept the parent's word for what is right" (Baumrind, 1972b, p. 179). Baumrind characterized permissive parents as those who believed that parents should "behave in an affirmative, acceptant, and benign manner" (Baumrind, 1972b, p. 179), that is, they should be available as a resource, rather than as active socializers who allow their children freedom of movement and expression. Nonconformist parents were also opposed to authority although they were "less passive and exerted more control than Permissive parents" (Baumrind, 1975, p. 14). Between the extreme patterns of authoritarian and permissive child rearing, a more moderate approach was observed in a group of parents whose behavior was described as authoritative. These parents were notable for their "attempts to direct the child's activities in a rational issue-oriented manner" (Baumrind, 1972b, p. 177); that is, they encouraged independence while also valuing conformity to cultural norms.

Baumrind assumed that these parenting styles were based, in part, on variations in parents' sensitivity to their children's maturational and developmental level. According to Baumrind, neither authoritarian nor permissive parents realistically evaluated their children's competencies.

> Both Authoritarian and Permissive parents saw their child as dominated by egotistic and primitive forces. . . . Few parents from either pattern took very much into account, on the one hand, the child's stage-appropriate desire to be good and to conform to parental expectations nor, on the other hand, the child's impulsivity and use of concrete reasoning which often interfered with his efforts to behave maturely. Thus, these parents appeared to construct a fiction about what their child was like and relate to that fiction. (Baumrind, 1973, p. 42)

Despite divergent child-rearing philosophies and practices, authoritarian and permissive parents are similar in that neither provide their children with opportunities to be effective agents in their own socialization. Authoritarian parents, for example, strictly require that their children conform to their expectations, whereas permissive parents place too few constraints on their children's behavior, but, in both cases, parents fail to provide their children with opportunities to experience rational, issue-oriented, cooperative interactions. Conversely, authoritative parents are sensitive to and facilitate their children's changing sense of self. Furthermore, by allowing themselves to learn from their children, authoritative parents become more effective socializers themselves and teach their children, as authoritarian and permissive parents do not, that social competence emerges within a context of interpersonal give-and-take.

Studying the association between child-rearing patterns and children's social competence, Baumrind found that daughters of authoritative parents tended to be socially responsible, as well as independent, whereas sons, though socially responsible, were no more independent than average. Both permissive and authoritarian styles were associated with less achievement orientation and independence in girls and more hostility in boys. Daughters of nonconformist parents resembled daughters of authoritarian and permissive parents, whereas sons of nonconformists were significantly more independent and achievement oriented. Baumrind (1970) has speculated that the similarity between the children of permissive and authoritarian parents is due to the fact that both types of parents tend to protect their children from stress, thus inhibiting the development of assertiveness and frustration tolerance. Authoritative parents, by contrast, value self-assertion, willfulness, and independence, and foster these goals by assuming active and rational parental roles. Typically, the children of authoritative parents are socially responsible because their parents clearly communicate realistic demands that are intellectually stimulating as well as moderately tension producing (Baumrind, 1967, 1972c).

Many of Baumrind's conclusions have been supported by other researchers. In an observational study of 2 ½-year-old children, for example, Lytton and Zwirner (1975) found that compliance with immediate parental demands was maximized by power-assertive techniques involving physical control, punishment, and commands, whereas compliance occurred less frequently following positive action or reasoning. Furthermore, there was a significant correlation between the probability of compliance with parental rules and evidence of compliance with internalized rules, suggesting that these toddlers behaved appropriately even when there was no direct instruction to do so. These findings support Baumrind's claims about the effectiveness of authoritative practices, although the finding that reasoning strategies were not effective suggests that before the later preschool years children have not acquired the cognitive skills necessary to understand them. On the other hand, Hoffman (1970) reported that inductive disciplinary techniques enhance the internalization of social rules and thus encourage socially competent moral behavior more effectively than power-assertive techniques. Inductive techniques involve withdrawal of love or explanations of the effects that personal misbehavior may have on others, whereas power-assertive techniques constitute commands and the verbal or physical punishment of misbehavior. Because Hoffman's subjects were mostly elementary school children rather than preschoolers, his findings, viewed in the context of Baumrind's and Lytton and Zwirner's results, suggest that appropriate child-rearing practices may change as children grow older.

Contrary to what permissive parents in her studies believed, Baumrind found that firm control did not inhibit social maturity and independence, provided that it was part of a pattern in which individuality, independence, arbitrariness, and restrictiveness (authoritarianism) were not associated with instrumental competence. In addition, children of parents who were passively permissive and overprotective exhibited heightened dependence, a finding that is consistent with those of several other studies. Independence and achievement motivation, for example, appear to be facilitated by the parents' rejection of dependent behavior (Crandall, 1972; Rosen & D'Andrade, 1959) and their reliance on disciplinary practices that might be described as coercive (Hoffman, Rosen, & Lippitt, 1960). Some degree of parental rejection and punitiveness may be especially important for girls whose parents tend to overemphasize nurturing and supportive behavior.

What does this imply about the effectiveness of punishment? Although many parents, particularly White, middle-class parents, prefer not to punish their children, negative sanctions — often involving corporal punishment — are employed by almost all parents. Baumrind has shown that parents of instrumentally competent children frequently punish their children. Even authoritative parents (who were most effective) included corporal punishment and other negative sanctions in their repertoires of disciplinary practices. Clearly, punishment is an effective means of controlling children's behavior, given that (a) it occurs shortly after the transgression, (b) it is consistently applied, and (c) it is coupled with indications of what behaviors would be more appropriate (see Aronfreed, 1968). Conversely, punishment that is inconsistently applied in the context of a repressive or hostile relationship may result in antisocial aggression (Hetherington, Stouwie, & Ridberg, 1971), as well as passivity, dependence, and withdrawal (Kagan & Moss, 1962). By the same token, parental warmth is not beneficial in the absence of firm control (Baumrind, 1975).

Baumrind (1991) has recently attempted to define parental styles among the parents of adolescents and to examine their influences on older children's development and performance. Based on previous research, Baumrind defined four dimensions of parental behavior, and then used scores on these dimensions in order to define seven types of parents. The first of these dimensions is called *directive* or *conventional control,* characterized by restrictive control and conventional values. The second dimension, *assertive control,* is characterized by firm nonrestrictive monitoring and a willingness to tolerate confrontation in order to enforce rules. The third dimension, *supportive control,* is defined by consideration, responsive discipline, the principled use of rational explanation, the provision of intellectual stimulation, and the encouragement of adolescent individuation (as reflected by autonomy or independence in the context of continued emotional closeness to parents; see Grotevant & Cooper, 1986).

The fourth dimension, *intrusiveness,* was defined by officiousness, over-control, and subversion of children's independence.

Based on the scores assigned to parents on these four dimensions, Baumrind then defined seven parenting styles: *Authoritative* parents had high scores on assertive control as well as high scores on supportive control; *democratic* parents had medium scores on assertive control, scored high on supportive control and not high on directive conventional control; *good enough* parents obtained medium-high to medium-low scores on assertive control, supportive control, and directive conventional control; *non-directive* parents obtained low scores on both directive conventional control and assertive control, and medium-high to high scores on supportive control; *unengaged* parents obtained low to medium-low scores on both supportive control and assertive control; *directive authoritarian* parents obtained high to medium-high scores on intrusiveness, medium to high scores on directive conventional control and assertive control, and relatively high scores on supportive control; and *directive non-authoritarian* parents had medium scores on intrusiveness, medium to high scores on directive conventional control, and assertive control, and medium to low scores on supportive control.

Having characterized parents in this fashion, Baumrind (1991) then assessed adolescents' adjustment and concluded that:

> adolescents' developmental progress is held back by directive, officious, or unengaged practices and facilitated by reciprocal, balanced interactions characteristic of both Authoritative and Democratic parents. Directive parents who are authoritarian generate internalizing problem behaviors and are less successful at curtailing drug use. Directive parents who are not authoritarian effectively promote positive competence. (p. 753)

In another study, Dornbusch, Ritter, Leiderman, Roberts, and Fraleigh (1987) found that adolescents with authoritative parents had higher grades in school than adolescents whose parents were rated authoritarian or permissive. The relationship between parental styles and school performance, however, may be mediated by adolescent psychosocial maturity, work orientations, and socioemotional adjustment (Steinberg, Elmen, & Mounts, 1989; Wentzel, Feldman, & Weinberger, in press).

Johnson, Shulman, and Collins (in press) have also defined dimensions of parental styles and related them to adolescent adjustment. Students in 5th, 8th, and 11th grade completed Schaefer's Child Report of Parental Behavior Inventory (CRPBI; Schaefer, 1965), and data were collected on their self-esteem, school adaptation, and school achievement. Four patterns of parenting were defined on the basis of factor analysis of the CRPBI scores: *authoritative; permissive; incongruent-mother authoritarian or rejecting; and incongruent-father authoritarian or rejecting.* As children grew older, their parents were less likely to be rated as authoritative and increasingly likely to report different maternal and paternal styles. Incongruent parenting adversely affected children's self-esteem, school adaptation, and school achievement, suggesting that it may be inappropriate to use a single category to represent the styles of both parents in a family.

Summary. The validity and utility of Baumrind's description of four basic parental disciplinary styles has been well established. Baumrind and others have demonstrated that an authoritative parenting style facilitates the socialization of children in middle-class American two-parent families. Although authoritative parents foster a sense of independence in their children, they also inculcate a value system characterized by conformity to cultural and societal norms by balancing the use of both reasoning and punishment. Parents of adolescents tend to use increasingly complex variations of these basic patterns when faced with the unique challenges and changes characteristic of the adolescent period. Mothers and fathers do not necessarily have similar parenting styles, and these discrepancies may have as important an influence on children's and adolescents' adjustment as does the type of parenting style.

OTHER ISSUES IN PARENT–CHILD RELATIONSHIPS

Gender Differences

Gender has a pervasive influence on parent–child interaction. From the day their children are born, parents tend to perceive sex-stereotyped proclivities in their babies. For example, parents (especially fathers) describe their sons with terms like "sturdy," "handsome," and "strong," and their daughters with terms like "dainty," "pretty," and "fragile" (Rubin, Provenzano, & Luria, 1974). John and Sandra Condry (1976) even found that the behavior of the same infant in the same videotape was described differently depending on whether raters thought the child was a girl or a boy: When the child was identified as John, "he" was perceived as inquisitive and adventurous, whereas when the child in the same film was identified as Mary, "she" was considered fearful and anxious.

Regardless of whether innate sex differences exist, however, there are only a few differences in the ways in which boys and girls are treated by their parents during the first year of life, although from birth on fathers interact preferentially with sons and mothers with daughters (Parke &

O'Leary, 1976; Parke & Sawin, 1980). From the beginning of the second year of life, however, parents become increasingly concerned about the gender appropriateness of their infants' behavior. This sudden concern is most clearly observed in the behavior of fathers, who sharply increase the amount of interaction they have with their sons (Lamb, 1977b; Rendina & Dickerscheid, 1976). During the second year, fathers become increasingly involved with their sons — fathers, for example, play more games with sons than with daughters (Fagot, 1974; Parke, 1979) — whereas mothers, who generally do not differentiate between male and female infants in this fashion, encourage independence and discourage affection in their sons (Clarke-Stewart & Hevey, 1981; Huston, 1983). Whatever their motivations for treating boys and girls differently, there is ample evidence that fathers continue to spend more time with their sons than with their daughters and engage in a greater variety of activities with their sons (Lamb, 1986; Lamb et al., 1987). These different modes of interaction are apparently evident to infants. At 12 months, few infants have established clear and consistent preferences for either parent, whereas by 24 months of age, eight of nine male infants in one intensive longitudinal study had developed preferences for their fathers (Lamb, 1977b). The establishment of preferences for the same-sex parent — especially in boys — may play an important role in the acquisition of gender identity, even in infancy.

Recently, researchers have also described some interesting differences in the ways in which mothers and fathers relate to their male and female adolescents (Collins & Russell, in press; Steinberg, 1987, 1990). In their review, Collins and Russell summarized research on gender differences during the transition from middle childhood to adolescence in dual parent middle-class families. They focused on three dimensions of parent–child relationships: *interactions* (measured by frequency, extent, and structure), *affect* (indexed by the degree of positive affect, closeness, and cohesion), and *cognition* (indexed by discrepancies between parents' and children's perceptions of their relationships).

As in infancy, mothers engage in more frequent interaction with children in middle childhood and adolescence (especially interactions involving caretaking and routine family tasks) than fathers do: Most father–child interactions involve play, recreation, and goal-oriented actions and tasks (Montemayor & Brownlee, 1987; Russell & Russell, 1987). Mothers and fathers are equivalently involved in activities related to their children's scholastic and extracurricular performance and achievement (Youniss & Smollar, 1985), however, and both parents frequently engage in nurturant caretaking in middle childhood (Russell & Russell, 1987). In most interactional domains, in fact, the differences between mothers and fathers are neither as large nor as consistent as many theorists believe.

Although distance between parents and children generally increases around puberty, distancing takes different forms in mother–child and father–child relationships, so that pubertal children perceived fathers as less assertive, less emotionally expressive, less knowledgeable about their adolescents' lives, and less approachable than mothers (Barnes & Olson, 1985; Youniss & Ketterlinus, 1987). At this time, mothers, but not fathers, report less satisfaction and increased concern over identity issues (Silverberg, 1989). As Collins and Russell point out, however, most researchers have employed cross-sectional designs, and have failed to take into account potential confounds such as the fact that many parents might have been dealing with their own mid-life crises at the same time that their children were dealing with puberty and the transition to adolescence. Finally, some research suggests that the degree of discrepancy between parents' perceptions of their children and children's perceptions of their parents tends to increase with age, especially in father–child dyads (Collins, 1990).

In a number of recent studies, dyadic and systemic aspects of parent-adolescent relationships were examined instead of individuals (Steinberg, 1990). These studies have shown that mothers tend to engage in more shared activities with daughters than with sons, although both relations are marked by relatively high levels of both closeness and discord. Fathers, by contrast, tend to be more engaged with their sons, have little contact with daughters, and generally have more distant relationships with their children than mothers do (Montemayor & Brownlee, 1987; Youniss & Ketterlinus, 1987). In an observational study, Gjerde (1986) found that mother–son interactions were less stormy when fathers were present than when mothers and sons were observed alone, whereas father–son interactions were of poorer quality in the triadic than in the dyadic setting.

In another study, Noller and Callan (1988) videotaped 41 mother–father-adolescent triads discussing the adolescents' behavior and then had trained observers, the interactants, and members of other mother–father–child triads rate the degree of anxiety, dominance, involvement, and friendliness shown by each of the interactants. The ratings made by the experts were very similar to those made by members of other families. Interactants rated other members of their families more negatively than they rated themselves, although the ratings by participant and nonparticipant parents were more divergent than ratings by adolescents who were and were not involved. Both Gjerde's and Noller and Callan's studies illustrate innovative techniques for studying parent–adolescent relationships.

Summary.   From birth, boys and girls are treated differently by their mothers and fathers, who hold deep-seated attitudes and beliefs about gender roles and inherent sex differences in abilities and propensities. In addition to parents, peers, the media, and society at large also direct the course of gender-role socialization, particularly during the period spanning puberty and late adolescence, making it difficult to distinguish the formative roles of parents and these other socializers. During this period, the distance between parents and children grows, although relationships between fathers and daughters are affected most adversely, whereas relationships between mothers and children take on increased importance. Most researchers have attributed these changes in the nature of parent–adolescent relationships to the increasing involvement with peers. Like the other research on parent–adolescent relationships, however, research on gender differences has been conducted primarily in middle-class, two-parent families. In the next two subsections, we examine the effects of sociocultural and family structure differences on the nature and quality of parent–child relationships.

Sociocultural and Cross-Cultural Differences

Despite the multicultural nature of contemporary society, most information on the socioemotional development of children has been derived from studies of White, middle-class Americans. Ethnocentricity in developmental psychology has limited the generalizability and universality of developmental principles and norms, while restricting our understanding of the variations in human behavior and experiences across cultures and subcultures. By the mid-1990s, more than 30% of all young Americans will be from minority groups. African-Americans make up an increasing proportion of the total population of young people, while the numbers of Hispanic youths and of children born to immigrants are growing rapidly. In addition, children in the United States are increasingly likely to grow up in poverty, which presumably has important effects on the nature and quality of parent–child relationships. Conditions of family hardship, for example, are associated with less responsive, patient, and nurturant parental behavior toward children and adolescents (Lempers, Clark-Lempers, & Simons, 1989) and these changes in parenting quality can accentuate normative processes and patterns of influence (Elder, Van Nguyen, & Caspi, 1985; Flanagan, 1990; Steinberg & Silverberg, 1986). Research on diverse cultural groups can enhance our knowledge of the association between differing experiences and developmental outcomes. Consequently, there have been increasing demands by social scientists to include culture and cultural experiences as critical variables in research on human development.

In fact, some of the most provocative work on Strange Situation behavior has been conducted outside the United States. As shown in Table 8.1, the distribution of infants across the A–B–C categories in many other countries differs from that typically found in American samples, suggesting that factors other than the quality of parental behavior may account for variations in Strange Situation behavior (Campos, Barrett, Lamb, Gold-

TABLE 8.1
Distribution of Infants across Attachment Types (in Percentages)

Country	Reference	A	B	C
United States	Ainsworth et al. (1978)	20	65	13
Japan	Miyake et al. (1985) and			
	unpublished data	0	77	23
West Germany	Grossmann et al. (1981)			
	unpublished data	46	43	8
Israel	Sagi et al. (1985)	8	55	33
Netherlands	van IJzendoorn et al. (1984)	24	72	4
Sweden	Lamb et al. (1982)	22	76	4
Puerto Ricans and Dominicans in USA	Fracasso et al. (1987)	30	50	20

smith, & Stenberg, 1983; Lamb et al., 1985; see also Cole, Chap. 13, this volume). For example, the high degrees of stress manifested by Japanese and Kibbutz-reared Israeli babies in the Strange Situation may have led to increases in the proportion of infants classified as Type C. Japanese infants appear inordinately distressed because they have much less experience with separations from their mothers than do American infants, whereas infants growing up on Israeli kibbutzim do not experience many encounters with strangers, resulting in expressions of great distress in the Strange Situation. Therefore, even though the procedure is structurally the same for Japanese, Israeli, and American infants, the procedure appears to have very different psychological meaning for infants from each culture. In addition, Miyake et al. (1985) reported that Japanese infants who were classified as Type C were temperamentally more irritable than Type B infants from birth. Therefore, it appears that culture-specific rearing practices and/or temperamental differences account for at least some of the variance in Strange Situation classifications across cultures. More recently, research has been conducted on Hispanics living within the United States (Fracasso, Busch-Rossnagel, & Fisher, 1987). As in the other studies reported in this section, the distribution across attachment classifications differed from that reported in studies of middle-class Americans. In addition, the maternal behavior that distinguished mothers of securely and insecurely attached infants was also different, and there were dramatic sex differences: Although two-thirds of the boys were securely attached, two-thirds of the girls were insecurely attached. These results lend further support to the suggestion that the mother–infant relationship must be evaluated in the context of culturally defined goals.

Some studies on parental disciplinary styles also demonstrate the significance of sociocultural factors. Baumrind (1972a), for example, found that associations between patterns of parental behavior and children's personalities were different in African-American and White families from comparable social class backgrounds. Although the findings for boys were unclear, it appeared that African-American girls raised by authoritarian (rather than authoritative) parents were most self-assertive and independent.

There have been relatively few studies comparing parent–adolescent relationships in different countries. Kroger (1985) found that U.S., New Zealand, and British adolescents from Grades 6, 8, 10, and 12 all had similar attitudes toward parental authority. Although U.S. girls of all ages felt more favorably about their parents, New Zealand girls, who had positive attitudes toward their parents in the early grades, held less favorable attitudes as they grew older. In a series of studies, Feldman and her colleagues (Feldman & Rosenthal, in press; Feldman, Rosenthal, Mont-Reynaud, Leung, & Lau, 1991), found that although Hong Kong Chinese adolescents reported more misbehavior and expected to achieve behavioral autonomy later than did Australian and U.S. youth, levels of misconduct and expectations of behavioral autonomy were related in similar ways to family environments and adolescent values in both Chinese and Western cultures.

Summary. Although the number of studies is small, research on sociocultural and cross-cultural differences suggests that the nature and quality of parent–child relationships must be considered in ecological context. Research on infant–mother attachment suggests that either sociocultural factors influence the development of attachment behavior, or that the validity of the Strange Situation varies from culture to culture. The sociocultural context should also be taken into account when reaching conclusions about the development of parent–child relationships and their effects on child adjustment.

Divorce and Single Parenthood

Between 1960 and 1981, divorce rates in the United States increased dramatically (Cherlin, 1981), such that the proportion of children experiencing divorce rose from 22% in the 1960s to almost 50% in the 1980s (Bumpass, 1984). Although divorce rates appeared to level off in the 1980s (Hernandez, 1988), about 50% of the children born today can expect to experience at least one family disruption by their 16th birthday (Bumpass & Castro, 1987).

In the 2 years immediately following divorce, both boys and girls frequently experience emotional distress, psychological and behavioral problems, and psychosomatic symptoms. Academic achievement and intellectual performance usually decline (Shinn, 1978), antisocial behavior increases (Dornbusch et al., 1985; Hetherington, Cox, & Cox, 1978), and peer interaction skills decline (Guidubaldi, Cleminshaw, Perry, & McLoughlin, 1983; Hetherington, Cox, & Cox, 1979; Hodges, Buchsbaum, & Tierney, 1983; Stolberg & Anker, 1983). In addition, adolescents from divorced families frequently act out sexually (Hetherington, 1972).

Although most children are acutely distressed and fantasize about the reconciliation of their parents, there are age differences in the short-term effects of parental separation and divorce. According to Wallerstein and Kelly (1980), for example, preschool children show intense separation anxiety and fear abandonment by both parents, which leads to regression and self-blaming. In elementary school, children react with anxiety, depression, worry, loyalty conflicts, guilt, and anger at one (or both) parents for deciding to divorce. Although initially anxious and upset about the divorce, adolescents appear to be least affected by parental separation and divorce (Allison & Furstenberg, 1989; Kurdek & Berg, 1983; Zill & Peterson, 1983). This may reflect their relative maturity and the availability of emotional support from peers and group activities (Crouter, Belsky, & Spanier, 1984; Hetherington, 1989; Steinberg & Silverberg, 1986).

Following divorce, many parents become more demanding, less nurturant, less sensitive, less available, and less able to maintain household routines while struggling with new emotional and practical burdens (Wallerstein & Kelly, 1980). Their discipline becomes less consistent, and is marked by harsh, punitive reactions to misbehavior (Hetherington, Cox, & Cox, 1982). As expected, a decline in the quality of parent–child relationships is associated with problem behavior in children (Guidubaldi et al., 1983; Santrock & Warshak, 1979).

Two years following divorce, many parents have consolidated their custody arrangements, some have remarried, and most have adjusted their lifestyles to suit the new circumstances. As a result, most children appear to rebound successfully from the initial impact of their parents' divorce (Hetherington, Cox, & Cox, 1982, 1985; Wallerstein & Kelly, 1980). According to Chase-Lansdale and Hetherington (1990), however:

> Behavior problems persist in young boys in nonremarried mother-custody homes for as long as 6 years. Girls seem to recover fully during elementary school years, but at the onset of adolescence they may show a variety of socioemotional problems. Remarriage seems to have positive effects on younger boys, but not on younger girls. Suggestive evidence indicated negative effects for both boys and girls if mother's remarriage occurs at the onset of adolescence. In adulthood, young women from families of marital disruption are more likely to experience divorce themselves. (p. 105)

Long-term effects are difficult to interpret, however, because many events can occur between the time of the initial disruption and the time of assessment, making it difficult to determine how much of the variance in outcome is attributable to divorce rather than other changing circumstances.

Unfortunately, there is a paucity of research on the quality of child–stepparent relationships and on the effects of remarriage on adjustment among both children and adolescents (Furstenberg & Nord, 1985; Youniss & Ketterlinus, 1987). Boys and girls of all ages find the early stages of remarriage difficult and stressful, and older children may suffer extended psychological problems (Bray, 1988; Peterson & Zill, 1986). In reconstituted families, furthermore, the quality of the marital relationship may have significant effects on parent–child relationships. Marital closeness and the active involvement of stepfathers, for example, are associated with high levels of conflict between stepchildren (especially girls) and the two parents (Brand, Clingempeel, & Bowen-Woodward, 1988; Bray, 1988).

Early research on the effects of divorce focused on the adverse affects of father absence but it has become clear that many boys and girls develop quite normally in the absence of their fathers, suggesting the importance of such factors as the absence of a co-parent (Maccoby, Depner, & Mnookin, 1988), the economic stress that accompanies single parenthood, especially single motherhood (Norton & Glick, 1986), the emotional stress occasioned by social isolation and disapproving social attitudes (Hetherington et al., 1982), and pre- and postdivorce marital conflict and hostility (Lamb, 1981b; Rutter, 1971, 1979; Wolkind & Rutter, 1985). By contrast, children who have had good relationships with both parents before and after the divorce tend to be better adjusted than those who do not (Hess & Camara, 1979; Wierson, Forehand, Fauber, & McCombs, 1989), as are those whose parents have a nonadversarial, close relationship (Bane, 1976; Goetting, 1981; Herzog & Sudia, 1971; Hess & Camara, 1979; Ketterlinus & Sloane, 1986; Rutter & Madge, 1976; Wallerstein & Kelly, 1980).

Family Violence

In the United States, most incidents of serious and less serious physical violence occur among family members in the home (Straus et al., 1980; Straus & Gelles, 1986). Because no standardized data collection techniques or consensual definitions exist, however, estimates of the prevalence of child maltreatment vary between 200,000 to 4 million cases per year, with approximately 1 million cases of serious abuse and 2,000 to 5,000 fatalities per year (American Association for Protecting Children [AAPC], 1986; Cohn, 1983). Various factors (such as the child's age, gender, and sociodemographic status) are related to the incidence of abuse.

Young children are overrepresented in samples of abused children; 14%

of all cases involve children under 1 year of age, 25% involve children under 2 years, and more than 60% involve children over 6 years of age (Gil, 1970). Preadolescents and adolescents may be at greater risk of maltreatment than was once believed, however. National and clinic studies show that between 24% and 47% of recognized victims of maltreatment are between the ages of 12 and 17 (AAPC, 1986; Burgdorf, 1980; Lourie, 1977, 1979; Olsen & Holmes, 1983; Powers & Eckenrode, 1988); according to Straus et al. (1980), 54% of 10- to 14-year-old children and 33% of 15- to 17-year-old adolescents were struck at least once by their parents during a 1-year period. In addition, adolescents are much more likely than younger children to direct violence at their parents (Gelles & Cornell, 1985; Straus et al., 1980), and several researchers have suggested that teenage parents are more likely to abuse their children than are adult parents (Bolton & Belsky, 1986; Gelles, 1986; Kinard, 1980).

Researchers have found a variety of environmental risk factors (such as low socioeconomic status, single parenthood, stress, marital conflict, and interspousal physical violence) associated with the incidence of child abuse. Gil (1970) estimated that 37% of abusive families reported receiving some form of public assistance at the time of the reported incident, over 29% were headed by single mothers, 12% of the abusive parents were unemployed at a time when the national average was only 3.2%, only 52% of the abusive parents had been steadily employed throughout the year prior to the report, and the rate of divorce and single parenthood was higher than in the general population. Gil found that young boys were slightly more likely than young girls to experience abuse, whereas among older children and adolescents, girls were more likely than boys to be abused; data from the Second National Violence Survey, however, revealed no significant sex differences in the prevalence of physical punishment (Wauchope & Straus, 1989).

The consequences of child abuse are pervasive. In addition to neurodevelopmental and psychological impairment (Lynch & Roberts, 1982; Oates, Peacock, & Forrest, 1984), socioemotional and psychological damage is also common. Social learning theorists contend that physical abuse leads to later aggression because aggressive responses are frequently modeled and often have desirable consequences (Dodge, Bates, & Pettit, 1990; Emery, 1989). Abused and maltreated children have poor relations with peers (George & Main, 1979; Wolfe & Mosk, 1983), with whom they behave aggressively (Bousha & Twentyman, 1984; Egeland & Sroufe, 1981; George & Main, 1979), and suffer from deficits in social cognition (Barahal, Waterman, & Martin, 1981), lack of empathy (Main & George, 1985), depression (Kazdin, Moser, Colbus, & Bell, 1985; Sternberg et al., 1991), poor performance on cognitive tasks (Hoffman-Plotkin & Twentyman, 1984), and aggressive, noncompliant acting-out (Pianta, Egeland, & Erickson, 1989; Sternberg et al., in press). Maltreated children are also more likely to develop insecure attachments (Carlson, Cicchetti, Barnett, & Braunwald, 1989; Crittenden, 1988; Crittenden & Ainsworth, 1989; Lamb, Gaensbauer, Malkin, & Shultz, 1985) because they have come to see the world as a threatening place. Abused children become overly attentive to hostile cues, misinterpreting the behavior of others, and responding with aggression (Dodge et al., 1990).

Maltreated adolescents exhibit more anger and conflict with their family, are more aggressive with their peers, and exhibit more internalizing and externalizing behavior problems than nonmaltreated adolescents do (Youngblade & Belsky, 1990). Abused and neglected children are also more likely than are matched controls to be arrested for delinquency, to become adult criminals, and to exhibit violent criminal behavior (Widom, 1989). Not all abused or neglected children suffer these negative consequences, however, although researchers have yet to discern why some adolescents are more resilient than others. Factors such as age of onset and seriousness of abuse and neglect probably play a role in determining long-term outcomes.

No single behavioral or emotional characteristic is common to abused children, and other aspects of the child's environment may be highly influential (Emery, 1989). In comparison with nonabused children, abused children of all ages manifest many psychological deviations, but there is no one-to-one relation between incidents and symptoms (Ammerman, Cassisi, Hersen, & Van Hasselt, 1986).

CONCLUSION

Thanks in large part to Sigmund Freud's insightful focus on the formative significance of parent–child relationships, students of social and personality development have studied parent–child relationships throughout much of the century. Over time, they have come to place less emphasis on the critical importance of early experiences and relationships, choosing instead to view relationships at various stages of the life span as significant, albeit changing, aspects of the formative social environment. As we have noted in this chapter, the focal contents of parent–child relationships change as children grow older and, presumably, as their parents mature as well. Initially, the parents provide a context in which children learn that their behaviors have consequences, developing conceptions of their own effectance and trust in others' reliable responsiveness. Thereafter, parents instill standards of behavior and self-control, before becoming foils for their children's pursuit of independence and autonomy as adolescence unfolds. Needless to say, parents differ in their ability to respond sensitively to their children's individual needs and characteristics, and in the way in which they strive to discipline and socialize their children. These differences affect the quality of parent–child relationships and may in turn have long-term influences on the children's behavior and adjustment, although their relative importance, in the context of the many other influential events children experience, remains to be determined. Certainly, researchers today see parent–child relationships as dynamic systems that vary in quality depending on individual, familial, societal, and cultural circumstances.

REFERENCES

Acock, A. C., & Bengtson, V. L. (1978). On the relative influence of mothers and fathers: A covariance analysis of political and religious socialization. *Journal of Marriage and the Family, 40,* 519–530.

Adamson, L. B., & Bakeman, R. (1984). Mothers' communicative acts: Changes during infancy. *Infant Behavior and Development, 7,* 467–478.

Ainsworth, M. D. S. (1979). Attachment as related to mother–infant interaction. In J. S. Rosenblatt, R. A. Hinde, C. Beer, & M. Busnel (Eds.), *Advances in the study of behavior* (Vol. 9, pp. 1–51). New York: Academic Press.

Ainsworth, M. D. S., Bell, S. M., & Stayton, D. J. (1974). Infant mother attachment and social development: "Socialization" as a product of reciprocal responsiveness to signals. In M. P. M. Richards (Ed.), *The integration of a child into a social world* (pp. 91–135). Cambridge: Cambridge University Press.

Ainsworth, M. D. S., Blehar, M. C., Waters, E., & Wall, S. (1978). *Patterns of attachment.* Hillsdale, NJ: Lawrence Erlbaum Associates.

Ainsworth, M. D. S., & Wittig, B. A. (1969). Attachment and exploratory behavior of one-year olds in a strange situation. In B. M. Foss (Ed.), *Determinants of infant behaviour* (Vol. 4, pp. 111–136). London: Methuen.

Allison, P. D., & Furstenberg, F. F., Jr. (1989). How marital dissolution affects children: Variations by age and sex. *Developmental Psychology, 25,* 540–549.

Ambrose, A. (Ed.). (1969). *Stimulation in early infancy.* New York: Academic Press.

American Association for Protecting Children. (1986). *Highlights of Official Child Neglect and Abuse Reporting 1984.* Denver, CO: American Humane Association.

Ammerman, R. T., Cassisi, J. E., Hersen, M., & Van Hasselt, V. B. (1986). *Clinical Psychology Review, 6,* 291–310.

Anderson, J. W. (1972). Attachment behavior out of doors. In N. Blurton Jones (Ed.), *Ethological studies of child behavior.* Cambridge: Cambridge University Press.

Arend, R., Gove, F. L., & Sroufe, L. A. (1979). Continuity of individual adaptation from infancy to kindergarten: A predictive study of ego-resiliency and curiosity in preschoolers. *Child Development, 50,* 950–959.

Aronfreed, J. (1968). *Conduct and conscience.* New York: Academic Press.

Bachman, J. G. (1970). *Youth in transition: The impact of family background and intelligence on tenth-grade boys.* Ann Arbor, MI: Survey Research Center, Institute for Social Research.

Bachman, J. G., Green, S., & Wirtanen, I. D. (1971). *Youth in transition: Dropping out — problem or symptom?* Ann Arbor, MI: Survey Research Center, Institute for Social Research.

Bandura, A. (1969). *Principles of behavior modification.* New York: Holt, Rinehart & Winston.

Bandura, A. (1977). Self-efficacy: Toward a unifying theory of behavioral change. *Psychological Review, 84,* 191–215.

Bane, M. (1976). Marital disruption and the lives of children. *Journal of Social Issues, 32,* 103–116.

Barahal, R. M., Waterman, J., & Martin, H. P. (1981). The social cognitive development of abused children. *Journal of Consulting and Clinical Psychology, 49,* 508–516.

Barnes, G. (1984). Adolescent alcohol abuse and other problem behaviors: Their relationship and common parental influences. *Journal of Youth and Adolescence, 13,* 329–348.

Barnes, H., & Olson, D. (1985). Parent-adolescent communication and the circumflex model. *Child Development, 56,* 438–447.

Bates, J. E., Maslin, L. A., & Frankel, K. A. (1985). Attachment security, mother–child interaction, and temperament as predictors of behavior problem ratings at age three years. In I. Bretherton & E. Waters (Eds.), *Growing points of attachment theory and research* (pp. 167–193). Monographs of the Society for Research in Child Development.

Baumrind, D. (1967). Child care practices anteceding three patterns of preschool behavior. *Genetic Psychology Monographs, 75,* 43–88.

Baumrind, D. (1970). Socialization and instrumental competence in young children. *Young Children, 26,* 154–169.

Baumrind, D. (1971). Current patterns of parental authority. *Developmental Psychology Monographs, 4,* 1–103.

Baumrind, D. (1972a). An exploratory study of socialization effects on black children: Some black–white comparisons. *Child Development, 43,* 261–267.

Baumrind, D. (1972b). From each according to her ability. *School Review, 80,* 161–197.

Baumrind, D. (1972c). Some thoughts about childrearing. In U. Bronfenbrenner (Ed.), *Readings in the development of human behavior.* New York: Dryden.

Baumrind, D. (1973). The development of instrumental competence through socialization. In A. Pick (Ed.), *Minnesota symposium on child psychology* (Vol. 7, pp. 3–46). Minneapolis: University of Minnesota Press.

Baumrind, D. (1975). *Early socialization and the discipline controversy.* Morristown, NJ: General Learning Press.

Baumrind, D. (1991). Parenting styles and adolescent development. In R. M. Lerner, A. C. Petersen, & J. Brooks-Gunn (Eds.), *Encyclopedia of adolescence* (Vol. 2, pp. 746–758). New York: Garland Publishing.

Baumrind, D., & Black, A. E. (1967). Socialization practices associated with dimensions of competence in preschool boys and girls. *Child Development, 38,* 291–327.

Bell, S. M., & Ainsworth, M. D. (1972). Infant crying and maternal responsiveness. *Child Development, 43,* 1171–1190.

Belsky, J., Gilstrap, B., & Rovine, M. (1984). The Pennsylvania Infant and Family Development Project, I: Stability and change in mother–infant and father–infant interaction in a family setting 1- to 3- to 9-months. *Child Development, 55,* 692–705.

Belsky, J., Rovine, M., & Taylor, D. (1984). The Pennsylvania Infant and Family Development Project, III: The origins of individual differences in infant–mother attachment: Maternal and infant contributions. *Child Development, 55,* 718–728.

Berndt, T. J. (1979). Developmental changes in conformity to peers and parents. *Developmental Psychology, 15,* 608–616.

Block, J. H., & Block, J. (1980). The role of ego-control and ego-resiliency in the organization of behavior. In W. A. Collins (Ed.), *Minnesota Symposium on Child Psychology* (Vol. 13, pp. 39–101). Hillsdale, NJ: Lawrence Erlbaum Associates.

Blos, P. (1979). *The adolescent passage.* New York: International Universities Press.

Blyth, D. A., Hill, J. P., & Thiel, K. S. (1982). Early adolescents' significant others: Grade and gender differences in perceived relationships with familial and nonfamilial adults and young people. *Journal of Youth and Adolescence, 11,* 425–449.

Bohlin, G., Hagekull, B., Germer, M., Andersson, K., & Lindberg, I. (1989). Avoidant and resistant reunion behaviors as predicted by maternal interactive behavior and infant temperament. *Infant Behavior and Development, 12,* 105–117.

Bolton, F. G. Jr., & Belsky, J. (1986). Adolescent fatherhood and child maltreatment. In A. Elster & M. E. Lamb (Eds.), *Adolescent fatherhood* (pp. 123–140). Hillsdale, NJ: Lawrence Erlbaum Associates.

Bousha, D. M., & Twentyman, C. T. (1984). Mother–child interactional style in abuse, neglect, and control groups: Naturalistic observations in the home. *Journal of Abnormal Psychology, 93,* 106–114.

Bowlby, J. (1969). *Attachment and loss. Vol. 1: Attachment.* New York: Basic.

Bowlby, J. (1973). *Attachment and loss. Vol. 2: Separation: Anxiety and anger.* New York: Basic.

Brand, E., Clingempeel, W. E., & Bowen-Woodward, K. (1988). Family relationships and children's psychological adjustment in stepmother and stepfather families: Findings and conclusions from the Philadelphia Stepfamily Research Project. In E. M. Hetherington & J. D. Arasteh (Eds.), *Impact of divorce, single parenting, and stepparenting on children* (pp. 299–324). Hillsdale, NJ: Lawrence Erlbaum Associates.

Bray, J. H. (1988). Children's development during early remarriage. In E. M. Hetherington & J. D. Arasteh (Eds.), *Impact of divorce, single parenting, and stepparenting on children* (pp. 279–298). Hillsdale, NJ: Lawrence Erlbaum Associates.

Bretherton, I. (1985). Attachment theory: Retrospect and prospect. In I. Bretherton & E. Waters (Eds.), *Growing points in attachment theory and research* (pp. 3–38). Monographs of the Society for Research in Child Development, *50,* (1–2, serial #209).

Bretherton, I. (1990). Open communication and internal working models: Their role in the development of attachment relationships. In R. A. Thompson (Ed.), *Socioemotional development* (pp. 57–114). Lincoln, NB: University of Nebraska Press.

Brittain, C. V. (1963). Adolescent choices and parent–peer cross-preferences. *American Sociological Review, 28,* 385–391.

Buhrmester, D. P., & Furman, W. C. (1990). Perceptions of sibling relationships during middle childhood and adolescence. *Child Development, 61,* 1387–1398.

Bumpass, L. L. (1984). Children and marital disruption: A replication and update. *Demography, 21,* 71–82.

Bumpass, L. L., & Castro, T. (1987). Recent trends and differentials in marital disruption. *Center for Demography and Ecology Working Paper 87-20.* Madison, WI: University of Wisconsin.

Burgdorf, K. (1980). *Recognition and reporting of child maltreatment: Findings from the National Incidence and Severity of Child Abuse and Neglect Study.* Report prepared for the National Center on Child Abuse and Neglect, Washington, DC.

Burr, W. R., Reige, G. K., Day, R. D., & Constantine, J. (1979). Symbolic interaction and the family. In W. R. Burr, R. Hill, F. I. Nye, & I. L. Reiss (Eds.), *Contemporary theories about the family* (Vol. 2, pp. 91–123). New York: Free Press.

Buss, A. G., & van IJzendoorn, M. H. (1988). Mother–child interactions, attachment, and emergent literacy: A cross-sectional study. *Child Development, 59,* 1262–1272.

Campos, J. J., Barrett, K. C., Lamb, M. E., Goldsmith, H. H., & Stenberg, C. (1983). Socioemotional development. In P. H. Mussen (Series Ed.) & M. M. Haith & J. J. Campos (Vol. Eds.), *Handbook of child psychology: Vol. 2, Infancy and developmental psychobiology* (pp. 783–915). New York: Wiley.

Carlson, V., Cicchetti, D., Barnett, D., & Braunwald, K. G. (1989). Finding order in disorganization: Lessons from research on maltreated infants' attachment to their caregivers. In D. Cicchetti & V. Carlson (Eds.), *Child maltreatment: Theory and research on the causes and consequences of child abuse and neglect* (pp. 494–528). Cambridge, MA: Cambridge University Press.

Cassidy, J. (1988). Child–mother attachment and the self in six-year-olds. *Child Development, 59,* 121–134.

Cernoch, J. M., & Porter, R. H. (1985). Recognition of maternal axillary odors by infants. *Child Development, 56,* 1593–1598.

Chase-Lansdale, P. L., & Hetherington, E. M. (1990). The impact of divorce on life-span development: Short and long term effects. In P. B. Baltes, D. L. Featherman, & R. M. Lerner (Eds.), *Life-span development and behavior* (Vol. 10, pp. 105–150). Hillsdale, NJ: Lawrence Erlbaum Associates.

Cherlin, A. (1981). *Marriage, divorce, remarriage: Changing patterns in the post-war United States.* Cambridge, MA: Harvard University Press.

Clarke-Stewart, K. A. (1980). The father's contribution to children's cognitive and social development in early childhood. In F. A. Pedersen (Ed.), *The father–infant relationship: Observational studies in a family setting* (pp. 111–146). New York: Praeger Special Publications.

Clarke-Stewart, K. A., & Hevey, C. M. (1981). Longitudinal relations in repeated observations of mother–child interaction from 1 to 2 ½ years. *Developmental Psychology, 17,* 127–145.

Cohn, A. H. (1983). *An approach to preventing child abuse.* Chicago: National Committee for the Prevention of Child Abuse.

Cohn, J. F., & Tronick, E. Z. (1983). Three-month-old infants' reactions to simulated maternal depression. *Child Development, 54,* 185–193.

Cohn, J. F., & Tronick, E. Z. (1988). Mother–infant interaction: Influence is bidirectional and unrelated to periodic cycles in either partner's behavior. *Developmental Psychology, 24,* 386–392.

Coleman, J. S. (1961). *The adolescent society: The social life of the teenager and its impact on education.* New York: Basic.

Coleman, J. C. (1974). *Relationships in adolescence.* London: Routledge & Kegan Paul.

Coleman, J. C. (1977). Current contradictions in adolescent theory. *Journal of Youth and Adolescence, 7,* 1–11.

Collins, W. A. (1990). Parent–child relationships in the transition to adolescence: Continuity and change in interaction, affect, and cognition. In R. Montemayor, G. Adams, & T. Gullotta (Eds.), *From childhood to adolescence: A transitional period? Advances in adolescent development* (Vol. 2, pp. 85–106). Beverly Hills, CA: Sage.

Collins, W. A., & Russell, G. (in press). Mother–child and father–child relationships in middle childhood and adolescence. *Developmental Review.*

Condry, J., & Condry, S. (1976). Sex differences: A study of the eye of the beholder. *Child Development, 47,* 812–819.

Connell, D. B. (1976). *Individual differences in attachment: An investigation into stability, implications, and relationships to structure of early language development.* Unpublished doctoral dissertation, Syracuse University, Syracuse, New York.

Crandall, V. (1972). *Progress report on NIMH grant No. MH-02238.* Yellow Springs, OH: Fels Institute.

Crittenden, P. M. (1988). Relationship at risk. In J. Belsky & J. Nezworski (Eds.), *Clinical implications of attachment* (pp. 136–176). Hillsdale, NJ: Lawrence Erlbaum Associates.

Crittenden, P. M., & Ainsworth, M. D. S. (1989). Child maltreatment and attachment theory. In D. Cicchetti & V. Carlson (Eds.), *Child maltreatment: Theory and research on the causes and consequences of child abuse and neglect* (pp. 432–463). Cambridge, MA: Cambridge University Press.

Crouter, A. C., Belsky, J., & Spanier, G. B. (1984). The family context of child development: Divorce and maternal employment. *Annals of Child Development, 1,* 201–238.

Crouter, A. C., MacDermid, S. M., McHale, S. M., & Perry-Jenkins, M. (1990). Parental monitoring and perceptions of children's school performance and conduct in dual- and single-earner families. *Developmental Psychology, 26,* 649–657.

Curtis, R. L. (1975). Adolescent orientations toward parents and peers: Variations by sex, age, and socioeconomic status. *Adolescence, 10,* 483–494.

Damon, W. (1977). *The social world of the child.* San Francisco: Jossey-Bass.

Damon, W. (1983). *Social and personality development.* New York: Norton.

DeCasper, D., & Fifer, W. (1980). Of human bonding: Newborns prefer their mothers' voices. *Science, 208,* 1174–1176.

Dodge, K. A., Bates, J. E., & Pettit, G. S. (1990). Mechanisms in the cycle of violence. *Science, 250,* 1678–1683.

Dornbusch, S. M., Carlsmith, J. M., Bushwall, S. J., Ritter, R. L., Leiderman, H., Hastorf, A. H., & Gross, R. T. (1985). Single parents, extended households, and the control of adolescents. *Child Development, 56,* 326–341.

Dornbusch, S. M., Ritter, R. L., Leiderman, H., Roberts, D., & Fraleigh, M. (1987). The relation of parenting style to adolescent school performance. *Child Development, 58,* 1244–1257.

Douvan, E., & Adelson, J. (1966). *The adolescent experience.* New York: Wiley.

Duncan, D. F. (1978). Attitudes towards parents and delinquency in suburban adolescent males. *Adolescence, 13,* 365–369.

Easterbrooks, M. A., & Goldberg, W. A. (1990). Security of toddler–parent attachment: Relation to children's sociopersonality functioning during kindergarten. In M. T. Greenberg, D. Cicchetti, & E. M. Cummings (Eds.), *Attachment in the preschool years: Theory, research, and intervention* (pp. 221–244). Chicago: University of Chicago Press.

Easterbrooks, M. A., & Lamb, M. E. (1979). The relationship between quality of infant–mother attachment and infant competence in initial encounters with peers. *Child Development, 50,* 380–387.

Egeland, B., & Farber, E. A. (1984). Infant–mother attachment: Factors related to its development and changes over time. *Child Development, 55,* 753–771.

Egeland, B., & Sroufe, L. A. (1981). Attachment and early maltreatment. *Child Development, 52,* 44–52.

Elder, G. H., Jr., Van Nguyen, T., & Caspi, A. (1985). Linking family hardship to children's lives. *Child Development, 56,* 361–375.

Emde, R. N., & Robinson, J. (1979). The first two months: Recent research in developmental psychology and the changing view of the newborn. In J. Noshpitz & J. Call (Eds.), *Basic handbook of child psychiatry.* New York: Basic.

Emery, R. E. (1989). Family violence. *American Psychologist, 44,* 312–329.

Emmerich, H. J. (1978). The influence of parents and peers on choices made by adolescents. *Journal of Youth and Adolescence, 7,* 175–180.

Erickson, M. F., Sroufe, L. A., & Egeland, B. (1985). The relationship between quality of attachment and behavior problems in preschool in a high-risk sample. In I. Bretherton & E. Waters (Eds.), *Growing points in attachment theory and research* (pp. 147–166). Monographs of the Society for Research in Child Development.

Fagot, B. I. (1974). Sex differences in toddlers' behavior and parental reaction. *Developmental Psychology, 10,* 554–558.

Feldman, S. S., & Rosenthal, D. A. (in press). Age expectations of behavioral autonomy in Hong Kong, Australian, and American youth: The influence of family variables and adolescents' values. *International Journal of Psychology.*

Feldman, S. S., Rosenthal, D. A., Mont-Reynaud, R. Leung, K., & Lau, S. (1991). Ain't misbehavin': Adolescent values and family environments as correlates of misconduct in Australia, Hong Kong, and the United States. *Journal of Research on Adolescence, 1,* 109–134.

Field, T. M. (1978). Interaction behaviors of primary versus secondary caretaker fathers. *Developmental Psychology, 14,* 183–184.

Flanagan, C. A. (1990). Families and schools in hard times. In V. C. McLoyd & C. A. Flanagan (Eds.), Economic stress: Effects on family life and child development. *New directions in child development* (Vol. 46, pp. 7–26). San Francisco: Jossey-Bass.

Flavell, J. H. (1963). *The developmental psychology of Jean Piaget*. New York: Van Nostrand.

Fracasso, M. P., Busch-Rossnagel, N. A., & Fisher, C. B. (1987, August). *Quality of attachment in Puerto Rican and Dominican infants*. Paper presented at the Annual Conference of the American Psychological Association, New York.

Frankel, K. A., & Bates, J. E. (1990). Mother–toddler problem solving: Antecedents in attachment, home behavior and temperament. *Child Development, 61*, 810–819.

Freud, A. (1958). Adolescence. *Psychoanalytic Study of the Child, 16*, 255–278.

Frodi, A. M., Lamb, M. E., Leavitt, L. A., & Donovan, W. L. (1978). Fathers' and mothers' responses to infant smiles and cries. *Infant Behavior and Development, 1*, 187–198.

Furman, W. C., & Buhrmester, D. P. (1985). Children's perceptions of the qualities of sibling relationships. *Child Development, 56*, 448–461.

Furstenberg, F. F. (1990). Coming of age in a changing family system. In S. S. Feldman & G. R. Elliott (Eds.), *At the threshold: The developing adolescent* (pp. 147–170). Cambridge, MA: Harvard University Press.

Furstenberg, F. F., & Nord, C. W. (1985). Parenting apart: Patterns of childbearing after martial disruption. *Journal of Marriage and the Family, 47*, 893–904.

Garvey, C., & Hogan, R. (1973). Social speech and social interaction: Egocentrism revisited. *Child Development, 44*, 562–568.

Gelles, R. J. (1986). School-age parents and child abuse. In J. B. Lancaster & B. A. Hamburg (Eds.), *School-aged pregnancy and parenthood: Biosocial dimensions* (pp. 347–359). New York: Aldine De Greyter.

Gelles, R. J., & Cornell, C. P. (1985). *Intimate violence in families. Family studies text series 2*. Beverly Hills, CA: Sage.

George, C., & Main, M. (1979). Social interactions of young abused children: Approach avoidance and aggression. *Child Development, 50*, 306–318.

Gil, D. (1970). *Violence against children: Physical child abuse in the United States*. Cambridge, MA: Harvard University Press.

Gjerde, P. F. (1986). The interpersonal structure of family interaction settings: Parent–adolescent relations in dyads and triads. *Developmental Psychology, 22*, 297–304.

Goetting, A. (1981). Divorce outcome research: Issues and perspectives. *Journal of Family Issues, 2*, 350–378.

Goodenough, F. W. (1931). *Anger in young children*. Minneapolis: University of Minnesota Press.

Goodnow, J. J. (1985). Change and variation in parents' ideas about childhood and parenting. In I. E. Sigel (Ed.), *Parental belief systems* (pp. 235–270). Hillsdale, NJ: Lawrence Erlbaum Associates.

Goodnow, J. J. (1988). Children's household work: Its nature and functions. *Psychological Bulletin, 103*, 5–26.

Green, J. A., Gustafson, G. E., & West, M. J. (1980). Effects of infant development on mother–infant interactions. *Child Development, 51*, 199–207.

Greenberg, M. T., Cicchetti, D., & Cummings, E. M. (Eds.). (1990). *Attachment in the preschool years: Theory, research, and intervention*. Chicago, IL: University of Chicago Press.

Greenberg, M. T., & Speltz, M. (1988). Attachment and the ontogeny of conduct problems. In J. Belsky & T. Nezworski (Eds.), *Clinical implications of attachment* (pp. 177–218). Hillsdale, NJ: Lawrence Erlbaum Associates.

Grossmann, K. E., Grossmann, K., Huber, F., & Wartner, V. (1981). German children's behavior toward their mothers at 12 months and their fathers at 18 months in Ainsworth's Strange Situation. *International Journal of Behavioral Development, 4,* 157–181.

Grossmann, K., Grossmann, K. E., Spangler, G., Suess, G., & Unzner, L. (1985). Maternal sensitivity and newborns' orientation responses as related to quality of attachment in northern Germany. In I. Bretherton & E. Waters (Eds.), *Growing points of attachment theory and research* (pp. 233–256). Monographs of the Society for Research in Child Development, 50 (Serial No. 209).

Grotevant, H., & Cooper, C. (1986). Individuation in family relationships. *Human Development, 29,* 82–100.

Guidubaldi, J., Cleminshaw, H. K., Perry, J. D., & McLoughlin, C. S. (1983). The impact of parental divorce on children: Report of the nationwide NASP study. *Study Psychology Review, 12,* 300–323.

Hall, G. S. (1904). *Adolescence: Its psychology and its relations to physiology, anthropology, sociology, sex, crime, religion, and education* (Vols. 1 & 2). New York: Appleton.

Hamburg, B. A. (1985). Early adolescence: A time of transition and stress. *Journal of Early Adolescence, 78,* 158–167.

Hauser, S., Book, B. Houlihan, J., Powers, S., Weiss-Perry, B., Follansbee, D., Jacobson, A., & Noam, G. (1987). Sex differences within the family: Studies of adolescent and parent family interactions. *Journal of Youth and Adolescence, 16,* 199–220.

Hayman, R. (1986). *Adolescence: A survival guide to the teenage years.* New York: Gower.

Hernandez, D. J. (1988). Demographic trends and the living arrangements of children. In E. M. Hetherington & J. D. Arasteh (Eds.), *Impact of divorce, single parenting, and stepparenting on children* (pp. 3–22). Hillsdale, NJ: Lawrence Erlbaum Associates.

Herzog, E., & Sudia, C. (1971). *Boys in fatherless families.* Washington, DC: U.S. Department of Health, Education, and Welfare, Children's Bureau.

Hess, R. D., & Camara, K. A. (1979). Post-divorce family relationships as mediating factors in the consequences of divorce for children. *Journal of Social Issues, 35,* 79–96.

Hetherington, E. M. (1972). Effects of father absence on personality development in adolescent daughters. *Developmental Psychology, 7,* 313–326.

Hetherington, E. M. (1988). Parents, children, and siblings six years after divorce. In R. Hinde & J. Stevenson-Hinde (Eds.), *Relationships within families: Mutual influences.* Cambridge: Cambridge University Press.

Hetherington, E. M. (1989). Coping with family transitions: Winners, losers, and survivors. *Child Development, 60,* 1–14.

Hetherington, E. M., Cox, M., & Cox, R. (1978). The aftermath of divorce. In J. H. Stevens & M. Matthews (Eds.), *Mother-child, father-child relations* (pp. 149–176) Washington, DC: National Association for the Education of Young Children.

Hetherington, E. M., Cox, M., & Cox, R. (1979). Play and social interactions in children following divorce. *Journal of Social Issues, 35,* 26–49.

Hetherington, E. M., Cox, M., & Cox, R. (1982). Effects of divorce on parents and children. In M. E. Lamb (Ed.), *Nontraditional families: Parenting and child development* (pp. 233–288). Hillsdale, NJ: Lawrence Erlbaum Associates.

Hetherington, E. M., Cox, M., & Cox, R. (1985). Long-term effects of divorce and remarriage on the adjustment of children. *Journal of the American Academy of Child Psychiatry, 24,* 518–530.

Hetherington, E. W., Stouwie, R. J., & Ridberg, E. H. (1971). Patterns of family interaction and child-rearing attitudes related to three dimensions of juvenile delinquency. *Journal of Abnormal Psychology, 78,* 160–176.

Hill, J. (1988). Adapting to menarche: Familial control and conflict. In M. Gunnar (Ed.), *21st Minnesota Symposium on Child Psychology* (pp. 43–77). Hillsdale, NJ: Lawrence Erlbaum Associates.

Hill, J., & Holmbeck, G. N. (1987). Familial adaptation to biological change during adolescence. In R. M. Lerner & T. Foch (Eds.), *Biological-psychosocial interactions in early adolescence: A life-span perspective* (pp. 207-223). Hillsdale, NJ: Lawrence Erlbaum Associates.

Hill, J., Holmbeck, G. N., Marlow, L., Green, T., & Lynch, M. (1985). Menarcheal status and parent-child relations in families of seventh grade girls. *Journal of Youth and Adolescence, 14,* 314-330.

Hirschi, T. (1969). *Causes of delinquency.* Berkeley, CA: University of California Press.

Hodges, W. F., Buchsbaum, H. H., & Tierney, C. W. (1983). Parent-child relationships and adjustment in preschool children in divorced and intact families. *Journal of Divorce, 7,* 43-58.

Hoffman, L. W. (1970). Conscience, personality, and socialization technique. *Human Development, 13,* 90-126.

Hoffman, L. W., Rosen, S., & Lippitt, R. (1960). Parental coerciveness, child autonomy, and child's role at school. *Sociometry, 23,* 1-22.

Hoffman-Plotkin, D., & Twentyman, C. T. (1984). A multimodal assessment of behavioral and cognitive deficits in abused and neglected preschoolers. *Child Development, 55,* 794-802.

Holden, G. W. (1985). How parents create a social environment via proactive behavior. In T. Garling & J. Valsiner (Eds.), *Children within environments* (pp. 193-216). New York: Plenum.

Hunter, F. T. (1984). Socializing procedures in parent-child and friendship relations during adolescence. *Developmental Psychology, 20,* 1092-1099.

Huston, A. C. (1983). Sex typing. In P. H. Mussen (Series Ed.) & E. M. Hetherington (Vol. Ed.), *Handbook of child psychology: Vol. 4. Socialization, personality, and social development* (4th ed., pp. 387-467). New York: Wiley.

Isabella, R. A., & Belsky, J. (1990). Interactional synchrony and the origins of infant-mother attachment: A replication study. *Child Development, 61,* 1-38.

Isabella, R. A., Belsky, J., & von Eye, A. (1989). Origins of infant-mother attachment: An examination of interactional synchrony during infant's first year. *Developmental Psychology, 25,* 12-21.

Jacobson, J. L., & Wille, D. E. (1984, April). *The influence of attachment patterns in peer interaction at 2 and 3 years.* Paper presented to the International Conference of Infant Studies, New York.

Jacobson, J. L., & Wille, D. E. (1986). The influence of attachment pattern on development changes in peer interaction from the toddler to the preschool period. *Child Development, 57,* 338-347.

Jacobson, J. L., Wille, D. E., Tianen, R. L., & Aytch, D. M. (1983, April). *The influence of infant-mother attachment on toddler sociability with peers.* Paper presented to the Society for Research in Child Development, Detroit, MI.

Jessor, S. L., & Jessor, R. (1977). *Problem behavior and psychological development.* New York: Academic Press.

Johnson, B. M., Shulman, S., & Collins, A. W. (in press). Systemic patterns of parenting as reported by adolescents: Developmental differences and implications for preschool outcomes. *Journal of Adolescent Research.*

Josselson, R. (1980). Ego development in adolescence. In J. Adelson (Ed.), *Handbook of adolescent psychology* (pp. 188-210). New York: Wiley.

Kagan, J., & Moss, H. A. (1962). *Birth to maturity.* New York: Wiley.

Kandel, D. B., Kessler, R. C., & Margulies, R. Z. (1978). Antecedents of adolescent initiation into stages of drug use: A developmental analyses. *Journal of Youth and Adolescence, 7,* 13-40.

Kandel, D. B., & Lesser, R. C. (1972). *Youth in two worlds.* San Francisco: Jossey-Bass.

Kaye, K. (1979). Thickening thin data: The maternal role in developing communication with language. In M. Bullowa (Ed.), *Before speech.* Cambridge: Cambridge University Press.

Kaye, K. (1982). *The mental and social life of babies: How parents create persons.* Chicago: University of Chicago Press.

Kazdin, A. E., Moser, J., Colbus, D., & Bell, R. (1985). Depressive symptoms among physically abused and psychiatrically disturbed children. *Journal of Abnormal Psychology, 94,* 298-307.

Keller, H., Scholmerich, A., & Eibl-Eibesfeldt, I. (1989). Communication-patterns in adult-infant interactions in western and non-western cultures. *Journal of Cross-Cultural Psychology, 23,* 62-67.

Ketterlinus, R. D. (1987). *Transformations in adolescents' relationships with parents, friends, and peers, and their behavioral correlates.* Unpublished doctoral dissertation, The Catholic University of America, Washington, D. C. (University Microfilms International #8717091.)

Ketterlinus, R. D., & Sloane, D. M. (1986, April). *The effects of family structure and closeness on delinquency: A log-linear analysis.* Paper presented at the biennial meeting of the Society of Research on Adolescence, Madison, WI.

Kinard, E. M. (1980). Emotional development in physically abused children. *American Journal of Orthopsychiatry, 50,* 686-695.

Kobak, R., & Sceery, A. (1988). Attachment in late adolescence: Working models, affect regulation, and representation of self and others. *Child Development, 59,* 135-146.

Koester, L. S., Papousek, H., & Papousek, M. (1989). Patterns of rhythmic stimuli by mothers with three month olds: A cross modal comparison. *International Journal of Behavioral Development, 12,* 143-154.

Korner, A. F., & Thoman, E. B. (1966). Visual alertness as related to soothing in neonates: Implications for maternal stimulation and early deprivation. *Child Development, 37,* 867-876.

Korner, A. F., & Thoman, E. G. (1970). Visual alertness in neonates as evoked by maternal care. *Journal of Experimental Child Psychology, 10,* 67-78.

Korner, A. F., & Thoman, E. G. (1972). The relative efficacy of contact and vestibular-proprioceptive stimulation in soothing neonates. *Child Development, 43,* 443-453.

Kroger, J. (1985). Relationships during adolescence: A cross-national study of New Zealand and United States teenagers. *Journal of Adolescence, 8,* 47-56.

Kuczynski, L. (1984). Socialization goals and mother-child interactions: Strategies for long-term and short-term compliance. *Developmental Psychology, 22,* 1061-1073.

Kuczynski, L., Kochanska, G., Radke-Yarrow, M., & Girnius-Brown, O. (1987). A developmental interpretation of young children's noncompliance. *Developmental Psychology, 23,* 799-806.

Kurdek, L. A., & Berg, B. (1983). Correlates of children's adjustment to their parents' divorces. In L. A. Kurdek (Ed.), *Children and divorce* (pp. 47-60). San Francisco: Jossey-Bass.

Lamb, M. E. (1976a). Effects of stress and cohort on mother- and father-infant interaction. *Developmental Psychology, 12,* 435-443.

Lamb, M. E. (1976b). Interactions between eight-month-old children and their fathers and mothers. In M. E. Lamb (Ed.), *The role of the father in child development* (pp. 307-328). New York: Wiley.

Lamb, M. E. (1976c). Twelve-month-olds and their parents. Interaction in a laboratory playroom. *Developmental Psychology, 12,* 237-244.

Lamb, M. E. (1977a). The development of mother-infant attachments in the second year of life. *Developmental Psychology, 13,* 637-648.

Lamb, M. E. (1977b). The development of parental preferences in the first two years of life. *Sex Roles, 3,* 495-497.

Lamb, M. E. (1977c). Father–infant and mother–infant interaction in the first year of life. *Child Development, 48,* 167–181.

Lamb, M. E. (1981a). Developing trust and perceived effectancies in infancy. In L. P. Lipsitt (Ed.), *Advances in infancy research* (Vol. 1, pp. 101–130). Norwood, NJ: Ablex.

Lamb, M. E. (1981b). The development of father–infant relationships. In M. E. Lamb (Ed.), *The role of the father in child development* (2nd ed., pp. 459–488). New York: Wiley.

Lamb, M. E. (1981c). The development of social expectations in the first year of life. In M. E. Lamb & L. R. Sherrod (Eds.), *Infant social cognition: Empirical and theoretical considerations* (pp. 155–176). Hillsdale, NJ: Lawrence Erlbaum Associates.

Lamb, M. E. (1986). The changing roles of fathers. In M. E. Lamb (Ed.), *The father's role: Applied perspectives* (pp. 3–28). New York: Wiley.

Lamb, M. E., & Baumrind, D. (1978). Socialization and personality development in the preschool years. In M. E. Lamb (Ed.), *Social and personality development* (pp. 50–69). New York: Holt, Rinehart & Winston.

Lamb, M. E., Frodi, A. M., Frodi, M., & Hwang, C. P. (1982). Characteristics of maternal and paternal behavior in traditional and nontraditional Swedish families. *International Journal of Behavioral Development, 5,* 131–141.

Lamb, M. E., Frodi, A. M., Hwang, C. P., Frodi, M., & Stenberg, C. (1982). Mother and father–infant interactions involving play and holding in traditional and nontraditional Swedish families. *Developmental Psychology, 18,* 215–221.

Lamb, M. E., Gaensbauer, T. J., Malkin, C. M., & Shultz, L. (1985). The effects of abuse and neglect on security of infant–adult attachment. *Infant Behavior and Development, 8,* 35–45.

Lamb, M. E., Hwang, C. P., Frodi, A. M., & Frodi, M. (1982). Security of mother- and father-infant attachment and its relation to sociability with strangers in traditional and nontraditional Swedish families. *Infant Behavior and Development, 5,* 355–367.

Lamb, M. E., & Malkin, C. M. (1986). The development of social expectations in distress relief sequence: A longitudinal study. *International Journal of Behavioral Development, 9,* 235–249.

Lamb, M. E., Morrison, D. C., & Malkin, C. M. (1987). The development of infant social experiences in face-to-face interaction. *Merrill-Palmer Quarterly, 33,* 241–254.

Lamb, M. E., Pleck, J. H., Charnov, E. L., & Levine, J. A. (1987). A biosocial perspective on paternal behavior and involvement. In J. B. Lancaster, J. Altman, A. Rossi, & L. Sherrod (Eds.), *Parenting across the life span: Biosocial perspectives* (pp. 111–142). Hawthorne, NY: Aldine DeGruter.

Lamb, M. E., Thompson, R. A., Gardner, E. L., & Charnov, E. L. (1985). *Infant–mother attachment: The origins and development significance of individual differences in Strange Situation behavior.* Hillsdale, NJ: Lawrence Erlbaum Associates.

Lamb, M. E., Thompson, R. A., Gardner, W. P., Charnov, E. L., & Estes, D. (1984). Security of infantile attachment as assessed in the Strange Situation: Its study and biological interpretation. *Behavioral and Brain Sciences, 7,* 127–147.

Lamb, M. E., & Urberg, K. A. (1978). The development of gender role and gender identity. In M. E. Lamb (Ed.), *Social and personality development* (pp. 178–199). New York: Holt, Rinehart & Winston.

Larson, L. E. (1972). The influence of parents and peers during adolescence: The situation hypothesis revisited. *Journal of Marriage and the Family, 34,* 67–74.

Lempers, J. D., Clark-Lempers, D., & Simons, R. L. (1989). Economic hardship, parenting, and distress in adolescence. *Child Development, 60,* 25–39.

Lerner, J. V. (1984). The import of temperament for psychosocial functioning: Tests of a "goodness of fit" model. *Merrill-Palmer Quarterly, 30,* 177–188.

Lerner, J. V., & Lerner, R. M. (1983). Temperament and adaptation across life: Theoretical and empirical issues. In P. B. Baltes & O. G. Brim (Eds.), *Life-span development and behavior* (Vol. 5, pp. 198–233). New York: Academic Press.

Lerner, R. M., Lerner, J. V., Windle, M., Hooker, K., Lenerz, K., & East, P. L. (1986). Children and adolescents in their contexts: Tests of a goodness of fit model. In R. Plomin & J. Dunn (Eds.), *The study of temperament: Changes, continuities and challenges* (pp. 99–114). Hillsdale, NJ: Lawrence Erlbaum Associates.

Lewis, M., & Feiring, C. (1989). Infant, mother and mother–infant interaction behavior and subsequent attachment. *Child Development, 60,* 831–837.

Lewis, M., Feiring, C., McGuffog, C., & Jaskir, J. (1984). Predicting psychopathology in 1-year-olds from early social relations. *Child Development, 55,* 123–136.

Libbey, P., & Bybee, R. (1979). The physical abuse of adolescents. *Journal of Social Issues, 35,* 101–126.

Londerville, S., & Main, M. (1981). Security of attachment, compliance, and maternal training methods in the second year of life. *Developmental Psychology, 17,* 289–299.

Lourie, I. (1977). The phenomenon of the abused adolescent: A clinical study. *Victimology, 2,* 268–276.

Lourie, I. (1979). Family dynamics and abuse of adolescents: A case for a developmental phase specific model of child abuse. *Child Abuse and Neglect, 3,* 967–974.

Lynch, M., & Roberts, J. (1982). *Consequences of child abuse.* London: Academic Press.

Lynn, D. B., & Cross, A. R. (1974). Parent preferences of preschool children. *Journal of Marriage and the Family, 36,* 555–559.

Lytton, H., & Zwirner, W. (1975). Compliance and its controlling stimuli observed in a natural setting. *Developmental Psychology, 11,* 769–779.

Maccoby, E. (1984). Middle childhood in the context of the family. In W. A. Collins (Ed.), *Development during middle childhood: The years from six to twelve* (pp. 184–239). Washington, DC: National Academy of Sciences Press.

Maccoby, E. E., Depner, C. E., & Mnookin, R. H. (1988). Custody of children following divorce. In E. M. Hetherington & J. D. Arasteh (Eds.), *Impact of divorce, single parenting, and stepparenting on children* (pp. 91–114). Hillsdale, NJ: Lawrence Erlbaum Associates.

Maccoby, E., & Martin, J. A. (1983). Socialization in the context of the family: Parent–child interaction. In P. H. Mussen (Series Ed.), & E. M. Hetherington (Vol. Ed.), *Handbook of child psychology: Vol. 4. Socialization, personality, and social development* (4th ed., pp. 1–102). New York: Wiley.

MacDonald, K., & Parke, R. D. (1984). Bridging the gap: Parent–child play interaction and peer interactive competence. *Child Development, 55,* 1265–1277.

Macfarlane, A. (1975). Olfaction in the development of social references in the human neonate. In M. A. Hofer (Ed.), *Parent–infant interaction.* Amsterdam: Elsevier.

Macfarlane, A. (1977). *The psychology of childbirth.* Cambridge, MA: Harvard University Press.

Mahler, M. S., Pine, F., & Bergman, A. (1975). *The psychological birth of the human infant.* New York: Basic.

Main, M. (1983). Exploration, play, and cognitive functioning related to infant–mother attachment. *Infant Behavior and Development, 6,* 167–174.

Main, M., & George, C. (1985). Response of abused and disadvantaged toddlers to distress in age mates: A study in the day care setting. *Developmental Psychology, 21,* 407–412.

Main, M., Kaplan, N., & Cassidy, J. (1985). Security in infancy, childhood, and adulthood: A move to the level of representation. In I. Bretherton & E. Waters (Eds.), *Growing points of attachment theory and research* (pp. 66–106). Monographs of the Society for Research in Child Development, 50, (1–2, Serial No. 209).

Main, M., & Weston, D. R. (1981). Security of attachment to mother and father: Related to conflict behavior and the readiness to establish new relationships. *Child Development, 52,* 932–940.

Marvin, R. S. (1977). An ethological-cognitive model for the attenuation of mother–child attachment behavior. In T. M. Alloway, L. Krames, & P. Pliner (Eds.), *Advances in the study of communication and affect, Vol. 3.: The development of social attachment* (pp. 25-60). New York: Plenum.

Marvin, R. S., & Greenberg, M. T. (1982). Preschoolers' changing conceptions of their mothers: A social-cognitive study of mother–child attachment. In D. Forbes & M. T. Greenberg (Eds.), *New directions in child development: Children's planning strategies* (Vol. 18). San Francisco: Jossey-Bass.

Matas, L., Arend, R. A., & Sroufe, L. A. (1978). Continuity of adaptation in the second year: The relationship between quality of attachment and later competence. *Child Development, 49,* 547-556.

Miyake, K., Chen, S. J., & Campos, J. J. (1985). Infant temperament, mother's mode of interaction, and attachment in Japan: An interim report. In I. Bretherton & E. Waters (Eds.), *Growing points of attachment theory and research* (pp. 276-297). Monographs of the Society for Research in Child Development, *50* (Serial No. 209).

Montemayor, R. (1982a, October). *Parent-adolescent conflict: A critical review of the literature.* Paper presented at the first biennial conference on Adolescent Research, Tucson, AZ.

Montemayor, R. (1982b). The relationship between parent–adolescent conflict and the amount of time adolescents spend alone and with their parents and peers. *Child Development, 53,* 1512-1519.

Montemayor, R. (1983). Parents and adolescents in conflict: All families some of the time and some families most of the time. *Journal of Early Adolescence, 3,* 83-103.

Montemayor, R. (1986). Family variation in parent–adolescent storm and stress. *Journal of Adolescent Research, 1,* 15-31.

Montemayor, R., & Brownlee, J. (1987). Fathers, mothers, and adolescents: Gender based differences in parental roles during adolescence. *Journal of Youth and Adolescence, 16,* 281-291.

Mueller, E., & Lucas, T. (1975). A developmental analysis of peer interaction among toddlers. In M. Lewis & L. Rosenblum (Eds.), *Friendship and peer relations* (pp. 223-257). New York: Wiley.

Murray, A. D. (1979). Infant crying as an elicitor of parental behavior: An examination of two models. *Psychological Bulletin, 86,* 191-215.

Nitz, K., Lerner, R. M., Lerner, J. V., & Talwar, R. (1988). Parental and peer ethnotheory demands, temperament, and early adolescent adjustment. *Journal of Early Adolescence, 8,* 243-263.

Noller, P., & Callan, V. J. (1986). Adolescent and parent perceptions of family cohesion and adaptability. *Journal of Adolescence, 9,* 97-106.

Noller, P., & Callan, V. J. (1988). Understanding parent-adolescent interactions: Perceptions of family members and outsiders. *Developmental Psychology, 24,* 707-714.

Norton, A. J., & Glick, P. C. (1986). One parent families: A social and economic profile. *Family Relations, 35,* 9-17.

Nye, F. I. (1958). *Family relationships and delinquent behavior.* New York: Wiley.

Oates, K., Peacock, A., & Forrest, D. (1984). The development of abused children. *Developmental Medicine and Child Neurology, 26,* 649-659.

Offer, D., & Offer, J. B. (1975). *From teenage to young manhood.* New York: Basic.

Offer, D., Ostrov, E., & Howard, K. (1981). *The adolescent: A psychological self-portrait.* New York: Basic.

Olsen, L., & Holmes, W. (1983). *Youth at risk: Adolescents and maltreatment.* Boston: Center for Applied Social Research.

Papousek, M., & Papousek, H. (1989). Forms and function of vocal matching interactions between mother and their precanonical infants. *First Language, 9* (Special Issue), 137-158.

Papousek, M., & Papousek, H. (1991). Early verbalizations as precursors of language development. In M. E. Lamb & H. Keller (Eds.), *Infant development: Perspectives from German-speaking countries* (pp. 299–328). Hillsdale, NJ: Lawrence Erlbaum Associates.

Parke, R. D. (1975). Rules, roles, and resistance to deviation: Recent advances in punishment, discipline and self-control. In A. D. Pick (Ed.), *Minnesota symposia on child psychology* (Vol. 8, pp. 111–143). Minneapolis: University of Minnesota Press.

Parke, R. D. (1979). Perspectives on father–infant interaction. In J. D. Osofsky (Ed.), *Handbook of infant development* (pp. 549–590). New York: Wiley.

Parke, R. D., & O'Leary, S. E. (1976). Family interaction in the newborn period: Some findings, some observations, and some unresolved issues. In K. Riegal & J. Meacham (Eds.), *The developing infant in a changing world.* Vol. 2: *Social and environmental issues.* The Hague: Mouton.

Parke, R. D., & Sawin, D. B. (1980). The family in early infancy: Social interactional and attitudinal analyses. In F. A. Pederson (Ed.), *The father–infant relationship: Observational studies in the family setting* (pp. 44–70). New York: Praeger Special Studies.

Pastor, D. L. (1981). The quality of mother–infant attachment and its relationship to toddlers' initial sociability with peers. *Developmental Psychology, 17,* 326–335.

Patterson, G. R. (1975). The aggressive child: Victim and architect of a coercive system. In L. A. Hamelynch, L. C. Handy, & E. J. Mash (Eds.), *Behavior modification and families.* New York: Brunner/Mazell.

Patterson, G. R. (1982). *Coercive family processes.* Eugene, OR: Castalia Press.

Patterson, G. R., & Dishion, T. J. (1988). A mechanism for transmitting the antisocial trait across generations. In R. Hinde & J. Stevenson-Hinde (Eds.), *Relations between relationships within families.* Oxford: Oxford University Press.

Pederson, F. A. (1980). *The father–infant relationship: Observational studies in a family setting.* New York: Praeger Special Studies.

Peterson, J. L., & Zill, N. (1986). Marital disruption, parent–child relationships, and behavior problems in children. *Journal of Marriage and the Family, 48,* 295–307.

Piaget, J. (1965). *The moral judgment of the child.* New York: Van Nostrand. (Original work published 1932)

Pianta, R., Egeland, B., & Erickson, M. F. (1989). The antecedents of maltreatment: Results of the Mother–Child Interaction Research Project. In D. Cicchetti & V. Carlson (Eds.) *Child Maltreatment: Theory and research on the causes and consequences of child abuse and neglect* (pp. 203–253). Cambridge: Cambridge University Press.

Powers, J. L., & Eckenrode, J. (1988). The maltreatment of adolescents. *Child Abuse and Neglect, 12,* 189–199.

Rendina, I., & Dickerscheid, J. D. (1976). Father involvement with first-born infants. *Family Coordinator, 25,* 373–378.

Rheingold, H., & Eckerman, C. (1970). The infant separates himself from his mother. *Science, 168,* 78–83.

Roggman, L. A. (1987). Mothers, infants, and toys: Social play correlates of attachment. *Infant Behavior and Development, 10,* 233–237.

Roopnarine, J. L., Taluker, E., Jain, D., Joshi, P., & Srivastavi, P. (1990). Characteristics of holding, pattern of play, and social behavior between parents and infants in New Delhi, India. *Developmental Psychology, 26,* 667–673.

Rosen, B. C., & D'Andrade, R. (1959). The psychological origins of achievement motivation. *Sociometry, 22,* 185–218.

Rubin, J., Provenzano, F., & Luria, Z. (1974). The eye of the beholder: Parent's view of sex of newborns. *American Journal of Orthopsychiatry, 43,* 720–731.

Russell, G., & Russell, A. (1987). Mother–child and father–child relationships in middle childhood. *Child Development, 58,* 1573–1585.

Rutter, M. (1971). Parent–child separation: Psychological effects on the child. *Journal of Psychology and Psychiatry, 12,* 233–260.

Rutter, M. (1979). Maternal deprivation, 1972–1978: New findings, new concepts, new approaches. *Child Development, 50,* 283–305.

Rutter, M., Graham, P., Chadwick, O. F. D., & Yule, W. (1976). Adolescent turmoil: Fact or fiction? *Journal of Child Psychology and Psychiatry, 17,* 35–56.

Rutter, M., & Madge, N. (1976). *Cycles of disadvantage: A review of research.* London: Heinemann.

Sagi, A., Lamb, M. E., Lewkowicz, K., Shoham, R., Dvir, R., & Estes, D. (1985). Security of infant–mother–father, and metapelet attachments among kibbutz-reared Israeli children. In I. Bretherton & E. Waters (Eds.), *Growing points of attachment theory and research* (pp. 257–275). Monographs of the Society for Research in Child Development, 50 (Serial No. 209).

Santrock, J. W., & Warshak, R. A. (1979). Father custody and social development in boys and girls. *Journal of Social Issues, 35,* 112–125.

Schaefer, E. S. (1965). Children's reports of parental behavior: An inventory. *Child Development, 36,* 413–425.

Schaefer, E. S. (1989). Dimensions of mother–infant interaction: Measurement, stability, and predictive validity. *Infant Behavior and Development, 12,* 379–393.

Sebald, H. (1977). *Adolescence: A social psychological analysis* (2nd ed.). Englewood Cliffs, NJ: Prentice-Hall.

Shantz, C. U. (1975). The development of social cognition. In E. M. Hetherington (Ed.), *Review of child development research* (Vol. 5, pp. 257–323). Chicago: University of Chicago Press.

Shinn, M. (1978). Father absence and children's cognitive development. *Psychological Bulletin, 85,* 295–324.

Silverberg, S. (1989, July). *A longitudinal look at parent adolescent relations and parents' evaluations of life and self.* Paper presented at the 10th biennial meeting of the International Society for the Study of Behavioral Development, Jyvaskyla, Finland.

Silverberg, S. B., & Steinberg, L. (1987). Adolescent autonomy, parent–adolescent conflict and parental well-being. *Journal of Youth and Adolescence, 16,* 293–312.

Simmons, R. G., & Blyth, D. A. (1987). *Moving into adolescence: The impact of pubertal change and school context.* Hawthorne, NY: Aldine de Gruyter.

Slough, N. (1988). *Assessment of attachment in five-year-olds: Relationship among separation, the internal representation, and mother-child functioning.* Unpublished doctoral dissertation, University of Washington, Seattle.

Smetana, J. G. (1983). Social-cognitive development: Domain distinctions and coordinations. *Developmental Review, 3,* 131–147.

Smetana, J. G. (1988a). Adolescents' and parents' conceptions of parental authority. *Child Development, 59,* 321–335.

Smetana, J. G. (1988b). Concepts of self and social conventions: Adolescents' and parents' reasoning about hypothetical and actual family conflicts. In M. R. Gunnar & W. A. Collins (Eds.), *Transitions to adolescence: The Minnesota Symposia on Child Psychology* (Vol. 21, pp. 79–122). Hillsdale, NJ: Lawrence Erlbaum Associates.

Smetana, J. G. (1989). Adolescents' and parents' reasoning about actual family conflict. *Child Development, 60,* 1052–1067.

Smetana, J. G. (in press). Doing what you say, and saying what you do: Reasoning about adolescent–parent conflict in interviews and interactions. *Journal of Adolescent Research.*

Smith, P. B., & Pederson, D. R. (1988). Maternal sensitivity and patterns of infant–mother attachment. *Child Development, 59,* 1097–1101.

Sroufe, L. A. (1977). Wariness of strangers and the study of infant development. *Child Development, 48,* 731-746.

Sroufe, L. A. (1983). Individual patterns of adaptation from infancy to preschool. In M. Perlmutter (Ed.), *Development and policy concerning children with special needs. Minnesota Symposium on Child Psychology* (Vol. 16, pp. 41-83). Hillsdale, NJ: Lawrence Erlbaum Associates.

Sroufe, L. A. (1985). Attachment classification from the perspective of infant-caregiver relationships and infant temperament. *Child Development, 56,* 1-14.

Sroufe, L. A. (1988). The role of infant-caregiver attachment in development. In J. Belsky & R. Nezworski (Eds.), *Clinical implications of attachment* (pp. 18-40). Hillsdale, NJ: Lawrence Erlbaum Associates.

Sroufe, L. A., Schork, E., Motti, F., Lawroski, N., & LaFreniere, P. (1984). The role of affect in social competence. In C. E. Izard, J. Kagan, & R. J. Zajonc (Eds.), *Affect, cognition, and behavior.* New York: Plenum.

Steinberg, L. (1981). Transformations in family relationships at puberty. *Developmental Psychology, 17,* 833-840.

Steinberg, L. (1987). Impact of puberty on family relations: Effects of pubertal status and pubertal timing. *Developmental Psychology, 23,* 451-460.

Steinberg, L. (1988). Reciprocal relations between parent-child distance and pubertal maturation. *Developmental Psychology, 24,* 122-128.

Steinberg, L. (1990). Interdependence in the family: Autonomy, conflict, and harmony in the parent-adolescent relationship. In S. S. Feldman & G. Elliott (Eds.), *At the threshold: The developing adolescent* (pp. 255-276). Cambridge, MA: Harvard University Press.

Steinberg, L., Elmen, J. D., & Mounts, N. S. (1989). Authoritative parenting, psychosocial maturity, and academic success among adolescents. *Child Development, 60,* 1424-1436.

Steinberg, L., & Silverberg, S. (1986). The vicissitudes of autonomy in early adolescence. *Child Development, 57,* 841-851.

Stern, D. (1977). *The first relationship.* Cambridge, MA: Harvard University Press.

Sternberg, K. J., Lamb, M. E., Greenbaum, C., Cicchetti, D., Dawud, S., Cortes, R. M., Krispin, O., & Lorey, F. (in press). Effects of domestic violence on children's behavior problems and depression. *Developmental Psychology.*

Stevenson, M. B., Leavitt, L. A., Thompson, R. A., & Roach, R. A. (1988). A social relations model analysis of parent and child play. *Developmental Psychology, 24,* 101-107.

Stevenson, M. B., Roach, M. A., verHoeve, J. N., & Leavitt, L. A. (1990). Rhythms in the dialogue of infant feeding: Preterm & term infants. *International Journal of Behavioral Development, 13,* 51-70.

Stolberg, A. L., & Anker, J. M. (1983). Cognitive-behavioral changes in children resulting from divorce and consequent environmental changes. *Journal of Divorce, 7,* 231-241.

Straus, M. A., & Gelles, R. J. (1986). Change in family violence from 1975-1985. *Journal of Marriage and the Family, 48,* 465-479.

Straus, M. A., Gelles, R. J., & Steinmetz, S. K. (1980). *Behind closed doors: Violence in the American family.* New York: Doubleday/Anchor.

Thoman, E. B. (1990). Sleeping and waking states in infants: A functional perspective. *Neuroscience & Biobehavioral Reviews, 14,* 93-107.

Thomas, A., & Chess, S. (1977). *Temperament and development.* New York: Brunner/Mazel.

Thompson, R. A., & Lamb, M. E. (1983). Security of attachment and stranger sociability in infancy. *Developmental Psychology, 19,* 184-191.

Thompson, R. A., & Lamb, M. E. (1986). Infant-mother attachment: New directions for theory and research. In P. Baltes, D. Featherman, & R. M. Lerner (Eds.), *Lifespan development and behavior* (Vol. 7, pp. 1-42). Hillsdale, NJ: Lawrence Erlbaum Associates.

Thompson, R. A., Lamb, M. E., & Estes, D. (1982). Stability of infant-mother attachment and its relationship to changing life circumstances in an unselected middle-class sample. *Child Development, 53,* 144–148.

Tronick, E. Z. (1989). Emotions and emotional communication in infants. *American Psychologist, 44,* 112–119.

Uhlenberg, P., & Eggebeen, D. (1986). The declining well being of American adolescents. *Public Interest, 82,* 25–38.

van IJzendoorn, M. H., Goosens, F. A., Kroonenberg, P. M., & Tavecchio, L. W. C. (1984, April). *Dependant attachment: A characterization of B children.* Paper presented to the International Conference on Infant Studies, New York.

Vaughn, B., Egeland, B., Sroufe, L. A., & Waters, E. (1979). Individual differences in infant–mother attachment at twelve and eighteen months: Stability and change in families under stress. *Child Development, 50,* 971–975.

Wallerstein, J. S., & Kelly, J. B. (1980). *Surviving the break-up: How children and parents cope with divorce.* New York: Basic.

Waters, E. (1978). The reliability and stability of individual differences in infant–mother attachment. *Child Development, 49,* 483–494.

Waters, E., Wippman, J., & Sroufe, L. A. (1979). Attachment, positive affect, and competence in the peer group: Two studies in construct validation. *Child Development, 50,* 821–829.

Wauchope, B., & Straus, M. A. (1989). Age, gender and class differences in physical punishment and physical abuse of American children. In M. A. Straus & R. J. Gelles (Eds.), *Physical violence in American families: Risk factors and adaptations in 8,145 families* (pp. 133–148). New Brunswick, NJ: Transaction Books.

Wentzel, K. R., Feldman, S. S., & Weinberger, D. A. (in press). Parental childrearing and academic achievement in boys: The mediational role of social-emotional adjustment. *Journal of Early Adolescence.*

Weston, D. R., & Richardson, E. (1985). *Children's world views: Working models and quality of attachment.* Poster presented at the biennial meeting of the Society of Research in Child Development, Toronto, Canada.

Widom, C. P. (1989). The cycle of violence. *Science, 244,* 160–166.

Wierson, M., Forehand, R., Fauber, R., & McCombs, A. (1989). Buffering young male adolescents against negative parental divorce influences: The role of good parent-adolescent relations. *Child Study Journal, 19,* 101–115.

Wolfe, D. A., & Mosk, M. D. (1983). Behavioral comparisons of children from abusive and distressed families. *Journal of Consulting and Clinical Psychology, 51,* 702–708.

Wolkind, S., & Rutter, M. (1985). Sociocultural factors. In M. Rutter & L. Hersov (Eds.), *Child and adolescent psychiatry: Modern approaches* (2nd ed., pp. 82–100). Oxford: Blackwell Scientific.

Yogman, M. W. (1982). Development of the father–infant relationship. In H. E. Fitzgerald, B. M. Lester, & M. W. Yogman (Eds.), *Theory and research in behavioral pediatrics* (Vol. 1). New York: Plenum.

Youngblade, L., & Belsky, J. (1990). The social and emotional consequences of maltreatment. In R. Ammerman & M. Herser (Eds.), *Children at risk: An evaluation of factors contributing to child abuse and neglect.* New York: Plenum.

Youniss, J. (1980). *Parents and peers in social development.* Chicago: University of Chicago Press.

Youniss, J. (1988). *Mutuality in parent-adolescent relationships.* Washington, DC: William T. Grant Commission on Work, Family, and Citizenship.

Youniss, J., & Ketterlinus, R. D. (1987). Communication and connectedness in mother- and father–adolescent relationships. *Journal of Youth and Adolescence, 16,* 265–280.

Youniss, J., & Smollar, J. (1985). *Adolescent relations with mothers, fathers, and friends.*

Chicago: University of Chicago Press.

Zaslow, M., Rabinovich, B., Suwalsky, J., & Klein, R. (1988). The role of social context in the prediction of secure and insecure-avoidant infant–mother attachment. *Journal of Applied Developmental Psychology, 9,* 287–299.

Zill, N., & Peterson, J. (1983). *Marital disruption and children's need for psychological help* (NIMH paper No. 6). Washington, DC: Child Trends, Inc.

9 Peer Relationships in Childhood

Kenneth H. Rubin
Robert J. Coplan
University of Waterloo

INTRODUCTION

It has long been argued that adaptive and maladaptive outcomes stem largely, if not mostly, from the quality of the child's relationship with his or her parents and from the types of socialization practices that the parents demonstrate. This primary focus on the developmental significance of the parent–child relationship and of parenting practices was taken early by Freud (1933) in his theory of psychosexual development, by Sears, Maccoby, and Levin (1957) in their seminal research on the significance of discipline variability and social learning, and by Bowlby (1958) in his influential treatise on the long-term developmental importance of the mother–infant attachment relationship. By and large, each of these theorists argued for the long-term developmental significance of early parent–child relationships and parenting practices. A review of these theories and the research emanating from them is described in Lamb, Ketterlinus, and Fracasso (Chap. 8, this volume).

Without denying the veracity of these claims, it is nevertheless the case that children spend an enormous amount of their time, both in and out of home, relating to and interacting with many others of potential influence. These significant others include their siblings, teachers or out-of-home caregivers, and peers. It is this latter group, children's peers, that is the focus of this chapter.

PEER RELATIONSHIPS RESEARCH:
HISTORY AND THEORY

History. It is interesting to note that the study of children's peer relationships has a relatively long history within the discipline of human development. As early as the turn of the century, Cooley (1902) maintained that children's peers, or their "primary groups," were important socialization agents, especially insofar as the development of the self system was concerned (see Chap. 7, this volume by Damon and Hart for a systematic review of this research). Yet, it was not until the 1920s, when the first child welfare research stations blossomed throughout North America, that the empirical study of children's peer relationships and social skills garnered a large and influential following. In these new research laboratories, investigators developed novel methodologies to examine developmental and individual differences in children's sociability and social participation (Parten, 1932), assertiveness (Dawe, 1934), sympathetic and altruistic behaviors (Murphy, 1937), aggression (Goodenough, 1931), group dynamics (Lewin, Lippit, & White, 1938), peer acceptance and group composition (Moreno, 1934), and the correlates of individual differences in social skills and competence (Jack, 1934; Koch, 1935).

By the beginning of the World War II, however, research concerned with child's play and children's playmates fell by the wayside. Those who had studied children turned their attention to performing war-related tasks and the number of personnel working at child welfare research stations was depleted (see Renshaw, 1981, for an excellent review of the peer relationships research conducted prior to 1940). Following the 1940s, the cold war fostered less research concern about children and their extrafamilial social relationships. Attention was directed to children's academic and intellectual prowess. Indeed, with the launching of the first earth-orbiting satellite by the U.S.S.R. in 1957, the pressures to train children to become achievement oriented and skilled in academic domains at earlier ages and at faster rates than ever before moved developmental researchers away from the earlier focus on children's social worlds. Nonetheless, the parent–child relationship remained a critical area of inquiry; after all, parents were viewed as primarily responsible for the socialization of achievement motives and behavior (e.g., Rosen & D'Andrade, 1959). Thus, while the study of social relationships remained part of the experimental repertoire for developmental psychologists, the examination of peer relationships was afforded limited attention.

The rediscovery of the developmental theory of Jean Piaget by North American psychologists in the 1960s likely led to a further disinclination to study children's peer relationships and social skills. North American researchers were considerably critical of many Piagetian premises concerning the development of cognitive operations. As such, archival journals were filled with descriptions of attempts to disprove Piaget by (a) altering the traditional Genevan research paradigms, or (b) attempting to train children to conserve, classify, or seriate. These paradigm shifts and training exercises were designed to demonstrate that the cognitive operations of reversibility and decentration could be taught or that they could be demonstrated at earlier ages than those proposed initially by Piaget and his Genevan colleagues. The research mandate to demonstrate earlier and faster learning of cognitive operations fit well within the achievement orientation of the times. Yet, while not believing Piaget about the trainability of cognitive operations, researchers in the 1960s and early 1970s nonetheless appeared to accept the premise that young children were primarily egocentric and neither willing, nor able, to understand the thoughts, feelings, and spatial perspectives of their peers. Egocentrism also stood in the way of making mature moral judgments and decisions (Kohlberg, 1963). Given these assumptions, it followed that studying children's peer relationships would do little good, at least until the mid-elementary school ages when concrete operations emerged and when egocentric thought vanished.

Finally, while the study of achievement and cognition dominated the field of child development, an important sociopolitical event occurred. President Lyndon Johnson proclaimed a "War on Poverty" in the United States. This war led to the development of early education prevention and intervention programs known as Head Start and Follow Through. The primary foci of these programs were cognitive and language development and the development of an achievement orientation in young children. Consequently, preschool programs were designed to prepare children for the academic "3Rs" of elementary school (reading, writing, and 'rithmetic). These novel curricula were often compared with the traditional social play-oriented nursery school in attempts to prove the efficacy of the former programs in training cognitive and language competencies. The traditional nursery fell out of favor because of its focus on social development and its purported neglect of cognitive and language development. As an aside, it is of no small interest to note that despite having been developed initially for children at socioeconomic and educational risk, cognitively-oriented preschool programs (e.g., Montessori), became increasingly favored by the achievement-oriented middle classes of the 1960s and 1970s.

Despite the emphasis on early cognitive and language development, the preschool and day-care movements of the 1960s and 1970s may have been more than a little responsible for the reemergence of peer relationships research. For one, the enormous growth in the numbers of early education and care centers in North America was dictated, not only by the need to prevent educational failure among the socioeconomically impoverished, but also by the need for out-of-home care for dual income middle-class households. Indeed, by 1985, approximately one of every two women with an infant younger than 12 months was employed (Belsky, 1988)!

Given that dual income and single-parent families require nonmaternal infant and early child care, and given that such care has increasingly taken the form of institutionalized day care and preschool, it is safe to say that children in North America are now entering organized peer group settings at earlier ages than ever before. Moreover, given the growing significance of education for life success, today's children remain with peers in age-segregated schools for more years than their cohorts of previous generations. Thus, it would have been shortsighted and irresponsible for developmental researchers to ignore the importance of children's peer relationships and social skills.

The bottom line, then, is that despite the primacy of cognitive and language developmental goals in institutionalized care and school settings, there has been a growing recognition that these more academic goals will not be met if the classroom constituents cannot get along with their peers, if they violate or are victimized by their peers, and if they feel inadequate in the company of their peers. Indeed, by the late 1970s, one of the earliest proponents of early intervention programs, Edward Zigler, wrote that "social competence, rather than IQ, should be the major source of intervention programs such as Head Start" (Zigler & Trickett, 1978, p. 793). Furthermore, it is now known that one of the best predictors of academic failure and high school drop-out is social rejection by the peer group in childhood (see Kupersmidt, Coie, & Dodge, 1990; Parker & Asher, 1987, for reviews).

Given the overview just presented, the purpose of this chapter is to describe the nature and significance of children's peer relationships. It is our intention to argue that such relationships represent contexts within which a significant degree of adaptive development occurs, and that without the experience of normal peer relationships, maladaptive development is likely to follow. We begin by providing a brief overview of the theoretical perspectives dominating the literature on children's peer relationships.

Theoretical Perspectives.   Ironically, one of the major theoretical figures in the study of children's peer relationships is Jean Piaget. In one of his first books, Piaget (1932) suggested that children's relationships with peers could be distinguished clearly, in form and function, from their relationships with adults. The latter relationships could be construed as being complementary, asymmetrical, and falling along a vertical plane of dominance and power assertion. Children normally accept adults' rules, not necessarily because they understand them, but rather because obedience is required. Alternately, adults are far less likely to follow the dictates of children.

On the other hand, children's peer relationships were portrayed as being balanced, egalitarian, and as falling along a more-or-less horizontal plane of power assertion and dominance. As such, it was within the peer context that Piaget believed children could experience opportunities to examine conflicting ideas and explanations, to negotiate and discuss multiple perspectives, to decide to compromise with or to reject the notions held by peers. These peer interactive experiences were posited to result in positive and adaptive developmental outcomes for children. For example, positive outcomes included, among other things, the ability to understand others' thoughts, emotions, and intentions (e.g., Doise & Mugny, 1981; Selman & Schultz, 1990).

Armed with these new social understandings, children were believed able to think about the consequences of their social behaviors, not only for themselves, but also for others. The abilities to take into account the perspectives of others and to identify the potential consequences of one's social actions have long been posited to result in the production of socially competent behavior (Dodge & Feldman, 1990). The relative lack of such skills, conversely, has been thought to predict incompetent social behavior. These Piagetian derived notions have influenced a good deal of contemporary research concerning children's peer relationships (e.g., Dodge & Feldman, 1990; Doise & Mugny, 1981; Rubin & Krasnor, 1986; Rubin & Rose-Krasnor, in press; Selman, 1985; Selman & Schultz 1990). One of the principal offshoots of this research has been the examination of relations among social cognition, social behavior, and the quality of children's peer relationships.

Another highly cited theoretical perspective on peer relations stems from the writings of Harry Stack Sullivan (1953). Like Piaget, Sullivan believed that the concepts of mutual respect, equality, and reciprocity developed from peer relationships. Sullivan, however, emphasized the significance of special relationships—chumships and friendships—for the emergence of these concepts. In the early school years, whether friends or not, Sullivan thought children were basically insensitive to their peers. During the juvenile years (late elementary school), however, children were thought to be able to recognize and value each other's personal qualities; as a consequence, peers gained power as personality shaping agents. Peers were thought to help each other understand the constructs of cooperation, competition, and social roles such as deference and dominance. Sullivan suggested that during preadolescence, children gained a more complex understanding of social relationships as the concepts of equality, mutuality, and reciprocity became central to their own close friendships. Once acquired between friends, these concepts were thought to be extended to other relationships. Sullivan's theory has proven influential insofar as the contemporary study of children's friendships is concerned (e.g., Berndt & Perry, 1986; Burhmester, 1990; Burhmester & Furman, 1987; Hartup, 1989; Parker & Gottman 1989; Youniss & Smollar, 1985).

Building on the turn-of-the-century notions of Cooley (1902), George Herbert Mead (1934) developed yet another influential theory implicating the significance of peer relationships in normal development. Like Piaget, Mead emphasized the importance of the development of perspective-taking through peer interaction. In his theory of symbolic interactionism, Mead suggested that the ability to reflect on the self developed gradually over the early years of life, primarily as a function of peer play and social interaction experiences. Participation in rule-governed games and activities with peers was believed to lead children to understand and coordinate the perspectives of others with relation to the self. Thus, perspective-taking experiences led to the conceptualization of the *generalized other* or the organized perspective of the social group, which in turn led to the emergence of an organized sense of self. In short, according to Mead, peer interaction was essential for the development, not only of perspective-taking skills, but also for the development of the self-system. This theoretical position has been highly influential in contemporary research concerning the relations between the quality of children's peer relationships and the organization of the self-system (e.g., Asher, Parkhurst, Hymel, & Williams, 1990; Damon & Hart, 1982; Damon & Hart, Chap. 7, this volume; Hymel & Franke, 1985; Mannarino, 1978).

Learning and social learning theory is yet another approach that has guided current research on children's peer relationships. It was suggested originally, and subsequently established empirically, that children learn about their social worlds, and how to behave within these contexts, through direct peer tutelage and indirect observation of peers in action (Bandura & Walters, 1963). From this perspective, peers are viewed as behavior control and behavior change agents for each other. Children punish or ignore non-normative social behavior and reward or reinforce positively those behaviors viewed as culturally appropriate and competent.

Social learning theory has been extraordinarily influential in the study of children's social behavior and their peer relationships. Over the years, for example, researchers have found that prosocial, agonistic, and sex-typed behaviors can be learned directly from peers as well as learned indirectly by observing these social behaviors and their consequences when enacted by peer models (see Hartup, 1983, for an extensive review of this research). In turn, the social behaviors learned and taught by peers have some bearing on the establishment, maintenance, and disruption of peer relationships.

Finally, ethological theory has proven influential insofar as the study of children's peer relationships is concerned. The ethological perspective suggests that there is a relation between biology and the ability to initiate, maintain, or disassemble particular relationships. It is a central tenet of ethological theory that social behavior and organizational structure are limited by biological constraints and by their serving an adaptive evolutionary function (Hinde & Stevenson-Hinde, 1976; Suomi, in press).

A basic focus of contemporary human ethological research has been the provision of detailed descriptions of the organization and structure of social behaviors and groups (Strayer, 1989). For example, prosocial, playful, and agonistic displays have been examined within the contexts of attachment, dominance, and affiliative relationships. Those who have studied children's social behaviors from an ethological perspective have focused their attention on the organizational structure and functions of children's peer groups.

THE DEVELOPMENTAL COURSE
OF PEER INTERACTION

It is not surprising that children become increasingly interactive and competent at initiating and maintaining social exchanges as they grow older. What might be surprising is how extremely young children are when they can be first observed demonstrating socially directed behaviors toward peers.

Given obvious motoric, cognitive, and verbal limitations, one might not expect much peer interaction when observing young infants. Indeed, Buhler (1935), in one of the first studies of peer interaction in infancy, suggested that prior to 6 months, babies were fairly oblivious to each other's presence. More recently, however, both Field (1979) and Fogel (1979) have reported that infants demonstrate social interest toward peers during the first half-year of life. Social interest is inferred from the presence of behaviors such as smiling, vocalizing, and reaching toward peers.

During the third quarter of the first year of life, infants produce clear manifestations of social interest in peers. When in the social company of age-mates, they watch, vocalize, reach toward, and smile at peers (Hay, Pederson, & Nash, 1982; Maudry & Nekula, 1939; Vandell, Wilson, & Buchanan, 1980). These socially oriented behaviors increase with age over the first year of life. Moreover, the tendency to respond to social overtures increases dramatically during the final quarter of the first year (Jacobson, 1981).

Despite the apparent sociability of the infant, it seems fairly clear that social interaction with peers occurs relatively rarely and that when interactive bouts do occur, they are not for lengthy periods of time. Nevertheless, rudimentary social acts are practiced, and become systematized and coordinated during the first year of life.

During the second year, toddlers take giant steps in advancing their social repertoires. With the emergence of locomotion and the ability to speak, social interchanges become increasingly complex. From the reaches, touches, and smiles of infancy, the toddler begins to demonstrate complementarity and reciprocity in his or her interactive behavior. Complementary roles can be observed in bouts of offer-and-receive and run-and-chase activities (Eckerman & Stein, 1982; Ross, Lollis, & Elliott, 1982). Thus, from the somewhat unpredictable social response sequences observed between infants, interactive exchanges and sequences in the toddler period can be characterized as more predictable, more complex, more coordinated, and lengthier (Baudonniere, Garcia-Werebe, Michel, & Liegois, 1989, Eckerman, Davis, & Didow, 1989; Eckerman & Stein, 1982, 1990; Goldman & Ross, 1978; Ross, 1982; Ross & Conant, in press; Ross & Kay, 1980; Ross et al., 1982). Some researchers believe that the roles demonstrated by children in their toddler games indicate the existence of an elementary cognitive understanding of rules concerning social exchange (Eckerman, in press; Goldman & Ross, 1978).

The major social interactive advance in the third year of life is the ability for children to share symbolic meanings through social pretense (Howes, 1985, 1988; Howes, Unger, & Seidner, 1989). This rather remarkable accomplishment for children spontaneously to take on complementary roles, none of which matches their real-world situations, and to agree on the adoption of these imaginary roles within a rule-governed context can be seen in the peer play of many 24- to 48-month-olds. At the same time, *prosocial* behavior (helping, sharing) is observed to increase from the early toddler to the early preschool years (Radke-Yarrow, Zahn-Waxler, & Chapman, 1983).

Yet, despite the advances noted above, it is clearly the case, then, when infants and toddlers are brought together in social groups, they spend most of their time alone, or near, or watching others and not in coordinated, complex social exchanges. Indeed, in the early 1930s, a classic study by Parten made evident the progression from nonsocial to social participation during the early- to mid-childhood period. We describe this progression in the following section.

Social Participation. In 1932, Parten published a manuscript in which she described six sequential social participation categories: unoccupied behavior, solitary play, onlooker behavior (the child observes others but does not participate in the activity), parallel play (plays beside but not with other children), associative play (plays and shares with others), and cooperative play (social play in which there is a defined division of labor). From her data, Parten concluded that children between the ages of 2 and 5 years engage in increasing frequencies of associative and cooperative play and in decreasing frequencies of idle, solitary, and onlooker behavior.

Parten's social participation scale and her reported findings dominated the literature concerning children's play and sociability for almost 50 years. Yet, her data base derived from samples of only 40 children attending a single university laboratory preschool. Furthermore, conclusions based on her data were overly simplistic. For example, the 3-year-old preschooler was characterized as a solitary or parallel player; the 5-year-old was described as spending the most time in associative or cooperative play.

A more critical reading of Parten's study and of those in which replications have been attempted (e.g., Barnes, 1971; Rubin, Maioni, & Horning, 1976; Rubin, Watson, & Jambor, 1978) suggests a more complex set of conclusions. First, even at 5 years of age children spend less of their free play time in classroom settings interacting with others than being alone or near others. Second, the major developmental changes in the play of preschoolers concern the cognitive maturity of their solitary, parallel, and group interactive activities (Rubin et al., 1978). Solitary–sensorimotor behaviors become increasingly rare over the preschool years, while the relative frequency of solitary–construction or exploration remains the same. Furthermore, the only types of social interactive activity to increase with age are sociodramatic play and games with rules. Taken together, the data extant reveal *age differences* only for particular forms of solitary and group behavior. In a later section, we discuss *individual differences* characterizing children's play in different types of solitary and social activity, and how such differences relate to the quality of children's relationships in the peer group.

Other Developmental Differences. On the prosocial side, 4-year-olds direct approval and affection to their peers more often than 3-year-olds (Charlesworth & Hartup, 1967). Aggression also increases with age; however, the proportion of aggressive to friendly interactions actually decreases with age (Hartup, 1983; see also Pepler & Rubin, 1991, for a relevant review).

Finally, older preschool-age children direct more speech to their peers than do their younger counterparts; however, regardless of age, two-thirds of preschoolers' socially directed speech is comprehensible and has a successful outcome (Levin & Rubin, 1983; Mueller, 1972). These data certainly raise questions concerning Piaget's assumption that the speech of preschoolers is characterized primarily by egocentric utterances.

Development Beyond the Preschool Period. The literature concerning quantitative and qualitative changes in social interaction beyond the preschool years is remarkably thin in scope. Communicative competence and the ability to persuade others to carry out one's own desired goals does appear to improve with age (see Levin & Rubin, 1983, for a review). The ability to resolve interpersonal dilemmas likewise improves with age (Rubin & Krasnor, 1986). Furthermore, with age children become better able to engage in the rule-governed competitive games (Hartup, Brady, & Newcomb, 1983). Finally, there are age-related increases in altruistic behavior (Radke-Yarrow et al., 1983) from early to middle and late childhood.

The age-related differences just described are generally thought to derive from intra- and interindividual sources. First, with cognitive development children become better able to understand others' thoughts, intentions, and emotions (Schultz & Selman, 1989; Selman, 1980; Selman & Schultz, 1990). With the development of decentration skills, children simultaneously come to understand their own and others' perspectives or to comprehend that the same social situation may demand both cooperation and competition (as in a rule-governed team sport). Second, parents assuredly play a role in the socialization of children's social skills and interactive behaviors. We briefly describe the relations among parenting behavior, parent-child relationships and children's social skills and peer relationships in a later section of this chapter.

CHILDREN AND THEIR FRIENDS

The establishment and maintenance of close friendships with peers represent challenging and rewarding tasks throughout development. In childhood, however, the constituent factors associated with friendship formation and maintenance change with age; indeed, the very meaning of friendship undergoes developmental change. Consequently, it is not surprising that children's friendships have been the focus of a large body of research. In the following sections we discuss the functions of friendship, children's changing understandings of friendship, children's interactive behaviors in friend and nonfriend peer groups, and the friendship formation process. An overriding theme will be the significance of friendship in children's social and emotional development.

Functions of Friendship.   Friendship reflects the presence of a close, mutual, and dyadic bilateral relationship. This distinguishes friendship from popularity, which refers to the experience of being liked or accepted by one's peers (Bukowski & Hoza, 1989). Friendship also reflects reciprocity and a feeling of perceived equality between individuals. In its simplest definition, reciprocity refers to the return of like behavior between partners, and is an essential component of any definition of friendship.

The functions of friendship have been subjected to theoretical enquiry for several decades. Sullivan (1953), for example, suggested that friendships in childhood serve to (a) offer consensual validation of interests, hopes, and fears; (b) bolster feelings of self-worth; (c) provide affection and opportunities for intimate disclosure; (d) promote the growth of interpersonal sensitivity; and (e) offer prototypes for later romantic, marital, and parental relationships. It is interesting to note that Sullivan argued, on the basis of his clinical experience, that children did not form true friendships until they reached age 9 or 10 years.

In recent years, it has been suggested that friendships serve functions additional to those offered by Sullivan. For example, friendships have been thought to (a) provide instrumental aid; (b) promote a sense of reliable alliance; (c) provide companionship; (d) provide a staging area for behavior; and (e) offer a forum for the transmission of social norms and knowledge (Bukowski & Hoza, 1989; Fine, 1981; Furman & Buhrmester, 1985; Furman & Robbins, 1985; Hartup & Sancilio, 1986; Lewis & Feiring, 1989). Perhaps most important of all, friendship offers children an extrafamilial base of security from which they may explore the effects of their behaviors on themselves, their peers, and their environments.

Parker and Gottman (1989) have argued that friendship is at the nucleus of developmental growth in social and emotional competence, and serves different functions for children at different points in development. For the young child, friendship serves to maximize excitement and amusement levels in play, and helps to organize behavior in the face of arousal. In middle childhood, friendships aid in acquiring knowledge about behavioral norms, and help children learn the skills necessary for successful self-presentation and impression management. These skills become crucial in middle childhood when anxiety about peer relationships develops. Finally, in adolescence, friendships serve to assist children in their quest for self-exploration, and to help them integrate logic and emotions.

Although Parker and Gottman base their speculations on a series of observational studies of friendship interaction and friendship formation begun in 1975 (see Gottman & Parker, 1986), they freely admit that their model is "unabashedly speculative, based on inferences drawn from coding and analysis of friendship conversations" (Parker & Gottman, 1989, p. 125). Despite this fact, their model merits further and more substantive empirical investigation, as it succeeds in synthesizing many previous theories of friendship functions.

Children's Conceptions of Friendship. One of the most productive areas of inquiry has been the study of children's conceptions of friendship and how such conceptions may change with development. Generally, these conceptions are assessed by asking children questions such as "What is a best friend?" (Youniss, 1980), or "What do you expect from a best friend?" (Bigelow, 1977). Based on interviews with Canadian and Scottish first through eighth graders, Bigelow (1977; Bigelow & LaGaipa, 1975) suggested that children's friendship conceptions progress through three broad stages. In the *reward-cost* stage (7–8 years of age), a friend is a companion who lives nearby, has nice toys, and shares the child's expectations about play activities. In the *normative stage* (10–11 years), shared values and rules become important, and friends are expected to stick up for, and be loyal to, each other. Finally, in the *empathetic stage* (11–13 years), friends are seen as sharing similar interests, making active attempts to understand each other, and being willing to engage in self-disclosure.

Other researchers have emphasized different aspects of the development of friendship conceptions. Selman (1976, 1980; Selman & Schultz, 1990), for example, argued that the key to developmental change in children's friendship conceptions is *perspective taking* ability. Young children do not yet realize that other people feel or think about things differently from themselves. As children grow older, they gradually begin to be able to take on the viewpoints of others, moving from egocentrism to a mutual perspective. As a final step, children/adolescents are able to mentally stand outside of the system itself and to view themselves and their relationships with others from a third person perspective. This shift in how children see others is thought to be manifested in their understanding of friendships. In one set of studies, for example, Selman (1981) has demonstrated that children who were cognitively advanced perspective-takers were also likely to have more sophisticated and mature ideas about friendship.

Youniss (1980; Youniss & Volpe, 1978) argued that children's friendship expectations develop in conjunction with the child's understanding of reciprocity. Young children, who believe that their own contribution to a friendship is the most important, are more likely to understand friendship in terms of momentary interactions, and how they themselves are affected. By the time children reach adolescence, friendship is perceived as an ongoing relationship, and friends are people on whom children can count for continuing understanding and intimate social support.

According to Selman, Youniss, and Bigelow, among others, children's ideas about relationships in general, and about friendship in particular, develop in a hierarchical, stagelike manner. Thus, it is assumed that the understanding of relationships is progressive, unidirectional and nonreversible, hierarchical, and qualitatively different from one stage to the next. In other words, all children are thought to progress through the same sequence of friendship understanding. Regression to earlier levels of cognitive structure or skipping levels are inconsistent with such structural models of social-cognitive development. Furthermore, each stage is considered qualitatively different in that progressive change involves a restructuring in the way an individual views social relationships.

Evidence in support of this stagelike model of friendship conceptions emanates largely from the work of Selman (1980). He suggested that children's ideas about friendship formation, trust, intimacy, conflict, and termination evolve in a stagelike manner. To support this claim, Selman has demonstrated that, at any given time, a child's ideas of friendship can generally be coded at, or around, a single stage or level. Furthermore, longitudinal research indicates that the development of friendship conceptions is generally progressive and invariant. Over a 2-year longitudinal period, Selman (1980) found that 83% of his sample demonstrated progressive change; the remaining 17% of the sample maintained their original levels of conceptual development.

Berndt (1981b), however, has argued that children's conceptions of friendship relationships do not change in a stagelike manner but rather represent the cumulative assimilation of basically unrelated themes or dimensions, such as commonalities in play interests and self-disclosure. According to Berndt, children do not abandon initial notions about play and mutual association when they eventually recognize the importance of intimacy and loyalty. This intriguing notion deserves further research as the current empirical evidence does not preclude the possibility that understanding about friendship develops cumulatively as opposed to hierarchically.

Although the jury is still out in terms of what may be the underlying mechanisms by which the understanding of friendships develops, certain generalizations are plausible. Essentially, children's conceptions about friendship reflect their own transitions from the world of the concrete to the world of the abstract. What children may require and desire in a friendship develops as a function of their growing understanding of the world and in conjunction with their own expanding social needs. Beginning in early childhood, the social world is cognitively differentiated, becoming more so as time goes on (Berndt & Perry, 1986). Eventually, children begin to realize that a friendship can serve potentially as both a resource and as a context that differs from the conditions that exist with nonfriends.

Similarities Between Friends.   The aforementioned theoretical perspectives on the development of children's friendship conceptions generate several predictions about the quality of children's friendships at various ages, along with how children will behave with their friends. For example, it would be consistent with these models if children's friendships actually demonstrated more stability, prosocial responding, psychological similarity, and intimate personal knowledge over time.

In actuality, friendships at all ages show remarkable stability. In the preschool years, two-thirds of children who identify one another as friends do so again 4 to 6 months later (Gershman & Hayes, 1983). Berndt and Hoyle (1985), however, found an increase in stability in mutual friendship from age 5 years to age 10 years but not from age 10 years to age 14 years.

Given that friendships are relatively stable phenomena, one important question concerns why it is that children are drawn into close relationships with each other. A facile first response is that age and sex are important magnets serving to pull children together (Duck, 1975; Kandel, 1978b). In addition, friends tend to be of the same racial or ethnic background (Singleton & Asher, 1979). Thus, it can be concluded that from an early age children tend to choose friends who are like themselves in observable characteristics. By adolescence, however, stable friendship pairs, as opposed to friendships that dissolve, are more likely to be similar in school attitudes and aspirations, attitudes toward the use of drugs and alcohol, and similar to each other concerning their attitudes about normative behaviors in the teen culture (Kandel 1978a, 1978b).

It also appears that friends know each other better as individuals as they get older. A study by Diaz and Berndt (1982) demonstrated that although knowledge of physical characteristics (e.g., birth date and phone number) did not show an age-related increase, older children were more capable than younger ones of accurately characterizing their friends' personalities, preferences, typical behaviors, and emotional responses (determined by comparing the child's responses with the friend's responses).

Behaviors Between Friends. Behaviorally, friends interact with each other differently than nonfriends. Positive social exchanges and mutuality occur more among friends than nonfriends of all ages (Baudonniere, 1987; Baudonniere et al., 1989; Hartup, 1983, 1989). Children as young as 3 ½ years of age direct more social overtures, engage in more social interaction, and play in more complex ways with their friends than with non-friends (Delormier, Tessier, Doyle, & Lebeau, 1991; Doyle, 1982). As well, preschool-aged friends tend to be more cooperative with each other during play (Charlesworth & LaFreniere, 1983).

Developmentally, it has been shown that altruistic acts, particularly generosity, cooperation, and helpfulness between friends, increase with age (Berndt, 1981a, 1985; see Hartup, 1989, for a review). Indeed, these increases in prosocial interchanges continue into adolescence (Berndt & Perry, 1986; Furman & Bierman, 1984).

This research is generally supportive of the predictions made by theorists concerned with children's developing conceptions of friendship. For example, the behavioral data indicate that there is an increase, with age, in the stability of friendships, in the exchange of intimate personal knowledge, and in the frequency of reciprocal prosocial acts between friends. Yet, in contrast to theoretical expectations, early friendships are somewhat more stable than originally proposed.

Other aspects of children's friendships have not presented a clear picture. Conflict, for example, appears to demonstrate a complex relation with friendship. Friends differ from nonfriends not only by engaging in more friendly interactions, but also by demonstrating more quarreling, active hostility (assaults and threats), and reactive hostility (refusals and resistance) between pairs (Green, 1933; Hinde, Titmus, Easton, & Tamplin, 1985). As well, Gottman (1983) found that initially unfamiliar pairs of children between the ages of 3 and 9 who became friends were more likely to give reasons for disagreements, to issue weak demands, and to avoid extended chains of disagreement in their conversations than those children who did not hit it off and become friends.

Hartup and his colleagues (Hartup & Laursen, in press; Hartup, Laursen, Stewart, & Eastenson, in press) demonstrated that nursery school children engaged in more conflicts overall with their friends than with neutral associates. Most likely, this can be attributed to the fact that friends spend much more time actually interacting with each other than do nonfriends. Hartup and his colleagues did report qualitative differences in how friends and non-friends resolved conflicts, and in what the outcomes of these conflicts were likely to be. Friends, as compared with nonfriends, made more use of negotiation and disengagement, relative to standing firm, in their resolution of conflicts. In terms of conflict outcomes, friends were more likely to have equal resolutions, relative to win or lose occurrences. Also, following conflict resolution, friends were more likely than neutral associates to stay in physical proximity and continue to engage in interactions. Older school-age friends also appear to resolve conflicts in qualitatively different manners than nonfriends, explaining themselves more, but also criticizing one another more, when resolving a conflict about social rules (Nelson & Aboud, 1985).

Sex differences also appear to bear a complex relation to friendship. Certain key differences in boys' and girls' peer cultures and in the nature of their interactions have been noted. For example, social networks are larger among boys than among girls, and relationships are less exclusive (Eder & Hallinan, 1978). As well, in their interactions with one another, boys tend to use commands more frequently than girls, who tend to use more suggestions and turntaking (Maccoby, 1986). In a recent study, Werebé and Baudonniere (in press) found that preschool girls engaged in almost twice as much sociodramatic play with their friends than did boys. Finally, boys tend to be more competitive than girls, both in within-group and between-group settings (Maccoby & Jacklin, 1974). It is important to study sex differences in children's behavior with their friends in order to assess properly whether experimental findings are generalizable to the population. In many ways, friendship experiences seem to be qualitatively different for boys and girls, and clearly more research is required in order to investigate this prospect.

In summary, children appear to behave differently in the company of friends than nonfriends. When children are interacting with friends, they tend to engage in more prosocial behaviors as well as more conflicts than when with nonfriends. These conflicts are most likely to be resolved through negotiation, and the outcomes are usually equitable. These differences suggest that children do view friendship as a unique context, separate and qualitatively different from their experiences with nonfriends.

Friendship Formation.   Many of the variables that have been used to characterize the nature of friendship interactions in children have also been used to describe and predict friendship formation. Children who are becoming friends engage in mutually directed affect and reciprocal interactions (Howes, 1983), and will ask each other questions in order to determine common ground (Furman & Childs, 1981). In his longitudinal study of 3- to 9-year-old children, Gottman (1983) found that children who were in the process of becoming friends were more likely to communicate clearly, self-disclose more often, have more positive exchanges, and resolve conflicts more effectively than children who would not become friends. Thus, it would appear as if friendships form when partners are able to establish some sense of commonality and community. This is accomplished through clear channels of mutual communication, thus allowing full understanding, and the avoidance or resolution of conflicts.

Children Without Friends.   Some children may be consistently unsuccessful in their attempts to make friends. Peer rejection may put these children at risk for later maladjustment (Kupersmidt et al., 1990; Parker & Asher 1987). It should be noted however, that children who are rejected by their peers are not necessarily friendless (Cairns, Cairns, Neckerman, Gest, & Garieppy, 1988). This leads to some interesting questions regarding the possible moderating or mediating effects of a close friend on the risk factors associated with peer rejection. It may be that a single close friend may serve to alleviate the negative effects of being disliked and isolated by the majority of one's peers.

Summary.   In summary, friendships serve many important and changing functions for a child as he or she develops. Children's conceptions of friendship progress from the concrete to the abstract with age, and this change is reflected in their behavior with their friends. With age, children's friendships demonstrate more stability, more reciprocal altruism, and more intimate personal knowledge. Friends engage in qualitatively different types of interactions than nonfriends at all ages, and the characteristics of these interactions can be used to describe and predict the friendship formation process. Children who are in the process of becoming friends are more likely to communicate clearly, self disclose more often, and resolve conflicts more effectively than children who will not become friends. From the data extant, it appears reasonable to conclude that childhood friendships, or the lack thereof, play a highly significant role in social development by providing children with settings and contexts within which to learn about themselves, their peers, and the world around them.

THE STRUCTURE OF CHILDREN'S GROUPS

Thus far, we have emphasized developmental trends in social interaction and the significance of dyadic peer relationships (friendship). Yet, as mentioned earlier, children spend much of their time in formal and informal group settings in which membership is not defined solely by friendship. In the following sections we (a) explore the functions of the peer group, (b) examine the processes that are involved in group formation, and (c) discuss briefly the nature of intra- and intergroup dynamics.

Definition and Functions of Peer Groups.   It is not uncommon to see groups of three to a dozen preschool children playing together in the classroom, the schoolyard, or the neighborhood. When children of this young age are observed together, for the most part, their behaviors are independently oriented, and their concerns are with their own immediate ends (Isaacs, 1933). Somewhere in middle childhood, however, a change occurs. This change can be characterized as a transformation from a group of peers to a peer group.

According to Hartup (1983), peer groups are characterized by peer participants who feel a strong desire to belong to a social unit, generate shared norms or rules of conduct beyond those maintained by society at large, and develop a hierarchical social structure of roles and relationships that govern their interaction with one another. Some researchers (e.g., Strayer, 1989; Strayer & Strayer, 1976) believe that the characteristics of a group can be represented by the additive effects of a specific behavior (e.g., dominance) from each member on one another. Another school of thought (see Ross, Cheyne, & Lollis, 1988) holds the position that it is necessary to demonstrate the characteristics of a group are emergent, that is, not reducible to the characteristics of the individuals who compose the group. Here the emphasis is on the nonadditivity of the individual's behaviors. Moreover, it has also been suggested that groups are more than just an aggregation of individuals; because every member has some relationship with every other member, these entities are best conceived of as aggregations of relationships, or as social systems (Hinde, 1976, 1987).

We have shown that close friendships serve several important and changing functions for a growing child. Also, experiences in multimember social groups provide children with a unique context for social learning. Fine (1980, 1987) suggested several important functions of the peer group. The group serves to teach children how to engage in cooperative activity aimed at collective rather than individual goals. Through the experiences associated with group membership, children also gain first-hand knowledge about social structures, practice the skills associated with leadership and followship, master control of hostile impulses toward fellow members, and learn to mobilize aggression in the service of group loyalty by directing it toward outsiders.

It is apparent that the peer group setting allows children to explore many other important aspects of social interaction that extend well beyond dyadic relationships. How peer groups are formed and the nature of the interactions both within- and between-groups are examined in the following sections.

Peer Group Formation.   We begin by describing a classic study by Sherif and his colleagues (1961), commonly referred to as the Robbers Cave Experiment. In a summer camp setting, observations were conducted on two groups of 10- and 11-year-old boys who were initially unaware of the other group's presence. During the first phase of the experiment, the 11-year-old boys in each group engaged in activities planned by the camp staff that required cooperation and interdependent activity. From the initial friendly intermingling among group members, a strong and cohesive group structure emerged. Soon each group evolved common goals, distinct names (the Rattlers and the Eagles), a sense of belonging, and a social organization. Over time, shifting patterns of leaders and followers stabilized from one activity to the next. Within each group there emerged a leader and some prestigious associates. Also, some members were of intermediate status and influence, while still others found themselves at the bottom of the social influence hierarchy. Norms for appropriate in-group behavior were slowly established, and it was not long before there was little need for corrective measures (e.g., reprimands or ridicule) to ensure behavioral conformity to these norms.

Sherif and his colleagues constructed *sociograms,* or graphs of the sociometric relationships among all the group members. These sociograms portrayed all the members of the group in relation to all others by indicating one-way choices, reciprocated choices, and one-way dislikes. It is interesting to note that these sociograms were the precursors to present-day sociometric scales, described in some detail later.

In the second phase of the Robbers Cave Experiment, the two groups "accidentally" discovered each other. Sherif was interested in how group norms and structures would evolve further, based on the groups' relationships with outsiders. A tournament of competitive activities was arranged between the two groups. This friendly competition between the groups soon deteriorated into a hard fought battle, and, consequently, had two striking effects. First, conflicts within groups increased. The consequence of losing was devastating for the solidarity of each group. Members began blaming one another for defeat as well as scapegoating. A social restructuring took place, with new leaders emerging, and new normative behaviors based on intergroup rivalry and hostility started to develop. More important, conflict between groups intensified enormously. "We" and "They" became salient frames of reference and animosities, hostile attacks, and retaliations between the groups escalated further.

In the final phase of the experiment, Sherif attempted to reconcile the two groups. The organization of some pleasurable joint recreational activities (a trip to the movies and fireworks), only served as new opportunities and settings for members of the two groups to berate each other. These first attempts were disastrous. The camp counselors preaching cooperation was also to no avail. Finally, the staff arranged activities with superordinate goals that each group desired but neither could achieve without the cooperation of the other (e.g., repairing the water supply and retrieving a stalled truck containing food for the campers). Only these circumstances, which required interdependent action among all the boys to solve a common problem, were able to achieve a reduction in intergroup hostility and an establishment of intergroup harmony.

This experiment neatly and clearly illustrates many of the important concepts involved in the study of social groups. Peer groups form when individuals perceive a commonality of shared goals. Shared motivations encourage the emergence of group norms, role structures, and social organization. As the group's goals may change, these basic determinants of its cohesion may be further modified in order to better adapt to the new situation. Group functioning also can be influenced by situational factors external to the group. It is important to note that these original findings have since been replicated in other natural peer group settings. Fine (1987) reported similar observations vis-à-vis the emergence of norms, roles, and structure in, for example, Little League baseball teams.

One of the most important and influential findings of the Robbers Cave Experiment suggests that activities with superordinate goals that one group cannot achieve without the aid of the other reduce intergroup hostilities and foster positive feelings and attitudes. These results have been substantiated further by applying these basic principles in different settings. For example, Aronson (1978) found that the best intervention for integrating handicapped and nonhandicapped students in classrooms involve (a) an active and necessary role for every child, (b) cooperative effort, and (c) a superordinate goal.

Many of the principles explored in the Robbers Cave Experiment have been examined more recently within a somewhat different theoretical framework, namely, ethology. The ethological perspective has provided an alternative vista for the examination of peer groups.

The Ethological Perspective.   Ethology is concerned with understanding the adaptive value of behavior and its evolutionary history. According to Markovits and Strayer (1982), ethology is often inappropriately defined simply as a behavioral science discipline involving the direct observation of naturally occurring behavior. A common focus in all ethological research is the commitment to provide a detailed description of behavioral patterns observed for a given species, and to answer questions concerning the organization or structure of the behavioral phenomena (Hinde, 1987). In addition, ethologists advocate the study of different species, in order to place the study of children in a comparative perspective.

Social ethology is concerned with the examination of individual social activity within the context of group social organization (Strayer, 1989). It is believed that individual growth and development take place within the dynamic context of group social organization (Attili, 1989; Crook, 1970; Hinde, 1987). Within the context of this social organization, group members differ along the dimensions of power or status. Ethologists have studied the bases on which group hierarchies emerge and how these hierarchical structures are related to cohesive forms of social activity.

Most research concerning group structure and hierarchies has focused on the importance of *dominance* (toughness and assertiveness) in determining ranks within the group. According to Markovits and Strayer (1982), social dominance essentially involves asymmetrical relationships. They distinguish between *dyadic dominance,* which refers to the balance of social power between two individuals in a social group, and *group dominance structures,* which refer to the organizational system that summarizes the coordination of all such dyadic relationships. These group dominance structures are more commonly referred to as *dominance hierarchies.* Essentially, dominance hierarchies are a stable ordering of individuals that serve to predict who will prevail under conditions of conflict between group members.

Many researchers have found that even in the preschool years, social dominance hierarchies are an important organizational feature of the peer group (e.g., Abramovitch, 1976; Strayer & Strayer, 1976; Vaughn & Waters, 1981). The observations of exchanges between children in which physical attacks, threats, and object conflicts occur reveal a consistent pattern of winners and losers. It is interesting to note, however, that although dominance relations are observable in the interactive behaviors of preschoolers, the children themselves cannot articulate their existence. Researchers have found that, when asked, preschoolers cannot agree on who is the toughest or strongest in their classrooms, and often nominate themselves (Edelman & Omark, 1973; Sluckin & Smith, 1977; Strayer, Chapeskie, & Strayer, 1978; Strayer, Moss, & Blicharski, 1988).

Social dominance hierarchies become increasingly stable during middle childhood (Strayer, 1989; Strayer & Strayer, 1976), especially among boys (Savin-Williams, 1979). Further ethological research has indicated that social dominance is a consistently contributing unifying aspect of peer group social organization throughout the grade school and adolescent periods (Savin-Williams, 1976; Weisfeld, 1980; Weisfeld, Omark, & Cronin, 1980). Agreements among individual group members as to which children are dominant and submissive is first evident in kindergarten and gradually increases with age (Edelman & Omark, 1973).

Another series of studies has examined how dominance affects cohesive forms of social activities and interactions. Research has shown that dominance is directly related to patterns of peer friendship and popularity (Strayer, 1980, 1989). Also, dominant children are looked at and imitated more often than nondominant children (Savin-Williams, 1980; Strayer, 1980; Vaughn & Waters, 1981). Additionally, Hartup (1983) reported that children are more likely to conform to the opinions and behavior of high-status peers.

In keeping with a central tenet of the ethological perspective, researchers have investigated the adaptive functions of dominance hierarchies. First, dominance hierarchies reduce overt aggression among members of the group, from preschool through to adolescence (La Freniere & Charlesworth 1983; Savin-Williams, 1976; Strayer, 1984; Weisfeld, 1980; Weisfeld et al., 1980). When hostility does occur between group members, it is usually very restrained, often taking the form of playfully delivered verbal insults (Fine, 1980; Savin-Williams, 1980). Dominance hierarchies also serve to help divide up, not only the tasks and labor of the group, but its resources as well. It is most often the case that "rank has its privileges," with lower status members assuming most of the work and high-status members benefiting the most from limited resources (Savin-Williams, 1979).

Some researchers, however, have questioned the central role of dominance as an organizing principle for the peer group (Vaughn & Waters, 1981). Savin-Williams (1980), for example, argued that during adolescence, group structures are less dependent on physical size and prowess, and more dependent on characteristics that support a group's present normative activities. These characteristics include athletic ability, intelligence, and engagement in friendly or sociable behaviors. These results are consistent with children's changing conceptions of friendship, discussed in some detail in the previous section. Hartup (1983) neatly sums up the situation by asserting that as groups may vary in their normative orientations, social power among group members will concordantly be distributed differently in different social situations.

There is also evidence that children's peer groups can be characterized along dimensions that are initially orthogonal to the dominance structures prevalent in the peer group. LaFreniere and Charlesworth (1983) found that children's peer groups were organized along multidimensional structures, including dominance, affiliation, and attention. These structures appear to converge with age (Strayer & Trudel, 1984).

Ethological research into the nature of group structures offers a unique and insightful perspective into intergroup dynamics. Peer groups from preschool to adolescence are organized and unified by dominance hierarchies among group members. These hierarchies serve the adaptive purpose of reducing intergroup aggression and assisting in the allocation of both group tasks and resources. There is some evidence that group structures may also be influenced by other member characteristics, including athletic ability, intelligence, and sociability, and some researchers believe that group structures are very much situation specific. LaFreniere and Charlesworth (1983) distinguish among two broad types of social power in children's peer groups. First, there is power that is expressed explicitly and forcefully and thereby elicits fear, submission, or compliance. Second, there is power that is implicit and stems from a recognition of status or competence and thereby depends on acceptance by subordinates. Longitudinal research is called for in which dominant- or high-power children are followed from preschool into middle childhood. It would be interesting to investigate the means by which they may maintain or lose their dominant status. The long-term consequences of both types of social power may well vary; this is certainly a testable hypothesis, and is one that merits investigation.

Notwithstanding the controversy surrounding some aspects of the study of peer groups, it is clear that peer groups offer children yet another unique context for learning about themselves and others. Children's initial dyadic experiences with friends assist them in acquiring the appropriate social skills necessary for peer acceptance. Once children are accepted by their peers, they are afforded the opportunity to explore the group setting. It is in this milieu where they learn about common goals, cooperation, and the complex interrelationships that comprise a group's structure.

PEER ACCEPTANCE AND REJECTION

According to Barker and Wright (1955), during the 1950s children between the ages of 7 and 11 spent over 40% of their waking hours with peers. It is likely that with the advent of increased and improved child care and with significant increases in dual-income households, the 40% figure noted by Barker and Wright now represents a severe underestimate. Given that this may be the case, the potential significance of being accepted and liked by one's peers is clear.

The experience of being liked and accepted by the peer group is known as popularity. This construct reflects the view of the group vis-à-vis any given individual (Bukowski & Hoza, 1989). Presumably, children who are not accepted by their peers experience some difficulty in their interactions with their peers. In the following sections, we examine the methods used by researchers to assess children's difficulties and/or acceptance within the peer group. We also describe findings concerning the possible determinants of peer acceptance, and the outcomes that persistent difficulties with peers may entail.

Assessing the Quality of Children's Peer Relationships

A quick glance at recent issues of the archival journals in developmental psychology (e.g., *Child Development* or *Developmental Psychology*) would reveal a mind-boggling array of procedures designed to assess the quality of children's peer relationships. Basically, these procedures may be subdivided into categories corresponding to two questions posed by Parker and Asher (1987): (a) Is the child liked? (b) What is the child like?

These questions are generally addressed by accessing information from one of three sources: the child's peers, his or her teachers, and behavioral observations. The methodological variants have led to a plethora of labels assigned to children who are nominated, rated, or observed by peers, teachers, and researchers. From these procedures, researchers are now able to identify children as "popular," "sociable," "withdrawn," "isolated," "neglected," "unpopular," "rejected," "aggressive," "controversial," and "average."

In the following section, we wade our way through the methods used to identify children to whom these labels are attached.

Peer Assessments. Children are excellent at indicating who in their peer group has qualitatively good or poor relationships. As insiders, peers can identify characteristics of children and of relationships that are considered relevant from the perspectives of those who ultimately determine a child's social status and integration within the peer group. Moreover, the judgments of peers are based on many extended and varied experiences with those being evaluated. For example, peers may be able to consider low-frequency but psychologically significant events (e.g., a punch in the nose or taking someone's valued possession) that lead to the establishment and maintenance of particular social reputations. These latter events may be unknown to nonpeer outsiders. Finally, peer assessments of children's behaviors and relationships represent the perspectives of many observers with whom the target child has had a variety of personal relationships. Taken together, it is not surprising that most contemporary research concerning the quality, the correlates, and the determinants of children's peer relationships is dominated by peer assessment methodology.

The two major peer assessment techniques are sociometric measures of peer acceptance and assessments of social behavior. The former procedure addresses the question of likeability; the latter procedure addresses the issue of identifying social behavioral characteristics.

Sociometric Nominations.   Sociometry has a long and rich history. Beginning with Moreno (1934), sociometry was viewed as a way to examine the structure or organization of the peer group. More recently, sociometric procedures have been used to identify children who are popular or disliked in a specific group.

The sociometric nomination procedure involves asking children to nominate a number of peers (usually three to five) according to some specified positive and/or negative criteria ("Name three classmates you really like" or "Name up to three classmates with whom you do not like to play").

Nomination techniques typically result in classifying children into one of several possible sociometric categories. A variety of classification systems has been used over the years (see Hymel & Rubin, 1985; Newcomb & Bukowski, 1983, for reviews), but according to Crick and Ladd (1989), researchers now use most frequently the classification system developed originally by Coie, Dodge, and Coppotelli (1982). The groups identified by this procedure include: (a) *popular* children—children who receive many positive nominations and few negative nominations; (b) *average* children—children who receive an average number of positive and negative nominations; (c) *neglected* children—children who receive few positive and negative nominations; (d) *rejected* children—children who receive few positive nominations and many negative nominations; and (e) *controversials*—children who receive many positive and many negative nominations.

Over the years, researchers have found that the more extreme sociometric classifications are relatively stable over time. Popular children tend to remain popular, rejected children tend to remain rejected (Coie & Dodge, 1983; Newcomb & Bukowski, 1983). When changes do occur it is usually from popular to average and vice-versa, or from neglected to average. Rarely do popular children become rejected, and even more rarely do rejected children become popular.

The tendency to classify children into presumably orthogonal sociometric categories has proven tempting to many. So, too, has the tendency to assume that each category of peer acceptance corresponds to particular behavioral profiles (see review following). Yet, it is important to note that, on close examination, particular sociometric classifications appear to be inhabited by children who are behaviorally quite distinct from one another. Specifically, there appear to be subcategories of under- and overcontrolled rejected children who may be characterized by impulsivity, disruptiveness, and aggression on the one hand, and by wariness, anxiety, and social withdrawal on the other hand (e.g., French, 1988, 1990; Rubin, Hymel, LeMare, & Rowden, 1989).

Thus, although it may be important to distinguish between sociometrically popular, rejected, neglected, and average children, it is equally important to acknowledge that the developmental causal pathways to and from each of these status classifications may vary. Children may arrive at a particular social status for many different reasons. Furthermore, it may be that information about children's placement in some of these classifications may be more significant and developmentally revealing than placement in other classifications. For example, it may be more important to identify children who are rejected than those who are neglected by their peers. We return to these points in a later section.

Sociometric Rating Scales. Another type of sociometric evaluation involves rating scales. In this case, each child is asked to rate all of his or her classmates on a Likert-type scale, with regard to some specified criteria ("How much do you like this person?" or "How much do you like to play or work with this person?"). The average rating received from peers is taken as an index of peer acceptance or popularity. The rating scale has several advantages over the nomination technique. For one, although rating-scale scores and nomination sociometric scores have been found to be highly correlated (Asher & Hymel 1981; Asher, Singleton, Tinsley, & Hymel, 1979; Bukowski & Hoza, 1989; Hoza, Bukowski, & Gold, 1987), rating scales have been shown to be more reliable or stable over time than nomination scores (Asher et al., 1979), especially with younger children (Hymel, 1983). Second, in contrast to nomination scores, rating-scale scores are based on perceptions of all peers by all peers within the group.

A disadvantage of rating scale scores, however, is that they do not permit distinctions between subclasses of unpopular children. For example, both rejected and neglected children, as identified via the nomination procedure, may receive low preference rating scores. Thus, Bukowski and Hoza (1989) suggest that rating scales are best conceptualized as a type of composite measure of popularity, simultaneously representing both the dimensions of acceptance and rejection.

Although sociometric measures can be used to obtain both valid and reliable information concerning the extent to which particular children are accepted or rejected by their peers, they do possess certain limitations. For one, sociometric measures do not lend themselves to repeated or continuous assessment; more important, they do not provide any information whatsoever about the factors that may contribute to peer status. In other words, sociometric procedures only answer the question, "Is the child liked?" and not "What is the child like?" The methods designed to identify the behavioral characteristics of children are examined in the next section.

Peer Assessments of Social Behavior. In general, peer assessment procedures involve asking children to nominate peers on the basis of a variety of behavioral roles or character descriptions provided ("Who in your class is a good leader?", "Who gets into fights?", or "Who likes to play alone?"). Nominations received from peers are summed in various ways to provide indices of a child's typical social behavior or reputation within the peer group. Two commonly used peer assessment techniques are the Revised Class Play (Masten, Morison, & Pellegrini, 1985) and the Pupil Evaluation Inventory (PEI; Pekarik, Prinz, Liebert, Weintraub, & Neale, 1976). Factor analysis of children's nominations using these two measures has yielded three similar behavioral factors. For the PEI, the factors obtained were Likeability, Aggression, and Withdrawal. The factors obtained for the Revised Class Play are labeled Sociability–Leadership, Aggressive–Disruptive, and Sensitive–Isolated.

By and large, peer assessments of behavior have proved stable. Longitudinal investigations have demonstrated, however, that peer assessments of sociability and aggression are more stable than those of social withdrawal (e.g., Moskowitz, Schwartzman, & Ledingham, 1985; Olweus, 1984). This finding has been viewed by some as a reflection of the normalcy and salience of particular constellations of social behavior at different points in childhood. For example, from very early in childhood, aggression is viewed as deviant and unacceptable (e.g., Rubin, LeMare, & Lollis, 1990). Social withdrawal, however, is not viewed negatively by peers until the later years of childhood (Rubin et al., 1990; Younger & Boyko, 1987; Younger & Piccinin, 1989). Consequently, the instability of peer assessments of social withdrawal may be attributed to the inability of young children to conceptualize these behaviors accurately. This would suggest the testable hypothesis that adult-assessed or -observed withdrawal should prove more stable than peer assessments of the phenomenon taken during the same period of time. It would behoove researchers to examine this possibility empirically.

Teacher Assessments of Peer Acceptance.   Teachers are a second source of information concerning children's peer relationships and social behaviors. Teachers spend an enormous amount of time with children; thus, like peers, teachers may provide useful and rich data concerning low-frequency social exchanges that may contribute toward the quality of a child's peer relationships. One advantage that teacher assessments have over peer assessments is that the collection of data from them is much more efficient and less time-consuming. One need not require precious classroom time in order to gather the assessment data. A second advantage is that teachers may prove to be more objective than peers in their assessments of social behavior. Teachers are not part of the group structure or behavioral schemes being evaluated: thus, they may be valuable, objective sources of information. On the other hand, teachers may bring with them an adultomorphic perspective that carries with it value judgments about social behaviors that might differ from those of children. This possibility has not received much attention in the existing literature.

Teacher *referrals* are often utilized in the initial screening of children experiencing social difficulties (Gresham, 1981; Michelson & Wood, 1981; Strain, Cooke, & Apolloni, 1976; Strain & Kerr, 1981). Reliance on teacher judgments is obviously an efficient, economical way to identify target children as aggressive or withdrawn from an initially large pool of potential candidates. However, potential bias may exist in teacher nominations or referrals of children experiencing social difficulties. Indeed, as Strain and Kerr (1981) noted, there is considerable evidence that teachers are more likely to refer socially aggressive as opposed to socially isolated or withdrawn children. Further, there is evidence to suggest that teacher perceptions of the social behaviors contributing to peer acceptance may vary depending on the sex of the child (La Greca, 1981). To date, the validity of teacher referrals has not been examined empirically, and researchers have relied on more structured teacher assessment procedures in order to assess children's social difficulties.

Given the pros and cons of using teacher assessments, it is interesting to note that teachers generally agree with peers concerning the rating of childhood acceptance. Typically, teachers are asked to rank order or rate children in terms of their relative popularity or preference as playmates (Connolly & Doyle, 1981; Green, Forehand, Beck, & Vosk, 1980; Vosk, Forehand, Parker, & Rickard, 1982). In general, these ratings correlate in the .40 to .60 range with peer sociometric measures (Connolly & Doyle, 1981; Green et al., 1980).

Like peer sociometric techniques, however, teacher ratings of social status tell us little about the associated behaviors that accompany or predict the general quality of children's peer relationships. Also, they do not allow distinctions to be made among peer popularity, rejection, and isolation.

Teacher Assessments of Social Behavior. It is not uncommon for psychologists to request teachers to assess the social and emotional characteristics of their students. Many standardized measures presently exist (see Hymel & Rubin, 1985; Michelson, Foster & Richey, 1981; Rubin et al., 1990, for reviews). Generally, these measures can be broken down into several socioemotional clusters or factors that fall along dimensions of sociability–likeability–leadership, aggression–hostility–conduct disorder, hyperactivity–impulsivity, and anxiety–fearfulness–withdrawal.

It is interesting that the relationships between teacher and peer assessments of children's social behavior are generally quite strong, especially as concerns aggression and sociability (Ledingham, Younger, Schwartzman, & Bergeron, 1982). Moreover, the relationships between teacher and peer assessments of social withdrawal increase with age from early-to-late childhood, becoming equivalent to the peer–teacher relationships, insofar as aggression is concerned, by late childhood and early adolescence (Hymel, Rubin, Rowden, & LeMare, 1990; Ledingham et al., 1982). It is likely that the increased correspondence between peer- and teacher-derived information concerning social withdrawal emanates from the increased salience that the phenomenon takes on for peers with increasing age.

Behavioral Observations of Social Behavior. It has been suggested that behavioral observations represent the standard against which all other forms of social behavioral assessment must be measured. Yet, relative to the use of peer and teacher assessment, behavioral observations remain infrequently used.

Several factors conspire against the use of observational methodology. First, observations are time-, energy-, and money-consuming. Whereas peer and teacher assessments can be conducted in minutes or hours, observations can require weeks or months of data collection. Second, as children get older it becomes increasingly difficult to observe them during free play. Third, observations may be reactive; for example, children who are aware that they are being observed may behave atypically, perhaps suppressing negative behaviors or increasing the production of prosocial behaviors.

Nevertheless, a true picture of aggression, withdrawal, or socially competent behavior is probably best painted from observations of children in naturalistic settings. From these observations, age and sex norms can be established for the production of particular forms of social behavior. From these norms, procedures may be developed to identify children who deviate from their age-mates or from children of the same gender.

For example, Rubin and colleagues (e.g., Rubin et al., 1990; Rubin & Krasnor, 1986) have developed a norm-based time-sampling procedure to identify extremely withdrawn and extremely aggressive children. In this procedure, a variety of play behaviors is coded within a free-play context (see Fig. 9.1). In preschools and kindergartens, children are observed during classroom freeplay (e.g., Rubin, 1982a, 1982b; Rubin & Daniels-Beirness, 1983). In elementary schools, children are invited to play with three same-sex age-mates for four free-play sessions in a laboratory playroom. Each child's playmates differ in each of the four sessions, thus allowing observations to be made with 12 different playmates (Rubin, 1985; Rubin & Mills, 1988; Hymel et al., 1990).

Behaviors are coded on a checklist that includes the cognitive play categories of functional–sensorimotor, exploratory, constructive, dramatic, and games-with-rules behaviors nested within the social participation categories of solitary, parallel, and group activities mentioned earlier. In addition, aggression, rough-and-tumble play, unoccupied and onlooker behaviors, and conversations with peers are recorded. Generally, children are observed for 10-second time samples.

FOCAL CHILD'S NAME OR I.D. #_____

TIME SAMPLE

	1	2	3	4	5	6	7
UNOCCUPIED							
ONLOOKER							
CONVERSATIONS							
ROUGH & TUMBLE							
AGGRESSION							
TRANSITIONAL							
SOLITARY:							
OCCUPIED							
FUNCTIONAL							
EXPLORATORY							
CONSTRUCTIVE							
DRAMATIC							
GAMES							
PARALLEL:							
OCCUPIED							
FUNCTIONAL							
EXPLORATORY							
CONSTRUCTIVE							
DRAMATIC							
GAMES							
GROUP:							
OCCUPIED							
FUNCTIONAL							
EXPLORATORY							
CONSTRUCTIVE							
DRAMATIC							
GAMES							
PROXIMITY:							
DIRECT CONTACT							
W-IN ARM'S LENGTH (CODE ADULT OR CHILD)							
ORIENTED TO							
NOT ORIENTED TO							
BEYOND ARMS LENGTH							
ORIENTED TO							
NOT ORIENTED TO							
ANXIOUS BEHAVIOURS							
ATTEMPTED TO LEAVE ROOM							
OUT OF ROOM							

CONVERSING/INTERACTING WITH: 1._____ 2._____
3._____ 4._____
5._____ 6._____
7._____

FIG. 9.1.   The play observation scale (Rubin, 1989).

From these data, age norms can be produced for social withdrawal and aggression. *Socially withdrawn* children are those whose solitary, unoccupied, and onlooker activity exceeds the age-group mean by one standard deviation and whose social play is less than one standard from the mean. *Aggressive* children are those whose aggressive behavior exceeds the age-group mean by one standard deviation.

Observational procedures such as those described above are useful in targeting children whose behaviors deviate from age-group norms. In addition, such procedures can be used to validate peer and teacher assessments of children's social behavior. Yet, because of prohibitive costs, observations are used rarely to target children as socially skilled, aggressive, or withdrawn.

To summarize, many different methods have been used to assess children's functioning within peer groups. Sociometric techniques are useful indications of how children feel about a specific child, that is, "is the child liked." This does not, however, inform us about the behaviors associated with, or contributing to, these assessments. Conversely, assessments and behavioral observations of children's social behaviors describe "what the child is like" but fail to inform us about their standing in the peer group. In the following section, we examine the relations between peer acceptance and children's social behaviors.

CORRELATES AND DETERMINANTS
OF PEER ACCEPTANCE

Who are the children that have qualitatively good or poor peer relationships? What are they like? These two questions have been subjected to countless numbers of studies for almost half a century (e.g., Bonney, 1942; Grossman & Wrighter, 1948; Northway, 1944). For the most part, researchers have focused on the behavioral correlates of peer acceptance and rejection. Thus, right from the start, we must issue two cautions to the reader. First, because the data described stem from correlational studies, one must not assume that the behaviors associated with peer acceptance or rejection necessarily cause children's social status. Second, not all correlates and potential causes of peer acceptance and rejection are behavioral in nature. For example, popularity is positively associated with academic competence (Coie & Krehbiel, 1984) and physical attractiveness (Langlois & Stephan, 1981); it is negatively associated with having an uncommon name (see Hartup, 1983, for a relevant review). Nevertheless, a minimal amount of variance appears to be accounted for by physical appearance and uncommon names; consequently, the variables that are most highly associated with status in the peer group include children's social behaviors and their ways of thinking about social phenomena.

Behavioral Correlates of Peer Acceptance

If one is to accept the classification scheme currently in vogue vis-à-vis the study of children's peer relationships, one might expect to find different and distinct behaviors associated with popular, rejected, neglected, and average peer status. Indeed, several researchers have adopted a rather simplistic perspective; they associate particular sociometric classifications with specific behavioral clusters. Thus, popular children have been viewed as cooperative and altruistic, rejected children as aggressive, and neglected children as socially withdrawn. We argue here, however, that children may acquire any particular peer reputation in a multitude of different ways.

Popular children are skilled at initiating and maintaining qualitatively positive relationships. When entering a new peer situation, popular children are more likely than members of other sociometric status groups to consider the frame of reference common to the ongoing playgroup, and to establish themselves as sharing in this frame of reference (Putallaz & Wasserman, 1990). It is as if they ask themselves "What's going on?" and then, "How can I fit in?" Popular children are also less likely to draw unwarranted attention to themselves when entering ongoing playgroups. That is, they do not talk exclusively or overbearingly about themselves and their own social goals or desires, and they are not disruptive of the group activity (Dodge, Schulundt, Schocken, & Delugach, 1983). Popular children are also viewed as cooperative, friendly, sociable, and sensitive by peers, teachers and behavioral observers (e.g., Coie et al., 1982; Coie, Dodge, & Kupersmidt, 1990; Rubin et al., 1989). In short, popular children appear to be socially competent.

Neglected children, those who receive few peer nominations of any kind, have typically been described as shy and withdrawn (e.g., Coie et al., 1982; Coie & Kupersmidt, 1983; Dodge, Murphy, & Buchsbaum, 1984). This characterization has led to a number of problematic and unfortunate conclusions.

First, it has been held traditionally that social withdrawal does not represent a long-term risk factor for children (Morris, Soroker, & Burruss, 1954; Robins, 1966). This clinical perspective has recently been questioned by several researchers who have demonstrated that childhood social withdrawal and its concomitants are predictive of subsequent psychological difficulty (e.g., Olweus, in press; Rubin & Mills, 1991). Thus, the conclusion that sociometric neglect is akin to social withdrawal suggests that neither phenomenon is of psychological significance, particularly insofar as long-term risk is concerned (e.g., Coie & Kupersmidt, 1983).

Second, the assumption that neglected children are socially withdrawn is not particularly accurate. The suggestion appears accurate if the reference against which neglected children are compared is the popular sociometric group. By and large, however, neglected children are no more shy and withdrawn than children identified as average in sociometric status (Coie et al., 1982; Dodge, 1983; Rubin et al., 1989). Indeed, neglected children are not even rated as less popular than peers of average sociometric status (Asher & Wheeler; 1985; French & Waas, 1985; Rubin et al., 1989). These latter findings are especially damaging insofar as the risk status of sociometric neglect is concerned; they do not, however, even begin to address the question of the risk status of social withdrawal. Thus, we must conclude that the often-cited equation of sociometric neglect and behavioral withdrawal is unwarranted. Whether neglected children differ from their average peers in ways other than their social behaviors is substance for further study. From our perspective, however, it would appear as if sociometrically neglected children are basically average on most dimensions of psychological significance.

To further confuse the issue, it appears as if extremely withdrawn children, especially in the mid-to-late years of childhood, are sociometrically rejected, and not neglected (Hymel & Rubin, 1985; Rubin & Chen, 1991; Rubin et al., 1989, 1990). Rejected children are described as more anxiously withdrawn (French, 1988, 1990; Rubin et al., 1990) and as more likely to play in inappropriate solitary manners than other sociometric groups (Coie & Kupersmidt, 1983; Dodge, Coie, & Brakke, 1982). Withdrawn preschoolers and kindergartners, however, do not appear to be rejected by their peers (Rubin, 1982a). Thus, it seems that when social withdrawal becomes salient to the peer group, it is judged as a marker of social deviance, and subsequently becomes associated with peer rejection (Younger, Gentile, & Burgess, in press).

Nonetheless, the most commonly cited correlate of peer rejection is aggression. This finding emerges regardless of whether peer evaluations (Cantrell & Prinz, 1985; Carlson, Lahey, & Neeper, 1984; Coie et al., 1982; Rubin et al., 1989), teacher ratings (Coie & Kupersmidt, 1983; Dodge, 1983; Dodge et al., 1982), or direct observations (Coie & Kupersmidt, 1983; Dodge, 1983) are used to evaluate children's social behavior.

It is important to reiterate at this point that the data we have described here are correlational. In two ground-breaking studies, however, Dodge (1983) and Coie and Kupersmidt (1983) observed the interactions of unfamiliar peers with one another. These interactions took place over several days. Gradually some of the children became popular, whereas others were rejected. The behavior that most clearly predicted peer rejection was aggression!

All in all, the findings just reported, when taken together with the more recent data concerning the association between peer rejection and social withdrawal, suggest that this particular sociometric category is heterogeneous in character. Indeed, French (1988, 1990) found two clusters of rejected boys and girls; one cluster may be best described as aggressive, the other as withdrawn. It would appear, then, that any form of social behavior considered deviant from normalcy is likely to be associated with peer rejection.

Social Cognitive Correlates of Peer Acceptance

Researchers have also investigated the relations between peer acceptance and social cognition. Generally, the argument has been that the ways in which children interpret and process information about their social worlds play a causal role in determining their production of social behaviors (Dodge, 1986; Rubin & Krasnor, 1986). In turn, these behaviors lead to peer acceptance or rejection.

An example of how social cognition may be implicated in the establishment of particular types of peer relationships is taken from a social information-processing model described by Rubin and Krasnor (1986). These authors speculated that when children face an interpersonal dilemma (e.g., making new friends or acquiring an object from someone else) their thinking follows a particular sequence. First, children may select a *social goal*. This entails the establishment of a representation of the desired *end state* of the problem-solving process. Second, they *examine the task environment;* this involves reading and interpreting all the relevant social cues. For example, boys and girls are likely to produce different solutions when faced with a social dilemma involving same-sex as opposed to opposite-sex peers (Rubin & Krasnor, 1983). The social status, familiarity, and age of the participants in the task environment also are likely to influence the child's goal and strategy selection (Krasnor & Rubin, 1983). Third, they *access and select strategies;* this process involves generating possible plans of action for achieving the perceived social goal, and choosing the most appropriate one for the specific situation. Fourth, they *implement the chosen strategy*. Finally, it is proposed that children *evaluate the outcome of the strategy;* this involves assessing the situation to determine the relative success of the chosen course of action in achieving the social goal. If the initial strategy is unsuccessful, the child may repeat it or he or she may select and enact a new strategy, or abandon the situation entirely. Dodge (1986) has proposed a similar social-cognitive model designed specifically to account for the production of aggression in children. This model also consists of five stages, namely, (a) the encoding of social cues, (b) the interpretation of encoded cues, (c) the accessing and generation of potential responses, (d) the evaluation and selection of responses, and (e) the enactment of the chosen response.

Aggressive and rejected children demonstrate characteristic deficits or qualitative differences in performance at various stages of these models. They are more likely than their nonaggressive and more popular counterparts to assume malevolent intent when they are faced with negative circumstances, even when the social cues are ambiguous (Dodge, 1986; Dodge & Feldman, 1990). Also, many researchers have demonstrated that aggressive and rejected children generate qualitatively different solutions, such as agonistic or bribe strategies, and are less likely than their nonaggressive or more popular counterparts to suggest prosocial strategies in response to social problems concerning object acquisition or friendship initiation (Rubin, Bream, & Rose-Krasnor, 1991; Rubin & Clark, 1983; Rubin, Moller, & Emptage, 1987; Walters & Peters, 1980).

Insofar as withdrawn children are concerned, in early childhood they suggest during interviews that they would use more adult-dependent and nonassertive social strategies to solve their interpersonal dilemmas (Rubin, 1982a; Rubin & Krasnor, 1986). Despite their actual production of unassertive strategies, withdrawn children are more often rebuffed by their peers than are nonwithdrawn children (Rubin & Borwick, 1984; Rubin & Krasnor, 1986). This finding suggests that withdrawn children, although not sociometrically rejected in the early years do experience qualitatively poor peer relationships as evidenced by the experience of behavioral rebuff (Rubin, 1985).

The social-cognitive profiles of elementary and middle school-age extremely withdrawn and extremely aggressive children are quite distinct. The latter group misinterprets ambiguous social stimuli, misblames others, and often responds with inappropriate anger-aggravated hostility (Dodge, 1986). There can be little doubt why such cognition-behavior sequences are associated with peer rejection. Withdrawn children, by the middle school years, do not appear to have difficulties in interpreting social cues and in generating competent solutions to interpersonal dilemmas. Their problem is in the production or enactment phase of the processing sequence (Rubin & Krasnor, 1986). Psychologists have speculated that social dilemmas evoke emotionally anxious–fearful reactions in withdrawn children; their inability to regulate and overcome their wariness is proposed to result in an unassertive, submissive social problem-solving style. It is interesting, however, that there has been little research in which the relations between emotion and affect regulation and social information processing have been studied.

Cognitions and Feelings About the Self and Peer Acceptance

Do children feel and think better about themselves when they experience positive peer relationships? Is there a relation between negative self-perceptions and peer rejection? These important questions have attracted research attention in recent years.

Perceived social competence was first defined and assessed by Harter (1982) as an index of children's awareness of their own peer acceptance or social skillfulness. In general, children with higher perceived social competence tend to be more popular with peers, and there is also a trend for the magnitude of this relation to increase with age (Harter, 1982; Kurdek & Krile, 1982; Ladd & Price, 1986; Rubin, 1985).

Rejected children do think more poorly about their own social competencies than do their more popular age-mates; however, this conclusion appears to be true only for that group of rejected children described as anxious–withdrawn (e.g., Boivin & Bégin, 1989). Rejected–aggressive children do not report thinking poorly about their social relationships with peers (Patterson, Kupersmidt, & Griesler, 1990). These findings are in keeping with the results of recent studies concerning extremely withdrawn and extremely aggressive children; it is only the former group that reports having difficulty with social skills and peer relationships (Rubin, 1985; Rubin & Chen, 1991).

Self-efficacy has been defined as the degree to which children believe they can successfully perform behaviors that are necessary for achieving desired outcomes (Bandura, 1977). In general, positive correlations have been found between children's social self-efficacy perceptions and positive sociometric nomination scores (Ladd & Price, 1986; Wheeler & Ladd, 1982). More recent research has demonstrated that aggressive and socially withdrawn children differ with regard to their perceived social self-efficacy. First, aggressive and nonaggressive children do not differ from each other concerning their self-efficacy perceptions of prosocial behaviors; aggressive children, however, report higher efficacy for enacting verbally and physically aggressive acts than do their peers. In contrast, withdrawn children report lower efficacy for enacting verbally and physically aggressive behaviors relative to peers (Crick & Dodge, 1990; Perry, Perry, & Rasmussen, 1986; Quiggle, Panak, & Garber, 1989).

Finally, rejected children report feeling more isolated and lonely than do their more well-accepted peers (see Asher et al., 1990 for a review). Asher and colleagues have reported consistently that it is only the rejected group that reports feeling lonely relative to average and popular children; neglected children are no more lonely or dissatisfied with their social circumstances than sociometrically average children (Asher & Wheeler, 1985; Asher & Williams, 1987). Furthermore, it appears as if it is only the rejected–submissive/timid/withdrawn subgroup that reports being more lonely than their more accepted peers; rejected–aggressive children do not express negative feelings in this regard (Boivin, Thomassin, & Alain, 1989; Parkhurst & Asher, 1987; Williams & Asher, 1987).

In summary, the data extant lead to two clear conclusions. First, rejected children internalize their social difficulties with peers; they report that they are less competent, less efficacious, and less satisfied vis-à-vis their social skills and peer relationships. Second, this conclusion is true only for that subset of rejected children who can be described as withdrawn, timid, or submissive. This latter conclusion demonstrates the importance of treating peer rejection as a heterogeneous entity.

Finally, it is probable that having a good friend can go a long way in preventing the development of negative feelings about one's social life. This suggestion has received support recently in a study by Bukowski and Newcomb (1987). These researchers found that having one mutual friend in a class buffered unpopular children from feeling poorly about themselves. These data may help serve to explain the finding that rejected–aggressive children do not report difficulties with the self system. Although this group is generally disliked by classmates, aggressive children do tend to affiliate with others like them (Cairns & Cairns, 1991). The social support available to them, albeit from a deviant subgroup, may buffer aggressive children from developing negative self perceptions and loneliness.

Summary.   In this section we described the characteristics of popular, rejected, and neglected children. Of these groups, only the rejected children appear to have substantive problems. They are unskilled socially and social-cognitively, and they think poorly of themselves and of their social relationships and skills. Rejected-aggressive children can best be characterized as behaviorally hostile and as having a limited social-cognitive repertoire insofar as dealing with interpersonal problems. Rejected-withdrawn children can best be characterized as behaviorally submissive and as thinking and feeling poorly about themselves. Given these characterizations, it behooves us to ask whether peer rejection can be used as a red flag to identify children who may be at risk for developing negative psychological outcomes as adolescents or adults. We address this question in the following section.

OUTCOMES OF PEER
RELATIONSHIP DIFFICULTIES

What are the known predictive correlates of peer rejection, aggression, and withdrawal? Generally, this question has been addressed by employing one of two research strategies. Most studies have been of a *follow-back* nature. This design usually begins with the identification, in adolescence or adulthood, of a particular target group (e.g., school dropouts, schizophrenics, or those with a record of delinquent crime). The target group is matched with a sample of nonsymptomatic subjects. Data obtained in childhood, usually from school or professional records, are examined in order to discover between-group differences. The data relevant to this section are pieces of information obtained retroactively concerning the quality of children's peer relationships and social skills.

The much less often used, but more revealing methodological strategy is labeled the *follow-forward* design. Such procedures typically involve following, longitudinally, a group of children from elementary school to high school or college age. Given the serious methodological problems associated with follow-back designs (e.g., distortions in retrospective memory, selective subject loss, and the use of inadequate and psychometrically questionable measures to assess peer relations at the earlier time period; see Parker & Asher, 1987, for a critique of such developmental designs), the literature reviewed herein stems only from follow-forward designs.

For the most part, the best and most consistent predictive outcomes of childhood peer rejection are school related. Being disliked in childhood predicts academic difficulties, truancy, and high school dropout (e.g., Barclay, 1966; Ullman, 1957). The predictive connection between experiencing poor peer relationships in elementary school and academic difficulties later on makes a good deal of sense. Academia must assuredly lose its luster when many of a child's peers demonstrate and target their negative feelings toward her or him. This is likely to be the case, not only for the child who was doing poorly in school to begin with, but also for the intellectually competent child. Withdrawing via truancy or by dropping out may serve as the escape route for children who are consistently the butt of peer rejection.

Another predictive outcome of peer rejection is adolescent delinquency. Recently, Kupersmidt and Coie (1990) reported the findings of a longitudinal study in which they followed-forward a group of fifth-grade children for 7 years. Children identified as sociometrically rejected were twice as likely to be delinquent (35%) in adolescence than was the case for the sample base rate (17%). Finally, Coie, Christopoulos, Terry, Dodge, and Lochman (1989) reported that peer rejection in the fourth grade was predictively associated with maternal reports of internalizing and externalizing difficulties in early adolescence.

The results of these follow-forward studies provide initial substance for the notion that qualitatively poor peer relationships in childhood represent an index of developmental risk. The risk outcomes appear to be school difficulties, adolescent criminality and externalizing problems, and psychological difficulties of an internalizing nature (e.g., anxiety or depression).

The negative outcomes just mentioned, however, are actually far more strongly predicted by behavioral assessments in childhood. For example, childhood aggression, as assessed by peers or teachers, is the strongest predictor, by far, of adolescent crime and delinquency (e.g., Farrington,

1991; Kupersmidt & Coie, 1990; Parker & Asher, 1987). Aggression in childhood also predicts academic failure and school dropout. Childhood aggression is also an antecedent of adult psychiatric problems, especially those of an externalizing nature (see Pepler & Rubin, 1991, for extensive reviews of the predictive outcomes of childhood aggression).

Only recently have longitudinal data become available for children identified as passively withdrawn. Rubin and colleagues followed-forward a group of children from kindergarten (age 5 years) to the ninth grade (age 15 years). They reported that passive withdrawal in kindergarten and Grade 2 predicted self-reported feelings of depression, loneliness, and negative self-worth, and teacher ratings of anxiety in the fifth grade (age 11 years; Hymel et al., 1990; Rubin & Mills, 1988). In turn, social withdrawal in the fifth grade predicted self-reports of loneliness, depression, negative self-evaluations of social competence, feelings of not belonging to a peer group that could be counted on for social support, and parental assessments of internalizing problems in the ninth grade (Rubin & Mills, 1991). In short, in one of the few follow-forward studies of normal school-attending children, the demonstration of anxious–passive social withdrawal has been shown to predict outcomes of an internalizing nature during adolescence.

Recently Caspi and colleagues have capitalized on the existence of the archival data set from the classic Berkeley Guidance Study (Macfarlane, Allen, & Honzik, 1954). Participants in the study, begun in 1928, were followed-forward from late childhood to adulthood. The particular focus of Caspi and colleagues' work was the life course of children who either "moved against the world" (Caspi, Elder, & Bem, 1987) or "moved away from the world" (Caspi, Elder, & Bem, 1988). The former group may best be described as aggressive and ill-tempered; the latter group as shy, passive, and withdrawn. Children who moved against the world continued to be ill-tempered as adults. The men with histories of ill-temperedness in childhood had lower occupational status, more erratic work lives, and less stable marriages than their more average counterparts. Women with histories of ill-temperedness married men of lower occupational status and had less stable marriages (Caspi et al., 1987). Children who moved away from the world also experienced negative outcomes in adulthood. Males continued to be shy or withdrawn into adulthood. In addition, they were delayed, relative to the norm, in marrying, becoming fathers, and establishing stable careers. Sociologically, they could best be described as being normatively off-time in their transitions to age-graded roles (Caspi et al., 1988). Finally, childhood shyness and passivity had an indirect and significant effect on occupational instability and low achievement in adulthood. Furthermore, it was linked indirectly with divorce by mid-life. Females also continued to be withdrawn into adulthood. But unlike their male counterparts, they led prototypically sex role-appropriate life patterns of marriage and homemaking. Taken together then, the Berkeley data suggest different outcomes for socially withdrawn males and females; only males appear to suffer negative outcomes. However, it is important to note that with their increased entry into post-secondary education and the previously male-dominated work force, women may be at similar occupational and marital risk as men, should they be submissive, shy, and withdrawn in childhood. This is, of course, a testable hypothesis of the generational or cohort effects of a given social–behavioral pattern in childhood.

In summary, children who have difficulty in their peer relationships appear to experience negative life-course outcomes. Specifically, peer rejection strongly predicts academic failure and school dropout. Aggression predicts externalizing difficulties and a life-course of criminality and occupational and marital instability. Recent studies indicate that social withdrawal may be a risk factor for the development of internalizing problems. However, the costs of being socially submissive and withdrawn may be greater for males than females. It is important to conclude that further longitudinal studies of rejection, aggression, and withdrawal are necessary before the findings described here can be accepted with some confidence.

ORIGINS OF CHILDREN'S
PEER RELATIONSHIPS AND SOCIAL SKILLS

By now, it should be obvious that children's peer relationships and social skills are of central importance to their experience of everyday life. Popular and socially competent children feel and think well of themselves, and they fare better in school than their less popular and skilled age-mates. Rejected children, on the other hand, tend to lead less successful lives.

Given the contemporaneous and long-term significance of children's peer relationships and social skills, it seems reasonable to ask questions about their origins. It is surprisingly that, to date, relatively little is known about this topic. The quality of children's extrafamilial social lives is likely a product of factors internal and external to the child. For example, it seems reasonable to suggest that biological or dispositional factors (e.g., temperament) may influence the quality of children's peer relationships. It is equally plausible to attribute the social well-being of children to their parent–child relationships and to their parents' socialization beliefs and behaviors. In the following section, we present a brief review of dispositional and parenting factors that may influence children's peer relationships.

Temperament and Peer Relationships. Despite the general lack of research relating dispositional factors and children's peer relationships, it is not difficult to imagine how such factors may be influential. Take, for example, three infant characteristics that have received a good deal of research attention—difficult temperament, activity level, and inhibition-sociability. *Difficult temperament* refers to the frequent and intense expression of negative affect (Thomas & Chess, 1977). Fussiness and irritability would be characteristic of a difficult infant. The highly *active* baby is one who is easily excited and motorically facile. Infants who are timid, vigilant, and fearful when faced with novel social stimuli are labeled *inhibited;* those who are outgoing and open in response to social novelty are described as *sociable* (Kagan, 1989).

Each of these temperamental characteristics appears to be stable, and each is related to particular constellations of social behaviors that we have described earlier as characteristic of popular and rejected children. For example, difficult and active temperament in infancy and toddlerhood are associated predictively with developmental problems of undercontrol in early childhood (e.g., aggression; Bates, Maslin, & Frankel, 1985). In turn, undercontrolled, impulsive and aggressive behavior is characteristic and predictive of peer rejection (Bates, Bayles, Bennet, Ridge, & Brown, 1991).

Similarly, infant inhibition predicts social withdrawal in early and middle childhood (Kagan, 1989). As mentioned earlier, social withdrawal in mid-childhood is a strong correlate of peer rejection. Finally, sociability is a significant correlate of popularity in childhood.

Taken together, infant temperament may set the stage for the development of parent–child relationships and social behavioral profiles that ultimately predict the quality of children's peer relationships. Although plausible, this notion has undergone little, if any, empirical scrutiny.

Parenting and Peer Relationships. Individual traits or dispositions do not develop in a vacuum. Children usually grow up living with their parents and one or more siblings. Moreover, their families bring with them societal and cultural expectations and values, and stressors and supports that must influence children's social repertoires.

The developmental theories we described earlier have all had something to say about the role parents play in their children's social development. Thus, psychoanalytic (see Maccoby & Martin, 1983, for a review), ethological (e.g., Ainsworth, 1973, Sroufe, 1983), and social learning (e.g., Bandura, 1977; Radke-Yarrow & Zahn-Waxler, 1986) theorists have strongly implicated parenting behaviors and the quality of parent–child relationships in the development of children's social skills and peer relationships (see also Lamb et al., Chap. 8, this volume, for a relevant review).

The classic developmental theories have provided, historically, the basis for a number of studies assessing the relations between parenting behaviors and children's social relationships and skills (Baldwin, 1955; Baumrind, 1967; Sears, 1961; Sears et al., 1957). For example, Putallaz (1987) recently found that mothers of popular children were less demanding, less disagreeable, more feelings oriented, and more likely to positively address their children when communicating, than mothers of less popular children. Parental use of reasoning and explanations has also been associated positively with popularity (Roopnarine, 1987; Roopnarine & Adams, 1987).

A second research stream focuses on the quality of the parent–child relationship. This research has generally demonstrated a reliable association between the quality of the parent–infant relationship and the subsequent demonstration of social skills in the child's peer group (Booth, Rose-Krasnor, & Rubin, 1991; Sroufe & Fleeson, 1986). Although promising, longitudinal data supportive of this link are only slowly beginning to accumulate.

In summary, there is at present, little research addressed to relations among parent–child relationships, parental behavior, and the quality of children's peer relationships. This is clearly an area in need of further study (see Putallaz & Heflin, 1990, for a review of the research extant). There is a larger body of research concerning the relations between parenting behaviors and childhood aggression. Generally, it is found that physically punitive parents, and parents who are both critical and disapproving of their children, while also demonstrating too much permissiveness, have children who are aggressive in the peer group (Baumrind, 1967, 1971; Patterson, 1983). In addition, it has been suggested that parental overcontrol, as evidenced in authoritarian patterns of socialization, is associated with social withdrawal in the peer group (Baumrind, 1971; Hetherington & Martin, 1986; Rubin & Mills, 1990). These latter speculations are also in need of further empirical attention.

A MODEL OF THE DEVELOPMENT
OF POPULARITY AND REJECTION

Drawing largely from relevant developmental theory, and from disparate areas of child developmental research, we have described a number of models of pathways to peer acceptance and rejection (Rubin et al., 1990; Rubin & Mills, 1991). These models are highly speculative and, as yet, empirically untested. Yet they provide heuristics for considering the development of social acceptance and rejection.

A Pathway to Peer Acceptance.   We begin with two assumptions. First, acceptance by peers is largely a function of the child's social skills; in normal circumstances, all else is secondary. Second, the development of social skills and subsequent peer acceptance derives from the interaction of intraindividual, interindividual, and macro-systemic forces. More specifically, social competence is probably the joint product of the child's dispositional and biologically based characteristics, his or her parents' socialization practices, the quality of relationships within and outside of the family, and the forces of culture, stress, and social support impinging on the child and the family.

In the most positive scenario, a combination of (a) an even-tempered, easy disposition, (b) the experience of sensitive and responsive parenting, and (c) the general lack of major stresses or crises during infancy and early childhood is hypothesized to predict the development of secure parent–child attachment relationships (Rubin et al., 1990; Rubin & Mills, 1991). In turn, these secure primary relationships are hypothesized to predict the development of social competence (e.g., Grossmann & Grossmann, in press; Sroufe, 1983).

This viewpoint derives from our understanding of some of the general functions of parent–child relationships (Hartup, 1985). First, parent–child relationships constitute emotional and cognitive resources that allow children to explore their social and nonsocial worlds. Second, the early parent–child relationship may serve as the precursor or model of all subsequent relationships (e.g., Bowlby, 1973). Given these perspectives, it is not difficult to understand how secure parent–child relationships, once established, can contribute to behavioral competence.

Most infants and toddlers have relatively easygoing dispositions (Thomas & Chess, 1977), and most come to develop secure relationships with their parents (Ainsworth, Blehar, Waters, & Wall, 1978). These relationships appear to be caused and maintained, in part, by sensitive and responsive parenting (Spieker & Booth, 1988). We should note, parenthetically, that it is probably easiest to behave in a responsive and sensitive manner (a) when one's infant is relatively easygoing, (b) when the infant was planned and desired, and (c) when the family unit is relatively stress-free.

Within the context of a secure relationship, then, a conceptual link to the development of social competence can be suggested. This link draws its underpinnings from the notion that a primary attachment relationship results in the child's development of a belief system that incorporates the parent as available and responsive to his or her needs. This "internal working model" allows the child to feel secure, confident, and self-assured when introduced to novel settings, and this sense of "felt security" fosters the child's active exploration of the social environment (Sroufe, 1983). In turn, exploration of the social milieu allows the child to address a number of significant other-directed questions such as "What are the properties of this other person?", "What is she/he like?", and "What can and does she/he do?" Once these exploratory questions are answered, the child can begin to address self-directed questions such as "What can I do with this person?" Thus, from our perspective, *felt security* is a central construct in the development of competence. It enhances social exploration, and exploration results in peer play (Rubin, Fein, & Vandenberg, 1983).

As we noted earlier, it is during play with peers that children experience the interpersonal exchange of ideas, perspectives, roles, and actions. From social negotiation, discussion, and conflict with peers, children learn to understand others' thoughts, emotions, motives, and intentions (e.g., Doise & Mugny, 1981). In turn, armed with these new social understandings, children are able to think about the consequences of their social behaviors, not only for themselves but also for others. The development of these social-cognitive abilities is thought to result in the production of socially competent behaviors (e.g., Selman, 1985; Selman & Schultz, 1990).

Once socially competent behavior is demonstrated by the child and recognized by the parent, the secure parent–child relationship will be nurtured and maintained by the dialectic between (a) the child who is willing and able to explore and play competently in a social milieu, and who is able to benefit social-cognitively and socially from peer interactive experiences and (b) a competent parent who is emotionally available, sharply attuned to social situations and to the thoughts and emotions of her or his child, able to anticipate the child's behaviors and the consequences of the child's actions, and able to predict the outcomes of her or his own actions for the child. This secure relationship system serves both parent and child well, and, barring any undue circumstances, an outcome of social competence can be predicted. A significant outcome of the production of competent social behaviors will be the establishment of a positive reputation among peers. Peer acceptance enables the child to continue to interact with age-mates and schoolmates in positive ways. Furthermore, the demonstration of competence is likely to gain the child close friendship relations, supportive relationships that will provide the child with confidence and security in the extrafamilial milieu.

Unfortunately, not all children are socially competent and popular. We have also described two possible developmental pathways to peer rejection and social isolation (see Rubin et al., 1990; Rubin, Hymel, Mills, & Rose-Krasnor, 1991).

Pathway 1 to Isolation and Peer Rejection. One developmental pathway to peer rejection begins with an infant who is perceived by his or her parents as being of difficult temperament. Certainly, we do not suggest that all such babies are at risk; however, one might predict that babies who are viewed by parents as fussy and overactive and who are born into less than desirable situations may receive less than optimal care. Consistent with these speculations are the findings of Egeland and Farber (1984), and Spieker and Booth (1988). These researchers have shown that temperamentally difficult infants often have mothers who are more aggressive, less nurturant, more anxious, and less responsive than mothers of nondifficult babies. The conditions in which families live, however, may be critical mediating factors; for example, Crockenberg (1981) reported that mothers of temperamentally difficult babies who have social and financial support are less negative in their interactions with their infants than high-risk mothers. For some families, then, the interaction between infant dispositional characteristics and ecological setting conditions may promote parenting practices that result in the establishment of insecure, perhaps hostile, early parent–child relationships (Engfer, 1986).

Existing data do suggest that there is a group of insecure babies who have already established hostile relationships with their primary caregivers by 12 or 18 months. Researchers have found that when these insecure babies reach preschool age, they often direct their hostility, anger, and aggression against peers (Sroufe, 1983). Furthermore, as noted earlier, aggression is a highly salient, determining cause of peer rejection or dislike (Coie & Kupersmidt, 1983). It follows logically and empirically that children who are initially sociable but at the same time aggressive will be rejected by their peers and not allowed to play with them (Dodge, 1983). Thus, one pathway to social rejection and social isolation may be determined by the display of anger and hostility in the peer group founded initially on the interplay among dispositional, parent–child relationships and ecological factors.

Pathway 2 to Isolation and Peer Rejection. In Pathway 1, social solitude could best be construed as imposed by others. A second pathway begins with newborns who may be biologically predisposed to have a low threshold for arousal when confronted with social (or nonsocial) stimulation and novelty. Recent research by Kagan and colleagues (e.g., Kagan, Reznick, & Snidman, 1987; Kagan, Reznick, & Gibbons, 1989) and others supports this perspective. During infancy, when faced with uncertainty, these babies may experience physical and physiological changes that may make them extremely difficult to soothe and comfort. It is possible that some mothers (and fathers) may find such infantile responses aversive (Kagan, Reznick, Clarke, Snidman, & Garcia-Coll, 1984); consequently, they may react to their babies with insensitivity, nonresponsivity and/or neglect. Each of these parental variables is predictive of insecure attachment relationships at 12 and 18 months. Furthermore, many of these negative socialization practices are associated with environmental and personal stressors such as poverty, unemployment, premature birth of the infant, marital satisfaction, and maternal depression (e.g., Engfer & Gavranidou, 1987).

As noted in Pathway 1, the interplay of endogenous, socialization, and early relationship factors described earlier, in addition to negative setting conditions, may lead to a sense of felt insecurity in toddlerhood and early childhood. In temperamentally inhibited children, however, this felt insecurity may further exacerbate behavioral wariness and inhibition in novel social and interpersonal settings. Behavioral wariness in the face of novelty is clearly consistent with the description of the play behaviors of many insecurely attached babies (Calkins & Fox, in press; Thompson, Connel, & Bridges, 1988). It also describes the behaviors of toddlers who have been identified as behaviorally inhibited. In novel settings these babies cling to their parents and refrain from exploring both people and objects. One might predict that these children will avoid the peer milieu when they first enter school, and, as such, they may be those who are eventually identified as socially withdrawn.

Reticence to explore novel, out-of-home settings precludes (a) the possibility of establishing normal social relationships, (b) the experience of normal social interactive play behaviors, and (c) the development of those social and cognitive skills that are supposedly encouraged by peer relationships and social play. Thus, it is easy to imagine a developmental sequence in which an anxious, insecure child withdraws from his or her social world of peers, fails to develop those skills derived from peer interaction and, because of this, becomes increasingly anxious and isolated from the peer group.

It is important to note also that during the early years of childhood, solitary or nonsocial activity is actually quite normal (Rubin et al., 1983). Consequently, there is little reason for nonsocial players to be singled out by their peers as displaying behaviors deviant from age-group play norms. As we indicated earlier, however, children do become increasingly sociable with age (Greenwood, Todd, Hops, & Walker, 1982; Parten, 1932). This increase in sociability and the concomitant decline in solitary activity with age may account for the finding that during the mid and late years of childhood, children who are socially withdrawn become increasingly salient to their age-mates (Younger et al., in press). Their deviance from age-appropriate social norms may well result in the establishment of negative peer reputations. Indeed, as we noted earlier, by the mid to late years of childhood, social withdrawal and anxiety are as strongly correlated with peer rejection and unpopularity as is aggression (Hymel et al., 1990; Rubin et al., 1989). Thus, this second developmental pathway, like the first described, concludes with a child who is socially isolated and rejected by his or her peers.

Whether endogenous or parent–child relationship factors predict, or for that matter determine, the quality of children's peer relationships remains a question. But the possibility that they are determining factors suggests that the question is worth answering.

SUMMARY AND CONCLUSIONS

In this chapter, we have reviewed literature concerning children's peer relationships. The topics covered need not be summarized extensively; rather, we review them in the context of setting agendas for future research.

There is developing an extensive literature concerning extrafamilial social relationships in very young children. Much of this work is normative and centers on the emergent social repertoires of infants and toddlers. For example, in our review we indicated that by the end of the second year of life, toddlers are able to engage in complementary and reciprocal interactive behaviors with peers (Ross et al., 1988). Unlike the research we described concerning the social skills and peer relationships of preschool-age and older children, however, little attention has been addressed to individual differences in social competence and peer relationships in the toddler period (e.g., Howes, 1988). This vacuum may be a product of thinking that social skills are range restricted or that qualitative differences in peer relationships are impossible to sort out at this period of childhood. Yet, if dispositional and socialization factors vary in infancy, it seems likely that individual differences may be present in the second and third years of life—differences that may predict and/or lead to adaptation or maladaption to the developmental milestone of preschool or kindergarten entry. Given the normative base extant vis-à-vis the emergent social skills of toddlers, the question of early individual differences now appears timely.

We then presented a brief overview of the significance of children's friendships. We indicated that children's friendships serve a variety of functions, including the provision of emotional and social support. We also noted that children's ideas about friendship become increasingly abstract with age. Furthermore, children's friendships are posited to play an increasingly important role with age. Yet little is known about the potential adaptive effects of friendship, or about when in childhood friendship can serve as an accelerator, promotor, or inhibitor of adaptation or as a buffer against the ill effects of parental or peer neglect or rejection. This issue of the functional significance of friendship may prove very helpful in the planning of intervention programs for children who have poorly developed social skills and peer relationships.

Our review of the literature on the structure of children's groups centered primarily on inter- and intragroup dynamics. We indicated that from as early as 3 years of age, children's groups can be characterized by stable and rigid dominance hierarchies. The main function of these hierarchies appears to be to reduce conflict and aggression among peer group members. In the early years of childhood, the most dominant members of the peer group are the most popular and most highly imitated in their peer group. Yet, dominance status in these earliest years of childhood is gained through consistent victory in interpersonal conflict. The route to dominance status in the middle and later years of childhood is, as yet, uncharted. It remains to be seen whether the relations between dominance status and peer acceptance remain consistent throughout childhood.

Over the years, there has emerged a literature on sex differences in social behavior and development. Yet not much is known about the possibility that the peer culture can play different functions for boys and girls. Furthermore, virtually nothing is known about the causes and consequences of peer acceptance and rejection for boys and girls. Given that for much of childhood, children interact primarily with same-sex peers, and given that boys and girls characteristically display rather different social behaviors (see Huston, 1983, for a review), it would not be surprising to discover that there might be sex differences in the forms and functions of peer groups. Again, this question should be added to the research agenda.

Finally, in this chapter we provided an extensive review of the determinants, correlates, and outcomes of peer acceptance and rejection. Generally, it is known that sociable and socially skilled behaviors lead to and maintain popularity among peers. From the earliest years of childhood, aggression is found to cause and maintain peer rejection. When passive, submissive, and withdrawn behavior becomes salient to the peer group (at around 7–8 years), it, too, becomes strongly associated with peer rejection. Childhood aggression is found to forecast problems of an externalizing nature in adolescence (e.g., delinquency); recent longitudinal research suggests that withdrawal is predictive of internalizing problems in adolescence (e.g., loneliness, depression).

What we know about the correlates, causes, and outcomes of peer acceptance and rejection, however, is constrained by the cultures in which we study these phenomena. By far the vast majority of the published literature in peer relationships is derived from studies conducted in North America and Western Europe. There is virtually no consensus about the definition of social competence or incompetence in Western cultures (Rubin & Rose-Krasnor, in press), let alone in other cultures. We also do not know very much about the significance of peer acceptance, rejection, and friendship in non-Western cultures. Thus, cross-cultural work should clearly be added to our research agenda.

These are only some of the areas of research that require our attention in the future. We have also suggested other investigatory possibilities throughout the chapter. As the reader will note, much work remains to be done in our search for a better understanding of the developmental significance of peer relationships in childhood.

REFERENCES

Abramovitch, R. (1976). The relation of attention and proximity rank in the preschool children. In M. Chance & R. Larsen (Eds.), *The social structure of attention*. London: Wiley.

Ainsworth, M. D. S. (1973). The development of infant–mother attachment. In B. Caldwell & H. Ricciuti (Eds.), *Review of child development research* (Vol. 3, pp. 1–94). Chicago: University of Chicago Press.

Ainsworth, M. D. S., Blehar, M. C., Waters, E., & Wall, S. (1978). *Patterns of attachment*. Hillsdale, NJ: Lawrence Erlbaum Associates.

Aronson, E. (1978). *The jigsaw classroom*. Beverly Hills, CA: Sage.

Asher, S. R., & Hymel, S. (1981). Children's social competence in peer relations: Sociometric and behavioral assessment. In J. D. Wine & M. D. Smye (Eds.), *Social competence*. New York: Guilford Press.

Asher, S. R., Parkhurst, J. T., Hymel, S., & Williams, G. A. (1990). Peer rejection and loneliness in childhood. In S. R. Asher & J. D. Coie (Eds.), *Peer rejection in childhood* (pp. 253–273). New York: Cambridge University Press.

Asher, S. R., Singleton, L. C., Tinsley, B. R., & Hymel, S. (1979). A reliable sociometric measure for preschool children. *Developmental Psychology, 15*, 443–444.

Asher, S. R., & Wheeler, V. A. (1985). Children's loneliness: A comparison of rejected and neglected peer status. *Journal of Consulting and Clinical Psychology, 53*, 500–505.

Asher, S. R. & Williams, G. A. (1987, April). New approaches to identifying rejected children of school. In G. W. Ladd (Chair), *Identification and treatment of socially rejected children in school settings*. Symposium conducted at the annual meeting of the American Educational Research Association, Washington, DC.

Attili, G. (1989). Social competence versus emotional security: The link between home relationships and behavior problems in preschool. In B. H. Schneider, G. Attili, J. Nadel, & R. P. Weissberg (Eds.), *Social competence in developmental perspective*. Boston: Kluwer.

Baldwin, J. (1955). *Behavior and development in childhood*. New York: Dreyden.

Bandura, A. (1977). *Social learning theory*. Englewood Cliffs, NJ: Prentice-Hall.

Bandura, A., & Walters, R. H. (1963). *Social learning and personality development*. New York: Holt, Rinehart & Winston.

Barclay, J. R. (1966). Sociometric choices and teacher ratings as predictors of school dropout. *Journal of Consulting and Clinical Psychology, 53*, 500–505.

Barker, R. G., & Wright, H. F. (1955). *The Midwest and its children*. New York: Harper & Row.

Barnes, K. E. (1971). Preschool play norms: A replication. *Developmental Psychology, 5*, 99–103.

Bates, J. E., Bayles, K., Bennet, D. S., Ridge, B., & Brown, M. (1991). Origins of externalizing behavior problems at eight years of age. In D. J. Pepler & K. H. Rubin (Eds.), *The development and treatment of childhood aggression*. Hillsdale, NJ: Lawrence, Erlbaum Associates.

Bates, J. E., Maslin, C. A., & Frankel, K. A. (1985). Attachment security, mother–infant interaction and temperament as predictors of behavior problem ratings at age three years. In I. Bretherton & E. Waters (Eds.), *Growing points of attachment theory and research: Monographs of the Society for Research in Child Development* (Serial No. 209, pp. 167–193).

Baudonniere, P. (1987). Dyadic interaction between 4-year-old children: Strangers, acquaintances, and friends. The influence of familiarity. *International Journal of Psychology, 22*, 347–362.

Baudonniere, P., Garcia-Werebe, M., Michel, J., & Liegois, J. (1989). Development of communicative competencies in early childhood: A model and results. In B. H. Schneider, G. Attili, J. Nadel, & R. P. Weissberg (Eds.), *Social competence in developmental perspective*. Boston: Kluwer.

Baumrind, D. (1967). Child care patterns anteceding three patterns of preschool behavior. *Genetic Psychology Monographs, 75,* 43–88.

Baumrind, D. (1971). Current patterns of parental authority. *Developmental Psychology Monograph, 4,* (No. 1, Pt. 2).

Belsky, J. (1988). The "effects" of day care reconsidered. *Early Childhood Research Quarterly, 3,* 235–272.

Berndt, T. J. (1981a). The effects of friendship on prosocial intentions and behavior between friends. *Developmental Psychology, 17,* 408–416.

Berndt, T. J. (1981b). Relations between social cognition, nonsocial cognition, and social behavior: The case of friendship. In J. H. Flavell & L. Ross (Eds.), *Social cognitive development* (pp. 176–199). Cambridge, England: Cambridge University Press.

Berndt, T. J. (1985). Prosocial behavior between friends in middle childhood and early adolescence. *Journal of Adolescence, 5,* 307–313.

Berndt, T. J., & Hoyle, S. G. (1985). Stability and change in childhood and adolescent friendships. *Developmental Psychology, 21,* 1007–1015.

Berndt, T. J., & Perry, T. B. (1986). Children's perceptions of friendships as supportive relationships. *Developmental Psychology, 22,* 640–648.

Bigelow, B. J. (1977). Children's friendship expectations: A cognitive developmental study. *Child Development, 48,* 246–253.

Bigelow, B. J., & LaGaipa, J. J. (1975). Children's written descriptions of friendship: A multidimensional analysis. *Developmental Psychology, 11,* 857–858.

Boivin, M., & Bégin, G. (1989). Peer status and self-perception among early elementary school children: The case of rejected children. *Child Development, 60,* 591–596.

Boivin, M., Thomassin, L., & Alain, M. (1989). Peer rejection and self-perceptions among early elementary school children: Aggressive rejectees versus withdrawn rejectees. In B. H. Schneider, G. Attili, J. Nadel, & R. P. Weissberg (Eds.), *Social competence in developmental perspective* (pp. 392–393). Boston: Kluwer Academic.

Bonney, M. E. (1942). A study of social status on the second grade level. *Journal of Genetic Psychology, 60,* 271–305.

Booth, C., Rose-Krasnor, L., & Rubin, K. H. (1991). Relating preschooler's social competence and their mothers' parenting behaviors to early attachment security and high risk status. *Journal of Social and Personal Relationships, 8,* 363–382.

Bowlby, J. (1958). The nature of the child's tie to his mother. *International Journal of Psychoanalysis, 39,* 350–373.

Bowlby, J. (1973). *Attachment and loss: Vol. 2.: Separation, anxiety, and anger.* New York: Basic Books.

Buhler, C. (1935). *From birth to maturity: An outline of the psychological development of the child.* London: Routledge & Kegan Paul.

Buhrmester, D. (1990). Intimacy of friendship, interpersonal competence, and adjustment during preadolescence and adolescence. *Child Development, 61,* 1101–1111.

Buhrmester, D., & Furman, W. (1987). The development of companionship and intimacy. *Child Development, 58,* 1101–1113.

Bukowski, W. M., & Hoza, B. (1989). Popularity and Friendship: Issues in theory, measurement, and outcome. In T. J. Berndt & G. W. Ladd (Eds.), *Peer relations in child development* (pp. 15–45). New York: Wiley-Interscience.

Bukowski, W. M., & Newcomb, A. F. (1987, April). *Friendship quality and the "self" during early adolescence.* Paper presented at the biennial meeting of the Society for Research in Child Development, Baltimore, MD.

Cairns, R. B., & Cairns, B. D. (1991). Social cognition and social networks: A developmental perspective. In D. J. Pepler & K. H. Rubin (Eds.), *The development and treatment of childhood aggression* (pp. 249–278). Hillsdale, NJ: Lawrence Erlbaum Associates.

Cairns, R. B., Cairns, B. D., Neckerman, H. J., Gest, S., & Garieppy, J. L. (1988). Peer networks and aggressive behavior: Peer support or peer rejection? *Developmental Psychology, 24,* 815–823.

Calkins, S., & Fox, N. (in press). The relations between infant temperament, security of attachment and behavioral inhibition at 24 months. *Child Development.*

Cantrell, S., & Prinz, R. J. (1985) Multiple perspectives of rejected, neglected, and accepted children: Relationship between sociometric status and behavioral characteristics. *Journal of Consulting and Clinical Psychology, 53,* 884–889.

Carlson, C. L., Lahey, B. B., & Neeper, R. (1984). Peer assessment of social behavior of accepted, rejected, and neglected children. *Journal of Abnormal Child Psychology, 12,* 189–198.

Caspi, A., Elder, G. H., Jr., & Bem, J. J. (1987). Moving against the world: Life-course patterns of explosive children. *Developmental Psychology, 22,* 303–308.

Caspi, A., Elder, G. H., Jr., & Bem, D. J. (1988). Moving away from the world: Life-course patterns of shy children. *Developmental Psychology, 24,* 824–831.

Charlesworth, R., & Hartup, W. W. (1967). Positive social reinforcement in the nursery school peer group. *Child Development, 38,* 993–1002.

Charlesworth, W. R., & LaFreniere, P. (1983). Dominance, friendship, and resource utilization in preschool children's groups. *Ethology and Sociobiology, 4,* 175–186.

Coie, J. D., Christopoulos, C., Terry, R., Dodge, K. A., & Lochman, J. E. (1989). Types of aggressive relationships, peer rejection, and developmental consequences. In B. H. Schneider, G. Attili, J. Nadel, & R. P. Weissberg (Eds.), *Social competence in developmental perspective.* Dordrecht: Kluwer.

Coie, J. D., & Dodge, K. (1983). Continuities and changes in children's social status: A five year longitudinal study. *Merrill-Palmer Quarterly, 29,* 261–282.

Coie, J. D., Dodge, K. A., & Coppotelli, H. (1982). Dimensions of types of social status: A cross-age perspective. *Developmental Psychology, 18,* 557–560.

Coie, J. D., Dodge, K. A., & Kupersmidt, J. B. (1990). Peer group behavior and social status. In S. R. Asher & J. D. Coie (Eds.), *Peer rejection in childhood.* New York: Cambridge University Press.

Coie, J. D., & Krehbiehl, G. (1984). Effects of academic tutoring on the social status of low-achieving, socially rejected children. *Child Development, 55,* 1465–1478.

Coie, J. D., & Kupersmidt, J. (1983). A behavioral analysis of emerging social status in boys' groups. *Child Development, 54,* 1400–1416.

Connolly, J., & Doyle, A. (1981). Assessment of social competence in preschoolers: Teachers versus peers. *Developmental Psychology, 17,* 454–462.

Cooley, C. H. (1902). *Human nature and the social order.* New York: Scribner's.

Crick, N. R., & Dodge, K. A. (1990). Children's perceptions of peer entry and conflict situations: Social strategies, goals, and outcome expectations. In B. Schneider, J. Nadel, G. Atteli, & R. Weissberg (Eds.), *Social competence in developmental perspective.* Dordrecht: Kluwer Press.

Crick, N. R., & Ladd, G. W. (1989). Nominator attrition: Does it affect the accuracy of children's sociometric classifications? *Merrill-Palmer Quarterly, 35,* 197–207.

Crockenberg, S. B. (1981). Infant irritability, mother responsiveness, and social support influences on the security of mother–infant attachment. *Child Development, 52,* 857–865.

Crook, J. H. (1970). Social organization and the environment: Aspects of contemporary social ethology. *Animal Behaviors, 18,* 197–209.

Damon, W., & Hart, D. (1982). The development of self-understanding from infancy through adolescence. *Child Development, 53,* 841–864.

Dawe, H. C. (1934). Analysis of two hundred quarrels of preschool children. *Child Development, 5,* 135–157.

Delormier, S., Tessier, O., Doyle, A., & Lebeau, J. (1991, April). *The temporal impact of peer relationships on dyadic free play.* Paper presented at the Biennial Meeting of the Society for Research in Child Development, Seattle, WA.

Diaz, R. M., & Berndt, T. J. (1982). Children's knowledge of a best friend: Fact or fancy. *Developmental Psychology, 18,* 787–794.

Dodge, K. A. (1983). Behavioral antecedents of peer social status. *Child Development, 54,* 1386–1399.

Dodge, K. A. (1986). A social information processing model of social competence in children. In M. Perlmutter (Ed.), *Minnesota symposium on child psychology* (Vol. 18, pp. 77–125). Hillsdale, NJ: Lawrence Erlbaum Associates.

Dodge, K. A., Coie, J. D., & Brakke, N. P. (1982). Behavioral patterns of socially rejected and neglected preadolescents: The roles of social approach and aggression. *Journal of Abnormal Child Psychology, 10,* 389–409.

Dodge, K. A., & Feldman, E. (1990). Issues in social cognition and sociometric status. In S. R. Asher & J. D. Coie (Eds.), *Peer rejection in childhood: Origins, consequences and intervention.* New York: Cambridge University Press.

Dodge, K. A., Murphy, R. R., & Buchsbaum, K. (1984). The assessment of intention–cue detection skills in children: Implications for developmental psychopathology. *Child Development, 55,* 163–173.

Dodge, K. A., Schlundt, D. G., Schocken, I., & Delugach, J. D. (1983). Social competence and children's social status: The role of peer group entry strategies. *Merrill-Palmer Quarterly, 29,* 309–336.

Doise, W., & Mugny, G. (1981). *Le développement social de l'intelligence* [The social development of intelligence]. Paris: Inter Editions.

Doyle, A. (1982). Friends, acquaintances, and strangers: The influence of familiarity and ethnolinguistic background on social interaction. In K. H. Rubin & H. S. Ross (Eds.), *Peer relations and social skills in childhood.* New York: Springer-Verlag.

Duck, S. W. (1975). Personality similarity and friend choices by adolescents. *European Journal of Social Psychology, 5,* 351–365.

Eckerman, C. O. (in press). Toddler's achievement of coordinated conspecifics: A dynamic systems perspective. In L. B. Smith & E. Thelen (Eds.), *Dynamic systems in development: Applications.* Cambridge, MA: Bradford Books, MIT Press.

Eckerman, C. O., Davis, C. C., & Didow, S. M. (1989). Toddlers' emerging ways of achieving social coordinations with a peer. *Child Development, 60,* 440–453.

Eckerman, C. O., & Stein, M. R. (1982). The toddler's emerging interactive skills. In K. H. Rubin & H. S. Ross (Eds.), *Peer relationships and social skills in childhood.* New York: Springer-Verlag.

Eckerman, C. O., & Stein, M. R. (1990). How imitation begets imitation and toddler's generation of games. *Developmental Psychology, 26,* 370–378.

Edelman, M. S., & Omark, D. R. (1973). Dominance hierarchies in young children. *Social Science Information, 12,* 1.

Eder, D., & Hallinan, M. T. (1978). Sex differences in children's friendships. *American Sociological Review, 43,* 237–250.

Egeland, B., & Farber, E. A. (1984). Infant–toddler attachment: Factors related to its development and change over time. *Child Development, 55,* 753–771.

Engfer, A. (1986). Antecedents of behavior problems in infancy. In G. A. Kohnstamm (Ed.), *Temperament discussed: Temperament and development in infancy and childhood* (pp. 155–180). Amsterdam: Stwets & Zeitlinger.

Engfer, A., & Gavranidou, M. (1987). Antecedents and consequences of maternal sensitivity:

A longitudinal study. In H. Rauh & H. Steinhausen (Eds.), *Psychobiology and early development* (pp. 71–99). North Holland: Elsevier.

Farrington, D. F. (1991). Childhood aggression and adult violence: Early precursors and later life outcomes. In D. J. Pepler & K. H. Rubin (Eds.), *The development and treatment of childhood aggression* (pp. 5–30). Hillsdale, NJ: Lawrence Erlbaum Associates.

Field, T. (1979). Infant behaviors directed towards peers and adults in the presence and absence of mother. *Infant Behavior and Development, 2*, 47–54.

Fine, G. A. (1980). The natural history of preadolescent male friendship groups. In H. C. Foot, A. J. Chapman, & J. R. Smith (Eds.), *Friendship and social relations in children* (pp. 293–320). Chichester, England: Wiley.

Fine, G. A. (1981). Friends, impression management, and preadolescent behavior. In S. R. Asher & J. M. Gottman (Eds.), *The development of children's friendships* (pp. 29–52). New York: Cambridge University Press.

Fine, G. A. (1987). *With the boys: Little league baseball and preadolescent culture.* Chicago: University of Chicago Press.

Fogel, A. (1979). Peer- vs. mother-directed behavior in 1- to 3-month old infants. *Infant Behavior and Development, 2*, 215–226.

French, D. C. (1988). Heterogeneity of peer rejected boys: Aggressive and nonaggressive subtypes. *Child Development, 59*, 976–985.

French, D. C. (1990). Heterogeneity of peer rejected girls. *Child Development, 61*, 2028–2031.

French, D. C. & Waas, G. A. (1985). Behavior problems of peer-neglected and peer-rejected elementary-age children: Parent and teacher perspectives. *Child Development, 56*, 246–252.

Freud, S. (1933). *New introductory lectures on psychoanalysis.* New York: Norton.

Furman, W., & Bierman, K. L. (1984). Children's conceptions of friendship: A multimethod study of developmental changes. *Developmental Psychology, 20*, 925–931.

Furman, W., & Buhrmester, D. (1985). Children's perceptions of the personal relationships in their social networks. *Developmental Psychology, 21*, 1016–1022.

Furman, W., & Childs, M. K. (1981, April). *A temporal perspective on children's friendships.* Paper presented at the biennial meeting of the Society for Research in Child Development, Boston, MA.

Furman, W., & Robbins, P. (1985). What's the point: Selection of treatment objectives. In B. Schneider, K. H. Rubin, & J. E. Ledingham (Eds.), *Children's peer relations: Issues in assessment and intervention* (pp. 41–54). New York: Springer-Verlag.

Gershman, E. S., & Hayes, D. S. (1983). Differential stability of reciprocal friendships and unilateral relationships among preschool children. *Merrill-Palmer Quarterly, 29*, 169–177.

Goldman, B. D., & Ross, H. S. (1978). Social skills in action: An analysis of early peer games. In J. Glick & K. A. Clarke-Stewart (Eds.), *Studies in social and cognitive development (Vol. 1): The development of social understanding.* New York: Gardner.

Goodenough, F. L. (1931). *Anger in young children.* Minneapolis: University of Minnesota Press.

Gottman, J. M. (1983). How children become friends. *Monographs of the Society for Research in Child Development, 48* (3, Serial No. 201).

Gottman, J. M., & Parker, J. G. (1986). *Conversation of friends.* Cambridge, England: Cambridge University Press.

Green, E. H. (1933). Friendships and quarrels among preschool children. *Child Development, 4*, 237–252.

Green, K., Forehand, R., Beck, S., & Vosk, B. (1980). An assessment of the relationship among measures of children's social competence and children's academic achievement. *Child Development, 51*, 1149–1156.

Greenwood, G. R., Todd, N. M., Hops, H., & Walker, H. M. (1982). Behavior change targets in the assessment and treatment of socially withdrawn preschool children. *Behavioral Assessment, 4*, 273–297.

Gresham, F. (1981). Validity of social skills measures for assessing social competence in low-status children: A multivariate investigation. *Developmental Psychology, 17,* 390–398.

Grossman, K. E., & Grossman, K. (in press). Attachment quality as an organizer of emotional and behavioral responses. In P. Harris, J. Stevenson-Hinde, & C. Parkes (Eds.), *Attachment across the life cycle.* New York: Rutledge.

Grossman, B., & Wrighter, J. (1948). The relationship between selection–rejection and intelligence, social status, and personality among sixth grade children. *Sociometry, 11,* 346–355.

Harter, S. (1982). The perceived competence scale for children. *Child Development, 53,* 89–97.

Hartup, W. W. (1983). Peer relations. In P. H. Mussen (Series Ed.) & E. M. Hetherington (Vol. Ed.), *Handbook of child psychology: Vol. 4. Socialization, personality and social development* (4th ed., pp. 103–196). New York: Wiley.

Hartup, W. W. (1985). Relationships and their significance in cognitive development. In R. A. Hinde, A. Perret-Clermont, & J. Stevenson-Hinde (Eds.), *Social relationships and cognitive development* (pp. 66–82). Oxford: Clarendon Press.

Hartup, W. W. (1989). Behavioral manifestations of children's friendships. In T. J. Berndt & G. W. Ladd (Eds.), *Peer relationships in child development.* New York: Wiley.

Hartup, W. W., Brady, J. E., & Newcomb, A. F. (1983). Social cognition and social interaction in childhood. In E. T. Higgins, D. N. Ruble, & W. W. Hartup (Eds.), *Social cognition and social development.* New York: Cambridge University Press.

Hartup, W. W., & Laursen, B. (in press). Conflict and context in peer relations. In C. H. Hart (Ed.), *Children on playgrounds.* Ithaca, NY: State University of New York Press.

Hartup, W. W., Laursen, B., Stewart, M. A., & Eastenson, A. (in press). Conflicts and the friendship relations of young children. *Child Development.*

Hartup, W. W., & Sancilio, M. F. (1986). Children's friendships. In E. Schopler & G. B. Mesibov (Eds.), *Social behavior in autism* (pp. 61–80). New York: Plenum.

Hay, D. F., Pedersen, J., & Nash, A. (1982). Dyadic interaction in the first year of life. In K. H. Rubin & H. S. Ross (Eds.), *Peer relationships and social skills in childhood.* New York: Springer-Verlag.

Hetherington, E. M., & Martin, B. (1986). Family factors and psychopathology in children. In H. C. Quay & J. S. Werry (Eds.), *Psychopathological disorders of childhood* (3rd ed., pp. 332–390). New York: Wiley.

Hinde, R. A. (1976). On describing relationships. *Journal of Child Psychology and Psychiatry, 17,* 1–19.

Hinde, R. A. (1987). *Individuals, relationships and culture.* Cambridge: Cambridge University Press.

Hinde, R. R. & Stevenson-Hinde, J. (1976). Toward understanding relationships: Dynamic stability. In P. Bateson & R. Hinde (Eds.), *Growing points in ethology* (pp. 451–479). Cambridge: Cambridge University Press.

Hinde, R. A., Titmus, G., Easton, D., & Tamplin, A. (1985). Incidence of "friendship" and behavior with strong associates versus non-associates in preschoolers. *Child Development, 56,* 234–245.

Howes, C. (1983). Patterns of friendship. *Child Development, 54,* 1041–1053.

Howes, C. (1985). Sharing fantasy: Social pretend play in toddlers. *Child Development, 56,* 1253–1258.

Howes, C. (1988). Peer interaction of young children. *Monographs of the Society for Research in Child Development, 53* (No. 217).

Howes, C., Unger, O., & Seidner, L. B. (1989). Social pretend play in toddlers: Parallels with social pretend play and solitary pretend. *Child Development, 60,* 77–84.

Hoza, B., Bukowski, W. M., & Gold, J. A. (1987). *A reexamination of the associates between nomination and rating-scale sociometric techniques.* Unpublished manuscript.

Huston, A. C. (1983). Sex-typing. In E. M. Hetherington (Ed.), *Handbook of Child*

Psychology (Vol. 4). New York: Wiley.

Hymel, S. (1983). Preschool children's peer relations: Issues in sociometric assessment. *Merrill-Palmer Quarterly, 29,* 237–260.

Hymel, S., & Franke, S. (1985). Children's peer relations: Assessing self-perceptions. In B. Scheider, K. H., Rubin, & J. E. Ledingham (Eds.), *Children's peer relationships: Issues in assessment and intervention* (pp. 75–92). New York: Springer-Verlag.

Hymel, S., & Rubin, K. H. (1985). Children with peer relationship and social skills problems: Conceptual, methodological, and developmental issues. In G. J. Whitehurst (Ed.), *Annals of child development* (Vol. 2). Greenwich, CT: JAI.

Hymel, S., Rubin, K. H., Rowden, L., & LeMare, L. (1990). Children's peer relationships: Longitudinal predictions of internalizing and externalizing problems from middle to late childhood. *Child Development, 61,* 2004–2021.

Isaacs, S. (1933). *Social development in young children: A study of beginnings.* London: Routledge.

Jack, L. M. (1934). An experimental study of ascendant behavior in preschool children. *University of Iowa Studies in Child Welfare, 9*(3), 9–65.

Jacobson, J. L. (1981). The role of inanimate objects in early peer interaction. *Child Development, 52,* 618–626.

Kagan, J. (1989). *Unstable ideas: Temperament, cognition and self.* Cambridge, MA: Harvard University Press.

Kagan, J., Reznick, S. J., Clarke, C., Snidman, N., & Gracia-Coll, C. (1984). Behavioral inhibition to the unfamiliar. *Child Development, 55,* 2212–2225.

Kagan, J., Reznick, J. S., & Gibbons, J. (1989). Inhibited and uninhibited types of children. *Child Development, 60,* 838–345.

Kagan, J., Reznick, J. S., & Snidman, N. (1987). The physiology and psychology of behavioral inhibition in children. *Child Development, 58,* 1459–1473.

Kandel, D. B. (1978a). Homophily, selection and socialization in adolescent friendships. *American Journal of Sociology, 84,* 427–436.

Kandel, D. B. (1978b). Similarity in real-life adolescent friendship pairs. *Journal of Personality and Social Psychology, 36,* 306–312.

Koch, H. (1935). Popularity among preschool children: Some related factors and technique for its measurement. *Child Development, 4,* 164–175.

Kohlberg, L. (1963). Moral development and identification. In H. W. Stevenson (Ed.), *Child psychology* (62nd Yearbook of the National Society for the Study of Education). Chicago: University of Chicago Press.

Krasnor, L., & Rubin, K. H. (1983). Preschool social problem solving: Attempts and outcomes in naturalistic interaction. *Child Development, 54,* 1545–1558.

Kupersmidt, J. B., & Coie, J. D. (1990). Preadolescent peer status, aggression, and school adjustment as predictors of externalizing problems in adolescence. *Child Development, 61,* 1350–1362.

Kupersmidt, J. B., Coie, J. D., & Dodge, K. A. (1990). The role of poor peer relationships in the development of disorder. In S. R. Asher & J. D. Coie (Eds.), *Peer rejection in childhood.* Cambridge: Cambridge University Press.

Kurdek, L. A., & Krile, D. (1982). A developmental analysis of the relation between peer acceptance and both interpersonal understanding and perceived social self-competence. *Child Development, 53,* 1485–1491.

LaFreniere, P. J., & Charlesworth, W. R. (1983). Dominance, attention, and affiliation in a preschool group: A nine-month longitudinal study. *Ethology and Sociobiology, 4*(2), 55–67.

La Greca, A. (1981). Peer acceptance: The correspondence between children's sociometric scores and teacher's ratings of peer interventions. *Journal of Abnormal Child Psychology, 9,* 167–178.

Ladd, G. W., & Price, J. M. (1987). Predicting children's social and school adjustments following the transition from preschool to kindergarten. *Child Development, 58,* 1168–1189.

Langlois, J. H. & Stephan, C. W. (1981). Beauty and the beast: The role of physical attraction in peer relationships and social behavior. In S. S. Brehm, S. M. Kassin, & S. X. Gibbans (Eds.), *Developmental social psychology: Theory and research* (pp. 152–168). New York: Oxford University Press.

Ledingham, J., Younger, A., Schwartzman, A., & Bergeron, G. (1982). Agreement among teacher, peer and self-ratings of children's aggression, withdrawal and likeability. *Journal of Abnormal Child Psychology, 10,* 363–372.

Levin, E. & Rubin, K. H. (1983). Getting others to do what you wanted them to do: The development of children's requestive strategies. In K. Nelson (Ed.), *Child language* (Vol. 4). Hillsdale, NJ: Lawrence Erlbaum Associates.

Lewin, K., Lippitt, R., & White, R. K. (1938). Patterns of aggressive behavior in experimentally created "social climates." *Journal of Social Psychology, 10,* 271–299.

Lewis, M. & Feiring, C. (1989). Early predictors of childhood friendship. In T. J. Berndt & G. W. Ladd (Eds.), *Peer relationships in child development.* New York: Wiley.

Maccoby, E. E. (1986). Social groupings in childhood: Their relationship to prosocial and antisocial behavior in boys and girls. In D. Olweus, J. Block, & M. Radke-Yarrow (Eds.), *Development of antisocial and social behavior* (pp. 263–284). New York: Academic Press.

Maccoby, E. E., & Jacklin, C. N. (1974). *The psychology of sex differences.* Stanford, CA: Stanford University Press.

Maccoby, E. E., & Martin, J. A. (1983). Socialization in the context of the family: Parent child interaction. In P. H. Mussen (Series Ed.) & E. M. Hetherington (Vol. Ed.), *Handbook of child psychology: Vol. 4. Socialization, personality, and social development* (4th ed., pp. 1–101). New York: Wiley.

Macfarlane, J. W., Allen, L. & Honzik, M. P. (1954). *A developmental study of the behavioral problems of children between twenty-one months and fourteen years.* Berkeley: University of California Press.

Mannarino, A. P. (1978). Friendship patterns and self-concept development in preadolescent mates. *Journal of Genetic Psychology, 133,* 105–110.

Markovits, H., & Strayer, F. F. (1982). Toward an applied social ethology: A case study of social skills among blind children. In K. H. Rubin & H. S. Ross (Eds.), *Peer relationships and social skills in childhood* (pp. 301–322). New York: Springer-Verlag.

Masten, A. S., Morison, P., & Pellegrini, D. S. (1985). A revised class play method of peer assessment. *Developmental Psychology, 3,* 523–533.

Maudry, M., & Nekula, M. (1939). Social relations between children of the same age during the first two years of life. *Journal of Genetic Psychology, 54,* 193–215.

Mead, G. H. (1934). *Mind, self, and society.* Chicago: University of Chicago Press.

Michelson, L., Foster, S. L., & Richey, W. L. (1981). Social-skills assessment of children. In B. B. Lahey & A. E. Kazdin (Eds.), *Advances in clinical child psychology* (Vol. 4, pp. 119–165). New York: Plenum.

Michelson, L., & Wood, R. (1981). Behavioral assessment and training of children's social skills. In M. Hersen, R. Eisler, & P. Miller (Eds.), *Progress in behavior modification* (Vol. 2, pp. 241–292). New York: Academic Press.

Moreno, J. L. (1934). *Who shall survive? A new approach to the problem of human interrelations.* Washington, DC: Nervous and Mental Disease Publishing.

Morris, D. P., Soroker, E., & Burruss, G. (1954). Follow-up studies of shy, withdrawn, children—I: Evaluation of later adjustment. *American Journal of Orthopsychiatry, 24,* 743–754.

Moskowitz, D. S., Schwartzman, A. E., & Ledingham, J. E. (1985). Stability and change in aggression and withdrawal in middle childhood and early adolescence. *Journal of Abnormal Psychology, 94,* 30–41.

Mueller, E. (1972). The maintenance of verbal exchanges between young children. *Child Development, 43,* 930–938.

Murphy, L. B. (1937). *Social behavior and child psychology: An exploratory study of some roots of sympathy.* New York: Columbia University Press.

Nelson, J., & Aboud, F. E. (1985). The resolution of social conflict between friends. *Child Development, 56,* 1009–1017.

Newcomb, A. F., & Bukowski, W. M. (1983). Social impact and social preference as determinants of children's peer group status. *Developmental Psychology, 19,* 856–867.

Northway, M. L. (1944). Outsiders: A study of the personality patterns of children least acceptable to their age mates. *Sociometry, 7,* 10–25.

Olweus, D. (1984). Stability in aggressive and withdrawn, inhibited behavior patterns. In R. M. Kaplan, V. J. Konecni, & R. W. Novaco (Eds.), *Aggression in children and youth* (pp. 104–136). The Hague: Nijhoff.

Olweus, D. (in press). Victimization and inhibited/withdrawal personality patterns: Antecedents, concurrent correlates, and long-term characteristics. In K. H. Rubin & J. Asendorpf (Eds.), *Social withdrawal, inhibition, and shyness in children.* Chicago: University of Chicago Press.

Parker, J. G., & Asher, S. R. (1987). Peer relations and later personal adjustment: Are low-accepted children at risk? *Psychological Bulletin, 102,* 357–389.

Parker, J. G., & Gottman, J. M. (1989). Social and emotional development in a relational context: Friendship interaction from early childhood to adolescence. In T. J. Berndt & G. W. Ladd (Eds.), *Peer relations in child development* (pp. 15–45). New York: Wiley.

Parkhurst, J. T., & Asher, S. R. (1987, April). The social concerns of aggressive-rejected children. In J. D. Coie (Chair), *Types of aggression and peer status: The social functions and consequences of children's aggression.* Symposium conducted at the Biennial meeting of the Society for Research in Child Development, Baltimore, MD.

Parten, M. B. (1932). Social participation among preschool children. *Journal of Abnormal and Social Psychology, 27,* 243–269.

Patterson, G. R. (1983). Stress: A change agent for family process. In N. Garmezy & M. Rutter (Eds.), *Stress, coping, and development in children* (pp. 235–264). New York: McGraw Hill.

Patterson, G. R., Kupersmidt, J. B., & Griesler, P. C. (1990). Children's perceptions of self and of relations with others as a function of sociometric status. *Child Development, 61,* 1335–1349.

Pekarik, E. G., Prinz, R. J., Liebert, D. E., Weintraub, S., & Neale, J. M. (1976). The Pupil Evaluation Inventory: A sociometric technique for assessing children's social behavior. *Journal of Abnormal Child Psychology, 4,* 83–97.

Pepler, D. J., & Rubin, K. H. (Eds.). (1991). *The development and treatment of childhood aggression.* Hillsdale, NJ: Lawrence Erlbaum Associates.

Perry, D. G., Perry, L. C., & Rasmussen, P. (1986). Cognitive social learning mediators of aggression. *Child Development, 57,* 700–711.

Piaget, J. (1932). *The moral judgment of the child.* Glencoe, IL: Free Press.

Putallaz, M. (1987). Maternal behavior and sociometric status. *Child Development, 58,* 324–340.

Putallaz, M., & Heflin, H. (1990). Parent child interaction. In S. P. Asher & J. D. Coie. (Eds.), *Peer rejection in childhood.* New York: Cambridge University Press.

Putallaz, M., & Wasserman, A. (1990). Children's entry behaviors. In S. R. Asher & J. D. Coie (Eds.), *Peer rejection in childhood.* New York: Cambridge University Press.

Quiggle, N., Panak, W. F., & Garber, J. (1989, April). *Social information processing in aggressive and depressed children.* Paper presented at the meeting of the Society for Research in Child Development, Kansas City, KS.

Radke-Yarrow, M., & Zahn-Waxler, C. (1986). The role of familial factors in the development of prosocial behavior: Research findings and questions. In D. Olweus, J. Block, & M.

Radke-Yarrow (Eds.), *Development of antisocial and prosocial behavior* (pp. 207–234). Orlando, FL: Academic Press.

Radke-Yarrow, M., Zahn-Waxler, C., & Chapman, M. (1983). Children's prosocial dispositions and behavior. In P. H. Mussen (Series Ed.) & E. M. Hetherington (Vol. Ed.), *Handbook of child psychology: Vol. 3. Social development.* New York: Wiley.

Renshaw, P. E. (1981). The roots of peer interaction research: A historical analysis of the 1930's. In S. R. Asher & J. M. Gottman (Eds.), *The development of children's friendships.* New York: Cambridge University Press.

Robins, L. N. (1966). *Deviant children grown up.* Baltimore, MD: Williams & Wilkins.

Roopnarine, J. L. (1987). Social interaction in the peer group: Relationship to perceptions of parenting and to children's interpersonal awareness and problem-solving ability. *Journal Applied Development Psychology, 8,* 351–362.

Roopnarine, J. L., & Adams, G. R. (1987). The interactional teaching patterns of mothers and fathers with their popular, moderately popular, or unpopular children. *Journal of Abnormal Child Psychology, 15,* 125–136.

Rosen, B. C., & D'Andrade, R. (1959). The psychosocial origins of achievement motivation. *Sociometry, 22,* 185–218.

Ross, H. S. (1982). The establishment of social games amongst toddlers. *Developmental Psychology, 18,* 509–518.

Ross, H. S., Cheyne, J. A., & Lollis, S. P. (1988). Defining and studying reciprocity in young children. In S. Duck (Ed.), *Handbook of personal relationships: Theory, research, and interventions.* New York: Wiley.

Ross, H. S., & Conant, C. L. (in press). The social structure of early conflict: Interactions, relationships, and alliances. In C. U. Shantz & W. W. Hartup (Eds.), *Conflict in child and adolescent development.* Cambridge: Cambridge University Press.

Ross, H. S., & Kay, D. A. (1980). The origins of social games. In K. H. Rubin (Ed.), *Children's play: New directions for child development* (Vol. 9). San Francisco: Jossey-Bass.

Ross, H. S., Lollis, S. P., & Elliot, C. (1982). Toddler-peer communication. In K. H. Rubin & H. S. Ross (Eds.), *Peer relationships and social skills in childhood.* New York: Springer-Verlag.

Rubin, K. H. (1982a). Non-social play in preschoolers: Necessary evil? *Child Development, 53,* 651–657.

Rubin, K. H. (1982b). Social and social-cognitive developmental characteristics of young isolate, normal and sociable children. In K. H. Rubin & H. S. Ross (Eds.), *Peer relationships and social skills in childhood* (pp. 353–374). New York: Springer-Verlag.

Rubin, K. H. (1985). Socially withdrawn children: An "at risk" population? In B. Schneider, K. H. Rubin, & J. Ledingham (Eds.), *Children's peer relations: Issues in assessment and intervention* (pp. 125–139). New York: Springer-Verlag.

Rubin, K. H., & Borwick, D. (1984). The communication skills of children who vary with regard to sociability. In H. Sypher & J. Applegates (Eds.), *Social cognition and communication.* Hillsdale, NJ: Lawrence Erlbaum Associates.

Rubin, K. H., Bream, L., & Rose-Krasnor, L. (1991). Social problem solving and aggression in childhood. In D. J. Pepler & K. H. Rubin (Eds.), *The development and treatment of childhood aggression* (pp. 219–248). Hillsdale, NJ: Lawrence Erlbaum Associates.

Rubin, K. H., & Chen, X. (1991, April). *Socio-emotional characteristics of extremely aggressive and extremely withdrawn children.* Paper presented at the Biennial Meeting of the Society for Research in Child Development, Seattle, WA.

Rubin, K. H., & Clark, M. L. (1983). Preschool teachers' ratings of behavioral problems: Observational, sociometric and social-cognitive correlates. *Journal of Abnormal Child Psychology, 11,* 273–285.

Rubin, K. H., & Daniels-Beirness, T. (1983). Concurrent and predictive correlates of sociometric status in kindergarten and grade 1 children. *Merrill-Palmer Quarterly, 29,* 337–351.

Rubin, K. H., Fein, G., & Vandenberg, B. (1983). Play. In P. H. Mussen (Series Ed.) & E. M. Hetherington (Vol. Ed.), *Handbook of child psychology: Vol. 4. Socialization, personality and social development* (4th ed.). New York: Wiley.

Rubin, K. H., Hymel, S., LeMare, L. J., & Rowden, L. (1989). Children experiencing social difficulties: Sociometric neglect reconsidered. *Canadian Journal of Behavioral Science, 21,* 94–111.

Rubin, K. H., Hymel, S., Mills, R. S. L., & Rose-Krasnor, L. (1991). Conceptualizing different pathways to and from social isolation in childhood. In D. Cicchetti & S. Toth (Eds.), *The Rochester Symposium on Developmental Psychopathology, Vol. 2. Internalizing and externalizing expressions of dysfunction.* Hillsdale, NJ: Lawrence Erlbaum Associates.

Rubin, K. H., & Krasnor, L. R. (1983). Age and gender differences in the development of a representative social problem solving skill. *Journal of Applied Developmental Psychology, 4,* 463–475.

Rubin, K. H., & Krasnor, L. R. (1986). Social-cognitive and social behavioral perspectives on problem solving. In M. Perlmutter (Ed.), *Cognitive perspectives on children's social and behavioral development. The Minnesota Symposia on Child Psychology* (Vol. 18, pp. 1–68). Hillsdale, NJ: Lawrence Erlbaum Associates.

Rubin, K. H., LeMare, L. J., & Lollis, S. (1990). Social withdrawal in childhood: Developmental pathways to peer rejection. In S. R. Asher & J. D. Cole (Eds.), *Peer rejection in childhood* (pp. 77–249). New York: Cambridge University Press.

Rubin, K. H., Maioni, T. L., & Hornung, M. (1976). Free play behaviors in middle and lower class preschoolers: Parten and Piaget revisited. *Child Development, 47,* 414–419.

Rubin, K. H., & Mills, R. S. L. (1988). The many faces of social isolation in childhood. *Journal of Consulting and Clinical Psychology, 6,* 916–924.

Rubin, K. H., & Mills, R. S. L. (1990). Maternal beliefs about adaptive and maladaptive social behaviors in normal, aggressive, and withdrawn preschoolers. *Journal of Abnormal Child Psychology, 18,* 419–435.

Rubin, K. H., & Mills, R. S. L. (1991). Conceptualizing developmental pathways to internalizing disorders in childhood. *Canadian Journal of Behavioural Science, 23,* 300–317.

Rubin, K. H., Moller, L., & Emptage, A. (1987). The Preschool Behavior Questionnaire: A useful index of behaviors in elementary school-age children? *Canadian Journal of Behavioral Science, 19,* 86–100.

Rubin, K. H., & Rose-Krasnor, L. (in press). Interpersonal problem solving. In V. B. Van Hassel & M. Hersen (Eds.), *Handbook of social development.* New York: Plenum.

Rubin, K. H., Watson, K., & Jambor, T. (1978). Free play behaviors in preschool and kindergarten children. *Child Development, 49,* 534–536.

Savin-Williams, R. C. (1976). An ethological study of dominance formation and maintenance in a group of human adolescents. *Child Development, 47,* 972–979.

Savin-Williams, R. C. (1979). Dominance hierarchies in groups of early adolescents. *Child Development, 50,* 142–151.

Savin-Williams, R. C. (1980). Dominance hierarchies in groups of middle to late adolescent males. *Journal of Youth and Adolescence, 9,* 75–85.

Schultz, L. H., & Selman, R. L. (1989). Bridging the gap between interpersonal thought and action in early adolescence. *Development and Psychopathology, 1,* 133–152.

Sears, R. R. (1961). Relation of early socialization experiences to aggression in middle childhood. *Journal of Abnormal and Social Psychology, 63,* 466–492.

Sears, R. R., Maccoby, E., & Levin, H. (1957). *Patterns of child rearing.* Evanston, IL: Row, Peterson.

Selman, R. L. (1976). Social-cognitive understanding: A guide to educational and clinical practice. In T. Lickona (Ed.), *Moral development and behavior: Theory, research, and social issues* (pp. 299–316). New York: Holt, Rinehart & Winston.

Selman, R. L. (1980). *The growth of interpersonal understanding.* New York: Cambridge University Press.

Selman, R. L. (1981). The child as a friendship philosopher. In S. R. Asher & J. M. Gottman (Eds.), *The development of friendships* (pp. 242–272). New York: Cambridge University Press.

Selman, R. L. (1985). The use of interpersonal negotiation strategies and communicative competences: A clinical-developmental exploration in a pair of troubled early adolescents. In R. A. Hinde, A. Perret-Clermont, & J. Stevenson-Hinde (Eds.), *Social relationships and cognitive development* (pp. 208–232). Oxford: Clarendon.

Selman, R. L., & Schultz, L. H. (1990). Children's strategies for interpersonal negotiation with peers: An interpretive/empirical approach to the study of social development. In T. J. Berndt & G. W. Ladd (Eds.), *Peer relationships in child development.* New York: Wiley.

Sherif, M., Harvey, O. J., White, B. J., Hood, W. R., & Sherif, C. W. (1961). *Inter-group conflict and cooperation: The Robbers Cave experiment.* Norman, OK: University of Oklahoma Press.

Singleton, L. C., & Asher, S. R. (1979). Racial integration and children's peer preferences: An investigation of developmental and cohort differences. *Child Development, 50,* 936–941.

Sluckin, A., & Smith, P. (1977). Two approaches to the concept of dominance in preschool children. *Child Development, 48,* 917–923.

Spieker, S. J. & Booth, C. L. (1988). Maternal antecedents of attachment quality. In J. Belsky & T. Nezworski (Eds.), *Clinical implications of attachment* (pp. 95–135). Hillsdale, NJ: Lawrence Erlbaum Associates.

Sroufe, L. A. (1983). Infant–caregiver attachment and patterns of adaptation in preschool: The roots of maladaptation. In M. Perlmutter (Ed.), *Minnesota symposia on child psychology* (Vol. 16, pp. 41–83). Hillsdale, NJ: Lawrence Erlbaum Associates.

Sroufe, L. A., & Fleeson, J. (1986). Attachment and the construction of relationships. In W. Hartup & Z. Rubin (Eds.), *The nature and development of relationships.* Hillsdale, NJ: Lawrence Erlbaum Associates.

Strain, P., Cooke, T., & Apolloni, T. (1976). *Teaching exceptional children: Assessing and modifying social behavior.* New York: Academic Press.

Strain, P., & Kerr, M. (1981). Modifying children's social withdrawal: Issues in assessment and clinical intervention. In M. Hersen, R. Eisler, & P. Miller (Eds.), *Progress in behavior modification* (Vol. 2, pp. 203–248). New York: Academic Press.

Strayer, F. F. (1980). Current problems in the study of human dominance. In D. Omark, F. F. Strayer, & D. Freedman (Eds.), *Dominance relations.* New York: Garland.

Strayer, F. F. (1984). Biological approaches to the study of the family. In R. D. Parke, R. Emde, H. Macadoo, & G. P. Sackett (Eds.), *Review of child development research, Vol. 7: The family.* Chicago: University of Chicago Press.

Strayer, F. F. (1989). Co-adaptation within the early peer group: A psychobiological study of social competence. In B. H. Schneider, G. Attili, J. Nadel, & R. Weissberg (Eds.), *Social competence in developmental perspective* (pp. 145–174). Dordrecht, Netherlands: Kluwer.

Strayer, F. F., Chapeskie, T. R., & Strayer, J. (1978). The perception of preschool dominance relations. *Aggressive Behavior, 4,* 183–192.

Strayer, F. F., Moss, E., & Blicharski, T. (1988). Bio-social bases of representational activity during early childhood. In T. Winegar (Ed.), *Social interaction and the development of children's understanding.* Hillsdale, NJ: Lawrence Erlbaum Associates.

Strayer, F. F., & Strayer, J. (1976). An ethological analysis of social agonism and dominance relations among preschool children. *Child Development, 47,* 980–989.

Strayer, F. F., & Trudel, M. (1984). Developmental changes in the nature and function of social dominance among young children. *Ethology and Sociobiology, 5,* 279–295.

Sullivan, H. S. (1953). *The interpersonal theory of psychiatry.* New York: Norton.

Suomi, S. J. (in press). Uptight and laid-back monkeys: Individual differences in the response to social challenges. In S. Brauth, W. Hall, & R. Dooling (Eds.), *Plasticity of development*. Cambridge, MA: MIT Press.

Thomas, A., & Chess, S. (1977). *Temperament and development*. New York: Brunner/Mazel.

Thompson, R. A., Connell, J., & Bridges, L. J. (1988). Temperament, emotional, and social interactive behavior in the strange situation: An analysis of attachment functioning. *Child Development, 59*, 1102–1110.

Ullman, C. A. (1957). Teachers, peers, and tests as predictors of adjustment. *Journal of Educational Psychology, 48*, 257–267.

Vandell, D. L., Wilson, K. S., & Buchanan, N. R. (1980). Peer interaction in the first year of life: An examination of its structure, content, and sensitivity to toys. *Child Development, 51*, 481–488.

Vaughn, B., & Waters, E. (1981). Attention structure, sociometric status, and dominance: Interrelations, behavioral correlates and relationships to social competence. *Developmental Psychology, 17*, 275–288.

Vosk, B., Forehand, R., Parker, J., & Rickard, K. (1982). A multi-method comparison of popular and unpopular children. *Developmental Psychology, 18*, 571–575.

Walters, J., & Peters, R. D. (1980, June). *Social problem solving in aggressive boys*. Paper presented at the annual meeting of the Canadian Psychological Association, Calgary.

Weisfeld, G. E. (1980). Social dominance and human motivation. In D. R. Omark, F. F. Strayer, & D. G. Freedman (Eds.), *Dominance relations: An ethological view of human conflict and social interaction*. New York: Garland STPM.

Weisfeld, G. E., Omark, D. R., & Cronin, C. L. (1980). A longitudinal and cross-sectional study of dominance in boys. In D. R. Omark, F. F. Strayer, & D. G. Freedman (Eds.), *Dominance relations: An ethological view of human conflict and social interaction*. New York: Garland STPM.

Werebé, M. J. G., & Baudonniere, P. M. (in press). Social pretend play among friends and familiar preschoolers. *International Journal of Behavioral Development*.

Wheeler, V. A., & Ladd, G. W. (1982). Assessment of children's self-efficacy for social interactions with peers. *Developmental Psychology, 18*, 795–805.

Williams, G. A., & Asher, S. R. (1987, April). *Peer- and self-perceptions of peer rejected children: Issues in classification and subgrouping*. Paper presented at the biennial meeting of the Society for Research in Child Development, Baltimore, MD.

Younger, A. J., & Boyko, K. A. (1987). Aggression and withdrawal as social schemas underlying children's peer perceptions. *Child Development, 58*, 1094–1100.

Younger, A. J., Gentile, C., & Burgess, K. (in press). Children's perceptions of withdrawal: Changes across age. In K. H. Rubin & J. Asendorpf (Eds.), *Social withdrawal inhibition, and shyness in childhood*. Hillsdale, NJ: Lawrence Erlbaum Associates.

Younger, A. J., & Piccinin, A. M. (1989). Children's recall of aggressive and withdrawn behaviors: Recognition memory and likeability judgements. *Child Development, 60*, 580–590.

Youniss, J. (1980). *Parents and peers in social development: A Piaget-Sullivan perspective*. Chicago: University of Chicago Press.

Youniss, J., & Smollar, J. (1985). *Adolescent relations with mothers, fathers, and friends*. Chicago: University of Chicago Press.

Youniss, J., & Volpe, J. (1978). A relational analysis of children's friendships. In W. Damon (Ed.), *New directions for child development* (No. 1, pp. 1–22). San Francisco: Jossey-Bass.

Zigler, E., & Trickett, P. (1978). IQ, social competence, and evaluation of early childhood intervention programs. *American Psychologist, 33*, 789–798.

10 The Child at School

Deborah Stipek
University of California, Los Angeles

INTRODUCTION

Among the many institutions that affect children's development, next to the family, school is the most important. As the primary source of information concerning one's competencies and as a major force in socializing expectations and values associated with achievement in many domains, school experiences shape the life children will have as adults.

Schooling influences are strong, in part, because schools offer experiences that most children do not have elsewhere. In school children experience a large group of same-aged peers, formal instruction, and publicly evaluated performance. Nowhere else is performance stressed so consistently and in so many domains. Although to some degree school mediates family effects, its unique characteristics give it special importance in children's development.

This chapter focuses on domains of development in which school plays a critical role. Developmental changes that appear to be universal in this culture, as well as factors that affect the development of stable individual differences, are discussed. The first section summarizes theory and research on children's beliefs about their competencies and talents — their answer to a set of interrelated questions: "What am I good at?" "Will I succeed?" "What factors determine whether I succeed or fail?" These judgments that children make in school influence the activities they choose, how much effort they exert, how long they persist when they encounter difficulty, and other behaviors that affect their level of success in achievement settings. Judgments about competence also influence the domains of achievement that children pursue (e.g., athletic, musical, intellectual) in school and throughout their lives.

The second section discusses achievement-related values — the answers to the questions, "What do I *want* to be good at and why?" Values are important because even when children expect to succeed they will not engage in activities that are not important to them. Values, like beliefs about competencies, influence children's choice of activities and the intensity of their effort in achievement settings.

Educational and occupational aspirations — children's answers to the question, "What do I want to do when I grow up?" — evolve partly out of their beliefs about their competencies and achievement-related values. These and other factors that influence occupational aspirations — such as gender stereotyping and social class — are discussed in the third section.

Not many years ago school entry was one of the most important junctures in children's lives. Now, with 56% of mothers of children under 6 in the work force and the majority of children having some formal group peer experience before they enter kindergarten, the transition from home to school is less abrupt (Hayes, Palmer, & Zaslow, 1990). Nevertheless, the academic focus initially encountered in kindergarten or first grade still brings with it myriad new experiences that have long-lasting significance in the development of children's beliefs and values.

ACHIEVEMENT-RELATED BELIEFS

In school, and other contexts that involve performance and competition, children formulate a set of interrelated beliefs about their competencies. In any particular situation children make judgments about what causes success and failure and how likely their effort is to lead to success and to be rewarded. At a more global level, they make judgments about how competent they are in various domains.

These judgments and beliefs are not necessarily conscious. They nevertheless have important effects on children's emotional well-being, as well as their behavior in achievement settings. Self-esteem, for example, is strongly associated with perceptions of competence (Harter, 1987). Research has shown also that individuals who believe they lack competence and have low expectations for success, or who attribute past failures to factors that they do not control, avoid achievement tasks when they can, and when they cannot avoid them, they exert less effort and persist less than individuals who have more positive beliefs (see Stipek, 1988, for a review).

Systematic age differences in children's beliefs have been found — differences that have important implications for how children behave in school and other achievement settings and that moderate the effect of school experiences on children. The next sections summarize what is known about developmental changes in children's expectations, perceptions of competence, and perceptions of the causes of achievement outcomes. Also discussed are factors associated with stable, individual differences that have been observed in these beliefs.

Perceptions of Competence and Expectations for Success

Age-related changes have been found in children's judgments of their own and others' competence and in the ways they conceptualize and assess competence. These changes are described and then explained in terms of changes in cognitive-processing abilities and changes in educational environments that are associated with age.

Age-Related Changes in Ability and Expectancy Judgments. When asked about their academic ability, most kindergarten-age children claim to be the smartest in their class. In many studies of self-perceptions of competence, children's ratings are near the top of the scale through the early elementary grades and decline, on average, thereafter (Benenson & Dweck, 1986; Eccles, 1983; Eshel & Klein, 1981; Nicholls, 1978, 1979; Pintrich & Blumenfeld, 1985; Stipek, 1981; Stipek & Tannatt, 1984). Spontaneous, self-congratulatory statements made in the classroom also decline over the elementary grades (Frey & Ruble, 1987). There is some evidence for a particularly steep decline in competence judgments as well as self-esteem in early adolescence (Eccles, 1983; Simmons, Blyth, Van Cleave, & Bush, 1979; Simmons, Rosenberg, & Rosenberg, 1973), although this decline is not consistently found (see Eccles et al., 1989).

As they decline, self-perceptions of ability become more accurate in the sense that they correlate more strongly with external indices (e.g., teacher's ratings; Eshel & Klein, 1981; Newman, 1984; Nicholls, 1978, 1979). It is also noteworthy that the strong positive bias found among young children applies to judgments about the self but not to judgments about others (e.g., Stipek & Tannatt, 1984), and it appears to be more prominent when children make global ratings than when they rate specific skills (see Stipek & Mac Iver, 1989). These findings suggest that even young children are able, under some circumstances, to make competence judgments that are based on objective information.

The decline in competence ratings is paralleled by an age-related decline in expectations to succeed in particular task situations. Experimental research suggests that young children typically overestimate their future performance and that performance predictions decrease, on average, with age. Until the age of about 6 or 7 years, children frequently maintain high expectations for success on experimental tasks regardless of their previous performance. In a study by Stipek and Hoffman (1980b), for example, preschool-age children almost invariably predicted optimal performance on an experimental task (getting a metal box attached to a string to the top of a tower without a ball falling off it), even when they had performed badly on four previous trials. Second and third graders, and to some degree kindergartners and first graders, adjusted their predictions for future performance as a function of their past performance on the task. In a later study by Stipek, Roberts, and Sanborn (1984), preschool-age children adjusted their predictions downward when past failure was made very salient, but they were nevertheless inclined toward optimism. They appeared to confuse to some degree their desires with their expectations — they expected to achieve what they hoped to achieve.

Children's expectancy judgments, like their competence judgments, become more realistic with age (see Stipek, 1984a, 1984c, for reviews). From preschool to the early elementary grades, children appear to develop an increasingly better understanding of the implications of past performance for future performance and their tendency toward optimism declines.

The typically strong positive bias in young children and the ensuing decline in perceived competence and expectations for success can be explained, in part, by changes in children's conceptions of academic competence and the criteria they use to assess competence. Research on these topics is summarized next.

Age-Related Changes in Conceptions of Ability.   Children's conceptions of competence become increasingly differentiated with age. Thus, for example, academic ability becomes conceptually differentiated from social ability (Stipek & Daniels, 1990; Yussen & Kane, 1985) and from work habits and effort on school tasks (Blumenfeld, Pintrich, Meece, & Wessels, 1982; Stipek & Tannatt, 1984); and competence ratings in different academic domains become increasingly differentiated (Marsh, Barnes, Cairns, & Tidman, 1984).

Research by Nicholls (1978; see also Nicholls & Miller, 1984) suggests that ability is not fully differentiated conceptually from effort until early adolescence. Nicholls and colleagues studied children's conceptions of ability by showing them films of children doing math problems with varying levels of effort and success. The youngest children (aged 5 and 6 years) did not distinguish among effort, ability, and outcome; they reasoned that if a person succeeded, he must be smart and he must have tried hard. If two children in the film received the same score but differed in effort, young subjects often invented effort-related explanations (e.g., she must have started earlier, or he must have been thinking while fiddling). Children from about the age of 7 to 10 years distinguished effort and outcome as a cause and effect, but ability "in the sense of capacity which can increase or limit the effectiveness of effort" was not understood (Nicholls & Miller, 1984, p. 195).

Nicholls (1978) suggested that a mature understanding of ability, distinct from effort, requires the formal operational capacity to coordinate proportional relations (Inhelder & Piaget, 1958; see Kuhn, Chap. 4, this volume). He pointed out that an understanding of the inverse relation between effort and ability is analogous to achieving equilibrium in Inhelder and Piaget's balance problem. The outcome in the balance task can only be predicted accurately by combining, proportionally, weight and distance of weight from the fulcrum, just as outcomes on achievement tasks can only be predicted by combining, proportionally, effort and ability.

In summary, children in preschool (and to some degree in the first or second year of elementary school) have a global concept of ability that includes social behavior, conduct, work habits, and effort. Over the elementary years children's definition of academic ability becomes narrower and more differentiated by subject matter. However, not until early adolescence do children have a concept of ability, in the sense of capacity, that is fully differentiated from their concept of effort.

Age-Related Changes in the Criteria Used for Assessing Competence. Information relevant to one's competence comes in many forms. Systematic age differences have been found in the type of information children attend to most, in how they process different types of information, and in their propensity to make judgments based on intra- versus interindividual comparisons.

Interview studies suggest that preschool-age children, and children in the first few grades of elementary school, focus on *effort expended* (Harter & Pike, 1984), *personal mastery* (Blumenfeld, Pintrich, & Hamilton, 1986; Stipek 1981), and *social reinforcement* (Lewis, Wall, & Aronfreed, 1963; Spear & Armstrong, 1978) in their ability assessments. Emphasis on these sources of information declines with age, and the way children interpret this kind of information changes.

Consider effort, for example. Harter and Pike (1984) reported that about one third of the preschool through second-grade children they interviewed explained high self-perceptions of cognitive competence by citing habitual engagement in activities that foster skill development (e.g., "I practice a lot"). But other studies have shown that older children, who presumably understand the inverse relation between effort and ability given equal outcomes, consider high effort, in some circumstances, as evidence of relatively low ability (Nicholls & Miller, 1984b; see also Kun, 1977; Kun, Parsons, & Ruble, 1974).

Young children cite mastery as evidence of their competence, but unlike older children, they tend not to accept nonmastery as evidence of incompetence. As was found in studies of children's expectations for success, developmental research reveals that repeatedly failing to demonstrate mastery on a task does not undermine perceptions of competence for preschool-age children as much as it does for older children (see Stipek, 1984a).

The way children process social feedback also changes with age. Meyer and colleagues (1979, Experiment 2) found in an experimental study that adults and students in the eighth grade or above interpreted praise for success on an easy task to indicate low ability. Younger children accepted praise at face value; they assumed that praise indicated high ability regardless of the task. Barker and Graham (1987) found, similarly, that an angry teacher response following a child's failure was interpreted by 11- and 12-year-olds to indicate high ability and by younger children to indicate low ability.

These findings on children's interpretation of teacher feedback are no doubt related to developmental changes in their understanding that success on easy tasks requires less ability than success on difficult tasks, and that, given equal outcomes, effort and ability are inversely related. Both young and older children understand that teachers praise success and express anger for failure when they perceive a child to have exerted high or low effort, respectively (Harari & Covington, 1981). But apparently only older children infer low ability when success on an easy task requires high effort (and is thus praiseworthy) or when failure on an easy task is not attributed to low effort (and therefore is not responded to with anger). Children may, therefore, become increasingly attentive to the context in which praise is given (e.g., the difficulty of the task and whether other children are praised) and to teachers' emotional reactions to their performance.

While effort, mastery, and social feedback decline in importance as indicators of academic competence and change in their implications, children pay increasing attention to grades (Blumenfeld et al., 1986; Nicholls, 1978, 1979), and they become more sensitive to differential treatment by teachers (see following). The most important developmental change in the ability-assessment process, however, concerns the use of social comparative information.

Social Comparison.   Children as young as preschool age make social comparisons and competitive, "besting" verbal statements (Mosatche & Bragonier, 1981). By the age of 3 ½, children also react differently to winning and losing a competition (Heckhausen, 1984).

The evidence suggests, however, that although preschool-age children may make simple comparisons with one other individual, they do not use group normative information (i.e., their own performance compared to the performance of a group of age-mates) to assess their competence until later (Aboud, 1985; Boggiano & Ruble, 1979; Nicholls, 1978; Ruble, Boggiano, Feldman, & Loebl, 1980; Ruble, Parsons, & Ross, 1976). For example, in a study by Ruble and colleagues (1980) first- and second-grade children were given tasks in groups of four. The outcome of the task was ambiguous so that the experimenter could give children predetermined but believable information about their own and the other three children's performances. Subjects were either told that they had succeeded or that they had failed; in each of the success and failure conditions children were either given no information about the other children's performance, were told that all of the other children had succeeded, or were told that all of the other children had failed. The first graders' subsequent ratings of their ability on the task were affected by whether they succeeded or failed, but not by the information about other children's performance. Second graders' ratings were influenced both by their own outcome and the normative information.

The evidence on whether children use normative information to evaluate their competence in the first few grades in school is inconsistent (Levine, Snyder, & Mendez-Caratini, 1982; Morris & Nemcek, 1982; Ruble et al., 1980). But it is clear that dramatic changes occur between kindergarten and about the second or third grade (Aboud, 1985; France-Kaatrude & Smith, 1985; Ruble et al., 1980; Stipek & Tannatt, 1984). By the third grade children's ability judgments are consistently affected by normative information, and they begin to explain their self-perceptions of ability in social-comparative terms. Older children are also more skilled than younger children at interpreting social comparative information (Aboud, 1985; Ruble, 1983). For example, in one study, fifth but not second graders considered differences in the amount of time they and a peer were given to work on a test in judging their performance relative to the peer (Aboud, 1985).

Students' attention to social comparison information increases even more on entry into junior high school (Feldlaufer, Midgley, & Eccles, 1988). During the junior and senior high school years students also place their achievement into an increasingly broader social context. Elementary school children compare themselves primarily with classmates. In junior high children begin to pay attention to grade point averages, which can be compared schoolwide. By the final years of high school, outcomes of scholarship competitions, college admissions, and other indicators of achievement relative to national norms probably figure into some students' judgments of their competence. Analogous changes are likely to apply to athletic and other spheres of performance. Although younger children most likely compare their performance to teammates, as they get older children presumably begin to assess their own competence in comparison to children on other teams, and eventually, for some, to national records.

The shift toward using normative criteria to judge ability is undoubtedly a major factor in the average decline observed in children's ratings of their ability. Children's own competencies, in an absolute sense, are constantly improving. Focusing on mastery and accepting praise at face value assures most young children of positive judgments of their competence. In contrast, social comparison inevitably leads to some negative judgments because half of the children in a class must, by definition, perform below average.

The role of cognitive development has been emphasized in the literature on age-related changes in children's ability judgments and expectations for success (e.g., Nicholls, 1978; Nicholls & Miller, 1984b; Surber, 1984). Some developmental theorists have suggested, for example, that accurate ability and expectancy judgments require the concrete operational ability to seriate (Nicholls, 1978). Also, as mentioned earlier, understanding of the inverse relationship between effort and ability when performance is held constant has been linked to the development of formal operations. However, age-related changes in children's definitions of competence, self-ratings of ability, and predictions for success are to some degree a consequence of systematic shifts in the organizational, instructional, and evaluation practices that children are exposed to in school (see Stipek & Mac Iver, 1989). Some of these changes are described next.

Age-Related Changes in Achievement Contexts.   Preschool teachers usually accept a child's product as satisfactory as long as the child has worked on it for a reasonable amount of time, and most children end up receiving positive feedback on tasks they complete (Apple & King, 1978; see also Blumenfeld et al., 1982). Tasks are typically done individually or in small groups, and comparable information about classmates' performance is not readily available. Under these circumstances, it is not surprising that preschool-age children are little inclined to compare their performance with peers and are able to maintain positive perceptions of their competence.

But children are not long protected from the potentially harsh effects of academic competition. The nature of tasks, competence feedback, and student–teacher relationships change gradually over the early elementary school years, and sometimes dramatically when children enter junior high.

Several changes in school tasks and evaluation practices presumably contribute to a more differentiated concept of ability. Throughout the early elementary grades teachers tend to emphasize effort and work habits, even in report card grades (Blumenfeld, Hamilton, Bossert, Wessels, & Meece, 1983; Brophy & Evertson, 1978). Effort figures less prominently in report card grades, however, as children move through elementary school (Entwisle & Hayduk, 1978), and by junior high, grades tend to be based more narrowly on test performance (Gullickson, 1985). Tasks, too, become more focused on intellectual skills as children advance in grade, and in junior high school, teacher–student relationships become much more formal and centered on school performance (Midgley, Feldlaufer, & Eccles, 1988, 1989). Accordingly, children's concept of ability shifts from a poorly differentiated construct that includes effort and work habits to a more narrowly defined construct that focuses on performance on academic tasks.

Many changes in the nature of instruction and evaluation foster interest in social comparison. Over the elementary school years children are increasingly given tasks in which there is a single right answer (Eccles, Midgley & Adler, 1984; Higgins & Parsons, 1983; Rosenholtz & Simpson 1984). They also encounter ability grouping (Hallinan & Sorensen, 1983) and other public evidence (e.g., star charts) of their own and classmates' skills (Higgins & Parsons, 1983). Assignments become more uniform across children and over time (Eccles & Midgley, 1989), and older children experience more whole-group and less individualized and small-group instruction than younger children (Brophy & Evertson, 1978).

Social comparison is more salient as a result of these changes because uniform task structures reduce intraindividual variation in performance across time and make inequalities in performance across students more interpretable. When tasks do not vary much from day to day, children perform more consistently than when the format and nature of tasks vary. When all students do the same task at the same time, performance is more comparable, more salient, and more public than when tasks vary or are individualized (e.g., Blumenfeld et al., 1982; Marshall & Weinstein, 1984; Rosenholtz & Simpson, 1984).

The amount of positive social reinforcement declines as children advance in grade (Pintrich & Blumenfeld, 1985) and grades are given more frequently. Partly because grades are increasingly based on relative performance (i.e., a normal curve) — a criterion that requires some children to do poorly — they decline, on average (Blumenfeld et al., 1983; Gullickson, 1985; Hill & Wigfield, 1984; Nottlemann, 1987). Because grades are easily comparable, these changes in evaluation practices no doubt contribute to children's interest in social comparative information, as well as the decline in average self-ratings.

In summary, the nature and diversity of tasks, evaluation practices, and relations with teachers change as children progress through school in ways that increasingly emphasize individual differences in performance on academic tasks. These changes make it difficult for average- and below-average students to maintain positive perceptions of competence. Changes in instructional and evaluation practices occur in conjunction with changes in children's information-processing abilities. We do not know, therefore, to what degree an increased emphasis on social comparison and declines in ability and expectancy judgments are an inevitable consequence of cognitive development, or primarily of changes in school experiences. Studies of classroom effects suggest that educational environments play more than a trivial role (see Stipek, 1988).

Perceptions of the Cause of Achievement Outcomes

In school, more often than in almost any other setting, children receive performance feedback that can be construed as success or failure. When individuals succeed or fail to achieve a goal or meet a standard of performance, they often make judgments about the cause of the outcome. Thus, for example, a child who gets a bad grade or strikes out in a baseball game considers possible explanations for her performance: "Am I incompetent? "Was I not trying or not paying attention?" "Or was I just unlucky?" Whether or not individuals are aware of their causal judgments, these judgments have important implications for expectations and behaviors in future achievement situations.

Weiner (1986) proposed a three-dimensional model to differentiate possible causes. The first dimension, *locus,* refers to the source of the cause, that is, whether outcomes are contingent on an individual's characteristics or behaviors (internal) or on some external variable. The *control* dimension concerns the degree of control individuals have over the cause. The *stability* dimension differentiates causes on the basis of their duration. Ability, for example, is usually considered a relatively stable trait, whereas effort, luck, or mood can vary from moment to moment.

The development of children's judgments about the cause of achievement outcomes on these three dimensions is important to understand because of the implications these judgments have for behavior. This is illustrated in the concept of *learned helplessness.* Dweck and her colleagues have shown that individuals who attribute achievement failure primarily to controllable causes — such as effort or strategy — typically persist and use effective problem-solving strategies to overcome failure. Individuals who attribute failure to causes that they do not control — such as lack of ability, or a biased teacher — tend to react to initial failure with maladaptive or helpless behavior (e.g., they employ strategies that have already failed or they give up; see Diener & Dweck, 1978; Dweck, 1975; Dweck & Elliott, 1983; Dweck & Reppucci, 1973).

Rotter (1966) and others have demonstrated further that individuals develop, partly as a consequence of experiences in school, generalized perceptions of the cause of outcomes — referred to as *locus of control.* These generalized beliefs are associated with such disparate psychological reactions as defensiveness, resilience, submission to authority, anxiety, and depression (Lefcourt, 1976).

Age Differences in Attributions. Age differences have been found in children's understanding of the causes of achievement and other outcomes with regard to the controllability and stability dimensions. Weisz (1986; Weisz & Stipek, 1982) pointed out that control requires both a perception of *contingency* (a belief that the outcome is causally dependent on variations in the individual's behavior) and *competence* (a belief in one's competence to produce the behavior on which the desired outcome is contingent). His research (summarized in Weisz, 1986, 1990) suggests that young children have exaggerated perceptions of contingency. This is evident, for example, in a study in which kindergarten children, much more than fourth graders, believed that outcomes in an experimental game of chance would be affected by age, practice, intelligence, and effort (Weisz, 1980). When asked to explain their own favorable outcomes at chance tasks, young children often claimed that they had tried hard, or they had previous experience with similar games—answers that indicated they believed effort and practice affected their outcome (Weisz & Cameron, 1985; see also Nicholls, 1987; Weisz, 1981; Weisz, Yeates, Robertson, & Beckham, 1982). Consistent with Piaget's (1930) observations, young children appeared to lack a concept of noncontingency or chance events.

Weisz (1986) noted that although illusory contingency declines in intensity with development, it persists to some degree even into adulthood. There may be an adaptive quality to illusory contingency or believing that one has control over events in one's life. For example, it may foster optimism and self-esteem, and guard against depression.

Children's exaggerated perceptions of control may, in addition to being affected by their poor understanding of chance events, be traced to their failure to differentiate ability from effort. Consistent with Nicholls and Miller's (1984) observations, Stipek and DeCotis (1988) found that when 6- and 7-year-olds rated the controllability of different causes, they did not differentiate among effort, luck, and ability. Thus, young children perceive contingency where it does not exist, and they assume that they control their ability in the same way that they do their effort.

Weisz (1986) pointed out that although perceptions of control require both beliefs in contingency and competence, perceptions of responsibility require only beliefs in contingency. Children sometimes believe that rewards (e.g., grades, winning a race) are contingent on their behavior (whether they give correct answers, run fast), but that they lack the competence to produce the behavior required for the reward. Because the competence component is missing, they do not believe they control the outcome. But the perceived lack of competence does not protect them from a feeling of responsibility for the outcome. Young children's tendency to overestimate contingency could make them especially vulnerable to self-blame for events they did not cause (e.g., the death of a loved one, their parents' divorce, a bad grade from a biased teacher or on an assignment that was too difficult for them). Weisz's observations, therefore, have implications for clinicians who are trying to help young children cope with stressful events, as well as for teachers.

Developmental research relevant to the stability dimension suggests that young children are less likely than older children to attribute outcomes to stable dispositions or traits (see Bar-Tal, Ravgad, & Zilberman, 1981). Studies have shown, for example, that young children tend not to describe themselves or another in terms of underlying stable dispositions (Livesley & Bromley, 1973; Peevers & Secord, 1973).

In summary, the research related to children's perceptions of the causes of success and failure suggest systematic changes in the judgments children make. These changes have implications for children's behavior. That young children are less likely to attribute failure to uncontrollable or stable causes, for example, may explain why they are less prone to giving up when they fail than are older children (Miller, 1985; Rholes, Blackwell, Jordan, & Walters, 1980).

Individual Differences in Achievement-Related Beliefs

In addition to the systematic developmental shifts described in the previous section, stable individual differences in achievement-related beliefs are manifest early and continue to develop throughout childhood. Experiences in school play a major role in the development of individual differences. School performance history is perhaps the most significant factor in children's beliefs about their competencies, expectations, and causal attributions, although it is certainly not the only one.

Among the many other variables associated with individual differences in achievement-related beliefs (e.g., social class, race), gender has attracted the most attention. Girls, on average, have been found in many studies to have lower perceptions of their ability (V. C. Crandall, 1969; Deaux, 1976; Eccles, 1983; Fennema & Sherman, 1977; Frey & Ruble, 1987; Ladd & Price, 1986; Parsons, Ruble, Hodges & Small, 1976) and lower expectations for success (Entwisle & Baker, 1983; Hanna & Sonnenschein, 1985). Likewise, many studies have found that females are less likely than males to attribute success to their own high ability and more likely to attribute failure to low ability (Dweck & Reppucci, 1973; Eccles, 1983; Nicholls, 1975, 1979, 1980; Stipek, 1984b; Stipek & Gralinski, 1991; see Sohn, 1982, for a meta-analysis). These gender differences in achievement-related beliefs are not always found, but they are usually found with regard to domains, such as math and science, that are gender-stereotyped as male (Gitelson, Petersen & Tobin-Richards, 1982; Ryckman & Peckham, 1987; Stipek, 1984b; Stipek

& Gralinski, 1991). Findings from a few studies suggest that gender differences may be particularly prominent among the brightest, highest-performing students (Stipek & Hoffman, 1980a).

Many of the studies on factors affecting individual differences in achievement-related beliefs have focused on gender differences. To the degree that a factor explains differences between genders, however, it should also explain variation within a gender. We turn now to research on factors believed to explain why some children seem predisposed to make positive judgments about their abilities, expect success, and perceive themselves to be in control of achievement outcomes, whereas others tend to make more negative and maladaptive judgments.

Performance History. To a considerable degree, individual differences in achievement-related beliefs are realistic. Some children perform better in school than others. Their higher perceptions of competence and expectations for success are, therefore, simply reflections of their experience in school of consistent high performance. Thus, studies have shown that children who have a history of good performance have higher perceptions of their competence and they are more likely to expect success (Newman, 1984; Stipek & Hoffman, 1980a). Children who consistently do well in school typically develop a concept of themselves as academically competent, and are therefore more likely to attribute success to internal causes (e.g., high ability) and failure to external causes (e.g., bad luck, an unfair test; Greene, 1985; Marsh, 1984; Stipek & Hoffman, 1980), and to perceive themselves in control of achievement outcomes (see Stipek & Weisz, 1981). Retarded children, who presumably experience frequent failure, are more likely to blame themselves for their failure than are nonretarded children (Chan & Keogh, 1974; MacMillan & Keogh, 1971), and they are more likely to manifest helpless behavior in task situations (Weisz, 1979).

Parent Socialization. Early work on achievement motivation, although not always generating consistent findings, suggested a positive relationship between parents' expectations for their children's achievement and children's achievement striving (e.g., V. C. Crandall, 1969; Rosen & D'Andrade, 1959; Winterbottom, 1958) and performance (see Seginer, 1983). Researchers have found that parents tend to have more favorable perceptions of boys' than girls' competence in math (Eccles, Jacobs, & Harold, 1990), higher educational aspirations for boys, and lower satisfaction with boys' performance in math (suggesting higher standards for boys; Holloway, 1986). Yee and Eccles (1988) found some of the same gender differences in parents' attributions for their children's performance that have been found for children's own attributions. Parents of boys rated natural talent as a more important reason for their children's math successes than did parents of girls; parents of girls rated effort as a more important reason for their math successes. Phillips and Zimmerman (1990) found, in addition, that girls perceived lower parental expectations than boys.

The effect of parental expectations on children's own perceptions of ability was demonstrated in Parsons, Adler, and Kaczala's (1982) large-scale study of parents and their children in Grades 5 to 11. These investigators proposed two ways parents might influence children's beliefs about their ability in math—by modeling particular beliefs and behaviors, and by directly socializing their children. They found little evidence for the modeling hypothesis. Neither parents' self-reports nor children's perceptions of their parents' own math use were strong predictors of children's self-perceptions, task perceptions, or performance in math.

Support was strong for the direct socialization hypothesis. Parents', especially mothers', perceptions of their children's math aptitude and potential were more powerful predictors of children's self-perceptions than were objective indicators of ability, such as grades and test scores (see also Phillips, 1987). Parsons, Adler, and Kaczala (1982) concluded that parents have their major impact as conveyors of expectancies regarding their children's ability, and, unfortunately, some parents hold gender-stereotyped beliefs regarding their children's achievement potential in math.

Teacher Expectations and Behaviors. Teacher expectations for students' success are assumed to affect children's learning directly—because teachers provide different kinds of tasks and learning opportunities for high- and low-expectancy children—and indirectly, by influencing children's perceptions of their competence and other achievement-related beliefs. Rosenthal and Jacobson's (1966) classic *self-fulfilling prophecy* study was the first to demonstrate expectancy effects on learning. Teachers were told at the beginning of the year that some of the children in their classes showed unusual potential for intellectual gains. In the first and second grades (but not in the upper grades) these "high-expectancy" students showed significantly greater gains in IQ than did the remaining students, even though they had actually been selected at random.

This study inspired hundreds of teacher-expectancy studies, many of which have tried to identify teacher behaviors that influence children's achievement-related beliefs and performance (see Dusek, 1975, 1985, for reviews). Good (1987) summarized teaching behaviors that have often been observed to covary with performance expectations. Teachers have been found, for example, to (a) wait less time for low achievers to answer questions, (b) not stay as long with low achievers in failure situations, (c) criticize low achievers more frequently, (d) pay less attention to low achievers, and (e) seat low achievers farther from themselves.

The findings are occasionally counterintuitive. For example, some studies have found that teachers praise children for whom they have low expectations more than high-expectancy children (Good, 1987). According to the research mentioned earlier, children above the age of about 10 years who observe that they are being praised more than other children for the same or a lower level of performance may conclude that the teacher has lower expectations for them (see Meyer et al., 1979).

Graham (1990) suggested that teachers also reveal low versus high expectations through their emotional expressions. In one study, she found that sixth graders who received a sympathetic response when they did poorly on a task were more likely to attribute their failure to low ability and had lower expectations for future success than children who received an angry response. The angry response resulted in high expectations presumably because children assumed that the teacher would be angry only if they had control over the outcome (i.e., the poor performance was caused by low effort, which they could increase, rather than low ability, which they do not control; see Barker & Graham, 1987; Graham, 1984).

Weinstein and her colleagues have studied children's awareness of differential teacher behavior (Brattesani, Weinstein, & Marshall, 1984; see Weinstein, 1985, 1989). Teachers vary considerably in the degree to which they behave differently toward high- and low-expectancy children. Children's own expectations were strongly related to teachers' expectations only in classrooms in which differential teacher behavior was perceived. Again, however, there were age differences in children's processing of teacher feedback. Weinstein, Marshall, Sharp, and Botkin (1987) report that children were aware in the early elementary grades that teachers treat high-ability students differently from low-ability students, but not until fifth grade did children perceive negative teacher treatment to themselves. Perhaps young children's bias toward positive beliefs about their competencies protected them from incorporating the more negative view that teachers conveyed in their behavior toward low achievers.

Taken together, the research on teacher expectations suggests that teachers do convey information about their expectations for students' performance, and these expectations influence children's own achievement-related beliefs. However, teachers' expectations are largely based on children's actual performance (Dusek, 1975), and to a considerable degree differential teacher behavior is an appropriate pedagogical response to children's different skill levels. There is some dispute about how much teachers' expectations themselves influence children's achievement-related beliefs and performance, and the degree to which teachers' differential behavior is unnecessary and harmful (see Dusek, 1975, 1985 for reviews).

The work of Weinstein (1985) and her colleagues suggests that the answer varies considerably from teacher to teacher. Good and Brophy (1980) concluded that about one-third of the teachers they had observed in several studies behaved in a way that appeared to exaggerate the initial deficiencies of low achievers. Thus, although teacher expectations are based primarily on children's performance, in some classrooms teacher expectancies have an independent effect on children's achievement-related beliefs and learning.

Classroom studies have not yielded consistent evidence on teacher expectations and behaviors that might foster systematic *gender differences* in children's achievement-related beliefs. Dweck and her colleagues proposed that girls may develop lower perceptions of competence, in part, because a larger proportion of the negative feedback that they receive concerns the quality of their academic performance. They observed in fourth- and fifth-grade classrooms that boys were criticized more than girls, but most of the criticism the boys received concerned conduct or failure to follow directions. In contrast to the boys, most of the small amount of criticism the girls received concerned the quality of their academic performance (Dweck, Davidson, Nelson, & Enna, 1978). They suggested that boys may not view negative feedback as relevant to their intellectual abilities. Because a much larger proportion of the negative feedback girls received concerned their academic performance, they may have been less able to disregard the relevance of teacher feedback to their intellectual abilities.

Parsons, Kaczala, and Meece (1982) studied gender differences in teacher expectations and associated teacher–student interaction patterns in math classrooms in Grades 5, 6, 7, and 9. They found that student gender was only modestly related to student–teacher interaction patterns, and not in the manner predicted by Dweck and colleagues (1978). In those classrooms in which girls had lower expectancies than boys, high-achieving girls were not praised as much as high-achieving boys. This study suggested that differential teacher praise, not criticism, was a more likely explanation of gender differences in achievement-related beliefs.

Classroom observation studies suggest that differential treatment of girls and boys in math and science is more prominent in the upper than in the lower grades. Findings of studies of elementary- and middle-school children are mixed. A few studies have found that girls receive less academic contact than boys (e.g., Leinhardt, Seewald, & Engel, 1979), but other studies report few or no differences in the ways boys and girls are treated (Kimball, 1989). In contrast to the early grades, differences are consistently found in high school classes. Researchers have found that teachers talk to, call on, give more corrective feedback to, and praise boys more than girls (e.g. Becker, 1981; Morse & Handley, 1985; Stallings, 1985). Becker observed, for example, that although there were no differences in student-initiated interactions with teachers in a sample of geometry classes, 63% of the teacher-initiated academic contacts were with boys. Girls received 30% of the encouraging comments and 84% of the discouraging comments (see Kimball, 1989).

These differential behaviors toward girls and boys are likely to affect boys' and girls' perceptions of competence and expectations, as well as their math learning. Researchers have been concerned about gender differences in achievement-related beliefs in math and science primarily because females take fewer high-level courses than males, and females are underrepresented in math and science professions. Relatively low perceptions of competence and low expectations for success, along with differences in values associated with gender-stereotyping of academic domains and professions, discussed later, are assumed to inhibit females from pursuing careers in math and science.

Cultural Factors

There is evidence for cultural differences in beliefs about the causes of achievement outcomes that presumably are transmitted to children by parents, teachers, and other socializing agents (e.g., the media). Compared to Americans, Japanese mothers and children have been found to emphasize effort more and ability less than their American counterparts (see Holloway, 1988; Holloway, Kashiwagi, Hess, & Azuma, 1986; Stevenson, Lee, & Stigler, 1986). Observers of Chinese culture suggest that Chinese, likewise, emphasize effort as a cause of performance (see Chen & Uttal, 1988). This emphasis is consistent with traditional Chinese philosophy that assumes malleability in humans and stresses striving for improvement. Thus, systematic, stable differences in achievement-related beliefs are seen not only among individuals within a culture, but also between individuals in different cultures. It is possible that the emphasis on effort contributes to Japanese students' relatively high academic skills.

Achievement-related beliefs are important to understand because they influence individuals' behavior in achievement situations — including behaviors, such as choosing courses, that have long-term implications for occupational options. School is the primary place in which these beliefs are manifested, and school, along with parents and cognitive-developmental factors, plays a critical role in the development of achievement-related beliefs. We turn now to another domain of development in which school figures prominently — achievement-related values.

VALUES

Individuals at all age levels forego opportunities to engage in achievement-related activities — not because they expect to fail, but because they simply do not value success. Values also affect how much effort people put into activities and how they feel about outcomes, and they have implications for life-long professional commitments. Thus, for example, children who value athletic performance more than academic performance may exert more effort on the field than in the classroom, experience greater pride and shame as a consequence of performance in athletic competitions than as a consequence of report card results, and aspire to an occupation requiring athletic skills. Some children learn to value musical or other artistic competencies, or popularity among peers, or serving the community. Even within the academic domain, there is variation in the degree to which children value competence and success in different subject areas.

Values also, in combination with perceptions of competence, affect individuals' self-esteem. This was demonstrated in a study reported in Harter (1987); perceptions of low competence in domains that children valued highly had more negative effects on self-esteem than perceptions of low competence in domains that they valued less.

School is a place in which achievement-related values are manifested, and school experiences play an important role in shaping them. This section describes different ways achievement-related values have been conceptualized and what is known about factors that influence their development.

Eccles (1983) proposed three kinds of values relevant to achievement: (a) *attainment value*—the subjective importance of doing well on a task or in an achievement domain, determined by how a task or the domain fulfills the individual's needs; (b) *intrinsic value*—the immediate enjoyment one gets from doing a task, and (c) *utility value*—the usefulness of a task as a means to achieve goals that might not be related to the task itself.

A fourth way to conceptualize value is in terms of *anticipated emotions*. In accordance with a hedonistic view of human motivation, individuals are assumed to seek opportunities to experience pleasurable emotions, such as pride, and to avoid situations in which they are likely to experience unpleasant emotions, such as shame or embarrassment (Weiner, 1980). Achievement situations expected to generate pride, therefore, are perceived to have more value than situations believed likely to produce feelings of shame.

Developmental research on anticipated emotions is described first because this is how value was originally conceptualized by achievement-motivation theorists (Atkinson, 1964; McClelland, 1951). This review is followed by a discussion of development related to attainment and intrinsic value, respectively.

Anticipated Emotions

Anticipated emotions have been conceptualized both in terms of unconscious motives and in relation to achievement-related beliefs (e.g., expectations for success and causal attributions for success and failure) that engender different emotional reactions. Recent developmental research has focused primarily on the latter, and is therefore discussed in more detail.

Unconscious Motives.   In early theoretical work, McClelland (1951; McClelland, Atkinson, Clark, & Lowell, 1953) proposed a motive to achieve success, which he conceptualized as a stable disposition reflecting an individual's capacity for experiencing pride in success. Atkinson (1964) added a second unconscious motive—a negative anticipatory goal reaction to failure—conceptualized in terms of anticipated shame. He assumed that achievement situations arouse both of these unconscious motives, and whether an individual approaches or avoids an achievement situation is determined, in part, by the relative strength of these two motives.

Both McClelland and Atkinson believed that achievement situations arouse motives, which, in turn, energize behavior. The motive aroused in a particular situation depends on emotional associations to achievement situations (e.g., pride in accomplishment and shame in failure) that are formed in early childhood as a function of parental behaviors. Many studies have, accordingly, been conducted to assess the effect of parents' child-rearing practices on children's (usually boys') achievement motives. Although some studies indicated that early independence training (Winterbottom, 1958) and high parental expectations (Rosen & D'Andrade, 1959) fostered a strong motive to achieve success in children, taken together, findings have been too inconsistent to suggest any general principles (see V. C. Crandall, 1967; V. J. Crandall, 1963; Trudewind, 1982, for reviews).

Emotions as a Function of Expectations.   Atkinson also assumed that the incentive value—which he defined as anticipated pride or shame—of success or failure in particular achievement situations affects behavior. Incentive value is determined entirely, in his theory, by expectations for success; individuals are assumed to expect to feel less proud of achieving success on an easy task (i.e., one on which they expect to succeed) than on a difficult task, and more shame as the result of failing an easy than a difficult task.

Developmental research suggests that children understand the inverse relationship between perceived probability of success or failure and incentive value by the age of 7 years. Studies have shown, for example, that sometime between the ages of 4 and 7 years, depending in part on the nature of the task, children begin to claim that success on a difficult task would please the teacher more than success on an easy task (Heckhausen, 1984; Nicholls, 1978, 1980). Younger children appear to value success on an easy task as much as success on a difficult task. This may explain why preschool-age children, unlike older children, nearly always select a task described as "easy" when given different difficulty levels from which to choose (Heckhausen, 1984).

Emotions as a Function of Attributions. Weiner (1980, 1985, 1986) also emphasized emotions as determinants of behavior. For Weiner, like Atkinson, anticipated pride and shame (as well as other emotions) push individuals toward or away from achievement situations. However, whereas Atkinson focused on relations between anticipated emotions and expectations, Weiner focused on relations between emotions and perceptions of the cause of outcomes.

Weiner differentiated between emotions (e.g., happy, sad) that are based on the outcome (success or failure) alone, and emotions that are based on the individual's perception of the cause of the outcome. Pride and shame, for example, occur only when an outcome is attributed to some internal cause, such as effort or ability, and guilt occurs only when failure is attributed to lack of effort or some other controllable cause. The value of success (e.g., a good grade) on a school task, therefore, depends in part on the degree to which individuals can attribute success to personal attributes or behaviors. Anything that reduces a child's perception of personal responsibility (e.g., unnecessary help from the teacher or a classmate) could undermine the value of success.

Children's understanding of the linkages adults make between attributions and emotions have been assessed in several studies. Thompson (1987, 1989) concluded that in early elementary school children focus primarily on global outcome-dependent emotions (e.g., happy, sad) when interpreting others' and their own achievement outcomes because outcome-dependent emotions require a less complex appraisal of situations (see also Weiner, Kun, & Benesh-Weiner, 1980). Studies suggest also that because young children do not interpret specific causes the same way that adults usually do (e.g., they believe ability and luck are controllable) they associate different emotional consequences with some causes. Stipek and DeCotis (1988), for example, found that kindergarten-age children expected to feel as much pride for success attributable to luck as for success attributable to effort.

In summary, several theorists have proposed that the value of achievement outcomes is based, in part, on the expected emotional consequences of performance outcomes. The evidence is inconsistent with regard to factors that affect the development of general dispositions or capacities to experience pride and shame in achievement contexts. Research assessing relations between anticipated pride and shame and two achievement-related beliefs — expectations for success and causal attributions — have demonstrated important developmental changes that have implications for the value of achievement outcomes. In general, research suggests that the value of success in school may be less dependent on other factors—such as the difficulty level of the task and whether help was received—for young (preoperational) than for older children.

Attainment Value

Attainment value concerns the relevance of an activity to an individual's self-concept. Children presumably engage in activities and develop competencies that are consistent with their concept of themselves (e.g., as feminine, musically talented, socially deviant). School offers opportunities for children to pursue activities in many domains (both sanctioned and unsanctioned), and school experiences have important effects on the attainment value of success in different domains.

There has been little research on developmental changes in attainment values. However, one large longitudinal study of children in sixth and seventh grade found that success in the social domain was considered most important, followed by success in math, and then English (Eccles et al., 1989). Sports were rated, on average, to be the least important. The attainment value of both social and math competence declined over the 2-year period, but because the decline in math was much greater, the relative importance of social competence over math competence was steeper at the end of seventh grade than at the beginning of sixth grade. The decline observed during adolescence in the perceived value of math (but not English) is consistent with other studies (Brush, 1980; Eccles et al., 1984, 1989).

Most of the research on attainment value has focused on gender differences. Cognitive theorists claim that gender-role identity influences achievement behavior by influencing perceptions of the attainment value of tasks (see Eccles, 1983). Consistent with this perspective, studies have shown that gender labeling of tasks affects students' choice and performance (e.g., Montemayor, 1974; Sherman, 1979). Research also suggests that, with age, males increasingly value achievement in school and females become more concerned about potential conflicts between academic and social goals (Sherman, 1979).

Discussions of gender differences in attainment value in school activities have centered primarily on differential course taking in mathematics. However, Eccles (1983) pointed out that the perceived value of math courses will only be affected by gender-typing if one's gender-role identity is a critical and salient component of one's self-concept. Thus, for example, the attainment value of math achievement should be low for females who perceive math courses as a masculine activity and avoid masculine activities as a way to affirm their femininity.

The evidence for an effect of gender typing on female's perceptions of the attainment value of math courses is weak. Males are more likely than females to see math courses as a male achievement domain and females usually do not characterize participation in math courses as unfeminine (see Eccles, 1983).

It is possible, however, that although females do not see math courses as a male domain, they do see math-related occupations as unfeminine. Eccles suggested that if females are less likely to aspire to a profession in mathematics, math courses would have less utility value than they would for males. Consistent with this claim, a study by Stevenson and Newman (1986) found that 10th-grade boys had higher expectancies for success in a career that required mathematical ability and perceived math to have greater utility in daily life than girls. Gender typing of careers may, therefore, be a more important mediator of sex differences in the perceived value of advanced math courses than sex typing of math courses. Gender stereo-typing of occupations is discussed in some detail later.

Attainment values in the achievement domain have not received nearly so much attention from developmental psychologists as the intrinsic value of tasks. We turn now to this topic.

Intrinsic Value

Eccles' (1983) concept of intrinsic value—although applicable to tasks encountered in school and any other achievement context—actually comes from a construct used to understand infants' mastery behavior. Long before children enter school—indeed, from the first day of life—infants are actively engaged in learning behaviors. To explain such infant behaviors as exploration and mastery attempts, motivation theorists have assumed that humans are *naturally disposed* to seek opportunities to practice newly developing competencies and that learning is (or at least can be) intrinsically pleasurable (Piaget, 1952; White, 1959). White pointed out that in humans, unlike in lower animals, few competencies are innately provided and much has to be learned about dealing with the environment. Thus, a drive to develop competence has considerable adaptive value.

Young infants are believed to be intrinsically motivated to engage in such simple behaviors as looking at and grasping objects. Intrinsic motivation continues to play a role in older children's achievement-related activities, although the particular learning activities children engage in change with age. Harter (1978) pointed out that in the preoperational stage, a need to practice the newly developed capacity for symbolic thought and newly developing physical abilities explains children's preoccupation with fantasy play and interest in physical activities. With the onset of concrete-operational thought, children become preoccupied with rules, social roles, and hobbies that involve the collection and categorization of objects. With formal operational thinking comes interest in discussing abstract issues, such as religion and politics. Children are, according to the theory, intrinsically motivated to practice any skill that they are developing but have not entirely mastered.

Developmental change has been observed in the strength of intrinsic motivation — at least related to academic tasks — as well as in the nature of the activities it stimulates. Harter (1981b) developed a questionnaire measure of five components of intrinsic motivation. Scores on the subscales measuring *preference for challenge, curiosity and interest,* and *independent mastery* declined from third through ninth grade; scores on the *independent judgment* (versus reliance on teacher judgment) and the *internal criteria for success/failure* (versus external criteria) subscales increased. Other investigators have reported declines in the perceived value and enjoyment of academic activities in math (Brush, 1980; Eccles, 1983). Thus, with age and experience in achievement contexts, children tend to become less motivated to engage in academic activities for their own pleasure, but better able to rely on their own judgment of the quality of their performance. Research on classroom factors that affect children's intrinsic motivation, discussed later in the chapter, provide some explanations for these declines.

Individual Differences. The intrinsic motivational force that compels the organism to engage in competence-developing behavior is assumed, by most theorists, to be innate. A few researchers, however, have found individual differences in the degree to which this motive is manifested in behavior in children as young as 1 year of age (see Morgan & Harmon, 1984, for a review). Individual differences in intrinsic interest in achievement tasks may increase as children get older as a consequence of increasingly divergent experiences in achievement contexts. Researchers have investigated both home and school factors that might account for the stable differences among children that have been revealed by Harter's and others' measures (Harter & Connell, 1984).

Several theorists have assumed that individual differences in mastery motivation are explained, in part, by parents' behavior toward children, especially in the early years. Harter proposes that reinforcing mastery efforts, modeling approving responses, and not reinforcing children for dependent behavior sustain or enhance children's intrinsic motivation to engage in activities that contribute to their cognitive and physical competencies. Criticizing independent mastery attempts, modeling disapproval, and reinforcing adult-dependent behavior are presumed to inhibit intrinsic motivation. Harter's (1978) point is reminiscent of Erikson's (1963) earlier warning to parents that if they react negatively to children's exploratory and achievement efforts, they could make children feel inadequate and doubtful of their competencies, which would inhibit spontaneous achievement striving.

School experiences undoubtedly play a major role in the degree to which achievement activities are intrinsically valued. Perceived intellectual competence—which is largely based on school performance—is one of the most important factors in children's intrinsic interest in academic tasks (Boggiano & Ruble, 1979; Harter, 1981a; Harter & Connell, 1984; see Ryan, Connell, & Deci, 1985). Children who feel competent in a domain are more likely to be intrinsically motivated to complete tasks related to that domain than children who believe they lack competence. Analogously, achievement situations that contribute to feelings of competence tend to enhance intrinsic motivation, and situations that result in feelings of incompetence tend to diminish intrinsic motivation.

This effect is illustrated in a study by Mac Iver, Stipek, and Daniels (1991); junior- and senior-high students who, from the beginning to the end of the semester gained self-confidence in their ability to perform well in a class, became more intrinsically interested in the subject area over the course of the semester, and children whose self-confidence eroded became less interested in the subject area. Children's performance and other variables that influence their perceptions of their competence, therefore, strongly affect their intrinsic interest in academic tasks and presumably in other domains. The declines in perceptions of academic competence, described earlier, may, therefore, contribute to the age-related declines observed in intrinsic interest in school tasks.

Individual differences in intrinsic interest in academic tasks can also be traced to the instructional and evaluation practices their teachers use. Instructional practices may, as well, contribute to differences in intrinsic motivation within children over time and across different performance domains (e.g., academic, music, athletic) and school subjects.

Systematic changes in instructional practices that are associated with age may explain the decline that has been observed in children's intrinsic interest in school tasks. Consider, for example, the use of extrinsic rewards, especially grades. Researchers have demonstrated that when extrinsic rewards are offered for tasks that children are naturally disposed (intrinsically motivated) to do, children's attention shifts from the intrinsic value of the task to the more salient extrinsic reward. When the extrinsic reward is withdrawn, children discount the intrinsic value of the task and cease engaging in it (Lepper, Greene, & Nisbett, 1973; see reviews by Bates, 1979; Deci & Ryan 1985; Notz, 1975). In a classic study by Lepper and colleagues (1973), preschool-age children who had not been previously rewarded for drawing pictures persisted longer at drawing when they were later given a choice than children who had previously been rewarded for drawing pictures. The intrinsic interest of the nonrewarded children apparently remained intact, whereas the intrinsic interest of the rewarded children declined.

Further research has shown, however, that rewards do not always undermine intrinsic motivation. Deci and Ryan (1985), for example, pointed out that extrinsic rewards have both a *controlling* and an *informational* aspect. When the informational value is stressed ("You got an A, you must really understand this"), a reward enhances an individual's perception of his or her competence, which in turn enhances intrinsic motivation. It is when the controlling function is stressed (e.g., "If you get to work immediately and do this correctly you'll get a good grade"), that rewards undermine intrinsic motivation; under these conditions students begin to perceive the reward, rather than their intrinsic interest in the task, as the reason for their effort. The degree to which rewards are stressed in an educational environment, therefore, should affect children's intrinsic interest in school tasks. The average decline in children's intrinsic interest in school tasks may be partly a consequence of the increased salience of extrinsic rewards, especially grades, used to control behavior.

Instruction-related variables that have been shown to positively affect intrinsic motivation may also decline over the school years. Choice, for example, enhances intrinsic motivation (see Deci, Nezlek, & Sheinman, 1981; Morgan, 1984; Zuckerman, Porac, Lathin, Smith, & Deci, 1978). Most preschool-age children have considerable choice in the kinds of activities they engage in, but as children move through the elementary grades and into junior high, time allocated to recess and freeplay is reduced, and the proportion of time that is spent in teacher-directed instruction and on teacher-designed assignments increases. Studies suggest a decline from elementary to junior high school in the amount of autonomy students are allowed and in opportunities to participate in decision making (Midgley & Feldlaufer, 1987). Competition, which has been shown to inhibit intrinsic motivation (Deci, Betley, Kahle, Abrams, & Porac, 1981), also increases as children get older.

The decline in individualized and small-group instruction and the more uniform tasks given in the upper grades, discussed previously, may indirectly undermine intrinsic motivation. Individualized instruction allows children to work on tasks that are *optimally challenging*—that require some effort and may involve initial failure, but that are not too difficult and generate a real feeling of competence or mastery when success is achieved. The same task given to all students in a class will inevitably be too easy for some, too difficult for others, and appropriately challenging for those in the middle. For only these fortunate few in the middle will the task be intrinsically interesting.

Summary

Values must be considered in any attempt to predict or understand children's behavior in achievement settings. Children will not approach a task or activity—even if they believe they will succeed—unless they also want to succeed or develop competence in that domain. Achievement-related values are manifested in school, perhaps more than in any other context, and school experiences play a major role in their development.

Like expectations and related beliefs about competence, achievement-related values change in systematic ways with age, and individual differences evolve as a function of socializing agents and experience in achievement settings. Systematic age-related changes were described in factors (e.g., difficulty level of tasks, perceptions of the cause of outcomes) that affect the emotional value of achievement outcomes. Attainment value has been studied primarily in an attempt to understand gender differences in participation in math-related activities. Finally, research suggesting that school experiences are more likely to undermine intrinsic interest in academic tasks than to increase it was reviewed.

As children formulate answers to the questions "What am I good at?" and "What do I want to be good at?" their long-range educational and occupational plans take shape. School experiences play a critical role in these decisions which, although not irreversible, have important implications for life-long opportunities. School is particularly important for youth who do not go on to college, although even for college-bound youth, experiences in high school and even in the early grades both limit and create options. Thus, to a significant degree, children's experiences in school influence the course of their entire lives. In the next section research on children's answers to the question, "What do I want to do when I grow up?" and factors that affect their answers are reviewed.

OCCUPATIONAL ASPIRATIONS

Experience in school is a major factor in students' perceptions of the accessibility and desirability of different occupations. Students are exposed in school to different domains of intellectual inquiry and occupational options. Their own expectations and aspirations are influenced by teachers, counselors, and peers encountered in school. Performance in school and courses taken also limit or facilitate preparation for further schooling and different professions in very real ways. Students who do poorly academically, or who do not take college prerequisite courses, have more limited options than high-achieving students in the college track.

Research on occupational aspirations has focused on gender stereotypes and racial and social class inequities. Although considerable progress has been made in the number of individuals entering nontraditional occupations, many occupations remain underrepresented by either men or women. Children's race and social class also continue to be significant predictors of the type of occupations they will pursue.

There are two points of view on the role of schools in these inequities. Taking an optimistic perspective, schools might be expected to serve as change agents — weakening gender stereotyping and racial and social-class constraints on opportunities. Schools might, for example, encourage students to participate in activities or training that would prepare them for nontraditional occupations or occupations to which their family experience might not direct them. A more pessimistic view is that schools perpetuate and even reinforce gender stereotypes and racial and social class inequities found in the larger society. Unfortunately, the weight of the evidence — some of which is summarized in the following section — is on the negative side.

Gender Stereotypes

By the time children enter school they are already able to assign gender-stereotypic labels to occupations (Franken, 1983; Garrett, Ein, & Tremaine, 1977; Papalia & Tennent, 1975), and they employ linguistic markers to refer to individuals in nontraditional occupations (e.g., lady doctor; Rosenthal & Chapman, 1982). Children also engage in play related to gender-typed occupations early in the preschool years. Boys are more involved with transportation toys and carpentry, girls with housekeeping and doll play (Etaugh, Collins, & Gerson, 1975; Sanders & Harper, 1976).

Children's awareness of social stereotypes related to achievement and occupations continues to increase throughout childhood and adolescence. Athletic, spatial, quantitative, scientific, and mechanical skills become stereotyped as masculine; verbal, artistic, and social skills are considered feminine (Huston, 1983; Kaminski & Sheridan, 1984; Raymond & Benbow, 1986).

It is generally believed that early gender typing is, in part, a consequence of the development of *gender identity* (Kohlberg, 1966). Children categorize themselves as boys or girls by the age of 3, and gradually (between the ages of about 4 and 7) develop the concept of *gender constancy* (the understanding of the unchangeability of gender). The development of these concepts is assumed to promote differential valuations and a desire to behave in a way that is consistent with their own gender label. Support for these claims comes from studies that have found a relation between children's understanding of gender constancy and gender role stereotyping (Kuhn, Nash, & Brucken, 1978; O'Keefe & Hyde, 1983; see Stangor &

Ruble, 1987 for a review). Findings that children choose stereotypical occupations for themselves even before they have a concept of gender constancy, however, suggest that gender constancy may not be necessary for gender stereotyping (O'Keefe & Hyde, 1983). These findings are consistent with the view of some theorists, that gender identity is sufficient to motivate and guide behavior (Martin & Halverson, 1981).

Children's knowledge of gender stereotypes increases with age. Kohlberg proposed, however, that gender roles are the most rigid at about the age of 6 or 7 — just as a fully developed concept of gender identity is achieved — and decline somewhat thereafter (Kohlberg & Ullman, 1974). Consistent with his claim, research suggests that children's acceptance of stereotypes as inflexible or morally appropriate declines after the preschool and early elementary grades (Carter & Patterson, 1982; Cummings & Taebel, 1980; Franken, 1983; O'Keefe & Hyde, 1983; Stoddart & Turiel, 1985; see Stangor & Ruble, 1987).

It has long been recognized that gender typing of occupations inhibits individuals from aspiring to nontraditional occupations — a phenomenon referred to as "occupational foreclosure" (Miller, 1986). Perceptions of the compatibility of an occupation with one's gender label appears to be the most important factor in occupational aspirations among early elementary school-aged children. Later, other factors become important. Between the ages of about 9 and 13 children also begin to rule out occupations on the basis of their perceptions of their abilities and social class. Thus, all girls may rule out being a truck driver at age 6 "because girls do not drive trucks." At 10, a girl from a high social-status family may also rule out being a bank teller, and a girl from a low social-status family may rule out being a doctor because these professions are not compatible with her social class background or her perceptions of her academic achievement (which is strongly associated with social class; Miller, 1986). Not until adolescence do children begin to select occupations that are compatible with their personal interests and values (which are also influenced by gender stereotypes and social class; Gottfredson, 1981).

School-Related Influences. Clearly parents, the media, and other cultural institutions influence the development of gender-stereotypic beliefs and behavior related to achievement and occupations. However, school experiences reinforce and expand on these other influences. School plays a role, in part, through its effect on perceptions of competence and values related to different domains of achievement. Gender differences in achievement-related beliefs and values associated with math and science were discussed earlier in this chapter. School also contributes to gender differences in occupational plans by socializing gender stereotypes and reinforcing behavior consistent with these stereotypes. Evidence for these effects is discussed next.

Teacher behavior toward students is presumed to socialize particular behaviors (e.g., conformity, independence) in students—behaviors that have implications for later achievements. In early research on gender-role development preschools and elementary schools were viewed as feminine environments in which teachers preferred and reinforced feminine characteristics in all children (see Brophy, 1985). Feshbach (1969), for example, found that teachers preferred students described as conforming and orderly (characteristics typically associated with girls) to students described as independent, active, and assertive (characteristics typically associated with boys). Fagot and Patterson (1969) observed, accordingly, that teachers reinforced feminine behaviors in both boys and girls. Early researchers were, therefore, concerned about the feminization of boys and other potentially negative effects of being in an environment in which female characteristics are valued.

Studies have since found that girls and boys are treated differently by some teachers. The differences are often small, but the pattern is fairly consistent. For example, in many studies teachers have been observed to have more interactions with boys than with girls, especially related to discipline (e.g., Blumenfeld et al., 1983; Eccles & Blumenfeld, 1985; Serbin, O'Leary, Kent, & Tonick, 1973; Stake & Katz, 1982; see Brophy, 1985). Research assessing student perceptions has also shown that both boys and girls perceive girls to be better behaved and to receive better teacher treatment (Kaminski & Sheridan, 1984).

Although in some respects girls in the elementary grades appear to be favored, researchers have expressed concern that differential treatment of girls and boys could, in the long-run, render girls less effective in the more competitive, achievement-oriented environment of the upper grades and in the work place. Observation studies of preschool-age children have found, for example, that teachers give girls more attention and approval (e.g., Etaugh et al., 1975) and reinforce dependent behaviors in girls more than boys (e.g., Serbin et al., 1973). Serbin and colleagues also found that teachers were more likely to give boys than girls positive attention when they engaged in task-relevant behavior. Thus, girls were reinforced for remaining close to the teacher, and boys for engaging in tasks. Experimental studies suggest that these differential teacher behaviors contribute to gender differences in children's behavior, at least in the short term. Serbin, Connor, and Citron (1978), for example, reported that the more teachers reinforced independent task persistence and ignored help seeking and proximity, the less children sought attention in an experimental setting.

Research suggests that *teachers' beliefs* about girls and boys underlie teachers' differential behavior. For example, in the early grades teachers perceive boys as having more discipline, learning, and emotional problems in school (see Minuchin & Shapiro, 1983; Weisz, Suwanlert, Chaiyasit, & Weiss, 1989). In another study teachers expected girls to be more persistent, cooperative, and attentive (Brophy & Evertson, with Anderson, Baum & Crawford, 1981). Elementary teachers' greater contact with boys may, therefore, reflect a perceived need to monitor boys' behavior more closely than girls.

Meta-analyses of *teacher expectancy* studies are consistent with the conclusion, based on observation studies, that teachers tend to expect better performance from girls in the elementary grades, primarily because they are perceived to be easier to manage and more obedient (Dusek & Joseph, 1983). However, this conclusion does not apply to the later grades. Studies have demonstrated that teachers in the later grades associate masculine characteristics with intelligence, independence, and success in school, and feminine characteristics with interpersonal skills (e.g., Benz, Pfeiffer, & Newman, 1981; Bernard, 1979). Teachers have also been found to rate written work more highly when it is attributed to a man than when it is attributed to a woman (see Archer & McCarthy, 1988). These beliefs may contribute to the differential behavior toward boys and girls in math and science courses, which was discussed earlier.

There are also subtle forms of teacher behavior that can reinforce gender-stereotyped behavior. Delamont (1980) observed that teachers often used competition between boys and girls to control boys' behavior. Boys, for example, were admonished for letting girls beat them and for being sissies. Classroom responsibilities were sometimes gender stereotyped. Girls were asked to be class secretaries and boys to be team captains.

Children also learn gender-appropriate behavior and gender roles in school through textbooks and other curriculum materials. Gender-related stereotyping in the presentation of males and females in curriculum materials has declined, but still exists (Hoffman, 1982; Minuchin & Shapiro, 1983; Smith, Greenlaw, & Scott, 1987; Vaughn-Robertson, Tompkins, Hitchcock, & Oldham, 1989). Occupational roles are more evident and varied for men than for women, who are often shown as homemakers or as engaged in a limited and conventional set of occupations. And women are not usually portrayed as working and raising a family, suggesting a lag between educational materials and social reality.

Although males are shown in more varied roles than females, depictions of males also convey limited options. This is illustrated in a study of elementary level basal readers in which males were less likely to be portrayed in nontraditional roles than females (Scott, 1981). Of the main characters in nontraditional roles, 70% were females, and 76% of the main characters in traditional roles were males. The relatively low frequency of males depicted in nontraditional roles mirrors the lower number of male than female high school students who plan to enter nontraditional occupations (Gerstein, Lichtman, & Barokas, 1988).

Gender-stereotyped role models are also encountered in school. Although progress toward greater equity has been made in recent years, elementary school teachers are much more likely to be women than men (Ferris & Winkler, 1986), and principals are more likely to be men (Feldman, Jorgensen, & Poling, 1988). In 1982, 87% of school administrators were men (Metha, 1983). The pattern in schools can be compared to other fields in which women hold more than 20% of managerial and administrative positions (U.S. Department of Labor, 1979). More men teach at the secondary than the elementary level, but there are gender-stereotypical differences in the subject matter taught by men and women. About two-thirds of high school humanities, business education, foreign languages, and English teachers are women and two-thirds of the math, science, and vocational teachers are men (Meece, 1987).

Children's exposure and preparation for occupations is also gender stereotyped in school. In addition to gender differences in the number and level of math and science courses taken, there are differences in vocational courses. Despite a considerable reduction in official constraints on course participation, girls are much more likely to engage in training related to homemaking, health, or office work, and boys in agriculture, trade, or industry (Farmer & Sidney, 1985; National Center for Education Statistics, 1984a; Stockard et al., 1980). Differential participation in vocational courses is largely a result of students' own preferences, but it may be reinforced by gender-stereotypic advice given by counselors (Eccles & Hoffman, 1984; Haring & Beyard-Tyler, 1984; Ratzlaff & Kahn, 1983).

Extracurricular school activities are also gender stereotyped. Girls' participation in sports increased dramatically, in part as the result of Title IX of the Educational Amendments passed by Congress in 1972. Title IX mandates that no person can be denied participation in programs or activities receiving Federal financial assistance. Thus, the percentage of interscholastic high school female athletes increased from 7% in 1971 to 35% in 1981. The number of high schools with interscholastic female basketball teams jumped from under 5,000 to over 17,000 (Eccles & Hoffman, 1984). Even with these gains, however, sports experiences in school are typically more varied and extensive for boys. Boys outnumber girls in athletic programs by a ratio of 3:1 (Meece, 1987).

Some authors have suggested that boys learn to be competitive, in part, because of the opportunities available to compete in sports, although they point out also that boys may suffer from an excessive emphasis on competition rather than pleasure and mastery (e.g., Stockard et al., 1980). These suggestions have not been carefully tested, but correlational studies suggest a link between participation in sports and success in the business world (Hennig & Jardim, 1977).

Boys are also more likely to participate in extracurricular activities that involve math and science (Kahle, Matyas, & Cho, 1985), computers, and farming (Meece, 1987). Girls are more involved in intellectual activities, such as honorary or subject matter clubs, student government, school newspaper or yearbook, and performing arts (National Center for Education Statistics, 1984b).

In summary, schools reflect social values and perceptions of the larger culture, and in subtle and not-so-subtle ways they transmit these values to children. Indeed, one reviewer of research on teacher behavior and attitudes concluded that schools have been slow to adapt to recent changes in men's and women's roles, and may be exposing children ". . . to masculine and feminine images that are even more rigid and more polarized than those currently held in the wider society" (Meece, 1987, p. 67). Eccles and Blumenfeld's (1985) conclusions are slightly more generous. They conclude that, "although teachers do not appear to be the major source of these beliefs, they also do very little to change them or to provide boys and girls with the types of information that might lead them to reevaluate their gender-stereotyped beliefs" (p. 80).

Experiences in school undoubtedly facilitate the development of nontraditional occupational plans for some children. Intervention studies suggest, moreover, that with special training teachers can reduce gender stereotyping of occupations and foster greater interest in nontraditional occupations (Kourilsky & Campbell, 1984; Mason & Kahle, 1989). Such training is unusual, however, and research indicates that schools primarily reinforce gender stereotypes found in the larger society. Studies on social class differences in occupational aspirations, reviewed next, lead us to a similar conclusion.

Social Class Differences

Educational and occupational aspirations are strongly associated with social class (and race, to the considerable degree that race is confounded with social class; see Campbell, 1983; Marjoribanks, 1985). Research on the causes and consequences of these aspirations has been dominated by the Wisconsin model of status attainment (see Campbell, 1983; Cook & Alexander, 1980). This model assumes that school experiences primarily mediate the effects of the home. In essence, family socioeconomic status (SES) affects academic achievement, which influences students' experiences in school—including the courses they take and the nature of their peer groups. These school experiences, in turn, influence students' educational and occupational plans, and ultimately their status attainment. The model has been replicated in several large samples, and although it has been criticized by some researchers and fine-tuned by others, it has generally held up fairly well in multivariate causal analyses of large, nationally representative samples (see Campbell, 1983; Cook & Alexander, 1980; Hauser, Tsai, & Sewell, 1983; Looker & Pineo, 1983; Marjoribanks, 1985).

The model is also supported by studies that have examined single pathways. Thus, from an early age ethnic minority children and children whose parents are relatively less educated have, on average, lower achievement in school than White children and children with better-educated parents (Alexander & Entwisle, 1988). Asian-American students, particularly Japanese, are one exception to the general finding that minority students have lower achievement levels than White students (Pang, 1990).

Studies also support the assumption in the Wisconsin model that academic performance affects future plans directly (e.g., by limiting options) and indirectly, by influencing track placement and friendship choices. Poor and minority students are more likely than middle-class students to be placed in lower ability groups in elementary school (Haller, 1985) and in the general (noncollege-bound) or vocational track in high school. Research indicates that academic achievement is the primary determinant of ability group and track placement (Alexander & Cook, 1982; Haller, 1985; Wolfe, 1985). But the placement itself affects achievement gains, which affect occupational aspirations. Thus, when children with equal achievement levels are assigned to different ability groups (e.g., Weinstein, 1976) or different tracks (Natriello, Pallas, & Alexander, 1989), the children assigned to the higher level, on average, learn more. The differences in achievement gains have been explained partly by qualitative differences in teaching (see Good, 1987). Students in different tracks also take different courses and, as a consequence, achieve different levels of competence in academic domains, especially math and science (Ekstrom, Goertz, & Rock, 1988; Gamoran, 1987) Track placement also has a small but significant effect on educational and occupational aspirations, after academic achievement is controlled (Alexander & Cook, 1982; Hotchkiss, 1984).

Social class also influences students' choice of friends both directly and through its effect on academic achievement and track. Students are more likely to develop friendships with students in the same track or at roughly the same achievement level. The friends that children make in school, in turn, influence their values related to achievement and their long-term educational and occupational plans. Research suggests that although family SES is, by far, the strongest predictor of occupational aspirations, friends exercise their own influence, especially for girls (Cohen, 1983; Davies & Kandel, 1981; Epstein, 1983).

Teachers may exacerbate academic performance differences associated with social class and race, and therefore reinforce relatively low occupational aspirations among poor, minority students. Teacher expectancy studies have shown that, on average, teachers have more favorable expectations for White and middle-class children than for poor and minority children (Dusek & Joseph, 1983). A few studies have found that when race or social class are manipulated experimentally (e.g., by providing equivalent written information on students varying only in social class and/or race), teachers favor White children in terms of performance judgments (e.g., McCombs & Gay, 1988) and placements in special education (e.g., Lanier & Wittmer, 1977; Prieto & Zucker, 1981; Zucker & Prieto, 1977).

Teachers' expectations and other judgments, like ability group placement and track, however, are strongly associated with students' achievement level. Although the results of some studies using hypothetical children suggest racial prejudice, it is not clear from classroom research to what degree teachers react to individual differences in children's behavior and performance versus stereotypes unrelated to children's behavior. The importance of achievement in their judgments does not rule out the existence of social class or racial biases. But to the degree that social class and race are associated with academic achievement, different educational opportunities will occur regardless of explicit teacher biases.

In conclusion, there are undoubtedly students who, as the result of an extraordinary or interested teacher or counselor, or because of exposure or experiences in school, raise their aspirations beyond what would be expected on the basis of their social class. Nevertheless, taken together, research supports the view that school experiences are more likely to reinforce than to reverse family effects.

This is not to say that poor, minority children would be better off not going to school (although they often reach that conclusion themselves). Dropping out of school for poor, minority students may mean moving from an environment that fails to foster high aspirations to an environment that forecloses high status options altogether.

CONCLUSIONS

Success in adulthood is to a considerable degree based on the level of skills—in academic and other domains—that are developed in school. Skill, however, may not be the most important factor in individuals' achievements as adults. Achievement-related beliefs about competencies, achievement-related values, and occupational aspirations are major determinants of adults' behavior and success in the workplace and other achievement contexts. School plays a critical role in the development of these beliefs, values, and aspirations.

School effects interact with and are mediated by the many age-related changes that are described in this chapter. Explanations for achievement-related behavior become increasingly complex as children advance in age. Infants are believed to be motivated exclusively by an innate predisposition to engage in activities that contribute to their competence. Later, children begin to make a set of interrelated cognitive judgments—about their competence, the cause of outcomes, and the probability of succeeding on particular tasks. Preschool-age children are typically optimistic about their performance and they appear to exaggerate their control over outcomes. As a result of improved abilities in processing performance feedback, in combination with systematic changes in the nature of instruction and evaluation in school that are associated with age, children's perceptions of their competence and their expectations for success decline and become more strongly associated with objective indices (e.g., teacher ratings).

Achievement-related values also change with age. Toddlers and preschoolers continue, as they did in infancy, to engage primarily in competence-building tasks because they have intrinsic value. With age, however, the significance of the intrinsic motive to develop competence declines as an explanation of achievement-related behavior. The desire to obtain external rewards and attainment value play increasingly important roles. As children advance in age, most engage in learning-related activities for their own sake less and to achieve some other end more.

Occupational plans of preschool and early elementary school-age children are strongly affected by gender stereotypical beliefs. By the upper elementary grades children's perceptions of their abilities and their social class influence aspirations, and in adolescence personal interests and values—which are strongly associated with gender and social class—begin to play a role. Most of the evidence supports the view that schools primarily reinforce gender stereotypes and social-class and ethnic differences found in the larger society.

The developmental changes in achievement-related beliefs and values described in this chapter are not inevitable outcomes of age and attendant developments in cognitive processing abilities. To a significant degree developments related to both beliefs and values are consequences of instructional practices used in schools. School also does not, by necessity, reinforce cultural stereotypes. Although teachers do not have the power to reverse, altogether, beliefs, behaviors, and outcomes that are strongly embedded in the larger society, training programs could help teachers move in that direction. The better we understand how school experiences foster negative achievement-related beliefs and values and how they perpetuate gender stereotypes and social class and ethnic inequities, the better able we will be to design school programs that will have a positive effect on children's development and life opportunities.

REFERENCES

Aboud, F. (1985). The development of a social comparison process in children. *Child Development, 56,* 682–688.

Alexander, K., & Cook, M. (1982). Curricula and coursework: A surprise ending to a familiar story. *American Sociological Review, 47,* 626–640.

Alexander, K., & Entwisle, D. (1988). Achievement in the first 2 years of school: Patterns and processes. *Monographs of the Society for Research in Child Development, 53* (2, Serial No. 218).

Archer, J., & McCarthy, B. (1988). Personal biases in student assessment. *Educational Research, 30,* 142–145.

Atkinson, J. W. (1964). *An introduction to motivation.* Princeton, NJ: Van Nostrand.

Apple, M., & King, N. (1978). What do schools teach? In G. Willis (Ed.), *Qualitative evaluation: Concepts and cases in curriculum criticism* (pp. 444–465). Berkeley, CA: McCutchan.

Barker, G., & Graham, S. (1987). Developmental study of praise and blame as attributional cues. *Journal of Educational Psychology, 79,* 62–66.

Bar-Tal, D., Ravgad, N., & Zilberman, D. (1981). Development of causal perception of success and failure. *Educational Psychology, 1,* 347–358.

Bates, J. (1979). Extrinsic reward and intrinsic motivation: A review with implications for the classroom. *Review of Educational Research, 49,* 557–576.

Becker, J. (1981). Differential treatment of females and males in mathematics classes. *Journal for Research in Mathematics Education, 12,* 40–53.

Benenson, J., & Dweck, C. (1986). The development of trait explanations and self-evaluations in the academic and social domains. *Child Development, 57,* 1179–1187.

Benz, C., Pfeiffer, I., & Newman, I. (1981). Sex role expectations of classroom teachers, Grades 1–12. *American Educational Research Journal, 18,* 289–302.

Bernard, M. (1979). Does sex role behavior influence the way teachers evaluate students? *Journal of Educational Psychology, 71,* 553–562.

Blumenfeld, P., Hamilton, V., Bossert, S., Wessels, K., & Meece, J. (1983). Teacher talk and student thought: Socialization into the student role. In J. M. Levine & M. C. Wang (Eds.), *Teacher and student perceptions: Implications for learning* (pp. 143–192). Hillsdale, NJ: Lawrence Erlbaum Associates.

Blumenfeld, P., Pintrich, P., & Hamilton, V. (1986). Children's concepts of ability, effort, and conduct. *American Educational Research Journal, 23,* 95–104.

Blumenfeld, P., Pintrich, P., Meece, J., & Wessels, K. (1982). The formation and role of self-perceptions of ability in elementary classrooms. *Elementary School Journal, 82,* 401–420.

Boggiano, A. K., & Ruble, D. N. (1979). Competence and the overjustification effect: A developmental study. *Journal of Personality and Social Psychology, 37,* 1462–1468.

Brattesani, K., Weinstein, R., & Marshall, H. (1984). Student perceptions of differential teacher treatment as moderators of teacher expectation effects. *Journal of Educational Psychology, 76,* 236–247.

Brush, L. (1980). *Encouraging girls in mathematics: The problem and the solution.* Cambridge, MA: Abt Books.

Brophy, J. (1985). Interactions of male and female students with male and female teachers. In L. Wilkinson & C. Marrett (Eds.), *Gender influences in classroom interaction* (pp. 115–142). Orlando, FL: Academic Press.

Brophy, J., & Evertson, C. (1978). Context variables in teaching. *Educational Psychologist, 12,* 310–316.

Brophy, J., & Evertson, C., with Anderson, I., Baum, M., & Crawford, J. (1981). *Student characteristics and teaching.* New York: Longman.

Campbell, R. (1983). Status attainment research: End of the beginning or beginning of the end? *Sociology of Education, 56,* 47–62.

Carter, D., & Patterson, C. (1982). Sex roles as social conventions: The development of children's conceptions of sex-role stereotypes. *Developmental Psychology, 18,* 812–824.

Chan, K., & Keogh, B. (1974). Interpretation of task interruption and feelings of responsibility for failure. *Journal of Special Education, 8,* 175–178.

Chen, C., & Uttal, D. (1988). Cultural values, parents' beliefs, and children's achievement in the United States and China. *Human Development, 31,* 351–358.

Cohen, J. (1983). Peer influence on college aspirations with initial aspirations controlled. *American Sociological Review, 48,* 728–734.

Cook, M., & Alexander, K. (1980). Design and substance in educational research: Adolescent attainments, a case in point. *Sociology of Education, 53,* 187–202.

Crandall, V. C. (1967). Achievement behavior in young children. In W. W. Hartup & N. L. Smothergill (Eds.), *The young child* (pp. 165–185). Washington, DC: National Association for the Education of Young Children.

Crandall, V. C. (1969). Sex differences in expectancy of intellectual and academic reinforcement. In C. P. Smith (Ed.), *Achievement-related motives in children* (pp. 11–45). New York: Russell Sage Foundation.

Crandall, V. J. (1963). Achievement. In H. Stevenson (Ed.), *Child psychology: Sixty-second yearbook of the National Society for the Study of Education* (pp. 416–459). Chicago: University of Chicago Press.

Cummings, S., & Taebel, D. (1980). Sexual inequality and the reproduction of consciousness: An analysis of sex-role stereotyping among children. *Sex Roles, 6,* 631–644.

Davies, M., & Kandel, D. (1981). Parental and peer influences on adolescents' educational plans: Some further evidence. *American Journal of Sociology, 87,* 363–387.

Deaux, K. (1976). Sex: A perspective on the attributional process. In J. Harvey, W. Ickes, & R. Kidd (Eds.), *New directions in attribution research* (Vol. 1; pp. 335–352). Hillsdale, NJ: Lawrence Erlbaum Associates.

Deci, E. L., Betley, G., Kahle, J., Abrams, L., & Porac, J. (1981). When trying to win: Competition and intrinsic motivation. *Personality and Social Psychology Bulletin, 7,* 79–83.

Deci, E. L., Nezlek, J., & Sheinman, L. (1981). Characteristics of the rewarder and intrinsic motivation of the rewardee. *Journal of Personality and Social Psychology, 40,* 1–10.

Deci, E. L., & Ryan, R. M. (1985). *Intrinsic motivation and self-determination in human behavior.* New York: Plenum.

Delamont, S. (1980). *Sex roles and the school.* London: Methuen.

Diener, C., & Dweck, C. (1978). An analysis of learned helplessness: Continuous changes in performance, strategy, and achievement cognitions following failure. *Journal of Personality and Social Psychology, 36,* 451–462.

Dusek, J. (1975). Do teachers bias children's learning? *Review of Educational Research, 45,* 661–684.

Dusek, J. (Ed.). (1985). *Teacher expectancies.* Hillsdale, NJ: Lawrence Erlbaum Associates.

Dusek, J., & Joseph, G. (1983). The bases of teacher expectancies: A meta-analysis. *Journal of Educational Psychology, 75,* 327–346.

Dweck, C. (1975). The role of expectations and attributions in the alleviation of learned helplessness. *Journal of Personality and Social Psychology, 31,* 674–685.

Dweck, C., Davidson, W., Nelson, S., & Enna, B. (1978). Sex differences in learned helplessness: II: The contingencies of evaluation feedback in the classroom, and III: An experimental analysis. *Developmental Psychology, 14,* 268–276.

Dweck, C. S., & Elliott, E. S. (1983). Achievement motivation. In P. Mussen (Ed.), *Handbook of child psychology, Vol. IV: Socialization, personality, and social development*. New York: Wiley.

Dweck, C., & Reppucci, N. (1973). Learned helplessness and reinforcement responsibility in children. *Journal of Personality and Social Psychology, 25,* 109–116.

Eccles, J. S. (1983). Expectancies, values, and academic behavior. In J. T. Spence (Ed.), *Achievement and achievement motives: Psychological and sociological approaches* (pp. 77–146). San Francisco: Freeman.

Eccles, J., & Blumenfeld, P. (1985). Classroom experiences and student gender: Are there differences and do they matter? In L. Wilkinson & C. Marrett (Eds.). *Gender influences in classroom interactions* (pp. 79–114). New York: Academic Press.

Eccles, J., & Hoffman, L. (1984). Sex roles, socialization, and occupational behavior. In H. Stevenson & A. Siegel (Eds.), *Child development research and social policy.* Chicago: University of Chicago Press.

Eccles, J., Jacobs, J., & Harold, R. (1990). Gender-role stereotypes, expectancy effects, and parents' socialization of gender differences. *Journal of Social Issues, 46,* 183–201.

Eccles, J., & Midgley, C. (1989). Stage environment fit: Developmentally appropriate classrooms for early adolescents. In R. Ames & C. Ames (Eds.), *Research on motivation in education. Vol. 3: Goals and cognitions* (pp. 139–186). New York: Academic Press.

Eccles, J., Midgley, C., & Adler, T. (1984). Grade-related changes in the school environment: Effects on achievement motivation. In J. G. Nicholls (Ed), *Advances to motivation and achievement: Vol. 3. The development of achievement motivation* (pp. 283–331). Greenwich, CT: JAI Press.

Eccles, J., Wigfield, A., Flanagan, C., Miller, C., Reuman, D., & Yee, D. (1989). Self-concepts, domain values, and self-esteem: Relations and changes at early adolescence. *Journal of Personality, 57,* 283–310.

Ekstrom, R., Goertz, M., Rock, D. (1988). *Education & American youth.* New York: Falmer Press.

Entwisle, D. R., & Baker, D. P. (1983). Gender and young children's expectations for performance in arithmetic. *Developmental Psychology, 19,* 200–209.

Entwisle, D., & Hayduk, L. (1978). *Too great expectations: Young children's academic outlook.* Baltimore, MD: Johns Hopkins University Press.

Epstein, J. (1983). The influence of friends on achievement and affective outcomes. In J. Epstein & N. Karweit (Eds.), *Friends in school: Patterns of selection and influence in secondary schools* (pp. 177–200). New York: Academic Press.

Erikson, E. (1963). *Childhood and society.* New York: Norton.

Eshel, Y., & Klein, Z. (1981). Development of academic self-concept of lower-class and middle-class primary school children. *Journal of Educational Psychology, 73,* 287–293.

Etaugh, C., Collins, G., & Gerson, A. (1975). Reinforcement of sex-typed behaviors of two-year-old children in a nursery school setting. *Developmental Psychology, 11,* 255.

Fagot, B., & Patterson, G. (1969). An *in vivo* analysis of reinforcing contingencies for sex-role behaviors in the preschool child. *Developmental Psychology, 1,* 563–568.

Farmer, H., & Sidney, J. (1985). Sex equity in career and vocational education. In S. Klein (Ed.), *Handbook for achieving sex equity through education.* Baltimore, MD: Johns Hopkins University Press.

Feldlaufer, H., Midgley, C., & Eccles, J. S. (1988). Student, teacher, and observer perceptions of the classroom environment before and after the transition to junior high school. *Journal of Early Adolescence, 8,* 133–156.

Feldman, J., Jorgensen, M., & Poling, E. (1988). Illusions: Women in educational administration. In A. O'Brien Carelli (Ed.), *Sex equity in education: Readings and strategies.* (pp. 335–354). Springfield, IL: Charles Thomas.

Fennema, E., & Sherman, J. (1977). Sex-related differences in mathematics achievement, spatial visualization and affective factors. *American Education Research Journal, 14,* 51–71.

Ferris, J., & Winkler, D. (1986). Teacher compensation and the supply of teachers. *Elementary School Journal, 86,* 389–403.

Feshbach, N. D. (1969). Student teacher preferences for elementary school pupils varying in personality characteristics. *Journal of Educational Psychology, 60,* 126–132.

France-Kaatrude, A., & Smith, W. (1985). Social comparison, task motivation, and the development of self-evaluative standards in children. *Developmental Psychology, 21,* 1080–1089.

Franken, M. (1983). Sex role expectations in children's vocational aspirations and perceptions of occupations. *Psychology of Women Quarterly, 8,* 59–68.

Frey, K. S., & Ruble, D. N. (1987). What children say about classroom performance: Sex and grade differences in perceived competence. *Child Development, 58,* 1066–1078.

Gamoran, A. (1987). The stratification of high school learning opportunities, *Sociology of Education, 60,* 135–155.

Garrett, C., Ein, P., & Tremaine, L. (1977). The development of gender stereotyping of adult occupations in elementary school children. *Child Development, 48,* 507–512.

Gerstein, M., Lichtman, M., & Barokas, J. (1988). Occupational plans of adolescent women compared to men: A cross-sectional examination. *The Career Development Quarterly, 36,* 222–230.

Gitelson, I., Petersen, A., & Tobin-Richards, M. (1982). Adolescents' expectancies of success, self-evaluations, and attributions about performance on spatial and verbal tasks. *Sex Roles, 8,* 411–419.

Good, T. (1987). Teacher expectations. In D. Berliner & B. Rosenshine (Eds.), *Talks to teachers* (pp. 159–200). New York: Random House.

Good, T., & Brophy, J. (1980). *Educational psychology: A realistic approach* (2nd ed.). New York: Holt, Rinehart, Winston.

Gottfredson, L. (1981). Circumscription and compromise: A developmental theory of occupational aspirations. *Journal of Counseling Psychology, 28,* 545–579.

Graham, S. (1984). Communicating sympathy and anger to black and white children: The cognitive (attributional) consequences of affective cues. *Journal of Personality and Social Psychology, 47,* 40–54.

Graham, S. (1990). Communicating low ability in the classroom: Bad things good teachers sometimes do. In S. Graham & V. Folkes (Eds.), *Attribution theory: Applications to achievement, mental health, and interpersonal conflict* (pp. 17–36). Hillsdale, NJ: Lawrence Erlbaum Associates.

Greene, J. C. (1985). Relationships among learning and attribution theory motivation variables. *American Educational Research Journal, 22,* 65–78.

Gullickson, A. (1985). Student evaluation techniques and their relationship to grade and curriculum. *Journal of Educational Research, 79,* 96–100.

Haller, E. (1985). Pupil race and elementary school ability grouping: Are teachers biased against black children? *American Educational Research Journal, 22,* 465–483.

Hallinan, M., & Sorensen, A. (1983). The formation and stability of instructional groups. *American Sociological Review, 48,* 838–851.

Hanna, G., & Sonnenschein, J. (1985). Relative validity of the Orleans–Hanna Algebra Prognosis Test in the prediction of girls' and boys' grades in first-year algebra. *Educational and Psychological Measurement, 45,* 361–368.

Harari, O., & Covington, M. (1981). Reactions to achievement from a teacher and a student perspective: A developmental analysis. *American Educational Research Journal, 18,* 15–28.

Haring, M., & Beyard-Tyler, K. (1984). Counseling with women: The challenge of nontraditional careers. *The School Counselor, 31,* 301–309.

Harter, S. (1978). Effectance motivation reconsidered: Toward a developmental model. *Human Development, 21,* 34–64.

Harter, S. (1981a). A model of mastery motivation in children: Individual differences and developmental change. In W. Collins (Ed.), *Aspects of the development of competence: The Minnesota symposia on child psychology* (Vol. 14; pp. 215–255). Hillsdale, NJ: Lawrence Erlbaum Associates.

Harter, S. (1981b). A new self-report scale of intrinsic versus extrinsic orientation in the classroom: Motivational and informational components. *Developmental Psychology, 17,* 300–312.

Harter, S. (1987). The determinants and mediational role of global self-worth in children. In N. Eisenberg (Ed.), *Contemporary topics in developmental psychology* (pp. 219–241). New York: Wiley.

Harter, S., & Connell, J. P. (1984). A model of children's achievement and related self-perceptions of competence, control, and motivational orientation. In J. Nicholls (Ed.), *Advances in motivation and achievement* (Vol. 3; pp. 219–250). Greenwich, CT: JAI Press.

Harter, S., & Pike, R. (1984). The pictorial scale of perceived competence and social acceptance for young children. *Child Development, 55,* 1969–1982.

Hauser, R., Tsai, S-L., & Sewell, W. (1983). A model of stratification with response error in social and psychological variables. *Sociology of Education, 56,* 20–46.

Hayes, C., Palmer, J., & Zaslow, M. (1990). *Who cares for America's Children: Child care policy for the 1990s.* Washington, DC: National Academy Press.

Heckhausen, H. (1984). Emergent achievement behavior: Some early developments. In J. Nicholls (Ed.), *Advances in motivation and achievement: Vol. 3. The development of achievement motivation* (pp. 1–32). Greenwich, CT: JAI Press.

Hennig, M., & Jardim, A. (1977). *The managerial woman.* Garden City, NY: Doubleday Anchor.

Hill, K., & Wigfield, A. (1984). Test anxiety: A major educational problem and what can be done about it. *Elementary School Journal. 85,* 105–126.

Higgins, E., & Parsons, J. (1983). Social cognition and the social life of the child. Stages as subcultures. In E. T. Higgins, D. N. Ruble, & W. W. Hartup (Eds.), *Social cognition and social development: A sociocultural perspective* (pp. 15–62). New York: Cambridge University Press.

Hoffman, L. (1982). Empirical findings concerning sexism in our schools. *Corrective and Social Psychiatry and Journal of Behavior Technology, Methods and Therapy, 28,* 100–108.

Holloway, S. (1986). The relationship of mothers' beliefs to children's mathematics achievement: Some effects of sex differences. *Merrill-Palmer Quarterly, 32,* 231–250.

Holloway, S. (1988). Concepts of ability and effort in Japan and the United States. *Review of Educational Research, 58,* 327–345.

Holloway, S., Kashiwagi, K., Hess, R. D., & Azuma, H. (1986). Causal attributions by Japanese and American mothers and children about performance in mathematics. *International Journal of Psychology, 21,* 269–286.

Hotchkiss, L. (1984). *Effects of schooling on cognitive, attitudinal, and behavioral outcomes.* Technical Report. ERIC ED 269572.

Huston, A. (1983). Sex-typing. In P. H. Mussen (Series Ed.) & E. M. Hetherington (Vol. Ed.), *Handbook of child psychology: Vol. 4. Socialization, personality, and social development* (4th ed., pp. 387–467). New York: Wiley.

Inhelder, B., & Piaget, J. (1958). *The growth of logical thinking from childhood to adolescence.* New York: Basic.

Kahle, J., Matyas, M., & Cho, H. (1985). An assessment of the impact of science experiences on the career choices of male and female biology students. *Journal of Research in Science Teaching, 22,* 385–394.

Kaminski, D., & Sheridan, M. (1984). Children's perceptions of sex stereotyping: A five-year study. *International Journal of Women's Studies, 7,* 24–36.

Kourilsky, M., & Campbell, M. (1984). Sex differences in a simulated classroom economy: Children's beliefs about entrepreneurship. *Sex Roles, 10,* 53–66.

Kimball, M. M. (1989). A new perspective on women's math achievement. *Psychological Bulletin, 105,* 198–214.

Kohlberg, L. (1966). A cognitive-developmental analysis of children's sex-role concepts and attitudes. In E. Maccoby (Ed.), *The development of sex differences* (pp. 82–173). Stanford, CA: Stanford University Press.

Kohlberg, L., & Ullman, D. (1974). Stages in the development of psychosexual concepts and attitudes. In R. Friedman, R. Richart, & R. Vande Wiele (Eds.), *Sex differences in behavior* (pp. 209–222). New York: Wiley.

Kuhn, D., Nash, S., & Brucken, L. (1978). Sex role concepts of two- and three-year-olds. *Child Development, 49,* 445–451.

Kun, A. (1977). Development of the magnitude-covariation and compensation schemata in ability and effort attributions of performance. *Child Development, 48,* 862–873.

Kun, A., Parsons, J. E., & Ruble, D. N. (1974). Development of integration processes using ability and effort information to predict outcome. *Developmental Psychology, 10,* 721–732.

Ladd, G. W., & Price, J. M. (1986). Promoting children's cognitive and social competences: The relation between parents' perceptions of task difficulty and children's perceived and actual competence. *Child Development, 57,* 446–460.

Lanier, J., & Wittmer, J. (1977). Teacher prejudice in referral of students to EMR programs. *School Counselor, 24,* 165–170.

Lefcourt, H. (1976). *Locus of control: Current trends in theory and research.* Hillsdale, NJ: Lawrence Erlbaum Associates.

Leinhardt, G., Seewald, A., & Engel, M. (1979). Learning what's taught: Sex differences in instruction. *Journal of Educational Psychology, 71,* 432–439.

Lepper, M., Greene, D., & Nisbett, R. (1973). Undermining children's intrinsic interest with extrinsic rewards: A test of the overjustification hypothesis. *Journal of Personality and Social Psychology, 28,* 129–137.

Levine, J., Snyder, H., & Mendez-Caratini, G. (1982). Task performance and interpersonal attraction in children. *Child Development, 53,* 359–371.

Lewis, M., Wall, M., & Aronfreed, J. (1963). Developmental change in the relative values of social and nonsocial reinforcement. *Journal of Experimental Psychology, 66,* 133–137.

Livesley, W. J., & Bromley, D. B. (1973). *Person perception in childhood & adolescence.* New York: Wiley.

Looker, E., & Pineo, P. (1983). Social psychological variables and their relevance to the status attainment of teenagers. *American Journal of Sociology, 88,* 1195–1219.

Mac Iver, D., Stipek, D., & Daniels, D. (1991). Explaining within-semester changes in student effort in junior and senior high school courses. *Journal of Educational Psychology, 83,* 201–211.

MacMillan, D., & Keogh, B. (1971). Normal and retarded children's expectancy for failure. *Developmental Psychology, 4,* 343–348.

Marjoribanks, K. (1985). Ecological correlates of adolescents' aspirations: Gender-related differences. *Contemporary Educational Psychology, 10,* 329–341.

Marsh, H. W. (1984). Relations among dimensions of self-attribution, dimensions of self-concept, and academic achievement. *Journal of Educational Psychology, 76,* 3–32.

Marsh, H., Barnes, J., Cairns, L., & Tidman, M. (1984). Self-description questionnaire: Age and sex effects in the structure and level of self-concept for preadolescent children. *Journal of Educational Psychology, 76,* 940–956.

Marshall, H., & Weinstein, R. (1984). Classroom factors affecting students' self-evaluation: An interactional model. *Review of Educational Research, 54,* 301-325.

McClelland, D. C. (1951). *Personality.* New York: William Sloane.

McClelland, D. C., Atkinson, J. W., Clark, R. W., & Lowell E. L. (1953). *The achievement motive.* New York: Appleton-Century-Crofts.

McCombs, R., & Gay, J. (1988). Effects of race, class, and IQ information on judgments of parochial grade school teachers. *Journal of Social Psychology, 128,* 647-652.

Martin, C., & Halverson, C. (1981). A schematic processing model of sex typing and stereotyping in children. *Child Development, 52,* 755-790.

Mason, C., & Kahle, J. (1989). Student attitudes toward science and science-related careers: A program designed to promote a stimulating gender-free learning environment. *Journal of Research in Science Teaching, 26,* 25-39.

Meece, J. (1987). The influence of school experiences on the development of gender schemata. *New Directions for Child Development: Children's Gender Schemata, 38,* 57-73.

Metha, A. (1983). Decade since Title IX: Some implications for teacher education. *Actions in Teacher Education, 5,* 21-27.

Meyer, W., Bachmann, M., Biermann, V., Hempelmann, P., Ploger, F., & Spiller, H. (1979). The informational value of evaluative behavior: Influence of praise and blame on perceptions of ability. *Journal of Educational Psychology, 71,* 259-268.

Midgley, C., & Feldlaufer, H. (1987). Students' and teachers' decision-making fit before and after the transition to junior high school. *Journal of Early Adolescence, 7,* 225-241.

Midgley, C., Feldlaufer, H., & Eccles, J. (1988). The transition to junior high school: Beliefs of pre- and posttransition teachers. *Journal of Youth and Adolescence, 17,* 544-562.

Midgley, C., Feldlaufer, H., & Eccles, J. (1989). Student/teacher relations and attitudes toward mathematics before and after the transition to junior high school. *Child Development, 60,* 981-992.

Miller, A. (1985). A developmental study of the cognitive basis of performance impairment after failure. *Journal of Personality and Social Psychology, 49,* 529-538.

Miller, R. (1986). Reducing occupational circumscription. *Elementary School Guidance and Counseling, 20,* 250-254.

Minuchin, P., & Shapiro, E. (1983). The school as a context for social development. In P. H. Mussen (Series Ed.) & E. M. Hetherington (Vol. Ed.), *Handbook of child psychology: Vol. 4. Socialization, personality, and social development* (4th ed., pp. 197-274). New York: Wiley.

Montemayor, R. (1974). Children's performance in a game and their attraction to it as a function of sex-typed labels. *Child Development, 45,* 152-156.

Morgan, G. (1984). Reward-induced decrements and increments in intrinsic motivation. *Review of Educational Research, 54,* 5-30.

Morgan, G., & Harmon, R. (1984). Developmental transformations in mastery motivation: Measurement and validation. In R. Emde & R. Harmon (Eds.), *Continuities and discontinuities in development* (pp. 263-291). New York: Plenum Press.

Morris, W., & Nemcek, D. (1982). The development of social comparison motivation among preschoolers: Evidence of a stepwise progression. *Merrill-Palmer Quarterly, 28,* 413-425.

Morse, L., & Handley, H. (1985). Listening to adolescents: Gender differences in science classroom interaction. In L. Wilkinson & C. Marrett (Eds.), *Gender influences in classroom interaction* (pp. 37-56). Orlando, FL: Academic Press.

Mosatche, H., & Bragonier, P. (1981). An observational study of social comparison in preschoolers. *Child Development, 52,* 376-378.

National Center for Education Statistics. (1984a). *High school seniors: A comparative study of the classes of 1972 and 1980.* Washington, DC: U.S. Government Printing Office.

National Center for Education Statistics. (1984b). *Science and mathematics education in*

American high schools: Results from the high school and beyond. Washington, DC: U.S. Department of Education.

Natriello, G., Pallas, A., & Alexander, K. (1989). On the right track? Curriculum and academic achievement. *Sociology of Education, 62,* 109–118.

Newman, R. (1984). Children's achievement and self-evaluations in mathematics: A longitudinal study. *Journal of Educational Psychology, 76,* 857–873.

Nicholls, J. G. (1975). Causal attributions and other achievement-related cognitions: Effects of task outcome, attainment value, and sex. *Journal of Educational Psychology, 31,* 379–389.

Nicholls, J. G. (1978). The development of the concepts of effort and ability perception of academic attainment, and the understanding that difficult tasks require more ability. *Child Development, 49,* 800–814.

Nicholls, J. (1979). Development of perception of own attainment and causal attributions for success and failure in reading. *Journal of Educational Psychology, 71,* 94–99.

Nicholls, J. (1980). A re-examination of boys' and girls' causal attributions for success and failure based on New Zealand data. In L. Fyans (Ed.), *Achievement motivation: Recent trends in theory and research* (pp. 266–288). New York: Plenum.

Nicholls, J. (1987). Conceptions of ability across the school years: Reflections on method. In F. Halisch & J. Kuhl (Eds.), *Motivation, intention, and volition* (201–210). Berlin: Springer-Verlag.

Nicholls, J. (1984). Conceptions of ability and achievement motivation. In R. Ames & C. Ames (Eds.), *Research on motivation in education: Vol. 1: Student motivation* (pp. 39–73). New York: Academic Press.

Nicholls, J., & Miller, A. (1984). Development and its discontents: The differentiation of the concept of ability. In J. Nicholls (Ed.), *Advances in motivation and achievement: Vol. 3. The development of achievement motivation* (pp. 219–250). Greenwich, CT: JAI Press.

Notz, W. (1975). Work motivation and the negative effects of extrinsic rewards. A review with implications for theory and practice. *American Psychologist, 30,* 804–891.

Nottlemann, E. (1987). Competence and self-esteem during transition from childhood to adolescence. *Developmental Psychology, 23,* 441–450.

O'Keefe, E., & Hyde, J. (1983). The development of occupational sex-role stereotypes: The effects of gender stability and age. *Sex Roles, 9,* 481–492.

Pang, V. (1990). Asian-American children: A diverse population. *The Educational Forum, 55,* 49–65.

Papalia, D., & Tennent, S. (1975). Vocational aspirations in preschoolers: A manifestation of early sex role stereotyping. *Sex Roles, 1,* 197–199.

Parsons, J., Adler, T., & Kaczala, C. (1982). Socialization of achievement attitudes and beliefs: Parental influences. *Child Development, 53,* 310–321.

Parsons, J., Kaczala, C., & Meece, J. (1982). Socialization of achievement attitudes and beliefs: Classroom influences. *Child Development, 53,* 322–339.

Parsons, J., Ruble, D., Hodges, K., & Small, A. (1976). Cognitive-developmental factors in emerging sex differences in achievement-related expectancies. *Journal of Social Issues, 32,* 47–61.

Peevers, B. H., & Secord, P. F. (1973). Developmental changes in attribution of descriptive concepts to persons. *Journal of Personality and Social Psychology, 27,* 120–128.

Phillips, D. (1987). Socialization of perceived academic competence among highly competent children. *Child Development, 58,* 1308–1320.

Phillips, D., & Zimmerman, M. (1990). The developmental course of perceived competence and incompetence among competent children. In J. Kolligian & R. Sternberg (Eds.), *Competence considered* (pp. 41–66). New Haven, CT: Yale University Press.

Piaget, J. (1930). *The child's conception of physical causality*. London: Routledge & Kegan Paul.

Piaget, J. (1952). *The origins of intelligence in children*. New York: Norton.

Pintrich, P., & Blumenfeld, P. (1985). Classroom experience and children's self-perceptions of ability, effort, and conduct. *Journal of Educational Psychology, 77,* 646–657.

Prieto, A., & Zucker, S. (1981). Teacher perception of race as a factor in the placement of behaviorally disordered children. *Behavioral Disorders, 7,* 34–38.

Ratzlaff, H., & Kahn, S. (1983). Occupational gender bias revisited: Methodological improvements. *Canadian Counsellor, 17,* 118–123.

Raymond, C., & Benbow, C. (1986). Gender differences in mathematics: A function of parental support and student sex typing? *Developmental Psychology, 22,* 808–819.

Rholes, W., Blackwell, J., Jordan, C., & Walters, C. (1980). A developmental study of learned helplessness. *Developmental Psychology, 16,* 616–624.

Rosen, B., & D'Andrade, R. C. (1959). The psychosocial origins of achievement motivation. *Sociometry, 22,* 185–218.

Rosenholtz, S., & Simpson, C. (1984). The formation of ability conceptions: Developmental trend or social construction? *Review of Educational Research, 54,* 31–63.

Rosenthal, D., & Chapman, D. (1982). The lady spaceman: Children's perceptions of sex-stereotyped occupations. *Sex Roles, 8,* 959–965.

Rosenthal, R., & Jacobson, L. (1966). Teachers' expectancies: Determinants of pupils' IQ gains. *Psychological Reports, 19,* 115–118.

Rotter, J. (1966). Generalized expectancies for internal versus external control of reinforcement. *Psychological Monographs, 1,* (Whole No. 609).

Ruble, D. (1983). The development of social comparison processes and their role in achievement-related self-socialization. In E. T. Higgins, D. N. Ruble, & W. W. Hartup (Eds.), *Social cognition and social development: Asociocultural perspective* (pp. 134–157). New York: Cambridge University Press.

Ruble, D., Boggiano, A., Feldman, N., & Loebl, J. (1980). A developmental analysis of the role of social comparison in self-evaluation. *Developmental Psychology, 16,* 105–115.

Ruble, D., Parsons, J., & Ross, J. (1976). Self-evaluative responses of children in an achievement setting. *Child Development, 47,* 990–997.

Ryan, R., Connell, J., & Deci, E. (1985). A motivational analysis of self-determination and self-regulation. In C. Ames & R. Ames (Eds.), *Research on motivation in education: Vol. 12, The classroom* (pp. 13–51). New York: Academic Press.

Ryckman, D. B., & Peckham, P. D. (1987). Gender differences in attributions for success and failure. *Journal of Early Adolescence, 7,* 47–63.

Sanders, K., & Harper, L. (1976). Free play fantasy behavior in pre-school children: Relations among gender, age, season and location. *Child Development, 47,* 1182–1185.

Scott, K. (1981). Whatever happened to Jane and Dick: Sexism in texts re-examined. *Peabody Journal of Education, 58,* 135–140.

Seginer, R. (1983). Parents' educational expectations and children's academic achievements: A literature review. *Merrill-Palmer Quarterly, 29,* 1–23.

Serbin, L., Connor, J., & Citron, C. (1978). Environmental control of independent and dependent behaviors in preschool girls and boys: A model for early independence training. *Sex Roles, 4,* 867–875.

Serbin, L., O'Leary, K., Kent, R., & Tonick, I. (1973). A comparison of teacher response to the pre-academic and problem behavior of boys and girls. *Child Development, 44,* 796–804.

Sherman, J. (1979). Predicting mathematics performance in high school girls and boys. *Journal of Educational Psychology, 71,* 242–249.

Simmons, R., Blyth, D., Van Cleave, E., & Bush, D. (1979). Entry into early adolescence: The impact of school structure, puberty, and early dating on self-esteem. *American Sociological Review, 44,* 948–967.

Simmons, R., Rosenberg, M., & Rosenberg, F. (1973). Disturbance in the self-image at adolescence. *American Sociological Review, 39,* 553–568.

Smith, N., Greenlaw, J., & Scott, C. (1987). Making the literate environment equitable. *Reading Teacher, 40,* 400–407.

Sohn, D. (1982). Sex differences in achievement self-attributions: An effect-size analysis. *Sex Roles, 8,* 345–357.

Spear, P., & Armstrong, S. (1978). Effects of performance expectancies created by peer comparison as related to social reinforcement, task difficulty, and age of child. *Journal of Experimental and Child Psychology, 25,* 254–266.

Stake, J., & Katz, J. (1982). Teacher-pupil relationships in the elementary school classroom: Teacher-gender and pupil-gender differences. *American Educational Research Journal, 19,* 465–471.

Stallings, J. (1985). School, classroom, and home influences on women's decisions to enroll in advanced mathematics courses. In S. Chipman, L. Brush, & D. Wilson (Eds.), *Women and mathematics: Balancing the equation* (pp. 199–223). Hillsdale, NJ: Lawrence Erlbaum Associates.

Stangor, C., & Ruble, D. (1987). Development of gender role knowledge and gender constancy. *New Directions for Child Development: Children's Gender Schemata, 38,* 5–22.

Stevenson, H., Lee, S., & Stigler, J. (1986). Mathematics achievement of Chinese, Japanese, and American children. *Science, 231,* 693–699.

Stevenson, H., & Newman, R. (1986). Long-term prediction of achievement and attitudes in mathematics and reading. *Child Development, 57,* 646–659.

Stipek, D. (1981). Children's perceptions of their own and their classmates' ability. *Journal of Educational Psychology, 73,* 404–410.

Stipek, D. (1984a). Developmental aspects of motivation in children. In R. Ames & C. Ames (Eds.), *Research on motivation in education: Vol. 1. Student motivation* (pp. 145–174). New York: Academic Press.

Stipek, D. (1984b). Sex differences in children's attributions for success and failure on math and spelling tests. *Sex Roles, 11,* 969–981.

Stipek, D. (1984c). Young children's performance expectations: Logical analysis or wishful thinking? In J. Nicholls (Ed.), *The development of achievement motivation* (pp. 33–56). Greenwich, CT: JAI Press.

Stipek, D. (1988). *Motivation to learn: From theory to practice.* Englewood Cliffs, NJ: Prentice Hall.

Stipek, D., & Daniels, D. (1990). Children's use of dispositional attributions in predicting the performance and behavior of classmates. *Journal of Applied Developmental Psychology, 11,* 13–28.

Stipek, D., & DeCotis, K. (1988). Children's understanding of the implications of causal attributions for emotional experiences. *Child Development, 59,* 1601–1616.

Stipek, D., & Gralinski, H. (1991). Gender differences in children's achievement-related beliefs and emotional responses to success and failure in math. *Journal of Educational Psychology, 83,* 361–371.

Stipek, D., & Hoffman, J. (1980a). Children's achievement-related expectancies as a function of academic performance histories and sex. *Journal of Educational Psychology, 72,* 861–865.

Stipek, D., & Hoffman, J. (1980b). Development of children's performance-related judgments. *Child Development, 51,* 912–914.

Stipek, D., & Mac Iver, D. (1989). Developmental change in children's assessment of intellectual competence. *Child Development, 60,* 521–538.

Stipek, D., Roberts, T., & Sanborn, M. (1984). Preschool-age children's performance expectations for themselves and another child as a function of the incentive value of success and the salience of past performance. *Child Development, 55,* 1983–1989.

Stipek, D., & Tannatt, L. (1984). Children's judgments of their own and their peers' academic competence. *Journal of Educational Psychology, 76,* 75–84.

Stipek, D., & Weisz, J. (1981). Perceived personal control and academic achievement. *Review of Educational Research, 51,* 101–137.

Stockard, J., Schmuck, P., Kempner, K., Williams, P., Edson, S., & Smith, M. (1980). *Sex equity in education.* New York: Academic Press.

Stoddart, T., & Turiel, E. (1985). Children's concepts of cross-gender activities. *Child Development, 56,* 1241–1252.

Surber, C. (1984). The development of achievement-related judgment process. In J. Nicholls (Ed.), *The development of achievement motivation* (pp. 137–184). Greenwich, CT: JAI Press.

Thompson, R. (1987). Development of children's inferences of the emotions of others. *Developmental Psychology, 23,* 124–131.

Thompson, R. (1989). Causal attributions and children's emotional understanding. In C. Saarni & P. Harris (Eds.), *Children's understanding of emotions* (pp. 117–150). Cambridge: Cambridge University Press.

Trudewind, C. (1982). The development of achievement motivation and individual differences: Ecological determinants. In W. Hartup (Ed.), *Review of Child Development Research, Vol. 6.* (pp. 669–703). Chicago: University of Chicago Press.

U.S. Department of Labor. (1979). *Women in the labor force: Some new data sources.* Washington, DC: Bureau of Labor Statistics.

Vaughn-Robertson, C., Tompkins, G., & Hitchcock, M., & Oldham, M. (1989). Sexism in basal readers: An analysis of male main characters. *Journal of Research in Childhood Education, 4,* 62–68.

Weiner, B. (1980). The role of affect in rational (attributional) approaches to human motivation. *Educational Researcher, 9,* 4–11.

Weiner, B. (1985). An attributional theory of achievement motivation and emotion. *Psychological Review, 92,* 548–573.

Weiner, B. (1986). *An attributional theory of motivation and emotion.* New York: Springer-Verlag.

Weiner, B., Kun, A., & Benesh-Weiner, M. (1980). The development of mastery emotions, and morality from an attributional perspective. In W. A. Collins (Ed). *Development of cognition, affect, and social relations. Minnesota Symposium on Child Psychology* (Vol. 13; pp. 103–129). Hillsdale, NJ: Lawrence Erlbaum Associates.

Weinstein, R. (1976). Reading group membership in first grade: Teacher behaviors and pupil experience over time. *Journal of Educational Psychology, 68,* 103–116.

Weinstein, R. (1985). Student mediation of classroom expectancy effects. In J. Dusek (Ed.), *Teacher expectations.* Hillsdale, NJ: Lawrence Erlbaum Associates.

Weinstein, R. (1989). Perceptions of classroom processes and student motivation: Children's views of self-fulfilling prophecies. In C. Ames & R. Ames (Eds.), *Research on motivation in education, Vol. 3: Goals and cognitions* (pp. 187–221). New York: Academic Press.

Weinstein, R., Marshall, H., Sharp, L., & Botkin, M. (1987). Pygmalion and the student: Age and classroom differences in children's awareness of teacher expectations. *Child Development, 58,* 1079–1093.

Weisz, J. R. (1979). Perceived control and learned helplessness among mentally retarded and nonretarded children: A developmental analysis. *Developmental Psychology, 15,* 311–319.

Weisz, J. R. (1980). Developmental change in perceived control: Recognizing noncontingency in the laboratory and perceiving it in the world. *Developmental Psychology, 16,* 385–390.

Weisz, J. R. (1981). Illusory contingency in children at the state fair. *Developmental Psychology, 17,* 481–489.

Weisz, J. R. (1986). Understanding the developing understanding of control. In M. Perlmutter (Ed.), *Cognitive perspectives on children's social and behavioral development: The Minnesota symposia on child psychology* (Vol. 18; pp. 219–278). Hillsdale, NJ: Lawrence Erlbaum Associates.

Weisz, J. (1990). Development of control-related beliefs, goals, and styles in childhood and adolescence: A clinical perspective. In K. Schaie, J. Rodin, & C. Schooler (Eds.), *Self-directedness: Cause and effects throughout the life course* (pp. 103–145). Hillsdale, NJ: Lawrence Erlbaum Associates.

Weisz, J., & Cameron, A. (1985). Individual differences in the student's sense of control. In C. Ames & R. Ames (Eds.). *Research on motivation in education. Vol. 2: The classroom milieu* (pp. 93–140). Academic Press: Orlando, FL.

Weisz, J., & Stipek, D. (1982). Competence, contingency and the development of perceived control. *Human Development, 25,* 250–281.

Weisz, J., Suwanlert, S., Chaiyasit, W., & Weiss, B. (1989). Epidemiology of behavioral and emotional problems among Thai and American children: Teacher reports for ages 6–11. *Journal of Child Psychology and Psychiatry and Allied Disciplines, 30,* 471–484.

Weisz, J. R., Yeates, K. O., Robertson, D., & Beckham, J. C. (1982). Perceived contingency of skill and chance events: A developmental analysis. *Developmental Psychology, 18,* 898–905.

White, R. (1959). Motivation reconsidered: The concept of competence. *Psychological Review, 66,* 297–333.

Winterbottom, M. (1958). The relation of need for achievement to learning experiences in independence and mastery. In J. Atkinson (Ed.), *Motives in fantasy, action, and society.* Princeton: Van Nostrand.

Wolfe, L. (1985). Postsecondary educational attainment among whites and blacks. *American Educational Research Journal, 22,* 501–526.

Yee, D., & Eccles, J. (1988). Parent perceptions and attributions for children's math achievement. *Sex Roles, 19,* 317–333.

Yussen, S., & Kane, P. (1985). Children's conception of intelligence. In S. R. Yussen (Ed.), *The growth of reflection in children* (pp. 207–241). Orlando FL: Academic Press.

Zucker, S., & Prieto, A. (1977). Ethnicity and teacher bias in educational decisions. *Journal of Instructional Psychology, 4,* 2–5.

Zuckerman, M., Porac, J., Lathin, D., Smith, R., & Deci, E. L. (1978). On the importance of self-determination for intrinsically motivated behavior. *Personality and Social Psychology Bulletin, 4,* 443–446.

IV PERSPECTIVES ON DEVELOPMENT

This final section of the text concerns itself with three broad and diverse perspectives on development—atypical development, applied issues, and cross-cultural approaches. In Chapter 11, Thomas Achenbach recounts the history of attempts to characterize the disturbed behavior of children and to develop a common language to be used to describe pathological behavior. Only now, he shows, are psychologists becoming more adept at describing developmental psychopathology and differentiating among developmental disorders. Reliable and widely applied systems of description and classification are, of course, essential when developing and evaluating sensitive, appropriate, and successful modes of treatment.

As noted in many of the preceding chapters, developmental psychology is not simply a subdiscipline in which scientists seek basic knowledge of developmental processes. The developing individuals at the focus of developmental research face real problems and challenges, and the results of that research often have implications for the design of intervention programs and for the development of social policy. An increasing proportion of developmental research is focused on applied as well as basic research issues and, in Chapter 12, Edward Zigler and Matia Finn-Stevenson illustrate the ways in which developmental thinking and research affect social policy.

Finally, in Chapter 13 Michael Cole provides a sweeping

account of understanding and wisdom to be gleaned from studying development in the context of culture. The author reviews central issues in the psychology of culture and then recounts specific relations between culture and different realms of development. As Cole convincingly shows, culture influences virtually all aspects of human growth, and therefore developmentalists must be constantly attentive to its pervasive and diverse effects.

11 Developmental Psychopathology

Thomas M. Achenbach
University of Vermont

INTRODUCTION

Unlike most topics in this book, the developmental study of psychopathology is not an established subspeciality of developmental psychology. Instead, it draws on many specialties, such as developmental, clinical, and cognitive psychology; genetics; psychiatry; epidemiology; biology; and education. This chapter therefore deals with ways of understanding psychopathology from diverse perspectives related to development. Because I assume the reader is already familiar with developmental theories, I emphasize the study of psychopathology rather than the details of particular developmental theories.

For those who are attracted by the challenge of shaping new paradigms, this is an exciting period when a few committed researchers can significantly improve our ways of helping troubled children. Yet, it will require patience and tolerance of ambiguity to fashion the disparate pieces into a coherent whole. It will also require a readiness to span academic psychology, the study of psychopathology, and clinical applications. These otherwise separate enterprises can all contribute to the developmental understanding of psychopathology.

A developmental approach to psychopathology views maladaptive behavior in relation to developmental tasks, processes, and sequences. It constitutes a way of looking at maladaptive behavior that highlights the following issues.

1. To judge whether an individual's behavior is *deviant,* we need to know what is typical for comparable individuals at the same level of

development. This requires normative data on large representative samples, stratified by important demographic variables and assessed by methods geared to each developmental level.

2. To judge whether an individual's behavior is *pathological,* we need to know the likely outcome of the behavior in subsequent developmental periods. This requires longitudinal or follow-up studies to determine which behaviors have especially unsatisfactory outcomes.

3. To understand *maladaptive behavior,* we must view it in relation to the individual's previous developmental history, the developmental tasks the individual faces, and the progress of important adaptive competencies. This requires knowledge of normal development in such areas as biological maturation, cognition, emotional functioning, social competencies, and academic skills.

4. To design appropriate interventions, we need to know how to facilitate development rather than merely to alleviate discomforts, remove symptoms, or restore a previous level of functioning. This requires knowledge of developmental processes and mechanisms of behavioral change.

5. To evaluate the effects of interventions, we need long-term comparisons of the outcomes of specific interventions and no-treatment control conditions. Evaluations of outcomes must assess not only the problems that initially prompted the interventions, but also developmental progress in other areas.

All of these issues are relevant to the study of psychopathology at all stages of the life cycle. They could well provide guidelines for a life-span developmental psychopathology that includes adult development and aging. It is in the period from birth to maturity, however, that the need for a developmental approach is most compelling, for the following reasons:

1. Conspicuous developmental changes occur much more rapidly in so many more areas during this period than during adulthood: 6-month-olds, 4-year-olds, 8-year-olds, and 16-year-olds differ far more dramatically from each other in physical, cognitive, social, emotional, and educational development than do adults who are separated by almost any span of years.

2. The period from birth to maturity is marked by a host of conspicuous developmental milestones, such as walking, talking, bowel control, the onset of schooling, learning to read, involvement in peer groups, puberty, and school graduation. Although there are also adult developmental milestones, they are less explicit and more

variable in nature and timing, depending heavily on differences in occupation, marriage, parenting, and so forth.

3. Children's problems, competencies, and needs must be judged in light of their requirements for further development. Most adults, by contrast, reach plateaus in their physical, cognitive, social, and educational development.

4. The judgment that a child needs help is usually made by others, such as parents and teachers, whereas adults often seek help for themselves, formulate their own referral complaints, and spontaneously assume the role of patient.

5. Because children are so dependent on their families, family functioning has a more decisive impact on children's problems and on what is done about them than is true for most adults, who are freer to alter their family circumstances.

6. There are marked differences between childhood disorders—which typically involve exaggerations of normal behavior or failures to develop important behaviors—and adult disorders—which more often involve marked declines from attained levels or the emergence of behavior that is clearly pathognomonic (i.e., indicative of pathology).

Many approaches to childhood disorders rest on assumptions derived from adult disorders. Such assumptions may unduly bias the study of psychopathology during the period of rapid development. I therefore try to distinguish aspects of each approach that may facilitate the developmental study of psychopathology from those aspects that may hinder it. After considering the major approaches, I address current challenges for the developmental study of psychopathology.

NOSOLOGICAL APPROACHES

Efforts to categorize abnormal behaviors as specific disease entities evolved during the 19th century as a result of two related factors. One was the movement to provide large-scale institutional care. This necessitated arrangements for different types of management problems, such as violent versus depressed behavior. A second factor was the growth of research on the organic causes of disease and the extension of organic disease models to mental disorders. This became enshrined in the dogma that mental diseases are brain diseases, as it was expressed in Wilhelm Griesinger's influential psychiatric textbook of 1845 (see Griesinger, 1867).

The institutional management needs and organic disease model both stimulated efforts to distinguish among types of disorders. It was hoped that descriptions of symptom syndromes would ultimately distinguish between different disease entities, each of which would then be found to have a specific organic cause.

The most successful prototype of the organic disease model was *general paralysis* (later called *paresis*, i.e., incomplete paralysis). Progressively more precise descriptions between 1798 and the 1840s converged on a syndrome defined mainly by mental symptoms, such as memory loss and irrationality, combined with physical symptoms of motor impairment, usually ending in death. From the 1840s through the 1870s, research revealed inflamed brain tissue in most patients who died of paresis. By the end of the 19th century, syphilitic infection was confirmed as the cause of paresis.

Organic abnormalities also helped to define certain syndromes of mental retardation. *Down syndrome,* for example, was first described in 1866 by Langdon Down, an Englishman who thought the mongoloid facial features reflected an evolutionary throwback to the Mongol race. In this case, however, it took nearly a century to discover that an extra chromosome was responsible (Lejeune, Gautier, & Turpin, 1959/1963).

Kraepelin's Nosology

Aside from a few clear-cut syndromes having salient physical correlates, efforts to distinguish between types of mental disorders yielded a melange of conflicting descriptions, based on diverse assumptions and conceptual principles. As it became clear that most psychopathology was not manifest in the form of self-evident syndromes, efforts were made to integrate case descriptions into classification systems, or *taxonomies,* that were intended to capture the important differences among types of disorders.

The most influential taxonomy was published by Emil Kraepelin in 1883, who progressively revised and expanded it over the next 40 years. Kraepelin's first edition was based on the assumption that all mental disorders, like paresis, are caused by brain pathology. The goal of taxonomy was thus to provide descriptive categories for discriminating between disease entities for which different organic etiologies could then be sought. It was a *nosology* (classification of diseases) in the sense that each category was assumed to represent a distinctive disease entity.

In later editions, Kraepelin added psychological processes and the course of the disorder to descriptions of symptoms as defining criteria. For example, *dementia praecox* ("insanity of the young," renamed schizophrenia by Eugen Bleuler in 1911) was distinguished from manic-depressive psychosis on the basis of psychological differences between them and the more favorable outcomes observed in manic-depressive conditions than in schizophrenia.

By 1915, Kraepelin also added disorders assumed to have psychological rather than organic causes, plus a category of personality disorders bordering between illness and ordinary eccentricity. Despite this broadening to include disorders not assumed to have organic causes, plus disorders that deviated in other ways from the disease model, Kraepelin's 19th-century nosological paradigm continues to have a major impact on views of psychopathology. In the following sections, we consider contemporary variations on the nosological theme.

The Diagnostic and Statistical Manual of Mental Disorders

The American Psychiatric Association's (APA) *Diagnostic and Statistical Manual* (the DSM) is widely used to classify mental disorders for purposes of medical records and third party payments. The DSM is a nosology in which each disorder is presented as a separate diagnostic entity. In the first edition of the DSM (DSM-I; APA, 1952), there were only two main categories for child and adolescent disorders: *Adjustment Reaction* and *Schizophrenic Reaction, Childhood Type.* Adjustment reaction referred to problems interpreted as relatively transient responses to stress, whereas schizophrenic reaction referred to severe psychopathology not likely to be transient. Although adult diagnoses could also be applied to children, 70% of children seen in mental health clinics were either undiagnosed or were diagnosed as having adjustment reactions (Achenbach, 1966; Rosen, Bahn, & Kramer, 1964). The second edition of the DSM (DSM-II; APA, 1968) added several behavior disorders of childhood, such as *Hyperkinetic Reaction* and *Withdrawing Reaction,* but adjustment reaction remained the most common diagnosis at least through 1980 (American Academy of Child Psychiatry, 1983). The third edition of the DSM (DSM-III; APA, 1980) departed in several ways from the earlier editions, as well as adding many new disorders of infancy, childhood, and adolescence. The overall structure was retained in a subsequent revision of DSM-III (DSM-III-R; APA, 1987), although the categories of childhood disorders were significantly altered in DSM-III-R. A major DSM-III innovation was the listing of criteria that have to be met for each diagnosis. These criteria involve yes-or-no judgments as to the presence of each feature required for each diagnosis.

Beside specifying criteria for each disorder, DSM-III provided the following five dimensions or axes:

Axis I: a. Clinical syndromes (e.g., Conduct Disorder)
          b. Conditions that are not attributable to a mental disorder but are a focus of attention or treatment (e.g., parent–child

problem, such as a conflict between parents and an adolescent's choice of friends)

Axis II: a. Personality disorders (e.g., Schizoid Personality)
          b. Specific Developmental Disorders (e.g., Developmental Reading Disorder)

Axis III: Physical disorders and conditions

Axis IV: A 7-point rating scale for severity of psychosocial stressors

Axis V: A 5-point rating scale for highest level of adaptive functioning during the past year (changed in DSM–III–R to separate 90-point ratings for current functioning and highest level in the past year).

DSM–III was designed to make diagnostic criteria more explicit and reliable and to broaden diagnosis by taking account of medical conditions, life stresses, and adaptive functioning. It reflected efforts to free diagnostic classification from unsubstantiated theoretical inferences, such as psychoanalytic interpretations of neurotic behavior. In effect, DSM–III constituted a return to the ideals of early Kraepelinian nosology in striving for noninferential descriptions of disorders of unknown etiology.

DSM–III also returned to another aspect of 19th-century nosological thinking: the medical disease model for psychopathology. Early drafts of DSM–III held that all mental disorders are medical disorders. This claim was moderated in the final version, but DSM–III repeatedly referred to disorders as "illnesses," although this was generally changed to "disorders" in DSM–III–R. Based on the nosological concept of categorical disease entities, the architects of DSM–III formulated each category by starting from:

> . . . a clinical concept for which there is some degree of face validity. Face validity is the extent to which the description of a particular category seems on the face of it to describe accurately the characteristic features of persons with a particular disorder. It is the result of clinicians agreeing on the identification of a particular syndrome or pattern of clinical features as a mental disorder. Initial criteria are generally developed by asking the clinicians to describe what they consider to be the most characteristic features of the disorder. (Spitzer & Cantwell, 1980, p. 369)

The clinical concepts of most of DSM–III's adult disorders, such as schizophrenia, date from Kraepelin's nosology. In defining their categories, the DSM–III committee was able to draw on existing research diagnostic criteria (RDC) for the major categories of adult disorders. Unlike the adult disorders, however, many of the child and adolescent disorders had no counterparts in previous nosologies or RDC. Spitzer and Cantwell's reference to "face validity" therefore concerns the diagnostic concepts held by those who formulated DSM–III's categories of child and adolescent disorders. Their formulations of these disorders were not validated in any other way.

Subsequent research on the DSM–III child and adolescent categories showed that some did, in fact, correspond to empirically derived taxonomic distinctions (Achenbach, 1991a; Edelbrock & Costello, 1988; Weinstein, Noam, Grimes, Stone, & Schwab-Stone, 1990). However, the reliability of the DSM–III child and adolescent diagnoses was too low to inspire much confidence. Two studies showed that DSM–III diagnoses made from standardized case histories were no more reliable than DSM–II diagnoses, which were themselves not very reliable (Mattison, Cantwell, Russell, & Will, 1979; Mezzich, Mezzich, & Coffman, 1985). Furthermore, the DSM–III *Manual* (APA, 1980) reported lower reliability for diagnoses of children than adults on Axes I, II, IV, and V (reliability was not reported for Axis III).

Although two studies of inpatients obtained overall interjudge kappas of .74 and .71 for child and adolescent diagnoses, both used an early draft of DSM–III (Strober, Green, & Carlson, 1981; Werry, Methven, Fitzpatrick, & Dixon, 1983). The data reported in the DSM–III *Manual* showed a decline in the reliability of child and adolescent diagnoses from this early draft to a later draft of the DSM–III, in contrast to the increasing reliability of adult diagnoses on all four axes. The possible benefits of the rejuvenated nosological approach for adult disorders were thus not evident for children's disorders. The DSM–III–R (APA, 1987) made numerous changes in the childhood categories, but there is little published support for the reliability or validity of the revised categories. A new edition, DSM–IV, is scheduled to be published in 1993.

Clinically Identified Syndromes

Beside their effects on formal taxonomies, nosological assumptions have affected views of individual syndromes. The following three disorders illustrate contemporary disease entity concepts of child psychopathology.

Early Infantile Autism.   This syndrome was proposed by Leo Kanner in 1943 after he had seen 11 children who shared certain striking peculiarities. Kanner summarized their peculiarities in terms of two cardinal symptoms: (a) extreme self-isolation, evident from the first years of life; and (b) obsessive insistence on the preservation of sameness (Eisenberg & Kanner, 1956).

The children Kanner diagnosed as autistic also avoided eye contact with others *(gaze aversion)* and showed speech abnormalities, ranging from a complete lack of speech or delayed onset through echolalia (exact repetition or *echoing* of others' speech), reversal of personal pronouns (substitution of "you" for "I"), and metaphorical speech that lacked communicative intent. Long-term follow-ups of 96 of Kanner's cases showed that, despite signs of high intelligence in many, only 11 achieved adequate social adjustment. Even these 11 remained severely limited in interpersonal relationships (Eisenberg & Kanner, 1956; Kanner, 1971; Kanner, Rodrigues, & Ashenden, 1972). Other follow-up studies agree with Kanner's finding that few autistic children achieve good social adjustments in later life (Chung, Luk, & Lee, 1990; Howlin & Rutter, 1987; Lotter, 1978).

Kanner's (1943) initial hypothesis was that autistic children have an "innate inability to form the usual, biologically provided affective contact with people" (p. 250). Despite Kanner's careful descriptions and his hypothesis of an organic etiology, however, others quickly extended the concept of autism to children having few of the abnormalities he described. Furthermore, psychoanalytic theorists blamed autism on parental behavior and unconscious attitudes, singling out mothers who were said to be immature, narcissistic, overintellectual, and incapable of mature emotional relationships (Despert, 1947; Rank, 1949). Indictments were also leveled at mothers who "wish that [their] child should not exist" (Bettelheim, 1967, p. 125) and "parents [who] inadvertently hated one another and used the child emotionally" (Wolman, 1970, p. vii).

There has recently been a marked reaction against the psychodynamic views and a return to organic hypotheses about autism. Yet, even when autism was interpreted in psychoanalytic terms, it was conceived as a generic entity that the sensitive clinician could detect lurking beneath diverse phenotypes. The striking behavior of autistic children, its very early onset, its imperviousness to a variety of environmental regimens, and its persistence into adulthood certainly argue for a diseaselike condition. Nevertheless, varied interpretations of the putative underlying disease and varied criteria for diagnosing it have continued to limit agreement among diagnosticians (Siegel, Anders, Ciaranello, Bienenstock, & Kraemer, 1986).

Hyperactivity. Like autism, hyperactivity has become a popular nosological construct. In contrast to the extreme deviance and rarity of autism, however, hyperactivity involves behaviors that most children show occasionally. Furthermore, hyperactivity typically becomes a cause for clinical concern during the elementary school years rather than during the very early years. And, once hyperactivity is evident, it seldom remains such a devastating lifetime affliction as autism. Why, then, has hyperactivity been viewed as a diseaselike condition?

Two early findings helped make hyperactivity an especially tempting candidate for nosological categorization. One was Bradley's (1937) observation that the amphetamine *Benzedrine* seemed to reduce overactivity in disturbed children. This suggested a specific organic defect underlying hyperactivity. The other finding grew out of efforts by Strauss, Lehtinen, and Werner to develop methods for diagnosing and educating brain-damaged children (Strauss & Lehtinen, 1947). Normal children, retarded children with brain damage, and retarded children without known brain damage were compared on a battery of perceptual and cognitive tasks. Behavioral differences between the brain-damaged and other children were then interpreted as signs of brain damage.

Largely from this research, a picture of the brain-damaged child emerged that included the following features: hyperactivity, impulsivity, distractibility, short attention span, emotional lability, perceptual–motor deficits, and clumsiness. Children who had these problems but no direct evidence of brain damage were assumed to have subtle brain damage, designated as: *Strauss syndrome, diffuse brain damage, minimal brain damage, minimal brain dysfunction,* or *minimal cerebral dysfunction.* "MBD" (minimal brain damage or dysfunction) soon became a synonym for hyperactivity. Some workers not only equated MBD with hyperactivity, but with the terms LD (learning disability) and SLD (specific learning disability; e.g., Ochroch, 1981).

As with autism, the nosological constructs of MBD and hyperactivity seemed to expand far beyond the observations on which they were based. The absence of operational criteria allowed the diagnosis to be made in idiosyncratic ways. Analysis of clinicians' use of a standardized set of case materials, for example, showed differences in the cues the clinicians used, their weighing of the cues, and their awareness of the diagnostic policies guiding their judgments (Ullman et al., 1981).

When psychiatric nosology first became differentiated with respect to childhood disorders (in the DSM–II; APA, 1968), hyperactivity was represented as "Hyperkinetic reaction of childhood (or adolescence)," characterized by "overactivity, restlessness, distractibility, and short attention span" (p. 50). DSM–II made a distinction between the behavioral phenotype and organic brain damage: "If this behavior is caused by organic brain damage, it should be diagnosed under the appropriate non-psychotic *organic brain syndrome*" (APA, 1968, p. 50). Furthermore, research during the 1970s and 1980s showed that most hyperactive children are probably not brain-damaged and that brain damage does not necessarily result in hyperactivity (e.g., Brown, Chadwick, Shaffer, Rutter, & Traub, 1981; Shaffer, McNamara, & Pincus, 1974). As brain damage became a less viable explanation for hyperactivity, other organic causes were sought. These have included neurotransmitter abnormalities, abnormalities of arousal in the central nervous system, food sensitivities, allergies, developmental delays, and constitutional patterns of temperament (Barkley, 1991; Goodman & Stevenson, 1989; Marshall, 1989).

In formulating its child categories, the DSM–III committee decided that attention deficits were more primary than overactivity in what DSM-II had called the Hyperkinetic Reaction. DSM-III therefore replaced the Hyperkinetic Reaction with the category of Attention Deficit Disorders (ADD), having two subtypes: (a) ADD with Hyperactivity, and (b) ADD without Hyperactivity.

DSM-III-R replaced the two ADD categories with a single one called Attention Deficit-Hyperactivity Disorder. Whereas the DSM-III diagnostic criteria required certain numbers of problems from separate lists representing inattention, impulsivity, and hyperactivity, DSM-III-R provided a single list of problems from which a specified number must be present in order to qualify for the diagnosis. The DSM-III-R thus moved toward a more unidimensional descriptive criterion for this disorder, in which clinical deviance was defined in terms of a specified number of problems on a dimension (APA, 1987). The DSM-III-R wording of each problem also implied quantitative assessment, as exemplified by the following items: "*Often* talks excessively," "is *easily* distracted by extraneous stimuli," and "*often* interrupts or intrudes on others" (APA, 1987, p. 52; italics added). Yet, each problem still had to be judged as either present or absent, and the overall criterion had to be met in a yes-or-no fashion.

Thus, even though the wording of the items and the requirement of a certain number of items from a list imply quantification, the decision rules imposed a categorical nosological construct on the diagnostic process: Each child was diagnosed as either having the disorder or not having it. However, the disorder could be described as mild, moderate, or severe according to the extent to which the number of symptoms and degree of impairment exceeded the categorical criteria. Later sections of this chapter deal with the implications of the categorical model for common behaviors that vary in degree like those used to diagnose problems of attention and hyperactivity.

Childhood Depression.   Interest in childhood depression has followed a course quite different from interest in autism and hyperactivity. Despite early reports of manic-depressive disorders in children (Kasanin & Kaufman, 1929), the psychoanalytic theory dominant from the 1930s through the 1960s held that true depressive disorders were impossible before the superego was fully internalized during adolescence (see Kashani et al., 1981). Following the spread of drug therapies and growing enthusiasm for biological explanations of adult depression in the 1960s, however, the quest for childhood depression was renewed.

As neither DSM-I nor DSM-II included childhood depression, and children do not spontaneously complain of depression, one approach was to infer depression from a variety of other problems. In arguing for the use of antidepressant drugs with children, Frommer (1967), for example, inferred depression in

. . . children who complain of non-specific recurrent abdominal pain, head-ache, sleep difficulties and irrational fears or mood disturbances such as irritability, unaccountable tearfulness, and associated outbursts of temper. Such children often develop sudden difficulty in social adjustments, which previously were normal; they may either withdraw themselves from the family circle and former friends or display outright aggressive and antisocial behavior. (p. 729)

Other advocates of antidepressant medication diagnosed children as depressed if they showed dysphoric (unhappy, irritable, hypersensitive, or negative) mood and self-deprecatory thoughts, plus at least two of the following: aggression, sleep disturbance, change in school performance, diminished socialization, change in attitude toward school, loss of usual energy, unusual change in appetite and/or weight (Weinberg, Rutman, Sullivan, Penick, & Dietz, 1973). Based on assessment of these symptoms by a pediatric neurologist who informally interviewed children and their parents, Weinberg and colleagues diagnosed 63% of children referred to an educational clinic as suffering from a "depressive illness."

Childhood depression was further broadened by the concept of *masked depression*—depression inferred from aggressive, hyperactive, and other troublesome behavior used defensively "to ward off the unbearable feelings of despair" (Cytryn & McKnew, 1979, p. 327). Psychophysiological reactions, truancy, running away, sexual promiscuity, and fire setting were also added as signs of masked depression (see Kovacs & Beck, 1977). The zealous quest for depression underlying so many different behaviors and the resulting reports of epidemics of previously undiagnosed depressive illness prompted one observer to dub childhood depression "the MBD of the 1980s" (Loney, personal communication).

Although the concept of masked depression has since been retracted by its authors (Cytryn, McKnew, & Bunney, 1980), the search for even unmasked depression as a generic entity among children is still plagued by a lack of agreement among various categorical criteria (Fleming & Offord, 1990). One reason for disagreements is that broad, inferential criteria classify a much larger proportion of children as depressed than more stringent criteria do. Carlson and Cantwell (1982), for example, found that the Weinberg et al. (1973) criteria produced considerably more diagnoses of depression than did the DSM–III criteria for a major depressive disorder in the same children. (The DSM–III criteria were written for adult disorders but include some extrapolations downward to children.) However, as neither set of criteria was quantified, the more stringent criteria could not be calibrated to the less stringent criteria in any systematic way: Not all children diagnosed by the more stringent criteria are included in the group diagnosed by the less stringent criteria. Furthermore, the two sets of criteria could not be made more congruent by adjusting cutoff points on quantitative dimensions, because they did not employ any. It was therefore difficult to advance the diagnosis of depression by combining results from the two sets of criteria.

Conclusion

In the 19th century, it was assumed that a descriptive nosology would identify diseases for which different organic etiologies could then be found. Current nosological approaches imply that disorders exist as categorical entities, each of which has a specific etiology. Although this view need not imply exclusively organic etiologies, as psychoanalytic interpretations of autism did not, it currently tends to assume organic etiologies.

In considering three popular candidates for the status of nosological entities, we saw that early infantile autism seems most like a disease entity, featuring very early onset and enduring abnormalities that do not appear to be situational or quantitative variations of normal behavior. Nevertheless, different conceptions of the disorder continue to produce diagnostic disagreements. The second candidate we considered, hyperactivity (called Attention Deficit–Hyperactivity Disorder in DSM–III–R), has been blamed on a variety of organic abnormalities, but involves situational and quantitative variations of behaviors that most children show in some degree. The overt problem behavior is relatively easy to identify, but the imposition of unvalidated categorical constructs on quantitative variations in the behavior provokes continuing diagnostic disagreements. The third candidate we considered, childhood depression, has been summarily cast into the nosological mold without prior refinement of the phenotypic picture. Whereas the application of the nosological paradigm to hyperactivity raises problems in categorizing quantitative variations of behavior, current nosological constructs of childhood depression still face problems of what phenomena to include as criteria and how to tailor the criteria to major developmental differences in expressions of affect.

MULTIVARIATE APPROACHES

Faced with a dearth of well-defined disorders on which to focus their efforts, researchers turned to statistical methods for empirically identifying syndromes of behavioral and emotional problems that tend to occur together in children. After some rudimentary efforts in the 1940s and 1950s, the advent of electronic computers spawned a host of multivariate studies in the 1960s and 1970s. In most of these studies, ratings obtained on behavior checklists were factor analyzed to identify syndromes of problems that tended to occur together. Despite differences in the rating instruments, raters, samples of children, and methods of analysis, there has been considerable convergence on certain syndromes (see Achenbach 1985, 1991a; Quay, 1986). There has also been convergence among findings obtained with different instruments in different samples and cultures (Achenbach, Conners, Quay, Verhulst, & Howell, 1989). Moreover, substantial correlations have been obtained between syndromes scored from different checklists (Achenbach, 1991b, 1991c). Some of the empirically identified syndromes resemble those that are evident in the nosological approaches, although there is no clear correspondence between other syndromes identified by the two approaches. When nosological syndromes have been scored in a quantitative fashion, some show a strong association with scores on empirically derived syndromes (Edelbrock & Costello, 1988; Weinstein et al., 1990). Figure 11.1 illustrates findings on relations between empirically derived syndromes and quantitatively scored DSM syndromes.

Contrasts Between Multivariate and Nosological Approaches

Even where there are similarities between the multivariate and nosological syndromes, there are also some important differences:

1. Official nosologies, such as the DSM and the World Health Organization's (WHO, 1978) *International Classification of Diseases* (ICD), are based on negotiated formulations of clinicians' concepts of disorders. Multivariate syndromes, by contrast, are derived statistically from covariation among scores on items rated for samples of children.

2. The criterial attributes of the nosological categories must be assessed according to yes-or-no judgments, whereas the criterial attributes of multivariate syndromes are usually assessed in terms of quantitative gradations.

3. Based on yes-or-no judgments of each criterial attribute, a nosological diagnosis culminates in a yes-or-no decision about whether a child has a particular disorder. Multivariate syndromes, on the other hand, are scored in terms of the degree to which a child manifests the characteristics of a syndrome. This is because quantitative indices of each criterial attribute are combined into a summary index of how strongly the child manifests the syndrome. However, cut points can also be established on the distribution of syndrome scores in order to discriminate categorically among particular classes of children, if desired.

4. The criteria for nosological diagnoses imply comparisons with normal age-mates, but they specify no operations for determining how a particular child compares with normal age-mates. The quantification of multivariate

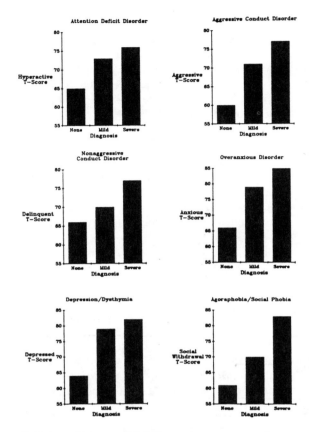

FIG. 11.1. Relations between DSM-III syndrome scores from a structured clinical interview (DISC-P) and T scores on corresponding scales of the Child Behavior Profile (Data from Edelbrock & Costello, 1988).

syndromes, by contrast, provides a metric for comparing a child with other children, such as normal age-mates.

5. Because nosological categories are defined in terms of discrete types of disorders, children who show characteristics of several types must either get multiple diagnoses or must be placed in a single category according to rules for preempting one diagnosis with another, often with no empirical basis for doing so. The multivariate approach, by contrast, lends itself to a profile format for describing a child in terms of his or her standing on multiple syndromes, without requiring forced-choices as to which ones preempt the others.

6. By cluster analyzing profiles, we can construct a taxonomy of patterns of scores obtained on all the syndromes of the profile. We can also quantify the degree of a child's resemblance to each profile type, further reducing

reliance on categorical forced choices (Edelbrock & Achenbach, 1980, provide detailed examples).

Syndromes Identified Through Multivariate Analyses

All efforts to identify syndromes of co-occurring problems are affected by the samples of children studied, the assessment instruments employed, the sources of assessment data, and the methods used to combine data. Children seen in a particular caseload are unlikely to provide a representative sample of disturbed children in general, because each caseload is affected by such factors as its catchment area, referral patterns, costs to clients, treatment philosophy, and image in the community. To obtain more representative samples of clinically referred children, it is therefore necessary to include children from many different clinical services.

The data obtained for analysis are affected by the assessment instruments employed, as instruments differing in items, scoring scales, or instructions may yield different results for the same subject samples. Because children's behavior varies from one context and interaction partner to another, the correlations between data obtained from different informants are generally modest. Meta-analyses have shown correlations averaging .60 between informants who play generally similar roles with respect to the subjects (e.g., mothers vs. fathers; teachers vs. teachers); .28 between pairs of informants who play different roles with respect to the subjects (e.g., parents vs. teachers; teachers vs. mental health workers); and .22 between the subjects themselves and people who know them, such as parents, teachers, and mental health workers (Achenbach, McConaughy, & Howell, 1987). Because each source may contribute reliable and valid—but different—data, multiple sources are necessary to support firm conclusions about childhood disorders. Because there is no single gold standard for combining data from multiple variables and multiple sources, it is helpful to compare findings that are combined by different methods.

Comparisons of multivariate studies using different samples, instruments, informants, and analytic methods have identified similarities in a number of empirically derived syndromes (Achenbach, 1985, and Quay, 1986, provide reviews). Table 11.1 summarizes findings from samples in which particular syndromes were derived by multivariate analyses of data obtained from case histories, mental health workers, parents, teachers, interviews, and self-reports. As is evident from Table 11.1, a large proportion of the samples yielded versions of the following eight syndromes, with the number of samples indicated in parentheses: Aggressive Behavior (27); Delinquent Behavior (22); Depressed (20); Attention Problems–Hyperactivity (22); Social Problems (13); Somatic Complaints (18);

TABLE 11.1
Number of Samples in Which Syndromes Were Identified Through Multivariate Analyses

	Case Histories	Mental Health Workers	Teachers	Parents	Interviews & Self-Reports	Total
Broad-Band Groupings						
Internalizing	2	1	9	6	3	21
Externalizing	3	3	9	7	3	25
Syndromes						
Academic Disability	—	1	—	3	—	4
Aggressive Behavior	3	4	5	12	3	27
Anxious	1	2	2	2	1	8
Attention Problems-Hyperactivity	3	2	5	11	1	22
Delinquent Behavior	3	1	5	11	2	22
Depressed	2	1	5	9	3	20
Immature	—	1	1	3	—	5
Obsessive-Compulsive	1	—	1	2	—	4
Sexual Problems	1	2	—	6	—	9
Sleep Problems	—	—	—	3	—	3
Social Problems	—	—	4	6	3	13
Somatic Complaints	1	—	4	11	2	18
Thought Problems (Schizoid)	3	4	4	9	2	22
Withdrawn	1	1	5	9	—	16

Based on Achenbach (1985, 1991a), Achenbach et al. (1989), McConaughy and Achenbach (1990).

Thought Problems (22); and Withdrawn (16). Other syndromes were less common, and some were found only for one sex or a particular age group.

In addition to the syndromes listed in Table 11.1, two broad-band groupings of problems corresponding to particular subsets of the syndromes have been identified in most studies that have included analyses capable of detecting such groupings. These broad-band groupings are designated as Externalizing and Internalizing at the top of Table 11.1, but they have also been given other labels, such as undercontrolled versus overcontrolled (Achenbach & Edelbrock, 1978), conduct problem versus personality problem (Peterson, 1961), and aggression versus inhibition (Miller, 1967). The Externalizing grouping typically includes problems from the Aggressive and Delinquent syndromes, and often from the Attention Problems–Hyperactivity syndrome as well. The Internalizing grouping, by contrast, typically includes problems from the Anxious, Depressed, Somatic Complaints, and Withdrawn syndromes.

Cross-Informant Syndrome Constructs

The syndromes listed in Table 11.1 as having counterparts in multiple samples were generally similar enough to be reliably categorized together

(Achenbach & Edelbrock, 1978). However, there was also considerable variation among the versions of each syndrome obtained from different samples, informants, instruments, and analytic procedures. Although statistically significant agreement has been obtained between different versions of particular syndromes, the agreement has been far from perfect.

In order to provide operationally defined taxa that represent the common elements of a particular syndrome across different samples and informants, we have developed *cross-informant syndrome constructs* for the eight syndromes that were found most often in the samples summarized in Table 11.1. We have done this by performing principal components/varimax analyses of large clinical samples scored by parents, teachers, and—for adolescents—the subjects themselves (Achenbach, 1991a).

To take account of sex and age variations, we performed separate analyses for each sex at ages 4 to 5, 6 to 11, and 12 to 18 on the parent instrument (the Child Behavior Checklist—CBCL; Achenbach, 1991b); ages 5 to 11 and 12 to 18 on the teacher instrument (Teacher's Report Form—TRF; Achenbach, 1991c); and 11 to 18 on the self-report instrument (Youth Self-Report—YSR; Achenbach, 1991d). Separately for each instrument, we then identified syndromes that had counterparts in a majority of the sex/age groups for that instrument. For each of these syndromes, we constructed a *core syndrome* that consisted of the items that occurred together in a majority of the sex/age groups for which the syndrome was found on a particular instrument. For example, versions of the Aggressive Behavior syndrome were found on the CBCL for both sexes at ages 4 to 5, 6 to 11, and 12 to 18. The items that had factor loadings of at least .40 on each version of the syndrome were printed out next to the items that had loadings of at least .40 on each of the other versions. Items that loaded ≥ .40 on at least four of the six versions were retained for the CBCL core Aggressive Behavior syndrome.

After we had identified core syndromes from the CBCL, TRF, and YSR, we placed the corresponding core syndromes from the three instruments side-by-side. We then identified items that were present in the corresponding core syndromes for at least two of the three instruments. For example, we placed the core aggressive syndromes from the CBCL, TRF, and YSR side-by-side. The items that were present in at least two of the three core syndromes were used to define a cross-informant syndrome construct for the Aggressive Behavior syndrome. This construct represents what is common to the different versions of the Aggressive Behavior syndrome that were derived empirically from each sex/age group on each of the three instruments. In statistical terms, it can be viewed as a latent variable. In terms of categorical concepts, it serves as a prototype (Rosch, 1978), consisting of correlated features that define a particular category of problems.

Each of the three instruments (CBCL, TRF, YSR) can be used to score children on syndrome scales that comprise the items of the cross-informant constructs. Because certain problems are evident only to particular informants, a few items besides those that define the cross-informant constructs are included in some syndrome scales. For example, the item *Disobedient at home* had high loadings on the versions of the Aggressive Behavior syndrome derived from the CBCL for all six sex/age groups. This item is not on the TRF and did not load highly on the Aggressive Behavior syndrome derived from the YSR. However, in recognition of its strong association with the Aggressive Behavior syndrome in parents' ratings, it is included on the scale for scoring the Aggressive Behavior syndrome from the CBCL.

To take account of sex, age, and informant variations in base rates for reported problems, the syndrome scales have been normed separately for each sex within particular age ranges for each type of informant. To facilitate comparisons between a child's problems in the different areas represented by each syndrome, the syndrome scales are displayed in a profile format. The profile provides percentiles and standard scores for normative samples of the child's sex and age. It also indicates normal, borderline, and clinical ranges for scores on each scale. Because the profiles scored from the CBCL, TRF, and YSR all display the same eight syndrome scales in the same order, a child's standing on each syndrome can easily be compared with normative samples as seen by each type of informant. In addition, Externalizing and Internalizing scores are computed from the items of the syndromes comprising these groupings, and competence scales are scored from items designed to tap various competencies on the CBCL, TRF, and YSR. A cross-informant computer program is available that scores and compares data obtained on CBCLs from both parents, the TRF, and the YSR (see Achenbach, 1991a). Figure 11.2 summarizes the steps by which the syndromes were derived from assessment data obtained with the three instruments and how the obtained syndromes are then used to assess individual children.

Conclusion

Lacking a differentiated nosology of childhood disorders, researchers have employed multivariate analyses to identify syndromes of covarying behaviors. Despite differences in rating instruments, raters, subject samples, and analytic methods, these analyses show considerable convergence on certain syndromes and two broad groupings of these syndromes. Multivariate syndromes utilize quantitative variations in criterial attributes and in aggregates of features rather than yes-or-no judgments of each feature and of the syndromes themselves.

Besides preserving quantitative variations, multivariate syndromes lend

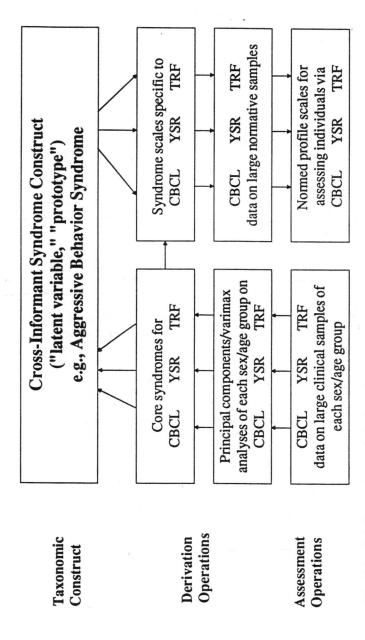

FIG. 11.2. Relations between derivation of syndromes, formulation of cross-informant syndrome constructs, and construction of profile scales (from Achenbach, 1991a).

647

themselves to profile formats that reveal children's patterns across all syndromes. These patterns provide a more comprehensive basis for phenotypic taxonomies than categorical nosologies do. By viewing a child's scores across a profile in relation to those of his or her age-mates, it is possible to assess the child's deviance for each syndrome, rather than making categorical judgments of each syndrome in isolation and without an operational basis for comparison with age norms.

GENERAL THEORETICAL APPROACHES TO PSYCHOPATHOLOGY

As we saw in preceding sections, the nosological and the multivariate approaches identify types of disorders without explaining them according to a single theory. The approaches considered in this section, by contrast, attempt to explain psychopathology on the basis of general theories of psychological functioning. We consider here only the two global theoretical approaches that have had the most impact on views of the development of psychopathology in children—psychoanalytic theory and learning theory. Because space restrictions preclude comprehensive treatment of these theories, the emphasis is on aspects having the most relevance to developmental psychopathology, but other aspects of these theories are considered in later sections.

Psychoanalytic Theory

Sigmund Freud's psychoanalytic theory grew out of his attempts to treat hysterical neuroses in the 1880s and 1890s. His patients displayed dramatic physical symptoms, such as paralyses, that violated the known principles of anatomy. Freud hypothesized that the symptoms were caused by conflicts between forbidden impulses seeking expression and psychological defenses against the impulses. His concept of conflicting psychological forces is the cornerstone of *psychodynamic* theory.

Libido Theory and Psychosexual Development. In investigating his patients' psychological conflicts, Freud concluded that the forbidden impulses were usually of a sexual nature. By urging patients to relax and say whatever came to mind—a process he called *free association*—Freud found that the patients' thoughts usually led back to childhood sexual experiences, especially seductions by adults. At first, Freud thought that repression of these memories was the basis for adult neurosis. He later concluded, however, that many of the seductions could not actually have occurred, although critics hold that childhood seductions were more common than Freud acknowledged (Masson, 1984). Current revelations of widespread sexual abuse also suggest that many of the seductions may in fact have occurred.

Why did so many patients "recall" sexual experiences that supposedly did not happen? Freud (1905/1953) inferred that the experiences were childhood fantasies triggered by sexual desires directed toward adults, especially the child's parent of the opposite sex. The desires themselves, he hypothesized, originated in the biologically determined sex drive, which was the source of affective excitation he termed *libido*. From patients' free associations, Freud inferred that libido was at first centered in the *oral* area, then the *anal* area, and then, between the ages of about 3 and 5, in the *phallic* area — the penis of the boy and the clitoris of the girl.

It was during the phallic phase that sexual desires toward the opposite-sex parent became intense. As a result, the child became hostile toward the same-sex parent, who was seen as a competitor. The typical outcome of this Oedipal situation was that the same-sex parent responded with punitive threats, which caused the child to repress the sexual impulses. Repression was enforced by a process of *identification* with the same-sex parent — by striving to emulate the same-sex parent, the child symbolically won the opposite-sex parent while reducing threats from the same-sex parent. Internalized prohibitions associated with the same-sex parent helped hold sexual impulses at bay during the latency period, until puberty intensified genital sexual urges, reawakened Oedipal conflicts, and provoked the *Sturm und Drang* of adolescence. Freud's portrayal of the sequence of libidinal phases from birth through adolescence is known as his *theory of psychosexual development*.

Personality Structure and Development. Also relevant to developmental psychopathology is Freud's theory of personality structure and development. As Freud's concepts of conflicting psychological forces grew more complex, he organized them in terms of three aspects of personality structure: the *id*, encompassing impulses arising from biological drives; the *ego*, encompassing the executive functions of personality that mediate between id impulses and external reality; and the *superego*, consisting of the ideals and prohibitions internalized via identification with the same-sex parent as a resolution of the Oedipal conflict. These three constructs have retained key roles in psychoanalytic views of development and psychopathology. The ego, in particular, became the centerpiece of later theory, as it was assigned ever wider functions in construing reality, detecting threats, experiencing anxiety, and activating defenses against anxiety. Anxiety came to be viewed as the *bête noire* of psychopathology, with different disorders being interpreted as reflecting different psychodynamic responses to it.

Implications of Psychoanalytic Theory for Developmental Psychopathology. Whereas Kraepelin provided the nosology, Freud provided the most popular explanations for psychopathology. Like Kraepelin, Freud focused on adult disorders, but his theory dealt with their developmental origins, inferred largely from adult recollections of childhood. Although Anna Freud and others psychoanalyzed children, their reports dealt mainly with elaborations of analytic theory, illustrated with anecdotal observations. Anna Freud's (1965) *Developmental Profile* for psychoanalytically assessing children has been illustrated in several case histories, but no reliability or validity data have been published (see Achenbach, 1985, for details).

The nature of psychoanalytic theory makes decisive tests difficult. However, a longitudinal study of the development of children's behavior disorders suggests that many of Freud's developmental inferences may have mistakenly imputed a causal role to intrapsychic variables that were actually effects of other problems.

> . . . in the young child, anxiety has not been evident as an initial factor preceding and determining symptom development. . . . However, intrapsychic conflict and psychodynamic defenses, as well as anxiety, have been evident in older children as later developments in the child's response to the unfavorable and sometimes threatening consequences of an initial maladaptation. . . . The painfulness of severe anxiety . . . makes it a striking symptom which may dominate our perceptions of the clinical picture. The elaborate psychological techniques utilized to minimize or avoid distress may also contribute dramatically to the elaboration of pathological behavior or thought. It is, therefore, not surprising that in retrospective studies that begin when the child already presents with an elaborated psychological disturbance, the prominent phenomena of anxiety and psychodynamic defenses dominate clinical thinking, and come to be labeled as primary, rather than as secondary, influences on the genesis of behavior disturbance. (Thomas, Chess, & Birch, 1968, pp. 188–189)

Learning Theories

As a major alternative to psychodynamic explanations for the development of child psychopathology, learning theories are distinguished from the psychoanalytic approach by the following features.

1. Learning theories originated with laboratory studies of learning, primarily in animals, rather than with clinical studies of psychopathology.
2. Learning theories focus mainly on observable environmental stimuli and observable responses by the organism, rather than on inferred mental events.

3. Learning theories attempt to explain most behavioral change at most ages with a single set of principles, rather than invoking a theory of development per se.
4. Learning theories emphasize environmental rather than biological and intrapsychic causes of psychopathology.

Origins of Learning Theories.   Systematic learning theories arose at about the same time as psychoanalytic theory, with laboratory studies by Pavlov, Bekhterev, and Thorndike suggesting general principles that were then extrapolated to a variety of human behavior. John B. Watson (1913, 1919), called the Father of Behaviorism, became the leading proponent of learning theory explanations for personality and psychopathology. He argued that most fears and other behavior problems resulted from faulty conditioning. Although initially sympathetic to the psychoanalytic advocacy of freer attitudes toward sex and the discussion of personal problems, Watson eventually contended that behaviorist studies of children would replace psychoanalysis, which was "based largely upon religion, introspective psychology, and Voodooism" (1924, p. 18).

Whereas psychoanalysis began as a therapy for adults and was later extended to children, most early applications of learning theory to behavior problems were with children. In a classic case, for example, Mary Cover Jones (1924) applied various conditioning principles to the treatment of a 2-year-old boy's phobia of rabbits. Holmes (1936) reinforced children for coping with their fear of the dark, while Mowrer and Mowrer (1938) used an alarm triggered by urine on a bed pad to cure children of bedwetting. It was not until the 1960s, however, that therapies based on learning theories became widespread.

Subsequent Development of Learning Theories.   What happened between the burst of enthusiasm for learning-based therapies in the 1920s and their revival in the 1960s? A great deal of laboratory research and refinement of learning theory was carried out by Clark Hull, B. F. Skinner, Neal Miller, and others. By the 1950s, efforts to apply more sophisticated learning theories to psychopathology became widespread. However, rather than attempting to change problem behavior, these efforts mainly translated the clinical theory and lore of psychoanalysis into learning theory terms.

The most ambitious of the translations was *Personality and Psychotherapy,* by John Dollard and Neal Miller (1950). Dedicating their book to "Freud and Pavlov and their students," Dollard and Miller sought "to combine the vitality of psychoanalysis, the rigor of the natural-science laboratory, and the facts of culture" (p. 3). They called psychotherapy a "window to higher mental life" and "the process by which *normality is created*" (pp. 3, 5). Thus accepting psychoanalytic views of psychopathology and its treatment, Dollard and Miller mainly sought to state these views in more rigorous terms derived from laboratory research on learning. Despite the basic contrasts listed earlier, psychoanalytic and learning theories converged in several ways.

1. Both explained mental processes largely in terms of principles of *association,* whereby sequences of thoughts are governed by previous contiguities among ideas, similarity of content, and other shared features. This associationistic view of mental processes was the basis for the psychoanalytic technique of free association, as well as the psychoanalytic theory of mental symbols.
2. Psychoanalytic theories and most learning theories postulated that reduction of organically based drives promoted the learning of important responses, attitudes, and emotions.
3. Psychoanalytic theory and learning theories made anxiety a central explanatory construct for psychopathology.
4. Psychoanalytic theory and learning theories blamed childhood experiences for most adult psychopathology but did not actually test the longitudinal/predictive relations that were assumed.

Conclusion

As of the 1950s, laboratory-based learning theories and clinical psychoanalytic theory seemed likely to converge on a sophisticated general theory of psychopathology, its development, and its treatment. This did not happen, however. Instead, the late 1950s and 1960s saw both a flowering of new therapies and an upsurge of developmental theory that took very different directions. In the following sections, we first consider the therapies and then the developmental theory. It is important to point out here, however, that learning and psychoanalytic theories both implied developmental etiologies for psychopathology. Yet, neither the theories nor their synthesis were based on direct study of human development, nor did they generate therapies whose efficacy was empirically demonstrated. Instead, they were rich heuristic systems whose appeal lay in their apparent ability to explain a wide variety of phenomena.

THERAPEUTIC APPROACHES EMERGING
SINCE THE ERA OF GRAND THEORIES

Following the era of comprehensive theories of all psychopathology and its treatment, diverse new therapies have emerged that embody specific techniques for dealing with limited classes of problems. Those used most widely with children include behavioral, cognitive, pharmacological, and family therapies.

Behavior Therapies

Despite the efforts of Dollard, Miller, and others to promote a synthesis of learning theory and psychoanalysis, most behavior therapies emerged as reactions against psychodynamic approaches. For example, in *Psychotherapy by Reciprocal Inhibition,* which heralded the renaissance of behavior therapies, Joseph Wolpe (1958) described himself as originally "a staunch follower of Freud." But Wolpe became skeptical of the universality of the Oedipus complex and the efficacy of psychoanalysis beyond the production of comforting insights. Drawing concepts from Pavlov and Hull, Wolpe defined neurotic behavior as ". . . any persistent habit of unadaptive behavior acquired by learning in a physiologically normal organism. Anxiety is usually the central constituent of this behavior, being invariably present in the causal situation. . . . By anxiety is meant the autonomic response pattern or patterns that are characteristically part of the organism's response to noxious stimulation" (pp. 32–34).

Unlike other extrapolations of learning concepts to psychopathology at that time, Wolpe applied his directly to the removal of neurotic symptoms. He did this by training more favorable responses that would reciprocally inhibit anxiety responses to particular stimuli. In Wolpe's main method, known as *systematic desensitization,* patients first construct *anxiety hierarchies* in which they rank stimulus situations from those that make them most anxious down to those that make them only slightly anxious. The patient is then taught relaxation responses that Wolpe believes are antagonistic to anxiety. Thereafter, the patient is induced to imagine the anxiety stimuli one-by-one, starting with the least threatening in the hierarchy. As each stimulus is imagined, the patient is to inhibit anxiety by making relaxation responses. Although young children may not be able to do everything required for this procedure, the same principles have been applied to *in vivo desensitization* of children by presenting the actual feared stimuli in a graded sequence while the child is engaged in pleasurable activities (e.g., Lazarus, Davison, & Polefka, 1965).

Other behavioral methods derive from Skinner's operant conditioning paradigm. Rather than attempting to extinguish anxiety by pairing threatening stimuli with nonfearful responses, operant methods change the reinforcement contingencies of the target behavior. For example, positive reinforcing consequences are made contingent on responses that are to be strengthened, whereas negative consequences are made contingent on responses that are to be weakened.

Behavior therapists at first implied that their techniques were rigorously derived from "modern learning theory." However, paradoxes arose from the apparent success of methods that were theoretically contradictory. A method known as *implosive therapy* or *flooding*, for example, is exactly opposite to Wolpe's systematic desensitization: It presents massive doses of the feared stimuli under the assumption that anxiety responses will quickly extinguish when no harm results from facing the feared stimuli. And there is evidence that implosive therapy can work with very fearful children (e.g., Ollendick & Gruen, 1972). Many other behavioral techniques likewise had ambiguous ties to general learning theories (see Achenbach, 1982, for further details).

In an article entitled "The End of Ideology in Behavior Modification," London (1972) argued that the ideology of learning theory had been a useful source of metaphors, paradigms, analogies, and a sense of theoretical identity, but that a technological orientation had become more appropriate than an ideological orientation. By this, London meant that the mechanical gadgetry and therapeutic techniques of behavior modification were developing faster than any integrative theory. Proving that each innovation was derived from learning theory was therefore less important than finding useful guides wherever possible. As this view spread, behavioral techniques were increasingly combined with other approaches, such as biofeedback, residential treatment, family therapy, group therapy, drug therapy, psychodynamic approaches, and educational approaches. As a result, behavioral technology is now used in diverse mental health services to children and adults, but not as a direct derivative of any general learning theory. Instead, the technology has a life of its own that generates ad hoc miniature theories and trial-and-error applications to many specific problems.

Cognitive–Behavioral Therapies

Another therapeutic approach emerging in recent years seeks to weaken cognitions that hinder adaption and strengthen those that are more adaptive. Although the focus on cognition may seem antithetical to behavioral views, behavior therapies have been a major impetus to certain varieties of cognitive therapy, known as *cognitive-behavioral therapies* (Kendall, 1991). Some of the most prominent behavior therapies, such as systematic desensitization, make use of imagined stimuli and covert cognitive responses for dealing with such stimuli. Although this was originally viewed as a convenience for manipulating anxiety-evoking stimuli and anxiety responses in the context of therapy, it assumed that behavioral principles derived from overt stimuli and responses were applicable to mental phenomena.

Because particular types of childhood problems—such as impulsivity and poor social skills—imply that the child lacks knowledge about appropriate behavior, these problems have been the focus of some of the most extensive efforts to apply behavioral principles to cognitions. *Self-instructional training,* for example, is designed to teach impulsive children to give themselves verbal instructions while they perform tasks slowly and carefully (Kendall & Braswell, 1985). Through modeling and guidance by the therapist, the making and repetition of overt verbal responses by the child, and reinforcement by the therapist, behavioral principles are used to teach impulsive children more effective strategies for doing school work and similar tasks.

A related approach, called *interpersonal problem-solving training,* is directed at improving social skills. Based largely on Spivak and Shure's (1982) analyses of social cognition, it uses behavioral principles to help children identify interpersonal problems, generate possible solutions, predict the consequences of different actions, and describe the feelings of other people involved in the situation.

Cognitive approaches are especially appealing from a developmental perspective, because they are intended to mesh with a child's current cognitive level and to promote new cognitive skills feasible for children at a particular level. Several reviews, however, have concluded that cognitive therapies affect performance on cognitive measures and some aspects of behavior in nonclinical groups, but that research has not demonstrated much influence on significant clinical problems (Abikoff, 1985; Beidel & Turner, 1986; Kazdin, 1985). This does not necessarily mean that the approach is wrong, but that much remains to be done in making it powerful enough to help truly troubled children.

Pharmacotherapies

During the 1950s, it was discovered that certain drugs initially developed for other purposes seemed to reduce florid psychotic symptoms in seriously disturbed adults. Further refinement of these drugs led to a revolution in the care of adult mental patients: Major tranquilizers—such as chlorpromazine (Thorazine)—made it possible to reduce physical restraints and to release violent and excited patients from hospitals; antidepressants—such as imipramine (Tofranil)—stimulated the functioning of severely depressed patients. Milder psychoactive drugs, such as Valium, became popular for prescription by physicians and in heavily advertised nonprescription forms. Although the biological mechanisms were not well understood, the apparent benefits of pharmacotherapy spurred psychiatry to turn toward psychopharmacology and away from psychoanalysis.

As discussed earlier, Bradley's (1937) report that amphetamines reduced hyperactivity contributed to the nosological conception of hyperactivity.

Few children, however, manifest the florid psychotic or depressive symptoms for which major tranquilizers and antidepressants are prescribed. Despite the occasional use of adult drugs with children, the drugs used for severe adult disorders showed little efficacy with childhood disorders (Campbell & Small, 1978).

Even the efficacy of stimulant drugs in reducing overactive behavior has not been followed by long-term improvements in the social and academic functioning of hyperactive children (Barkley, Fischer, Edelbrock, & Smallish, 1990; Weiss & Hechtman, 1986). Nevertheless, as we saw earlier in this chapter, enthusiasm for the psychopharmacological models spawned by adult drug therapies has inspired a hunt for childhood versions of pharmacologically treatable disorders, especially those involving depression and anxiety. Whether such disorders exist remains to be seen, but it seems clear that pharmacotherapies, like behavior therapies, now have a life of their own that cannot be credited to any particular theory.

Conjoint Family Therapy

Most therapies for children include work with the child's family, but this usually means that the therapist meets separately with the parents and child. In *conjoint family therapy,* all members of the family meet together with one or two therapists. In one of the first published illustrations, Bell (1961) portrayed conjoint family therapy as a way of dealing more quickly and effectively with problems imputed to a child (the identified patient). Bell outlined four phases of the therapy:

1. The *child-centered phase,* in which the therapist builds a relationship with the children of a family by being especially attentive to them, supporting their requests for changes in parental behavior, and tending to ignore parental criticism.
2. The *parent–child interaction phase,* in which parents' complaints about the child are prominent and the parents and child tend to talk about each other instead of to each other.
3. The *father–mother interaction phase,* in which parents express conflicts with each other that are assumed to cause the child's problems.
4. The *termination phase,* in which emphasis on parental interaction and the identified patient gives way to an emphasis on the interactions among all family members.

Family therapists view the family as a social system in which each member's behavior is a function of pressures existing in the system as a whole (Combrinck-Graham, 1990). The problems of the identified patient are viewed as symptoms of family stress. Because these symptoms serve a definite function in the family, removing them without other changes in the family is expected to produce symptoms in other family members or dissolution of the family system.

Despite their shared emphasis on the family as a system, family therapists vary widely in their therapeutic philosophies and techniques. Some see the parents alone for a couple of sessions and obtain a family history, whereas others see the parents and identified patient together from the beginning. Still others insist on seeing all family members together at all times.

Although family therapy has generated a large literature and many schools of thought, controlled research is meager. In one of the few adequately controlled studies, Wellisch, Vincent, and Ro-Trock (1976) found a significantly lower rate of rehospitalization for adolescents who had received family therapy during psychiatric hospitalization than for a control group receiving individual psychotherapy. Yet a comparison of outcomes for adolescent delinquents receiving three types of family therapy or a no-treatment control condition showed that not all forms of family therapy produce the same results (Klein, Barton, & Alexander, 1980). The conditions were: (a) *behavioral family therapy* (family members were prompted and reinforced for clearly communicating their thoughts and for negotiating contractual compromises), (b) *client-centered family therapy,* (c) *psychodynamic family therapy,* and (d) *no-treatment control.* Follow-ups showed a recidivism rate of 26% for delinquents receiving behavioral family therapy, which was significantly better than for the client-centered therapy (47%), the psychodynamic therapy (73%), and the no-treatment control condition (50%). Furthermore, significantly fewer siblings of adolescents in the behavioral therapy group later had court contacts (20%) than in the no-treatment (40%), client-centered (59%), or psychodynamic (63%) groups. This suggested that family systems were favorably altered by behavioral methods, but not by the other approaches to family therapy. Within the groups receiving the behavioral approach, however, those having therapists with the best skills in interpersonal relations had the best outcomes of all (Alexander, Barton, Schiavo, & Parsons, 1976). Not only the method of therapy, but the therapists' skills thus played an important role.

Conclusion

After being dominated by psychodynamic approaches, child and adolescent therapies have been augmented by a variety of new techniques. Although behavior therapies were nominally rooted in learning theory, they rapidly assumed diverse forms that were not dictated by any particular learning theory and could not be integrated within a single theory. The serendipitous discovery of the effects of certain drugs on adult psychotic symptoms helped stimulate biological research, but the initial discoveries did not result from theories of psychopathology. Conjoint family therapy has likewise been a source of miniature theories more than being derived from a single general theory. Aside from being relatively independent of grand theories, these therapies share another important feature: They are not very developmental, in that they focus neither on the developmental history of disorders, nor on differences in the developmental levels of the children treated, nor on subsequent developmental needs. Instead, they focus on the current status of each disorder and seek to change it by ameliorating environmental contingencies, biochemical variables, or family systems. How can knowledge of development improve our understanding and treatment of psychopathology?

DEVELOPMENTAL APPROACHES

Most of what we have considered so far has concerned psychopathology, rather than development. Where developmental considerations arose, they were secondary to other concerns. For example, the psychoanalytic theory of psychosexual development was constructed from adult recollections in order to explain the origins of neurosis. Likewise, learning theories blamed much of adult psychopathology on childhood learning experiences. Learning principles were assumed to be the same for children and adults, although certain variables, such as verbal labels, were assumed to acquire new roles at certain ages (Dollard & Miller, 1950; Kendler & Kendler, 1970).

Whereas the major therapeutic approaches have not dealt much with development, the major developmental theories have not dealt much with treatment of psychopathology. We turn now to two developmental theories that are potentially relevant to psychopathology.

Piaget's Theory

Without recounting all the important aspects of Jean Piaget's theory (see Kuhn, Chapter 4, this volume), let us consider some features most relevant to the developmental study of psychopathology.

Cognitive Developmental Periods.   The best known feature of Piaget's theory is its sequence of cognitive developmental periods: the *sensorimotor* period, *preoperational* period, *concrete operational* period, and *formal operational* period. The hypothesized characteristics of these periods are familiar to most students of developmental psychology. Whether or not the periods embody precisely the cognitive systems claimed by Piaget, they certainly reflect important differences in the way children process information. Yet, none of the major nosological, theoretical, or therapeutic approaches to psychopathology takes account of these differences. Although all approaches implicitly recognize differences between infancy and later childhood, they do not take account of the differences between the level of language, reasoning powers, logical assumptions, and use of information that distinguish 4-year-olds, 8-year-olds, and adolescents, for example.

Figurative Versus Operative Aspects of Cognition.   Another feature of Piaget's (1977) theory relevant to the developmental study of psychopathology first becomes crucial around the age of 18 months. At this age, Piaget hypothesized, the sensorimotor period is brought to a close by the child's increasing ability to form mental representations. According to Piaget, the process of mental representation has two aspects: The *figurative* aspect encompasses mental signifiers, such as images, symbols, and words, that stand for particular stimuli. These signifiers are roughly analogous to the contents of mental life hypothesized by other theories, such as the mental symbols of psychoanalytic theory and the covert mediating responses of learning theories. Piaget called these mental signifiers *schemas.* Prior to about 18 months of age, Piaget hypothesized that the only schemas are percepts evoked by sensory stimulation. After about 18 months, however, mental schemas can be generated with increasing independence of perceptual input. It is this capacity for purposefully representing stimuli via mental schemas that marks the transition from sensorimotor to preoperational thought.

Piaget called the second aspect of mental representation the *operative* aspect. In contrast to the mental signifiers of the figurative aspect, the operative aspect refers to organized mental *activities* analogous to behavioral *schemes* evident during the sensorimotor period; in early infancy, for example, the sucking scheme is an organized series of actions encompassing the recognition, grasp, and sucking of suckable objects. Sensorimotor schemes are physical activities, but *mental* schemes are cognitive activities whereby the contents (schemas) of thought are manipulated. (Translations of Piaget's work often use the terms *schema* and *scheme* interchangeably, but in the 1960s Piaget clarified that *schemas* are mental signifiers belonging to the figurative aspect of thought, whereas *schemes* are organized mental activities belonging to the operative aspect.) Piaget's distinction between operative and figurative aspects of thought has no clear counterpart in other developmental theories. Yet, according to Piaget, cognitive development consists mainly of changes in the operative aspect of thought. Even during the sensorimotor period—from birth to about 18 months—Piaget noted significant changes in overt schemes that he divided into six stages. More pervasive changes in operative functioning are marked by the transition to the concrete operational period between the ages of about 5 and 7 years, and the transition to the formal operational period at about the age of 11. Aside from the advent of mental signifiers at the end of the sensorimotor period, Piaget did not ascribe major developmental changes to the figurative aspect of thought. Nevertheless, the progressive acquisition of new signifiers, such as words, and the growth of operative powers to use signifiers in new ways continue to contribute to the development of mental functioning.

The distinction between the figurative and operative aspects of thought enabled Piaget to provide a far more differentiated picture of mental development than did psychoanalytic or learning theorists, whose preoccupation with the *contents* of thought left little room for changes in the *operations* and *structure* of thought. However, despite applications of Piagetian concepts to social thinking under the banner of *social cognition* (e.g., Flavell & Ross, 1981), a large gap remains to be bridged between the differentiated Piagetian picture of cognition and the developmental study of psychopathology.

Causes of Development. Piaget hypothesized four major sources of development: (a) *organic maturation,* (b) *experience* gained through interactions with the physical world, whereby the child observes phenomena and actively experiments to find out how things happen, (c) *transmission of information* from other people by language, modeling, and teaching, and (d) *equilibration.* The first three contributors to development — maturation, experience, and social transmission — have counterparts in most theories. But Piaget believed that these three were not enough to explain cognitive development. Instead, cognitive development involves *construction* of new mental representations when a child's existing concepts prove inadequate. The process of *equilibration* is especially crucial in the major transitions from one period of cognitive development to the next. It brings together the other contributors to development in the construction of higher-order cognitive structures from lower-order structures that have reached their limits. To use a computer analogy, cognitive structures resemble computer programs, whereas schemes are like subroutines of these programs, and schemas are like the encoded data that the programs manipulate and transform. Unlike computers, however, living organisms can create for themselves new cognitive challenges to which they respond through the process of equilibration by constructing new representations and operations. Although Piaget never fully clarified the equilibration process, it represents a crucial aspect of cognition and adaptive activity in general. The essence of this activity is the struggle to overcome gaps and contradictions in our comprehension of the world and ourselves. Such activity is an essential part of healthy development that deserves far more attention in the developmental study of psychopathology.

Erikson's Theory

Erik H. Erikson's (1963, 1980) theory of *psychosocial development* was an outgrowth of Freud's theory of psychosexual development. Erikson, however, stressed the social aspects of development rather than the distribution of libido or the origins of adult neurosis. The interface between society and the developing individual is highlighted in his basic assumptions:

> (1) that the human personality in principle develops according to steps predetermined in the growing person's readiness to be driven toward, to be aware of, and to interact with, a widening social radius; and (2) that society, in principle, tends to be so constituted as to meet and invite this succession of potentialities for interaction and attempts to safeguard and to encourage the proper rate and the proper sequence of their unfolding. (Erikson, 1963, p. 270)

Stages of Psychosocial Development.   Although Erikson divided childhood development into stages approximating Freud's phases of libidinal development, his stages are defined not only in terms of ascendant erogeneous zones, but also in terms of *modes of action* employed by the child and the *modalities of social interaction* characterizing interpersonal exchanges at each stage. The initial stage, for example, is dominated by a general incorporative mode that includes incorporation of stimuli through the sense organs, as well as through the mouth. Erikson therefore called this stage the *oral–sensory stage,* rather than just the oral stage, as Freud called it. The dominant mode of action at this stage is *incorporation* of input from the outside world. Because infants' social interactions center on getting others to provide for their needs and receiving what others give, the social modality is called *getting.* The four subsequent psychosocial stages are a *second oral–sensory stage* in which more active incorporation is the child's dominant mode and *taking* is the social modality; the *anal–urethral–muscular stage;* the *locomotor and infantile genital stage;* and the *rudimentary genital stage.*

Erikson did not specify why development progresses from one stage to the next, but he maintained that failure of the appropriate mode to dominate a stage may disrupt subsequent stages. If a baby repeatedly vomits, for example, this premature dominance of the *eliminative mode* (which normally dominates the anal–urethral–muscular stage) may hinder learning of the social modality of getting. Such disruptions can affect later personality development.

Nuclear Conflicts. Erikson is probably best known for the *developmental crises* or *nuclear conflicts* he ascribed to particular stages. The two oral sensory stages, for example, raise conflicts over the development of *basic trust versus mistrust.* A resolution in favor of basic trust depends on the mother's success in satisfying the child's needs, thereby instilling in the child a sense of trust in the mother and the world she represents. Erikson's conceptions of later conflicts, especially the adolescent conflict over *identity versus role confusion,* have received abundant attention in the developmental and psychodynamic literature and have influenced psychotherapy with children and adolescents (Greenspan & Pollock, 1980).

Although Erikson's theory has not produced a distinctive therapeutic method or testable explanations for psychopathology, several studies have found evidence for sequences of conflictual concerns like those that Erikson hypothesizes (e.g., Ciaccio, 1971; Constantinople, 1969; Waterman, Geary, & Waterman, 1974). Even though the hypothesized conflicts do seem to exist, however, these studies have suggested that some conflicts typically remain salient even as later ones rise and fall.

Conclusion

Developmental theories have provided a rich picture of various aspects of development. An interweaving of Piaget's theory and Erikson's theory, in particular, can provide a sense of understanding normal development and its problems. Table 11.2 offers a capsule summary of the relations between these theories and Freud's theory of psychosexual development, as well as the normal achievements, common behavior problems, and clinical disorders characterizing each period.

 Despite the value of comprehensive overviews of development, the sense of understanding bestowed by global theories has not revealed the causes nor provided efficacious methods for the treatment or prevention of most childhood disorders. We therefore turn now to major problems facing developmental research on psychopathology.

CURRENT PROBLEMS AND ISSUES

As we have seen, there is great diversity among the approaches that touch on the developmental study of psychopathology, but no approach deals comprehensively with it. Instead, there are nosological approaches to psychopathology in general based largely on medical models for severe adult disorders but not of much demonstrated value for children's disorders. As an alternative to nosological approaches, there are multivariate approaches for extracting syndromes from the quantitative covariation

TABLE 11.2

Relations Between Developmental Theories, Achievements, Behavior Problems, and Clinical Disorders (from Achenbach, 1982, p. 67)

Approximate Age	Cognitive Period	Psychosexual Phase	Psychosocial Conflict	Normal Achievements	Common Behavior Problems[a]	Clinical Disorders
0–2	Sensory-Motor	Oral	Basic Trust vs. Mistrust	Eating, digestion, sleeping, social responsiveness, attachment, motility, sensory-motor organization	Stubbornness, temper, toileting	Organically based dysfunctions, anaclitic depression, autism, failure to thrive
2–5	Pre-Operational	Anal	Autonomy vs. Shame and Doubt	Language, toileting, self-care skills, safety rules, self-control, peer relationships	Argues, brags, demands attention, disobedient, jealous, fears,[c] prefers older children, overactive, resists bedtime, shows off, shy,[c] stubborn, talks too much, temper, whines	Speech and hearing problems, phobias, unsocialized behavior
		Phallic-Oedipal	Initiative vs. Guilt			
6–11	Concrete Operational	Latency	Industry vs. Inferiority	Academic skills, school rules, rule-governed games, hobbies, monetary exchange, simple responsibilities	Argues, brags,[b] can't concentrate,[b] self-conscious, shows off, talks too much[c]	Hyperactivity, learning problems, school phobia, aggression, withdrawal
12–20	Formal Operational	Genital	Identity vs. Role Confusion	Relations with opposite sex, vocational preparation, personal identity, separation from family, adult responsibilities	Argues, brags[b]	Anorexia, delinquency, suicide attempts, drug and alcohol abuse, schizophrenia, depression

[a]Problems reported for at least 45% of children in nonclinical samples.

[b]Indicates problem reported for ≥45% of boys only.

[c]Indicates ≥45% of girls only.

663

among reported behaviors. In the absence of known etiologies, multivariate approaches can utilize phenotypic data more efficiently than the arbitrary decision rules imposed by categorical nosological approaches. Multivariate approaches also lend themselves to profile formats for providing comprehensive descriptions of behavior that can serve as a basis for taxonomies of behavior patterns. So far, multivariate behavioral descriptions have been cross-sectional, although comparisons of the syndromes found at different ages suggest developmental differences that are worth testing in longitudinal studies, as discussed later.

Aside from the nosological and multivariate approaches to the identification of disorders, we considered two general theoretical approaches to the understanding of psychopathology: Psychoanalytic theory and learning theory, both of which implied developmental origins for psychopathology, but were not based on the direct study of children's development. Although both have had major impacts on views of psychopathology, and efforts were made to join them in a grand synthesis, they gave way to a variety of new therapeutic approaches that were not dictated by any general theory.

Just as the major approaches to psychopathology have not been based on developmental research, the major approaches to development have not involved much research on child psychopathology. In the case of Piaget's theory, this is understandable, because Piaget sought to construct a genetic epistemology rather than to explain psychopathology. However, Piaget's picture of developmental sequences and processes, and his distinction between operative and figurative aspects of thought, are important for all aspects of development, maladaptive as well as adaptive. When we try to help a troubled child, it is always important to understand the child's level of cognitive functioning, the limits and possibilities characterizing that level, and the child's potential for further growth.

Erikson applied his developmental theory to psychopathology, but mainly to illustrate his general developmental principles. Unlike Piaget, he did not provide extensive methodologies for empirically testing his concepts.

In light of where we have been, where should we be going? Although many approaches are pertinent to the development of psychopathology, they do not share a systematic program of research. The following sections highlight issues that must be faced in order to systematize the developmental study of psychopathology.

Operationally Defining Disorders

The paucity of accepted operational definitions for disorders of childhood and adolescence has prevented different approaches from converging on a common set of target phenomena. As applied to childhood disorders, the nosological approach has been handicapped by the lack of a taxonomic data base on which to build its categories and by a precommitment to diagnostic constructs that must be judged as present or absent. Although the DSM now provides explicit decision rules for each diagnostic category, the rules for the common disorders of childhood have not been derived from data on differences among disorders in representative samples of children. Furthermore, the decision rules do not constitute operational definitions, because no assessment operations are specified for determining whether a child's behavior meets the specified criteria.

Multivariate approaches, by contrast, are designed to derive target disorders from empirical data and to quantify criterial attributes. Because disorders are defined in terms of scores on particular instruments, multivariate approaches also provide operational definitions. However, as with any taxonomic effort, multivariate approaches require decisions about what data to use in formulating taxa, what taxa are useful for what purposes, and what cut points should be used to discriminate between the normal and pathological range, as well as between one taxon and another. These are questions that should be answered through programmatic research. In the absence of known etiologies or clear-cut organic markers, this type of research is a form of psychometric bootstrapping—that is, trial-and-error revision of measures in order to strengthen their relations to each other and to admittedly imperfect validity criteria.

In some disorders, such as autism, the age of onset and clear-cut pathognomonic behavior argue for a taxon of the classical nosological type. Yet, even in these disorders, multivariate approaches can help to sharpen distinctions among children who meet the categorical criteria for the taxon (Siegel et al., 1986). In the more common disorders of childhood and adolescence, multivariate findings have recently converged on a set of syndromes derived from multiple sources of data (Achenbach, 1991a). These syndromes provide a firm basis for research on differential etiologies, responsiveness to treatment, course, and outcome.

Differential Clinical Assessment

Related to the problem of operationally defining disorders is the problem of differential clinical assessment. Although operational definitions specify procedures for determining which taxonomic criteria a child meets, clinical assessment must provide a more comprehensive picture than a taxonomy of disorders can. It is always important to know, for example, the child's family situation, developmental history, medical condition, level of cognitive functioning, school record, peer relations, social competencies, and important life stresses. Some of these may contribute to taxonomic decisions, but no taxonomy will ever be comprehensive enough to take detailed account of all of them. Instead, taxonomies overlook many individual characteristics in order to highlight a few that define classes of individuals.

In assessing a child, decisions may be needed in relation to several different taxonomies. For example, a boy's behavior may be deviant in a way that meets the criteria for a particular behavior disorder. The boy's IQ may be low enough to classify him as "mildly retarded." This, in turn, may classify him as eligible for special education. He might also have organic problems that classify him as having a perceptual–motor handicap. These multiple classifications serve different purposes and are not mutually contradictory. However, they alone cannot convey a detailed picture of the boy's specific needs.

In trying to help individual children, we need a comprehensive, idiographic picture of each child that cannot be derived from taxonomic criteria alone. In practice, clinicians have relied much more on idiographic assessment than on linking children to overarching taxonomies. Clinical interviews with children and their parents, a developmental history taken from the parents, comments by teachers, and cognitive, perceptual–motor, and personality tests are commonly used in deciding what is wrong and what to do about it. Even behaviorally oriented clinicians have relied much more on procedures of this sort than on the direct observations in natural environments that the behavioral literature espouses (Wade, Baker, & Hartmann, 1979). Yet, a weakness of this approach to assessment is that the data are obtained in ways that vary from case to case, are of unknown reliability and validity, and cannot be compared with normative baselines for a child's age.

Not only for taxonomic purposes, then, but also for purposes of formulating an idiographic picture of the child that distinguishes the child from other children, we need assessment procedures of proven reliability and validity, based on normative data. Interviews, reports by parents and teachers, self-reports, behavior samples, and cognitive, perceptual–motor, and other tests may all contribute valid assessment data. Yet, research is needed to determine what unique contribution each procedure can make and to standardize the best of these procedures for use across diverse settings.

Longitudinal Course of Adaptive and Maladaptive Behavior

The previous two sections dealt with research that is largely cross-sectional—operationally defining disorders and making differential assessments of children at a particular point in time. Although children's past histories are also relevant to the definitions of disorders and to broader clinical assessment, good operational definitions and differential assessment of current problems are needed to facilitate children's future development. But facilitating development requires knowledge of the typical outcomes of each disorder. And such knowledge, in turn, requires longitudinal research comparing the developmental course of children grouped according to type of disorder and other variables. Although etiological research is also important, the multidetermined nature of most childhood disorders means that longitudinal follow-up studies may yield quicker and surer benefits for troubled children than etiological research will.

As an example, suppose we start with 6- to 11-year-old children for whom parents and teachers have filled out standardized rating forms at intake into several mental health settings. Forms of this sort for obtaining data on children's problems and competencies are coming into widespread use. They have been subjected to multivariate analyses to produce empirically derived scales for scoring behavioral problems and competencies. The scales have been normed and cast in profile formats.

The profiles derived from parent and teacher ratings of large samples of children provide a good picture of the range of problems for which children are typically referred. The standardization of ratings and classification of children by profile types give us a starting point from which to compare outcomes for children differing in their initial problems and competencies, as seen by important adults in their natural environments.

If we have parents and teachers fill out the same rating forms again at regular intervals, such as every 6 months for 2 years, we can track the course of the child's problems and competencies as judged by these important adults. We can then determine whether the patterns of problems and competencies manifested at intake can predict outcomes over the 2 years. In particular, we can determine whether any patterns have much worse or better outcomes than others. Even if the clinical services are heterogeneous (as they are in most settings), findings of especially poor outcomes for a particular profile pattern would indicate that this was a group in need of close study to find out why their outcomes are so poor and what can be done to help them. Conversely, a group that had exceptionally good outcomes could be examined to identify the factors responsible. For example, were they especially well suited to the services offered? Or might they be especially competent and able to improve regardless of the services? Or might their problems have been specific to a particular developmental period?

Further variables can be readily added to a study of this type. For example, demographic and family data routinely obtained at intake (e.g., socioeconomic status, ethnicity, rural vs. suburban vs. urban residence, marital status of parents, number of siblings) may augment the predictive power of profile patterns. Other data, such as IQ and medical conditions, may also be important. However, the more variables included, the larger the samples need to be and the greater the risk of chance findings that must be controlled by adjusting significance levels. Furthermore, such studies should also incorporate cross-validation, either in new samples or by jackknife procedures or by splitting samples in half and testing the findings from one half on the other half of the sample.

In summary, it seems clear that even short-term longitudinal studies of the problems and competencies of children already identified as disturbed can be of great value for understanding childhood psychopathology and development. Moreover, such studies can improve services to children by pinpointing groups in need of help not now provided and by laying the groundwork for devising new ways to help these children. By first identifying those currently having the worst outcomes, we can also concentrate etiological research where it is most needed, instead of initiating etiological studies without knowing the usual outcomes of the disorders we are studying.

Experimental Intervention and Prevention

The most powerful strategy for testing causal relations is by experimentally manipulating the hypothesized causal variable to see whether it affects the dependent variable of interest. Drug therapies are tested in experimental studies that employ as a control condition inactive placebo drugs identical in appearance to the drug under test. Because the patients and evaluators are kept blind as to which is the placebo and which is the active drug, this is known as a *double-blind placebo-controlled procedure*. Experimental studies of this sort have shown that hyperactivity can be reduced with stimulant drugs (Weiss & Hechtman, 1986).

The double-blind placebo-controlled experiment is viewed as an ideal to be emulated in the evaluation of all therapies. Experimental studies have demonstrated significant benefits from some child therapies (Weisz, Weiss, Alicke, & Klotz, 1987). However, most nondrug therapies cannot approximate the double-blind placebo-controlled study for several reasons.

1. Placebo conditions cannot be created that are both ethical and convincing alternatives to the active treatment.
2. The differences between experimental and control conditions are too obvious to enable patients and evaluators to remain blind.
3. The onset and offset of the hypothesized therapeutic effects cannot be precisely controlled.
4. Treatments such as psychotherapy and family therapy aim to bring about general changes in functioning that are not assessable via short-term measures of specific behaviors.

Efforts at prevention face even greater obstacles, because the target disorders are not yet evident when the preventive intervention takes place. This means that experimental manipulations must be made with subjects who are not motivated by current distress and may never develop the target disorders. Furthermore, because the target disorders have not emerged when the preventive efforts are made, the evaluation of the interventions must last until well into the period at which the disorders would ordinarily emerge.

In light of the foregoing obstacles, it should not be surprising that there are few well-controlled experimental evaluations of interventions for child psychopathology other than drug and behavior therapies. Nevertheless, it is incumbent on advocates of therapeutic and preventive methods to demonstrate that they are safe and effective. How can this be done?

Because experimental studies are so costly, time-consuming, and methodologically difficult, they are likely to be worthwhile only after the tasks outlined in the preceding sections have been accomplished. That is, we should have reliable and valid operational definitions of the disorders, standardized procedures for differential clinical assessment, and longitudinal data on outcomes. If we have a good operational definition of a disorder, can reliably differentiate it from other disorders, and know that it usually has a poor outcome, then experimental studies of interventions for treating or preventing the disorder may be worthwhile.

The difficulty of creating appropriate placebo control conditions argues for comparing two different treatments in similar groups of children who have the target disorder, rather than a treatment versus a no-treatment group. One treatment might be the therapy that such children ordinarily receive. The second can be a new treatment based on close study of children having a pattern of problems found to have poor outcomes in longitudinal follow-ups.

Let us suppose, for example, that a behavior profile pattern having peaks on depression, social withdrawal, and aggression has especially poor outcomes among 6- to 11-year-old boys. Close study of boys manifesting this pattern indicates that they lack skill in making friends, are often rejected by others, cannot communicate their feelings verbally, and react to frustration with extreme aggression. A possible intervention may be to train them in skills required to make friends, avoid doing things that precipitate rejection, communicate their feelings verbally, and react more constructively to frustration.

After pilot research to perfect a social skills training program, an experimental study can be designed to compare it with one or more treatments ordinarily administered to these boys. For example, it may be possible to compare the new treatment with two commonly used treatments, such as individual psychotherapy and family therapy. The candidate subjects would be boys who at intake into a mental health service manifest profiles of problems that include peaks on depression, withdrawal, and aggression. Extensive differential assessment would be used to exclude boys who might be poor subjects because of major problems beyond the reach of the therapies to be tested, such as organic dysfunctions, very low cognitive ability, or extreme family instability.

If a boy met the criteria for the study and he and his family agreed to participate, a random procedure could be used to assign him to one of the three treatment conditions. Prior to treatment and again at 6-month intervals thereafter, behavior ratings by the boys' parents and teachers, self-reports by the boys, and standardized clinical interviews would be used to assess behavioral change. Boys receiving the three treatments would ultimately be compared on these variables, plus others such as achievement test performance, friendships, and trouble with the law. Ratings by evaluators such as teachers and clinical interviewers could be blind as to the treatment conditions. Other outcome variables, such as test performance and police records, would not be susceptible to influence by knowledge of treatment conditions.

A single-factor design of this sort could be expanded by comparing two groups who have different initial behavioral patterns across two types of intervention in a two-by-two design. The very few studies reporting adequate subject-by-treatment analyses have revealed unexpected interaction effects that greatly outweighed the main effects of treatment (e.g., Love & Kaswan, 1974; Miller, Barrett, Hampe, & Noble, 1972). Thus, certain treatments may be helpful to some kinds of children but harmful to others. Unless the interactions between child characteristics and treatment effects are assessed, however, we will not know what treatments are optimal for which children.

CONCLUSION

In summarizing approaches to development and psychopathology, we considered several key tasks requiring programmatic research to foster a developmental understanding of psychopathology. The first task was to construct reliable and valid operational definitions of disorders from empirical data. The second was to establish standardized assessment procedures that reliably and validly compare each child with other children. The third was to conduct longitudinal follow-ups aimed at determining the characteristic outcomes of particular patterns of adaptive and maladaptive behavior. Once we have reliable and valid operational definitions of disorders, standardized procedures for differential clinical assessment, and longitudinal data on outcomes, then it may be worth mounting experimental studies of interventions for preventing or treating disorders found to have poor outcomes. These tasks by no means exhaust the possibilities for significant developmental research on psychopathology, but they are of critical importance to almost all theories, disorders, and approaches to treatment.

Developmental perspectives are obviously essential for understanding the nature and course of psychopathology during the period of rapid development from birth to maturity. In addition, however, developmental perspectives may also be useful for understanding the interplay between psychopathology and the more subtle aspects of development characterizing adulthood and aging. A major challenge for developmental psychopathology will be to progressively extend its purview into these later developmental periods.

REFERENCES

Abikoff, H. (1985). Efficacy of cognitive training interventions in hyperactive children: A critical review. *Clinical Psychology Review, 5,* 479–512.

Achenbach, T. M. (1966). The classification of children's psychiatric symptoms: A factor-analytic study. *Psychological Monographs, 80* (Whole No. 615).

Achenbach, T. M. (1982). *Developmental psychopathology* (2nd ed.). New York: Wiley.

Achenbach, T. M. (1985). *Assessment and taxonomy of child and adolescent psychopathology.* Newbury Park, CA: Sage.

Achenbach, T. M. (1991a). *Integrative guide for the 1991 CBCL/4–18, YSR, and TRF Profiles.* Burlington, VT: University of Vermont Department of Psychiatry.

Achenbach, T. M. (1991b). *Manual for the Child Behavior Checklist and 1991 Profile.* Burlington, VT: University of Vermont Department of Psychiatry.

Achenbach, T. M. (1991c). *Manual for the Teacher's Report Form and 1991 Profile.* Burlington, VT: University of Vermont Department of Psychiatry.

Achenbach, T. M. (1991d). *Manual for the Youth Self-Report 1991 and Profile.* Burlington, VT: University of Vermont Department of Psychiatry.

Achenbach, T. M., Conners, C. K., Quay, H. C., Verhulst, F. C., & Howell, C. T. (1989). Replication of empirically derived syndromes as a basis for taxonomy of child/adolescent psychopathology. *Journal of Abnormal Child Psychology, 17,* 299–323.

Achenbach, T. M., & Edelbrock, C. (1978). The classification of child psychopathology: A review and analysis of empirical efforts. *Psychological Bulletin, 85,* 1275–1301.

Achenbach, T. M., McConaughy, S. H., & Howell, C. T. (1987). Child/adolescent behavioral and emotional problems: Implications of cross-informant correlations for situational specificity. *Psychological Bulletin, 101,* 213–232.

Alexander, J. F., Barton, C., Schiavo, R. S., & Parsons, B. V. (1976). Systems-behavioral intervention with families of delinquents: Therapist characteristics, family behavior, and outcome. *Journal of Consulting and Clinical Psychology, 44,* 636–644.

American Academy of Child Psychiatry. (1983). *Child psychiatry: A plan for the coming decades.* Washington, DC: Author.

American Psychiatric Association. (1952). *Diagnostic and statistical manual of mental disorders.* Washington, DC: Author.

American Psychiatric Association. (1968). *Diagnostic and statistical manual of mental disorders* (2nd ed.). Washington, DC: Author.

American Psychiatric Association. (1980). *Diagnostic and statistical manual of mental disorders* (3rd ed.). Washington, DC: Author.

American Psychiatric Association. (1987). *Diagnostic and statistical manual of mental disorders* (3rd ed., rev.). Washington, DC: Author.

Barkley, R. A. (1991). *Attention deficit hyperactivity disorder. A handbook for diagnosis and treatment.* New York: Guilford Press.

Barkley, R. A., Fischer, M., Edelbrock, C., & Smallish, L. (1990). The adolescent outcome of hyperactive children diagnosed by research criteria: I. An 8-year prospective follow-up study. *Academy of Child and Adolescent Psychiatry, 29,* 546–557.

Beidel, D. C., & Turner, S. M. (1986). A critique of the theoretical bases of cognitive–behavioral theories and therapy. *Clinical Psychology Review, 6,* 177–197.

Bell, J. E. (1961). Family group therapy. *Public Health Monograph* (No. 64). Washington, DC: United States Department of Health, Education, and Welfare.

Bettelheim, B. (1967). *The empty fortress.* New York: The Free Press.

Bradley, C. (1937). The behavior of children receiving benzedrine. *American Journal of Psychiatry, 94,* 577–585.

Brown, G., Chadwick, O., Shaffer, D., Rutter, M., & Traub, M. (1981). A prospective study of children with head injuries: III. Psychiatric sequelae. *Psychological Medicine, 11,* 63–78.

Campbell, M., & Small, A. M. (1978). Chemotherapy. In B. B. Wolman, J. Egan, & A. O. Ross (Eds.), *Handbook of treatment of mental disorders in childhood and adolescence.* Englewood Cliffs, NJ: Prentice-Hall.

Carlson, G. A., & Cantwell, D. P. (1982). Diagnosis of childhood depression: A comparison of the Weinberg and DSM–III criteria. *Journal of the American Academy of Child Psychiatry, 21,* 247–250.

Chung, S. Y., Luk, S. L., & Lee, P. W. H. (1990). A follow-up study of infantile autism in Hong Kong. *Journal of Autism and Developmental Disorders, 20,* 221–232.

Ciaccio, N. V. (1971). A test of Erikson's theory of ego epigenesis. *Developmental Psychology, 4,* 306–311.

Combrinck-Graham, L. (1990). Developments in family systems theory and research. *Journal of the American Academy of Child and Adolescent Psychiatry, 29,* 501–512.

Constantinople, A. (1969). An Eriksonian measure of personality development in college students. *Developmental Psychology, 1,* 357–372.

Cytryn, L., & McKnew, D. H. (1979). Affective disorders. In J. Noshpitz. (Ed.), *Basic handbook of child psychiatry* (Vol. 2, pp. 321–340). New York: Basic.

Cytryn, L., McKnew, D. H., & Bunney, W. E. (1980). Diagnosis of depression in children: A reassessment. *American Journal of Psychiatry, 137,* 22–25.

Despert, L. (1947). Psychotherapy in childhood schizophrenia. *American Journal of Psychiatry, 104,* 36–43.

Dollard, J., & Miller, N. (1950). *Personality and psychotherapy.* New York: McGraw-Hill.

Edelbrock, C., & Achenbach, T. M. (1980). A typology of Child Behavior Profile patterns: Distribution and correlates for disturbed children aged 6–16. *Journal of Abnormal Child Psychology, 8,* 441–470.

Edelbrock, C., & Costello, A. J. (1988). Convergence between statistically derived behavior problem syndromes and child psychiatric diagnoses. *Journal of Abnormal Child Psychology, 16,* 219–231.

Edelbrock, C., Costello, A. J., & Kessler, M. D. (1984). Empirical corroboration of the Attention Deficit Disorder. *Journal of the American Academy of Child Psychiatry, 23,* 285–290.

Eisenberg, L., & Kanner, L. (1956). Early infantile autism, 1943–1955. *American Journal of Orthopsychiatry, 26,* 556–566.

Erikson, E. H. (1963). *Childhood in society* (2nd ed.). New York: Norton.

Erikson, E. H. (1980). Elements of a psychoanalytic theory of psychosocial development. In S. I. Greenspan & G. H. Pollock (Eds.), *The course of life: Psychoanalytic contributions toward understanding personality development. Vol. I. Infancy and early childhood* (pp. 11–61). Adelphi, MD: NIMH Mental Health Study Center.

Flavell, J. H., & Ross, L. (Eds.). (1981). *Social cognitive development: Frontiers and possible futures.* New York: Cambridge University Press.

Fleming, J. E., & Offord, D. R. (1990). Epidemiology of childhood depressive disorders: A critical review. *Journal of the American Academy of Child and Adolescent Psychiatry, 29,* 571–580.

Freud, A. (1965). *Normality and pathology in childhood.* New York: International Universities Press.

Freud, S. (1953). Three essays on the theory of sexuality (1905). In *Standard edition of the complete psychological works of Sigmund Freud* (Vol. 7). London: Hogarth Press.

Frommer, E. A. (1967). Treatment of childhood depression with antidepressant drugs. *British Medical Journal, 1,* 729–732.

Goodman, R., & Stevenson, J. (1989). A twin study of hyperactivity — II. The aetiological role of genes, family relationships, and family adversity. *Journal of Child Psychology and Psychiatry, 30,* 691–709.

Greenspan, S. I., & Pollock, G. H. (Eds.). (1980). *The course of life: Psychoanalytic contributions toward understanding personality development.* Adelphi, MD: NIMH Mental Health Study Center.

Griesinger, W. (1867) *Mental pathology and therapeutics* (C. L. Robertson & J. Rutherford, Trans.). London: New Sydenham Society. (Original work published 1845).

Holmes, F. B. (1936). An experimental investigation of a method of overcoming children's fears. *Child Development, 7,* 6–30.

Howlin, P., & Rutter, M. (1987). *Treatment of autistic children.* Cichester, England: Wiley.

Jones, M. C. (1924). A laboratory study of fear: The case of Peter. *Pedagogical Seminary, 31,* 308–315.

Kanner, L. (1943). Autistic disturbances of affective contact. *Nervous Child, 2,* 217–250.

Kanner, L. (1971). Childhood psychosis: A historical overview. *Journal of Autism and Childhood Schizophrenia, 1,* 14–19.

Kanner, L., Rodrigues, A., & Ashenden, B. (1972). How far can autistic children go in matters of social adaptation? *Journal of Autism and Childhood Schizophrenia, 2,* 9–33.

Kasanin, J., & Kaufman, M. R. (1929). A study of the functional psychoses in childhood. *American Journal of Psychiatry, 9,* 307–384.

Kashani, J. M., Husain, A., Shekim, W. O., Hodges, K. K., Cytryn, L., & McKnew, D. H. (1981). Current perspectives on childhood depression: An overview. *American Journal of Psychiatry, 138,* 143–153.

Kazdin, A. E. (1985). *Treatment of antisocial behavior in children and adolescents.* Homewood, IL: Dorsey.

Kendall, P. C. (Ed.). (1991). *Child and adolescent therapy. Cognitive–behavioral approaches.* New York: Guilford.

Kendall, P. C., & Braswell, L. (1985). *Cognitive-behavioral therapy for impulsive children.* New York: Guilford.

Kendler, T. S., & Kendler, H. H. (1970). An ontogeny of optional shift behavior. *Child Development, 41,* 1–27.

Klein, N. C., Barton, C., & Alexander, J. F. (1980). Intervention and evaluation in family settings. In R. H. Price & P. E. Politser (Eds.), *Evaluation and action in the social environment.* New York: Academic Press.

Kovacs, M., & Beck, A. T. (1977). An empirical-clinical approach toward a definition of childhood depression. In J. G. Schulterbrandt & A. Raskin (Eds.), *Depression in childhood:*

Diagnosis, treatment, and conceptual models. New York: Raven.

Kraepelin, E. (1883). *Compendium der Psychiatrie* [Compendium of psychiatry]. Leipzig: Abel.

Lazarus, A. A., Davison, G. C., & Polefka, D. A. (1965). Classical and operant factors in the treatment of school phobia. *Journal of Abnormal Psychology, 70,* 225–229.

Lejeune, J., Gautier, M., & Turpin, R. (1963). Study of the somatic chromosomes of nine mongoloid idiot children. In S. H. Boyer (Ed.), *Papers on human genetics.* Englewood Cliffs, NJ: Prentice-Hall. (Original work published 1959).

London, P. (1972). The end of ideology in behavior modification. *American Psychologist, 27,* 913–920.

Lotter, V. (1978). Follow-up studies. In M. Rutter & E. Schopler (Eds.), *Autism: A reappraisal of concepts and treatment.* New York: Plenum.

Love, L. R., & Kaswan, J. W. (1974). *Troubled children: Their families, schools, and treatments.* New York: Wiley.

Marshall, P. (1989). Attention deficit disorder and allergy: A neurochemical model of the relation between the illnesses. *Psychological Bulletin, 106,* 434–446.

Masson, J. M. (1984). *The assault on truth: Freud's suppression of the seduction theory.* New York: Farrar, Straus, & Giroux.

Mattison, R., Cantwell, D. P., Russell, A. T., & Will, L. (1979). A comparison of DSM–II and DSM–III in the diagnosis of childhood psychiatric disorders. *Archives of General Psychiatry, 36,* 1217–1222.

Mezzich, A. C., Mezzich, J. E., & Coffman, G. A. (1985). Reliability of DSM–III vs. DSM–II in child psychopathology. *Journal of the American Academy of Child Psychiatry, 24,* 273–280.

Miller, L. C. (1967). Louisville Behavior Checklist for males 6–12. *Psychological Reports, 21,* 885–896.

Miller, L. C., Barrett, C. L., Hampe, E., & Noble, H. (1972). Comparison of reciprocal inhibition, psychotherapy, and waiting list control for phobic children. *Journal of Abnormal Psychology, 79,* 269–279.

Mowrer, O. H., & Mowrer, W. M. (1938). Enuresis: A method for its study and treatment. *American Journal of Orthopsychiatry, 8,* 436–459.

Ochroch, R. (1981). *The diagnosis and treatment of minimal brain dysfunction in children. A clinical approach.* New York: Human Sciences Press.

Ollendick, T., & Gruen, G. E. (1972). Treatment of a bodily injury phobia with implosive therapy. *Journal of Consulting and Clinical Psychology, 38,* 389–393.

Peterson, D. R. (1961). Behavior problems of middle childhood. *Journal of Consulting Psychology, 25,* 205–209.

Piaget, J. (1977). The role of action in the development of thinking. In W. F. Overton & J. M. Gallagher (Eds.), *Knowledge and development* (Vol. I). New York: Plenum.

Quay, H. C. (1986). Classification. In H. C. Quay & J. S. Werry (Eds.), *Psychopathological disorders of childhood* (3rd ed.). New York: Wiley.

Rank, B. (1949). Adaptation of the psychoanalytic technique for the treatment of young children with atypical development. *American Journal of Orthopsychiatry, 19,* 130–139.

Rosch, E. (1978). Principles of categorization. In E. Rosch & B. B. Lloyd (Eds.), *Cognition and categorization.* Hillsdale, NJ: Lawrence Erlbaum Associates.

Rosen, B. M., Bahn, A. K., & Kramer, M. (1964). Demographic and diagnostic characteristics of psychiatric clinic outpatients in the U.S.A. *American Journal of Orthopsychiatry, 34,* 455–468.

Shaffer, D., McNamara, N., & Pincus, J. H. (1974). Controlled observations on patterns of activity, attention, and impulsivity in brain-damaged and psychiatrically disturbed boys. *Journal of Psychological Medicine, 4,* 4–18.

Siegel, B., Anders, T. F., Ciaranello, R. D., Bienenstock, B., & Kraemer, H. C. (1986). Empirically derived subclassification of the autustic syndrome. *Journal of Autism and Developmental Disabilities, 16,* 275-293.

Spitzer, R. L., & Cantwell, D. P. (1980). The DSM-III classification of the psychiatric disorders of infancy, childhood, and adolescence. *Journal of the American Academy of Child Psychiatry, 19,* 356-370.

Spivak, G., & Shure, M. B. (1982). The cognition of social adjustment. In B. B. Lahey & A. E. Kazdin (Eds.), *Advances in clinical child psychology* (Vol. 5). New York: Plenum.

Strauss, A. A., & Lehtinen, L. E. (1947). *Psychopathology and education of the brain-injured child.* New York: Grune & Stratton.

Strober, M., Green, J., & Carlson, G. (1981). The reliability of psychiatric diagnosis in hospitalized adolescents: Inter-rater agreement using the DSM-III. *Archives of General Psychiatry, 38,* 141-145.

Thomas, A., Chess, S., & Birch, H. G. (1968). *Temperament and behavior disorders in children.* New York: New York University Press.

Ullman, D., Egan, D., Fiedler, N., Jurenec, G., Pliske, R., Thompson, P., & Doherty, M. E. (1981). The many faces of hyperactivity: Similarities and differences in diagnostic policies. *Journal of Consulting and Clinical Psychology, 49,* 694-704.

Wade, T. C., Baker, T. B., & Hartmann, D. T. (1979). Behavior therapists' self-reported views and practices. *The Behavior Therapist, 2,* 3-6.

Waterman, A. S., Geary, P. S., & Waterman, C. K. (1974). Longitudinal study of changes in ego identity status from the freshman to the senior year of college. *Developmental Psychology, 10,* 387-392.

Watson, J. B. (1913). Psychology as the behaviorist views it. *Psychological Review, 20,* 158-177.

Watson, J. B. (1919). *Psychology from the standpoint of a behaviorist.* Philadelphia: Lippincott.

Watson, J. B. (1924). *Behaviorism.* New York: People's Publishing.

Weinberg, W. A., Rutman, J., Sullivan, L., Penick, E. C., & Dietz, S. G. (1973). Depression in children referred to an educational diagnostic center: Diagnosis and treatment. *Journal of Pediatrics, 83,* 1065-1072.

Weinstein, S. R., Noam, G. G., Grimes, K., Stone, K., & Schwab-Stone, M. (1990). Convergence of DSM-III diagnoses and self-reported symptoms in child and adolescent inpatients. *Journal of the American Academy of Child and Adolescent Psychiatry, 29,* 627-634.

Weiss, G., & Hechtman, L. T. (1986). *Hyperactive children grown up: Empirical findings and theoretical considerations.* New York: Guilford.

Weisz, J. R., Weiss, B., Alicke, M. D., & Klotz, M. L. (1987). Effectiveness of psychotherapy with children and adolescents: A meta-analysis for clinicians. *Journal of Consulting and Clinical Psychology, 55,* 542-549.

Wellisch, D. K., Vincent, J., & Ro-Trock, G. K. (1976). Family therapy versus individual therapy: A study of adolescents and their parents. In D. H. L. Olson (Ed.), *Treating relationships.* Lake Mills, IA: Graphic Publications.

Werry, J. S., Methven, R. J., Fitzpatrick, J., & Dixon, H. (1983). The interrater reliability of DSM-III in children. *Journal of Abnormal Child Psychology, 11,* 341-354.

Wolman, B. B. (1970). *Children without childhood.* New York: Grune & Stratton.

Wolpe, J. (1958). *Psychotherapy by reciprocal inhibition.* Stanford, CA: Stanford University Press.

World Health Organization. (1978). *Mental disorders: Glossary and guide to their classification in accordance with the Ninth Revision of the International Classification of Diseases.* Geneva: Author.

12 Applied Developmental Psychology

Edward Zigler
Yale University

Matia Finn-Stevenson
Yale University

INTRODUCTION

Researchers in developmental psychology have become increasingly appreciative of the close link between basic research in child development and the applications of that research. Basic research is generally defined as any research that is motivated by the desire to expand knowledge. Applied research is defined as research that is conducted in an effort to solve a problem or in order to provide information that can be put to some specific use. Although these two types of research are distinct by definition, they actually overlap and contribute to each other, to the benefit of both.

Applied research in developmental psychology encompasses a broad array of studies, as the field has practical applications and relevance. For example, the research on a number of developmental topics in cognition, learning, and language acquisition may be considered applied research, as it is often used in educational settings in efforts to help parents and teachers in their task of educating children, or to enhance children's abilities to learn (Belmont, 1989; Dillon & Sternberg, 1986; Rice, 1989). Some of the research conducted on sex-role acquisition and gender differences also has applied uses. Such research is designed to enhance our understanding of how sex roles in this society influence career and other choices, values, and behaviors (Eccles & Hoffman, 1984; Jacklin, 1989; Stipek, Chap. 10, this volume). It also has implications for child-rearing practices in which both boys and girls are rewarded for displaying positive behaviors that are thought to be stereotypically male or stereotypically female. Because many such developmental topics are covered in other chapters in this book, we have chosen to focus in this chapter on the integration of child development research and social policy, and the increasing recognition among researchers that some of their work should be directed toward the understanding and solution of contemporary problems faced by children and families (Horowitz & O'Brien, 1989; Stevenson & Siegel, 1984; Zigler, Kagan, & Klugman, 1983).

Horowitz and O'Brien (1989) highlight this trend toward the integration of child development research and social policy, noting that many researchers are making a conscious effort to relate developmental topics — even those oriented toward basic research — directly to issues of the health and welfare of children as reflected in social policy. Several developments have precipitated this trend in the field, most notably the implementation during the 1960s and 1970s of federally sponsored social programs. The proliferation of a wide range of such programs provided an opportunity for developmental psychologists to apply their knowledge and training to new areas of study such as children's services, which had not previously received attention from the scientific community (Garwood, Phillips, Hartman, & Zigler, 1989; Salkind, 1983; Takanishi, DeLeon, & Pallak, 1983). Other developments that precipitated psychologists' involvement in social policy issues were: (a) the increased recognition among researchers of the reciprocity between basic and applied studies (Bryant, 1972; Garner, 1972; Zigler, 1980), and the need to utilize both of these types of research in the study of children (Weisz, 1978; Zigler, 1980); and (b) the realization that children are influenced not only by the people in their immediate social settings, but also by aspects of the larger and more remote social systems such as the school, the work place, the community, the government, and the mass media. As a result of this new understanding, developmental psychologists have broadened their research to include ecological studies that examine development within the wider social context (Bronfenbrenner, 1979). They have also begun to conduct studies on the impact of societal changes on the lives of children (Brim & Dustan, 1983; Hetherington, Hagan, & Anderson, 1989), examining such issues as maternal employment, infant day care, divorce, family violence, and teen pregnancy.

In this chapter we examine some of these areas of study and show how findings from the research may be used to clarify policy options and provide guidelines for the development and operation of programs designed to enhance child and family life. We also discuss the role of developmental psychologists in the policy arena, and the possibilities and problems inherent in the use of research in policy settings. The reader will see that although a number of opportunities exist for developmental psychologists to contribute to decisions about social policies, psychologists' effectiveness in this regard is dependent not only on their knowledge of scientific research, but also on their familiarity with the policy process and their ability to work with policy makers.

INTEGRATION OF CHILD DEVELOPMENT RESEARCH AND SOCIAL POLICY

Researchers' focus on social policy issues and the research they conduct on the impact of societal changes on the lives of children have important implications. The past 40 years have been a period of vast changes for American society as the result of now-familiar shifts in the economy and employment patterns, in family composition, and in the age structure of the population. In order to assess how these changes are influencing the growth and development of children, a number of researchers are compiling childhood social indicators. These are measures of the constancies and changes in the lives of children and of the health, achievement, behavior, and well-being of children themselves (Parke & Peterson, 1981; Zill, Sigal, & Brim, 1983). The systematic compilation of such indicators provides a knowledge base for understanding the factors that affect development, as well as valuable data that facilitate our ability to identify and respond to the needs of children and their families.

On the basis of such data, psychologists and others concerned about human welfare note that children face a number of problems in the areas of health and psychological well-being. It has been found, for example, that a large number of children experience serious mental health problems ranging from extreme depression and suicide to more moderate behavioral problems characterized by antisocial acts (Knitzer, 1982; Select Committee on Children, Youth and Families, 1987a). The Committee of the Institute of Medicine (1989) found that in the United States, 12% of children under the age of 18 (7.5 million children) have a diagnosable mental illness, and that many other children exhibit other indicators of mental health problems, including substance abuse, teen pregnancy, and school dropout. Although more research is needed to isolate the determinants of childhood mental illness, it is suggested that a variety of biological, psychological, social, and environmental factors are involved as causal agents, and that these factors may interact to exacerbate the vulnerability to mental disorders.

Of utmost importance to policy makers and others concerned with children's well-being are the social and environmental risk factors associated with the onset of mental dysfunction in increasing numbers of children (Tuma, 1989). Many of these risk factors, such as poverty (Garmezy, 1985; Rutter, 1976), physical or sexual abuse (Allen & Oliver, 1982; Kashani et al., 1987), and instability in the family environment (Rutter, 1987; Sameroff et al., 1987) can be significantly influenced by policy decisions, and therefore demand not only the attention of policy makers, but also the attention of developmental researchers.

Research on Social Changes Affecting Children

For developmental psychologists, the benefits of being involved in social policy issues include not only the opportunity to contribute to the well-being of children, but also the opportunity for research. The opportunity for research is exemplified by several areas of study that were generated by societal changes. Consider, for example, the research on fatherhood (e.g., Lamb, 1981, 1986; Pruett, 1987). Fathers have always played an important role in children's lives; however, it was not until recently that psychologists began to study the relationship between fathers and children and the ramifications of paternal involvement in the lives of children. Scientific interest in the topic of fatherhood was triggered in part by changes in the traditional roles assumed by men and women and the policy implications inherent in such changes.

Numerous other societal changes have also affected children and, at the same time, have provided opportunities for research. Although it is beyond the scope of this chapter to discuss all such changes, we will explore several of these as examples of areas in which developmental psychology research can help identify the problems children confront and the steps necessary to alleviate those problems.

Children in Poverty. One of the most significant social changes in the past decade has been the increase in the number of American children who live in poverty. The U.S. Census Bureau (1988b) estimates that one out of every four children lives in poverty. For African-American children, the situation is even worse; half of all African-American children under 5 years of age live in poverty (National Center for Children in Poverty, 1990). Several factors have contributed to the increasing numbers of children in poverty. One such factor is the declining economy, which results in low wages. A report published by the Economic Policy Institute (1986) notes that between 1973 and 1984, weekly wages, adjusted for inflation, declined by 14.5%, and that hourly wages declined by 10.1%. In an analysis of the U.S. job market, Reischauer (1987) found that only one out of three jobs pays enough to keep a family of four above the poverty line. With jobs paying so little, many women have had to join the labor force to help supplement the family income. But even among dual worker families, median family income, adjusted for inflation, declined by 3.1% between 1973 and 1984 (Economic Policy Institute, 1986); had it not been for the additional money brought home by women, the drop in family income would have been an even more severe 9.5%.

These economic problems are even worse for the growing number of single-parent families, because only one parent's income is available. For example, in 1988, 59% of single-parent families were below the poverty level, as compared with 10% of two-parent families. In single-parent families, it is often the woman who supports the family, a particularly important point because women's income tends to be much lower than men's. The median annual income of single-parent households is $13,500 if the mother works, and only $4,500 if she does not work (U.S. Department of Labor, 1988). The issue of single-parenting is not only an issue of gender; it is also an issue of race. About 70% of African-American and Hispanic single-parent families, compared with half of White single-parent families, live below the poverty level (U.S. Census Bureau, 1988a).

Another factor that has contributed to the increase in the number of poor children is the decrease in the amount of public money available for services to the poor. As a result, since 1981 numerous social service programs such as Medicaid and Aid to Families with Dependent Children (AFDC) have been altered by restrictions in eligibility criteria. Such restrictions contribute to an increase in the number of families who are poor but do not benefit from services that may buffer the effects of poverty (Garwood et al., 1989; Kimmich, 1985).

For children, the consequences of living in poverty are numerous and include assaults on their physical and psychological well-being. Researchers have found, for example, that poverty is associated with poor child health care (Margolis & Farran, 1985). Poor prenatal care, malnutrition, and low birth weight — factors that can result in developmental delays, learning disabilities, and other developmental problems — are also associated with poverty (National Center for Children in Poverty, 1988). The environmental stresses and feelings of powerlessness that accompany poverty have been linked to low achievement in school and mental dysfunction in children (Albee, 1986; Institute of Medicine, 1989; Rutter, 1976).

Understanding these and other consequences of living in poverty can provide a direction for policy. In addition, by examining the effects of poverty on children, researchers gain insights into other environmental effects on development. This point is highlighted by past research that has linked poverty with lack of prenatal care and infant mortality. For over a decade, researchers have noted that infant mortality among African-Americans is high because many poor pregnant African-American women do not receive prenatal care. However, a recent study of other ethnic groups suggests that other factors besides poverty and lack of prenatal care may play a role in infant mortality. A study conducted by The Centers for Disease Control (1990) found that pregnant Mexican-American women who have a low level of education, are poor, and receive little or no prenatal care, nevertheless have a lower rate of infant mortality than poor African-American women. Whereas for poor African-Americans, 18.7 out of every 1,000 infants die before their first birthday, for poor Mexican-Americans, the rate is only 9.0 per 1,000 infants. It is too early to determine the reasons underlying the difference in infant mortality rates between these two groups, but researchers suggest that dietary factors may play a role, as well as social support, which appears to be more prevalent in poor Mexican-American families than in poor African-American families.

Changes in Family Life. Besides the increase in the number of children in poverty, other striking societal changes have occurred in recent years, notable among which is the transformation in family life. Developmental psychologists generally agree that although the family has undergone radical changes during the past several decades, it remains the most important institution in influencing child growth and development. Researchers emphasize, however, the need to acknowledge and study the multiple forms that families may take. The traditional nuclear family, which includes the father as breadwinner, the mother as homemaker, and two or more children living at home, represents a small percentage of all families in the United States, and is therefore only one of several contexts necessary for the study of children. Some of the different forms that families now take are families with both parents as wage-earners, single-parent families, unrelated persons living together, and what have come to be called *blended families* (also known as reconstituted or new extended families) created by the divorce and subsequent remarriage of one or both parents (Hetherington et al., 1989; Lamb, 1982b).

Changes in family structure may not be, in and of themselves, necessarily stressful to children; rather, factors associated with these changes act as stressors. For example, whereas there may be no effects associated with living in a single-parent family per se, a significant number of such families are poor and under stress, and children of these families are at risk for experiencing the consequences of poverty detailed above. Single-parent families, although not necessarily homogeneous, are generally characterized by female heads of household, poverty, and the presence of young children (U.S. Census Bureau, 1988a). Currently, one out of every four children in the United States, and half of all African-American children, live in a single-parent family (U.S. Census Bureau, 1988b; National Center for Children in Poverty, 1988).

Although single-parent families in particular may be in need of social support, many two-parent families function in relative isolation and lack social support, as people today move frequently in search of employment (McCullough, 1987; Packard, 1972). As a result, many families do not have the support and counsel of their extended families and friends, nor the child care by relatives on which many families could at one time rely. Access to a support system is important because it often mediates the negative consequences of stress (Garmezy, 1985; Gore, 1980).

Divorce. Another change in family life is the growing prevalence of divorce. Although the divorce rate has stabilized somewhat in recent years, close to half of all marriages end in divorce (Cherlin, 1981), and in 60% of these marriages children are involved (Select Committee on Children, Youth, and Families, 1983). Glick and Lin (1986) estimated that 40% to 50% of children born in the late 1980s will experience the divorce of their parents, and that a majority of these children will also experience the remarriage of one or both parents.

Some researchers regard divorce positively, noting that the high rate of divorce per se is not a matter of concern because it means that there are now fewer unhappy, destructive families that stay together for the sake of the children or for some other reason (Bane, 1976). Although divorce may be considered a positive solution to destructive family life, it is also a critical experience that can have negative consequences for the entire family, especially the children. This point is made on the basis of several reports that have been issued by two major research projects on the impact of divorce on children; Mavis Hetherington and her colleagues head one project, while the other is headed by Judith Wallerstein and Joan Kelly from the Marin County (California) Mental Health Center. Several other researchers have contributed to our knowledge of the impact of divorce on children; among them are Joseph Goldstein, Anna Freud, and Albert Solnit, whose work, described later in this chapter, is a vivid example of the synthesis of theoretical principles organized in such a way that they are applicable to specific practical situations.

To summarize the research findings to date, it appears that for children, the divorce of their parents is not a single event but rather a sequence of experiences, each one representing a transition and each requiring adjustments (Wallerstein, 1985; Wallerstein & Kelly, 1979). The transitions center around the shift from the family life prior to the divorce; the disequilibrium and disorganization immediately following the divorce; the experimentation with a variety of coping mechanisms, living arrangements, and relationships; and the eventual reorganization, and attainment of equilibrium. Households in which divorce has occurred are characterized by increased disorganization and by marked changes in the management of children, including inconsistency of discipline, diminished communication and nurturance, and the holding of fewer expectations of mature behavior from the children (Hetherington, Cox, & Cox, 1978, 1981).

Almost all children are found to experience divorce and the transition periods that follow it as painful experiences (Hetherington et al., 1989; Guidubaldi, Cleminshaw, Perry, & McLoughlin, 1983; Kurdek & Sieski, 1980). Even children who eventually recognize the divorce of their parents as constructive initially undergo considerable stress with the breakup of the family. Children vary widely in their reaction and adjustment to divorce: Some are actively negative, whereas others are more subdued in their reaction, and some also change in their school performance during the adjustment period following the divorce (Kurdek & Siesky, 1979, 1980). In addition, some children seem to adjust well to the divorce in its early stages, but show negative effects of the divorce over time (Wallerstein & Corbin, 1991; Wallerstein, Corbin, & Lewis, 1988). Developmental consequences seem to be worse for children who experience divorce as one of multiple stressors. For example, for some children divorce brings not only emotional pain, changes in living arrangements, and changes in time spent with the noncustodial parent, but also changes in income if the noncustodial parent fails to pay for child support (Hernandez, 1988). The fact that so many children in this nation are involved in divorce, and that divorce has become socially acceptable, has not been found to alleviate the pain; this point was documented in a book by and for the children of divorce (Rofes, 1980).

Parents also undergo emotional, psychological, and economic stresses following the divorce (Kurdek & Blisk, 1983). Researchers have found, for example, that some parents experience such acute distress that they neglect to attend to the children, to recognize their children's painful experience with the divorce, and to prepare the children for the marital breakup. This is especially so when young children are involved (Hetherington et al., 1989; Kurdek & Siesky, 1979). Researchers further note that the intensity and duration of the emotional and psychological distress a child may suffer due to the divorce are related to the psychological status of the custodial parent, and the availability and involvement of the noncustodial parent (Guidubaldi, Cleminshaw, Perry, Natasi, & Lightel, 1986; Hess & Camara, 1979).

The most vulnerable children of divorce are those who are involved in legal battles between their divorcing parents on *custody issues* and *visitation rights*. These legal battles can continue indefinitely because any decision on any of the issues is modifiable by the courts. The courts attempt to make custody decisions on the basis of the "best interests of the child"; however, in practice, the explication of this principle is far from easy. Judges and lawyers often are not trained to determine what the best interests of the child may be (Wallerstein, 1986), and they have little help in this regard because few psychologists or other mental health professionals look on the court as an arena of their interest. When the courts have psychological services attached to them, they are often understaffed or staffed by people who are not trained to work with children (Wallerstein & Kelly, 1979). Goldstein, Freud, and Solnit (1973, 1979) have made some attempt to provide guidance for decisions on custody issues. On the basis of principles of developmental psychology and psychiatry, the authors recommend, for example, that decisions regarding child custody be resolved in accelerated proceedings instead of long, drawn-out procedures; that they have final effect and not be reversible; and that they award full custody of the children to the *psychological parent*. However, there is difficulty in applying some of these ideas because the terms used (e.g., psychological parent) are not sufficiently explicit (Thompson, 1986). In addition, there is controversy surrounding Goldstein and colleagues' recommendations (e.g., Benedek & Benedek, 1977); some psychologists emphasize the value inherent in the child's maintaining a close relationship with both parents (Guidubaldi et al., 1986), a point that contradicts the suggestions made by Goldstein and colleagues. Although the work of these authors is not fully accepted in practice, their efforts are important, as they have paved the way for others to think about the use of knowledge and theoretical principles in establishing some criteria for such practical decisions as those involved in child custody cases.

What we have described is admittedly only a brief summary of the research literature on the impact of divorce on children. Numerous other issues related to divorce have been studied, and there are several important research questions that remain to be investigated (see Hetherington et al., 1989). However, the brief review presented here should be sufficient for the reader to realize that the research on divorce has widespread implications. An understanding of how and when divorce affects children is important not only to research and clinical psychologists but also to others who come in contact with children and families. Teachers, for instance, need to be alerted to these findings so that they can be sensitive to any changes in children's behavior in school, and can offer children and parents appropriate advice and guidelines about possible ways they can cope with the changes going on in their lives (Kurdek, 1981; Kurdek & Siesky, 1979). Hetherington and colleagues (1989) note that schools and other settings such as child care centers that "provide a warm, structured and predictable environment can offer stability to children experiencing chaotic household routines, an altered parent, and inconsistent parenting" (p. 309). They further note that teachers, child care providers, and other adults who interact with children can help validate the self-worth of children of divorce.

Pediatricians can also be a source of support for children and should be alerted to these findings from the research, for the same reasons. Also, lawyers and judges who have primary and extensive involvement in divorce cases should be made aware of the research and its implications. Ideally, psychological support for parents and children should be offered immediately when divorce proceedings are begun. An important development in divorce cases is the use of mediators rather than lawyers, and the settling of cases outside the confines of the courtroom wherever possible (Bahr, 1981; Wallerstein, 1991). The increasing use of mediators, who are often psychologists or social workers with access to legal advice, is admittedly due to the high costs of divorce. Families who have used divorce mediation, however, consider the psychological support associated with the method—for the parents as well as the children—to be one of its major benefits (Bahr, 1981; Wallerstein & Corbin, 1991).

Given the research on the many stressors on divorcing parents and their inability to care for their children appropriately, it is also important to develop support for children outside the home. Keeping teachers, child care providers, and pediatricians informed of the ways they can help children of divorce is one important method, but policy makers can also take a more active role by instituting support services to buffer the psychological stresses of divorce. There are several successful support programs of this kind in schools across the United States (Weiss, 1989). Their number, however, is not nearly large enough to meet the needs of the children who need their services.

Maternal Employment.   Another recent change in family life that has had far-reaching social implications is the increase in the number of women who are working outside of the home. This change is largely due to economic necessity and changes in attitudes about women's roles. Whereas mothers tended in the past to be employed part time and to move in and out of the labor force depending on the ages of their children, many mothers today are employed full time even when their children are very young. Currently over 62% of women with children are employed outside the home (U.S. Census Bureau, 1988b). This figure represents a tenfold increase in maternal employment since the end of World War II, and it has not yet peaked.

Hoffman (1989) noted that maternal employment is not a new phenomenon among mothers with school-age children; for the past 20 years, almost 70% of these mothers worked outside the home. However, during the past few years we have witnessed an enormous increase in the number of employed mothers of young children. The fastest growing subgroup of employed mothers is currently mothers with children under 1 year of age. In fact, one out of two infants under 1 year of age has a working mother, and the percentage of mothers with children under age 6 has increased from 12% in 1950 to 57% in 1987 (U.S. Census Bureau, 1988b). The potential impact of this trend on children is enormous, as families have to rely on out-of-home care for their children, and in increasing numbers, they relegate the rearing of the children to people who are not related.

For older children, maternal employment has not been shown, in and of itself, to be harmful (Greenberger, 1989; Hoffman, 1989). What does seem to have negative effects on children are parental attitudes to the mother's employment (Hoffman, 1986, 1989). With infants, however, there is concern that child care may interfere with the attachment relationship between the parent and child (Belsky, 1986, 1987), although researchers still disagree on this issue (Phillips, McCartney, Scarr, & Howes, 1987) and suggest that more research is needed before we can come to any conclusions (Clarke-Stewart, 1989).

Some researchers also point out that a key factor in the effects of infant day care is the quality of the out-of-home care (Phillips et al., 1987). Others note, too, that infants in out-of-home care differ, some of them experiencing stressful family life. Gamble and Zigler (1986), in a review of the research on infant day care, note that infants in out-of-home care who experience stress in the family are more likely than nonstressed infants in out-of-home care to be negatively affected by the day-care experience.

For many infants and children in out-of-home care, stressful family life is a reality. Although women are working outside of the home, they have not given up the primary responsibility of child rearing, which creates a great deal of stress (Hoffman, 1989; Moen & Dempster, 1987) and guilt about their competency as mothers. In dual-worker families, men also experience stress, guilt, and difficulty balancing work and family life. Friedman (1987) found that 40% of employed parents—men and women— report that they experience severe conflict, guilt, and stress.

Increased Demand for Child Care. For many employed parents, the stress associated with the attempt to balance work and family life is heightened by lack of child-care services. Recently there has been a great deal of concern among policy makers, parents, and legislators concerning the availability of good quality, affordable child care. Demand for child care has exceeded supply, particularly for infants and toddlers and for children who are disabled or economically disadvantaged (Hayes, Palmer, & Zaslow, 1990), and for school-age children, creating, in effect, a national crisis (Zigler & Lang, 1990).

Although the issue has received extensive attention in the past 2 or 3 years, the lack of child-care services has been a problem for quite some time. In 1970, at the White House Conference on Children, it was noted that the need for more child care of good quality was the number one priority for our nation to address (White House Conference on Children, 1970). This need, however, not only continues, but has been exacerbated, and has only been partially addressed by recent federal legislation. This legislation, enacted in 1990, represents the first child-care policy for our nation, and child-care advocates have worked for 20 years to accomplish it.

There are several reasons why the fundamental need for child care has been overlooked in the policy arena for so many years. First, some researchers and lay people have questioned the advantages of child care by nonrelatives, and others have been ideologically opposed to child care outside of the home (Nelson, 1982). Whether this type of care compares to care by a mother is a complex and controversial issue, but crucial to this debate should be a consideration of the reality of the matter: In a time when families are finding it an economic necessity for both parents or the single parent to work outside the home, care by nonrelatives is not an option — it is a necessity.

Another problem that stood in the way of a national child-care policy was the lack of public awareness of the need for child-care services (Zigler & Lang, 1990); however, as more families have experienced difficulties finding good quality, affordable child care, the media has paid increasing attention to the issue. For a time between 1987 and 1990, stories on the child-care issue appeared with regularity in the popular media. As a result, legislators at the federal and state levels began to consider the issue and have enacted policies that partially address the need for child care, for example, subsidizing the cost of child care for low-income families.

Availability of Care.   Researchers have investigated several aspects of the child-care issue. One such issue, the availability of care, is controversial; some researchers note that enough services exist to meet the demand (Haskins, 1989) and others contend otherwise (Child Care Action Campaign, 1988). However, there is agreement that in at least two aspects of child care — care for infants and care for school-age children — the demand exceeds supply.

When parents cannot find child care, children are sometimes left alone at home, often in the care only of siblings not much older than they are. Such self-care is an especially acute problem with school-age children. Estimates of the number of children engaged in self-care (also referred to as latch-key children) vary widely, because parents seem to be reluctant to admit that their children are left alone, but all estimates count millions of children caring for themselves (Hayes et al., 1990). There are conflicting reports about whether self-care is harmful or beneficial to school-age children. Some researchers note that they found no difference between children in self-care and supervised children on various measures such as self-esteem, susceptibility to negative peer pressure, and achievement measures (Rodman, Pratto, & Nelson, 1985; Steinberg, 1985). Others argue that self-care may even have positive effects, such as the development of independence (e.g., Korchin, 1981).

Yet some studies support the view that self-care is potentially harmful. Long and Long (1983) and Ginter (1981) found that self-care children are more fearful and lonely than children cared for by adults. Garbarino (1981) emphasized the safety hazards that confront children who are home alone. In a study in Detroit, for instance, an investigator discovered that one-sixth of the residential fires in that city involved an unattended child (Smock, 1977). In addition, in one of the most recent and largest studies on the issue, Richardson and colleagues (1989) found that children in self-care were more susceptible to substance abuse (alcohol, cigarettes, and marijuana) than supervised children. This difference held for children in dual-parent, high-income families, as well as for children who earned good grades and those who played sports.

Cost of Care. Another aspect of the child-care issue is the high cost of care. The cost of child care varies depending on the location, the type of care (e.g., family day-care provider vs. nursery school), the age of the child, and the quality of the care. Although the cost of care varies, it is estimated that child-care costs are between $1,500 and $10,000 per year per child, depending on the quality of care and the age of the child. Care for younger children is more expensive; full-time care for a preschooler is estimated at $3,000 per year on average, whereas full-time child care for an infant can be as high as $9,600. Clearly, child-care costs represent a major expenditure for families, and this burden is heaviest for low-income families. Although low-income families may spend less on child care in absolute terms than do higher-income families, the percentage of their income allocated for child care is much greater, often as high as 30% (Friedman, 1987; Hayes et al., 1990). Another cost that is not easily quantified is the loss of wages to parents who would work outside the home if given the opportunity to place their children in good quality, affordable care. One study found that 26% of nonworking mothers with preschool children would look for work if affordable child care was available (National Research Council, 1990).

Quality of Care. Higher-income families can afford better quality child care than low- and middle-income families, a fact that is cause for much concern, considering the very large portion of time children spend in child care. Although more research needs to be done to analyze the effects of child care in general, researchers agree that many aspects of children's development are influenced by the quality of their day-care environment (McCartney, 1984; McCartney, Scarr, Phillips, Grajek, & Schwarz, 1982), and that children will be negatively affected by poor quality care (McCartney et al., 1982; National Center for Children in Poverty, 1988).

Using the knowledge from the research, developmental psychologists have made strides in defining good quality care. Phillips (1988) made the distinction between developmentally appropriate care that is responsive to the individual needs of children and care that is merely custodial and irresponsive to the needs of the child. Howes and Rubenstein (1985) found that the quality of care children receive, whether at home, in family day care, or in a day-care center, depends on the caregiver's ability to attend to the children's individual needs and to provide them with meaningful social interactions. Other, more easily quantified measures of the quality of care include an appropriate staff-to-child ratio, depending on the age of the children, the number of children in a group, and the level of training of the child-care provider (Phillips, 1988; Roupp, Travers, Glantz, & Coelen, 1979).

Although it is not known exactly how many children experience good or poor quality care, a national study of child-care centers in five cities indicates that a significant number of children may not be receiving good quality care (Whitbrook, Phillips, & Howes, 1990). This study focused only on licensed child-care centers; however, the majority of children are not in center-based care, but in family day-care homes in which an individual, often a mother, looks after several children in her own home (Finn-Stevenson & Ward, 1990). Between 60% and 90% of family day-care homes are unlicensed and are therefore not accountable to public authority, making reliable data on children's actual day-care experiences difficult to obtain (Kamerman & Kahn, 1987). In fact, even among licensed day-care facilities, standards for the quality of care provided are often lax or unenforced (Morgan, 1987; Young & Zigler, 1986), so the fact that children are in a licensed day-care setting does not necessarily provide an assurance that they receive good quality care. For example, in some states it is permissible for one adult to care for as many as 10 infants, despite the fact that this staff-to-child ratio is not only potentially harmful in view of infants' need for individual attention, but also dangerous. In the case of fire, for instance, how could one caregiver bring 10 infants to safety?

Another aspect of good quality care is provider training. The long-term consequences of day care, especially infant day care, are not yet known as more research on the issue needs to be conducted (Clarke-Stewart, 1989). However, from the research of the past few decades (e.g., Dennis, 1973), we know that an important factor in a child's development is the quality of interaction that the child has with the adults in his or her life. Children need to be reared in an environment that is not just safe but is nurturant as well. In the same vein, parents must be assured that their infants and young children are supervised by adults who are trained and competent in the task of child care. Studies have found that child-care providers who receive training in child development provide better quality care and interact with children more positively than providers who do not have such training (Hayes et al., 1990; Roupp et al., 1979). It is interesting to note that it is not the number of years of experience working with children that separates nurturant from merely custodial providers; rather, it is the presence of training in child development (Roupp et al., 1979).

In order to address the need for trained child-care providers, in 1972 the U.S. Office of Child Development, with the support of national organizations concerned with child development and welfare, established a consortium that set out to upgrade the quality of care children receive in day-care centers. Known then as the Child Development Associate Consortium (CDAC), and now known as the CDA National Credential Program, this nonprofit organization — with the help of leading psychologists and early childhood educators — developed an assessment and credential system for child-care workers (Ward, 1976).

The CDA effort is now being directed by the National Association for the Education of Young Children (NAEYC). NAEYC has expanded its child-care training activities to include not only the CDA, but also efforts such as the creation of a developmentally appropriate curriculum guide for use by child-care workers (Bredekamp, 1989). Another NAEYC effort is the development of criteria to be used for the credentialing of child-care centers (Bredekamp, 1989). These efforts, in bringing research knowledge to bear on an emerging social problem, exemplify the interface between social policy and child development research. Providing adequate and appropriate training for caregivers in order to ensure quality care for children is a major task facing policy makers. Through the CDA and NAEYC activities, progress has been made in delineating the skills and competence necessary for the care of preschool children in groups, and in delineating quality criteria for the operation of child-care facilities. In addition, these efforts have served as catalysts for further research to ascertain what constitutes quality care and to examine the role of staff training and other factors in the overall quality of care provided in a day-care setting.

Research as a Guide to Policy and Institutional Change

It is evident, given our discussion thus far, that many decisions regarding the type and quality of child day-care facilities can be made on the basis of knowledge from child development research. As we have shown, the knowledge from the research can help clarify policy options (Zigler & Lang, 1990) as well as provide guidelines for the operation of programs (Provence, 1982).

Changes in the Work Place.   Also, research knowledge can serve as a guide for institutional changes. This is evident in changes in the workplace. Most businesses do not make provisions to help employees coordinate their work and family life, and although there have been some recent changes in this regard, few corporations regard the family as a relevant issue. However, with the two-paycheck family now the norm rather than the exception, and with the increase in single-parent households, the impact of the workplace on family life becomes a relevant issue. The relation between the two institutions has been the subject of several studies that emphasize an important point: Work and family life are not separate worlds as had been assumed, but are, rather, interdependent and overlapping, with functions and behavioral rules in each system influencing processes in the other (Fernandez, 1986; Kanter, 1977; Pleck & Staines, 1985; Staines & Pleck, 1983). This interplay between the worlds of work and family life, and its effect on children, are very much within the realm of concern of developmental psychologists.

There have been some corporate attempts to address the child-care needs of employees. These attempts include the development of on-site care centers, some of which partially offset the cost of child care for employees. Another way that corporations can support families with children is to allow flexible schedules (Bureau of National Affairs, 1986; Kuhne & Blair, 1978), part-time work opportunities (Schwartz, 1974), and job-sharing (Olmstead, 1979), all of which alternatives can provide time for child rearing. These initiatives have been shown to act as a buffer against the stresses associated with work and family life (Staines & Pleck, 1986).

The majority of corporations, however, do not provide such options to their employees (Friedman, 1987; Kamerman, 1983). Researchers can help these corporations address this issue by disseminating the results of studies that measure the productivity, satisfaction, and turnover of employees who are allowed to work on a flexible schedule. Kanter (1977) has shown that worker satisfaction and productivity have been found to be a function of family stability and other processes within the family system. It therefore behooves industry to create policies that can help families.

Related to the issue of flexible work schedules are parental leave policies that would enable parents to spend time with their infants for the first several months after birth. The first few months of a child's life is an important period during which the infant and parent become acquainted with one another, laying the foundations for a secure attachment. It is also a stressful time for parents, who have to get used to the new baby and adjust to the demands of parenting.

Parental leave is necessary not only to allow the mother adequate time to recover physically from the delivery, but also to enable parents to adjust to the changes in their family and to give the infant the care he or she needs for adequate development (Hopper & Zigler, 1988). Yet advocates of parental leave argue that the need for a "bonding period" is only one reason for parental leave. Also important for parents is the opportunity to take time off from work to care for children when they are ill, or to care for a newborn adopted child.

Opponents of parental leave agree on the fundamental importance of caring for newborn and ill children, but argue that employers should not have to bear the responsibility for employees' needs. Trzcinski and Finn-Stevenson (1991) pointed out that this type of thinking goes hand-in-hand with the ideological belief in the United States that the way to protect American families is to protect the companies for which they work, and that when a conflict arises between industry and families, industry's needs should be protected. This idea has been rejected in other countries; the United States and South Africa are the only two industrialized nations that do not have a national parental leave policy. Even maternity leave, which is generally available for only 6 weeks after birth for the mother to recover physically, is structured so that only employers who provide a medical disability leave policy are required to provide maternity leave, thereby excluding many women (Finn-Stevenson, Emmel, & Barbuto, 1988).

Although there is much to be done to bring U.S. policies up to standards other countries now hold, evidence from psychiatrists, developmental psychologists, and pediatricians concerning the need for parental leave is so uniformly persuasive (Finn-Stevenson et al., 1988; Zigler & Frank, 1988) that some states decided not to wait for Federal action on the issue but rather have taken legislative steps to institute a leave policy. Currently 14 states have parental or family leave statutes. Although state action on the matter is encouraging, such leave policies vary in amount of time parents are allowed to take a leave of absence from work, and all of the policies mandate only unpaid leave. By far the most progressive state parental leave bill is that passed in Connecticut. In 1987, Connecticut legislators voted to allow state employees up to 6 months of unpaid leave to care for a newborn or adopted child, or a seriously ill family member (Finn-Stevenson et al., 1988). In 1989, they enacted another law to require employers in the private sector to provide up to 6 months unpaid leave to employees who have a newborn, adopted, or ill child, or seriously ill family member. According to Kamerman and Kahn (1988), European nations, in order to facilitate child rearing, make provisions for 6 to 12 months of maternity or paternity leave with pay, and facilities for child care are available in cases in which both parents choose to work.

Changes in the Use of the School.   Using the knowledge from the research as a guide to policy and program development, a number of other recommendations for institutional changes have been made in an effort to enhance the lives of children and families.

Some of these recommendations focus on the use of schools and school personnel. Comer (1991), for example, in an effort to address the mental health needs of low-income children, developed plans for schoolwide reform that emphasize parent involvement, teacher and principal empowerment, and acceptance of the diverse cultural backgrounds of children and families served. Through such school reforms, the program seeks to raise students' achievement and self-esteem, as well as boost teachers' morale.

The School of the 21st Century.   Another recommendation, embodied in the School of the 21st Century program (Zigler, 1987), is the use of the school as the coordinating base for child care and family support services. Designed as a comprehensive program that is available for all children from birth to age 12, the School of the 21st Century is made up of two child-care components and three outreach services. The child-care components consist of year-round child care in the school for children ages 3, 4, and 5, and year-round before- and after-school care in the schools for children ages 6 to 12.

Advantages of school-based child care are numerous: Child care is more accessible for parents; it familiarizes young children with the school setting, thus possibly reducing later anxiety about school; older children are located in the same building, therefore reducing transportation needs and providing opportunity for interactions between young and older children. In addition to these benefits, the prevalence of self-care for children who are not ready to care for themselves is reduced. Also, the use of the school building itself is cost-effective, because it is used year round for before- and after-school child care and summer and vacation care.

There have, however, been some concerns about the use of the school for the care of young children, with opponents contending that schools would focus on promoting academic skills at the expense of enabling children to engage in play (National Black Child Development Institute, 1988). However, the School of the 21st Century is based on several principles, two of which are the importance of providing developmentally appropriate care to young children and the emphasis on providing the children with opportunities to engage in play and social interactions. For older children in the program, it is recommended that children be able to make choices about whether to play, do homework, or participate in other activities. Quality child care in the School of the 21st Century is further ensured through recommendations for staff trained in child development, high staff-to-child ratios, small groups of children, and appropriate pay and benefits for employees to prevent staff turnover. In addition, the School of the 21st Century guidelines include recommendations for parent involvement, as this has been proven an important aspect of successful programs for young children (Honig, 1988).

The outreach services of the School of the 21st Century program include a family support home visitation program. Modeled after the Parents as Teachers Program, the service begins at the birth of the child and extends through the third year of life. Other outreach services include support and training for family day-care providers in the community, and an information and referral service to answer parents' questions regarding child care and other services. The outreach programs are designed to make the school a hub of information and services that connects the family and child-care providers to the services they may need. Parent educators in the home visitation program visit parents, often beginning during pregnancy, providing them with information about the developmental needs of their child, social support, and assessment of the child's development. The program also seeks to address the needs of family day-care providers in the community by providing them with opportunities for training, social support, and other services they may need. Such opportunities not only address the needs of providers, but also have the potential to enhance the quality of care they provide to the children in their care (Zigler & Finn-Stevenson, 1989).

Although the School of the 21st Century program is based on a relatively new idea, it has moved rapidly from concept to reality and has been implemented in school districts in Missouri, Connecticut, Colorado, and Wyoming. Variations of the program are in the process of being implemented in several other states, including Florida, Texas, Oklahoma, and Kentucky. In Kentucky, program implementation began in over 130 schools in July of 1991.

There are several reasons for the widespread interest in the School of the 21st Century program. First, the program seeks to address the child-care crisis many parents are facing by providing affordable, good quality child care for all children who need such services, regardless of income (Zigler & Lang, 1990). This is achieved by a sliding scale fee system and subsidies to low-income families. Second, many parents see the school as a safe and accessible place for child care; in a national survey conducted by Louis Harris and Associates, Inc. (1989), 62% of parents indicated that they would like to see public schools offer child care. Third, during the past decade, educators and school board members have become increasingly accepting of young children and appreciative of the fact that they can enhance children's ability to succeed in school if they provide a variety of services to families, as well as intervening during the child's early years. This trend is evident not only in the use of the school for the provision of child care and family support services, but also in the increase in school-based intervention programs for preschool children (Marx & Seligson, 1988; National Association of State Boards of Education, 1988; Schweinhart, 1988).

Family Support Programs.   Although school-based child care and parental leave policies have the potential to have pervasive and dramatic
effects on many children and families, such policies are not as yet widely
institutionalized across the country. Other forms of family support, however, have been more prevalent. The need for family support is diverse;
families often experience different stressful experiences that can be allevi-
ated by outside help. Numerous families—for example, those with preterm
babies (Friedman & Sigman, 1980; Goldberg & DiVitto, 1983), handicapped
children (Field, Goldberg, Stern, & Sostek, 1980), or families who have
experienced the illness, divorce, or death of family members, or who are
struggling with financial problems—have difficulty coping with and adjusting to the circumstances in their lives, and are in need of some type of
support. Likewise, there are many people who need assistance if they are to
discipline effectively, but at the same time nurture, their children; or if they
are to cope with helping their teenagers with problems such as drug abuse
(York & York, 1983).

In response to the widespread need for such assistance, a host of family
support programs has been developed and implemented in recent years. The
programs range from informal, grass-roots, self-help services such as
Parents Anonymous and Parents Without Partners (Whittaker & Garbarino, 1983), to more formal types of services that include professional
assistance. Often these programs are referred to as a new breed of programs
in that they are rooted in the premise that the most effective way to create
and sustain benefits for children is to improve their family and community
environment. However, Zigler and Freedman (1987b) point out that this
premise is hardly new and can be traced to Project Head Start (discussed in
detail in the next section).

Project Head Start was initiated over two decades ago in an effort to
enhance the lives of young children. It was and continues to be an
innovative program that includes a cycle of experimentation and revision
that helps ascertain which types of services are best suited for and have the
most impact on which children. As a result of this cycle of experimentation
and revision, and of recent research interest in the ecological approach to
the study of children, the conventional wisdom about how to enhance
children's growth and development has shifted from child-centered programs to programs that focus on the family as a whole (Bronfenbrenner &
Weiss, 1983; Zigler & Berman, 1983).

Although the development of family support programs is conceptually
traced to previously developed social programs, family support programs
differ from other types of programs in a number of ways. The most
important difference is that many family support programs were not
created through government initiative, as in the case of Project Head Start
and many other social programs; rather, they began as grass-roots efforts

initiated and sustained by people in response to stressful situations in their lives, and in the absence of any other form of social support. In discussing the development of such programs, Zigler and Weiss (1985) note that although these programs are diverse, differing in the types of service they render and the populations they serve, they share a commitment to provide emotional, informational, and instrumental assistance to family members, thus enabling them to cope with whatever problems they may have.

In helping individuals in these ways, family support programs exemplify a *primary prevention* strategy that focuses on preventing mental health disorders from arising (Caplan, 1974). Primary prevention includes an attempt to reduce the risk factors that can lead to problems, (Cowen, 1980; Grant, 1991), and it is distinct from other forms of intervention in that it is not a treatment. In the intervention spectrum there is also *secondary prevention,* which focuses on the early identification of a problem, and *tertiary prevention,* which involves rehabilitation.

In the attempt to prevent problems from arising, the focus has been on identifying risk focus factors that increase the likelihood of a child developing a disorder. High levels of stress have been found, for example, to place an individual—child or adult—at risk for mental health disorders.

Several other studies have also helped establish that both personal and situational variables may mediate this relation, and may enable individuals who are vulnerable to life stresses to become better able to cope (Dohrenwend, 1978; Sandler, 1980). One such variable is social support, which has been found to improve an individual's ability to withstand stress (Cassel, 1976), to mediate the consequences of life crises (Gore, 1980), and to enhance general adjustment and well-being. Such social support systems, according to Caplan (1974), should not be conceived of as the propping up of someone who is in danger of falling; rather, they refer to efforts to augment an individual's strengths in order to facilitate mastery of the environment. Caplan (1974) further pointed out that social support as a means of primary prevention in mental health does not denote a one-time intervention but rather an enduring pattern of continuous or intermittent ties that help maintain the psychological and physical integrity of the individual.

Families, like individuals, have a certain life course in that, at particular points, stresses and crises are the natural state of affairs. At those times, support programs can be invaluable in helping family members to utilize their strengths, and rally to cope with problems, thus warding off severe family dysfunction and mental health disorders (Riessman, 1986). Although family support programs have this primary prevention potential, the question of whether or not they prevent mental health disorders, and if so, to what extent, is as yet unanswered. The fact is, the growth and proliferation of such programs has not been matched by evaluations of their efficacy. Weiss (1985) and Zigler and Freedman (1987a) suggested that one reason for this may be that these programs were not recognized by researchers until recently and have been, in fact, one of the best-kept secrets of our nation (Whittaker & Garbarino, 1983).

The lack of evaluation data is a characteristic not only of family support programs but of other types of primary prevention programs as well. This point is made by Cowen (1986) in his review of a monograph on the evaluation of prevention programs (Price & Smith, 1985). Cowen pointed out in this review that evaluation data are imperative and are necessary to separate some of the many good and effective preventive programs now being tried from others that may be less effective and simply "maintained by inertia or falsely placed conviction" (Cowen, 1986, p. ii). Addressing problems posed by the lack of evaluation data regarding family support programs, Zigler and Freedman (1987a) point out that although these programs are growing at a rapid rate, they are doing so without any clear indication as to which direction their course of growth should take. On an even more practical level, Cowen (1986) noted that the future of prevention programs in general and family support programs in particular depends on evaluations of their effectiveness, as the funding of programs is often based on a single issue: Are these programs beneficial?

The evaluation of family support and other prevention programs is not a simple task, however. In many cases, these programs have no explicitly stated goals, thus rendering evaluation difficult (Weiss & Jacobs, 1988; Zigler & Freedman, 1987b). In other cases, the programs are still in the formative stage, which also renders evaluation difficult (Campbell, 1987). These and other problems associated with the evaluation of social programs are discussed in detail in the following section. Suffice it to add here that these problems are not insurmountable but instead represent new vistas for research, and a challenge to developmental psychologists to contribute to, as well as learn from, the partnership between research and practice.

DESIGN AND EVALUATION
OF SOCIAL PROGRAMS

Project Head Start

The fact that developmental psychologists can contribute to, as well as learn from, the partnership between research and practice is especially evident in the use of social science research in the design and evaluation of social programs. Beginning in the 1960s, a wide range of such programs has been implemented, many having the general goal of improving children's lives. It is beyond the scope of this chapter to describe many of the programs that have been developed. (For a historical perspective on the field of early intervention, see Haskins, 1989; Salkind, 1983; Zigler & Berman, 1983.) However, much of our discussion focuses on one such program, Project Head Start, because its wide scope and commitment to experimentation have permitted an evolutionary approach to the task of designing effective interventions for children and families, and have allowed it to serve as a stable base from which to develop a number of early intervention service models and methods. Head Start has also been evaluated extensively, and in those Head Start programs that deliver high quality services, has been credited with increasing children's chances of becoming literate and graduating from high school and with decreasing their chances of requiring special education (Berrueta-Clement, Schweinhart, Barnett, Epstein, & Weikart, 1984).

Project Head Start began in the summer of 1965 as part of the War on Poverty, which was a massive effort to eradicate social class inequities in the United States (Zigler & Muenchow, in press; Zigler & Valentine, 1979). One facet of this effort was preschool intervention, which, it was hoped, would provide young children with an inoculation against the ills resulting from poverty. Project Head Start differed from other intervention efforts of the early 1960s in that its planners were careful to avoid using a deficit model based on the notion of cultural deprivation or cultural disadvantage (Zigler & Berman, 1983). The focus in the deficit model is to provide poor children with learning experiences supposedly lacking in their impoverished environments. In contrast, Project Head Start focused on a cultural relativistic approach that respected the children's many cultures (Zigler & Muenchow, 1983). One way this was achieved was through parent participation (Valentine & Stark, 1979). This included parents' work in the daily activities of the program, and their involvement in the planning and administration of Head Start centers in the community. Parent participation has by now become an important and often required aspect of programs for children (Honig, 1988); in the early years of Head Start, however, parent participation was regarded as a significant break from past practices in which paid professionals dictated the operation of programs.

Several incidental benefits of parent involvement have been realized ("A review of Head Start research," 1982). One such benefit is suggested by a finding of the Coleman report (Coleman et al., 1966) that children's school performance improved when they felt more control over their lives. Children's locus of control was associated first with family background and second with variance in school performance. It was found that because parents' attitudes are likely to influence those of their children, parental participation in decision making could promote both parents' and children's feelings of control and lead to increased effort, performance, and self-satisfaction on the part of the children.

Head Start has further differed from other early intervention efforts in that it has been a source of learning for developmental psychologists and for scientists from other disciplines, and is often regarded as a national laboratory for the design of effective programs for children and adults (Zigler & Seitz, 1982b). Continued experimentation in Head Start has led to a number of innovative approaches to early intervention, exemplified in the changes that have taken place in the program since its inception. Over the years there has been, for instance, disillusionment with early childhood as a critical period for intervention (e.g., Clarke & Clarke, 1976). By extending the provision of Head Start services to include earlier as well as later stages of development, which was made possible by Head Start's Home Start and Follow Through efforts (Rhine, 1981), we have come to appreciate the importance of continuous intervention from one stage of life to the next (Seitz, 1982). Another example is the Child and Family Resource Program (CFRP), which was a Head Start demonstration project that has contributed to the emergence of the family support programs discussed earlier. The underlying concepts of the CFRP are that children need to be served at different developmental stages, and that effective early intervention rests not in a single program designed to aid children, or to remediate any one particular problem, but in a host of family support services (Comptroller General of the United States, 1979). Thus, the CFRP was designed to serve families with children from the prenatal period through age 8 by linking them to existing community services, depending on the families' particular needs. Although the CFRP was a short-lived demonstration effort, the concept has been applied to other services for children and families.

Other Head Start innovations that have made significant contributions to services and programs for children include the Head Start Handicapped Children's Effort, an attempt to deal sensitively with mainstreaming handicapped children even before they reach school age. Head Start has also been a source of innovation in its adoption of the Child Development Associate program as the basis on which to train and assess child-care workers. Finally, as becomes apparent in the next section, a major contribution of Project Head Start can be seen in its focus on evaluation, which resulted in the use of social competence instead of IQ score changes as the criterion by which to evaluate the success of early intervention programs.

Evaluation of Head Start and Other Social Programs.   Indeed, the evaluation of Head Start and other social programs has been an important element of such programs and has been used to justify their usefulness. For many years, the argument for the need for early intervention programs for certain populations and the question of how effective these are have been addressed in academic journals of developmental psychology and other disciplines and have constituted primarily a scientific interest (Salkind, 1983) in the effects of programs on children's growth and development. Over the years, however, we have learned that this perspective alone is not sufficient: We should also include in any evaluation effort a policy perspective (Haskins, 1989). That is, we should address the concerns of taxpayers and policy makers about the costs and benefits of such programs.

Researchers' recognition of the need to address both the scientific and policy issues inherent in social program evaluation has greatly increased our understanding of the ways in which these programs affect children, and has improved our ability to document these through a variety of evaluation methodologies. Several methods have thus emerged that have been applied to evaluation research, and some problems have been encountered in that area. These problems are important in that they have resulted not only in the search for and application of more valid evaluation methodologies and more realistic expectations of what evaluation studies can and cannot tell us, but also in changes in theoretical issues related to children's development (Travers & Light, 1982).

Methods in Evaluation Research.   Given the different perspectives associated with the evaluation of social programs, a useful definition of evaluation, incorporating both the scientific and policy perspectives, is offered by Travers and Light (1982). They define evaluation as the systematic inquiry into the operations of a program, the services it delivers, the processes by which those services are provided, the costs involved, the characteristics of the population served, and the outcome or the impact of the program on its participants. There are two types of evaluation associated with social services. The first is called *process evaluation.* Process evaluation refers to the assessment of the actual implementation of a program or service. An example of this is the monitoring effort in Head Start programs to guarantee that each Head Start center delivers the services mandated by the program. This type of evaluation should begin when the programs are first initiated, as it can provide valuable feedback to administrators and staff about how the program is working and what changes may be made to improve it. The second type of evaluation, *outcome evaluation,* involves an assessment of the verifiable impact of the program or service, and is important as a source of knowledge and direction. It provides us with information about which programs work and which do not. This information is especially relevant to policy makers who are faced with the many unmet needs of America's children, and the limited public funds for helping them, and who must decide whether to continue existing programs or to allocate funds to new ones that hold the promise of achieving a specific end.

The classic design for outcome evaluation studies has been the experimental model. In this model, an experimental and a control group—one group that receives a program and another that does not—are chosen at random from the target population. Measures are taken of the relevant criterion variable (e.g., IQ score) both before the program starts and after it ends. Any differences between the two groups at the end of the program are used to determine the program's success or failure. The experimental model presents some restrictions in the evaluation of social programs as these programs are not always developed or implemented in such a way as to allow for sufficient control of all the variables (Abt, 1974). What is more, the exclusive use of this model may fail to yield important or useful information that cannot be derived from experimental studies: What are the needs of the participants? Has the program secured community acceptance? The need for answers to these and other questions has led to the use of a variety of quasi-experimental and nonexperimental designs in the evaluation of programs (Campbell & Erlebacher, 1970).

Besides the changes in the design of evaluation studies, the validity and utility of evaluation studies have also been improved through the use of different methods of analysis. One of these methods is known as *secondary analysis* (Cook, 1974), which is the reanalysis of data for purposes of answering the original research question with better statistical techniques, or of answering new questions with old data; *primary analysis,* on the other hand, is the original analysis of data in a research study. Another method is *meta-analysis* (Glass, McGraw, & Smith, 1981), which is the statistical analysis of the summary of findings of many empirical studies. An example is the study by the System Development Corporation (Coulson et al., 1972) of data collected by regional Head Start Evaluation and Research Centers between 1966 and 1968. The data used in the study came from nine quasi-experimental programs that were part of a systematic planned variation study originally designed to assess the effects of different approaches in Head Start programs on children of different characteristics. The analysis showed that children who participated in the 1966 to 1969 full-year Head Start programs showed statistically reliable and relatively large gains in task orientation, social adjustment, and achievement orientation. Both these methods of analysis provide an added dimension to evaluation research, thus enhancing the ability of researchers to document some of the strengths and weaknesses of social programs.

Other evaluation methodologies have been developed because of recognition of the need to address the concerns of taxpayers and policy makers about programs. Examples of such evaluation methodologies are cost-effectiveness analysis and cost–benefit analysis. Salkind (1983) discussed these two methodologies, noting the differences between them. Cost-effectiveness analysis is used when the outcomes or benefits of a program or policy cannot be measured in dollars. Karnes, Teska, Hodgins, and Badger

(1970), for example, reported a positive change in parents' ratings of their children's school performance as a function of participation in an early childhood program. This change is considered a beneficial outcome because it indicates greater parent involvement in the child's education, and greater understanding of the child's school performance; but effectiveness in this case can be measured only in units other than dollars. Cost–benefit analysis looks at both the costs of the program and the benefits associated with the program in terms of dollars, usually expressed as the "amount of money invested" and the "amount of money returned."

In response to economic realities and the pressure to demonstrate to taxpayers and policy makers the return to society of public investments, social scientists have become involved in the development of cost–benefit analyses that have proved to be meaningful to both psychologists and legislators. One of these is the Economic Analysis of the Ypsilanti Perry Preschool Project (Barnett, 1985). In one such analysis (Weber, Foster, & Weikart, 1978), the benefits and costs for the experimental group were compared with those of the control group, using the human capital approach of economics. The economic benefits of the preschool program were quantified; then, by comparing the costs of the program with these economic benefits, the rate of return on the investment was calculated. The study was based on a small sample, and, the researchers note, the computations required making some broad assumptions about the applicability of census data to the studied cohorts. Nonetheless, the results showed that the benefits to society outweighed the costs of the program. The economic benefits to society were derived from: (a) less costly education (i.e., fewer children of the experimental group repeated a grade and/or were placed in special education programs); (b) higher projected lifetime earnings for this group; and (c) time release from child-care responsibilities for the parents of the children in the experimental group. In another cost–benefit analysis of the Perry Preschool Program, data collected revealed that children who participated in the program were involved in fewer crimes and were less likely than the control group children to be on welfare. Taking these benefits into account, Barnett (1985) included money saved on welfare payments and crimes, and found that for every dollar spent on the program, $5 can be saved.

Similar findings on other intervention programs were obtained by the Consortium for Longitudinal Studies (1981), which pooled the information from several of the older and more complete early childhood education studies and, using the Economic Analysis described above, demonstrated the cost–effectiveness of such programs in the long run. In another compilation of the program findings, longitudinal data, and cost measures of selected early intervention programs, Antley (1982) also demonstrated the cost-effectiveness of several early intervention programs. We should note, however, that there is danger in generalizing these findings to other programs. The Perry Preschool Project included high quality center-based care as well as weekly home visits by the program staff (Haskins, 1989). However, not all preschool programs deliver high quality services, and many do not include, in addition to center-based programs, a home visitation component. Any effort to expand the availability of preschool programs should therefore focus on good quality care and a range of services.

Principles From Evaluation Research.   In addition to having refined evaluation methodologies, psychologists have delineated what are now known to be essential elements in any effective evaluation study (see Guttentag & Struening, 1975; Struening & Guttentag, 1974). As it is beyond the scope of this chapter to enumerate these elements, we briefly highlight several of the major principles that have emerged over the past 20 years of evaluations of early intervention.

The first principle is that programs must be evaluated broadly rather than by laboratory measures only. As noted by Travers and Light (1982), the choice of measures and/or research designs should be based on an assessment of the full range of possibilities in light of the goals and circumstances of the particular program under evaluation. To this end, researchers are urged to give careful consideration to several types of information that may illuminate the working of programs. Examples of such information are the characteristics of the quality of life of the children in these programs; descriptions of their social environment, such as the adults they come in contact with, who have the greatest potential for enhancing or thwarting the children's development; and the relationships between program clients and staff. This type of information not only yields important data on the actual operation of the program but also enhances our understanding of the variations in effectiveness within and across programs. An interesting example is the evaluation of the Perry preschool programs discussed earlier (Schweinhart, Weikart, & Larner, 1986). In the course of revealing that program benefits may extend to such developmental aspects as the reduction in the rate of crime and juvenile delinquency, the evaluation showed also that a particular model of preschool intervention (namely, the open framework model, which encourages children to engage in self-initiated activities) is more successful than are other models (such as those that require children to respond to activities planned and initiated by the teacher).

Related to the aforementioned is a second principle: the necessity of both process and outcome evaluations. As defined earlier, process evaluation is a check to determine whether services are actually delivered, and how this is done. Outcome evaluation is an assessment of the impact of programs.

Neither type of evaluation by itself is sufficient. For example, despite the fact that Head Start centers vary enormously from one locale to another, researchers in early studies compared on a national basis graduates of Head Start with children who had not attended Head Start (Cicirelli, 1969). There was undoubtedly as much variation within the groups as there was between them, but the studies failed to document this. Over the years, it has become common practice to monitor the activities that actually occur in intervention programs and to compare differences within programs (e.g., Huston-Stein, Friedrich-Cofer, & Susman, 1977), because the use of both process evaluation and outcome evaluation can yield valuable lessons about the intervention.

The third principle is that, because the effects of early intervention are complex, oversimplification in their assessment must be avoided. As becomes apparent in the following section, researchers, using what has since come to be regarded as a narrow interpretation of evaluation results, hastened to declare that early intervention programs such as Head Start were failures. However, we now know that program evaluation is not a simple matter. Indeed, researchers, in their quest to find out not only *if* a social program is a success or failure, but *why* it is a success or failure, are learning to specify particular populations, particular ages, and particular modes of service delivery systems, and what the particular intervention means in relation to such mediating factors, rather than expecting to find that the program is either a success or a failure.

What We Have Learned From Program Evaluation. Besides learning a great deal about how to design and interpret the results of evaluation studies, developmental psychologists have also been able to clarify and enhance their understanding of a number of developmental issues. In our discussion of what psychologists have learned in this regard, we focus on the evaluation of Project Head Start, which in many ways became the test of whether early intervention efforts could be successful. The most noted of Head Start evaluations was the Westinghouse report (Westinghouse Learning Corporation, 1969), which was the first large-scale study to examine the impact of Head Start on later school achievement. There were shortcomings to this evaluation. First, the evaluation criteria did not reflect the fundamental goals of Head Start; and second, as we have now come to appreciate, the evaluation's reliance on the IQ as a measure of success presented problems.

The Westinghouse study involved the assessment of children enrolled in summer Head Start programs between 1965 and 1968. Much has been written about the study and its impact (e.g., Cicirelli, 1974; Datta, 1974, 1979). Briefly summarized, the findings of the study indicated that the IQ improvements associated with children's participation in Head Start programs tend to fade out. Although the Westinghouse study had numerous methodological problems (see Campbell & Erlebacher, 1970; Smith & Bissel, 1970; White, 1970), many people were quick to declare, on the basis of this one study, that public spending on early intervention was a waste of resources. So strong was the negative feeling generated by the Westinghouse study in regard to early intervention programs, that evidence about Head Start's positive outcomes rarely came to light. For example, even though a later study (Kirschner Associates, 1970) pointed to several important contributions of the Head Start program, these findings were not widely acknowledged at the time.

Since the Westinghouse report, there has accumulated an extensive amount of literature discussing and even refuting its findings (e.g., Campbell & Erlebacher, 1970; Ryan, 1974). The problems associated with the study, however, have led to our greater understanding of evaluation research in general and the refinement of the methodologies involved. We have come to appreciate, for example, that our ability to perform outcome evaluation depends on the degree to which the goals of the program are well presented and held constant throughout the life of the program (Zigler & Trickett, 1978). The programs included in the cost–benefit analyses mentioned earlier had stated, at the outset, the explicit educational goals to be attained by the children involved. However, in the case of Project Head Start, the goals originally presented were vague, and were later changed; and various of its most promising components were not highlighted.

The same problem arose with another social program, the supplemental food program for Women, Infants, and Children (WIC). Approximately $200 million a year is spent in this program for the provision of dairy products to pregnant women and young children. Numerous evaluations of this program have attested to its effectiveness and importance in reducing developmental disabilities among children (Hicks, Langham, & Takenaka, 1982; Kotelchuck, Schwartz, Anderka, & Finison, 1981, 1984). However, for a time, researchers and advocates of the WIC program have had difficulties convincing policy makers of the effectiveness of the program as a result of the failure to enunciate at the outset what WIC's circumscribed and measurable goal might be — whether to improve the nutritional status of pregnant women and young children, thereby preventing the serious disorders associated with malnutrition, or whether to eliminate poverty (Solkoff, 1977).

Another problem that has emerged in relation to evaluation is the selection of outcome measures. The most often utilized outcome measure during the past 20 years of early childhood intervention programs has been the IQ score, or the magnitude of change in a child's IQ score. Using the IQ score as a measure in the evaluation of programs afforded the opportunity to avoid the rigors of goal-sensitive outcome evaluation by concluding that a program was a success if it resulted in higher IQs, and a failure if it did not (Zigler & Trickett, 1978). Various theoretical and methodological problems are associated with the use of the IQ score in this way (Cronbach, 1971; McClelland, 1973), but although reservations have been voiced about the use of the IQ score as an outcome measure, it is still widely used in evaluation efforts.

There are several reasons for the initial popularity of the IQ score and for its continued use. One such reason is historic; early intervention efforts, in many cases, were initiated in order to examine the degree to which IQ scores can be influenced by life experiences (e.g., Garber & Heber, 1977; Gordon, 1973; Gray & Klaus, 1965; Karnes et al., 1970; Levenstein & Sunley, 1968; Skeels, 1966). Another reason for the popularity of the IQ score is that standard IQ tests are well-developed instruments. Their psychometric properties are well documented, a factor that allows a user to avoid difficult measurement problems. The IQ test is also readily available and easy to administer, an advantage that is further enhanced if other tests are employed (e.g., the Peabody Picture Vocabulary Test, the Otis-Lennon Mental Ability Test), because high correlation is found between such 10-minute tests and the longer Stanford-Binet Intelligence Scale or the Weschler Intelligence Scale for Children.

Also, no other test has been found to be related to so many behaviors of theoretical and practical significance (Kohlberg & Zigler, 1967; Mischel, 1968). Because early childhood intervention programs are popularly regarded as efforts to prepare children for school, the fact that the IQ is the best available predictor of school performance is a compelling rationale for its use as an assessment criterion. Beyond the school issue, if compensatory education programs are directed at correcting deficiencies across a broad array of cognitive abilities, the best single measure of the success of such programs is improvement on the IQ test, which reflects a broad spectrum of abilities. Finally, once it became obvious that the most common outcome of just about any intervention program was a 10-point increase in the IQ score, the IQ test became an instant success as a tool for demonstrating the effectiveness of early intervention. However, over the years developmental psychologists have acquired more insight into the cause of the IQ changes resulting from participation in early childhood intervention programs such as Head Start. Considerable empirical evidence has shown that these changes in IQ reflect motivational changes that influence test performance, rather than changes in the actual nature of formal cognitive functioning (Seitz, Abelson, Levine, & Zigler, 1975; Zigler, Abelson, & Seitz, 1973; Zigler, Abelson, Trickett, & Seitz, 1980; Zigler & Butterfield, 1968).

Given some of the advantages associated with the use of the IQ score as an outcome measure, it is useful at this point to reflect on what the IQ test actually measures, as well as on some of its limitations. As is elaborated in other contexts (see Zigler & Trickett, 1978), the IQ test should not be viewed solely as a measure of formal cognition, but rather as a measure of behavior that is influenced by three empirically related but conceptually distinct collections of variables. First, the IQ test measures formal cognitive processes such as abstracting ability, reasoning, and speed of visual information processing. Second, the IQ test is an achievement test that is highly influenced by the child's particular experiences. This is an important point because in some situations the child's experiences are a major disadvantage. For example, if we ask children what a "gown" is and they reply that they do not know, it is easy to assume that there is something inadequate about their memory storage and/or retrieval systems that are aspects of their formal cognitive systems. If, however, the children have never in their experience encountered a gown, they will fail the item even though there may be nothing wrong with their memory. Also, as Laosa (1984) pointed out, disadvantaged children's poor performance on measures of abilities is often evident at a young age and may be attributed to a combination of influences associated with their low socioeconomic level and, in the case of Chicano children in particular, their language minority status.

Intelligence test performance is also influenced by a variety of motivational and/or personality variables that have little to do with either formal cognition or achievement variables (Weinberg, 1989). This point is made on the basis of studies with infants and preschool children. Lamb (1982a), for example, noted that there is a correlation between infant sociability and cognitive performance, although he acknowledged that no firm conclusions regarding the relation can yet be made. Zigler and colleagues (1973) tested disadvantaged preschool children and found that children's familiarity with the examiner and with the testing situation significantly affected their performance on the test. Zigler and Trickett (1978) explain that among economically disadvantaged children there is a tendency to answer questions with the standard reply "I don't know." This reply is not necessarily reflective of a lack of ability, nor of a lack of knowledge, but may be indicative of the children's desire to terminate or minimize their interactions with the examiner. Why this is so is not exactly clear, but it could be because the children dislike the examiner, or because they dislike the testing situation, or both. Clearly, given the demands of our society, children who adopt the "I don't know" strategy are not likely to utilize their cognitive systems optimally; moreover, if they continue with this strategy, they are unlikely to obtain those rewards, such as high grades in school and desirable jobs after school, that society dispenses to those who behave in the manner it prefers.

Policy Implications.   It is this tripartite conception of IQ test performance that explains why performance on the test is a successful predictor of a wide variety of behaviors and thus, if conceptualized and used properly, may be useful in the evaluation of programs. However, along with some of the disadvantages we have highlighted that are associated with use of the IQ test, there is a controversy surrounding its use in the evaluation and prediction of children's performance (e.g., Jensen, 1979). Therefore, alternative assessment instruments have been considered and to some extent developed. An example of these is the *generative test* developed to assess the value and impact of the High/Scope Cognitively Oriented Curriculum (Weikart, 1982). In generative tests, which were created in order to avoid some of the testing problems associated with the use of IQ tests with disadvantaged children, the children themselves provide both questions and answers, and have full control over the sophistication of their responses. Another example is the Learning Potential Assessment Device (Feuerstein, 1980), which is an approach to the assessment of the cognitive modifiability of children.

In addition, it has been proposed (Zigler, 1970, 1973) that social competence rather than IQ should be used as the major measure of the success of early intervention efforts. The relation between IQ and social competence has been made explicit in other contexts (e.g., Zigler & Trickett, 1978) and is implied in our preceding discussion on what the IQ test measures. There are, however, problems associated with the use of social competence measures. One of these is a definitional problem that stems from the lack of agreement among psychologists as to what social competence is (Anderson & Messick, 1974), and therefore of what a social competence index should consist. Despite these problems, some psychologists contend that we have sufficient knowledge of human development to warrant at the very least an arbitrary definition of social competence. It is suggested (Zigler & Seitz, 1982a; Zigler & Trickett, 1978) that a social competence index should include the following: first, measures of physical health and well-being, including appropriate weight for age, inoculation history, and so on; second, a measure of formal cognitive ability; third, achievement measures such as the Caldwell Preschool Inventory or the Peabody Individual Achievement Test and/or a variety of school-age achievement tests; and fourth, measurement of motivational and emotional variables that may include (a) effectance motivation, including indicators of preference for challenging tasks, curiosity, variation-seeking, and mastery motivation; (b) outer-directedness and degree of imitation in problem solving; (c) positive responsiveness to social reinforcement; (d) comfort around adults; (e) verbal attention-seeking behavior; (f) locus of control, measured for both parents and children; (g) expectancy of success; (h) aspects of self-image and measures of learned helplessness; and (i) attitude toward school.

Zigler and his colleagues (Zigler & Seitz, 1982a; Zigler & Trickett, 1978) emphasize not only the importance of developing and utilizing a social competence measure, but also the policy implications entailed in the use of such a measure in evaluating social programs. They note in particular that such a measure is needed as an alternative to the use of IQ tests in determining the effectiveness of programs aimed at a disadvantaged population.

THE RECIPROCAL LINK BETWEEN
CHILD DEVELOPMENT RESEARCH
AND SOCIAL POLICY

Numerous other psychologists include in their research reports not only findings of studies, but also the policy implications of their work (Horowitz & O'Brien, 1989). In his studies on young Chicano children, Laosa (1984), for example, made a link between research and policy as he underscores "the urgent need for an effective implementation of policies aimed at eliminating ethnic group inequalities in socioeconomic levels" (p. 1196). His recommendation is made on the basis of research with Chicano and non-Hispanic White preschool children, which has shown that even before they enter school, Chicano children are at a disadvantage on a number of characteristics such as verbal skills, which are required for successful adaptation to the school environment (Laosa, 1982, 1984). It is Laosa's contention that a policy approach, if it is to be effective, must attempt to implement not only programs that serve to eliminate ethnic group inequalities, but also programs designed to overcome the disadvantages associated with language. He stressed, in fact, that "policies that accomplish one but not the other of these [policy] goals, no matter how effectively, will fail to completely eliminate the ethnic group's disparity in children's performance" (Laosa, 1984, p. 1196).

These recommendations for policies made on the basis of research findings exemplify researchers' increased involvement in the policy arena and their recognition of the reciprocity that exists between research and policy (Horowitz & O'Brien, 1989). DeLone (1982) emphasized this reciprocity, noting that any policy designed to facilitate human development must be based on a good theory and an understanding of what development is and how it occurs; and that it must be a theory that can be translated into action, which he defined as a set of resource allocations and decisions that will lead to the desired outcomes provided by the theory. It is his contention that, in relation to policy, a theory is no better than its application, and vice versa. Acknowledging the axiom that social policy should be based on science, Bronfenbrenner (1974) proposed that, particularly in the field of developmental psychology, science also needs social policy, not only as a guide for organizational activities but also to provide what he regards as the two essential elements in any scientific endeavor, *vitality and validity.*

However, although an increasing number of developmental psychologists work at the intersection of research and policy, there is still a gap between what is known about human development and the application of that knowledge. The gap between research knowledge and its application is exemplified in the foster care system. We know from many years of accumulated research that a child suffers in the absence of a sense of continuity and consistency in his or her environment. When children need out-of-home placements, therefore, it is important that their lives be stabilized and that permanent and supportive homes for them be found. Beneficial programs for children at risk within their own family situations would include preventive family support services. If children must be removed from their families, they should be placed in the least restrictive environments, preferably with relatives and near their families. Reviews of children in the foster care system should be made periodically, and, if the children are not returned to their families, termination of parental rights should be hastened and adoption of those children encouraged (Cranston, 1979). Despite these possible solutions and the fact that they are cost-effective (Zigler & Finn, 1982), many children remain adrift in the foster care system in this country where they are subject to being moved from one home to another for indefinite periods. Recent improvements in this regard have been made as the result of the enactment of the Child Welfare Act of 1980, which ensures modifications in the way foster children are treated (Edna McConnell Clark Foundation, 1985). Still, there are numerous communities in which this act is not enforced (National Black Child Development Institute, 1989).

This gap between research and application is evident in the increasing number of children who, as noted earlier in the chapter, have a diagnosable mental health problem (Institute of Medicine, 1989). In a review of several effective programs, Price and colleagues (1988), Hamburg (1982), and Schorr and Schorr (1988) note not only that we have the knowledge to improve the quality of life of many children at risk, but also that it is not necessary to change every stressor (e.g., neighborhood, environment, family income) in order to make a significant difference in the well-being of children at risk. Rather, there are several programmatic approaches, such as the provision of social support and home visitations, that have been evaluated and proven effective.

Understanding Problems in the Utilization of Research in the Policy Arena

Several problems impede the utilization of research knowledge in policy and contribute to the wide gap between research knowledge and its applications.

One major problem is the inadequate allocation of funds for child and family services. This problem is present even when programs have been demonstrated to produce dramatic changes in problems affecting children. A recent study (Infant Health Development Program, 1990) that demonstrated the effects of early intervention on premature infants clearly highlights the issue. The study involved 985 infants who weighed less than 5 ½ pounds at birth and whose gestational age was less than 37 weeks. The infants were divided into an intervention and a control group. Infants in the intervention group were given intensive services that included home visits and parental guidance, and they also attended a high quality child development program. The results of the intervention were quite impressive. Infants in the intervention group were less likely to have IQ scores in the mentally retarded range, and their mothers reported fewer behavioral problems in the children than did mothers of comparison group children. These findings provide a great deal of support for the impact that interventions can have on the lives of children who are at risk for later problems. However, they raise the omnipresent issue of cost. The Gross and colleagues study spanned 4 years and cost $33 million to complete. Although part of these costs were incurred as a result of the evaluation of the intervention, the intervention itself was extremely costly per infant. Given these kinds of costs, policy makers and voters must make difficult choices about the allocation of resources to competing programs.

Besides lack of financial resources, Maccoby, Kahn, and Everett (1983) suggest another factor that contributes to the gap between research knowledge and its application:

> The relationship between researchers and policymakers is essentially an uneasy one. Policymakers sometimes see researchers as impractical, and may be skeptical about policy recommendations coming from researchers who seem not to understand the complexities of achieving a consensus among rival constituencies or administering programs once they have been legislated. Researchers, on the other hand, often see policymakers as disingenuous and too willing to compromise on matters where compromise does not seem justified on the basis of research evidence. (p. 80)

Maccoby and colleagues further note that often social scientists are perceived as unable to provide clear answers to policy questions. Or, looked at from another perspective, that policy makers are not asking questions in a way that would lead to valid and reliable research. This problem arises because of unrealistic expectations on the part of policy makers about the types of questions that social science can answer, and the number of studies that need to be conducted to arrive at appropriate answers. Those who expect a single study to have an impact on policy are likely to be disappointed, for the effects of such studies are usually small or nonexistent (Cohen & Garet, 1975; Cohen & Weiss, 1977; Rich & Caplan, 1976). Nevertheless, there are times when studies on a particular topic can illuminate a policy direction. For instance, the studies conducted by the Children's Defense Fund on foster care provided a clear policy option, the provision of financial subsidies to encourage the adoption of children in foster care, which was eventually enacted into law as The Child Welfare Act of 1980.

In addition to the problems just noted, another contributing factor to the gap between researchers' knowledge and the practical application of that knowledge is that policy makers often do not have a chance to judge, and therefore apply, research on a program's effectiveness, because the information is not shared with the public or policy makers. Despite the fact that a crucially important value of science is that it be used to better the lives of society, it is estimated that out of each dollar spent on research, only one cent is allocated for the distribution and utilization of research findings (Havelock, 1975).

There are several problems with the dissemination of valuable research findings, one of these being that there is no established system for researchers to distribute their findings to policy makers. Some researchers are frequently consulted in policy decisions, but this process is not systematized, and the distribution of research to the public through the media is characterized by many errors on the part of both researchers and reporters. McCall (1987) notes that although social science research is more popular than physical science research in media coverage, it is also less respected, and more likely to be covered by inexperienced reporters who lack the training to report it in its complexity. Also, the competitive and timely nature of news coverage is such that only findings that are "catchy," unusual, and those that can be described in one study are likely to be reported. In addition, researchers are generally not accustomed to explaining the details of complex methodologies and results so that lay people can easily comprehend them. The use of jargon and the tendency to go into too much detail can lead to errors in reporting and a misunderstanding of the results of research findings (McCall, 1987).

Although it is preferable to await conclusive findings before attempting to publicize studies, there are times when research findings, even if not entirely conclusive, must be acted on because of the timeliness of the issue. The child care issue is an example. The research on the consequences of infant day care is as yet inconclusive and requires additional longitudinal studies (Clarke-Stewart, 1989; National Center for Children in Poverty, 1988). However, as Clarke-Stewart (1989) noted:

Infant day care policy must proceed from reality. Maternal employment is a reality. The issue today, therefore, is not whether infants should be in day care. It is how to make their day care experiences there and at home supportive of their development and of the parents' peace of mind. (p. 271)

Another problem that arises in the dissemination of research in the popular media and in the policy arena in general is that some researchers use their positions to advance their own agendas. This point was brought to light in the recent debate over the long-term impact of out-of-home care of children. As we note in the previous paragraph, the research on the issue is as yet inconclusive, yet several researchers have waged a debate in the context of the popular media, some contending that there are no negative influences associated with child care, and others contending the opposite. In their scientific writings, researchers on both sides of the research (Belsky, 1987; Phillips et al., 1987) would have had the opportunity to discuss the limitations of the available data and other methodological problems that prevent our forming any conclusions about the effects of out-of-home care on infants. However, in the media, they presented their opinions as if they were confirmed by research, leading to widespread public confusion.

Guidelines for the Use of Research in Policy.   Understanding some of these and other problems that may impede the use of research in policy is important if research is to be utilized and to have a major impact on policies. This point is made by Lindblom (1986), who has identified four general guidelines for researchers to follow in order to encourage more widespread use of research in policy:

1. Researchers should be concerned in a nonpartisan way with the values and interests of the whole society rather than with one segment of it;
2. They should take a practical approach and suggest policies that are feasible and have a chance of winning political support;
3. They must become cognizant of and responsible to the policy process; and
4. They should respond to the needs of policy makers and provide them with recommendations for action on the basis of available research.

Strategies for Change

Others (e.g., Task Force on Psychology and Public Policy, 1986) make similar recommendations. It is also suggested that social scientists should participate in a broad-based lobby in behalf of children (Blom, Keith, &

Tomber, 1984), and should identify appropriate leverage points within government and work through these to develop and implement policies for children (Takanishi et al., 1983; Zigler & Finn, 1981). These suggestions are made in light of the fact that while federal efforts on behalf of children and their families are extensive and varied, it is difficult to identify any overarching and consistent goals of the support of children in America. Programs have been enacted piecemeal over an extended period of time, with little apparent attention to their collective impact or their interrelations. As Steiner noted (1976), "public involvement in [this] field is federal agency-by-federal agency, congressional committee-by-congressional committee" (p. vii). This state of affairs exists also in state and local policies and services for children and families. Another important problem is the lack of replication of quality programs to larger numbers of children. When programs are replicated, their benefits are often reduced in order to serve as many children as possible (Zigler et al., 1980). These diluted programs need to be monitored to assure that they are delivering the benefits they are expected to provide.

It is also important that social scientists inform the general public regarding the needs of children (McCall, Gregory, & Murray, 1984; Zigler & Finn, 1981). No society acts until it has a sense of the immediacy of a particular problem. This has been illustrated in the founding of what was called, in the mid-1960s, the Great Society. During that time, social issues were covered in major newspapers and were in the forefront of national attention. There were daily stories on welfare mothers, reports on poverty, and expositions on hunger in the United States. Hence, there was sympathy for the poor and support for the War on Poverty and its associated programs.

There are indications that developmental psychologists are becoming aware of the need for public education on issues related to children (McCall et al., 1984). However, for many years it has been our pattern as researchers to function in isolation and to discuss human problems, as well as possible solutions for them, with each other either at professional conferences or by means of professional journals. Most researchers' assumptions about the audience they wished to reach and their potential influence were probably fairly modest. That is, they hoped their colleagues would notice their work, appreciate the implications, and carry the ideas one step further. Now this approach is changing. Researchers in the field of developmental psychology are acknowledging the need to disseminate their knowledge in the context of the popular media, not only by presenting research findings to policy makers but also indirectly, through addressing more general changes in viewpoint regarding a topic or an issue (McCall, 1987; Stevenson & Siegel, 1984). An example of this type of activity by researchers is the creation of a committee chaired by Robert McCall on the role of research and the media within the Society for Research in Child Development. McCall and his colleagues (1984) have summarized some of the procedures in the knowledge dissemination process and have illuminated the sorts of skills researchers need in order to communicate research findings to the public or other interested parties. Carol Weiss (1985) also documented the recognition among social scientists of the need to disseminate research findings in the popular media, noting that scientists seem to be generally satisfied with the way journalists represent research findings.

Finally, in delineating the role of applied researchers in the area of social science and social policy, Ballard, Brosz, and Parker (1981) note that there are several requirements of the successful application of knowledge to social problems. Among these are the need for early and continued collaboration between researchers and policy makers in order to establish and maintain trust, and the need for scientific credibility on the part of the researchers. This latter requirement cannot be overemphasized. Whereas applied researchers must pay attention to approaches toward the utilization of their research, they must also maintain credibility in the scientific community. Academic credibility facilitates the application of social science knowledge, including theories, methods, and data bases, to social problems. In an effort to ensure the use of our research in practical ways that can help children and families, we must always ensure that we maintain a disciplinary and professional identity as scientists.

INTEGRATION OF CHILD DEVELOPMENT RESEARCH AND SOCIAL POLICY: BEYOND THE PUBLIC SECTOR

Thus far in this chapter we have illustrated the link between child development research and social policy largely as it is relevant to policies made at the federal government level. During the past three decades, the federal government was responsible for most of the initiatives related to programs for children and families. Since the early 1980s, however, the role of the federal government has been diminished and many more responsibilities have shifted to the states (Garwood et al., 1989). However, even here there are trends such that in the future, government in general will play less of a role in addressing the needs of children. These trends include the deficits in the national budget, the political temper of the times to allocate increasingly smaller amounts of money for social services, and public support in favor of less government intervention.

These developments mean that we must look beyond the public sector for the support of needy children and families (Finn, 1981). As we noted earlier, there are several opportunities for the private sector to help enhance family life. Assistance with child care and the provision of leaves of absence for employees who have newborn or ill family members are examples of such opportunities.

The decline in public funds for the support of social services has also highlighted the use of volunteers. The volunteer sector has traditionally been an integral aspect of the philanthropic community. Well-known programs such as Meals on Wheels were initiated and implemented by volunteers. More recently, Zigler and Finn-Stevenson (1988) prepared plans for volunteer initiatives to address issues pertaining to family day care.

Family day-care homes are utilized by a large number of families needing out of home care for young children (U.S. Census Bureau, 1987). There are numerous benefits associated with good quality family day-care homes. For example, the small group size and individual attention children can receive in such settings are conducive to optimal development of children. However, family day-care providers are often isolated from others in the child care community and they do not have the opportunities to participate in training and other activities from which they may derive support and assistance. The sheer number of family day-care providers, who care for an estimated 5 million children (U.S. Census Bureau, 1987), and their location in small neighborhoods across the nation, prohibits any large-scale federal or state program that would address their needs. In conceptualizing volunteer initiatives for family day care, Zigler and Finn-Stevenson (1988) note that the savings in staff costs inherent in the use of volunteers, as well as their accessibility to local neighborhoods, are important in any effort to address the family day-care issue.

On the basis of their plans, The National Council of Jewish Women (NCJW), a major national volunteer organization, implemented the National Family Day Care Project in over 30 communities across the United States (Finn-Stevenson & Ward, 1990). An initial evaluation of the project indicates that over a 2-year project implementation period, the volunteers contributed to the formation of 700 new family day-care homes, and they also provided financial and other resources (e.g., mobile libraries) to existing family day-care homes in 24 communities. In addition, NCJW has created and implemented several educational campaigns that enhanced public awareness of the need of family day-care providers (Modigliani, 1991). Although the National Family Day Care Project is only one example of a volunteer initiative, it highlights the possibility of systematically using a volunteer corp to address social issues and enhance the lives of children and families in the various communities.

SUMMARY AND CONCLUSIONS

In our discussion of applied developmental psychology, we have described the reciprocity that exists between applied and basic research, and we have highlighted the opportunities for new learning that are offered by applied settings as well as the contributions that developmental psychologists can make in the arena of policy. Our discussion has centered on the need for policy changes to improve the often difficult conditions under which children in this country live; the possibilities for research into children's development in view of the economic and demographic changes our society is experiencing; and on research related to the design and evaluation of social programs.

It is clear from this discussion not only that developmental psychologists have opportunities to learn from research in social settings, but also that, if they are to be effective, applied developmental psychologists cannot work entirely within their own discipline. This is true of both the acquisition and the implementation of knowledge wherein the principles taken from basic research and the collaboration with policy makers can significantly influence applied developmental psychology, and the potential inherent in the field to help meet the needs of children.

It is also evident from our discussion that there are tensions and uncertainties in the emerging efforts to integrate child developmental research and social policy. Although these are not insurmountable (Masters, 1983), they nonetheless influence decisions by researchers to address policy issues in their work or to consider the social relevance of their research (Thompson, 1986). Fortunately, there is considerable encouragement and support today for developmental psychologists to engage in research that has social utility and to focus on the practical implications of their studies. This trend is evidenced, for example, by the growing number of child development and social policy centers in several universities (Masters, 1983), as well as in the inclusion of policy courses in numerous graduate and undergraduate programs in developmental psychology (Thompson, 1985). The purpose in both these cases is to provide comprehensive training for developmental psychologists and other professionals in issues related to policy.

The effort to train researchers at the intersection of child development research and social policy has given impetus to more widespread initiatives among researchers to resolve the needs of children and families by participating in the policy process, or by delineating the policy implications inherent in their research (Horowitz & O'Brien, 1989). As to the direction such efforts would take, our suggestions include, first, the collaboration of developmental psychologists with the public, private, and volunteer sector policy makers in the development of programs and policies based on principles taken from child development research; and, second, recognizing that our role as psychologists includes not only generating new knowledge through research but also sharing it with the general public. Through such activities we can anticipate, over time, an enhancement of our understanding of human development and an increased awareness of our obligation to be responsive to the developmental needs of children and families.

REFERENCES

Abt, C. C. (1974). Social programs evaluation: Research allocation strategies for maximizing policy payoffs. In C. C. Abt (Ed.), *The evaluation of social programs* (pp. 49–73). Beverly Hills, CA: Sage.

Albee, G. W. (1986). Toward a just society: Lessons from observations on the primary prevention of psychopathology. *American Psychologist, 41,* 891–898.

Allen, R. E., & Oliver, J. M. (1982). The effects of child maltreatment on language development. *Child Abuse and Neglect, 6,* 299–305.

Anderson, S., & Messick, S. (1974). Social competency in young children. *Developmental Psychology, 10,* 282–293.

Antley, T. R. (1982). *A case for early intervention: Summary of program findings, longitudinal data and cost effectiveness.* Seattle, WA: Model Preschool Center Outreach Program, Experimental Education Unit.

Bahr, S. J. (1981, Winter). Divorce mediation: An evaluation of an alternative divorce policy. *The Networker, 2*(2), 1. (Available from the Bush Center in Child Development and Social Policy, Yale University, New Haven, CT).

Ballard, S. C., Brosz, A. R., & Parker, L. B. (1981). Social science and social policy: Roles of the applied researcher. In J. Grum & S. Wasby (Eds.), *The analysis of policy impact.* Lexington, MA: Lexington Books.

Bane, M. J. (1976). Marital disruption and the lives of children. *Journal of Social Issues, 32,* 103–117.

Barnett, W. S. (1985). *The Perry Preschool Program and its longterm effects: A benefit–cost analysis.* Ypsilanti, MI: High/Scope.

Belmont, J. M. (1989). Cognitive strategies and strategic learning: The socio-instructional approach. *American Psychologist, 44*(2), 142–148.

Belsky, J. (1986). Infant day care: A cause for concern. *Zero to Three 6*(5), 1–9.

Belsky, J. (1987). Infant day care: Risks remain. *Zero to Three, 7*(3), 22–24.

Benedek, R. S., & Benedek, E. P. (1977). Post divorce visitation: A child's right. *Journal of the American Academy of Child Psychiatry, 16,* 256–271.

Berrueta-Clement, J., Schweinhart, L. J., Barnett, W. S., Epstein, A. S., & Weikart, D. P. (1984). *Changed lives. Effects of the Perry Preschool Program on youths through age 19.* Ypsilanti, MI: High/Scope Press.

Blom, G. E., Keith, J. G., & Tomber, I. (1984). Child and family advocacy: Addressing the rights and responsibilities of child, family, and society. In R. P. Boger, G. E. Blom, & L. E. Lezotte (Eds.), *Child nurturance: Vol. 4. Child nurturing in the 1980s.* New York: Plenum.

Bredekamp, S. (Ed.). (1989). *Developmentally appropriate practice in early childhood programs serving children from birth through age 8.* Washington, DC: National Association for the Education of Young Children.

Brim, O. G., & Dustan, J. (1983). Translating research into policy for children: The private foundation experience. *American Psychologist, 38,* 85–90.

Bronfenbrenner, U. (1974). Developmental research, public policy, and the ecology of childhood. *Child Development, 45,* 1–5.

Bronfenbrenner, U. (1979). *The ecology of human development.* Cambridge, MA: Harvard University Press.

Bronfenbrenner, U., & Weiss, H. (1983). Beyond policies without people: An ecological perspective on child and family policy. In E. Zigler, S. L. Kagan, & E. Klugman (Eds.), *Children, families, and government: Perspectives on American policy* (pp. 79–91). Cambridge, MA: Harvard University Press.

Bryant, G. (1972). Evaluation of basic research in the context of mission orientation. *American Psychologist, 27,* 947–950.

Bureau of National Affairs. (1986). *Special report; Work and family: A changing dynamic.* Rockville, MD: Author.

Campbell, D. T. (1987). An experimenting society in the interface between evaluation and service provider. In S. Kagan, D. Powell, B. Weissbourd, & E. Zigler (Eds.), *Family support programs: The state of the art.* New Haven, CT: Yale University Press.

Campbell, D. T., & Erlebacher, A. (1970). How regression artifacts in quasi-experimental evaluations can mistakenly make compensatory education look harmful. In J. Hellmuth (Ed.), *The disadvantaged child: Vol. 3. Compensatory education: A national debate.* New York: Brunner/Mazel.

Caplan, G. (1974). *Support systems and community mental health.* New York: Behavioral Publications.

Cassel, J. (1976). The contributions of the social environment to host resistance. *American Journal of Epidemiology, 104,* 107–123.

Centers for Disease Control. (1990). *Unpublished data. Infant mortality rates: Breakdown by ethnicity.* Atlanta, GA: Author.

Cherlin, A. J. (1981). *Marriage, divorce, remarriage.* Cambridge, MA: Harvard University Press.

Child Care Action Campaign. (1988). *Child care: The bottom line.* New York: Author.

Cicirelli, V. G. (1969). *The impact of Head Start: An evaluation of the effects of Head Start on children's cognitive and affective development.* Washington, DC: National Bureau of Standards, Institute for Applied Technology.

Cicirelli, V. G. (1974). Westinghouse summary—The impact of Head Start. In C. C. Abt (Ed.), *The evaluation of social programs* (pp. 25–48). Beverly Hills, CA: Sage.

Clarke, A. M., & Clarke, A. O. B. (1976). *Early experience: Myth and evidence.* London: Open Books.

Clarke-Stewart, K. A. (1989). Infant day care: Maligned or malignant? *American Psychologist, 44*(2), 266–273.

Cohen, D. K., & Garet, M. A. (1975). Reforming education policy with applied social research. *Harvard Educational Review, 45,* 17–43.

Cohen, D. K., & Weiss, J. A. (1977). Social science and social policy: Schools and race. In C. H. Weiss (Ed.), *Using social research in public policy making.* Lexington, MA: Lexington Books.

Coleman, J. S., Campbell, E., Hobson, C., McPartland, J., Mood, A., Weinfeld, F., & York, R. (1966). *Equality of educational opportunity.* Washington, DC: U.S. Government Printing Office.

Comer, J. P. (1991). African-American children and the school. In M. Lewis (Ed.), *Child and adolescent psychiatry: A comprehensive textbook.* Baltimore, MD: Williams & Wilkins.

Comptroller General of the United States. (1979). *Report to the Congress: Early childhood and family development programs improve the quality of life for low income families.* (Document No. [HRD] 79–40). Washington, DC: U.S. Government Printing Office.

Consortium for Longitudinal Studies. (1981). Lasting effects of early education. *Monographs of the Society for Research in Child Development.*

Cook, T. D. (1974). The potential and limitations of secondary evaluations. In M. A. Apple (Ed.), *Educational evaluation: Analysis and responsibility.* Berkeley, CA: McCutchan.

Coulson, J. M. (1972). *Effects of different Head Start program approaches on children of different characteristics: A report on analyses of data from 1966–67 and 1967–68 national evaluations.* Technical Memorandum TM-4862-001/00 (EDO-70859). Santa Monica, CA: Systems Development Corporations.

Cowen, E. L. (1980). The wooing of primary prevention. *American Journal of Community Psychology, 5,* 258-284.

Cowen, E. L. (1986). Expanding horizons in prevention research. *Contemporary Psychology, 31,* 260-261.

Cranston, A. (1979). *Proposals related to social and child welfare services, adoption assistance and foster care.* (Testimony). Senate Committee on Finance, Subcommittee on Public Assistance. Ninety-sixth Congress.

Cronbach, L. I. (1971). Five decades of public controversy over mental testing. *American Psychologist, 30,* 1-14.

Datta, L. (1974). The impact of the Westinghouse/Ohio evaluation of Project Head Start: An examination of the immediate and long term effects and how they came about. In C. C. Abt (Ed.), *The evaluation of social programs.* Beverly Hills, CA: Sage.

Datta, L. (1979). Another spring and other hopes: Some findings from national evaluations of Project Head Start. In E. Zigler & J. Valentine (Eds.), *Project Head Start: A legacy of the War on Poverty.* New York: Free Press.

DeLone, R. H. (1982). Early childhood development as a policy goal: An overview of choices. In L. Bond & J. Joffe (Eds.), *Facilitating infant and early childhood development.* Hanover, NH: University Press of New England.

Dennis, W. (1973). *Children of the crèche.* New York: Appleton-Century-Crofts.

Dillon, R. F., & Sternberg, R. J. (1986). *Cognition and instruction.* New York: Academic Press.

Dohrenwend, B. S. (1978). Social stress and community psychology. *American Journal of Community Psychology, 6,* 1-14.

Eccles, J. A., & Hoffman, L. W. (1984). Sex roles, socialization, and occupational behavior. In H. W. Stevenson & A. E. Siegel (Eds.), *Child development research and social policy.* Chicago: University of Chicago Press.

Economic Policy Institute. (1986). Family income in america. Washington, DC: Author.

Edna McConnell Clark Foundation. (1985). *Keeping families together: The case for family preservation.* New York: Author.

Fernandez, J. (1986). *Child care and corporate productivity.* Lexington, MA: Heath.

Feuerstein, R. (1980). *Instrumental enrichment: An intervention program for cognitive and modifiability.* Baltimore, MD: University Park Press.

Field, T. M., Goldberg, S., Stern, S., & Sostek, A. M. (Eds.). (1980). *High risk infants and children: Adult and peer interaction.* New York: Academic Press.

Finn, M. (1981). Surviving the budget cuts: A public policy report. *Young Children, 37,* 1.

Finn-Stevenson, M., Emmel, B. & Barbuto, J. (1988). Issues of parental leave: Its practice, availability, and future feasibility in the state of Connecticut. *Report to the Connecticut Task Force to study work and family roles.* New Haven, CT: Bush Center in Child Development & Social Policy, Yale University.

Finn-Stevenson, M., & Ward, P. (1990). Outreach to family day care: A national volunteer initiative. *Zero to Three, 10*(3), 18-21.

Friedman, D. (1987). *Family supportive policies: The corporate decision making process.* New York: The Conference Board.

Friedman, S. L., & Sigman, M. (Eds.). (1980). *Preterm birth and psychological development.* New York: Academic Press.

Gamble, T. J., & Zigler, E. (1986). Effects of infant day care: Another look at the evidence. *American Journal of Orthopsychiatry, 56,* 26-42.

Garbarino, J. (1981, February) Latchkey children: How much of a problem? *Education Digest,* 14-16.

Garber, H., & Heber, R. (1977). The Milwaukee Project. In P. Mittler (Ed.), *Research to practice in mental retardation.* Baltimore, MD: University Park Press.

Garmezy, M. (1985). Stress resistant children: The search for protective factors. In J. E. Stevenson (Ed.), *Recent research in developmental psychopathology* (pp. 213–233). Oxford: Pergamon.

Garner, R. (1972). The acquisition and application of knowledge: A symbiotic relation. *American Psychologist, 27,* 941–946.

Garwood, S. G., Phillips, D., Hartman, A., & Zigler, E. (1989). As the pendulum swings: Federal agency programs for children. *American Psychologist, 44*(2), 434–440.

Ginter, M. A. (1981). *An exploratory study of the "latchkey child": Children who care for themselves.* Unpublished manuscript, Yale University, New Haven, CT.

Glass, G. V., McGraw, B., & Smith, M. (1981). *Meta-analysis in social research.* Beverly Hills, CA: Sage.

Glick, P. C., & Lin, S. (1986). Recent changes in divorce and remarriage. *Journal of Marriage and the Family, 48,* 737.

Goldberg, S., & DiVitto, B. A. (1983). *Born too soon: Pre-term birth and early development.* New York: Freeman.

Goldstein, J., Freud, A., & Solnit, A. (1973). *Beyond the best interests of the child.* New York: Free Press.

Goldstein, J., Freud, A., & Solnit, A. (1979). *Before the best interests of the child.* New York: Free Press.

Gordon, I. J. (1973). *An early intervention project: A longitudinal look.* Gainesville, FL: University of Florida, Institute for Development of Human Resources.

Gore, S. (1980). Stress buffering functions of social supports: An appraisal and clarification of research models. In B. S. Dohrenwend & B. P. Dohrenwend (Eds.), *Stressful life events: Their nature and effects.* New York: Wiley.

Grant, N. I. R. (1991). Primary prevention. In M. Lewis (Ed.), *Child and adolescent psychiatry. A comprehensive textbook* (pp. 918–929). Baltimore, MD: Williams & Wilkins.

Gray, S. W., & Klaus, R. A. (1965). An experimental preschool program for culturally deprived children. *Child Development, 36,* 887–898.

Greenberger, E. (1989, August 11). *Bronfenbrenner et al. revisited: Maternal employment and the perception of young children.* Paper presented to the 97th annual convention of the American Psychological Association, New Orleans, LA.

Guidubaldi, J., Cleminshaw, H. K., Perry, J. D., & McLoughlin, C. S. (1983). The effects of divorce on child development. *School Psychology Review, 12,* 300–323.

Guidubaldi, J., Cleminshaw, H. D., Perry, J. D., Natasi, B. K., & Lightel, J. (1986). The role of selected family environment factors in children's post-divorce adjustment. *Family Relations, 34,* 35–41.

Guttentag, M., & Struening, E. L. (1975). *Handbook of evaluation research* (Vol. 2). Beverly Hills, CA: Sage.

Hamburg, D. (1982). An outlook on stress research and health. In G. Elliot & C. Eisdorfer (Eds.), *Stress and human health.* New York: Springer.

Harris, Louis and Associates, Inc. (1989). *The Philip Morris Companies Inc. Family Survey II: Child care.* New York: Author.

Haskins, R. (1989). Beyond the metaphor: The efficacy of early childhood education. *American Psychologist, 44*(2), 274–282.

Havelock, R. G. (1975). Research on the utilization of knowledge. In M. Kochen (Ed.), *Information for action.* New York: Academic Press.

Hayes, C. D., Palmer, J. L., & Zaslow, M. J. (Eds.). (1990). *Who cares for America's children? Child care policy for the 1990s.* Washington, DC: National Academy Press.

Hernandez, D. J. (1988). Demographic trends and the living arrangements of children. In E. M. Hetherington & J. Arsteh (Eds.), *Impact of divorce, simple parenting and stepparenting on children.* Hillsdale, NJ: Lawrence Erlbaum Associates.

Hess, R. D., & Camara, K. A. (1979). Post divorce relationships as mediating factors in the consequences of divorce for children. *Journal of Social Issues, 35,* 79–96.

Hetherington, E. M., Cox, M., & Cox, R. (1978). The aftermath of divorce. In J. Stevens & M. Mathews (Eds.), *Mother–child/father–child relationships.* Washington, DC: National Association for the Education of Young Children.

Hetherington, E. M., Cox, M., & Cox, R. (1981). *Divorce and remarriage.* Paper presented at the meeting of the Society for Research in Child Development, Boston, MA.

Hetherington, E. M., Hagan, M. S., & Anderson, E. R. (1989). Marital transitions: A child's perspective. *American Psychologist, 44*(2), 303–312.

Hicks, L. E., Langham, R. A., & Takenaka, J. (1982). Cognitive and health measures following early nutritional supplementation: A sibling study. *American Journal of Public Health, 72*(10) 1110–1118.

Hoffman, L. W. (1986). Work, family and the child. In M. S. Pallak & R. O. Perloff (Eds.), *Psychology and work: Productivity, change, and employment.* Washington, DC: American Psychological Association Press.

Hoffman, L. W. (1989). Effects of maternal employment in the two-parent family. *American Psychologist, 44*(2), 283–292.

Honig, A. S. (1988). *Parent involvement in early childhood education.* Washington, DC: National Association for the Education of Young Children.

Hopper, P., & Zigler, E. (1988). The medical and social science basis for a national infant care leave policy. *American Journal of Orthopsychiatry, 58,* 324–338.

Horowitz, F. D., & O'Brien, M. (1989). Introduction to the special issue: Children and their development: Knowledge base, research agenda, and social policy applications. *American Psychologist, 44*(2), 95–96.

Howes, C., & Rubinstein, J. L. (1985). Determinants of toddlers' experience in day care: Age of entry and quality of setting. *Child Care Quarterly, 14,* 140–151.

Huston-Stein, A., Friedrich-Cofer, & Susman, E. J. (1977). The relation of classroom structure to social behavior, imaginative play and self-regulation of economically disadvantaged children. *Child Development, 48,* 908–916.

Infant Health Development Program. (1990). Enhancing the outcomes of low-birthweight premature infants. *Journal of the American Medical Association, 263,* 3035–3042.

Institute of Medicine. (1989). *Research on children and adolescents with mental, behavioral, and developmental disorders.* Washington, DC: National Academy Press.

Jacklin, C. N. (1989). Female and male: Gender issues. *American Psychologist, 44*(2), 127–133.

Jensen, A. R. (1979). *Educational differences.* London: Methuen.

Kamerman, S. B. (1983). Child care services: A national picture. *Monthly Labor Review,* 448–464.

Kamerman, S. B., & Kahn, A. J. (1987). *The unresponsive workplace: Employers and a changing labor force.* New York: Columbia University Press.

Kamerman, S. B., & Kahn, A. J. (1988). *Mothers alone: Strategies for a time of change.* Dover, MA: Auburn House.

Kanter, R. M. (1977). *Work and family in the United States: A critical review and agenda for research and policy.* New York: Russell Sage Foundation.

Karnes, M. B., Teska, J. A., Hodgins, A., & Badger, E. (1970). Educational intervention at home for mothers of disadvantaged infants. *Child Development, 41,* 925–935.

Kashani, J. H., Beck, N. C., & Hoepper, E. W. (1987). Psychiatric disorders in a community sample of adolescents. *American Journal of Psychiatry, 144,* 584–589.

Kimmich, M. (1985). *America's children: Who cares: Growing needs and declining assistance in the Reagan era.* New York: University Press of America.

Kirschner Associates. (1970, May). *A national survey of the impacts of Head Start centers on community institutions.* (EDO45195). Washington, DC: Office of Economic Opportunity.

Knitzer, J. (1982). *Unclaimed children.* Washington, DC: Children's Defense Fund.

Kohlberg, L., & Zigler, E. (1967). The impact of cognitive maturity on the development of sex role attitudes in the years four to eight. *Genetic Psychology Monographs, 75,* 89–165.

Korchin, S. (1981, February 16). Quoted in *Newsweek,* p. 97.

Kotelchuck, M., Schwartz, J. B., Anderka, N. T., & Finison, K. F. (1981). *Final Report: 1980 Massachusetts Special Supplemental Food Program for Women, Infants and Children Evaluation Project.* Submitted to Food and Nutrition Service, U.S. Department of Agriculture, Washington, DC.

Kotelchuck, M., Schwartz, J. B., Anderka, N. T., & Finison, K. F. (1984, October). WIC participation and pregnancy outcomes: Massachusetts Statewide Evaluation Project. *American Journal of Public Health, 74,* 1084–1092.

Kuhne, R., & Blair, C. (1978, April). Changing the workweek. *Business Horizons, 21*(2), 2–4.

Kurdek, L. A. (1981). An integrative perspective on children's divorce adjustment. *American Psychologist, 36,* 856–866.

Kurdek, L. A., & Blisk, D. (1983). Dimensions and correlates of mother's divorce experiences. *Journal of Divorce, 6,* 1–24.

Kurdek, L. A., & Siesky, A. E., Jr. (1979). An interview study of parents' perceptions of their children's reactions and adjustments to divorce. *Journal of Divorce, 3,* 5–17.

Kurdek, L. A., & Siesky, A. E., Jr. (1980). Effects of divorce on children: The relationship between parent and child perspectives. *Journal of Divorce, 4,* 85–99.

Lamb, M. E. (1981). The development of father–infant relationships. In M. E. Lamb (Ed.), *The role of the father in child development* (2nd ed.). New York: Wiley.

Lamb, M. E. (1982a). Individual differences in infant sociability: Their origins and implications for cognitive development. In H. W. Reese & L. P. Lipsitt (Eds.), *Advances in child development and behavior* (Vol. 16, pp. 213–239). New York: Academic Press.

Lamb, M. E. (Ed.). (1982b). *Nontraditional families: Parenting and childrearing.* Hillsdale, NJ: Lawrence Erlbaum Associates.

Lamb, M. E. (Ed.). (1986). *The father's role: Applied perspectives.* New York: Wiley.

Laosa, L. M. (1982). School, occupation, culture, and family: The impact of parental schooling on the parent–child relationship. *Journal of Educational Psychology, 74,* 791–827.

Laosa, L. M. (1984). Ethnic, socioeconomic, and home language influences upon early performance on measures of ability. *Journal of Educational Psychology, 76,* 1178–1198.

Levenstein, P., & Sunley, R. (1968). Stimulation of verbal interaction between disadvantaged mothers and children. *American Journal of Orthopsychiatry, 38,* 116–121.

Lindblom, C. E. (1986). Who needs what social research for policymaking? *Knowledge: Creation, Diffusion, Utilization, 7,* 345–366.

Long, L., & Long, T. (1983). *The handbook for latchkey children and their parents.* New York: Arbor House.

Maccoby, E. E., Kahn, A. J., & Everett, B. A. (1983). The role of psychological research in the formation of policies affecting children. *American Psychologist, 38,* 80–84.

Margolis, L., & Farran, D. (1985). Consequences of unemployment. *The Networker, 4,* 1–3.

Marx, F., & Seligson, M. (1988). *The public school early childhood study: The state survey.* New York: Bank Street College of Education.

Masters, J. C. (1983). Models for training and research in child development and social policy. In G. Whitehurst (Ed.), *Annals of child development* (Vol. 1). Greenwich, CT: JAI Press.

McCall, R. B. (1987). The media, society, and child development research. In J. D. Osofsky (Ed.), *Handbook of infant development.* New York: Wiley.

McCall, R. B., Gregory, T. G., & Murray, J. P. (1984). Communicating developmental research results to the general public through television. *Developmental Psychology, 20,* 45–54.

McCartney, K. (1984). Effect of quality of day care environment on children's language development. *Developmental Psychology, 20,* 244–260.

McCartney, K., Scarr, S., Phillips, D., Grajek, S., & Schwartz, J. C. (1982). Environmental differences among day care centers and their effects on children's development. In E. Zigler & E. Gordon (Eds.), *Day care: Scientific and social policy issues.* Boston: Auburn House.

McClelland, D. C. (1973). Testing for competence rather than for intelligence. *American Psychologist, 28,* 1–14.

McCullough, M. (1987). Testimony presented before Select Committee on Children, Youth and Families (One Hundredth Congress, First Session). In *Children's mental health: Promising responses to neglected problems.* Washington, DC: U.S. Government Printing Office.

Mischel, W. (1968). *Personality and assessment.* New York: Wiley.

Modigliani, K. (1991). *The National Family Day Care Project: Accomplishments.* New York: National Council of Jewish Women.

Moen, P., & Dempster, M. C. (1987). Employed parent: Roles strain, work time and preferences for working less. *Journal of Marriage and Family, 49,* 579.

Morgan, G. (1987). *The national state of child care regulations, 1986.* Watertown, MA: Work/Family Directions.

National Association of State Boards of Education. (1988). *Right from the start.* Alexandria, VA: Author.

National Black Child Development Institute. (1988). *Safeguards: Guidelines for four-year-olds in the public schools.* Washington, DC: Author.

National Black Child Development Institute. (1989). *Who will care when parents can't?: A study of black children in foster care.* Washington, DC: Author.

National Center for Children in Poverty. (1990). *Five million children.* Washington, DC: Author.

Nelson, J. R., Jr. (1982). The politics of federal day care regulation. In E. Zigler & E. Gordon (Eds.), *Day care: Scientific and social policy issues.* Boston: Auburn House.

Olmsted, B. (1979, May–June). Job sharing: An emerging work-style. *International Labour Review, 118*(3), 9–11.

Packard, V. (1972). *A nation of strangers.* New York: Simon & Schuster.

Parke, R., & Peterson, J. L. (1981). Indicators of social change: Developments in the United States. *Accounting Organization and Society, 6,* 323–329.

Phillips, D. (1988, June). *Quality child care.* The A. L. Mailman Family Foundation Conference, White Plains, NY. Paper presented at symposium on dimensions of quality in programs for children. White Plains, NY.

Phillips, D., McCartney, K., Scarr, S. & Howes, C. (1987). Selective review of infant day care research: A cause for concern. *Zero to Three, 7,* 3.

Pleck, J., & Staines, G. L. (1985). Work schedules and family life in two-earner couples. *Journal of Family Issues, 6,* 61–82.

Price, R. H., Cowen, E. L., & Lorion, R. P. (1988). *Fourteen ounces of prevention: A casebook for practitioners.* Washington, DC: American Psychological Association Press.

Price, R. H., & Smith, S. (1985). *A guide to evaluating prevention programs in mental health.* Rockville, MD: National Institute of Mental Health.

Provence, S. (1982). Infant day care: The relationship between theory and practice: In E. Zigler & E. Gordon (Eds.), *Day care: Scientific and social policy issues.* Boston: Auburn House.

Pruett, K. (1987). *The nurturing father.* New York: Warner Books.

Reischauer, R. (1987). *An analysis of the U.S. job market.* Washington, DC: Congressional Budget Office.

A Review of Head Start Research Since 1970. (1982). Prepared by C.S.R. Inc. for the Administration for Children, Youth and Families, Department of Health and Human

Services, Contract #185-81-C-026. Draft Copy.

Rhine, W. R. (1981). *Making schools more effective: New directions from Follow Through.* New York: Academic Press.

Rice, M. L. (1989). Children's language acquisition. *American Psychologist, 44*(2), 149–156.

Rich, R. F., & Caplan, N. (1976). *Instrumental and conceptual use of social science knowledge in policy making at the national level: Means/ends matching versus understanding.* Unpublished manuscript, University of Michigan, Ann Arbor, MI.

Richardson, J. L., Dwyer, K., McGuigan, K., Hansen, W. B., Dent, C., Johnson, C. A., Sussman, S. Y., Brannon, B., & Flay, B. (1989). Substance use among eighth-grade students who take care of themselves after school. *Pediatrics, 84*(3), 556–560.

Riessman, F. (1986). Support groups as preventive intervention, In M. Kessler & S. E. Goldston (Eds.), *A decade of progress in primary prevention.* Hanover, NH: University Press of New England.

Rodman, H., Pratto, D. J., & Nelson, R. S. (1985). Child care arrangements and children's functioning: A comparison of self-care and adult-care children. *Development Psychology, 21,* 413–418.

Rofes, E. (Ed.). (1980). *The kids' book of divorce: By, for and about kids.* New York: Vintage Books.

Roupp, R., Travers, J., Glantz, F., & Coelen, C. (1979). *Children at the center: Final report of the National Day Care Study* (Vol. 1). Cambridge, MA: Abt Books.

Rutter, M. (1976). Institute of psychiatry department of child and adolescent psychiatry. *Psychological Medicine, 6,* 505–516.

Rutter, M. (1987). Parental mental disorder as a psychiatric risk factor. In R. Hales & A. Frances (Eds.), *American Psychiatric Association Annual Review, 6,* 647–633.

Ryan, S. (Ed.). (1974). *A report on longitudinal evaluations of preschool programs: Vol. 1 Longitudinal evaluation* (Pub. No. [OTTO] 72-54). Washington, DC: U.S. Department of Health, Education, and Welfare.

Salkind, N. J. (1983). The effectiveness of early intervention. In E. M. Goetz & K. E. Allen (Eds.), *Early childhood education: Special environment, policy, and legal considerations.* Gaithersburg, MD: Aspen Systems Corp.

Sameroff, A. J., Seifer, R., & Zax, M. (1987). Early indicators of developmental risk: The Rochester longitudinal study. *Schizophrenia Bulletin, 13,* 383–394.

Sandler, I. N. (1980). Social support resources, stress and maladjustment of poor children. *American Journal of Community Psychology, 8,* 41–52.

Schorr, L. B., & Schorr, D. (1988). *Within our reach: Breaking the cycle of disadvantage.* New York: Doubleday.

Schwartz, F. N. (1974, May). New work patterns for better use of womanpower. *Management Review,* 4–12.

Schweinhart, L. J. (1988). *A school administrator's guide to early childhood programs.* Ypsilanti, MI: High/Scope.

Schweinhart, L. J., Weikart, D. P., & Larner, M. B. (1986). Program report on the consequences of three preschool curriculum models through age 15. *Early Childhood Research Quarterly, 1,* 15–45.

Seitz, V. (1982). A methodological comment on "the problem of infant day care." In E. Zigler & E. Gordon (Eds.), *Day care: Scientific and social policy issues.* Boston: Auburn House.

Seitz, V., Abelson, W. D., Levine, E., & Zigler, E. (1975). Effects of place testing on the Peabody Picture Vocabulary Test scores of disadvantaged Head Start and non-Head Start children. *Child Development, 46,* 481–486.

Select Committee on Children, Youth, and Families. (1983, May). *U.S. children and their families: Current conditions and recent trends.* Washington, DC: U.S. Government Printing Office.

Select Committee on Children, Youth, and Families. (1987). *Children's mental health:*

Promising responses to neglected problems. Washington, DC: U.S. Government Printing Office.

Skeels, H. M. (1966). Adult status of children with contrasting early life experiences: A follow-up study. *Monographs of the Society for Research in Child Development, 31*(3, Serial No. 105).

Smith, M. S., & Bissell, J. S. (1970). Report analysis: The impact of Head Start. *Harvard Educational Review, 40*, 51–104.

Smock, S. M. (1977). *The children: The shape of child care*. Detroit: Wayne State University Press.

Solkoff, J. (1977, June 11). Strictly from hunger. *New Republic*, pp. 13–15.

Staines, G. L., & Pleck, J. H. (1983). *The impact of work schedules on the family*. Ann Arbor, MI: Institute for Social Research.

Staines, G. L., & Pleck, J. H. (1986). Work schedule flexibility and family life. *Journal of Occupational Behaviour, 7*, 147–153.

Steinberg, L. (1985). *Latchkey children and susceptibility to peer pressure*. Unpublished manuscript, University of Wisconsin, Madison, WI.

Steiner, G. (1976). *The children's cause*. Washington, DC: Brookings Institution.

Stevenson, H. W., & Siegel, A. E. (Eds.). (1984). *Child development research and social policy*. Chicago: University of Chicago Press.

Struening, E. L., & Guttentag, M. (Eds.). (1974). *Handbook of evaluation research* (Vol. 1). Beverly Hills, CA: Sage.

Takanishi, R., DeLeon, P., & Pallak, M. S. (1983). Psychology and public policy affecting children, youth and families. *American Psychologist, 38*, 67–69.

Task Force on Psychology and Public Policy. (1986). Psychology and public policy. *American Psychologist, 41*, 914–921.

Thompson, R. A. (1985, Winter). Teaching child development courses from a social policy perspective. *The Networker, 6*(2), 1, 6. (Available from the Bush Center in Child Development and Social Policy, Psychology Dept., Box 11A Yale Station, New Haven, CT.).

Thompson, R. A. (1986, Summer). Applying research insights to legal policy issues. *The Networker, 7*(4), 1, 8. (Available from the Bush Center in Child Development and Social Policy, Psychology Dept., Box 11A Yale Station, New Haven, CT.).

Travers, J. R., & Light, R. J. (Eds.). (1982). *Learning from experience: Evaluating early childhood demonstration programs*. Washington, DC: National Academy Press.

Trzcinski, E., & Finn-Stevenson, M. (1991). Public policy issues surrounding parental leave: A state-by-state analysis of parental leave legislation. *Journal of Marriage and the Family, 53*, 2.

Tuma, J. M. (1989). Mental health services for children. *American Psychologist, 44*, 188–199.

U.S. Census Bureau. (1987). *Who's minding the kids?* Current population reports, Series P–70, No. 9. Washington, DC: U.S. Department of Commerce.

U.S. Census Bureau. (1988a). *Money, income, and poverty status in the United States: 1987*. Current populations reports, Series P–60, No. 161. Washington, DC: U.S. Department of Commerce.

U.S. Census Bureau. (1988b). *Poverty in the United States 1986*. Current population reports, Series P–60, No. 160. Washington, DC: U.S. Department of Commerce.

U.S. Department of Labor. (1988). *Child care: A workforce issue*. Report of the Secretary's Task Force. Washington, DC: Author.

Valentine, J., & Stark, E. (1979). The social context of parent involvement in Head Start. In E. Zigler & J. Valentine (Eds.), *Project Head Start: A legacy of the War on Poverty*. New York: Free Press.

Wallerstein, J. S. (1985). Children of divorce: Preliminary report of a ten year follow-up of older children and adolescents. *Journal of the American Academy of Child Psychiatry, 24*, 545–553.

Wallerstein, J. S. (1986). Child of divorce: An overview. *Behavioral Science and Law, 4,* 105–118.

Wallerstein, J. S., & Corbin, S. B. (1991). The child and the vicissitudes of divorces. In M. Lewis (Ed.), *Child and adolescent psychiatry: A comprehensive textbook.* Baltimore, MD: Williams & Wilkins.

Wallerstein, J. S., Corbin, S., & Lewis, J. M. (1988). Children of divorce: A ten year study. In E. M. Hetherington & J. Arsteh (Eds.), *Impact of divorce, single parenting, and stepparenting on children.* Hillsdale, NJ: Lawrence Erlbaum Associates.

Wallerstein, J. S., & Kelly, J. B. (1979). Children and divorce: A review. *Social Work, 24,* 468–475.

Ward, E. H. (1976). CDA: Credentials for day care. *Voice for Children, 9*(5), 15.

Weber, C. U., Foster, P. S., & Weikart, D. P. (1978). An economic analysis of the Ypsilanti Perry Preschool Project. *Monographs of the High/Scope Educational Research Foundation* (Series No. 5).

Weikart, D. (1982). Preschool education for disadvantaged children. In J. Travers & R. Light (Eds.), *Learning from experience: Evaluating early childhood demonstration programs.* Washington, DC: National Academy Press.

Weinberg, R. A. (1989). Intelligence and IQ: Landmark issues and great debates. *American Psychologist, 44*(2), 98–104.

Weiss, C. H. (1985). Media report card for social science. *Society, 22*(3), 39–47.

Weiss, H. B. (1989). *State leadership in family support programs.* Cambridge, MA: Harvard Family Research Project, Harvard University.

Weiss, H. B. & Jacobs, F. H. (1988). *Evaluating family programs.* New York: Aldine De Gruyter.

Weisz, J. R. (1978). Transcontextual validity in developmental research. *Child Development, 49,* 1–12.

Westinghouse Learning Corporation. (1969, June). *The impact of Head Start: An evaluation of the effects of Head Start on children's cognitive and affective development.* Executive Summary (EDO 36321). Washington, DC: Clearinghouse for Federal, Scientific and Technical Information.

Whitbrook, M. D., Phillips, D., & Howes, C. (1990). *Who cares? Child care teachers and the quality of care in America.* Executive Summary, National Child Care Staffing Study. Oakland, CA: Child Care Employee Project.

White, S. (1970). The national impact study of Head Start. In J. Hellmuth (Ed.), *The disadvantaged child: Vol. 3. Compensatory education: A national debate.* New York: Brunner/Mazel.

White House Conference on Children. (1970). *Report to the president.* Washington, DC: U.S. Government Printing Office.

Whittaker, J., & Garbarino, J. (1983). *Social support networks: Informal helping in the human services.* New York: Aldine.

York, P., & York, D. (1983). *Toughlove: A self-help manual for parents troubled by teenage behavior.* Sellersville, PA: Community Service Foundation.

Young, K. T., & Zigler, E. (1986). Infant and toddler day care: Regulations and policy implications. *American Journal of Orthopsychiatry, 56,* 43–55.

Zigler, E. (1970). The environmental mystique: Training the intellect versus development of the child. *Childhood Education, 46,* 402–414.

Zigler, E. (1973). Project Head Start: Success or failure? *Learning, 1,* 43–47.

Zigler, E. (1980). Welcoming a new journal. *Journal of Applied Developmental Psychology, 1*(1), 1–6.

Zigler, E. (1987). A solution to the nation's child care crisis: The school of the twenty-first century. In Parents as Teachers National Center (Ed.), *Investing in the beginning.* St. Louis, MO: Parents as Teachers National Center.

Zigler, E., Abelson, W. D., & Seitz, V. (1973). Motivational factors in the performance of economically disadvantaged children on the Peabody Picture Vocabulary Test. *Child Development, 44,* 294–303.

Zigler, E., Abelson, W. D., Trickett, P. E., & Seitz, V. (1980). *Is intervention really necessary to raise disadvantaged children's IQ scores?* Unpublished manuscript, Yale University, New Haven, CT.

Zigler, E., & Berman, W. (1983). Discerning the future of early childhood intervention. *American Psychologist, 38,* 894–906.

Zigler, E., & Butterfield, E. C. (1968). Motivational aspects of changes in IQ test performance of culturally deprived nursery school children. *Child Development, 39,* 1–14.

Zigler, E., & Finn, M. (1981, May). From problem to solution: Changing public policy as it affects children and families. *Young Children, 36,* 31–32, 55–59.

Zigler, E., & Finn, M. (1982). A vision of child care in the 1980s. In L. Bond & J. Joffe (Eds.), *Facilitating infant and early childhood development* (pp. 443–465). Hanover, NH: University Press of New England.

Zigler, E., & Finn-Stevenson, M. (1988). *Windows on day care revisited: Plans for volunteer action on family day care.* Concept paper prepared for the National Council of Jewish Women.

Zigler, E., & Finn-Stevenson, M. (1989). Child care in America: From problem to solution. *Education Policy, 3,* 313–329.

Zigler, E., & Frank, M. (Eds.). (1988). *The parental leave crisis: Toward a national policy.* New Haven, CT: Yale University Press.

Zigler, E., & Freedman, J. (1987a). Evaluating family support programs. In S. Kagan, D. Powell, B. Weissbourd, & E. Zigler (Eds.), *Family support programs: The state of the art.* New Haven, CT: Yale University Press.

Zigler, E., & Freedman, J. (1987b). Head Start: A pioneer of family support. In S. Kagan, D. Powell, B. Weissbourd, & E. Zigler (Eds.), *Family support programs: The state of the art.* New Haven, CT: Yale University Press.

Zigler, E., Kagan, S. L., & Klugman, E. (Eds.). (1983). *Children, families and government: Perspectives on American social policy.* New York: Cambridge University Press.

Zigler, E., & Lang, M. (1990). *Child care choices: Balancing the needs of children, families & society.* New York: Free Press.

Zigler, E., & Muenchow, S. (1983). Infant day care and infant-care leaves: A policy vacuum. *American Psychologist, 38,* 91–94.

Zigler, E., & Muenchow, S. (1992). *The inside story of Head Start.* New York: Basic.

Zigler, E., & Seitz, V. (1982a). Future research on socialization and personality development. In E. Zigler, M. Lamb, & I. Child (Eds.), *Socialization and personality development* (2nd ed.). New York: Oxford University Press.

Zigler, E., & Seitz, V. (1982b, May). Head Start as a national laboratory. *Annals of the American Academy of Political and Social Science, 461,* 81–90.

Zigler, E., & Trickett, P. E. (1978). IQ, social competence, and evaluation of early childhood intervention programs. *American Psychologist, 33,* 789–798.

Zigler, E., & Valentine, J. (Eds.). (1979). *Project Head Start: A legacy of the War on Poverty.* New York: Free Press.

Zigler, E., & Weiss, H. (1985). Family support systems: An ecological approach to child development. In N. Rapoport (Ed.), *Children, youth and families: The action–research relationship.* New York: Cambridge University Press.

Zill, N., Sigal, H., & Brim, O. G., Jr. (1983). Development of childhood social indicators. In E. Zigler, S. L. Kagan, & E. Klugman (Eds.), *Children, families and government: Perspectives on American social policy.* New York: Cambridge University Press.

13 Culture in Development

Michael Cole
University of California, San Diego

INTRODUCTION

Although it is generally agreed that the distinctive characteristic of human beings as a species is their ability to inhabit a culturally organized environment, it is a curious fact that the topic of culture and human nature is little represented in basic texts, either of general or developmental psychology. To appreciate just how markedly absent culture is, all one has to do is to scan the indices of leading texts and journals. In a great many cases there will be no citation for culture at all. In some cases there will be references to cross-cultural research in a few, restricted, domains: IQ testing, Piagetian conservation tasks, Kohlbergian moral dilemmas, and perhaps the question of the origins of emotion or aggression. (Lonner took the trouble to collect systematic data to prove the point, as reported in Segall, Dasen, Berry, & Poortinga, 1990, p. 372.)

Implicit in even the limited treatment of culture available in the psychological literature is the notion that culture is synonymous with cultural differences. This assumption is embodied in the contents of various handbook chapters on cultural psychology (e.g., De Vos & Hippler, 1969; Kluckhohn, 1954; Price-Williams, 1985) whose authors promise to treat of culture and behavior or cultural psychology but whose presentations are restricted to cross-cultural studies. The assumption that culture refers to cultural difference is made explicitly by Hinde (1987) who argued that culture is "better regarded as a convenient label for many of the diverse ways in which human practices and beliefs *differ between groups*" (pp. 3–4).

This emphasis on culture-as-difference overlooks the fact that the capacity to inhabit a culturally organized environment is the universal, species-specific characteristic of homo sapiens, of which particular cultures represent special cases. A full understanding of culture in human development requires both a specification of its universal mechanisms and the specific forms that it assumes in particular historical circumstances.

In my discussion of these issues I proceed as follows. I begin in the first section with a summary of three classical views about the nature of development and suggest a fourth that places cultural mediation at its center. I then turn to examine alternative conceptions of culture based largely, but not entirely, on the work of anthropologists, for whom it is a foundational concept. In the course of this discussion, I contrast two schools of 19th century anthropological thought about culture and development and then specify a concept of culture that I believe holds special promise for the modern study of human development. In the second section, I select especially informative examples of research on culture and development from different periods of childhood. This survey draws both on intra-cultural and cross-cultural studies to emphasize both the theoretical point that cultural mediation of development is a universal process expressed in historically specific circumstances and the methodological problems associated with the study of cultural mediation, both intra-culturally and cross-culturally.[1] I end by returning to discuss the general theoretical and methodological implications of evidence about culture for psychological theories of development in general.

THREE DUALISTIC THEORIES
AND A CULTURAL ALTERNATIVE

Figure 13.1 contains a schematic representation of the three positions that have dominated theorizing about development in this century (see also Dixon & Lerner, Chap. 1, this volume), along with a fourth approach in which the category of culture has been added as third force. The uppermost line in the figure represents the view articulated in the first half of this century by Arnold Gesell, according to whom endogenous factors dominate development, which goes through a series of invariant stages, characterized by qualitatively different structures of the organism and qualitatively different patterns of interaction between organism and environment. Gesell wrote, for example,

---

[1]There have been several excellent, and still up-to-date discussions focused on the methodological problems of conducting cross-cultural research on development (e.g., Bornstein, 1980; Rogoff, Gauvain, & Ellis, 1984). The strategy of this chapter is intended to complement, not replace, these earlier discussions.

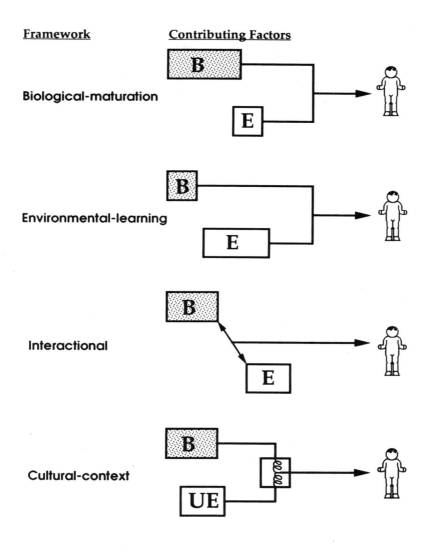

Framework   Contributing Factors

Biological-maturation

Environmental-learning

Interactional

Cultural-context

B = Biological
E = Environmental
UE = Universal features of environment
ℓℓℓ = Culture (historically specific features of environment)

FIG. 13.1. Four theoretical frameworks for interpreting the sources of development and the major ways in which they interact. In the first three frameworks, development is seen as the interaction of two factors; the theories differ in the weight they give to each and the mode of their interaction. The fourth approach assumes that the two factors included in the first three frameworks interact indirectly through the medium of culture.

733

> Environment . . . determines the occasion, the intensity, and the correlation of many aspects of behavior, but it does not engender the basic progressions of behavior development. These are determined by inherent, maturational mechanisms. (1940, p. 13)

Elsewhere he added,

> Neither physical nor cultural environment contains any architechtonic arrangements like the mechanisms of growth. Culture accumulates; it does not grow. The glove goes on the hand; the hand determines the glove. (1945, p. 358)

Gesell's ideas went out of fashion in the 1950s, but in recent years there has been a significant revival of interest in innate biological constraints on development (Carey, 1985; Gelman, 1990; Plomin, 1986).

The view that the environment provides the major impetus for developmental change is represented in row two of Fig. 13.1. An extreme version of this view was put forward by B. F. Skinner, whose views were summarized in the following striking paragraph:

> Operant conditioning shapes behavior as a sculptor shapes a lump of clay. Although at some point the sculptor seems to have produced an entirely novel object, we can always follow the process back to the original undifferentiated lump, and we can make the successive stages by which we return to this condition as small as we wish. At no point does anything emerge which is very different from what preceded it. The final product seems to have a special unity or integrity of design, but we cannot find a point at which this suddenly appears. In the same sense, an operant is not something which appears full grown in the behavior of the organism. It is the result of a continuous shaping process. (Skinner, 1953, p. 91)

In this view, it is not the past, coded in the genetic makeup, that is the active agent in development; rather it is the environment, the sculptor, that is the source not only of the minute changes that gradually modify the lump of clay, but of the new forms that emerge from this process in a continuous fashion. Contemporary psychologists sympathetic to an environmentalist perspective may consider Skinner's position somewhat exaggerated. The analogy between the organism and a lump of clay is especially unfortunate, because it implies a totally passive organism (contrary to Skinner's own principles!), but his emphasis on the dominant role of the environment in shaping development continues to have many adherents (e.g., Bandura, 1986; Zimmerman, 1983).

Jean Piaget, perhaps the most influential developmental theorist of the 20th century, argued forcefully for the equal weight of endogenous and exogenous factors in development. On the one hand, he asserted that "Mental growth is inseparable from physical growth; maturation of the nervous and endocrine systems, in particular, continue until the age of sixteen" (Piaget & Inhelder, 1969, p. viii).

At the same time, Piaget, like those who adopt an environmental-shaping perspective, argued that the role of environmental input goes well beyond determining the occasioning, intensity, and correlation of behavioral aspects.

> The human being is immersed right from birth in a social environment which affects him just as much as his physical environment. Society, even more, in a sense, than the physical environment, changes the very structure of the individual. . . . Every relation between individuals (from two onwards) literally modifies them. . . . (Piaget, 1973, p. 156)

Piaget's view is often contrasted with the maturational and environmental shaping views by his emphasis on the crucial role of the active organism, who constructs her or his own development through attempts to adapt to the environment.

Although they differ in the weights that they assign to phylogenetic constraints or ontogenetic experiences and the importance of children's active modifications of their environments, the adherents of all three positions conceive of development as an interaction between two juxtaposed forces. Although Gesell, Skinner, and Piaget all implicitly or explicitly suggest that the environmental side of the equation can be partitioned into culture or social factors versus the physical environment, these distinctions are not well developed in their writings.

The fourth row of Fig. 13.1 explicitly includes culture as a separable constituent of development. According to this cultural context view, the two factors labeled *biology* and *the environment* or *the individual* and *the society* in the previously described approaches do not interact directly. Rather, their interaction is mediated through a third factor, culture. In order to develop this fourth perspective more fully, it is necessary to pause briefly to consider the concept of culture in more detail.

Conceptions of Culture

In thinking about culture as it relates to development, I have found it useful to begin with the intuitive notion underlying this word, as it has evolved since entering English from Latin many centuries ago. As Williams noted, the core features that coalesce in modern conceptions of culture originate in terms that refer to the process of helping things to grow. "Culture," Williams wrote, "in all of its early uses was a noun of process: the tending of, something, basically crops or animals" (1973, p. 87). From earliest times, the notion of culture included a general theory for how to promote development: Create an artificial environment in which young organisms could be provided optimal conditions for growth. Such tending required tools, perfected over generations and designed for the special tasks to which they were put.

Although it would be foolish to overinterpret the metaphorical parallels between the theory and practice of growing next generations of crops and next generations of children, the exercise has considerable heuristic value. To begin with, the properties that one associates with gardens bear an obvious affinity to one broad class of definitions of culture offered by anthropologists. For example, E. B. Tylor, in his classic book, *Primitive Culture* (1874) defined culture as "that complex whole which includes knowledge, belief, art, morals, law, custom, and any other capabilities and habits acquired by man as a member of society" (p. 1). A garden as an artificial-environment-for-growing-things is also a "complex whole," and gardening requires knowledge, beliefs, and the like, as an integral part of the process. The root English conception fits just as well with Herskovitz's (1948) definition of culture as "the man made part of the environment" (p. 17).

The garden metaphor for culture also reminds us that gardeners must attend not only to a specialized form of environment created inside the garden but also to the ecological circumstances surrounding the garden. These two classes of concern often seem to be addressable independently of each other, but in reality are interdependent. Inside the garden one must consider the quality of the soil, the best way to till the soil, the right kinds of nutrients to use, the proper amount of moisture, as well as the best time to plant and nurture the seeds, and the need to protect the growing plants against predators, disease, and so forth. Each of these tasks has its own material needs, associated tools, beliefs, and knowledge. The theory and practice of development at this level focuses on finding exactly the right combination of factors to promote development within the garden walls.

In thinking about development it is necessary to consider the conditions outside of the garden or culture as well as those within it. It is possible to raise any plant anywhere in the world, given the opportunity first to arrange the appropriate set of conditions, but it is not always possible to create the right conditions, even for a short while. If one is interested in the creation of conditions that sustain and even enhance the needed properties of the artificial environment, then it is as important to attend to the ways that the system in which the garden is embedded shapes the properties of the garden itself. This common sense understanding fits well with ecocultural approaches to the study of culture and development (Berry, 1976; B. Whiting,

1980), which trace relations among physical ecology, economic activities and institutions, and the organization of children's experience.

Humanizing the Garden Metaphor

Although the garden metaphor is useful for thinking about culture and development because it emphasizes the fact that human beings live in an artificial environment, and that cultures exist within, are shaped by, and in turn shape their ecological settings, it fails to capture several aspects of modern conceptions of culture that need to be elaborated in the study of development. One point of elaboration occurred in the 16th century when the word "culture" began to apply to the rearing of children.[2] When this occurred, both the gardener and the plants were now seen to be from the same species, and, therefore, we are pushed to ask the question, What is the general property of an organism that can inhabit an artificial environment in the process of creating and recreating both itself and its environment?" That is, "what are the specifically human characteristics of both culture and human development?"

To deal with these questions it is helpful to think of the garden in which human beings live as an environment transformed by the artifacts of prior generations, extending back to the beginning of the species (Geertz, 1973; Leontiev, 1981; Luria, 1979; Sahlins, 1976). The basic function of these artifacts is to coordinate human beings with the physical world and each other; in the aggregate, culture is then seen as the species-specific medium of human development.

Because artifact mediation was present hundreds of thousands of years prior to the emergence of homo sapiens, it is not appropriate to juxtapose human biology and human culture. The human brain and body co-evolved over a long period of time with our species' increasingly complex cultural environment. The implications of the co-evolution of human culture and human biology have been succinctly summarized by Washburn (1960).

> Selection is based on successful behavior, and in man-apes the beginnings of the human way of life depended on the learned skills of tool-using. The success of the new way of life based on the use of tools changed the selection pressures on many parts of the body, notably the teeth, hands and brain, as well as on the pelvis. (p. 69)

---

[2]The botanical metaphor continues to exist, of course, in the notion of a kindergarten, a special environment for children that protects them against the harsher elements of human society.

Geertz (1973) points out that as a result of their tangled relations in the course of human phylogeny, culture and biology are equally tangled in the course of human ontogeny.

> Rather than culture acting only to supplement, develop, and extend organically based capacities logically and genetically prior to it, it would seem to be ingredient to those capacities themselves. A cultureless human being would probably turn out to be not an intrinsically talented though unfulfilled ape, but a wholly mindless and consequently unworkable monstrosity. (p. 68)

This long-term, phylogenetic perspective is important to keep in mind when considering the ontogeny of children, for it reminds us that causal influences do not run unidirectionally from biology to culture.

One essential property of culture-as-medium is that the artifacts that constitute culture are simultaneously ideal (conceptual) and material. They are ideal in that they contain in coded form the interactions of which they were previously a part and that they mediate in the present (e.g., the structure of a pencil carries within it the history of certain means of representing spoken language in a different medium). They are material in that they are embodied in material artifacts, whether in the morphology of a spoken or written or signed word, or in a solid object such as a pencil. This principle applies with equal force whether one is considering language and speech or the more usually noted forms of artifacts, such as tables and knives, that constitute material culture. What differentiates a word, such as "language" from, say, a table, is the relative prominence of their material and ideal aspects. No word exists apart from its material instantiation (as a configuration of sound waves, or hand movements, or as writing, or as neuronal activity), whereas every table embodies an order imposed by thinking human beings. (The anthropologist, D'Andrade, 1986, made this point when he said that "Material culture—tables and chairs, buildings and cities—is the reification of human ideas in a solid medium" [p. 22]. As a consequence of the dual material–ideal nature of the systems of artifacts that are the cultural medium of their existence, human beings live in a double world, simultaneously natural and artificial.

This conception of the relation between culture and the special properties of human nature was expressed in particularly powerful language by the American anthropologist, White (1942), half a century ago.

> Man differs from the apes, and indeed all other living creatures so far as we know, in that he is capable of symbolic behavior. With words man creates a new world, a world of ideas and philosophies. In this world man lives just as truly as in the physical world of his senses. . . . This world comes to have a continuity and a permanence that the external world of the senses can never

have. It is not made up of present only but of a past and a future as well. Temporally, it is not a succession of disconnected episodes, but a continuum extending to infinity in both directions, from eternity to eternity. (p. 372)[3]

Among other properties White here attributed to culture, his emphasis on the way it creates an (artificial) continuity between past and future merits special attention, as I attempt to show later. It is also significant that both White and Soviet cultural–historical psychologists (e.g., Luria, 1928; Vygotsky, 1987) emphasize that, as mediators of human action, all artifacts can be considered tools. As White (1959) expressed the relationship:

> An axe has a subjective component; it would be meaningless without a concept and an attitude. On the other hand, a concept or attitude would be meaningless without overt expression, in behavior or speech (which is a form of behavior). Every cultural element, every cultural trait, therefore, has a subjective and an objective aspect. (p. 236)

Identifying Structured Units Within the Medium

The properties of culture-as-medium discussed so far—its foundation in artifact mediation, the dual material–ideal nature of artifacts, the close relation (perhaps identity) of artifact and tool, and the unique time extension provided by the medium—are all important to understanding the relation between culture and development. But one additional fact about culture that is implicit in the garden metaphor also needs to be emphasized: While artifact creation and artifact or tool mediation are central to culture, culture is not a random assemblage of such artifacts. With respect to gardens, we can note that, in addition to having a wall separating them from their surroundings, they also have internal organization; different plants are not scattered at random within the garden walls. And so it is with culture. As Geertz (1973) put the matter, "It is through culture patterns, ordered clusters of significant symbols, that man makes sense of the events through which he lives" (p. 363). Super (1987) made a similar point when he commented that,

> Rarely in the developmental sciences . . . does theory acknowledge that environments have their own structure and internal rules of operation, and

---

[3]It would be an error, in view of recent decades of work on proto-cultural features among primates (Cheney & Seyfarth, 1990; Goodall, 1986; Kawamura, 1963; Premack & Premack, 1983; Tomasello, 1989), to overstate the discontinuities between homo sapiens and other species. Robert Hinde (1987) argued that these phenomena do not imply culture in the way in which human beings have culture. I concur, even though I disagree with his identification of culture only with difference.

thus, that what the environment contributes to development is not only isolated, unidimensional pushes and pulls but also structure. (p. 5)

There are a great many suggestions about the units in terms of which culture operates as a constituent of human activity. One well-known formulation offered by Geertz is that culture should be conceived of by analogy with a recipe or a computer program that he referred to as "control mechanisms." Significantly (as these mechanisms might seem to be located entirely inside people's heads and therefore entirely ideal), Geertz (1973) goes on to write in a manner that links up neatly with the notion of artifact mediation:

> The "control mechanism" view of culture begins with the assumption that human thought is basically both social and public — that its natural habitat is the house yard, the marketplace, and the town square. Thinking consists not of "happenings in the head" (though happenings there and elsewhere are necessary for it to occur) but of traffic in what have been called, by G. H. Mead and others, significant symbols — words for the most part but also gestures, drawings, musical sounds, mechanical devices like clocks. . . . (p. 45)

A complementary notion of structured ensembles within the overall medium of culture is offered by D'Andrade who suggested the term *cultural schemas* to refer to units that organize entire sets of conceptual–material artifacts. In D'Andrade's (1984) terms:

> Typically such schemas portray simplified worlds, making the appropriateness of the terms that are based on them dependent on the degree to which these schemas fit the actual worlds of the objects being categorized. Such schemas portray not only the world of physical objects and events, but also more abstract worlds of social interaction, discourse, and even word meaning. (p. 93)

Finally, psychologists such as Bruner (1990) and Nelson (1981) identify event schemas, embodied in narratives, as basic organizers of both culture and cognition. Referred to as scripts by Nelson, these generalized event schemas specify the people who participate in an event, the social roles that they play, the objects that are used during the event, the sequences of actions required, the goals to be attained, and so on. Nelson's account of scripted activity is similar in many ways to Geertz's and D'Andrade's suggestions for basic units of cultural structure. Her emphasis on the fact that children grow up inside of other people's scripts, which serve as guides to action before the children are ready to understand and execute culturally appropriate actions on their own, leads naturally to her conclusion that "the acquisition of scripts is central to the acquisition of culture" (Nelson, 1981, p. 110).

Culture or Cultures?

So far I have been emphasizing universal features of culture as a species-specific medium. Before proceeding to the issue of how this structured medium enters into the process of ontogenetic development, I need to address the question of cultural variability, and especially the issue of cultural evolution.

During the 18th century, the concept of culture as applied to human affairs began to differentiate quantitatively: Some people came to be considered more cultured or cultivated than others. This differentiation was associated with attempts to formulate a universal history of humankind, which in the 19th century became intertwined with attempts to formulate unilinear schemes of cultural evolution (see Harris, 1968, for an acerbic, but interesting review).

Tylor (1874), whose notion of culture was discussed earlier, believed that cultures could be classified according to their level of development, characterized by the sophistication of their technology, the complexity of their social organization, and similar criteria, a view referred to in the literature as *cultural evolution*. He assumed in addition that all people are born with the same potential to use culture (an assumption dubbed *the doctrine of psychic unity* in anthropology), but that certain societies had developed more fully than others, with industrialized societies at the top of the heap. Combining these two assumptions with the assumption that the cultural traits observed in various cultures were arrived at through a process of independent invention, Tylor believed that he could reconstruct the stages of development of humankind through a comparative analysis of societies at different levels of cultural development.[4]

Tylor's view is of more than historical interest to psychologists because it was combined with the view that there is an intimate link between culture and thought. As he put it on the opening page of his 1784 monograph, "the condition of culture among various societies of mankind . . . is a subject apt for the study of laws of human thought and action" (p. 1). This line of thinking (discussed at greater length in Jahoda, 1982, 1989; Laboratory of Comparative Human Cognition [LCHC], 1983) both fit with and gave respectability to the idea that the members of societies judged to be at an earlier stage of cultural evolution were also at an earlier stage of mental

---

[4]Tylor (1874) acknowledged, but did not build on, the fact that "if not only knowledge and art, but at the same time moral and political excellence be taken into consideration, it becomes more difficult to scale societies from lower to higher stages of culture" (p. 29).

development. Captured in the colorful phrase that "primitives think like children," this belief in the mental superiority of people living in industrially advanced countries was held by a vast majority of 19th- and early 20th-century psychologists, anthropologists, and sociologists, and remains a serious issue in the study of culture and development to this day.

Despite general agreement that there is an intimate relation between culture and thought, this unilinear theory of cultural–mental evolution has long had its critics, starting with Herder (1784/1803) who argued that the history of a culture can only be understood with respect to the specific development of single peoples and communities; general comparisons are deceiving. This idea of the historical specificity of cultures came into modern anthropology largely through the work of Franz Boas (1911), one of the first major figures in anthropology to do fieldwork in societies outside of Europe (see Stocking, 1968, for an outstanding interpretive account of Boas's contribution to modern thinking about culture).

Boas conducted research among the peoples of the American and Canadian Northwest with the objective of obtaining first-hand evidence about their technology, language use, art, custom, and myth to determine the empirical validity of evolutionary theorizing. His findings shattered his initial expectations. On the basis of comparative ethnographic data, Boas concluded that borrowing from other groups was a major source of cultural traits among the peoples he studied, undermining the basis for historical reconstruction. Moreover, the within-society heterogeneity of cultural traits contradicted either a simple diffusionist or independent-invention account of cultural change: Tribes with the same basic languages were found to have quite different customs and beliefs, and tribes with quite different languages were found to have very similar customs and beliefs. Assignment of societies to particular cultural levels was undermined by the great heterogeneity of levels of complexity in different domains of life in a single society. Among the Kwakiutl, for example, the graphic arts revealed a quite abstract way of representing natural forms while the technology was relatively unsophisticated.

From these and other observations, Boas concluded that each culture represents a combination of locally developed and borrowed features, the configurations of which are adaptations to the special historical circumstances of the group. Because all societies are characterized by heterogeneous constituent elements with respect to any single criterion of development, and because all societies can be considered equally valid responses to the historically posed problems of survival, there can be no basis for comparisons across societies with respect to general levels of development. Such comparisons illegitimately tear aspects of a culture out of their appropriate context as if they played an equivalent role in the life of the people being compared, when they do not.

Adopting Boas' position has direct implications for how one studies culture and development. It means that if we want to understand a behavior being manifested in any particular cultural context, we need to know the way that this context fits into the pattern of life experiences of the individuals being studied, as well as into the past history of interactions between and within cultures that have shaped the contexts where we make our observations. To fail to consider a behavior in its cultural context is to risk misinterpreting its meaning, and hence its overall psychological significance for the people involved. (See Rogoff, Gauvain, & Ellis, 1984, for an elaboration of this point.)

From this rather truncated discussion of anthropological conceptions of culture, we can abstract the following essential points:

1. Culture is the residue in the present of past human activity in which human beings have transformed nature to suit their own ends and passed the cumulated artifacts down to succeeding generations in the form of tools, rituals, beliefs, and ways of conceiving of the world in general.

2. Culture is not a random assortment of artifacts; it comes packaged in the form of conceptual systems, social institutions, and a multitude of acceptable ways of behaving.

3. Culture is a medium, not an "independent variable."

However, varieties of cultural configurations, associated with different historical experiences (where "history" is assumed to extend back to the first creatures dubbed homo sapiens although we have deliberate recordings dating back only a few thousand years) allow us to treat cultures as *independent variables*. When cultural variations are studied, the fact that cultures are organized patterns of artifacts means that it will prove difficult or impossible to unpackage them to determine precisely which aspects of culture contribute to the development of particular behavioral outcomes (B. Whiting, 1976, referred to culture used in this way as a *packaged variable*). In the sections that follow, I illustrate these and other psychologically important aspects of culture in development.

TRACKING A DYNAMICAL SYSTEM OVER TIME

One enormous challenge facing students of development in general, and human development in particular, is that they seek to explain the lawful changes in the properties of a complex, interacting system in which different aspects of the system are themselves developing at different rates. As a means of orienting ourselves in attempting to describe this process of growth, it is useful to employ a framework proposed by Emde, Gaensbauer, and Harmon (1976) who in turn were influenced by what Spitz (1958) called *genetic field theory.* Emde and colleagues' basic proposal was to study developmental change as the emergent synthesis of several major factors interacting over time. In the course of their interactions, the dynamic relations among these factors appears to give rise to qualitative rearrangements in the organization of behavior that Emde and his colleagues referred to as *bio-behavioral shifts.* Cole and Cole (1989) expanded on this notion by referring to *bio-social-behavioral shifts* because, as the work of Emde and colleagues shows quite clearly, every bio-behavioral shift involves changes in relations between children and their social world as an integral part of the changing relations between their biological makeup and their behavior. Cole and Cole also emphasized that the interactions out of which development emerges always occur in cultural contexts, thereby implicating all of the basic contributors to development that a cultural approach demands.

In this section, I present a series of examples illustrating how culture enters into the process of development, focusing on major developmental periods and bio-social-behavioral shifts between periods. In order to keep this chapter within the scope of normal developmental study, I choose my examples from broad age periods that, while perhaps not universal stages of development, are very widely recognized as such in a variety of cultures (B. Whiting & Edwards, 1988). The examples have been chosen for a variety of reasons. In some cases, my goal is to illustrate one or another universal process through which culture enters into the constitution of developmental stages and the process of change. In other cases, my examples are chosen to highlight the particular impact of particular configurations of cultural mediation. Yet other examples highlight the special difficulties psychologists must cope with when they focus on culture in development.

Prenatal Development

It might seem capricious to begin an examination of cultural influences on development with the prenatal period. After all, the child does not appear to be in contact with the environment until birth. This view is implicit in Leiderman, Tulkin, and Rosenfeld's (1977) introduction to *Culture and Infancy,* which begins with the assertion that "the human environment is inescapably social. From the moment of birth, human infants are dependent on others for biological survival" (p. 1). A moment's reflection will reveal that the same can be said of prenatal development, with the proviso that the child's experience is, for the most part, mediated by the biological system of the mother. We need the proviso "for the most part" because there is increasing evidence that prenatal humans are sensitive to, and are modified by, the language spoken in the environment of the mother

(DeCasper & Spence, 1986; Mehler, Lambertz, Jusczyk, & Amiel-Tison, 1986).

The best documented way in which the cultural organization of the mother's experience influences the development of her child is through the selection of food and other substances that she ingests. Current public attention to the devastating effects of alcohol, cigarette, and drug ingestion provides an obvious and painful reminder of cultural effects on prenatal development with long-term consequences (Fricker, Hindermann, & Bruppacher, 1989).

At a more mundane level, research in both industrialized and nonindustrialized societies demonstrates that beliefs about appropriate foods for expectant mothers are quite variable in ways that are likely to influence such important indicators of development as birthweight and head size. In one of the few intra-cultural studies on this topic, Jeans, Smith, and Stearns (1955) compared the health of babies born to mothers whose diets were judged as either "fair to good" or "poor to very poor." The women were all from a single rural area and did not differ in any indices of social class; it was their choice of foods that differed. The mothers judged as having fair to good diets had markedly healthier babies.

In a survey of the eating habits of people from nonindustrialized societies, Mead and Newton (1967) report on a number of cases in which beliefs about pregnancy reduced the supply of protein and other food that modern medicine considers important to prenatal growth. In some societies the banning of food extends to kinds that we consider staples including various kinds of meat, eggs, fish, and milk. For example, the Siriono of South America do not allow women to eat the meat of various animals and birds that are a part of other people's diets because they are afraid that characteristics of the animals women eat while pregnant will be transferred to their unborn children (Holmburg, 1950, cited in Mead & Newton, 1967).

There is also reasonably good evidence that pregnant women who inhabit stressful environments have more irritable babies (see Chisholm, 1989; Chisholm & Heath, 1987, for useful summaries). For example, Chisholm has shown that Navajo women who live within Navajo communities have less irritable babies. Chisholm provided suggestive data implicating high blood pressure resulting from the stress of living in fast-paced and generally unsupportive urban centers dominated by Anglos as the cause of increased infant irritability.

With the advent of modern medical technologies there is an obvious new source of cultural influence on prenatal development through genetic screening techniques, especially the ability to learn the sex of the expected child. In a number of countries selective abortion of females is being reported, where previously female infanticide practices were delayed until the child made its appearance.

Birth: The First Major Bio-Social-Behavioral Shift

The realignment of biological, behavioral, and social factors at birth makes it perhaps the most dramatic bio-social-behavioral shift in all of development. Whereas there is evidence of great cultural variation in the organization of the birthing process, it is also the case that this fundamental transition provides some of the clearest evidence of universal mechanisms relating culture to development (Richardson & Guttmacher, 1967).

Little needs to be said about the biological and behavioral changes that accompany birth. Suffice it to recall that when babies emerge from the birth canal and the umbilical cord is cut, their automatic supply of oxygen and nutrients comes to an abrupt halt. In adjusting to these changed conditions, the blood flow reverses direction, beginning a pattern that will last the rest of their lives. Out in the world, the babies now see, hear, and feel in new ways. And, very significantly, they are seen, heard, and felt in a new way by others.

From existing ethnographic evidence, we know that both the mother's and child's experiences at birth vary considerably across societies of the world according to cultural traditions that prescribe the procedures to be followed in preparation for, during, and after the birth. In a few societies, birthing is treated as a natural process that requires no special preparation or care. Shostak (1981) recorded the autobiography a !Kung woman living in the Kalahari desert in the middle of this century who reported that she observed her mother simply walk a short way out of the village, sit down against a tree, and give birth to her brother. In most societies, however, birthing is treated as dangerous (and in some places as an illness), requiring specialized help (see Cole & Cole, 1989, p. 108ff, for examples and additional references).

Rather than concentrate on the potential consequences of these cultural variations in birthing practices, I focus on the way that birth provides evidence of a universal mechanism of cultural mediation of development — the process through which the ideal side of culture is transformed into material–cultural organization of the child's environment. This example (taken from the work of pediatrician Aiden Mcfarlane, 1977) also demonstrates in a particularly clear fashion White's point that culture provides a specifically human form of temporal continuity.

Figure 13.2 presents in schematic form five different time scales simultaneously operating at the moment at which parents see their newborn for the first time. The vertical elipse represents the events immediately surrounding birth, which occurs at the point marked by the vertical line. At the top of the figure is what might be called physical time, or the history of the universe that long precedes the appearance of life on earth.

The bottom four time lines correspond to the developmental domains

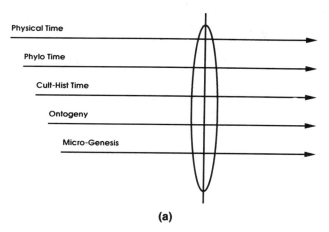

(a)

FIG. 13.2a. The five kinds of time in effect at the moment a child is born (marked by the vertical line).

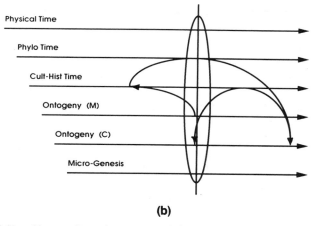

(b)

FIG. 13.2b. How culture is converted from an ideational or conceptual property of the mother into a material or interactional organization of the baby's environment. Note that there are two ontogenies included, the mother's and the baby's. The curved lines depict the sequence of influences: The mother thinks about what she knows about girls from her (past) cultural experience; she projects that knowledge into the *child's* future (indicated by remarks such as "It will never be a rugby player"); this ideal or conceptual future is then embodied materially in the way the mother interacts with the child.

(Wertsch, 1985) that, according to the cultural framework espoused here, simultaneously serve as major constraints for human development. The second line represents phylogenetic time, the history of life on earth, a part of which constitutes the biological history of the newborn individual. The third line represents cultural–historical time, the residue of which is the child's cultural heritage. The fourth line represents ontogeny, the history of a single human being, which is the usual object of psychologists' interest. The fifth line represents the moment-to-moment time of lived human experience, the event called "being born" (from the perspective of the child) or "having a baby" (from the perspective of the parents) in this case. Four kinds of genesis are involved: phylogenesis, culturogenesis, ontogenesis, and microgenesis, with each lower level embedded in the level above it.

Macfarlane's example reminds us to keep in mind that not one but two ontogenies must be represented in place of the single ontogeny in Fig. 13.2a. That is, at a minimum one needs a mother and a child interacting in a social context for the process of birth to occur and for development to proceed. These two ontogenies are coordinated in time by the simultaneous structuration provided by phylogeny and culture (Fig. 13.2b).

Now consider the behaviors of the adults when they first catch sight of their newborn child and discover if it is male or female. Typical comments include "I shall be worried to death when she's eighteen" or "She can't play rugby." In each of these examples, the adults interpret the biological characteristics of the child in terms of their own past (cultural) experience. In the experience of English men and women living in the mid-20th century, it could be considered common knowledge that girls do not play rugby and that when they enter adolescence they will be the object of boys' sexual attention, putting them at various kinds of risk. Using this information derived from their cultural past and assuming that the world will be very much for their daughters what it has been for them, parents project probable futures for their children. This process is depicted in Fig. 13.2b by following the arrows from the mother to the cultural past of the mother to the cultural future of the baby to the present adult treatment of the baby.

Of crucial importance to understanding the contribution of culture in constituting development is the fact that the parents' (purely ideal) projection of their children's future, derived from their memory of their cultural past becomes a fundamentally important material constraint organizing the child's life experiences in the present. This rather abstract, nonlinear process is what gives rise to the well-known phenomenon that even adults totally ignorant of the real gender of a newborn will treat the baby quite differently depending on its symbolic or cultural gender. Adults literally create different material forms of interaction based on conceptions of the world provided by their cultural experience when, for example, they bounce boy infants (those wearing blue diapers) and attribute manly virtues to them while they treat girl infants (those wearing pink diapers) in a gentle manner and attribute beauty and sweet temperaments to them (Rubin, Provezano, & Luria, 1974).

Macfarlane's example also demonstrates an important distinction between the social and the cultural, which are generally conflated in two factor theories of development, such as those presented schematically in Fig. 13.1. Culture in this case refers to remembered forms of activity deemed appropriate to one's gender as an adolescent and as an infant, while social refers to the people whose behavior is conforming to the given cultural pattern. This example also motivates the special emphasis placed on the social origins of higher psychological functions by developmental psychologists who adopt the notion of culture presented here (Cole, 1988; Rogoff, 1989, Valsiner, 1988; Vygotsky, 1987; Wertsch, 1985). As Macfarlane's transcripts clearly demonstrate, human nature is social in a sense different from the sociability of other species. Only a culture-using human being can reach into the cultural past, project it into the (ideal or conceptual) future, and then carry that ideal or conceptual future back into the present to create the sociocultural environment of the newcomer.

This example also helps us to understand the ways in which culture contributes to both continuity and discontinuity in individual development. In thinking about their babies' futures these parents are assuming that the "way things have always been is the way things will always be" calling to mind White's telling image that temporally, the culturally constituted mind "is not a succession of disconnected episodes, but a continuum extending to infinity in both directions, from eternity to eternity." In this manner, culture is the medium that allows people to project the past into the future, providing an essential basis of psychological continuity.

This assumption, of course, is sometimes wrong. The invention of new ways to exploit energy or new media of representation, or simple changes in custom, may sufficiently disrupt the existing cultural order to be a source of significant developmental discontinuity. As an example, in the 1950s American parents who assumed that their daughters would not be soccer players at the age of 16, would have been correct. But in 1990, a great many American girls play soccer.

I know of no recordings equivalent to Macfarlane's from very different cultures, but an interesting account of birthing among the Zinacanteco of south-central Mexico appears to show similar processes at work. In their summary of developmental research among the Zinacanteco, Greenfield, Brazelton, and Childs (1989) report a man's account of his son's birth at which the son "was given three chilies to hold so that it would . . . know to buy chili when it grew up. It was given a billhood, a digging stick, an axe, and a [strip of] palm so that it would learn to weave palm" (p. 177).

Baby girls are given an equivalent set of objects associated with adult female status. The future orientation of differential treatment of the babies is not only present in ritual; it is coded in the Zinacantecan saying, "For in the newborn baby is the future of our world."

Infancy

It has long been recognized that there is an intimate link between relative immaturity of the human newborn, which will require years of nurturing before it can approach something akin to self-sufficiency, and that fact that human beings inhabit a culturally mediated environment. Both facts are distinctive characteristics of our species. Infancy (from a Latin word meaning one who does not speak) is widely, if not universally, considered a distinctive period of development that extends from birth until approximately the age of 2 ½.[5]

Getting on a Schedule. The earliest, essential condition for continued development following birth is that the child and those who care for him or her must become coordinated in such a manner that the adults are able to accumulate enough resources to accommodate the newcomer. In this process, there is an intricate interplay between the initial characteristics of children and the cultural environment into which they are born, resulting in what Super and Harkness (1982, 1986) refer to as the developmental niche.

A clear-cut example of a cultural influence on the way the process of coordination is achieved is afforded by the contrasting patterns of sleep in the months following birth by American urban dwelling and rural Kenyan (Kipsigis) children (Super & Harkness, 1982). Among children in the United States, there is a marked shift toward the adult day/night cycle a few weeks after birth; by the end of the second week, they are averaging about 8 ½ hours of sleep between the hours of 7 p.m. and 7 a.m. Between 4 and 8 months the longest sleep episode increases from about 4 to 8 hours a night. The pressures toward sleeping through the night are not difficult to identify. American urban dwellers live by the clock. In an era in which a very large proportion of mothers as well as fathers have jobs outside the home, they must leave the house at a specified time, and the child must be ready at that time. As a consequence of the child's need for sleep, the adults' needs to get to work, and the adults' desires to spend some leisure time without the child to worry about, they are likely to push as hard as possible for the child to eat and sleep when it is convenient for them.

Among the Kipsigis infants, the course of getting on a schedule is very

---

[5]Because babies begin to acquire their first words well before the age of 2 ½, it seems most appropriate to interpret the link between infancy and speaking by interpreting it to mean the ability to engage in a conversation.

different. At night they sleep with their mothers and are permitted to nurse on demand. During the day they are strapped to their mothers' backs, accompanying them on their daily rounds of farming, household chores, and social activities. They do a lot of napping while their mothers go about their work. At one month, the longest period of sleep reported for babies in the Kipsigis sample was 3 hours, and their longest sleep episode increases little during the first 8 months of postnatal life.

At one level these observations are banal. They show only that children fit into the community into which they are born. But a seemingly simple case can be useful when it comes to analyzing more complex cases, and even this simple case contains some important lessons. First, the shaping process that produces different patterns of sleeping is indicative of more than a temporary convenience. As adults, assuming there is little change in Kipsigis life circumstances, the children socialized into a flexible sleep schedule will themselves be more flexible than their American counterparts. Second, the rather rigid schedule imposed by modern industrialized lifestyles may be pushing the limits of what the immature human brain can sustain; hence, while the length of a longest sleep period may be a good indicator of physical maturity, pushing those limits may be a source of stress with negative consequences for children who cannot measure up to parental expectations (Konner & Super, 1987).

From Sucking to Nursing. In the 1940s Margaret Mead and Frances Macgregor (1951) set out to test Gesell's ideas about the relation between growth (maturation) and learning through cross-cultural research. They argued that basic principles of the way that cultures interweave learning and maturation can be seen in the way that the change from reflex sucking to nursing is organized and in the long-term behavioral implications of this organization.

Some cultures, they noted, take advantage of the sucking reflex by putting the baby to the mother's breast immediately to stimulate the flow of milk, although the baby remains hungry; others provide a wet nurse, others will give the baby a bottle, and so on. In an immediate sense, all of these routes to mature nursing are equally adequate. However, they have various different implications in the short, and even the long, run. Mead and Macgregor point to one potential short-run effect; babies who are bottle fed until their mother's milk comes in may elaborate nursing behaviors that interfere with breast-feeding, changing both short-run nutritional and social–interactional experiences.

Longer term effects arise from the interconnection of the adults' choice of feeding method and larger life patterns. For example, if a mother who stays at home gives her baby a bottle because she believes that bottled milk is more nutritious, the use of a bottle rather than breast-feeding may have no differential impact on the development of social relations between mother and child (although it may produce a tendency to obesity, which can have other long-term effects). However, if the baby is bottle fed because the mother works at a factory and must return to work in a week and knows that the baby will be placed in infant day care, the bottle feeding at birth will become part of a life pattern in which the mother and baby have a less intimate relationship and the baby becomes accustomed at an early age to social interactions with peers and several caretakers.

The Future in the Present: A Cross-Cultural Example

To link the mechanisms of cultural mediation displayed in Macfarlane's conversations of parents greeting their newborns to examples of cultural effects discussed in later sections, I selected an example from work by Bornstein and his colleagues on the interactions between American and Japanese mothers with their 5-month-old offspring (Bornstein, Toda, Azuma, Tamis-LeMonda, & Ogino, 1990; Bornstein, Tal, & Tamis-LeMonda, 1991; see Nugent, Lester, & Brazelton, 1989, for another set of articles).

The focus of this work was the way that mothers living in New York and in Tokyo respond to their infants' orientations to events in the environment or to the mothers themselves. Using a variety of measures of infant behaviors (level of activity, the rate at which they habituate to the sight of their mothers' faces or objects in the environment, the level of vocalization of various kinds) Bornstein and his colleagues established the fact that infants in the two cultures behaved in similar manners and in this important sense, provided similar starting points for their mothers' responses to them. Of particular importance in light of maternal behaviors, infants from the two societies displayed equal levels of orientation to their mothers and to physical objects in the environment.

Despite the fact that these infants represented equivalent stimuli in the objective sense provided by the researchers' behavioral measurements, there was a distinctive difference in the way that the mothers responded to their infants. American mothers were more responsive when their children oriented to physical objects in the environment; Japanese mothers were more responsive when their infants oriented to them. Moreover, the mothers made overt attempts to change the locus of their infants' orientation when it did not fit their preference; American mothers diverted children's attention from themselves to objects, while Japanese mothers showed the opposite pattern.

Once again we see a pervasive feature of cultural influences on development. Japanese maternal behavior is part of a system that highly values a strong dependence of the child on the mother while American maternal behavior is part of a system that values independence. These different value orientations make little difference to the welfare of the children at 5 months of age; both forms of interaction are caring and supportive. But they are part of a system of constraints on the children that do make a difference as the child grows older. Bornstein and his colleagues note that as toddlers, Japanese and American children do not differ in their global language and play skills. But they do differ in the kinds of language and the kinds of play they are best at in ways that correspond to the differences evident in their mothers' behaviors at the age of 5 months. We see other ways in which they differ in the following sections.

A Shift in Socioemotional and Cognitive Development at 6 to 9 Months. The period from 6 to 9 months of age is strategically useful for illustrating several points about culture and development for several reasons. First, there is a good deal of evidence pointing to a universal and distinctive reorganization of the overall way in which children interact with their environments at this time, illustrating the stage-transformation process that we referred to earlier as a bio-social-behavioral shift (Cole & Cole, 1989, Chap. 6). Second, there is a good deal of cross-cultural data that allow us to address both general and culture-specific ways in which this change occurs. The cross-cultural data are also interesting for the general method-ological problems of cross-cultural research that they raise as for their substantive contributions to understanding the role of culture in develop-ment.

The universal changes occurring at 6 to 9 months of age are apparent in all parts of the bio-social-behavioral shift. With respect to the biological strand, we find that new patterns of electrical activity, associated with increased levels of myelinization, arise in several parts of the brain (Dreyfus-Brisac, 1978; Goldman-Rakic, 1987). The affected areas include the frontal lobes (which play a crucial role in deliberate action and planning), the cerebellum (which is important in controlling movement and balance), and the hippocampus (important in memory). In addition, the muscles have become stronger and the bones harder than they were at birth, providing support for increasingly vigorous movement.

Increased motor skills associated with these changes allow children to move around objects, pick them up, taste them, and attempt to use them for various purposes. This increased exploratory capacity has been shown to have important psychological consequences because they are important in enabling the infant to discover the invariant properties of objects. Berten-thal and Campos (1990), for example, showed that children given extensive experience moving around in babywalkers before they could locomote on their own displayed improved performance on Piagetian object permanence tests.

For these new forms of experience to have a cumulative impact, infants must be able to remember them. Evidence from a number of sources (Kagan, Kearsley, & Zelazo, 1978; Mandler, 1984; Schacter & Moskovitch, 1984) indicates that between 6 and 9 months of age children show a markedly enhanced ability to recall prior events without being reminded of them. Closely related is a shift in the propensity to categorize artificially constructed arrays of objects (Ruff, 1978; Starkey, 1981). Taken together, these increased memory and categorizing abilities increase the degree to which children can structure information from past experience, enabling them to deal more effectively with current circumstances.

The combination of increased mobility and increased remembering also brings increased awareness of the dangers and discomforts the world has in store. These changes, in turn, are associated with changes in children's social relationships with caretakers about whom children have begun to build stable expectations.

Once children begin to crawl and walk, caretakers can no longer directly prevent mishaps, no matter how carefully they arrange the environment. Newly mobile babies keep a watchful eye on their caretakers for feedback about how they are doing — called *social referencing* (Campos & Stenberg, 1981). At the same time, children become wary of strangers and become upset when their primary caretakers leave them. This complex of apparently related social behaviors has led a number of psychologists to hypothesize that a new quality of emotional relationship between caretaker and child emerges, called attachment.

Attachment. Although various aspects of the complex of changes that occur between 6 and 9 months of age have been investigated cross-culturally (e.g., Kagan, 1977, reported data supporting the hypothesis of cross-cultural universals with respect to various aspects of remembering and object permanence), by far the greatest amount of data has been collected on cultural contributions to attachment, so it is on this issue that I focus in attempting to specify the role of culture in overall behavior at this time. Despite the fact that there are competing theories to account for how and why children form special emotional bonds with their caretakers (see Cole & Cole, 1989, for a summary), current research appears to be motivated primarily by ideas put forth by Bowlby (1969). The starting point for Bowlby's work on attachment was his attempt to explain why extended periods of separation from parents were so upsetting to small children, even though they were maintained in perfectly adequate circumstances from a purely physical point of view. His explanation, briefly stated, was that one has to interpret contemporary forms of behavior in terms of the environment of evolutionary adaptedness into which our species evolved. Behaviors that might seem irrational today were once crucial to survival, becoming a part of the human biological repertoire through natural selection.

Bowlby based his ideas about the environment of evolutionary adaptedness of attachment behaviors in part on what is known about mother–infant interactions among currently existing large, ground-living apes. These presumed phylogenetic cousins share their environment with predators from whom they protect themselves by banding together. Owing to their relatively long immaturity, the offspring of these apes must remain close to their mothers to survive. This need for proximity and safety is counterbalanced by the equally strong need to explore and play, which separates offspring and parent. Bowlby hypothesized that attachment arises during the first year of life as a way of maintaining a dynamic equilibrium between safety and exploration controlled by the mother–child dyad. When the distance between mother and child is too great, one or the other gets upset and seeks the other out. When there is too much proximity, one of the partners gets bored or annoyed, resulting in increased distance.

Described in this way, the development of attachment would seem to be a necessary, universal biological requirement to be found in all cultures under normal circumstances because it is a species-specific consequence of our phylogenetic heritage. However, the fact of universality (should it be demonstrated) would in no way contradict the principle of cultural mediation. Rather, it forces a closer look at precisely how the formation of attachment is mediated and how that pattern of mediation fits into the overall life course of human beings reared in varying cultural–historical circumstances. During the past two decades, there has been an increasingly heated dispute on precisely this point. This dispute is worth examining in some detail because it is typical of difficulties facing the use of cross-cultural approaches to culture and development in a great many other cases.

Appropriately, the studies that began the modern debate on culture and attachment arose from comparison of the behaviors mother–child pairs observed in their homes in the United States and Uganda by Mary Ainsworth (Ainsworth, 1967; Ainsworth, Blehar, Waters, & Wall, 1978). Ainsworth was struck by the fact that children in both cultural groups exhibited similar patterns of attachment-related behavior (distress during brief, everyday, separation from their mothers, fear of strangers, and use of the mother as a secure base from which to explore). However, the Ugandan children seemed to express these behavior patterns more readily and intensely than did the American children Ainsworth studied. As a means of provoking attachment-related behaviors in American children, Ainsworth devised the Strange Situation, a sequence of interactional episodes acted out by the mother in a specially designed laboratory environment that typically resembles a doctor's waiting room. It is important to note that she assumed that this artificial situation would evoke levels of anxiety in American children roughly comparable to those evoked among Ugandan children in the everyday settings she had observed so that she could have comparable phenomena to study.

The standardized Strange Situation consists of eight phases, each of which lasts 3 minutes or less: After giving instructions (Phase 1), the experimenter leaves the child and caregiver alone (Phase 2). Then the experimenter returns (Phase 3), the caregiver leaves (Phase 4), the caregiver returns (Phase 5), and then leaves the child alone (Phase 6), after which the experimenter returns (Phase 7), and finally the caregiver returns (Phase 8).

During the 1970s and continuing to the present time there has been a great deal of research on the behavior produced in this situation, its antecedents, and its sequelae (see Bretherton & Waters, 1985, or the entire issue of *Human Development,* 1990, No. 1, for reviews and references to additional primary sources of information). Slowly at first, and with increasing frequency in the past 5 years, the Strange Situation has been used in cross-cultural research. This time (ironically in light of the reasons that Ainsworth introduced it in the first place) it was used as a standardized research instrument, to be administered to all subjects in all cultures in precisely the same way, instead of as a procedure for creating slightly discrepant series of events designed to model and assess development in relation to its cultural origins.

As a way to establish the antecedents and consequences of different qualities of attachment, Ainsworth and her colleagues constructed three categories, based heavily on how the infant reacts when the caretaker returns after an absence:

Type A (anxious–avoidant) children turn away or look away when their caregivers return, instead of seeking closeness and comfort.

Type B (securely attached) children go to their caregivers, calm down quickly after their early upset, and soon resume playing.

Type C (anxious–resistant) children are often upset while their mothers are with them just as a result of being in the strange environment. They become very upset when their caregivers leave, and they simultaneously seek closeness and resist contact when the caregivers return.

Use of these categories in cross-cultural research is significant because the distribution of children among categories is used to underpin the claim that it is possible to identify precursors of habitual socioemotional characteristics of children and their relationships to their caregivers that have developmental consequences that last for months, and perhaps years (see e.g., the articles by Grossmann & Grossmann, 1990; Main, 1990). The primary antecedent to varying degrees of attachment has been assumed to be maternal sensitiveness, the degree to which the caretaker responds reliably and satisfactorily to the infant's behavior; the main consequence has been thought of as increased sociocognitive competence.

Grossmann and Grossmann's (1990) summary of the research literature captures well one view of the results of this work:

> Caretakers' responsiveness to infants' signals of insecurity seems to be the main determinant of secure versus avoidantly or ambivalently insecure infant behaviors to mothers or fathers at 1 year of age. An individual's "inner working model," resulting from differential dyadic attachment history, may determine how inner emotional conflicts are resolved. On the basis of existing longitudinal data, the following emotional response styles appear to be prevalent: Individuals with secure attachment histories pay attention to the full range of external causes for conflicting emotions and they tolerate contradictory emotions. Individuals with insecure attachment histories, in contrast, pay attention only to selected fractions of their emotional reactions at any given time, and they tend to lose sight of the full range of external causes for potentially conflicting emotions. These developmental sequences appear to be universal. Cultural differences may exist in terms of frequency and difficulty of potentially conflicting challenges. (p. 31)

Clearly, if this summary is taken at face value, secure attachment, especially secure attachment as manifested in the Strange Situation, is important to the future well-being of the child, and populations in which secure attachment occurs infrequently ought to be concerned. Because rather wide cross-national variations in the proportion of children assigned to the three major attachment categories have been reported in the literature, it should come as no surprise that the Grossmann's view is somewhat controversial.

To begin with, consider the data in Table 13.1, which are taken from four

TABLE 13.1
Patterns of Attachment from Four Cultural Samples

Country	Anxious/Avoidant	Secure	Anxious/Resistant
USA (n = 105)[a]	21	67	12
Germany (n = 46)[b]	52	35	13
Israel (n = 82)[c]	7	57	34
Japan (n = 60)[d]	0	68	32

[a]From Ainsworth, Blehar, Waters, & Wall, 1978
[b]From Grossmann, Grossmann, Huber, & Wartner, 1981
[c]From Sagi et al., 1985
[d]From Takahashi, 1986

(These studies were selected as benchmarks owing to the selection by Van IJzendoorn & Kroonenberg's, 1988, use of them in this capacity in their meta-analysis.)

widely cited studies of attachment using the Strange Situation (from IJzendoorn & Kroonenberg, 1988). The top line is from an early study by Ainsworth and colleagues that has often been taken as a standard of comparison. Roughly two thirds of the children are assessed as securely attached. In contrast, only one third of children tested in northern Germany are assessed as secure, with fully half assessed as anxious–avoidant. In Israel and Japan, the proportions of securely attached children are roughly equivalent to that in the U.S. sample, but there are almost three times as many children assessed as anxious–resistant as in the other two samples.

What are we to make of such variation? When interpretation is based on the distribution of types of attachment behaviors manifested in the Strange Situation alone, two lines of explanation are offered. The first assumes that the Strange Situation is a valid index of a universal form of emotional reaction that is distributed differently in different cultures. The second assumes that although standardized, the Strange Situation is really a different situation in different cultural circumstances, in that it takes on different meanings for the participants.[6]

As LeVine and Miller (1990) point out, the assumption that the meaning of the Strange Situation is a culture-neutral and valid indicator of a universal form of relationship called *attachment* leads to the further assumption that the American pattern is a universal norm and the conclusion (for example) that, in northern Germany, a high proportion of the children will display various forms of incompetence owing to deficient attachment formation in early childhood. Precisely such interpretations have been given in the case of American subpopulations, such as families in which there are high levels of conflict and child abuse (Vaughn, Egeland, Sroufe, & Waters, 1979). An alternative strategy of explanation, which retains the notion that the Strange Situation is a valid indicator of attachment, retains the categories and measuring criteria, but redefines the meaning of the categories according to the local culture. This is what the Grossmanns and their colleagues did (Grossmann, Grossmann, Spangler, Suess, & Unzner, 1985; Grossmann & Grossmann, 1990) when they suggested that vis-à-vis the American standard, northern German parents emphasize autonomy at an early age, which induces their children to show autonomy in this situation (perhaps a slight, but certainly a significant, reinterpretation of anxious–avoidant).

The other choice is to assume, as does Takahashi (1990) for example, that

---

[6]As van IJzendoorn (1990) pointed out, the complexity of reaching conclusions about cultural variations in attachment is complicated by the fact that there is a good deal of variation *within* societies in the distribution of attachment behaviors observed. This added level of variation might reflect either variations across subcultures within a society (e.g., northern vs. southern German samples) or secular changes in culture associated with rapid urbanization or other factors.

although standardized, the Strange Situation is really a different situation in different cultural circumstances, in that it has different meaning for the participants. For example, in Japan children are almost never away from their mothers during the first year of life, so the Strange Situation is indeed very strange, and the resulting stress pushes children from the secure to the anxious–resistant category. In Israel, the children are often away from their parents, but always with one of a small set of familiar caretakers, so they, like the Japanese, are especially stressed by the Strange Situation because it exposes them, perhaps for the first time in their lives, to separation from their major attachment figure(s). These explanations have one thing in common: They assume that the fit between the Strange Situation and children's prior experience differs systematically from culture to culture and that differences in Strange Situation behaviors are a function of this difference. The only way to obtain functional equivalence of Strange Situations in different cultures, it would seem, would be to create a different assessment instrument for each culture; this is, in effect, what Ainsworth did when she took her appearance in a village as the criterial situation of Ugandan infants and the artificially created Strange Situation as the functionally equivalent situation for the American children with whom she worked. However, using a different observational setting for each cultural group would immediately undermine the equivalence of procedures that is the foundation of standardization needed by the those who seek to establish the universal validity of the Strange Situation.

As Grossmann and Grossmann (1990) and LeVine and Miller (1990) point out, the dilemma of standardization (literal equivalence of the test environment) versus culture-contingent standardization (functional equivalence of the test environment; see Frijda & Jahoda, 1966) cannot be solved using the Strange Situation alone. Detailed analyses of the cultures under study is required to determine the normative life courses of members that shape the everyday interactions of child–caregiver relationships. This line of action also requires psychologists to study individuals in a way that not only includes their behaviors in the Strange Situation, but that traces back to their earlier life experiences and follows them forward to later behaviors in a variety of culturally common circumstances for each culture involved. In the work of the Grossmanns and Main, a variety of ingenious techniques, including ratings of the quality of mother–child interaction in later years, the quality of children's communication with other children in different settings, and even adult memories of their own childhoods, has been used to establish the longitudinal predictiveness of different qualities of behavior in the Strange Situation in some cultures. However, in other cases, such as that reported by Takahashi (1990) for Japanese children, it appears that while behavior in the Strange Situation is predictive of such characteristics as curiosity toward unfamiliar objects and social competence for about 1 year, the behavioral difference between babies categorized as securely and insecurely attached disappeared by the time the children were 3 years of age. These findings indicate that it will require culturally sensitive longitudinal research to tease apart the universal and culture-specific aspects of the socioemotional development presumably indexed by the Strange Situation.

It should also be pointed out that recent culturally sensitive longitudinal research using the Strange Situation has yet to be extended to nonindustrial societies in which very different values relating to desirable infant behaviors may exist. For example, Greenfield and colleagues (1989) report that among Zinacantecans there is a strong emphasis on socializing children to maintain old traditions; exploration, experimentation, and novelty are negatively valued. In line with this value system, infants are breast-fed at the slightest hint of any activity on their part as a way of quieting, and, Greenfield and colleagues speculate, as a way to teach them to allow their elders to take the initiative. There is no doubt that this is sensitive responding on the part of the mother, but its effects on infant behavior can be expected to be quite different from any of the societies in which the ontogenetic implications of attachment have thus far been studied.

Language.   No area of culture and human development has attracted as much scholarly attention as the interrelation among culture, language, and development. Two major, and related, questions have organized discussion in the field. First, the acquisition of language has been one of the major battlefields on which the nature–nurture controversy has been fought: Must language be acquired through a process of culturally mediated learning or constructive interaction like any other human cognitive capacity, or is language a specialized, bounded domain (module) that needs only to be triggered to spring into action? (See Bruner, 1983; Piatelli-Palmerini, 1980; Wanner & Gleitman, 1982, for excellent discussions of the contending viewpoints.) Second, what role does the acquisition of language play in the development of thought? If language is a structurally distinct module, then there should be no particular relation between language and thought. On the other hand, in so far as culturally organized experience is seen to be essential to the acquisition of language, then language, thought, and development are likely to be intimately connected.

In contrast with the research on attachment, but like the research on the earliest adaptations of infants to the culturally scripted schedules into which they must fit, the research on language depends more on the study of natural variations in cultural circumstances, and less on standardized test procedures.

Hardly anyone believes that language can be acquired in the total absence of interaction with other human beings who speak a language. Rather, the position of those who adopt a nativist position with respect to language assumes that its development proceeds akin to the development of any bodily organ: Any environment that sustains the life of the social group is adequate to produce the development of language without any special attention needing to be paid to the process.

With respect to human beings, the environment that sustains life is one that exists in the medium of culture, which leads one to attempt to specify more carefully what minimum conditions of culturally mediated interaction between children and adults are sufficient to support development of the language organ.

Two categories of cases in which children are reared in conditions that systematically reduce their immersion in culture help to specify the universal lower limits of cultural support needed to sustain language development. The first is the well-known case of Genie, studied by Susan Curtiss (1977). Genie was locked in a room by herself sometime before her second birthday. She lived chained by day to a potty and trussed up in a sleeping bag at night for 11 years, during which time she had virtually no normal linguistic input and only a minimum of social interactions that could be considered culturally normal in any culture.

When she was liberated from these horrible circumstances at the age of 13 she was in pitiful shape: She was emaciated and very short. She could not walk normally, rarely made a sound, and was not toilet trained. Although on testing she showed remarkable skills for spatial analysis, she had failed to acquire language. Nor did she recover from her many years of severely deprived existence; she acquired a small vocabulary and some forms of appropriate social interaction, but her behavior remained abnormal, despite attempts at therapeutic intervention.

There are several intermediate cases between the extreme deprivation resulting in development without language or culture (the case of Genie) and the situation of the vast majority of children. One particularly instructive situation arises among children born deaf to hearing parents who do not believe that it is useful for their children to sign, insisting instead that they learn to interact through oral language (Goldin-Meadow, 1985). These children are reared in an environment that is rich in culturally mediated social interactions (including linguistic mediation), which include the child and proceed very much as they would if the child could hear; people eat meals together, the children are given baths and put to bed, they go to the store, and are toilet trained. Thus, they live in a world suffused with meaning; it is only the linguistic behavior that fills the gaps between movements and provides accounts of the rationale and prior history of those actions that they are missing.

Under these circumstances, children are known spontaneously to begin to employ *home sign,* a kind of communication through pantomime. Goldin-Meadow showed that home sign acquired in these circumstances exhibits a number of properties also found in the early stages of natural language acquisition. Children who start signing in the absence of adult sign language knowers begin to make two, three, and longer sign sequences around their second birthdays, at about the same time that hearing children create multiword sentences. Most significantly, Goldin-Meadow reported that these deaf children were able to embed sign sentences within each other ("You/Susan give me/Abe cookie round"). This kind of behavior reveals that the children could engage in recursion, a form of communicative behavior that is characteristic of all human languages and absent from the communicative system of chimpanzees or other creatures, even following extensive training.

However, their language development comes to a halt at this point. The cultural medium is simply too thin to support the development of fully mature language. It appears that unless such children are provided access to some form of language as a part of the culturally organized environments they participate in, they will not develop the more subtle features of language on which sustainable cultural formations depend.

It is important to add that at the other extreme, where children have access to language, but not to culturally organized activity, language development also fails to take place. Children who have been left alone for a long time with a television set broadcasting in a foreign language do not acquire that language (Snow et al., 1976).

It seems an inescapable conclusion from this kind of evidence that in order for children to acquire more than the barest rudiments of language, they must not only hear (or see) language but they must also participate in the activities that that language is helping to create. In everyday activity, words are essential material-ideal artifacts, by means of which people establish and maintain coordination, filling in the gaps between gestures and other actions, and making possible the fine tuning of expectations and interpretations.

Bruner (1982) referred to the social interactional constraints of ongoing everyday activities as *formats*. The format, he wrote

> is a rule-bound microcosm in which the adult and child *do* things to and with each other. In its most general sense, it is the instrument of patterned human interaction. Since formats pattern communicative interaction between infant and caretaker before lexico-grammatical speech begins, they are crucial vehicles in the passage from communication to language.

Later he added that once they become conventionalized, formats seem to have a kind of exteriority that allows them to act as constraints on the actions that occur within them. In this respect, Bruner's notion of format is very similar to Nelson's (1981, 1986) concept of generalized event schemas called *scripts,* "sequentially organized structures of causally and temporally linked acts with the actors and objects specified in the most general way" (Nelson, 1981, p. 101). In effect, these event-level cultural artifacts, embodied in the vocabulary and habitual actions of adults, act as structured media within which children can experience the covariation of language and action while remaining coordinated in a general way with culturally organized forms of behavior. In the process of negotiating such events with enculturated caregivers, children discover the vast range of meanings encoded in their language at the same time as they find new ways to carry out their own intentions.

Bruner (1982) captured the cultural view of language development when he wrote that language acquisition cannot be reduced to

> either the virtuoso cracking of a linguistic code, or the spinoff of ordinary cognitive development, or the gradual takeover of adults' speech by the child through some impossible inductive *tour de force.* It is rather, a subtle process by which adults artificially arrange the world so that the child can succeed culturally by doing what comes naturally, and with others similarly inclined. (p. 15)

Cross-cultural research on language interaction supplements intra-cultural studies by laying bare the incredible diversity of cultural modes of involving children in adult-run activities, such that they come to acquire language.

Arguments over the importance of the environment in language acquisition gave rise to a large literature on the different ways that parents structure children's activities (see, e.g., de Villiers & de Villiers, 1978; Chap. 6, this volume). Parents in many societies adopt something akin to a baby-talk mode when speaking to their children, before and while the children are acquiring language. Evidence available at the time led Ferguson (1977) to speculate that a special *baby talk register* (using higher pitch and intonation, simplified vocabulary, grammatically less complex sentences, and utterances designed to highlight important aspects of the situation) is a universal, acquisition-enhancing form of adult language socialization behavior. Cross-cultural data have shown that although adults everywhere speak to young children differently than they speak to older children and adults, the particular form of baby talk involving simplified grammar and vocabulary characteristic of middle-class American parents is not universal. There is some evidence that other features of baby talk, such as the use of distinctive pitch and intonation, may be universal, but the data on cultural variation remain sparse (Fernald, 1989).

In many societies, adults deliberately teach vocabulary, styles of address, and other linguistic features. The Kaluli of Papua, New Guinea, for example, are reported to hold their small infants facing away from them and toward other people while the mothers speak for them. There are also subcultures within the United States (e.g., working class people in Baltimore, Maryland; Miller, 1982) in which it is firmly believed that children must be explicitly taught vocabulary, using quite rigid frames of the sort "How do you call this?" (See Schieffelin & Ochs, 1986, for a wide range of examples.) However, although the adults involved in such practices may believe that such special tailoring is helpful to their children's language acquisition, the data indicate that significant benefits associated with variations in cultural patterns of mother–infant interactions involving language are found rather rarely and in restricted domains (Snow & Ferguson, 1977).

The most secure overall generalization at this point is that culturally organized joint activity that incorporates the child into the scene as a novice participant is one necessary ingredient in language acquisition. As children in such activities struggle to understand objects and social relations in order to gain control over their environments and themselves, they recreate the culture into which they are born, even as they reinvent the language of their forbearers.

The Future in the Present During Early Childhood

In contrast to infancy, which is a good candidate for a universally acknowledged stage of development, there is some uncertainty about how one should treat children of ages from 2 ½ to 6 years. Whiting and Edwards (1988), following Mead (1935), divide this period into two parts: 2- to 3-year-olds are referred to as knee children, who are kept close at hand but not continuously on the mother's lap or in a crib; 4- to 5-year-olds are referred to as yard children, because they can leave their mothers' sides but are not allowed to wander far. In many modern, industrialized countries, children between 3 and 5 to 6 years of age spend part of every day in an environment designed to prepare them for school, which has led this time of life to be called the preschool period.

The example of culture in development for children of this age provides another clear illustration of how adults bring the future into the present in shaping children's experiences. Tobin, Wu, and Davidson (1989) conducted a comparative study of preschool socialization in Hawaii, Japan, and China. They recorded classroom interactions that they then showed to teachers and other audiences in all three countries, to evoke their interpretations and basic cultural schemata relevant to the preschool child. Only the Japanese and American data are discussed here.

When Tobin and his colleagues videotaped a day in the life of a Japanese preschool, young Hiroki was acting up. He greeted the visitors by exposing his penis and waving it at them. He initiated fights, disrupted other children's games, and made obscene comments. When American preschool teachers observed the videotape they disapproved of Hiroki's behavior, his teacher's handling of it, and of many aspects of life in the Japanese classroom, in general. His teacher and other Japanese observers had a quite different interpretation. Starting first with the overall ambience of the classroom, Americans were scandalized by the fact that there were 30 preschoolers and only one teacher in the classroom. How could this be in an affluent country like Japan? They could not understand why Hiroki was not isolated as punishment.

The Japanese had a very different interpretation. First, while teachers acknowledged that it would be very pleasant for them to have a smaller classroom, they believed it would be bad for the children, who "need to have the experience of being in a large group in order to learn to relate to lots of children in lots of kinds of situations" (Tobin et al., 1989, p. 37). When asked about their ideal notion of class size, the Japanese teachers generally named 15 or more students per teacher in contrast with the 4 to 8 preferred by American preschool teachers. When Japanese preschool teachers observed a tape of an American preschool they worried for the children. "A class that size seems kind of sad and underpopulated," one remarked. Another added, "I wonder how you teach a child to become a member of a group in a class that small" (p. 38).

Members of the two cultures also had very different interpretations of the probable reasons for Hiroki's behavior. One American speculated that Hiroki misbehaved because he was intellectually gifted and easily became bored. Not only did the Japanese reject this notion (on the grounds that speed is not the same as intelligence), but they offered a different interpretation. To them, such words as smart and intelligent are almost synonymous with well-behaved and praiseworthy, neither of which apply to Hiroki. Hiroki, they believed, had a *dependency disorder*. Owing to the absence of a mother in the home, he did not know how to be properly dependent and consequently, how to be sensitive to others and obedient. Isolating Hiroki, they reasoned, would not help. Rather, he needed to learn to get along in his group and develop the proper understanding in that context.

Tobin and his colleagues (1989) comment on the Japanese view of their preschool system and Hiroki's behavior as follows:

> . . . Japanese teachers and Japanese society place [great value] on equality and the notion that children's success and failure and their potential to become successful versus failed adults has more to do with effort and character and thus with what can be learned and taught in school than with raw inborn ability. (p. 24)

The Japanese who watched the tape disapproved of the promotion of individualism that they observed in tapes of an American classroom, believing that "A child's humanity is realized most fully not so much in his ability to be independent from the group as his ability to cooperate and feel part of the group" (p. 39). One Japanese school administrator added:

> For my tastes there is something about the American approach [where children are asked to explain their feelings when they misbehave] that is a bit too heavy, too adultlike, too severe and controlled for young children. (p. 53)

There are many interesting implications to be drawn from these observations, only a tiny fraction of which I have touched on here. However, in the present context my purpose is to relate them to the situation such children will encounter as adults, in particular the situation that Japanese boys will face should they pursue a career in the American pastime of baseball.

My source in this case is a fascinating account of the fate of American baseball players who play in the Japanese major leagues (R. Whiting, 1989). Despite their great skill, experience, and physical size, American ballplayers generally have a very difficult time in Japan. There are many reasons for their difficulties, but crucial is a completely different understanding of keys to success in this team sport, a difference that mirrors differences in preschool education in the two cultures to an amazing degree. The title of the book, *You Gotta Have Wa*, pinpoints one key difference. *Wa* is the Japanese word for group harmony, and, according to Whiting, it is what most clearly differentiates Japanese baseball from the American game. Although American ballplayers maintain that individual initiative and innate ability are the key ingredients to success, the Japanese emphasize that "the individual was nothing without others and that even the most talented people need constant direction" (p. 70). Linked to the emphasis on group harmony is an equivalent emphasis on *doryoku,* the ability to persevere in the face of adversity as the key to success, whereas Americans emphasized individual talent.

Whiting pointed out that the ideals of wa and doryoku are cornerstones not only of Japanese baseball, but of Japanese business as well.

> **Wa** is the motto of large multinational corporations, like Hitachi, while Sumimoto, Toshiba, and other leading Japanese firms send junior executives on outdoor retreats, where they meditate and perform spirit-strengthening exercises, wearing only loin-cloths and headband with **doryoku** emblazoned on them. (p. 74)

Despite their acknowledged talent, American players, whose understanding of the sources of success, the cultivation of which can clearly be seen in their preschool education, are generally unable to submit to the Japanese way of doing things. In a remark that echoes poignantly on the Japanese disapproval of the American emphasis on verbalizing and valuing personal feelings over group harmony, one American ballplayer who had a long and acrimonious public dispute with his manager was led to ask in desperation, "Don't you think that's going too far? What about my feelings? I have my pride you know." To which the manager replied, "I understand your feelings, however there are more important things."

Here again we see how culture operating on young children creates an effect conditioned not by present necessity, but by deep beliefs about "how things work"; an effect that has relatively minor consequences in the present life of the child, but major effects in terms of the long-term organization of his or her behavior.

Middle Childhood

One of the most pervasive changes in the cultural organization of children's lives is the new social arrangements that a wide variety of societies institute when their children reach the age of 5 to 7 years (Harkness & Super, 1985; Rogoff, Sellers, Pirrotta, Fox, & White, 1975). Given evidence of concomitant changes in biological, behavioral, and social characteristics of children sometime around their sixth birthday makes this transition an excellent candidate for a major bio-social-behavioral shift.[7]

In modern industrialized societies, this is the period during which children begin formal schooling. But even in societies in which there is no schooling, marked changes in children's activities are likely to occur. For example, among the Ngoni of Malawi in Central Africa (when Read, 1960, worked there), the boys, who have been living and socializing with other children of both sexes and their mothers, must leave the protection of the women, stop playing childish games, and move into dormitories where they must submit to male authority and begin to engage in at least rudimentary forms of adult work.

When we contrast the experiences of children who spend several hours a day, 5 days a week, attending formal schools with comparable children who remain at home helping their mothers with cooking, childcare, or gardening; or who accompany their fathers into the fields or forests to assist in farming, hunting, or making mortar bricks with which to build houses, certain prominent characteristics of the classroom experience stand out quite clearly.

---

[7]Here we restrict ourselves largely to changes in cognitive capacities in relation to the cultural organization of children's activities. For a more extensive treatment of this topic see Cole and Cole (1989, Part IV).

1. The settings in which schooling occurs are distinctive in that they are removed from contexts of practical activity; students are trained in the use of mediational means such as writing and provide dense exposure to the conceptual content of various cultural domains, which are supposed to provide the means later productive activity.

2. There is a peculiar social structure to formal schooling, in which a single adult interacts with many (often as many as 40 or 50, sometimes as many as 400) students at a time. Unlike most other settings for socialization, this adult is unlikely to have any familial ties to the learner, rendering the social relations relatively impersonal.

3. There is a peculiar value system associated with schooling that sets educated people above their peers and that, in secular education, values change and discontinuity over tradition and community.

4. There is a special mediational skill, writing, that is essential to the activity of schooling. Writing is used to represent both language and physical systems (e.g., mathematics).

5. All of these factors taken together result in a situation in which language is used in quite distinctive ways. Perhaps the best documented example of this distinction is the pattern of interaction in which teachers ask children to answer questions, the answers to which the teachers already know (Mehan, 1978).

This characterization of the distinctive nature of the activity settings associated with formal schooling does not do justice to all the differences between formal schooling and other socialization settings that might be considered educational in the broad sense. (For more extended discussions see Greenfield & Lave, 1982; Scribner & Cole, 1973.) However, it is sufficient to see that cultural discontinuities occurring during middle childhood present an especially attractive proving ground for testing theories about culture and cognitive development (for reviews see LCHC, 1983; Rogoff, 1981; Segall et al., 1990). From the many specific developmental phenomena that might be chosen for illustration, I discuss two here, the development of logical operations as interpreted by Piaget, and the development of memory, as interpreted by American cognitive psychologists. The topic of logic is of special interest because it assumes no special role of culture, but a universal pattern of age-related development. The topic of memory is interesting because it is one in which traditional theorizing hypothesized an advantage to cultures that do not use writing systems.

Schooling and the Development of Logical Operations.   For purposes of discussion, I assume the logical operations in question are those that form the basis for Piagetian theory within which it is assumed that concrete operations consist of organized systems (classifications, serial ordering, correspondences, etc.) that allow children to think through the consequences of an action (such as pouring water from one pitcher into another) and mentally to reverse that action. However, such operations remain limited in the sense that they proceed from one partial link to the next in a step-by-step fashion, without relating each partial link to all the others and they must be carried out on actual objects. Formal operations differ in that all of the possible combinations are considered, they can be carried out without reference to actual objects, and each partial link is grouped in relation to the "structured whole" (Inhelder & Piaget, 1958, p. 16).

It is an odd fact that when Piaget (1974) began to address the issue of cultural variations and cognitive development in the 1960s he did so with no reference whatsoever to his earlier speculations about traditional–conformist and modern–differentiated societies. Rather, he assumed that the sequence of cognitive changes that he had observed in Geneva was universal, and he restricted his attention to various factors that might modify the rate at which children progressed.

Three potential cultural differentia were selected for discussion (see LCHC, 1983, for more extended discussion). The key factor was the amount of *operational exercise,* the constant interplay of assimilation and accommodation that drives the system to higher, more inclusive, levels of equilibration (see Kuhn, Chap. 4, this volume).

Piaget saw two major sources of such exercise. First, in so far as children are encouraged to ask questions, work together, argue, and so on, they will be provided opportunities to notice different aspects of the same situation and achieve additional operational exercise through the need to reconcile different points of view. Second, it is possible that through such social institutions as formal schooling, some societies provide greater opportunities for operational exercise by helping children to confront and think about their environment with greater frequency. However, he was dubious about the extent to which schooling actually accomplished this task, in light of an authority structure that discouraged equilibration.

So, it would seem that here is a case in which the cross-cultural method is well suited to answering important questions about culture and development more generally. However, the history of this line of research has proved as much a cautionary tale, demonstrating how difficult it is to conduct cross-cultural research, as a way to answer the initial question.

The difficulties confronting researchers are well illustrated by research initiated by Greenfield and Bruner (Greenfield, 1966; Greenfield & Bruner, 1969). Working in rural Senegal, Greenfield and Bruner observed the steady development of conservation among schooled children and its absence among about half of the noneducated adults in their sample, leading naturally to speculation that schooling might actually be necessary for the development of concrete operations. This kind of result was picked up by Hallpike (1979) who claimed that adults in nonliterate societies, as a rule, fail to develop beyond preoperational thought (a conclusion hotly denied by, among others, Jahoda, 1980).

The crucial ambiguity in this research is similar to that which we have already encountered in the work on attachment: When a social context representing a test situation with particular meanings in one cultural system is imported into another, how do we know that the subjects have understood the problem in the way the experimenter intended?

For at least some of the research on schooling and the development of concrete operations in which unschooled children fail to conserve, the results point clearly to the fact that the subjects failed to enter into the framework of the problem as intended by the experimenter, although they complied in a surface way with instructions. Thus, for example, in the study by Greenfield (1966) among the Wolof of Senegal, it appeared that unless children attended school, many of them failed to achieve conservation of volume. However, in a follow-up study, Irvine (1978) asked subjects to play the role of an informant whose task it was to clarify for the experimenter the meaning of the Wolof terms for equivalence and resemblance. In their roles as subjects, these individuals gave nonconserving responses when liquid was poured from one beaker into another. However, in their roles as linguistic informants, they indicated that while the water in one beaker had increased as a result of pouring, the amounts were the same (using different vocabulary to make the appropriate distinctions). Greenfield's own research also pointed to interpretational factors that interfere with conservation judgments; when she permitted Wolof children to pour water themselves, conservation comprehension improved markedly.

Two additional lines of evidence support the conclusion that problems in interpreting the Piagetian interview situation, not a failure to develop concrete operations, accounts for cases in which cultures appear to differ. First, Siegal (1991) demonstrated that even 4- to 5-year-old children display an understanding of conservation principles but misunderstand what is being asked of them by the experimenter. Second, in a number of instances no differences between the conservation performance of schooled and unschooled children from third-world countries has been observed when the experimenter was a member of the cultural group in question (Kamara & Easley, 1977; Nyiti, 1978).

A number of years ago Dasen (1977a, 1977b) suggested that performance factors might interfere with the expression of concrete operational competence. As a consequence, he has advocated the use of training procedures that, in effect, teach subjects the framework within which they were expected to perform. If the failure to perform had come about because subjects were not familiar with the language game of the experiment, the training would remove the deficit. In many (but not all) cases, modest amounts of conservation training were sufficient to improve performance markedly; in those cases in which training failed, it remained an open question whether or not different kinds of training or more training would permit the hypothesized competence (Dasen, Ngini, & Lavallee, 1979). Although some ambiguities remain in this research, it appears most sensible to conclude that concrete operational thinking is not influenced by schooling; what is influenced by schooling is subjects' ability to understand the language of testing and the presuppositions of the testing situation itself.

The situation is less clear with respect to formal operations. Inhelder and Piaget distinguished formal operations, which they believed emerge by age 12, from concrete operations, which are characteristic of middle childhood, in the following way:

> Although concrete operations consist of organized systems (classifications, serial ordering, correspondences, etc.), [children in the concrete operational stage] proceed from one partial link to the next in step-by-step fashion, without relating each partial link to all the others. Formal operations differ in that all of the possible combinations are considered in each case. Consequently, each partial link is grouped in relation to the whole; in other words, reasoning moves continually as a function of a "structured whole." (Inhelder & Piaget, 1958, p. 16)

In this view formal operational thinking is the kind of thinking needed by anyone who has to solve problems systematically. This new ability would be needed by the owner of a gasoline station who, in order to make a profit, has to take into account the current price he pays for gasoline, the kinds of customers that pass by his station, the kinds of services he needs to offer, the hours he needs to stay open, and the cost of labor. Or it might apply to a lawyer, who lays out a course of action that takes into account a wide variety of complications and who develops a far-reaching scenario for her client.

At different times in his career, Piaget adopted different positions on the universality of formal operational thinking. Within his general framework, the acquisition of formal operations should be universal, reflecting universal properties of biological growth and social interaction. Nonetheless, he entertained the notion that "in extremely disadvantageous conditions, [formal operational thought] will never really take shape" (Piaget, 1972, p. 7). This is the position that Inhelder and Piaget adopted in their monograph on formal operations:

> The age of about 11 to 12 years, which in our society we found to mark the beginning of formal thinking, must be extremely relative, since the logic of the

so-called primitive societies appears to be without such structures. (1958, p. 337)

In such statements we see explicit rejection of formal operations as a universal cognitive ability by Piaget, coupled with a claim about differences in development between cultures.

An alternative possibility, which Piaget also entertained, is to envisage a difference in speed of development without any modification of the order of succession of the stages. These different speeds would be due to the quality and frequency of intellectual stimulation received from adults or obtained from the possibilities available to children for spontaneous activity in their environment (1972). This position, which Piaget preferred toward the end of his life, led him to conclude that all normal people attain the level of formal operations. "However," he wrote, "they reach this stage in different areas according to their aptitudes and their professional special-izations (advanced studies or different types of apprenticeship for the various trades): the way in which these formal structures are used, however, is not necessarily the same in all cases" (1972, p. 10).

The cross-cultural evidence is unclear with respect to the universality of formal operations. Generally speaking, when Piagetian tasks have been used as the proper measure of formal operations, Third World peoples who have not attended school fail, and even those who have attended several years of formal schooling rarely display formal operations (see Segall, Dasen, Berry, & Poortinga, 1990, for a review and additional sources).

However, if one allows for evidence of systematic manipulation of variables, even if less than "all and only" the relevant variables are considered, it is possible to find evidence of formal operations in all cultures where anyone has thought to inquire into them (see Cole & Cole, 1989, for examples and discussion).

Perhaps the most reasonable conclusion given present evidence is that formal operations conceived of as thinking in (mentally) closed systems of logical relations are to be found routinely only where people have developed notation systems of some kind to help keep track of required manipula-tions. Since such notation systems are used even in modern, technologically sophisticated societies, only restricted contexts, Piaget's later speculations about the context-specificity of formal operations, would appear far more plausible than any notion of their universality across cultures and across contexts within cultures.

Memory. The basic expectation underlying research on culture and memory is quite different from that of work on logical operations. The mental operations that underpin performance in Piagetian conservation tasks are presumed to be universal, as they are believed to reflect the logic of everyday action in any culture. In the case of memory, there are three different sets of expectations growing out of three different academic traditions. The first, which traces its history to Bartlett (1932), assumes that memory processes are universal; memory will be effective in so far as the to-be-remembered materials fit preexisting mental schemas of the people involved.

Bartlett pointed out that cultures are made up of organized collectivities of people with shared customs, institutions, and values. Strong sentiments form around culturally valued activities that guide people's selection of information from the environment. These socially determined psychological tendencies to select certain kinds of information to be remembered and the knowledge assimilated through their operation constitute the schemas on which reconstructive remembering processes operate. In content domains in which the schemas are richly elaborated, recall will be better than in domains that are less valued, and, hence, in which fewer schemas are available, guide recall. In domains in which there are no preexisting schemas to guide recall, Bartlett assumed that simple temporal order would serve as the organizing principle, resulting in rote recapitulation. In effect, Bartlett asserted that the processes of remembering are culturally mediated and universal. Cultural differences would reside in the differences in strong sentiments and associated social tendencies that provide the supply of widely used schemas.

A second tradition, which one finds most often represented among anthropologists and philologists, assumes that nonliterate cultures, precisely because they cannot depend on the written word, will have highly developed powers of memory (Havelock, 1963; Levy-Bruhl, 1966; Rivers, 1901, 1903).

A third tradition, associated with the Soviet cultural–historical school, takes a dual-process approach to the question of culture and memory (Leontiev, 1981). In a manner similar to Bartlett, the Soviet theorists assume that there is a natural kind of memory, akin to contemporary notions of incidental remembering, in which there is no special intention to remember and no special strategy involved; such memories may or may not be evoked later depending on how directly the subsequent experience is linked to the earlier one. In addition, there is a cultural, mediated kind of remembering that involves the creation of artificial stimuli (either externally in the form of the proverbial string tied to one's finger or the Inca "quipu" — see Ascher & Ascher, 1981 — or internally, in the form of mnemonic strategies). This culturally mediated kind of remembering is intentional and has been greatly amplified by the invention and diffusion of writing systems and their information-storing sequelae. Crudely speaking, this line of theorizing leads to the expectation of universality for those kinds of events that people remember naturally, and cultural differences in remembering for those events that rely on culturally elaborated mediational means.

The existing evidence does not support the notion that the advent of writing systems decreases the ability to remember because, as Riesman (1956) put it, "they can afford to be careless with the spoken word, backstopped as they are by the written one" (p. 9). On the contrary, the psychological literature using experimental tests of remembering in different societies indicates that when people are asked to commit a sizeable body of arbitrarily selected material to memory, those who are literate and have attended school exhibit superior performance (see Cole & Scribner, 1977; LCHC, 1983, Scribner & Cole, 1981, for reviews).

Some combination of the positions developed by Bartlett and the Soviet cultural–historical theorists seems to fair best. In an early study, Nadel (1937) compared recall of a story constructed to be familiar in form and general content to members of two Nigerian groups, the Yoruba and the Nupe. On the basis of prior ethnographic analysis, Nadel predicted that the Yoruba would emphasize the logical structure of the story, whereas the Nupe would emphasize circumstantial facts and details because these two emphases fit their dominant sociocultural tendencies and associated schemas. His results confirmed his expectations.

Many years later, Deregowski (1970) obtained similar results comparing rural and urban Zambian adolescents. He predicted, correctly, that the urban subjects would emphasize temporal items built into the stories more than their rural brethren because clock time and dates had become such a prominent aspect of their lives. For nontemporal aspects of the stories, there were negligible recall differences between the groups, but for the key temporal items, the urban subjects displayed superior recall.

Turning to the question of the special forms of deliberate remembering and their associated *mnemotechnic means,* most research has used comparison between schooled and unschooled people of different ages as a method of investigation. The reason is obvious. School confronts children with specialized information-processing tasks such as committing large amounts of esoteric information to memory in a short time, and producing lengthy written discourses on the basis of memorized information. These, and similar tasks that are a routine part of schooling, have few analogies in the lives of people from societies in which there is no formal schooling. Hence, it is only to be expected that when confronted with such tasks, which carry within them highly specialized histories and associated practices, there would be marked differences in performance, and there are.

For example, a number of studies show that schooling promotes the ability to remember unrelated materials (Cole & Scribner, 1977; Stevenson, 1982; Wagner, 1982). Specific results include the following.

1. When a list of common items that fall into culturally recognized categories are presented repeatedly to children who are asked to recall as many of them as possible in any order (Cole, Gay, Glick & Sharp, 1971), those children who have completed 6 or more years of schooling remember more and cluster items in recall more than nonschooled comparison groups.

2. Short-term recall of item location increases as a function of schooling, but not age (Wagner, 1982).

3. Paired-associate learning of randomly paired items increases with schooling (Sharp, Cole, & Lave, 1979). In addition, Stevenson (1982) reports a modest positive effect of very small amounts of schooling on a battery of tasks that included various kinds of memory problems as well as visual analysis.

By contrast, schooling effects are generally absent in tests of recall of well-structured stories (Mandler, Cole, Scribner, & de Forest, 1980). They are also absent when the items to be paired in a paired-associate task are strongly associated with each other (Sharp, et al., 1979). Short-term memory also seems unaffected by schooling; in Wagner's studies, most recently probed locations show no education effects (Wagner, 1974, 1978).

With respect to the methodological issues of conducting cross-cultural research, the data on schooling's effects on the development of memory (schooling being a manifestly nonuniversal form of the cultural organization of children's lives during middle childhood) raises some interesting new questions about cross-cultural methods and the role of culture in development. In a somewhat different way from the research on attachment, the cross-cultural research on schooling evokes skepticism about the generality of the conclusions that one can draw. The difficulty amounts to the following: schooling effects turn up in those cases in which the form of talk, the content, and the structuring of the content of various tests of memory are very similar to those found in school. How are we to determine if anything general about the development of remembering is indexed by these results? Presumably what we would need is to find some sort of remembering activity that is engaged in equally often by those who have been to school and those who have not and see if schooling changes the way that common remembering activity is accomplished. Such conditions are approximated in cases such as recall of stories, and in those cases there appears to be little in the way of schooling effects. Yet, it could be argued, those cases are "easy" because they provide a ready-made structure for remembering and it is exactly the creation of such structures that is what schooling teaches (so-called meta-memory strategies). So we need an everyday remembering task that requires the imposition of structure on unstructured, or covertly structured materials. But this kind of experience is special to schooling! It is a vicious circle that has yet to be broken.

In summary, there is little doubt that there are vast differences in children's experiences during middle childhood and it seems altogether plausible that one should observe equally vast differences in the psychological characteristics of children during this age period. However, cross-cultural research appears to be limited in the degree to which it can lay bear these differences in a scientific manner.

The most positive thing that can be said about the cross-cultural work on schooling and development is that it has revealed that a good deal of developmental research conducted in industrialized countries on age and cognitive development has, in fact, resulted in an indexing of the number of years in school and has not revealed any broad cultural effect. In short, we are learning something about our own cultural practices that should make us more cautious in our claims about the cognitive benefits of schooling, independent of the value we place on the specific abilities that children acquire there. Very similar remarks apply to children's social behavior, where the data are, if anything, less compelling (see Price-Williams, 1985; Segall et al., 1990, for useful summaries).

Adolescence: Stage or Transition?

One of the most famous examples of the use of cross-cultural research to determine the influence of culture on the dynamics of developmental change was Mead's research on the socioemotional changes associated with adolescence (Mead, 1928). Mead sought to determine the validity of claims by various American and European scholars that high levels of emotional stress and intergenerational conflict were associated with adolescence "as inevitably as teething is a period of misery for the small baby" (p. 109). She concluded that the conflict and stress associated with adolescence is a cultural-bound phenomenon that is virtually absent in Samoa because the Samoans take a more relaxed attitude toward adolescent sexuality and are more casual in general. Many years later, her conclusions were disputed by Freeman (1983), who claimed that Mead's own data revealed signs of conflict that she had overlooked or misinterpreted. What neither Freeman nor Mead question was the existence among Samoans of a distinct psychological stage called adolescence, with associated psychological and social characteristics. Yet there is no word in the Samoan language corresponding to the popular contemporary notion of adolescence. This linguistic fact raises an interesting psychological question: There may be a universal transition from childhood to adulthood, but is there a distinctive stage of adolescence independent of cultural or historical circumstances?

The stage versus transition discussion is more than an empty academic argument because it speaks to the basic question of the existence of, and sources of, discontinuity in development. As ordinarily used by psychologists, the terms transition and stage are not synonymous. A stage is a more or less stable, patterned, and enduring system of interactions between the organism and the environment; a transition is a period of flux, when the "ensemble of the whole" that makes up one stage has disintegrated and a new stage is not firmly in place. According to this set of ideas, can adolescence be considered a stage, even in societies that give it a name and treat it as one? Or is it, despite popular understanding, best considered a transition between childhood and adulthood?

What is indisputable is that some time around the end of a decade of life (the exact onset time depends greatly on nutritional and other factors), a cascade of biochemical events begins that will alter the size, the shape, and the functioning of the human body. The most revolutionary of the changes that will occur is the development of the entirely new potential for individuals to engage in biological reproduction (Katchadourian, 1989). These biological changes have profound social implications for the simple reason that reproduction cannot be accomplished by a single human being. As their reproductive organs reach maturity, boys and girls begin to engage in new forms of social behavior because they begin to find the opposite sex attractive. According to Piaget and many other psychologists, some combination of biological changes in brain and changed social circumstances give rise to new cognitive capacities.

Consistent with this line of reasoning, some scholars argue that adolescence is indeed a universal and necessary stage of development, with its own special characteristics. Bloch and Niederhoffer (1958), for example, suggest one of the universal features shared by both the notion of a "transition to adulthood" and "adolescence": a struggle for adult status. In all societies, the old eventually give way to the young. It is not easy for those in power to give it up, so it is natural to expect that, to some degree, the granting of adult status, and with it adult power, will involve a struggle. A good candidate for a second universal feature of the transition from childhood to adulthood that arouses tension, but that is necessary for the continuation of human society, is the necessity for children, who have long identified strongly with members of their own sex, to become attached to a member of the opposite sex. Whether or not these necessary changes require an entire stage of development for their realization remains, however, to be demonstrated.

Often the argument for the universality of adolescence as a stage of development is based on historical evidence, such as the following:

> The young are in character prone to desire and ready to carry any desire they may have formed into action. Of bodily desires it is the sexual to which they are most disposed to give way, and in regard to sexual desire they exercise no self-restraint. They are changeful too, and fickle in their desires, which are as

> transitory as they are vehement. . . . They are passionate, irascible, and apt to be carried away by their impulses. . . . They regard themselves as omniscient and are positive in their assertions; this is, in fact, the reason for their carrying everything too far. . . . Finally, they are fond of laughter and consequently facetious, facetiousness being disciplined insolence. (quoted in Kiell, 1964, pp. 18–19)

This description has a certain timeless quality to it. It could be a description of members of a high school clique in almost any modern city or town, or it might be a description of Romeo and his friends in medieval Verona. In fact, it is a description of youth in the fourth-century B.C., written by the philosopher Aristotle. Combining such historical evidence with similar accounts from various nonindustrialized societies around the world today leads naturally to a belief that the experience of adolescence is universal. However, the universality of adolescence as a unified stage is by no means clearly established on the basis of these data.

First, there is a noticeable shortcoming in the evidence cited from ancient societies; women are largely excluded. In Aristotle's description of adolescents, and in similar descriptions from other ancient societies (Kiell, 1964), the people being talked about are clearly males. Moreover, they are urban males of the monied classes who did indeed undergo a period of extended training, often including formal schooling, which created a delay between puberty and full adult status. Generally speaking, women and most members of the lower classes did not undergo such specialized training, nor is there evidence that they were ever included in the category of adolescents.

Second, the evidence from other cultures may support the idea that the transition to adult status is universally fraught with anxiety and uncertainty, but it provides equally strong evidence that adolescence, as the term is used in modern industrialized societies, exists only under particular cultural circumstances (Whiting, Burbank, & Ratner, 1982).

Among the Inuit Eskimos of the Canadian Arctic at the turn of the century, for example, special terms were used to refer to boys and girls when they entered puberty, but these terms did not coincide with western notions of adolescence (Condon, 1987). Young women were considered fully grown (adult) at menarche, a change in status marked by the fact that they were likely to be married by this time and ready to start bearing children within a few years. Young men were not considered fully grown until they were able to build a snowhouse and hunt large game unassisted. This feat might occur shortly after the onset of puberty, but it was more likely for boys to achieve adult status somewhat later because they had to prove first that they could support themselves and their families. In view of the different life circumstances of these people, it is not surprising that they developed no special concept corresponding to adolescence that applied to boys and girls alike; such a concept did not correspond to their reality.

When we consider the actual organization of life in ancient Greece, Europe in the middle ages, or in contemporary nonindustrialized societies in terms of the role of culture in development, we are reminded that the process of biological reproduction by itself is insufficient for the continuation of our species. It must be complemented by the process of cultural reproduction (education, broadly conceived), which ensures that the designs for living evolved by the group will be transmitted to the next generation. According to this view, adolescence will exist as a distinctive period of life only under specific cultural or historical circumstances (Aries, 1962; Demos & Demos, 1969).

In the United States and other industrialized societies, a gap of 7 to 9 years typically separates the biological changes that mark the onset of sexual maturity and the social changes that confer adult status (such as the right to marry without parental consent or to run for elective office).[8] This lengthy period is necessary because of the time it takes to acquire the many skills that will ensure economic independence and cultural reproduction.

Matters can be expected to be different in those societies in which there is little or no gap between the beginning of sexual maturity and the beginning of adulthood (J. Whiting, Burbank, & Ratner, 1982). These are often societies in which the level of technology is relatively low and in which biological maturity occurs relatively late by our standards. By the time biological reproduction becomes possible, which is about the age of 15 in many nonindustrial societies, young people already know how to farm, weave cloth, prepare food, and care for children. Although they still have a good deal to learn (a fact that their elders impress on them, often with considerable force), they are capable of the basics of cultural reproduction. In such societies, there may be no commonly acknowledged stage of development equivalent to adolescence.

CONCLUSION: INCLUDING CULTURE IN DEVELOPMENT

At the outset of this chapter, I noted the seeming paradox that, although there is consensus that the use, creation, and transmission of culture is the unique characteristic of our species, there is little discussion of culture's role in human development. Having provided some background on various approaches to the concept of culture and its inclusion in developmen-

---

[8]It should be noted that the onset of puberty is itself shaped by cultural forces that govern the eating habits and health care of children. Depending on circumstances, the onset of menarche may vary by as much as 8 years or more (Khatchadourian, 1989).

tal–psychological research, we are in a better position to understand why culture receives relatively little attention among psychologists and what sorts of changes in theory and methodology would be necessary to bring about a major change in the status quo.

To begin with, there is a very instructive parallel between the difficulties of conducting convincing cross-cultural research in the late 20th century and the dispute between Boas and evolutionary anthropologists such as Tylor in the 19th century. Recall that Tylor believed he could rank cultures with respect to level of development using a standardized criterion such as "extent of scientific knowledge" or "complexity of social organization." Boas demurred, insisting that the very meaning of these terms shifted with its cultural context and that heterogeneity of functioning depending on the domain studied had to be taken into account. Like Tylor, cross-cultural psychologists who use standardized instruments that they carry from place to place can rank subjects with respect to developmental level. However, as Boas would have predicted, their conclusions are suspect because the meaning of their criterial instruments changes with its cultural context. Eventually they must engage in local ethnographic work to establish the relation of their testing procedures to the local culture and the kinds of experiences that people undergo over their life spans. It is a giant undertaking, for which there are only a few extended examples on which to draw.

Nor is success guaranteed. Some critics of the cross-cultural enterprise claim that it will fail in principle. For example, in a recent essay, Shweder (1990) wrote:

Cross-cultural psychology has lived on the margins of general psychology as a frustrated gadfly, and it is not too hard to understand why. For one thing, cross-cultural psychology offers no substantial challenge to the core Platonic interpretive principle of general psychology (the principle of psychic unity). Moreover, if you are a general psychologist cum Platonist (and a principled one, at that) there is no theoretical benefit in learning more and more about the quagmire of appearances—the retarding effects of environment on the development of the central processing mechanism, the noise introduced by translation of differences in the understanding of the test situation or by cultural variations in the norms regulating the asking and the answering of questions.

Rather, if you are a general psychologist, you will want to transcend those appearances and reach for the imagined abstract forms and processes operating behind intrinsic crutches and restraints and distortions of this or that performance environment. Perhaps that is why, in the circles of general psychology, cross-cultural psychology has diminutive status, and why its research literature tends to be ignored. Not surprisingly, developmental psychology—the study of age-graded differences in performance on psychological tests and tasks—has suffered a similar fate, and for similar reasons. (pp. 11–12)

My own view is less gloomy than this. Despite its shortcomings, cross-cultural methods can (as in the case of the effects of forced change toward prolonged sleep episodes in early infancy) help us to understand the contributions of particular kinds of experience to the development of particular kinds of characteristics. Cross-cultural research alerts us to the possibility that the very existence of certain stages of development may be the consequence of particular cultural–historical circumstances and not universal, as in the case of adolescence. It also achieves the important function of getting us to question the sources of age-related differences observed in our own culture, as indicated by the research on the effects of schooling in middle childhood. The fact that we are left wondering about the generality of the resulting changes in many cases (the schooling effects being a major case in point) is disappointing of course, but the good news is that it puts us on our guard against the ever-present danger of overgeneralizing the results of work conducted in our own societies.

When we turn from cross-cultural research, where culture is considered as an independent variable, and begin to take seriously the garden metaphor of culture-as-medium (what Valsiner, 1989, referred to as an organizing variable), entirely new avenues of research are opened up, posing major challenges to developmental psychologists. When we make the move from cross-cultural to cultural psychology, we stand the usual relationship between everyday experience and experimentation on its head. Instead of starting with presumably culture-free measures of psychological process, we begin with observation of everyday activities as part of a culturally organized sequence with its own internal logic and goals. Experiments then become ways to model conveniently existing cultural practices in order to externalize their inner workings. When we begin in this way, we come across such new (theoretically speaking) phenomena as the revelation of the projection of ideal or mental models of past gender relations onto ideal or mental models of a child's future and the transformation of this ideal model into concrete reality. Or we are led into an analysis of the organization of everyday conversations between mothers and children to understand how their structure is related to the society's world view (Bornstein, 1989; Goodnow, 1984), or school activities to determine how to make instruction developmentally beneficial (Newman, Griffin, & Cole, 1989).

Such analyses are often, from the perspective of experimental psychology, messy and difficult. However, a growing literature on this topic, only a small part of which I have been able to touch on in this chapter, suggests that it holds great promise for the future development of the science of human development.

ACKNOWLEDGMENTS

This chapter was prepared during a year spent at the Center for Advanced Study in the Social Sciences, Stanford, California. I acknowledge the support of the Spencer Foundation through a grant to the Center. I also thank Marc Bornstein for his astute editorial comments.

REFERENCES

Ainsworth, M. D. (1967). *Infancy in Uganda; Infant care and the growth of love.* Baltimore, MD: Johns Hopkins Press.

Ainsworth, M. D., Blehar, M. C., Waters, E., & Wall, S. (1978). *Patterns of attachment.* Hillsdale, NJ: Lawrence Erlbaum Associates.

Aries, P. (1962). *Centuries of childhood: A social history of family life.* New York: Vintage Books.

Ascher, M., & Ascher, S. R. (1981). *Code of the quipu.* Ann Arbor, MI: University of Michigan Press.

Bandura, A. (1986). *Social foundations of thought and action: A social cognitive theory.* Englewood Cliffs, NJ: Prentice-Hall.

Bartlett, F. C. (1932). *Remembering.* Cambridge: Cambridge University Press.

Berry, J. (1976). *Human ecology and cultural style.* New York: Sage-Halstead.

Bertenthal, B. I., & Campos, J. J. (1990). A systems approach to the organizing effects of self-produced locomotion during infancy. In Rovee-Collier & L. P. Lipsitt (Eds.), *Advances in infancy research* (Vol. 6). Norwood, NJ: Ablex.

Bloch, H. A., & Niederhoffer, A. (1958). *The gang: A study in adolescent behavior.* New York: Philosophical Library.

Boas, F. (1911). *The mind of primitive man.* New York: Macmillan.

Bornstein, M. (1980). Cross-cultural developmental psychology. In M. H. Bornstein (Ed.), *Comparative methods in psychology.* Hillsdale, NJ: Lawrence Erlbaum Associates.

Bornstein, M. H. (1989). Cross-cultural comparisons: The case of Japanese-American infant and mother activities and interactions. What we know, what we need to know, and why we need to know. *Developmental Review, 9,* 171–204.

Bornstein, M. H., Tal, J., & Tamis-LeMonda, C. S. (1991). Parenting in cross-cultural perspective: The United States, France, and Japan. In M. H. Bornstein (Ed.), *Cultural approaches to parenting* (pp. 69–90). Hillsdale, NJ: Lawrence Erlbaum Associates.

Bornstein, M. H., Toda, S., Azuma, H., Tamis-LeMonda, C. S., & Ogino, M. (1990). Mother and infant activity and interaction in Japan and in the United States: II. A comparative microanalysis of naturalistic exchanges focused on the organization of infant attention. *International Journal of Behavioral Development, 13,* 289–308.

Bowlby, J. (1969). *Attachment and loss: Vol. 1. Attachment.* New York: Basic.

Bretherton, I., & Waters, E. (Eds.). (1985). Growing points in attachment theory. *Monographs of the Society for Research in Child Development, 50,* (1–2, Serial No. 209).

Bruner, J. S. (1982). The formats of language acquisition. *American Journal of Semiotics, 1,* 1–16.

Bruner, J. S. (1983). *Child's talk.* New York: Norton.

Bruner, J. S. (1990). *Acts of meaning.* Cambridge, MA: Harvard University Press.

Campos, J. J., & Stenberg, C. R. (1981). Perception, appraisal, and emotion: The onset of social referencing. In M. E. Lamb & L. R. Sherrod (Eds.), *Infants social cognition: Empirical and social considerations*. Hillsdale, NJ: Lawrence Erlbaum Associates.

Carey, S. (1985). *Conceptual change in childhood*. Cambridge, MA: MIT Press.

Cheney, D. L., & Seyfarth, R. M. (1990). *How monkeys perceive the world*. New York: Cambridge University Press.

Chisholm, J. S. (1989). Biology, culture, and the development of temperament: A Navajo example. In J. K. Nugent, B. M. Lester, & T. B. Brazelon (Eds.), *The cultural context of infancy* (Vol. 1) Norwood, NJ: Ablex.

Chisholm, D. L., & Heath, G. (1987). Evolution and pregnancy: A biosocial view of prenatal influences. In C. Super (Ed.), *The role of culture in developmental disorder*. New York: Academic Press.

Cole, M. (1988). Cross-cultural psychology in the sociohistorical tradition. *Human Development, 31,* 137-157.

Cole, M., & Cole, S. (1989). *The development of children*. New York: Scientific American Books.

Cole, M., Gay, J., Glick, J. A., & Sharp, D. W. (1971). *The cultural context of learning and thinking*. New York: Basic.

Cole, M., & Scribner, S. (1977). Cross-cultural studies of memory and cognition. In R. V. Kail & J. W. Hagen (Eds.), *Perspectives on the development of memory and cognition*. Hillsdale, NJ: Lawrence Erlbaum Associates.

Condon, R. G. (1987). *Inuit youth*. New Brunswick, NJ: Rutgers University Press.

Curtiss, S. (1977). *Genie: A psychological study of a modern-day wild child*. New York: Academic Press.

D'Andrade, R. (1984). Cultural meaning systems. In R. A. Shweder & R. A. LeVine (Eds.), *Culture theory: Essays on mind, self, and emotion*. New York: Cambridge University Press.

D'Andrade, R. (1986). Three scientific world views and the covering law model. In D. Fiske & R. Shweder (Eds.), *Meta-theory in the social sciences*. Chicago: University of Chicago Press.

Dasen, P. R. (1977a). Are cognitive processes universal? A contribution to cross-cultural Piagetian psychology. In N. Warren (Ed.), *Studies in cross-cultural psychology* (Vol. 1). London: Academic Press.

Dasen, P. R. (1977b). *Piagetian psychology: Cross cultural contributions*. New York: Gardner.

Dasen, P. R., Ngini, L., & Lavalee, M. (1979). Cross-cultural training studies of concrete operations. In L. H. Eckenberger, W. J. Lonner, & Y. H. Poortinga (Eds.), *Cross-cultural contributions to psychology*. Amsterdam: Swets & Zeilinger.

DeCasper, A. J., & Spence, M. J. (1986). Prenatal maternal speech influences newborn's perception of speech sounds. *Infant Behavior and Development, 9,* 133-150.

Demos, J., & Demos, V. (1969). Adolescence in historical perspective. *Journal of Marriage and the Family, 31,* 632-638.

Deregowski, J. (1970). Effect of cultural value of time upon recall. *British Journal of Social and Clinical Psychology, 9,* 37-41.

de Villiers, J. G., & de Villiers, P. A. (1978). *Language acquisition*. Cambridge, MA: Harvard University Press.

DeVos, G. A., & Hippler, A. E. (1969). Cultural psychology: Comparative studies of human behavior. In G. Lindzey & E. Aronson, (Eds.), *The handbook of social psychology* (Vol. 4, 2nd ed.). Reading, MA: Addison-Wesley.

Dreyfus-Brisac, C. (1978). Ontogenesis of brain bioelectrical activity and sleep organization in neonates and infants. In F. Falkner & J. M. Tanner (Eds.), *Human growth: Vol. 3 Neurobiology and nutrition*. New York: Plenum.

Emde, R. N., Gaensbauer, T. J., & Harmon, R. J. (1976). Emotional expression in infancy: A behavioral study. *Psychological Issues Monograph Series, 10* (1, Serial No. 37). New York: International Universities Press.

Fernald, A. (1989). Intonation and communicative intent in mothers' speech to infants: Is the melody the message? *Child Development, 60,* 1497–1510.

Freeman, D. (1983). *Margaret Mead and Samoa.* Cambridge, MA: Harvard University Press.

Fricker, H. S., Hindermann, R., & Bruppacher, R. (1989). The Aarau study on pregnancy and the newborn: An epidemiological investigation of the course of pregnancy in 996 Swiss women, and its influence on newborn behavior using the Brazelton scale. In J. K. Nugent, B. M. Lester, & T. B. Brazelton (Eds.), *The cultural context of infancy* (Vol. 1). Norwood, NJ: Ablex.

Frijda, N., & Jahoda, G. (1966). On the scope and methods of cross-cultural research. *International Journal of Psychology, 1,* 110–127.

Furgeson, C. (1977). Baby talk as a simplified register. In C. Snow & C. Furgeson (Eds.), *Talking to children.* Cambridge: Cambridge University Press.

Geertz, C. (1973). *The interpretation of cultures.* New York: Basic.

Gelman, R. (1990). First principles affect learning and transfer in children. *Cognitive Science, 14,* 79–107.

Gesell, A. (1940). *The first five years of life* (9th ed.). New York: Harper & Row.

Gesell, A. (1945). *The embryology of behavior.* New York: Harper & Row.

Goldin-Meadow, S. (1985). Language development under atypical learning conditions. In K. E. Nelson (Ed.), *Children's language* (Vol. 5). Hillsdale, NJ: Lawrence Erlbaum Associates.

Goldman-Rakic, P. S. (1987). Development of cortical circuitry and cognitive function. *Child Development, 58,* 601–622.

Goodall, J. (1986). *The chimpanzees of Gombe: Patterns of behavior.* Cambridge: Harvard University Press.

Goodnow, J. (1984) Parents' ideas about parenting and development. In A. L. Brown & B. Rogoff (Eds.), *Advances in developmental psychology* (Vol. 3). Hillsdale, NJ: Lawrence Erlbaum Associates.

Greenfield, P. M. (1966). On culture and conservation. In J. S. Bruner, R. P. Olver, & P. M. Greenfield (Eds.), *Studies in cognitive growth.* New York: Wiley.

Greenfield, P. M., Brazelton, T. B., & Childs, C. P. (1989). From birth to maturity in Zinacantan: Ontogenesis in cultural context. In V. Bricker & G. Gossen (Eds.), *Ethnographic encounters in southern Mesoamerica: Celebratory essays in honor of Evon Z. Vogt.* Albany: Institute of Mesoamerican Studies, State University of New York.

Greenfield, P. M., & Bruner, J. S. (1969). Culture and cognitive growth. In D. A. Goslin (Ed.), *Handbook of socialization theory and research.* New York: Rand McNally.

Greenfield, P. M., & Lave, J. (1982). Cognitive aspects of informal education. In D. A. Wagner & H. E. Stevenson (Eds.), *Cultural perspectives on child development.* New York: Freeman.

Grossmann, K. E., & Grossmann, K. (1990). The wider concept of attachment in cross-cultural research. *Human Development, 33,* 31–47.

Grossmann, K. E., Grossmann, K., Huber, F., & Wartner, U. (1981). Children's behavior towards their mothers at 12 months and their fathers at 18 months in Ainsworth's Strange Situation. *International Journal of Behavioral Development, 4,* 157–181.

Grossmann, K., Grossmann, K. E., Spangler, S., Suess, G., & Unzner, L. (1985). Maternal sensitivity and newborn orientation responses as related to quality of attachment in northern Germany. In I. Bretherton & E. Waters (Eds.), Growing points of attachment theory. *Monographs of the Society for Research in Child Development, 50* (1–2 Serial No. 209).

Hallpike, C. R. (1979). *The foundations of primitive thought*. Oxford: Clarendon Press.

Harkness, S., & Super, C. (1985). The cultural context of gender segregation in children's peer groups. *Child Development, 56*, 219–224.

Harris, M. (1968). *The rise of anthropological theory*. New York: Crowell.

Havelock, E. A. (1963). *Preface to Plato*. Cambridge, MA: Harvard University Press.

Herder, J. G. V. (1784/1803). *Outlines of a philosophy of the history of man*. London: Luke Hansard.

Herskovitz, M. J. (1948). *Man and his works: The science of cultural anthropology*. New York: Knopf.

Hinde, R. (1987). *Individuals, relationships, and culture*. Cambridge: Cambridge University Press.

Holmberg, A. R. (1950). *Nomads of the long bow: The Siriono of eastern Bolivia*. Publication No. 10, Smithsonian Institute. Institute of Social Anthropology. Washington, DC.

Inhelder, B., & Piaget, J. (1958). *The growth of logical thinking from childhood to adolescence*. New York: Basic.

Irvine, J. (1978). Wolof "magical thinking": Culture and conservation revisited. *Journal of Cross-Cultural Psychology, 9*, 38–47.

Jahoda, G. (1980). Theoretical and systematic approaches in cross-cultural psychology. In H. C. Triandis & W. W. Lambert (Eds.), *Handbook of cross-cultural psychology* (Vol. 1). Boston: Allyn and Bacon.

Jahoda, G. (1982). *Psychology and anthropology: A psychological perspective*. London: Academic Press.

Jahoda, G. (1989). Our forgotten ancestors. In J. J. Berman (Ed.), *Cross-cultural perspectives: Nebraska symposium on motivation, 1989*. Lincoln, NE: University of Nebraska Press.

Jeans, P. C., Smith, M. B., & Stearns, G. (1955). Incidence of prematurity in relation to maternal nutrition. *Journal of the American Dietary Association, 31*, 576–581.

Kagan, J. (1977). The uses of cross-cultural research in early development. In P. H. Liederman, S. Tulkin, & A. Rosenfeld (Eds.), *Culture and infancy: Variations in the human experience*. New York: Academic Press.

Kagan, J., Kearsley, R. B., & Zelazo, P. (1978). *Infancy: Its place in human development*. Cambridge, MA: Harvard University Press.

Kamara, A. I., & Easley, J. A. (1977). Is the rate of cognitive development uniform across cultures? A methodological critique with new evidence from Themne children. In P. R. Dasen (Ed.), *Piagetian psychology: Cross-cultural contributions*. New York: Gardner.

Katchadourian, H. A. (1989). *Fundamentals of human sexuality* (5th ed.). Fort Worth, TX: Holt, Rinehart & Winston.

Kawamura, S. (1963). The process of sub-culture propagation among Japanese macaques. In C. H. Southwick (Ed.), *Primate social behavior*. New York: Van Nostrand.

Kiell, N. (1964). *The universal experience of adolescence*. New York: International Universities Press.

Kluckhohn, C. (1954). Culture and behavior. In G. Lindzey (Ed.), *Handbook of social psychology* (Vol. 2). Cambridge: Addison-Wesley.

Konner, M. J., & Super, C. (1987). Sudden infant death syndrome: An anthropological hypothesis. In C. Super (Ed.), *The role of culture in developmental disorder*. New York: Academic Press.

Laboratory of Comparative Human Cognition. (1983). Culture and development. In P. H. Mussen (Series Ed.) & W. Kessen (Vol. Ed.), *Handbook of child psychology: Vol. 1. History, theory, and methods*. New York: Wiley.

Leiderman, P. H., Tulkin, S., & Rosenfeld, A. (Eds.). (1977). *Culture and infancy: Variations in the human experience.* New York: Academic Press.

Leontiev, A. N. (1981). *Problems of the development of the mind.* Moscow: Progress Publishers.

LeVine, R. A., & Miller, P. M. (1990). Commentary. *Human Development, 33,* 73–80.

Levy-Bruhl, L. (1966). *How natives think* (L. A. Clare, Trans.). New York: Washington Square Press. (Original work published 1910)

Luria, A. R. (1928). The problem of the cultural development of the child. *Journal of Genetic Psychology, 35,* 493–506.

Luria, A. R. (1979). *The making of mind.* Cambridge, MA: Harvard University Press.

Macfarlane, A. (1977). *The psychology of childbirth.* Cambridge, MA: Harvard University Press.

Main, M. (1990). Cross-cultural studies of attachment organization: Recent studies, changing methodologies, and the concept of conditional strategies. *Human Development, 33,* 48–61.

Mandler, J. (1984). Representation and recall in infancy. In M. Moscovitch (Ed.), *Infant memory.* New York: Plenum.

Mandler, J., Scribner, S., Cole, M., & de Forest, M. (1980). Cross-cultural invariance in story recall. *Child Development, 51,* 19–26.

Mead, M. (1928). *Coming of age in Samoa.* New York: American Museum of Natural History.

Mead, M. (1935). *Sex and temperament in three primitive societies.* New York: William Morrow.

Mead, M., & Macgregor, F. C. (1951). *Growth and culture.* New York: Putnam.

Mead, M., & Newton, N. (1967). Cultural patterning of perinatal behavior. In S. Richardson & A. Guttmacher (Eds.), *Childbearing: Its social and psychological aspects.* Baltimore, MD: Williams & Wilkins.

Mehan, H. (1978). *Learning lessons.* Cambridge, MA: Harvard University Press.

Mehler, J., Lambertz, G., Jusczyk, P., & Amiel-Tison, C. (1986). Discrimination de la langue maternelle par le nouveau-ne (Discrimination of maternal language in the neonate). *Comptes Rendus de l'Academie de Science, 303,* Serie III, 637–640.

Miller, P. (1982). *Amy, Wendy and Beth: Learning language in south Baltimore.* Austin, TX: University of Texas Press.

Nadel, S. F. (1937). Experiments on culture psychology. *Africa, 10,* 421–435.

Nelson, K. (1981). Social cognition in a script framework. In J. H. Flavell & L. Ross (Eds.), *Social cognitive development.* Cambridge: Cambridge University Press.

Nelson, K. (1986). *Event knowledge: Structure and function in development.* Hillsdale, NJ: Lawrence Erlbaum Associates.

Newman, D., Griffin, P., & Cole, M. (1989). *The construction zone: Working for cognitive change in the school.* New York: Cambridge University Press.

Nugent, J. K., Lester, B. M., & Brazelton, T. B. (1989). *The cultural context of infancy, Vol. 1: Biology, culture, and infant development.* Norwood, NJ: Ablex.

Nyiti, R. (1978). The development of conservation in the Meru children of Tanzania. *Child Development, 47,* 1122–1129.

Piaget, J. (1972). Intellectual evolution from adolescence to adulthood. *Human Development, 15,* 1–12.

Piaget, J. (1973). *The psychology of intelligence.* Totowa, NJ: Littlefield & Adams.

Piaget, J., & Inhelder, B. (1969). *The psychology of the child.* New York: Basic.

Piattelli-Palmerini, M. (1980). *Language and learning.* Cambridge, MA: Harvard University Press.

Plomin, R. (1986). *Development, genetics, and psychology.* Hillsdale, NJ: Lawrence Erlbaum Associates.

Premack, D., & Premack, A. J. (1983). *The mind of an ape.* New York: Norton.

Price-Williams, D. (1985). Cultural psychology. In G. Lindzey & E. Aronson (Eds.),

Handbook of social psychology (Vol. 2, 3rd ed.). New York: Random House.

Read, M. (1960). *Children of their fathers: Growing up among the Ngoni of Malawi.* New York: Holt, Rinehart & Winston.

Richardson, S. A., & Guttmacher, A. F. (1967). *Childbearing: Its social and psychological aspects.* Baltimore, MD: Williams & Wilkins.

Riesman, D. (1956). *The oral tradition, the written word and the screen image.* Yellow Springs, OH: Antioch Press.

Rivers, W. H. R. (1901). Introduction and vision. In A. C. Haddon (Ed.), *Reports of the Cambridge anthropological expedition to the Torres Stratis* (Vol. 2, Pt. 1). Cambridge: Cambridge University Press.

Rivers, W. H. R. (1903). Observations of the senses of the Todas. *British Journal of Psychology, 1,* 321–396.

Rogoff, B. (1981). Schooling and the development of cognitive skills. In H. C. Triandis & A. Heron (Eds.), *Handbook of cross-cultural psychology* (Vol. 4). Boston: Allyn & Bacon.

Rogoff, B. (1989). *Apprenticeships in thinking.* New York: Oxford University Press.

Rogoff, B., Gauvain, M., & Ellis, S. (1984). Development viewed in its cultural context. In M. H. Bornstein & M. E. Lamb (Eds.), *Developmental psychology.* Hillsdale, NJ: Lawrence Erlbaum Associates.

Rogoff, B., Sellers, M. J., Pirrotta, S., Fox, N., & White, S. H. (1975). Age of assignment of roles and responsibilities to children. A cross-cultural survey. *Human Development, 18,* 353–369.

Rubin, J. Z., Provezano, F. J., & Luria, Z. (1974). The eye of the beholder: Parents' view on sex of newborns. *American Journal of Orthopsychiatry, 44,* 512–519.

Ruff, H. (1978). Infant recognition of the invariant form of objects. *Child Development, 16,* 293–306.

Sagi, A., Lamb, M. E., Lewkowicz, K. S., Shoham, K. R., Dvir, R., & Estes, D. (1985). Security of infant–mother, father, metapelet, attachments among kibbutz-raised Israeli children. In I. Bretherton & K. Waters (Eds.), Growing points of attachment theory. *Monographs of the Society for Research in Child Development, 50*(1–2, Serial No. 209), 257–275.

Sahlins, M. (1976). *Culture and practical reason.* Chicago: University of Chicago Press.

Schacter, D. L., & Moscovitch, M. (1984). Infants, amnesics, and dissociable memory systems. In M. Moscovitch (Ed.), *Infant memory.* New York: Plenum.

Schieffelin, B., & Ochs, E. (1986). *Language socialization across cultures.* New York: Cambridge University Press.

Scribner, S., & Cole, M. (1973). Cognitive consequences of formal and informal education. *Science, 182,* 553–559.

Scribner, S., & Cole, M. (1981). *The psychology of literacy.* Cambridge, MA: Harvard University Press.

Segall, M. H., Dasen, P. R., Berry, J. W., & Poortinga, Y. (1990). *Human behavior in global perspective.* New York: Pergamon.

Sharp, D. W., Cole, M., & Lave, C. (1979). Education and cognitive development: The evidence from experimental research. *Monographs of the Society for Research in Child Development, 4*(1–2, Serial No. 178).

Shostak, M. (1981). *Nissa: The life and words of a !Kung Woman.* Cambridge, MA: Harvard University Press.

Shweder, R. (1990). Cultural psychology—What is it? In J. W. Stigler, R. A. Shweder, & G. Herdt (Eds.), *Cultural psychology: Essays on comparative human development.* New York: Cambridge University Press.

Siegal, M. (1991). A clash of conversational worlds: Interpreting cognitive development through communication. In J. M. Levine & L. B. Resnick (Eds.), *Socially shared cognition.*

Washington, DC: American Psychological Association.

Skinner, B. F. (1953). *Science and human behavior.* New York: Macmillan.

Snow, C. E., Arlman-Rupp, A., Hassing, Y., Jobse, J., Joosken, J., & Vorster, J. (1976). Mother's speech in three social classes. *Journal of Psycholinguistic Research, 5,* 1–20.

Snow, C. E., & Ferguson, C. A. (Eds.). (1977). *Talking to children.* Cambridge: Cambridge University Press.

Special topic: Cross-cultural validity of attachment theory. (1990). *Human Development* (Whole Issue No. 1).

Spitz, R. (1958). *A genetic field theory of ego development.* New York: International Universities Press.

Starkey, D. (1981). The origins of concept formation: Object sorting and object preference in early infancy. *Child Development, 52,* 489–497.

Stevenson, H. W. (1982). Influences of schooling on cognitive development. In D. A. Wagner & H. W. Stevenson (Eds.), *Cultural perspectives on child development.* San Francisco. Freeman.

Stocking, G. (1968). *Race, culture, and evolution.* New York: Free Press.

Super, C. (1987). The role of culture in developmental disorder. In C. Super (Ed.), *The role of culture in developmental disorder.* New York: Academic Press.

Super, C. M., & Harkness, S. (1982). The infant's niche in rural Kenya and metropolitan America. In L. Adler (Ed.), *Issues in cross-cultural research.* New York: Academic Press.

Super, C. M., & Harkness, S. (1986). The developmental niche: A conceptualization at the interface of child and culture. *International Journal of Behavioral Development, 9,* 545–569.

Takahashi, H. (1986). Examining the Strange Situation procedure with Japanese mothers and 12-month-old infants. *Developmental Psychology, 19,* 184–191.

Takahashi, K. (1990). Are the key assumptions of the "Strange Situation" procedure universal? *Human Development, 33,* 23–30.

Tobin, J. J., Wu, D. Y. H., & Davidson, D. H. (1989). *Preschool in three cultures.* New Haven, CT: Yale University Press.

Tomasello, M. (1989, Winter). Chimpanzee culture. *SRCD Newsletter,* 1–3.

Tylor, E. B. (1874). *Primitive culture: Researches into the development of mythology, philosophy, religion, language, art, and custom.* London: J. Murray.

Valsiner, J. (1988). *Developmental psychology in the Soviet Union.* Bloomington, IN: Indiana University Press.

Valsiner, J. (1989). From group comparisons to knowledge: Lessons from cross-cultural psychology. In J. P. Forgas & J. M. Innes (Eds.), *Recent advances in social psychology: An international perspective* (pp. 501–510). Amsterdam: North Holland.

van IJzendoorn, M. H. (1990). Developments in cross-cultural research on attachment: Some methodological notes. *Human Development, 33,* 3–9.

van IJzendoorn, M. H., & Kroonenberg, P. M. (1988). Cross-cultural patterns of attachment: A meta-analysis of the strange situation. *Child Development, 59,* 147–156.

Vaughn, B., Egeland, B., Sroufe, L. A., & Waters, E. (1979). Individual differences in infant–mother attachment at twelve and eighteen months: Stability and change in families under stress. *Child Development, 50,* 971–975.

Vygotsky, L. S. (1987). Thinking and speech. In N. Minick (Ed. & Trans.), *The collected works of L. S. Vygotsky: Vol 1. Problems of general psychology.* New York: Plenum.

Wagner, D. A. (1974). The development of short-term and incidental memory: A cross cultural study. *Child Development, 48,* 389–396.

Wagner, D. A. (1978). Memories of Morocco: The influence of age, schooling, and environment on memory. *Cognitive Psychology, 10,* 1–28.

Wagner, D. A. (1982). Ontogeny in the study of culture and cognition. In D. A. Wagner & H.

W. Stevenson (Eds.), *Cultural perspectives on child development*. San Francisco: Freeman.

Wanner, E., & Gleitman, L. R. (Eds.). (1982). *Language acquisition: State of the art.* Cambridge: Cambridge University Press.

Washburn, S. L. (1960). Tools and human evolution. *Scientific American, 203,* 63–73.

Wertsch, J. (1985). *Vygotsky and the social formation of mind.* Cambridge, MA: Harvard University Press.

White, L. (1942). On the use of tools by primates. *Journal of Comparative Psychology, 34,* 369–374.

White, L. (1959). The concept of culture. *American Anthropologist, 61,* 227–251.

Whiting, B. B. (1976). The problem of the packaged variable. In K. F. Riegel & J. A. Meacham (Eds.), *The developing individual in a changing world* (Vol. 1). Chicago: Aldine.

Whiting, B. B. (1980). Culture and social behavior: A model for development of social behaviors. *Ethos, 8,* 95–116.

Whiting, B. B., & Edwards, C. P. (1988). *Children of different worlds: The formation of social behavior.* Cambridge, MA: Harvard University Press.

Whiting, J. W. M., Burbank, V. K., & Ratner, M. S. (1982). *The duration of maidenhood.* Paper presented at the Social Science Conference on School Age Pregnancies and Parenthood, Elkridge, MD.

Whiting, R. (1989). *You gotta have wa.* New York: Macmillan.

Williams, R. (1973). *Keywords.* New York: Oxford University Press.

Zimmerman, B. J. (1983). Social learning theory: A contextualist account of cognitive functioning. In C. Brainard (Ed.), *Recent advances in cognitive developmental theory.* New York: Springer-Verlag.

About the Authors

Thomas M. Achenbach, is professor of psychiatry and psychology, and director of the Center for Children, Youth, and Families at the University of Vermont Department of Psychiatry. A graduate of Yale, he received his PhD from the University of Minnesota and was a postdoctoral fellow at the Yale Child Study Center. Before moving to the University of Vermont, he taught at Yale and was a research psychologist at the National Institute of Mental Health. He has been a DAAD fellow at the University of Heidelberg, Germany, a SSRC senior faculty fellow at Jean Piaget's Centre d'Épistémologie Génétique in Geneva, Chair of the American Psychological Association's Task Force on Classification of Children's Behavior, and a member of the American Psychiatric Association's Advisory Committee on *DSM-III-R*. He is author of *Developmental Psychopathology; Research in Developmental Psychology: Concepts, Strategies, Methods; Assessment and Taxonomy of Child and Adolescent Psychopathology; Manuals* for the Child Behavior Checklist, Teacher's Report Form, and Youth Self-Report Form, and (with Stephanie McConaughy) *Empirically Based Assessment of Child and Adolescent Psychopathology.*

Marc H. Bornstein is senior research scientist and head of Child and Family Research at the National Institute of Child Health and Human Development. He was awarded a BA from Columbia College and MS and PhD degrees from Yale University. Bornstein has received the C. S. Ford Cross-Cultural Research Award from the Human Relations Area Files and the B. R. McCandless Young Scientist Award from the American Psychological Association. He was a J. S. Guggenheim Foundation fellow, and he received a Research Career Development Award from the NICHD. Bornstein has held academic appointments at Princeton University and New York University as well as visiting appointments in Munich, London, Paris, New York, and Tokyo. He has administered both federal and foundation grants, sits on the editorial boards of several professional journals, is fellow in a number of scholarly societies in a variety of disciplines, and consults for governments, foundations, universities, publishers, scientific journals, the media, and UNICEF. Bornstein is author or editor of more than a dozen books, including the children's books *Wide World* and *Wide World in Action,* and he has contributed numerous scientific papers in the areas of human experimental, methodological, comparative, developmental, cross-cultural, and aesthetic psychology.

Michael Cole is professor of communication and psychology and a member of the Laboratory of Comparative Human Cognition at the University of California, San Diego. Cole received his BA from UCLA and his PhD from Indiana University. He has been the editor of *Soviet Psychology* since 1969 and is the founder and currently serves on the editorial board of the *Quarterly Newsletter of the Laboratory of Comparative Human Cognition.* His research has centered on the role of culture in human development. He is the co-author of several books including *The Cultural Context of Learning and Thinking, Comparative Studies of How People Think, The Psychology of Literacy,* and *The Development of Children.* Cole is a member of the National Academy of Education and the American Academy of Arts and Sciences.

Robert J. Coplan is a graduate student in developmental psychology at the University of Waterloo. He received his BSc from McGill University and is currently pursuing his PhD. Coplan is interested in social and emotional development, especially social withdrawal, aggression, play, and social cognition in childhood.

William Damon is professor and chair of the Education Department at Brown University. He received a BA in social relations from Harvard and his doctorate in developmental psychology from the University of California at Berkeley. Damon is editor in chief of *New Directions for Child Development* and has authored *The Social World of the Child, Social and Personality Development, The Moral Child,* and (with Daniel Hart) *Self-Understanding in Childhood and Adolescence.*

Jill de Villiers is a professor of psychology and philosophy at Smith College. Her BA is from Reading University in England, and her PhD in experimental psychology from Harvard, where she also taught. She has co-authored two books, *Early Language* and *Language Acquisition,* co-edited *Language Processing and Language Acquisition,* and has written extensively on these topics. Her current work is on the acquisition of syntax, particularly questions, and lies at the intersection of linguistics and psychology.

Peter de Villiers is professor of psychology at Smith College. He received BAs from Rhodes University in South Africa and Oxford University, and his PhD in experimental psychology from Harvard. He taught at Harvard before coming to Smith College. He has co-authored two books, *Early Language* and *Language Acquisition,* and many articles on the topic of language development, and his current work focuses on the development of English language and literacy skills in deaf children.

Roger A. Dixon is professor of psychology at the University of Victoria in British Columbia, Canada. He received an MA from the University of Chicago and an MS and PhD from The Pennsylvania State University. Dixon is currently on the editorial boards of *Developmental Psychology* and *Psychology and Aging.* His research interests include the development of cognitive competence and compensatory processes in adulthood and aging, as well as history and theory in developmental psychology.

Matia Finn-Stevenson earned her PhD from The Ohio State University. She is a research scientist at Yale University, with a joint appointment at the Department of Psychology and the School of Medicine's Child Study Center. She is also a member of the faculty and associate director of the Yale Bush Center in Child Development and Social Policy, and was formerly the editor of the *Networker,* a newsletter on child and family policy issues. Finn-Stevenson has done extensive research on child development, children's services, and work and family life issues. Her special research interests include infant development and behavior, parent training, and program development and evaluation. She is the author, co-author, or editor of scholarly publications, the most recent of which are related to child care, parental leave policies, and family support programs. In her current research she also focuses on school's involvement in the area of child care and is a co-principal investigator on a longitudinal outcome evaluation of a school-based child care and family support program. Finn-Stevenson serves as an advisor to local school districts, state departments of education, and several national organizations and foundations. Between 1988 and 1991 she served as consultant on domestic policy issues to the staff of the White House Office of Policy Development and Congressional committees on child care and other work/family issues.

Maria P. Fracasso is a National Research Council research associate in the Section on Social and Emotional Development at the National Institute of Child Health and Human Development. She received her BS in psychology and Spanish from Fordham College in the Bronx, New York and her PhD from the Graduate School of Arts and Sciences at Fordham University. Her research is concerned with social and emotional development in infancy and early childhood, and her interests incorporate the role and influence of Spanish culture on mother–infant attachment. Her studies focus on the ecology of parent–infant interactions with recently migrated Central American families and the physiological and experiential origins of temperamental differences in infancy.

Daniel A. Hart is associate professor of psychology at Rutgers University, Camden, New Jersey, and is currently a visiting scientist at the MacArthur Foundation's Program on Conscious and Unconscious Mental Process. He received his doctorate from the Laboratory of Human Development at Harvard University. Hart is co-author of *Self-Understanding in Childhood and Adolescence,* and author of the forthcoming *Becoming Men: The Development of Aspirations, Values, and Adaptational Styles.*

Donald Hartmann received his BA at the University of Minnesota and his PhD from Stanford University. He is professor at the University of Utah, where he has been affiliated with both the clinical and developmental programs in the Department of Psychology, and with the Department of Family and Consumer Studies and the College of Nursing. He has served as editor or associate editor of *Behavioral Assessment, Behavior Therapy,* and the *Journal of Applied Behavior Analysis,* and as a member of the board of editors of numerous journals. He also served as a member of the NIMH Life Course Prevention Research Review Committee, the AABT Publication Board, and the AABT Committee Regarding APA Standards for Educational and Psychological Testing. He is the co-author of *Child Behavior: Analysis and Therapy,* and editor of *New Directions for the Methodology of Behavioral Sciences: Using Observers to Study Behavior.* His primary research interests include behavioral assessment and modification with children, measurement, statistics, and research design, children's prosocial behavior, and peer interactions.

Robert D. Ketterlinus is a staff fellow in the Section on Social and Emotional Development at the National Institute of Child Health and Human Development. Ketterlinus received his BA from The Pennsylvania State University, and his MA and PhD degrees in developmental psychology from The Catholic University of America. Dr. Ketterlinus and his collaborators are engaged in secondary analysis research on adolescent problem behaviors. They focus on the interrelations between sexual and nonsexual problem behaviors, adolescents and AIDS, and the effects of early child care and home-rearing environments on later development. He is the co-author of many articles and book chapters and is co-editor of *Adolescent Problem Behaviors.*

David Klahr is professor of psychology at Carnegie Mellon University where he has been department head since 1983. He received his BS in electrical engineering from the Massachusetts Institute of Technology, and his PhD from Carnegie Mellon University in the area of organizations and social behavior. He has been a visiting research fellow at the University of Stirling (Scotland) and a Fulbright lecturer at the London Graduate School of Business Studies. Klahr is a charter fellow of the American Psychological Society and a fellow of the American Psychological Association (Division 7). He has published widely in major cognitive and developmental journals and has served on their editorial boards. Klahr's book, *Cognitive Development, An Information Processing View* (with J. G. Wallace), pioneered the application of information-processing analysis to questions of cognitive development. He has edited *Cognition and Instruction* and co-edited *Production System Models of Learning and Development* and *Complex Information Processing: The Impact of Herbert A. Simon.* His current research interests include children's problem-solving behavior, the cognitive consequences of learning how to program, and the development of scientific discovery processes.

Deanna Kuhn is a professor of psychology at Teachers College, Columbia University. She received a BS from the University of Illinois and a PhD from the University of California, Berkeley, and taught previously at Harvard University. Kuhn has published widely in cognitive development and is the editor of *Human Development.* Her most recent books are *The Development of Scientific Thinking Skills* and *The Skills of Argument.*

Michael Lamb is head of the Section on Social and Emotional Development at the National Institute of Child Health and Human Development, where he directs research on the origins and developmental significance of individual differences in infant, child, and adolescent development. Longitudinal projects involving children and families from various cultural and national backgrounds are concerned with the effects of varying home and out-of-home care experiences, the physiological and experiential origins of temperamental differences in infancy, the characteristics of adolescent parents and their children, patterns of childrearing in various cultures and subcultures, the effects of domestic violence on children's development, and the effects of contrasting early life experiences on social and emotional development. Lamb has written or edited some 30 books and several hundred articles.

Richard M. Lerner, director of the Institute for Children, Youth, and Families, is a professor of Family and Child Ecology, Psychology, and Pediatrics and Human Development at Michigan State University. A developmental psychologist, Lerner received his PhD from the City University of New York. He has taught at Hunter College, Eastern Michigan University, and Pennsylvania State University. He has also been a fellow at the Center for Advanced Study in the Behavioral Sciences and is a fellow of the American Association for the Advancement of Science, the American Psychological Association, and the American Psychological Society. Lerner is the author or editor of more than 25 books and 150 scholarly articles and chapters, and is known for his theory of, and research about, relations between human development and contextual or ecological change. He currently serves as membership secretary of the International Society for the Study of Behavioral Development and is the founding editor of the *Journal of Research on Adolescence.*

Kenneth H. Rubin is professor of psychology at the University of Waterloo. He received his BA from McGill University and his MS and PhD from Pennsylvania State University. Rubin has been associate editor of *Child Development.* He has been the coordinator (president) of the Developmental Division of the Canadian Psychological Association and is currently General Secretary-Treasurer of the International Society for the Study of Behavioral Development and chairman of the graduate program in developmental psychology at the University of Waterloo. Rubin is interested in social, emotional, and personality development in infancy, childhood, and early adolescence. He has written extensively on the topics of social competence, social cognition, play, and parent–child relationships. Rubin was recently awarded a Killam Research Fellowship from the Canada Council.

Deborah Stipek is professor of education at the University of California, Los Angeles. She received her doctorate in developmental psychology from Yale University and spent a year working in the U.S. Senate as a Society for Research in Child Development Congressional Science fellow. Stipek's research is on the development of achievement-related emotions and cognitions and instructional variables that influences their development. She authored *Motivation to Learn.*

Edward F. Zigler earned his PhD from The University of Texas at Austin. A former chairman of the Department of Psychology at Yale University, he is currently Sterling Professor of Psychology, head of the psychology section of the Child Study Center, and director of the Bush Center in Child Development and Social Policy at Yale University. He is the author, co-author, or editor of numerous scholarly publications and has conducted extensive investigations on topics related to normal child development, as well as psychopathology and mental retardation. Zigler is also well known for his role in the shaping of national policies for children and families. He regularly testifies as an expert witness before congressional committees, and has served as a consultant to a number of cabinet rank officers. He was one of the planners of Project Head Start. Between 1970 and 1972, Zigler served as the first director of the Office of Child Development (now the Administration for Children, Youth and Families), and as chief of the U.S. Children's Bureau. In 1980, President Carter named him chair of the 15th anniversary of the Head Start program. Zigler is the recipient of several awards, the most recent of which are from the American Psychological Association, the American Academy of Pediatrics, the Society for Research in Child Development, the American Academy of Child and Adolescent Psychiatry, the American Academy on Mental Retardation, and the American Orthopsychiatric Association.

Author Index

797

Subject Index